ILLINOIS CRIMINAL LAW AND PROCEDURE

Statutes, Cases and Commentary

2016

J. Steven Beckett

ISBN 978-1-60904-575-3

Published by

Stipes Publishing L.L.C.
204 W. University Ave.
Champaign, Illinois 61820

TABLE OF CONTENTS

Foreword

Criminal law and procedure in Illinois had pioneer beginnings. The Illinois territory was sparsely populated and the courts were crude, so it goes without saying that the law was fairly crude as well. English common law was the controlling authority on matters of crimes and court procedure. It is against this backdrop that the territorial and state legislatures first considered adopting statutes that were codified or were different from the common law.

The first Illinois Criminal Code was adopted in 1827. Thereafter, from time to time, the General Assembly would enact statutes with criminal penalties, often without regard to the effect and confusion that any sort of *ad hoc* legislation causes on a system of justice. Decades would go by and a conglomeration of crimes and procedures would be created. Yeoman-like efforts to organize the criminal statutes would be made – usually with limited success.

Finally, in 1961, the Code of Criminal Law and Procedure was adopted following the leadership of University of Illinois Law Professor, Charles Bowman. This comprehensive and logical organization of the statutes defining crimes and setting forth detailed criminal procedures was a masterpiece of legislative draftsmanship. This code has served Illinois well for 50 years.

However, as with all good things, time wears away the solid foundation. In the past 35 years, the well-intended politics of "get tough on crime" has led to repeated enactment of statutes defining new crimes or amending old ones. Sometimes responsive to recognized interest groups, sometimes created based on societal changes in the area of technological advances, and sometimes based on questionable logic, the Illinois Criminal Code has again morphed itself to resemble the hodge-podge of statutes that existed a century or more ago.

With this background, this book attempts to examine all the major criminal offenses under Illinois law and all of the important steps involved in investigating crimes through conviction or acquittal of the accused. It is a significant journey for law enforcement, the lawyers and judges, the victims and defendants and for Illinois citizens. This work is intended to simplify some of the complexity, or at least put the issues in a light of common sense and understanding, remembering the history of our state and the very legislation under scrutiny.

Case Citations. Illinois cases have traditionally been referred to by "official reports" citations, with a parallel citations to a West publication, either the North Eastern reporter or Illinois Decisions. The practice is continued with this text until the time that the Illinois Supreme Court adopted a new "public domain" citation process. "Public domain" citations exist now and that is the way of the future. All Illinois citations using public domain citations, in this edition, use the new system of citation. I have used the "official" citations of all cases, but there is no longer a parallel citation.

Readers should be reminded that cases sometime have temporary lives – there is often a chance for further review. I have tried to utilize the most recent cases on points of law that can be used, but this often means that cases decided by the Illinois Appellate Court in one of the five appellate districts could still be reviewed by the Illinois Supreme Court. And of course, Illinois Supreme Court decisions that involve constitutional claims may be reviewed by the United States Supreme Court. Over the course of my career, I have learned to avoid predicting what the higher courts are going to do about points of law. While the case decisions I have selected to illustrate Illinois legal principles are on point now, time may change the import of some of those decisions.

2016 Edition. It is my hope that updating this book by adding newly enacted statutes and by discussing recent decisions will keep students current on Illinois criminal law and procedure. Hopefully this will promote further discussion and research into the needs of the criminal justice system for those embarking on careers that concern criminal law. I have included the appropriate criminal legislation enacted since July1, 2014 through June 30, 2016. More than 40 additional (and recent) cases have been added to the commentary in this, my fourth edition, of the text – including all major criminal cases decided by the United States Supreme Court and Illinois Supreme Court from July, 2014 to June, 2016. In the case of the former, the cases are only those that would affect the Illinois criminal justice system.

Acknowledgments. The task of preparing this text continues to require a significant commitment in time and effort. I want to acknowledge the remarkable research and editing efforts of Audrey Thompson (Illinois Law '17). Her work has been thorough, steadfast and significant. I also want to acknowledge the editing work and guidance of a helpful faculty assistant at the University of Illinois, College of Law, Molly Lindsey. Most of all, I am even more thankful than ever for my wife, Barbara, for her incredible patience with my varied projects, including this book.

J. Steven Beckett
Director of Trial Advocacy (ret.)
University of Illinois College of Law
becketts@illinois.edu

Beckett & Webber PC
Urbana IL 61801
steve@beckettwebber.com

July, 2016

TABLE OF CASES

Illinois Criminal Offense Classifications
Basic Range of Sentences[1]

Offense Class	Imprisonment Range	Probation	Maximum Fine
FELONIES			
1st Degree Murder	20 – 60 years	No	$ 25,000
2nd Degree Murder[2]	4 – 15 years	Yes	$ 25,000
Class X	6 – 30 years	No	$ 25,000
Class 1	4 – 15 years	48 months	$ 25,000
Class 2	3 – 7 years	48 months	$ 25,000
Class 3	2 – 5 years	30 months	$ 25,000
Class 4	1 – 3 years	30 months	$ 25,000
MISDEMEANORS			
Class A	365 days (county jail)	24 months	$ 2,500
Class B	180 days (county jail)	24 months	$ 1,500
Class C	30 days (county jail)	24 months	$ 1,500
Petty offenses	No	6 months	$ 1,000

ENHANCEMENTS[3]

Extended Term Sentencing (prior conviction of same class or greater class within 10 years)

1st Degree Murder	60 – 100 years
Class X	30 – 60 years
Class 1	15 – 30 years
Class 2	7 – 14 years
Class 3	5 – 10 years
Class 4	3 – 6 years

---

[1] Sentences for criminal offenses may be specified in the statute defining that offense and can vary substantially from the basic sentencing ranges of imprisonment and fines. Specific offenses can also have mandatory minimum prison sentences.

[2] 2nd Degree Murder is a Class 1 Felony.

[3] There are many sentencing enhancements under Illinois law. Some enhancements are set forth in the statute defining the elements of the crime. Additional enhancements are set forth in the Code of Corrections 730 ILCS 5/5-1 *et seq.*

Chapter 1: Criminal Offenses and the Criminal Code of 1961
Title I: General Provisions

Article 1 – Title and Construction of Act – State Jurisdiction
720 ILCS 5/1-1 *et seq.*

§ 1-1. Short Title. This Act shall be known and may be cited as the "Criminal Code of 1961".

§ 1-2. General Purposes. The provisions of this Code shall be construed in accordance with the general purposes hereof, to:

(a) Forbid and prevent the commission of offenses;

(b) Define adequately the act and mental state which constitute each offense, and limit the condemnation of conduct as criminal when it is without fault;

(c) Prescribe penalties which are proportionate to the seriousness of offenses and which permit recognition of differences in rehabilitation possibilities among individual offenders;

(d) Prevent arbitrary or oppressive treatment of persons accused or convicted of offenses.

§ 1-3. Applicability of Common Law. No conduct constitutes an offense unless it is described as an offense in this Code or in another statute of this State. However, this provision does not affect the power of a court to punish for contempt or to employ any sanction authorized by law for the enforcement of an order or civil judgment.

Commentary – Criminal Conduct and Mental State

Criminal Offenses. All criminal offenses have two components to them. First, there must be prohibited conduct. This conduct could be physical acts, such as an assault or battery (defined later). The conduct could be in the form of speech, such as obstructing a police officer by giving a false name. The conduct could be in the form of an omission from acting, such as an adult failing to prevent harm to a child that the adult has a duty to protect. The second component of a criminal offense is a mental state or *mens rea*, such as "knowingly" or "intentionally" (mental states will be addressed later). For an offense to have been committed, when the actor engages in the criminal conduct (i.e. an act or omission from a duty to act), it must be shown that he had the required criminal mental state for a crime to have occurred. Once a crime has been established after trial or by plea, the offender is subject to sanction in some form from a judge. This part of a criminal case is when the offender – as a criminal defendant – receives a sentence from the court.

Guide to Interpretation. Section 1-2 reminds the courts of the principles to be applied in interpreting the provisions of the criminal code. Apart from the identified statutory factors, another tenet used by courts in interpreting criminal statutes is to resolve all ambiguity in favor of the criminal defendant. The rules of interpretation apply to the delineation of crimes and the prescribed penalties.

No Common Law Crimes. Section 1-3 notes that all conduct to be prosecuted as a crime in Illinois must be identified as a crime in the Criminal Code of 1961. This simply means that there are no "common law" crimes in Illinois. Common Law crimes come from English law and were the result of court decisions over centuries. Once Illinois became a territory and had a legislature, crimes were defined by legislative act. The history of legislative enactment has continued to the present – each legislative session produces amendments to statutes which set forth the elements of existing crimes or which define new crimes. Certainly our Illinois ancestors could not have predicted the issues raised by the technology of ATM's and the internet. But instead of having courts re-define the meaning of criminal statutes (as would happen in common law jurisdictions), our system of government requires that the legislature take on this task. The criminal statutes become law when signed by the Illinois Governor and then are interpreted by Illinois Courts in the context of facts of specific cases. Of course, there seem to always be exceptions in the law, and in this instance there is one offense, criminal contempt, that is not defined by legislative act. In that sense it is a "common law" survivor, based on the court's inherent authority to enforce its orders by indirect criminal contempt (where willful criminal conduct occurs in whole or in part outside of the judge's presence). The court also has summary inherent authority to preserve the dignity of court proceeding by direct criminal contempt to sanction a party or an attorney for conduct that undermines the significance and majesty of court proceedings.

§ 1-4. Civil Remedies Preserved. This Code does not bar, suspend, or otherwise affect any right or liability to damages, penalty, forfeiture, or other remedy authorized by law to be recovered or enforced in a civil action, for any conduct which this Code makes punishable; and the civil injury is not merged in the offense.

Commentary – Criminal versus Civil

The fact that there can be a criminal prosecution with attendant punishment, including an order of restitution, does not mean that a civil remedy could not be pursued under the same factual situation. Thus, a victim injured by the criminal acts of an intoxicated person in a bar could pursue civil claims against the same criminal defendant and could also pursue a Dram Shop Act claim of liability for damages against the tavern owner for selling the beer that caused the defendant's intoxication. The burden of proof in a criminal case is "beyond a reasonable doubt", while the burden of proof of a plaintiff in a civil case is the lesser burden of "preponderance of the evidence". When a criminal defendant is acquitted, he may still face civil liability for his acts. A verdict of "not guilty" does not necessarily mean that a defendant is "not liable" for injuries caused.

Criminal remedies do not preclude or serve as a substitute for civil remedies. In *People ex rel. Difanis v. Boston*, 92 Ill. App. 3d 962, 416 N.E.2d 333 (Ill. App. Ct. 4th Dist. 1981), the Court held that it was lawful to pursue a civil injunction against a place of prostitution even though the individual acts of prostitution could be prosecuted as criminal offenses.

§ 1-5. State criminal jurisdiction. (a) A person is subject to prosecution in this State for an offense which he commits, while either within or outside the State, by his own conduct or that of another for which he is legally accountable, if:

(1) The offense is committed either wholly or partly within the State; or

(2) The conduct outside the State constitutes an attempt to commit an offense within the State; or

(3) The conduct outside the State constitutes a conspiracy to commit an offense within the State, and an act in furtherance of the conspiracy occurs in the State; or

(4) The conduct within the State constitutes an attempt, solicitation or conspiracy to commit in another jurisdiction an offense under the laws of both this State and such other jurisdiction.

(b) An offense is committed partly within this State, if either the conduct which is an element of the offense, or the result which is such an element, occurs within the State. In a prosecution pursuant to paragraph (3) of subsection (a) of Section 9-1, the attempt or commission of a forcible felony other than second degree murder within this State is conduct which is an element of the offense for which a person is subject to prosecution in this State. In homicide, the "result" is either the physical contact which causes death, or the death itself; and if the body of a homicide victim is found within the State, the death is presumed to have occurred within the State.

(c) An offense which is based on an omission to perform a duty imposed by the law of this State is committed within the State, regardless of the location of the offender at the time of the omission.

Commentary – Jurisdiction

Jurisdiction in Illinois. For a criminal offense to be prosecuted in Illinois there must be some nexus with Illinois. In Illinois criminal cases, the concept of jurisdiction is very broad. If the commission of a crime has a factual connection with Illinois, this gives Illinois the legal and constitutional authority to apply its criminal law to a defendant and to impose criminal remedies against that defendant, including the possibility of imprisonment. Jurisdiction gives the court judicial power to address and resolve the issue of whether a defendant has committed a crime. Without jurisdiction, a court has no power. Section 1-5 is the legislative recognition of this fundamental concept. Jurisdiction always has geographic implications in that acts that occur within Illinois give its courts criminal judicial power. The prosecution must prove jurisdiction exists beyond a reasonable doubt.

When the criminal conduct occurs within Illinois, the jurisdictional analysis is simple. However, the analysis becomes complex when the criminal conduct is in another state and the nexus to Illinois is less obvious. In *People v. Ruppenthal,* 771 N.E.2d 1002 (Ill. App. Ct. 1st Dist. 2002), the defendant in California was charged with solicitation of a minor. He argued that the crime with which he was charged was not committed wholly or partly within Illinois because the only element of the offense of indecent solicitation of a child - the utterance of words of solicitation - occurred in California. He claimed that the prosecution did not have to prove that his words of solicitation were communicated to an Illinois resident and that therefore no part of the offense took place in Illinois. However, the court found that the fact that the target child was in Illinois was enough to give Illinois courts territorial jurisdiction.

Part of conduct in another state. What if the criminal conduct occurs in Illinois and the results occur in another state? In *People v. Alexander,* 354 Ill.App.3d 832, 838-839, 822 N.E.2d 496, 502-503 (Ill. App. Ct. 5th Dist. 2004), the victim was kidnapped and beaten in Illinois, but was left on a Missouri highway where he was hit by a car and killed. The Court denied defendant's appeal claiming the State failed to prove that the crime occurred in Illinois and that Illinois lacked jurisdiction. "A defendant is subject to prosecution in Illinois for a criminal offense if it is committed either wholly or partly within the state, pursuant to [Section 1-5(a)(1)] or if conduct within Illinois constitutes an attempt, solicitation, or conspiracy to commit an offense in another state that is a criminal offense in both states. [Section 1-5(a)(4)]. An offense is committed partly in Illinois if either the conduct or a result that constitutes an element of the offense occurs within Illinois. [Section 1-5(b)] (2002)."

§ 1-6. Place of trial. (a) Generally. Criminal actions shall be tried in the county where the offense was committed, except as otherwise provided by law. The State is not required to prove during trial that the alleged offense occurred in any particular county in this State. When a defendant contests the place of trial under this Section, all proceedings regarding this issue shall be conducted under Section 114-1 of the Code of Criminal Procedure of 1963. All objections of improper place of trial are waived by a defendant unless made before trial.

(b) Assailant and Victim in Different Counties. If a person committing an offense upon the person of another is located in one county and his victim is located in another county at the time of the commission of the offense, trial may be had in either of said counties.

(c) Death and Cause of Death in Different Places or Undetermined. If cause of death is inflicted in one county and death ensues in another county, the offender may be tried in either county. If neither the county in which the cause of death was inflicted nor the county in which death ensued are known before trial, the offender may be tried in the county where the body was found.

(d) Offense Commenced Outside the State. If the commission of an offense commenced outside the State is consummated within this State, the offender shall be tried in the county where the offense is consummated.

(e) Offenses Committed in Bordering Navigable Waters. If an offense is committed on any of the navigable waters bordering on this State, the offender may be tried in any county adjacent to such navigable water.

(f) Offenses Committed while in Transit. If an offense is committed upon any railroad car, vehicle, watercraft or aircraft passing within this State, and it cannot readily be determined in which county the offense was committed, the offender may be tried in any county through which such railroad car, vehicle, watercraft or aircraft has passed.

(g) Theft. A person who commits theft of property may be tried in any county in which he exerted control over such property.

(h) Bigamy. A person who commits the offense of bigamy may be tried in any county where the bigamous marriage or bigamous cohabitation has occurred.

(i) Kidnapping. A person who commits the offense of kidnaping may be tried in any county in which his victim has traveled or has been confined during the course of the offense.

(j) Pandering. A person who commits the offense of pandering as set forth in Section 11-14.3 may be tried in any county in which the prostitution was practiced or in any county in which any act in furtherance of the offense shall have been committed.

(k) Treason. A person who commits the offense of treason may be tried in any county.

(l) Criminal Defamation. If criminal defamation is spoken, printed or written in one county and is received or circulated in another or other counties, the offender shall be tried in the county where the defamation is spoken, printed or written. If the defamation is spoken, printed or written outside this state, or the offender resides outside this state, the offender may be tried in any county in this state in which the defamation was circulated or received.

(m) Inchoate Offenses. A person who commits an inchoate offense may be tried in any county in which any act which is an element of the offense, including the agreement in conspiracy, is committed.

(n) Accountability for Conduct of Another. Where a person in one county solicits, aids, abets, agrees, or attempts to aid another in the planning or commission of an offense in another county, he may be tried for the offense in either county.

(o) Child Abduction. A person who commits the offense of child abduction may be tried in any county in which his victim has traveled, been detained, concealed or removed to during the course of the offense. Notwithstanding the foregoing, unless for good cause shown, the preferred place of trial shall be the county of the residence of the lawful custodian.

(p) A person who commits the offense of narcotics racketeering may be tried in any county where cannabis or a controlled substance which is the basis for the charge of narcotics racketeering was used; acquired; transferred or distributed to, from or through; or any county where any act was performed to further the use; acquisition, transfer or distribution of said cannabis or controlled substance; any money, property, property interest, or any other asset generated by narcotics activities was acquired, used, sold, transferred or distributed to, from or through; or, any enterprise interest obtained as a result of narcotics racketeering was acquired, used, transferred or distributed to, from or through, or where any activity was conducted by the enterprise or any conduct to further the interests of such an enterprise.

(q) A person who commits the offense of money laundering may be tried in any county where any part of a financial transaction in criminally derived property took place or in any county where any money or monetary instrument which is the basis for the offense was acquired, used, sold, transferred or distributed to, from or through.

(r) A person who commits the offense of cannabis trafficking or controlled substance trafficking may be tried in any county.

(s) A person who commits the offense of online sale of stolen property, online theft by deception, or electronic fencing may be tried in any county where any one or more elements of the offense took place, regardless of whether the element of the offense was the result of acts by the accused, the victim or by proper venue for all of the violations another person, and regardless of whether the defendant was ever physically present within the boundaries of the county.

(t) A person who commits the offense of identity theft or aggravated identity theft may be tried in any one of the following counties in which: (1) the offense occurred; (2) the information used to commit the offense was illegally used; or (3) the victim resides.
If a person is charged with more than one violation of identity theft or aggravated identity theft and those violations may be tried in more than one county, any of those counties is a

Commentary – Place of Trial

Venue. Where should the criminal trial be held? If all the acts that constitute the crime occur in one county, that answer is simple – the trial is to be held in that county. The concept of the place of the trial is described as the venue of the trial. Section 1-6(a) notes that venue, unlike jurisdiction, need not be proved by the prosecution in a criminal case. In controversial, highly publicized cases, a defendant can try to change the place of trial (transferring venue) pursuant to Section 114-1 to assure a fair trial.

When the acts that constitute the crime occur in more than one county, the trial can be held in any of the counties involved. Sections 1-6(b) through 1-6(t) detail the possible trial locations for different types of offenses.

In the past, venue was a material element that had to be proved by the prosecution. In *People v. Jones* 219 Ill.2d 1, 845 N.E.2d 598 (Ill. Sup. Ct. 2006), the defendant was convicted of murder; however, the victim's body was discovered outside Illinois. The Court held that venue is proper for a crime in any county where an element of the offense occurred and that the then required proof of venue could be based on circumstantial evidence. Remember that venue is not jurisdiction and jurisdiction is not venue – each has a distinct purpose: jurisdiction to establish judicial power and venue to determine the place of trial.

Article 2 – General Definitions
720 ILCS 5/2-0.5 et seq.

2-0.5. Definitions. For the purposes of this Code, the words and phrases described in this Article have the meanings designated in this Article, except when a particular context clearly requires a different meaning.

Commentary - Definitions

The Illinois criminal code has its own "official" definitions. These definitions are used by courts when interpreting the various provisions of the code unless the context of a particular statutory provision dictates otherwise. In some instances, courts use common or dictionary meanings for words or phrases. For example, in *People v. Comage* 241 Ill.2d 139, 946 N.E.2d 313 (Ill. S. Ct. 2011), the Court used the dictionary definition from Webster's Third International Dictionary of "conceal" where the obstructing justice statute had no definition for interpretation purposes.

§ 2-1. "Acquittal". "Acquittal" means a verdict or finding of not guilty of an offense, rendered by a legally constituted jury or by a court of competent jurisdiction authorized to try the case without a jury.

§ 2-2. "Act". "Act" includes a failure or omission to take action.

Commentary – Criminal Code Definitions

Criminal Code Definitions. An example of how an official definition may differ from a common definition is the word "act", which under Section 2—2 is described as "including an omission to act". A dictionary definition of "act" would not include a concept of "not acting". (See www.dictionary.com for "act" which defines the word when a noun, in part, as "anything done, being done or to be done" or as a verb, in part, as "to do something"). In *People v. Caruso* 119 Ill.2d 376, 619 N.E.2d 440 (Ill. S. Ct. 1987), the defendant kidnapped his children and held them out of state in violation of a court order providing custody to his spouse. He claimed that he had performed no act within Illinois that would provide jurisdiction to Illinois courts. The court noted that Illinois has eliminated the distinction between an act and an omission to act and that jurisdiction may be based on an omission to act that is based on a duty imposed by Illinois law. Thus the defendant had a duty to comply with an Illinois child custody order and his failure to return the children was an omission to act, based on a violation of that duty.

§ 2-3. "Another". "Another" means a person or persons as defined in this Code other than the offender.

§ 2-3.5. "Community policing volunteer" means a person who is summoned or directed by a peace officer or any person actively participating in a community policing program and who is engaged in lawful conduct intended to assist any unit of government in enforcing any criminal or civil law. For the purpose of this Section, "community policing program" means any plan, system or strategy established by and conducted under the auspices of a law enforcement agency in which citizens participate with and are guided by the law enforcement agency and work with members of that agency to reduce or prevent crime within a defined geographic area.

§ 2-3.6. "Armed with a firearm". Except as otherwise provided in a specific Section, a person is considered "armed with a firearm" when he or she carries on or about his or her person or is otherwise armed with a firearm.

§ 2-4. "Conduct". "Conduct" means an act or a series of acts, and the accompanying mental state.

§ 2-5. "Conviction". "Conviction" means a judgment of conviction or sentence entered upon a plea of guilty or upon a verdict or finding of guilty of an offense, rendered by a legally constituted jury or by a court of competent jurisdiction authorized to try the case without a jury.

Commentary - Conviction

Conviction. A conviction occurs when a judge enters a judgment of conviction or a sentencing judgment. the verdict of guilty by a jury after a trial or a finding of guilty by a judge after a trial or upon a plea of guilty is not alone a conviction. Indeed there are some case dispositions (Court supervision or First Offender Probation) that are desirable because no judgment of conviction is entered against the defendant. In the case of Driving Under the Influence of Alcohol, the absence of a judgment of conviction means that no revocation of an Illinois driver's license occurs. A juvenile adjudication in a delinquency case is not a conviction. See *People v. Taylor* 221 Ill.2d 157, 850 N.E.2d 134 (Ill. S. Ct. 2006).

§ 2-5.1. Day care center. "Day care center" has the meaning ascribed to it in Section 2.09 of the Child Care Act of 1969.

§ 2-5.2. Day care home. "Day care home" has the meaning ascribed to it in Section 2.18 of the Child Care Act of 1969.

§ 2-6. "Dwelling". (a) Except as otherwise provided in subsection (b) of this Section, "dwelling" means a building or portion thereof, a tent, a vehicle, or other enclosed space which is used or intended for use as a human habitation, home or residence.

(b) For the purposes of Section 19-3 of this Code, "dwelling" means a house, apartment, mobile home, trailer, or other living quarters in which at the time of the alleged offense the owners or occupants actually reside or in their absence intend within a reasonable period of time to reside.

Commentary - Dwelling

Dwelling. An example of a word having differing meanings based on the context of a statute is the word "dwelling", which has a general and broad definition in Section 2 – 6(a), meaning a structure of some type, including a vehicle "used or intended for use as a . . . . . home or residence" and in Section 2-6(b) when considered for the crime of Residential Burglary, means a structure where "owners or occupants actually reside or intend . . . within a reasonable period of time to reside." In *People v. McGee* 398 Ill.App.3d 789, 924 N.E.2d 612 (Ill. App. Ct. 1st Dist. 2010), the evidence was sufficient to support the conviction of the defendant who had entered a house that had been damaged by fire. The resident had lived in the house for over 20 years and stated that she intended to move back in at the earliest practicable time, even though, after the burglary, the house had gone into foreclosure and she had not, in fact, moved back in. This satisfied the meaning of "dwelling" under Section 2-6(b) for purposes of the defendant's conviction for Residential Burglary.

§ 2-6.5. Emergency medical technician. "Emergency medical technician-ambulance", "emergency medical technician-intermediate", and "emergency medical technician-paramedic" have the meanings ascribed to them in the

Emergency Medical Services (EMS) Systems Act.

§ 2-6.6. Emergency management worker. "Emergency management worker" shall include the following:

(a) any person, paid or unpaid, who is a member of a local or county emergency services and disaster agency as defined by the Illinois Emergency Management Agency Act, or who is an employee of the Illinois Emergency Management Agency or the Federal Emergency Management Agency;

(b) any employee or volunteer of the American Red Cross;

(c) any employee of a federal, State, county, or local government agency assisting an emergency services and disaster agency, the Illinois Emergency Management Agency, or the Federal Emergency Management Agency through mutual aid or as otherwise requested or directed in time of disaster or emergency; and

(d) any person volunteering or directed to assist an emergency services and disaster agency, the Illinois Emergency Management Agency, or the Federal Emergency Management Agency.

§ 2-7. "Felony". "Felony" means an offense for which a sentence to death or to a term of imprisonment in a penitentiary for one year or more is provided.

§ 2-7.1. "Firearm" and "firearm ammunition". "Firearm" and "firearm ammunition" have the meanings ascribed to them in Section 1.1 of the Firearm Owners Identification Card Act.

§ 2-7.5. "Firearm". Except as otherwise provided in a specific Section, "firearm" has the meaning ascribed to it in Section 1.1 of the Firearm Owners Identification Card Act.

Commentary - Firearm

Firearm. The official definition of "firearm" is found in the Firearm Owners Identification Act (FOID) 430 ILCS 65/1.1 which states that "'Firearm' means any device . . . which is designed to expel a projectile . . . by the action of an explosion, expansion of gas or escape of gas" but excludes pneumatic guns, BB guns, paint ball guns, antique weapons (as found by the Illinois State Police) and other such non-weapon devices. Similarly, the FOID Act states, "'Firearm ammunition' means any self-contained cartridge or shotgun shell . . . which is designed to be used or adaptable to use in a firearm" but excludes studs or rivets from an industrial device or safety flares.

§ 2-8. "Forcible felony". "Forcible felony" means treason, first degree murder, second degree murder, predatory criminal sexual assault of a child, aggravated criminal sexual assault, criminal sexual assault, robbery, burglary, residential burglary, aggravated arson, arson, aggravated kidnaping, kidnaping, aggravated battery resulting in great bodily harm or permanent disability or disfigurement and any other felony which involves the use or threat of physical force or violence against any individual.

Commentary – Forcible Felony

Forcible Felony. Having a conviction for a forcible felony can result in a more serious criminal charge or can be an enhancement for sentencing purposes. What a forcible is felony also plays a role in use of deadly force under Article 7 of the Criminal Code by police and citizens in response to conduct that constitutes the commission of a forcible felony. The Aggravated Battery offenses that meet the definition of forcible felony can have a great impact. There are multiple aggravating factors under Section 12-4 that can enhance a Battery offense to Aggravated Battery (committed on a public way, in a public or privately owned sports arena, a passenger of a transportation system, a taxi driver, etc.). Treating all aggravating factors the same would mean that deadly force (i.e. gunplay) would be arguably available as a response to any Battery offenses that could be argued to be "aggravated". The definition under Section 2-8 limits the qualifying Aggravated Battery offenses to those involving (1) great bodily harm, (2) permanent disability or (3) disfigurement. Thus in *In re Angelique E.* 389 Ill.App.3d 430, 907 N.E.2d 59 (Ill App. Ct. 2nd Dist. 2009), the Court found error in an adjudicated juvenile receiving a mandatory minimum 5 years probation based on the commission of a forcible felony - Aggravated Battery. Her offense consisted of resisting a municipal pool patrol officer who received only an abrasion and did not seek medical treatment. The Court noted that Aggravated Battery offenses as forcible felonies were limited to the three listed categories.

Identified Forcible Felonies. The enumerated offenses may seem obvious (treason, first degree murder, etc.), however, Illinois courts have grappled with the phrase "any other felony which involves the use or threat of force or violence against any individual". One of the potential applications of the forcible felony concept is charging First Degree Murder under the felony-murder doctrine, where the death of another individual occurs during the commission of a forcible felony. In *People v. Belk* 203 Ill.2d 187, 784 N.E.2d 825 (Ill. S. Ct. 2003), the defendant stole a van and fled from the police reaching speeds of over 100 miles per hour on city streets during business hours. He eventually crashed into the rear end of another vehicle, killing its two occupants. He was convicted of First Degree Murder under the felony murder rule, with the forcible felony being the commission of the offense of Aggravated Possession of a Stolen Vehicle. The Illinois Supreme Court noted that "any other felony" under the definition of forcible felony requires a finding that a threat of force or violence to an individual is present. Since no such facts existed in *Belk*, there could be no qualifying felony under the felony-murder doctrine and the defendant's murder conviction had to be reversed. In *People v. Schmidt* 392 Ill.App.3d 689, 924, N.E.2d 998 (Ill. App. Ct. 2009), the defendant was convicted of First Degree Murder. The defendant was driving a stolen SUV and accidentally struck a police officer in the arm with the mirror, who tried to stop him. During the flight from the officer, the defendant struck some pedestrians causing death. The predicate "forcible felony" for purposes of the felony-murder rule was the Aggravated Battery to the police officer. The Court reversed finding that the qualifying Aggravated Battery offense (great bodily harm, disability or disfigurement to the police officer) did not apply, and that the "other felony" rule likewise did not apply under the *Belk* rule, where there was no force or threat of force or violence to the police officer.

Attempted Murder as Forcible Felony. In *People v. Thomas* 407 Ill.App.3d 136, 943 N.E.2d 179 (Ill. App. Ct. 1st Dist. 2011), the Court construed the term "forcible felony" within the context of the Armed Habitual Criminal statute (720 ILCS 5/24-1.7) to include attempted murder as a qualifying offense. The court noted that attempted murder was not a specifically listed offense under the definition of forcible felony, but reasoned that since every attempted murder included an element of intent to cause death, it necessarily involved the use or threat of physical force or violence.

§ 2-8.1. Group day care home. "Group day care home" has the meaning ascribed to it in Section 2.20 of the Child Care Act of 1969.

§ 2-9. "Included offense". "Included offense" means an offense which (a) Is established by proof of the same or less than all of the facts or a less culpable mental state (or both), than that which is required to establish the commission of the offense charged, or (b) Consists of an attempt to commit the offense charged or an offense included therein.

§ 2-10. "Includes". "Includes" or "including" means comprehending among other particulars, without limiting the generality of the foregoing word or phrase.

§2-10.1. "Person with a severe or profound intellectual disability" means a person (i) whose intelligence quotient does not exceed 40 or (ii) whose intelligence quotient does not exceed 55 and who suffers from significant mental illness to the extent that the person's ability to exercise rational judgment is impaired. In any proceeding in which the defendant is charged with committing a violation of Section 10-2, 10-5, 11-1.30, 11-1.60, 11-14.4, 11-15.1, 11-19.1, 11-19.2, 11-20.1, 11-20.1B, 11-20.3, 12-4.3, 12-14, or 12-16, or subdivision (b)(1) of Section 12-3.05, of this Code against a victim who is alleged to be a person with a severe or profound intellectual disability, any findings concerning the victim's status as a person with a severe or profound intellectual disability, made by a court after a judicial admission hearing concerning the victim under Articles V and VI of Chapter IV of the Mental Health and Developmental Disabilities Code shall be admissible.

§ 2-10.2. Laser or laser device. "Laser" or "laser device" means any small or hand-held battery powered device which converts incident electromagnetic radiation of mixed frequencies to one or more discrete frequencies of highly amplified and coherent visible radiation or light. Proof that a particular device casts a small red dot or other similar small and discrete image or small and discrete visual signal upon a target surface at least 15 feet away creates a rebuttable presumption that the device is a laser. Flashlights and similar lamps, lanterns, lights, and penlights are not laser devices.

§ 2-10.3. Laser gunsight. "Laser gunsight" means any battery powered laser device manufactured to function as a firearm aiming device or sold as a firearm aiming device.

§ 2-11. "Misdemeanor". "Misdemeanor" means any offense for which a sentence to a term of imprisonment in other than a penitentiary for less than one year may be imposed.

§ 2-12. "Offense". "Offense" means a violation

of any penal statute of this State.

§ 2-12.1. Part day child care facility. "Part day child care facility" has the meaning ascribed to it in Section 2.10 of the Child Care Act of 1969.

§ 2-13. "Peace officer". "Peace officer" means (i) any person who by virtue of his office or public employment is vested by law with a duty to maintain public order or to make arrests for offenses, whether that duty extends to all offenses or is limited to specific offenses, or (ii) any person who, by statute, is granted and authorized to exercise powers similar to those conferred upon any peace officer employed by a law enforcement agency of this State.

For purposes of Sections concerning unlawful use of weapons, for the purposes of assisting an Illinois peace officer in an arrest, or when the commission of any offense under Illinois law is directly observed by the person, and statutes involving the false personation of a peace officer, false personation of a peace officer while carrying a deadly weapon, and aggravated false personation of a peace officer, then officers, agents, or employees of the federal government commissioned by federal statute to make arrests for violations of federal criminal laws shall be considered "peace officers" under this Code, including, but not limited to all criminal investigators of:

(1) the United States Department of Justice, the Federal Bureau of Investigation, the Drug Enforcement Agency and the Department of Immigration and Naturalization;

(2) the United States Department of the Treasury, the Secret Service, the Bureau of Alcohol, Tobacco and Firearms and the Customs Service;

(3) the United States Internal Revenue Service;

(4) the United States General Services Administration;

(5) the United States Postal Service;

(6) all United States Marshals or Deputy United States Marshals whose duties involve the enforcement of federal criminal laws; and

(7) the United States Department of Defense.

§ 2-14. "Penal institution". "Penal institution" means a penitentiary, state farm, reformatory, prison, jail, house of correction, or other institution for the incarceration or custody of persons under sentence for offenses or awaiting trial or sentence for offenses.

§ 2-15. "Person". "Person" means an individual, natural person, public or private corporation, government, partnership, unincorporated association, or other entity.

§ 2-15.5. "Personally discharged a firearm". A person is considered to have "personally discharged a firearm" when he or she, while armed with a firearm, knowingly and intentionally fires a firearm causing the ammunition projectile to be forcefully expelled from the firearm.

§ 2-15a. "Person with a physical disability". "Person with a physical disability" means a person who suffers from a permanent and disabling physical characteristic, resulting from disease, injury, functional disorder, or congenital condition.

§ 2-15b. "Place of worship" means a church, synagogue, mosque, temple, or other building, structure, or place used primarily for religious worship and includes the grounds of a place of worship.

§ 2-16. "Prosecution". "Prosecution" means all legal proceedings by which a person's liability for an offense is determined, commencing with the return of the indictment or the issuance of the information, and including the final disposition of the case upon appeal.

§ 2-17. "Public employee". "Public employee" means a person, other than a public officer, who is authorized to perform any official function on behalf of, and is paid by, the State or any of its political subdivisions.

§ 2-18. "Public officer". "Public officer" means

a person who is elected to office pursuant to statute, or who is appointed to an office which is established, and the qualifications and duties of which are prescribed, by statute, to discharge a public duty for the State or any of its political subdivisions.

§ 2-19. "Reasonable belief". "Reasonable belief" or "reasonably believes" means that the person concerned, acting as a reasonable man, believes that the described facts exist.

§ 2-19.5. "School" means a public, private, or parochial elementary or secondary school, community college, college, or university and includes the grounds of a school.

§ 2-20. "Solicit". "Solicit" or "solicitation" means to command, authorize, urge, incite, request, or advise another to commit an offense.

§ 2-21. "State". "State" or "this State" means the State of Illinois, and all land and water in respect to which the State of Illinois has either exclusive or concurrent jurisdiction, and the air space above such land and water. "Other state" means any state or territory of the United States, the District of Columbia and the Commonwealth of Puerto Rico.

§ 2-22. "Statute". "Statute" means the Constitution or an Act of the General Assembly of this State.

Article 3 – Rights Of Defendant
720 ILCS 5/3-1 *et seq.*

§ 3-1. Presumption of Innocence and Proof of Guilt. Every person is presumed innocent until proved guilty. No person shall be convicted of any offense unless his guilt thereof is proved beyond a reasonable doubt.

Commentary – Defendant Rights

Fundamental Rights of a Criminal Defendant. Section 3-1 codifies the fundamental rights of a criminal defendant. He is presumed to be innocent of any charges brought against him. The prosecution must prove him guilty beyond a reasonable doubt. While stated as statutory law, in fact, these principles of criminal procedure are due process protections of constitutional magnitude. *In re Winship 397* U.S. 357, 90 S.Ct. 1068 (U.S. S. Ct. 1970). Each element of a criminal offense must be proved beyond a reasonable doubt to establish the defendant's guilt. Thus, identity as an element of a crime must be proved beyond a reasonable doubt. *People v. Slim* 127 Ill.2d 302, 537 N.E.2d 317 (1989)(single witness identification of defendant sufficient for conviction in spite of alibi evidence). The concept of reasonable doubt needs no definition and it is error to have a jury instruction that attempts to do so. *People v. Cagle* 41 Ill.2d 528, 244 N.E.2d 200 (1969)(jury instruction which stated, in part, "the Court instructs the jury that a doubt, to justify acquittal, must be reasonable" was reversible error because it appeared to give a burden to the defendant to prove his innocence and was inconsistent with the presumption of innocence).

Single Witness Identification. Identity is often a key issue in proof beyond a reasonable doubt in a criminal case. In Illinois, a single witness' identification of the defendant as the perpetrator has been held to be sufficient evidence, beyond a reasonable doubt, on the issue of identify. *People v. Tatum* 389 Ill.App.3d 656, 906 N.E.2d 695 (Ill. App. Ct. 1st Dist. 2009)(claim that witness' identification of defendant was from seeing him the neighborhood reject, one good identification from a witness is sufficient to establish identify as an element of the crime).

§ 3-2. Affirmative defense. (a) "Affirmative defense" means that unless the State's evidence raises the issue involving the alleged defense, the defendant, to raise the issue, must present some evidence thereon.

(b) If the issue involved in an affirmative defense, other than insanity, is raised then the State must sustain the burden of proving the defendant guilty beyond a reasonable doubt as to that issue together with all the other elements of the offense. If the affirmative defense of insanity is raised, the defendant bears the burden of proving by clear and convincing evidence his insanity at the time of the offense.

Commentary – Affirmative Defense

Affirmative Defense. If the evidence at trial raises the issue of an affirmative defense, the burden is on the prosecution to negate that defense by proof beyond a reasonable doubt. The most common affirmative defenses are justifiable use of force (self-defense) and entrapment (the defendant's criminal conduct was wrongfully induced by the police). When the defendant's evidence raises the issue of entrapment, it is the prosecution's burden to prove the absence of entrapment. If the defendant's claim of entrapment is not refuted, he is entitled to an acquittal. *People v. Dollen* 53 Ill.2d 280, 290 N.E.2d 879 (1972)(drug conviction reversed where defendant's testimony that police informant asked him to sell narcotics left in a taxi cab was not rebutted). The requirement that the defendant produce "some evidence" of the affirmative defense is often described as a burden to come forward with evidence, as opposed to having a burden of proof.

Historically, insanity was an affirmative defense that followed the same principles of burden of proof. After the attempted assassination of President Reagan and the acquittal of John David Hinckley by reason of insanity, Illinois along with many other states, modified the affirmative defense requirements by imposing the burden of proof on the affirmative defense of insanity on the defendant. Although the burden of proof was initially "preponderance of the evidence", the statute was amended in 1995 to require the defendant to prove insanity by "clear and convincing" evidence.

§ 3-3. Multiple Prosecutions for Same Act. (a) When the same conduct of a defendant may establish the commission of more than one offense, the defendant may be prosecuted for each such offense.

(b) If the several offenses are known to the proper prosecuting officer at the time of commencing the prosecution and are within the jurisdiction of a single court, they must be prosecuted in a single prosecution, except as provided in Subsection (c), if they are based on the same act.

(c) When 2 or more offenses are charged as required by Subsection (b), the court in the interest of justice may order that one or more of such charges shall be tried separately.

Commentary – Multiple Prosecutions

Multiple Offenses. The course of conduct by a defendant on one occasion may result in the prosecution for multiple offenses. All of those offenses, if arising out of that course of conduct (i.e. the "same act"), must be joined for trial in the same court at the same time. In *People v. Izquierdo-Flores* 367 Ill.App.3d 377, 854 N.E.2d 1156 (Ill. App. 1st Dist. 2006), the Court recognized that charges of First Degree Murder and Second Degree Murder arising from the same facts must be charged together. However, under Section 3-3(b), a court does have discretion to order separate trials of offenses if it is in the interest of justice. In *People v. Collins* 214 Ill.App.3d 98, 573 N.E.2d 346 (Ill. App. Ct. 4th Dist. 1991), additional charges of sexual abuse were properly tried separately even though related to other sexual offense charges.

§ 3-4. Effect of former prosecution. (a) A prosecution is barred if the defendant was formerly prosecuted for the same offense, based upon the same facts, if that former prosecution:

(1) resulted in either a conviction or an acquittal or in a determination that the evidence was insufficient to warrant a conviction;

(2) was terminated by a final order or judgment, even if entered before trial, that required a determination inconsistent with any fact or legal proposition necessary to a conviction in the subsequent prosecution; or

(3) was terminated improperly after the jury was impaneled and sworn or, in a trial before a court without a jury, after the first witness was sworn but before findings were rendered by the trier of facts, or after a plea of guilty was accepted by the court.

A conviction of an included offense, other than through a plea of guilty, is an acquittal of the offense charged.

(b) A prosecution is barred if the defendant was formerly prosecuted for a different offense, or for the same offense based upon different facts, if that former prosecution:

(1) resulted in either a conviction or an acquittal, and the subsequent prosecution is for an offense of which the defendant could have been convicted on the former prosecution; or was for an offense with which the defendant should have been charged on the former prosecution, as provided in Section 3-3 of this Code (unless the court ordered a separate trial of that charge); or was for an offense that involves the same conduct, unless each prosecution requires proof of a fact not required on the other prosecution, or the offense was not consummated when the former trial began;

(2) was terminated by a final order or judgment, even if entered before trial, that required a determination inconsistent with any fact necessary to a conviction in the subsequent prosecution; or

(3) was terminated improperly under the circumstances stated in subsection (a), and the subsequent prosecution is for an offense of which the defendant could have been convicted if the former prosecution had not been terminated improperly.

(c) A prosecution is barred if the defendant was formerly prosecuted in a District Court of the United States or in a sister state for an offense that is within the concurrent jurisdiction of this State, if that former prosecution:

(1) resulted in either a conviction or an acquittal, and the subsequent prosecution is for the same conduct, unless each prosecution requires proof of a fact not required in the other prosecution, or the offense was not consummated when the former trial began; or

(2) was terminated by a final order or judgment, even if entered before trial, that required a determination inconsistent with any fact necessary to a conviction in the prosecution in this State.

(d) A prosecution is not barred within the meaning of this Section 3-4, however, if the former prosecution:

(1) was before a court that lacked jurisdiction over the defendant or the offense; or

(2) was procured by the defendant without the knowledge of the proper prosecuting officer, and with the purpose of avoiding the sentence that otherwise might be imposed; or if subsequent proceedings resulted in the invalidation, setting aside, reversal, or vacating of the conviction, unless the defendant was thereby adjudged not guilty.

Commentary – Former Prosecution

Double Jeopardy. The purpose of Section 3-4 is to codify the constitutional principles against double jeopardy. Generally speaking, under the Fifth Amendment to the U.S. Constitution, a defendant is not required to face the same criminal charges more than once. If a trial has commenced by a jury being selected or witnesses being sworn, the law says that "jeopardy" has attached. If the defendant is acquitted, he cannot be tried again for the same conduct. However, if the new charge is based on different facts, the principles of jeopardy and this statute would not prevent a second prosecution. In *People v. Mueller* 109 Ill.2d 378, 488 N.E2d 523 (1985, the defendant was charged with murder for shooting two victims at his Cass County farm, but acquitted based on a claim of self-defense. Thereafter, he was charged and convicted of Concealment of a Homicide for hiding the bodies in a creek in Scott County. In affirming his conviction, the Court reasoned that the additional facts regarding the concealment offense were separate from the facts of the murder charges.

If the trial is terminated based on improper conduct of the prosecution, it is possible that a re-trial could be barred if it could be shown, for example, that a mistrial was caused by the prosecution engaging in conduct to provoke the termination of the trial.

§ 3-5. General Limitations. (a) A prosecution for: (1) first degree murder, attempt to commit first degree murder, second degree murder, involuntary manslaughter, reckless homicide, leaving the scene of a motor vehicle accident involving death or personal injuries under Section 11-401 of the Illinois Vehicle Code, failing to give information and render aid under Section 11-403 of the Illinois Vehicle Code, concealment of homicidal death, treason, arson, aggravated arson, forgery, child pornography under paragraph (1) of subsection (a) of Section 11-20.1, aggravated child pornography under paragraph (1) of subsection (a) of Section 11-20.1B, or (2) any offense involving sexual conduct or sexual penetration, as defined by Section 11-0.1 of this Code in which the DNA profile of the offender is obtained and entered into a DNA database within 10 years after the commission of the offense, may be commenced at any time. Clause (2) of this subsection (a) applies if either: (i) the victim reported the offense to law enforcement authorities within 3 years after the commission of the offense unless a longer period for reporting the offense to law enforcement authorities is provided in Section 3-6 or (ii) the victim is murdered during the course of the offense or within 2 years after the commission of the offense.

(b) Unless the statute describing the offense provides otherwise, or the period of limitation is extended by Section 3-6, a prosecution for any offense not designated in Subsection (a) must be commenced within 3 years after the commission of the offense if it is a felony, or within one year and 6 months after its commission if it is a misdemeanor.

§ 3-6. Extended limitations. The period within which a prosecution must be commenced under the provisions of Section 3-5 or other applicable statute is extended under the following conditions:

(a) A prosecution for theft involving a breach of a fiduciary obligation to the aggrieved person may be commenced as follows:

(1) If the aggrieved person is a minor or a person under legal disability, then during the minority or legal disability or within one year after the termination thereof.

(2) In any other instance, within one year after the discovery of the offense by an aggrieved person, or by a person who has legal capacity to represent an aggrieved person or has a legal duty to report the offense, and is not himself or herself a party to the offense; or in the absence of such discovery, within one year after the proper prosecuting officer becomes aware of the offense. However, in no such case is the period of limitation so extended more than 3 years beyond the expiration of the period otherwise applicable.

(b) A prosecution for any offense based upon misconduct in office by a public officer or employee may be commenced within one year after discovery of the offense by a person having a legal duty to report such offense, or in the absence of such discovery, within one year after the proper prosecuting officer becomes aware of the offense. However, in no such case is the period of limitation so extended more than 3 years beyond the expiration of the period otherwise applicable.

(c) (Blank).

(d) A prosecution for child pornography, aggravated child pornography, indecent solicitation of a child, soliciting for a juvenile prostitute, juvenile pimping, exploitation of a child, or promoting juvenile prostitution except for keeping a place of juvenile prostitution may be commenced within one year of the victim attaining the age of 18 years. However, in no such case shall the time period for prosecution expire sooner than 3 years after the commission of the offense. When the victim is under 18 years of age, a prosecution for criminal sexual abuse may be commenced within one year of the victim attaining the age of 18 years. However, in no such case shall the time period for prosecution expire sooner than 3 years after the commission of the offense.

(e) Except as otherwise provided in subdivision (j), a prosecution for any offense involving sexual conduct or sexual penetration, as defined in Section 11-0.1 of this Code, where the defendant was within a professional or fiduciary relationship or a purported professional or fiduciary relationship with the victim at the time of the commission of the offense may be commenced within one year after the discovery of the offense by the victim.

(f) A prosecution for any offense set forth in Section 44 of the "Environmental Protection Act", approved June 29, 1970, as amended,1 may be commenced within 5 years after the discovery of such an offense by a person or agency having the legal duty to report the offense or in the absence of such discovery, within 5 years after the proper prosecuting officer becomes aware of the offense.

(f-5) A prosecution for any offense set forth in Section 16-30 of this Code may be commenced within 5 years after the discovery of the offense by the victim of that offense.

(g) (Blank).

(h) (Blank).

(i) Except as otherwise provided in subdivision (j), a prosecution for criminal sexual assault, aggravated criminal sexual assault, or aggravated criminal sexual abuse may be commenced within 10 years of the commission of the offense if the victim reported the offense to law enforcement authorities within 3 years after the commission of the offense.

Nothing in this subdivision (i) shall be construed to shorten a period within which a prosecution must be commenced under any other provision of this Section.

(i-5) A prosecution for armed robbery, home invasion, kidnapping, or aggravated kidnaping may be commenced within 10 years of the commission of the offense if it arises out of the same course of conduct and meets the criteria under one of the offenses in subsection (i) of this Section.

(j) When the victim is under 18 years of age at the time of the offense, a prosecution for criminal sexual assault, aggravated criminal sexual assault, predatory criminal sexual assault of a child, aggravated criminal sexual abuse, or felony criminal sexual abuse, or a prosecution for failure of a person who is required to report an alleged or suspected commission of any of these offenses under the Abused and Neglected Child Reporting Act may be commenced within 20 years after the child victim attains 18 years of age. When the victim is under 18 years of age at the time of the offense, a prosecution for misdemeanor criminal sexual abuse may be commenced within 10 years after the child victim attains 18 years of age.

Nothing in this subdivision (j) shall be construed to shorten a period within which a prosecution must be commenced under any other provision of this Section.

(k) A prosecution for theft involving real

property exceeding $100,000 in value under Section 16-1, identity theft under subsection (a) of Section 16-30, aggravated identity theft under subsection (b) of Section 16-30, or any offense set forth in Article 16H or Section 17-10.6 may be commenced within 7 years of the last act committed in furtherance of the crime.

(1) A prosecution for any offense set forth in Section 26-4 of this Code may be commenced within one year after the discovery of the offense by the victim of that offense.

3-7. Periods excluded from limitation. (a) The period within which a prosecution must be commenced does not include any period in which:

(1) the defendant is not usually and publicly resident within this State; or

(2) the defendant is a public officer and the offense charged is theft of public funds while in public office; or

(3) a prosecution is pending against the defendant for the same conduct, even if the indictment or information which commences the prosecution is quashed or the proceedings thereon are set aside, or are reversed on appeal; or

(4) a proceeding or an appeal from a proceeding relating to the quashing or enforcement of a Grand Jury subpoena issued in connection with an investigation of a violation of a criminal law of this State is pending. However, the period within which a prosecution must be commenced includes any period in which the State brings a proceeding or an appeal from a proceeding specified in this paragraph (4); or

(5) a material witness is placed on active military duty or leave. In this paragraph (5) "material witness" includes, but is not limited to, the arresting officer, occurrence witness, or the alleged victim of the offense; or

(6) the victim of unlawful force or threat of imminent bodily harm to obtain information or a confession is incarcerated, and the victim's incarceration, in whole or in part, is a consequence of the unlawful force or threats; or .

(7) the sexual assault evidence is collected and submitted to the Department of State Police until the completion of the analysis of the submitted evidence.

(b) For the purposes of this Section:
"Completion of the analysis of the submitted evidence" means analysis of the collected evidence and conducting of laboratory tests and the comparison of the collected evidence with the genetic marker grouping analysis information maintained by the Department of State Police under Section 5-4-3 of the Unified Code of Corrections and with the information contained in the Federal Bureau of Investigation's National DNA database.
"Sexual assault" has the meaning ascribed to it in Section 1a of the Sexual Assault Survivors Emergency Treatment Act.
"Sexual assault evidence" has the meaning ascribed to it in Section 5 of the Sexual Assault Evidence Submission Act.

§ 3-8. Limitation on offense based on series of acts. When an offense is based on a series of acts performed at different times, the period of limitation prescribed by this Article starts at the time when the last such act is committed.

Commentary - Limitations

Statute of Limitations. Most criminal offenses must be charged within a limitations period, commonly referred to as a statute of limitations. The ordinary limitations period set forth in Section 3-5(b) is three years from the commission of the offense for a felony and one year and six (6) months from the commission of the offense for a misdemeanor. If an offense is not charged within the applicable statute of limitations, prosecution is forever barred and the filing of charges beyond the time limit prescribed by law would be subject to a motion to dismiss.

Section 3-5(a)(1) notes the exception to general limitations that there is no limitations period for the enumerated offenses and they may be brought at any time. Among those offenses are the crimes of First Degree Murder, Attempted First Degree Murder, Second Degree Murder, Involuntary Manslaughter, Reckless Homicide, Treason and Concealment of a Homicidal Death. Section 3(a)(2) identifies offenses where there is no limitations period when certain events have occurred – such as the report of a sexual assault within three years of its occurrence or the entry of DNA into a law enforcement data bank within 10 years of the assault.

The time for filing charges can be "extended" (Section 3-6) or "tolled" (Section 3-7) under certain circumstances. For example under, Section 3-6, if a sexual assault occurred between family members and the victim was a minor, the limitations period could be extended to one year past the victim's 18th birthday. Or under Section 3-5, if charges were pending on appeal or the subject of appeal, and additional offenses were charged thereafter, the time period during which charges were pending would be excluded (i.e. "tolled") from the calculation of the limitations period. In *People v. Gray* 396 Ill.App.3d 216, 924 N.E.2d 1109 (Ill. App. Ct. 4th Dist. 2009), the defendant was charged in 2001 with criminal sexual assault of his 11 and 12 year old daughters for conduct alleged to have occurred in 1999. Thereafter, in June 2006, he was charged and convicted of predatory criminal sexual assault for the same conduct, after both his daughters had turned 18 and one year had passed. His claim that the second set of charges should be dismissed as beyond the statute of limitations was rejected because the time the charges were pending was excluded from the limitations period.

Title II. Principles of Criminal Liability

Article Four – Criminal Act and Mental State
720 ILCS 5/4-1 *et seq.*

§ 4-1. Voluntary act. A material element of every offense is a voluntary act, which includes an omission to perform a duty which the law imposes on the offender and which he is physically capable of performing.

§ 4-2. Possession as voluntary act. Possession is a voluntary act if the offender knowingly procured or received the thing possessed, or was aware of his control thereof for a sufficient time to have been able to terminate his possession.

Commentary – Voluntary Act

Voluntary Act. Remembering that a criminal offense has two elements – an act and an accompanying mental state – suggests that crimes ordinarily are not committed involuntarily or by accident. The conduct must be voluntary – a product of the will of the person who is charged. In the same sense, possession of a drug or a gun or other contraband must be voluntary. The law does recognize that one can have exclusive control over such contraband in the voluntary sense by having actual or constructive possession – the ability to control the location or movement of the object.

§ 4-3. Mental state. (a) A person is not guilty of an offense, other than an offense which involves absolute liability, unless, with respect to each element described by the statute defining the offense, he acts while having one of the mental states described in Sections 4-4 through 4-7 [720 ILCS 5/4-4 through 720 ILCS 5/4-7].

(b) If the statute defining an offense prescribed a particular mental state with respect to the offense as a whole, without distinguishing among the elements thereof, the prescribed mental state applies to each such element. If the statute does not prescribe a particular mental state applicable to an element of an offense (other than an offense which involves absolute liability), any mental state defined in Sections 4-4, 4-5 or 4-6 [720 ILCS 5/4-4, 720 ILCS 5/4-5 or 720 ILCS 5/4-6] is applicable.

(c) Knowledge that certain conduct constitutes an offense, or knowledge of the existence, meaning, or application of the statute defining an offense, is not an element of the offense

unless the statute clearly defines it as such.

§ 4-4. **Intent**. A person intends, or acts intentionally or with intent, to accomplish a result or engage in conduct described by the statute defining the offense, when his conscious objective or purpose is to accomplish that result or engage in that conduct.

§ **4-5. Knowledge.** A person knows, or acts knowingly or with knowledge of:

(a) The nature or attendant circumstances of his or her conduct, described by the statute defining the offense, when he or she is consciously aware that his or her conduct is of that nature or that those circumstances exist. Knowledge of a

material fact includes awareness of the substantial probability that the fact exists.

(b) The result of his or her conduct, described by the statute defining the offense, when he or she is consciously aware that that result is practically certain to be caused by his conduct. Conduct performed knowingly or with knowledge is performed willfully, within the meaning of a statute using the term "willfully", unless the statute clearly requires another meaning.

When the law provides that acting knowingly suffices to establish an element of an offense, that element also is established if a person acts intentionally.

§ **4-6. Recklessness.** A person is reckless or acts recklessly when that person consciously disregards a substantial and unjustifiable risk that circumstances exist or that a result will follow, described by the statute defining the offense, and that disregard constitutes a gross deviation from the standard of care that a reasonable person would exercise in the situation. An act performed recklessly is performed wantonly, within the meaning of a statute using the term "wantonly", unless the statute clearly requires another meaning.

§ **4-7. Negligence**. A person is negligent, or acts negligently, when that person fails to be aware of a substantial and unjustifiable risk that circumstances exist or a result will follow, described by the statute defining the offense, and that failure constitutes a substantial deviation from the standard of care that a reasonable person would exercise in the situation.

4-8. Ignorance or Mistake. (a) A person's ignorance or mistake as to a matter of either fact or law, except as provided in Section 4-3(c) above, is a defense if it negatives the existence of the mental state which the statute prescribes with respect to an element of the offense.

(b) A person's reasonable belief that his conduct does not constitute an offense is a defense if:
(1) The offense is defined by an administrative regulation or order which is not known to him and has not been published or otherwise made reasonably available to him, and he could not have acquired such knowledge by the exercise of due diligence pursuant to facts known to him; or

(2) He acts in reliance upon a statute which later is determined to be invalid; or

(3) He acts in reliance upon an order or opinion of an Illinois Appellate or Supreme Court, or a United States appellate court later overruled or reversed;

(4) He acts in reliance upon an official interpretation of the statute, regulation or order defining the offense, made by a public officer or agency legally authorized to interpret such statute.

(c) Although a person's ignorance or mistake of fact or law, or reasonable belief, described in this Section 4-8 is a defense to the offense charged, he may be convicted of an included offense of which he would be guilty if the fact or law were as he believed it to be.

(d) A defense based upon this Section 4-8 is an affirmative defense.

§ 4-9. Absolute liability. A person may be guilty of an offense without having, as to each element thereof, one of the mental states described in Sections 4-4 through 4-7 if the offense is a misdemeanor which is not punishable by incarceration or by a fine exceeding $1,000, or the statute defining the offense clearly indicates a legislative purpose to impose absolute liability for the conduct described.

Commentary – Mental States

Mental State. Sections 4-3 to 4-9 address the second element of a criminal offense – the actor's mental state. Every crime that can result in incarceration for a misdemeanor or felony conviction must have one of the mental states set forth in Sections 4-4 through 4-7. To be guilty, the defendant must have acted with intent, knowledge, recklessness or negligence as to the required elements of each criminal offense. The importance of the second element of an offense was relied upon in *People v. Madrigal* 241 Ill.2d 463, 948 N.E.2d 591 (Ill. S. Ct. 2011), where the Court found facially unconstitutional a section of the Identity Theft statute, 720 ILCS 5/16G-15(a)(7), because it failed to have the requirement of a culpable criminal *mens rea*, and thus would criminalize otherwise innocent conduct. This section of the felony statute criminalized the knowing use of name, date of birth, telephone number or other identifying information to obtain "any record of actions taken, communications made or received, or other activities or transactions of that person". Innocent activities such as a husband checking on the status of his wife's car at a repair shop or a wife checking to see if a husband had checked into a hotel would be arguably criminal under such a statute that lacked a mental state about the criminal purpose behind the knowing use of the personal identification records. A statute is facially unconstitutional if it does not rationally reach the targeted criminal conduct and where, as here, it potentially subjected someone to criminal penalty for wholly innocent conduct.

Ignorance of the Law. Section 4-8 provides that it is not a defense to a criminal charge that the defendant did not actually know the law or was mistaken as to what the law actually provides, unless he acted in reliance on an administrative regulation, a statute that was later determined to be invalid, a decision of a court that was later overruled or an interpretation of the law by a public officer who had the authority to make an interpretation. Ignorance or mistake of law in these limited circumstances is an affirmative defense.

Absolute Liability Offenses. Section 4-9 describes that certain offenses that are fine-only, not exceeding $1000, can be "absolute liability" offenses, for which no mental state can be prescribed. These would be described as petty offenses. The Illinois legislature could also expressly define an offense as an absolute liability offense as a matter of public policy.

Intent. Intent, under Section 4 – 4, is the conscious purpose to perform acts underlying the offense to obtain a result or conscious objective. Circumstantial evidence is most often used to prove intent (and other mental states) but often the defendant's own words are the best evidence of intent. In *People v. Felton* 376 Ill.App.3d 1041, 879 N.E.2d 350 (Ill. App. Ct. 2nd Dist. 2007), the defendant was charged with obstruction of justice for providing false information to the police with the intent to prevent the apprehension of Marcus Jones, who had been a passenger in the defendant's car. The defendant had loaned the car to her cousin, Carl King. The defendant, when interviewed by the police, told them she did not permit anyone to use her car and had not permitted anyone to drive it on the relevant date. Carl King testified for the prosecution that he had driven the defendant's car with her approval and that Marcus Jones, a passenger in the car, had been in an altercation at a convenience store. Felton's claim that the prosecution had failed to prove criminal intent was rejected.

Knowledge. Knowledge, under Section 4-5, is the awareness that facts or circumstances exist, or that actions or omissions create a strong probability that a result will occur. In Illinois, knowingly and willfully are considered the same thing. Something that is done intentionally by a person is also done knowingly, but something done knowingly is not necessarily done intentionally. In *People v. Lessade* 403 Ill.App.3d 609, 935 N.E.2d 1041 (Ill. App. Ct. 2nd Dist. 2010), the defendant was convicted of unlawful restraint (720 ILCS 5/10-3 - the knowing detention of another without lawful authority) when he held his former girlfriend by the throat and forced her back on a couch during an incident where he removed their two children from her home. The defendant claimed that he did not act knowingly because his conduct constituted a domestic battery not the victim's detention. The court noted that knowledge is often proved by the surrounding circumstances and that the defendant had to realize the practical certainty that his grasp of the victim's throat and refusal to release her was a detention. On the other hand, in *People v. Hinton* 402 Ill.App.3d 181, 931 N.E.3d 939 (Ill. App. Ct. 3rd. Dist. 2010), the defendant was charged with criminal violation of an order of protection (720 ILCS 5/12-30 – violation of the terms of an order of a protection with notice or actual knowledge of its existence). The defendant, while in jail in October 2007, had been served with an emergency order of protection that prohibited his contact with a specific address. The defendant was not released from custody until January, 2008 and was arrested at the prohibited address on February 24, 2008. The emergency order had been extended as a plenary order for two years at a hearing on November 14, 2008. In reversing the defendant's conviction the court noted that there was no evidence the defendant had been served with the November 14 plenary order thus failing to meet the "notice or actual knowledge" requirement.

Recklessness. Recklessness, under Section 4–6, is conduct done with a conscious disregard of a substantial and unjustifiable risk – a gross deviation from what a reasonable person would ordinarily do or not do. A person acting recklessly is not acting with knowledge or intent under the criminal code. In each of the three mental states – intent, knowledge and recklessness – there is an awareness of risk. In "intent", the risk is the conscious purpose of the conduct; in "knowledge", there is an accompanying strong probability that the risk's results will ensue; but in "recklessness", there is a conscious disregard of the probable consequences of the risk. Each mental state thus differs from the other. *People v. Hulitt* 361 Ill.App.3d 634, 838 N.E.2d 148 (Ill App. Ct. 1st Dist. 2005)(where the defendant tied the hands of her crying child and put a stocking in her mouth causing her death, her conduct constituted murder because it was knowing and was not involuntary manslaughter done recklessly). Indiscriminately pointing or shooting a loaded gun can be reckless conduct. Driving under the influence of alcohol, driving at excessive speeds, erratic driving changing lanes or running through traffic controls are all typical patterns of conduct that support findings of recklessness. The focus is on the gross deviation from what a reasonable person would do. However, the intentional or knowing deviation, such as firing into a crowd with a gun, is not recklessness. In *People v. Kolzow* 301 Ill.App.3d 1, 703 N.E.2d 424 (Ill. App. Ct. 1st Dist. 1998), the defendant's conduct was found to be reckless where she left her 3 month-old son in a car for three hours with the windows up in August, causing heat stroke, and was convicted of involuntary manslaughter.

Negligence. Negligence, under Section 4-7, is the failure to be aware of the presence of a substantial or unjustifiable risk and that failure is a substantial deviation of the standard of care of a reasonable person. There are few offenses based on criminal negligence.

Article Five – Parties to Crime
720 ILCS 5/5-1 *et seq.*

§ 5-1. Accountability for Conduct of Another. A person is responsible for conduct which is an element of an offense if the conduct is either that of the person himself, or that of another and he is legally accountable for such conduct as provided in Section 5-2, or both.

§ 5-2. When accountability exists. A person is legally accountable for the conduct of another when:

(a) having a mental state described by the statute defining the offense, he or she causes another to perform the conduct, and the other person in fact or by reason of legal incapacity lacks such a mental state;

(b) the statute defining the offense makes him or her so accountable; or

(c) either before or during the commission of an offense, and with the intent to promote or facilitate that commission, he or she solicits, aids, abets, agrees, or attempts to aid that other person in the planning or commission of the offense.

When 2 or more persons engage in a common criminal design or agreement, any acts in the furtherance of that common design committed by one party are considered to be the acts of all parties to the common design or agreement and all are equally responsible for the consequences of those further acts. Mere presence at the scene of a crime does not render a person accountable for an offense; a person's presence at the scene of a crime, however, may be considered with other circumstances by the trier of fact when determining accountability.

A person is not so accountable, however, unless the statute defining the offense provides otherwise, if:

(1) he or she is a victim of the offense committed;

(2) the offense is so defined that his or her conduct was inevitably incident to its commission; or

(3) before the commission of the offense, he or she terminates his or her effort to promote or facilitate that commission and does one of the following: (i) wholly deprives his or her prior efforts of effectiveness in that commission, (ii) gives timely warning to the proper law enforcement authorities, or (iii) otherwise makes proper effort to prevent the commission of the offense.

§ 5-3. Separate Conviction of Person Accountable. A person who is legally accountable for the conduct of another which is an element of an offense may be convicted upon proof that the offense was committed and that he was so accountable, although the other person claimed to have committed the offense has not been prosecuted or convicted, or has been convicted of a different offense or degree of offense, or is not amenable to justice, or has been acquitted.

§ 5-4. Responsibility of corporation. (a) A corporation may be prosecuted for the commission of an offense if, but only if:

(1) The offense is a misdemeanor, or is defined by Sections 11-20, 11-20.1 or 24-1 of this Code, or Section 44 of the "Environmental Protection Act", approved June 29, 1970, as amended1 or is defined by another statute which clearly indicates a legislative purpose to impose liability on a corporation; and an agent of the corporation performs the conduct which is an element of the offense while acting within the scope of his or her office or employment and in behalf of the corporation, except that any limitation in the defining statute, concerning the corporation's accountability for certain agents or under certain circumstances, is applicable; or

(2) The commission of the offense is authorized, requested, commanded, or performed, by the

board of directors or by a high managerial agent who is acting within the scope of his or her employment in behalf of the corporation.

(b) A corporation's proof, by a preponderance of the evidence, that the high managerial agent having supervisory responsibility over the conduct which is the subject matter of the offense exercised due diligence to prevent the commission of the offense, is a defense to a prosecution for any offense to which Subsection (a)(1) refers, other than an offense for which absolute liability is imposed. This Subsection is inapplicable if the legislative purpose of the statute defining the offense is inconsistent with the provisions of this Subsection.

(c) For the purpose of this Section:

(1) "Agent" means any director, officer, servant, employee, or other person who is authorized to act in behalf of the corporation.

(2) "High managerial agent" means an officer of the corporation, or any other agent who has a position of comparable authority for the formulation of corporate policy or the supervision of subordinate employees in a managerial capacity.

§ 5-5. Accountability for Conduct of Corporation. (a) A person is legally accountable for conduct which is an element of an offense and which, in the name or in behalf of a corporation, he performs or causes to be performed, to the same extent as if the conduct were performed in his own name or behalf.

(b) An individual who has been convicted of an offense by reason of his legal accountability for the conduct of a corporation is subject to the punishment authorized by law for an individual upon conviction of such offense, although only a lesser or different punishment is authorized for the corporation.

Commentary – Criminal Responsibility for Acts or Crimes of Another

Accountability. Crimes are often the result of multiple people acting together to achieve a criminal objective. Sections 5–1 through 5-5 describe the circumstances where the liability for the commission of an offense can be shared based on the participatory roles in the crime. In general, the person or persons with direct responsibility for the crime who perform the acts to complete the crime are called principals. Others who help them before or during the commission of the crime are called aiders and abettors. Each one of the people who participate in the commission of the crime with the goal or understanding that the crime will be committed is guilty of the crime. This criminal liability of the aider or abettor is called accountability.

Sections 5-1 and 5-2 establish criminal liability for one who aids, abets, solicits or attempts to do so in the planning or commission of the crime. When several individuals act in concert, the act of any one of them is the act of all of them. There is a form of criminal agency at work where it is expected that each member of the criminal team is acting on behalf of the entire team when his conduct moves the crime toward ultimate commission. But in each scenario, the person who is being reviewed for liability based on accountability must have either the mental state required by the statute that defines the crime or must have the specific intent when acting that the crime be committed. Not everyone who assists in the commission of the crime has accountability – the ordinary postman who delivers the drugs certainly aids in the commission of the offense, but he lacks a criminal mental state since he knows nothing of what is in the package he is delivering. The victim of a crime certainly is no part of the criminal team, and someone who participated in the planning or early stages of the crime can avoid liability by stopping the effort and (1) removing any effect of what he had done before withdrawal from the enterprise; or (2) notifying law enforcement to report the crime or (3) making a serious effort to stop the crime from happening. The statute specifically notes that mere presence at the scene of a crime does not make one a criminal, but presence at the scene is one of the circumstantial factors that can be considered in deciding accountability. In *People v. Perez* 189 Ill.2d 254, 725 N.E.2d 1258 (2000), the defendant, Perez, stopped his car, got out and exchanged words with the victim (Gonzalez) about gang membership. The defendant got back into his car and drove away as Gonzalez was being shot and killed by another gang member. Perez's conviction on the basis of accountability was reversed because there was no showing that he had intent to participate in the shooting. Even his gang association and flight from the scene did not establish that Perez was part of any common design, effort or encouragement that the crime be committed.

Section 5-3 provides that a person guilty on the basis of accountability is just as guilty as the main perpetrator of the offense. The accountable person faces criminal liability for a range of offenses that his conduct supports, even if others involved in the crime are found guilty of different offenses, or if others (including the principal actor) are not charged, have the charges dismissed or are found not guilty. Prosecution of the criminal combination of many people addresses the danger of criminals who avoid detection by dividing responsibility. The seemingly innocent acts of different individuals can add up to the planning and commission of the crime.

In the model armed robbery, one could case the convenience store and serve as a lookout, one could be the driver, one could enter the store disguised as a utility worker and take care of the security cameras and finally, one could enter the store with a gun and actually threaten the clerk and take the money. The plan would be to divide the criminal proceeds. Assuming all were charged with armed robbery, all would be equally guilty even though there was only one actor with a gun who took the money. In fact, there could be a mastermind who did nothing but come up with the plan and convince the others to execute it. If the actual robber shot and killed the clerk, each of the aiders and abettors could be held criminally responsible for murder because it was done to further the criminal scheme and was foreseeable. This example closely tracks the facts and holdings in *People v. Sangster* 91 Ill.2d 260, 437 N.E.2d 625 (1982), *People v. Lewis (Cornelius)* 88 Ill.2d 128, 430 N.E.2d. 1346 (1981) and *People v. Lewis (Bernice)* 88 S.Ct. 429, 430 N.E.2d 994 (1981) where convictions of three defendants for murder, armed robbery and aggravated kidnapping were upheld where the facts established roles as the mastermind (Willie Sangster), the assistant (Bernice Lewis) and the kidnapper and shooter (Cornelius Lewis). Indeed consistent with Section 5-3, a fourth actor, the lookout and get-away driver (Maurice Farris) received immunity and was not prosecuted. Sangster, under principles of accountability, was liable for all the offenses although he planned only the robbery and recruited the Lewis brother and sister to commit it, because the common design of the scheme would include all crimes committed that were incident to the robbery's completion – including the murder and kidnapping.

In *People v. Fernandez* 2014 IL 115527 ¶18, the Defendant was convicted, after a bench trial, of Burglary and Aggravated Discharge of a Firearm under an accountability theory. The defendant admitted that he was guilty of Burglary but contended he lacked specific, concurrent intent to commit the firearm offense where there was no evidence he was aware that his co-defendant was armed. In affirming the firearm offense conviction, the Court confirmed the common law principle of "common design". The Court noted that "where one aids another in the planning or commission of an offense, that person is legally accountable for the conduct of the person he aids; and that the word 'conduct' encompasses any criminal act done in furtherance of the planned and intended act".

In *People v. Malcolm* 2015 IL (1st) 133406 the Defendant's convictions for murder and robbery were affirmed under an accountability theory, where he had video recorded the killing on a cell phone. The Defendant claimed that the incident was spontaneous and that he played no role in the crime because it was spontaneous. The Court noted that the video contained the statement of a co-defendant that he was "going to knock the motherf**ker out" and with the later posting of the video on Facebook, the Defendant's actions and knowledge were sufficient to establish the elements of accountability. The Court stated:

> This is a case of first impression, which involves the recording of a crime and the accountability of the person doing the recording. After reviewing all the facts of the case at hand, the applicable Illinois statutes and supporting case law, this court affirms the trial court's decision to convict the defendant of first-degree murder and robbery based on the theory of accountability and we hold that a rational trier of fact could have found the essential elements of the crimes beyond a reasonable doubt.
>
> *People v. Malcolm* 2015 IL App (1st) 133406 at ¶53.

Corporate responsibility. Corporations are "persons" for purposes of criminal and civil liability and are created by act of law. Corporations commit crimes through the actions of its agents and Section 5-4 recognizes criminal liability for a corporation for acts authorized by its board of director or by a high managerial agent. In *People v. Universal Pub. Transp., Inc.* 2012 IL App (1st) 073303-B, 974 N.E.2d 251, the defendant company provided transportation services for Medicaid recipients and falsely billed for trips by increasing mileage and other devices. Because one of its principal agents was found guilty of theft by this scheme, the corporation was also criminally liable. Under 720 ILCS 5/16-1(a)(5)(A), the company committed theft when its high managerial agent had knowingly exercised unauthorized control of funds of the State of Illinois with the intent to permanently deprive Illinois of the benefit of those funds.

Article Six – Responsibility
720 ILCS 5/6-1 *et seq.*

§ 6-1. Infancy. No person shall be convicted of any offense unless he had attained his 13th birthday at the time the offense was committed.

§ 6-2. Insanity.

(a) A person is not criminally responsible for conduct if at the time of such conduct, as a result of mental disease or mental defect, he lacks substantial capacity to appreciate the criminality of his conduct.

(b) The terms "mental disease or mental defect" do not include an abnormality manifested only by repeated criminal or otherwise antisocial conduct.

(c) A person who, at the time of the commission of a criminal offense, was not insane but was suffering from a mental illness, is not relieved of criminal responsibility for his conduct and may be found guilty but mentally ill.

(d) For purposes of this Section, "mental illness" or "mentally ill" means a substantial disorder of thought, mood, or behavior which afflicted a person at the time of the commission of the offense and which impaired that person's judgment, but not to the extent that he is unable to appreciate the wrongfulness of his behavior.

(e) When the defense of insanity has been presented during the trial, the burden of proof is on the defendant to prove by clear and convincing evidence that the defendant is not guilty by reason of insanity. However, the burden of proof remains on the State to prove beyond a reasonable doubt each of the elements of each of the offenses charged, and, in a jury trial where the insanity defense has been presented, the jury must be instructed that it may not consider whether the defendant has met his burden of proving that he is not guilty by reason of insanity until and unless it has first determined that the State has proven the defendant guilty beyond a reasonable doubt of the offense with which he is charged.

§ 6-3. Intoxicated or drugged condition. A person who is in an intoxicated or drugged condition is criminally responsible for conduct unless such condition is involuntarily produced and deprives him of substantial capacity either to appreciate the criminality of his conduct or to conform his conduct to the requirements of law.

§ 6-4. Affirmative Defense. A defense based upon any of the provisions of Article 6 is an affirmative defense except that mental illness is not an affirmative defense, but an alternative plea or finding that may be accepted, under appropriate evidence, when the affirmative defense of insanity is raised or the plea of guilty but mentally ill is made.

Commentary – Incapacity and Insanity

Minor's Incapacity. Section 6-1 notes that children under age 13 by law are incapable of committing criminal acts in Illinois. Infancy is a defense to all criminal offenses. Children under age 13 are subject to the terms of the Juvenile Court Act and could be prosecuted as juveniles.

Insanity. Section 6-2 addresses the defense of insanity. Insanity was an affirmative defense to a criminal offense at common law. At common law, just as with other affirmative defenses, once the defendant adduced some evidence on the issue of his insanity, the prosecution had the burden of proving the defendant's sanity beyond a reasonable doubt. This was the legislated procedure that was followed in Illinois and was continued under the 1961 Code of Criminal Law and Procedure. Following the assassination attempt on President Reagan and the verdict of not-guilty-by-reason-of-insanity of John David Hinckley, the Illinois procedure was changed and the burden of proof as to insanity was placed on the defendant to prove by a preponderance of the evidence. In 1995, the burden of proof requirement was changed to "by clear and convincing evidence", a burden that is greater that a preponderance burden but less than "beyond a reasonable doubt. Section 6-2(d) confirms that the prosecution still must prove the elements of the charged offense(s) beyond a reasonable doubt while the defendant must prove his own insanity as a defense to that charge.

Insanity is a legal term, not a medical one and has two components. The elements of insanity have evolved over time by legislative action and amendment. The test for insanity requires proof that at the time of the criminal conduct the defendant (1) as a result of a mental disease or defect (2) lacked substantial capacity to appreciate the criminality of his behavior. In layman's terms this means that the defendant had a diagnosable mental disease or disorder that kept him from understanding the wrongfulness of his behavior in committing the crime. to prove insanity, the defense must have expert testimony in the form of opinion that the defendant's mental disease or disorder meets the criteria of the Diagnostic and Statistical Manuel of Mental Disorders – Fifth Edition ("DSM V") and that the DSM V mental disease or disorder had a causal relationship with the criminal conduct committed by the defendant that prevented the defendant from appreciating the wrongfulness of his behavior.

The 1995 amendments effectively narrow the utility of insanity as a successful defense in other ways. Section 6-2(b) limits the mental disease or defect - not permitting reliance on the defendants mental health history of repeated criminal or anti-social conduct as evidence of mental abnormality. Also, Section 6-2(c) provides the possible verdict of "guilty but mentally ill" as an alternative to a finding of insanity. Section 6-2(d) defines a "mental Illness" as a "substantial disorder" of thought, mood or behavior that would impair the judgment at the time of the criminal conduct but not prevent the defendant from appreciating his wrongfulness. a verdict of "guilty but mentally ill" does not alter the punishment for the convicted defendant, while a verdict of not-guilty-by-reason-of-insanity (NGRI) places the defendant for court ordered treatment of his mental disease. In *People v. Harrison* 366 Ill.App.3d, 210, 851 N.E.2d 152 (Ill.

App. Ct. 1st Dist. 2005), the defendant was charged with 1st degree murder, however the expert opinion evidence established the defendant suffered from paranoid-type schizophrenia which caused him to lack the required substantial capacity to appreciate his criminal conduct. The trial court in a bench trial entered a NGRI finding and then ordered the defendant to be sent to the Department of Health and Human Services for mental health treatment. The defendant sought to appeal but the appellate court noted that a NGRI finding is an "acquittal" of the charged criminal conduct so there could be no appeal seeking to raise criminal trial issues.

A qualified expert's opinion (normally a psychiatrist or psychologist) that the defendant suffers from a DSM - V mental disease or disorder that substantially impaired his ability to appreciate his criminal conduct need not be accepted by the trier-of-fact (court or jury), although many times cases involving the claim of insanity devolve into a battle of the experts where the defendant's expert testimony is rebutted by prosecution expert testimony on the insanity issue. In recent times, the incidence of "guilty but mentally ill verdicts" is a fairly common result, while the not-guilty-by-reason-of-insanity result is rare. in *People v. Urdiales* Ill.2d , N.E.2d (2007), the defendant attempted to have the court accept a guilty but mentally ill plea or find him NGRI in a bench proceeding and then determine his eligibility for death sentence consideration, to be ultimately determined by a jury. Extensive contested expert testimony was presented at the bench proceeding, in which the trial court rejected the guilty but mentally ill plea, found the defendant guilty of 1st degree murder and found him eligible for the death penalty. after a further contested trial hearing with a jury, which included information about the defendant's eight prior murders, testimony from a victim of a prior sexual assault which included sadistic behavior, and contested expert opinion on the defendant's mental health history and condition at the time of the offense, and mitigation evidence about the defendant's family and social history, the jury returned a verdict that death was the appropriate sentence. The Illinois Supreme Court affirmed, and just as the trial court had done, some exert testimony was found persuasive and some was rejected as not persuasive. The Urdiales opinion is lengthy and illustrates the serious complexity in the interplay of guilty, guilty but mentally ill and NGRI issues.

Insanity is different than "fitness for trial" which focuses on the defendant's then-present ability to understand the charges brought against him and his ability to communicate and work with his defense attorney. Fitness for trial is addressed under 725 ILCS 5/104.

Article Seven – Justifiable Use of Force; Exoneration
720 ILCS 5/7-1 *et seq.*

§ 7-1. Use of force in defense of person. (a) A person is justified in the use of force against another when and to the extent that he reasonably believes that such conduct is necessary to defend himself or another against such other's imminent use of unlawful force. However, he is justified in the use of force which is intended or likely to cause death or great bodily harm only if he reasonably believes that such force is necessary to prevent imminent death or great bodily harm to himself or another, or the commission of a forcible felony.

(b) In no case shall any act involving the use of force justified under this Section give rise to any claim or liability brought by or on behalf of any person acting within the definition of "aggressor" set forth in Section 7-4 of this Article, or the estate, spouse, or other family member of such a person, against the person or estate of the person using such justified force, unless the use of force involves willful or wanton misconduct.

§ 7-2. Use of force in defense of dwelling. (a) A person is justified in the use of force against another when and to the extent that he reasonably believes that such conduct is necessary to prevent or terminate such other's unlawful entry into or attack upon a dwelling. However, he is justified in the use of force which is intended or likely to cause death or great bodily harm only if:

(1) The entry is made or attempted in a violent, riotous, or tumultuous manner, and he reasonably believes that such force is necessary to prevent an assault upon, or offer of personal violence to, him or another then in the dwelling, or

(2) He reasonably believes that such force is necessary to prevent the commission of a felony in the dwelling.

(b) In no case shall any act involving the use of force justified under this Section give rise to any claim or liability brought by or on behalf of any person acting within the definition of "aggressor" set forth in Section 7-4 of this Article, or the estate, spouse, or other family member of such a person, against the person or estate of the person using such justified force, unless the use of force involves willful or wanton misconduct.

§ 7-3. Use of force in defense of other property. (a) A person is justified in the use of force against another when and to the extent that he reasonably believes that such conduct is necessary to prevent or terminate such other's trespass on or other tortious or criminal interference with either real property (other than a dwelling) or personal property, lawfully in his possession or in the possession of another who is a member of his immediate family or household or of a person whose property he has a legal duty to protect. However, he is justified in the use of force which is intended or likely to cause death or great bodily harm only if he reasonably believes that such force is necessary to prevent the commission of a forcible felony.

(b) In no case shall any act involving the use of force justified under this Section give rise to any claim or liability brought by or on behalf of any person acting within the definition of "aggressor" set forth in Section 7-4 of this Article, or the estate, spouse, or other family member of such a person, against the person or estate of the person using such justified force, unless the use of force involves willful or wanton misconduct.

§ 7-4. Use of Force by Aggressor. The justification described in the preceding Sections of this Article is not available to a person who:

(a) Is attempting to commit, committing, or escaping after the commission of, a forcible felony; or

(b) Initially provokes the use of force against himself, with the intent to use such force as an excuse to inflict bodily harm upon the assailant; or

(c) Otherwise initially provokes the use of force against himself, unless:

(1) Such force is so great that he reasonably believes that he is in imminent danger of death or great bodily harm, and that he has exhausted every reasonable means to escape such danger other than the use of force which is likely to cause death or great bodily harm to the assailant; or

(2) In good faith, he withdraws from physical contact with the assailant and indicates clearly to the assailant that he desires to withdraw and terminate the use of force, but the assailant continues or resumes the use of force.

§ 7-5. Peace officer's use of force in making arrest. (a) A peace officer, or any person whom he has summoned or directed to assist him, need not retreat or desist from efforts to make a lawful arrest because of resistance or threatened resistance to the arrest. He is justified in the use of any force which he reasonably believes to be necessary to effect the arrest and of any force which he reasonably believes to be necessary to defend himself or another from bodily harm while making the arrest. However, he is justified in using force likely to cause death or great bodily harm only when he reasonably believes that such force is necessary to prevent death or great bodily harm to himself or such other person, or when he reasonably believes both that:

(1) Such force is necessary to prevent the arrest

from being defeated by resistance or escape; and

(2) The person to be arrested has committed or attempted a forcible felony which involves the infliction or threatened infliction of great bodily harm or is attempting to escape by use of a deadly weapon, or otherwise indicates that he will endanger human life or inflict great bodily harm unless arrested without delay.

(b) A peace officer making an arrest pursuant to an invalid warrant is justified in the use of any force which he would be justified in using if the warrant were valid, unless he knows that the warrant is invalid.

§7-5.5. Prohibited use of force by a peace officer. (a) A peace officer shall not use a chokehold in the performance of his or her duties, unless deadly force is justified under Article 7 of this Code.

(b) A peace officer shall not use a chokehold, or any lesser contact with the throat or neck area of another in order to prevent the destruction of evidence by ingestion.

(c) As used in this Section, "chokehold" means applying any direct pressure to the throat, windpipe, or airway of another with the intent to reduce or prevent the intake of air. "Chokehold" does not include any holding involving contact with the neck that is not intended to reduce the intake of air.

§ 7-6. Private person's use of force in making arrest. (a) A private person who makes, or assists another private person in making a lawful arrest is justified in the use of any force which he would be justified in using if he were summoned or directed by a peace officer to make such arrest, except that he is justified in the use of force likely to cause death or great bodily harm only when he reasonably believes that such force is necessary to prevent death or great bodily harm to himself or another.

(b) A private person who is summoned or directed by a peace officer to assist in making an arrest which is unlawful, is justified in the use of any force which he would be justified in using if the arrest were lawful, unless he knows that the arrest is unlawful.

§ 7-7. Private person's use of force in resisting arrest. A person is not authorized to use force to resist an arrest which he knows is being made either by a peace officer or by a private person summoned and directed by a peace officer to make the arrest, even if he believes that the arrest is unlawful and the arrest in fact is unlawful.

§ 7-8. Force likely to cause death or great bodily harm. (a) Force which is likely to cause death or great bodily harm, within the meaning of Sections 7-5 and 7-6 includes:

(1) The firing of a firearm in the direction of the person to be arrested, even though no intent exists to kill or inflict great bodily harm; and

(2) The firing of a firearm at a vehicle in which the person to be arrested is riding.

(b) A peace officer's discharge of a firearm using ammunition designed to disable or control an individual without creating the likelihood of death or great bodily harm shall not be considered force likely to cause death or great bodily harm within the meaning of Sections 7-5 and 7-6.

§ 7-9. Use of force to prevent escape. (a) A peace officer or other person who has an arrested person in his custody is justified in the use of such force to prevent the escape of the arrested person from custody as he would be justified in using if he were arresting such person.

(b) A guard or other peace officer is justified in the use of force, including force likely to cause death or great bodily harm, which he reasonably believes to be necessary to prevent the escape from a penal institution of a person whom the officer reasonably believes to be lawfully detained in such institution under sentence for an offense or awaiting trial or commitment for an offense.

§ 7-10. Execution of death sentence. A public officer who, in the exercise of his official duty, puts a person to death pursuant to a sentence of a court of competent jurisdiction, is justified if he acts in accordance with the sentence pronounced and the law prescribing the procedure for execution of a death sentence.

§ 7-11. Compulsion. (a) A person is not guilty of an offense, other than an offense punishable with death, by reason of conduct that he or she performs under the compulsion of threat or menace of the imminent infliction of death or great bodily harm, if he or she reasonably believes death or great bodily harm will be inflicted upon him or her, or upon his or her spouse or child, if he or she does not perform that conduct.

(b) A married woman is not entitled, by reason of the presence of her husband, to any presumption of compulsion or to any defense of compulsion, except that stated in subsection (a).

§ 7-12. Entrapment. A person is not guilty of an offense if his or her conduct is incited or induced by a public officer or employee, or agent of either, for the purpose of obtaining evidence for the prosecution of that person. However, this Section is inapplicable if the person was pre-disposed to commit the offense and the public officer or employee, or agent of either, merely affords to that person the opportunity or facility for committing an offense.

§ 7-13. Necessity. Conduct which would otherwise be an offense is justifiable by reason of necessity if the accused was without blame in occasioning or developing the situation and reasonably believed such conduct was necessary to avoid a public or private injury greater than the injury which might reasonably result from his own conduct.

§ 7-14. Affirmative defense. A defense of justifiable use of force, or of exoneration, based on the provisions of this Article is an affirmative defense.

Commentary – Justifiable Use of Force

Defending Yourself or Another. Section 7-1 provides for the justified use of force or self-defense as an affirmative defense in Illinois criminal law. In essence a person is justified in using force against the imminent use of unlawful force against him or another. However, a person's degree or amount of force used that could cause death or great bodily harm is limited. Such "deadly force" can only be use in the circumstance when deadly force is threatened by the aggressor and the responding force may also be deadly force. The measure of force in each circumstance is the amount of force a reasonable person faced with the same threat of unlawful force against him or another would use to defend against that level of force. The elements of a claim of self-defense include (1) there is a threat of unlawful forces against someone, (2) the threatened person is not the aggressor, (3) danger or harm is impending, (4) responding with force is required to meet the threat, (5) the threatened person really believed force was needed, and (6) his belief is objectively reasonable, *People v. Lee* 213 Ill.2d 218, 821 N.E.2d 307 (2004). Someone's acts are "objectively reasonable" if a reasonable person under the same or similar circumstances would act in the same way. this is to be contrasted with acts that are "subjectively reasonable", where a person honestly believes that he must act in a certain manner, but that is only his own belief, while a reasonable person would not agree that his conduct was reasonable. A typical self-defense scenario would be a fist fight where the aggressor attacks or threatens to attack the defendant. The defendant may reasonably respond with the same level of force (i.e. hand-to-hand combat). If the aggressor were to threaten the use of a weapon (e.g. knife, gun or club) or use the weapon against the defendant, the latter would be justified in responding with deadly force to protect him. As in the non-deadly force scenario, the ultimate issue is whether a reasonable person would respond with the level of force the defendant used. There is no duty to retreat when threatened with force, even deadly force, and one may respond to the threat of force with appropriate responding force. A person is no longer acting with justification if he responds with too much force, for such excessive force makes him the aggressor. If threatened with a fist, the defendant responded with a knife or a gun and stabbed or shot his attacker, the amount of force used would be considered as retaliation. Such retaliatory force would be excessive and unreasonable. Issues of reasonableness and the defendant's belief in the need for force are questions for the jury.

In *People v. Morris* 162 Ill.App.3d 1062, 516 N.E.2d 412 the defendant (Morris) and Thomas had fought each other hand-to-hand with Thomas the aggressor. Thomas left and returned to the apartment with a gun and shot it. Morris' sister had screamed "don't shoot me" inside the apartment. Morris had confronted the victim Thomas who had fired his gun in the apartment. Morris then followed Thomas out the door, when Thomas fired shots at Morris. Morris shot at Thomas and killed him. When the defendant testified, the trial court sustained the prosecution's objections to questions and answers that addressed what the defendant thought was going to happen when he fired his gun and why he pulled the gun. The appellate court ruled that the trial court erred in not permitting the defendant to testify about his thoughts when using deadly force.

Force is also permitted against imminent force that responds to the commission of a forcible felony (as explained in Section 2-15 above). Deadly force is recognized as permissible in the forcible felony.

Since justified use of force is an affirmative defense, in the event there is some evidence introduced tending to raise the issue of the defendant's justified use of force, the burden is on the prosecution to prove beyond a reasonable doubt that the defendant was not justified in his conduct in responding to an aggressor's force. Evidence of the victims prior aggressive and violent acts are not admissible until some evidence supporting defendant's claim of self-defense is introduced. This evidence of the victim's violent character can be used to explain the defendant's reaction to the perceived acts of the victim, and in such case the other character evidence will only be admitted if it can be shown the defendant had knowledge of the victim's prior acts. On the other hand, if there is a conflict in the evidence about who was the aggressor under conflicting versions of fact, the victim's prior aggressive character may be admitted regardless of the defendant's knowledge of such conduct. People v. Guyton 2014 IL App (1st) 110450, ¶¶49-52(trial court's admission of evidence of victim's violent character was properly limited until defendant introduced evidence of self-defense in the defense case.)

Justifiable use of force has been held to not apply as an affirmative defense to criminal trespass not to criminal damage to property or disorderly conduct. *People v. Brant* 394 Ill.App.3d 663, 916 N.E.2d 144 (Ill. App. Ct. 2nd Dist. 2009)(self-defense is not available where the only issue is authority to enter property); *People v. McLennon* 2011 IL App (2d) 091299 (no self-defense claim available where defendant broke EKG wire during attempt at emergency room treatment and his out-of-control behavior frightened medical personnel).

Defending Your Home. Section 7-2 recognizes that a person may respond to the unlawful entry or attack upon his dwelling to terminate the unlawful conduct with the use of force. However deadly force may only be resorted to if the entry or attack upon the dwelling is done in a "violent, riotous or tumultuous manner" to if a reasonable person would use such force to prevent an assault on him or another in the dwelling or to prevent the commission of a felony in the dwelling. The "defense of dwelling" principle is to protect people – not the property. In *People v. Sawyer* 115 Ill.2d 184, 503 N.E.2d 331 (1986), the victim (Kennedy) had previously slapped the defendant's (Sawyer) girlfriend in her apartment and threatened her a second time. Kennedy then left the apartment and had a conversation with Sawyer outside. When Kennedy re-entered the apartment without permission, he did so by walking in past Sawyer. Kennedy and Sawyer exchanged words and then fought. Sawyer reached for a knife he had left on the desk behind him and stabbed Kennedy in the course of the ensuing struggle, causing Kennedy's death. Sawyer was convicted of voluntary manslaughter. His claim of use of force in defense of dwelling was rejected by the jury and the courts on appeal. Kennedy's entry had not been "riotous" and Sawyers subjective belief that deadly force was necessary was unreasonable. Kennedy had no weapon. Any prior threat of unlawful force was past. the prospect of further use of force by Kennedy was not imminent.

Since justified use of force is an affirmative defense, in the event there is some evidence introduced tending to raise the issue of the defendant's justified use of force, the burden is on the prosecution to prove beyond a reasonable doubt that the defendant was not justified in his conduct in responding to an aggressor's force. In *People v. Tally* 2014 IL App (5th) 120349, the defendant's murder conviction was reversed where the trial court's refusal to permit the defendant present evidence of his self-defense claim as a discovery sanction was found to be an abuse of discretion..

Defending Other Property. Section 7-3 recognizes that a person may use reasonable non-deadly force to prevent or stop unlawful possession of or threatened damage to ("trespass on or other tortuous or criminal interference") personal property or real estate other than a dwelling. However, deadly force can only be used when defending against the commission of a forcible felony.

Aggressor's Use of Force. As Section 7-4 explains an aggressor my not use unlawful force and then claim that he was justified in doing so. An aggressor is a person who is committing a forcible felony, who initially provokes the use of force as an excuse to retaliate with force. Criminals caught in the act or fleeing felons have no right to self-defense. Nor can someone start a fight with the hope of claiming self-defense. In *People v. Sloan* 111 Ill.2d 571, 490 N.E.2d 560 (1986), the defendant (Sloan) went to his former girlfriend's apartment armed with a sawed-off shotgun. According to Sloan, he confronted Wilson, not knowing if Wilson was armed, and Wilson resisted the show of force by coming at Sloan. In rejecting Sloan's claim of self-defense the court noted that Sloan was the aggressor and had provoked whatever response Wilson made. Common sense tells one that ordinarily a criminal cannot provoke the use of force and then claim justification to respond to that level of force.

Police Use of Force in Making Arrest. A peace officer may use whatever level of force that is reasonably necessary to make an arrest, but may only use deadly force if he reasonably believes (1) he is confronted with the imminent use of deadly force (force likely to cause death or great bodily harm) or (2) he believes such force is necessary to prevent escape (a) by a person who has committed or is attempting to commit a forcible felony involving the infliction or threat of great bodily harm, or (b) the person escaping is attempting to do so by use of a deadly weapon or (3) the person escaping will endanger human life unless arrested immediately. In *People v. Sims* 374 Ill.App.3d 427, 871 N.E.2d 453 (Ill. App. Ct. 3rd Dist. 2007), the defendant was being arrested on an outstanding warrant and claimed in his presentation of evidence that arresting officers used excessive force on him and also beat his girlfriend who was present, after Sims had surrendered to the officers on the warrant. Photographs of Sims were consistent with his claims. Sims was granted a new trial where the trial judge refused to instruct the jury on Sims' claim of self-defense.

Entrapment. Section 7 – 12 sets forth the affirmative defense of entrapment. A person is not guilty of a crime, if he is induced to commit the crime by an agent of the government in an effort to create evidence that the defendant is committing the crime. A person who has the predisposition to commit a crime cannot be entrapped. In raising the affirmative defense of entrapment, the defendant is admitting that the crime occurred but claiming that he would not have engaged in the criminal conduct if not incited to do so by the government. It is contrary to good public policy to have the government provoke criminal behavior.

Entrapment is frequently raised as a defense in cases involving drugs or prostitution. In drug enforcement cases, informants are often used to make cases. Informants often cooperate with police to work off arrests or pending cases for possession of drugs. Typically informants will identify others who make a drug deal with them. A friend might at first waffle about a possible drug transaction, but persistent attempts may result in a drug transaction. These operations are often the subject of surveillance, including audio or visual recording techniques. Since it is clear the deal has taken place and provable, the defendant will claim that he only bought or sold the drugs because the police coaxed him to do so. In response the prosecution will show that defendant had prior involvement in drug trafficking. This proves that the drug deal was in the defendant's idea, not the creation of an undercover police sting.

People v. Bonner 385 Ill.App.3d 141, 895 N.E.2d 99 (Ill. App. Ct. 2nd Dist. 2008) provides a good example of entrapment. The appellate court found that the defendant (Bonner) had been entrapped, as a matter of law, and reversed his conviction. Bonner was a drug addict. A woman (Vedros) asked him to sell crack cocaine to a friend (Arres) but Bonner refused. Vedros asked several times and finally offered to have sex with Bonner if he would do so. Arres was an undercover police officer and Vedros had two pending cases and received benefit from helping the police with Bonner. With the first two drug deals Vedros was present and had sex with Bonner afterward. Bonner had two more deals with Arres in which the amount of drugs was increased. Despite evidence of Bonner's drug addiction, his knowledge of drugs and drug lingo and a prior drug conviction, the court held that Bonner would not have committed these crimes without being lured to do so by the promise and fact of sex by a government agent, Vedros.

Title III. Specific Offenses
Part A – Inchoate Offenses

Article 8 – Solicitation, Conspiracy and Attempt
720 ILCS 5/8-1 *et seq.*

§ 8-1. Solicitation and solicitation of murder.
(a) Solicitation. A person commits the offense of solicitation when, with intent that an offense be committed, other than first degree murder, he or she commands, encourages, or requests another to commit that offense.

(b) Solicitation of murder. A person commits the offense of solicitation of murder when he or she commits solicitation with the intent that the offense of first degree murder be committed.

(c) Sentence. A person convicted of solicitation may be fined or imprisoned or both not to exceed the maximum provided for the offense solicited, except that the penalty shall not exceed the corresponding maximum limit provided by subparagraph (c) of Section 8-4 of this Code. Solicitation of murder is a Class X felony, and a person convicted of solicitation of murder shall be sentenced to a term of imprisonment of not less than 15 years and not more than 30 years, except that a person convicted of solicitation of murder when the person solicited was a person under the age of 17 years shall be sentenced to a term of imprisonment of not less than 20 years and not more than 60 years.

§ 8-1.2. Solicitation of murder for hire. (a) A person commits the offense of solicitation of murder for hire when, with the intent that the offense of first degree murder be committed, he or she procures another to commit that offense pursuant to any contract, agreement, understanding, command, or request for money or anything of value.

(b) Sentence. Solicitation of murder for hire is a Class X felony, and a person convicted of solicitation of murder for hire shall be sentenced to a term of imprisonment of not less than 20 years and not more than 40 years, except that a person convicted of solicitation of murder for hire when the person solicited was a person under the age of 17 years shall be sentenced to a term of imprisonment of not less than 25 years and not more than 60 years.

§ 8-2. Conspiracy. (a) Elements of the offense. A person commits the offense of conspiracy when, with intent that an offense be committed, he or she agrees with another to the commission of that offense. No person may be convicted of conspiracy to commit an offense unless an act in furtherance of that agreement is alleged and proved to have been committed by him or her or by a co-conspirator.

(b) Co-conspirators. It is not a defense to conspiracy that the person or persons with whom the accused is alleged to have conspired:

(1) have not been prosecuted or convicted,

(2) have been convicted of a different offense,

(3) are not amenable to justice,

(4) have been acquitted, or

(5) lacked the capacity to commit an offense.

(c) Sentence.

(1) Except as otherwise provided in this subsection or Code, a person convicted of conspiracy to commit:

(A) a Class X felony shall be sentenced for a Class 1 felony;

(B) a Class 1 felony shall be sentenced for a Class 2 felony;

(C) a Class 2 felony shall be sentenced for a Class 3 felony;

(D) a Class 3 felony shall be sentenced for a Class 4 felony;

(E) a Class 4 felony shall be sentenced for a Class 4 felony; and

(F) a misdemeanor may be fined or imprisoned or both not to exceed the maximum provided for the offense that is the object of the conspiracy.

(2) A person convicted of conspiracy to commit any of the following offenses shall be sentenced for a Class X felony:

(A) aggravated insurance fraud conspiracy when the person is an organizer of the conspiracy (720 ILCS 5/46-4); or

(B) aggravated governmental entity insurance fraud conspiracy when the person is an organizer of the conspiracy (720 ILCS 5/46-4).

(3) A person convicted of conspiracy to commit any of the following offenses shall be sentenced for a Class 1 felony:

(A) first degree murder (720 ILCS 5/9-1); or

(B) aggravated insurance fraud (720 ILCS 5/46-3) or aggravated governmental insurance fraud (720 ILCS 5/46-3).

(4) A person convicted of conspiracy to commit insurance fraud (720 ILCS 5/46-3) or governmental entity insurance fraud (720 ILCS 5/46-3) shall be sentenced for a Class 2 felony.

(5) A person convicted of conspiracy to commit any of the following offenses shall be sentenced for a Class 3 felony:

(A) soliciting for a prostitute (720 ILCS 5/11-14.3(a)(1));

(B) pandering (720 ILCS 5/11-14.3(a)(2)(A) or 5/11-14.3(a)(2)(B));

(C) keeping a place of prostitution (720 ILCS 5/11-14.3(a)(1));

(D) pimping (720 ILCS 5/11-14.3(a)(2)(C));

(E) unlawful use of weapons under Section 24-1(a)(1) (720 ILCS 5/24-1(a)(1));

(F) unlawful use of weapons under Section 24-1(a)(7) (720 ILCS 5/24-1(a)(7));

(G) gambling (720 ILCS 5/28-1);

(H) keeping a gambling place (720 ILCS 5/28-3);

(I) registration of federal gambling stamps violation (720 ILCS 5/28-4);

(J) look-alike substances violation (720 ILCS 570/404);

(K) miscellaneous controlled substance violation under Section 406(b) (720 ILCS 570/406(b)); or

(L) an inchoate offense related to any of the principal offenses set forth in this item (5).

§ 8-3. Defense. It is a defense to a charge of solicitation or conspiracy that if the criminal object were achieved the accused would not be guilty of an offense.

§ 8-4. Attempt. (a) Elements of the offense. A person commits the offense of attempt when, with intent to commit a specific offense, he or she does any act that constitutes a substantial step toward the commission of that offense.

(b) Impossibility. It is not a defense to a charge of attempt that because of a misapprehension of the circumstances it would have been impossible for the accused to commit the offense attempted.

(c) Sentence. A person convicted of attempt may be fined or imprisoned or both not to exceed the maximum provided for the offense attempted but, except for an attempt to commit the offense defined in Section 33A-2 of this Code:

(1) the sentence for attempt to commit first degree murder is the sentence for a Class X felony, except that

(A) an attempt to commit first degree murder when at least one of the aggravating factors specified in paragraphs (1), (2), and (12) of subsection (b) of Section 9-1 is present is a Class X felony for which the sentence shall be a term of imprisonment of not less than 20 years and not more than 80 years;

(B) an attempt to commit first degree murder while armed with a firearm is a Class X felony for which 15 years shall be added to the term of imprisonment imposed by the court;

(C) an attempt to commit first degree murder during which the person personally discharged a firearm is a Class X felony for which 20 years shall be added to the term of imprisonment imposed by the court;

(D) an attempt to commit first degree murder during which the person personally discharged a firearm that proximately caused great bodily harm, permanent disability, permanent disfigurement, or death to another person is a Class X felony for which 25 years or up to a term of natural life shall be added to the term of imprisonment imposed by the court; and

(E) if the defendant proves by a preponderance of the evidence at sentencing that, at the time of the attempted murder, he or she was acting under a sudden and intense passion resulting from serious provocation by the individual whom the defendant endeavored to kill, or another, and, had the individual the defendant endeavored to kill died, the defendant would have negligently or accidentally caused that death, then the sentence for the attempted murder is the sentence for a Class 1 felony;

(2) the sentence for attempt to commit a Class X felony is the sentence for a Class 1 felony;

(3) the sentence for attempt to commit a Class 1 felony is the sentence for a Class 2 felony;

(4) the sentence for attempt to commit a Class 2 felony is the sentence for a Class 3 felony; and

(5) the sentence for attempt to commit any felony other than those specified in items (1), (2), (3), and (4) of this subsection (c) is the sentence for a Class A misdemeanor.

§ 8-5. Multiple Convictions. No person shall be convicted of both the inchoate and the principal offense.

Commentary – Inchoate Offenses

Inchoate Offenses. There is a category conduct that is considered criminal even if the crime itself is not completed. In other words it is a crime to begin to commit a crime even if it is not completed. These offenses are solicitation, conspiracy and attempt. The inchoate offenses are separate from the principal offenses – an attempted murder charge is distinct from a murder charge. A defendant could be acquitted of murder of Smith but convicted of solicitation to commit the murder of Smith, even in separate indictments. A "not guilty" of murder does not prevent a "guilty" of solicitation to commit murder - the elements of the offenses are different. Under Section 8 – 5, if the defendant is found guilty of both the inchoate offense and the principal offense, the inchoate offense is said to "merge" with the main crime. For example, if a defendant was found guilty of murder and conspiracy to commit murder, he would only be sentenced on the murder conviction.

Solicitation. Section 8-1 defines the separate crime of solicitation, essentially asking another person to commit a crime. While there may appear to be some overlap with criminal accountability, this is a "stand alone" offense where there is a crime even if the solicited crime is never committed. See *People v. Boyce* 2015 IL 117108 (defendant's conviction of attempted solicitation of murder was upheld where his letter seeking commission of the crime was intercepted by prison officials. Solicitation of murder is a specific offense and thus attempted solicitation is no an "attempt to attempt" but rather is an attempt to commit a specific crime). The separate crime of solicitation to commit murder recognizes the seriousness of that offense in comparison with other solicitation effort. one convicted of solicitation can be sentenced within the same maximum and minimum penalties as the solicited offense, again except for murder which has a Class X designation and has the minimum penalty of 15 years imprisonment and 30 years maximum imprisonment. The penalty faced increases if a minor is solicited to commit the murder. Of the same nature is solicitation to commit murder for hire in Section 8-1.2 which has even greater penalties for arranging the first degree murder of another for money or other thing of value.

Conspiracy. Section 8-2 provides that a person who agrees with another to commit a crime with intent that the crime be committed is guilty of conspiracy. However, at least one act in furtherance of the conspiracy must be committed for a conspiracy charge to be successful. The essential elements are (1) an agreement to commit a crime; (2) intent by the defendant that the conspiracy be completed; (3) an overt act in furtherance of the conspiracy. The "act in furtherance" can be proved to have been committed by any of the co-conspirators, not just the defendant, and need not be a criminal act, only an act that advances the purpose of the unlawful agreement. The defendant can be convicted even if none of the other co-conspirators were charged or convicted and even if one of the other co-conspirators was acquitted. However, the defendant cannot be guilty of conspiracy if there is no co-conspirator – so for example if an undercover officer enters into an agreement with the defendant to commit a crime and the defendant made a phone call in furtherance of that agreement, there still would be no conspiracy because all conspiracies require the existence of an agreement between the conspirators and in this case there was a false agreement on the undercover officer's part. As with other inchoate offenses, the crime consists of the agreement and an act and is complete at that time, regardless of the completion of the main offense. A person may be found guilty of conspiracy to commit robbery even if the robbery never occurs.

The crime of conspiracy exists to address the evil presented by individuals combining in a criminal agreement or enterprise to commit a crime – such criminal behavior often occurs in secrecy and is difficult to detect. Society should not have to wait until the crime is committed to arrest, stop and punish the criminals who have agreed to engage in the criminal behavior and harm others. Conspiracy is an attractive charge to bring because the charges can be brought in any county where an act in furtherance occurred, the statute of limitations continues for as long as the conspiracy continues so that conduct outside a limitations period can be joined as proof of the existence of a continuing agreement between the same parties and statements made by co-conspirators are admissible against each of the co-conspirators at trial. (See Illinois Rules of Evidence (IRE) 801(d)(2)(E)). A conspiracy is normally proved by circumstantial evidence including statements and conduct of the parties from which a conspiracy can be inferred. Under what is known as "Wharton's Rule" there can be no conspiracy if number of co-conspirators equals the number of individuals necessary to complete the intended offense. There can be no conspiracy to distribute cocaine where the only individuals involved in the criminal agreement are the seller and buyer of the drugs. There could be no distribution crime without the seller and buyer.

Attempt. Even though criminal conduct does not result in a completed crime, there is a separate criminal offense in attempting to do so. Section 8 – 4 points out that the crime of Attempt (i.e. Attempted Arm Robbery, Attempted Sexual Assault, Attempted Murder, etc.) occurs when a defendant takes a substantial step toward the completion of the underlying offense and intends to commit that offense. This would require proof that the essential elements of the underlying offense would be proved if the crime had been successful. For example, if the proof shows that the defendant fired a shot at someone and missed, and in fact, intended to shoot the would-be victim, the defendant has committed attempted murder. In *People v. Douglas* 371 Ill.App.3d 21, 861 N.E.2d 1096 (Ill. App. Ct. 1st Dist. 2007), the defendant shot at two men standing on a corner doing a "pat down" of a member of his gang. He was convicted of Attempt 1st Degree Murder of a Peace Officer. Understandably, shooting at the men, who were known to the defendant, was a substantial step towards the commission of 1st Degree Murder. See also *People v. Petermon* 2014 IL App (1st) 113536 (Defendant shot at police officer and missed but hit another man. Shooting at the police officer was a substantial step and the shooting also supported the inference of intent to kill, hitting the other victim with the shot along with transferred intent supported both convictions for attempted First Degree Murder).

It is not a defense to the crime of attempt that the defendant's plan would not have been successful (i.e. it was "impossible" for the offense to have occurred).

Inchoate Offense Sentencing. Inchoate offenses are generally punished one step or grade lower than the underlying offense, unless there is specific sentencing language associated with the inchoate offense. Thus an attempted Class X felony, upon conviction, will be sentenced as a Class 1 felony and an attempted Class 1 felony will be sentenced as a Class 2 felony, and so on.

Part B – Offenses Directed Against the Person

Article 9 – Homicide
720 ILCS 5/9-1 *et seq.*

§ 9-1. First degree Murder–Death penalties–Exceptions–Separate Hearings–Proof–Findings–Appellate procedures–Reversals.

(a) A person who kills an individual without lawful justification commits first degree murder if, in performing the acts which cause the death:

(1) he either intends to kill or do great bodily harm to that individual or another, or knows that such acts will cause death to that individual or another; or

(2) he knows that such acts create a strong probability of death or great bodily harm to that individual or another; or

(3) he is attempting or committing a forcible felony other than second degree murder.

(b) Aggravating Factors. A defendant who at the time of the commission of the offense has attained the age of 18 or more and who has been found guilty of first degree murder

may be sentenced to death if:

(1) the murdered individual was a peace officer or fireman killed in the course of performing his official duties, to prevent the performance of his official duties, or in retaliation for performing his official duties, and the defendant knew or should have known that the murdered individual was a peace officer or fireman; or

(2) the murdered individual was an employee of an institution or facility of the Department of Corrections, or any similar local correctional agency, killed in the course of performing his official duties, to prevent the performance of his official duties, or in retaliation for performing his official duties, or the murdered individual was an inmate at such institution or facility and was killed on the grounds thereof, or the murdered individual was otherwise present in such institution or facility with the knowledge and approval of the chief administrative officer thereof; or

(3) the defendant has been convicted of murdering two or more individuals under subsection (a) of this Section or under any law of the United States or of any state which is substantially similar to subsection (a) of this Section regardless of whether the deaths occurred as the result of the same act or of several related or unrelated acts so long as the deaths were the result of either an intent to kill more than one person or of separate acts which the defendant knew would cause death or create a strong probability of death or great bodily harm to the murdered individual or another; or

(4) the murdered individual was killed as a result of the hijacking of an airplane, train, ship, bus or other public conveyance; or

(5) the defendant committed the murder pursuant to a contract, agreement or understanding by which he was to receive money or anything of value in return for committing the murder or procured another to commit the murder for money or anything of value; or

(6) the murdered individual was killed in the course of another felony if:

(a) the murdered individual:(i) was actually killed by the defendant, or(ii) received physical injuries personally inflicted by the defendant substantially contemporaneously with physical injuries caused by one or more persons for whose conduct the defendant is legally accountable under Section 5-2 of this Code, and the physical injuries inflicted by either the defendant or the other person or persons for whose conduct he is legally accountable caused the death of the murdered individual; and

(b) in performing the acts which caused the death of the murdered individual or which resulted in physical injuries personally inflicted by the defendant on the murdered individual under the circumstances of subdivision (ii) of subparagraph (a) of paragraph (6) of subsection (b) of this Section, the defendant acted with the intent to kill the murdered individual or with the knowledge that his acts created a strong probability of death or great bodily harm to the murdered individual or another; and

(c) the other felony was an inherently violent crime or the attempt to commit an inherently violent crime. In this subparagraph (c), "inherently violent crime" includes, but is not limited to, armed robbery, robbery, predatory criminal sexual assault of a child, aggravated criminal sexual assault, aggravated kidnapping, aggravated vehicular hijacking, aggravated arson, aggravated stalking, residential burglary, and home invasion; or

(7) the murdered individual was under 12 years of age and the death resulted from exceptionally brutal or heinous behavior indicative of wanton cruelty; or

(8) the defendant committed the murder with intent to prevent the murdered individual from testifying or participating in any criminal investigation or prosecution or giving material assistance to the State in any investigation or prosecution, either against the defendant or another; or the defendant committed the murder because the murdered individual was a witness in any prosecution or gave material assistance to the State in any investigation or prosecution, either against the defendant or another; for purposes of this paragraph (8), "participating in any criminal investigation or prosecution" is intended to include those appearing in the proceedings in any capacity such as trial judges, prosecutors, defense attorneys, investigators, witnesses, or jurors; or

(9) the defendant, while committing an offense punishable under Sections 401, 401.1, 401.2, 405, 405.2, 407 or 407.1 or subsection (b) of Section 404 of the Illinois Controlled Substances Act,1 or while engaged in a conspiracy or solicitation to commit such offense, intentionally killed an individual or counseled, commanded, induced, procured or caused the intentional killing of the murdered individual; or

(10) the defendant was incarcerated in an institution or facility of the Department of Corrections at the time of the murder, and while committing an offense punishable as a felony under Illinois law, or while engaged in a conspiracy or solicitation to commit such offense, intentionally killed an individual or counseled, commanded, induced, procured or caused the intentional killing of the murdered individual; or

(11) the murder was committed in a cold, calculated and premeditated manner pursuant to a preconceived plan, scheme or design to take a human life by unlawful means, and the conduct of the defendant created a reasonable expectation that the death of a human being would result therefrom; or

(12) the murdered individual was an emergency medical technician--ambulance, emergency medical technician--intermediate, emergency medical technician--paramedic, ambulance driver, or other medical assistance or first aid personnel, employed by a municipality or other governmental unit, killed in the course of performing his official duties, to prevent the performance of his official duties, or in retaliation for performing his official duties, and the defendant knew or should have known that the murdered individual was an emergency medical technician--ambulance, emergency medical technician--intermediate, emergency medical technician--paramedic, ambulance driver, or other medical assistance or first aid personnel; or

(13) the defendant was a principal administrator, organizer, or leader of a calculated criminal drug conspiracy consisting of a hierarchical position of authority superior to that of all other members of the conspiracy, and the defendant counseled, commanded, induced, procured, or caused the intentional killing of the murdered person; or

(14) the murder was intentional and involved the infliction of torture. For the purpose of this Section torture means the infliction of or subjection to extreme physical pain, motivated by an intent to increase or prolong the pain, suffering or agony of the victim; or

(15) the murder was committed as a result of the intentional discharge of a firearm by the defendant from a motor vehicle and the victim was not present within the motor vehicle; or

(16) the murdered individual was 60 years of age or older and the death resulted from exceptionally brutal or heinous behavior indicative of wanton cruelty; or

(17) the murdered individual was a person with a disability and the defendant knew or should have known that the murdered individual was a person with a disability. For purposes of this paragraph (17), "person with a disability" means a person who suffers from a permanent physical or mental impairment resulting from disease, an injury, a functional disorder, or a congenital condition that renders the person incapable of adequately providing for his or her own health or personal care; or

(18) the murder was committed by reason of any person's activity as a community policing volunteer or to prevent any person from engaging in activity as a community policing volunteer; or

(19) the murdered individual was subject to an order of protection and the murder was committed by a person against whom the same order of protection was issued under the Illinois Domestic Violence Act of 1986; or

(20) the murdered individual was known by the defendant to be a teacher or other person employed in any school and the teacher or other employee is upon the grounds of a school or grounds adjacent to a school, or is in any part of a building used for school purposes; or

(21) the murder was committed by the defendant in connection with or as a result of the offense of terrorism as defined in Section 29D-14.9 of this Code.

(b-5) Aggravating Factor; Natural Life Imprisonment. A defendant who has been found guilty of first degree murder and who at the time of the commission of the offense had attained the age of 18 years or more may be sentenced to natural life imprisonment if (i) the murdered individual was a physician, physician assistant, psychologist, nurse, or advanced practice nurse, (ii) the defendant knew or should have known that the murdered individual was a physician, physician assistant, psychologist, nurse, or advanced practice nurse, and (iii) the murdered individual was killed in the course of acting in his or her capacity as a physician, physician assistant, psychologist, nurse, or advanced practice nurse, or to prevent him or her from acting in that capacity, or in retaliation for his or her acting in that capacity.

(c) Consideration of factors in Aggravation and Mitigation.

The court shall consider, or shall instruct the jury to consider any aggravating and any mitigating factors which are relevant to the imposition of the death penalty. Aggravating factors may include but need not be limited to those factors set forth in subsection (b). Mitigating factors may include but need not be limited to the following:

(1) the defendant has no significant history of prior criminal activity;

(2) the murder was committed while the defendant was under the influence of extreme mental or emotional disturbance, although not such as to constitute a defense to prosecution;

(3) the murdered individual was a participant in the defendant's homicidal conduct or consented to the homicidal act;

(4) the defendant acted under the compulsion of threat or menace of the imminent infliction of death or great bodily harm;

(5) the defendant was not personally present during commission of the act or acts causing death;

(6) the defendant's background includes a history of extreme emotional or physical abuse;

(7) the defendant suffers from a reduced mental capacity.

(d) Separate sentencing hearing.

Where requested by the State, the court shall

conduct a separate sentencing proceeding to determine the existence of factors set forth in subsection (b) and to consider any aggravating or mitigating factors as indicated in subsection (c). The proceeding shall be conducted:

(1) before the jury that determined the defendant's guilt; or

(2) before a jury impanelled for the purpose of the proceeding if:

A. the defendant was convicted upon a plea of guilty; or

B. the defendant was convicted after a trial before the court sitting without a jury; or

C. the court for good cause shown discharges the jury that determined the defendant's guilt; or

(3) before the court alone if the defendant waives a jury for the separate proceeding.

(e) Evidence and Argument.

During the proceeding any information relevant to any of the factors set forth in subsection (b) may be presented by either the State or the defendant under the rules governing the admission of evidence at criminal trials. Any information relevant to any additional aggravating factors or any mitigating factors indicated in subsection (c) may be presented by the State or defendant regardless of its admissibility under the rules governing the admission of evidence at criminal trials. The State and the defendant shall be given fair opportunity to rebut any information received at the hearing.

(f) Proof. The burden of proof of establishing the existence of any of the factors set forth in subsection (b) is on the State and shall not be satisfied unless established beyond a reasonable doubt.

(g) Procedure--Jury. If at the separate sentencing proceeding the jury finds that none of the factors set forth in subsection (b) exists, the court shall sentence the defendant to a term of imprisonment under Chapter V of the Unified Code of Corrections.3 If there is a unanimous finding by the jury that one or more of the factors set forth in subsection (b) exist, the jury shall consider aggravating and mitigating factors as instructed by the court and shall determine whether the sentence of death shall be imposed. If the jury determines unanimously, after weighing the factors in aggravation and mitigation, that death is the appropriate sentence, the court shall sentence the defendant to death. If the court does not concur with the jury determination that death is the appropriate sentence, the court shall set forth reasons in writing including what facts or circumstances the court relied upon, along with any relevant documents, that compelled the court to non-concur with the sentence. This document and any attachments shall be part of the record for appellate review. The court shall be bound by the jury's sentencing determination.

If after weighing the factors in aggravation and mitigation, one or more jurors determines that death is not the appropriate sentence, the court shall sentence the defendant to a term of imprisonment under Chapter V of the Unified Code of Corrections.

(h) Procedure--No Jury. In a proceeding before the court alone, if the court finds that none of the factors found in subsection (b) exists, the court shall sentence the defendant to a term of imprisonment under Chapter V of the Unified Code of Corrections.

If the Court determines that one or more of the factors set forth in subsection (b) exists, the Court shall consider any aggravating and mitigating factors as indicated in subsection (c). If the Court determines, after weighing the factors in aggravation and mitigation, that death is the appropriate sentence, the Court shall sentence the defendant to death.

If the court finds that death is not the appropriate sentence, the court shall sentence the defendant to a term of imprisonment under Chapter V of the Unified Code of Corrections.

(h-5) Decertification as a capital case.

In a case in which the defendant has been found guilty of first degree murder by a judge or jury, or a case on remand for resentencing, and the State seeks the death penalty as an appropriate sentence, on the court's own motion or the written motion of the defendant, the court may decertify the case as a death penalty case if the court finds that the only evidence supporting the defendant's conviction is the uncorroborated testimony of an informant witness, as defined in Section 115-21 of the Code of Criminal Procedure of 1963, concerning the confession or admission of the defendant or that the sole evidence against the defendant is a single eyewitness or single accomplice without any other corroborating evidence. If the court decertifies the case as a capital case under either of the grounds set forth above, the court shall issue a written finding. The State may pursue its right to appeal the decertification pursuant to Supreme Court Rule 604(a)(1). If the court does not decertify the case as a capital case, the matter shall proceed to the eligibility phase of the sentencing hearing.

(i) Appellate Procedure. The conviction and sentence of death shall be subject to automatic review by the Supreme Court. Such review shall be in accordance with rules promulgated by the Supreme Court. The Illinois Supreme Court may overturn the death sentence, and order the imposition of imprisonment under Chapter V of the Unified Code of Corrections if the court finds that the death sentence is fundamentally unjust as applied to the particular case. If the Illinois Supreme Court finds that the death sentence is fundamentally unjust as applied to the particular case, independent of any procedural grounds for relief, the Illinois Supreme Court shall issue a written opinion explaining this finding.

(j) Disposition of reversed death sentence. In the event that the death penalty in this Act is held to be unconstitutional by the Supreme Court of the United States or of the State of Illinois, any person convicted of first degree murder shall be sentenced by the court to a term of imprisonment under Chapter V of the Unified Code of Corrections.

In the event that any death sentence pursuant to the sentencing provisions of this Section is declared unconstitutional by the Supreme Court of the United States or of the State of Illinois, the court having jurisdiction over a person previously sentenced to death shall cause the defendant to be brought before the court, and the court shall sentence the defendant to a term of imprisonment under Chapter V of the Unified Code of Corrections.

(k) Guidelines for seeking the death penalty. The Attorney General and State's Attorneys Association shall consult on voluntary guidelines for procedures governing whether or not to seek the death penalty. The guidelines do not have the force of law and are only advisory in nature.

Commentary – First Degree Murder

First Degree Murder – Death Penalty Abolished. The most serious criminal offenses are homicides. Historically this was the only offense in Illinois punishable by a sentence of death. In March, 2011 the death penalty was abolished in Illinois. First Degree Murder has a general range of imprisonment from 20 to 60 years in the Department of Corrections, but there are many sentencing enhancements that can be charged to increase the possible penalties (e.g. use of a firearm by the defendant who shot and killed the victim is a "25 year-to-life" possible imprisonment enhancement). a defendant may still also be sentenced to natural life in prison if the charge of 1st Degree Murder includes the presence of qualifying aggravating factors as set forth in Section 9-1(b-5). The procedure for prosecuting a murder case as a potential "natural life" case is currently in a state of flux because the death penalty procedures that are outlined in Section 9-1(b) – (h) would appear to be no longer applicable. Sections 9-1(g-5) and (j) would appear to direct all 1st Degree Murder cases for sentencing under the normal sentence procedures under Chapter V of the Illinois Code of Corrections.

There are several formulations of the crime of murder in Illinois. Murder requires conduct that

that is not legally justified which causes the death of another human being. Murder is the killing of a human being without justification, with a certain mental state. The law requires the defendant intend or know that his acts will cause death or present a significant chance that someone's death will be caused. Death by accidental means is not a murder.

Murder – Intent or Knowledge. Section 9-1(a)(1) provides that one can be convicted of murder if he caused the death of another individual and (1) he intended to kill the victim or another; (2) he intended to do great bodily harm and death ensues; or (3) he knew that his conduct would cause death or great bodily harm to the victim or another.

Murder – Knowledge of Strong Probability of Death or Great Bodily Harm. Section 9-1(a)(2) defines another type of 1st degree murder when the defendant's acts caused the death of another. At the time of the killing the defendant must have known his conduct created a strong probability of death or great bodily harm to the victim or another.

Felony Murder. Section 9-1(a)(3) identifies the third type of 1st degree murder in Illinois where the defendant caused the death of another while attempting to commit or committing a forcible felony. The felony murder rule accepts the notion that if a felony is committed that involves the concept of force; it is natural to expect that a death could be caused under the circumstances of the commission of that offense. See *People v. Brown* 2015 IL App (1st) 131552 (defendant properly convicted under the felony murder doctrine where following the commission of a burglary his co-defendant recklessly drove during the escape from the crime scene, crashed the get-away car and caused the death of another.)

Illustrative Murder cases. The prosecution must prove that the defendant's conduct was a cause of the death and also prove the criminal nature of the defendant's acts. In *People v. Sims* 374 Ill.App.3d 231, 869 N.E.2d 1115 (Ill. App. Ct. 1st Dist. 2007)(reversed on other grounds) the defendant was convicted of armed robbery and 1st Degree Murder. The victim, a restaurant manager, had died 5 ½ hours after the armed robbery of the restaurant based on a stress-induced heart attack. The Court rejected the argument that the evidence was insufficient to support the murder conviction holding that the defendant's conduct did not have to be the sole cause, and instead could be a contributing proximate cause of the victim's death.

In *People v. Smith* 233 Ill.2d 1, 906 N.E.2d 529 (2009), the court noted that there is only one offense of 1st degree murder but multiple ways to charge the offense and obtain a conviction (e.g. intentional, knowing or felony murder). The two scenarios involved in *Smith* involved an armed robbery and the shooting-death of a bar patron, as well as a case where a pizza deliveryman was shot, killed and robbed. In each case, the defendants (Smith and Titus) were charged with intentional murder, knowing murder and felony murder in a three-count indictment. In holding that Smith and Titus were entitled to separate verdict forms as to each type of murder charged, the court noted:

> "While our statute describes three "types" of murder, first degree murder is a single offense. As we have explained on numerous occasions, the different theories embodied in the first degree murder statute are merely different ways to commit the same crime.' in other words, "subsections (a)(1), (a)(2), and (a)(3) of section 9-1 of the Criminal Code, defining intentional murder, knowing murder and felony murder, delineate only the mental state or conduct that must accompany the acts that cause a death . . . (case citations and punctuation omitted)
>
> *People v. Smith* 233 Ill.2d at 16, 906 N.E.2d 537-538.

While one ordinarily thinks of murder on the basis of personal acts of violence with a gun, knife or other physical acts of the perpetrator, murder is actually a much broader term. In *People v.*

Alsup 373 Ill.App.3d 745, 869 N.E.2d 157 (Ill. App. Ct. 5th Dist. 2007), the defendant stole a van near St. Louis, Missouri and led police on a high-speed chase into Illinois for 28 miles, running through traffic control devices, going the wrong way on highways and finally broad-siding a car in Granite City, Illinois killing its driver. The defendant's conviction for1st Degree Murder was upheld on the basis that he caused the death of the victim and that he knew that his conduct created the strong probability of death or great bodily harm to another.

Justified Use of Force. Justified use of force is a defense to the offense of 1st Degree Murder. Self-defense is a factual question for the trier-of-fact (judge or jury). Evidence that the defendant believed he was justified in using the force he used to cause the death of the victim puts the burden on the prosecution to prove beyond a reasonable doubt that the killing was without lawful justification. Evidence may raise a reasonable doubt that the defendant's belief that he needed to defend himself was objectively reasonable (a reasonable person would believe under the circumstances that the force used was necessary). If so the jury would find the defendant not guilty. This form of justification is commonly referred to as "perfect self-defense". It is "perfect" because the defendant's belief in the need to resort to force is deemed reasonable. "Imperfect self-defense" can lead to a conviction for 2nd degree murder.

§ 9-2. Second degree murder. (a) A person commits the offense of second degree murder when he or she commits the offense of first degree murder as defined in paragraph (1) or (2) of subsection (a) of Section 9-1 of this Code and either of the following mitigating factors are present:

(1) at the time of the killing he or she is acting under a sudden and intense passion resulting from serious provocation by the individual killed or another whom the offender endeavors to kill, but he or she negligently or accidentally causes the death of the individual killed; or

(2) at the time of the killing he or she believes the circumstances to be such that, if they existed, would justify or exonerate the killing under the principles stated in Article 7 of this Code, but his or her belief is unreasonable.

(b) Serious provocation is conduct sufficient to excite an intense passion in a reasonable person.

(c) When evidence of either of the mitigating factors defined in subsection (a) of this Section has been presented, the burden of proof is on the defendant to prove either mitigating factor by a preponderance of the evidence before the defendant can be found guilty of second degree murder. The burden of proof, however, remains on the State to prove beyond a reasonable doubt each of the elements of first degree murder and, when appropriately raised, the absence of circumstances at the time of the killing that would justify or exonerate the killing under the principles stated in Article 7 of this Code.

(d) Sentence. Second degree murder is a Class 1 felony.

Commentary – Second Degree Murder

2nd Degree Murder. There are several forms of homicide that are less serious than First Degree Murder. These offenses recognize that not all killings are murder and that circumstances exist that diminish the nature of the conduct to allow for proportionately lesser penalties. Second Degree Murder is one of the lesser homicide offenses. Concepts of mitigating circumstances and an altered burden of proof make this a unique criminal offense.

Section 9-2(a) identifies 2nd degree murder as a 1st degree murder with mitigating circumstances. If the 1st Degree Murder occurred under circumstances where the defendant acted because of (1) sudden and intense passion from serious provocation by the victim or another person who the perpetrator was trying to kill or (2) the subjective belief that the perpetrator was justified in using the force used but that belief was unreasonable, then the defendant would be guilty of 2nd Degree Murder.

To be guilty of 2nd Degree murder the defendant must be proved guilty of 1st degree murder. The twist is that Section 9-2(c) places the burden of proof that the mitigating circumstances exist on the defendant who must prove the mitigating factor(s) by a preponderance of the evidence. Being convicted of 2nd Degree Murder would be far preferable to being convicted of 1st Degree Murder since as a Class 1 Felony, the possible sentence is 4 to 15 years imprisonment and the offender can be sentenced to probation.

Mitigating Circumstances – Sudden and Intense Passion as a Result of Serious Provocation. A murder that is committed in the heat of the moment is of lesser degree that one that is contemplated. Section 9-2(a)(1) recognizes that such acts of passion, while not a defense to murder, indeed lessen its seriousness. Section 9-2(b) recognizes that serious provocation is an objective test not a subjective one (a reasonable person would have been provoked). A person who resorts to force and causes another's death must act because of the sudden excitement of that moment. Illinois cases have recognized four categories of such serious provocation (1) physical injury or assault; (2) mutual combat; (3) illegal arrest or (4) adultery by one's spouse. *People v. Gomez* 402 Ill.App.3d 945, 931 N.E.2d 1235 (Ill. App. Ct. 1st Dist. 2010)(rejecting a fifth type based on subjective claim of fear by defendant). Certainly words alone are not enough for a reasonable person to use deadly force that causes another's death. There must be immediacy about the acts that cause death, so that in instances involving adultery, the defendant-spouse must have killed the victim during or immediately before or after the act of adultery. A delay in time of acting does not support a claim of 2nd degree murder. *People v. Chevalier* 131 Ill.2d 65, 544 N.E.2d 942 (1989)(killings of spouses are murder since there was no reasonable claim of serious provocation even in the presence of sudden and intense passion that rose following admission of and arguments about marital infidelity.).

Mitigating Circumstances – Subjective Belief in Justified Use of Force. As explained in 1st Degree Murder, if the defendant's conduct was what a reasonable person under the same facts might do, he would be not guilty of 1st degree murder. However, if the defendant actually believed that he was justified in defending himself but he was wrong (i.e. his subjective belief that he need to use that force was unreasonable) he is not guilty of 1st degree murder but is guilty of 2nd degree murder. The defendant must prove actual, subjective belief. If the jury rejects the claim that the defendant believed he needed to use force to defend himself, the defendant is guilty of 1st degree murder. This form of reduction from 1st degree murder to 2nd degree murder is commonly referred to as "imperfect self-defense", because while the defendant believed in his resort to force, his belief was objectively unreasonable (a reasonable person would conclude that the use of this force was not reasonable.)

The Illinois Supreme Court has held that where the evidence supports a claim of self-defense for the use of deadly force, an instruction for the lesser-included offense of 2nd Degree Murder must be given. *People v. Washington* 2012 IL 110283 (Ill. S. Ct. 2012)(defendant testified that victim reached for gun in his belt and that he shot him as a result, justifying deadly force self-defense instructions but mandating the trial court giving of 2nd Degree Murder "reasonable belief" instructions.)

In *People v. Billups* 404 Ill.App.3d 1, 935 N.E.2d 1046 (Ill. App. Ct. 1st Dist. 2010), the defendant shot and killed Charlie Thompson in an alley. Thompson had two gunshot wounds to his chest from a distance and one gunshot wound to the back of his head where the gun muzzle was right next to the wound. Billups testified that he had wrested a gun away from Thompson who was attempting to rob him and acted in self-defense, and denied that he had shot Thompson in the back of the head. The trial court refused to consider a claim of imperfect self-defense and that refusal was upheld on appeal. In affirming the jury verdict, the court noted that Billups was either guilty of murder or not guilty of murder under these facts, stating:

> When a claim of perfect self-defense is made, the dispositive question is not whether the use of force by the defendant is reasonable or unreasonable under the circumstances but, rather, which set of opposing *circumstances* presented by the parties existed at the time of the incident based upon all of the evidence: the one urged by the defendant that the decedent was the aggressor or true criminal or the one urged by the prosecution that the defendant killed the decedent in a senseless act. The circumstances existed as the defendant testified or they did not. The jury could conclude only one of two things: either the circumstances were as the defendant testified, which means his claim of self-defense is perfect, or the circumstances were as the prosecution witnesses testified, which means the defendant is guilty of first degree murder.
>
> *People v. Billups* 404 Ill.App.3d at 10, 935 N.E.2d at 1054.

§ 9-2.1. Voluntary Manslaughter of an Unborn Child. (a) A person who kills an unborn child without lawful justification commits voluntary manslaughter of an unborn child if at the time of the killing he is acting under a sudden and intense passion resulting from serious provocation by another whom the offender endeavors to kill, but he negligently or accidentally causes the death of the unborn child.

Serious provocation is conduct sufficient to excite an intense passion in a reasonable person.

(b) A person who intentionally or knowingly kills an unborn child commits voluntary manslaughter of an unborn child if at the time of the killing he believes the circumstances to be such that, if they existed, would justify or exonerate the killing under the principles stated in Article 7 of this Code, but his belief is unreasonable.

(c) Sentence. Voluntary Manslaughter of an unborn child is a Class 1 felony.

(d) For purposes of this Section, (1) "unborn child" shall mean any individual of the human species from fertilization until birth, and (2) "person" shall not include the pregnant woman whose unborn child is killed.

(e) This Section shall not apply to acts which cause the death of an unborn child if those acts were committed during any abortion, as defined in Section 2 of the Illinois Abortion Law of 1975, as amended,1 to which the pregnant woman has consented. This Section shall not apply to acts which were committed pursuant to usual and customary standards of medical practice during diagnostic testing or therapeutic treatment.

§ 9-3. Involuntary Manslaughter and Reckless Homicide. (a) A person who unintentionally kills an individual without lawful justification commits involuntary manslaughter if his acts whether lawful or unlawful which cause the death are such as are likely to cause death or great bodily harm to some individual, and he performs them recklessly, except in cases in which the cause of the death consists of the driving of a motor vehicle or operating a snowmobile, all-terrain vehicle, or watercraft, in which case the person commits reckless homicide. A person commits reckless homicide if he or she unintentionally kills an individual while driving a vehicle and using an incline in a roadway, such as a railroad crossing, bridge approach, or hill, to cause the vehicle to become airborne.

(b) (Blank)

(c) (Blank)

(d) Sentence.

(1) Involuntary manslaughter is a Class 3 felony.

(2) Reckless homicide is a Class 3 felony.

(e-2) Except as provided in subsection (e-3), in cases involving reckless homicide in which the offense is committed upon a public thoroughfare where children pass going to and from school when a school crossing guard is performing official duties, the penalty is a Class 2 felony, for which a person, if sentenced to a term of imprisonment, shall be sentenced to a term of not less than 3 years and not more than 14 years.

(e-3) In cases involving reckless homicide in which (i) the offense is committed upon a public thoroughfare where children pass going to and from school when a school crossing guard is performing official duties and (ii) the defendant causes the deaths of 2 or more persons as part of a single course of conduct, the penalty is a Class 2 felony, for which a person, if sentenced to a term of imprisonment, shall be sentenced to a term of not less than 6 years and not more than 28 years.

(e-5) (Blank).

(e-7) Except as otherwise provided in subsection (e-8), in cases involving reckless homicide in which the defendant: (1) was driving in a construction or maintenance zone, as defined in Section 11-605.1 of the Illinois Vehicle Code, or (2) was operating a vehicle while failing or refusing to comply with any lawful order or direction of any authorized police officer or traffic control aide engaged in traffic control, the penalty is a Class 2 felony, for which a person, if sentenced to a term of imprisonment, shall be sentenced to a term of not less than 3 years and not more than 14 years.

(e-8) In cases involving reckless homicide in which the defendant caused the deaths of 2 or more persons as part of a single course of conduct and: (1) was driving in a construction or maintenance zone, as defined in Section 11-605.1 of the Illinois Vehicle Code, or (2) was operating a vehicle while failing or refusing to comply with any lawful order or direction of any authorized police officer or traffic control aide engaged in traffic control, the penalty is a Class 2 felony, for which a person, if sentenced to a term of imprisonment, shall be sentenced to a term of not less than 6 years and not more than 28 years.

(e-9) In cases involving reckless homicide in which the defendant drove a vehicle and used an incline in a roadway, such as a railroad crossing, bridge approach, or hill, to cause the vehicle to become airborne, and caused the deaths of 2 or more persons as part of a single course of conduct, the penalty is a Class 2 felony.

(e-10) In cases involving involuntary manslaughter or reckless homicide resulting in the death of a peace officer killed in the performance of his or her duties as a peace officer, the penalty is a Class 2 felony.

(e-11) In cases involving reckless homicide in which the defendant unintentionally kills an individual while driving in a posted school zone, as defined in Section 11-605 of the Illinois Vehicle Code, while children are present or in a construction or maintenance zone, as defined in Section 11-605.1 of the Illinois Vehicle Code, when construction or maintenance workers are present the trier of fact may infer that the defendant's actions were performed recklessly where he or she was also either driving at a speed of more than 20 miles per hour in excess of the posted speed limit or violating Section 11-501 of the Illinois Vehicle Code.

(e-12) Except as otherwise provided in subsection (e-13), in cases involving reckless homicide in which the offense was committed as result of a violation of subsection (c) of Section 11-907 of the Illinois Vehicle Code, the penalty is a Class 2 felony, for which a person, if sentenced to a term of imprisonment, shall be sentenced to a term of not less than 3 years and not more than 14 years.

(e-13) In cases involving reckless homicide in which the offense was committed as result of a violation of subsection (c) of Section 11-907 of the Illinois Vehicle Code and the defendant caused the deaths of 2 or more persons as part of a single course of conduct, the penalty is a Class 2 felony, for which a person, if sentenced to a term of imprisonment, shall be sentenced to a term of not less than 6 years and not more than 28 years.

(e-14) In cases involving reckless homicide in which the defendant unintentionally kills an individual, the trier of fact may infer that the defendant's actions were performed recklessly where he or she was also violating subsection (c) of Section 11-907 of the Illinois Vehicle Code. The penalty for a reckless homicide in which the driver also violated subsection (c) of Section 11-907 of the Illinois Vehicle Code is a Class 2 felony, for which a person, if sentenced to a term of imprisonment, shall be sentenced to a term of not less than 3 years and not more than 14 years.

(f) In cases involving involuntary manslaughter in which the victim was a family or household member as defined in paragraph (3) of Section 112A-3 of the Code of Criminal Procedure of 1963, the penalty shall be a Class 2 felony, for which a person if sentenced to a term of imprisonment, shall be sentenced to a term of not less than 3 years and not more than 14 years.

Commentary – Involuntary Manslaughter

Involuntary manslaughter. The unintentional killing of another human being is the crime of involuntary manslaughter when the defendant's acts cause the death of another, are unintentional, are likely to cause death or great bodily harm and are preformed recklessly. Recklessness is action in the face of a known and unjustifiable risk of danger, such as shooting a gun into the dark, dropping rocks from a bridge when the road below cannot be seen but traffic is known to be there or shaking a crying baby to attempt to calm it. In each of these circumstances there is a recognizable danger and risk of death, even if the acts themselves (shooting a gun, dropping a rock or shaking a baby) may or may not be legal, depending on the circumstances. Recklessness as a mental state is the main focus. In *People v. Wright* 111 Ill.2d 18, 488 N.E.2d 972 (1986), the defendant's murder conviction had been reduced to involuntary manslaughter following a post conviction proceeding. The defendant shot her daughter when intoxicated on drugs and alcohol. The defendant, in the past, shot a gun in the ceiling at her home to quell an argument. Handling a gun while intoxicated is reckless conduct. The Supreme Court accepted (as not manifestly erroneous) a trial court finding that the defendant's conduct amounted to recklessness - not intentional or knowing conduct as required for a murder conviction.

In *People v. Beasley* 2014 IL App (4th) 120774, the defendant drew his gun when in a confrontation with a large crowd and told people not to move. The evidence was in dispute about the decedent's actions toward the defendant but no witness said the defendant pointed his gun at the victim. Although charged with 1st Degree Murder, the trial court agreed to give 2nd Degree Murder jury instructions consistent with the defendant's claim that he believed he was justified in using deadly force, but that his belief might be found to be unreasonable; however, the trial court refused the defendant's request that the jury be instructed about the lesser-included offense of involuntary manslaughter The jury found the defendant guilty of 2nd Degree Murder. The appellate court reversed the conviction finding the disputed evidence sufficient to support the defendant's request for involuntary manslaughter instructions because the jury could have found from the evidence that the defendant's conduct was reckless and therefore unintentional. See also *People v. Lengyel* 2015 IL App (1st) 131022 (Defendant's conviction for 2nd Degree Murder reduced to involuntary manslaughter where the victim (defendant's father) grabbed and ripped defendant's shirt during an argument, and defendant struck his father with his fists to get away from his grasp. Defendant's actions were reckless, not intentional or knowing, so under the evidence, the conviction for 2nd Degree Murder would be reversed and a judgment of conviction for involuntary manslaughter would be entered instead.)

Reckless Homicide. Reckless Homicide is the reckless and unintentional killing of another while driving a vehicle. In this context recklessness is not negligence. Ordinary traffic violations of speeding, driving too fast for conditions or improper lane usage are not reckless acts;

however, gross and excessive speed violations, multiple driving offenses during a high speed chase and most commonly, intoxication, are all evidence that support a finding of recklessness for purposes of reckless homicide when a death has been caused. The combination of driving behaviors must constitute a conscious disregard that presents a substantial and unjustifiable risk of death or great bodily harm.

In *People v. Gancarz* 309 Ill.App.3d 154, 859 N.E.2d 1127 (Ill. App. Ct. 2nd Dist. 2006) the defendant's conviction of reckless homicide was upheld. The evidence showed the defendant, while under the influence of cannabis, accelerated his semi-truck to attempt to make a yellow light, as it turned red, and struck a left turning car in an intersection. The car's driver was killed in the collision. The combination of all the circumstances supported findings of recklessness and the unintentional yet foreseeable killing of the driver of the other car.

§ 9-3-1.5. Concealment of death. (a) For purposes of this Section, "conceal" means the performing of some act or acts for the purpose of preventing or delaying the discovery of a death. "Conceal" means something more than simply withholding knowledge or failing to disclose information.

(b) A person commits the offense of concealment of death when he or she knowingly conceals the death of any other person who died by other than homicidal means.

(c) A person commits the offense of concealment of death when he or she knowingly moves the body of a dead person from its place of death, with the intent of concealing information regarding the place or manner of death of that person, or the identity of any person with information regarding the death of that person. This subsection shall not apply to any movement of the body of a dead person by medical personnel, fire fighters, law enforcement officers, coroners, medical examiners, or licensed funeral directors, or by any person acting at the direction of medical personnel, fire fighters, law enforcement officers, coroners, medical examiners, or licensed funeral directors.

(d) Sentence. Concealment of death is a Class 4 felony.

§ 9-3.2. Involuntary Manslaughter and Reckless Homicide of an Unborn Child. (a) A person who unintentionally kills an unborn child without lawful justification commits involuntary manslaughter of an unborn child if his acts whether lawful or unlawful which cause the death are such as are likely to cause death or great bodily harm to some individual, and he performs them recklessly, except in cases in which the cause of death consists of the driving of a motor vehicle, in which case the person commits reckless homicide of an unborn child.

(b) Sentence.

(1) Involuntary manslaughter of an unborn child is a Class 3 felony.

(2) Reckless homicide of an unborn child is a Class 3 felony.

(c) For purposes of this Section, (1) "unborn child" shall mean any individual of the human species from fertilization until birth, and (2) "person" shall not include the pregnant woman whose unborn child is killed.

(d) This Section shall not apply to acts which cause the death of an unborn child if those acts were committed during any abortion, as defined in Section 2 of the Illinois Abortion Law of 1975, as amended,1 to which the pregnant woman has consented. This Section shall not apply to acts which were committed pursuant to usual and customary standards of medical practice during diagnostic testing or therapeutic treatment.

(e) The provisions of this Section shall not be construed to prohibit the prosecution of any person under any other provision of law, nor shall it be construed to preclude any civil cause of action.

§ 9-3.3. Drug-induced homicide. (a) A person who violates Section 401 of the Illinois Controlled Substances Act1 or Section 55 of the Methamphetamine Control and Community Protection Act by unlawfully delivering a controlled substance to another, and any person's death is caused by the injection, inhalation, absorption, or ingestion of any amount of that controlled substance, commits the offense of drug-induced homicide.

(b) Sentence. Drug-induced homicide is a Class X felony.

(c) A person who commits drug-induced homicide by violating subsection (a) or subsection (c) of Section 401 of the Illinois Controlled Substances Act or Section 55 of the Methamphetamine Control and Community Protection Act commits a Class X felony for which the defendant shall in addition to a sentence authorized by law, be sentenced to a term of imprisonment of not less than 15 years and not more than 30 years or an extended term of not less than 30 years and not more than 60 years.

§ 9-3.4. Concealment of homicidal death.

(a) A person commits the offense of concealment of homicidal death when he or she knowingly conceals the death of any other person with knowledge that such other person has died by homicidal means.

(b) Nothing in this Section prevents the defendant from also being charged with and tried for the first degree murder, second degree murder, or involuntary manslaughter of the person whose death is concealed.

(b-5) For purposes of this Section:

"Conceal" means the performing of some act or acts for the purpose of preventing or delaying the discovery of a death by homicidal means. "Conceal" means something more than simply withholding knowledge or failing to disclose information.

"Homicidal means" means any act or acts, lawful or unlawful, of a person that cause the death of another person.

(c) Sentence. Concealment of homicidal death is a Class 3 felony.

Commentary – Concealment of Death and Homicidal Death

Concealment offenses. If one knows about the death of a human being, or knows of a death caused by homicide, he must report those deaths. Section 9-3-1.5 defines the lesser offense of concealment of death - committed if the acts undertaken by the defendant knowingly prevented or delayed discovery of a dead body in a non-homicidal death. Concealment of Death is a Class 4 Felony.

Concealment of a Homicidal Death. Concealment of a homicide under Section 9-4 is often charged with another homicide offense. It is not unusual for someone who has killed another to dispose of the body to prevent or delay the discovery of the crime. The offense requires proof of a mental state element - that the offender knowingly concealed the death, but had also had knowledge that the death was by homicidal means Concealment of a homicidal death is a Class 3 Felony. A conviction for homicide and concealment require consecutive sentences.

In *People v. Jennings* 343 Ill.App.3d 717, 798 N.E.2d 1211 (Ill. App. Ct. 5th Dist. 2003), the defendant killed the victim after catching him engaged in a sexual act with his wife. The defendant tied coffee cans full of concrete to the victim's body and put the body into Lake Shelbyville where it was discovered by a fisherman. The defendant was sentenced to 15 years imprisonment for the 2nd Degree Murder conviction and 5 years imprisonment on the conviction for Concealment of a Homicidal Death. In affirming the conviction for 2nd Degree Murder and Concealment of a Homicidal Death, the Court noted that the trial court was required to impose a consecutive sentence for the concealment offense.

Article 10 – Kidnapping and Related Offenses
720 ILCS 5/10-1 *et seq.*

§ 10-1. Kidnapping. (a) A person commits the offense of kidnapping when he or she knowingly:

(1) and secretly confines another against his or her will;

(2) by force or threat of imminent force carries another from one place to another with intent secretly to confine that other person against his or her will; or

(3) by deceit or enticement induces another to go from one place to another with intent secretly to confine that other person against his or her will.

(b) Confinement of a child under the age of 13 years, or of a person with a severe or profound intellectual disability, is against that child's or person's will within the meaning of this Section if that confinement is without the consent of that child's or person's parent or legal guardian.

(c) Sentence. Kidnapping is a Class 2 felony.

§ 10-2. Aggravated kidnapping. (a) A person commits the offense of aggravated kidnapping when he or she commits kidnapping and:

(1) kidnaps with the intent to obtain ransom from the person kidnapped or from any other person;

(2) takes as his or her victim a child under the age of 13 years, or a person with a severe or profound intellectual disability;

(3) inflicts great bodily harm, other than by the discharge of a firearm, or commits another felony upon his or her victim;

(4) wears a hood, robe, or mask or conceals his or her identity;

(5) commits the offense of kidnapping while armed with a dangerous weapon, other than a firearm, as defined in Section 33A-1 of this Code;

(6) commits the offense of kidnapping while armed with a firearm;

(7) during the commission of the offense of kidnapping, personally discharges a firearm; or

(8) during the commission of the offense of kidnapping, personally discharges a firearm that proximately causes great bodily harm, permanent disability, permanent disfigurement, or death to another person.

As used in this Section, "ransom" includes money, benefit, or other valuable thing or concession.
(b) Sentence. Aggravated kidnapping in violation of paragraph (1), (2), (3), (4), or (5) of subsection (a) is a Class X felony. A violation of subsection (a)(6) is a Class X felony for which 15 years shall be added to the term of imprisonment imposed by the court. An offender under the age of 18 years at the time of the commission of aggravated kidnaping in violation of paragraphs (1) through (8) of subsection (a) shall be sentenced under Section 5-4.5-105 of the Unified Code of Corrections.

A person who has attained the age of 18 years at the time of the commission of the offense and who is convicted of a second or subsequent offense of aggravated kidnaping shall be sentenced to a term of natural life imprisonment; except that a sentence of natural life imprisonment shall not be imposed under this Section unless the second or subsequent offense was committed after conviction on the first offense. An offender under the age of 18 years at the time of the commission of the second or subsequent offense shall be sentenced under Section 5-4.5-105 of the Unified Code of Corrections.

Commentary – Kidnapping Offenses

Section 10-1 defines the crime of kidnapping under three theories when someone exercises non-consensual control over another by knowingly committing acts of (1) asportation (carrying away a person from one place to another), (2) secret confinement or (3) deceitful inducement. Section 10-2 defines aggravated kidnapping with aggravating factors when a defendant kidnaps with (1) intent to obtain ransom, (2) a victim under age 13 or with disability, (3) causes bodily harm or commits a felony on the victim, (4) the use of disguises such as masks or hoods or (5) possession or use of a firearm or other dangerous weapon during the crime.

Asportation. Asportation is the carrying away of a person or object from one location to another - generally used to describe the first type of kidnapping. In *People v. Siguenza-Brito* 235 Ill.2d 213, 920 N.E.2d 233 (2009), the defendant forced the victim into a car, drove her a short distance to a garage where he removed her from the car and sexually assaulted her. He was convicted of Aggravated Kidnapping as well as Aggravated Criminal Sexual Assault, a kidnapping under the asportation or confinement elements of the statute. Despite the short distance travelled and the short time involved in the kidnapping, the evidence was sufficient proof of the carrying away of the victim from one location to another. The sexual assault of the victim was an aggravating factor for the more serious kidnapping conviction. In *People v. Johnson* 2015 IL App (1st) 123249, the Court found sufficient evidence to support asportation where the Defendant committed a sexual assault in a vacant lot and then moved the victim to a nearby alley between two buildings where he committed a second sexual assault. The Defendant's claim that the movement was incidental to the crime of sexual assault was rejected.

Secret Confinement. A second kidnapping theory is the secret confinement of the victim against his will. In *People v. Gonzalez* 239 Ill.2d 431, 942 N.E.2d 1246 (Ill. S. Ct. 2011), the defendant was convicted of aggravated kidnapping after a jury trial where she took a neighbor's baby in a hospital waiting room and walked away, down the street and to another hospital where she was apprehended. The kidnapping was based on a confinement theory and the aggravation was the age of the victim (less than 13 years old). The defendant had a tubal ligation and was unable to have children, nonetheless she had told her husband she was pregnant and had gone to the hospital to take the baby, as described. The appellate court had reversed the conviction for aggravated kidnapping based on a lack of showing of a secret confinement of the victim – the defendant had the victim on the street and in a hospital – at all times in public view. In reversing the appellate court and affirming the defendant's conviction, the Illinois Supreme Court noted that "secret" confinements are those that are hidden or concealed, and stated:

> Reviewing this evidence in the light most favorable to the State, we conclude that a trier of fact could reasonably find that defendant's conduct isolated the baby from meaningful contact with the public. The baby was unable to escape, cry out, or call attention to her plight. The evidence also suggested that defendant took the baby without the parents' permission or knowledge and sought to pass the baby off as her own, unbeknownst to anyone who saw defendant with the baby. Consequently, defendant's actions isolated the baby from the public even though defendant kept the baby in public view.
>
> *People v. Gonzalez* 239 Ill.2d at 80-81, 942 N.E.2d at 1252.

In *People v. Calderon* 393 Ill.App.3d 1, 911 N.E.2d 1115 (Ill App. Ct. 1st Dist. 2009), the defendant's conviction for aggravated kidnapping on the basis of secret confinement was upheld where he had kept his victim inside a car by threat of force for 1 ½ hours against his will and then forced him to drive to another location, even though it was daytime, the car windows were clear and there were members of the public at a nearby gas station. The aggravating factor was the robbery of the victim. What constitutes secret confinement or intent to secretly confine depends on the circumstances of each case.

Kidnapping as a Separate Offense. Sometimes it may be difficult to determine whether a kidnapping occurred because the continuity of the conduct led to the commission of another offense. courts look to four factors in making the determination about whether the asportation or detention can be conduct associated with the separate offense or the commission of the crime of kidnapping: (1) the duration of the asportation or detention; (2) whether the asportation or detention occurred during the commission of the separate offense; (3) whether the asportation or detention is inherent in the commission of the separate offense and (4) whether the asportation or detention threatened harm to the victim independent of the harm threatened by the commission of the other offense. In *People v. Ware* 323 Ill.App.3d 47, 751 N.E.2d 81 (Ill. App. Ct. 1st Dist. 2001), the defendant worked at a restaurant and forced the victim, a former co-worker, into the men's restroom, where he sexually assaulted her. Even though the duration of the unlawful movement from the hallway to the rest room was short, it occurred before the sexual assault, was independent of the sexual assault and created the possibility of a different kind of harm to the victim.

Dangerous Weapon. An aggravating factor for the offense of Aggravating Kidnapping is the use of a dangerous weapon. "Dangerous Weapon" is a broad term that include a variety of weapons; however, a mace canister is not a dangerous weapon for purposes of this offense. See *People v. Dressler* 317 Ill.App.3d 379, 739 N.E.2d 630 (Ill. App. Ct. 3rd Dist. 2000)

§ 10-3. Unlawful restraint. (a) A person commits the offense of unlawful restraint when he or she knowingly without legal authority detains another.

(b) Sentence. Unlawful restraint is a Class 4 felony.

§ 10-3.1. Aggravated unlawful restraint. (a) A person commits the offense of aggravated unlawful restraint when he or she commits unlawful restraint while using a deadly weapon.

(b) Sentence. Aggravated unlawful restraint is a Class 3 felony.

§ 10-4. Forcible Detention. (a) A person commits the offense of forcible detention when he holds an individual hostage without lawful authority for the purpose of obtaining performance by a third person of demands made by the person holding the hostage, and

(1) the person holding the hostage is armed with

a dangerous weapon as defined in Section 33A-1 of this Code, or

(2) the hostage is known to the person holding him to be a peace officer or a correctional employee engaged in the performance of his official duties.

(b) Forcible detention is a Class 2 felony.

§ 10-5. Child abduction. (a) For purposes of this Section, the following terms have the following meanings:

(1) "Child" means a person who, at the time the alleged violation occurred, was under the age of 18 or was a person with a severe or profound intellectual disability.

(2) "Detains" means taking or retaining physical custody of a child, whether or not the child resists or objects.

(2.1) "Express consent" means oral or written permission that is positive, direct, and unequivocal, requiring no inference or implication to supply its meaning.

(2.2) "Luring" means any knowing act to solicit, entice, tempt, or attempt to attract the minor.

(3) "Lawful custodian" means a person or persons granted legal custody of a child or

entitled to physical possession of a child pursuant to a court order. It is presumed that, when the parties have never been married to each other, the mother has legal custody of the child unless a valid court order states otherwise. If an adjudication of paternity has been completed and the father has been assigned support obligations or visitation rights, such a paternity order should, for the purposes of this Section, be considered a valid court order granting custody to the mother.

(4) “Putative father” means a man who has a reasonable belief that he is the father of a child born of a woman who is not his wife.

(5) "Unlawful purpose" means any misdemeanor or felony violation of State law or a similar federal or sister state law or local ordinance.

(b) A person commits the offense of child abduction when he or she does any one of the following:

(1) Intentionally violates any terms of a valid court order granting sole or joint custody, care, or possession to another by concealing or detaining the child or removing the child from the jurisdiction of the court.

(2) Intentionally violates a court order prohibiting the person from concealing or detaining the child or removing the child from the jurisdiction of the court.

(3) Intentionally conceals, detains, or removes the child without the consent of the mother or lawful custodian of the child if the person is a putative father and either: (A) the paternity of the child has not been legally established or (B) the paternity of the child has been legally established but no orders relating to custody have been entered. Notwithstanding the presumption created by paragraph (3) of subsection (a), however, a mother commits child abduction when she intentionally conceals or removes a child, whom she has abandoned or relinquished custody of, from an unadjudicated father who has provided sole ongoing care and custody of the child in her absence.

(4) Intentionally conceals or removes the child from a parent after filing a petition or being served with process in an action affecting marriage or paternity but prior to the issuance of a temporary or final order determining custody.

(5) At the expiration of visitation rights outside the State, intentionally fails or refuses to return or impedes the return of the child to the lawful custodian in Illinois.

(6) Being a parent of the child, and if the parents of that child are or have been married and there has been no court order of custody, knowingly conceals the child for 15 days, and fails to make reasonable attempts within the 15-day period to notify the other parent as to the specific whereabouts of the child, including a means by which to contact the child, or to arrange reasonable visitation or contact with the child. It is not a violation of this Section for a person fleeing domestic violence to take the child with him or her to housing provided by a domestic violence program.

(7) Being a parent of the child, and if the parents of the child are or have been married and there has been no court order of custody, knowingly conceals, detains, or removes the child with physical force or threat of physical force.

(8) Knowingly conceals, detains, or removes the child for payment or promise of payment at the instruction of a person who has no legal right to custody.

(9) Knowingly retains in this State for 30 days a child removed from another state without the consent of the lawful custodian or in violation of a valid court order of custody.

(10) Intentionally lures or attempts to lure a child under the age of 16 into a motor vehicle, building, housetrailer, or dwelling place without the consent of the child's parent or lawful custodian for other than a lawful purpose. For the purposes of this item (10), the trier of fact may infer that luring or attempted luring of a child under the age of 16 into a motor vehicle, building, housetrailer, or dwelling place without the express consent of the child's parent or lawful custodian or with the intent to avoid the express consent of the child’s parent or lawful

custodian was for other than a lawful purpose.

(11) With the intent to obstruct or prevent efforts to locate the child victim of a child abduction, knowingly destroys, alters, conceals, or disguises physical evidence or furnishes false information.

(c) It is an affirmative defense to subsections (b)(1) through (b)(10) of this Section that:

(1) the person had custody of the child pursuant to a court order granting legal custody or visitation rights that existed at the time of the alleged violation;

(2) the person had physical custody of the child pursuant to a court order granting legal custody or visitation rights and failed to return the child as a result of circumstances beyond his or her control, and the person notified and disclosed to the other parent or legal custodian the specific whereabouts of the child and a means by which the child could be contacted or made a reasonable attempt to notify the other parent or lawful custodian of the child of those circumstances and made the disclosure within 24 hours after the visitation period had expired and returned the child as soon as possible;

(3) the person was fleeing an incidence or pattern of domestic violence; or

(4) the person lured or attempted to lure a child under the age of 16 into a motor vehicle, building, housetrailer, or dwelling place for a lawful purpose in prosecutions under paragraph (10) of subsection (b).

(d) A person convicted of child abduction under this Section is guilty of a Class 4 felony. A person convicted of child abduction under subsection (b)(10) shall undergo a sex offender evaluation prior to a sentence being imposed. A person convicted of a second or subsequent violation of paragraph (10) of subsection (b) of this Section is guilty of a Class 3 felony. A person convicted of child abduction under subsection (b)(10) when the person has a prior conviction of a sex offense as defined in the Sex Offender Registration Act or any substantially similar federal, Uniform Code of Military Justice, sister state, or foreign government offense is guilty of a Class 2 felony. It is a factor in aggravation under subsections (b)(1) through (b)(10) of this Section for which a court may impose a more severe sentence under Section 5-8-1 (730 ILCS 5/5-8-1) or Article 4.5 of Chapter V of the Unified Code of Corrections1 if, upon sentencing, the court finds evidence of any of the following aggravating factors:

(1) that the defendant abused or neglected the child following the concealment, detention, or removal of the child;

(2) that the defendant inflicted or threatened to inflict physical harm on a parent or lawful custodian of the child or on the child with intent to cause that parent or lawful custodian to discontinue criminal prosecution of the defendant under this Section;

(3) that the defendant demanded payment in exchange for return of the child or demanded that he or she be relieved of the financial or legal obligation to support the child in exchange for return of the child;

(4) that the defendant has previously been convicted of child abduction;

(5) that the defendant committed the abduction while armed with a deadly weapon or the taking of the child resulted in serious bodily injury to another; or

(6) that the defendant committed the abduction while in a school, regardless of the time of day or time of year; in a playground; on any conveyance owned, leased, or contracted by a school to transport students to or from school or a school related activity; on the real property of a school; or on a public way within 1,000 feet of the real property comprising any school or playground. For purposes of this paragraph (6), "playground" means a piece of land owned or controlled by a unit of local government that is designated by the unit of local government for use solely or primarily for children's recreation; and "school" means a public or private elementary or secondary school, community college, college, or university.

(e) The court may order the child to be returned to the parent or lawful custodian from whom the child was concealed, detained, or removed. In addition to any sentence imposed, the court may assess any reasonable expense incurred in searching for or returning the child against any person convicted of violating this Section.

(f) Nothing contained in this Section shall be construed to limit the court's contempt power.

(g) Every law enforcement officer investigating an alleged incident of child abduction shall make a written police report of any bona fide allegation and the disposition of that investigation. Every police report completed pursuant to this Section shall be compiled and recorded within the meaning of Section 5.1 of the Criminal Identification Act.2

(h) Whenever a law enforcement officer has reasons to believe a child abduction has occurred, she or he shall provide the lawful custodian a summary of her or his rights under this Code, including the procedures and relief available to her or him.

(i) If during the course of an investigation under this Section the child is found in the physical custody of the defendant or another, the law enforcement officer shall return the child to the parent or lawful custodian from whom the child was concealed, detained, or removed, unless there is good cause for the law enforcement officer or the Department of Children and Family Services to retain temporary protective custody of the child pursuant to the Abused and Neglected Child Reporting Act.

§ 10-5.1. Luring of a minor. (a) A person commits the offense of luring of a minor when the offender is 21 years of age or older and knowingly contacts or communicates electronically to the minor:

(1) knowing the minor is under 15 years of age;

(2) with the intent to persuade, lure or transport the minor away from his or her home, or other location known by the minor's parent or legal guardian to be the place where the minor is to be located;

(3) for an unlawful purpose;

(4) without the express consent of the person's parent or legal guardian;

(5) with the intent to avoid the express consent of the person's parent or legal guardian;

(6) after so communicating, commits any act in furtherance of the intent described in clause (a)(2); and

(7) is a stranger to the parents or legal guardian of the minor.

(b) A person commits the offense of luring of a minor when the offender is at least 18 years of age but under 21 years of age and knowingly contacts or communicates electronically to the minor:

(1) knowing the minor is under 15 years of age;

(2) with the intent to persuade, lure, or transport the minor away from his or her home or other location known by the minor's parent or legal guardian, to be the place where the minor is to be located;

(3) for an unlawful purpose;

(4) without the express consent of the person's parent or legal guardian;

(5) with the intent to avoid the express consent of the person's parent or legal guardian;

(6) after so communicating, commits any act in furtherance of the intent described in clause (b)(2); and

(7) is a stranger to the parents or legal guardian of the minor.

(c) Definitions. For purposes of this Section:

(1) "Emergency situation" means a situation in which the minor is threatened with imminent bodily harm, emotional harm or psychological harm.

(2) "Express consent" means oral or written permission that is positive, direct, and unequivocal, requiring no inference or

implication to supply its meaning.

(3) “Contacts or communicates electronically” includes but is not limited to, any attempt to make contact or communicate telephonically or through the Internet or text messages.

(4) “Luring” shall mean any knowing act to solicit, entice, tempt, or attempt to attract the minor.

(5) “Minor” shall mean any person under the age of 15.

(6) “Stranger” shall have its common and ordinary meaning, including but not limited to, a person that is either not known by the parents of the minor or does not have any association with the parents of the minor.

(7) “Unlawful purpose” shall mean any misdemeanor or felony violation of State law or a similar federal or sister state law or local ordinance.

(d) This Section may not be interpreted to criminalize an act or person contacting a minor within the scope and course of his employment, or status as a volunteer of a recognized civic, charitable or youth organization.

(e) This Section is intended to protect minors and to help parents and legal guardians exercise reasonable care, supervision, protection, and control over minor children.

(f) Affirmative defenses.

(1) It shall be an affirmative defense to any offense under this Section 10-5.1 that the accused reasonably believed that the minor was over the age of 15.

(2) It shall be an affirmative defense to any offense under this Section 10-5.1 that the accused is assisting the minor in an emergency situation.

(3) It shall not be a defense to the prosecution of any offense under this Section 10-5.1 if the person who is contacted by the offender is posing as a minor and is in actuality an adult law enforcement officer.

(g) Penalties.

(1) A first offense of luring of a minor under subsection (a) shall be a Class 4 felony. A person convicted of luring of a minor under subsection (a) shall undergo a sex offender evaluation prior to a sentence being imposed. An offense of luring of a minor under subsection (a) when a person has a prior conviction in Illinois of a sex offense as defined in the Sex Offender Registration Act, or any substantially similar federal, Uniform Code of Military Justice, sister state, or foreign government offense, is guilty of a Class 2 felony.

(2) A first offense of luring of a minor under subsection (b) is a Class B misdemeanor.

(3) A second or subsequent offense of luring of a minor under subsection (a) is a Class 3 felony. A second or subsequent offense of luring of a minor under subsection (b) is a Class 4 felony. A second or subsequent offense when a person has a prior conviction in Illinois of a sex offense as defined in the Sex Offender Registration Act, or any substantially similar federal, Uniform Code of Military Justice, sister state, or foreign government offense, is a Class 1 felony. A defendant convicted a second time of an offense under subsection (a) or (b) shall register as a sexual predator of children pursuant to the Sex Offender Registration Act.

(4) A third or subsequent offense is a Class 1 felony. A third or subsequent offense when a person has a prior conviction in Illinois of a sex offense as defined in the Sex Offender Registration Act, or any substantially similar federal, Uniform Code of Military Justice, sister state, or foreign government offense, is a Class X felony.

(h) For violations of subsection (a), jurisdiction shall be established if the transmission that constitutes the offense either originates in this State or is received in this State and does not apply to emergency situations. For violations of subsection (b), jurisdiction shall be established in any county where the act in furtherance of the commission of the offense is committed, in the county where the minor resides, or in the county where the offender resides.

§ 10-5.5. Unlawful visitation or parenting time interference. (a) As used in this Section, the terms "child", "detain", and "lawful custodian" have the meanings ascribed to them in Section 10-5 of this Code.

(b) Every person who, in violation of the visitation, parenting time, or custody time provisions of a court order relating to child custody, detains or conceals a child with the intent to deprive another person of his or her rights to visitation, parenting time, or custody time commits the offense of unlawful visitation or parenting time interference.

(c) A person committing unlawful visitation or parenting time interference is guilty of a petty offense. Any person violating this Section after 2 prior convictions of unlawful visitation interference or unlawful visitation or parenting time interference, however, is guilty of a Class A misdemeanor.

(d) Any law enforcement officer who has probable cause to believe that a person has committed or is committing an act in violation of this Section shall issue to that person a notice to appear.

(e) The notice shall:

(1) be in writing;

(2) state the name of the person and his or her address, if known;

(3) set forth the nature of the offense;

(4) be signed by the officer issuing the notice; and

(5) request the person to appear before a court at a certain time and place.

(f) Upon failure of the person to appear, a summons or warrant of arrest may be issued.

(g) It is an affirmative defense that:

(1) a person or lawful custodian committed the act to protect the child from imminent physical harm, provided that the defendant's belief that there was physical harm imminent was reasonable and that the defendant's conduct in withholding visitation rights, parenting time, or custody time was a reasonable response to the harm believed imminent;

(2) the act was committed with the mutual consent of all parties having a right to custody and visitation of the child or parenting time with the child; or

(3) the act was otherwise authorized by law.

§ 10-6. Harboring a runaway. (a) Any person, other than an agency or association providing crisis intervention services as defined in Section 3-5 of the Juvenile Court Act of 1987,1 or an operator of a youth emergency shelter as defined in Section 2.21 of the Child Care Act of 1969,2 who, without the knowledge and consent of the minor's parent or guardian, knowingly gives shelter to a minor, other than a mature minor who has been emancipated under the Emancipation of Minors Act,3 for more than 48 hours without the consent of the minor's parent or guardian, and without notifying the local law enforcement authorities of the minor's name and the fact that the minor is being provided shelter commits the offense of harboring a runaway.

(b) Any person who commits the offense of harboring a runaway is guilty of a Class A misdemeanor.

§ 10-7. Aiding or abetting child abduction.(a) A person violates this Section when, before or during the commission of a child abduction as defined in Section 10-5 and with the intent to promote or facilitate such offense, he or she intentionally aids or abets another in the planning or commission of child abduction, unless before the commission of the offense he or she makes proper effort to prevent the commission of the offense.

(b) Sentence. A person who violates this Section commits a Class 4 felony.

§ 10-8. Unlawful sale of a public conveyance travel ticket to a minor. (a) A person commits the offense of unlawful sale of a public conveyance travel ticket to a minor when the person sells a ticket for travel on any public conveyance to an unemancipated minor under 17 years of age without the consent of the minor's parents or guardian for passage to a destination outside this state and knows the minor's age or fails to take reasonable measures to ascertain the minor's age.

(b) Evidence. The fact that the defendant demanded, was shown, and reasonably relied upon written evidence of a person's age in any transaction forbidden by this Section is competent evidence, and may be considered in any criminal prosecution for a violation of this Section.

(c) Definition. "Public Conveyance", includes an airplane, boat, bus, railroad, train, taxicab or other vehicle used for the transportation of passengers for hire.

(d) Sentence. Unlawful sale of a public conveyance travel ticket to a minor is a Class C misdemeanor.

§ 10-8.1. Unlawful sending of a public conveyance travel ticket to a minor. (a) In this Section, "public conveyance" has the meaning ascribed to it in Section 10-8 of this Code.

(b) A person commits the offense of unlawful sending of a public conveyance travel ticket to a minor when the person without the consent of the minor's parent or guardian:

(1) knowingly sends, causes to be sent, or purchases a public conveyance travel ticket to any location for a person known by the offender to be an unemancipated minor under 17 years of age or a person he or she believes to be a minor under 17 years of age, other than for a lawful purpose under Illinois law; or

(2) knowingly arranges for travel to any location on any public conveyance for a person known by the offender to be an unemancipated minor under 17 years of age or a person he or she believes to be a minor under 17 years of age, other than for a lawful purpose under Illinois law.

(b-5) Telecommunications carriers, commercial mobile service providers, and providers of information services, including, but not limited to, Internet service providers and hosting service providers, are not liable under this Section, except for willful and wanton misconduct, by virtue of the transmission, storage, or caching of electronic communications or messages of others or by virtue of the provision of other related telecommunications, commercial mobile services, or information services used by others in violation of this Section.

(c) Sentence. Unlawful sending of a public conveyance travel ticket to a minor is a Class A misdemeanor. A person who commits unlawful sending of a public conveyance travel ticket to a minor who believes that he or she is at least 5 years older than the minor is guilty of a Class 4 felony.

§ 10-9. Trafficking in persons, involuntary servitude, and related offenses. (a) Definitions. In this Section:

(1) "Intimidation" has the meaning prescribed in Section 12-6.

(2) "Commercial sexual activity" means any sex on account of which anything of value is given, promised to, or received by any person.

(3) "Financial harm" includes intimidation that brings about financial loss, criminal usury, or employment contracts that violate the Frauds Act.
(4) (Blank). "

(5) "Labor" means work of economic or financial value.
(6) "Maintain" means, in relation to labor or services, to secure continued performance thereof, regardless of any initial agreement on the part of the victim to perform that type of service.

(7) "Obtain" means, in relation to labor or services to secure performance thereof.

(7.5) “Serious harm” means any harm, whether physical or nonphysical, including psychological, financial, or reputational harm, that is sufficiently serious, under all the surrounding circumstances, to compel a reasonable person of the same background and in the same circumstances to perform or to continue performing labor or services in order to avoid incurring that harm.

(8) "Services" means activities resulting from a relationship between a person and the actor in which the person performs activities under the supervision of or for the benefit of the actor. Commercial sexual activity and sexually-explicit performances are forms of activities that are "services" under this Section. Nothing in this definition may be construed to legitimize or legalize prostitution.

(9) "Sexually-explicit performance" means a live, recorded, broadcast (including over the Internet), or public act or show intended to arouse or satisfy the sexual desires or appeal to the prurient interests of patrons.

(10) "Trafficking victim" means a person subjected to the practices set forth in subsection (b), (c), or (d).

(b) Involuntary servitude. A person commits involuntary servitude when he or she knowingly subjects, attempts to subject, or engages in a conspiracy to subject another person to labor or services obtained or maintained through any of the following means, or any combination of these means:

(1) causes or threatens to cause physical harm to any person;

(2) physically restrains or threatens to physically restrain another person;

(3) abuses or threatens to abuse the law or legal process;

(4) knowingly destroys, conceals, removes, confiscates, or possesses any actual or purported passport or other immigration document, or any other actual or purported government identification document, of another person;

(5) uses intimidation, or exerts financial control over any person; or

(6) uses any scheme, plan, or pattern intended to cause the person to believe that, if the person did not perform the labor or services, that person or another person would suffer serious harm or physical restraint. Sentence. Except as otherwise provided in subsection (e) or (f), a violation of subsection (b)(1) is a Class X felony, (b)(2) is a Class 1 felony, (b)(3) is a Class 2 felony, (b)(4) is a Class 3 felony, (b)(5) and (b)(6) is a Class 4 felony.

(c) Involuntary sexual servitude of a minor. A person commits involuntary sexual servitude of a minor when he or she knowingly recruits, entices, harbors, transports, provides, or obtains by any means, or attempts to recruit, entice, harbor, provide, or obtain by any means, another person under 18 years of age, knowing that the minor will engage in commercial sexual activity, a sexually-explicit performance, or the production of pornography, or causes or attempts to cause a minor to engage in one or more of those activities and:

(1) there is no overt force or threat and the minor is between the ages of 17 and 18 years;
(2) there is no overt force or threat and the minor is under the age of 17 years; or

(3) there is overt force or threat. Sentence. Except as otherwise provided in subsection (e) or (f), a violation of subsection (c)(1) is a Class 1 felony, (c)(2) is a Class X felony, and (c)(3) is a Class X felony.

(d) Trafficking in persons. A person commits trafficking in persons when he or she knowingly: (1) recruits, entices, harbors, transports, provides, or obtains by any means, or attempts to recruit, entice, harbor, transport, provide, or obtain by any means, another person, intending or knowing that the person will be subjected to involuntary servitude; or (2) benefits, financially or by receiving anything of value, from participation in a venture that has engaged in an act of involuntary servitude or involuntary sexual servitude of a minor. Sentence. Except as otherwise provided in subsection (e) or (f), a violation of this subsection is a Class 1 felony.

(e) Aggravating factors. A violation of this Section involving kidnapping or an attempt to kidnap, aggravated criminal sexual assault or an attempt to commit aggravated criminal sexual assault, or an attempt to commit first degree murder is a Class X felony.

(f) Sentencing considerations.

(1) Bodily injury. If, pursuant to a violation of this Section, a victim suffered bodily injury, the defendant may be sentenced to an extended-term sentence under Section 5-8-2 of the Unified Code of Corrections. The sentencing court must take into account the time in which the victim was held in servitude, with increased penalties for cases in which the victim was held for between 180 days and one year, and increased penalties for cases in which the victim was held for more than one year.

(2) Number of victims. In determining sentences within statutory maximums, the sentencing court should take into account the number of victims, and may provide for substantially increased sentences in cases involving more than 10 victims.

(g) Restitution. Restitution is mandatory under this Section. In addition to any other amount of loss identified, the court shall order restitution including the greater of (1) the gross income or value to the defendant of the victim's labor or services or (2) the value of the victim's labor as guaranteed under the Minimum Wage Law and overtime provisions of the Fair Labor Standards Act (FLSA) or the Minimum Wage Law, whichever is greater.

(h) Trafficking victim services. Subject to the availability of funds, the Department of Human Services may provide or fund emergency services and assistance to individuals who are victims of one or more offenses defined in this Section.

(i) Certification. The Attorney General, a State's Attorney, or any law enforcement official shall certify in writing to the United States Department of Justice or other federal agency, such as the United States Department of Homeland Security, that an investigation or prosecution under this Section has begun and the individual who is a likely victim of a crime described in this Section is willing to cooperate or is cooperating with the investigation to enable the individual, if eligible under federal law, to qualify for an appropriate special immigrant visa and to access available federal benefits. Cooperation with law enforcement shall not be required of victims of a crime described in this Section who are under 18 years of age. This certification shall be made available to the victim and his or her designated legal representative.

(j) A person who commits involuntary servitude, involuntary sexual servitude of a minor, or trafficking in persons under subsection (b), (c), or (d) of this Section is subject to the property forfeiture provisions set forth in Article 124B of the Code of Criminal Procedure of 1963.

Commentary – Other Crimes of Restraint

Unlawful Restraint. Section 10-3 defines the crime of Unlawful Restraint which - essentially where a person knowingly prevents someone's movement without authority to do so. In *People v. Lissade* 403 Ill.App.3d 609, 935, N.E.2d 1041 (Ill. App. Ct. 2nd Dist. 2010), the defendant came to his ex-girlfriend's home and grabbed her by the throat as she sat on the couch and refused to let her go, holding on to her and forcing her to stay on the couch until a third party intervened and he let go. This is the essence of an unlawful restraint. An Aggravated Unlawful Restraint (Section 10-3.1) occurs when a deadly weapon is used during the offense.

Child Abduction. Section 10-5 is meant to protect children from unlawful abduction. Section 10-5(b)(1) defines the crime as the intentional violation of a court order regarding custody by detaining or concealing a child or removing a child from the jurisdiction of the court without the consent of the custodial parent. A child is detained when he is within the physical control of another, regardless of the child's consent to that control.

Under Section 10(5)(b)(3) child abduction may also occur when no court order regarding custody has been entered where the perpetrator, and the father of the child, intentionally detains or conceals the child from the child's mother, who has provided the primary care for the child. Note the presumption under this section in favor of the natural mother of a child.

Under Section 10-5(b)(10) child abduction can also occur when the perpetrator intentionally lures the child into a vehicle, building or dwelling for other than a lawful purpose. In *People v. Woodrum* 223 Ill.2d 286, 860 N.E.2d 259 (2006), the defendant admitted that he lured children into his home by videotaping them and replaying the video. His purpose was to enhance his own sexual excitement. He claimed that he was wrongfully convicted for his personal thoughts, as opposed to actually doing anything to harm the children. The Illinois Supreme Court stated:

> the offense of child abduction is complete upon luring a child into a dwelling with the requisite unlawful purpose. The State is not required to prove that defendant completed his unlawful purpose or intended offense after luring the children inside. The completion or attempted completion of the unlawful purpose would result in a prosecution for a separate offense. Thus, contrary to defendant's argument, the State was not required to prove that a separate crime or attempt occurred inside the residence to sustain the charge of child abduction.
>
> *People v. Woodrum* 223 Ill.2d at 306, 860 N.E. 2d at 273.

There are other charging variations of the unlawful detention or concealment of the child under this section but the essence is often the recognition that the normal living circumstances of the child have been defeated by the surreptitious behavior of the perpetrator who wants to keep the child within his control for unlawful purposes or away from the child's parent.

Luring a Child. Section 10-5.1 is a crime of technology. Section 10-5.1(a) covers persons over 21 years of age that by telephone, texting, or internet use communicate with children under 15 and seek to entice them to make personal contact with the perpetrator without the children's parents consent. This is a Class 4 felony. Section 10-5.1(b) is a Class B misdemeanor and addresses the same conduct by a person over age 18 years and under 21 years who tries to electronically lure a child under 15 years of age. It is not a defense to this charge that a police officer was pretending to be a minor under age 15.

As of this writing there are no reported cases interpreting this statute.

Unlawful Visitation Interference. Section 10-5.5 addresses visitation and custody disputes that occur when one party to a visitation or custody order detains or conceals a child with the intent to deprive the other parent of visitation or custody time. As a petty offense, police officers are directed to give a Notice to Appear to the alleged offending party, and not make an arrest. However, if there is a pattern of interference (two prior convictions) unlawful visitation interference can be charged as a Class A misdemeanor.

Affirmative Defenses. There are some affirmative defenses to these child-related offenses (sections 10-5, 10-5.1 and 10-5.5). If the defendant can present evidence to show that a custody order permitted the detention or if defendant can show that he was acting in an emergency circumstance to protect the child, he has not committed an offense, If age is an element of the offense and the defendant can show that he reasonably believed the child to be of legal age, he is not guilty of an offense.

Article 11 – Sexual Offenses
720 ILCS 5/11-0.1 *et seq.*

Subdivision 1. General Definitions

§ 11-0.1. Definitions. In this Article, unless the context clearly requires otherwise, the following terms are defined as indicated:

"Accused" means a person accused of an offense prohibited by Section 11-1.20, 11-1.30, 11-1.40, 11-1.50, or 11-1.60 of this Code or a person for whose conduct the accused is legally responsible under Article 5 of this Code.

"Adult obscenity or child pornography Internet site". See Section 11-23.

"Advance prostitution" means:

(1) Soliciting for a prostitute by performing any of the following acts when acting other than as a prostitute or a patron of a prostitute:

(A) Soliciting another for the purpose of prostitution.
(B) Arranging or offering to arrange a meeting of persons for the purpose of prostitution.

(C) Directing another to a place knowing the direction is for the purpose of prostitution.

(2) Keeping a place of prostitution by controlling or exercising control over the use of any place that could offer seclusion or shelter for the practice of prostitution and performing any of the following acts when acting other than as a prostitute or a patron of a prostitute:

(A) Knowingly granting or permitting the use of the place for the purpose of prostitution.

(B) Granting or permitting the use of the place under circumstances from which he or she could reasonably know that the place is used or is to be used for purposes of prostitution.
(C) Permitting the continued use of the place after becoming aware of facts or circumstances from which he or she should reasonably know that the place is being used for purposes of prostitution.

"Agency". See Section 11-9.5.

"Arranges". See Section 11-6.5.

"Bodily harm" means physical harm, and includes, but is not limited to, sexually transmitted disease, pregnancy, and impotence.

"Care and custody". See Section 11-9.5.

"Child care institution". See Section 11-9.3.

"Child pornography". See Section 11-20.1.

"Child sex offender". See Section 11-9.3.

"Community agency". See Section 11-9.5.

"Conditional release". See Section 11-9.2.

"Consent". See Section 11-1.70.

"Custody". See Section 11-9.2.

"Day care center". See Section 11-9.3.

"Depict by computer". See Section 11-20.1.

"Depiction by computer". See Section 11-20.1.

"Disseminate". See Section 11-20.1.

"Distribute". See Section 11-21.

"Family member" means a parent, grandparent, child, aunt, uncle, great-aunt, or great-uncle, whether by whole blood, half-blood, or adoption, and includes a step-grandparent, step-parent, or step-child. "Family member" also means, if the victim is a child under 18 years of age, an accused who has resided in the household with the child continuously for at least 6 months.

"Force or threat of force" means the use of force or violence or the threat of force or violence, including, but not limited to, the following situations:

(1) when the accused threatens to use force or violence on the victim or on any other person, and the victim under the circumstances reasonably believes that the accused has the ability to execute that threat; or

(2) when the accused overcomes the victim by use of superior strength or size, physical restraint, or physical confinement.

"Harmful to minors". See Section 11-21.

"Loiter". See Section 9.3.

"Material". See Section 11-21.

"Minor". See Section 11-21.

"Nudity". See Section 11-21.

"Obscene". See Section 11-20.

"Part day child care facility". See Section 11-9.3.

"Penal system". See Section 11-9.2.

"Person responsible for the child's welfare". See Section 11-9.1A.

"Person with a disability". See Section 11-9.5.

"Playground". See Section 11-9.3.

"Probation officer". See Section 11-9.2.

"Produce". See Section 11-20.1.

"Profit from prostitution" means, when acting other than as a prostitute, to receive anything of value for personally rendered prostitution services or to receive anything of value from a prostitute, if the thing received is not for lawful consideration and the person knows it was earned in whole or in part from the practice of prostitution.

"Public park". See Section 11-9.3.

"Public place". See Section 11-30.

"Reproduce". See Section 11-20.1.

"Sado-masochistic abuse". See Section 11-21.

"School". See Section 11-9.3.

"School official". See Section 11-9.3.

"Sexual abuse". See Section 11-9.1A.

"Sexual act". See Section 11-9.1.
"Sexual conduct" means any knowing touching or fondling by the victim or the accused, either directly or through clothing, of the sex organs, anus, or breast of the victim or the accused, or any part of the body of a child under 13 years of age, or any transfer or transmission of semen by the accused upon any part of the clothed or unclothed body of the victim, for the purpose of sexual gratification or arousal of the victim or the accused.

"Sexual excitement". See Section 11-21.

"Sexual penetration" means any contact, however slight, between the sex organ or anus of one person and an object or the sex organ, mouth, or anus of another person, or any intrusion, however slight, of any part of the body of one person or of any animal or object into the sex organ or anus of another person, including, but not limited to, cunnilingus, fellatio, or anal penetration. Evidence of emission of semen is not required to prove sexual penetration.

"Solicit". See Section 11-6.

"State-operated facility". See Section 11-9.5.

"Supervising officer". See Section 11-9.2.

"Surveillance agent". See Section 11-9.2.

"Treatment and detention facility". See Section 11-9.2.

"Victim" means a person alleging to have been subjected to an offense prohibited by Section 11-1.20, 11-1.30, 11-1.40, 11-1.50, or 11-1.60 of this Code.

Subdivision 5. Major Sex Offenses

§ 11-1.10. General provisions concerning offenses described in Sections 11-1.20 through 11-1.60. (a) No person accused of violating Section 11-1.20, 11-1.30, 11-1.40, 11-1.50, or 11-1.60 of this Code shall be presumed to be incapable of committing an offense prohibited by Section 11-1.20, 11-1.30, 11-1.40,11-1.50, or 11-1.60 of this Code because of age, physical condition or relationship to the victim. Nothing in this Section shall be construed to modify or abrogate the affirmative defense of infancy under Section 6-1 of this Code or the provisions of Section 5-805 of the Juvenile Court Act of 1987.

(b) Any medical examination or procedure which is conducted by a physician, nurse, medical or hospital personnel, parent, or caretaker for purposes and in a manner consistent with reasonable medical standards is not an offense under Section 11-1.20, 11-1.30, 11-1.40, 11-1.50, or 11-1.60 of this Code.

(c) (Blank).
(d) (Blank).

(e) The prosecuting attorney shall seek an order from the court to compel the accused to be tested for any sexually transmissible disease, including a test for infection with human immunodeficiency virus (HIV), within 48 hours.
(1) after a finding at a preliminary hearing that there is probable cause to believe that an accused has committed a violation of Section 11-1.20, 11-1.30, or 11-1.40 of this Code, or
(2) after an indictment is returned charging an accused with a violation of Section 11-1.20, 11-1.30, or 11-1.40 of this Code, or
(3) after a finding that a defendant charged with a violation of Section 11-1.20, 11-1.30, or 11-1.40 of this Code is unfit to stand trial pursuant to Section 104-16 of the Code of Criminal Procedure of 1963 where the finding is made prior to preliminary hearing, or
(4) after the request of the victim of the violation of Section 11-1.20, 11-1.30, or 11-1.40.

The medical tests shall be performed only by appropriately licensed medical practitioners. The testing shall consist of a test approved by the Illinois Department of Public Health to determine the presence of HIV infection, based upon recommendations of the United States Centers for Disease Control and Prevention; in the event of a positive result, a reliable supplemental test based upon recommendations of the United States Centers for Disease Control and Prevention shall be administered. The results of the tests and any follow-up tests shall be kept strictly confidential by all medical personnel involved in the testing and must be personally delivered in a sealed envelope to the victim, to the defendant, to the State's Attorney, and to the judge who entered the order, for the judge's inspection in camera. The judge shall provide to the victim a referral to the Illinois Department of Public Health HIV/AIDS toll-free hotline for counseling and information in connection with the test result. Acting in accordance with the best interests of the victim and the public, the judge shall have the discretion to determine to whom, if anyone, the result of the testing may be revealed; however, in no case shall the identity of the victim be disclosed. The court shall order that the cost of the tests shall be paid by the county, and shall be taxed as costs against the accused if convicted.

(f) Whenever any law enforcement officer has reasonable cause to believe that a person has been delivered a controlled substance without his or her consent, the law enforcement officer shall advise the victim about seeking medical treatment and preserving evidence.

(g) Every hospital providing emergency hospital services to an alleged sexual assault survivor, when there is reasonable cause to believe that a person has been delivered a controlled substance without his or her consent, shall designate personnel to provide:

(1) An explanation to the victim about the nature and effects of commonly used controlled substances and how such controlled substances are administered.

(2) An offer to the victim of testing for the presence of such controlled substances.

(3) A disclosure to the victim that all controlled substances or alcohol ingested by the victim will be disclosed by the test.

(4) A statement that the test is completely voluntary.

(5) A form for written authorization for sample analysis of all controlled substances and alcohol ingested by the victim.

A physician licensed to practice medicine in all its branches may agree to be a designated person under this subsection.

No sample analysis may be performed unless the victim returns a signed written authorization within 30 days after the sample was collected.

Any medical treatment or care under this subsection shall be only in accordance with the order of a physician licensed to practice medicine in all of its branches. Any testing under this subsection shall be only in accordance with the order of a licensed individual authorized to order the testing.

§ 11-1.20. Criminal Sexual Assault. (a) a person commits criminal sexual assault if that person commits an act of sexual penetration and:

(1) uses force or threat of force;

(2) knows that the victim is unable to understand the nature of the act or is unable to give knowing consent;

(3) is a family member of the victim, and the victim is under 18 years of age; or

(4) is 17 years of age or over and holds a position of trust, authority, or supervision in relation to the victim, and the victim is at least 13 years of age but under 18 years of age.

(b) Sentence. (1) Criminal sexual assault is a Class 1 felony, except that:

(A) a person who is convicted of the offense of criminal sexual assault as defined in paragraph (a)(1) or (a)(2) after having previously been convicted of the offense of criminal sexual assault or the offense of exploitation of a child, or who is convicted of the offense of criminal sexual assault as defined in paragraph (a)(1) or (a)(2) after having previously been convicted under the laws of this State or any other state of an offense that is substantially equivalent to the offense of criminal sexual assault or to the offense of exploitation of a child, commits a Class X felony for which the person shall be sentenced to a term of imprisonment of not less than 30 years and not more than 60 years. , except that if the person is under the age of 18 years at the time of the offense, he or she shall be sentenced under Section 5-4.5-105 of the Unified Code of Corrections. The commission of the second or subsequent offense is required to have been after the initial conviction for this paragraph (A) to apply.

(B) A person who has attained the age of 18 years at the time of the commission of the offense and who is convicted of the offense of criminal sexual assault as defined in paragraph (a)(1) or (a)(2) after having previously been convicted of the offense of aggravated criminal sexual assault or the offense of predatory criminal sexual assault of a child, or who is convicted of the offense of criminal sexual assault as defined in paragraph (a)(1) or (a)(2) after having previously been convicted under the laws of this State or any other state of an offense that is substantially equivalent to the offense of aggravated criminal sexual assault or the offense of predatory criminal sexual assault of a child shall be sentenced to a term of natural life imprisonment. The commission of the second or subsequent offense is required to have been after the initial conviction for this paragraph (B) to apply. An offender under the age of 18 years at the time of the commission of the offense covered by this subparagraph (B) shall be sentenced under Section 5-4.5-105 of the Unified Code of Corrections.

(C) a second or subsequent conviction for a violation of paragraph (a)(3) or (a)(4) or under any similar statute of this State or any other state for any offense involving criminal sexual assault that is substantially equivalent to or more serious than the sexual assault prohibited under paragraph (a)(3) or (a)(4) is a Class X felony.

§ 11-1.30. Aggravated Criminal Sexual Assault. (a) a person commits aggravated criminal sexual assault if that person commits criminal sexual assault and any of the following aggravating circumstances exist during the commission of the offense or, for purposes of paragraph (7), occur as part of the same course of conduct as the commission of the offense:

(1) the person displays, threatens to use, or uses a dangerous weapon, other than a firearm, or any other object fashioned or used in a manner that leads the victim, under the circumstances, reasonably to believe that the object is a dangerous weapon;

(2) the person causes bodily harm to the victim, except as provided in paragraph (10);

(3) the person acts in a manner that threatens or endangers the life of the victim or any other person;

(4) the person commits the criminal sexual assault during the course of committing or attempting to commit any other felony;

(5) the victim is 60 years of age or older;

(6) the victim is a person with a physical disability;

(7) the person delivers (by injection, inhalation, ingestion, transfer of possession, or any other means) any controlled substance to the victim without the victim's consent or by threat or deception for other than medical purposes;

(8) the person is armed with a firearm;

(9) the person personally discharges a firearm during the commission of the offense; or

(10) the person personally discharges a firearm during the commission of the offense, and that discharge proximately causes great bodily harm, permanent disability, permanent disfigurement, or death to another person.

(b) A person commits aggravated criminal sexual assault if that person is under 17 years of age and:

(i) commits an act of sexual penetration with a victim who is under 9 years of age; or

(ii) commits an act of sexual penetration with a victim who is at least 9 years of age but under 13 years of age and the person uses force or threat of force to commit the act.

(c) a person commits aggravated criminal sexual assault if that person commits an act of sexual penetration with a victim who is a person with a severe or profound intellectual disability.

(d) Sentence. (1) Aggravated criminal sexual assault in violation of paragraph (2), (3), (4), (5), (6), or (7) of subsection (a) or in violation of subsection (b) or (c) is a Class X felony. A violation of subsection (a)(1) is a Class X felony for which 10 years shall be added to the term of imprisonment imposed by the court. A violation of subsection (a)(8) is a Class X felony for which 15 years shall be added to the term of imprisonment imposed by the court. A violation of subsection (a)(9) is a Class X felony for which 20 years shall be added to the term of imprisonment imposed by the court. A violation of subsection (a)(10) is a Class X felony for which 25 years or up to a term of natural life imprisonment shall be added to the term of imprisonment imposed by the court. An offender under the age of 18 years at the time of the commission of aggravated criminal sexual assault in violation of paragraphs (1) through (10) of subsection (a) shall be sentenced under Section 5-4.5-105 of the Unified Code of Corrections.

(2) A person who has attained the age of 18 and who is convicted of a second or subsequent offense of aggravated criminal sexual assault, or who is convicted of the offense of aggravated criminal sexual assault after having previously been convicted of the offense of criminal sexual assault or the offense of predatory criminal sexual assault of a child, or who is convicted of the offense of aggravated criminal sexual assault after having previously been convicted under the laws of this or any other state of an offense that is substantially equivalent to the offense of criminal sexual assault, the offense of aggravated criminal sexual assault or the offense of predatory criminal sexual assault of a child, shall be sentenced to a term of natural life imprisonment. The commission of the second or subsequent offense is required to have been after the initial conviction for this paragraph (2) to apply. An offender under the age of 18 years at the time of the commission of the offense covered by this subparagraph (2) shall be sentenced under Section 5-4.5-105 of the Unified Code of Corrections.

§ 11-1.40. Predatory criminal sexual assault of a child. (a) a person commits predatory criminal sexual assault of a child if that person is 17 years of age or older and commits an act of contact, however slight, between the sex organ or anus of one person and the part of body of another for the purpose of sexual gratification or arousal of the victim or the accused, or an act of sexual penetration, and:

(1) the victim is under 13 years of age; or
(2) the victim is under 13 years of age and that person:
- (A) is armed with a firearm;
- (B) personally discharges a firearm during the commission of the offense;
- (C) causes great bodily harm to the victim that:
  - (i) results in permanent disability; or
  - (ii) is life threatening; or
- (D) delivers (by injection, inhalation, ingestion, transfer of possession, or any other means) any controlled substance to the victim without the victim's consent or by threat or deception, for other than medical purposes.

(b) Sentence. (1) A person convicted of a violation of subsection (a)(1) commits a Class X felony, for which the person shall be sentenced to a term of imprisonment of not less than 6 years and not more than 60 years. A person convicted of a violation of subsection (a)(2)(A) commits a Class X felony for which 15 years shall be added to the term of imprisonment imposed by the court. A person convicted of a violation of subsection (a)(2)(B) commits a Class X felony for which 20 years shall be added to the term of imprisonment imposed by the court. A person who has attained the age of 18 at the time of the commission of the offense and who is convicted of a violation of subsection (a)(2)(C) commits a Class X felony for which the person shall be sentenced to a term of imprisonment of not less than 50 years or up to a term of natural life subsection (a)(2)(C) commits a Class X felony for which the person shall be sentenced to a term of imprisonment of not less than 50 years or up to a term of natural life imprisonment. An offender under the age of 18 years at the time of the commission of predatory criminal sexual assault of a child in violation of subsections (a)(1), (a)(2)(A), (a)(2)(B), and (a)(2)(C) shall be sentenced under Section 5-4.5-105 of the Unified Code of Corrections.

(1.1) A person convicted of a violation of subsection (a)(2)(D) commits a Class X felony for which the person shall be sentenced to a term of imprisonment of not less than 50 years and not more than 60 years. An offender under the age of 18 years at the time of the commission of predatory criminal sexual assault of a child in violation of subsection (a)(2)(D) shall be sentenced under Section 5-4.5-105 of the Unified Code of Corrections.

(1.2) A person who has attained the age of 18 years at the time of the commission of the offense and convicted of predatory criminal sexual assault of a child committed against 2 or more persons regardless of whether the offenses occurred as the result of the same act or of several related or unrelated acts shall be sentenced to a term of natural life imprisonment and an offender under the age of 18 years at the time of the commission of the offense shall be sentenced under Section 5-4.5-105 of the Unified Code of Corrections.

(2) A person who has attained the age of 18 years at the time of the commission of the offense and who is convicted of a second or subsequent offense of predatory criminal sexual assault of a child, or who is convicted of the offense of predatory criminal sexual assault of a child after having previously been convicted of the offense of criminal sexual assault or the offense of aggravated criminal sexual assault, or who is convicted of the offense of predatory criminal sexual assault of a child after having previously been convicted under the laws of this State or any other state of an offense that is substantially equivalent to the offense of predatory criminal sexual assault of a child, the offense of aggravated criminal sexual assault or the offense of criminal sexual assault, shall be sentenced to a term of natural life imprisonment. The commission of the second or subsequent offense is required to have been after the initial conviction for this paragraph (2) to apply. An offender under the age of 18 years at the time of the commission of the offense covered by this paragraph (2) shall be sentenced under Section 5-4.5-105 of the Unified Code of Corrections.

§ 11-1.50. Criminal sexual abuse. (a) A person commits criminal sexual abuse if that person :

(1) commits an act of sexual conduct by the use of force or threat of force; or

(2) commits an act of sexual conduct and knows that the victim is unable to understand the nature of the act or is unable to give knowing consent.

(b) a person commits criminal sexual abuse if that person is under 17 years of age and commits an act of sexual penetration or sexual conduct with a victim who is at least 9 years of age but under 17 years of age.

(c) a person commits criminal sexual abuse if that person commits an act of sexual penetration or sexual conduct with a victim who is at least 13 years of age but under 17 years of age and the person is less than 5 years older than the victim.

(d) Sentence. Criminal sexual abuse for a violation of subsection (b) or (c) of this Section is a Class A misdemeanor. Criminal sexual abuse for a violation of paragraph (1) or (2) of subsection (a) of this Section is a Class 4 felony.

A second or subsequent conviction for a violation of subsection (a) of this Section is a Class 2 felony. For purposes of this Section it is a second or subsequent conviction if the accused has at any time been convicted under this Section or under any similar statute of this State or any other state for any offense involving sexual abuse or sexual assault that is substantially equivalent to or more serious than the sexual abuse prohibited under this Section.

§ 11-1.60. Aggravated Criminal Sexual Abuse. (a) a person commits aggravated criminal sexual abuse if that person commits criminal sexual abuse and any of the following aggravating circumstances exist (i) during the commission of the offense or (ii) for purposes of paragraph (7), as part of the same course of conduct as the commission of the offense:

(1) the person displays, threatens to use, or uses a dangerous weapon or any other object fashioned or used in a manner that leads the victim, under the circumstances, reasonably to believe that the object is a dangerous weapon;
(2) the person causes bodily harm to the victim;
(3) the victim is 60 years of age or older;
(4) the victim is a person with a physical disablity;
(5) the person acts in a manner that threatens or endangers the life of the victim or any other person;
(6) the person commits the criminal sexual abuse during the course of committing or attempting to commit any other felony; or
(7) the person delivers (by injection, inhalation, ingestion, transfer of possession, or any other means) any controlled substance to the victim for other than medical purposes without the victim's consent or by threat or deception.

(b) a person commits aggravated criminal sexual abuse if that person commits an act of sexual conduct with a victim who is under 18 years of age and the person is a family member.

(c) a person commits aggravated criminal sexual abuse if:

(1) that person is 17 years of age or over and:
(i) commits an act of sexual conduct with a victim who is under 13 years of age; or
(ii) commits an act of sexual conduct with a victim who is at least 13 years of age but under 17 years of age and the person uses force or threat of force to commit the act; or

(2) that person is under 17 years of age and: (i) commits an act of sexual conduct with a victim who is under 9 years of age; or
(ii) commits an act of sexual conduct with a victim who is at least 9 years of age but under 17 years of age and the person uses force or threat of force to commit the act.

(d) a person commits aggravated criminal sexual abuse if that person commits an act of sexual penetration or sexual conduct with a victim who is at least 13 years of age but under 17 years of age and the person is at least 5 years older than the victim.

(e) a person commits aggravated criminal sexual abuse if that person commits an act of sexual conduct with a victim who is a person with a severe or profound intellectual disability.

(f) a person commits aggravated criminal sexual abuse if that person commits an act of sexual conduct with a victim who is at least 13 years of age but under 18 years of age and the person is 17 years of age or over and holds a position of trust, authority, or supervision in relation to the victim.

(g) Sentence. Aggravated criminal sexual abuse is a Class 2 felony.

§ 11-1.70. Defenses with respect to offenses described in Sections 11-1.20 through 11-1.60.
(a) It shall be a defense to any offense under Section 11-1.20, 11-1.30, 11-1.40, 11-1.50, or 11-1.60 of this Code where force or threat of force is an element of the offense that the victim consented. "Consent" means a freely given agreement to the act of sexual penetration or sexual conduct in question. Lack of verbal or physical resistance or submission by the victim resulting from the use of force or threat of force by the accused shall not constitute consent. The manner of dress of the victim at the time of the offense shall not constitute consent.

(b) It shall be a defense under subsection (b) and subsection (c) of Section 11-1.50 and subsection (d) of Section 11-1.60 of this Code that the accused reasonably believed the person to be 17 years of age or over.
(c) A person who initially consents to sexual penetration or sexual conduct is not deemed to have consented to any sexual penetration or sexual conduct that occurs after he or she withdraws consent during the course of that sexual penetration or sexual conduct.

§ 11-1.80. Civil Liability. [Omitted.]

Commentary – Sexual Assault and Sexual Abuse Offenses

Legislative updates. Effective July 1, 2011, all sexual offenses were re-codified. Prior to that time they were found in Article 12 (crimes against the person). Although re-numbered, they have essentially remained the same offenses.

Sexual penetration and sexual conduct. An act of sexual penetration (Section 11-0.1) is contact (no matter how slight) between the sex organs of the defendant and the sex organs, mouth or anus of the victim. The difference between sexual assault crimes and sexual abuse crimes is that the latter are based on an act or acts of sexual conduct (Section 11-0.1). Sexual conduct is the offender's knowing touching of the sexual organs, breasts or anus of the victim, or any portion of the body of a child under age 13, either directly or through clothing, for purposes of sexual arousal of the offender.

In *People v. Ostrowski* 394 Ill.App.3d 82, 914 N.E.2d 558 (Ill. App. Ct. 2nd Dist. 2009), the defendant was convicted of aggravated criminal sexual abuse. The defendant was the grandfather of the 4-year-old victim, and took her to a town festival to watch fireworks. While in this public setting he was observed kissing his grandchild on several occasions for periods from 4 to 15 seconds. The defendant was also intoxicated and had no shirt on. The grandfather and granddaughter were observed rolling around on the ground playfully, and the victim's mother noted that the child often kissed family members - always on the lips. The trial court concluded the kissing was for purposes of the defendant's sexual arousal. The appellate court disagreed and found the evidence did not prove the kissing was for sexual arousal. The court noted that the conduct was in public, was between a grandfather and grandchild the kisses were normal kisses (as opposed to a "French kiss"). The incident was of relatively short duration and was unaccompanied by any other suggestive sexual movement or contact. Without evidence that proved sexual conduct, the aggravated criminal sexual abuse conviction was reversed.

In *People v. Guerrero* 2011 IL App (2d) 090972, the defendant was charged with multiple counts of criminal sexual assault of his 14 year old daughter. The defendant had sent his daughter to live with her mother, the defendant's ex-wife. The girl was returned to her father's home and her mother told the defendant that the girl had had an illicit relationship with another man. The defendant ordered the victim to undress so he could check her out for infection, and then inserted his fingers into her vagina. He then inserted his penis. He pulled out and ejaculated on her pubic hair. He took a q-tip swab and told the girl he was taking liquid from her and sperm from him to a laboratory. Based on this evidence, the defendant was convicted of criminal sexual assault for the acts of penetration with the victim, including (1) inserting his fingers into the victim's vagina (2) inserting his penis into the victim's vagina and (3) inserting the q-tip into the victims vagina. The convictions based on the first two acts of penetration were affirmed on appeal; however, the appellate court reviewed in detail the testimony of the victim about the q-tip. the court found that the evidence showed that while there was contact with the victim's pubic hair, there was insufficient proof that there was any touching of the victim's vagina with the q-tip to prove a third act of vaginal penetration. The court reversed the criminal sexual assault conviction only as to that charge.

Force and Consent. If a sexual assault is charged on the basis of a claimed "force or threat of force" then proof of the consent of the victim is a complete defense to the charge. Under Section 11-1.70 consent is the freely given agreement of the victim to the act of sexual conduct or sexual penetration. The lack of physical or verbal resistance to the acts is not consent. The manner in which the victim is dressed is also not evidence of consent. If there is consent at the beginning of the sexual activity and the victim withdraws consent, any forced sexual conduct or penetration thereafter would be an act of criminal sexual assault (or abuse). Proof that force was used contradicts the claim that there was consent. See *People v. Mims* 403 Ill.App.3d 884, 934 N.E.2d 666 (Ill. App. Ct. 1st Dist. 2010)

Force (Section 11-.01) means the use or threat of violence is in fact used, or that a reasonable victim would believe the violent act could be accomplished by the offender. Force is also using greater physical size or strength to accomplish the sexual act.

In *People v. Denbo* 372 Ill.App.3d 994, 868 N.E.2d 347 (Ill. App. Ct. 4th Dist. 2007), the defendant and victim had a lesbian relationship. They had engaged in sexual relations three times before the event that formed the basis of the charges. The defendant had showered, was wearing a negligee, the lights were off in her bedroom where there was candlelight and music when the victim (who was hearing-impaired) came into the bedroom. The alleged victim got into bed with the defendant. The two women started kissing and defendant, with the victim's consent, removed her clothing including her bra and panties. Defendant digitally penetrated the victim who responded by pushing the defendant twice. After the second push the defendant withdrew. The victim went to the bathroom where she observed vaginal bleeding. When she returned to the bed, the defendant was crying and apologizing. The victim spent the rest of the night sleeping in bed with defendant, had breakfast and stayed for some time the next morning. The defendant wrote letters apologizing to the victim for hurting her. Five weeks after the incident the victim complained to law enforcement about the incident. A jury convicted the defendant of aggravated criminal sexual assault (vaginal penetration by threat of force causing bodily harm), but the conviction was reversed on appeal. The court reasoned that the first penetration of the victim's vagina was not by force, since force cannot be the amount of physical effort necessary to perform the sexual act – thus the only act of vaginal penetration was consensual. A reasonable person would not have understood that the victim had withdrawn consent until the second push. The second push was the first clear indication from the victim that she had withdrawn consent, and the sexual penetration ceased after that push. In the absence of force, there was consent.

In *People v. Mpulamasaka* 2016 IL App (2d) 130703 the Defendant was convicted of Aggravated Criminal Sexual Assault based on use of force or threat of force. However the defense cross examination established that the victim had repositioned herself because she was uncomfortable and admitted that she was on top of Defendant in the back seat of a car in a restaurant parking lot during early morning business hours. She made no complaint to restaurant employees or patrons and went home instead of to the police station or the hospital despite vaginal bleeding. The Court on appeal reversed the conviction finding the evidence insufficient to prove force or threat of force.

Criminal sexual assault. Section 11-1.20 defines the crime of sexual assault – this is the commission of an act of sexual penetration (1) by force or threat of force, (2) upon a victim who is not capable of consenting to the act; (3) to a victim under 18 years old, who is a family member of the defendant or (4) to a victim between the ages of 13 and 18 by the adult defendant (18 or older) who is in a position of trust or supervision over the victim. Criminal sexual assault is a general intent crime since it has no specified mental state, thus proof that the defendant's conduct was "knowing or intentional" is sufficient to support a sexual assault conviction of any type.

In *People v. Gutierrez* 402 Ill.App.3d 866, 932 N.E.2d 139 (Ill. App. Ct. 1st Dist. 2010), the defendant lived above a funeral home where he had been a worker. He stabbed and strangled another employee and hid her body in the floorboards of his apartment. The post-mortem autopsy showed no injury to her vagina, but did disclose the presence of semen. DNA tests were botched but the male fraction of the sample could not exclude the defendant, whose DNA was found on the victim's underpants. After conviction, on appeal, the defendant contended that the state had failed to prove a sexual assault because there was no proof the victim was alive at the time of sexual penetration. The court held that the defendant had murdered and sexually assaulted the victim as part of the same criminal episode. The evidence was sufficient to prove guilt of both offenses.

Aggravated criminal sexual assault. Section 11-1.30 sets forth the aggravating factors to enhance sexual assault offenses to a higher classified felony. the primary factors concern circumstances during the commission of the criminal sexual assault and include (1) the use, display or threat of use of a dangerous weapon other than a firearm, during the commission of the sexual assault; (2) causing bodily harm to the victim; (3) threatening or endangering the victim's life, (4) committing another felony offense, (5) the victim is over 60 years old, physically handicapped or profoundly retarded, (7) being armed with a firearm, discharging a firearm or causing great bodily harm or permanent disfigurement or disability by discharging a firearm, (8) the victim is under 9 years old or (9) the victim is between 9 and 13 years old and the sexual assault committed by force or threat of force.

In *People v. Bishop* 218 Ill.2d 232, 843 N.E.2d 365 (Ill. S. Ct. 2006), the defendant was convicted of four counts of criminal sexual assault and four counts of aggravated criminal sexual assault of his teenage daughter. The evidence showed that the defendant had vaginal and anal sex with his daughter over the course of several years. He was charged in eight counts with (1) aggravated criminal sexual assault (vaginal act of sexual penetration causing bodily injury), (2) aggravated criminal sexual assault (vaginal act of sexual penetration by threat of force causing bodily harm (pregnancy)), (3) criminal sexual assault (act of sexual penetration to the anus by threat of force), (4) criminal sexual assault (act of sexual penetration to the anus by threat of force), (5) criminal sexual assault (vaginal act of sexual penetration on a family member under age 18), (6) aggravated criminal sexual assault (vaginal act of sexual penetration by force or threat of force on a family member under age 18), (7) criminal sexual assault (act of sexual penetration to the anus on a family member under age 18), and (8) aggravated criminal sexual assault (act of sexual penetration to the anus by force or threat of force on a family member under age 18). He was convicted on all counts and received concurrent sentences on each count of 30 years for aggravated criminal sexual assault and 15 years for criminal sexual assault. The Court vacated one count of conviction based on injury from vaginal penetration because the evidence was that the victim was only pregnant once. The Court also noted that the other offenses were actually three separate aggravated criminal sexual assaults with each crime including criminal sexual assaults as lesser-included offenses. Each of the three sets of sexual crimes was based on the same acts. The trial court had erred in giving sentences for the lesser included offenses and but, also giving concurrent sentences for the three separate sexual acts, when consecutive sentences were required for each sexual act. There should have been three sentences for three aggravated sexual assault convictions with each sentence of imprisonment consecutive to the other two convictions.

In *People v. Giraud* 2012 IL 113116, the defendant was convicted of Aggravated Criminal Sexual Assault on the basis that this sexual assault caused the victim to become infected with HIV virus and thus endangered or threatened the victim's life. The Court held this was an improper interpretation of 720 ILCS 5/11-1.30(a)(3), which instead was limited to a defendants conduct during the commission of the sexual assault. The defendant's conviction was reduced to one of Criminal Sexual Assault.

Predatory criminal sexual assault of a child. Section 11-1.40 criminally proscribes acts of sexual penetration between (1) an adult offender (18 or over) and a child that is under age 13 and (2) an adult offender and a child under age 13 where the perpetrator armed with a firearm, discharges the firearm and causes great bodily harm or permanent disfigurement or disability.

In *People v. Letcher* 386 Ill.App.3d 412, 899 N.E.2d 315 (Ill. App. Ct. 2nd Dist. 2008), the defendant was charged with 14 counts of predatory criminal sexual assault of a six year old girl. The defendant admitted to having to acts of oral sexual penetration with the girl, but denied the other claimed acts of digital and penile contact with the girl's vagina and anus. He was convicted of eight counts of predatory assault, and sentenced to 20 years consecutive with each count. The defendant claimed that the evidence against him was not specific, as to date and type of sexual act, and made it difficult it not impossible to defend. He asserted that the child's testimony was a generic description of molestation, without dates, times and places. the young girl, who was in third grade at the time of the bench trial was unable to be specific about the number of times the defendant assaulted her, except to say that he had touched her with his penis on her vagina and her bottom, in her old house and in her new house, and that the defendant tried to put his penis in her mouth and had also licked her vagina. The appellate court noted the difficulty with predatory criminal sexual assault cases involving young children. The children may very well have been subjected to monthly, weekly or even daily assaults but would not be able to describe with detail the numbers of incidents, the places or the particulars of each sexual assault. Recognizing that the penalties are substantial, the prosecution should be careful to not overcharge, but the court should make reasonable inferences from the evidence that substantiates the molestation that has been charged. The court affirmed six of the eight counts of conviction.

In *People v. Raymond* 404 Ill.App.3d 1028, 938 N.E.2d 131 (Ill. App. Ct. 1st Dist. 2010), the defendant, who had been convicted of predatory criminal sexual criminal sexual assault of a child, claimed that evidence was insufficient to prove that he had committed an act of sexual penetration. Two police officers came into an abandoned building and entered a second floor bedroom where they saw the defendant on top of a young girl. Both the defendant and the girl were naked from the waist down and the defendant was moving in a humping or thrusting motion while between the girl's legs. When ordered to stand by the officers, the defendant arose. He had an erect, wet penis. The girl did not testify at trial and there was also no medical evidence of contact between the participants. In rejecting the defendant's claim, the court noted that while there was no evidence of direct contact between the sex organ of the defendant and the sex organ of the girl, reasonable inferences drawn from the direct and circumstantial evidence supported the conclusion there was sexual penetration by contact, however slight.

Criminal sexual abuse. Section 11-1.50 (a) provides that criminal sexual abuse occurs when an offender commits an act of sexual conduct (1) by the use or threat of force, or (2) on someone who is incapable of giving consent. Thus this type of criminal sexual abuse is non-consensual conduct, is thus more serious and classified as a Class 4 felony for the first offender.

Section 11-1.50(b) and (c) also address acts of sexual conduct or sexual penetration that are consensual - but nonetheless are defined as criminal - the offender has consensual sexual contact with the victim but (1) the offender is less than17 years old and the victim is between the ages of 9 and 17, or (2) the victim is between the ages 13 and 17 and the offender is less than 5 years older than the victim. Criminal sexual abuse could be referred to as "statutory rape" because the actual consent given by the victim does not mitigate the behavior of the offender. The law assumes that the age and lack of maturity of the victim requires protection from the offender who is older and more mature. This type of criminal sexual abuse is considered less serious. It is classified as a Class A misdemeanor for a first offender. A 16 year old boy who fondled a 12 year old girl commits sexual abuse (but would be prosecuted as a juvenile) and an 18 year old girl who has sexual intercourse with a 16 year old boy would violate the criminal abuse statute (as would the 16 year old boy who had intercourse with a 16 year old girl!)

Aggravated criminal sexual abuse. Section 11-1.60 sets forth the aggravating factors to enhance sexual abuse offenses to a higher classified felony. the primary factors concern circumstances during the commission of the criminal sexual abuse and include (1) the use, display or threat of use of a dangerous weapon other than a firearm, during the commission of the sexual abuse; (2) causing bodily harm to the victim; (3) threatening or endangering the victim's life, (4) committing another felony offense, (5) the victim is over 60 years old, physically handicapped or profoundly retarded, (7) being armed with a firearm, discharging a firearm or causing great bodily harm or permanent disfigurement or disability by discharging a firearm, (8) the victim is under 9 years old or (9) the victim is between 9 and 13 years old and the sexual abuse was committed by force or threat of force.

In *People v.* Kolton 219 Ill.2d 353, 848 N.E.2d 950 (Ill. S. Ct. 2006), the defendant was 49 years old and was found with a 12 year old girl. The young girl testified that she was offered money by the defendant who placed his finger in her vagina. although charged with predatory sexual assault, the trial court in a bench trial, in the absence of medical evidence of penetration, found the defendant guilty of aggravated criminal sexual abuse - he was older than 17. The victim was under age 13, and his sexual conduct (even without proof of penetration) was for purposes of his own sexual arousal. His conviction was affirmed on appeal.

In *People v. Mack* 2016 IL App (5th) 130294 the 44 year old Defendant was charged and convicted of Aggravated Criminal Sexual Abuse for rubbing the vagina was a 15 year old girl while she was asleep. The victim awoke and screamed and her screams were heard by her mother. The Defendant admitted contact with the victim but claimed it was not sexual in nature, also claiming that the offense was a charge that was easily made and hard to disprove. The Court affirmed his conviction finding that the evidence considered in the light most favorable to the prosecution supported the jury's verdict of guilty.

Age - Mistake of Age. In *People v. Lloyd* 2013 IL 113510 (Ill. S. Ct. 2013), the 41 year-old defendant was charged with Aggravated Criminal Sexual Assault under 720 ILCS 5/11-1.20(a)(2) under the prosecution theory that the defendant knew that the 13 year- old victim was not capable of understanding the nature of the sexual acts or to give knowing consent. The prosecutor argued that defendant's knowledge that the victim was 13 years –old, was sufficient to satisfy the "knowing consent" element. In reversing the Defendant's conviction, the Illinois Supreme Court reviewed the "age elements" of sexual assault and sexual abuse offenses and noted that there were many age-based sex offenses where age differential between the defendant and the victim was an element of the crime. The Court also noted that all reported Illinois cases had applied the "knowing consent" element to offenses where the victim was mentally disable, was asleep, was under the influence of alcohol or had some other external condition or circumstance, other than age, that reflected the Defendant knowingly using the condition to perpetrate the crime. The Court also noted an anomaly from the prosecution's use of the Criminal Sexual Assault statute inferring lack of knowing consent:

> the State's construction would cause havoc to our statutory scheme by allowing, for example, the State to prosecute under the criminal sexual assault provision a 17–year–old girl who has sexual intercourse with her willing 16–year–old boyfriend, assuming that the State could prove, as it most certainly could, that she knew his age. This offense would constitute a Class 1 felony [720

ILCS 5/11-1.20(a)(3)] even though the legislature has determined elsewhere in the Code that such conduct would fall within the criminal sexual abuse provision . . . [720 ILCS 5/11-1.50(a)], a Class A misdemeanor . . . [720 ILCS 5/11-1.50(d)]. Our legislature could not have intended such a result that would require a court to impose a sentence of years (730 ILCS 5/5–4.5–30 (West 2008)) for conduct it has specifically determined elsewhere in the Code constitutes a misdemeanor.

People v. Lloyd 2013 IL 113510, ¶38.

Section 11-1.70(b) has provided for a limited defense of mistake of age to certain sexual abuse offenses - Sections 11-1.50(b) and (c) and aggravated criminal sexual abuse as set forth in Section 11-1.60(d). In each of these sections, the defendant's reasonable belief that the victim was older than 17 years of age or older would be a complete defense.

In *People v. Douglas* 381 Ill.App.3d 1067, 886 N.E.2d 1232 (Ill. App. Ct. 2nd Dist. 2008), a 31 year old defendant had sexual intercourse with a 12 year old girl, who at the time, the defendant believed to be 15 years old. The trial court granted the state's motion *in limine* and barred the defendant from introducing evidence as to his belief in the age of the victim since it was not a defense to the charge of predatory criminal sexual assault and on appeal the defendant claimed it was error to prevent him from presenting this defense. If the defendant's testimony had been accepted, he would have been guilty of the lesser offense of aggravated criminal sexual abuse, not predatory criminal sexual assault. The appellate court affirmed the defendant's conviction holding that the only mental state required to be proved was that related to the voluntary act of sexual penetration. Since the statute (now Section 11-1.50) had no stated mental state, under 720 ILCS 5/4-4 a mental state of knowledge or intent would be inferred as to the voluntary act, but that no knowledge of the age of the victim need be proved. The serious nature of each of the sexual offenses where mistaken belief of age is not a defense supports the legislative action.

Propensity evidence. Sexual offenses are the one category of offense that permits the admission of propensity evidence. In America the notion of a fair criminal trial is that the defendant will be convicted or acquitted on the basis of evidence that he or she committed the specific crime charged and not on the basis that the defendant had been in trouble before, had a criminal record or in general was a bad person. Sexual offenses are the one exception to the rule and both the Federal Rules of Evidence (Rules 413 and 414) and Illinois law (724 ILCS 5/115-7.3) permit introduction of prior similar crimes committed by the sexual offender to prove guilt in his pending case.

In *People v. Roberson* 401 Ill.App.3d 758, 927 N.E.2d 1277 (Ill. App. Ct. 4th Dist. 2010), the defendant was convicted of aggravated criminal sexual abuse and indecent liberties with a child. The female victim in the case was a 16 year old girl while the defendant was 39 years old. He invited her to his apartment, touched her butt several times, asked her to have sex with him, and then when she was ready to leave in her car, reached in and grabbed her crouch. Evidence was introduced at trial that when the defendant was 31 years old he had sexual intercourse on several occasions (including in his apartment) with a 14 year old girl. Although the prior incident was eight years prior to the incident in the case on trial, the appellate court agreed with the trial court that the prior evidence of sexual crimes was properly admitted as propensity evidence.

§ 11-6. Indecent solicitation of a child. (a) A person of the age of 17 years and upwards commits indecent solicitation of a child if the person, with the intent that the offense of aggravated criminal sexual assault, criminal sexual assault, predatory criminal sexual assault of a child, or aggravated criminal sexual abuse be committed, knowingly solicits a child or one whom he or she believes to be a child to perform an act of sexual penetration or sexual conduct as defined in Section 11-0.1 of this Code.

(a-5) A person of the age of 17 years and upwards commits indecent solicitation of a child if the person knowingly discusses an act of sexual conduct or sexual penetration with a child or with one whom he or she believes to be a child by means of the Internet with the intent that the offense of aggravated criminal sexual assault, predatory criminal sexual assault of a child, or aggravated criminal sexual abuse be committed.

(a-6) It is not a defense to subsection (a-5) that the person did not solicit the child to perform sexual conduct or sexual penetration with the person.

(b) Definitions. As used in this Section:

"Solicit" means to command, authorize, urge, incite, request, or advise another to perform an act by any means including, but not limited to, in person, over the phone, in writing, by computer, or by advertisement of any kind.

"Child" means a person under 17 years of age.

"Internet" has the meaning set forth in Section 16J-5 of this Code .

"Sexual penetration" or "sexual conduct" are defined in Section 11-0.1 of this Code.

(c) Sentence. Indecent solicitation of a child under subsection (a) is:

(1) a Class 1 felony when the act, if done, would be predatory criminal sexual assault of a child or aggravated criminal sexual assault;

(2) a Class 2 felony when the act, if done, would be criminal sexual assault;

(3) a Class 3 felony when the act, if done, would be aggravated criminal sexual abuse.

Indecent solicitation of a child under subsection (a-5) is a Class 4 felony.

§ 11-6.5. Indecent solicitation of an adult. (a) A person commits indecent solicitation of an adult if the person knowingly:

(1) Arranges for a person 17 years of age or over to commit an act of sexual penetration as defined in Section 11-0.1 with a person:

(i) Under the age of 13 years; or
(ii) Thirteen years of age or over but under the age of 17 years; or

(2) Arranges for a person 17 years of age or over to commit an act of sexual conduct as defined in Section 11-0.1
with a person:

(i) Under the age of 13 years; or

(ii) Thirteen years of age or older but under the age of 17 years.
(b) Sentence.

(1) Violation of paragraph (a)(1)(i) is a Class X felony.

(2) Violation of paragraph (a)(1)(ii) is a Class 1 felony.

(3) Violation of paragraph (a)(2)(i) is a Class 2 felony.
(4) Violation of paragraph (a)(2)(ii) is a Class A misdemeanor.

(c) For the purposes of this Section, "arranges" includes but is not limited to oral or written communication and communication by telephone, computer, or other electronic means. "Computer" has the meaning ascribed to it in Section 16D-2 of this Code.

§ 11-6.6. Solicitation to meet a child. (a) A person of the age of 18 or more years commits the offense of solicitation to meet a child if the person while using a computer, cellular telephone, or any other device, with the intent to meet a child or one whom he or she believes to be a child, solicits, entices, induces, or arranges with the child to meet at a location without the knowledge of the child's parent or guardian and the meeting with the child is arranged for a

purpose other than a lawful purpose under Illinois law.
(b) Sentence. Solicitation to meet a child is a Class A misdemeanor. Solicitation to meet a child is a Class 4 felony when the solicitor believes he or she is 5 or more years older than the child.

(c) For purposes of this Section, "child" means any person under 17 years of age; and "computer" has the meaning ascribed to it in Section 16D-2 of this Code.

Subdivision 10. Vulnerable Victim Offenses

§ 11-9.1. Sexual exploitation of a child. (a) a person commits sexual exploitation of a child if in the presence or virtual presence, or both, of a child and with knowledge that a child or one whom he or she believes to be a child would view his or her acts, that person:

(1) engages in a sexual act; or
(2) exposes his or her sex organs, anus or breast for the purpose of sexual arousal or gratification of such person or the child or one whom he or she believes to be a child.

(a-5) A person commits sexual exploitation of a child who knowingly entices, coerces, or persuades a child to remove the child's clothing for the purpose of sexual arousal or gratification of the person or the child, or both.

(b) Definitions. As used in this Section:

"Sexual act" means masturbation, sexual conduct or sexual penetration as defined in Section 11-0.1 of this Code.
"Sex offense" means any violation of Article 11 of this Code or Section 12-16.2 of this Code.

"Child" means a person under 17 years of age.

"Virtual presence" means an environment that is created with software and presented to the user and or receiver via the Internet, in such a way that the user appears in front of the receiver on the computer monitor or screen or hand held portable electronic device, usually through a web camming program. "Virtual presence" includes primarily experiencing through sight or sound, or both, a video image that can be explored interactively at a personal computer or hand held communication device, or both.

"Webcam" means a video capturing device connected to a computer or computer network that is designed to take digital photographs or live or recorded video which allows for the live transmission to an end user over the Internet.

(c) Sentence.

(1) Sexual exploitation of a child is a Class A misdemeanor. A second or subsequent violation of this Section or a substantially similar law of another state is a Class 4 felony.

(2) Sexual exploitation of a child is a Class 4 felony if the person has been previously convicted of a sex offense.

(3) Sexual exploitation of a child is a Class 4 felony if the victim was under 13 years of age at the time of the commission of the offense.

(4) Sexual exploitation of a child is a Class 4 felony if committed by a person 18 years of age or older who is on or within 500 feet of elementary or secondary school grounds when children are present on the grounds.

§ 11-9.1A. Permitting sexual abuse of a child. (a) A person responsible for a child's welfare commits permitting sexual abuse of a child if the person has actual knowledge of and permits an act of sexual abuse upon the child, or permits the child to engage in prostitution as defined in Section 11-14 of the Criminal Code of 1961.
(b) In this Section:

"Actual knowledge" includes credible allegations made by the child.

"Child" means a minor under the age of 17 years.

"Person responsible for the child's welfare" means the child's parent, step-parent, legal guardian, or other person having custody of a child, who is responsible for the child's care at the time of the alleged sexual abuse.

"Prostitution" means prostitution as defined in Section 11-14 of the Criminal Code of 1961.

"Sexual abuse" includes criminal sexual abuse or criminal sexual assault as defined in Section 11-1.20, 11-1.30, 11-1.40, 11-1.50, or 11-1.60 of the Criminal Code of 1961.

(c) This Section does not apply to a person responsible for the child's welfare who, having reason to believe that sexual abuse has occurred, makes timely and reasonable efforts to stop the sexual abuse by reporting the sexual abuse in conformance with the Abused and Neglected Child Reporting Act or by reporting the sexual abuse, or causing a report to be made, to medical or law enforcement authorities or anyone who is a mandated reporter under Section 4 of the Abused and Neglected Child Reporting Act.

(d) Whenever a law enforcement officer has reason to believe that the child or the person responsible for the child's welfare has been abused by a family or household member as defined by the Illinois Domestic Violence Act of 1986, the officer shall immediately use all reasonable means to prevent further abuse under Section 112A-30 of the Code of Criminal Procedure of 1963.

(e) An order of protection under Section 111-8 of the Code of Criminal Procedure of 1963 shall be sought in all cases where there is reason to believe that a child has been sexually abused by a family or household member. In considering appropriate available remedies, it shall be presumed that awarding physical care or custody to the abuser is not in the child's best interest.

(f) A person may not be charged with the offense of permitting sexual abuse of a child under this Section until the person who committed the offense is charged with criminal sexual assault, aggravated criminal sexual assault, predatory criminal sexual assault of a child, criminal sexual abuse, aggravated criminal sexual abuse, or prostitution.

(g) A person convicted of permitting the sexual abuse of a child is guilty of a Class 1 felony. As a condition of any sentence of supervision, probation, conditional discharge, or mandatory supervised release, any person convicted under this Section shall be ordered to undergo child sexual abuse, domestic violence, or other appropriate counseling for a specified duration with a qualified social or mental health worker.

(h) It is an affirmative defense to a charge of permitting sexual abuse of a child under this Section that the person responsible for the child's welfare had a reasonable apprehension that timely action to stop the abuse or prostitution would result in the imminent infliction of death, great bodily harm, permanent disfigurement, or permanent disability to that person or another in retaliation for reporting.

§ 11-9.1B. Failure to report sexual abuse of a child. (a) For the purposes of this Section:

"Child" means any person under the age of 13.

"Sexual abuse" means any contact, however slight, between the sex organ or anus of the victim or the accused and an object or body part, including but not limited to, the sex organ, mouth, or anus of the victim or the accused, or any intrusion, however slight, of any part of the body of the victim or the accused or of any animal or object into the sex organ or anus of the victim or the accused, including, but not limited to, cunnilingus, fellatio, or anal penetration. Evidence of emission of semen is not required to prove sexual abuse.

(b) A person over the age of 18 commits failure to report sexual abuse of a child when he or she personally observes sexual abuse, as defined by this Section, between a person who he or she knows is over the age of 18 and a person he or she knows is a child, and knowingly fails to report the sexual abuse to law enforcement.

(c) This Section does not apply to a person who makes timely and reasonable efforts to stop the sexual abuse by reporting the sexual abuse in conformance with the Abused and Neglected Child Reporting Act or by reporting the sexual abuse or causing a report to be made, to medical or law enforcement authorities or anyone who is a mandated reporter under Section 4 of the Abused and Neglected Child Reporting Act.

(d) A person may not be charged with the offense of failure to report sexual abuse of a child under this Section until the person who committed the offense is charged with criminal sexual assault, aggravated criminal sexual assault, predatory criminal sexual assault of a child, criminal sexual abuse, or aggravated criminal sexual abuse.

(e) It is an affirmative defense to a charge of failure to report sexual abuse of a child under this Section that the person who personally observed the sexual abuse had a reasonable apprehension that timely action to stop the abuse would result in the imminent infliction of death, great bodily harm, permanent disfigurement, or permanent disability to that person or another in retaliation for reporting.

(f) Sentence. A person who commits failure to report sexual abuse of a child is guilty of a Class A misdemeanor for the first violation and a Class 4 felony for a second or subsequent violation.

(g) Nothing in this Section shall be construed to allow prosecution of a person who personally observes the act of sexual abuse and assists with an investigation and any subsequent prosecution of the offender.

§ 11-9.2. Custodial sexual misconduct. (a) A person commits custodial sexual misconduct when: (1) he or she is an employee of a penal system and engages in sexual conduct or sexual penetration with a person who is in the custody of that penal system or (2) he or she is an employee of a treatment and detention facility and engages in sexual conduct or sexual penetration with a person who is in the custody of that treatment and detention facility.

(b) A probation or supervising officer or surveillance agent commits custodial sexual misconduct when the probation or supervising officer or surveillance agent engages in sexual conduct or sexual penetration with a probationer, parolee, or release or person serving a term of conditional release who is under the supervisory, disciplinary, or custodial authority of the officer or agent so engaging in the sexual conduct or sexual penetration.

(c) Custodial sexual misconduct is a Class 3 felony.

(d) Any person convicted of violating this Section immediately shall forfeit his or her employment with a penal system, treatment and detention facility, or conditional release program.

(e) For purposes of this Section, the consent of the probationer, parolee, release, or inmate in custody of the penal system or person detained or civilly committed under the Sexually Violent Persons Commitment Act shall not be a defense to a prosecution under this Section. A person is deemed incapable of consent, for purposes of this Section, when he or she is a probationer, parolee, release, or inmate in custody of a penal system or person detained or civilly committed under the Sexually Violent Persons Commitment Act.

(f) This Section does not apply to:

(1) Any employee, probation or supervising officer, or surveillance agent who is lawfully married to a person in custody if the marriage occurred before the date of custody.

(2) Any employee, probation or supervising officer, or surveillance agent who has no knowledge, and would have no reason to believe, that the person with whom he or she engaged in custodial sexual misconduct was a person in custody.

(g) In this Section:

(1) "Custody" means:

(i) pretrial incarceration or detention;

(ii) incarceration or detention under a sentence or commitment to a State or local penal institution;
(iii) parole or mandatory supervised release;
(iv) electronic home detention;
(v) probation;

(vi) detention or civil commitment either in secure care or in the community under the Sexually Violent Persons Commitment Act.
(2) "Penal system" means any system which includes institutions as defined in Section 2-14 of this Code or a county shelter care or detention home established under Section 1 of the County Shelter Care and Detention Home Act.

(2.1) "Treatment and detention facility" means any Department of Human Services facility established for the detention or civil commitment of persons under the Sexually Violent Persons Commitment Act.

(2.2) "Conditional release" means a program of treatment and services, vocational services, and alcohol or other drug abuse treatment provided to any person civilly committed and conditionally released to the community under the Sexually Violent Persons Commitment Act;

(3) "Employee" means:

(i) an employee of any governmental agency of this State or any county or municipal corporation that has by statute, ordinance, or court order the responsibility for the care, control, or supervision of pretrial or sentenced persons in a penal system or persons detained or civilly committed under the Sexually Violent Persons Commitment Act;

(ii) a contractual employee of a penal system as defined in paragraph (g)(2) of this Section who works in a penal institution as defined in Section 2-14 of this Code;

(iii) a contractual employee of a "treatment and detention facility" as defined in paragraph (g)(2.1) of this Code or a contractual employee of the Department of Human Services who provides supervision of persons serving a term of conditional release as defined in paragraph (g)(2.2) of this Code.

(4) "Sexual conduct" or "sexual penetration" means any act of sexual conduct or sexual penetration as defined in Section 11-0.1 of this Code.

(5) "Probation officer" means any person employed in a probation or court services department as defined in Section 9b of the Probation and Probation Officers Act.

(6) "Supervising officer" means any person employed to supervise persons placed on parole or mandatory supervised release with the duties described in Section 3-14-2 of the Unified Code of Corrections.

(7) "Surveillance agent" means any person employed or contracted to supervise persons placed on conditional release in the community under the Sexually Violent Persons Commitment Act.

§ 11-9.3. Presence within school zone by child sex offenders prohibited; approaching, contacting, residing with, or communicating with a child within certain places by child sex offenders prohibited. (a) It is unlawful for a child sex offender to knowingly be present in any school building, on real property comprising any school, or in any conveyance owned, leased, or contracted by a school to transport students to or from school or a school related activity when persons under the age of 18 are present in the building, on the grounds or in the conveyance, unless the offender is a parent or guardian of a student attending the school and the parent or guardian is:

(i) attending a conference at the school with school personnel to discuss the progress of his or her child academically or socially,

(ii) participating in child review conferences in which evaluation and placement decisions may be made with respect to his or her child regarding special education services, or

(iii) attending conferences to discuss other student issues concerning his or her child such as retention and promotion and notifies the principal of the school of his or her presence at the school or unless the offender has permission to be present from the superintendent or the school board or in the case of a private school from the principal. In the case of a public school, if permission is granted, the superintendent or school board president must inform the principal of the school where the sex offender will be present.

Notification includes the nature of the sex offender's visit and the hours in which the sex offender will be present in the school. The sex offender is responsible for notifying the principal's office when he or she arrives on school property and when he or she departs from school property. If the sex offender is to be present in the vicinity of children, the sex offender has the duty to remain under the direct supervision of a school official.

(a-5) It is unlawful for a child sex offender to knowingly be present within 100 feet of a site posted as a pick-up or discharge stop for a conveyance owned, leased, or contracted by a school to transport students to or from school or a school related activity when one or more persons under the age of 18 are present at the site.

(a-10) It is unlawful for a child sex offender to knowingly be present in any public park building or on real property comprising any public park when persons under the age of 18 are present in the building or on the grounds and to approach, contact, or communicate with a child under 18 years of age, unless the offender is a parent or guardian of a person under 18 years of age present in the building or on the grounds.

(b) It is unlawful for a child sex offender to knowingly loiter within 500 feet of a school building or real property comprising any school while persons under the age of 18 are present in the building or on the grounds, unless the offender is a parent or guardian of a student attending the school and the parent or guardian is:

(i) attending a conference at the school with school personnel to discuss the progress of his or her child academically or socially,

(ii) participating in child review conferences in which evaluation and placement decisions may be made with respect to his or her child regarding special education services, or

(iii) attending conferences to discuss other student issues concerning his or her child such as retention and promotion and notifies the principal of the school of his or her presence at the school or has permission to be present from the superintendent or the school board or in the case of a private school from the principal. In the case of a public school, if permission is granted, the superintendent or school board president must inform the principal of the school where the sex offender will be present.

Notification includes the nature of the sex offender's visit and the hours in which the sex offender will be present in the school. The sex offender is responsible for notifying the principal's office when he or she arrives on school property and when he or she departs from school property. If the sex offender is to be present in the vicinity of children, the sex offender has the duty to remain under the direct supervision of a school official.

(b-2) It is unlawful for a child sex offender to knowingly loiter on a public way within 500 feet of a public park building or real property comprising any public park while persons under the age of 18 are present in the building or on the grounds and to approach, contact, or communicate with a child under 18 years of age, unless the offender is a parent or guardian of a person under 18 years of age present in the building or on the grounds.

(b-5) It is unlawful for a child sex offender to knowingly reside within 500 feet of a school building or the real property comprising any school that persons under the age of 18 attend. Nothing in this subsection (b-5) prohibits a child sex offender from residing within 500 feet of a school building or the real property comprising any school that persons under 18 attend if the property is owned by the child sex offender and was purchased before July 7, 2000 (The effective date of Public Act 91-911).

(b-10) It is unlawful for a child sex offender to knowingly reside within 500 feet of a playground, child care institution, day care center, part day child care facility, day care home, group day care home, or a facility providing programs or services exclusively directed toward persons under 18 years of age.

Nothing in this subsection (b-10) prohibits a child sex offender from residing within 500 feet of a playground or a facility providing programs or services exclusively directed toward persons under 18 years of age if the property is owned by the child sex offender and was purchased before July 7, 2000.

Nothing in this subsection (b-10) prohibits a child sex offender from residing within 500 feet of a child care institution, day care center, or part day child care facility if the property is owned by the child sex offender and was purchased before June 26, 2006.

Nothing in this subsection (b-10) prohibits a child sex offender from residing within 500 feet of a day care home or group day care home if the property is owned by the child sex offender and was purchased before August 14, 2008 (the effective date of Public Act 95-821).

(b-15) It is unlawful for a child sex offender to knowingly reside within 500 feet of the victim of the sex offense. Nothing in this subsection (b-15) prohibits a child sex offender from residing within 500 feet of the victim if the property in which the child sex offender resides is owned by the child sex offender and was purchased before August 22, 2002.

This subsection (b-15) does not apply if the victim of the sex offense is 21 years of age or older.

(b-20) It is unlawful for a child sex offender to knowingly communicate, other than for a lawful purpose under Illinois law, using the Internet or any other digital media, with a person under 18 years of age or with a person whom he or she believes to be a person under 18 years of age, unless the offender is a parent or guardian of the person under 18 years of age.
(c) It is unlawful for a child sex offender to knowingly operate, manage, be employed by, volunteer at, be associated with, or knowingly be present at any:

(i) facility providing programs or services exclusively directed toward persons under the age of 18;

(ii) day care center;

(iii) part day child care facility;

(iv) child care institution;

(v) school providing before and after school programs for children under 18 years of age;

(vi) day care home; or

(vii) group day care home. This does not prohibit a child sex offender from owning the real property upon which the programs or services are offered or upon which the day care center, part day child care facility, child care institution, or school providing before and after school programs for children under 18 years of age is located, provided the child sex offender refrains from being present on the premises for the hours during which: (1) the programs or services are being offered or (2) the day care center, part day child care facility, child care institution, or school providing before and after school programs for children under 18 years of age, day care home, or group day care home is operated.

(c-2) It is unlawful for a child sex offender to participate in a holiday event involving children under 18 years of age, including but not limited to distributing candy or other items to children on Halloween, wearing a Santa Claus costume on or preceding Christmas, being employed as a department store Santa Claus, or wearing an Easter Bunny costume on or preceding Easter. For the purposes of this subsection, child sex offender has the meaning as defined in this Section, but does not include as a sex offense under paragraph (2) of subsection (d) of this Section, the offense under subsection (c) of Section 11-1.50 of this Code. This subsection does not apply to a child sex offender who is a parent or guardian of children under 18 years of age that are present in the home and other non-familial minors are not present.

(c-5) It is unlawful for a child sex offender to knowingly operate, manage, be employed by, or be associated with any county fair when persons under the age of 18 are present.

(c-6) It is unlawful for a child sex offender who owns and resides at residential real estate to knowingly rent any residential unit within the same building in which he or she resides to a person who is the parent or guardian of a child or children under 18 years of age. This subsection shall apply only to leases or other rental arrangements entered into after January 1, 2009 (the effective date of Public Act 95-820).

(c-7) It is unlawful for a child sex offender to knowingly offer or provide any programs or services to persons under 18 years of age in his or her residence or the residence of another or in any facility for the purpose of offering or providing such programs or services, whether such programs or services are offered or provided by contract, agreement, arrangement, or on a volunteer basis.

(c-8) It is unlawful for a child sex offender to knowingly operate, whether authorized to do so or not, any of the following vehicles: (1) a vehicle which is specifically designed, constructed or modified and equipped to be used for the retail sale of food or beverages, including but not limited to an ice cream truck; (2) an authorized emergency vehicle; or (3) a rescue vehicle.

(d) Definitions. In this Section:

(1) "Child sex offender" means any person who:

(i) has been charged under Illinois law, or any substantially similar federal law or law of another state, with a sex offense set forth in paragraph (2) of this subsection (d) or the attempt to commit an included sex offense, and the victim is a person under 18 years of age at the time of the offense and:

(A) is convicted of such offense or an attempt to commit such offense; or

(B) is found not guilty by reason of insanity of such offense or an attempt to commit such offense; or

(C) is found not guilty by reason of insanity pursuant to subsection (c) of Section 104-25 of the Code of Criminal Procedure of 1963 of such offense or an attempt to commit such offense; or

(D) is the subject of a finding not resulting in an acquittal at a hearing conducted pursuant to subsection (a) of Section 104-25 of the Code of Criminal Procedure of 1963 for the alleged commission or attempted commission of such offense; or

(E) is found not guilty by reason of insanity following a hearing conducted pursuant to a federal law or the law of another state substantially similar to subsection (c) of Section 104-25 of the Code of Criminal Procedure of 1963 of such offense or of the attempted commission of such offense; or

(F) is the subject of a finding not resulting in an acquittal at a hearing conducted pursuant to a federal law or the law of another state substantially similar to subsection (a) of Section 104-25 of the Code of Criminal Procedure of 1963 for the alleged violation or attempted commission of such offense; or

(ii) is certified as a sexually dangerous person pursuant to the Illinois Sexually Dangerous Persons Act, or any substantially similar federal law or the law of another state, when any conduct giving rise to such certification is committed or attempted against a person less than 18 years of age; or

(iii) is subject to the provisions of Section 2 of the Interstate Agreements on Sexually Dangerous Persons Act.

Convictions that result from or are connected with the same act, or result from offenses committed at the same time, shall be counted for the purpose of this Section as one conviction. Any conviction set aside pursuant to law is not a conviction for purposes of this Section.

(2) Except as otherwise provided in paragraph (2.5), "sex offense" means:

(i) A violation of any of the following Sections of the Criminal Code of 1961: 10-4 (forcible detention), 10-7 (aiding or abetting child abduction under Section 10-5(b)(10)), 10-5(b)(10) (child luring), 11-1.40 (predatory criminal sexual assault of a child), 11-6 (indecent solicitation of a child), 11-6.5 (indecent solicitation of an adult), 11-9.1 (sexual exploitation of a child), 11-9.2 (custodial sexual misconduct), 11-9.5 (sexual misconduct with a person with a disability), 11-11 (sexual relations within families), 11-14.3(a)(1) (promoting prostitution by advancing prostitution), 11-14.3(a)(2)(A) (promoting prostitution by profiting from prostitution by compelling a person to be a prostitute), 11-14.3(a)(2)(C) (promoting prostitution by profiting from prostitution by means other than as described in subparagraphs (A) and (B) of paragraph (2) of subsection (a) of Section 11-14.3),11-14.4 (promoting juvenile prostitution), 11-18.1 (patronizing a juvenile prostitute), 11-20.1 (child pornography), 11-20.1B (aggravated child pornography), 11-21 (harmful material), 11-25 (grooming), 11-26 (traveling to meet a minor), 12-33 (ritualized abuse of a child), 11-20 (obscenity) (when that offense was committed in any school, on real property comprising any school, in any conveyance owned, leased, or contracted by a school to transport students to or from school or a school related activity, or in a public park) ,11-30 (public indecency) (when committed in a school, on real property comprising a school, in any conveyance owned, leased, or contracted by a school to transport students to or from school or a school related activity, or in a public park). an attempt to commit any of these offenses.

(ii) A violation of any of the following Sections of the Criminal Code of 1961, when the victim is a person under 18 years of age: 11-1.20 (criminal sexual assault), 11-1.30 (aggravated criminal sexual assault), 11-1.50 (criminal sexual abuse), 11-1.60 (aggravated criminal sexual abuse). An attempt to commit any of these offenses.

(iii) A violation of any of the following Sections of the Criminal Code of 1961, when the victim is a person under 18 years of age and the defendant is not a parent of the victim:

10-1 (kidnapping),

10-2 (aggravated kidnapping),

10-3 (unlawful restraint),
10-3.1 (aggravated unlawful restraint),

11-9.1(A) (permitting sexual abuse of a child).

An attempt to commit any of these offenses.

(iv) A violation of any former law of this State substantially equivalent to any offense listed in clause (2)(i) of subsection (d) of this Section.

(2.5) For the purposes of subsections (b-5) and (b-10) only, a sex offense means:

(i) A violation of any of the following Sections of the Criminal Code of 1961:

10-5(b)(10) (child luring), 10-7 (aiding or abetting child abduction under Section 10-5(b)(10)), 11-1.40 (predatory criminal sexual assault of a child), 11-6 (indecent solicitation of a child), 11-6.5 (indecent solicitation of an adult), 11-9.2 (custodial sexual misconduct), 11-9.5 (sexual misconduct with a person with a disability), 11-11 (sexual relations within families), 11-14.3(a)(1) (promoting prostitution by advancing prostitution), 11-14.3(a)(2)(A) (promoting prostitution by profiting from prostitution by compelling a person to be a prostitute), 11-14.3(a)(2)(C) (promoting prostitution by profiting from prostitution by means other than as described in subparagraphs (A) and (B) of paragraph (2) of subsection (a) of Section 11-14.3), 11-14.4 (promoting juvenile prostitution), 11-18.1 (patronizing a juvenile prostitute), 11-20.1 (child pornography), 11-20.1B (aggravated child pornography), 11-25 (grooming), 11-26 (traveling to meet a minor), or 12-33 (ritualized abuse of a child). An attempt to commit any of these offenses.

(ii) A violation of any of the following Sections of the Criminal Code of 1961, when the victim is a person under 18 years of age: 11-1.20 (criminal sexual assault), 11-1.30 (aggravated criminal sexual assault), 11-1.60 (aggravated criminal sexual abuse), and subsection (a) of Section 11-1.50 (criminal sexual abuse). An attempt to commit any of these offenses.

(iii) A violation of any of the following Sections of the Criminal Code of 1961, when the victim is a person under 18 years of age and the defendant is not a parent of the victim:

10-1 (kidnapping),

10-2 (aggravated kidnapping),

10-3 (unlawful restraint),

10-3.1 (aggravated unlawful restraint),

11-9.1(A) (permitting sexual abuse of a child).

An attempt to commit any of these offenses.

(iv) A violation of any former law of this State substantially equivalent to any offense listed in this paragraph (2.5) of this subsection.

(3) A conviction for an offense of federal law or the law of another state that is substantially equivalent to any offense listed in paragraph (2) of subsection (d) of this Section shall constitute a conviction for the purpose of this Section. A finding or adjudication as a sexually dangerous person under any federal law or law of another state that is substantially equivalent to the Sexually Dangerous Persons Act shall constitute an adjudication for the purposes of this Section.

(4) "Authorized emergency vehicle", "rescue vehicle", and "vehicle" have the meanings ascribed to them in Sections 1-105, 1-171.8 and 1-217, respectively, of the Illinois Vehicle Code.

(5) "Child care institution" has the meaning ascribed to it in Section 2.06 of the Child Care Act of 1969.

(6) "Day care center" has the meaning ascribed to it in Section 2.09 of the Child Care Act of 1969.

(7) "Day care home" has the meaning ascribed to it in Section 2.18 of the Child Care Act of 1969.

(8) "Facility providing programs or services directed towards persons under the age of 18" means any facility providing programs or services exclusively directed towards persons under the age of 18.

(9) "Group day care home" has the meaning ascribed to it in Section 2.20 of the Child Care Act of 1969.

(10) "Internet" has the meaning set forth in Section 16J-5 of this Code.

(11) "Loiter" means:

(i) Standing, sitting idly, whether or not the person is in a vehicle, or remaining in or around school or public park property.

(ii) Standing, sitting idly, whether or not the person is in a vehicle, or remaining in or around school or public park property, for the purpose of committing or attempting to commit a sex offense.

(iii) Entering or remaining in a building in or around school property, other than the offender's residence.

(12) "Part day child care facility" has the meaning ascribed to it in Section 2.10 of the Child Care Act of 1969.

(13) "Playground" means a piece of land owned or controlled by a unit of local government that is designated by the unit of local government for use solely or primarily for children's recreation.

(14) "Public park" includes a park, forest preserve, bikeway, trail, or conservation area under the jurisdiction of the State or a unit of local government.

(15) "School" means a public or private preschool or elementary or secondary school.

(16) "School official" means the principal, a teacher, or any other certified employee of the school, the superintendent of schools or a member of the school board.

(e) for the purposes of this Section, the 500 feet distance shall be measured from: (1) the edge of the property of the school building or the real property comprising the school that is closest to the edge of the property of the child sex offender's residence or where he or she is loitering, and (2) the edge of the property comprising the public park building or the real property comprising the public park, playground, child care institution, day care center, part day child care facility, or facility providing programs or services exclusively directed toward persons under 18 years of age, or a victim of the sex offense who is under 21 years of age, to the edge of the child sex offender's place of residence or place where he or she is loitering.

(f) Sentence. A person who violates this Section is guilty of a Class 4 felony.

§ 11-9.4-1. Sexual predator and child sex offender; presence or loitering in or near public parks prohibited. (a) For the purposes of this Section:

"Child sex offender" has the meaning ascribed to it in subsection (d) of Section 11-9.3 of this Code [720 ILCS 5/11-9.3], but does not include as a sex offense under paragraph (2) of subsection (d) of Section 11-9.3 [720 ILCS 5/11-9.3], the offenses under subsections (b) and (c) of Section 12-15 of this Code [720 ILCS 5/15].

"Public park" includes a park, forest preserve, bikeway, trail, or conservation area under the jurisdiction of the State or a unit of local government.

"Loiter" means:

(i) Standing, sitting idly, whether or not the person is in a vehicle or remaining in or around public park property.

(ii) Standing, sitting idly, whether or not the person is in a vehicle or remaining in or around public park property, for the purpose of committing or attempting to commit a sex offense.

"Sexual predator" has the meaning ascribed to it in subsection (E) of Section 2 of the Sex Offender Registration Act [730 ILCS 150/2].

(b) It is unlawful for a sexual predator or a child sex offender to knowingly be present in any public park building or on real property comprising any public park.

(c) It is unlawful for a sexual predator or a child sex offender to knowingly loiter on a public way within 500 feet of a public park building or real property comprising any public park. For the purposes of this subsection (c), the 500 feet distance shall be measured from the edge of the property comprising the public park building or the real property comprising the public park.

(d) Sentence. A person who violates this Section is guilty of a Class A misdemeanor, except that a second or subsequent violation is a Class 4 felony.

Commentary – Child Sexual Offender and Sexual Predator Restraint Laws

Sections 11-9.3, 11-9.4 and 11-9.4-1 establish prohibitions against persons who have been subject of Sexual Registry laws or have been convicted of certain sexual offenses from having contact with or being present near minors (i.e. under the age of 18). This modern trend of banishment laws is meant to protect children from harm by sexual recidivists. As one might expect schools and parks are off-limits to a child sex offender, as are contact with any child under age 18 unless it is the child of the sex offender. Activities such as renting homes or apartments to families with children under age 18 are also prohibited. Loitering within 500 feet of a park by a child sex offender or sexual predator is likewise criminalized. In fact, it is a crime for a child sex offender or sexual predator to contact or attempt to contact a minor by telephone, text or internet (unless it is the person's own child).

In *People v. Diestelhorst* 344 Ill.App.3d 1172, 801 N.E.2d 1146 (Ill. App. Ct. 5th Dist. 2007), the defendant was a child sex offender, having been convicted of sexual assault by an act of sexual penetration on a male child under 13 years of age. He went to a park and watched a high school baseball team practice, making comments to players, shagging foul balls and returning a dropped glove to one of the players. He was convicted of approaching and making contact with a child less than 18 years of age, when he was not a parent of the child. His claims that words like "approach" and "contact" were impermissibly vague were rejected, with the court noting that the purpose of such laws was not punishment of the prior-convicted offender but to diminish contact between children and such offenders for protection of the children.

In *People v. Pollard* 2016 IL App (5th) 130514 the Defendant had been convicted of Predatory Criminal Sexual Assault of a Child and attacked the validity of provisions of the Sex Offender Registration Act (SORA) 730 ILCS 150/1 *et seq* and the criminalization of activities of child sex offenders under 720 ILCS 5/11-9.3 and 5/11-9.4.1 (no residence within 500 feet of a school, no presence in public parks, or schools, prohibited employment, etc.) The Defendant claimed the lifetime SORA registration requirement and the restraints on permissible activities and living arrangements violation due process and other provisions of the U. S. and Illinois Constitutions. In rejecting the claims, the court found no violation of fundamental rights and that the protection of children was a rational basis for the statutory scheme, including imposing criminal penalties.

§ 11-9.5. Sexual misconduct with a person with a disability. (a) Definitions. As used in this Section:

(1) "Person with a disability" means:

(i) a person diagnosed with a developmental disability as defined in Section 1-106 of the Mental Health and Developmental Disabilities Code; or

(ii) a person diagnosed with a mental illness as defined in Section 1-129 of the Mental Health and Developmental Disabilities Code.

(2) "State-operated facility" means:

(i) a developmental disability facility as defined in the Mental Health and Developmental Disabilities Code; or
(ii) a mental health facility as defined in the Mental Health and Developmental Disabilities Code.

(3) "Community agency" or "agency" means any community entity or program providing residential mental health or developmental disabilities services that is licensed, certified, or funded by the Department of Human Services and not licensed or certified by any other human service agency of the State such as the Departments of Public Health, Healthcare and Family Services, and Children and Family Services.

(4) "Care and custody" means admission to a State-operated facility.

(5) "Employee" means:

(i) any person employed by the Illinois Department of Human Services;

(ii) any person employed by a community agency providing services at the direction of the owner or operator of the agency on or off site; or

(iii) any person who is a contractual employee or contractual agent of the Department of Human Services or the community agency. This includes but is not limited to payroll personnel, contractors, subcontractors, and volunteers.

(6) "Sexual conduct" or "sexual penetration" means any act of sexual conduct or sexual penetration as defined in Section 11-0.1 of this Code.

(b) A person commits sexual misconduct with a person with a disability when:

(1) he or she is an employee and knowingly engages in sexual conduct or sexual penetration with a person with a disability who is under the care and custody of the Department of Human Services at a State-operated facility; or

(2) he or she is an employee of a community agency funded by the Department of Human Services and knowingly engages in sexual conduct or sexual penetration with a person with a disability who is in a residential program operated or supervised by a community agency.

(c) For purposes of this Section, the consent of a person with a disability in custody of the Department of Human Services residing at a State-operated facility or receiving services from a community agency shall not be a defense to a prosecution under this Section. A person is deemed incapable of consent, for purposes of this Section, when he or she is a person with a disability and is receiving services at a State-operated facility or is a person with a disability who is in a residential program operated or supervised by a community agency.

(d) This Section does not apply to:

(1) any State employee or any community agency employee who is lawfully married to a person with a disability in custody of the Department of Human Services or receiving services from a community agency if the marriage occurred before the date of custody or the initiation of services at a community agency; or

(2) any State employee or community agency employee who has no knowledge, and would have no reason to believe, that the person with whom he or she engaged in sexual misconduct was a person with a disability in custody of the Department of Human Services or was receiving services from a community agency.

(e) Sentence. Sexual misconduct with a person with a disability is a Class 3 felony.
(f) Any person convicted of violating this Section shall immediately forfeit his or her employment with the State or the community agency.

§ 11-11. Sexual Relations Within Families.
(a) A person commits sexual relations within families if he or she:

(1) Commits an act of sexual penetration as defined in Section 11-0.1 of this Code; and

(2) The person knows that he or she is related to the other person as follows: (i) Brother or sister, either of the whole blood or the half blood; or (ii) Father or mother, when the child, regardless of legitimacy and regardless of whether the child was of the whole blood or half-blood or was adopted, was 18 years of age or over when the act was committed; or (iii) Stepfather or stepmother, when the stepchild was 18 years of age or over when the act was committed; or (iv) Aunt or uncle, when the niece or nephew was 18 years of age or over when the act was committed; or (v) Great-aunt or great-uncle, when the grand-niece or grand-nephew was 18 years of age or over when the act was committed; or (vi) Grandparent or step-grandparent, when the grandchild or step-

grandchild was 18 years of age or over when the act was committed.

(b) Sentence. Sexual relations within families is a Class 3 felony.

Subdivision 15. Prostitution Offenses

§ 11-14. Prostitution. (a) Any person who knowingly performs, offers or agrees to perform any act of sexual penetration as defined in Section11-0.1 of this Code for anything of value, or any touching or fondling of the sex organs of one person by another person, for anything of value, for the purpose of sexual arousal or gratification commits an act of prostitution.

(b) Sentence. A violation of this Section is a Class A misdemeanor.

(c) (Blank).

(c-5) It is an affirmative defense to a charge under this Section that the accused engaged in or performed prostitution as a result of being a victim of involuntary servitude or trafficking in persons as defined in Section 10-9 of this Code.

(d) Notwithstanding the foregoing, if it is determined, after a reasonable detention for investigative purposes, that a person suspected of or charged with a violation of this Section is a person under the age of 18, that person shall be immune from prosecution for a prostitution offense under this Section, and shall be subject to the temporary protective custody provisions of Sections 2-5 and 2-6 of the Juvenile Court Act of 1987. Pursuant to the provisions of Section 2-6 of the Juvenile Court Act of 1987, a law enforcement officer who takes a person under 18 years of age into custody under this Section shall immediately report an allegation of a violation of Section 10-9 of this Code to the Illinois Department of Children and Family Services State Central Register, which shall commence an initial investigation into child abuse or child neglect within 24 hours pursuant to Section 7.4 of the Abused and Neglected Child Reporting Act.

§ 11-14.1. Solicitation of a sexual act. (a) Any person who offers a person not his or her spouse any money, property, token, object, or article or anything of value for that person or any other person not his or her spouse to perform any act of sexual penetration as defined in Section 11-0.1 of this Code, or any touching or fondling of the sex organs of one person by another person for the purpose of sexual arousal or gratification, commits solicitation of a sexual act.

(b) Sentence. Solicitation of a sexual act is a Class A misdemeanor. Solicitation of a sexual act from a person who is under the age of 18 or who is a person with a severe or profound intellectual disability is a Class 4 felony. If the court imposes a fine under this subsection (b), it shall be collected and distributed to the Specialized Services for Survivors of Human Trafficking Fund in accordance with Section 5-9-1.21 of the Unified Code of Corrections.

(b-5) It is an affirmative defense to a charge of solicitation of a sexual act with a person who is under the age of 18 or who is a person with a severe or profound intellectual disability that the accused reasonably believed the person was of the age of 18 years or over or was not a person with a severe or profound intellectual disability at the time of the act giving rise to the charge.

§ 11-14.2. First offender; felony prostitution. (a) Whenever any person who has not previously been convicted of or placed on probation for felony prostitution or any law of the United States or of any other state relating to felony prostitution pleads guilty to or is found guilty of felony prostitution, the court, without entering a judgment and with the consent of such person, may sentence the person to probation.

(b) When a person is placed on probation, the court shall enter an order specifying a period of probation of 24 months and shall defer further proceedings in the case until the conclusion of the period or until the filing of a petition alleging violation of a term or condition of probation.

(c) The conditions of probation shall be that the person: (1) not violate any criminal statute of any jurisdiction; (2) refrain from possessing a firearm or other dangerous weapon; (3) submit to periodic drug testing at a time and in a manner as ordered by the court, but no less than 3 times during the period of the probation, with the cost of the testing to be paid by the probationer; and (4) perform no less than 30 hours of community service, provided community service is available in the jurisdiction and is funded and approved by the county board.

(d) The court may, in addition to other conditions, require that the person:

(1) make a report to and appear in person before or participate with the court or such courts, person, or social service agency as directed by the court in the order of probation;

(2) pay a fine and costs;

(3) work or pursue a course of study or vocational training;

(4) undergo medical or psychiatric treatment; or treatment or rehabilitation by a provider approved by the Illinois Department of Human Services;

(5) attend or reside in a facility established for the instruction or residence of defendants on probation;

(6) support his or her dependents;

(7) refrain from having in his or her body the presence of any illicit drug prohibited by the Cannabis Control Act or the Illinois Controlled Substances Act, unless prescribed by a physician, and submit samples of his or her blood or urine or both for tests to determine the presence of any illicit drug;

(8) (blank).

(e) Upon violation of a term or condition of probation, the court may enter a judgment on its original finding of guilt and proceed as otherwise provided.

(f) Upon fulfillment of the terms and conditions of probation, the court shall discharge the person and dismiss the proceedings against him or her.

(g) A disposition of probation is considered to be a conviction for the purposes of imposing the conditions of probation and for appeal, however, discharge and dismissal under this Section is not a conviction for purposes of this Act or for purposes of disqualifications or disabilities imposed by law upon conviction of a crime.

(h) There may be only one discharge and dismissal under this Section.

(i) If a person is convicted of prostitution within 5 years subsequent to a discharge and dismissal under this Section, the discharge and dismissal under this Section shall be admissible in the sentencing proceeding for that conviction as evidence in aggravation.

§ 11-14.3. Promoting prostitution. (a) Any person who knowingly performs any of the following acts commits promoting prostitution:

(1) advances prostitution as defined in Section 11-0.1;

(2) profits from prostitution by:

(A) compelling a person to become a prostitute;

(B) arranging or offering to arrange a situation in which a person may practice prostitution; or

(C) any means other than those described in subparagraph (A) or (B), including from a person who patronizes a prostitute. This paragraph (C) does not apply to a person engaged in prostitution who is under 18 years of age. A person cannot be convicted of promoting prostitution under this paragraph (C) if the practice of prostitution underlying the offense consists exclusively of the accused's own acts of prostitution under Section 11-14 of this Code.

(b) Sentence. (1) A violation of subdivision (a)(1) is a Class 4 felony, unless committed within 1,000 feet of real property comprising a school, in which case it is a Class 3 felony. A second or subsequent violation of subdivision (a)(1), or any combination of convictions under subdivision (a)(1), (a)(2)(A), or (a)(2)(B) and Section 11-14 (prostitution), 11-14.1 (solicitation of a sexual act), 11-14.4 (promoting juvenile prostitution), 11-15 (soliciting for a prostitute), 11-15.1 (soliciting for a juvenile prostitute), 11-16 (pandering), 11-17 (keeping a place of prostitution), 11-17.1 (keeping a place of juvenile prostitution), 11-18 (patronizing a prostitute), 11-18.1 (patronizing a juvenile prostitute), 11-19 (pimping), 11-19.1 (juvenile pimping or aggravated juvenile pimping), or 11-19.2 (exploitation of a child), is a Class 3 felony.

(2) A violation of subdivision (a)(2)(A) or (a)(2)(B) is a Class 4 felony, unless committed within 1,000 feet of real property comprising a school, in which case it is a Class 3 felony.

(3) A violation of subdivision (a)(2)(C) is a Class 4 felony, unless committed within 1,000 feet of real property comprising a school, in which case it is a Class 3 felony. A second or subsequent violation of subdivision (a)(2)(C), or any combination of convictions under subdivision (a)(2)(C) and subdivision (a)(1), (a)(2)(A), or (a)(2)(B) of this Section (promoting prostitution), 11-14 (prostitution), 11-14.1 (solicitation of a sexual act), 11-14.4 (promoting juvenile prostitution), 11-15 (soliciting for a prostitute), 11-15.1 (soliciting for a juvenile prostitute), 11-16 (pandering), 11-17 (keeping a place of prostitution), 11-17.1 (keeping a place of juvenile prostitution), 11-18 (patronizing a prostitute), 11-18.1 (patronizing a juvenile prostitute), 11-19 (pimping), 11-19.1 (juvenile pimping or aggravated juvenile pimping), or 11-19.2 (exploitation of a child), is a Class 3 felony.

§ 11-14.4. Promoting juvenile prostitution.
(a) Any person who knowingly performs any of the following acts commits promoting juvenile prostitution:
(1) advances prostitution as defined in Section 11-0.1, where the minor engaged in prostitution, or any person engaged in prostitution in the place, is under 18 years of age or is a person with a severe or profound intellectual disability at the time of the offense;
(2) profits from prostitution by any means where the prostituted person is under 18 years of age or is a person with a severe or profound intellectual disability at the time of the offense;
(3) profits from prostitution by any means where the prostituted person is under 13 years of age at the time of the offense;
(4) confines a child under the age of 18 or a person with a severe or profound intellectual disability against his or her will by the infliction or threat of imminent infliction of great bodily harm or permanent disability or disfigurement or by administering to the child or a person with a severe or profound intellectual disability, without his or her consent or by threat or deception and for other than medical purposes, any alcoholic intoxicant or a drug as defined in the Illinois Controlled Substances Act or the Cannabis Control Act or methamphetamine as defined in the Methamphetamine Control and Community Protection Act and:

(A) compels the child or a person with a severe or profound intellectual disability to engage in prostitution;

(B) arranges a situation in which the child or a person with a severe or profound intellectual disability may practice prostitution; or

(C) profits from prostitution by the child or a person with a severe or profound intellectual disability.

(b) For purposes of this Section, administering drugs, as defined in subdivision (a)(4), or an alcoholic intoxicant to a child under the age of 13 or a person with a severe or profound intellectual disability shall be deemed to be without consent if the administering is done without the consent of the parents or legal guardian or if the administering is performed by the parents or legal guardian for other than medical purposes.

(c) If the accused did not have a reasonable opportunity to observe the prostituted person, it is an affirmative defense to a charge of promoting juvenile prostitution, except for a charge under subdivision (a)(4), that the accused reasonably believed the person was of the age of

18 years or over or was not a person with a severe or profound intellectual disability at the time of the act giving rise to the charge.

(d) Sentence. A violation of subdivision (a)(1) is a Class 1 felony, unless committed within 1,000 feet of real property comprising a school, in which case it is a Class X felony.

A violation of subdivision (a)(2) is a Class 1 felony. A violation of subdivision (a)(3) is a Class X felony. A violation of subdivision (a)(4) is a Class X felony, for which the person shall be sentenced to a term of imprisonment of not less than 6 years and not more than 60 years.
A second or subsequent violation of subdivision (a)(1), (a)(2), or (a)(3), or any combination of convictions under subdivision (a)(1), (a)(2), or (a)(3) and Sections 11-14 (prostitution), 11-14.1 (solicitation of a sexual act), 11-14.3 (promoting prostitution), 11-15 (soliciting for a prostitute), 11-15.1 (soliciting for a juvenile prostitute), 11-16 (pandering), 11-17 (keeping a place of prostitution), 11-17.1 (keeping a place of juvenile prostitution), 11-18 (patronizing a prostitute), 11-18.1 (patronizing a juvenile prostitute), 11-19 (pimping), 11-19.1 (juvenile pimping or aggravated juvenile pimping), or 11-19.2 (exploitation of a child) of this Code, is a Class X felony.

(e) Forfeiture. Any person convicted of a violation of this Section that involves promoting juvenile prostitution by keeping a place of juvenile prostitution or convicted of a violation of subdivision (a)(4) is subject to the property forfeiture provisions set forth in Article 124B of the Code of Criminal Procedure of 1963.

(f) For the purposes of this Section, "prostituted person" means any person who engages in, or agrees or offers to engage in, any act of sexual penetration as defined in Section 11-0.1 of this Code for any money, property, token, object, or article or anything of value, or any touching or fondling of the sex organs of one person by another person, for any money, property, token, object, or article or anything of value, for the purpose of sexual arousal or gratification.

§ 11-15. Soliciting for a prostitute. (a) Any person who performs any of the following acts commits soliciting for a prostitute:

(1) Solicits another for the purpose of prostitution; or

(2) Arranges or offers to arrange a meeting of persons for the purpose of prostitution; or

(3) Directs another to a place knowing such direction is for the purpose of prostitution.

(b) Sentence. Soliciting for a prostitute is a Class 4 felony. A person convicted of a second or subsequent violation of this Section, or of any combination of such number of convictions under this Section and Sections 11-14, 11-14.1, 11-15.1, 11-16, 11-17, 11-17.1, 11-18, 11-18.1, 11-19, 11-19.1, or 11-19.2 of this Code is guilty of a Class 3 felony. The fact of such prior conviction is not an element of the offense and may not be disclosed to the jury during trial unless otherwise permitted by issues properly raised during such trial.

(b-5) A person who violates this Section within 1,000 feet of real property comprising a school commits a Class 3 felony.

11-15.1. Soliciting for a minor engaged in prostitution. (a) Any person who violates any of the provisions of Section 11-15(a) of this Act commits soliciting for a minor engaged in prostitution where the person for whom such person is soliciting is under 18 years of age or is a severely or profoundly a person with an intellectual disability person.

(b) It is an affirmative defense to a charge of soliciting for a minor engaged in prostitution that the accused reasonably believed the person was of the age of 18 years or over or was not a severely or profoundly a person with an intellectual disability person at the time of the act giving rise to the charge.

(c) Sentence.

Soliciting for a minor engaged in prostitution is a Class 1 felony. A person convicted of a second or subsequent violation of this Section, or of any combination of such number of convictions under this Section and Sections 11-14, 11-14.1, 11-15, 11-16, 11-17, 11-17.1, 11-18, 11-18.1, 11-19, 11-19.1, or 11-19.2 of this Code, is guilty of a Class X felony. The fact of such prior conviction is not an element of the offense and may not be disclosed to the jury during trial unless otherwise permitted by issues properly raised during the trial.

(c-5) A person who violates this Section within 1,000 feet of real property comprising a school commits a Class X felony.

§ 11-16. Pandering. (a) Any person who performs any of the following acts for any money, property, token, object, or article or anything of value commits pandering:

(1) Compels a person to become a prostitute; or

(2) Arranges or offers to arrange a situation in which a person may practice prostitution.

(b) Sentence.

Pandering by compulsion is a Class 4 felony. Pandering other than by compulsion is a Class 4 felony.

(c) A person who violates this Section within 1,000 feet of real property comprising a school commits a Class 3 felony.

§ 11-17. Keeping a Place of Prostitution. (a) Any person who has or exercises control over the use of any place which could offer seclusion or shelter for the practice of prostitution who performs any of the following acts keeps a place of prostitution:

(1) Knowingly grants or permits the use of such place for the purpose of prostitution; or

(2) Grants or permits the use of such place under circumstances from which he could reasonably know that the place is used or is to be used for purposes of prostitution; or

(3) Permits the continued use of a place after becoming aware of facts or circumstances from which he should reasonably know that the place is being used for purposes of prostitution.

(b) Sentence. Keeping a place of prostitution is a Class 4 felony. A person convicted of a second or subsequent violation of this Section, or of any combination of such number of convictions under this Section and Sections 11-14, 11-14.1, 11-15, 11-15.1, 11-16, 11-17.1, 11-18, 11-18.1, 11-19, 11-19.1, or 11-19.2 of this Code, is guilty of a Class 3 felony. The fact of such conviction is not an element of the offense and may not be disclosed to the jury during trial unless otherwise permitted by issues properly raised during such trial. A person who violates this Section within 1,000 feet of real property comprising a school commits a Class 3 felony.

11-17.1. Keeping a Place of Juvenile Prostitution. (a) Any person who knowingly violates any of the provisions of Section 11-17 of this Act commits keeping a place of juvenile prostitution when any person engaged in prostitution in the place of prostitution is under 18 years of age or is a severely or profoundly a person with an intellectual disability person.

(b) If the accused did not have a reasonable opportunity to observe the person, it is an affirmative defense to a charge of keeping a place of juvenile prostitution that the accused reasonably believed the person was of the age of 18 years or over or was not a severely or profoundly a person with an intellectual disability person at the time of the act giving rise to the charge.

(c) Sentence. Keeping a place of juvenile prostitution is a Class 1 felony. A person convicted of a second or subsequent violation of this Section, or of any combination of such number of convictions under this Section and Sections 11-14, 11-14.1, 11-15, 11-15.1, 11-16, 11-17, 11-18, 11-18.1, 11-19, 11-19.1, or 11-19.2 of this Code, is guilty of a Class X felony.
(d) Forfeiture. Any person convicted under this Section is subject to the property forfeiture provisions set forth in Article 124B of the Code of Criminal Procedure of 1963.

§ 11-18. Patronizing a prostitute. (a) Any person who knowingly performs any of the following acts with a person not his or her spouse commits patronizing a prostitute:

(1) Engages in an act of sexual penetration as defined in Section 11-0.1 of this Code with a prostitute; or

(2) Enters or remains in a place of prostitution with intent to engage in an act of sexual penetration as defined in Section 11-0.1 of this Code; or

(3) Engages in any touching or fondling with a prostitute of the sex organs of one person by the other person, with the intent to achieve sexual arousal or gratification.

(b) Sentence.

Patronizing a prostitute is a Class 4 felony, unless committed within 1,000 feet of real property comprising a school, in which case it is a Class 3 felony. A person convicted of a second or subsequent violation of this Section, or of any combination of such number of convictions under this Section and Sections 11-14 (prostitution), 11-14.1 (solicitation of a sexual act), 11-14.3 (promoting prostitution), 11-14.4 (promoting juvenile prostitution), 11-15 (soliciting for a prostitute), 11-15.1 (soliciting for a juvenile prostitute), 11-16 (pandering), 11-17 (keeping a place of prostitution), 11-17.1 (keeping a place of juvenile prostitution), 11-18.1 (patronizing a juvenile prostitute), 11-19 (pimping), 11-19.1 (juvenile pimping or aggravated juvenile pimping), or 11-19.2 (exploitation of a child) of this Code, is guilty of a Class 3 felony.

§ 11-18.1. Patronizing a minor engaged in prostitution. (a) Any person who engages in an act of sexual penetration as defined in Section 11-0.1 of this Code with a person engaged in prostitution who is under 18 years of age or is a person with a severe or profound intellectual disability commits patronizing a minor engaged in prostitution.

(a-5) Any person who engages in any touching or fondling, with a person engaged in prostitution who either is under 18 years of age or is a person with a severe or profound intellectual disability, of the sex organs of one person by the other person, with the intent to achieve sexual arousal or gratification, commits patronizing a minor engaged in prostitution.

(b) It is an affirmative defense to the charge of patronizing a minor engaged in prostitution that the accused reasonably believed that the person was of the age of 18 years or over or was not a person with a severe or profound intellectual disability at the time of the act giving rise to the charge.

(c) Sentence. A person who commits patronizing a juvenile prostitute is guilty of a Class 3 felony, unless committed within 1,000 feet of real property comprising a school, in which case it is a Class 2 felony. A person convicted of a second or subsequent violation of this Section, or of any combination of such number of convictions under this Section and Sections 11-14 (prostitution), 11-14.1 (solicitation of a sexual act), 11-14.3 (promoting prostitution), 11-14.4 (promoting juvenile prostitution), 11-15 (soliciting for a prostitute), 11-15.1 (soliciting for a juvenile prostitute), 11-16 (pandering), 11-17 (keeping a place of prostitution), 11-17.1 (keeping a place of juvenile prostitution), 11-18 (patronizing a prostitute), 11-19 (pimping), 11-19.1 (juvenile pimping or aggravated juvenile pimping), or 11-19.2 (exploitation of a child) of this Code, is guilty of a Class 2 felony. The fact of such conviction is not an element of the offense and may not be disclosed to the jury during trial unless otherwise permitted by issues properly raised during such trial.

§ 11-19. Pimping. (a) Any person who receives any money, property, token, object, or article or anything of value from a prostitute or from a person who patronizes a prostitute, not for a lawful consideration, knowing it was earned or paid in whole or in part from or for the practice of prostitution, commits pimping. The foregoing shall not apply to a person engaged in prostitution who is under 18 years of age. A person cannot be convicted of pimping under this Section if the practice of prostitution underlying such offense consists exclusively of the accused's own acts of prostitution under Section 11-14 of this Code.

(b) Sentence. Pimping is a Class 4 felony. A

person convicted of a second or subsequent violation of this Section, or of any combination of such number of convictions under this Section and Sections 11-14, 11-14.1, 11-15, 11-15.1, 11-16, 11-17, 11-17.1, 11-18, 11-18.1, 11-19.1, or 11-19.2 of this Code is guilty of a Class 3 felony. The fact of such conviction is not an element of the offense and may not be disclosed to the jury during trial unless otherwise permitted by issues properly raised during such trial.

(c) A person who violates this Section within 1,000 feet of real property comprising a school commits a Class 3 felony.

§ 11-19.1. Juvenile Pimping and aggravated juvenile pimping. (a) A person commits the offense of juvenile pimping if the person knowingly receives any form of consideration derived from the practice of prostitution, in whole or in part, and

(1) the prostituted person was under the age of 18 at the time the act of prostitution occurred; or

(2) the prostitute was a severely or profoundly a person with an intellectual disability person at the time the act of prostitution occurred.

(b) A person commits the offense of aggravated juvenile pimping if the person knowingly receives any form of consideration derived from the practice of prostitution, in whole or in part, and the prostituted person was under the age of 13 at the time the act of prostitution occurred.

(c) If the accused did not have a reasonable opportunity to observe the prostituted person, it is an affirmative defense to a charge of juvenile pimping that the accused reasonably believed the person was of the age of 18 years or over or was not a severely or profoundly a person with an intellectual disability person at the time of the act giving rise to the charge.

(d) Sentence.

A person who commits a violation of subsection (a) is guilty of a Class 1 felony. A person convicted of a second or subsequent violation of this Section, or of any combination of such number of convictions under this Section and Sections 11-14, 11-14.1, 11-15, 11-15.1, 11-16, 11-17, 11-17.1, 11-18, 11-18.1, 11-19, or 11-19.2 of this Code, is guilty of a Class X felony. A person who commits a violation of subsection (b) is guilty of a Class X felony.

(e) For the purposes of this Section, "prostituted person" means any person who engages in, or agrees or offers to engage in, any act of sexual penetration as defined in Section 12-12 of this Code for any money, property, token, object, or article or anything of value, or any touching or fondling of the sex organs of one person by another person, for any money, property, token, object, or article or anything of value, for the purpose of sexual arousal or gratification.

§ 11-19.2. Exploitation of a child. (A) A person commits exploitation of a child when he or she confines a child under the age of 18 or a severely or profoundly a person with an intellectual disability person against his or her will by the infliction or threat of imminent infliction of great bodily harm, permanent disability or disfigurement or by administering to the child or severely or profoundly a person with an intellectual disability person without his or her consent or by threat or deception and for other than medical purposes, any alcoholic intoxicant or a drug as defined in the Illinois Controlled Substances Act1 or the Cannabis Control Act2 or methamphetamine as defined in the Methamphetamine Control and Community Protection Act and:

(1) compels the child or severely or profoundly a person with an intellectual disability person to engage in prostitution; or

(2) arranges a situation in which the child or severely or profoundly a person with an intellectual disability person may practice prostitution; or

(3) receives any money, property, token, object, or article or anything of value from the child or severely or profoundly a person with an intellectual disability person knowing it was obtained in whole or in part from the practice of prostitution.

(B) For purposes of this Section, administering drugs, as defined in subsection (A), or an alcoholic intoxicant to a child under the age of 13 or a severely or profoundly a person with an intellectual disability person shall be deemed to be without consent if such administering is done without the consent of the parents or legal guardian or if such administering is performed by the parents or legal guardians for other than medical purposes.

(C) Exploitation of a child is a Class X felony, for which the person shall be sentenced to a term of imprisonment of not less than 6 years and not more than 60 years.

(D) Any person convicted under this Section is subject to the property forfeiture provisions set forth in Article 124B of the Code of Criminal Procedure of 1963.

(A) A person commits exploitation of a child when he or she confines a child under the age of 18 or a severely or profoundly a person with an intellectual disability person against his or her will by the infliction or threat of imminent infliction of great bodily harm, permanent disability or disfigurement or by administering to the child or severely or profoundly a person with an intellectual disability person without his or her consent or by threat or deception and for other than medical purposes, any alcoholic intoxicant or a drug as defined in the Illinois Controlled Substances Act1 or the Cannabis Control Act2 or methamphetamine as defined in the Methamphetamine Control and Community Protection Act and:

(1) compels the child or severely or profoundly a person with an intellectual disability person to engage in prostitution; or

(2) arranges a situation in which the child or severely or profoundly a person with an intellectual disability person may practice prostitution; or

(3) receives any money, property, token, object, or article or anything of value from the child or severely or profoundly a person with an intellectual disability person knowing it was obtained in whole or in part from the practice of prostitution.

(B) For purposes of this Section, administering drugs, as defined in subsection (A), or an alcoholic intoxicant to a child under the age of 13 or a severely or profoundly a person with an intellectual disability person shall be deemed to be without consent if such administering is done without the consent of the parents or legal guardian or if such administering is performed by the parents or legal guardians for other than medical purposes.

(C) Exploitation of a child is a Class X felony, for which the person shall be sentenced to a term of imprisonment of not less than 6 years and not more than 60 years.

(D) Any person convicted under this Section is subject to the property forfeiture provisions set forth in Article 124B of the Code of Criminal Procedure of 1963.

§ 11-19.3. Vehicle impoundment. (a) In addition to any other penalty provided by law, a peace officer who arrests a person for a violation of Section 10-9, 11-14, 11-14. 1, 11-15, 11-15.1, 11-16, 11-17, 11-17.1, 11-18, 11-18.1, 11-19, 11-19.1, or 11-19.2 of this Code, may tow and impound any vehicle used by the person in the commission of the offense. The person arrested for one or more such violations shall be charged a $1,000 fee, to be paid to the unit of government that made the arrest. The person may recover the vehicle from the impound after a minimum of 2 hours after arrest upon payment of the fee.

(b) $500 of the fee shall be distributed to the unit of government whose peace officers made the arrest, for the costs incurred by the unit of government to tow and impound the vehicle. Upon the defendant's conviction of one or more of the offenses in connection with which the vehicle was impounded and the fee imposed under this Section, the remaining $500 of the fee shall be deposited into the DHS State Projects Fund and shall be used by the Department of Human Services to make grants to non-governmental organizations to provide services for persons encountered during the course of an investigation into any violation of Section 10-9,

11-14, 11-14.1, 11-15, 11-15.1, 11-16, 11-17, 11-17.1, 11-18, 11-18.1, 11-19, 11-19.1, or 11-19.2 of this Code, provided such persons constitute prostituted persons or other victims of human trafficking.

(c) Upon the presentation by the defendant of a signed court order showing that the defendant has been acquitted of all of the offenses in connection with which a vehicle was impounded and a fee imposed under this Section, or that the charges against the defendant for those offenses have been dismissed, the unit of government shall refund the $1,000 fee to the defendant.

Commentary – Prostitution, Pimping and Exploitation

Prostitution. The Illinois Criminal Code has detailed, if not complex, criminal proscriptions for prostitution and related offense. Prostitution is the performing of sexual acts for money, property or other things of value. (Section 11-14). It includes touching of the genitals of one person by another for purposes of sexual arousal or gratification. It is also a crime to solicit for a prostitute (Section 11-15), to solicit a minor for prostitution (Section 11-15.1), to keep a place of prostitution (Section 11-17), and to keep a place for juvenile prostitution, to patronize a prostitute (Section 11 – 18); to patronize a minor engaged in prostitution (Section 11-18.1). As might be expected, when minors are involved the crimes have more serious classifications, such as soliciting a minor or keeping a place of juvenile prostitution which are Class 1 felonies, where the adult companion statutes are Class 4 felonies.

Pandering and Pimping. Pandering (Section 11-16) is a crime of prostitution management. The panderer introduces the prostitute into the business of selling sex, arranges the meeting and details with the customer - including price, promised sex acts and location. In *People v. Wiler* 190 Ill.App.3d 47, 545 N.E.2d 1014 (Ill. App. Ct. 1st Dist. 1989), the defendant and a 15 year old prostitute crossed the street to approach an undercover officer. The defendant offered the girl to perform oral sex but the officer-customer asked for sexual intercourse. They agreed on a $50 price. They negotiated a meeting at a bar, and eventually the officer-customer agreed to take the girl to a motel. The defendant contended that he was only guilty of solicitation (a misdemeanor) but the Court noted that his activities were just the type of management that the pandering statute (a felony) sought to address.

Under Section 11-19 the crime of pimping is living off the earnings of a prostitute. The prostitute who earns the money cannot be found guilty of pimping - only the person who receives the money from the prostitute or the customer who patronized the prostitute. *People v. Russell* 69 Ill.App.3d 59, 396 N.E.2d 369 (Ill. App. Ct. 3rd Dist. 1979) recognized that pimping and pandering are two separate crimes with different elements.

Subdivision 20. Pornography Offenses

§ 11-20. Obscenity. (a) Elements of the Offense. A person commits obscenity when, with knowledge of the nature or content thereof, or recklessly failing to exercise reasonable inspection which would have disclosed the nature or content thereof, he or she:

(1) Sells, delivers or provides, or offers or agrees to sell, deliver or provide any obscene writing, picture, record or other representation or embodiment of the obscene; or

(2) Presents or directs an obscene play, dance or other performance or participates directly in that portion thereof which makes it obscene; or

(3) Publishes, exhibits or otherwise makes available anything obscene; or

(4) Performs an obscene act or otherwise presents an obscene exhibition of his or her body for gain; or

(5) Creates, buys, procures or possesses obscene matter or material with intent to disseminate it in violation of this Section, or of the penal laws or regulations of any other jurisdiction; or

(6) Advertises or otherwise promotes the sale of material represented or held out by him or her to be obscene, whether or not it is obscene.

(b) Obscene Defined.

Any material or performance is obscene if: (1) the average person, applying contemporary adult community standards, would find that, taken as a whole, it appeals to the prurient interest; and (2) the average person, applying contemporary adult community standards, would find that it depicts or describes, in a patently offensive way, ultimate sexual acts or sadomasochistic sexual acts, whether normal or perverted, actual or simulated, or masturbation, excretory functions or lewd exhibition of the genitals; and (3) taken as a whole, it lacks serious literary, artistic, political or scientific value.

(c) Interpretation of Evidence. Obscenity shall be judged with reference to ordinary adults, except that it shall be judged with reference to children or other specially susceptible audiences if it appears from the character of the material or the circumstances of its dissemination to be specially designed for or directed to such an audience.

Where circumstances of production, presentation, sale, dissemination, distribution, or publicity indicate that material is being commercially exploited for the sake of its prurient appeal, such evidence is probative with respect to the nature of the matter and can justify the conclusion that the matter is lacking in serious literary, artistic, political or scientific value.

In any prosecution for an offense under this Section evidence shall be admissible to show:

(1) The character of the audience for which the material was designed or to which it was directed;

(2) What the predominant appeal of the material would be for ordinary adults or a special audience, and what effect, if any, it would probably have on the behavior of such people;

(3) The artistic, literary, scientific, educational or other merits of the material, or absence thereof;

(4) The degree, if any, of public acceptance of the material in this State;

(5) Appeal to prurient interest, or absence thereof, in advertising or other promotion of the material;

(6) Purpose of the author, creator, publisher or disseminator.

(d) Sentence. Obscenity is a Class A misdemeanor. A second or subsequent offense is a Class 4 felony.

(e) Permissive Inference.

The trier of fact may infer an intent to disseminate from the creation, purchase, procurement or possession of a mold, engraved plate or other embodiment of obscenity specially adapted for reproducing multiple copies, or the possession of more than 3 copies of obscene material .

(f) Affirmative Defenses. It shall be an affirmative defense to obscenity that the dissemination:

(1) Was not for gain and was made to personal associates other than children under 18 years of age;

(2) Was to institutions or individuals having scientific or other special justification for possession of such material.

(g) Forfeiture of property. A person who has been convicted previously of the offense of obscenity and who is convicted of a second or subsequent offense of obscenity is subject to the property forfeiture provisions set forth in Article

124B of the Code of Criminal Procedure of 1963.

§ 11-20.1. Child pornography. (a) A person commits child pornography who:

(1) films, videotapes, photographs, or otherwise depicts or portrays by means of any similar visual medium or reproduction or depicts by computer any child whom he or she knows or reasonably should know to be under the age of 18 and at least 13 years of age or any person with a severe or profound intellectual disability where such child or person with a severe or profound intellectual disability is:

(i) actually or by simulation engaged in any act of sexual penetration or sexual conduct with any person or animal; or
(ii) actually or by simulation engaged in any act of sexual penetration or sexual conduct involving the sex organs of the child or severely or profoundly a person with an intellectual disability person and the mouth, anus, or sex organs of another person or animal; or which involves the mouth, anus or sex organs of the child or person with a severe or profound intellectual disability and the sex organs of another person or animal; or
(iii) actually or by simulation engaged in any act of masturbation; or
(iv) actually or by simulation portrayed as being the object of, or otherwise engaged in, any act of lewd fondling, touching, or caressing involving another person or animal; or
(v) actually or by simulation engaged in any act of excretion or urination within a sexual context; or
(vi) actually or by simulation portrayed or depicted as bound, fettered, or subject to sadistic, masochistic, or sadomasochistic abuse in any sexual context; or
(vii) depicted or portrayed in any pose, posture or setting involving a lewd exhibition of the unclothed or transparently clothed genitals, pubic area, buttocks, or, if such person is female, a fully or partially developed breast of the child or other person; or

(2) with the knowledge of the nature or content thereof, reproduces, disseminates, offers to disseminate, exhibits or possesses with intent to disseminate any film, videotape, photograph or other similar visual reproduction or depiction by computer of any child or person with a severe or profound intellectual disability whom the person knows or reasonably should know to be under the age of 18 and at least 13 years of age or to be a person with a severe or profound intellectual disability, engaged in any activity described in subparagraphs (i) through (vii) of paragraph (1) of this subsection; or

(3) with knowledge of the subject matter or theme thereof, produces any stage play, live performance, film, videotape or other similar visual portrayal or depiction by computer which includes a child whom the person knows or reasonably should know to be under the age of 18 and at least 13 years of age or a person with a severe or profound intellectual disability engaged in any activity described in subparagraphs (i) through (vii) of paragraph (1) of this subsection; or

(4) solicits, uses, persuades, induces, entices, or coerces any child whom he or she knows or reasonably should know to be under the age of 18 and at least 13 years of age or a person with a severe or profound intellectual disability to appear in any stage play, live presentation, film, videotape, photograph or other similar visual reproduction or depiction by computer in which the child or person with a severe or profound intellectual disability is or will be depicted, actually or by simulation, in any act, pose or setting described in subparagraphs (i) through (vii) of paragraph (1) of this subsection; or

(5) is a parent, step-parent, legal guardian or other person having care or custody of a child whom the person knows or reasonably should know to be under the age of 18 and at least 13 years of age or a person with a severe or profound intellectual disability and who knowingly permits, induces, promotes, or arranges for such child or severely or profoundly a person with an intellectual disability person to appear in any stage play, live performance, film, videotape, photograph or other similar visual presentation, portrayal or simulation or depiction by computer of any act or activity described in

subparagraphs (i) through (vii) of paragraph (1) of this subsection; or

(6) with knowledge of the nature or content thereof, possesses any film, videotape, photograph or other similar visual reproduction or depiction by computer of any child or person with a severe or profound intellectual disability whom the person knows or reasonably should know to be under the age of 18 and at least 13 years of age or to be a person with a severe or profound intellectual disability, engaged in any activity described in subparagraphs (i) through (vii) of paragraph (1) of this subsection; or

(7) solicits, or knowingly uses, persuades, induces, entices, or coerces, a person to provide a child under the age of 18 and at least 13 years of age or a person with a severe or profound intellectual disability to appear in any videotape, photograph, film, stage play, live presentation, or other similar visual reproduction or depiction by computer in which the child or person with a severe or profound intellectual disability will be depicted, actually or by simulation, in any act, pose, or setting described in subparagraphs (i) through (vii) of paragraph (1) of this subsection.

(b) (1) It shall be an affirmative defense to a charge of child pornography that the defendant reasonably believed, under all of the circumstances, that the child was 18 years of age or older or that the person was not a severely or profoundly a person with an intellectual disability person but only where, prior to the act or acts giving rise to a prosecution under this Section, he or she took some affirmative action or made a *bona fide* inquiry designed to ascertain whether the child was 18 years of age or older or that the person was not a severely or profoundly a person with an intellectual disability person and his or her reliance upon the information so obtained was clearly reasonable.

(1.5) Telecommunications carriers, commercial mobile service providers, and providers of information services, including, but not limited to, Internet service providers and hosting service providers, are not liable under this Section by virtue of the transmission, storage, or caching of electronic communications or messages of others or by virtue of the provision of other related telecommunications, commercial mobile services, or information services used by others in violation of this Section.

(2) (Blank).

(3) The charge of child pornography shall not apply to the performance of official duties by law enforcement or prosecuting officers or persons employed by law enforcement or prosecuting agencies, court personnel or attorneys, nor to *bona fide* treatment or professional education programs conducted by licensed physicians, psychologists or social workers.

(4) If the defendant possessed more than one of the same film, videotape or visual reproduction or depiction by computer in which child pornography is depicted, then the trier of fact may infer that the defendant possessed such materials with the intent to disseminate them.

(5) The charge of child pornography does not apply to a person who does not voluntarily possess a film, videotape, or visual reproduction or depiction by computer in which child pornography is depicted. Possession is voluntary if the defendant knowingly procures or receives a film, videotape, or visual reproduction or depiction for a sufficient time to be able to terminate his or her possession.

(6) Any violation of paragraph (1), (2), (3), (4), (5), or (7) of subsection (a) that includes a child engaged in, solicited for, depicted in, or posed in any act of sexual penetration or bound, fettered, or subject to sadistic, masochistic, or sadomasochistic abuse in a sexual context shall be deemed a crime of violence.

(c) If the violation does not involve a film, videotape, or other moving depiction, a violation of paragraph (1), (4), (5), or (7) of subsection (a) is a Class 1 felony with a mandatory minimum fine of $2,000 and a maximum fine of $100,000. If the violation involves a film, videotape, or other moving depiction, a violation of paragraph (1), (4), (5), or (7) of subsection (a) is a Class X felony with a mandatory minimum fine of $2,000 and a maximum fine of $100,000. If the violation does not involve a film, videotape, or other moving depiction, a violation of paragraph (3) of subsection (a) is a Class 1 felony with a mandatory minimum fine of $1500 and a maximum fine of $100,000. If the violation involves a film, videotape, or other moving depiction, a violation of paragraph (3) of subsection (a) is a Class X felony with a mandatory minimum fine of $1500 and a maximum fine of $100,000. If the violation does not involve a film, videotape, or other moving depiction, a violation of paragraph (2) of subsection (a) is a Class 1 felony with a mandatory minimum fine of $1000 and a maximum fine of $100,000. If the violation involves a film, videotape, or other moving depiction, a violation of paragraph (2) of subsection (a) is a Class X felony with a mandatory minimum fine of $1000 and a maximum fine of $100,000. If the violation does not involve a film, videotape, or other moving depiction, a violation of paragraph (6) of subsection (a) is a Class 3 felony with a mandatory minimum fine of $1000 and a maximum fine of $100,000. If the violation involves a film, videotape, or other moving depiction, a violation of paragraph (6) of subsection (a) is a Class 2 felony with a mandatory minimum fine of $1000 and a maximum fine of $100,000.

(d) If a person is convicted of a second or subsequent violation of this Section within 10 years of a prior conviction, the court shall order a presentence psychiatric examination of the person. The examiner shall report to the court whether treatment of the person is necessary.

(e) Any film, videotape, photograph or other similar visual reproduction or depiction by computer which includes a child under the age of 18 and at least 13 years of age or a severely or profoundly a person with an intellectual disability person engaged in any activity described in subparagraphs (i) through (vii) or paragraph 1 of subsection (a), and any material or equipment used or intended for use in photographing, filming, printing, producing, reproducing, manufacturing, projecting, exhibiting, depiction by computer, or disseminating such material shall be seized and forfeited in the manner, method and procedure provided by Section 36-1 of this Code for the seizure and forfeiture of vessels, vehicles and aircraft.

In addition, any person convicted under this Section is subject to the property forfeiture provisions set forth in Article 124B of the Code of Criminal Procedure of 1963.

(e-5) Upon the conclusion of a case brought under this Section, the court shall seal all evidence depicting a victim or witness that is sexually explicit. The evidence may be unsealed and viewed, on a motion of the party seeking to unseal and view the evidence, only for good cause shown and in the discretion of the court. The motion must expressly set forth the purpose for viewing the material. The State's attorney and the victim, if possible, shall be provided reasonable notice of the hearing on the motion to unseal the evidence. Any person entitled to notice of a hearing under this subsection (e-5) may object to the motion.

(f) Definitions. For the purposes of this Section:

(1) "Disseminate" means (i) to sell, distribute, exchange or transfer possession, whether with or without consideration or (ii) to make a depiction by computer available for distribution or downloading through the facilities of any telecommunications network or through any other means of transferring computer programs or data to a computer.

(2) "Produce" means to direct, promote, advertise, publish, manufacture, issue, present or show.

(3) "Reproduce" means to make a duplication or copy.

(4) "Depict by computer" means to generate or create, or cause to be created or generated, a computer program or data that, after being processed by a computer either alone or in

conjunction with one or more computer programs, results in a visual depiction on a computer monitor, screen, or display.

(5) "Depiction by computer" means a computer program or data that, after being processed by a computer either alone or in conjunction with one or more computer programs, results in a visual depiction on a computer monitor, screen, or display.

(6) "Computer", "computer program", and "data" have the meanings ascribed to them in Section 16D-2 of this Code.

(7) for the purposes of this Section, "child pornography "includes a film, videotape, photograph, or other similar visual medium or reproduction or depiction by computer that is, or appears to be, that of a person, either in part, or in total, under the age of 18 and at least 13 years of age or a severely or profoundly a person with an intellectual disability person, regardless of the method by which the film, videotape, photograph, or other similar visual medium or reproduction or depiction by computer is created, adopted, or modified to appear as such. "Child pornography "also includes a film, videotape, photograph, or other similar visual medium or reproduction or depiction by computer that is advertised, promoted, presented, described, or distributed in such a manner that conveys the impression that the film, videotape, photograph, or other similar visual medium or reproduction or depiction by computer is of a person under the age of 18 and at least 13 years of age or a severely or profoundly a person with an intellectual disability person.

(g) Re-enactment; findings; purposes. (1) The General Assembly finds and declares that:

(i) Section 50-5 of Public Act 88-680, effective January 1, 1995, contained provisions amending the child pornography statute, Section 11-20.1 of the Criminal Code of 1961. Section 50-5 also contained other provisions.

(ii) In addition, Public Act 88-680 was entitled "AN ACT to create a Safe Neighborhoods Law". (A) Article 5 was entitled JUVENILE JUSTICE and amended the Juvenile Court Act of 1987. (B) Article 15 was entitled GANGS and amended various provisions of the Criminal Code of 1961 and the Unified Code of Corrections. (C) Article 20 was entitled ALCOHOL ABUSE and amended various provisions of the Illinois Vehicle Code. (D) Article 25 was entitled DRUG ABUSE and amended the Cannabis Control Act and the Illinois Controlled Substances Act. (E) Article 30 was entitled FIREARMS and amended the Criminal Code of 1961 and the Code of Criminal Procedure of 1963. (F) Article 35 amended the Criminal Code of 1961, the Rights of Crime Victims and Witnesses Act, and the Unified Code of Corrections. (G) Article 40 amended the Criminal Code of 1961 to increase the penalty for compelling organization membership of persons. (H) Article 45 created the Secure Residential Youth Care Facility Licensing Act and amended the State Finance Act, the Juvenile Court Act of 1987, the Unified Code of Corrections, and the Private Correctional Facility Moratorium Act. (I) Article 50 amended the WIC Vendor Management Act, the Firearm Owners Identification Card Act, the Juvenile Court Act of 1987, the Criminal Code of 1961, the Wrongs to Children Act, and the Unified Code of Corrections.

(iii) On September 22, 1998, the Third District Appellate Court in People v. Dainty, 701 N.E. 2d 118, ruled that Public Act 88-680 violates the single subject clause of the Illinois Constitution (Article IV, Section 8 (d)) and was unconstitutional in its entirety. As of the time this amendatory Act of 1999 was prepared, People v. Dainty was still subject to appeal.

(iv) Child pornography is a vital concern to the people of this State and the validity of future prosecutions under the child pornography statute of the Criminal Code of 1961 is in grave doubt.

(2) It is the purpose of this amendatory Act of 1999 to prevent or minimize any problems relating to prosecutions for child pornography that may result from challenges to the constitutional validity of Public Act 88-680 by re-enacting the Section relating to child

pornography that was included in Public Act 88-680.

(3) This amendatory Act of 1999 re-enacts Section 11-20.1 of the Criminal Code of 1961, as it has been amended. This re-enactment is intended to remove any question as to the validity or content of that Section; it is not intended to supersede any other Public Act that amends the text of the Section as set forth in this amendatory Act of 1999. The material is shown as existing text (i.e., without underscoring) because, as of the time this amendatory Act of 1999 was prepared, People v. Dainty was subject to appeal to the Illinois Supreme Court.

(4) The re-enactment by this amendatory Act of 1999 of Section 11-20.1 of the Criminal Code of 1961 relating to child pornography that was amended by Public Act 88-680 is not intended, and shall not be construed, to imply that Public Act 88-680 is invalid or to limit or impair any legal argument concerning whether those provisions were substantially re-enacted by other Public Acts.

§11-20.1B. Aggravated child pornography.
(a) A person commits aggravated child pornography who:

(1) films, videotapes, photographs, or otherwise depicts or portrays by means of any similar visual medium or reproduction or depicts by computer any child whom he or she knows or reasonably should know to be under the age of 13 years where such child is:

(i) actually or by simulation engaged in any act of sexual penetration or sexual conduct with any person or animal; or

(ii) actually or by simulation engaged in any act of sexual penetration or sexual conduct involving the sex organs of the child and the mouth, anus, or sex organs of another person or animal; or which involves the mouth, anus or sex organs of the child and the sex organs of another person or animal; or

(iii) actually or by simulation engaged in any act of masturbation; or

(iv) actually or by simulation portrayed as being the object of, or otherwise engaged in, any act of lewd fondling, touching, or caressing involving another person or animal; or

(v) actually or by simulation engaged in any act of excretion or urination within a sexual context; or

(vi) actually or by simulation portrayed or depicted as bound, fettered, or subject to sadistic, masochistic, or sadomasochistic abuse in any sexual context; or

(vii) depicted or portrayed in any pose, posture or setting involving a lewd exhibition of the unclothed or transparently clothed genitals, pubic area, buttocks, or, if such person is female, a fully or partially developed breast of the child or other person; or

(2) with the knowledge of the nature or content thereof, reproduces, disseminates, offers to disseminate, exhibits or possesses with intent to disseminate any film, videotape, photograph or other similar visual reproduction or depiction by computer of any child whom the person knows or reasonably should know to be under the age of 13 engaged in any activity described in subparagraphs (i) through (vii) of paragraph (1) of this subsection; or

(3) with knowledge of the subject matter or theme thereof, produces any stage play, live performance, film, videotape or other similar visual portrayal or depiction by computer which includes a child whom the person knows or reasonably should know to be under the age of 13 engaged in any activity described in subparagraphs (i) through (vii) of paragraph (1) of this subsection; or

(4) solicits, uses, persuades, induces, entices, or coerces any child whom he or she knows or reasonably should know to be under the age of 13 to appear in any stage play, live presentation, film, videotape, photograph or other similar visual reproduction or depiction by computer in which the child or severely or profoundly a person with an intellectual disability person is or will be depicted, actually or by simulation, in

any act, pose or setting described in subparagraphs (i) through (vii) of paragraph (1) of this subsection; or

(5) is a parent, step-parent, legal guardian or other person having care or custody of a child whom the person knows or reasonably should know to be under the age of 13 and who knowingly permits, induces, promotes, or arranges for such child to appear in any stage play, live performance, film, videotape, photograph or other similar visual presentation, portrayal or simulation or depiction by computer of any act or activity described in subparagraphs (i) through (vii) of paragraph (1) of this subsection; or

(6) with knowledge of the nature or content thereof, possesses any film, videotape, photograph or other similar visual reproduction or depiction by computer of any child whom the person knows or reasonably should know to be under the age of 13 engaged in any activity described in subparagraphs (i) through (vii) of paragraph (1) of this subsection; or

(7) solicits, or knowingly uses, persuades, induces, entices, or coerces a person to provide a child under the age of 13 to appear in any videotape, photograph, film, stage play, live presentation, or other similar visual reproduction or depiction by computer in which the child will be depicted, actually or by simulation, in any act, pose, or setting described in subparagraphs (i) through (vii) of paragraph (1) of this subsection.

(b)(1) It shall be an affirmative defense to a charge of aggravated child pornography that the defendant reasonably believed, under all of the circumstances, that the child was 13 years of age or older, but only where, prior to the act or acts giving rise to a prosecution under this Section, he or she took some affirmative action or made a *bona fide* inquiry designed to ascertain whether the child was 13 years of age or older and his or her reliance upon the information so obtained was clearly reasonable.

(2) The charge of aggravated child pornography shall not apply to the performance of official duties by law enforcement or prosecuting officers or persons employed by law enforcement or prosecuting agencies, court personnel or attorneys, nor to *bona fide* treatment or professional education programs conducted by licensed physicians, psychologists or social workers.

(3) If the defendant possessed more than 3 of the same film, videotape or visual reproduction or depiction by computer in which aggravated child pornography is depicted, then the trier of fact may infer that the defendant possessed such materials with the intent to disseminate them.
(4) The charge of aggravated child pornography does not apply to a person who does not voluntarily possess a film, videotape, or visual reproduction or depiction by computer in which aggravated child pornography is depicted. Possession is voluntary if the defendant knowingly procures or receives a film, videotape, or visual reproduction or depiction for a sufficient time to be able to terminate his or her possession.

(5) Any violation of paragraph (1), (2), (3), (4), (5), or (7) of subsection (a) that includes a child engaged in, solicited for, depicted in, or posed in any act of sexual penetration or bound, fettered, or subject to sadistic, masochistic, or sadomasochistic abuse in a sexual context shall be deemed a crime of violence.

(c) Sentence: (1) A person who commits a violation of paragraph (1), (2), (3), (4), (5), or (7) of subsection (a) is guilty of a Class X felony with a mandatory minimum fine of $ 2,000 and a maximum fine of $ 100,000.

(2) A person who commits a violation of paragraph (6) of subsection (a) is guilty of a Class 2 felony with a mandatory minimum fine of $ 1000 and a maximum fine of $ 100,000.

(3) A person who commits a violation of paragraph (1), (2), (3), (4), (5), or (7) of subsection (a) where the defendant has previously been convicted under the laws of this State or any other state of the offense of child pornography, aggravated child pornography, aggravated criminal sexual abuse, aggravated

criminal sexual assault, predatory criminal sexual assault of a child, or any of the offenses formerly known as rape, deviate sexual assault, indecent liberties with a child, or aggravated indecent liberties with a child where the victim was under the age of 18 years or an offense that is substantially equivalent to those offenses, is guilty of a Class X felony for which the person shall be sentenced to a term of imprisonment of not less than 9 years with a mandatory minimum fine of $ 2,000 and a maximum fine of $ 100,000.

(4) A person who commits a violation of paragraph (6) of subsection (a) where the defendant has previously been convicted under the laws of this State or any other state of the offense of child pornography, aggravated child pornography, aggravated criminal sexual abuse, aggravated criminal sexual assault, predatory criminal sexual assault of a child, or any of the offenses formerly known as rape, deviate sexual assault, indecent liberties with a child, or aggravated indecent liberties with a child where the victim was under the age of 18 years or an offense that is substantially equivalent to those offenses, is guilty of a Class 1 felony with a mandatory minimum fine of $ 1000 and a maximum fine of $ 100,000.

(d) If a person is convicted of a second or subsequent violation of this Section within 10 years of a prior conviction, the court shall order a presentence psychiatric examination of the person. The examiner shall report to the court whether treatment of the person is necessary.

(e) Any film, videotape, photograph or other similar visual reproduction or depiction by computer which includes a child under the age of 13 engaged in any activity described in subparagraphs (i) through (vii) of paragraph (1) of subsection (a), and any material or equipment used or intended for use in photographing, filming, printing, producing, reproducing, manufacturing, projecting, exhibiting, depiction by computer, or disseminating such material shall be seized and forfeited in the manner, method and procedure provided by Section 36-1 of this Code for the seizure and forfeiture of vessels, vehicles and aircraft.

In addition, any person convicted under this Section is subject to the property forfeiture provisions set forth in Article 124B of the Code of Criminal Procedure of 1963.

(e-5) Upon the conclusion of a case brought under this Section, the court shall seal all evidence depicting a victim or witness that is sexually explicit. The evidence may be unsealed and viewed, on a motion of the party seeking to unseal and view the evidence, only for good cause shown and in the discretion of the court. The motion must expressly set forth the purpose for viewing the material. The State's attorney and the victim, if possible, shall be provided reasonable notice of the hearing on the motion to unseal the evidence. Any person entitled to notice of a hearing under this subsection (e-5) may object to the motion.

(f) Definitions. For the purposes of this Section:

(1) "Disseminate" means (i) to sell, distribute, exchange or transfer possession, whether with or without consideration or (ii) to make a depiction by computer available for distribution or downloading through the facilities of any telecommunications network or through any other means of transferring computer programs or data to a computer.
(2) "Produce" means to direct, promote, advertise, publish, manufacture, issue, present or show.
(3) "Reproduce" means to make a duplication or copy.
(4) "Depict by computer" means to generate or create, or cause to be created or generated, a computer program or data that, after being processed by a computer either alone or in conjunction with one or more computer programs, results in a visual depiction on a computer monitor, screen, or display.
(5) "Depiction by computer" means a computer program or data that, after being processed by a computer either alone or in conjunction with one or more computer programs, results in a visual depiction on a computer monitor, screen, or display.

(6) "Computer", "computer program", and "data" have the meanings ascribed to them in Section 16D-2 of this Code.
(7) For the purposes of this Section, "child" means a person, either in part or in total, under the age of 13, regardless of the method by which the film, videotape, photograph, or other similar visual medium or reproduction or depiction by computer is created, adopted, or modified to appear as such

(g) When a charge of aggravated child pornography is brought, the age of the child is an element of the offense to be resolved by the trier of fact as either exceeding or not exceeding the age in question. The trier of fact can rely on its own everyday observations and common experiences in making this determination.

§ 11-20.2. Duty of commercial film and photographic print processors or computer technicians to report sexual depiction of children. (a) Any commercial film and photographic print processor or computer technician who has knowledge of or observes, within the scope of his professional capacity or employment, any film, photograph, videotape, negative, slide, computer hard drive or any other magnetic or optical media which depicts a child whom the processor or computer technician knows or reasonably should know to be under the age of 18 where such child is:

(i) actually or by simulation engaged in any act of sexual penetration or sexual conduct with any person or animal; or

(ii) actually or by simulation engaged in any act of sexual penetration or sexual conduct involving the sex organs of the child and the mouth, anus, or sex organs of another person or animal; or which involves the mouth, anus or sex organs of the child and the sex organs of another person or animal; or

(iii) actually or by simulation engaged in any act of masturbation; or

(iv) actually or by simulation portrayed as being the object of, or otherwise engaged in, any act of lewd fondling, touching, or caressing involving another person or animal; or

(v) actually or by simulation engaged in any act of excretion or urination within a sexual context; or

(vi) actually or by simulation portrayed or depicted as bound, fettered, or subject to sadistic, masochistic, or sadomasochistic abuse in any sexual context; or

(vii) depicted or portrayed in any pose, posture or setting involving a lewd exhibition of the unclothed or transparently clothed genitals, pubic area, buttocks, or, if such person is female, a fully or partially developed breast of the child or other person; shall report or cause a report to be made pursuant to subsections (b) and (c) as soon as reasonably possible. Failure to make such report shall be a business offense with a fine of $ 1,000.

(b) Commercial film and photographic film processors shall report or cause a report to be made to the local law enforcement agency of the jurisdiction in which the image or images described in subsection (a) are discovered.
(c) Computer technicians shall report or cause the report to be made to the local law enforcement agency of the jurisdiction in which the image or images described in subsection (a) are discovered or to the Illinois Child Exploitation e-Tipline at reportchildporn@atg.state.il.us.

(d) Reports required by this Act shall include the following information:

(i) name, address, and telephone number of the person filing the report;

(ii) the employer of the person filing the report, if any;

(iii) the name, address and telephone number of the person whose property is the subject of the report, if known;

(iv) the circumstances which led to the filing of the report, including a description of the reported content.

(e) If a report is filed with the Cyber Tipline at the National Center for Missing and Exploited Children or in accordance with the requirements of 42 U.S.C. 13032, the requirements of this Act will be deemed to have been met.

(f) A computer technician or an employer caused to report child pornography under this Section is immune from any criminal, civil, or administrative liability in connection with making the report, except for willful or wanton misconduct.

(g) For the purposes of this Section, a "computer technician" is a person who installs, maintains, troubleshoots, repairs or upgrades computer hardware, software, computer networks, peripheral equipment, electronic mail systems, or provides user assistance for any of the aforementioned tasks.

§ 11-21. Harmful material. (a) As used in this Section:

"Distribute" means to transfer possession of, whether with or without consideration.

"Harmful to minors" means that quality of any description or representation, in whatever form, of nudity, sexual conduct, sexual excitement, or sado-masochistic abuse, when, taken as a whole, it (i) predominately appeals to the prurient interest in sex of minors, (ii) is patently offensive to prevailing standards in the adult community in the State as a whole with respect to what is suitable material for minors, and (iii) lacks serious literary, artistic, political, or scientific value for minors.

"Knowingly" means having knowledge of the contents of the subject matter, or recklessly failing to exercise reasonable inspection which would have disclosed the contents.

"Material" means (i) any picture, photograph, drawing, sculpture, film, video game, computer game, video or similar visual depiction, including any such representation or image which is stored electronically, or (ii) any book, magazine, printed matter however reproduced, or recorded audio of any sort.

"Minor" means any person under the age of 18.

"Nudity" means the showing of the human male or female genitals, pubic area or buttocks with less than a fully opaque covering, or the showing of the female breast with less than a fully opaque covering of any portion below the top of the nipple, or the depiction of covered male genitals in a discernably turgid state.

"Sado-masochistic abuse" means flagellation or torture by or upon a person clad in undergarments, a mask or bizarre costume, or the condition of being fettered, bound or otherwise physically restrained on the part of one clothed for sexual gratification or stimulation.

"Sexual conduct" means acts of masturbation, sexual intercourse, or physical contact with a person's clothed or unclothed genitals, pubic area, buttocks or, if such person be a female, breast.

"Sexual excitement" means the condition of human male or female genitals when in a state of sexual stimulation or arousal.

(b) A person is guilty of distributing harmful material to a minor when he or she:

(1) knowingly sells, lends, distributes, exhibits to, depicts to, or gives away to a minor, knowing that the minor is under the age of 18 or failing to exercise reasonable care in ascertaining the person's true age:

(A) any material which depicts nudity, sexual conduct or sado-masochistic abuse, or which contains explicit and detailed verbal descriptions or narrative accounts of sexual excitement, sexual conduct or sado-masochistic abuse, and which taken as a whole is harmful to minors;

(B) a motion picture, show, or other presentation which depicts nudity, sexual conduct or sado-masochistic abuse and is harmful to minors; or

(C) an admission ticket or pass to premises where there is exhibited or to be exhibited such a motion picture, show, or other presentation; or

(2) admits a minor to premises where there is exhibited or to be exhibited such a motion picture, show, or other presentation, knowing that the minor is a person under the age of 18 or failing to exercise reasonable care in ascertaining the person's true age.

(c) In any prosecution arising under this Section, it is an affirmative defense:

(1) that the minor as to whom the offense is alleged to have been committed exhibited to the accused a draft card, driver's license, birth certificate or other official or apparently official document purporting to establish that the minor was 18 years of age or older, which was relied upon by the accused;

(2) that the defendant was in a parental or guardianship relationship with the minor or that the minor was accompanied by a parent or legal guardian;

(3) that the defendant was a *bona fide* school, museum, or public library, or was a person acting in the course of his or her employment as an employee or official of such organization or retail outlet affiliated with and serving the educational purpose of such organization;

(4) that the act charged was committed in aid of legitimate scientific or educational purposes; or

(5) that an advertisement of harmful material as defined in this Section culminated in the sale or distribution of such harmful material to a child under circumstances where there was no personal confrontation of the child by the defendant, his or her employees, or agents, as where the order or request for such harmful material was transmitted by mail, telephone, Internet or similar means of communication, and delivery of such harmful material to the child was by mail, freight, Internet or similar means of transport, which advertisement contained the following statement, or a substantially similar statement, and that the defendant required the purchaser to certify that he or she was not under the age of 18 and that the purchaser falsely stated that he or she was not under the age of 18: "NOTICE: It is unlawful for any person under the age of 18 to purchase the matter advertised. Any person under the age of 18 that falsely states that he or she is not under the age of 18 for the purpose of obtaining the material advertised is guilty of a Class B misdemeanor under the laws of the State."

(d) The predominant appeal to prurient interest of the material shall be judged with reference to average children of the same general age of the child to whom such material was sold, lent, distributed or given, unless it appears from the nature of the matter or the circumstances of its dissemination or distribution that it is designed for specially susceptible groups, in which case the predominant appeal of the material shall be judged with reference to its intended or probable recipient group.

(e) Distribution of harmful material in violation of this Section is a Class A misdemeanor. A second or subsequent offense is a Class 4 felony.

(f) Any person under the age of 18 who falsely states, either orally or in writing, that he or she is not under the age of 18, or who presents or offers to any person any evidence of age and identity that is false or not actually his or her own with the intent of ordering, obtaining, viewing, or otherwise procuring or attempting to procure or view any harmful material is guilty of a Class B misdemeanor.

(g) A person over the age of 18 who fails to exercise reasonable care in ascertaining the true age of a minor, knowingly distributes to, or sends, or causes to be sent, or exhibits to, or offers to distribute, or exhibits any harmful material to a person that he or she believes is a minor is guilty of a Class A misdemeanor. If that person utilized a computer web camera, cellular telephone, or any other type of device to manufacture the harmful material, then each offense is a Class 4 felony.

(h) Telecommunications carriers, commercial mobile service providers, and providers of information services, including, but not limited to, Internet service providers and hosting service providers, are not liable under this Section, except for willful and wanton misconduct, by virtue of the transmission, storage, or caching of electronic communications or messages of others or by virtue of the provision of other related telecommunications, commercial mobile services, or information services used by others in violation of this Section.

§ 11-22. Tie-in Sales of Obscene Publications to Distributors. Any person, firm or corporation, or any agent, officer or employee thereof, engaged in the business of distributing books, magazines, periodicals, comic books or other publications to retail dealers, who shall refuse to furnish to any retail dealer such quantity of books, magazines, periodicals, comic books or other publications as such retail dealer normally sells because the retail dealer refuses to sell, or offer for sale, any books, magazines, periodicals, comic books or other publications which are obscene, lewd, lascivious, filthy or indecent is guilty of a petty offense. Each publication sold or delivered in violation of this Act shall constitute a separate petty offense.

§ 11-23. Posting of identifying or graphic information on a pornographic Internet site or possessing graphic information with pornographic material. (a) A person at least 17 years of age who knowingly discloses on an adult obscenity or child pornography Internet site the name, address, telephone number, or e-mail address of a person under 17 years of age at the time of the commission of the offense or of a person at least 17 years of age without the consent of the person at least 17 years of age is guilty of posting of identifying information on a pornographic Internet site.

(a-5) Any person who knowingly places, posts, reproduces, or maintains on an adult obscenity or child pornography Internet site a photograph, video, or digital image of a person under 18 years of age that is not child pornography under Section 11-20.1, without the knowledge and consent of the person under 18 years of age, is guilty of posting of graphic information on a pornographic Internet site. This provision applies even if the person under 18 years of age is fully or properly clothed in the photograph, video, or digital image.

(a-10) Any person who knowingly places, posts, reproduces, or maintains on an adult obscenity or child pornography Internet site, or possesses with obscene or child pornographic material a photograph, video, or digital image of a person under 18 years of age in which the child is posed in a suggestive manner with the focus or concentration of the image on the child's clothed genitals, clothed pubic area, clothed buttocks area, or if the child is female, the breast exposed through transparent clothing, and the photograph, video, or digital image is not child pornography under Section 11-20.1, is guilty of posting of graphic information on a pornographic Internet site or possessing graphic information with pornographic material.
(b) Sentence. A person who violates subsection (a) of this Section is guilty of a Class 4 felony if the victim is at least 17 years of age at the time of the offense and a Class 3 felony if the victim is under 17 years of age at the time of the offense. A person who violates subsection (a-5) of this Section is guilty of a Class 4 felony. A person who violates subsection (a-10) of this Section is guilty of a Class 3 felony.

(c) Definitions. For purposes of this Section:

(1) "Adult obscenity or child pornography Internet site" means a site on the Internet that contains material that is obscene as defined in Section 11-20 of this Code or that is child pornography as defined in Section 11-20.1 of this Code.

(2) "Internet" has the meaning set forth in Section 16J-5 of this Code .

Sec. 11-23.5. Non-consensual dissemination of private sexual images. (a) Definitions. For the purposes of this Section:

"Computer", "computer program", and "data" have the meanings ascribed to them in Section 17-0.5 of this Code.

"Image" includes a photograph, film, videotape, digital recording, or other depiction or portrayal of an object, including a human body.

"Intimate parts" means the fully unclothed, partially/unclothed or transparently clothed genitals, pubic area, anus, or if the person is female, a partially or fully exposed nipple, including exposure through transparent clothing.

"Sexual act" means sexual penetration, masturbation, or sexual activity.

"Sexual activity" means any:
(1) knowing touching or fondling by the victim or another person or animal, either directly or through clothing, of the sex organs, anus, or breast of the victim or another person or animal for the purpose of sexual gratification or arousal; or
(2) any transfer or transmission of semen upon any part of the clothed or unclothed body of the victim, for the purpose of sexual gratification or arousal of the victim or another; or
(3) an act of urination within a sexual context; or
(4) any bondage, fetter, or sadism masochism; or
(5) sadomasochism abuse in any sexual context.

(b) A person commits non-consensual dissemination of private sexual images when he or she:
(1) intentionally disseminates an image of another person:
(A) who is at least 18 years of age; and
(B) who is identifiable from the image itself or information displayed in connection with the image; and
(C) who is engaged in a sexual act or whose intimate parts are exposed, in whole or in part; and
(2) obtains the image under circumstances in which a reasonable person would know or understand that the image was to remain private; and
(3) knows or should have known that the person in the image has not consented to the dissemination.

(c) The following activities are exempt from the provisions of this Section:
(1) The intentional dissemination of an image of another identifiable person who is engaged in a sexual act or whose intimate parts are exposed when the dissemination is made for the purpose of a criminal investigation that is otherwise lawful.
(2) The intentional dissemination of an image of another identifiable person who is engaged in a sexual act or whose intimate parts are exposed when the dissemination is for the purpose of, or in connection with, the reporting of unlawful conduct.
(3) The intentional dissemination of an image of another identifiable person who is engaged in a sexual act or whose intimate parts are exposed when the images involve voluntary exposure in public or commercial settings.
(4) The intentional dissemination of an image of another identifiable person who is engaged in a sexual act or whose intimate parts are exposed when the dissemination serves a lawful public purpose.

(d) Nothing in this Section shall be construed to impose liability upon the following entities solely as a result of content or information provided by another person:
(1) an interactive computer service, as defined in 47 U.S.C. 230(f)(2);
(2) a provider of public mobile services or private radio services, as defined in Section 13-214 of the Public Utilities Act; or
(3) a telecommunications network or broadband provider.

(e) A person convicted under this Section is subject to the forfeiture provisions in Article 124B of the Code of Criminal Procedure of 1963.

(f) Sentence. Non-consensual dissemination of private sexual images is a Class 4 felony.

§ 11-24. Child photography by sex offender.
(a) In this Section:

"Child" means a person under 18 years of age.

"Child sex offender" has the meaning ascribed to it in Section 11-0.1 of this Code.

(b) It is unlawful for a child sex offender to knowingly:

(1) conduct or operate any type of business in which he or she photographs, videotapes, or takes a digital image of a child; or

(2) conduct or operate any type of business in which he or she instructs or directs another person to photograph, videotape, or take a digital image of a child; or

(3) photograph, videotape, or take a digital image of a child, or instruct or direct another person to photograph, videotape, or take a digital image of a child without the consent of the parent or guardian.

(c) Sentence. A violation of this Section is a Class 2 felony. A person who violates this Section at a playground, park facility, school, forest preserve, day care facility, or at a facility providing programs or services directed to persons under 17 years of age is guilty of a Class 1 felony.

§ 11-25. Grooming. (a) A person commits the offense of grooming when he or she knowingly uses a computer on-line service, Internet service, local bulletin board service, or any other device capable of electronic data storage or transmission to seduce, solicit, lure, or entice, or attempt to seduce, solicit, lure, or entice, a child, a child's guardian, or another person believed by the person to be a child or a child's guardian, to commit any sex offense as defined in Section 2 of the Sex Offender Registration Act to depict photographs of the sex organs of the child ,or to otherwise engage in any unlawful sexual conduct with a child or with another person believed by the person to be a child.

(b) Sentence. Grooming is a Class 4 felony.

§ 11-26. Traveling to meet a minor.
(a) A person commits the offense of traveling to meet a minor when he or she travels any distance either within this State, to this State, or from this State by any means, attempts to do so, or causes another to do so or attempt to do so for the purpose of engaging in any sex offense as defined in Section 2 of the Sex Offender Registration Act, or to otherwise engage in other unlawful sexual conduct with a child or with another person believed by the person to be a child after using a computer on-line service, Internet service, local bulletin board service, or any other device capable of electronic data storage or transmission to seduce, solicit, lure, or entice, or to attempt to seduce, solicit, lure, or entice, a child or a child's guardian, or another person believed by the person to be a child or a child's guardian, for such purpose.

(b) Sentence. Traveling to meet a minor is a Class 3 felony.

Commentary – Obscenity and Child Pornography

The internet communications explosion has led to an increase in criminal legislation creating offenses related to internet possession and distribution of sexually explicit materials. There is a clear demarcation between adult pornography and child pornography and the statutes designed to criminally regulate such material.

Obscenity. Section 11-20 criminalizes obscenity defined as sexually explicit material that appeals to a disgusting interest in sexual matters, that contains depictions or descriptions of sexual acts or lewd exhibition of genitals and which lacks serious value. Whether a specific movie, magazine, photo or other work is obscene is tied to "contemporary community standards" which in Illinois is a state-wide issue. The advent of internet availability of sexually explicit movies or photos has significantly diminished prosecutions under the obscenity statute and a counterpart under Section 11-21 which proscribes harmful materials that are disseminated to minors. On the other hand, there has been another explosion of criminal prosecutions in the internet age – cases involving the production, possession and distribution of child pornography. Illinois criminal law has followed this trend with amendments to existing statutes and new laws meant to address the evil such material presents.

Child Pornography Section 11-20.1 criminalizes the production, distribution, possession with intent to distribute and possession of child pornography. Child pornography is the actual or simulated depiction of sexual activity (including a focus of the genitals for a sexual purpose) of a child. The depiction must be of an actual child – not a "virtual child" (a computer image that is not a real child). *People v. Alexander* 204 Ill.2d 472, 791 N.E.2d 506 (2003) requires that child pornography prosecutions must be about actual children under age 18 not computer generated images of children who are not real. Otherwise, such a prosecution would be overbroad and violate the right of free speech under the First Amendment to the Constitution of the United States. No expert testimony or proof other than the images themselves is required and the trier-of-fact (judge or jury) may determine, based on common sense experience, whether the depicted children are "actual children" and whether they are under 18 years of age. See *People v. Phillips* 346 Ill.App.3d 487, 805 N.E.2d 667 (Ill. App. Ct. 3rd. Dist. 2004).

In *People v. Hollins* 2012 IL 112754, 971 N.E.2d 504 (Ill. S. Ct. 2012), the 32 year-old defendant had consensual sex with a 17 year-old girl and committed no crime in doing so, since a 16 years is the age of consent in Illinois. The parties memorialized their conduct in photographs which the young woman asked to be email to her. Her mother discovered the digital photos and contacted authorities, resulting in the defendant's prosecution, conviction and sentence of eight (8) years imprisonment for Child Pornography in violation of 720 ILCS 5/11-20.1(a). His argument on appeal was that since his sexual conduct was legal, it was unconstitutional to criminalize the consensual photographing of legal conduct. The Illinois Supreme Court rejected his arguments, upholding his conviction and sentence, finding a sound constitutional and public policy rational for the holding:

> The legitimate government purpose is protecting children from sexual abuse and exploitation, and the prohibition of photographing or videotaping minors engaged in sexual activity bears a rational relationship to protecting them from such abuse. Raising the age to 18, even though the age of consent for sexual activity is 17, is a reasonable means of accomplishing this legitimate government purpose as it aids the State in enforcing child pornography laws.
>
> *People v. Hollins* 2012 IL 112754 ¶ 24, 976 N.E.2d at 511.

In *People v. Wayman* 379 Ill.App.3d 1043, 885 N.E.2d 416 (Ill. App. Ct. 5th Dist. 2008), the defendant was charged with child pornography for taking nude photographs of his 10-year-step-daughter. His wife had observed the scanned photographs on a computer but had deleted them and so they were unavailable at time of trial. The appellate court held that the absence of the photographs did not preclude a prosecution for child pornography, but that the testimony describing the photographs failed to prove beyond a reasonable doubt that the photos constituted the lewd exhibition of the child's genitals, breast or buttocks. The Court reversed the defendant's conviction for child pornography.

Section 11-20.2 requires film processors or computer technicians who discover child pornography to notify local law enforcement agencies or in the case of computer technicians to the Illinois Child Exploitation e-Tipline at reportchildporn@atg.state.il.us.

Section 11-20.3 defines Aggravated Child Pornography as child pornography with depictions of children under age 13. Violation of this section is a Class X felony with a potential fine up to $100,000.

Subdivision 25. Other Offense

§11-30. Public indecency. (a) Any person of the age of 17 years and upwards who performs any of the following acts in a public place commits a public indecency:

(1) An act of sexual penetration or sexual conduct; or

(2) A lewd exposure of the body done with intent to arouse or to satisfy the sexual desire of the person.

Breast-feeding of infants is not an act of public indecency.

(b) "Public place" for purposes of this Section means any place where the conduct may reasonably be expected to be viewed by others.

(c) Sentence.

Public indecency is a Class A misdemeanor. A person convicted of a third or subsequent violation for public indecency is guilty of a Class 4 felony. Public indecency is a Class 4 felony if committed by a person 18 years of age or older who is on or within 500 feet of elementary or secondary school grounds when children are present on the grounds.

§ 11-35. adultery. (a) A person commits adultery when he or she has sexual intercourse with another not his or her spouse, if the behavior is open and notorious, and
(1) The person is married and knows the other person involved in such intercourse is not his spouse; or

(2) The person is not married and knows that the other person involved in such intercourse is married.

A person shall be exempt from prosecution under this Section if his liability is based solely on evidence he has given in order to comply with the requirements of Section 4-1.7 of "The Illinois Public Aid Code", approved April 11, 1967, as amended.

(b) Sentence. Adultery is a Class A misdemeanor.

§ 11-40. fornication. (a) a person commits fornication when he or she knowingly has sexual intercourse with another not his or her spouse if the behavior is open and notorious.

A person shall be exempt from prosecution under this Section if his liability is based solely on evidence he has given in order to comply with the requirements of Section 4-1.7 of "The Illinois Public Aid Code", approved April 11, 1967, as amended.
(b) Sentence. Fornication is a Class B misdemeanor.

§ 11-45. Bigamy and Marrying a bigamist.
(a) Bigamy. A person commits bigamy when that person has a husband or wife and subsequently knowingly marries another.

(a-5) Marrying a bigamist. An unmarried person commits marrying a bigamist when that person knowingly marries another under circumstances known to him or her which would render the other person guilty of bigamy under the laws of this State.

(b) It shall be an affirmative defense to bigamy and marrying a bigamist that:

(1) The prior marriage was dissolved or declared invalid; or

(2) The accused reasonably believed the prior spouse to be dead; or

(3) The prior spouse had been continually absent for a period of 5 years during which time the accused did not know the prior spouse to be alive; or
(4) The accused reasonably believed that he or she or the person he or she marries was legally eligible to be married.
(c) Sentence. Bigamy is a Class 4 felony. Marrying a bigamist is a Class A misdemeanor.

Article 12 – Bodily Harm
720 ILCS 5/12-0.1 *et seq.*

Subdivision 1. Definitions

§ 12-0.1. Definitions. In this Article, unless the context clearly requires otherwise:

"Bona fide labor dispute" means any controversy concerning wages, salaries, hours, working conditions, or benefits, including health and welfare, sick leave, insurance, and pension or retirement provisions, the making or maintaining of collective bargaining agreements, and the terms to be included in those agreements.

"Coach" means a person recognized as a coach by the sanctioning authority that conducts an athletic contest.

"Correctional institution employee" means a person employed by a penal institution.

"Emergency medical technician" includes a paramedic, ambulance driver, first aid worker, hospital worker, or other medical assistance worker.

"Family or household members" include spouses, former spouses, parents, children, stepchildren, and other persons related by blood or by present or prior marriage, persons who share or formerly shared a common dwelling, persons who have or allegedly have a child in common, persons who share or allegedly share a blood relationship through a child, persons who have or have had a dating or engagement relationship, persons with disabilities and their personal assistants, and caregivers as defined in Section 12-4.4a of this Code. For purposes of this Article, neither a casual acquaintanceship nor ordinary fraternization between 2 individuals in business or social contexts shall be deemed to constitute a dating relationship.

"In the presence of a child" means in the physical presence of a child or knowing or having reason to know that a child is present and may see or hear an act constituting an offense.

"Park district employee" means a supervisor, director, instructor, or other person employed by a park district.

"Physically handicapped person" means a person who suffers from a permanent and disabling physical characteristic, resulting from disease, injury, functional disorder, or congenital condition.

"Private security officer" means a registered employee of a private security contractor agency under the Private Detective, Private Alarm, Private Security, Fingerprint Vendor, and Locksmith Act of 2004.

"Probation officer" means a person as defined in the Probation and Probation Officers Act.

"Sports official" means a person at an athletic contest who enforces the rules of the contest, such as an umpire or referee.

"Sports venue" means a publicly or privately owned sports or entertainment arena, stadium, community or convention hall, special event center, or amusement facility, or a special event center in a public park, during the 12 hours before or after the sanctioned sporting event.

"Streetgang", "streetgang member", and "criminal street gang" have the meanings ascribed to those terms in Section 10 of the Illinois Streetgang Terrorism Omnibus Prevention Act.

"Transit employee" means a driver, operator, or employee of any transportation facility or system engaged in the business of transporting the public for hire.

"Transit passenger" means a passenger of any transportation facility or system engaged in the business of transporting the public for hire, including a passenger using any area designated by a transportation facility or system as a vehicle boarding, departure, or transfer location.

"Utility worker" means any of the following:

(1) A person employed by a public utility as defined in Section 3-105 of the Public Utilities Act.

(2) An employee of a municipally owned utility.

(3) An employee of a cable television company.

(4) An employee of an electric cooperative as defined in Section 3-119 of the Public Utilities Act.

(5) An independent contractor or an employee of an independent contractor working on behalf of a cable television company, public utility, municipally owned utility, or electric cooperative.

(6) An employee of a telecommunications carrier as defined in Section 13-202 of the Public Utilities Act, or an independent contractor or an employee of an independent contractor working on behalf of a telecommunications carrier.

(7) An employee of a telephone or telecommunications cooperative as defined in Section 13-212 of the Public Utilities Act, or an independent contractor or an employee of an independent contractor working on behalf of a telephone or telecommunications cooperative.

Subdivision 5. Assault and Battery

§ 12-1. Assault. (a) A person commits an assault when, without lawful authority, he or she knowingly engages in conduct which places another in reasonable apprehension of receiving a battery.

(b) Sentence. Assault is a Class C misdemeanor.

(c) In addition to any other sentence that may be imposed, a court shall order any person convicted of assault to perform community service for not less than 30 and not more than 120 hours, if community service is available in the jurisdiction and is funded and approved by the county board of the county where the offense was committed. In addition, whenever any person is placed on supervision for an alleged offense under this Section, the supervision shall be conditioned upon the performance of the community service.

This subsection does not apply when the court imposes a sentence of incarceration.

§ 12-2. Aggravated assault. (a) Offense based on location of conduct. A person commits aggravated assault when he or she commits an assault against an individual who is on or about a public way, public property, a public place of accommodation or amusement, or a sports venue.

(b) Offense based on status of victim. A person commits aggravated assault when, in committing an assault, he or she knows the individual assaulted to be any of the following:

(1) A person with a physical disability or a person 60 years of age or older and the assault is without legal justification.

(2) A teacher or school employee upon school grounds or grounds adjacent to a school or in any part of a building used for school purposes.

(3) A park district employee upon park grounds or grounds adjacent to a park or in any part of a building used for park purposes.

(4) A community policing volunteer, private security officer, or utility worker:
(i) performing his or her official duties;
(ii) assaulted to prevent performance of his or her official duties; or
(iii) assaulted in retaliation for performing his or her official duties.

(4.1) A peace officer, fireman, emergency management worker, or emergency medical technician:
(i) performing his or her official duties;
(ii) assaulted to prevent performance of his or her official duties; or

(iii) assaulted in retaliation for performing his or her official duties.

(5) A correctional officer or probation officer:

(i) performing his or her official duties;
(ii) assaulted to prevent performance of his or her official duties; or
(iii) assaulted in retaliation for performing his or her official duties.

(6) A correctional institution employee, Department of Human Services employee, Department of Human Services officer or employee of a subcontractor of the Department of Human Services supervising or controlling sexually dangerous persons or sexually violent persons:

(i) performing his or her official duties;

(ii) assaulted to prevent performance of his or her official duties; or

(iii) assaulted in retaliation for performing his or her official duties.

(7) An employee of the State of Illinois, a municipal corporation therein, or a political subdivision thereof, performing his or her official duties.

(8) A transit employee performing his or her official duties, or a transit passenger.

(9) A sports official or coach actively participating in any level of athletic competition within a sports venue, on an indoor playing field or outdoor playing field, or within the immediate vicinity of such a facility or field.

(c) Offense based on use of firearm, device, or motor vehicle. A person commits aggravated assault when, in committing an assault, he or she does any of the following:

(1) Uses a deadly weapon, an air rifle as defined in Section 24.8-0.1 of this Act, or any device manufactured and designed to be substantially similar in appearance to a firearm, other than by discharging a firearm.

(2) Discharges a firearm, other than from a motor vehicle.

(3) Discharges a firearm from a motor vehicle.
(4) Wears a hood, robe, or mask to conceal his or her identity.

(5) Knowingly and without lawful justification shines or flashes a laser gun sight or other laser device attached to a firearm, or used in concert with a firearm, so that the laser beam strikes near or in the immediate vicinity of any person.

(6) Uses a firearm, other than by discharging the firearm, against a peace officer, community policing volunteer, fireman, private security officer, emergency management worker, emergency medical technician, employee of a police department, employee of a sheriff's department, or traffic control municipal employee:

(i) performing his or her official duties;

(ii) assaulted to prevent performance of his or her official duties; or

(iii) assaulted in retaliation for performing his or her official duties.

(7) Without justification operates a motor vehicle in a manner which places a person, other than a person listed in subdivision (b)(4), in reasonable apprehension of being struck by the moving motor vehicle.

(8) Without justification operates a motor vehicle in a manner which places a person listed in subdivision (b)(4), in reasonable apprehension of being struck by the moving motor vehicle.

(9) Knowingly video or audio records the offense with the intent to disseminate the recording.

(d) Sentence. Aggravated assault as defined in subdivision (a), (b)(1), (b)(2), (b)(3), (b)(4), (b)(7), (b)(8), (b)(9), (c)(1), (c)(4), or (c)(9) is a Class A misdemeanor, except that aggravated assault as defined in subdivision (b)(4) and (b)(7) is a Class 4 felony if a Category I, Category II, or Category III weapon is used in the commission of the assault. Aggravated assault as defined in subdivision (b)(4.1), (b)(5), (b)(6), (c)(2), (c)(5), (c)(6), or (c)(7) is a Class 4 felony. Aggravated assault as defined in subdivision (c)(3) or (c)(8) is a Class 3 felony.

(e) For the purposes of this Section, "Category I weapon", "Category II weapon, and "Category III weapon" have the meanings ascribed to those terms in Section 33A-1 of this Code.

§ 12-3. Battery. (a) A person commits battery if he or she knowingly without legal justification by any means (1) causes bodily harm to an individual or (2) makes physical contact of an insulting or provoking nature with an individual.

(b) Sentence. Battery is a Class A misdemeanor.

§ 12-3.05. Aggravated battery. (a) Offense based on injury. A person commits aggravated battery when, in committing a battery, other than by the discharge of a firearm, he or she knowingly does any of the following:

(1) Causes great bodily harm or permanent disability or disfigurement.

(2) Causes severe and permanent disability, great bodily harm, or disfigurement by means of a caustic or flammable substance, a poisonous gas, a deadly biological or chemical contaminant or agent, a radioactive substance, or a bomb or explosive compound.

(3) Causes great bodily harm or permanent disability or disfigurement to an individual whom the person knows to be a peace officer, community policing volunteer, fireman, private security officer, correctional institution employee, or Department of Human Services employee supervising or controlling sexually dangerous persons or sexually violent persons:

(i) performing his or her official duties;

(ii) battered to prevent performance of his or her official duties; or

(iii) battered in retaliation for performing his or her official duties.

(4) Causes great bodily harm or permanent disability or disfigurement to an individual 60 years of age or older.

(5) Strangles another individual.

(b) Offense based on injury to a child or person with an intellectual disability. A person who is at least 18 years of age commits aggravated battery when, in committing a battery, he or she knowingly and without legal justification by any means:
(1) causes great bodily harm or permanent disability or disfigurement to any child under the age of 13 years, or to any person with a severe or profound intellectual disability; or
(2) causes bodily harm or disability or disfigurement to any child under the age of 13 years or to any person with a severe or profound intellectual disability.

(c) Offense based on location of conduct. A person commits aggravated battery when, in committing a battery, other than by the discharge of a firearm, he or she is or the person battered is on or about a public way, public property, a public place of accommodation or amusement, a sports venue, or a domestic violence shelter.

(d) Offense based on status of victim. A person commits aggravated battery when, in committing a battery, other than by discharge of a firearm, he or she knows the individual battered to be any of the following:

(1) A person 60 years of age or older.

(2) A person who is pregnant or has a physical disability.

(3) A teacher or school employee upon school grounds or grounds adjacent to a school or in any part of a building used for school purposes.

(4) A peace officer, community policing volunteer, fireman, private security officer, correctional institution employee, or Department

of Human Services employee supervising or controlling sexually dangerous persons or sexually violent persons:

(i) performing his or her official duties;

(ii) battered to prevent performance of his or her official duties; or

(iii) battered in retaliation for performing his or her official duties.

(5) A judge, emergency management worker, emergency medical technician, or utility worker:

(i) performing his or her official duties;

(ii) battered to prevent performance of his or her official duties; or

(iii) battered in retaliation for performing his or her official duties.

(6) An officer or employee of the State of Illinois, a unit of local government, or a school district, while performing his or her official duties.

(7) A transit employee performing his or her official duties, or a transit passenger.

(8) A taxi driver on duty.

(9) A merchant who detains the person for an alleged commission of retail theft under Section 16-26 of this Code and the person without legal justification by any means causes bodily harm to the merchant.

(e) Offense based on use of a firearm. A person commits aggravated battery when, in committing a battery, he or she knowingly does any of the following:

(1) Discharges a firearm, other than a machine gun or a firearm equipped with a silencer, and causes any injury to another person.

(2) Discharges a firearm, other than a machine gun or a firearm equipped with a silencer, and causes any injury to a person he or she knows to be a peace officer, community policing volunteer, person summoned by a police officer, fireman, private security officer, correctional institution employee, or emergency management worker:

(i) performing his or her official duties;

(ii) battered to prevent performance of his or her official duties; or

(iii) battered in retaliation for performing his or her official duties.

(3) Discharges a firearm, other than a machine gun or a firearm equipped with a silencer, and causes any injury to a person he or she knows to be an emergency medical technician employed by a municipality or other governmental unit:

(i) performing his or her official duties;

(ii) battered to prevent performance of his or her official duties; or

(iii) battered in retaliation for performing his or her official duties.

(4) Discharges a firearm and causes any injury to a person he or she knows to be a teacher, a student in a school, or a school employee, and the teacher, student, or employee is upon school grounds or grounds adjacent to a school or in any part of a building used for school purposes.

(5) Discharges a machine gun or a firearm equipped with a silencer, and causes any injury to another person.

(6) Discharges a machine gun or a firearm equipped with a silencer, and causes any injury to a person he or she knows to be a peace officer, community policing volunteer, person summoned by a police officer, fireman, private security officer, correctional institution employee or emergency management worker:

(i) performing his or her official duties;

(ii) battered to prevent performance of his or her official duties; or

(iii) battered in retaliation for performing his or her official duties.

(7) Discharges a machine gun or a firearm equipped with a silencer, and causes any injury to a person he or she knows to be an emergency medical technician employed by a municipality or other governmental unit:

(i) performing his or her official duties;
(ii) battered to prevent performance of his or her official duties; or

(iii) battered in retaliation for performing his or her official duties.
(8) Discharges a machine gun or a firearm equipped with a silencer, and causes any injury to a person he or she knows to be a teacher, or a student in a school, or a school employee, and the teacher, student, or employee is upon school grounds or grounds adjacent to a school or in any part of a building used for school purposes.

(f) Offense based on use of a weapon or device. A person commits aggravated battery when, in committing a battery, he or she does any of the following:

(1) Uses a deadly weapon other than by discharge of a firearm, or uses an air rifle as defined in the Air Rifle Act.
(2) Wears a hood, robe, or mask to conceal his or her identity.
(3) Knowingly and without lawful justification shines or flashes a laser gun sight or other laser device attached to a firearm, or used in concert with a firearm, so that the laser beam strikes upon or against the person of another.
(4) Knowingly video or audio records the offense with the intent to disseminate the recording.

(g) Offense based on certain conduct. A person commits aggravated battery when, other than by discharge of a firearm, he or she does any of the following:

(1) Violates Section 401 of the Illinois Controlled Substances Act by unlawfully delivering a controlled substance to another and any user experiences great bodily harm or permanent disability as a result of the injection, inhalation, or ingestion of any amount of the controlled substance.

(2) Knowingly administers to an individual or causes him or her to take, without his or her consent or by threat or deception, and for other than medical purposes, any intoxicating, poisonous, stupefying, narcotic, anesthetic, or controlled substance, or gives to another person any food containing any substance or object intended to cause physical injury if eaten.
(3) Knowingly causes or attempts to cause a correctional institution employee or Department of Human Services employee to come into contact with blood, seminal fluid, urine, or feces by throwing, tossing, or expelling the fluid or material, and the person is an inmate of a penal institution or is a sexually dangerous person or sexually violent person in the custody of the Department of Human Services.

(h) Sentence. Unless otherwise provided, aggravated battery is a Class 3 felony.

Aggravated battery as defined in subdivision (a)(4), (d)(4), or (g)(3) is a Class 2 felony.

Aggravated battery as defined in subdivision (a)(3) or (g)(1) is a Class 1 felony.

Aggravated battery under subdivision (a)(5) is a Class 1 felony if: (A) the person used or attempted to use a dangerous instrument while committing the offense; or

(B) the person caused great bodily harm or permanent disability or disfigurement to the other person while committing the offense; or

(C) the person has been previously convicted of a violation of subdivision (a)(5) under the laws of this State or laws similar to subdivision (a)(5) of any other state.

Aggravated battery as defined in subdivision (e)(1) is a Class X felony.

Aggravated battery as defined in subdivision (a)(2) is a Class X felony for which a person shall be sentenced to a term of imprisonment of a minimum of 6 years and a maximum of 45 years.

Aggravated battery as defined in subdivision (e)(5) is a Class X felony for which a person shall be sentenced to a term of imprisonment of a minimum of 12 years and a maximum of 45 years.

Aggravated battery as defined in subdivision (e)(2), (e)(3), or (e)(4) is a Class X felony for which a person shall be sentenced to a term of imprisonment of a minimum of 15 years and a maximum of 60 years.

Aggravated battery as defined in subdivision (e)(6), (e)(7), or (e)(8) is a Class X felony for which a person shall be sentenced to a term of imprisonment of a minimum of 20 years and a maximum of 60 years.

Aggravated battery as defined in subdivision (b)(1) is a Class X felony, except that:

(1) if the person committed the offense while armed with a firearm, 15 years shall be added to the term of imprisonment imposed by the court;

(2) if, during the commission of the offense, the person personally discharged a firearm, 20 years shall be added to the term of imprisonment imposed by the court;

(3) if, during the commission of the offense, the person personally discharged a firearm that proximately caused great bodily harm, permanent disability, permanent disfigurement, or death to another person, 25 years or up to a term of natural life shall be added to the term of imprisonment imposed by the court.

(i) Definitions. For the purposes of this Section:

"Building or other structure used to provide shelter" has the meaning ascribed to "shelter" in Section 1 of the Domestic Violence Shelters Act.

"Domestic violence" has the meaning ascribed to it in Section 103 of the Illinois Domestic Violence Act of 1986.

"Domestic violence shelter" means any building or other structure used to provide shelter or other services to victims or to the dependent children of victims of domestic violence pursuant to the Illinois Domestic Violence Act of 1986 or the Domestic Violence Shelters Act, or any place within 500 feet of such a building or other structure in the case of a person who is going to or from such a building or other structure.

"Firearm" has the meaning provided under Section 1.1 of the Firearm Owners Identification Card Act, and does not include an air rifle as defined by Section 24.8-0.1 of this Code.

"Machine gun" has the meaning ascribed to it in Section 24-1 of this Code.

"Merchant" has the meaning ascribed to it in Section 16-0.1 of this Code.
"Strangle" means intentionally impeding the normal breathing or circulation of the blood of an individual by applying pressure on the throat or neck of that individual or by blocking the nose or mouth of that individual.

§ 12-3.1. Battery of an unborn child; aggravated battery of an unborn child.(a) A person commits battery of an unborn child if he or she knowingly without legal justification and by any means causes bodily harm to an unborn child.

(a-5) A person commits aggravated battery of an unborn child when, in committing a battery of an unborn child, he or she knowingly causes great bodily harm or permanent disability or disfigurement to an unborn child.

(b) For purposes of this Section, (1) "unborn child" shall mean any individual of the human species from fertilization until birth, and (2) "person" shall not include the pregnant woman whose unborn child is harmed.

(c) Sentence. Battery of an unborn child is a Class A misdemeanor. aggravated battery of an unborn child is a Class 2 felony.

(d) This Section shall not apply to acts which cause bodily harm to an unborn child if those acts were committed during any abortion, as defined in Section 2 of the Illinois Abortion Law of 1975, as amended, to which the pregnant woman has consented. This Section shall not apply to acts which were committed pursuant to usual and customary standards of medical practice during diagnostic testing or therapeutic treatment.

§ 12-3.2. Domestic battery. (a) A person commits domestic battery if he or she knowingly without legal justification by any means:

(1) Causes bodily harm to any family or household member;

(2) Makes physical contact of an insulting or provoking nature with any family or household member.

((b) Sentence. Domestic battery is a Class A misdemeanor.

Domestic battery is a Class 4 felony if the defendant has any prior conviction under this Code for violation of an order of protection (Section 12-3.4 or 12-30), or any prior conviction under the law of another jurisdiction for an offense which is substantially similar.

Domestic battery is a Class 4 felony if the defendant has any prior conviction under this Code for first degree murder (Section 9-1), attempt to commit first degree murder (Section 8-4), aggravated domestic battery (Section 12-3.3), aggravated battery (Section 12-3.05 or 12-4), heinous battery (Section 12-4.1), aggravated battery with a firearm (Section 12-4.2), aggravated battery with a machine gun or a firearm equipped with a silencer (Section 12-4.2-5), aggravated battery of a child (Section 12-4.3), aggravated battery of an unborn child (subsection (a-5) of Section 12-3.1, or Section 12-4.4), aggravated battery of a senior citizen (Section 12-4.6), stalking (Section 12-7.3), aggravated stalking (Section 12-7.4), criminal sexual assault (Section 11-1.20 or 12-13), aggravated criminal sexual assault (Section 11-1.30 or 12-14), kidnapping (Section 10-1), aggravated kidnapping (Section 10-2), predatory criminal sexual assault of a child (Section 11-1.40 or 12-14.1), aggravated criminal sexual abuse (Section 11-1.60 or 12-16), unlawful restraint (Section 10-3), aggravated unlawful restraint (Section 10-3.1), aggravated arson (Section 20-1.1),or aggravated discharge of a firearm (Section 24-1.2), or any prior conviction under the law of another jurisdiction for any offense that is substantially similar to the offenses listed in this Section, when any of these offenses have been committed against a family or household member. Domestic battery is a Class 4 felony if the defendant has one or 2 prior convictions under this Code for domestic battery (Section 12-3.2), or one or 2 prior convictions under the law of another jurisdiction for any offense which is substantially similar. Domestic battery is a Class 3 felony if the defendant had 3 prior convictions under this Code for domestic battery (Section 12-3.2), or 3 prior convictions under the law of another jurisdiction for any offense which is substantially similar. Domestic battery is a Class 2 felony if the defendant had 4 or more prior convictions under this Code for domestic battery (Section 12-3.2), or 4 or more prior convictions under the law of another jurisdiction for any offense which is substantially similar. In addition to any other sentencing alternatives, for any second or subsequent conviction of violating this Section, the offender shall be mandatorily sentenced to a minimum of 72 consecutive hours of imprisonment. The imprisonment shall not be subject to suspension, nor shall the person be eligible for probation in order to reduce the sentence.

(c) Domestic battery committed in the presence of a child. In addition to any other sentencing alternatives, a defendant who commits, in the presence of a child, a felony domestic battery (enhanced under subsection (b)), aggravated domestic battery (Section 12-3.3), aggravated battery (Section 12-3.05 or 12-4), unlawful restraint (Section 10-3), or aggravated unlawful restraint (Section 10-3.1) against a family or household member shall be required to serve a mandatory minimum imprisonment of 10 days or perform 300 hours of community service, or both. The defendant shall further be liable for the cost of any counseling required for the child at the discretion of the court in accordance with subsection (b) of Section 5-5-6 of the Unified

Code of Corrections. For purposes of this Section, "child" means a person under 18 years of age who is the defendant's or victim's child or step-child or who is a minor child residing within or visiting the household of the defendant or victim.

(d) Upon conviction of domestic battery, the court shall advise the defendant orally or in writing, substantially as follows: "An individual convicted of domestic battery may be subject to federal criminal penalties for possessing, transporting, shipping, or receiving any firearm or ammunition in violation of the federal Gun Control Act of 1968 (18 U.S.C. 922(g)(8) and (9))."

A notation shall be made in the court file that the admonition was given.

§ 12-3.3. Aggravated domestic battery. (a) A person who, in committing a domestic battery, knowingly causes great bodily harm, or permanent disability or disfigurement commits aggravated domestic battery.

(a-5) A person who, in committing a domestic battery, strangles another individual commits aggravated domestic battery. For the purposes of this subsection (a-5), "strangle" means intentionally impeding the normal breathing or circulation of the blood of an individual by applying pressure on the throat or neck of that individual or by blocking the nose or mouth of that individual.

(b) Sentence. Aggravated domestic battery is a Class 2 felony. Any order of probation or conditional discharge entered following a conviction for an offense under this Section must include, in addition to any other condition of probation or conditional discharge, a condition that the offender serve a mandatory term of imprisonment of not less than 60 consecutive days. A person convicted of a second or subsequent violation of this Section must be sentenced to a mandatory term of imprisonment of not less than 3 years and not more than 7 years or an extended term of imprisonment of not less than 7 years and not more than 14 years.

(c) Upon conviction of aggravated domestic battery, the court shall advise the defendant orally or in writing, substantially as follows: "An individual convicted of aggravated domestic battery may be subject to federal criminal penalties for possessing, transporting, shipping, or receiving any firearm or ammunition in violation of the federal Gun Control Act of 1968 (18 U.S.C. 922(g)(8) and (9))."

A notation shall be made in the court file that the admonition was given.

§ 12-3.4. Violation of an order of protection. (a) A person commits violation of an order of protection if:

(1) He or she knowingly commits an act which was prohibited by a court or fails to commit an act which was ordered by a court in violation of:

(i) a remedy in a valid order of protection authorized under paragraphs (1), (2), (3), (14), or (14.5) of subsection (b) of Section 214 of the Illinois Domestic Violence Act of 1986,

(ii) a remedy, which is substantially similar to the remedies authorized under paragraphs (1), (2), (3), (14) or (14.5) of subsection (b) of Section 214 of the Illinois Domestic Violence Act of 1986, in a valid order of protection, which is authorized under the laws of another state, tribe or United States territory,

(iii) any other remedy when the act constitutes a crime against the protected parties as the term protected parties is defined in Section 112A-4 of the Code of Criminal Procedure of 1963; and

(2) Such violation occurs after the offender has been served notice of the contents of the order, pursuant to the Illinois Domestic Violence Act of 1986 or any substantially similar statute of another state, tribe or United States territory, or otherwise has acquired actual knowledge of the contents of the order.

An order of protection issued by a state, tribal or territorial court related to domestic or family violence shall be deemed valid if the issuing court had jurisdiction over the parties and matter under the law of the state, tribe or territory. There shall be a presumption of validity where an order is certified and appears authentic on its face. for purposes of this Section, an "order of protection" may have been issued in a criminal or civil proceeding.

(a-5) Failure to provide reasonable notice and opportunity to be heard shall be an affirmative defense to any charge or process filed seeking enforcement of a foreign order of protection.

(b) Nothing in this Section shall be construed to diminish the inherent authority of the courts to enforce their lawful orders through civil or criminal contempt proceedings.

(c) the limitations placed on law enforcement liability by Section 305 of the Illinois Domestic Violence Act of 1986 apply to actions taken under this Section.

(d) Violation of an order of protection is a Class A misdemeanor. Violation of an order of protection is a Class 4 felony if the defendant has any prior conviction under this Code for domestic battery (Section 12-3.2) or violation of an order of protection (Section 12-3.4 or 12-30).

Violation of an order of protection is a Class 4 felony if the defendant has any prior conviction under this Code for first degree murder (Section 9-1), attempt to commit first degree murder (Section 8-4), aggravated domestic battery (Section 12-3.3), aggravated battery (Section 12-3.05 or 12-4), heinous battery (Section 12-4.1), aggravated battery with a firearm (Section 12-4.2), aggravated battery with a machine gun or a firearm equipped with a silencer (Section 12-4.2-5) aggravated battery of a child (Section 12-4.3), aggravated battery of an unborn child (subsection (a-5) of Section 12-3.1, or Section 12-4.4), aggravated battery of a senior citizen (Section 12-4.6), stalking (Section 12-7.3), aggravated stalking (Section 12-7.4), criminal sexual assault (Section 12-13), aggravated criminal sexual assault (12-14), kidnapping (Section 10-1), aggravated kidnapping (Section 10-2), predatory criminal sexual assault of a child (Section 12-14.1), aggravated criminal sexual abuse (Section 12-16), unlawful restraint (Section 10-3), aggravated unlawful restraint (Section 10-3.1), aggravated arson (Section 20-1.1), aggravated discharge of a firearm (Section 24-1.2), or a violation of any former law of this State that is substantially similar to any listed offense, when any of these offenses have been committed against a family or household member as defined in Section 112A-3 of the Code of Criminal Procedure of 1963.

The court shall impose a minimum penalty of 24 hours imprisonment for defendant's second or subsequent violation of any order of protection; unless the court explicitly finds that an increased penalty or such period of imprisonment would be manifestly unjust.

In addition to any other penalties, the court may order the defendant to pay a fine as authorized under Section 5-9-1 of the Unified Code of Corrections or to make restitution to the victim under Section 5-5-6 of the Unified Code of Corrections.

In addition to any other penalties, including those imposed by Section 5-9-1.5 of the Unified Code of Corrections, the court shall impose an additional fine of $ 20 as authorized by Section 5-9-1.11 of the Unified Code of Corrections upon any person convicted of or placed on supervision for a violation of this Section. The additional fine shall be imposed for each violation of this Section.

§ 12-3.5. Interfering with the reporting of domestic violence. (a) A person commits interfering with the reporting of domestic violence when, after having committed an act of domestic violence, he or she knowingly prevents or attempts to prevent the victim of or a witness to the act of domestic violence from calling a 9-1-1 emergency telephone system, obtaining medical assistance, or making a report to any law enforcement official.

(b) For the purposes of this Section:

"Domestic violence" shall have the meaning ascribed to it in Section 112A-3 of the Code of Criminal Procedure of 1963.

(c) Sentence. Interfering with the reporting of domestic violence is a Class A misdemeanor.

§ 12-3.6. Disclosing location of domestic violence victim. (a) As used in this Section:

"Domestic violence" means attempting to cause or causing abuse of a family or household member or high-risk adult with disabilities, or attempting to cause or causing neglect or exploitation of a high-risk adult with disabilities which threatens the adult's health and safety.

"Family or household member" means a spouse, person living as a spouse, parent, or other adult person related by consanguinity or affinity, who is residing or has resided with the person committing domestic violence. "Family or household member" includes a high-risk adult with disabilities who resides with or receives care from any person who has the responsibility for a high-risk adult as a result of a family relationship or who has assumed responsibility for all or a portion of the care of an adult with disabilities voluntarily, by express or implied contract, or by court order.

"High-risk adult with disabilities" means a person aged 18 or over whose physical or mental disability impairs his or her ability to seek or obtain protection from abuse, neglect, or exploitation.

"Abuse", "exploitation", and "neglect" have the meanings ascribed to those terms in Section 103 of the Illinois Domestic Violence Act of 1986.

(b) A person commits disclosure of location of domestic violence victim when he or she publishes, disseminates or otherwise discloses the location of any domestic violence victim, without that person's authorization, knowing the disclosure will result in, or has the substantial likelihood of resulting in, the threat of bodily harm.

(c) Nothing in this Section shall apply to confidential communications between an attorney and his or her client.

(d) Sentence. Disclosure of location of domestic violence victim is a Class A misdemeanor.

Commentary – Assault and Battery Offenses

Assault and Battery. The basic offenses involving bodily harm are assault and battery. Section 12-1 defines assault as the knowing and unjustified threat of committing a battery by one person to another. The conduct by the defendant must be such to create a reasonable fear on the part of the victim. That fear must be objectively reasonable in that a reasonable person under the same circumstances would believe that a battery was imminent. Words alone are not enough, but the combination of words, inflection, movements and actions can lead a person to reasonably conclude that the threat of a battery is real. In *In re C.L.* 180 Ill.App.3d 173, 534 N.E.2d 1330 (Ill. App. Ct. 1st Dist. 1989), the respondent – juveniles (i.e. defendants in a juvenile delinquency case) said threatening words to the effect that one of them had a gun and would "pop" the victim, they wore gang colors, and move away from and back towards the victims' porch and one of them pulled gun. All of the circumstances, not just the words alone, would place a reasonable person in fear of a battery being committed.

Section 12-3 defines battery as conduct by the defendant where he made intentional contact with the victim that was (1) insulting or provoking or (2) caused bodily harm. Bodily harm is physical harm – harm that would cause pain or which would leave a bruise or mark on the victim. The contact cannot be accidental nor incidental, it must be intentional. In *People v. DeRosario* 397 Ill.App.3d 332, 921 N.E.2d 753 (Ill. App. Ct. 2nd Dist. 2009), the defendant and victim had a failed personal relationship the victim testified that although they had stopped dating, they worked in the same office complex and every day at lunch the defendant would come to a common building area and stare at her and make her feel uncomfortable. on the day of the offense, he sat down in a chair next to where the victim was seated and hit her back and hip with his knees. She left and called the police. In affirming the trial court conviction for battery, the Court noted that intentional conduct can be insulting or provoking depending on the context in which it occurred, and the defendant's contact with the victim based on the entirety of the evidence was not the same as incidental innocent bumping that humans experience every day, as the defendant had claimed.

Aggravated assault and Aggravated Battery. While assault and battery are sometimes called "simple" offenses, they are easily enhanced into more serious offenses by applying factors that aggravate the offenses. These factors include (1) the status of the victim, (2) the harm caused to the victim; (3) a weapon or other means used to commit the offense or (4) the location of the offense.

Location. Section 12-2(a) enhances an assault to an aggravated assault if the conduct occurred in a public place or on a public way. The aggravating factor changes the classification of the offense from a Class C misdemeanor to a Class A misdemeanor. The same "public place" location factor enhances a battery to an aggravated battery under Section 12-3.05(c) and changes the classification of offense from a Class A misdemeanor to a Class 3 felony. In *People v. Ojeda* 397 Ill.App.3d 285, 921 N.E.2d 490 (Ill. App. Ct. 2nd Dist. 2009), the defendant punched another student at Belvidere High School. Public high schools were public places, funded by taxes and a place of public events, even though attendance at schools was restricted during school days to permit attendance by only those students who were enrolled to attend school. In fact security officers were present to enforce the restrictions. Nevertheless the location of the simple battery properly enhanced the offense and supported a conviction for aggravated battery. See also *People v. Hill* 409 Ill.App.3d 451, 454, 494 N.E.2d, 1180.1184 (4th Dist. 2011)("public property" means "government owned property".)

Status of Victim. Sections 12-2(b)(1) – (9) and 12-3.05(d)(1) - (9) define aggravated assault and aggravated battery respectively based on the status of the victim. School teachers, police officers, state employees, coaches and sports official and others are all protected victims - committing an assault or battery on that class of victim is a more serious offense than other victims. In *People v. Wrencher* 2011 IL App (4th) 080619,959 N.E.2d 693, the defendant was arrested and dug his fingernails into one police officer's hand (Manzana) causing pain and a small cut on the officer's little finger. The defendant continued to struggle with officers and was sprayed with mace. When another officer (Briggs) tried to put the defendant into a squad car, the defendant spit a mouthful of blood and mace on the officer's shirt, on the chest and sleeve. The officer put the defendant's head down on the trunk of the car and eventually put a "spit hood" on him to prevent him from spitting on anyone. The defendant's two convictions for aggravated battery (one for causing bodily harm to Manzana and the other for contact of an insulting or provoking nature to Briggs) were affirmed.

Weapons and other Means of committing the offense. How the battery offense was committed can also be an aggravating factor. Section 12-1(c)(1) – (8) and 12-3.05(e) and (f) define the use of weapons, use of motor vehicles, the wearing of hoods and disguises and use of other devices in committing an assault or battery to enhance from a simple offense to a more serious offense. Shooting a firearm or brandishing a knife creates a very serious assault, of course and using a motor vehicle to strike someone is a very serious battery. In *People v. Blanks* 361 Ill.App.3d 400, 865 N.E.2d 1, (Ill. App. Ct. 1st Dist. 2005), a 2" x 2" stick that was approximately 30" long was held to be a deadly weapon for purposes of an aggravated battery conviction where it was brandished to strike a man's head.

Harm to the Victim. Another factor that can elevate a battery to aggravated battery is where the perpetrator's actions knowingly cause great bodily harm or permanent disfigurement to the victim. (Section 12-3.05(a)(1)) Great bodily harm has no precise definition. It can be decided by the fact-finder as a matter of common sense. Great bodily harm is more than the physical injury of "bodily harm." In *In re Keith C.* 378 Ill.App.3d 252, 880 N.E.2d 57 (Ill. App. Ct. 1st Dist. 2007), the court held that throwing a brick at an occupied car, breaking the windshield and causing the victim to lose consciousness and bleed from her ear was sufficient proof of knowingly causing great bodily harm. What constitutes "great bodily harm" depends on the injuries to the victim and not to the treatment the victim received.

In *People v. Edwards* 304 Ill.App.3d 250, 710 N.E.2d 507 (Ill. App. Ct. 2nd Dist. 1999), the victim received a gunshot wound to the leg but sought no medical treatment and cleaned the wound with a piece of gauze. At the time of the incident, there was no immediate pain, although the wound hurt a week later. The wound left a scar. This evidence was sufficient proof of great bodily harm.

Domestic Battery and Aggravated Domestic Battery. The more recent trend to specialize offenses is demonstrated in the legislative creation of the offense of domestic battery and its progeny. If a father, mother, son, daughter, brother or sister, without justification, knowingly caused injury or made contact of an insulting or provoking nature a battery on another family member, it could be criminally prosecuted as a battery. Rather than a simple battery prosecution, Illinois has a separate category of battery offenses, ostensibly to protect family members and others who live in the same household. *People v. Pickens* 354 Ill.App.3d 904, 822 N.E.2d 58 (Ill. App. Ct. 1st Dist. 2004)(evidence sufficient to support conviction for domestic battery where during argument over Thanksgiving plans husband shut door on wife's foot.) Section 12 – 3.2 defines domestic battery as a battery on a family or household member. Section 12-3.3 defines aggravated domestic battery as a domestic battery which causes great bodily harm or permanent disfigurement. A "family or household member" includes a victim who had a dating relationship with the assailant. In *People v. Irvine* 379 Ill.App.3d 116, 882 N.E.2d 1124 (Ill. App. Ct. 1st Dist. 2008), the court affirmed a conviction for domestic battery for the defendant who had a "full relationship" with the victim for 45 days and then a sexual relationship with the victim for another two weeks thereafter. Ex-boyfriends and ex-girlfriends, people related by blood or marriage, and people who used to live in the same dwelling are among those recognized to be "family or household members" as defined in 725 ILCS 5/112A-3. However, reasonable parental discipline may be justification for physical contact that otherwise would be a battery against a child. *People v. Roberts* 351 Ill.App.3d 684, 690, 814 N.E.2d 174, 179 (Ill. App. Ct. 4th Dist. 2004)(error for trial court to refuse to instruct jury that "a parent is legally justified in using reasonable force when necessary as part of reasonable discipline of a child" where evidence showed that defendant grabbed his daughter's hair in stopping a mother-daughter argument). However the use of corporal punishment must be reasonable, and normally does not include causing physical injury. *People v. Green* 2011 IL App (2d) 091123 (Ill. App. Ct. 2nd Dist. 2011)(it was unreasonable for defendant-mother to use corporal punishment with repeated blows to her son in school parking lot with a 2 ½ foot ice-scraper, continuing with the blows after a passerby asked her to stop and where her son pleaded with her to stop).

Prior Acts of Domestic Battery. The Code of Criminal Procedure 725 ILCS 5/115-7.4 permits the introduction of evidence of prior acts of domestic battery committed by the defendant as propensity evidence to prove the defendant's guilt of a domestic battery. The victims do not have to be identical, nor must the violence be the same type of misconduct. The trial court must hold a pretrial hearing to determine the admissibility of the evidence, over the objection of the defendant, to consider whether its probative value is substantially outweighed by undue prejudice. the Illinois Supreme Court upheld the statute and the procedure employed to admit prior acts of domestic violence against constitutional attack in *People v. Dabbs* 239 Ill.2d 77, 940 N.E.2d 1088 (2010).

Violation of an Order of Protection. a victim of domestic violence may obtain an "order of protection" in a civil proceeding under provisions of 725 ILCS Sections 5/112A-1 *et seq*, or 750 ILCS 60/101 *et seq.* (the Illinois Domestic Violence Act of 1986), after she alleges and proves the existence of a defined relationship with the civil defendant and prior acts or threats of violence against her. An order of protection is a civil court order which can be enforced by civil contempt powers inherent in a court's authority. However, Section 12-3.4 also provides for criminal sanctions against the civil defendant for violation of the same order of protection.

Subdivision 10. Endangerment

§ 12-4.4a. Abuse or criminal neglect of a long term care facility resident; criminal abuse or neglect of an elderly person or person with a disability. (a) Abuse or criminal neglect of a long term care facility resident.

(1) A person or an owner or licensee commits abuse of a long term care facility resident when he or she knowingly causes any physical or mental injury to, or commits any sexual offense in this Code against, a resident.

(2) A person or an owner or licensee commits criminal neglect of a long term care facility resident when he or she recklessly:

(A) performs acts that cause a resident's life to be endangered, health to be injured, or pre-existing physical or mental condition to deteriorate, or that create the substantial likelihood that an elderly person's or person with a disability's life will be endangered, health will be injured, or pre-existing physical or mental condition will deteriorate;

(B) fails to perform acts that he or she knows or reasonably should know are necessary to maintain or preserve the life or health of a resident, and that failure causes the resident's life to be endangered, health to be injured, or pre-existing physical or mental condition to deteriorate, or that create the substantial likelihood that an elderly person's or person with a disability's life will be endangered, health will be injured, or pre-existing physical or mental condition will deteriorate; or

(C) abandons a resident.

(3) A person or an owner or licensee commits neglect of a long term care facility resident when he or she negligently fails to provide adequate medical care, personal care, or maintenance to the resident which results in physical or mental injury or deterioration of the resident's physical or mental condition. An owner or licensee is guilty under this subdivision (a)(3), however, only if the owner or licensee failed to exercise reasonable care in the hiring, training, supervising, or providing of staff or other related routine administrative responsibilities.

(b) Criminal abuse or neglect of an elderly person or person with a disability.

(1) A caregiver commits criminal abuse or neglect of an elderly person or person with a disability when he or she knowingly does any of the following:

(A) performs acts that cause the person's life to be endangered, health to be injured, or pre-existing physical or mental condition to deteriorate;

(B) fails to perform acts that he or she knows or reasonably should know are necessary to maintain or preserve the life or health of the person, and that failure causes the person's life to be endangered, health to be injured, or pre-existing physical or mental condition to deteriorate;

(C) abandons the person;

(D) physically abuses, harasses, intimidates, or interferes with the personal liberty of the person; or

(E) exposes the person to willful deprivation.

(2) It is not a defense to criminal abuse or neglect of an elderly person or person with a disability that the caregiver reasonably believed that the victim was not an elderly person or person with a disability.

(c) Offense not applicable. (1) Nothing in this Section applies to a physician licensed to practice medicine in all its branches or a duly licensed nurse providing care within the scope of his or her professional judgment and within the accepted standards of care within the community.

(2) Nothing in this Section imposes criminal liability on a caregiver who made a good faith effort to provide for the health and personal care of an elderly person or person with a disability, but through no fault of his or her own was unable to provide such care.

(3) Nothing in this Section applies to the medical supervision, regulation, or control of the remedial care or treatment of residents in a long term care facility conducted for those who rely upon treatment by prayer or spiritual means in accordance with the creed or tenets of any well-recognized church or religious denomination as described in Section 3-803 of the Nursing Home Care Act or Section 3-803 of the MR/DD Community Care Act.

(4) Nothing in this Section prohibits a caregiver from providing treatment to an elderly person or person with a disability by spiritual means through prayer alone and care consistent therewith in lieu of medical care and treatment in accordance with the tenets and practices of any church or religious denomination of which the elderly person or person with a disability is a member.

(5) Nothing in this Section limits the remedies available to the victim under the Illinois Domestic Violence Act of 1986.

(d) Sentence. (1) Long term care facility. Abuse of a long term care facility resident is a Class 3 felony. Criminal neglect of a long term care facility resident is a Class 4 felony, unless it results in the resident's death in which case it is a Class 3 felony. Neglect of a long term care facility resident is a petty offense.

(2) Caregiver. Criminal abuse or neglect of an elderly person or person with a disability is a Class 3 felony, unless it results in the person's death in which case it is a Class 2 felony, and if imprisonment is imposed it shall be for a minimum term of 3 years and a maximum term of 14 years.

(e) Definitions. For the purposes of this Section:

"Abandon" means to desert or knowingly forsake a resident or an elderly person or person with a disability under circumstances in which a reasonable person would continue to provide care and custody.

"Caregiver" means a person who has a duty to provide for an elderly person or person with a disability's health and personal care, at the elderly person or person with a disability's place of residence, including, but not limited to, food and nutrition, shelter, hygiene, prescribed medication, and medical care and treatment, and includes any of the following:

(1) A parent, spouse, adult child, or other relative by blood or marriage who resides with or resides in the same building with or regularly visits the elderly person or person with a disability, knows or reasonably should know of such person's physical or mental impairment, and knows or reasonably should know that such person is unable to adequately provide for his or her own health and personal care.

(2) A person who is employed by the elderly person or person with a disability or by another to reside with or regularly visit the elderly person or person with a disability and provide for such person's health and personal care.

(3) A person who has agreed for consideration to reside with or regularly visit the elderly person or person with a disability and provide for such person's health and personal care.

(4) A person who has been appointed by a private or public agency or by a court of competent jurisdiction to provide for the elderly person or person with a disability's health and personal care.

"Caregiver" does not include a long-term care facility licensed or certified under the Nursing Home Care Act or a facility licensed or certified under the MR/DD Community Care Act, or any administrative, medical, or other personnel of such a facility, or a health care provider who is licensed under the Medical Practice Act of 1987 and renders care in the ordinary course of his or her profession.

"Elderly person" means a person 60 years of age or older who is incapable of adequately providing for his or her own health and personal care.

"Licensee" means the individual or entity licensed to operate a facility under the Nursing Home Care Act, the MR/DD Community Care Act, or the Assisted Living and Shared Housing Act.

"Long term care facility" means a private home, institution, building, residence, or other place, whether operated for profit or not, or a county home for the infirm and chronically ill operated pursuant to Division 5-21 or 5-22 of the Counties Code, or any similar institution operated by the State of Illinois or a political subdivision thereof, which provides, through its ownership or management, personal care, sheltered care, or nursing for 3 or more persons not related to the owner by blood or marriage. The term also includes skilled nursing facilities and intermediate care facilities as defined in Titles XVIII and XIX of the federal Social Security Act and assisted living establishments and shared housing establishments licensed under the Assisted Living and Shared Housing Act.

"Owner" means the owner a long term care facility as provided in the Nursing Home Care Act, the owner of a facility as provided in the MR/DD Community Care Act, or the owner of an assisted living or shared housing establishment as provided in the Assisted Living and Shared Housing Act.

"Person with a disability" means a person who suffers from a permanent physical or mental impairment, resulting from disease, injury, functional disorder, or congenital condition, which renders the person incapable of adequately providing for his or her own health and personal care.

"Resident" means a person residing in a long term care facility.

"Willful deprivation" has the meaning ascribed to it in paragraph (15) of Section 103 of the Illinois Domestic Violence Act of 1986.

§ 12-4.5. Tampering with food, drugs or cosmetics. (a) A person who knowingly puts any substance capable of causing death or great bodily harm to a human being into any food, drug or cosmetic offered for sale or consumption commits tampering with food, drugs or cosmetics.

(b) Sentence. Tampering with food, drugs or cosmetics is a Class 2 felony.

§ 12-4.9. Drug induced infliction of aggravated battery to a child athlete. (a) Any person who distributes to or encourages the ingestion of a drug by a person under the age of 18 with the intent that the person under the age of 18 ingest the drug for the purpose of a quick weight gain or loss in connection with participation in athletics is guilty of the offense of drug induced infliction of aggravated battery of a child athlete. This Section does not apply to care under usual and customary standards of medical practice by a physician licensed to practice medicine in all its branches nor to the sale of drugs or products by a retail merchant.

(b) Drug induced infliction of aggravated battery to a child athlete is a Class A misdemeanor. A second or subsequent violation is a Class 4 felony.

§ 12-5. Reckless conduct. (a) A person commits reckless conduct when he or she, by any means lawful or unlawful, recklessly performs an act or acts that:

(1) cause bodily harm to or endanger the safety of another person; or

(2) cause great bodily harm or permanent disability or disfigurement to another person.

(b) Sentence. Reckless conduct under subdivision (a)(1) is a Class A misdemeanor. Reckless conduct under subdivision (a)(2) is a Class 4 felony.

Commentary – Reckless Conduct

A person who harms or endangers someone recklessly commits the crime of reckless conduct. Reckless conduct is a misdemeanor unless the conduct causes great bodily harm or permanent disfigurement, in which case it is a Class 4 felony. Examples of reckless conduct include an intoxicated person firing a gun, or a person shooting a gun without any intent to harm, disregarding the chance that a ricochet would cause a bullet to strike another person.

In *People v. Martin* 401 Ill.App.3d 315, 927 N.E.2d 877 (Ill. App. Ct. 3rd Dist. 2010), the court affirmed the defendant's conviction for reckless conduct. The evidence showed that the defendant disconnected gas line end caps to a stove and a water heater in his pizza restaurant. His upstairs tenant smelled natural gas and contacted emergency authorities. the court held that the defendant performed acts (disconnecting the end caps to gas lines) which caused an endangerment (the accumulation of excess natural gas) of the safety of another (the building's other tenant) and that the actions in doing so were reckless (disregard of the known risk of releasing the natural gas.)

§ 12-5.01. Criminal transmission of HIV. (a) A person commits criminal transmission of HIV when he or she, knowing that he or she is infected with HIV:

(1) engages in intimate contact with another;

(2) transfers, donates, or provides his or her blood, tissue, semen, organs, or other potentially infectious body fluids for transfusion, transplantation, insemination, or other administration to another; or

(3) dispenses, delivers, exchanges, sells, or in any other way transfers to another any non-sterile intravenous or intramuscular drug paraphernalia.

(b) For purposes of this Section:

"HIV" means the human immunodeficiency virus or any other identified causative agent of acquired immunodeficiency syndrome.

"Intimate contact with another" means the exposure of the body of one person to a bodily fluid of another person in a manner that could result in the transmission of HIV.

"Intravenous or intramuscular drug paraphernalia" means any equipment, product, or material of any kind which is peculiar to and marketed for use in injecting a substance into the human body.

(c) Nothing in this Section shall be construed to require that an infection with HIV has occurred in order for a person to have committed criminal transmission of HIV.

(d) It shall be an affirmative defense that the person exposed knew that the infected person was infected with HIV, knew that the action could result in infection with HIV, and consented to the action with that knowledge.

(e) A person who commits criminal transmission of HIV commits a Class 2 felony.

§ 12-5.02. Vehicular endangerment. (a) a person commits vehicular endangerment when he or she strikes a motor vehicle by causing an object to fall from an overpass in the direction of a moving motor vehicle with the intent to strike a motor vehicle while it is traveling upon a highway in this State.

(b) Sentence. Vehicular endangerment is a Class 2 felony, unless death results, in which case vehicular endangerment is a Class 1 felony.

(c) Definitions. For purposes of this Section:

"Object" means any object or substance that by its size, weight, or consistency is likely to cause great bodily harm to any occupant of a motor vehicle.

"Overpass" means any structure that passes over a highway.

"Motor vehicle" and "highway" have the meanings as defined in the Illinois Vehicle Code.

§ 12-5.1. Criminal housing management. (a) A person commits criminal housing management when, having personal management or control of residential real estate, whether as a legal or equitable owner or as a managing agent or otherwise, he or she recklessly permits the physical condition or facilities of the residential real estate to become or remain in any condition which endangers the health or safety of a person other than the defendant.

(b) Sentence. Criminal housing management is a Class A misdemeanor, and a subsequent conviction is a Class 4 felony.

§ 12-5.1a. Aggravated criminal housing management. (a) A person commits aggravated criminal housing management when he or she commits criminal housing management and:

(1) the condition endangering the health or safety of a person other than the defendant is determined to be a contributing factor in the death of that person; and

(2) the person recklessly conceals or attempts to conceal the condition that endangered the health or safety of the person other than the defendant that is found to be a contributing factor in that death.

(b) Sentence. Aggravated criminal housing management is a Class 4 felony.

§ 12-5.2. Injunction in connection with criminal housing management or aggravated criminal housing management. (a) In addition to any other remedies, the State's Attorney of the county where the residential property which endangers the health or safety of any person exists is authorized to file a complaint and apply to the circuit court for a temporary restraining order, and such circuit court shall upon hearing grant a temporary restraining order or a preliminary or permanent injunction, without bond, restraining any person who owns, manages, or has any equitable interest in the property, from collecting, receiving or benefiting from any rents or other monies available from the property, so long as the property remains in a condition which endangers the health or safety of any person.

(b) The court may order any rents or other monies owed to be paid into an escrow account. The funds are to be paid out of the escrow account only to satisfy the reasonable cost of necessary repairs of the property which had been incurred or will be incurred in ameliorating the condition of the property as described in subsection (a), payment of delinquent real estate taxes on the property or payment of other legal debts relating to the property. The court may order that funds remain in escrow for a reasonable time after the completion of all necessary repairs to assure continued upkeep of the property and satisfaction of other outstanding legal debts of the property.

(c) The owner shall be responsible for contracting to have necessary repairs completed and shall be required to submit all bills, together with certificates of completion, to the manager of the escrow account within 30 days after their receipt by the owner.

(d) In contracting for any repairs required pursuant to this Section the owner of the property shall enter into a contract only after receiving bids from at least 3 independent contractors capable of making the necessary repairs. If the owner does not contract for the repairs with the lowest bidder, he shall file an affidavit with the court explaining why the lowest bid was not acceptable. At no time, under the provisions of this Section , shall the owner contract with anyone who is not a licensed contractor, except that a contractor need not be licensed if neither the State nor the county, township, or municipality where the residential real estate is located requires that the contractor be licensed. The court may order release of those funds in the escrow account that are in excess of the monies that the court determines to its satisfaction are needed to correct the condition of the property as described in subsection (a).

For the purposes of this Section, "licensed contractor" means: (i) a contractor licensed by the State, if the State requires the licensure of the contractor; or (ii) a contractor licensed by the county, township, or municipality where the residential real estate is located, if that jurisdiction requires the licensure of the contractor.

(e) The Clerk of the Circuit Court shall maintain a separate trust account entitled "Property Improvement Trust Account", which shall serve as the depository for the escrowed funds prescribed by this Section. The Clerk of the Court shall be responsible for the receipt, disbursement, monitoring and maintenance of all funds entrusted to this account, and shall provide to the court a quarterly accounting of the activities for any property, with funds in such account, unless the court orders accountings on a more frequent basis.

The Clerk of the Circuit Court shall promulgate rules and procedures to administer the provisions of this Act.

(f) Nothing in this Section shall in any way be construed to limit or alter any existing liability incurred, or to be incurred, by the owner or manager except as expressly provided in this Act. Nor shall anything in this Section be construed to create any liability on behalf of the Clerk of the Court, the State's Attorney's office or any other governmental agency involved in this action.

Nor shall anything in this Section be construed to authorize tenants to refrain from paying rent.

(g) Costs. As part of the costs of an action under this Section, the court shall assess a reasonable fee against the defendant to be paid to the Clerk of the Circuit court. This amount is to be used solely for the maintenance of the Property Improvement Trust Account. No money obtained directly or indirectly from the property subject to the case may be used to satisfy this cost.

(h) The municipal building department or other entity responsible for inspection of property and the enforcement of such local requirements shall, within 5 business days of a request by the State's Attorney, provide all documents requested, which shall include, but not be limited to, all records of inspections, permits and other information relating to any property.

§ 12-5.3. Use of a dangerous place for the commission of a controlled substance or cannabis offense. (a) A person commits use of a dangerous place for the commission of a controlled substance or cannabis offense when that person knowingly exercises control over any place with the intent to use that place to manufacture, produce, deliver, or possess with intent to deliver a controlled or counterfeit substance or controlled substance analog in violation of Section 401 of the Illinois Controlled Substances Act or to manufacture, produce, deliver, or possess with intent to deliver cannabis in violation of Section 5, 5.1, 5.2, 7, or 8 of the Cannabis Control Act and:

(1) the place, by virtue of the presence of the substance or substances used or intended to be used to manufacture a controlled or counterfeit

substance, controlled substance analog, or cannabis, presents a substantial risk of injury to any person from fire, explosion, or exposure to toxic or noxious chemicals or gas; or

(2) the place used or intended to be used to manufacture, produce, deliver, or possess with intent to deliver a controlled or counterfeit substance, controlled substance analog, or cannabis has located within it or surrounding it devices, weapons, chemicals, or explosives designed, hidden, or arranged in a manner that would cause a person to be exposed to a substantial risk of great bodily harm.

(b) It may be inferred that a place was intended to be used to manufacture a controlled or counterfeit substance or controlled substance analog if a substance containing a controlled or counterfeit substance or controlled substance analog or a substance containing a chemical important to the manufacture of a controlled or counterfeit substance or controlled substance analog is found at the place of the alleged illegal controlled substance manufacturing in close proximity to equipment or a chemical used for facilitating the manufacture of the controlled or counterfeit substance or controlled substance analog that is alleged to have been intended to be manufactured.

(c) As used in this Section, "place" means a premises, conveyance, or location that offers seclusion, shelter, means, or facilitation for manufacturing, producing, possessing, or possessing with intent to deliver a controlled or counterfeit substance, controlled substance analog, or cannabis.

(d) Use of a dangerous place for the commission of a controlled substance or cannabis offense is a Class 1 felony.

§ 12-5.5. Common carrier recklessness. (a) A person commits common carrier recklessness when he or she, having personal management or control of or over a public conveyance used for the common carriage of persons, recklessly endangers the safety of others.

(b) Sentence. Common carrier recklessness is a Class 4 felony.

Subdivision 15. Intimidation

§ 12-6. Intimidation. (a) A person commits intimidation when, with intent to cause another to perform or to omit the performance of any act, he or she communicates to another, directly or indirectly by any means , a threat to perform without lawful authority any of the following acts:

(1) Inflict physical harm on the person threatened or any other person or on property; or

(2) Subject any person to physical confinement or restraint; or

(3) Commit a felony or Class A misdemeanor; or

(4) Accuse any person of an offense; or

(5) Expose any person to hatred, contempt or ridicule; or

(6) Take action as a public official against anyone or anything, or withhold official action, or cause such action or withholding; or

(7) Bring about or continue a strike, boycott or other collective action.

(b) Sentence. intimidation is a Class 3 felony for which an offender may be sentenced to a term of imprisonment of not less than 2 years and not more than 10 years.

§ 12-6.2. Aggravated intimidation. (a) A person commits aggravated intimidation when he or she commits intimidation and:

(1) the person committed the offense in furtherance of the activities of an organized gang or because of the person's membership in or allegiance to an organized gang; or

(2) the offense is committed with the intent to prevent any person from becoming a community policing volunteer; or

(3) the following conditions are met:

(A) the person knew that the victim was a peace officer, a correctional institution employee, a fireman, or a community policing volunteer; and

(B) the offense was committed:
(i) while the victim was engaged in the execution of his or her official duties; or

(ii) to prevent the victim from performing his or her official duties;

(iii) in retaliation for the victim's performance of his or her official duties; or

(iv) by reason of any person's activity as a community policing volunteer.

(b) Sentence. Aggravated intimidation as defined in paragraph (a)(1) is a Class 1 felony. Aggravated intimidation as defined in paragraph (a)(2) or (a)(3) is a Class 2 felony for which the offender may be sentenced to a term of imprisonment of not less than 3 years nor more than 14 years.

(c) (Blank).

Commentary – Intimidation

Intimidation and aggravated intimidation. Section 12-6 creates the crime of intimidation which involves (1) the use of a threat of physical harm or restraint, (2) the threat to commit an offense, (3) the threat to accuse the victim of an offense or to publicly insult or ridicule the victim, with each to knowingly force the victim to do something or to refrain from doing something. The victim is intimidated to act or not act because of the threats.

Section 12 – 6.2 defines aggravated intimidation. Aggravating factors include: (1) intimidation by gang members; or (2) intimidation of a peace officer or correctional employee who is threatened to act or not act due to official duties.

In *People v. Young* 312 Ill.App.3d 428, 722 N.E.2d 386 (Ill. App. Ct. 2nd Dist. 2000), the defendant made threatening telephone calls to his estranged wife (who was in Ohio) that if she did not reconcile with him, he would kill her and their children. His conviction for intimidation was affirmed. The court noted that his placing the phone calls from Illinois to Ohio conferred jurisdiction on Illinois courts. The purpose of the intimidation statute, was present in *Young,* where the evidence demonstrated that the defendant threatened physical harm in an effort to get the victim to do something (reconcile) or not do something (proceed with a divorce).

§ 12-6.4. Criminal street gang recruitment on school grounds or public property adjacent to school grounds and criminal street gang recruitment of a minor. (a) A person commits criminal street gang recruitment on school grounds or public property adjacent to school grounds when on school grounds or public property adjacent to school grounds, he or she knowingly threatens the use of physical force to coerce, solicit, recruit, or induce another person to join or remain a member of a criminal street gang, or conspires to do so.
(a-5) A person commits the offense of criminal street gang recruitment of a minor when he or she threatens the use of physical force to coerce, solicit, recruit, or induce another person to join or remain a member of a criminal street gang, or conspires to do so, whether or not such threat is communicated in person, by means of the Internet, or by means of a telecommunications device.

(b) Sentence. Criminal street gang recruitment on school grounds or public property adjacent to school grounds is a Class 1 felony and criminal street gang recruitment of a minor is a Class 1 felony.

(c) In this Section:

"School grounds" means the building or buildings or real property comprising a public or private elementary or secondary school, community college, college, or university and includes a school yard, school playing field, or school playground.

"Minor" means any person under 18 years of age.

"Internet" means an interactive computer service or system or an information service, system, or access software provider that provides or enables computer access by multiple users to a computer server, and includes, but is not limited to, an information service, system, or access software provider that provides access to a network system commonly known as the Internet, or any comparable system or service and also includes, but is not limited to, a World Wide Web page, newsgroup, message board, mailing list, or chat area on any interactive computer service or system or other online service.

"Telecommunications device" means a device that is capable of receiving or transmitting speech, data, signals, text, images, sounds, codes, or other information including, but not limited to, paging devices, telephones, and cellular and mobile telephones.

§ 12-6.5. Compelling organization membership of persons. A person who knowingly, expressly or impliedly, threatens to do bodily harm or does bodily harm to an individual or to that individual's family or uses any other criminally unlawful means to solicit or cause any person to join, or deter any person from leaving, any organization or association regardless of the nature of such organization or association, is guilty of a Class 2 felony.

Any person of the age of 18 years or older who knowingly, expressly or impliedly, threatens to do bodily harm or does bodily harm to a person under 18 years of age or uses any other criminally unlawful means to solicit or cause any person under 18 years of age to join, or deter any person under 18 years of age from leaving, any organization or association regardless of the nature of such organization or association is guilty of a Class 1 felony.

A person convicted of an offense under this Section shall not be eligible to receive a sentence of probation, conditional discharge, or periodic imprisonment.

§ 12-7. Compelling confession or information by force or threat.
(a) A person who, with intent to obtain a confession, statement or information regarding any offense, knowingly inflicts or threatens imminent bodily harm upon the person threatened or upon any other person commits compelling a confession or information by force or threat.

(b) Sentence. Compelling a confession or information is a: (1) Class 4 felony if the defendant threatens imminent bodily harm to obtain a confession, statement, or information but does not inflict bodily harm on the victim, (2) Class 3 felony if the defendant inflicts bodily harm on the victim to obtain a confession, statement, or information, and (3) Class 2 felony if the defendant inflicts great bodily harm to obtain a confession, statement, or information.

§ 12-7.1. Hate crime. (a) A person commits hate crime when, by reason of the actual or perceived race, color, creed, religion, ancestry, gender, sexual orientation, physical or mental disability, or national origin of another individual or group of individuals, regardless of the existence of any other motivating factor or factors, he commits assault, battery, aggravated assault, misdemeanor theft, criminal trespass to residence, misdemeanor criminal damage to property, criminal trespass to vehicle, criminal trespass to real property, mob action or disorderly conduct as these crimes are defined in Sections 12-1, 12-2, 12-3(a), 16-1, 19-4, 21-1, 21-2, 21-3, 25-1, and 26-1 of this Code, respectively, or harassment by telephone as defined in Section 1-1 of the Harassing and Obscene Communications Act, or harassment through electronic communications as defined in clauses (a)(2) and (a)(4) of Section 1-2 of the Harassing and Obscene Communications Act.

(b) Except as provided in subsection (b-5), hate crime is a Class 4 felony for a first offense and a Class 2 felony for a second or subsequent offense.

(b-5) Hate crime is a Class 3 felony for a first offense and a Class 2 felony for a second or subsequent offense if committed:

(1) in a church, synagogue, mosque, or other building, structure, or place used for religious worship or other religious purpose;

(2) in a cemetery, mortuary, or other facility used for the purpose of burial or memorializing the dead;

(3) in a school or other educational facility, including an administrative facility or public or private dormitory facility of or associated with the school or other educational facility;

(4) in a public park or an ethnic or religious community center;

(5) on the real property comprising any location specified in clauses (1) through (4) of this subsection (b-5); or

(6) on a public way within 1,000 feet of the real property comprising any location specified in clauses (1) through (4) of this subsection (b-5).

(b-10) Upon imposition of any sentence, the trial court shall also either order restitution paid to the victim or impose a fine up to $1,000. In addition, any order of probation or conditional discharge entered following a conviction or an adjudication of delinquency shall include a condition that the offender perform public or community service of no less than 200 hours if that service is established in the county where the offender was convicted of hate crime. In addition, any order of probation or conditional discharge entered following a conviction or an adjudication of delinquency shall include a condition that the offender enroll in an educational program discouraging hate crimes if the offender caused criminal damage to property consisting of religious fixtures, objects, or decorations. The educational program may be administered, as determined by the court, by a university, college, community college, non-profit organization, or the Holocaust and Genocide Commission. Nothing in this subsection (b-10) prohibits courses discouraging hate crimes from being made available online. The court may also impose any other condition of probation or conditional discharge under this Section.

(c) Independent of any criminal prosecution or the result thereof, any person suffering injury to his person or damage to his property as a result of hate crime may bring a civil action for damages, injunction or other appropriate relief. The court may award actual damages, including damages for emotional distress, or punitive damages. A judgment may include attorney's fees and costs. The parents or legal guardians, other than guardians appointed pursuant to the Juvenile Court Act or the Juvenile Court Act of 1987, of an unemancipated minor shall be liable for the amount of any judgment for actual damages rendered against such minor under this subsection (c) in any amount not exceeding the amount provided under Section 5 of the Parental Responsibility Law.

(d) "Sexual orientation" has the meaning ascribed to it in paragraph (O-1) of Section 1-103 of the Illinois Human Rights Act

Commentary – Hate Crimes

If the reason for the commission of assault, battery and a number of other enumerated offenses is a person's race, ethnic or religious background, gender or sexual orientation or other defined status, it is a crime motivated in whole or in part by hate. "Hate" as utilized in Section 12-7.1 becomes an aggravating factor that causes a higher offense classification and higher potential penalty than the predicate offense. A misdemeanor battery when committed by reason of the victim's race becomes a Class 4 felony. While it is not a crime to have bigoted thoughts, it is a crime to act against a particular victim on the basis of the same bigotry.

In *People v. Davis* 285 Ill.App.3d 875, 674 N.E.2d 895 (Ill. App. Ct. 1st Dist. 1996), the defendant, who was white, battered the victim, who was African-American outside of a bar. The victim was with a white companion who was not assaulted. Before the victim was attacked the defendant yelled race-based insults at the victim. The evidence was sufficient to support a guilty verdict that the battery was committed based on the race of the victim.

§ 12-7.3. Stalking. (a) A person commits stalking when he or she knowingly engages in a course of conduct directed at a specific person, and he or she knows or should know that this course of conduct would cause a reasonable person to:

(1) fear for his or her safety or the safety of a third person; or

(2) suffer other emotional distress.

(a-3) A person commits stalking when he or she, knowingly and without lawful justification, on at least 2 separate occasions follows another person or places the person under surveillance or any combination thereof and:

(1) at any time transmits a threat of immediate or future bodily harm, sexual assault, confinement or restraint and the threat is directed towards that person or a family member of that person; or

(2) places that person in reasonable apprehension of immediate or future bodily harm, sexual assault, confinement or restraint to or of that person or a family member of that person.

(a-5) A person commits stalking when he or she has previously been convicted of stalking another person and knowingly and without lawful justification on one occasion:

(1) follows that same person or places that same person under surveillance; and

(2) transmits a threat of immediate or future bodily harm, sexual assault, confinement or restraint to that person or a family member of that person.

(b) Sentence. Stalking is a Class 4 felony; a second or subsequent conviction is a Class 3 felony.

(c) Definitions. For purposes of this Section:

(1) "Course of conduct" means 2 or more acts, including but not limited to acts in which a defendant directly, indirectly, or through third parties, by any action, method, device, or means follows, monitors, observes, surveils, threatens, or communicates to or about, a person, engages in other non-consensual contact, or interferes with or damages a person's property or pet. A course of conduct may include contact via electronic communications.

(2) "Electronic communication" means any transfer of signs, signals, writings, sounds, data, or intelligence of any nature transmitted in whole or in part by a wire, radio, electromagnetic, photoelectric, or photo-optical system. "Electronic communication" includes transmissions by a computer through the Internet to another computer.

(3) "Emotional distress" means significant mental suffering, anxiety or alarm.

(4) "Family member" means a parent, grandparent, brother, sister, or child, whether by whole blood, half-blood, or adoption and includes a step-grandparent, step-parent, step-brother, step-sister or step-child. "Family member" also means any other person who regularly resides in the household, or who, within the prior 6 months, regularly resided in the household.

(5) "Follows another person" means (i) to move in relative proximity to a person as that person moves from place to place or (ii) to remain in relative proximity to a person who is stationary

or whose movements are confined to a small area. "Follows another person" does not include a following within the residence of the defendant.

(6) "Non-consensual contact" means any contact with the victim that is initiated or continued without the victim's consent, including but not limited to being in the physical presence of the victim; appearing within the sight of the victim; approaching or confronting the victim in a public place or on private property; appearing at the workplace or residence of the victim; entering onto or remaining on property owned, leased, or occupied by the victim; or placing an object on, or delivering an object to, property owned, leased, or occupied by the victim.

(7) "Places a person under surveillance" means: (1) remaining present outside the person's school, place of employment, vehicle, other place occupied by the person, or residence other than the residence of the defendant; or (2) placing an electronic tracking device on the person or the person's property.

(8) "Reasonable person" means a person in the victim's situation.

(9) "Transmits a threat" means a verbal or written threat or a threat implied by a pattern of conduct or a combination of verbal or written statements or conduct.

(d) Exemptions.

(1) This Section does not apply to any individual or organization (i) monitoring or attentive to compliance with public or worker safety laws, wage and hour requirements, or other statutory requirements, or (ii) picketing occurring at the workplace that is otherwise lawful and arises out of a bona fide labor dispute, including any controversy concerning wages, salaries, hours, working conditions or benefits, including health and welfare, sick leave, insurance, and pension or retirement provisions, the making or maintaining of collective bargaining agreements, and the terms to be included in those agreements.

(2) This Section does not apply to an exercise of the right to free speech or assembly that is otherwise lawful.

(3) Telecommunications carriers, commercial mobile service providers, and providers of information services, including, but not limited to, Internet service providers and hosting service providers, are not liable under this Section, except for willful and wanton misconduct, by virtue of the transmission, storage, or caching of electronic communications or messages of others or by virtue of the provision of other related telecommunications, commercial mobile services, or information services used by others in violation of this Section.

(d-5) The incarceration of a person in a penal institution who commits the course of conduct or transmits a threat is not a bar to prosecution under this Section.

(d-10) A defendant who directed the actions of a third party to violate this Section, under the principles of accountability set forth in Article 5 of this Code, is guilty of violating this Section as if the same had been personally done by the defendant, without regard to the mental state of the third party acting at the direction of the defendant.

§ 12-7.4. Aggravated stalking. (a) A person commits aggravated stalking when he or she commits stalking and:

(1) causes bodily harm to the victim;

(2) confines or restrains the victim; or

(3) violates a temporary restraining order, an order of protection, a stalking no contact order, a civil no contact order, or an injunction prohibiting the behavior described in subsection (b)(1) of Section 214 of the Illinois Domestic Violence Act of 1986.

(a-1) A person commits aggravated stalking when he or she is required to register under the Sex Offender Registration Act or has been previously required to register under that Act and commits the offense of stalking when the victim of the stalking is also the victim of the offense for which the sex offender is required to register under the Sex Offender Registration Act or a family member of the victim.

(b) Sentence. Aggravated stalking is a Class 3 felony; a second or subsequent conviction is a Class 2 felony.

(c) Exemptions.

(1) This Section does not apply to any individual or organization (i) monitoring or attentive to compliance with public or worker safety laws, wage and hour requirements, or other statutory requirements, or (ii) picketing occurring at the workplace that is otherwise lawful and arises out of a bona fide labor dispute including any controversy concerning wages, salaries, hours, working conditions or benefits, including health and welfare, sick leave, insurance, and pension or retirement provisions, the managing or maintenance of collective bargaining agreements, and the terms to be included in those agreements.

(2) This Section does not apply to an exercise of the right of free speech or assembly that is otherwise lawful.

(3) Telecommunications carriers, commercial mobile service providers, and providers of information services, including, but not limited to, Internet service providers and hosting service providers, are not liable under this Section, except for willful and wanton misconduct, by virtue of the transmission, storage, or caching of electronic communications or messages of others or by virtue of the provision of other related telecommunications, commercial mobile services, or information services used by others in violation of this Section.

(d) A defendant who directed the actions of a third party to violate this Section, under the principles of accountability set forth in Article 5 of this Code, is guilty of violating this Section as if the same had been personally done by the defendant, without regard to the mental state of the third party acting at the direction of the defendant.

§ 12-7.5. Cyberstalking. (a) A person commits cyberstalking when he or she engages in a course of conduct using electronic communication directed at a specific person, and he or she knows or should know that would cause a reasonable person to:

(1) fear for his or her safety or the safety of a third person; or
(2) suffer other emotional distress.

(a-3) A person commits cyberstalking when he or she, knowingly and without lawful justification, on at least 2 separate occasions, harasses another person through the use of electronic communication and:
(1) at any time transmits a threat of immediate or future bodily harm, sexual assault, confinement, or restraint and the threat is directed towards that person or a family member of that person; or

(2) places that person or a family member of that person in reasonable apprehension of immediate or future bodily harm, sexual assault, confinement, or restraint; or

(3) at any time knowingly solicits the commission of an act by any person which would be a violation of this Code directed towards that person or a family member of that person.

(a-5) A person commits cyberstalking when he or she, knowingly and without lawful justification, creates and maintains an Internet website or webpage which is accessible to one or more third parties for a period of at least 24 hours, and which contains statements harassing another person and:

(1) which communicates a threat of immediate or future bodily harm, sexual assault, confinement, or restraint, where the threat is directed towards that person or a family member of that person, or

(2) which places that person or a family member of that person in reasonable apprehension of immediate or future bodily harm, sexual assault, confinement, or restraint, or

(3) which knowingly solicits the commission of an act by any person which would be a violation of this Code directed towards that person or a family member of that person.

(b) Sentence. Cyberstalking is a Class 4 felony; a second or subsequent conviction is a Class 3 felony.

(c) For purposes of this Section:

(1) "Course of conduct" means 2 or more acts, including but not limited to acts in which a defendant directly, indirectly, or through third parties, by any action, method, device, or means follows, monitors, observes, surveils, threatens, or communicates to or about, a person, engages in other non-consensual contact, or interferes with or damages a person's property or pet. The incarceration in a penal institution of a person who commits the course of conduct is not a bar to prosecution under this Section.

(2) "Electronic communication" means any transfer of signs, signals, writings, sounds, data, or intelligence of any nature transmitted in whole or in part by a wire, radio, electromagnetic, photoelectric, or photo-optical system. "Electronic communication" includes transmissions through an electronic device including, but not limited to, a telephone, cellular phone, computer, or pager, which communication includes, but is not limited to, e-mail, instant message, text message, or voice mail.

(3) "Emotional distress" means significant mental suffering, anxiety or alarm.

(4) "Harass" means to engage in a knowing and willful course of conduct directed at a specific person that alarms, torments, or terrorizes that person.

(5) "Non-consensual contact" means any contact with the victim that is initiated or continued without the victim's consent, including but not limited to being in the physical presence of the victim; appearing within the sight of the victim; approaching or confronting the victim in a public place or on private property; appearing at the workplace or residence of the victim; entering onto or remaining on property owned, leased, or occupied by the victim; or placing an object on, or delivering an object to, property owned, leased, or occupied by the victim.

(6) "Reasonable person" means a person in the victim's circumstances, with the victim's knowledge of the defendant and the defendant's prior acts.

(7) "Third party" means any person other than the person violating these provisions and the person or persons towards whom the violator's actions are directed.

(d) Telecommunications carriers, commercial mobile service providers, and providers of information services, including, but not limited to, Internet service providers and hosting service providers, are not liable under this Section, except for willful and wanton misconduct, by virtue of the transmission, storage, or caching of electronic communications or messages of others or by virtue of the provision of other related telecommunications, commercial mobile services, or information services used by others in violation of this Section.

(e) A defendant who directed the actions of a third party to violate this Section, under the principles of accountability set forth in Article 5 of this Code, is guilty of violating this Section as if the same had been personally done by the defendant, without regard to the mental state of the third party acting at the direction of the defendant.

Commentary – Stalking Offenses

Stalking. Section 12 – 7.3 criminalizes stalking. the crime is defined as a pattern of conduct by the perpetrator (two or more times) knowingly and without authority (1) following a particular person or communicating a threat on at least two separate occasions, with the intent to place the victim in fear of death, physical harm, sexual assault or confinement or (2) communicating threats of immediate or future death, sexual assault or confinement. Stalking can be done directly by the stalker or indirectly by commanding another person to commit the acts. Police officers have to "tail" suspects in investigations but such conduct is authorized by law. Although the statute does not have the phrase "without lawful authority", the Illinois Supreme Court interpreted the statute to include this requirement so that there would be no question that innocent conduct would not be considered stalking. *People v. Bailey* 167 Ill.2d 210, 657 N.E.2d 953 (1995)

Section 12-7.4 enhances stalking to aggravated stalking when the defendant causes bodily harm to the victim, confines the victim or violates an order of protection or other court order.

Cyberstalking. As our technology has advanced the ability of stalkers to harass victims by use of technology has increased – cell phones, texting, fax, e-mails and voice mail can all be used to harass victims. Section 12-7.5 is the offense of cyberstalking (1) using electronic communication to knowingly engage in a course of conduct directed to a specific victim that would cause that victim to fear for her own safety or the safety of another or cause emotional distress to the victim, or (2) using electronic communication to knowingly harass a specific victim and send a threat of immediate or future bodily harm, sexual assault or confinement or cause the victim or victim's family member fear of immediate or future harm or (3) soliciting another person to use electronic communication to do the harassment. Setting up a web page and leaving it in place for 24 hours to harass a victim is cyberstalking.

In *People v. Sucic* 401 Ill.App.3d 492, 928 N.E.2d 1231(Ill. App. Ct. 1st Dist. 2010), the defendant asked the victim to marry him but she broke off the relationship. On two separate occasions he came to her apartment to force interaction between them. On two separate occasions he sent threatening e-mails to her suggesting that she either marry him or he would kill her or see that she was sent to prison. On eight occasions he left voice mails on her telephone answering system to the same effect. His convictions for stalking and cyberstalking were affirmed. The court noted that there was no specific time period required for the defendant to remain at the victim's apartment to constitute surveillance. The defendant's use of e-mail and voice mail was more than adequate to meet the requirement that his harassment be done by electronic communication.

§ 12-7.6. Cross burning. (a) A person commits cross burning when he or she, with the intent to intimidate any other person or group of persons, burns or causes to be burned a cross.

(b) Sentence. Cross burning is a Class A misdemeanor for a first offense and a Class 4 felony for a second or subsequent offense.

(c) For the purposes of this Section, a person acts with the "intent to intimidate" when he or she intentionally places or attempts to place another person in fear of physical injury or fear of damage to that other person's property.

§ 12-9. Threatening public officials. (a) A person commits threatening a public official when:

(1) that person knowingly delivers or conveys, directly or indirectly, to a public official by any means a communication:

(i) containing a threat that would place the public official or a member of his or her immediate family in reasonable apprehension of immediate or future bodily harm, sexual assault, confinement, or restraint; or

(ii) containing a threat that would place the public official or a member of his or her

immediate family in reasonable apprehension that damage will occur to property in the custody, care, or control of the public official or his or her immediate family; and
(2) the threat was conveyed because of the performance or nonperformance of some public duty, because of hostility of the person making the threat toward the status or position of the public official, or because of any other factor related to the official's public existence.

(a-5) For purposes of a threat to a sworn law enforcement officer, the threat must contain specific facts indicative of a unique threat to the person, family or property of the officer and not a generalized threat of harm.

(b) For purposes of this Section:

(1) "Public official" means a person who is elected to office in accordance with a statute or who is appointed to an office which is established, and the qualifications and duties of which are prescribed, by statute, to discharge a public duty for the State or any of its political subdivisions or in the case of an elective office any person who has filed the required documents for nomination or election to such office. "Public official" includes a duly appointed assistant State's Attorney, assistant Attorney General, or Appellate Prosecutor, and a sworn law enforcement or peace officer.

(2) "Immediate family" means a public official's spouse or child or children.

(c) Threatening a public official is a Class 3 felony for a first offense and a Class 2 felony for a second or subsequent offense.

Subdivision 20. Mutilation

§ 12-10.2. Tongue splitting. (a) In this Section, "tongue splitting" means the cutting of a human tongue into 2 or more parts.

(b) A person may not knowingly perform tongue splitting on another person unless the person performing the tongue splitting is licensed to practice medicine in all its branches under the Medical Practice Act of 1987 or licensed under the Illinois Dental Practice Act.
(c) Sentence. Tongue splitting performed in violation of this Section is a Class A misdemeanor for a first offense and a Class 4 felony for a second or subsequent offense.

§ 12-10.3. False representation to a tattoo or body piercing business as the parent or legal guardian of a minor. (a) A person, other than the parent or legal guardian of a minor, commits the offense of false representation to a tattoo or body piercing business as the parent or legal guardian of a minor when he or she falsely represents himself or herself as the parent or legal guardian of the minor to an owner or employee of a tattoo or body piercing business for the purpose of:

(1) accompanying the minor to a business that provides tattooing as required under Section 12-10 of this Code (tattooing body of minor);

(2) accompanying the minor to a business that provides body piercing as required under Section 12-10.1 of this Code (piercing the body of a minor); or

(3) furnishing the written consent required under Section 12-10.1 of this Code (piercing the body of a minor).

(b) Sentence. False representation to a tattoo or body piercing business as the parent or legal guardian of a minor is a Class C misdemeanor.

§ 12-18.1. Civil Liability. [Omitted.]

§ 12-20. Sale of body parts. (a) Except as provided in subsection (b), any person who knowingly buys or sells, or offers to buy or sell, a human body or any part of a human body, is guilty of a Class A misdemeanor for the first conviction and a Class 4 felony for subsequent convictions.

(b) This Section does not prohibit:

(1) An anatomical gift made in accordance with the Illinois Anatomical Gift Act.

(2) (Blank).

(3) Reimbursement of actual expenses incurred by a living person in donating an organ, tissue or other body part or fluid for transplantation, implantation, infusion, injection, or other medical or scientific purpose, including medical costs, loss of income, and travel expenses.

(4) Payments provided under a plan of insurance or other health care coverage.

(5) Reimbursement of reasonable costs associated with the removal, storage or transportation of a human body or part thereof donated for medical or scientific purposes.

(6) Purchase or sale of blood, plasma, blood products or derivatives, other body fluids, or human hair.

(7) Purchase or sale of drugs, reagents or other substances made from human bodies or body parts, for use in medical or scientific research, treatment or diagnosis.

§ 12-20.5. Dismembering a human body. (a) A person commits dismembering a human body when he or she knowingly dismembers, severs, separates, dissects, or mutilates any body part of a deceased's body.

(b) This Section does not apply to:
(1) an anatomical gift made in accordance with the Illinois Anatomical Gift Act;

(2) (blank);

(3) the purchase or sale of drugs, reagents, or other substances made from human body parts, for the use in medical or scientific research, treatment, or diagnosis;

(4) persons employed by a county medical examiner's office or coroner's office acting within the scope of their employment while performing an autopsy;

(5) the acts of a licensed funeral director or embalmer while performing acts authorized by the Funeral Directors and Embalmers Licensing Code;

(6) the acts of emergency medical personnel or physicians performed in good faith and according to the usual and customary standards of medical practice in an attempt to resuscitate a life; or

(7) physicians licensed to practice medicine in all of its branches or holding a visiting professor, physician, or resident permit under the Medical Practice Act of 1987, performing acts in accordance with usual and customary standards of medical practice, or a currently enrolled student in an accredited medical school in furtherance of his or her education at the accredited medical school.

(c) It is not a defense to a violation of this Section that the decedent died due to natural, accidental, or suicidal causes.

(d) Sentence. Dismembering a human body is a Class X felony.

§ 12-21.6-5. Parent or guardian leaving custody or control of child with child sex offender. (a) For the purposes of this Section,

"minor" means a person under 18 years of age; and

"child sex offender" means a sex offender who is required to register under the Sex Offender Registration Act and is a child sex offender as defined in Sections 11-9.3 and 11-9.4 of this Code.

(b) It is unlawful for a parent or guardian of a minor to knowingly leave that minor in the custody or control of a child sex offender, or allow the child sex offender unsupervised access to the minor.

(c) This Section does not apply to leaving the minor in the custody or control of, or allowing unsupervised access to the minor by:

(1) a child sex offender who is the parent of the minor;

(2) a person convicted of a violation of subsection (c) of Section 12-15 of this Code; or

(3) a child sex offender who is married to and living in the same household with the parent or guardian of the minor. This subsection (c) shall not be construed to allow a child sex offender to knowingly reside within 500 feet of the minor victim of the sex offense if prohibited by subsection (b-6) of Section 11-9.4 of this Code.

(d) Sentence. A person who violates this Section is guilty of a Class A misdemeanor.

(e) Nothing in this Section shall prohibit the filing of a petition or the instituting of any proceeding under Article II of the Juvenile Court Act of 1987 relating to abused minors.

§ 12-30. Violation of an order of protection. (a) A person commits violation of an order of protection if:

(1) He or she commits an act which was prohibited by a court or fails to commit an act which was ordered by a court in violation of:

(i) a remedy in a valid order of protection authorized under paragraphs (1), (2), (3), (14), or (14.5) of subsection (b) of Section 214 of the Illinois Domestic Violence Act of 1986,

(ii) a remedy, which is substantially similar to the remedies authorized under paragraphs (1), (2), (3), (14) or (14.5) of subsection (b) of Section 214 of the Illinois Domestic Violence Act of 1986, in a valid order of protection, which is authorized under the laws of another state, tribe or United States territory,

(iii) any other remedy when the act constitutes a crime against the protected parties as the term protected parties is defined in Section 112A-4 of the Code of Criminal Procedure of 1963; and

(2) Such violation occurs after the offender has been served notice of the contents of the order, pursuant to the Illinois Domestic Violence Act of 1986 or any substantially similar statute of another state, tribe or United States territory, or otherwise has acquired actual knowledge of the contents of the order.

An order of protection issued by a state, tribal or territorial court related to domestic or family violence shall be deemed valid if the issuing court had jurisdiction over the parties and matter under the law of the state, tribe or territory. There shall be a presumption of validity where an order is certified and appears authentic on its face.

(a-5) Failure to provide reasonable notice and opportunity to be heard shall be an affirmative defense to any charge or process filed seeking enforcement of a foreign order of protection.

(b) For purposes of this Section, an "order of protection" may have been issued in a criminal or civil proceeding.

(c) Nothing in this Section shall be construed to diminish the inherent authority of the courts to enforce their lawful orders through civil or criminal contempt proceedings.

(d) Violation of an order of protection under subsection (a) of this Section is a Class A misdemeanor. Violation of an order of protection under subsection (a) of this Section is a Class 4 felony if the defendant has any prior conviction under this Code for domestic battery (Section 12-3.2) or violation of an order of protection (Section 12-30). Violation of an order of protection is a Class 4 felony if the defendant has any prior conviction under this Code for first degree murder (Section 9-1), attempt to commit first degree murder (Section 8-4), aggravated domestic battery (Section 12-3.3), aggravated battery (Section 12-4), heinous battery (Section 12-4.1), aggravated battery with a firearm (Section 12-4.2), aggravated battery of a child (Section 12-4.3), aggravated battery of an unborn child (Section 12-4.4), aggravated battery of a senior citizen (Section 12-4.6), stalking (Section 12-7.3), aggravated stalking (Section 12-7.4), criminal sexual assault

(Section 11-1.20 or 12-13), aggravated criminal sexual assault (Section 11-1.30 or 12-14), kidnapping (Section 10-1), aggravated kidnapping (Section 10-2), predatory criminal sexual assault of a child (Section 11-1.40 or 12-14.1), aggravated criminal sexual abuse (Section 11-1.60 or 12-16), unlawful restraint (Section 10-3), aggravated unlawful restraint (Section 10-3.1), aggravated arson (Section 20-1.1), or aggravated discharge of a firearm (Section 24-1.2), when any of these offenses have been committed against a family or household member as defined in Section 112A-3 of the Code of Criminal Procedure of 1963. The court shall impose a minimum penalty of 24 hours imprisonment for defendant's second or subsequent violation of any order of protection; unless the court explicitly finds that an increased penalty or such period of imprisonment would be manifestly unjust. In addition to any other penalties, the court may order the defendant to pay a fine as authorized under Section 5-9-1 of the Unified Code of Corrections or to make restitution to the victim under Section 5-5-6 of the Unified Code of Corrections. In addition to any other penalties, including those imposed by Section 5-9-1.5 of the Unified Code of Corrections, the court shall impose an additional fine of $ 20 as authorized by Section 5-9-1.11 of the Unified Code of Corrections upon any person convicted of or placed on supervision for a violation of this Section. The additional fine shall be imposed for each violation of this Section.

(e) The limitations placed on law enforcement liability by Section 305 of the Illinois Domestic Violence Act of 1986 apply to actions taken under this Section.

(f) A defendant who directed the actions of a third party to violate this Section, under the principles of accountability set forth in Article 5 of this Code, is guilty of violating this Section as if the same had been personally done by the defendant, without regard to the mental state of the third party acting at the direction of the defendant.

§ 12-32. Ritual mutilation. (a) A person commits ritual mutilation when he or she knowingly mutilates, dismembers or tortures another person as part of a ceremony, rite, initiation, observance, performance or practice, and the victim did not consent or under such circumstances that the defendant knew or should have known that the victim was unable to render effective consent.

(b) Ritual mutilation does not include the practice of male circumcision or a ceremony, rite, initiation, observance, or performance related thereto.

(c) Sentence. Ritual mutilation is a Class 2 felony.

§ 12-33. Ritualized abuse of a child. (a) A person commits ritualized abuse of a child when he or she knowingly commits any of the following acts with, upon, or in the presence of a child as part of a ceremony, rite or any similar observance:

(1) actually or in simulation, tortures, mutilates, or sacrifices any warm-blooded animal or human being;

(2) forces ingestion, injection or other application of any narcotic, drug, hallucinogen or an aesthetic for the purpose of dulling sensitivity, cognition, recollection of, or resistance to any criminal activity;

(3) forces ingestion, or external application, of human or animal urine, feces, flesh, blood, bones, body secretions, no prescribed drugs or chemical compounds;

(4) involves the child in a mock, unauthorized or unlawful marriage ceremony with another person or representation of any force or deity, followed by sexual contact with the child;

(5) places a living child into a coffin or open grave containing a human corpse or remains;

(6) threatens death or serious harm to a child, his or her parents, family, pets, or friends that instills a well-founded fear in the child that the threat will be carried out; or

(7) unlawfully dissects, mutilates, or incinerates a human corpse.

(b) The provisions of this Section shall not be construed to apply to:

(1) lawful agricultural, animal husbandry, food preparation, or wild game hunting and fishing practices and specifically the branding or identification of livestock;

(2) the lawful medical practice of male circumcision or any ceremony related to male circumcision;

(3) any state or federally approved, licensed, or funded research project; or

(4) the ingestion of animal flesh or blood in the performance of a religious service or ceremony.

(b-5) For the purposes of this Section, "child" means any person under 18 years of age.

(c) Ritualized abuse of a child is a Class 1 felony for a first offense. A second or subsequent conviction for ritualized abuse of a child is a Class X felony for which an offender who has attained the age of 18 years at the time of the commission of the offense may be sentenced to a term of natural life imprisonment and an offender under the age of 18 years at the time of the commission of the offense shall be sentenced under Section 5-4.5-105 of the Unified Code of Corrections.

(d) (Blank).

§ 12-34. Female genital mutilation. (a) Except as otherwise permitted in subsection (b), whoever knowingly circumcises, excises, or infibulates, in whole or in part, the labia majora, labia minora, or clitoris of another commits female genital mutilation. Consent to the procedure by a minor on whom it is performed or by the minor's parent or guardian is not a defense to a violation of this Section.

(b) A surgical procedure is not a violation of subsection (a) if the procedure is performed by a physician licensed to practice medicine in all its branches and:

(1) is necessary to the health of the person on whom it is performed; or
(2) is performed on a person who is in labor or who has just given birth and is performed for medical purposes connected with that labor or birth.

(c) Sentence. Female genital mutilation is a Class X felony.

Subdivision 25. Other Harm Offenses

§ 12-34.5. Inducement to commit suicide. (a) A person commits inducement to commit suicide when he or she does either of the following:

(1) Knowingly coerces another to commit suicide and the other person commits or attempts to commit suicide as a direct result of the coercion, and he or she exercises substantial control over the other person through (i) control of the other person's physical location or circumstances; (ii) use of psychological pressure; or (iii) use of actual or ostensible religious, political, social, philosophical or other principles.

(2) With knowledge that another person intends to commit or attempt to commit suicide, intentionally (i) offers and provides the physical means by which another person commits or attempts to commit suicide, or (ii) participates in a physical act by which another person commits or attempts to commit suicide.

For the purposes of this Section, "attempts to commit suicide" means any act done with the intent to commit suicide and which constitutes a substantial step toward commission of suicide.

(b) Sentence. Inducement to commit suicide under paragraph (a)(1) when the other person commits suicide as a direct result of the coercion is a Class 2 felony. Inducement to commit suicide under paragraph (a)(2) when the other person commits suicide as a direct result of the assistance provided is a Class 4 felony. Inducement to commit suicide under paragraph (a)(1) when the other person attempts to commit suicide as a direct result of the coercion is a Class 3 felony. Inducement to commit suicide under paragraph (a)(2) when the other person attempts to commit suicide as a direct result of the assistance provided is a Class A misdemeanor.

(c) The lawful compliance or a good-faith attempt at lawful compliance with the Illinois Living Will Act, the Health Care Surrogate Act, or the Powers of Attorney for Health Care Law is not inducement to commit suicide under paragraph (a)(2) of this Section.

§ 12-35. Sexual conduct or sexual contact with an animal. (a) A person may not knowingly engage in any sexual conduct or sexual contact with an animal.

(b) A person may not knowingly cause, aid, or abet another person to engage in any sexual conduct or sexual contact with an animal.

(c) A person may not knowingly permit any sexual conduct or sexual contact with an animal to be conducted on any premises under his or her charge or control.

(d) A person may not knowingly engage in, promote, aid, or abet any activity involving any sexual conduct or sexual contact with an animal for a commercial or recreational purpose.

(e) Sentence. A person who violates this Section is guilty of a Class 4 felony. A person who violates this Section in the presence of a person under 18 years of age or causes the animal serious physical injury or death is guilty of a Class 3 felony.
(f) In addition to the penalty imposed in subsection (e), the court may order that the defendant do any of the following:

(1) Not harbor animals or reside in any household where animals are present for a reasonable period of time or permanently, if necessary.

(2) Relinquish and permanently forfeit all animals residing in the household to a recognized or duly organized animal shelter or humane society.
(3) Undergo a psychological evaluation and counseling at defendant's expense.

(4) Reimburse the animal shelter or humane society for any reasonable costs incurred for the care and maintenance of the animal involved in the sexual conduct or sexual contact in addition to any animals relinquished to the animal shelter or humane society.

(g) Nothing in this Section shall be construed to prohibit accepted animal husbandry practices or accepted veterinary medical practices by a licensed veterinarian or certified veterinary technician.

(h) If the court has reasonable grounds to believe that a violation of this Section has occurred, the court may order the seizure of all animals involved in the alleged violation as a condition of bond of a person charged with a violation of this Section.

(i) In this Section:

"Animal" means every creature, either alive or dead, other than a human being.

"Sexual conduct" means any knowing touching or fondling by a person, either directly or through clothing, of the sex organs or anus of an animal or any transfer or transmission of semen by the person upon any part of the animal, for the purpose of sexual gratification or arousal of the person.

"Sexual contact" means any contact, however slight, between the sex organ or anus of a person and the sex organ, mouth, or anus of an animal, or any intrusion, however slight, of any part of the body of the person into the sex organ or anus of an animal, for the purpose of sexual gratification or arousal of the person. Evidence of emission of semen is not required to prove sexual contact.

§ 12-36. Possession of unsterilized or vicious dogs by felons prohibited. (a) For a period of 10 years commencing upon the release of a person from incarceration, it is unlawful for a person convicted of a forcible felony, a felony violation of the Humane Care for Animals Act, a felony violation of Section 26-5 of this Code, a felony violation of Article 24 of this Code, a felony violation of Class 3 or higher of the Illinois Controlled Substances Act, a felony violation of Class 3 or higher of the Cannabis Control Act, or a felony violation of Class 2or higher of the Methamphetamine Control and Community Protection Act, to knowingly own, possess, have custody of, or reside in a residence with, either:

(1) an unspayed or unneutered dog or puppy older than 12 weeks of age; or

(2) irrespective of whether the dog has been spayed or neutered, any dog that has been determined to be a vicious dog under Section 15 of the Animal Control Act.

(b) Any dog owned, possessed by, or in the custody of a person convicted of a felony, as described in subsection (a), must be microchipped for permanent identification.

(c) Sentence. A person who violates this Section is guilty of a Class A misdemeanor.

(d) It is an affirmative defense to prosecution under this Section that the dog in question is neutered or spayed, or that the dog in question was neutered or spayed within 7 days of the defendant being charged with a violation of this Section. Medical records from, or the certificate of, a doctor of veterinary medicine licensed to practice in the State of Illinois who has personally examined or operated upon the dog, unambiguously indicating whether the dog in question has been spayed or neutered, shall be prima facie true and correct, and shall be sufficient evidence of whether the dog in question has been spayed or neutered.

This subsection (d) is not applicable to any dog that has been determined to be a vicious dog under Section 15 of the Animal Control Act.

§ 12-37. Possession and sale of caustic and noxious substances. (a) Except as provided in subsection (b), it is unlawful for any person knowingly to have in his or her possession or to carry about any of the substances which are regulated by Title 16 CFR Section 1500.129 of the Federal Caustic Poison Act and are required to contain the words "causes severe burns" as the affirmative statement of principal hazard on its label.

(b) Provided that the product is not used to threaten, intimidate, injure, or cause distress to another, the restrictions of subsection (a) do not apply to:

(1) persons while engaged in the legitimate commercial manufacture, distribution, storage, or use of the specified substances;

(2) persons while engaged in legitimate scientific or medical research, study, teaching or treatment involving the use of such substances, including without limitation physicians, pharmacists, scientists, teachers, students, and employees of regularly established laboratories, manufacturing and wholesale pharmacies, retail pharmacies, medical treatment facilities, schools, colleges, and universities;

(3) persons who have procured any of the specified substances for medicinal purposes upon a prescription of a physician licensed to practice medicine in all its branches under the Medical Practice Act of 1987;

(4) commercial or consumer products that contain any of the specified substances found in subsection (a) including, but not limited to, batteries;
(5) production agriculture as defined in Section 3-5 of the Use Tax Act;

(6) persons while engaged in the possession or transportation, or both, of a commercial product containing any of the substances specified in subsection (a) for retail sale;

(7) persons while engaged in the possession, transportation, or use, unrelated to a retail sale, of any of the substances specified in subsection (a); or

(8) persons engaged in the possession, transportation, or use of a commercial product containing any of the substances specified in subsection (a).

(c) Sentence. A violation of this Section is a Class 4 felony.

(d) The regulation of the possession and carrying of caustic and noxious substances under this Section is an exclusive power and function of the State. A home rule unit may not regulate the possession and carrying of caustic and noxious substances and any ordinance or local law contrary to this Section is declared void. This is a denial and limitation of home rule powers and functions under subsection (h) of Section 6 of Article VII of the Illinois Constitution.

§ 12-38. Restrictions on purchase or acquisition of corrosive or caustic acid.

(a) A person seeking to purchase a substance which is regulated by Title 16 CFR Section 1500.129 of the Federal Caustic Poison Act and is required to contain the words "causes severe burns" as the affirmative statement of principal hazard on its label, must prior to taking possession:
(1) provide a valid driver's license or other government-issued identification showing the person's name, date of birth, and photograph; and

(2) sign a log documenting the name and address of the person, date and time of the transaction, and the brand, product name and net weight of the item.

(b) Exemption. The requirements of subsection (a) do not apply to batteries.
(c) Rules and Regulations. The Illinois Department of State Police shall have the authority to promulgate rules for the implementation and enforcement of this Section.

(d) Sentence. Any violation of this Section is a business offense for which a fine not exceeding $150 for the first violation, $500 for the second violation, or $1,500 for the third and subsequent violations within a 12-month period shall be imposed.
(e) Preemption. The regulation of the purchase or acquisition, or both, of a caustic or corrosive substance and any registry regarding the sale or possession, or both, of a caustic or corrosive substance is an exclusive power and function of the State. A home rule unit may not regulate the purchase or acquisition of caustic or corrosive substances and any ordinance or local law contrary to this Section is declared void. This is a denial and limitation of home rule powers and functions under subsection (h) of Section 6 of Article VII of the Illinois Constitution.

Article 12A – Violent Video Games
720 ILCS 5/12A-1 *et seq.*

Article 12B– Sexually Explicit Video Games
720 ILCS 5/12B-1 *et seq.*

[Author's Note: articles 12 and 12A were declared unconstitutional in *Entertainment Software Assn. v. Blagojevich* 404 F.Supp.2d 1051 (U. S. Dist. Ct. N. Dist. Ill. 2005) and are omitted.]

Article 12C – Harms to Children
720 ILCS 5/12C *et seq.*

§12C-5. Endangering the life or health of a child. (a) A person commits endangering the life or health of a child when he or she knowingly:

(1) causes or permits the life or health of a child under the age of 18 to be endangered; or

(2) causes or permits a child to be placed in circumstances that endanger the child's life or health. It is not a violation of this Section for a person to relinquish a child in accordance with the Abandoned Newborn Infant Protection Act.

(b) A trier of fact may infer that a child 6 years of age or younger is unattended if that child is left in a motor vehicle for more than 10 minutes.

(c) "Unattended" means either: (i) not accompanied by a person 14 years of age or older; or (ii) if accompanied by a person 14 years of age or older, out of sight of that person.

(d) Sentence. A violation of this Section is a Class A misdemeanor. A second or subsequent violation of this Section is a Class 3 felony. A violation of this Section that is a proximate cause of the death of the child is a Class 3 felony for which a person, if sentenced to a term of imprisonment, shall be sentenced to a term of not less than 2 years and not more than 10 years. A parent, who is found to be in violation of this Section with respect to his or her child, may be sentenced to probation for this offense pursuant to Section 12C-15.

§ 12C-10. Child Abandonment. (a) A person commits the offense of child abandonment when he or she, as a parent, guardian, or other person having physical custody or control of a child, without regard for the mental or physical health, safety, or welfare of that child, knowingly leaves that child who is under the age of13 without supervision by a responsible person over the age of 14 for a period of 24 hours or more, except that a person does not commit the offense of child abandonment when he or she relinquishes a child in accordance with the Abandoned Newborn Infant Protection Act.

(b) For the purposes of determining whether the child was left without regard for the mental or physical health, safety, or welfare of that child, the trier of fact shall consider the following factors:

(1) the age of the child;

(2) the number of children left at the location;

(3) special needs of the child, including whether the child is a person with a physical or mental disability, or otherwise in need of ongoing prescribed medical treatment such as periodic doses of insulin or other medications;

(4) the duration of time in which the child was left without supervision;

(5) the condition and location of the place where the child was left without supervision;

(6) the time of day or night when the child was left without supervision;

(7) the weather conditions, including whether the child was left in a location with adequate protection from the natural elements such as adequate heat or light;

(8) the location of the parent, guardian, or other person having physical custody or control of the child at the time the child was left without supervision, the physical distance the child was from the parent, guardian, or other person having physical custody or control of the child at the time the child was without supervision;

(9) whether the child's movement was restricted, or the child was otherwise locked within a room or other structure;

(10) whether the child was given a phone number of a person or location to call in the event of an emergency and whether the child

was capable of making an emergency call;

(11) whether there was food and other provision left for the child;

(12) whether any of the conduct is attributable to economic hardship or illness and the parent, guardian or other person having physical custody or control of the child made a good faith effort to provide for the health and safety of the child;

(13) the age and physical and mental capabilities of the person or persons who provided supervision for the child;

(14) any other factor that would endanger the health or safety of that particular child;

(15) whether the child was left under the supervision of another person.

(d) Child abandonment is a Class 4 felony. A second or subsequent offense after a prior conviction is a Class 3 felony.

§12C-15. Child abandonment or endangerment; probation. (a) Whenever a parent of a child as determined by the court on the facts before it, pleads guilty to or is found guilty of, with respect to his or her child, child abandonment under Section 12C-10 of this Article or endangering the life or health of a child under Section 12C-5 of this Article, the court may, without entering a judgment of guilt and with the consent of the person, defer further proceedings and place the person upon probation upon the reasonable terms and conditions as the court may require. At least one term of the probation shall require the person to cooperate with the Department of Children and Family Services at the times and in the programs that the Department of Children and Family Services may require.

(b) Upon fulfillment of the terms and conditions imposed under subsection (a), the court shall discharge the person and dismiss the proceedings. Discharge and dismissal under this Section shall be without court adjudication of guilt and shall not be considered a conviction for purposes of disqualification or disabilities imposed by law upon conviction of a crime. However, a record of the disposition shall be reported by the clerk of the circuit court to the Department of State Police under Section 2.1 of the Criminal Identification Act, and the record shall be maintained and provided to any civil authority in connection with a determination of whether the person is an acceptable candidate for the care, custody and supervision of children.

(c) Discharge and dismissal under this Section may occur only once.

(d) Probation under this Section may not be for a period of less than 2 years.
(e) If the child dies of the injuries alleged, this Section shall be inapplicable.

§12C-20. Abandonment of a school bus containing children. (a) A school bus driver commits abandonment of a school bus containing children when he or she knowingly abandons the school bus while it contains any children who are without other adult supervision, except in an emergency where the driver is seeking help or otherwise acting in the best interests of the children.

(b) Sentence. A violation of this Section is a Class A misdemeanor for a first offense, and a Class 4 felony for a second or subsequent offense.

§12C-25. Contributing to the dependency and neglect of a minor. (a) Any parent, legal guardian or person having the custody of a child under the age of 18 years commits contributing to the dependency and neglect of a minor when he or she knowingly:

(1) causes, aids, or encourages such minor to be or to become a dependent and neglected minor;

(2) does acts which directly tend to render any such minor so dependent and neglected; or
(3) fails to do that which will directly tend to prevent such state of dependency and neglect. It is not a violation of this Section for a person to relinquish a child in accordance with the Abandoned Newborn Infant Protection Act.

(b) "Dependent and neglected minor" means any child who, while under the age of 18 years, for any reason is destitute, homeless or abandoned; or dependent upon the public for support; or has not proper parental care or guardianship; or habitually begs or receives alms; or is found living in any house of ill fame or with any vicious or disreputable person; or has a home which by reason of neglect, cruelty or depravity on the part of its parents, guardian or any other person in whose care it may be is an unfit place for such child; and any child who while under the age of 10 years is found begging, peddling or selling any articles or singing or playing any musical instrument for gain upon the street or giving any public entertainments or accompanies or is used in aid of any person so doing.

(c) Sentence. A violation of this Section is a Class A misdemeanor.

(d) The husband or wife of the defendant shall be a competent witness to testify in any case under this Section and to all matters relevant thereto.

§12C-30. Contributing to the delinquency or criminal delinquency of a minor. (a) Contributing to the delinquency of a minor. A person commits contributing to the delinquency of a minor when he or she knowingly:

(1) causes, aids, or encourages a minor to be or to become a delinquent minor; or

(2) does acts which directly tend to render any minor so delinquent.

(b) Contributing to the criminal delinquency of a minor. A person of the age of 21 years and upwards commits contributing to the criminal delinquency of a minor when he or she, with the intent to promote or facilitate the commission of an offense solicits, compels or directs a minor in the commission of the offense that is either: (i) a felony when the minor is under the age of 17 years; or (ii) a misdemeanor when the minor is under the age of 18 years.

(c) "Delinquent minor" means any minor who prior to his or her 17th birthday has violated or attempted to violate, regardless of where the act occurred, any federal or State law or county or municipal ordinance, and any minor who prior to his or her 18th birthday has violated or attempted to violate, regardless of where the act occurred, any federal or State law or county or municipal ordinance classified as a misdemeanor offense.

(d) Sentence.

(1) A violation of subsection (a) is a Class A misdemeanor.

(2) A violation of subsection (b) is:

(i) a Class C misdemeanor if the offense committed is a petty offense or a business offense;

(ii) a Class B misdemeanor if the offense committed is a Class C misdemeanor;

(iii) a Class A misdemeanor if the offense committed is a Class B misdemeanor;

(iv) a Class 4 felony if the offense committed is a Class A misdemeanor;

(v) a Class 3 felony if the offense committed is a Class 4 felony;

(vi) a Class 2 felony if the offense committed is a Class 3 felony;

(vii) a Class 1 felony if the offense committed is a Class 2 felony; and

(viii) a Class X felony if the offense committed is a Class 1 felony or a Class X felony.

(3) A violation of subsection (b) incurs the same penalty as first degree murder if the committed offense is first degree murder.

(e) The husband or wife of the defendant shall be a competent witness to testify in any case under this Section and to all matters relevant thereto.

Sec. 12C-35. Tattooing the body of a minor.(a) A person, other than a person licensed to practice medicine in all its branches, commits tattooing the body of a minor when he or she knowingly or recklessly tattoos or offers to tattoo a person under the age of 18.

(b) A person who is an owner or employee of a business that performs tattooing, other than a person licensed to practice medicine in all its branches, may not permit a person under 18 years of age to enter or remain on the premises where tattooing is being performed unless the person under 18 years of age is accompanied by his or her parent or legal guardian.

(c) "Tattoo" means to insert pigment under the surface of the skin of a human being, by pricking with a needle or otherwise, so as to produce an indelible mark or figure visible through the skin.

(d) Subsection (a) of this Section does not apply to a person under 18 years of age who tattoos or offers to tattoo another person under 18 years of age away from the premises of any business at which tattooing is performed.

(d-5) Subsections (a) and (b) of this Section do not apply to the removal of a tattoo from a person under 18 years of age,who is a victim of a violation of Section 10-9 of this Code or who is or has been a streetgang member as defined in Section 10 of the Illinois Streetgang Terrorism Omnibus Prevention Act, if the removal of the tattoo is performed in an establishment or multi-type establishment which has received a certificate of registration from the Department of Public Health or its agent under the Tattoo and Body Piercing Establishment Registration Act and the removal of the tattoo is performed by the operator or an authorized employee of the operator of the establishment or multi-type establishment. For the purposes of this subsection (d-5), "tattoo" also means the indelible mark or figure visible through the skin created by tattooing.

(e) Sentence. A violation of this Section is a Class A misdemeanor.

§12C-40. Piercing the body of a minor.
(a)(1) A person commits piercing the body of a minor when he or she knowingly or recklessly pierces the body of a person under 18 years of age without written consent of a parent or legal guardian of that person. Before the oral cavity of a person under 18 years of age may be pierced, the written consent form signed by the parent or legal guardian must contain a provision in substantially the following form:

"I understand that the oral piercing of the tongue, lips, cheeks, or any other area of the oral cavity carries serious risk of infection or damage to the mouth and teeth, or both infection and damage to those areas, that could result but is not limited to nerve damage, numbness, and life threatening blood clots.".

A person who pierces the oral cavity of a person under 18 years of age without obtaining a signed written consent form from a parent or legal guardian of the person that includes the provision describing the health risks of body piercing, violates this Section.

(2) A person who is an owner or employed by a business that performs body piercing may not permit a person under 18 years of age to enter or remain on the premises where body piercing is being performed unless the person under 18 years of age is accompanied by his or her parent or legal guardian.

(b) "Pierce" means to make a hole in the body in order to insert or allow the insertion of any ring, hoop, stud, or other object for the purpose of ornamentation of the body. "Piercing" does not include tongue splitting as defined in Section 12-10.2. The term "body" includes the oral cavity.

(c) Exceptions. This Section may not be construed in any way to prohibit any injection, incision, acupuncture, or similar medical or dental procedure performed by a licensed health care professional or other person authorized to perform that procedure or the presence on the premises where that procedure is being performed by a health care professional or other person authorized to perform that procedure of a person under 18 years of age who is not accompanied by a parent or legal guardian. This Section does not prohibit ear piercing. This

Section does not apply to a minor emancipated under the Juvenile Court Act of 1987 or the Emancipation of Minors Act or by marriage. This Section does not apply to a person under 18 years of age who pierces the body or oral cavity of another person under 18 years of age away from the premises of any business at which body piercing or oral cavity piercing is performed.

(d) Sentence. A violation of this Section is a Class A misdemeanor.

§12C-45. Drug induced infliction of harm to a child athlete. (a) A person commits drug induced infliction of harm to a child athlete when he or she knowingly distributes a drug to or encourages the ingestion of a drug by a person under the age of 18 with the intent that the person under the age of 18 ingest the drug for the purpose of a quick weight gain or loss in connection with participation in athletics.

(b) This Section does not apply to care under usual and customary standards of medical practice by a physician licensed to practice medicine in all its branches or to the sale of drugs or products by a retail merchant.

(c) Drug induced infliction of harm to a child athlete is a Class A misdemeanor. A second or subsequent violation is a Class 4 felony.

§12C-50. Hazing. (a) A person commits hazing when he or she knowingly requires the performance of any act by a student or other person in a school, college, university, or other educational institution of this State, for the purpose of induction or admission into any group, organization, or society associated or connected with that institution, if:

(1) the act is not sanctioned or authorized by that educational institution; and

(2) the act results in bodily harm to any person.

(b) Sentence. Hazing is a Class A misdemeanor, except that hazing that results in death or great bodily harm is a Class 4 felony.

§12C-50.1. Failure to report hazing. (a) For purposes of this Section, "school official" includes any and all paid school administrators, teachers, counselors, support staff, and coaches and any and all volunteer coaches employed by a school, college, university, or other educational institution of this State.

(b) A school official commits failure to report hazing when:

(1) while fulfilling his or her official responsibilities as a school official, he or she personally observes an act which is not sanctioned or authorized by that educational institution;

(2) the act results in bodily harm to any person; and

(3) the school official knowingly fails to report the act to supervising educational authorities or, in the event of death or great bodily harm, to law enforcement.

(c) Sentence. Failure to report hazing is a Class B misdemeanor. If the act which the person failed to report resulted in death or great bodily harm, the offense is a Class A misdemeanor.

(d) It is an affirmative defense to a charge of failure to report hazing under this Section that the person who personally observed the act had a reasonable apprehension that timely action to stop the act would result in the imminent infliction of death, great bodily harm, permanent disfigurement, or permanent disability to that person or another in retaliation for reporting.

(e) Nothing in this Section shall be construed to allow prosecution of a person who personally observes the act of hazing and assists with an investigation and any subsequent prosecution of the offender.

§12C-60. Curfew. (a) Curfew offenses.

(1) A minor commits a curfew offense when he or she remains in any public place or on the premises of any establishment during curfew hours.

(2) A parent or guardian of a minor or other person in custody or control of a minor commits a curfew offense when he or she knowingly permits the minor to remain in any public place or on the premises of any establishment during curfew hours.

(b) Curfew defenses. It is a defense to prosecution under subsection (a) that the minor was:

(1) accompanied by the minor's parent or guardian or other person in custody or control of the minor;

(2) on an errand at the direction of the minor's parent or guardian, without any detour or stop;

(3) in a motor vehicle involved in interstate travel;

(4) engaged in an employment activity or going to or returning home from an employment activity, without any detour or stop;

(5) involved in an emergency;

(6) on the sidewalk abutting the minor's residence or abutting the residence of a next-door neighbor if the neighbor did not complain to the police department about the minor's presence;

(7) attending an official school, religious, or other recreational activity supervised by adults and sponsored by a government or governmental agency, a civic organization, or another similar entity that takes responsibility for the minor, or going to or returning home from, without any detour or stop, an official school, religious, or other recreational activity supervised by adults and sponsored by a government or governmental agency, a civic organization, or another similar entity that takes responsibility for the minor;

(8) exercising First Amendment rights protected by the United States Constitution, such as the free exercise of religion, freedom of speech, and the right of assembly; or

(9) married or had been married or is an emancipated minor under the Emancipation of Minors Act.

(c) Enforcement. Before taking any enforcement action under this Section, a law enforcement officer shall ask the apparent offender's age and reason for being in the public place. The officer shall not issue a citation or make an arrest under this Section unless the officer reasonably believes that an offense has occurred and that, based on any response and other circumstances, no defense in subsection (b) is present.

(d) Definitions. In this Section:

(1) "Curfew hours" means:
(A) Between 12:01 a.m. and 6:00 a.m. on Saturday;

(B) Between 12:01 a.m. and 6:00 a.m. on Sunday; and

(C) Between 11:00 p.m. on Sunday to Thursday, inclusive, and 6:00 a.m. on the following day.

(2) "Emergency" means an unforeseen combination of circumstances or the resulting state that calls for immediate action. The term includes, but is not limited to, a fire, a natural disaster, an automobile accident, or any situation requiring immediate action to prevent serious bodily injury or loss of life.

(3) "Establishment" means any privately-owned place of business operated for a profit to which the public is invited, including, but not limited to, any place of amusement or entertainment.

(4) "Guardian" means:

(A) a person who, under court order, is the guardian of the person of a minor; or

(B) a public or private agency with whom a minor has been placed by a court.

(5) "Minor" means any person under 17 years of age.

(6) "Parent" means a person who is:

(A) a natural parent, adoptive parent, or step-parent of another person; or

(B) at least 18 years of age and authorized by a parent or guardian to have the care and custody of a minor.

(7) "Public place" means any place to which the public or a substantial group of the public has access and includes, but is not limited to, streets, highways, and the common areas of schools, hospitals, apartment houses, office buildings, transport facilities, and shops.

(8) "Remain" means to:

(A) linger or stay; or

(B) fail to leave premises when requested to do so by a police officer or the owner, operator, or other person in control of the premises.

(9) "Serious bodily injury" means bodily injury that creates a substantial risk of death or that causes death, serious permanent disfigurement, or protracted loss or impairment of the function of any bodily member or organ.

(e) Sentence. A violation of this Section is a petty offense with a fine of not less than $10 nor more than $500, except that neither a person who has been made a ward of the court under the Juvenile Court Act of 1987, nor that person's legal guardian, shall be subject to any fine. In addition to or instead of the fine imposed by this Section, the court may order a parent, legal guardian, or other person convicted of a violation of subsection (a) of this Section to perform community service as determined by the court, except that the legal guardian of a person who has been made a ward of the court under the Juvenile Court Act of 1987 may not be ordered to perform community service. The dates and times established for the performance of community service by the parent, legal guardian, or other person convicted of a violation of subsection (a) of this Section shall not conflict with the dates and times that the person is employed in his or her regular occupation.

(f) County, municipal and other local boards and bodies authorized to adopt local police laws and regulations under the constitution and laws of this State may exercise legislative or regulatory authority over this subject matter by ordinance or resolution incorporating the substance of this Section or increasing the requirements thereof or otherwise not in conflict with this Section.

§12C-65. Unlawful transfer of a telecommunications device to a minor. (a) A person commits unlawful transfer of a telecommunications device to a minor when he or she gives, sells or otherwise transfers possession of a telecommunications device to a person under 18 years of age with the intent that the device be used to commit any offense under this Code, the Cannabis Control Act, the Illinois Controlled Substances Act, or the Methamphetamine Control and Community Protection Act.

(b) "Telecommunications device" or "device" means a device which is portable or which may be installed in a motor vehicle, boat or other means of transportation, and which is capable of receiving or transmitting speech, data, signals or other information, including but not limited to paging devices, cellular and mobile telephones, and radio transceivers, transmitters and receivers, but not including radios designed to receive only standard AM and FM broadcasts.

(c) Sentence. A violation of this Section is a Class A misdemeanor.

(d) Seizure and forfeiture of property. Any person who commits the offense of unlawful transfer of a telecommunications device to a minor as set forth in this Section is subject to the property forfeiture provisions in Article 124B of the Code of Criminal Procedure of 1963.

§Adoption Compensation Prohibited.
[Omitted in editing.]

Article 14 – Eavesdropping
720 ILCS 5/14-1 *et seq.*

§ 14-1. Definition. (a) Eavesdropping device. An eavesdropping device is any device capable of being used to hear or record oral conversation or intercept, retain, or transcribe electronic communications whether such conversation or electronic communication is conducted in person, by telephone, or by any other means; Provided, however, that this definition shall not include devices used for the restoration of the deaf or hard-of-hearing to normal or partial hearing.

(b) Eavesdropper. An eavesdropper is any person, including law enforcement officers, who is a principal, as defined in this Article, or who operates or participates in the operation of any eavesdropping device contrary to the provisions of this Article.

(c) Principal. A principal is any person who:

(1) Knowingly employs another who illegally uses an eavesdropping device in the course of such employment; or

(2) Knowingly derives any benefit or information from the illegal use of an eavesdropping device by another; or

(3) Directs another to use an eavesdropping device illegally on his behalf.

(d) Conversation. For the purposes of this Article, the term conversation means any oral communication between 2 or more persons regardless of whether one or more of the parties intended their communication to be of a private nature under circumstances justifying that expectation.

(e) Electronic communication. For purposes of this Article, the term electronic communication means any transfer of signs, signals, writing, images, sounds, data, or intelligence of any nature transmitted in whole or part by a wire, radio, pager, computer, electromagnetic, photo electronic or photo optical system, where the sending and receiving parties intend the electronic communication to be private and the interception, recording, or transcription of the electronic communication is accomplished by a device in a surreptitious manner contrary to the provisions of this Article. Electronic communication does not include any communication from a tracking device.

(f) Bait car. For purposes of this Article, the term bait car means any motor vehicle that is not occupied by a law enforcement officer and is used by a law enforcement agency to deter, detect, identify, and assist in the apprehension of an auto theft suspect in the act of stealing a motor vehicle.

§ 14-2. Elements of the offense; affirmative defense. (a) A person commits eavesdropping when he:

(1) Knowingly and intentionally uses an eavesdropping device for the purpose of hearing or recording all or any part of any conversation or intercepts, retains, or transcribes electronic communication unless he does so (A) with the consent of all of the parties to such conversation or electronic communication or (B) in accordance with Article 108A or Article 108B of the "Code of Criminal Procedure of 1963", approved August 14, 1963, as amended [725 ILCS 5/108A-1 et seq. or 725 ILCS 5/108B-1 et seq.]; or

(2) Manufactures, assembles, distributes, or possesses any electronic, mechanical, eavesdropping, or other device knowing that or having reason to know that the design of the device renders it primarily useful for the purpose of the surreptitious hearing or recording of oral conversations or the interception, retention, or transcription of electronic communications and the intended or actual use of the device is contrary to the provisions of this Article; or

(3) Uses or divulges, except as authorized by this Article or by Article 108A or 108B of the "Code of Criminal Procedure of 1963", approved August 14, 1963, as amended [725 ILCS 5/108A-1 et seq. or 725 ILCS 5/108B-1 et

seq.], any information which he knows or reasonably should know was obtained through the use of an eavesdropping device.

(b) It is an affirmative defense to a charge brought under this Article relating to the interception of a privileged communication that the person charged:

1. was a law enforcement officer acting pursuant to an order of interception, entered pursuant to Section 108A-1 or 108B-5 of the Code of Criminal Procedure of 1963 [725 ILCS 5/108A-1 et seq. or 725 ILCS 5/108B-1 et seq.]; and

2. at the time the communication was intercepted, the officer was unaware that the communication was privileged; and

3. stopped the interception within a reasonable time after discovering that the communication was privileged; and

4. did not disclose the contents of the communication.

(c) It is not unlawful for a manufacturer or a supplier of eavesdropping devices, or a provider of wire or electronic communication services, their agents, employees, contractors, or venders to manufacture, assemble, sell, or possess an eavesdropping device within the normal course of their business for purposes not contrary to this Article or for law enforcement officers and employees of the Illinois Department of Corrections to manufacture, assemble, purchase, or possess an eavesdropping device in preparation for or within the course of their official duties.

(d) The interception, recording, or transcription of an electronic communication by an employee of a penal institution is not prohibited under this Act, provided that the interception, recording, or transcription is:

(1) otherwise legally permissible under Illinois law;

(2) conducted with the approval of the penal institution for the purpose of investigating or enforcing a State criminal law or a penal institution rule or regulation with respect to inmates in the institution; and

(3) within the scope of the employee's official duties.

For the purposes of this subsection (d), "penal institution" has the meaning ascribed to it in clause (c)(1) of Section 31A-1.1.

(e) Nothing in this Article shall prohibit any individual, not a law enforcement officer, from recording a law enforcement officer in the performance of his or her duties in a public place or in circumstances in which the officer has no reasonable expectation of privacy. However, an officer may take reasonable action to maintain safety and control, secure crime scenes and accident sites, protect the integrity and confidentiality of investigations, and protect the public safety and order.

§ 14-3. Exemptions. The following activities shall be exempt from the provisions of this Article:

(a) Listening to radio, wireless and television communications of any sort where the same are publicly made;

(b) Hearing conversation when heard by employees of any common carrier by wire incidental to the normal course of their employment in the operation, maintenance or repair of the equipment of such common carrier by wire so long as no information obtained thereby is used or divulged by the hearer;

(c) Any broadcast by radio, television or otherwise whether it be a broadcast or recorded for the purpose of later broadcasts of any function where the public is in attendance and the conversations are overheard incidental to the main purpose for which such broadcasts are then being made;

(d) Recording or listening with the aid of any device to any emergency communication made in the normal course of operations by any federal, state or local law enforcement agency or institutions dealing in emergency services, including, but not limited to, hospitals, clinics, ambulance services, fire fighting agencies, any public utility, emergency repair facility, civilian defense establishment or military installation;

(e) Recording the proceedings of any meeting required to be open by the Open Meetings Act [5 ILCS 120/1 et seq.], as amended;

(f) Recording or listening with the aid of any device to incoming telephone calls of phone lines publicly listed or advertised as consumer "hotlines" by manufacturers or retailers of food and drug products. Such recordings must be destroyed, erased or turned over to local law enforcement authorities within 24 hours from the time of such recording and shall not be otherwise disseminated. Failure on the part of the individual or business operating any such recording or listening device to comply with the requirements of this subsection shall eliminate any civil or criminal immunity conferred upon that individual or business by the operation of this Section;

(g) With prior notification to the State's Attorney of the county in which it is to occur, recording or listening with the aid of any device to any conversation where a law enforcement officer, or any person acting at the direction of law enforcement, is a party to the conversation and has consented to it being intercepted or recorded under circumstances where the use of the device is necessary for the protection of the law enforcement officer or any person acting at the direction of law enforcement, in the course of an investigation of a forcible felony, a felony offense of involuntary servitude, involuntary sexual servitude of a minor, or trafficking in persons for forced labor or services under Section 10-9 of this Code, an offense involving prostitution, solicitation of a sexual act, or pandering, a felony violation of the Illinois Controlled Substances Act [720 ILCS 570/100 et seq.], a felony violation of the Cannabis Control Act [720 ILCS 550/1 et seq.], a felony violation of the Methamphetamine Control and Community Protection Act [720 ILCS 646/1 et seq.], any "streetgang related" or "gang-related" felony as those terms are defined in the Illinois Streetgang Terrorism Omnibus Prevention Act [740 ILCS 147/1 et seq.], or any felony offense involving any weapon listed in paragraphs (1) through (11) of subsection (a) of Section 24-1 of this Code [720 ILCS 5/24-1]. Any recording or evidence derived as the result of this exemption shall be inadmissible in any proceeding, criminal, civil or administrative, except (i) where a party to the conversation suffers great bodily injury or is killed during such conversation, or (ii) when used as direct impeachment of a witness concerning matters contained in the interception or recording. The Director of the Department of State Police shall issue regulations as are necessary concerning the use of devices, retention of tape recordings, and reports regarding their use;

(g-5) With approval of the State's Attorney of the county in which it is to occur, recording or listening with the aid of any device to any conversation where a law enforcement officer, or any person acting at the direction of law enforcement, is a party to the conversation and has consented to it being intercepted or recorded in the course of an investigation of any offense defined in Article 29D of this Code [720 ILCS 5/29D-5 et seq.]. In all such cases, an application for an order approving the previous or continuing use of an eavesdropping device must be made within hours of the commencement of such use. In the absence of such an order, or upon its denial, any continuing use shall immediately terminate. The Director of State Police shall issue rules as are necessary concerning the use of devices, retention of tape recordings, and reports regarding their use.

Any recording or evidence obtained or derived in the course of an investigation of any offense defined in Article 29D of this Code shall, upon motion of the State's Attorney or Attorney General prosecuting any violation of Article 29D, be reviewed in camera with notice to all parties present by the court presiding over the criminal case, and, if ruled by the court to be relevant and otherwise admissible, it shall be admissible at the trial of the criminal case.This subsection (g-5) is inoperative on and after January 1, 2005. No conversations recorded or monitored pursuant to this subsection (g-5) shall be inadmissible in a court of law by virtue of the repeal of this subsection (g-5) on January 1, 2005;

(g-6) With approval of the State's Attorney of the county in which it is to occur, recording or listening with the aid of any device to any conversation where a law enforcement officer, or any person acting at the direction of law enforcement, is a party to the conversation and has consented to it being intercepted or recorded in the course of an investigation of involuntary servitude, involuntary sexual servitude of a minor, trafficking in persons for forced labor or services, child pornography, aggravated child pornography, indecent solicitation of a child, child abduction, luring of a minor, sexual exploitation of a child, predatory criminal sexual assault of a child, aggravated criminal sexual abuse in which the victim of the offense was at the time of the commission of the offense under 18 years of age, criminal sexual abuse by force or threat of force in which the victim of the offense was at the time of the commission of the offense under 18 years of age, or aggravated criminal sexual assault in which the victim of the offense was at the time of the commission of the offense under 18 years of age. In all such cases, an application for an order approving the previous or continuing use of an eavesdropping device must be made within 48 hours of the commencement of such use. In the absence of such an order, or upon its denial, any continuing use shall immediately terminate. The Director of State Police shall issue rules as are necessary concerning the use of devices, retention of recordings, and reports regarding their use. Any recording or evidence obtained or derived in the course of an investigation of involuntary servitude, involuntary sexual servitude of a minor, trafficking in persons for forced labor or services, child pornography, aggravated child pornography, indecent solicitation of a child, child abduction, luring of a minor, sexual exploitation of a child, predatory criminal sexual assault of a child, aggravated criminal sexual abuse in which the victim of the offense was at the time of the commission of the offense under 18 years of age, criminal sexual abuse by force or threat of force in which the victim of the offense was at the time of the commission of the offense under 18 years of age, or aggravated criminal sexual assault in which the victim of the offense was at the time of the commission of the offense under 18 years of age shall, upon motion of the State's Attorney or Attorney General prosecuting any case involving involuntary servitude, involuntary sexual servitude of a minor, trafficking in persons for forced labor or services, child pornography, aggravated child pornography, indecent solicitation of a child, child abduction, luring of a minor, sexual exploitation of a child, predatory criminal sexual assault of a child, aggravated criminal sexual abuse in which the victim of the offense was at the time of the commission of the offense under 18 years of age, criminal sexual abuse by force or threat of force in which the victim of the offense was at the time of the commission of the offense under 18 years of age, or aggravated criminal sexual assault in which the victim of the offense was at the time of the commission of the offense under 18 years of age, be reviewed in camera with notice to all parties present by the court presiding over the criminal case, and, if ruled by the court to be relevant and otherwise admissible, it shall be admissible at the trial of the criminal case. Absent such a ruling, any such recording or evidence shall not be admissible at the trial of the criminal case;

(h) Recordings made simultaneously with the use of an in-car video camera recording of an oral conversation between a uniformed peace officer, who has identified his or her office, and a person in the presence of the peace officer whenever (i) an officer assigned a patrol vehicle is conducting an enforcement stop; or (ii) patrol vehicle emergency lights are activated or would otherwise be activated if not for the need to conceal the presence of law enforcement.

For the purposes of this subsection (h), "enforcement stop" means an action by a law enforcement officer in relation to enforcement and investigation duties, including but not limited to, traffic stops, pedestrian stops, abandoned vehicle contacts, motorist assists, commercial motor vehicle stops, roadside safety checks, requests for identification, or responses to requests for emergency assistance;

(h-5) Recordings of utterances made by a person while in the presence of a uniformed peace officer and while an occupant of a police vehicle including, but not limited to, (i) recordings made simultaneously with the use of an in-car video camera and (ii) recordings made in the presence of the peace officer utilizing video or audio systems, or both, authorized by the law enforcement agency;

(h-10) Recordings made simultaneously with a video camera recording during the use of a taser or similar weapon or device by a peace officer if the weapon or device is equipped with such camera;

(h-15) Recordings made under subsection (h), (h-5), or (h-10) shall be retained by the law enforcement agency that employs the peace officer who made the recordings for a storage period of 90 days, unless the recordings are made as a part of an arrest or the recordings are deemed evidence in any criminal, civil, or administrative proceeding and then the recordings must only be destroyed upon a final disposition and an order from the court. Under no circumstances shall any recording be altered or erased prior to the expiration of the designated storage period. Upon completion of the storage period, the recording medium may be erased and reissued for operational use;

(i) Recording of a conversation made by or at the request of a person, not a law enforcement officer or agent of a law enforcement officer, who is a party to the conversation, under reasonable suspicion that another party to the conversation is committing, is about to commit, or has committed a criminal offense against the person or a member of his or her immediate household, and there is reason to believe that evidence of the criminal offense may be obtained by the recording;

(j) The use of a telephone monitoring device by either (1) a corporation or other business entity engaged in marketing or opinion research or (2) a corporation or other business entity engaged in telephone solicitation, as defined in this subsection, to record or listen to oral telephone solicitation conversations or marketing or opinion research conversations by an employee of the corporation or other business entity when:

(i) the monitoring is used for the purpose of service quality control of marketing or opinion research or telephone solicitation, the education or training of employees or contractors engaged in marketing or opinion research or telephone solicitation, or internal research related to marketing or opinion research or telephone solicitation; and

(ii) the monitoring is used with the consent of at least one person who is an active party to the marketing or opinion research conversation or telephone solicitation conversation being monitored.

No communication or conversation or any part, portion, or aspect of the communication or conversation made, acquired, or obtained, directly or indirectly, under this exemption (j), may be, directly or indirectly, furnished to any law enforcement officer, agency, or official for any purpose or used in any inquiry or investigation, or used, directly or indirectly, in any administrative, judicial, or other proceeding, or divulged to any third party.

When recording or listening authorized by this subsection (j) on telephone lines used for marketing or opinion research or telephone solicitation purposes results in recording or listening to a conversation that does not relate to marketing or opinion research or telephone solicitation; the person recording or listening shall, immediately upon determining that the conversation does not relate to marketing or opinion research or telephone solicitation, terminate the recording or listening and destroy any such recording as soon as is practicable.

Business entities that use a telephone monitoring or telephone recording system pursuant to this exemption (j) shall provide current and prospective employees with notice that the monitoring or recordings may occur during the course of their employment. The notice shall include prominent signage notification within the workplace.

Business entities that use a telephone monitoring or telephone recording system pursuant to this exemption (j) shall provide their employees or agents with access to personal-only telephone lines which may be pay telephones, that are not subject to telephone monitoring or telephone recording.

For the purposes of this subsection (j), "telephone solicitation" means a communication through the use of a telephone by live operators:

(i) soliciting the sale of goods or services;

(ii) receiving orders for the sale of goods or services;

(iii) assisting in the use of goods or services; or

(iv) engaging in the solicitation, administration, or collection of bank or retail credit accounts.

For the purposes of this subsection (j), "marketing or opinion research" means a marketing or opinion research interview conducted by a live telephone interviewer engaged by a corporation or other business entity whose principal business is the design, conduct, and analysis of polls and surveys measuring the opinions, attitudes, and responses of respondents toward products and services, or social or political issues, or both;

(k) Electronic recordings, including but not limited to, a motion picture, videotape, digital, or other visual or audio recording, made of a custodial interrogation of an individual at a police station or other place of detention by a law enforcement officer under Section 5-401.5 of the Juvenile Court Act of 1987 [705 ILCS 405/5-401.5] or Section 103-2.1 of the Code of Criminal Procedure of 1963 [725 ILCS 5/103-2.1];

(l) Recording the interview or statement of any person when the person knows that the interview is being conducted by a law enforcement officer or prosecutor and the interview takes place at a police station that is currently participating in the Custodial Interview Pilot Program established under the Illinois Criminal Justice Information Act [20 ILCS 3930/1 et seq.];

(m) An electronic recording, including but not limited to, a motion picture, videotape, digital, or other visual or audio recording, made of the interior of a school bus while the school bus is being used in the transportation of students to and from school and school-sponsored activities, when the school board has adopted a policy authorizing such recording, notice of such recording policy is included in student handbooks and other documents including the policies of the school, notice of the policy regarding recording is provided to parents of students, and notice of such recording is clearly posted on the door of and inside the school bus.

Recordings made pursuant to this subsection (m) shall be confidential records and may only be used by school officials (or their designees) and law enforcement personnel for investigations, school disciplinary actions and hearings, proceedings under the Juvenile Court Act of 1987, and criminal prosecutions, related to incidents occurring in or around the school bus;

(n) Recording or listening to an audio transmission from a microphone placed by a person under the authority of a law enforcement agency inside a bait car surveillance vehicle while simultaneously capturing a photographic or video image;

(o) The use of an eavesdropping camera or audio device during an ongoing hostage or barricade situation by a law enforcement officer or individual acting on behalf of a law enforcement officer when the use of such device is necessary to protect the safety of the general public, hostages, or law enforcement officers or anyone acting on their behalf; and

(p) (Effective January 1, 2011) Recording or listening with the aid of any device to incoming telephone calls of phone lines publicly listed or advertised as the "CPS Violence Prevention Hotline," but only where the notice of recording is given at the beginning of each call as required by Section 34-21.8 of the School Code [105 ILCS 5/34-21.8]. The recordings may be retained only by the Chicago Police Department or other law enforcement authorities, and shall not be otherwise retained or disseminated.

and

q)(1) With prior request to and verbal approval

of the State's Attorney of the county in which the conversation is anticipated to occur, recording or listening with the aid of an eavesdropping device to a conversation in which a law enforcement officer, or any person acting at the direction of a law enforcement officer, is a party to the conversation and has consented to the conversation being intercepted or recorded in the course of an investigation of a drug offense. The State's Attorney may grant this verbal approval only after determining that reasonable cause exists to believe that a drug offense will be committed by a specified individual or individuals within a designated period of time.

(2) Request for approval. To invoke the exception contained in this subsection (q), a law enforcement officer shall make a written or verbal request for approval to the appropriate State's Attorney. This request for approval shall include whatever information is deemed necessary by the State's Attorney but shall include, at a minimum, the following information about each specified individual whom the law enforcement officer believes will commit a drug offense:

(A) his or her full or partial name, nickname or alias;

(B) a physical description; or

(C) failing either (A) or (B) of this paragraph (2), any other supporting information known to the law enforcement officer at the time of the request that gives rise to reasonable cause to believe the individual will commit a drug offense.

(3) Limitations on verbal approval. Each verbal approval by the State's Attorney under this subsection (q) shall be limited to:

(A) a recording or interception conducted by a specified law enforcement officer or person acting at the direction of a law enforcement officer;

(B) recording or intercepting conversations with the individuals specified in the request for approval, provided that the verbal approval shall be deemed to include the recording or intercepting of conversations with other individuals, unknown to the law enforcement officer at the time of the request for approval, who are acting in conjunction with or as co-conspirators with the individuals specified in the request for approval in the commission of a drug offense;

(C) a reasonable period of time but in no event longer than 24 consecutive hours.

(4) Admissibility of evidence. No part of the contents of any wire, electronic, or oral communication that has been recorded or intercepted as a result of this exception may be received in evidence in any trial, hearing, or other proceeding in or before any court, grand jury, department, officer, agency, regulatory body, legislative committee, or other authority of this State, or a political subdivision of the State, other than in a prosecution of:

(A) a drug offense;

(B) a forcible felony committed directly in the course of the investigation of a drug offense for which verbal approval was given to record or intercept a conversation under this subsection (q); or

(C) any other forcible felony committed while the recording or interception was approved in accordance with this Section (q), but for this specific category of prosecutions, only if the law enforcement officer or person acting at the direction of a law enforcement officer who has consented to the conversation being intercepted or recorded suffers great bodily injury or is killed during the commission of the charged forcible felony.

(5) Compliance with the provisions of this subsection is a prerequisite to the admissibility in evidence of any part of the contents of any wire, electronic or oral communication that has been intercepted as a result of this exception, but nothing in this subsection shall be deemed to prevent a court from otherwise excluding the evidence on any other ground, nor shall anything in this subsection be deemed to prevent a court from independently reviewing the admissibility of the evidence for compliance with the Fourth

Amendment to the U.S. Constitution or with Article I, Section 6 of the Illinois Constitution.

(6) Use of recordings or intercepts unrelated to drug offenses. Whenever any wire, electronic, or oral communication has been recorded or intercepted as a result of this exception that is not related to a drug offense or a forcible felony committed in the course of a drug offense, no part of the contents of the communication and evidence derived from the communication may be received in evidence in any trial, hearing, or other proceeding in or before any court, grand jury, department, officer, agency, regulatory body, legislative committee, or other authority of this State, or a political subdivision of the State, nor may it be publicly disclosed in any way.

(7) Definitions. For the purposes of this subsection (q) only:

"Drug offense" includes and is limited to a felony violation of one of the following: (A) the Illinois Controlled Substances Act, (B) the Cannabis Control Act, and (C) the Methamphetamine Control and Community Protection Act.

"Forcible felony" includes and is limited to those offenses contained in Section 2-8 of the Criminal Code of 1961 as of the effective date of this amendatory Act of the 97th General Assembly, and only as those offenses have been defined by law or judicial interpretation as of that date.

"State's Attorney" includes and is limited to the State's Attorney or an assistant State's Attorney designated by the State's Attorney to provide verbal approval to record or intercept conversations under this subsection (q).

(8) Sunset. This subsection (q) is inoperative on and after January 1, 2015. No conversations intercepted pursuant to this subsection (q), while operative, shall be inadmissible in a court of law by virtue of the inoperability of this subsection

(q) on January 1, 2015.

(r) Electronic recordings, including but not limited to, motion picture, videotape, digital, or other visual or audio recording, made of a lineup under Section 107A-2 of the Code of Criminal Procedure of 1963.

§ 14-3A. Recordings, records, and custody. (a) Any private oral communication intercepted in accordance with subsection (g) of Section 14-3 [720 ILCS 5/14-3] shall, if practicable, be recorded by tape or other comparable method. The recording shall, if practicable, be done in such a way as will protect it from editing or other alteration. During an interception, the interception shall be carried out by a law enforcement officer, and the officer shall keep a signed, written record, including:

(1) The day and hours of interception or recording;

(2) The time and duration of each intercepted communication;

(3) The parties, if known, to each intercepted communication; and

(4) A summary of the contents of each intercepted communication.

(b) Both the written record of the interception or recording and any and all recordings of the interception or recording shall immediately be inventoried and shall be maintained where the chief law enforcement officer of the county in which the interception or recording occurred directs. The written records of the interception or recording conducted under subsection (g) of Section 14-3 [720 ILCS 5/14-3] shall not be destroyed except upon an order of a court of competent jurisdiction and in any event shall be kept for 10 years.

14-3B. Notice of interception or recording. (a) Within a reasonable time, but not later than 60 days after the termination of the investigation for which the interception or recording was conducted, or immediately upon the initiation of criminal proceedings, the person who was the subject of an interception or recording under subsection (g) of Section 14-3 [720 ILCS 5/14-3] shall be served with an inventory that shall include:

(1) Notice to any person who was the subject of the interception or recording;

(2) Notice of any interception or recording if the defendant was arrested or indicted or otherwise charged as a result of the interception of his or her private oral communication;

(3) The date of the interception or recording;

(4) The period of interception or recording; and

(5) Notice of whether during the period of interception or recording devices were or were not used to overhear and record various conversations and whether or not the conversations are recorded.

(b) A court of competent jurisdiction, upon filing of a motion, may in its discretion make available to those persons or their attorneys for inspection those portions of the intercepted communications as the court determines to be in the interest of justice.

§ 14-4. Sentence. (a) Eavesdropping, for a first offense, is a Class 4 felony and, for a second or subsequent offense, is a Class 3 felony.

(b) The eavesdropping of an oral conversation or an electronic communication between any law enforcement officer, State's Attorney, Assistant State's Attorney, the Attorney General, Assistant Attorney General, or a judge, while in the performance of his or her official duties, if not authorized by this Article or proper court order, is a Class 1 felony.

§ 14-5. Evidence inadmissible. Any evidence obtained in violation of this Article is not admissible in any civil or criminal trial, or any administrative or legislative inquiry or proceeding, nor in any grand jury proceedings; provided, however, that so much of the contents of an alleged unlawfully intercepted, overheard or recorded conversation as is clearly relevant, as determined as a matter of law by the court in chambers, to the proof of such allegation may be admitted into evidence in any criminal trial or grand jury proceeding brought against any person charged with violating any provision of this Article.

§ 14-6. Civil remedies to injured parties. (1) Any or all parties to any conversation upon which eavesdropping is practiced contrary to this Article shall be entitled to the following remedies:

(a) To an injunction by the circuit court prohibiting further eavesdropping by the eavesdropper and by or on behalf of his principal, or either;

(b) To all actual damages against the eavesdropper or his principal or both;

(c) To any punitive damages which may be awarded by the court or by a jury;

(d) To all actual damages against any landlord, owner or building operator, or any common carrier by wire who aids, abets, or knowingly permits the eavesdropping concerned;

(e) To any punitive damages which may be awarded by the court or by a jury against any landlord, owner or building operator, or common carrier by wire who aids, abets, or knowingly permits the eavesdropping concerned.

(2) No cause of action shall lie in any court against any common carrier by wire or its officers, agents or employees for providing information, assistance or facilities in accordance with the terms of a court order entered under Article 108A of the Code of Criminal Procedure of 1963 [725 ILCS 5/108A-1 et seq.]

§ 14-7. Common carrier to aid in detection. Subject to regulation by the Illinois Commerce Commission, any common carrier by wire shall, upon request of any subscriber and upon responsible offer to pay the reasonable cost thereof, furnish whatever services may be within its command for the purpose of detecting any eavesdropping involving its wires which are used by said subscriber. All such requests by subscribers shall be kept confidential unless divulgence is authorized in writing by the requesting subscriber.

§ 14-8. Discovery of eavesdropping device by an individual, common carrier, private investigative agency or non-governmental corporation. Any agent, officer or employee of a private investigative agency or non-governmental corporation, or of a common carrier by wire, or any individual, who discovers any physical evidence of an eavesdropping device being used which such person does not know to be a legal eavesdropping device shall, within a reasonable time after such discovery disclose the existence of such eavesdropping device to the State's Attorney of the county where such device was found. The State's Attorney shall within a reasonable time notify the person or persons apparently being eavesdropped upon of the existence of that device if the device is illegal. A violation of this Section is a Business Offense for which a fine shall be imposed not to exceed $ 500.

§ 14-9. Discovery of eavesdropping device by common carrier by wire -- disclosure to subscriber. Any agent, officer or employee of any common carrier by wire who discovers any physical evidence of an eavesdropping device which such person does not know to be a legal eavesdropping device shall, within a reasonable time after such discovery, disclose the existence of the eavesdropping device to the State's Attorney of the County where such device was found. The State's Attorney shall within a reasonable time notify the person or persons apparently being eavesdropped upon of the existence of that device if the device is illegal. A violation of this Section is a Business Offense for which a fine shall be imposed not to exceed $ 500.

Commentary – Eavesdropping

Eavesdropping crime. Section 14-2 defines the crime of eavesdropping. In Illinois, the knowing recording of an audio conversation with an eavesdropping device without consent of all the parties to that conversation, unless otherwise authorized by law, is a crime. In fact, the crime is infrequently prosecuted; however, it is important to understand Illinois Eavesdropping law because the issue of the admissibility of recorded conversations recurs. As broad as the definition of prohibited eavesdropping seems to be, the reach of the statute is marked by exceptions. Section 14-2(b) notes an affirmative defense for police officers who are acting pursuant to an 725 ILCS 5/108A or 5/108B order who inadvertently record privileged conversations of the target of the investigation. If during the overhear, for example, the officer discovers the subject is talking to his attorney, he is to stop the recording and not disclose anything that has been overheard. the exemptions of Section 14-3 are quite broad and cover a variety of instances where recording of conversations routinely occur (jails, undercover investigations with informants who have consented to recording, traffic stops with video cameras, media broadcasts at public events, telephone marketing solicitations or service calls, scanners used to monitor emergency communications of public agencies and more). When the eavesdropping law does apply it can have significant consequences by preventing the admission of the contents into evidence (Section 14 – 5).

Instant messages. In *People v. Gariano* 366 Ill.App.3d 379, 852 N.E.2d 344 (Ill. App. Ct. 1st Dist. 2006), the Court held that no unlawful eavesdropping occurred when an officer pretending to be a 15 year-old boy saved and printed "instant messages" from an internet web service in a chat room with the defendant. The court held that the officer never intended that his chat conversation would be private and therefore it was not within the scope of the eavesdropping law, even if it appeared to fit within the language of the statute. In *People v. Coleman* 227 Ill.2d 426, 882 N.E.2d 1025 (2008), the Illinois Supreme Court approved a "joint investigation" exception to the inadmissibility of evidence obtained by eavesdropping that occurred in violation of Article 14 where the eavesdropping was conducted in cooperation with Federal law enforcement and was valid under federal law. Consent to eavesdropping can be express or implied. In *People v. Ceja* 204 Ill.2d 332, 789 N.E.2d 1228 (2003), the court found no violation of the eavesdropping statute because of implied consent where the defendant and a fellow gang member were in the detention area of a jail, the monitoring devices on the walls were in plain view and a supervising officer told the two men several times to keep quiet because she could hear their conversations through the monitoring devices.

Cell Phones and Speaker Phone Options: In *People v. Armbrust,* 2011 IL App (2d) 100955, the defendant filed a motion in limine to bar a phone call made to his wife threatening to kill her. The defendant's wife put the husband on speakerphone so her friend could hear the conversation. Defendant argued that the speakerphone option turned the cell phone into an eavesdropping device and the trial court agreed, excluding the evidence. On the State's appeal the trial court's ruling was reversed. The Court held that the use of a speakerphone option on a cell phone does not transform the cell phone into an eavesdropping device, instead only increasing the volume of the received sounds - similar to holding the receiver in a way so multiple people could hear. As such a cell phone's ability to transmit and receive sounds is unaltered, nor is the speakerphone a separate eavesdropping device. See also *People v. Jenkins* 2012 IL Lapp. (2d) 091168 (Ill. App. Ct. 2nd Dist. 2011) (unaltered cell phone is not an eavesdropping device and relevant testimony about conversation between two people that is overheard in the natural functioning of a cell phone is admissible.)

Criminal Eavesdropping Statute Held Unconstitutional. In *People v. Clark,* 2014 IL 115776, 6 N.E.3d 154 (Ill. S. Ct. 2014), the criminal provision of the Illinois Eavesdropping statute (720 ILCS 5/14-2(a)(1)) was found unconstitutionally overbroad in violation of the First Amendment. In so holding the court noted:

> If another person overhears what we say, we cannot control to whom that person may repeat what we said. That person may write down what we say and publish it, and this is not a violation of the eavesdropping statute. Yet if that same person records our words with an audio recording device, even if it is not published in any way, a criminal act has been committed. The person taking notes may misquote us or misrepresent what we said, but an audio recording is the best evidence of our words. Yet, the eavesdropping statute bars it. Understandably, many people do not want their voices broadcast to others or on the Internet to be heard around the world. But, to a certain extent this is beyond our control, given the ubiquity of devices like smartphones, with their video and audio recording capabilities and the ability to post such recordings instantly to the Internet. Illinois' privacy statute goes too far in its effort to protect individuals' interest in the privacy of their communications. Indeed, by removing all semblance of privacy from the statute in the 1994 amendments, the legislature has "severed the link between the eavesdropping statute's means and its end." . . . .The statute therefore burdens substantially more speech than is necessary to serve the interests the statute may legitimately serve. Accordingly, the statute does not meet the requirements necessary to satisfy intermediate scrutiny. We hold that section (a)(1)(A) of the eavesdropping statute is overbroad because a substantial number of its applications are unconstitutional, judged in relation to the statute's plainly legitimate sweep.
>
> *People v. Clark* 2014 IL 115776, ¶23. (internal citation omitted)

See also *People v. Melongo*, 2014 IL 114852 (Ill. S. Ct. 2014) where the Court explained further:

> When that policy criminalizes a wide range of innocent conduct, however, it cannot be sustained. The statute criminalizes the recording of conversations that cannot be deemed private: a loud argument on the street, a political debate on a college quad, yelling fans at an athletic event, or any conversation loud enough that the speakers should expect to be heard by others. None of these examples implicate privacy interests, yet the statute makes it a felony to audio record each one. Judged in terms of the legislative purpose of protecting conversational privacy, the statute's scope is simply too broad.
>
> *People v. Melongo, 2014 IL 114852, ¶29,* 6 N.E.3d at 126

The General Assembly replaced the eavesdropping statute. 38 states have one-party consent statutes. In some such statutes there are exemptions for law enforcement to be able to do audio or video recording without a warrant for specified criminal investigations such as crimes of violence, drug crimes, murder for hire or weapons offenses. The new Illinois statute provided exemptions as well. See §14-3 (above).

Part C: Offenses Directed Against Property

Article 15 – Definitions
720 ILCS 5/15-1 *et seq.*

§ 15-1. Property. As used in this Part C, "property" means anything of value. Property includes real estate, money, commercial instruments, admission or transportation tickets, written instruments representing or embodying rights concerning anything of value, labor, or services, or otherwise of value to the owner; things growing on, affixed to, or found on land, or part of or affixed to any building; electricity, gas and water; telecommunications services; birds, animals and fish, which ordinarily are kept in a state of confinement; food and drink; samples, cultures, microorganisms, specimens, records, recordings, documents, blueprints, drawings, maps, and whole or partial copies, descriptions, photographs, computer programs or data, prototypes or models thereof, or any other articles, materials, devices, substances and whole or partial copies, descriptions, photographs, prototypes, or models thereof which constitute, represent, evidence, reflect or record a secret scientific, technical, merchandising, production or management information, design, process, procedure, formula, invention, or improvement.

§ 15-2. Owner. As used in this Part C, "owner" means a person, other than the offender, who has possession of or any other interest in the property involved, even though such interest or possession is unlawful, and without whose consent the offender has no authority to exert control over the property.

§ 15-3. Permanent Deprivation. As used in this Part C, to "permanently deprive" means to:

(a) Defeat all recovery of the property by the owner; or

(b) Deprive the owner permanently of the beneficial use of the property; or

(c) Retain the property with intent to restore it to the owner only if the owner purchases or leases it back, or pays a reward or other compensation for its return; or
(d) Sell, give, pledge, or otherwise transfer any interest in the property or subject it to the claim of a person other than the owner.

§ 15-4. Deception. As used in this Part C, "deception" means knowingly to:

(a) Create or confirm another's impression which is false and which the offender does not believe to be true; or

(b) Fail to correct a false impression which the offender previously has created or confirmed; or
(c) Prevent another from acquiring information pertinent to the disposition of the property involved; or

(d) Sell or otherwise transfer or encumber property, failing to disclose a lien, adverse claim, or other legal impediment to the enjoyment of the property, whether such impediment is or is not valid, or is or is not a matter of official record; or

(e) Promise performance which the offender does not intend to perform or knows will not be performed. Failure to perform standing alone is not evidence that the offender did not intend to perform.

§ 15-5. Threat. As used in this Part C, "threat" means a menace, however communicated, to:

(a) Inflict physical harm on the person threatened or any other person or on property; or

(b) Subject any person to physical confinement or restraint; or

(c) Commit any criminal offense; or

(d) Accuse any person of a criminal offense; or

(e) Expose any person to hatred, contempt or ridicule; or

(f) Harm the credit or business repute of any person; or

(g) Reveal any information sought to be concealed by the person threatened; or
(h) Take action as an official against anyone or anything, or withhold official action, or cause such action or withholding; or

(i) Bring about or continue a strike, boycott or other similar collective action if the property is not demanded or received for the benefit of the group which he purports to represent; or

(j) Testify or provide information or withhold testimony or information with respect to another's legal claim or defense; or

(k) Inflict any other harm which would not benefit the offender.

§ 15-6. Stolen Property. As used in this Part C, "stolen property" means property over which control has been obtained by theft.

§ 15-7. Obtain. As used in this Part C, "obtain" means:

(a) In relation to property, to bring about a transfer of interest or possession, whether to the offender or to another, and

(b) In relation to labor or services, to secure the performance thereof.

§ 15-8. Obtains Control. As used in this Part C, the phrase "obtains or exerts control" over property, includes but is not limited to the taking, carrying away, or the sale, conveyance, or transfer of title to, or interest in, or possession of property.

§ 15-9. Value. As used in this Part C, the "value" of property consisting of any commercial instrument or any written instrument representing or embodying rights concerning anything of value, labor, or services or otherwise of value to the owner shall be:

(a) The "market value" of such instrument if such instrument is negotiable and has a market value; and

(b) The "actual value" of such instrument if such instrument is not negotiable or is otherwise without a market value. For the purpose of establishing such "actual value", the interest of any owner or owners entitled to part or all of the property represented by such instrument, by reason of such instrument, may be shown, even if another "owner" may be named in the complaint, information or indictment.

§ 15-10. Governmental property. As used in this Part C, "governmental property" means funds or other property owned by the State, a unit of local government, or a school district.

Commentary – Property Definitions

Part C of Title III of the criminal code deals with crimes against property. Article 15 contains definitions that apply to all offenses set forth in Part C.

In *People v. Perry* 224 Ill.2d 312, 864 N.E.2d 196 (2007), the defendant had stayed at an Embassy Suites in Lombard, Illinois with his family for three months without payment, he had given a false address and company for billing purposes and fraudulently used a credit card. the question was whether the use of a hotel room for the three month period constituted "property" for purposes of a section of the Theft statute. 720 ILCS 5/16-1(a)(2) (i.e. "theft by deception"). The Illinois Supreme Court noted the application to all Part C offenses including theft, robbery, computer crimes, arson and burglary. It concluded that the common law definition of property as something that could be taken and carried away from the owner was not the intended meaning of the present-day criminal code. The Court held that property was "anything of value" as set forth in Section 15-1. The court also noted that the hotel's loss of revenue for the use of the room over the three month period was a loss that amounted to "permanent deprivation" under Section 15-3.

Article 16 – Theft and Related Offenses
720 ILCS 5/16-1 *et seq.*

§ 16-0.1. Definitions. In this Article, unless the context clearly requires otherwise, the following terms are defined as indicated:

"Access" means to use, instruct, communicate with, store

data in, retrieve or intercept data from, or otherwise utilize

any services of a computer.

"Coin-operated machine" includes any automatic vending machine or any part thereof, parking meter, coin telephone, coin-operated transit turnstile, transit fare box, coin laundry machine, coin dry cleaning machine, amusement machine, music machine, vending machine dispensing goods or services, or money changer.

"Communication device" means any type of instrument, device, machine, or equipment which is capable of transmitting, acquiring, decrypting, or receiving any telephonic, electronic, data, Internet access, audio, video, microwave, or radio transmissions, signals, communications, or services, including the receipt, acquisition, transmission, or decryption of all such communications, transmissions, signals, or services provided by or through any cable television, fiber optic, telephone, satellite, microwave, radio, Internet-based, data transmission, or wireless distribution network, system or facility; or any part, accessory, or component thereof, including any computer circuit, security module, smart card, software, computer chip, electronic mechanism or other component, accessory or part of any communication device which is capable of facilitating the transmission, decryption, acquisition or reception of all such communications, transmissions, signals, or services.

"Communication service" means any service lawfully provided for a charge or compensation to facilitate the lawful origination, transmission, emission, or reception of signs, signals, data, writings, images, and sounds or intelligence of any nature by telephone, including cellular telephones or a wire, wireless, radio, electromagnetic, photo-electronic or photo-optical system; and also any service lawfully provided by any radio, telephone, cable television, fiber optic, satellite, microwave, Internet-based or wireless distribution network, system, facility or technology, including, but not limited to, any and all electronic, data, video, audio, Internet access, telephonic, microwave and radio communications, transmissions, signals and services, and any such communications, transmissions, signals and services lawfully provided directly or indirectly by or through any of those networks, systems, facilities or technologies.

"Communication service provider" means: (1) any person or entity providing any communication service, whether directly or indirectly, as a reseller, including, but not limited to, a cellular, paging or other wireless communications company or other person or entity which, for a fee, supplies the facility, cell site, mobile telephone switching office or other equipment or communication service; (2) any person or entity owning or operating any cable television, fiber optic, satellite, telephone, wireless, microwave, radio, data transmission or Internet-based distribution network, system or facility; and (3) any person or entity providing any communication service directly or indirectly by or through any such distribution system, network or facility.

"Computer" means a device that accepts, processes, stores, retrieves or outputs data, and includes but is not limited to auxiliary storage and telecommunications devices connected to computers.

"Continuing course of conduct" means a series of acts, and the accompanying mental state necessary for the crime in question, irrespective of whether the series of acts are continuous or intermittent.

"Delivery container" means any bakery basket of wire or plastic used to transport or store bread or bakery products, any dairy case of wire or plastic used to transport or store dairy products, and any dolly or cart of 2 or 4 wheels used to transport or store any bakery or dairy product.

"Document-making implement" means any implement, impression, template, computer file, computer disc, electronic device, computer hardware, computer software, instrument, or device that is used to make a real or fictitious or fraudulent personal identification document.

"Financial transaction device" means any of the following:

(1) An electronic funds transfer card.

(2) A credit card.

(3) A debit card.

(4) A point-of-sale card.

(5) Any instrument, device, card, plate, code, account number, personal identification number, or a record or copy of a code, account number, or personal identification number or other means of access to a credit account or deposit account, or a driver's license or State identification card used to access a proprietary account, other than access originated solely by a paper instrument, that can be used alone or in conjunction with another access device, for any of the following purposes:

(A) Obtaining money, cash refund or credit account, credit, goods, services, or any other thing of value.

(B) Certifying or guaranteeing to a person or business the availability to the device holder of funds on deposit to honor a draft or check payable to the order of that person or business.

(C) Providing the device holder access to a deposit account for the purpose of making deposits, withdrawing funds, transferring funds between deposit accounts, obtaining information pertaining to a deposit account, or making an electronic funds transfer.

"Full retail value" means the merchant's stated or advertised price of the merchandise. "Full retail value" includes the aggregate value of property obtained from retail thefts committed by the same person as part of a continuing course of conduct from one or more mercantile establishments in a single transaction or in separate transactions over a period of one year.

"Internet" means an interactive computer service or system or an information service, system, or access software provider that provides or enables computer access by multiple users to a computer server, and includes, but is not limited to, an information service, system, or access software provider that provides access to a network system commonly known as the Internet, or any comparable system or service and also includes, but is not limited to, a World Wide Web page, newsgroup, message board, mailing list, or chat area on any interactive computer service or system or other online service.

"Library card" means a card or plate issued by a library facility for purposes of identifying the person to whom the library card was issued as authorized to borrow library material, subject to all limitations and conditions imposed on the borrowing by the library facility issuing such card.

"Library facility" includes any public library or museum, or any library or museum of an educational, historical or eleemosynary institution, organization or society.

"Library material" includes any book, plate, picture, photograph, engraving, painting, sculpture, statue, artifact, drawing, map, newspaper, pamphlet, broadside, magazine, manuscript, document, letter, microfilm, sound recording, audiovisual material, magnetic or other tape, electronic data processing record or other documentary, written or printed material regardless of physical form or characteristics, or any part thereof, belonging to, or on loan to or otherwise in the custody of a library facility.

"Manufacture or assembly of an unlawful access device" means to make, produce or assemble an unlawful access device or to modify, alter, program or re-program any instrument, device, machine, equipment or software so that it is capable of defeating or circumventing any technology, device or software used by the provider, owner or licensee of a communication service or of any data, audio or video programs or transmissions to protect any such communication, data, audio or video services, programs or transmissions from unauthorized access, acquisition, disclosure, receipt, decryption, communication, transmission or re-transmission.

"Manufacture or assembly of an unlawful communication device" means to make, produce or assemble an unlawful communication or wireless device or to modify, alter, program or reprogram a communication or wireless device to be capable of acquiring, disrupting, receiving, transmitting, decrypting, or facilitating the acquisition, disruption, receipt, transmission or decryption of, a communication service without the express consent or express authorization of the communication service provider, or to knowingly assist others in those activities.

"Master sound recording" means the original physical object on which a given set of sounds were first recorded and which the original object from which all subsequent sound recordings embodying the same set of sounds are directly or indirectly derived.

"Merchandise" means any item of tangible personal property, including motor fuel.

"Merchant" means an owner or operator of any retail mercantile establishment or any agent, employee, lessee, consignee, officer, director, franchisee, or independent contractor of the owner or operator. "Merchant" also means a person who receives from an authorized user of a payment card, or someone the person believes to be an authorized user, a payment card or information from a payment card, or what the person believes to be a payment card or information from a payment card, as the instrument for obtaining, purchasing or receiving goods, services, money, or anything else of value from the person.

"Motor fuel" means a liquid, regardless of its properties, used to propel a vehicle, including gasoline and diesel.

"Online" means the use of any electronic or wireless device to access the Internet.

"Payment card" means a credit card, charge card, debit card, or any other card that is issued to an authorized card user and that allows the user to obtain, purchase, or receive goods, services, money, or anything else of value from a merchant.

"Person with a disability" means a person who suffers from a physical or mental impairment resulting from disease, injury, functional disorder or congenital condition that impairs the individual's mental or physical ability to independently manage his or her property or financial resources, or both.

"Personal identification document" means a birth certificate, a driver's license, a State identification card, a public, government, or private employment identification card, a social security card, a firearm owner's identification card, a credit card, a debit card, or a passport issued to or on behalf of a person other than the offender, or any document made or issued, or falsely purported to have been made or issued, by or under the authority of the United States Government, the State of Illinois, or any other state political subdivision of any state, or any other governmental or quasi-governmental organization that is of a type intended for the purpose of identification of an individual, or any such document made or altered in a manner that it falsely purports to have been made on behalf of or issued to another person or by the authority of one who did not give that authority.

"Personal identifying information" means any of the following information:

(1) A person's name.

(2) A person's address.

(3) A person's date of birth.

(4) A person's telephone number.

(5) A person's driver's license number or State of Illinois identification card as assigned by the Secretary of State of the State of Illinois or a similar agency of another state.

(6) A person's social security number.

(7) A person's public, private, or government employer, place of employment, or employment identification number.

(8) The maiden name of a person's mother.

(9) The number assigned to a person's depository account, savings account, or brokerage account.

(10) The number assigned to a person's credit or debit card, commonly known as a "Visa Card", "MasterCard", "American Express Card", "Discover Card", or other similar cards whether issued by a financial institution, corporation, or business entity.

(11) Personal identification numbers.

(12) Electronic identification numbers.

(13) Digital signals.

(14) User names, passwords, and any other word, number, character or combination of the same usable in whole or part to access information relating to a specific individual, or to the actions taken, communications made or received, or other activities or transactions of a specific individual.

(15) Any other numbers or information which can be used to access a person's financial resources, or to identify a specific individual, or the actions taken, communications made or received, or other activities or transactions of a specific individual.

"Premises of a retail mercantile establishment" includes, but is not limited to, the retail mercantile establishment; any common use areas in shopping centers; and all parking areas set aside by a merchant or on behalf of a merchant for the parking of vehicles for the convenience of the patrons of such retail mercantile establishment.

"Public water, gas, or power supply, or other public services" mean any service subject to regulation by the Illinois Commerce Commission; any service furnished by a public utility that is owned and operated by any political subdivision, public institution of higher education or municipal corporation of this State; any service furnished by any public utility that is owned by such political subdivision, public institution of higher education, or municipal corporation and operated by any of its lessees or operating agents; any service furnished by an electric cooperative as defined in Section 3.4 of the Electric Supplier Act; or wireless service or other service regulated by the Federal Communications Commission.

"Publish" means to communicate or disseminate information to any one or more persons, either orally, in person, or by telephone, radio or television or in writing of any kind, including, without limitation, a letter or memorandum, circular or handbill, newspaper or magazine article or book.

"Reencoder" means an electronic device that places encoded information from the magnetic strip or stripe of a payment card onto the magnetic strip or stripe of a different payment card.

"Retail mercantile establishment" means any place where merchandise is displayed, held, stored or offered for sale to the public.

"Scanning device" means a scanner, reader, or any other electronic device that is used to access, read, scan, obtain, memorize, or store, temporarily or permanently, information encoded on the magnetic strip or stripe of a payment card.

"Shopping cart" means those push carts of the type or types which are commonly provided by grocery stores, drug stores or other retail mercantile establishments for the use of the public in transporting commodities in stores and markets and, incidentally, from the stores to a place outside the store.

"Sound or audio visual recording" means any sound or audio visual phonograph record, disc, pre-recorded tape, film, wire, magnetic tape or other object, device or medium, now known or hereafter invented, by which sounds or images may be reproduced with or without the use of any additional machine, equipment or device.

"Theft detection device remover" means any tool or device specifically designed and intended to be used to remove any theft detection device from any merchandise.

“Under-ring" means to cause the cash register or other sales recording device to reflect less than the full retail value of the merchandise.

"Unidentified sound or audio visual recording" means a sound or audio visual recording without the actual name and full and correct street address of the manufacturer, and the name of the actual performers or groups prominently and legibly printed on the outside cover or jacket and on the label of such sound or audio visual recording.

"Unlawful access device" means any type of instrument, device, machine, equipment, technology, or software which is primarily possessed, used, designed, assembled, manufactured, sold, distributed or offered, promoted or advertised for the purpose of defeating or circumventing any technology, device or software, or any component or part thereof, used by the provider, owner or licensee of any communication service or of any data, audio or video programs or transmissions to protect any such communication, audio or video services, programs or transmissions from unauthorized access, acquisition, receipt, decryption, disclosure, communication, transmission or re-transmission.

"Unlawful communication device" means any electronic serial number, mobile identification number, personal identification number or any communication or wireless device that is capable of acquiring or facilitating the acquisition of a communication service without the express consent or express authorization of the communication service provider, or that has been altered, modified, programmed or reprogrammed, alone or in conjunction with another communication or wireless device or other equipment, to so acquire or facilitate the unauthorized acquisition of a communication service.

"Unlawful communication device" also means:

(1) any phone altered to obtain service without the express consent or express authorization of the communication service provider, tumbler phone, counterfeit or clone phone, tumbler microchip, counterfeit or clone microchip, scanning receiver of wireless communication service or other instrument capable of disguising its identity or location or of gaining unauthorized access to a communications or wireless system operated by a communication service provider; and (2) any communication or wireless device which is capable of, or has been altered, designed, modified, programmed or reprogrammed, alone or in conjunction with another communication or wireless device or devices, so as to be capable of, facilitating the disruption, acquisition, receipt, transmission or decryption of a communication service without

the express consent or express authorization of the communication service provider, including, but not limited to, any device, technology, product, service, equipment, computer software or component or part thereof, primarily distributed, sold, designed, assembled, manufactured, modified, programmed, reprogrammed or used for the purpose of providing the unauthorized receipt of, transmission of, disruption of, decryption of, access to or acquisition of any communication service provided by any communication service provider.

"Vehicle" means a motor vehicle, motorcycle, or farm implement that is self-propelled and that uses motor fuel for propulsion.

"Wireless device" includes any type of instrument, device, machine, or equipment that is capable of transmitting or receiving telephonic, electronic or radio communications, or any part of such instrument, device, machine, or equipment, or any computer circuit, computer chip, electronic mechanism, or other component that is capable of facilitating the transmission or reception of telephonic, electronic, or radio communications.

Subdivision 5. General Theft

§16-1. Theft. (a) A person commits theft when he or she knowingly:

(1) Obtains or exerts unauthorized control over property of the owner; or

(2) Obtains by deception control over property of the owner; or

(3) Obtains by threat control over property of the owner; or

(4) Obtains control over stolen property knowing the property to have been stolen or under such circumstances as would reasonably induce him or her to believe that the property was stolen; or

(5) Obtains or exerts control over property in the custody of any law enforcement agency which is explicitly represented to him by any law enforcement officer or any individual acting in behalf of a law enforcement agency as being stolen, and

(A) Intends to deprive the owner permanently of the use or benefit of the property; or

(B) Knowingly uses, conceals or abandons the property in such manner as to deprive the owner permanently of such use or benefit; or

(C) Uses, conceals, or abandons the property knowing such use, concealment or abandonment probably will deprive the owner permanently of such use or benefit.

(b) Sentence.

(1) Theft of property not from the person and not exceeding $ 500 in value is a Class A misdemeanor.

(1.1) Theft of property not from the person and not exceeding $ 500 in value is a Class 4 felony if the theft was committed in a school or place of worship or if the theft was of governmental property.

(2) A person who has been convicted of theft of property not from the person and not exceeding $ 500 in value who has been previously convicted of any type of theft, robbery, armed robbery, burglary, residential burglary, possession of burglary tools, home invasion, forgery, a violation of Section 4-103, 4-103.1, 4-103.2, or 4-103.3 of the Illinois Vehicle Code relating to the possession of a stolen or converted motor vehicle, or a violation of Section 17-36 of the Criminal Code of 1961 or Section 8 of the Illinois Credit Card and Debit Card Act is guilty of a Class 4 felony.

(3) (Blank).

(4) Theft of property from the person not exceeding $ 500 in value, or theft of property exceeding $ 500 and not exceeding $ 10,000 in value, is a Class 3 felony.

(4.1) Theft of property from the person not exceeding $ 500 in value, or theft of property exceeding $ 500 and not exceeding $ 10,000 in value, is a Class 2 felony if the theft was committed in a school or place of worship or if the theft was of governmental property.

(5) Theft of property exceeding $ 10,000 and not exceeding $ 100,000 in value is a Class 2 felony.

(5.1) Theft of property exceeding $ 10,000 and not exceeding $ 100,000 in value is a Class 1 felony if the theft was committed in a school or place of worship or if the theft was of governmental property.

(6) Theft of property exceeding $ 100,000 and not exceeding $ 500,000 in value is a Class 1 felony.

(6.1) Theft of property exceeding $ 100,000 in value is a Class X felony if the theft was committed in a school or place of worship or if the theft was of governmental property.

(6.2) Theft of property exceeding $ 500,000 and not exceeding $ 1,000,000 in value is a Class 1 non-probationable felony.

(6.3) Theft of property exceeding $ 1,000,000 in value is a Class X felony.

(7) Theft by deception, as described by paragraph (2) of subsection (a) of this Section, in which the offender obtained money or property valued at $ 5,000 or more from a victim 60 years of age or older is a Class 2 felony.

(8) Theft by deception, as described by paragraph (2) of subsection (a) of this Section, in which the offender falsely poses as a landlord or agent or employee of the landlord and obtains a rent payment or a security deposit from a tenant is a Class 3 felony if the rent payment or security deposit obtained does not exceed $ 500.

(9) Theft by deception, as described by paragraph (2) of subsection (a) of this Section, in which the offender falsely poses as a landlord or agent or employee of the landlord and obtains a rent payment or a security deposit from a tenant is a Class 2 felony if the rent payment or security deposit obtained exceeds $ 500 and does not exceed $ 10,000.

(10) Theft by deception, as described by paragraph (2) of subsection (a) of this Section, in which the offender falsely poses as a landlord or agent or employee of the landlord and obtains a rent payment or a security deposit from a tenant is a Class 1 felony if the rent payment or security deposit obtained exceeds $ 10,000 and does not exceed $ 100,000.

(11) Theft by deception, as described by paragraph (2) of subsection (a) of this Section, in which the offender falsely poses as a landlord or agent or employee of the landlord and obtains a rent payment or a security deposit from a tenant is a Class X felony if the rent payment or security deposit obtained exceeds $ 100,000.

(c) When a charge of theft of property exceeding a specified value is brought, the value of the property involved is an element of the offense to be resolved by the trier of fact as either exceeding or not exceeding the specified value.

§ 16-1.1. Theft by lessee; permissive evidence. The trier of fact may infer evidence that a person intends to deprive the owner permanently of the use or benefit of the property (1) if a lessee of the personal property of another fails to return it to the owner within 10 days after written demand from the owner for its return or (2) if a lessee of the personal property of another fails to return it to the owner within 24 hours after written demand from the owner for its return and the lessee had presented identification to the owner that contained a materially fictitious name, address, or telephone number. A notice in writing, given after the expiration of the leasing agreement, addressed and mailed, by registered mail, to the lessee at the address given by him and shown on the leasing agreement shall constitute proper demand.

§16-1.2.[Prima facie evidence of theft]. It shall be prima facie evidence of intent that a person "knowingly obtains by deception control over property of the owner" when he fails to return, within 45 days after written demand from the owner, the downpayment and any additional payments accepted under a promise, oral or in writing, to perform services for the owner for consideration of $3,000 or more, and the promisor willfully without good cause failed to substantially perform pursuant to the agreement after taking a downpayment of 10% or more of the agreed upon consideration. This provision shall not apply where the owner initiated the suspension of performance under the agreement, or where the promisor responds to the notice within the 45 day notice period. A notice in writing, addressed and mailed, by registered mail, to the promisor at the last known address of the promisor, shall constitute proper demand.

(d) Theft by lessee; permissive inference. The trier of fact may infer evidence that a person intends to deprive the owner permanently of the use or benefit of the property (1) if a lessee of the personal property of another fails to return it to the owner within 10 days after written demand from the owner for its return or (2) if a lessee of the personal property of another fails to return it to the owner within 24 hours after written demand from the owner for its return and the lessee had presented identification to the owner that contained a materially fictitious name, address, or telephone number. A notice in writing, given after the expiration of the leasing agreement, addressed and mailed, by registered mail, to the lessee at the address given by him and shown on the leasing agreement shall constitute proper demand.

(e) Permissive inference; evidence of intent that a person obtains by deception control over property. The trier of fact may infer that a person "knowingly obtains by deception control over property of the owner" when he or she fails to return, within 45 days after written demand from the owner, the downpayment and any additional payments accepted under a promise, oral or in writing, to perform services for the owner for consideration of $3,000 or more, and the promisor knowingly without good cause failed to substantially perform pursuant to the agreement after taking a down payment of 10% or more of the agreed upon consideration. This provision shall not apply where the owner initiated the suspension of performance under the agreement, or where the promisor responds to the notice within the 45-day notice period. A notice in writing, addressed and mailed, by registered mail, to the promisor at the last known address of the promisor, shall constitute proper demand.

(f) Offender's interest in the property. (1) It is no defense to a charge of theft of property that the offender has an interest therein, when the owner also has an interest to which the offender is not entitled. (2) Where the property involved is that of the offender's spouse, no prosecution for theft may be maintained unless the parties were not living together as man and wife and were living in separate abodes at the time of the alleged theft.

§ 16-2. Theft of Lost or Mislaid Property. A person commits theft of lost or mislaid property when he or she obtains control over the property and:

(a) Knows or learns the identity of the owner or knows, or is aware of, or learns of a reasonable method of identifying the owner, and

(b) Fails to take reasonable measures to restore the property to the owner, and

(c) Intends to deprive the owner permanently of the use or benefit of the property.

(d) Sentence. Theft of lost or mislaid property where:

(1) the value does not exceed $500 is a Class B misdemeanor;

(2) the value exceeds $500 but does not exceed $10,000is a Class A misdemeanor; and

(3) the value exceeds $10,000 is a Class 4 felony.

§ 16-3. Theft of labor or services or use of property. (a) A person commits theft when he or she knowingly obtains the temporary use of property, labor or services of another which are available only for hire, by means of threat or deception or knowing that such use is without the consent of the person providing the property, labor or services. For the purposes of this subsection, library material is available for hire.

(b) A person commits theft when after renting or leasing a motor vehicle, obtaining a motor vehicle through a "driveaway" service mode of transportation or renting or leasing any other type of personal property exceeding $500 in value, under an agreement in writing which provides for the return of the vehicle or other personal property to a particular place at a particular time, he or she knowingly without good cause fails to return the vehicle or other personal property to that place within the time specified, and is thereafter served or sent a written demand mailed to the last known address, made by certified mail return receipt requested, to return such vehicle or other personal property within 3 days from the mailing of the written demand, and who without good cause knowingly fails to return the vehicle or any other personal property to any place of business of the lessor within such period.

(c) A person commits theft when he or she borrows from a library facility library material which has an aggregate value of $50 or more pursuant to an agreement with or procedure established by the library facility for the return of such library material, and knowingly without good cause fails to return the library material so borrowed in accordance with such agreement or procedure, and further knowingly without good cause fails to return such library material within 30 days after receiving written notice by certified mail from the library facility demanding the return of such library material.
(d) Sentence. A person convicted of theft under subsection (a) is guilty of a Class A misdemeanor , except that the theft of library material where the aggregate value exceeds $300 is a Class 3 felony. A person convicted of theft under subsection (b) of this Section is guilty of a Class 4 felony. A person convicted of theft under subsection (c) is guilty of a petty offense for which the offender may be fined an amount not to exceed $500 and shall be ordered to reimburse the library for postage costs, attorney's fees, and actual replacement costs of the materials not returned, except that theft under subsection (c) where the aggregate value exceeds $300 is a Class 3 felony. For the purpose of sentencing on theft of library material, separate transactions totaling more than $300 within a 90-day period shall constitute a single offense.

§ 16-3.1. False Report of Theft and Other Losses. (a) A person who knowingly makes a false report of a theft, destruction, damage or conversion of any property to a law enforcement agency or other governmental agency with the intent to defraud an insurer is guilty of a Class A misdemeanor.

(b) A person convicted of a violation of this Section a second or subsequent time is guilty of a Class 4 felony.

§ 16-4. Offender's Interest in the Property. (a) It is no defense to a charge of theft of property that the offender has an interest therein, when the owner also has an interest to which the offender is not entitled.

(b) Where the property involved is that of the offender's spouse, no prosecution for theft may be maintained unless the parties were not living together as man and wife and were living in separate abodes at the time of the alleged theft.

Commentary – General Theft Offenses

Theft. Section 16-1 codifies the offense of theft. the basic conduct constituting theft falls into five categories (1) physical taking of the property from the owner without his consent, (2) taking the property from the owner by deceit, (3) taking the property from the owner by threat, (4) receiving stolen property knowing that it was stolen and (5) taking property from the custody of police after being told it was stolen property with the intent to permanently deprive the owner of the use or benefit of the property. There are dual mental states for each of these categories– "knowingly" which applies to all the elements except "permanent deprivation" where the actor must have the intent to permanently deprive.

Unauthorized control. In *People v. Gutman,* 401 Ill. App. 3d 199, 340 Ill. Dec. 342 (Ill. App. Ct. 1st Dist. 2010), the defendant was an agent company which provided transportation services for Medicaid recipients and falsely billed for trips by increasing mileage and other devices. under

Section 16-1(a)(a) the company through its agents had knowingly exercised unauthorized control of funds of the State of Illinois with the intent to permanently deprive Illinois of the benefit of those funds, causing overpayments of Medicaid funds to the company.

Deception. In *People v. Dupree* 339 Ill.App.3d 512, 793 N.E.2d 31 (Ill. App. Ct. 1st Dist. 2003), the defendant's conviction for theft by deception under Section 16-1(a)(2) was affirmed where the evidence showed that he posed as an attorney, received a $300 retainer and $500 to post as bond for a victim and then did not represent the victim nor return the $800.

Theft by receipt of stolen property. Section 16-1(a)(3) criminalizes receipt or possession of stolen property. An additional requirement in this offense is proof that the defendant knew the stolen character of the property. In *People v. Long* 391 Ill. 529, 63 N.E.2d 726 (1945), the defendant sold a .20 gauge Remington shotgun to Bourland. The gun was stolen from Bourland. The same month as the theft the defendant bought a .20 gauge Remington shotgun from Martin and had a bill of sale. The prosecution's evidence did not further identify the gun. The court held that knowledge that the property is stolen is an essential element of the crime of receipt of stolen property and although such knowledge may be proved by circumstantial evidence, the facts in the record were confused and insufficient for the conviction for theft by receipt of stolen property to stand.

Theft by threat of force. Section 16-1(a) (4) proscribes against theft by threat of force. Even if the victim consents to the taking of his property, if that consent was induced by threat of force a theft has occurred. In *People v. Rhodes* 38 Ill.2d 389, 231 N.E.2d 400 (1967), the defendant's attempted theft conviction was held proper where he told the victim that he had been sent to kill him and that if the victim gave the defendant $2750 the defendant would leave town.

Theft by Undercover Operation. Section 16-1(a)(5) was enacted to be utilized in sting operations by police officers in which the suspect is told that the property he is receiving is stolen, and still takes the property. This adds a third layer of mental state to the prosecution of the case. There is the general knowledge requirement but also a requirement of proof of the "intent to permanently deprive" requirement. However, section 16-1(a)(5) requires proof of knowledge that defendant gained from a law enforcement agent that the property was stolen property.

In *People v. Garmon* 394 Ill.App.3d 977, 916 N.E.2d 1191 (Ill. App. Ct. 1st Dist. 2009), the defendant ran a retail store that sold videos and cell phones. In an undercover sting operation, police officers working with a department store (Target), posed as sellers of cell phones that had been taken from the store. (In fact the phones were provided by the department store for use in the sting operation). An undercover officer told the defendant he had had trouble stealing phones the defendant commented that the seller must have been at Target and this was held to be sufficient to meet the requirement that explicit communication existed to prove knowledge that the phones were stolen - even though the word "stolen" was never mentioned by the undercover officers, nor were the phones stolen from the department store. In affirming the conviction the appellate court held that the "explicit representation" issue was to be determined by looking at the totality of the circumstances of the case.

Value and Sentencing. The value of property is its fair cash value. The exact value need not be proven only that the value of the property falls into one of the offense classification categories. The classification of theft as an offense is primarily based on the value of the stolen property. If the value is less than $500 then the offense is a Class a misdemeanor. If the value is greater than $500 but less than $10,000, the offense is a Class 3 felony and if the value is greater than $10,000 but less than $100,000, the offense is a Class 1 felony. theft of property of a value in excess of $100,000 is a Class X felony.

§ 16-5. Theft from coin-operated machine.
(a) A person commits theft from a coin-operated machine when he or she knowingly and without authority opens, breaks into, tampers with, triggers, or damages a coin-operated machine either:

(1) to operate or use the machine; or

(2) with the intent to commit a theft from the machine.

(b) Sentence. (1) A violation of subdivision (a)(1) is a Class B misdemeanor.

(2) A violation of subdivision (a)(2) is a Class A misdemeanor.

(3) A person who has been convicted of theft from a coin-operated machine and who has been previously convicted of any type of theft, robbery, armed robbery, burglary, residential burglary, possession of burglary tools, or home invasion is guilty of a Class 4 felony.

§ 16-6. Theft-related devices (a)(1) A person commits unlawful possession of a key or device for a coin-operated machine when he or she possesses a key, a drawing, print, mold of a key, a device, or substance designed to open, break into, tamper with, or damage a coin-operated machine, with intent to commit a theft from the machine.
(2) A person commits unlawful use of a key or device for a coin-operated machine when he or she with the intent to commit a theft from a coin-operated machine uses a key, drawing, print, mold of a key, device, or substance and causes damage or loss to the coin-operated machine of more than $300.

(b)(1) A person commits unlawful use of a theft detection shielding device when he or she knowingly manufactures, sells, offers for sale or distributes any theft detection shielding device.

(b)(2) A person commits unlawful possession of a theft detection shielding device when he or she knowingly possesses a theft detection shielding device with the intent to commit theft or retail theft.

(b)(3) A person commits unlawful possession of a theft detection device remover when he or she knowingly possesses a theft detection device remover with the intent to use such tool to remove any theft detection device from any merchandise without the permission of the merchant or person owning or holding the merchandise.

(c) A person commits use of a scanning device or reencoder to defraud when the person knowingly uses:

(1) a scanning device to access, read, obtain, memorize, or store, temporarily or permanently, information encoded on the magnetic strip or stripe of a payment card without the permission of the authorized user of the payment card and with the intent to defraud the authorized user, the issuer of the authorized user's payment card, or a merchant; or

(2) a reencoder to place information encoded on the magnetic strip or stripe of a payment card onto the magnetic strip or stripe of a different card without the permission of the authorized user of the card from which the information is being reencoded and with the intent to defraud the authorized user, the issuer of the authorized user's payment card, or a merchant.

(d) Sentence. A violation of subdivision (a)(1), (b)(1), (b)(2), or (b)(3) is a Class A misdemeanor. A second or subsequent violation of subdivision (b)(1), (b)(2), or (b)(3) is a Class 4 felony. A violation of subdivision (a)(2), (c)(1), or (c)(2) is a Class 4 felony. A second or subsequent violation of subdivision (c)(1) or (c)(2) is a Class 3 felony.

(e) The owner of a coin-operated machine may maintain a civil cause of action against a person engaged in the activities covered in subdivisions (a)(1) and (a)(2) and may recover treble actual damages, reasonable attorney's fees, and costs.

(f) As used in this Section, “substance” means a corrosive or acidic liquid or solid but does not include items purchased through a coin-operated machine at the location or acquired as condiments at the location of the coin-operated machine.

(g) For the purposes of this Section, "theft detection shielding device" means any laminated or coated bag or device peculiar to and marketed for shielding and intended to shield merchandise from detection by an electronic or magnetic theft alarm sensor.

§ 16-7. Unlawful use of recorded sounds or images. (a) A person commits unlawful use of recorded sounds or images when he:

(1) transfers or causes to be transferred without the consent of the owner, any sounds or images recorded on any sound or audio visual recording with the purpose of selling or causing to be sold, or using or causing to be used for profit the article to which such sounds or recordings of sound are transferred.
(2) sells, offers for sale, advertises for sale, uses or causes to be used for profit any such article described in subdivision (a)(1) without consent of the owner;

(3) offers or makes available for a fee, rental or any other form of compensation, directly or indirectly, any equipment or machinery for the purpose of use by another to reproduce or transfer, without the consent of the owner, any sounds or images recorded on any sound or audio visual recording to another sound or audio visual recording or for the purpose of use by another to manufacture any sound or audio visual recording in violation of Section 16-8.

(4) transfers or causes to be transferred without the consent of the owner, any live performance with the intent of selling or causing to be sold, or using or causing to be used for profit the sound or audio visual recording to which the performance is transferred.

(b) A person commits unlawful use of unidentified sound or audio visual recordings when he or she knowingly, recklessly, or negligently for profit manufacturers, sells, distributes, vends, circulates, performs, leases, possesses, or otherwise deals in and with unidentified sound or audio visual recordings or causes the manufacture, sale, distribution, vending, circulation, performance, lease, or other dealing in and with unidentified sound or audio visual recordings.

(c) For the purposes of this Section, "owner" means the person who owns the master sound recording on which sound is recorded and from which the transferred recorded sounds are directly or indirectly derived, or the person who owns the rights to record or authorize the recording of a live performance.
for the purposes of this Section, "manufacturer" means the person who actually makes or causes to be made a sound or audio visual recording. "Manufacturer" does not include a person who manufactures the medium upon which sounds or visual images can be recorded or stored, or who manufactures the cartridge or casing itself.

(d) Sentence. Unlawful use of recorded sounds or images or unidentified sound or audio visual recordings is a Class 4 felony; however:
(1) If the offense involves more than 100 but not exceeding 1000 unidentified sound recordings or more than 7 but not exceeding 65 unidentified audio visual recordings

during any 180 day period the authorized fine is up to $100,000; and
(2) If the offense involves more than 1,000 unidentified sound recordings or more than 65 unidentified audio visual recordings during any 180 day period the authorized fine is up to $250,000.

(e) Upon conviction of any violation of subsection (b), the offender shall be sentenced to make restitution to any owner or lawful producer of a master sound or audio visual recording, or to the trade association representing such owner or lawful producer, that has suffered injury resulting from the crime. The order of restitution shall be based on the aggregate wholesale value of lawfully manufactured and authorized sound or audio visual recordings corresponding to the non-conforming recorded devices involved in the offense, and shall include investigative costs relating to the offense.

(f) Subsection (a) of this Section shall neither enlarge nor diminish the rights of parties in private litigation.

(g) Subsection (a) of this Section does not apply to any person engaged in the business of radio or television broadcasting who transfers, or causes to be transferred, any sounds (other than from the sound track of a motion picture) solely for the purpose of broadcast transmission.

(h) Each individual manufacture, distribution or sale or transfer for a consideration of such recorded devices in contravention of subsection (a) of this Section constitutes a separate violation of this Section. Each individual manufacture, sale, distribution, vending, circulation, performance, lease, possession, or other dealing in and with an unidentified sound or audio visual recording under subsection (b) of this Section constitutes a separate violation of this Section.

(i) Any sound or audio visual recordings containing transferred sounds or a performance whose transfer was not authorized by the owner of the master sound recording or performance, or unidentified sound or audio visual recordings, in violation of this Section, or in the attempt to commit such violation as defined in Section 8-4, or in a conspiracy to commit such violation as defined in Section 8-2, or in a solicitation to commit such offense as defined in Section 8-1, may be confiscated and destroyed upon conclusion of the case or cases to which they are relevant, except that the court may enter an order preserving them as evidence for use in other cases or pending the final determination of an appeal.

(j) It is an affirmative defense to any charge of unlawful use of recorded sounds or images that the recorded sounds or images so used are public domain material. For purposes of this Section, recorded sounds are deemed to be in the public domain if the recorded sounds were copyrighted pursuant to the copyright laws of the United States, as the same may be amended from time to time, and the term of the copyright and any extensions or renewals thereof has expired.

(j) With respect to sound recordings (other than accompanying a motion picture or other audiovisual work), this Section applies only to sound recordings that were initially recorded before February 15, 1972.

§ 16-8. Unlawful use of unidentified sound or audiovisual recordings. (a) A person commits unlawful use of unidentified sound or audio visual recordings when he intentionally, knowingly, recklessly or negligently for profit manufactures, advertises or offers for sale, sells, distributes, transports, vends, circulates, performs, leases, or possesses for such purposes, unidentified sound or audio visual recordings or causes the manufacture, advertisement or offer for sale, sale, distribution, transportation, vending, circulation, performance, lease, or possession for such purposes, unidentified sound or audio visual recordings.

(b) Unlawful use of unidentified sound or audio visual recordings is a Class 4 felony; however:

(1) If the offense involves more than 100 but not exceeding 1000 unidentified sound recordings or more than 7 but not exceeding 65 unidentified audio visual recordings during any 180 day period the authorized fine is up to $100,000; and

(2) If the offense involves more than 1,000 unidentified sound recordings or more than 65 unidentified audio visual recordings during any 180 day period the authorized fine is up to $250,000.

(c) Each and every individual manufacture, advertisement or offer for sale, sale, distribution, transportation, vending, circulation, performance, lease, or possession for such purposes, an unidentified sound or audio visual recording constitutes a separate violation of this Section.

(c-5) Upon conviction of any violation of this Section, the offender shall be sentenced to make restitution to any owner or lawful producer of a master sound or audio visual recording, or to the trade association representing such owner or lawful producer, that has suffered injury resulting from the crime. The order of restitution shall be based on the aggregate wholesale value of lawfully manufactured and authorized sound or audio visual recordings corresponding to the non-conforming recorded devices involved in the offense, and shall include investigative costs relating to the offense.

(d) If any provision or item of this Section or the application thereof is held invalid, such invalidity shall not affect other provisions, items or applications of this Section which can be given effect without the invalid provisions, items or applications and to this end the provisions of this Section are hereby declared severable.

(e) Any unidentified sound or audio visual recording used in violation of this Section, or in the attempt to commit such violation as defined in Section 8-4, or in a conspiracy to commit such violation as defined in Section 8-2, or in a solicitation to commit such offense as defined in Section 8-1, may be confiscated and destroyed upon conclusion of the case or cases to which they are relevant, except that the Court may enter an order preserving them as evidence for use in other cases or pending the final determination of an appeal.

§ 16-14. Theft of utility services.

(a) A person commits theft of utility services when he or she knowingly, without authority, diverts or interferes with any public water, gas, power supply, or other public services or installs any device with the intent to divert or interfere with any public water, gas, power supply, or other public services without the authority of the owner or entity furnishing or transmitting such product or services.

(b) Sentence. (1) Except as provided in paragraph (3), a violation of this Section is a Class A misdemeanor unless the offense was committed for remuneration, in which case it is a Class 4 felony.

(2) Except as provided in paragraph (3), a second or subsequent violation of this Section is a Class 4 felony.

(3) If the offense causes disruption of the public utility services or delay in the restoration of the public utility services to 10 or more customers or affects an area of more than one square mile, a violation of this Section is a Class 2 felony.

(c) This Section does not apply to the theft of telecommunication services.

§ 16-17. Theft of advertising services.

(a) A person commits theft of advertising services when he or she knowingly attaches or inserts an unauthorized advertisement in a newspaper or periodical, and redistributes it to the public or has the intent to redistribute it to the public.

(b) This Section applies to any newspaper or periodical that is offered for retail sale or is distributed without charge.

(c) This Section does not apply if the publisher or authorized distributor of the newspaper or periodical consents to the attachment or insertion of the advertisement.

(d) In this Section, "unauthorized advertisement" means any form of representation or communication, including any handbill, newsletter, pamphlet, or notice that contains any letters, words, or pictorial representation that is attached to or inserted in a newspaper or periodical without a contractual agreement between the publisher and an advertiser.

(e) Sentence. Theft of advertising services is a Class A misdemeanor.

§ 16-18. Tampering with communication services; theft of communication services. (a) Injury to wires or obtaining service with intent to defraud. A person commits injury to wires or obtaining service with intent to defraud when he or she knowingly:

(1) displaces, removes, injures or destroys any telegraph or telephone line, wire, cable, pole or conduit, belonging to another, or the material or property appurtenant thereto; or

(2) cuts, breaks, taps, or makes any connection with any telegraph or telephone line, wire, cable or instrument belonging to another; or
(3) reads, takes or copies any message, communication or report intended for another passing over any such telegraph line, wire or cable in this State; or

(4) prevents, obstructs or delays by any means or contrivance whatsoever, the sending, transmission, conveyance or delivery in this State of any message, communication or report by or through any telegraph or telephone line, wire or cable; or

(5) uses any apparatus to unlawfully do or cause to be done any of the acts described in subdivisions (a)(1) through (a)(4) of this Section; or
(6) obtains, or attempts to obtain, any telecommunications service with the intent to deprive any person of the lawful charge, in whole or in part, for any telecommunications service:

(A) by charging such service to an existing telephone number without the authority of the subscriber thereto; or

(B) by charging such service to a nonexistent, false, fictitious, or counterfeit telephone number or to a suspended, terminated, expired, canceled, or revoked telephone number; or

(C) by use of a code, prearranged scheme, or other similar stratagem or device whereby said person, in effect, sends or receives information; or

(D) by publishing the number or code of an existing, canceled, revoked or nonexistent telephone number, credit number or other credit device or method of numbering or coding which is employed in the issuance of telephone numbers, credit numbers or other credit devices which may be used to avoid the payment of any lawful telephone toll charge; or

(E) by any other trick, stratagem, impersonation, false pretense, false representation, false statement, contrivance, device, or means.

(b) Theft of communication services. A person commits theft of communication services when he or she knowingly:

(1) obtains or uses a communication service without the authorization of, or compensation paid to, the communication service provider;

(2) possesses, uses, manufactures, assembles, distributes, leases, transfers, or sells, or offers, promotes or advertises for sale, lease, use, or distribution, an unlawful communication device:

(A) for the commission of a theft of a communication service or to receive, disrupt, transmit, decrypt, or acquire, or facilitate the receipt, disruption, transmission, decryption or acquisition, of any communication service without the express consent or express authorization of the communication service provider; or

(B) to conceal or to assist another to conceal from any communication service provider or from any lawful authority the existence or place of origin or destination of any communication;

(3) modifies, alters, programs or reprograms a communication device for the purposes described in subdivision (2)(A) or (2)(B);
(4) possesses, uses, manufactures, assembles, leases, distributes, sells, or transfers, or offers, promotes or advertises for sale, use or distribution, any unlawful access device; or

(5) possesses, uses, prepares, distributes, gives or otherwise transfers to another or offers, promotes, or advertises for sale, use or distribution, any:

(A) plans or instructions for making or assembling an unlawful communication or access device, with the intent to use or employ the unlawful communication or access device, or to allow the same to be used or employed, for a purpose prohibited by this subsection (b), or knowing or having reason to know that the plans or instructions are intended to be used for manufacturing or assembling the unlawful communication or access device for a purpose prohibited by this subsection (b); or
(B) material, including hardware, cables, tools, data, computer software or other information or equipment, knowing that the purchaser or a third person intends to use the material in the manufacture or assembly of an unlawful communication or access device for a purpose prohibited by this subsection (b).

(c) Sentence. (1) A violation of subsection (a) is a Class A misdemeanor; provided, however, that any of the following is a Class 4 felony:

(A) a second or subsequent conviction for a violation of subsection (a); or

(B) an offense committed for remuneration; or

(C) an offense involving damage or destruction of property in an amount in excess of $300 or defrauding of services in excess of $500.

(2) A violation of subsection (b) is a Class A misdemeanor, except that:

(A) A violation of subsection (b) is a Class 4 felony if:

(i) the violation of subsection (b) involves at least 10, but not more than 50, unlawful communication or access devices; or (ii) the defendant engages in conduct identified in subdivision (b)(3) of this Section with the intention of substantially disrupting and impairing the ability of a communication service provider to deliver communication services to its lawful customers or subscribers; or (iii) the defendant at the time of the commission of the offense is a pre-trial detainee at a penal institution or is serving a sentence at a penal institution; or (iv) the defendant at the time of the
commission of the offense is a pre-trial detainee at a penal institution or is serving a sentence at a penal institution and uses any means of electronic communication as defined in the Harassing and Obscene Communications Act for fraud, theft, theft by deception, identity theft, or any other unlawful purpose; or
(v) the aggregate value of the service obtained is $300 or more; or

(vi) the violation is for a wired communication service or device and the defendant has been convicted previously for an offense under subsection (b) or for any other type of theft, robbery, armed robbery, burglary, residential burglary, possession of burglary tools, home invasion, or fraud, including violations of the Cable Communications Policy Act of 1984 in this or any federal or other state jurisdiction.

(B) A violation of subsection (b) is a Class 3 felony if:

(i) the violation of subsection (b) involves more than 50 unlawful communication or access devices; or
(ii) the defendant at the time of the commission of the offense is a pre-trial detainee at a penal institution or is serving a sentence at a penal institution and has been convicted previously of an offense under subsection (b) committed by

the defendant while serving as a pre-trial detainee in a penal institution or while serving a sentence at a penal institution; or

(iii) the defendant at the time of the commission of the offense is a pre-trial detainee at a penal institution or is serving a sentence at a penal institution and has been convicted previously of an offense under subsection (b) committed by the defendant while serving as a pre-trial detainee in a penal institution or while serving a sentence at a penal institution and uses any means of electronic communication as defined in the Harassing and Obscene Communications Act for fraud, theft, theft by deception, identity theft, or any other unlawful purpose; or

(iv) the violation is for a wired communication service or device and the defendant has been convicted previously on 2 or more occasions for offenses under subsection (b) or for any other type of theft, robbery, armed robbery, burglary, residential burglary, possession of burglary tools, home invasion, or fraud, including violations of the Cable Communications Policy Act of 1984 in this or any federal or other state jurisdiction.

(C) A violation of subsection (b) is a Class 2 felony if the violation is for a wireless communication service or device and the defendant has been convicted previously for an offense under subsection (b) or for any other type of theft, robbery, armed robbery, burglary, residential burglary, possession of burglary tools, home invasion, or fraud, including violations of the Cable Communications Policy Act of 1984 in this or any federal or other state jurisdiction.

(3) Restitution. The court shall, in addition to any other sentence authorized by law, sentence a person convicted of violating subsection (b) to make restitution in the manner provided in Article 5 of Chapter V of the Unified Code of Corrections.
(d) Grading of offense based on prior convictions. For purposes of grading an offense based upon a prior conviction for an offense under subsection (b) or for any other type of theft, robbery, armed robbery, burglary, residential burglary, possession of burglary tools, home invasion, or fraud, including violations of the Cable Communications Policy Act of 1984 in this or any federal or other state jurisdiction under subdivisions (c)(2)(A)(i) and (c)(2)(B)(i) of this Section, a prior conviction shall consist of convictions upon separate indictments or criminal complaints for offenses under subsection (b) or for any other type of theft, robbery, armed robbery, burglary, residential burglary, possession of burglary tools, home invasion, or fraud, including violations of the Cable Communications Policy Act of 1984 in this or any federal or other state jurisdiction.

(e) Separate offenses. For purposes of all criminal penalties or fines established for violations of subsection (b), the prohibited activity established in subsection (b) as it applies to each unlawful communication or access device shall be deemed a separate offense.
(f) Forfeiture of unlawful communication or access devices. Upon conviction of a defendant under subsection (b), the court may, in addition to any other sentence authorized by law, direct that the defendant forfeit any unlawful communication or access devices in the defendant's possession or control which were involved in the violation for which the defendant was convicted.

(g) Venue. An offense under subsection (b) may be deemed to have been committed at either the place where the defendant manufactured or assembled an unlawful communication or access device, or assisted others in doing so, or the place where the unlawful communication or access device was sold or delivered to a purchaser or recipient. It is not a defense to a violation of subsection (b) that some of the acts constituting the offense occurred outside of the State of Illinois.

(h) Civil action. [Omitted in editing.]

Subdivision 10. Retail Theft

§ 16-25. Retail theft.(a) A person commits retail theft when he or she knowingly:

(1) Takes possession of, carries away, transfers or causes to be carried away or transferred any merchandise displayed, held, stored or offered for sale in a retail mercantile establishment with the intention of retaining such merchandise or with the intention of depriving the merchant permanently of the possession, use or benefit of such merchandise without paying the full retail value of such merchandise; or

(2) Alters, transfers, or removes any label, price tag, marking, indicia of value or any other markings which aid in determining value affixed to any merchandise displayed, held, stored or offered for sale in a retail mercantile establishment and attempts to purchase such merchandise at less than the full retail value with the intention of depriving the merchant of the full retail value of such merchandise; or

(3) Transfers any merchandise displayed, held, stored or offered for sale in a retail mercantile establishment from the container in or on which such merchandise is displayed to any other container with the intention of depriving the merchant of the full retail value of such merchandise; or

(4) Under-rings with the intention of depriving the merchant of the full retail value of the merchandise; or

(5) Removes a shopping cart from the premises of a retail mercantile establishment without the consent of the merchant given at the time of such removal with the intention of depriving the merchant permanently of the possession, use or benefit of such cart; or

(6) Represents to a merchant that he, she, or another is the lawful owner of property, knowing that such representation is false, and conveys or attempts to convey that property to a merchant who is the owner of the property in exchange for money, merchandise credit or other property of the merchant; or

(7) Uses or possesses any theft detection shielding device or theft detection device remover with the intention of using such device to deprive the merchant permanently of the possession, use or benefit of any merchandise displayed, held, stored or offered for sale in a retail mercantile establishment without paying the full retail value of such merchandise; or

(8) Obtains or exerts unauthorized control over property of the owner and thereby intends to deprive the owner permanently of the use or benefit of the property when a lessee of the personal property of another fails to return it to the owner, or if the lessee fails to pay the full retail value of such property to the lessor in satisfaction of any contractual provision requiring such, within 10 days after written demand from the owner for its return. A notice in writing, given after the expiration of the leasing agreement, by registered mail, to the lessee at the address given by the lessee and shown on the leasing agreement shall constitute proper demand.

(b) Theft by emergency exit. A person commits theft by emergency exit when he or she commits a retail theft as defined in subdivisions (a)(1) through (a)(8) of this Section and to facilitate the theft he or she leaves the retail mercantile establishment by use of a designated emergency exit.

(c) Permissive inference. If any person:

(1) conceals upon his or her person or among his or her belongings unpurchased merchandise displayed, held, stored or offered for sale in a retail mercantile establishment; and
(2) removes that merchandise beyond the last known station for receiving payments for that merchandise in that retail mercantile establishment, then the trier of fact may infer that the person possessed, carried away or transferred such merchandise with the intention of retaining it or with the intention of depriving the merchant permanently of the possession, use or benefit of such merchandise without paying the full retail value of such merchandise. To

"conceal" merchandise means that, although there may be some notice of its presence, that merchandise is not visible through ordinary observation.

(d) Venue. Multiple thefts committed by the same person as part of a continuing course of conduct in different jurisdictions that have been aggregated in one jurisdiction may be prosecuted in any jurisdiction in which one or more of the thefts occurred.

(e) For the purposes of this Section, "theft detection shielding device" means any laminated or coated bag or device designed and intended to shield merchandise from detection by an electronic or magnetic theft alarm sensor.

(f) Sentence. (1) A violation of any of subdivisions (a)(1) through (a)(6) and (a)(8) of this Section, the full retail value of which does not exceed $300 for property other than motor fuel or $150 for motor fuel, is a Class A misdemeanor. A violation of subdivision (a)(7) of this Section is a Class A misdemeanor for a first offense and a Class 4 felony for a second or subsequent offense. Theft by emergency exit of property, the full retail value of which does not exceed $300, is a Class 4 felony.

(2) A person who has been convicted of retail theft of property under any of subdivisions (a)(1) through (a)(6) and (a)(8) of this Section, the full retail value of which does not exceed $300 for property other than motor fuel or $150 for motor fuel, and who has been previously convicted of any type of theft, robbery, armed robbery, burglary, residential burglary, possession of burglary tools, home invasion, unlawful use of a credit card, or forgery is guilty of a Class 4 felony. A person who has been convicted of theft by emergency exit of property, the full retail value of which does not exceed $300, and who has been previously convicted of any type of theft, robbery, armed robbery, burglary, residential burglary, possession of burglary tools, home invasion, unlawful use of a credit card, or forgery is guilty of a Class 3 felony.

(3) Any retail theft of property under any of subdivisions (a)(1) through (a)(6) and (a)(8) of this Section, the full retail value of which exceeds $300 for property other than motor fuel or $150 for motor fuel in a single transaction, or in separate transactions committed by the same person as part of a continuing course of conduct from one or more mercantile establishments over a period of one year, is a Class 3 felony. Theft by emergency exit of property, the full retail value of which exceeds $300 in a single transaction, or in separate transactions committed by the same person as part of a continuing course of conduct from one or more mercantile establishments over a period of one year, is a Class 2 felony. When a charge of retail theft of property or theft by emergency exit of property, the full value of which exceeds $300, is brought, the value of the property involved is an element of the offense to be resolved by the trier of fact as either exceeding or not exceeding $300.

§ 16-26. Detention; affirmative defense.
(a) Detention. Any merchant who has reasonable grounds to believe that a person has committed retail theft may detain the person, on or off the premises of a retail mercantile establishment, in a reasonable manner and for a reasonable length of time for all or any of the following purposes:

(1) To request identification;

(2) To verify such identification;

(3) To make reasonable inquiry as to whether such person has in his possession unpurchased merchandise and to make reasonable investigation of the ownership of such merchandise;

(4) To inform a peace officer of the detention of the person and surrender that person to the custody of a peace officer;

(5) In the case of a minor, to immediately make a reasonable attempt to inform the parents, guardian or other private person interested in the welfare of that minor and, at the merchant's discretion, a peace officer, of this detention and to surrender custody of such minor to such person. A merchant may make a detention as permitted in this Section off the premises of a

retail mercantile establishment only if such detention is pursuant to an immediate pursuit of such person. A merchant shall be deemed to have reasonable grounds to make a detention for the purposes of this Section if the merchant detains a person because such person has in his or her possession either a theft detection shielding device or a theft detection device remover.

(b) Affirmative defense. A detention as permitted in this Section does not constitute an arrest or an unlawful restraint, as defined in Section 10-3 of this Code, nor shall it render the merchant liable to the person so detained.

(c) For the purposes of this Section, "minor" means a person who is less than 19 years of age, is unemancipated, and resides with his or her parent or parents or legal guardian.

§ 16-27. Civil liability.[Omitted in editing.]

§ 16-28. Delivery container theft. (a) A person commits delivery container theft when he or she knowingly does any of the following:

(1) Uses for any purpose, when not on the premises of the owner or an adjacent parking area, a delivery container of another person which is marked by a name or mark unless the use is authorized by the owner.

(2) Sells, or offers for sale, a delivery container of another person which is marked by a name or mark unless the sale is authorized by the owner.

(3) Defaces, obliterates, destroys, covers up or otherwise removes or conceals a name or mark on a delivery container of another person without the written consent of the owner.

(4) Removes the delivery container of another person from the premises, parking area or any other area under the control of any processor, distributor or retail establishment, or from any delivery vehicle, without the consent of the owner of the delivery container. If a person possesses any marked or named delivery container without the consent of the owner and while not on the premises, parking area or other area under control of a processor, distributor or retail establishment doing business with the owner, the trier of fact may infer that the person removed the delivery container in violation of this paragraph.

(b) Any common carrier or private carrier for hire, except those engaged in transporting bakery or dairy products to and from the places where they are produced, that receives or transports any delivery container marked with a name or mark without having in its possession a bill of lading or invoice for that delivery container commits the offense of delivery container theft.

(c) Sentence. Delivery container theft is a Class B misdemeanor. An offender may be sentenced to pay a fine of $150 for the first offense and $500 for a second or subsequent offense.

Commentary – Retail Theft

A special category of theft is retail theft which is committed when an offender takes merchandise from a retail store with the intent to permanently deprive the owner of the property without paying the face value (the amount on the price tag.) these shoplifting offenses can occur in several ways (1) simple taking of the merchandise: (2) changing price tags of merchandise; (3) putting merchandise into other containers; (4) under-ring the merchandise by a clerk when it is presented for payment; (5) taking a shopping cart from the retail store; (6) telling the owner that property belongs to the shopper that actually is the store's merchandise; (7) using a device to block the electronic functioning of a theft detection device and (8) failing to return retail rental property within 10 days of receipt of a notice that the property is due to be returned. Retail theft of property less that $300 is a Class A misdemeanor, retail theft of property greater than $300 is a Class 3 felony and retail theft with a prior theft or other identified convictions is a Class 4 felony.

Subdivision 15 Identity Theft

§ 16-30. Identity theft; aggravated identity theft. (a) A person commits identity theft when he or she knowingly:

(1) uses any personal identifying information or personal identification document of another person to fraudulently obtain credit, money, goods, services, or other property; or

(2) uses any personal identification information or personal identification document of another with intent to commit any felony not set forth in paragraph (1) of this subsection (a); or

(3) obtains, records, possesses, sells, transfers, purchases, or manufactures any personal identification information or personal identification document of another with intent to commit any felony; or

(4) uses, obtains, records, possesses, sells, transfers, purchases, or manufactures any personal identification information or personal identification document of another knowing that such personal identification information or personal identification documents were stolen or produced without lawful authority; or

(5) uses, transfers, or possesses document-making implements to produce false identification or false documents with knowledge that they will be used by the person or another to commit any felony; or

(6) uses any personal identification information or personal identification document of another to portray himself or herself as that person, or otherwise, for the purpose of gaining access to any personal identification information or personal identification document of that person, without the prior express permission of that person; or

(7) uses any personal identification information or personal identification document of another for the purpose of gaining access to any record of the actions taken, communications made or received, or other activities or transactions of that person, without the prior express permission of that person; or

(8) in the course of applying for a building permit with a unit of local government, provides the license number of a roofing or fire sprinkler contractor whom he or she does not intend to have perform the work on the roofing or fire sprinkler portion of the project; it is an affirmative defense to prosecution under this paragraph (8) that the building permit applicant promptly informed the unit of local government that issued the building permit of any change in the roofing or fire sprinkler contractor.

(b) Aggravated identity theft. A person commits aggravated identity theft when he or she commits identity theft as set forth in subsection (a) of this Section:

(1) against a person 60 years of age or older or a person with a disability; or

(2) in furtherance of the activities of an organized gang.

A defense to aggravated identity theft does not exist merely because the accused reasonably believed the victim to be a person less than 60 years of age. For the purposes of this subsection, "organized gang" has the meaning ascribed in Section 10 of the Illinois Streetgang Terrorism Omnibus Prevention Act.
(c) Knowledge shall be determined by an evaluation of all circumstances surrounding the use of the other person's identifying information or document.

(d) When a charge of identity theft or aggravated identity theft of credit, money, goods, services, or other property exceeding a specified value is brought, the value of the credit, money, goods, services, or other property is an element of the offense to be resolved by the trier of fact as either exceeding or not exceeding the specified value.

(e) Sentence. (1) Identity theft. (A) A person convicted of identity theft in violation of paragraph (1) of subsection (a) shall be sentenced as follows:

(i) Identity theft of credit, money, goods, services, or other property not exceeding $300 in value is a Class 4 felony. A person who has been previously convicted of identity theft of less than $300 who is convicted of a second or subsequent offense of identity theft of less than $300 is guilty of a Class 3 felony. A person who has been convicted of identity theft of less than $300 who has been previously convicted of any type of theft, robbery, armed robbery, burglary, residential burglary, possession of burglary tools, home invasion, home repair fraud, aggravated home repair fraud, or financial exploitation of an elderly person or person with a disability is guilty of a Class 3 felony. Identity theft of credit, money, goods, services, or other property not exceeding $300 in value when the victim of the identity theft is an active duty member of the Armed Services or Reserve Forces of the United States or of the Illinois National Guard serving in a foreign country is a Class 3 felony. A person who has been previously convicted of identity theft of less than $300 who is convicted of a second or subsequent offense of identity theft of less than $300 when the victim of the identity theft is an active duty member of the Armed Services or Reserve Forces of the United States or of the Illinois National Guard serving in a foreign country is guilty of a Class 2 felony. A person who has been convicted of identity theft of less than $300 when the victim of the identity theft is an active duty member of the Armed Services or Reserve Forces of the United States or of the Illinois National Guard serving in a foreign country who has been previously convicted of any type of theft, robbery, armed robbery, burglary, residential burglary, possession of burglary tools, home invasion, home repair fraud, aggravated home repair fraud, or financial exploitation of an elderly person or person with a disability is guilty of a Class 2 felony.
(ii) Identity theft of credit, money, goods, services, or other property exceeding $300 and not exceeding $2,000 in value is a Class 3 felony. Identity theft of credit, money, goods, services, or other property exceeding $300 and not exceeding $2,000 in value when the victim of the identity theft is an active duty member of the Armed Services or Reserve Forces of the United States or of the Illinois National Guard serving in a foreign country is a Class 2 felony.

(iii) Identity theft of credit, money, goods, services, or other property exceeding $2,000 and not exceeding $10,000 in value is a Class 2 felony. Identity theft of credit, money, goods, services, or other property exceeding $2,000 and not exceeding $10,000 in value when the victim of the identity theft is an active duty member of the Armed Services or Reserve Forces of the United States or of the Illinois National Guard serving in a foreign country is a Class 1 felony.

(iv) Identity theft of credit, money, goods, services, or other property exceeding $10,000 and not exceeding $100,000 in value is a Class 1 felony. Identity theft of credit, money, goods, services, or other property exceeding $10,000 and not exceeding $100,000 in value when the victim of the identity theft is an active duty member of the Armed Services or Reserve Forces of the United States or of the Illinois National Guard serving in a foreign country is a Class X felony.

(v) Identity theft of credit, money, goods, services, or other property exceeding $100,000 in value is a Class X felony.
(B) A person convicted of any offense enumerated in paragraphs (2) through (7) of subsection (a) is guilty of a Class 3 felony. A person convicted of any offense enumerated in paragraphs (2) through (7) of subsection (a) when the victim of the identity theft is an active duty member of the Armed Services or Reserve Forces of the United States or of the Illinois National Guard serving in a foreign country is guilty of a Class 2 felony.

(C) A person convicted of any offense enumerated in paragraphs (2) through (5) of subsection (a) a second or subsequent time is guilty of a Class 2 felony. A person convicted of any offense enumerated in paragraphs (2) through (5) of subsection (a) a second or subsequent time when the victim of the identity theft is an active duty member of the Armed Services or Reserve Forces of the United States or of the Illinois National Guard serving in a foreign country is guilty of a Class 1 felony.

(D) A person who, within a 12-month period, is found in violation of any offense enumerated in paragraphs (2) through (7) of subsection (a) with respect to the identifiers of, or other information relating to, 3 or more separate individuals, at the same time or consecutively, is guilty of a Class 2 felony. A person who, within a 12-month period, is found in violation of any offense enumerated in paragraphs (2) through (7) of subsection (a) with respect to the identifiers of, or other information relating to, 3 or more separate individuals, at the same time or consecutively, when the victim of the identity theft is an active duty member of the Armed Services or Reserve Forces of the United States or of the Illinois National Guard serving in a foreign country is guilty of a Class 1 felony.

(E) A person convicted of identity theft in violation of paragraph (2) of subsection (a) who uses any personal identification information or personal identification document of another to purchase methamphetamine manufacturing material as defined in Section 10 of the Methamphetamine Control and Community Protection Act with the intent to unlawfully manufacture methamphetamine is guilty of a Class 2 felony for a first offense and a Class 1 felony for a second or subsequent offense. A person convicted of identity theft in violation of paragraph (2) of subsection (a) who uses any personal identification information or personal identification document of another to purchase methamphetamine manufacturing material as defined in Section 10 of the Methamphetamine Control and Community Protection Act with the intent to unlawfully manufacture methamphetamine when the victim of the identity theft is an active duty member of the Armed Services or Reserve Forces of the United States or of the Illinois National Guard serving in a foreign country is guilty of a Class 1 felony for a first offense and a Class X felony for a second or subsequent offense.

(F) A person convicted of identity theft in violation of paragraph (8) of subsection (a) of this Section is guilty of a Class 4 felony.

(2) Aggravated identity theft. (A) Aggravated identity theft of credit, money, goods, services, or other property not exceeding $300 in value is a Class 3 felony.

(B) Aggravated identity theft of credit, money, goods, services, or other property exceeding $300 and not exceeding $10,000 in value is a Class 2 felony.

(C) Aggravated identity theft of credit, money, goods, services, or other property exceeding $10,000 in value and not exceeding $100,000 in value is a Class 1 felony.

(D) Aggravated identity theft of credit, money, goods, services, or other property exceeding $100,000 in value is a Class X felony.

(E) Aggravated identity theft for a violation of any offense enumerated in paragraphs (2) through (7) of subsection (a) of this Section is a Class 2 felony.

(F) Aggravated identity theft when a person who, within a 12-month period, is found in violation of any offense enumerated in paragraphs (2) through (7) of subsection (a) of this Section with identifiers of, or other information relating to, 3 or more separate individuals, at the same time or consecutively, is a Class 1 felony.
(G) A person who has been previously convicted of aggravated identity theft regardless of the value of the property involved who is convicted of a second or subsequent offense of aggravated identity theft regardless of the value of the property involved is guilty of a Class X felony.

§ 16-31. Transmission of personal identifying information. (a) A person commits transmission of personal identifying information if he or she is not a party to a transaction that involves the use of a financial transaction device and knowingly:

(i) secretly or surreptitiously photographs, or otherwise captures or records, electronically or by any other means, personal identifying information from the transaction without the consent of the person whose information is photographed or otherwise captured, recorded, distributed, disseminated, or transmitted, or

(ii) distributes, disseminates, or transmits, electronically or by any other means, personal identifying information from the transaction without the consent of the person whose information is photographed, or otherwise captured, recorded, distributed, disseminated, or transmitted.

(b) This Section does not:

(1) prohibit the capture or transmission of personal identifying information in the ordinary and lawful course of business;

(2) apply to a peace officer of this State, or of the federal government, or the officer's agent, while in the lawful performance of the officer's duties;

(3) prohibit a person from being charged with, convicted of, or punished for any other violation of law committed by that person while violating or attempting to violate this Section.

(c) Sentence. A person who violates this Section is guilty of a Class A misdemeanor.

§ 16-32. Facilitating identity theft. (a) A person commits facilitating identity theft when he or
she, in the course of his or her employment or official duties, has access to the personal information of another person in the possession of the State of Illinois, whether written, recorded, or on computer disk, and knowingly, with the intent of committing identity theft, aggravated identity theft, or any violation of the Illinois Financial Crime Law, disposes of that written, recorded, or computerized information in any receptacle, trash can, or other container that the public could gain access to, without shredding that information, destroying the recording, or wiping the computer disk so that the information is either unintelligible or destroyed.

(b) Sentence. Facilitating identity theft is a Class A misdemeanor for a first offense and a Class 4 felony for a second or subsequent offense.

(c) For purposes of this Section, "personal information" has the meaning provided in the Personal Information Protection
Act.

§ 16-33. Civil remedies. [Deleted in editing.]

§ 16-34. Offender's interest in the property; consent. (a) It is no defense to a charge of aggravated identity theft or identity theft that the offender has an interest in the credit, money, goods, services, or other property.

(b) It is no defense to a charge of aggravated identity theft or identity theft that the offender received the consent of any person to access any personal identification information or personal identification document, other than the person described by the personal identification information or personal identification document used by the offender.

§ 16-35. Mandating law enforcement agencies to accept and provide reports; judicial factual determination. (a) A person who has learned or reasonably suspects that his or her personal identifying information has been unlawfully used by another may initiate a law enforcement investigation by contacting the local law enforcement agency that has jurisdiction over his or her actual residence, which shall take a police report of the matter, provide the complainant with a copy of that report, and begin an investigation of the facts, or, if the suspected crime was committed in a different jurisdiction, refer the matter to the law enforcement agency where the suspected crime was committed for an investigation of the facts.

(b) A person who reasonably believes that he or she is the victim of financial identity theft may petition a court, or upon application of the prosecuting attorney or on its own motion, the court may move for an expedited judicial determination of his or her factual innocence, where the perpetrator of the financial identity theft was arrested for, cited for, or convicted of a crime under the victim's identity, or where a criminal complaint has been filed against the perpetrator in the victim's name, or where the victim's identity has been mistakenly associated with a criminal conviction. Any judicial determination of factual innocence made pursuant to this subsection may be heard and determined upon declarations, affidavits, police reports, or other material, relevant, and reliable information submitted by the parties or ordered to be part of the record by the court. If the court determines that the petition or motion is meritorious and that there is no reasonable cause to believe that the victim committed the offense for which the perpetrator of the identity theft was arrested, cited, convicted, or subject to a criminal complaint in the victim's name, or that the victim's identity has been mistakenly associated with a record of criminal conviction, the court shall find the victim factually innocent of that offense. If the victim is found factually innocent, the court shall issue an order certifying this determination.

(c) After a court has issued a determination of factual innocence under this Section, the court may order the name and associated personal identifying information contained in the court records, files, and indexes accessible by the public sealed, deleted, or labeled to show that the data is impersonated and does not reflect the defendant's identity.

(d) A court that has issued a determination of factual innocence under this Section may at any time vacate that determination if the petition, or any information submitted in support of the petition, is found to contain any material misrepresentation or fraud.

(e) Except for criminal and civil actions provided for by Sections 16-30 through 16-36, or for disciplinary or licensure-related proceedings involving the violation of Sections 16-30 through 16-36, no information acquired by, or as a result of, any violation of Section 16-30 shall be discoverable or admissible in any court or other proceeding, or otherwise subject to disclosure without the express permission of any person or persons identified in that information.

§ 16-36. Venue. In addition to any other venues provided for by statute or otherwise, venue for any criminal prosecution or civil recovery action under Sections 16-30 through 16-36 shall be proper in any county where the person described in the personal identification information or personal identification document in question resides or has his or her principal place of business. Where a criminal prosecution or civil recovery action under Sections 16-30 through 16-36 involves the personal identification information or personal identification documents of more than one person, venue shall be proper in any county where one or more of the persons described in the personal identification information or personal identification documents in question resides or has his or her principal place of business.

§ 16-37. Exemptions; relation to other laws.
(a) Sections 16-30 through 16-36 do not:

(1) prohibit the capture or transmission of personal identifying information in the ordinary and lawful course of business;

(2) apply to a peace officer of this State, or of the federal government, or the officer's agent, while in the lawful performance of the officer's duties;

(3) prohibit a licensed private detective or licensed private detective agency from representing himself, herself, or itself as another person, provided that he, she, or it may not portray himself, herself, or itself as the person whose information he, she, or it is seeking except as provided under Sections 16-30 through 16-36;
(4) apply to activities authorized under any other statute.

(b) No criminal prosecution or civil action brought under Sections 16-30 through 16-36 shall prohibit a person from being charged with, convicted of, or punished for any other violation of law committed by that person while violating or attempting to violate Sections 16-30 through 16-36.

Commentary – Identity Theft

Personal Identifying Information. Another crime that is of recent vintage is identity theft. Section 16G-15 *et seq.* makes it unlawful for a person to knowingly use the personal identifying information of another to fraudulently acquire credit, money, goods or services or use stolen information to commit a felony. Aggravated identity theft occurs when the identity theft victim is over 60 years of age or a disabled person, or if the transactions are part of gang-related activity. the class of the offense is also enhanced on the basis of the amount of money or property obtained by the conduct, with an ID theft in excess of $100,000 constituting a Class X felony.

In *People v. Montoya* 373 Ill.App.3d 78, 868 N.E.2d 389 (Ill. App. Ct. 2nd Dist. 2007), the defendant, an illegal immigrant, purchased a social security card for another woman and used that identity to obtain a job and related employment benefits, including health insurance. The defendant used the health insurance coverage to pay expenses of the birth of her child. When the hospital sent bills to the "real person" the defendant was portraying the police were called to investigate the identify theft. The defendant was charged with knowingly using the personal identifying information of another to obtain money (the salary from the employer) and services (the insurance coverage) and was convicted. On appeal, the defendant claimed that she did not commit identity theft as defined by the statute because she did not "fraudulently" obtain the goods and services – she earned them. The court rejected the argument in affirming the conviction noting that fraud is a knowing misrepresentation or concealment of a material fact – using someone else's name met that description. The victim was not the employer that had received the defendant's efforts, it was the "real person" whose identify had been stolen and used. The Court also noted that the statute (Section 16G-25) provided that it was not a defense that the ID thief had an interest in the property acquired by the fraud.

Subdivision 20. Miscellaneous Theft-Related Offenses

§ 16-40. Internet offenses. (a) Online sale of stolen property. A person commits online sale of stolen property when he or she uses or accesses the Internet with the intent of selling property gained through unlawful means.

(b) Online theft by deception. A person commits online theft by deception when he or she uses the Internet to purchase or attempt to purchase property from a seller with a mode of payment that he or she knows is fictitious, stolen, or lacking the consent of the valid account holder.

(c) Electronic fencing. A person commits electronic fencing when he or she sells stolen property using the Internet, knowing that the property was stolen. A person who unknowingly purchases stolen property over the Internet does not violate this Section.

(d) Sentence. A violation of this Section is a Class 4 felony if the full retail value of the stolen property or property obtained by deception does not exceed $300. A violation of this Section is a Class 2 felony if the full retail value of the stolen property or property obtained by deception exceeds $300.

Article 16C – Unlawful Sale of Household Appliances
720 ILCS 5/16C-1 *et seq.*

§ 16C-1. Definitions. For purposes of this Article the following words and phrases have the following meaning:

(1) "commercial context" means a continuing business enterprise conducted for profit by any person whose primary business is the wholesale or retail marketing of household appliances, or a significant portion of whose business or inventory consists of household appliances kept or sold on a wholesale or retail basis.

(2) "household appliance" means any gas or electric device or machine marketed for use as home entertainment or for facilitating or expediting household tasks or chores. The term shall include but not necessarily be limited to refrigerators, freezers, ranges, radios, television sets, vacuum cleaners, toasters, dishwashers, and other similar household items.

(3) "manufacturer's identification number" means any serial number or other similar numerical or alphabetical designation imprinted upon or attached to or placed, stamped, or otherwise imprinted upon or attached to a household appliance by the manufacturer for purposes of identifying a particular appliance individually or by lot number.

§ 16C-3. Continuation of prior law. The provisions of this Article, insofar as they are the same or substantially the same as those of Article 16 of this Code shall be construed as a continuation of such Article 16 and not as a new enactment

Article 16D – Computer Crime
720 ILCS 5/16D-1 *et seq.*

Article 16E - Delivery Container Crime
720 ILCS 5/16E-1 *et seq.*

Article 16F - Wireless Service Theft
720 ILCS 5/16F-1 *et seq.*

Article 16G - Identity Theft Law
720 ILCS 5/16G-1 *et seq.*

Article 16J - Online Property Offenses Article
720 ILCS 5/16J-1 *et seq.*

16K - Theft of Motor Oil
720 ILCS 5/16K-1 *et seq.*

[*Author's note: the*se articles were repealed effective July 1, 2011 and their provisions were renumbered and relocated in Article 17.]

Article 16H – Illinois Financial Crime Law
720 ILCS 5/16H-1 *et seq.*

[*Author's Note: article 16H was r*epealed, effective July 1, 2011. However another act rewrites §16H-50, §16H-51, and adds §16H-70, effective January 1, 2012.]

§ 16H-1. Short title. This Article may be cited as the Illinois Financial Crime Law.

§ 16H-5 to §16H- 45 [Omitted.]

§ 16H-50. Continuing financial crimes enterprise. A person commits the offense of a continuing financial crimes enterprise when the person knowingly, within an 18 month period, commits 3 or more separate offenses under this Article, or, if involving a financial institution, any other felony offenses established under this Code.

§ 16H-55. Organizer of a continuing financial crimes enterprise. (a) A person commits the offense of being an organizer of a continuing financial crimes enterprise when the person:

(1) with the intent to commit an offense under this Article, or, if involving a financial institution, any other felony offense established

under this Code, agrees with another person to the commission of that offense on 3 or more separate occasions within an 18 month period, and

(2) with respect to the other persons within the conspiracy, occupies a position of organizer, supervisor, or financier or other position of management.

(b) The person with whom the accused agreed to commit the 3 or more offenses under this Article, or, if involving a financial institution, any other felony offenses established under this Code, need not be the same person or persons for each offense, as long as the accused was a part of the common scheme or plan to engage in each of the 3 or more alleged offenses.

§ 16H-60. Sentence. (a) A financial crime, the full value of which does not exceed $500, is a Class A misdemeanor.

(b) A person who has been convicted of a financial crime, the full value of which does not exceed $500, and who has been previously convicted of a financial crime or any type of theft, robbery, armed robbery, burglary, residential burglary, possession of burglary tools, or home invasion, is guilty of a Class 4 felony. When a person has such prior conviction, the information or indictment charging that person shall state such prior conviction so as to give notice of the State's intention to treat the charge as a felony. The fact of such prior conviction is not an element of the offense and may not be disclosed to the jury during trial unless otherwise permitted by issues properly raised during such trial.

(c) A financial crime, the full value of which exceeds $500 but does not exceed $10,000, is a Class 3 felony. When a charge of financial crime, the full value of which exceeds $500 but does not exceed $10,000, is brought, the value of the financial crime involved is an element of the offense to be resolved by the trier of fact as either exceeding or not exceeding $500.

(d) A financial crime, the full value of which exceeds $10,000 but does not exceed $100,000, is a Class 2 felony. When a charge of financial crime, the full value of which exceeds $10,000 but does not exceed $100,000, is brought, the value of the financial crime involved is an element of the offense to be resolved by the trier of fact as either exceeding or not exceeding $10,000.

(e) A financial crime, the full value of which exceeds $100,000 but does not exceed $500,000, is a Class 1 felony. When a charge of financial crime, the full value of which exceeds $100,000 but does not exceed $500,000, is brought, the value of the financial crime involved is an element of the offense to be resolved by the trier of fact as either exceeding or not exceeding $100,000.

(f) A financial crime which is a financial institution robbery is a Class 1 felony.

(g) A financial crime which is a continuing financial crimes enterprise is a Class 1 felony.

(h) A financial crime which is the offense of being an organizer of a continuing financial crimes enterprise is a Class X felony.

(i) (Blank).

(j) A financial crime, the full value of which exceeds $500,000 but does not exceed $1,000,000, is a Class 1 non-probationable felony. When a charge of financial crime, the full value of which exceeds $500,000 but does not exceed $1,000,000, is brought, the value of the financial crime involved is an element of the offense to be resolved by the trier of fact as either exceeding or not exceeding $500,000.

(k) A financial crime, the full value of which exceeds $1,000,000, is a Class X felony. When a charge of financial crime, the full value of which exceeds $1,000,000, is brought, the value of the financial crime involved is an element of the offense to be resolved by the trier of fact as either exceeding or not exceeding $1,000,000.

§ 16H-65. Period of limitations. The period of limitations for prosecution of any offense defined in this Article begins at the time when the last act in furtherance of the offense is committed.

Sec. 16H-70. Forfeiture. Any violation of subdivision (2) of Section 16H-50 or subdivision (a)(1)(B) of Section 16H-55 of this Article shall be subject to the remedies, procedures, and forfeiture as set forth in subsections (f) through (s) of Section 29B-1 of this Code.

Article 17 – Deception and Fraud
720 ILCS 5/17-0.5 *et seq.*

Subdivision 1. General Definitions

§ 17-0.5. Definitions. In this Article:
"Altered credit card or debit card" means any instrument or device, whether known as a credit card or debit card, which has been changed in any respect by addition or deletion of any material, except for the signature by the person to whom the card is issued.

"Cardholder" means the person or organization named on the face of a credit card or debit card to whom or for whose benefit the credit card or debit card is issued by an issuer.

"Computer" means a device that accepts, processes, stores, retrieves, or outputs data and includes, but is not limited to, auxiliary storage and telecommunications devices connected to computers.

"Computer network" means a set of related, remotely connected devices and any communications facilities including more than one computer with the capability to transmit data between them through the communications facilities.

"Computer program" or "program" means a series of coded instructions or statements in a form acceptable to a computer which causes the computer to process data and supply the results of the data processing.

"Computer services" means computer time or services, including data processing services, Internet services, electronic mail services, electronic message services, or information or data stored in connection therewith.

"Counterfeit" means to manufacture, produce or create, by any means, a credit card or debit card without the purported issuer's consent or authorization.
"Credit card" means any instrument or device, whether known as a credit card, credit plate, charge plate or any other name, issued with or without fee by an issuer for the use of the cardholder in obtaining money, goods, services or anything else of value on credit or in consideration or an undertaking or guaranty by the issuer of the payment of a check drawn by the cardholder.

"Data" means a representation in any form of information, knowledge, facts, concepts, or instructions, including program documentation, which is prepared or has been prepared in a formalized manner and is stored or processed in or transmitted by a computer or in a system or network. Data is considered property and may be in any form, including, but not limited to, printouts, magnetic or optical storage media, punch cards, or data stored internally in the memory of the computer.

"Debit card" means any instrument or device, known by any name, issued with or without fee by an issuer for the use of the cardholder in obtaining money, goods, services, and anything else of value, payment of which is made against funds previously deposited by the cardholder. A debit card which also can be used to obtain money, goods, services and anything else of value on credit shall not be considered a debit card when it is being used to obtain money, goods, services or anything else of value on credit.

"Document" includes, but is not limited to, any document, representation, or image produced manually, electronically, or by computer.

"Electronic fund transfer terminal" means any machine or device that, when properly activated, will perform any of the following services:

(1) Dispense money as a debit to the cardholder's account; or

(2) Print the cardholder's account balances on a statement; or

(3) Transfer funds between a cardholder's accounts; or
(4) Accept payments on a cardholder's loan; or

(5) Dispense cash advances on an open end credit or a revolving charge agreement; or

(6) Accept deposits to a customer's account; or

(7) Receive inquiries of verification of checks and dispense information that verifies that funds are available to cover such checks; or

(8) Cause money to be transferred electronically from a cardholder's account to an account held by any business, firm, retail merchant, corporation, or any other organization.

"Electronic funds transfer system", hereafter referred to as "EFT System", means that system whereby funds are transferred electronically from a cardholder's account to any other account.

"Electronic mail service provider" means any person who (i) is an intermediary in sending or receiving electronic mail and (ii) provides to end-users of electronic mail services the ability to send or receive electronic mail.

"Expired credit card or debit card" means a credit card or debit card which is no longer valid because the term on it has elapsed.

"False academic degree" means a certificate, diploma, transcript, or other document purporting to be issued by an institution of higher learning or purporting to indicate that a person has completed an organized academic program of study at an institution of higher learning when the person has not completed the organized academic program of study indicated on the certificate, diploma, transcript, or other document.

"False claim" means any statement made to any insurer, purported insurer, servicing corporation, insurance broker, or insurance agent, or any agent or employee of one of those entities, and made as part of, or in support of, a claim for payment or other benefit under a policy of insurance, or as part of, or in support of, an application for the issuance of, or the rating of, any insurance policy, when the statement does any of the following:

(1) Contains any false, incomplete, or misleading information concerning any fact or thing material to the claim.

(2) Conceals (i) the occurrence of an event that is material to any person's initial or continued right or entitlement to any insurance benefit or payment or (ii) the amount of any benefit or payment to which the person is entitled.

"Financial institution" means any bank, savings and loan association, credit union, or other depository of money or medium of savings and collective investment.

"Governmental entity" means: each officer, board, commission, and agency created by the Constitution, whether in the executive, legislative, or judicial branch of State government; each officer, department, board, commission, agency, institution, authority, university, and body politic and corporate of the State; each administrative unit or corporate outgrowth of State government that is created by or pursuant to statute, including units of local government and their officers, school districts, and boards of election commissioners; and each administrative unit or corporate outgrowth of the foregoing items and as may be created by executive order of the Governor.

"Incomplete credit card or debit card" means a credit card or debit card which is missing part of the matter other than the signature of the cardholder which an issuer requires to appear on the credit card or debit card before it can be used by a cardholder, and this includes credit cards or debit cards which have not been stamped, embossed, imprinted or written on.

"Institution of higher learning" means a public or private college, university, or community college located in the State of Illinois that is authorized by the Board of Higher Education or the Illinois Community College Board to issue post-secondary degrees, or a public or private college, university, or community college located anywhere in the United States that is or has been legally constituted to offer degrees and instruction in its state of origin or incorporation.

"Insurance company" means "company" as defined under Section 2 of the Illinois Insurance Code.

"Issuer" means the business organization or financial institution which issues a credit card or debit card, or its duly authorized agent.

"Merchant" has the meaning ascribed to it in Section 16-0.1 of this Code.

"Person" means any individual, corporation, government, governmental subdivision or agency, business trust, estate, trust, partnership or association or any other entity.

"Receives" or "receiving" means acquiring possession or control.

"Record of charge form" means any document submitted or intended to be submitted to an issuer as evidence of a credit transaction for which the issuer has agreed to reimburse persons providing money, goods, property, services or other things of value.

"Revoked credit card or debit card" means a credit card or debit card which is no longer valid because permission to use it has been suspended or terminated by the issuer.

"Sale" means any delivery for value.

"Scheme or artifice to defraud" includes a scheme or artifice to deprive another of the intangible right to honest services.

"Self-insured entity" means any person, business, partnership, corporation, or organization that sets aside funds to meet his, her, or its losses or to absorb fluctuations in the amount of loss, the losses being charged against the funds set aside or accumulated.

"Social networking website" means an Internet website containing profile web pages of the members of the website that include the names or nicknames of such members, photographs placed on the profile web pages by such members, or any other personal or personally identifying information about such members and links to other profile web pages on social networking websites of friends or associates of such members that can be accessed by other members or visitors to the website. A social networking website provides members of or visitors to such website the ability to leave messages or comments on the profile web page that are visible to all or some visitors to the profile web page and may also include a form of electronic mail for members of the social networking website.

"Statement" means any assertion, oral, written, or otherwise, and includes, but is not limited to: any notice, letter, or memorandum; proof of loss; bill of lading; receipt for payment; invoice, account, or other financial statement; estimate of property damage; bill for services; diagnosis or prognosis; prescription; hospital, medical, or dental chart or other record, x-ray, photograph, videotape, or movie film; test result; other evidence of loss, injury, or expense; computer-generated document; and data in any form.

"Universal Price Code Label" means a unique symbol that consists of a machine-readable code and human-readable numbers.

"With intent to defraud" means to act knowingly, and with the specific intent to deceive or cheat, for the purpose of causing financial loss to another or bringing some financial gain to oneself, regardless of whether any person was actually defrauded or deceived. This includes an intent to cause another to assume, create, transfer, alter, or terminate any right, obligation, or power with reference to any person or property.

Subdivision 5. Deception

§ 17-1. Deceptive practices. (A) General deception. a person commits a deceptive practice when, with intent to defraud, the person does any of the following:

(1) He or she knowingly causes another, by deception or threat, to execute a document disposing of property or a document by which a pecuniary obligation is incurred.

(2) being an officer, manager or other person participating in the direction of a financial institution, he or she knowingly receives or permits the receipt of a deposit or other investment, knowing that the institution is insolvent.

(3) He or she knowingly makes a false or deceptive statement addressed to the public for the purpose of promoting the sale of property or services.

(B) Bad checks. A person commits a deceptive practice when:

(1) With intent to obtain control over property or to pay for property, labor or services of another, or in satisfaction of an obligation for payment of tax under the Retailers' Occupation

Tax Act or any other tax due to the State of Illinois, he or she issues or delivers a check or other order upon a real or fictitious depository for the payment of money, knowing that it will not be paid by the depository. the trier of fact may infer that the defendant knows that the check or other order will not be paid by the depository and that the defendant has acted with intent to defraud when the defendant fails to have sufficient funds or credit with the depository when the check or other order is issued or delivered, or when such check or other order is presented for payment and dishonored on each of 2 occasions at least 7 days apart. In this paragraph (B)(1) , "property" includes rental property (real or personal).

(2) He or she issues or delivers a check or other order upon a real or fictitious depository in an amount exceeding $ 150 in payment of an amount owed on any credit transaction for property, labor or services, or in payment of the entire amount owed on any credit transaction for property, labor or services, knowing that it will not be paid by the depository, and thereafter fails to provide funds or credit with the depository in the face amount of the check or order within 7 days of receiving actual notice from the depository or payee of the dishonor of the check or order.

(C) Bank-related fraud. (1) False Statement.

A person commits false statement bank fraud if he or she , with intent to defraud, makes or causes to be made any false statement in writing in order to obtain an account with a bank or other financial institution, or to obtain credit from a bank or other financial institution, or to obtain services from a currency exchange, knowing such writing to be false, and with the intent that it be relied upon.

For purposes of this subsection (C), a false statement means any false statement representing identity, address, or employment, or the identity, address, or employment of any person, firm, or corporation.

(2) Possession of stolen or fraudulently obtained checks.

A person commits possession of stolen or fraudulently obtained checks when he or she possesses, with the intent to obtain access to funds of another person held in a real or fictitious deposit account at a financial institution, makes a false statement or a misrepresentation to the financial institution, or possesses, transfers, negotiates, or presents for payment a check, draft, or other item purported to direct the financial institution to withdraw or pay funds out of the account holder's deposit account with knowledge that such possession, transfer, negotiation, or presentment is not authorized by the account holder or the issuing financial institution.

A person shall be deemed to have been authorized to possess, transfer, negotiate, or present for payment such item if the person was otherwise entitled by law to withdraw or recover funds from the account in question and followed the requisite procedures under the law. If the account holder, upon discovery of the withdrawal or payment, claims that the withdrawal or payment was not authorized, the financial institution may require the account holder to submit an affidavit to that effect on a form satisfactory to the financial institution before the financial institution may be required to credit the account in an amount equal to the amount or amounts that were withdrawn or paid without authorization.

(3) Possession of implements of check fraud.

A person commits possession of implements of check fraud when he or she possesses, with the intent to defraud and without the authority of the account holder or financial institution, any check imprinter, signature imprinter, or "certified" stamp.

(D) Sentence. (1) The commission of a deceptive practice in violation of this Section, except as otherwise provided by this subsection (D), is a Class A misdemeanor.

(2) For purposes of paragraphs (A)(1) and (B)(1):

(a) The commission of a deceptive practice in violation of paragraph (A)(1) or (B)(1), when the value of the property so obtained, in a single transaction or in separate transactions within a 90-day period, exceeds $ 150, is a Class 4 felony. In the case of a prosecution for separate transactions totaling more than $ 150 within a 90-day period, those separate transactions shall be alleged in a single charge and prosecuted in a single prosecution.

(b) The commission of a deceptive practice in violation of paragraph (B)(1) a second or subsequent time is a Class 4 felony.

(3) For purposes of paragraph (C)(2), a person who, within any 12-month period, violates paragraph (C)(2) with respect to 3 or more checks or orders for the payment of money at the same time or consecutively, each the property of a different account holder or financial institution, is guilty of a Class 4 felony.

(4) For purposes of paragraph (C)(3), a person who within any 12-month period violates paragraph (C)(3) as to possession of 3 or more such devices at the same time or consecutively is guilty of a Class 4 felony.

(E) Civil liability. [omitted.]

§ 17-1b. State's Attorney's bad check diversion program. [Omitted.]

Commentary – Deceptive Practices

Bad Checks. Section 17-1 addresses the offense of deceptive practices. It is much broader in scope than addressing “bad checks” as a crime, but of course, is used predominately to address the bad check scenario. the elements of the deceptive practice for “bad checks” are set forth in Section 17-1(B)(d) are (1) intent to obtain control over property or pay for property or services of another, (2) issues or delivers a check, (3) knowing there is insufficient funds in the bank to honor the check when presented and (4) intent to defraud. there is a presumption that the failure to have funds in the account to honor a check on two occasions over a seven day period is prima facie evidence that the defendant knew he had insufficient funds and that he intended to defraud. Deceptive Practices is ordinarily a Class A misdemeanor but can be elevated to Class 4 felony status by subsequent conviction after a prior conviction. Section 17-1(B)(e) proscribes the failure to pay a bad check of $150 or more within seven days after receiving actual notice that the check was dishonored.

In *People v. Butcher* 257 Ill.App.3d 1051, 630 N.E.2d 198 (Ill. App. Ct. 2nd Dist. 1994), the defendant was the high bidder for a computer at an auction and gave a check in payment. The check was present for payment but the account needed $580 to honor the check. The check was presented a second time but the defendant put a "stop payment" order on it. When the auctioneer contacted the defendant, she asked to return the computer but was reminded that the auction terms were that all sales were final. The computer was never returned nor the check paid. The defendant had made other payments and deposits on other accounts during this time period. In affirming the conviction the court noted that the state must still prove intent to defraud even in the face of the dishonor of the check on two occasions within 7 days. The court found other evidence besides the prima facie inference of intent to defraud in the defendant's "stop payment" order, the failure to return the computer and the fact that she had other transactions on other accounts to corroborate her intent to defraud.

§ 17-2. False personation; solicitation (a)(1) a person commits a false personation when he or she knowingly and falsely represents himself or herself to be a member or representative of any veterans' or public safety personnel organization or a representative of any charitable organization, or when he or she knowingly exhibits or uses in any manner any decal, badge or insignia of any charitable, public safety personnel, or veterans' organization when not authorized to do so by the charitable, public safety personnel, or veterans' organization. "Public safety personnel organization" has the meaning ascribed to that term in Section 1 of the Solicitation for Charity Act.

(2) a person commits a false personation when he or she knowingly and falsely represents himself or herself to be a veteran in seeking employment or public office. In this paragraph, "veteran" means a person who has served in the Armed Services or Reserve Forces of the United States.

(3) No person shall knowingly use the words " Police ", "Police Department", "Patrolman", " Sergeant ", " Lieutenant ", " Peace Officer", "Sheriff's Police", "Sheriff", "Officer", "Law Enforcement", "Trooper", "Deputy", "Deputy Sheriff", "State Police", or any other words to the same effect (i) in the title of any organization, magazine, or other publication without the express approval of the named public safety personnel organization's governing board or (ii) in combination with the name of any state, state agency, public university, or unit of local government without the express written authorization of that state, state agency, public university, or unit of local government.

(4) No person may knowingly claim or represent that he or she is acting on behalf of any public safety personnel organization when soliciting financial contributions or selling or delivering or offering to sell or deliver any merchandise, goods, services, memberships, or advertisements unless the chief of the police department, fire department, and the corporate or municipal authority thereof, or the sheriff has first entered into a written agreement with the person or with an organization with which the person is affiliated and the agreement permits the activity and specifies and states clearly and fully the purpose for which the proceeds of the solicitation, contribution, or sale will be used.

(5) No person, when soliciting financial contributions or selling or delivering or offering to sell or deliver any merchandise, goods, services, memberships, or advertisements may claim or represent that he or she is representing or acting on behalf of any nongovernmental organization by any name which includes "officer", "peace officer", "police", "law enforcement", "trooper", "sheriff", "deputy", "deputy sheriff", "State police", or any other word or words which would reasonably be understood to imply that the organization is composed of law enforcement personnel unless

(A) the person is actually representing or acting on behalf of the nongovernmental organization;

(B) the nongovernmental organization is controlled by and governed by a membership of and represents a group or association of active duty peace officers, retired peace officers, or injured peace officers; and

(C) before commencing the solicitation or the sale or the offers to sell any merchandise, goods, services, memberships, or advertisements, a written contract between the soliciting or selling person and the nongovernmental organization, which specifies and states clearly and fully the purposes for which the proceeds of the solicitation, contribution, or sale will be used, has been entered into.

(6) No person, when soliciting financial contributions or selling or delivering or offering to sell or deliver any merchandise, goods, services, memberships, or advertisements, may knowingly claim or represent that he or she is representing or acting on behalf of any nongovernmental organization by any name which includes the term "fireman", "fire fighter", "paramedic", or any other word or words which would reasonably be understood to imply that the organization is composed of fire fighter or paramedic personnel unless:

(A) the person is actually representing or acting on behalf of the nongovernmental organization;

(B) the nongovernmental organization is controlled by and governed by a membership of and represents a group or association of active duty, retired, or injured fire fighters (for the purposes of this Section, "fire fighter" has the meaning ascribed to that term in Section 2 of the Illinois Fire Protection Training Act) or active duty, retired, or injured emergency medical technicians - ambulance, emergency medical technicians - intermediate, emergency medical technicians - paramedic, ambulance drivers, or other medical assistance or first aid personnel; and

(C) before commencing the solicitation or the sale or delivery or the offers to sell or deliver any merchandise, goods, services, memberships, or advertisements, the soliciting or selling person and the nongovernmental organization have entered into a written contract that specifies and states clearly and fully the purposes for which the proceeds of the solicitation, contribution, or sale will be used.

(7) No person may knowingly claim or represent that he or she is an airman, airline employee, airport employee, or contractor at an airport in order to obtain the uniform, identification card, license, or other identification paraphernalia of an airman, airline employee, airport employee, or contractor at an airport.

(8) No person, firm, copartnership, or corporation (except corporations organized and doing business under the Pawners Societies Act) shall knowingly use a name that contains in it the words "Pawners' Society".

(b) False personation; judicial process. A person commits a false personation if he or she knowingly and falsely represents himself or herself to be any of the following:

(1) An attorney authorized to practice law for purposes of compensation or consideration. This paragraph (b)(1) does not apply to a person who unintentionally fails to pay attorney registration fees established by Supreme Court Rule.

(2) A public officer or a public employee or an official or employee of the federal government.

(2.3) A public officer, a public employee, or an official or employee of the federal government, and the false representation is made in furtherance of the commission of felony.

(2.7) A public officer or a public employee, and the false representation is for the purpose of effectuating identity theft as defined in Section 16G-15 of this Code.

(3) A peace officer.

(4) A peace officer while carrying a deadly weapon.

(5) A peace officer in attempting or committing a felony.

(6) A peace officer in attempting or committing a forcible felony.

(7) The parent, legal guardian, or other relation of a minor child to any public official, public employee, or elementary or secondary school employee or administrator.

(7.5) The legal guardian, including any representative of a State or public guardian, of a person with a disability appointed under Article XIa of the Probate Act of 1975.

8) A fire fighter.

(9) A fire fighter while carrying a deadly weapon.

(10) A fire fighter in attempting or committing a felony.

(11) An emergency management worker of any jurisdiction in this State.

(12) An emergency management worker of any jurisdiction in this State in attempting or committing a felony. For the purposes of this subsection (b), "emergency management worker" has the meaning provided under Section 2-6.6 of this Code.

(c) Fraudulent advertisement of a corporate name.

(1) A company, association, or individual commits fraudulent advertisement of a corporate name if he, she, or it, not being incorporated, puts forth a sign or advertisement and assumes, for the purpose of soliciting business, a corporate name.

(2) Nothing contained in this subsection (c) prohibits a corporation, company, association, or person from using a divisional designation or trade name in conjunction with its corporate name or assumed name under Section 4.05 of the Business Corporation Act of 1983 or, if it is a member of a partnership or joint venture, from doing partnership or joint venture business under the partnership or joint venture name.

The name under which the joint venture or partnership does business may differ from the names of the members. Business may not be conducted or transacted under that joint venture or partnership name, however, unless all provisions of the Assumed Business Name Act have been complied with. Nothing in this subsection (c) permits a foreign corporation to do business in this State without complying with all Illinois laws regulating the doing of business by foreign corporations. No foreign corporation may conduct or transact business in this State as a member of a partnership or joint venture that violates any Illinois law regulating or pertaining to the doing of business by foreign corporations in Illinois.

(3) The provisions of this subsection (c) do not apply to limited partnerships formed under the Revised Uniform Limited Partnership Act or under the Uniform Limited Partnership Act (2001).

(d) False law enforcement badges.

(1) A person commits false law enforcement badges if he or she knowingly produces, sells, or distributes a law enforcement badge without the express written consent of the law enforcement agency represented on the badge or, in case of a reorganized or defunct law enforcement agency, its successor law enforcement agency.

(2) It is a defense to false law enforcement badges that the law enforcement badge is used or is intended to be used exclusively:

(i) as a memento or in a collection or exhibit;

(ii) for decorative purposes; or

(iii) for a dramatic presentation, such as a theatrical, film, or television production.

(e) False medals. (1) A person commits a false personation if he or she knowingly and falsely represents himself or herself to be a recipient of, or wears on his or her person, any of the following medals if that medal was not awarded to that person by the United States Government, irrespective of branch of service: The Congressional Medal of Honor, The Distinguished Service Cross, The Navy Cross, The Air Force Cross, The Silver Star, The Bronze Star, or the Purple Heart.

(2) It is a defense to a prosecution under paragraph (e)(1) that the medal is used, or is intended to be used, exclusively:

(A) for a dramatic presentation, such as a theatrical, film, or television production, or a historical re-enactment; or

(B) for a costume worn, or intended to be worn, by a person under 18 years of age.

(f) Sentence.

(1) A violation of paragraph (a)(8) is a petty offense subject to a fine of not less than $ 5 nor more than $ 100, and the person, firm, co-partnership, or corporation commits an additional petty offense for each day he, she, or it continues to commit the violation. A violation of paragraph (c)(1) is a petty offense, and the company, association, or person commits an

additional petty offense for each day he, she, or it continues to commit the violation. A violation of subsection (e) is a petty offense for which the offender shall be fined at least $ 100 and not more than $ 200.

(2) A violation of paragraph (a)(1) or (a)(3) is a Class C misdemeanor.

(3) A violation of paragraph (a)(2), (a)(7), (b)(2), or (b)(7) or subsection (d) is a Class A misdemeanor. A second or subsequent violation of subsection (d) is a Class 3 felony.

(4) A violation of paragraph (a)(4), (a)(5), (a)(6), (b)(1), (b)(2.3), (b)(2.7), (b)(3), (b)(8), or (b)(11) is a Class 4 felony.

(5) A violation of paragraph (b)(4), (b)(9), or (b)(12) is a Class 3 felony.

(6) A violation of paragraph (b)(5) or (b)(10) is a Class 2 felony.

(7) A violation of paragraph (b)(6) is a Class 1 felony.

§ 17-2. False personation; use of title; solicitation; certain entities. (a) A person commits a false personation when he or she falsely represents himself or herself to be a member or representative of any veterans' or public safety personnel organization or a representative of any charitable organization, or when any person exhibits or uses in any manner any decal, badge or insignia of any charitable, public safety personnel, or veterans' organization when not authorized to do so by the charitable, public safety personnel, or veterans' organization. "Public safety personnel organization" has the meaning ascribed to that term in Section 1 of the Solicitation for Charity Act.

(a-5) A person commits a false personation when he or she falsely represents himself or herself to be a veteran in seeking employment or public office. In this subsection, "veteran" means a person who has served in the Armed Services or Reserve Forces of the United States.

(a-6) A person commits a false personation when he or she falsely represents himself or herself to be a recipient of, or wears on his or her person, any of the following medals if that medal was not awarded to that person by the United States government, irrespective of branch of service: the Congressional Medal of Honor, the Distinguished Service Cross, the Navy Cross, the Air Force Cross, the Silver Star, the Bronze Star, or the Purple Heart.
It is a defense to a prosecution under this subsection (a-6) that the medal is used, or is intended to be used, exclusively:

(1) for a dramatic presentation, such as a theatrical, film, or television production, or a historical re-enactment; or

(2) for a costume worn, or intended to be worn, by a person under 18 years of age.
(a-7) A person commits a false personation when he or she knowingly and falsely represents himself or herself to be:

(1) another actual person and does an act in such assumed character with intent to intimidate, threaten, injure, defraud, or to obtain a benefit from another; or

(2) a representative of an actual person or organization and does an act in such false capacity with intent to obtain a benefit or to injure or defraud another.

(b) No person shall use the words "Chicago Police," "Chicago Police Department," "Chicago Patrolman," "Chicago Sergeant," "Chicago Lieutenant," "Chicago Peace Officer" or any other words to the same effect in the title of any organization, magazine, or other publication without the express approval of the Chicago Police Board.

(b-5) No person shall use the words "Cook County Sheriff's Police" or "Cook County Sheriff" or any other words to the same effect in the title of any organization, magazine, or other publication without the express approval of the office of the Cook County Sheriff's Merit Board. The references to names and titles in this Section may not be construed as authorizing use of the names and titles of other organizations or public safety personnel organizations otherwise prohibited by this Section or the Solicitation for Charity Act.

(b-10) No person may use, in the title of any organization, magazine, or other publication, the words "officer", "peace officer", "police", "law enforcement", "trooper", "sheriff", "deputy", "deputy sheriff", or "state police" in combination with the name of any state, state agency, public university, or unit of local government without the express written authorization of that state, state agency, or unit of local government.

(c) (Blank).

(c-1) No person may claim or represent that he or she is acting on behalf of any police department, chief of a police department, fire department, chief of a fire department, sheriff's department, or sheriff when soliciting financial contributions or selling or delivering or offering to sell or deliver any merchandise, goods, services, memberships, or advertisements unless the chief of the police department, fire department, and the corporate or municipal authority thereof, or the sheriff has first entered into a written agreement with the person or with an organization with which the person is affiliated and the agreement permits the activity.

(c-2) No person, when soliciting financial contributions or selling or delivering or offering to sell or deliver any merchandise, goods, services, memberships, or advertisements may claim or represent that he or she is representing or acting on behalf of any nongovernmental organization by any name which includes "officer", "peace officer", "police", "law enforcement", "trooper", "sheriff", "deputy", "deputy sheriff", "State police", or any other word or words which would reasonably be understood to imply that the organization is composed of law enforcement personnel unless the person is actually representing or acting on behalf of the nongovernmental organization, and the nongovernmental organization is controlled by and governed by a membership of and represents a group or association of active duty peace officers, retired peace officers, or injured peace officers and before commencing the solicitation or the sale or the offers to sell any merchandise, goods, services, memberships, or advertisements, a written contract between the soliciting or selling person and the nongovernmental organization has been entered into.

(c-3) No person may solicit financial contributions or sell or deliver or offer to sell or deliver any merchandise, goods, services, memberships, or advertisements on behalf of a police, sheriff, or other law enforcement department unless that person is actually representing or acting on behalf of the department or governmental organization and has entered into a written contract with the police chief, or head of the law enforcement department, and the corporate or municipal authority thereof, or the sheriff, which specifies and states clearly and fully the purposes for which the proceeds of the solicitation, contribution, or sale will be used.

(c-4) No person, when soliciting financial contributions or selling or delivering or offering to sell or deliver any merchandise, goods, services, memberships, or advertisements, may claim or represent that he or she is representing or acting on behalf of any nongovernmental organization by any name which includes the term "fireman", "fire fighter", "paramedic", or any other word or words which would reasonably be understood to imply that the organization is composed of fire fighter or paramedic personnel unless the person is actually representing or acting on behalf of the nongovernmental organization, and the nongovernmental organization is controlled by and governed by a membership of and represents a group or association of active duty, retired, or injured fire fighters (for the purposes of this Section, "fire fighter" has the meaning ascribed to that term in Section 2 of the Illinois Fire Protection Training Act[2]) or active duty, retired, or injured emergency medical technicians--ambulance, emergency medical technicians--intermediate, emergency medical technicians--paramedic, ambulance drivers, or other medical assistance or first aid personnel, and before commencing the solicitation or the sale or delivery or the offers to sell or deliver any merchandise, goods, services, memberships, or advertisements, a written contract between the soliciting or selling person and the nongovernmental organization has been entered into.

(c-5) No person may solicit financial contributions or sell or deliver or offer to sell or deliver any merchandise, goods, services, memberships, or advertisements on behalf of a department or departments of fire fighters unless that person is actually representing or acting on behalf of the department or departments and has entered into a written contract with the department chief and corporate or municipal authority thereof which specifies and states clearly and fully the purposes for which the proceeds of the solicitation, contribution, or sale will be used.

(c-6) No person may claim or represent that he or she is an airman, airline employee, airport employee, or contractor at an airport in order to obtain the uniform, identification card, license, or other identification paraphernalia of an airman, airline employee, airport employee, or contractor at an airport.

(d) Sentence. False personation, unapproved use of a name or title, or solicitation in violation of subsection (a), (b), (b-5), or (b-10) of this Section is a Class C misdemeanor. False personation in violation of subsections (a-5), (a-7), and (c-6) is a Class A misdemeanor. False personation in violation of subsection (a-6) of this Section is a petty offense for which the offender shall be fined at least $100 and not exceeding $200. Engaging in any activity in violation of subsection (c-1), (c-2), (c-3), (c-4), or (c-5) of this Section is a Class 4 felony.

(e) A violation of this Section may be accomplished in person or by any means of communication, including but not limited to the use of an Internet website or any form of electronic communication.

§ 17-3. Forgery. (a) A person commits forgery when, with intent to defraud, he or she knowingly:

(1) makes a false document or alters any document to make it false and that document is apparently capable of defrauding; or

(2) issues or delivers such document knowing it to have been thus made or altered; or

(3) possesses, with intent to issue or deliver, any such document knowing it to have been thus made or altered; or

(4) unlawfully uses the digital signature, as defined in the Financial Institutions Electronic Documents and Digital Signature Act, of another; or

(5) unlawfully uses the signature device of another to create an electronic signature of that other person, as those terms are defined in the Electronic Commerce Security Act.

(b) (Blank).

(c) A document apparently capable of defrauding another includes, but is not limited to, one by which any right, obligation or power with reference to any person or property may be created, transferred, altered or terminated. A document includes any record or electronic record as those terms are defined in the Electronic Commerce Security Act. for purposes of this Section, a document also includes a Universal Price Code Label or coin.
(c-5) For purposes of this Section, "false document" or "document that is false" includes, but is not limited to, a document whose contents are false in some material way, or that purports to have been made by another or at another time, or with different provisions, or by authority of one who did not give such authority.
(d) Sentence. (1) Except as provided in paragraphs (2) and (3), forgery is a Class 3 felony.

(2) Forgery is a Class 4 felony when only one Universal Price Code Label is forged.

(3) Forgery is a Class A misdemeanor when an academic degree or coin is forged.

(e) It is not a violation of this Section if a false academic degree explicitly states "for novelty purposes only".

Commentary – Forgery

Section 17-3 sets forth the elements of the crime of forgery. forgery requires proof that a defendant (1)with intent to defraud (2)knowingly (3) made or altered (4) a document or a provision of a document that (5) purports to have been made by another or at another time and (6) was capable of defrauding another of money, property or other right or power. The statute has been amended in recent times to address the creation of computer generated documents or the creation or use of a digital signature for purposes of committing forgery. acting without authority, in creating a false deed to transfer property and signing someone else's name and having it recorded, in endorsing another payee's name on a check and cashing it, and signing someone else's name to an application for benefits would be a common forms of forgery. Note that the crime is complete once the forged document is created, possessed, delivered or presented and the intent to defraud is present. The potential transaction itself does not have to be completed for the crime to be complete. The forged document must purport to be made by someone else.

In *People v. De Filippo* 235 Ill.2d 377, 919 N.E.2d 921 (2009), the defendant sought retirement benefits based on a claim that he was sworn in as a deputy in 1981 and wrote a notarized letter to that effect. He used the letter with the sheriff and others on three separate occasions with that false date. His conviction for forgery was reversed however because he never represented the information in a document that purported to be from someone else – the statement about his swearing in date came only from him. Forgery deals with documents that appear to have been changed to reflect the action of another or reflect a change in time.

In *People v. Brown*, 2013 IL 114196, 1 N.E.3d 888 (Ill. S. Ct. 2013), the court reversed the defendant's conviction for forgery by making a counterfeit document, where the proof was that the defendant's conduct was limited to endorsing the document and presenting it for deposit.

In *People v. Olsen* 351 Ill.App.3d 534, 814 N.E.2d 211 (Ill. App. Ct. 2nd Dist. 2004), the defendant's conviction for forgery was upheld. She had inherited property in Wisconsin from her mother and had placed title in her name, her husband's name and her two daughters' names as joint tenants. After her husband died, the defendant remarried and sought to put her new husband's name on the property but her daughters would not sign the deed. The defendant created a quit-claim deed adding her new husband as a fourth joint tenant and signed her daughters' names to it, had it notarized and recorded it in Wisconsin. the document purported to be the act of her daughters, was capable of affecting the actions and rights of others (the notary, the recorder of deeds, her daughters and even future buyers of the property) and thus satisfied the "intent to defraud" requirement and other elements of forgery.

§ 17-3.5. Deceptive sale of gold or silver. (a) Whoever makes for sale, or sells, or offers to sell or dispose of, or has in his or her possession with intent to sell or dispose of, any article or articles construed in whole or in part, of gold or any alloy or imitation thereof, having thereon or on any box, package, cover, wrapper or other thing enclosing or encasing such article or articles for sale, any stamp, brand, engraving, printed label, trade mark, imprint or other mark, indicating or designed, or intended to indicate, that the gold, alloy or imitation thereof, in such article or articles, is different from or better than the actual kind and quality of such gold, alloy or imitation, shall be guilty of a petty offense and shall be fined in any sum not less than $ 50 nor more than $ 100.

(b) Whoever makes for sale, sells or offers to sell or dispose of or has in his or her possession, with intent to sell or dispose of, any article or articles constructed in whole or in part of silver or any alloy or imitation thereof, having thereon--or on any box, package, cover, wrapper or other thing enclosing or encasing such article or articles for sale--any stamp, brand, engraving, printed label, trademark, imprint or other mark, containing the words "sterling" or "sterling silver," referring, or designed or intended to refer, to the silver, alloy or imitation thereof in such article or articles, when such silver, alloy or imitation thereof shall contain less than nine hundred and twenty-five one-thousandths thereof of pure silver, shall be guilty of a petty offense and shall be fined in any sum not less than $ 50 nor more than $ 100.

(c) Whoever makes for sale, sells or offers to sell or dispose of or has in his or her possession, with intent to sell or dispose of, any article or articles constructed in whole or in part of silver or any alloy or imitation thereof, having thereon--or on any box, package, cover, wrapper or other thing enclosing or encasing such article or articles for sale--any stamp, brand, engraving, printed label, trademark, imprint, or other mark, containing the words "coin" or "coin silver," referring to or designed or intended to refer to, the silver, alloy or imitation thereof, in such article or articles, when such silver, alloy or imitation shall contain less than nine-tenths thereof pure silver, shall be guilty of a petty offense and shall be fined in any sum not less than $ 50 and not more than $ 100.

§ 17-5. Deceptive collection practices.
A collection agency as defined in the Collection Agency Act or any employee of such collection agency commits a deceptive collection practice when, with the intent to collect a debt owed to an individual or a corporation or other entity, he, she, or it does any of the following:

(a) Represents falsely that he or she is an attorney, a policeman, a sheriff or deputy sheriff, a bailiff, a county clerk or employee of a county clerk's office, or any other person who by statute is authorized to enforce the law or any order of a court.

(b) While attempting to collect an alleged debt, misrepresents to the alleged debtor or to his or her immediate family the corporate, partnership or proprietary name or other trade or business name under which the debt collector is engaging in debt collections and which he, she, or it is legally authorized to use.

(c) While attempting to collect an alleged debt, adds to the debt any service charge, interest or penalty which he, she, or it is not entitled by law to add.

(d) Threatens to ruin, destroy, or otherwise adversely affect an alleged debtor's credit rating unless, at the same time, a disclosure is made in accordance with federal law that the alleged debtor has a right to inspect his or her credit rating.

(e) accepts from an alleged debtor a payment which he, she, or it knows is not owed. Sentence. the commission of a deceptive collection practice is a Business Offense punishable by a fine not to exceed $ 3,000.

§ 17-5.5. Unlawful attempt to collect compensated debt against a crime victim. (a) a person or a vendor commits unlawful attempt to collect a compensated debt against a crime victim when, with intent to collect funds for a debt incurred by or on behalf of a crime victim, which debt has been approved for payment by the Court of Claims under the Crime Victims Compensation Act, but the funds are involuntarily withheld from the person or vendor by the Comptroller by virtue of an outstanding obligation owed by the person or vendor to the State under the Uncollected State Claims Act, the person or vendor:

(1) communicates with, harasses, or intimidates the crime victim for payment;

(2) contacts or distributes information to affect the compensated crime victim's credit rating as a result of the compensated debt; or

(3) takes any other action adverse to the crime victim or his or her family on account of the compensated debt.

(b) Sentence. Unlawful attempt to collect a compensated debt against a crime victim is a Class A misdemeanor.

(c) Nothing in this Code prevents the attempt to collect an uncompensated debt or an uncompensated portion of a compensated debt incurred by or on behalf of a crime victim and not covered under the Crime Victims Compensation Act.

(d) As used in this Section, "crime victim" means a victim of a violent crime or applicant as defined in the Crime Victims Compensation Act. "Compensated debt" means a debt incurred by or on behalf of a crime victim and approved for payment by the Court of Claims under the Crime Victims Compensation Act.

§ 17-5.7. Deceptive advertising. (a) Any person, firm, corporation or association or agent or employee thereof, who, with intent to sell, purchase, or in any wise dispose of, or to contract with reference to merchandise, securities, real estate, service, employment, money, credit or anything offered by such person, firm, corporation or association, or agent or employee thereof, directly or indirectly, to the public for sale, purchase, loan, distribution, or the hire of personal services, or with intent to increase the consumption of or to contract with reference to any merchandise, real estate, securities, money, credit, loan, service or employment, or to induce the public in any manner to enter into any obligation relating thereto, or to acquire title thereto, or an interest therein, or to make any loan, makes, publishes, disseminates, circulates, or places before the public, or causes, directly or indirectly, to be made, published, disseminated, circulated, or placed before the public, in this State, in a newspaper, magazine, or other publication, or in the form of a book, notice, handbill, poster, sign, bill, circular, pamphlet, letter, placard, card, label, or over any radio or television station, or in any other way similar or dissimilar to the foregoing, an advertisement, announcement, or statement of any sort regarding merchandise, securities, real estate, money, credit, service, employment, or anything so offered for use, purchase, loan or sale, or the interest, terms or conditions upon which such loan will be made to the public, which advertisement contains any assertion, representation or statement of fact which is untrue, misleading or deceptive, shall be guilty of a Class A misdemeanor.

(b) Any person, firm or corporation offering for sale merchandise, commodities or service by making, publishing, disseminating, circulating or placing before the public within this State in any manner an advertisement of merchandise, commodities, or service, with the intent, design or purpose not to sell the merchandise, commodities, or service so advertised at the price stated therein, or otherwise communicated, or with intent not to sell the merchandise, commodities, or service so advertised, may be enjoined from such advertising upon application for injunctive relief by the State's Attorney or Attorney General, and shall also be guilty of a Class A misdemeanor.

(c) Any person, firm or corporation who makes, publishes, disseminates, circulates or places before the public, or causes, directly or indirectly to be made, published, disseminated, circulated or placed before the public, in this State, in a newspaper, magazine or other publication published in this State, or in the form of a book, notice, handbill, poster, sign, bill, circular, pamphlet, letter, placard, card, or label distributed in this State, or over any radio or television station located in this State or in any other way in this State similar or dissimilar to the foregoing, an advertisement, announcement, statement or representation of any kind to the public relating to the sale, offering for sale, purchase, use or lease of any real estate in a subdivision located outside the State of Illinois may be enjoined from such activity upon application for injunctive relief by the State's Attorney or Attorney General and shall also be guilty of a Class A misdemeanor unless such advertisement, announcement, statement or representation contains or is accompanied by a clear, concise statement of the proximity of such real estate in common units of measurement to public schools, public highways, fresh water supply, public sewers, electric power, stores and shops, and telephone service or contains a statement that one or more of such facilities are not readily available, and name those not available.

(d) Subsections (a), (b), and (c) do not apply to any medium for the printing, publishing, or disseminating of advertising, or any owner, agent or employee thereof, nor to any advertising agency or owner, agent or employee thereof, nor to any radio or television station, or owner, agent, or employee thereof, for printing, publishing, or disseminating, or causing to be printed, published, or disseminated, such advertisement in good faith and without knowledge of the deceptive character thereof.

(e) No person, firm or corporation owning or operating a service station shall advertise or hold out or state to the public the per gallon price of gasoline, upon any sign on the premises of such station, unless such price includes all taxes, and unless the price, as so advertised, corresponds with the price appearing on the pump from which such gasoline is dispensed. Also, the identity of the product must be included with the price in any such advertisement, holding out or statement to the public. Any person who violates this subsection (e) shall be guilty of a petty offense.

Subdivision 10. Fraud on A Governmental Entity

§ 17-6. State benefits fraud. (a) A person commits State benefits fraud when he or she obtains or attempts to obtain money or benefits from the State of Illinois, from any political subdivision thereof, or from any program funded or administered in whole or in part by the State of Illinois or any political subdivision thereof through the knowing use of false identification documents or through the knowing misrepresentation of his or her age, place of residence, number of dependents, marital or family status, employment status, financial status, or any other material fact upon which his eligibility for or degree of participation in any benefit program might be based.

(b) Notwithstanding any provision of State law to the contrary, every application or other document submitted to an agency or department of the State of Illinois or any political subdivision thereof to establish or determine eligibility for money or benefits from the State of Illinois or from any political subdivision thereof, or from any program funded or administered in whole or in part by the State of Illinois or any political subdivision thereof, shall be made available upon request to any law enforcement agency for use in the investigation or prosecution of State benefits fraud or for use in the investigation or prosecution of any other crime arising out of the same transaction or occurrence.

Except as otherwise permitted by law, information disclosed pursuant to this subsection shall be used and disclosed only for the purposes provided herein. The provisions of this Section shall be operative only to the extent that they do not conflict with any federal law or regulation governing federal grants to this State.

(c) Any employee of the State of Illinois or any agency or political subdivision thereof may seize as evidence any false or fraudulent document presented to him or her in connection with an application for or receipt of money or benefits from the State of Illinois, from any political subdivision thereof, or from any program funded or administered in whole or in part by the State of Illinois or any political subdivision thereof.

(d) Sentence. (1) State benefits fraud is a Class 4 felony except when more than $ 300 is obtained, in which case State benefits fraud is a Class 3 felony.

(2) If a person knowingly misrepresents oneself as a veteran or as a dependent of a veteran with the intent of obtaining benefits or privileges provided by the State or its political subdivisions to veterans or their dependents, then State benefits fraud is a Class 3 felony when $ 300 or less is obtained and a Class 2 felony when more than $ 300 is obtained. For the purposes of this paragraph (2), benefits and privileges include, but are not limited to, those benefits and privileges available under the Veterans' Employment Act, the Viet Nam Veterans Compensation Act, the Prisoner of War Bonus Act, the War Bonus Extension Act, the Military Veterans Assistance Act, the Veterans' Employment Representative Act, the Veterans

Preference Act, the Service Member's Employment Tenure Act, the Housing for Veterans With Disabilities Act, the Under Age Veterans Benefits Act, the Survivors Compensation Act, the Children of Deceased Veterans Act, the Veterans Burial Places Act, the Higher Education Student Assistance Act, or any other loans, assistance in employment, monetary payments, or tax exemptions offered by the State or its political subdivisions for veterans or their dependents.

§ 17-6.3. WIC fraud. (a) For the purposes of this Section, the Special Supplemental Food Program for Women, Infants and Children administered by the Illinois Department of Public Health or Department of Human Services shall be referred to as "WIC".

(b) A person commits WIC fraud if he or she knowingly (i) uses, acquires, possesses, or transfers WIC Food Instruments or authorizations to participate in WIC in any manner not authorized by law or the rules of the Illinois Department of Public Health or Department of Human Services or (ii) uses, acquires, possesses, or transfers altered WIC Food Instruments or authorizations to participate in WIC.

(c) Administrative malfeasance.

(1) A person commits administrative malfeasance if he or she knowingly or recklessly misappropriates, misuses, or unlawfully withholds or converts to his or her own use or to the use of another any public funds made available for WIC.

(2) An official or employee of the State or a unit of local government who knowingly aids, abets, assists, or participates in a known violation of this Section is subject to disciplinary proceedings under the rules of the applicable State agency or unit of local government.

(d) Unauthorized possession of identification document. A person commits unauthorized possession of an identification document if he or she knowingly possesses, with intent to commit a misdemeanor or felony, another person's identification document issued by the Illinois Department of Public Health or Department of Human Services. For purposes of this Section, "identification document" includes, but is not limited to, an authorization to participate in WIC or a card or other document that identifies a person as being entitled to WIC benefits.

(e) Penalties. (1) If an individual, firm, corporation, association, agency, institution, or other legal entity is found by a court to have engaged in an act, practice, or course of conduct declared unlawful under subsection (a), (b), or (c) of this Section and:

(A) the total amount of money involved in the violation, including the monetary value of the WIC Food Instruments and the value of commodities, is less than $ 150, the violation is a Class A misdemeanor; a second or subsequent violation is a Class 4 felony;

(B) the total amount of money involved in the violation, including the monetary value of the WIC Food Instruments and the value of commodities, is $ 150 or more but less than $ 1,000, the violation is a Class 4 felony; a second or subsequent violation is a Class 3 felony;

(C) the total amount of money involved in the violation, including the monetary value of the WIC Food Instruments and the value of commodities, is $ 1,000 or more but less than $ 5,000, the violation is a Class 3 felony; a second or subsequent violation is a Class 2 felony;

(D) the total amount of money involved in the violation, including the monetary value of the WIC Food Instruments and the value of commodities, is $ 5,000 or more but less than $ 10,000, the violation is a Class 2 felony; a second or subsequent violation is a Class 1 felony; or

(E) the total amount of money involved in the violation, including the monetary value of the WIC Food Instruments and the value of commodities, is $ 10,000 or more, the violation is a Class 1 felony and the defendant shall be permanently ineligible to participate in WIC.

(2) A violation of subsection (d) is a Class 4 felony.

(3) The State's Attorney of the county in which the violation of this Section occurred or the Attorney General shall bring actions arising

under this Section in the name of the People of the State of Illinois.

(4) For purposes of determining the classification of an offense under this subsection (e), all of the money received as a result of the unlawful act, practice, or course of conduct, including the value of any WIC Food Instruments and the value of commodities, shall be aggregated.

(f) Seizure and forfeiture of property. (1) A person who commits a felony violation of this Section is subject to the property forfeiture provisions set forth in Article 124B of the Code of Criminal Procedure of 1963.

(2) Property subject to forfeiture under this subsection (f) may be seized by the Director of State Police or any local law enforcement agency upon process or seizure warrant issued by any court having jurisdiction over the property. The Director or a local law enforcement agency may seize property under this subsection (f) without process under any of the following circumstances:

(A) If the seizure is incident to inspection under an administrative inspection warrant.

(B) If the property subject to seizure has been the subject of a prior judgment in favor of the State in a criminal proceeding or in an injunction or forfeiture proceeding under Article 124B of the Code of Criminal Procedure of 1963.

(C) If there is probable cause to believe that the property is directly or indirectly dangerous to health or safety.

(D) If there is probable cause to believe that the property is subject to forfeiture under this subsection (f) and Article 124B of the Code of Criminal Procedure of 1963 and the property is seized under circumstances in which a warrantless seizure or arrest would be reasonable.

(E) In accordance with the Code of Criminal Procedure of 1963.

(g) Future participation as WIC vendor. A person who has been convicted of a felony violation of this Section is prohibited from participating as a WIC vendor for a minimum period of 3 years following conviction and until the total amount of money involved in the violation, including the value of WIC Food Instruments and the value of commodities, is repaid to WIC. This prohibition shall extend to any person with management responsibility in a firm, corporation, association, agency, institution, or other legal entity that has been convicted of a violation of this Section and to an officer or person owning, directly or indirectly, 5% or more of the shares of stock or other evidences of ownership in a corporate vendor.

§ 17-6.5. Persons under deportation order; ineligibility for benefits. (a) An individual against whom a United States Immigration Judge has issued an order of deportation which has been affirmed by the Board of Immigration Review, as well as an individual who appeals such an order pending appeal, under paragraph 19 of Section 241(a) of the Immigration and Nationality Act relating to persecution of others on account of race, religion, national origin or political opinion under the direction of or in association with the Nazi government of Germany or its allies, shall be ineligible for the following benefits authorized by State law:

(1) The homestead exemptions and homestead improvement exemption under Sections 15-170, 15-175, 15-176, and 15-180 of the Property Tax Code.

(2) Grants under the Senior Citizens and Persons With Disabilities Property Tax Relief and Pharmaceutical Assistance Act.

(3) The double income tax exemption conferred upon persons 65 years of age or older by Section 204 of the Illinois Income Tax Act.

(4) Grants provided by the Department on Aging.

(5) Reductions in vehicle registration fees under Section 3-806.3 of the Illinois Vehicle Code.

(6) Free fishing and reduced fishing license fees under Sections 20-5 and 20-40 of the Fish and Aquatic Life Code.

(7) Tuition free courses for senior citizens under the Senior Citizen Courses Act.

(8) Any benefits under the Illinois Public Aid Code.

(b) If a person has been found by a court to have knowingly received benefits in violation of subsection (a) and:

(1) the total monetary value of the benefits received is less than $ 150, the person is guilty of a Class A misdemeanor; a second or subsequent violation is a Class 4 felony;

(2) the total monetary value of the benefits received is $ 150 or more but less than $ 1,000, the person is guilty of a Class 4 felony; a second or subsequent violation is a Class 3 felony;

(3) the total monetary value of the benefits received is $ 1,000 or more but less than $ 5,000, the person is guilty of a Class 3 felony; a second or subsequent violation is a Class 2 felony;

(4) the total monetary value of the benefits received is $ 5,000 or more but less than $ 10,000, the person is guilty of a Class 2 felony; a second or subsequent violation is a Class 1 felony; or

(5) the total monetary value of the benefits received is $ 10,000 or more, the person is guilty of a Class 1 felony.

(c) For purposes of determining the classification of an offense under this Section, all of the monetary value of the benefits received as a result of the unlawful act, practice, or course of conduct may be accumulated.

(d) Any grants awarded to persons described in subsection (a) may be recovered by the State of Illinois in a civil action commenced by the Attorney General in the circuit court of Sangamon County or the State's Attorney of the county of residence of the person described in subsection (a).

(e) An individual described in subsection (a) who has been deported shall be restored to any benefits which that individual has been denied under State law pursuant to subsection (a) if (i) the Attorney General of the United States has issued an order cancelling deportation and has adjusted the status of the individual to that of an alien lawfully admitted for permanent residence in the United States or (ii) the country to which the individual has been deported adjudicates or exonerates the individual in a judicial or administrative proceeding as not being guilty of the persecution of others on account of race, religion, national origin, or political opinion under the direction of or in association with the Nazi government of Germany or its allies.

§ 17-8.3. False information on an application for employment with certain public or private agencies; use of false academic degree. (a) It is unlawful for an applicant for employment with a public or private agency that provides State funded services to persons with mental illness or developmental disabilities to knowingly furnish false information regarding professional certification, licensing, criminal background, or employment history for the 5 years immediately preceding the date of application on an application for employment with the agency if the position of employment requires or provides opportunity for contact with persons with mental illness or developmental disabilities.

(b) It is unlawful for a person to knowingly use a false academic degree for the purpose of obtaining employment or admission to an institution of higher learning or admission to an advanced degree program at an institution of higher learning or for the purpose of obtaining a promotion or higher compensation in employment.

(c) Sentence. A violation of this Section is a Class A misdemeanor.

§ 17-8.5. Fraud on a governmental entity. (a) Fraud on a governmental entity. A person commits fraud on a governmental entity when he or she knowingly obtains, attempts to obtain, or causes to be obtained, by deception, control over the property of any governmental entity by the making of a false claim of bodily injury or of damage to or loss or theft of property or by causing a false claim of bodily injury or of damage to or loss or theft of property to be made against the governmental entity, intending to deprive the governmental entity permanently of the use and benefit of that property.

(b) Aggravated fraud on a governmental entity. A person commits aggravated fraud on a governmental entity when he or she commits fraud on a governmental entity 3 or more times within an 18-month period arising out of separate incidents or transactions.

(c) Conspiracy to commit fraud on a governmental entity. If aggravated fraud on a governmental entity forms the basis for a charge of conspiracy under Section 8-2 of this Code against a person, the person or persons with whom the accused is alleged to have agreed to commit the 3 or more violations of this Section need not be the same person or persons for each violation, as long as the accused was a part of the common scheme or plan to engage in each of the 3 or more alleged violations.

(d) Organizer of an aggravated fraud on a governmental entity conspiracy. A person commits being an organizer of an aggravated fraud on a governmental entity conspiracy if aggravated fraud on a governmental entity forms the basis for a charge of conspiracy under Section 8-2 of this Code and the person occupies a position of organizer, supervisor, financer, or other position of management within the conspiracy.

For the purposes of this Section, the person or persons with whom the accused is alleged to have agreed to commit the 3 or more violations of subdivision (a)(1) of Section 17-10.5 or subsection (a) of Section 17-8.5 of this Code need not be the same person or persons for each violation, as long as the accused occupied a position of organizer, supervisor, financer, or other position of management in each of the 3 or more alleged violations.

Notwithstanding Section 8-5 of this Code, a person may be convicted and sentenced both for the offense of being an organizer of an aggravated fraud conspiracy and for any other offense that is the object of the conspiracy.

(e) Sentence.

(1) A violation of subsection (a) in which the value of the property obtained or attempted to be obtained is $ 300 or less is a Class A misdemeanor.

(2) A violation of subsection (a) in which the value of the property obtained or attempted to be obtained is more than $ 300 but not more than $ 10,000 is a Class 3 felony.

(3) A violation of subsection (a) in which the value of the property obtained or attempted to be obtained is more than $ 10,000 but not more than $ 100,000 is a Class 2 felony.

(4) A violation of subsection (a) in which the value of the property obtained or attempted to be obtained is more than $ 100,000 is a Class 1 felony.

(5) A violation of subsection (b) is a Class 1 felony, regardless of the value of the property obtained, attempted to be obtained, or caused to be obtained.

(6) The offense of being an organizer of an aggravated fraud conspiracy is a Class X felony.

(7) Notwithstanding Section 8-5 of this Code, a person may be convicted and sentenced both for the offense of conspiracy to commit fraud and for any other offense that is the object of the conspiracy.

(f) Civil damages for fraud on a governmental entity. A person who knowingly obtains, attempts to obtain, or causes to be obtained, by deception, control over the property of a governmental entity by the making of a false claim of bodily injury or of damage to or loss or theft of property, intending to deprive the governmental entity permanently of the use and benefit of that property, shall be civilly liable to the governmental entity that paid the claim or against whom the claim was made or to the subrogee of the governmental entity in an amount equal to either 3 times the value of the property wrongfully obtained or, if property was not wrongfully obtained, twice the value of the property attempted to be obtained, whichever amount is greater, plus reasonable attorney's fees.

(g) Determination of property value. For the purposes of this Section, if the exact value of the property attempted to be obtained is either not alleged by the claimant or not otherwise specifically set, the value of the property shall be the fair market replacement value of the property claimed to be lost, the reasonable costs of reimbursing a vendor or other claimant for services to be rendered, or both.

(h) Actions by State licensing agencies.

(1) All State licensing agencies, the Illinois State Police, and the Department of Financial and Professional Regulation shall coordinate enforcement efforts relating to acts of fraud on a governmental entity.

(2) If a person who is licensed or registered under the laws of the State of Illinois to engage in a business or profession is convicted of or pleads guilty to engaging in an act of fraud on a governmental entity, the Illinois State Police must forward to each State agency by which the person is licensed or registered a copy of the conviction or plea and all supporting evidence.

(3) Any agency that receives information under this Section shall, not later than 6 months after the date on which it receives the information, publicly report the final action taken against the convicted person, including but not limited to the revocation or suspension of the license or any other disciplinary action taken.

(i) Definitions. For the purposes of this Section, "obtain", "obtains control", "deception", "property", and "permanent deprivation" have the meanings ascribed to those terms in Article 15 of this Code.

§ 17-9. Public aid wire and mail fraud. (a) Whoever knowingly (i) makes or transmits any communication by means of telephone, wire, radio, or television or (ii) places any communication with the United States Postal Service, or with any private or other mail, package, or delivery service or system, such communication being made, transmitted, placed, or received within the State of Illinois, intending that such communication be made, transmitted, or delivered in furtherance of any plan, scheme, or design to obtain, unlawfully, any benefit or payment under the Illinois Public Aid Code, commits public aid wire and mail fraud.

(b) Whoever knowingly directs or causes any communication to be (i) made or transmitted by means of telephone, wire, radio, or television or (ii) placed with the United States Postal Service, or with any private or other mail, package, or delivery service or system, intending that such communication be made, transmitted, or delivered in furtherance of any plan, scheme, or design to obtain, unlawfully, any benefit or payment under the Illinois Public Aid Code, commits public aid wire and mail fraud.

(c) Sentence. A violation of this Section is a Class 4 felony.

§ 17-10.2. Businesses owned by minorities, females, and persons with disabilities; fraudulent contracts with governmental units. (a) In this Section:

"Minority person" means a person who is: (1) African American (a person having origins in any of the black racial groups in Africa); (2) Hispanic (a person of Spanish or Portuguese culture with origins in Mexico, South or Central America, or the Caribbean Islands, regardless of race); (3) Asian American (a person having origins in any of the original peoples of the Far East, Southeast Asia, the Indian Subcontinent or the Pacific Islands); or (4) Native American or Alaskan Native (a person having origins in any of the original peoples of North America).

"Female" means a person who is of the female gender.

"Person with a disability" means a person who is a person qualifying as having a disability.

"Disability" means a severe physical or mental disability that: (1) results from: amputation, arthritis, autism, blindness, burn injury, cancer, cerebral palsy, cystic fibrosis, deafness, head injury, heart disease, hemiplegia, hemophilia, respiratory or pulmonary dysfunction, intellectual disabilities, mental illness, multiple sclerosis, muscular dystrophy, musculoskeletal disorders, neurological disorders, including stroke and epilepsy, paraplegia, quadriplegia and other spinal cord conditions, sickle cell anemia, specific learning disabilities, or end stage renal failure disease; and (2) substantially limits one or more of the person's major life activities.

"Minority owned business" means a business concern that is at least 51% owned by one or more minority persons, or in the case of a corporation, at least 51% of the stock in which is owned by one or more minority persons; and the management and daily business operations of which are controlled by one or more of the minority individuals who own it.

"Female owned business" means a business concern that is at least 51% owned by one or more females, or, in the case of a corporation, at least 51% of the stock in which is owned by one or more females; and the management and daily business operations of which are controlled by one or more of the females who own it.

"Business owned by a person with a disability" means a business concern that is at least 51% owned by one or more persons with a disability and the management and daily business operations of which are controlled by one or more of the persons with disabilities who own it. A not-for-profit agency for persons with disabilities that is exempt from taxation under Section 501 of the Internal Revenue Code of 1986 is also considered a "business owned by a person with a disability".

"Governmental unit" means the State, a unit of local government, or school district.

(b) In addition to any other penalties imposed by law or by an ordinance or resolution of a unit of local government or school district, any individual or entity that knowingly obtains, or knowingly assists another to obtain, a contract with a governmental unit, or a subcontract or written commitment for a subcontract under a contract with a governmental unit, by falsely representing that the individual or entity, or the individual or entity assisted, is a minority owned business, female owned business, or business owned by a person with a disability is guilty of a Class 2 felony, regardless of whether the preference for awarding the contract to a minority owned business, female owned business, or business owned by a person with a disability was established by statute or by local ordinance or resolution.

(c) In addition to any other penalties authorized by law, the court shall order that an individual or entity convicted of a violation of this Section must pay to the governmental unit that awarded the contract a penalty equal to one and one-half times the amount of the contract obtained because of the false representation.

§ 17-10.3. Deception relating to certification of disadvantaged business enterprises. (a) Fraudulently obtaining or retaining certification. A person who, in the course of business, fraudulently obtains or retains certification as a minority owned business or female owned business commits a Class 2 felony.

(b) Willfully making a false statement. A person who, in the course of business, willfully makes a false statement whether by affidavit, report or other representation, to an official or employee of a State agency or the Minority and Female Business Enterprise Council for the purpose of influencing the certification or denial of certification of any business entity as a minority owned business or female owned business commits a Class 2 felony.

(c) Willfully obstructing or impeding an official or employee of any agency in his or her investigation. Any person who, in the course of business, willfully obstructs or impedes an official or employee of any State agency or the Minority and Female Business Enterprise Council who is investigating the qualifications of a business entity which has requested certification as a minority owned business or a female owned business commits a Class 2 felony.

(d) Fraudulently obtaining public moneys reserved for disadvantaged business enterprises. Any person who, in the course of business, fraudulently obtains public moneys reserved for, or allocated or available to minority owned businesses or female owned businesses commits a Class 2 felony.

(e) Definitions. As used in this Article, "minority owned business", "female owned business", "State agency" and "certification" shall have the meanings ascribed to them in Section 2 of the Business Enterprise for Minorities, Females, and Persons with Disabilities Act.

Subdivision 15. Fraud on a Private Entity

§ 17-10.5. Insurance fraud. (a)(1) A person commits insurance fraud when he or she knowingly obtains, attempts to obtain, or causes to be obtained, by deception, control over the property of an insurance company or self-insured entity by the making of a false claim or by causing a false claim to be made on any policy of insurance issued by an insurance company or by the making of a false claim or by causing a false claim to be made to a self-insured entity, intending to deprive an insurance company or self-insured entity permanently of the use and benefit of that property.

(2) A person commits health care benefits fraud against a provider, other than a governmental unit or agency, when he or she knowingly obtains or attempts to obtain, by deception, health care benefits and that obtaining or attempt to obtain health care benefits does not involve control over property of the provider.

(b) Aggravated insurance fraud.
(1) A person commits aggravated insurance fraud on a private entity when he or she commits insurance fraud 3 or more times within an 18-month period arising out of separate incidents or transactions.

(2) A person commits being an organizer of an aggravated insurance fraud on a private entity conspiracy if aggravated insurance fraud on a private entity forms the basis for a charge of conspiracy under Section 8-2 of this Code and the person occupies a position of organizer, supervisor, financer, or other position of management within the conspiracy.

(c) Conspiracy to commit insurance fraud. If aggravated insurance fraud on a private entity forms the basis for charges of conspiracy under Section 8-2 of this Code, the person or persons with whom the accused is alleged to have agreed to commit the 3 or more violations of this Section need not be the same person or persons for each violation, as long as the accused was a part of the common scheme or plan to engage in each of the 3 or more alleged violations.

If aggravated insurance fraud on a private entity forms the basis for a charge of conspiracy under Section 8-2 of this Code, and the accused occupies a position of organizer, supervisor, financer, or other position of management within the conspiracy, the person or persons with whom the accused is alleged to have agreed to commit the 3 or more violations of this Section need not be the same person or persons for each violation as long as the accused occupied a position of organizer, supervisor, financer, or other position of management in each of the 3 or more alleged violations.

(d) Sentence.

(1) A violation of paragraph (a)(1) in which the value of the property obtained, attempted to be obtained, or caused to be obtained is $ 300 or less is a Class A misdemeanor.

(2) A violation of paragraph (a)(1) in which the value of the property obtained, attempted to be obtained, or caused to be obtained is more than $ 300 but not more than $ 10,000 is a Class 3 felony.

(3) A violation of paragraph (a)(1) in which the value of the property obtained, attempted to be obtained, or caused to be obtained is more than $ 10,000 but not more than $ 100,000 is a Class 2 felony.

(4) A violation of paragraph (a)(1) in which the value of the property obtained, attempted to be obtained, or caused to be obtained is more than $ 100,000 is a Class 1 felony.

(5) A violation of paragraph (a)(2) is a Class A misdemeanor.

(6) A violation of paragraph (b)(1) is a Class 1 felony, regardless of the value of the property obtained, attempted to be obtained, or caused to be obtained.

(7) A violation of paragraph (b)(2) is a Class X felony.

(8) A person convicted of insurance fraud, vendor fraud, or a federal criminal violation associated with defrauding the Medicaid program shall be ordered to pay monetary restitution to the insurance company or self-insured entity or any other person for any financial loss sustained as a result of a violation of this Section, including any court costs and attorney's fees. An order of restitution shall include expenses incurred and paid by the State of Illinois or an insurance company or self-insured entity in connection with any medical evaluation or treatment services.

(9) Notwithstanding Section 8-5 of this Code, a person may be convicted and sentenced both for the offense of conspiracy to commit insurance fraud and for any other offense that is the object of the conspiracy.

(e) Civil damages for insurance fraud.

(1) A person who knowingly obtains, attempts to obtain, or causes to be obtained, by deception, control over the property of any insurance company by the making of a false claim or by causing a false claim to be made on a policy of insurance issued by an insurance company, or by the making of a false claim or by causing a false claim to be made to a self-insured entity, intending to deprive an insurance company or self-insured entity permanently of the use and benefit of that property, shall be civilly liable to the insurance company or self-insured entity that paid the claim or against whom the claim was made or to the subrogee of that insurance company or self-insured entity in an amount equal to either 3 times the value of the property wrongfully obtained or, if no property was wrongfully obtained, twice the value of the property attempted to be obtained, whichever amount is greater, plus reasonable attorney's fees.

(2) An insurance company or self-insured entity that brings an action against a person under paragraph (1) of this subsection in bad faith shall be liable to that person for twice the value of the property claimed, plus reasonable attorney's fees. In determining whether an insurance company or self-insured entity acted in bad faith, the court shall relax the rules of evidence to allow for the introduction of any facts or other information on which the insurance company or self-insured entity may have relied in bringing an action under paragraph (1) of this subsection.

(f) Determination of property value. For the purposes of this Section, if the exact value of the property attempted to be obtained is either not alleged by the claimant or not specifically set by the terms of a policy of insurance, the value of the property shall be the fair market replacement value of the property claimed to be lost, the reasonable costs of reimbursing a vendor or other claimant for services to be rendered, or both.

(g) Actions by State licensing agencies.

(1) All State licensing agencies, the Illinois State Police, and the Department of Financial and Professional Regulation shall coordinate enforcement efforts relating to acts of insurance fraud.

(2) If a person who is licensed or registered under the laws of the State of Illinois to engage in a business or profession is convicted of or pleads guilty to engaging in an act of insurance fraud, the Illinois State Police must forward to each State agency by which the person is

licensed or registered a copy of the conviction or plea and all supporting evidence.

(3) Any agency that receives information under this Section shall, not later than 6 months after the date on which it receives the information, publicly report the final action taken against the convicted person, including but not limited to the revocation or suspension of the license or any other disciplinary action taken.

(h) Definitions. For the purposes of this Section, "obtain", "obtains control", "deception", "property", and "permanent deprivation" have the meanings ascribed to those terms in Article 15 of this Code.

§ 17-10.6. Financial institution fraud.
(a) Misappropriation of financial institution property. A person commits misappropriation of a financial institution's property whenever he or she knowingly obtains or exerts unauthorized control over any of the moneys, funds, credits, assets, securities, or other property owned by or under the custody or control of a financial institution, or under the custody or care of any agent, officer, director, or employee of such financial institution.

(b) Commercial bribery of a financial institution.

(1) A person commits commercial bribery of a financial institution when he or she knowingly confers or offers or agrees to confer any benefit upon any employee, agent, or fiduciary without the consent of the latter's employer or principal, with the intent to influence his or her conduct in relation to his or her employer's or principal's affairs.

(2) An employee, agent, or fiduciary of a financial institution commits commercial bribery of a financial institution when, without the consent of his or her employer or principal, he or she knowingly solicits, accepts, or agrees to accept any benefit from another person upon an agreement or understanding that such benefit will influence his or her conduct in relation to his or her employer's or principal's affairs.

(c) Financial institution fraud. A person commits financial institution fraud when he or she knowingly executes or attempts to execute a scheme or artifice:

(1) to defraud a financial institution; or

(2) to obtain any of the moneys, funds, credits, assets, securities, or other property owned by or under the custody or control of a financial institution, by means of pretenses, representations, or promises he or she knows to be false.

(d) Loan fraud. A person commits loan fraud when he or she knowingly, with intent to defraud, makes any false statement or report, or overvalues any land, property, or security, with the intent to influence in any way the action of a financial institution to act upon any application, advance, discount, purchase, purchase agreement, repurchase agreement, commitment, or loan, or any change or extension of any of the same, by renewal, deferment of action, or otherwise, or the acceptance, release, or substitution of security.

(e) Concealment of collateral. A person commits concealment of collateral when he or she, with intent to defraud, knowingly conceals, removes, disposes of, or converts to the person's own use or to that of another any property mortgaged or pledged to or held by a financial institution.

(f) Financial institution robbery. A person commits robbery when he or she knowingly, by force or threat of force, or by intimidation, takes, or attempts to take, from the person or presence of another, or obtains or attempts to obtain by extortion, any property or money or any other thing of value belonging to, or in the care, custody, control, management, or possession of, a financial institution.

(g) Conspiracy to commit a financial crime.

(1) A person commits conspiracy to commit a financial crime when, with the intent that any violation of this Section be committed, he or she agrees with another person to the commission of that offense.

(2) No person may be convicted of conspiracy to commit a financial crime unless an overt act or acts in furtherance of the agreement is alleged and proved to have been committed by that person or by a co-conspirator and the accused is a part of a common scheme or plan to engage in the unlawful activity.

(3) It shall not be a defense to conspiracy to commit a financial crime that the person or persons with whom the accused is alleged to have conspired:

(A) has not been prosecuted or convicted;
(B) has been convicted of a different offense;
(C) is not amenable to justice;
(D) has been acquitted; or
(E) lacked the capacity to commit the offense.
(h) Continuing financial crimes enterprise. A person commits a continuing financial crimes enterprise when he or she knowingly, within an 18-month period, commits 3 or more separate offenses under this Section or, if involving a financial institution, any other felony offenses under this Code.
(i) Organizer of a continuing financial crimes enterprise.

(1) A person commits being an organizer of a continuing financial crimes enterprise when he or she:

(A) with the intent to commit any offense under this Section, or, if involving a financial institution, any other felony offense under this Code, agrees with another person to the commission of that offense on 3 or more separate occasions within an 18-month period; and

(B) with respect to the other persons within the conspiracy, occupies a position of organizer, supervisor, or financier or other position of management.

(2) The person with whom the accused agreed to commit the 3 or more offenses under this Section, or, if involving a financial institution, any other felony offenses under this Code, need not be the same person or persons for each offense, as long as the accused was a part of the common scheme or plan to engage in each of the 3 or more alleged offenses.

(j) Sentence.

(1) Except as otherwise provided in this subsection, a violation of this Section, the full value of which:
(A) does not exceed $ 500, is a Class A misdemeanor;

(B) does not exceed $ 500, and the person has been previously convicted of a financial crime or any type of theft, robbery, armed robbery, burglary, residential burglary, possession of burglary tools, or home invasion, is guilty of a Class 4 felony;
(C) exceeds $ 500 but does not exceed $ 10,000, is a Class 3 felony;
(D) exceeds $ 10,000 but does not exceed $ 100,000, is a Class 2 felony;
(E) exceeds $ 100,000, is a Class 1 felony.

(2) A violation of subsection (f) is a Class 1 felony.
(3) A violation of subsection (h) is a Class 1 felony.

(4) A violation for subsection (i) is a Class X felony.

(k) A "financial crime" means an offense described in this Section.

(l) Period of limitations. The period of limitations for prosecution of any offense defined in this Section begins at the time when the last act in furtherance of the offense is committed.

§ 17-10.7. Insurance claims for excessive charges. (a) A person who sells goods or services commits insurance claims for excessive charges if:
(1) the person knowingly advertises or promises to provide the goods or services and to pay:

(A) all or part of any applicable insurance deductible; or
(B) a rebate in an amount equal to all or part of any applicable insurance deductible;

(2) the goods or services are paid for by the consumer from proceeds of a property or casualty insurance policy; and

(3) the person knowingly charges an amount for the goods or services that exceeds the usual and customary charge by the person for the goods or services by an amount equal to or greater than all or part of the applicable insurance deductible paid by the person to an insurer on behalf of an insured or remitted to an insured by the person as a rebate.

(b) A person who is insured under a property or casualty insurance policy commits insurance claims for excessive charges if the person knowingly:

(1) submits a claim under the policy based on charges that are in violation of subsection (a) of this Section; or

(2) knowingly allows a claim in violation of subsection (a) of this Section to be submitted, unless the person promptly notifies the insurer of the excessive charges.

(c) Sentence. A violation of this Section is a Class A misdemeanor.

Subdivision 20. Fraudulent Tampering

§ 17-11. Odometer or hour meter fraud. a person commits odometer or hour meter fraud when he or she disconnects, resets, or alters, or causes to be disconnected, reset, or altered, the odometer of any used motor vehicle or the hour meter of any used farm implement to conceal or change the actual miles driven or hours of operation with the intent to defraud another. A violation of this Section is a Class A misdemeanor. A second or subsequent violation is a Class 4 felony. This Section does not apply to legitimate practices of automotive or implement parts recyclers who recycle used odometers or hour meters for resale.

§ 17-11.2. Installation of object in lieu of air bag. a person commits installation of object in lieu of airbag when he or she, for consideration, knowingly installs or reinstalls in a vehicle any object in lieu of an air bag that was designed in accordance with federal safety regulations for the make, model, and year of the vehicle as part of a vehicle inflatable restraint system. A violation of this Section is a Class A misdemeanor.

§ 17-11.5. Tampering with a security, fire, or life safety system. (a) A person commits tampering with a security, fire, or life safety system when he or she knowingly damages, sabotages, destroys, or causes a permanent or temporary malfunction in any physical or electronic security, fire, or life safety system or any component part of any of those systems including, but not limited to, card readers, magnetic stripe readers, Wiegand card readers, smart card readers, proximity card readers, digital keypads, keypad access controls, digital locks, electromagnetic locks, electric strikes, electronic exit hardware, exit alarm systems, delayed egress systems, biometric access control equipment, intrusion detection systems and sensors, burglar alarm systems, wireless burglar alarms, silent alarms, duress alarms, hold-up alarms, glass break detectors, motion detectors, seismic detectors, glass shock sensors, magnetic contacts, closed circuit television (CCTV), security cameras, digital cameras, dome cameras, covert cameras, spy cameras, hidden cameras, wireless cameras, network cameras, IP addressable cameras, CCTV camera lenses, video cassette recorders, CCTV monitors, CCTV consoles, CCTV housings and enclosures, CCTV pan-and-tilt devices, CCTV transmission and signal equipment, wireless video transmitters, wireless video receivers, radio frequency (RF) or microwave components, or both, infrared illuminators, video motion detectors, video recorders, time lapse CCTV recorders, digital video recorders (DVRs), digital image storage systems, video converters, video distribution amplifiers, video time-date generators, multiplexers, switchers, splitters, fire alarms, smoke alarm systems, smoke detectors, flame detectors, fire detection systems and sensors, fire sprinklers, fire suppression systems, fire extinguishing systems, public address systems, intercoms, emergency telephones, emergency call boxes, emergency pull stations, telephone entry systems, video entry equipment, annunciators, sirens, lights, sounders, control panels and components, and all associated computer hardware, computer software, control panels, wires, cables, connectors, electromechanical components, electronic modules, fiber optics, filters, passive components, and power sources including batteries and back-up power supplies.

(b) Sentence. A violation of this Section is a Class 4 felony.

§ 17-13. Fraud in transfers of real and personal property. (a) Conditional sale; sale without consent of title holder. (720 ILCS 5/17-30) (was No person purchasing personal property under a conditional sales contract shall, during the existence of such conditional sales contract and before the conditions thereof have been fulfilled, knowingly sell, transfer, conceal, or in any manner dispose of such property, or cause or allow the same to be done, without the written consent of the holder of title.

(b) Acknowledgment of fraudulent conveyance. No officer authorized to take the proof and acknowledgment of a conveyance of real or personal property or other instrument shall knowingly certify that the conveyance or other instrument was duly proven or acknowledged by a party to the conveyance or other instrument when no such acknowledgment or proof was made, or was not made at the time it was certified to have been made, with intent to injure or defraud or to enable any other person to injure or defraud.

(c) Fraudulent land sales. No person, after once selling, bartering, or disposing of a tract or tracts of land or a town lot or lots, or executing a bond or agreement for the sale of lands or a town lot or lots, shall again knowingly and with intent to defraud sell, barter, or dispose of the same tract or tracts of land or town lot or lots, or any part of those tracts of land or town lot or lots, or knowingly and with intent to defraud execute a bond or agreement to sell, barter, or dispose of the same land or lot or lots, or any part of that land or lot or lots, to any other person for a valuable consideration.

(d) Sentence. A violation of subsection (a) of this Section is a Class A misdemeanor. A violation of subsection (b) of this Section is a Class 4 felony. A violation of subsection (c) of this Section is a Class 3 felony.

§ 17-17. Fraud in stock transactions. (a) No officer, director, or agent of a bank, railroad, or other corporation, nor any other person, shall knowingly, and with intent to defraud, issue, sell, transfer, assign, or pledge, or cause or procure to be issued, sold, transferred, assigned, or pledged, any false, fraudulent, or simulated certificate or other evidence of ownership of a share or shares of the capital stock of a bank, railroad, or other corporation.

(b) No officer, director, or agent of a bank, railroad, or other corporation shall knowingly sign, with intent to issue, sell, pledge, or cause to be issued, sold, or pledged, any false, fraudulent, or simulated certificate or other evidence of the ownership or transfer of a share or shares of the capital stock of that corporation, or an instrument purporting to be a certificate or other evidence of the ownership or transfer, the signing, issuing, selling, or pledging of which by the officer, director, or agent is not authorized by law.

(c) Sentence. a violation of this Section is a Class 3 felony.

§ 17-20. Obstructing gas, water, or electric current meters. A person commits obstructing gas, water, or electric current meters when he or she knowingly, and with intent to injure or defraud a company, body corporate, copartnership, or individual, injures, alters, obstructs, or prevents the action of a meter provided for the purpose of measuring and registering the quantity of gas, water, or electric current consumed by or at a burner, orifice, or place, or supplied to a lamp, motor, machine, or appliance, or causes, procures, or aids the injuring or altering of any such meter or the obstruction or prevention of its action, or makes or causes to be made with a gas pipe, water pipe, or electrical conductor any connection so as to conduct or supply illumination or inflammable gas, water, or electric current to any burner, orifice, lamp, motor, or other machine or appliance from which the gas, water, or electricity may be consumed or utilized without passing through or being registered by a meter or without the consent or acquiescence of the company, municipal corporation, body corporate, copartnership, or individual furnishing or transmitting the gas, water, or electric current through the gas pipe, water pipe, or electrical conductor.

A violation of this Section is a Class B misdemeanor.

§ 17-21. Obstructing service meters. A person commits obstructing service meters when he or she knowingly, and , with the intent to defraud, tampers with, alters, obstructs or prevents the action of a meter, register, or other counting device that is a part of a mechanical or electrical machine, equipment, or device that measures service, without the consent of the owner of the machine, equipment, or device.

A violation of this Section is a Class B misdemeanor.

§ 17-24. Mail fraud and wire fraud. (a) Mail fraud. A person commits mail fraud when he or she:

(1) devises or intends to devise any scheme or artifice to defraud, or to obtain money or property by means of false or fraudulent pretenses, representations, or promises, or to sell, dispose of, loan, exchange, alter, give away, distribute, supply, or furnish or procure for unlawful use any counterfeit obligation, security, or other article, or anything represented to be or intimated or held out to be such a counterfeit or spurious article; and

(2) with the intent to execute such scheme or artifice or to attempt to do so, does any of the following:

(A) Places in any post office or authorized depository for mail matter within this State any matter or thing to be delivered by the United States Postal Service, according to the direction on the matter or thing.

(B) Deposits or causes to be deposited in this State any matter or thing to be sent or delivered by mail or by private or commercial carrier, according to the direction on the matter or thing.

(C) Takes or receives from mail or from a private or commercial carrier any such matter or thing at the place at which it is directed to be delivered by the person to whom it is addressed.

(D) Knowingly causes any such matter or thing to be delivered by mail or by private or commercial carrier, according to the direction on the matter or thing.

(b) Wire fraud. a person commits wire fraud when he or she:

(1) devises or intends to devise a scheme or artifice to defraud or to obtain money or property by means of false pretenses, representations, or promises; and

(2) for the purpose of executing the scheme or artifice, transmits or causes to be transmitted any writings, signals, pictures, sounds, or electronic or electric impulses by means of wire, radio, or television communications:

(A) from within this State; or

(B) so that the transmission is received by a person within this State; or

(C) so that the transmission may be accessed by a person within this State.

(c) Jurisdiction.

(1) Mail fraud using a government or private carrier occurs in the county in which mail or other matter is deposited with the United States Postal Service or a private commercial carrier for delivery, if deposited with the United States Postal Service or a private or commercial carrier within this State, and the county in which a person within this State receives the mail or other matter from the United States Postal Service or a private or commercial carrier.

(2) Wire fraud occurs in the county from which a transmission is sent, if the transmission is sent from within this State, the county in which a person within this State receives the transmission, and the county in which a person who is within this State is located when the person accesses a transmission.

(d) Sentence. A violation of this Section is a Class 3 felony. The period of limitations for prosecution of any offense defined in this Section begins at the time when the last act in furtherance of the scheme or artifice is committed.

§ 17-26. Misconduct by a corporate official.
(a) A person commits misconduct by a corporate official when:

(1) being a director of a corporation, he or she knowingly, with the intent to defraud, concurs in any vote or act of the directors of the corporation, or any of them, which has the purpose of:

(A) making a dividend except in the manner provided by law;
(B) dividing, withdrawing or in any manner paying any stockholder any part of the capital stock of the corporation except in the manner provided by law;

(C) discounting or receiving any note or other evidence of debt in payment of an installment of capital stock actually called in and required to be paid, or with purpose of providing the means of making such payment;

(D) receiving or discounting any note or other evidence of debt with the purpose of enabling any stockholder to withdraw any part of the money paid in by him or her on his or her stock; or

(E) applying any portion of the funds of such corporation, directly or indirectly, to the purchase of shares of its own stock, except in the manner provided by law; or

(2) being a director or officer of a corporation, he or she, with the intent to defraud:

(A) issues, participates in issuing, or concurs in a vote to issue any increase of its capital stock beyond the amount of the capital stock thereof, duly authorized by or in pursuance of law;

(B) sells, or agrees to sell, or is directly interested in the sale of any share of stock of such corporation, or in any agreement to sell such stock, unless at the time of the sale or agreement he or she is an actual owner of such share, provided that the foregoing shall not apply to a sale by or on behalf of an underwriter or dealer in connection with a bona fide public offering of shares of stock of such corporation;

(C) executes a scheme or attempts to execute a scheme to obtain any share of stock of such corporation by means of false representation; or

(3) being a director or officer of a corporation, he or she with the intent to defraud or evade a financial disclosure reporting requirement of this State or of Section 13(A) or 15(D) of the Securities Exchange Act of 1934, as amended, *15 U. S. C. 78M*(A) or 78O(D):

(A) causes or attempts to cause a corporation or accounting firm representing the corporation or any other individual or entity to fail to file a financial disclosure report as required by State or federal law; or

(B) causes or attempts to cause a corporation or accounting firm representing the corporation or any other individual or entity to file a financial disclosure report, as required by State or federal law, that contains a material omission or misstatement of fact.

(b) Sentence. If the benefit derived from a violation of this Section is $ 500,000 or more, the violation is a Class 2 felony. If the benefit derived from a violation of this Section is less than $ 500,000, the violation is a Class 3 felony.

§ 17-27. Fraud on creditors. (a) Fraud in insolvency. a person commits fraud in insolvency when , knowing that proceedings have or are about to be instituted for the appointment of a receiver or other person entitled to administer property for the benefit of creditors, or that any other composition or liquidation for the benefit of creditors has been or is about to be made, he or she:

(1) destroys, removes, conceals, encumbers, transfers, or otherwise deals with any property or obtains any substantial part of or interest in the debtor's estate with the intent to defeat or obstruct the claim of any creditor, or otherwise to obstruct the operation of any law relating to administration of property for the benefit of creditors;

(2) knowingly falsifies any writing or record relating to the property; or

(3) knowingly misrepresents or refuses to disclose to a receiver or other person entitled to administer property for the benefit of creditors, the existence, amount, or location of the property, or any other information which the actor could be legally required to furnish in relation to such administration.

Sentence. If the benefit derived from a violation of this subsection (a) is $ 500,000 or more, the violation is a Class 2 felony. If the benefit derived from a violation of this subsection (a) is less than $ 500,000, the violation is a Class 3 felony.

(b) Fraud in property transfer. A person commits fraud in property transfer when he or she transfers or conveys any interest in property with the intent to defraud, defeat, hinder, or delay his or her creditors. A violation of this subsection (b) is a business offense subject to a fine not to exceed $ 1,000.

§ 17-30. Defaced, altered, or removed manufacturer or owner identification number. (a) Unlawful sale of household appliances. a person commits unlawful sale of household appliances when he or she knowingly, with the intent to defraud or deceive another, keeps for sale, within any commercial context, any household appliance with a missing, defaced, obliterated, or otherwise altered manufacturer's identification number.

(b) Construction equipment identification defacement. A person commits construction equipment identification defacement when he or she knowingly changes, alters, removes, mutilates, or obliterates a permanently affixed serial number, product identification number, part number, component identification number, owner-applied identification, or other mark of identification attached to or stamped, inscribed, molded, or etched into a machine or other equipment, whether stationary or mobile or self-propelled, or a part of such machine or equipment, used in the construction, maintenance, or demolition of buildings, structures, bridges, tunnels, sewers, utility pipes or lines, ditches or open cuts, roads, highways, dams, airports, or waterways or in material handling for such projects.

The trier of fact may infer that the defendant has knowingly changed, altered, removed, or obliterated the serial number, product identification number, part number, component identification number, owner-applied identification number, or other mark of identification, if the defendant was in possession of any machine or other equipment or a part of such machine or equipment used in the construction, maintenance, or demolition of buildings, structures, bridges, tunnels, sewers, utility pipes or lines, ditches or open cuts, roads, highways, dams, airports, or waterways or in material handling for such projects upon which any such serial number, product identification number, part number, component identification number, owner-applied identification number, or other mark of identification has been changed, altered, removed, or obliterated.

(c) Defacement of manufacturer's serial number or identification mark. A person commits defacement of a manufacturer's serial number or identification mark when he or she knowingly removes, alters, defaces, covers, or destroys the manufacturer's serial number or any other manufacturer's number or distinguishing identification mark upon any machine or other article of merchandise, other than a motor vehicle as defined in Section 1-146 of the Illinois Vehicle Code or a firearm as defined in the Firearm Owners Identification Card Act, with the intent of concealing or destroying the identity of such machine or other article of merchandise.

(d) Sentence.

(1) A violation of subsection (a) of this Section is a Class 4 felony if the value of the appliance or appliances exceeds $ 1,000 and a Class B misdemeanor if the value of the appliance or appliances is $ 1,000 or less.
(2) A violation of subsection (b) of this Section is a Class A misdemeanor.

(3) A violation of subsection (c) of this Section is a Class B misdemeanor.

(e) No liability shall be imposed upon any person for the unintentional failure to comply with subsection (a) .
(f) Definitions. In this Section:

"Commercial context" means a continuing business enterprise conducted for profit by any person whose primary business is the wholesale or retail marketing of household appliances, or a significant portion of whose business or inventory consists of household appliances kept or sold on a wholesale or retail basis.

"Household appliance" means any gas or electric device or machine marketed for use as home entertainment or for facilitating or expediting household tasks or chores. The term shall include but not necessarily be limited to refrigerators, freezers, ranges, radios, television sets, vacuum cleaners, toasters, dishwashers, and other similar household items.

"Manufacturer's identification number" means any serial number or other similar numerical or alphabetical designation imprinted upon or attached to or placed, stamped, or otherwise imprinted upon or attached to a household appliance or item by the manufacturer for purposes of identifying a particular appliance or item individually or by lot number.

Subdivision 25. Credit and Debit Card Fraud

§ 17-31. False statement to procure credit or debit card. A person commits false statement to procure credit or debit card when he or she makes or causes to be made, either directly or indirectly, any false statement in writing, knowing it to be false and with the intent that it be relied on, respecting his or her identity, his or her address, or his or her employment, or that of any other person, firm, or corporation, with the intent to procure the issuance of a credit card or debit card. A violation of this Section is a Class 4 felony.

§ 17-32. Possession of another's credit, debit, or identification card. (a) Possession of another's identification card. A person commits possession of another's identification card when he or she, with the intent to defraud, possesses any check guarantee card or key card or identification card for cash dispensing machines without the authority of the account holder or financial institution.

(b) Possession of another's credit or debit card. A person commits possession of another's credit or debit card when he or she receives a credit card or debit card from the person, possession, custody, or control of another without the cardholder's consent or if he or she, with knowledge that it has been so acquired, receives the credit card or debit card with the intent to use it or to sell it, or to transfer it to a person other than the issuer or the cardholder. The trier of fact may infer that a person who has in his or her possession or under his or her control 2 or more such credit cards or debit cards each issued to a cardholder other than himself or herself has violated this Section.

(c) Sentence.

(1) A violation of subsection (a) of this Section is a Class A misdemeanor. A person who, within any 12-month period, violates subsection (a) of this Section at the same time or consecutively with respect to 3 or more cards, each the

property of different account holders, is guilty of a Class 4 felony. A person convicted under subsection (a) of this Section, when the value of property so obtained, in a single transaction or in separate transactions within any 90-day period, exceeds $ 150 is guilty of a Class 4 felony.

(2) A violation of subsection (b) of this Section is a Class 4 felony. A person who, in any 12-month period, violates subsection (b) of this Section with respect to 3 or more credit cards or debit cards each issued to a cardholder other than himself or herself is guilty of a Class 3 felony.

§ 17-33. Possession of lost or mislaid credit or debit card. A person who receives a credit card or debit card that he or she knows to have been lost or mislaid and who retains possession with intent to use it or to sell it or to transfer it to a person other than the issuer or the cardholder is guilty of a Class 4 felony.

A person who, in a single transaction, violates this Section with respect to 3 or more credit cards or debit cards each issued to different cardholders other than himself or herself is guilty of a Class 3 felony.

§ 17-34. Sale of credit or debit card. A person other than the issuer who sells a credit card or debit card, without the consent of the issuer, is guilty of a Class 4 felony.

A person who knowingly purchases a credit card or debit card from a person other than the issuer, without the consent of the issuer, is guilty of a Class 4 felony.

A person who, in a single transaction, makes a sale or purchase prohibited by this Section with respect to 3 or more credit cards or debit cards each issued to a cardholder other than himself or herself is guilty of a Class 3 felony.

§ 17-35. Use of credit or debit card as security for debt. A person who, with intent to defraud either the issuer, or a person providing an item or items of value, or any other person, obtains control over a credit card or debit card as security for debt or transfers, conveys, or gives control over a credit card or debit card as security for debt is guilty of a Class 4 felony.

§ 17-36. Use of counterfeited, forged, expired, revoked, or unissued credit or debit card. a person who, with intent to defraud either the issuer, or a person providing an item or items of value, or any other person,
(i) uses, with the intent to obtain an item or items of value, a credit card or debit card obtained or retained in violation of this Subdivision 25 or without the cardholder's consent, or a credit card or debit card which he or she knows is counterfeited, or forged, or expired, or revoked or

(ii) obtains or attempts to obtain an item or items of value by representing without the consent of the cardholder that he or she is the holder of a specified card or by representing that he or she is the holder of a card and such card has not in fact been issued is guilty of a Class 4 felony if the value of all items of value obtained or sought in violation of this Section does not exceed $ 300 in any 6-month period; and is guilty of a Class 3 felony if the value exceeds $ 300 in any 6-month period. The trier of fact may infer that knowledge of revocation has been received by a cardholder 4 days after it has been mailed to him or her at the address set forth on the credit card or debit card or at his or her last known address by registered or certified mail, return receipt requested, and, if the address is more than 500 miles from the place of mailing, by air mail. The trier of fact may infer that notice was received 10 days after mailing by registered or certified mail if the address is located outside the United States, Puerto Rico, the Virgin Islands, the Canal Zone, and Canada.

§ 17-37. Use of credit or debit card with intent to defraud. a cardholder who uses a credit card or debit card issued to him or her, or allows another person to use a credit card or debit card issued to him or her, with intent to defraud the issuer, or a person providing an item or items of value, or any other person is guilty of a Class A misdemeanor if the value of all items of value does not exceed $ 150 in any 6-month period; and is guilty of a Class 4 felony if the value exceeds $ 150 in any 6-month period.

§ 17-38. Use of account number or code with intent to defraud; possession of record of charge forms. (a) A person who, with intent to defraud either an issuer, or a person providing an item or items of value, or any other person, utilizes an account number or code or enters information on a record of charge form with the intent to obtain an item or items of value is guilty of a Class 4 felony if the value of the item or items of value obtained does not exceed $ 150 in any 6-month period; and is guilty of a Class 3 felony if the value exceeds $ 150 in any 6-month period.

(b) A person who, with intent to defraud either an issuer or a person providing an item or items of value, or any other person, possesses, without the consent of the issuer or purported issuer, record of charge forms bearing the printed impression of a credit card or debit card is guilty of a Class 4 felony. The trier of fact may infer intent to defraud from the possession of such record of charge forms by a person other than the issuer or a person authorized by the issuer to possess record of charge forms.

§ 17-39. Receipt of goods or services. A person who receives an item or items of value obtained in violation of this Subdivision 25, knowing that it was so obtained or under such circumstances as would reasonably induce him or her to believe that it was so obtained, is guilty of a Class A misdemeanor if the value of all items of value obtained does not exceed $ 150 in any 6-month period; and is guilty of a Class 4 felony if the value exceeds $ 150 in any 6-month period.

§ 17-40. Signing another's card with intent to defraud. A person other than the cardholder or a person authorized by him or her who, with intent to defraud either the issuer, or a person providing an item or items of value, or any other person, signs a credit card or debit card is guilty of a Class A misdemeanor.

§ 17-41. Altered or counterfeited card. (a) A person commits an offense under this Section when he or she, with intent to defraud either a purported issuer, or a person providing an item or items of value, or any other person, commits an offense under this Section if he or she: (i) alters a credit card or debit card or a purported credit card or debit card, or possesses a credit card or debit card or a purported credit card or debit card with knowledge that the same has been altered; or (ii) counterfeits a purported credit card or debit card, or possesses a purported credit card or debit card with knowledge that the card has been counterfeited.

(b) Sentence. A violation of item (i) of subsection (a) is a Class 4 felony. A violation of item (ii) of subsection (a) is a Class 3 felony. The trier of fact may infer that possession of 2 or more credit cards or debit cards by a person other than the issuer in violation of subsection (a) is evidence that the person intended to defraud or that he or she knew the credit cards or debit cards to have been so altered or counterfeited.

§ 17-42. Possession of incomplete card. A person other than the cardholder possessing an incomplete credit card or debit card, with intent to complete it without the consent of the issuer or a person possessing, with knowledge of its character, machinery, plates, or any other contrivance designed to reproduce instruments purporting to be credit cards or debit cards of an issuer who has not consented to the preparation of such credit cards or debit cards is guilty of a Class 3 felony. The trier of fact may infer that a person other than the cardholder or issuer who possesses 2 or more incomplete credit cards or debit cards possesses those cards without the consent of the issuer.

§ 17-43. Prohibited deposits. (a) A person who, with intent to defraud the issuer of a credit card or debit card or any person providing an item or items of value, or any other person, deposits into his or her account or any account, via an electronic fund transfer terminal, a check, draft, money order, or other such document, knowing such document to be false, fictitious, forged, altered, counterfeit, or not his or her lawful or legal property, is guilty of a Class 4 felony.

(b) A person who receives value as a result of a false, fictitious, forged, altered, or counterfeit check, draft, money order, or other such document having been deposited into an account via an electronic fund transfer terminal, knowing at the time of receipt of the value that the document so deposited was false, fictitious, forged, altered, counterfeit, or not his or her lawful or legal property, is guilty of a Class 4 felony.

§ 17-44. Fraudulent use of electronic transmission. (a) A person who, with intent to defraud the issuer of a credit card or debit card, the cardholder, or any other person, intercepts, taps, or alters electronic information between an electronic fund transfer terminal and the issuer, or originates electronic information to an electronic fund transfer terminal or to the issuer, via any line, wire, or other means of electronic transmission, at any junction, terminal, or device, or at any location within the EFT System, with the intent to obtain value, is guilty of a Class 4 felony.

(b) Any person who, with intent to defraud the issuer of a credit card or debit card, the cardholder, or any other person, intercepts, taps, or alters electronic information between an electronic fund transfer terminal and the issuer, or originates electronic information to an electronic fund transfer terminal or to the issuer, via any line, wire, or other means of electronic transmission, at any junction, terminal, or device, or at any location within the EFT System, and thereby causes funds to be transferred from one account to any other account, is guilty of a Class 4 felony.

§ 17-45. Payment of charges without furnishing item of value. (a) No person shall process, deposit, negotiate, or obtain payment of a credit card charge through a retail seller's account with a financial institution or through a retail seller's agreement with a financial institution, card issuer, or organization of financial institutions or card issuers if that retail seller did not furnish or agree to furnish the item or items of value that are the subject of the credit card charge.

(b) No retail seller shall permit any person to process, deposit, negotiate, or obtain payment of a credit card charge through the retail seller's account with a financial institution or the retail seller's agreement with a financial institution, card issuer, or organization of financial institutions or card issuers if that retail seller did not furnish or agree to furnish the item or items of value that are the subject of the credit card charge.

(c) Subsections (a) and (b) do not apply to any of the following:

(1) A person who furnishes goods or services on the business premises of a general merchandise retail seller and who processes, deposits, negotiates, or obtains payment of a credit card charge through that general merchandise retail seller's account or agreement.
(2) A general merchandise retail seller who permits a person described in paragraph (1) to process, deposit, negotiate, or obtain payment of a credit card charge through that general merchandise retail seller's account or agreement.
(3) A franchisee who furnishes the cardholder with an item or items of value that are provided in whole or in part by the franchisor and who processes, deposits, negotiates, or obtains payment of a credit card charge through that franchisor's account or agreement.
(4) A franchisor who permits a franchisee described in paragraph (3) to process, deposit, negotiate, or obtain payment of a credit card charge through that franchisor's account or agreement.
(5) The credit card issuer or a financial institution or a parent, subsidiary, or affiliate of the card issuer or a financial institution.
(6) A person who processes, deposits, negotiates, or obtains payment of less than $ 500 of credit card charges in any one-year period through a retail seller's account or agreement. The person has the burden of producing evidence that the person transacted less than $ 500 in credit card charges during any one-year period.
(7) A telecommunications carrier that includes charges of other parties in its billings to its subscribers and those other parties whose charges are included in the billings of the telecommunications carrier to its subscribers.

(d) A person injured by a violation of this Section may bring an action for the recovery of damages, equitable relief, and reasonable attorney's fees and costs.

(e) A person who violates this Section is guilty of a business offense and shall be fined $ 10,000 for each offense.

Each occurrence in which a person processes, deposits, negotiates, or otherwise seeks to obtain payment of a credit card charge in violation of subsection (a) constitutes a separate offense.

(f) The penalties and remedies provided in this Section are in addition to any other remedies or penalties provided by law.

(g) As used in this Section:
"Franchisor" and "franchisee" have the same meanings as in Section 3 of the Franchise Disclosure Act of 1987.

"Retail seller" has the same meaning as in Section 2.4 of the Retail Installment Sales Act.

"Telecommunications carrier" has the same meaning as in Section 13-202 of the Public Utilities Act.

§ 17-46. Furnishing items of value with intent to defraud. A person who is authorized by an issuer to furnish money, goods, property, services or anything else of value upon presentation of a credit card or debit card by the cardholder, or any agent or employee of such person, who, with intent to defraud the issuer or the cardholder, furnishes money, goods, property, services or anything else of value upon presentation of a credit card or debit card obtained or retained in violation of this Code or a credit card or debit card which he knows is counterfeited, or forged, or expired, or revoked is guilty of a Class A misdemeanor, if the value furnished in violation of this Section does not exceed $ 150 in any 6-month period; and is guilty of a Class 4 felony if such value exceeds $ 150 in any 6-month period.

§ 17-47. Failure to furnish items of value. A person who is authorized by an issuer to furnish money, goods, property, services or anything else of value upon presentation of a credit card or debit card by the cardholder, or any agent or employee of such person, who, with intent to defraud the issuer or the cardholder, fails to furnish money, goods, property, services or anything else of value which he represents in writing to the issuer that he has furnished is guilty of a Class A misdemeanor if the difference between the value of all money, goods, property, services and anything else of value actually furnished and the value represented to the issuer to have been furnished does not exceed $ 150 in any 6-month period; and is guilty of a Class 4 felony if such difference exceeds $ 150 in any 6-month period.

§ 17-48. Repeat offenses. Any person convicted of a second or subsequent offense under this Subdivision 25 is guilty of a Class 3 felony. For purposes of this Section, an offense is considered a second or subsequent offense if, prior to his or her conviction of the offense, the offender has at any time been convicted under this Subdivision 25, or under any prior Act, or under any law of the United States or of any state relating to credit card or debit card offenses.

§ 17-49. Severability. If any provision of this Subdivision 25 or its application to any person or circumstances is held invalid, the invalidity shall not affect other provisions or applications of this Subdivision 25 which can be given effect without the invalid provision or application, and to this end the provisions of this Subdivision 25 are declared to be severable.

§ 17-49.5. Telephone Charge Fraud Act unaffected. Nothing contained in this Subdivision 25 shall be construed to repeal, amend, or otherwise affect the Telephone Charge Fraud Act.

Subdivision 30. Computer Fraud

§ 17-50. Computer fraud. (a) A person commits computer fraud when he or she knowingly:

(1) Accesses or causes to be accessed a computer or any part thereof, or a program or data, with the intent of devising or executing any scheme or artifice to defraud, or as part of a deception;

(2) Obtains use of, damages, or destroys a computer or any part thereof, or alters, deletes, or removes any program or data contained therein, in connection with any scheme or artifice to defraud, or as part of a deception; or

(3) Accesses or causes to be accessed a computer or any part thereof, or a program or data, and obtains money or control over any such money, property, or services of another in connection with any scheme or artifice to defraud, or as part of a deception.
(b) Sentence.

(1) A violation of subdivision (a)(1) of this Section is a Class 4 felony.

(2) A violation of subdivision (a)(2) of this Section is a Class 3 felony.

(3) A violation of subdivision (a)(3) of this Section: (i) is a Class 4 felony if the value of the money, property, or services is $ 1,000 or less; or

(ii) is a Class 3 felony if the value of the money, property, or services is more than $ 1,000 but less than $ 50,000; or

(iii) is a Class 2 felony if the value of the money, property, or services is $ 50,000 or more.

(c) forfeiture of property. Any person who commits computer fraud as set forth in subsection (a) is subject to the property forfeiture provisions set forth in Article 124B of the Code of Criminal Procedure of 1963.

§ 17-51. Computer tampering. (a) A person commits computer tampering when he or she knowingly and without the authorization of a computer's owner or in excess of the authority granted to him or her:

(1) Accesses or causes to be accessed a computer or any part thereof, a computer network, or a program or data;

(2) Accesses or causes to be accessed a computer or any part thereof, a computer network, or a program or data, and obtains data or services;

(3) Accesses or causes to be accessed a computer or any part thereof, a computer network, or a program or data, and damages or destroys the computer or alters, deletes, or removes a computer program or data;

(4) Inserts or attempts to insert a program into a computer or computer program knowing or having reason to know that such program contains information or commands that will or may:

(A) damage or destroy that computer, or any other computer subsequently accessing or being accessed by that computer;

(B) alter, delete, or remove a computer program or data from that computer, or any other computer program or data in a computer subsequently accessing or being accessed by that computer; or

(C) cause loss to the users of that computer or the users of a computer which accesses or which is accessed by such program; or
(5) Falsifies or forges electronic mail transmission information or other routing information in any manner in connection with the transmission of unsolicited bulk electronic mail through or into the computer network of an electronic mail service provider or its subscribers.
(a-5) Distributing software to falsify routing information. It is unlawful for any person

knowingly to sell, give, or otherwise distribute or possess with the intent to sell, give, or distribute software which:

(1) is primarily designed or produced for the purpose of facilitating or enabling the falsification of electronic mail transmission information or other routing information;

(2) has only a limited commercially significant purpose or use other than to facilitate or enable the falsification of electronic mail transmission information or other routing information; or

(3) is marketed by that person or another acting in concert with that person with that person's knowledge for use in facilitating or enabling the falsification of electronic mail transmission information or other routing information.

(a-10) For purposes of subsection (a), accessing a computer network is deemed to be with the authorization of a computer's owner if:

(1) the owner authorizes patrons, customers, or guests to access the computer network and the person accessing the computer network is an authorized patron, customer, or guest and complies with all terms or conditions for use of the computer network that are imposed by the owner; or

(2) the owner authorizes the public to access the computer network and the person accessing the computer network complies with all terms or conditions for use of the computer network that are imposed by the owner.

(b) Sentence.

(1) A person who commits computer tampering as set forth in subdivision (a)(1) or (a)(5) or subsection (a-5) of this Section is guilty of a Class B misdemeanor.

(2) A person who commits computer tampering as set forth in subdivision (a)(2) of this Section is guilty of a Class A misdemeanor and a Class 4 felony for the second or subsequent offense.
(3) A person who commits computer tampering as set forth in subdivision (a)(3) or (a)(4) of this Section is guilty of a Class 4 felony and a Class 3 felony for the second or subsequent offense.

(4) If an injury arises from the transmission of unsolicited bulk electronic mail, the injured person, other than an electronic mail service provider, may also recover attorney's fees and costs, and may elect, in lieu of actual damages, to recover the lesser of $ 10 for each unsolicited bulk electronic mail message transmitted in violation of this Section, or $ 25,000 per day. The injured person shall not have a cause of action against the electronic mail service provider that merely transmits the unsolicited bulk electronic mail over its computer network.

(5) If an injury arises from the transmission of unsolicited bulk electronic mail, an injured electronic mail service provider may also recover attorney's fees and costs, and may elect, in lieu of actual damages, to recover the greater of $ 10 for each unsolicited electronic mail advertisement transmitted in violation of this Section, or $ 25,000 per day.

(6) The provisions of this Section shall not be construed to limit any person's right to pursue any additional civil remedy otherwise allowed by law.

(c) Whoever suffers loss by reason of a violation of subdivision (a)(4) of this Section may, in a civil action against the violator, obtain appropriate relief. In a civil action under this Section, the court may award to the prevailing party reasonable attorney's fees and other litigation expenses.

§ 17-52. Aggravated computer tampering.
(a) A person commits aggravated computer tampering when he or she commits computer tampering as set forth in paragraph (a)(3) of Section 17-51 and he or she knowingly:

(1) causes disruption of or interference with vital services or operations of State or local government or a public utility; or

(2) creates a strong probability of death or great bodily harm to one or more individuals.

(b) Sentence.
(1) A person who commits aggravated computer tampering as set forth in paragraph (a)(1) of this Section is guilty of a Class 3 felony.

(2) A person who commits aggravated computer tampering as set forth in paragraph (a)(2) of this Section is guilty of a Class 2 felony.

§ 17-52.5. Unlawful use of encryption.
(a) For the purpose of this Section:

"Computer" means an electronic device which performs logical, arithmetic, and memory functions by manipulations of electronic or magnetic impulses and includes all equipment related to the computer in a system or network.

"Computer contaminant" means any data, information, image, program, signal, or sound that is designated or has the capability to: (1) contaminate, corrupt, consume, damage, destroy, disrupt, modify, record, or transmit; or (2) cause to be contaminated, corrupted, consumed, damaged, destroyed, disrupted, modified, recorded, or transmitted, any other data, information, image, program, signal, or sound contained in a computer, system, or network without the knowledge or consent of the person who owns the other data, information, image, program, signal, or sound or the computer, system, or network.

"Computer contaminant" includes, without limitation: (1) a virus, worm, or Trojan horse; (2) spyware that tracks computer activity and is capable of recording and transmitting such information to third parties; or (3) any other similar data, information, image, program, signal, or sound that is designed or has the capability to prevent, impede, delay, or disrupt the normal operation or use of any component, device, equipment, system, or network.

"Encryption" means the use of any protective or disruptive measure, including, without limitation, cryptography, enciphering, encoding, or a computer contaminant, to: (1) prevent, impede, delay, or disrupt access to any data, information, image, program, signal, or sound; (2) cause or make any data, information, image, program, signal, or sound unintelligible or unusable; or (3) prevent, impede, delay, or disrupt the normal operation or use of any component, device, equipment, system, or network.

"Network" means a set of related, remotely connected devices and facilities, including more than one system, with the capability to transmit data among any of the devices and facilities. The term includes, without limitation, a local, regional, or global computer network.

"Program" means an ordered set of data representing coded instructions or statements which can be executed by a computer and cause the computer to perform one or more tasks.

"System" means a set of related equipment, whether or not connected, which is used with or for a computer.

(b) A person shall not knowingly use or attempt to use encryption, directly or indirectly, to:

(1) commit, facilitate, further, or promote any criminal offense;

(2) aid, assist, or encourage another person to commit any criminal offense;

(3) conceal evidence of the commission of any criminal offense; or
(4) conceal or protect the identity of a person who has committed any criminal offense.

(c) Telecommunications carriers and information service providers are not liable under this Section, except for willful and wanton misconduct, for providing encryption services used by others in violation of this Section.
(d) Sentence. A person who violates this Section is guilty of a Class A misdemeanor, unless the encryption was used or attempted to be used to commit an offense for which a greater penalty is provided by law. If the encryption was used or attempted to be used to commit an offense for which a greater penalty is provided by law, the person shall be punished as prescribed by law for that offense.

(e) A person who violates this Section commits a criminal offense that is separate and distinct from any other criminal offense and may be prosecuted and convicted under this Section whether or not the person or any other person is or has been prosecuted or convicted for any other criminal offense arising out of the same facts as the violation of this Section.

§ **17-54. Evidence of lack of authority.** for the purposes of Sections 17-50 through 17-52, the trier of fact may infer that a person accessed a computer without the authorization of its owner or in excess of the authority granted if the person accesses or causes to be accessed a computer, which access requires a confidential or proprietary code which has not been issued to or authorized for use by that person.

§ 17-55. Definitions. For the purposes of Sections 17-50 through 17-53:
In addition to its meaning as defined in Section 15-1 of this Code, "property" means: (1) electronic impulses; (2) electronically produced data; (3) confidential, copyrighted, or proprietary information; (4) private identification codes or numbers which permit access to a computer by authorized computer users or generate billings to consumers for purchase of goods and services, including but not limited to credit card transactions and telecommunications services or permit electronic fund transfers; (5) software or programs in either machine or human readable form; or (6) any other tangible or intangible item relating to a computer or any part thereof.

"Access" means to use, instruct, communicate with, store data in, retrieve or intercept data from, or otherwise utilize any services of, a computer, a network, or data.

"Services" includes but is not limited to computer time, data manipulation, or storage functions.
"Vital services or operations" means those services or operations required to provide, operate, maintain, and repair network cabling, transmission, distribution, or computer facilities necessary to ensure or protect the public health, safety, or welfare. Those services or operations include, but are not limited to, services provided by medical personnel or institutions, fire departments, emergency services agencies, national defense contractors, armed forces or militia personnel, private and public utility companies, or law enforcement agencies.

Commentary – Computer Fraud

As technology advances, so must the criminal code keep pace. When a person uses a computer in some fashion to accomplish a theft, the crime could be charged as a theft. Illinois, on the other hand, has recognized the particular types of illicit conduct associated with computers and created a separate category of crime called computer fraud. This meant the creation of a list of definitions attributable to this type of conduct and proscription of the acts which make up the elements of the crime. One commits computer fraud if he knowingly uses a computer as a part of a scheme to defraud someone out of money or property.

In *People v. Davis* 353 Ill.App.3d 790, 819 N.E.2d 1195 (Ill. App. Ct. 2nd Dist. 2004), the defendant obtained customer information at a Radio Shack where he worked. He used that personal information to apply online for credit cards issued in his name and in the customer's name and then used those credit cards to obtain cash and goods in excess of $12,000. He was convicted of offenses including computer fraud and theft and argued that his theft and computer fraud convictions should merge because they were the same offense. The court disagreed noting that computer fraud required access to a computer as a separate element while theft had no such element.

§ 17-56. Financial exploitation of an elderly person or a person with a disability.
(a) A person commits financial exploitation of an elderly person or a person with a disability when he or she stands in a position of trust or confidence with the elderly person or a person with a disability and he or she knowingly and by deception or intimidation obtains control over the property of an elderly person or a person with a disability or illegally uses the assets or resources of an elderly person or a person with a disability.

(b) Sentence. Financial exploitation of an elderly person or a person with a disability is: (1) a Class 4 felony if the value of the property is $ 300 or less, (2) a Class 3 felony if the value of the property is more than $ 300 but less than $ 5,000, (3) a Class 2 felony if the value of the property is $ 5,000 or more but less than $ 50,000, and (4) a Class 1 felony if the value of the property is $ 50,000 or more or if the elderly person is over 70 years of age and the value of the property is $ 15,000 or more or if the elderly person is 80 years of age or older and the value of the property is $ 5,000 or more.
(c) for purposes of this Section: (1) "Elderly person" means a person 60 years of age or older.
(2) "Person with a disability" means a person who suffers from a physical or mental impairment resulting from disease, injury, functional disorder or congenital condition that impairs the individual's mental or physical ability to independently manage his or her property or financial resources, or both.

(3) "Intimidation" means the communication to an elderly person or a person with a disability that he or she shall be deprived of food and nutrition, shelter, prescribed medication or medical care and treatment.

(4) "Deception" means, in addition to its meaning as defined in Section 15-4 of this Code, a misrepresentation or concealment of material fact relating to the terms of a contract or agreement entered into with the elderly person or person with a disability or to the existing or pre-existing condition of any of the property involved in such contract or agreement; or the use or employment of any misrepresentation, false pretense or false promise in order to induce, encourage or solicit the elderly person or person with a disability to enter into a contract or agreement.

The illegal use of the assets or resources of an elderly person or a person with a disability includes, but is not limited to, the misappropriation of those assets or resources by undue influence, breach of a fiduciary relationship, fraud, deception, extortion, or use of the assets or resources contrary to law.
A person stands in a position of trust and confidence with an elderly person or person with a disability when he (i) is a parent, spouse, adult child or other relative by blood or marriage of the elderly person or person with a disability, (ii) is a joint tenant or tenant in common with the elderly person or person with a disability, (iii) has a legal or fiduciary relationship with the elderly person or person with a disability, or (iv) is a financial planning or investment professional.

(d) Limitations. Nothing in this Section shall be construed to limit the remedies available to the victim under the Illinois Domestic Violence Act of 1986.

(e) Good faith efforts. Nothing in this Section shall be construed to impose criminal liability on a person who has made a good faith effort to assist the elderly person or person with a disability in the management of his or her property, but through no fault of his or her own has been unable to provide such assistance.

(f) Not a defense. It shall not be a defense to financial exploitation of an elderly person or person with a disability that the accused reasonably believed that the victim was not an elderly person or person with a disability.

(g) Civil Liability. A civil cause of action exists for financial exploitation of an elderly person or a person with a disability as described in subsection (a) of this Section. A person against whom a civil judgment has been entered for financial exploitation of an elderly person or person with a disability shall be liable to the victim or to the estate of the victim in damages of treble the amount of the value of the property obtained, plus reasonable attorney fees and court costs. In a civil action under this subsection, the burden of proof that the defendant committed financial exploitation of an elderly person or a person with a disability as described in subsection(a) of this Section shall be by a preponderance of the evidence. This subsection shall be operative whether or not the defendant has been charged or convicted of the criminal offense as described insubsection (a) of this Section. This subsection (g) shall not limit or affect the right of any person to bring any cause of action or seek any remedy available under the common law, or other applicable law, arising out of the financial exploitation of an elderly person or a person with a disability.

§ 17-57. Defrauding drug and alcohol screening tests. (a) It is unlawful for a person to:

(1) manufacture, sell, give away, distribute, or market synthetic or human substances or other products in this State or transport urine into this State with the intent of using the synthetic or human substances or other products to defraud a drug or alcohol screening test;

(2) substitute or spike a sample or advertise a sample substitution or other spiking device or measure, with the intent of attempting to foil or defeat a drug or alcohol screening test;
(3) adulterate synthetic or human substances with the intent to defraud a drug or alcohol screening test; or
(4) manufacture, sell, or possess adulterants that are intended to be used to adulterate synthetic or human substances with the intent of defrauding a drug or alcohol screening test.

(b) the trier of fact may infer intent to violate this Section if a heating element or any other device used to thwart a drug or alcohol screening test accompanies the sale, giving, distribution, or marketing of synthetic or human substances or other products or instructions that provide a method for thwarting a drug or alcohol screening test accompany the sale, giving, distribution, or marketing of synthetic or human substances or other products.

(c) Sentence. A violation of this Section is a Class 4 felony for which the court shall impose a minimum fine of $ 1,000.

(d) For the purposes of this Section, "drug or alcohol screening test" includes, but is not limited to, urine testing, hair follicle testing, perspiration testing, saliva testing, blood testing, fingernail testing, and eye drug testing.

§ 17-58. Fraudulent production of infant. A person who fraudulently produces an infant, falsely pretending it to have been born of parents whose child would be entitled to a share of a personal estate, or to inherit real estate, with the intent of intercepting the inheritance of the real estate, or the distribution of the personal property from a person lawfully entitled to the personal property, is guilty of a Class 3 felony.

§ 17-59. Criminal usury. (a) a person commits criminal usury when, in exchange for either a loan of money or other property or forbearance from the collection of such a loan, he or she knowingly contracts for or receives from an individual, directly or indirectly, interest, discount, or other consideration at a rate greater than 20% per annum either before or after the maturity of the loan.

(b) When a person has in his or her personal or constructive possession records, memoranda, or other documentary record of usurious loans, the trier of fact may infer that he or she has violated subsection (a) of this Section.

(c) Sentence. Criminal usury is a Class 4 felony.

(d) Non-application to licensed persons. This Section does not apply to any loan authorized to be made by any person licensed under the Consumer Installment Loan Act or to any loan permitted by Sections 4, 4.2 and 4a of the Interest Act or by any other law of this State.

§ 17-60. Promotion of pyramid sales schemes. (a) A person who knowingly sells, offers to sell, or attempts to sell the right to participate in a pyramid sales scheme commits a Class A misdemeanor.

(b) the term "pyramid sales scheme" means any plan or operation whereby a person, in exchange for money or other thing of value, acquires the opportunity to receive a benefit or thing of value, which is primarily based upon the inducement of additional persons, by himself or others, regardless of number, to participate in the same plan or operation and is not primarily contingent on the volume or quantity of goods, services, or other property sold or distributed or to be sold or distributed to persons for purposes of resale to consumers. For purposes of this subsection, "money or other thing of value" shall not include payments made for sales demonstration equipment and materials furnished on a nonprofit basis for use in making sales and not for resale.

§ 17-61. Unauthorized use of university stationery. (a) No person, firm or corporation shall use the official stationery or seal or a facsimile thereof, of any State supported university, college or other institution of higher education or any organization thereof unless approved in writing in advance by the university, college or institution of higher education affected, for any private promotional scheme wherein it is made to appear that the organization or university, college or other institution of higher education is endorsing the private promotional scheme.

(b) A violation of this Section is a petty offense.

§ 17-62. Unlawful possession of device for manufacturing a false universal price code label. It is unlawful for a person to knowingly possess a device the purpose of which is to manufacture a false, counterfeit, altered, or simulated universal price code label. A violation of this Section is a Class 3 felony.

Article 18 – Robbery
720 ICLS 5/18-1 *et seq.*

§ 18-1. Robbery. (a) A person commits robbery when he or she takes property, except a motor vehicle covered by Section 18-3 or 18-4 from the person or presence of another by the use of force or by threatening the imminent use of force.

(b) Sentence.

Robbery is a Class 2 felony. However, if the victim is 60 years of age or over or is a person with a physical disability, or if the robbery is committed in a school, day care center, day care home, group day care home, or part day child care facility, or place of worship, robbery is a Class 1 felony.

(c) Regarding penalties prescribed in subsection (b) for violations committed in a day care center, day care home, group day care home, or part day child care facility, the time of day, time of year, and whether children under 18 years of age were present in the day care center, day care home, group day care home, or part day child care facility are irrelevant.

§ 18-2. Armed robbery. (a) A person commits armed robbery when he or she violates Section 18-1; and

(1) he or she carries on or about his or her person, or is otherwise armed with a dangerous weapon other than a firearm; or

(2) he or she carries on or about his or her person or is otherwise armed with a firearm; or

(3) he or she, during the commission of the offense, personally discharges a firearm; or

(4) he or she, during the commission of the offense, personally discharges a firearm that proximately causes great bodily harm, permanent disability, permanent disfigurement, or death to another person.

(b) Sentence.

Armed robbery in violation of subsection (a)(1) is a Class X felony. A violation of subsection (a)(2) is a Class X felony for which 15 years shall be added to the term of imprisonment imposed by the court. A violation of subsection (a)(3) is a Class X felony for which 20 years shall be added to the term of imprisonment imposed by the court. A violation of subsection (a)(4) is a Class X felony for which 25 years or up to a term of natural life shall be added to the term of imprisonment imposed by the court

Commentary – Robbery Offenses

Robbery. Section 18-1 proscribes against the crime of robbery. A person commits robbery when he knowingly or intentionally takes property (other than a motor vehicle) from the personal presence of another person by use of force or threat of imminent use of force. Robbery generally is distinguished from armed robbery (Section 18-2) because of the lack of use of a weapon and is distinguished from aggravated robbery (Section 18-5) because there is no threat of the use of a weapon. Robbery is distinguished from the offense vehicular hijacking which involves the use or threat of force to take a motor vehicle from the personal presence of the victim – this conduct is specifically excluded from the robbery statute.

Use or threat of force. The taking of the property must be accompanied by the use of force or threat of imminent force. Use of force or threat of force is the difference between commission of a robbery and a theft. Snatching an object and running away is a theft, not a robbery, but a struggle over the taking of the property is the use of force, and words during the taking or struggle can convey the imminent threat of force.

In *People v. DeBerry* 375 Ill.App.3d 822, 875 N.E.2d 1 (Ill. App. Ct. 4th Dist. 2007), the defendant was talking with the victim when his friend Woods grabbed the victim. The victim fell to the ground and Woods took a cell phone and money from the victim's pocket. The defendant and Woods walked away. The defendant then gave Woods a ride home. This evidence was sufficient to support the conviction of the defendant for knowingly taking property from the victim by the use of force.

In *People v. Hay* 362 Ill.App.3d 459, 840 N.E.2d 835 (Ill. App. Ct. 2nd Dist. 2005), a clerk at a jewelry store was asked by a man to see two rings. After she took the rings from a display case and held one in each of her hands, the perpetrator grabbed the rings and attempted to go out the door, however, it was buzz-latched. Another employee attempted to stop him and he said to her that if she did not stop he would hurt her. He left through a back door forcing his way out of the building. The defendant was identified as the culprit. While the defendant did not use force to get the rings, he did use force to escape from the scene, he did threaten to hurt an employee who tried to stop him and his departure was an essential part of the robbery. This evidence was sufficient to affirm his conviction.

General intent. Robbery is a general intent crime. Proof of a specific intent to commit the robbery, to harm the victim or threaten the victim is not required. See *People v. Lewis* 165 Ill.2d 305, 651 N.E.2d 72 (1995). Note that since §18-1 has no assigned mental state, a mental state (knowledge, intent or recklessness) will be implied for the offense under 720 ILCS 5/4-3(b). See *People v. Thomas 217* Ill.App.3d 698, 577 N.E.2d 831 (Ill. App. Ct. 5th Dist. 1991)(Defendant's claim that §18-1violates due process for having no express mental state is rejected.)

Armed robbery. Armed robbery is almost literally a robbery while armed. The types of armed robbery involve a robbery where the defendant (1) uses or possesses a dangerous weapon, (2) uses or possesses a firearm, (3) personally discharges a firearm during the robbery or (4) personally discharges a firearm and causes great bodily harm, permanent disability or disfigurement or death. Offense classification (sentencing enhancements) depends on which section is charged and proved. As one might expect, the largest enhancement of 25 years to life imprisonment applies to the last category where serious injury or death has been caused during the commission of the offense.

Dangerous weapon. The weapon is the feature that elevates a robbery to armed robbery and other than a firearm, the weapon must be a "dangerous weapon" (Section 18-1(a)). The offender need only have the weapon on him, he does not have to tell the victim he has the weapon, he does not have to show the weapon to the victim and he does not have to use the weapon to be guilty of an armed robbery. The term "dangerous weapon" is not defined by the statute and is an issue for the trier-of-fact to resolve. Certainly proof of the offender's possession of a knife or a loaded gun during the robbery or proof of the actual use of the object as a weapon during the robbery would suffice, but ultimately the question must be resolved as a matter of fact by the jury or judge. The state must prove that the object was a dangerous weapon as an element of the offense.

In *People v. Lampton* 385 Ill.App.3d 507, 898 N.E.2d 680 (Ill. App. Ct. 4th Dist. 2008), the court held that the defendant's possession of pepper spray during the commission of a robbery was properly considered as a "dangerous weapon" in his conviction for armed robbery. The defendant never threatened the bank employees with the pepper spray, never displayed it and never used it. The employees did not know that he had the pepper spray but it was on his person when he was apprehended immediately after he left the bank and admitted that he had taken it with him initially to use. Nonetheless, the record supported the jury's conclusion the defendant was armed with a dangerous weapon during the robbery.

In *People v. Ross* 229 Ill.2d 255 891 N.E.2d 265 (2008), the defendant pointed a small gun at the victim during a robbery. The victim thought it was a real gun. In fact it was a BB gun. The gun was not admitted into evidence. No picture of the gun was presented. There was no evidence the gun was loaded with BB pellets. The court noted that some weapons are dangerous in and of themselves (loaded guns and knives) and some are dangerous in the way that the manner in which they are used (unloaded gun used as a bludgeon). Proof that a gun is unloaded can rebut a presumption that it is a dangerous weapon. The court concluded that the evidence did not support the required element that the defendant used a dangerous weapon during the armed robbery, and that he would have to be re-sentenced on the basis of a conviction for simple robbery. The fact that the victim thought it was a real gun is not conclusive on the dangerous weapon issue. However, in *People v. Washington* 2012 IL 107993 (Ill. S. Ct. 2012), the Court upheld the defendant's conviction for armed robbery where no weapon was recovered and presented in evidence, but where there was evidence the victim had a clear unobstructed view of the weapon held to his head and described it as a gun.

§ 18-3. Vehicular hijacking. (a) A person commits vehicular hijacking when he or she takes a motor vehicle from the person or the immediate presence of another by the use of force or by threatening the imminent use of force.

(b) For the purposes of this Article, the term "motor vehicle" shall have the meaning ascribed to it in the Illinois Vehicle Code [*625 ILCS 5/1-100* et seq.].

(c) *Sentence.* Vehicular hijacking is a Class 1 felony.

§ 18-4. Aggravated vehicular hijacking. (a) A person commits aggravated vehicular hijacking when he or she violates Section 18-3 [*720 ILCS 5/18-4*]; and

(1) the person from whose immediate presence the motor vehicle is taken is a person with a physical disabilitu or a person 60 years of age or over; or

(2) a person under 16 years of age is a passenger in the motor vehicle at the time of the offense; or

(3) he or she carries on or about his or her person, or is otherwise armed with a dangerous weapon, other than a firearm; or

(4) he or she carries on or about his or her person or is otherwise armed with a firearm; or

(5) he or she, during the commission of the offense, personally discharges a firearm; or

(6) he or she, during the commission of the offense, personally discharges a firearm that proximately causes great bodily harm, permanent disability, permanent disfigurement, or death to another person.

(b) Sentence. Aggravated vehicular hijacking in violation of subsections (a)(1) or (a)(2) is a Class X felony. Aggravated vehicular hijacking in violation of subsection (a)(3) is a Class X felony for which a term of imprisonment of not less than 7 years shall be imposed. Aggravated vehicular hijacking in violation of subsection (a)(4) is a Class X felony for which 15 years shall be added to the term of imprisonment imposed by the court. Aggravated vehicular hijacking in violation of subsection (a)(5) is a Class X felony for which 20 years shall be added to the term of imprisonment imposed by the court. Aggravated vehicular hijacking in violation of subsection (a)(6) is a Class X felony for which 25 years or up to a term of natural life shall be added to the term of imprisonment imposed by the court

Commentary – Vehicular Hijacking Offenses

Vehicular Hijacking. Section 18-3 criminalizes the taking of a motor vehicle from the immediate presence of another by force or threat of force. It is the equivalent of robbery where the property taken is a motor vehicle. To commit hijacking the defendant must actually take over control of the vehicle by dispossessing the vehicle from another person, even if the person remains in the vehicle. It is not a hijacking to force someone else to drive the vehicle. See *People v. Reese* 2015 IL App (1st) 131147, (defendant's conviction for Aggravated Vehicular Hijacking reversed where evidence showed that he forced the driver to operate the vehicle and never took possession himself).

Aggravated vehicular hijacking. Similar to the difference between armed robbery and robbery, aggravated vehicular hijacking occurs when the offender during the commission of the hijacking has a dangerous weapon, has a firearm, shoots the firearm, or shoots the firearm and causes great bodily harm, permanent disability or disfigurement or death. However, aggravated vehicular hijacking has three other aggravating factors – the age (over 60) or physical disability (handicapped) of the victim or the presence of a child under 16 as a passenger in the vehicle.

Immediate presence of another. The recurring issue in hijacking cases is whether the vehicle was taken from the immediate presence of another (the victim). Unlike robbery which requires proof that the taking be "from the person or presence of another", Section 18-3(a) requires the taking be "from the person or immediate presence of another." What is meant by "immediate presence"?

In *In re Ricardo A.* 356 Ill.App.3d 980, 827 N.E.2d 894 (Ill. App. Ct. 1st Dist. 2005), the victim got out of his car and was jumped by six individuals who beat him, threw bottles at him and hit him with baseball bats taking his wallet and car keys. The attack took place right beside his car. When he was walking about 20 to 25 feet away from his car, he realized it had been started and was being driven by Ricardo who pulled within one foot of the victim before leaving. The court affirmed the guilt of Ricardo finding that being in the immediate vicinity of the victim when the car was being taken was within the "immediate presence" for purposes of the charge of vehicular hijacking.

In *People v. Robinson* 383 Ill.App.3d 160, 892 N.E.2d 39 (Ill. App. Ct. 1st Dist. 2008), the defendant confronted the victim on the street where a struggle ensued. The defendant was armed with a hammer and struck the victim in the head. The defendant took the victim's car keys. The victim ran down the street towards her home and was three houses away when she saw the defendant driving away in her car. The court reversed the defendant's conviction for vehicular hijacking where the hijacked vehicle was some distance away from the scene of the attack between the victim and the defendant as not being in the immediate presence of the victim.

§ 18-5. Aggravated robbery. (a) A person commits aggravated robbery when he or she takes property from the person or presence of another by the use of force or by threatening the imminent use of force while indicating verbally or by his or her actions to the victim that he or she is presently armed with a firearm or other dangerous weapon, including a knife, club, ax, or bludgeon. This offense shall be applicable even though it is later determined that he or she had no firearm or other dangerous weapon, including a knife, club, ax, or bludgeon, in his or her possession when he or she committed the robbery.

(a-5) A person commits aggravated robbery when he or she takes property from the person or presence of another by delivering (by injection, inhalation, ingestion, transfer of possession, or any other means) to the victim without his or her consent, or by threat or deception, and for other than medical purposes, any controlled substance.

(b) *Sentence.* Aggravated robbery is a Class 1 felony.

Commentary – Aggravated Robbery

Section 18-5(a) enhances the offense robbery in the circumstance of the offender threatening force by saying that he is armed with a firearm or other dangerous weapon, even though there is no proof the defendant was actually armed with a weapon. the fear induced in the victim by the veiled threat of a weapon is sufficient justification for the aggravating factor, but the threat of force by the spoken words must be objective (it would be reasonable to believe the defendant was armed) not subjective (the victim stated he believed the defendant was armed). An additional and different aggravating factor under Section 18-5(a-d) is the use of controlled substances on a victim to create a context for a robbery to occur. Aggravated robbery is an intermediate offense – while simple robbery is a Class 2 felony and a basic armed robbery offense (dangerous weapon) is a Class X felony, aggravated robbery is a Class 1 felony.

In *People v. Hall* 352 Ill.App.3d.537, 816 N.E.2d 703 (Ill. App. Ct. 1st Dist. 2005), the defendant approached a clerk in a video store and asked if the clerk had ever been shot, if the clerk was wearing a bulletproof vest and if the clerk wanted to be shot. The defendant then reached toward his own waist two or three times and asked if the clerk was going to cooperate. The defendant pulled out two plastic bags and had the clerk put in 50 DVD's and also took two video tapes and left the store, telling the clerk not to call the police. The defendant was later apprehended with the two video tapes in his possession. The court affirmed the defendant's conviction for aggravated robbery finding the conduct was supported by objective evidence.

§18-6. Vehicular invasion. (a) A person commits vehicular invasion when he or she knowingly, by force and without lawful justification, enters or reaches into the interior of a motor vehicle while the motor vehicle is occupied by another person or persons, with the intent to commit therein a theft or felony.
(b) Sentence. Vehicular invasion is a Class 1 felony.

Article 19 – Burglary
720 ILCS 5/19-1 *et seq.*

§ 19-1. Burglary. (a) A person commits burglary when without authority he knowingly enters or without authority remains within a building, housetrailer, watercraft, aircraft, motor vehicle as defined in The Illinois Vehicle Code [625 ILCS 5/1-100 et seq.], railroad car, or any part thereof, with intent to commit therein a felony or theft. This offense shall not include the offenses set out in Section 4-102 of The Illinois Vehicle Code [625 ILCS 5/4-102].

(b) Sentence.
Burglary is a Class 2 felony. A burglary committed in a school, day care center, day care home, group day care home, or part day child care facility, or place of worship is a Class 1 felony, except that this provision does not apply to a day care center, day care home, group day care home, or part day child care facility operated in a private residence used as a dwelling.

(c) Regarding penalties prescribed in subsection (b) for violations committed in a day care center, day care home, group day care home, or part day child care facility, the time of day, time of year, and whether children under 18 years of age were present in the day care center, day care home, group day care home, or part day child care facility are irrelevant.

§ 19-2. Possession of burglary tools. (a) A person commits the offense of possession of burglary tools when he possesses any key, tool, instrument, device, or any explosive, suitable for use in breaking into a building, housetrailer, watercraft, aircraft, motor vehicle as defined in The Illinois Vehicle Code [625 ILCS 5/1-100 et seq.], railroad car, or any depository designed for the safekeeping of property, or any part thereof, with intent to enter any such place and with intent to commit therein a felony or theft. The trier of fact may infer from the possession of a key designed for lock bumping an intent to commit a felony or theft; however, this inference does not apply to any peace officer or other employee of a law enforcement agency, or to any person or agency licensed under the Private Detective, Private Alarm, Private Security, Fingerprint Vendor, and Locksmith Act of 2004 [225 ILCS 447/5-5 et seq.]. For the purposes of this Section, "lock bumping" means a lock picking technique for opening a pin tumbler lock using a specially-crafted bumpkey.

(b) Sentence. Possession of burglary tools in violation of this Section is a Class 4 felony.

§ 19-2.5. Unlawful sale of burglary tools. (a) For the purposes of this Section:

"Lock bumping" means a lock picking technique for opening a pin tumbler lock using a specially-crafted bumpkey.

"Motor vehicle" has the meaning ascribed to it in the Illinois Vehicle Code [625 ILCS 5/].

(b) A person commits the offense of unlawful sale of burglary tools when he or she knowingly sells or transfers any key, including a key designed for lock bumping, or a lock pick specifically manufactured or altered for use in breaking into a building, housetrailer, watercraft, aircraft, motor vehicle, railroad car, or any depository designed for the safekeeping of property, or any part of that property.

(c) This Section does not apply to the sale or transfer of any item described in subsection (b) to any peace officer or other employee of a law enforcement agency, or to any person or agency licensed as a locksmith under the Private Detective, Private Alarm, Private Security, Fingerprint Vendor, and Locksmith Act of 2004 [225 ILCS 447/], or to any person engaged in the business of towing vehicles, or to any person engaged in the business of lawful repossession of property who possesses a valid Repossessor-ICC Authorization Card.

(d) Sentence. Unlawful sale of burglary tools is a Class 4 felony.

§ 19-3. Residential burglary. (a) A person commits residential burglary who knowingly and without authority enters or knowingly and without authority remains within the dwelling place of another, or any part thereof, with the intent to commit therein a felony or theft. This offense includes the offense of burglary as defined in Section 19-1 [720 ILCS 5/19-1].

(a-5) A person commits residential burglary who falsely represents himself or herself, including but not limited to falsely representing himself or herself to be a representative of any unit of government or a construction, telecommunications, or utility company, for the purpose of gaining entry to the dwelling place of another, with the intent to commit therein a felony or theft or to facilitate the commission therein of a felony or theft by another.

(b) Sentence. Residential burglary is a Class 1 felony.

Commentary – Burglary and Related Offenses

Burglary. Section 19-1 defines burglary as the knowing, unauthorized entry into a building (or other defined location – trailer, motor vehicle, watercraft, etc.) with the intent to commit a theft or another felony. Simple burglary is in any building that is not a dwelling, residential burglary under Section 19-3 is a burglary of a dwelling. A burglary offense cannot occur when the initial entry into the location was authorized because the location is open to the public. Thus one commits a burglary if he enters a business during regular hours, and either (1) hides and waits for the business to close, (2) enters an unauthorized area of the business or (3) remains after being told to leave, and with the intent to commit the predicate theft or felony. However a person who enters a building lawfully and shoplifts merchandise in a public area of the business and then leaves during business hours is guilty of ordinary retail theft, not burglary. See *People v. Bradford* 2016 IL 118674 (Ill. St. Ct. 2016)

In *People v. Richardson*, 2011 IL App (5th) 090663, the defendant was charged with burglary after he was observed walking out of the "Employees Only" section of a liquor store. His conviction for burglary based on "remaining" is the store with intent to commit a theft was affirmed. Evidence at trial included security camera videotape showing the defendant entering the store and leaving after opening two large safes, removing items from both safes, and putting the items in his pockets before walking out. Because the defendant had authority to enter the store, but no authority to go to or remain in the office sections, his guilt of burglary was evident.

In *People v. Beauchamp* 241 Ill.2d 1, 944 N.E.2d 319 (Ill. S. Ct. 2011), the defendants were convicted of burglary based on entry to an SUV when the rear hatch-back window had been stolen. The window was later recovered in the back seat of the defendants' car. The hydraulic arms on the hatch-back window had been damaged when it was removed from the SUV. The victim (the SUV owner) had seen the defendants standing by her car. The appellate court had reversed the defendants' conviction on the basis that no "entry" had been made into the SUV with intent to commit a theft. The Supreme Court held the evidence was sufficient to support the conclusion that there was a knowing entry, without authority to a motor vehicle for purposes of committing a theft. The court noted that "breaking the close" of a protect space, such as the interior of a car is all that is required for a burglary to have occurred. Here the hydraulic arms were attached on the inside and were broken, and one was lying on the ground – sufficient evidence to support the burglary conviction.

In *People v. Singleton* 367 Ill.App.3d 182, 854 N.E.2d 326 (Ill. App. Ct. 4th Dist. 2006), the defendant and an accomplice entered a garage to commit a theft but ran when the burglar alarm sounded. The defendant and the same accomplice entered an auto repair garage and stole tools, killing a watch dog. The defendant and the accomplice then entered a farm shed and stole a van. The accomplice pleaded to a lesser office and testified against the defendant. While the defendant claimed an alibi defense, the evidence was sufficient to affirm his three burglary and other convictions in each instance, he had entered the building, without authority, with the intent to commit a theft.

Residential Burglary. Under Section 19-3, the knowing entry (or remaining) into the dwelling place of another with the intent to commit a theft or other felony constitutes a residential burglary. As contrasted with simple burglary (Class 2 felony), residential burglary is a Class 1 felony. A dwelling place is a residential unit where people live. An attached garage is not a dwelling place. See *People v. Mata* 243 Ill. App. 3d 365, 611 N.E.2d 1235 (Ill. App. Ct. 1st Dist. 1993).

In *People v. McGee* 398 Ill.App.3d 789, 924 N.E.2d 612 (Ill. App. Ct. 2010), the defendant was found inside a residence with stolen property in his hands. The house had been damaged by fire. The property was in foreclosure, but its owner kept the premises locked and checked on it every day. Her furniture and appliances remained in the house. The owner testified that she intended to move back into the home once it was repaired after a settlement with the insurance company; however, in fact the house was sold at the foreclosure sale. The defendant's conviction for residential burglary was affirmed with the court holding that the property had not been abandoned, had been used as a dwelling place (as defined in 720 ILCS 5/2-6(b)). The defendant knew or should have known the building was a dwelling place.

Entry without authority. The state must prove that the defendant did not have authority to be in the building or other location. Entering a building only for the purpose of committing a theft is far different than entering a location for the purpose the building or location exists. While a store open to the public can be entered by anyone who wants to shop at that store, a person who enters the building to commit a theft does not have authority to enter and can be held criminally responsible for the offense of burglary.

In *People v. Hopkins* 229 Ill.App.3d 665, 593 N.E.2d 1028 (Ill. App. Ct. 1992), a man and women entered Central Supply, a retail store, and conversed with the owner about his goods, causing the owner to leave the area of the cash register. When the owner looked to the front of his store at the cash register, he saw the defendant behind the counter with the cash register drawer open, making grasping motions at the money. The owner announced he was going to call the police and the defendant fled. The original couple left shortly thereafter and the three were stopped by police nearby in the same car. The defendant contended that since the store was a retail store open to the public, he could not be convicted of burglary because anyone had authority to enter, and that he could have decided to commit the theft after he was inside the building. The owner had testified that while he was open to the public no one who entered to steal from him had his authority to enter. In upholding the defendant's burglary conviction, the court stated:

> The burglary charge before the court in this case is not typical because it involves no locked doors and no entry by stealth. Instead, this charge involves a retail establishment, open for business at the time of the alleged burglary, which invited potential customers to come in off the street, look around at the stocks within, and (the store's owner hopes) make a purchase. As shown by defendant's arguments in the present case, this charge of burglary-commonly known throughout central Illinois as a "Jones burglary"-often raises serious questions regarding both the accused burglar's intent to steal at the time he entered the store and his lack of authority to enter.
>
> *People v. Hopkins* 229 Ill.App.3d at 771, 593 N.E.2d at 1032.

The court assessed the evidence and held that a rational jury could conclude that none of the three people who entered Central Supply that day had any intent to buy products and instead entered with the intent to steal. Thus there was no authority to enter the building.

Burglary tools. Section 19-2 requires the state to prove these elements for a conviction for possession of burglary tools (1) knowing possession of (2) any tool or device suitable for use (3) in committing a burglary. The fact that no burglary had been committed is not a defense if the proof of the elements is otherwise present. Having common tools in ones' possession that could be used in a burglary is insufficient evidence to convict someone of the crime in the absence of proof of intent to commit a burglary.

In *People v. Ramirez* 151 Ill.App.3d 731, 502 N.E.2d 1237 (Ill. App. Ct. 5th Dist. 1986), the defendant was found outside a grocery store that was burglarized and near a car that had screwdrivers, a hydraulic spreader, socket wrenches and pipes in the trunk. The court reversed the defendant's conviction for possession of burglary tools because there was no evidence showing that these items were not common tools, that they were used in any burglary or that the defendant had any intent to commit a burglary.

In *People v. Wahn* 169 Ill.App.3d 264, 523 N.E.2d 1318 (Ill. App. Ct. 5th Dist. 1988), the defendants were charged and convicted of possession of burglary tools – a screwdriver. They were passengers in a van and within their area of immediate control there was a screwdriver, stocking caps, brown gloves, penlights and a radio scanner, although some items were in various compartments of the seats and glove box. The driver of the van testified that he was asked to drive to a location where no one was home to pick up a lawn tractor. As the van approached the location, there was a police call on the scanner that the van was to be stopped. Wahn said that everything needed to be stashed and that is why the things were found where they were in the van. The court held that the driver's testimony and the circumstantial evidence were sufficient to prove that the defendants knew the character of the screwdriver as a burglary too, that it was suitable for use in a burglary and that there was intent to commit a burglary.

§ 19-4. Criminal trespass to a residence. (a)(1) A person commits the offense of criminal trespass to a residence when, without authority, he knowingly enters or remains within any residence, including a house trailer.

(2) A person commits the offense of criminal trespass to a residence when, without authority, he or she knowingly enters the residence of another and knows or has reason to know that one or more persons is present or he or she knowingly enters the residence of another and remains in the residence after he or she knows or has reason to know that one or more persons is present.

(3) For purposes of this Section, in the case of a multi-unit residential building or complex, "residence" shall only include the portion of the building or complex which is the actual dwelling place of any person and shall not include such places as common recreational areas or lobbies.

(b) Sentence.

(1) Criminal trespass to a residence under paragraph (1) of subsection (a) is a Class A misdemeanor.

(2) Criminal trespass to a residence under paragraph (2) of subsection (a) is a Class 4 felony.

Commentary – Criminal Trespass to Residence

Section 19-4 proscribes against criminal trespass to residence. This crime is committed where the offender knowingly and without authority enters or remains in the residence of another. Section 19-4(a)(1) is a Class A misdemeanor. Section 19-4(a)(2) is a Class 4 felony with the enhancing element that the criminal trespasser knows or has reason to know that one or more persons is present in the residence. Note that other criminal trespass offenses are in Article 21 of the Criminal Code.

In *People v. Brant* 394 Ill.App.3d 663, 916 N.E.2d 144 (Ill. App. Ct. 2nd Dist. 2009), the defendant drove a friend (Nowrat) to a residence to confront another woman. The defendant parked and remained in the car, as Nowrat went to the front door of the house. The defendant observed Nowrat shoved by another woman, grabbed by the hair and dragged inside the house. The defendant got out of the car, pushed her way into the house and struggled with several women trying to get Nowrat free so that she could leave the residence. The defendant's conviction for felony criminal trespass to residence was affirmed because there was no dispute that the defendant did not have authority from the homeowner or any other occupant to enter the residence. The claim of the right to defend another did not confer authority on the defendant to enter the home.

In *People v. Davis* 2012 IL App (2d) 100934 (Ill. App. Ct. 2nd Dist. 2012), the defendant entered a private residence during the day and walked around the home. A nanny, a drapery hanger and others were present in the home observing the defendant move about. He did not take any with and looked as if he were in a museum looking around. The defendant was convicted of Trespass to Residence and sentenced to prison. On appeal he claimed the evidence did not prove that he knew had lacked authority to be in the residence. This claim was rejected because the crime is complete with entry without authority. The prosecution need not prove the defendant's knowledge of lack of authority.

§ 19-5. Criminal fortification of a residence or building. (a) A person commits criminal fortification of a residence or building when, with the intent to prevent the lawful entry of a law enforcement officer or another, he or she maintains a residence or building in a fortified condition, knowing that the residence or building is used for the unlawful manufacture, storage, with intent to deliver or manufacture, delivery, or trafficking of cannabis, controlled substances, or methamphetamine as defined in the Cannabis Control Act, the Illinois Controlled Substances Act, or the Methamphetamine Control and Community Protection Act [720 ILCS 550/1 et seq., 720 ILCS 570/100 et seq., or 720 ILCS 646/1 et seq.].

(b) "Fortified condition" means preventing or impeding entry through the use of steel doors, wooden planking, crossbars, alarm systems, dogs video surveillance, motion sensing devices, booby traps, or other similar means. If video surveillance is the sole component of the fortified condition, the video surveillance must be with the intent to alert an occupant to the presence of a law enforcement officer for the purpose of interfering with the official duties of a law enforcement officer, allowing removal or destruction of evidence, or facilitating the infliction of harm to a law enforcement officer. For the purposes of this Section, "booby trap" means any device, including but not limited to any explosive device, designed to cause physical injury or the destruction of evidence, when triggered by an act of a person approaching, entering, or moving through a structure.

(c) Sentence. Criminal fortification of a residence or building is a Class 3 felony.

(d) This Section does not apply to the fortification of a residence or building used in the manufacture of methamphetamine as described in Sections 10 and 15 of the Methamphetamine Control and Community Protection Act [720 ILCS 646/10 and 720 ILCS 646/15].

§ 19-6. Home Invasion. (a) A person who is not a peace officer acting in the line of duty commits home invasion when without authority he or she knowingly enters the dwelling place of another when he or she knows or has reason to know that one or more persons is present or he or she knowingly enters the dwelling place of another and remains in such dwelling place until he or she knows or has reason to know that one or more persons is present or who falsely represents himself or herself, including but not limited to, falsely representing himself or herself to be a representative of any unit of government or a construction, telecommunications, or utility company, for the purpose of gaining entry to the dwelling place of another when he or she knows or has reason to know that one or more persons are present and

(1) While armed with a dangerous weapon, other than a firearm, uses force or threatens the imminent use of force upon any person or persons within such dwelling place whether or not injury occurs, or

(2) Intentionally causes any injury, except as provided in subsection (a)(5), to any person or persons within such dwelling place, or

(3) While armed with a firearm uses force or threatens the imminent use of force upon any person or persons within such dwelling place whether or not injury occurs, or

(4) Uses force or threatens the imminent use of force upon any person or persons within such dwelling place whether or not injury occurs and during the commission of the offense personally discharges a firearm, or

(5) Personally discharges a firearm that proximately causes great bodily harm, permanent disability, permanent disfigurement, or death to another person within such dwelling place, or

(6) Commits, against any person or persons within that dwelling place, a violation of Section 11-1.20, 11-1.30, 11-1.40, 11-1.50, 11-1.60, 12-13, 12-14, 12-14.1, 12-15, or 12-16 of the Criminal Code of 1961.

(b) It is an affirmative defense to a charge of home invasion that the accused who knowingly enters the dwelling place of another and remains in such dwelling place until he or she knows or has reason to know that one or more persons is present either immediately leaves such premises or surrenders to the person or persons lawfully present therein without either attempting to cause or causing serious bodily injury to any person present therein.

(c) Sentence. Home invasion in violation of subsection (a)(1), (a)(2)or (a)(6) is a Class X felony. A violation of subsection (a)(3) is a Class X felony for which 15 years shall be added to the term of imprisonment imposed by the court. A violation of subsection (a)(4) is a Class X felony for which 20 years shall be added to the term of imprisonment imposed by the court. A violation of subsection (a)(5) is a Class X felony for which25 years or up to a term of natural life shall be added to the term of imprisonment imposed by the court.

(d) For purposes of this Section, "dwelling place of another" includes a dwelling place where the defendant maintains a tenancy interest but from which the defendant has been barred by a divorce decree, judgment of dissolution of marriage, order of protection, or other court order.

Commentary – Home Invasion

Section 12-11 sets forth the elements of home invasion to require proof of (1) knowing entry into the dwelling of another, (2) knowing or having reason to know that one or more persons are present (or remains in the dwelling of another until he knows or has reason to know that one or more persons are present and (3) (a) armed with a dangerous weapon or a firearm threatens use of force or (b) intentionally injures anyone in the home or (c) armed with a firearm and using or threatening force or (c) shoots a firearm while threatening the use of force or (d) shoots a firearm and causes great bodily harm, permanent disfigurement or disability or death or (e) commits a violation of listed criminal sexual assault and abuse offenses. the entry into the house must be proved to be without authority.

In *People v. Thomas* 384 Ill.App.3d 895, 894 N.E.2d 940 (Ill. App. Ct. 1st Dist. 2010), the defendant and his cohorts waited outside a residence until the victim and her children came home. As the victim family was entering the home, the offenders grabbed them and forced them inside the house, where invaders demanded money and one of the men fired a gunshot into the floor. The defendant's conviction for home invasion was affirmed (as were other convictions for armed robbery and aggravated kidnapping offenses). As to the home invasion, his claim that there was no one in the home at the time of entry was rejected, where the entry of the family and the criminal actors was simultaneous.

Article 20 – Arson
720 ILCS 5/20-1 *et seq.*

§ 20-1. Arson. A person commits arson when, by means of fire or explosive, he knowingly:

(a) Damages any real property, or any personal property having a value of $ 150 or more, of another without his consent; or

(b) With intent to defraud an insurer, damages any property or any personal property having a value of $ 150 or more.

Property "of another" means a building or other property, whether real or personal, in which a person other than the offender has an interest which the offender has no authority to defeat or impair, even though the offender may also have an interest in the building or property.

(c) Sentence. Arson is a Class 2 felony.

§ 20-1.1. Aggravated Arson. (a) A person commits aggravated arson when in the course of committing arson he or she knowingly damages, partially or totally, any building or structure, including any adjacent building or structure, including all or any part of a school building, house trailer, watercraft, motor vehicle, or railroad car, and (1) he knows or reasonably should know that one or more persons are present therein or (2) any person suffers great bodily harm, or permanent disability or disfigurement as a result of the fire or explosion or (3) a fireman, policeman, or correctional officer who is present at the scene acting in the line of duty is injured as a result of the fire or explosion. For purposes of this Section, property "of another" means a building or other property, whether real or personal, in which a person other than the offender has an interest that the offender has no authority to defeat or impair, even though the offender may also have an interest in the building or property; and "school building" means any public or private preschool, elementary or secondary school, community college, college, or university.

(b) Sentence. Aggravated arson is a Class X felony.

§ 20-1.2. Residential arson. (a) A person commits the offense of residential arson when, in the course of committing an arson, he or she knowingly damages, partially or totally, any building or structure that is the dwelling place of another.

(b) Sentence. Residential arson is a Class 1 felony.

§ 20-1.3. Place of worship arson. (a) A person commits the offense of place of worship arson when, in the course of committing an arson, he or she knowingly damages, partially or totally, any place of worship.

(b) Sentence. Place of worship arson is a Class 1 felony.

§ 20-2. Possession of explosives or explosive or incendiary devices. (a) A person commits the offense of possession of explosives or explosive or incendiary devices in violation of this Section when he or she possesses, manufactures or transports any explosive compound, timing or detonating device for use with any explosive compound or incendiary device and either intends to use such explosive or device to commit any offense or knows that another intends to use such explosive or device to commit a felony.

(b) Sentence. Possession of explosives or explosive or incendiary devices in violation of this Section is a Class 1 felony for which a person, if sentenced to a term of imprisonment, shall be sentenced to not less than 4 years and not more than 30 years.

Commentary – Arson

Arson. Section 20-1 delineates the offense of arson. an offender who (1) knowingly, without consent, damages real property or personal property having a value in excess of $150, of another, by means of fire or explosion or (2) with intent to defraud an insurance company damages any real property, or personal property having a value in excess of $150 by means of fire or explosion commits arson. Arson is a Class 2 felony.

Aggravated Arson. Arson becomes "aggravated arson" under Section 20-1.1 when (1) the defendant commits arson to a building and knows or should reasonably know that someone is in the building, or (2) the arson's fire or explosion causes great bodily harm, permanent disability or disfigurement or death to a person or (3) a fireman or police who responds to the fire event in the line of duty is injured as a result. Aggravated arson is a Class X felony. Even when the injury to a policeman or fireman is not directly caused by the fire, a defendant can be convicted of aggravated arson because the fireman was injured in the line of duty by falling and breaking his leg fighting the arson fire set by the defendant. See *People v. Herman* 347 Ill. App.3d 525, 807 N.E.2d 1036 (Ill. App. Ct. 2nd Dist. 2004).

Property. Property can be of any type - real or personal, including motor vehicles. See *People v. Carmona-Olvara* 363 Ill.App.3d 162, 842 N.E.2d 313 (Ill. App. Ct. 1st Dist. 2009) (evidence was sufficient to support a re-trial for arson to a motor vehicle in spite of other trial errors). The fact that the defendant may have an interest in the property damaged by the fire or explosion is not a defense if there is some other person who also has an interest in the property that is damaged or destroyed. The $150 amount in Section 20-1(a) relates to the value of the personal property that is damaged, not the amount of damage to the personal property and does not apply to damage to real property.

Residential Arson. Section 20-2 proscribes against residential arson where the property that is damaged by fire or explosion is a dwelling place of another person. Residential arson is a Class 1 felony.

Cases. In *People v. Stewart* 406 Ill.App.3d 518, 940 N.E.2d 273 (Ill. App. Ct. 1st Dist. 2010), the defendant was convicted after jury trial of arson and aggravated arson. A fire was started with gasoline at an abandoned building and a 27 mph wind blew embers to an adjacent residence starting the roof on fire. There were people living in the adjacent residence. The only proof of ownership of the abandoned building was a death certificate of Willie Jones, dated eight months before the fire, with an address which matched the building's address. the defendant contended that his conviction for aggravated arson (as to the occupied building) should be reversed claiming there was insufficient proof that he knowingly damaged the property of another because it was not foreseeable that the fire would spread nor that it would spread to an occupied building. The court concluded that a rational trier-of-fact could determine based on the proximity of the buildings and the wind conditions that (1) the fire could spread to a near-by building and (2) that the defendant knew or should have known that people would be present in the second location that was damaged by the fire. The court did reverse the defendant's conviction for arson to the unoccupied building. While the state had charged arson as the knowing damage to property of Willie Jones, the death certificate was not proof that Willie Jones had an interest in the property on the day of the offense.

In *People v. Bauer* 393 Ill.App.3d 414, 913 N.E.2d 1132 (Ill. App. Ct. 2nd Dist. 2009), the defendant's convictions for aggravated arson were affirmed. The defendant and her boyfriend stayed up drinking and arguing until 4 a.m. the defendant left the townhouse that she shared with her boyfriend and another male friend, but returned at 8 a.m. when the other two occupants were in bed. She sprayed lighter fluid on the dining room table and rug, and sprayed more down the stairs to the outside entryway. She lit three matches and threw them at the lighter fluid-soaked area, but did not think that it had actually started on fire, and then left. A fire ensued causing smoke and other damage. Defendant's claim that she did not actually know there was a fire was not a defense to aggravated arson.

Article 21 – Damage and Trespass to Property
720 ILCS 5/21-1 *et seq.*

§ 21-1. Criminal damage to property.
(a) A person commits criminal damage to property when he or she:

(1) knowingly damages any property of another;

(2) recklessly by means of fire or explosive damages property of another:

(3) knowingly starts a fire on the land of another:

(4) knowingly injures a domestic animal of another without his consent;

(5) knowingly deposits on the land or in the building of another, any stink bomb or any offensive smelling compound and thereby intends to interfere with the use by another of the land or building;

(6) knowingly damages any property, other than as described in subsection (2) of subsection (a) of Section 20-1 [720 ILCS 5/20-1], with intent to defraud an insurer;
(7) knowingly shoots a firearm at any portion of a railroad train;
(8) knowingly, without proper authorization, cuts, injures, damages, defaces, destroys, or tampers with any fire hydrant or any public or private fire fighting equipment, or any apparatus appertaining to fire fighting equipment; or

(9) intentionally, without proper authorization, opens any fire hydrant.

(b) When the charge of criminal damage to property exceeding a specified value is brought, the extent of the damage is an element of the offense to be resolved by the trier of fact as either exceeding or not exceeding the specified value.

(c) It is an affirmative defense to a violation of item (a), (c), or (e) of this Section that the owner of the property or land damaged consented to such damage.

Commentary – Criminal Damage to Property

Elements. Section 21-1 sets forth the alternative ways of committing criminal damage to property which include the (a) knowing damage to property of another, or (b) reckless damage to property of another by fire or explosion, or (c) knowing lighting of a fire on someone else's land, or (d) knowing injury to someone else's animal, (e) causing interference with the use of property or a building by a stink bomb, or (f) damage to property with intent to defraud an insurance company, or (g) knowingly shooting at a railroad train. the classification of offense depends on the amount of damage (i.e. cost of repair) to the property, so that damage of less than $300 under Section 21-1(a), (b), (c), (e) and (f) is a Class A misdemeanor, but damage of less than $300 under these sections that occur at a school, place of worship or to farm equipment or buildings are Class 4 felonies. Other classification enhancements involve the value of the damage (cost of repair or replacement) or location of the property (school or place of worship or farm building) or type of property (farm equipment).

In *People v. Kyles* 303 Ill.App.3d 338, 708 N.E.2d 391 (Ill. App. Ct. 1st Dist. 1998), the defendant, an inmate in the Cook County Jail, set his bedding, mattress and other items in his cell on fire. He was charged with attempted aggravated arson, but the trial court found him guilty of the lesser-included offense of misdemeanor criminal damage to property without specifying which subsection of 21-1 that was being relied on as supporting the conviction. in affirming the trial court, the appellate court noted that the defendant was guilty of criminal damage to property under three separate sections – (1) Section 21-1(a) for knowing damage to property of another; (2) Section 21-1(b) for reckless damage to property of another by means of fire or (3) Section 21-1(c) for starting a fire on the land of another without his consent – finding that the requisite acts and mental states for each was supported by the evidence.

In *People v. Berrier* 362 Ill.App.3d 1153, 848 N.E.2d 1117 (Ill. App. Ct. 2nd Dist. 2006), the victim had car trouble and pulled his Explorer to the side of an expressway and later returned in another vehicle to repair the Explorer. When he returned he saw a blue van parked right behind his Explorer with the rear passenger window broken and the defendant reaching inside the vehicle. While the defendant claimed that he had accidently broken the window, the court held the evidence supported the verdict that the defendant had knowingly damaged the victim's property.

In *People v. Hauschild* 364 Ill.App.3d 202, 845 N.E.2d 74 (Ill. App. Ct. 2nd Dist. 2006), the defendant was charged with home invasion and other crimes including criminal damage to property for shooting a Labrador retriever causing damage in excess of $300. The charge required the state to prove that the defendant knowingly injured the dog as well as the damage amount. The evidence showed that the defendant came into the victim's darkened bedroom and heard a dog bark. The defendant began blindly shooting his gun and hit the dog. The court upheld his conviction noting the circumstantial evidence supported the notion that he knew or should have known that his conduct in spraying shots in the room could injure the animal.

Affirmative defense. Consent of the property owner is an affirmative defense. If the defendant puts forth some evidence that he had permission or authority to damage the property, the state must prove lack of consent beyond a reasonable doubt.

§ 21-1.1. Criminal Damage of Fire Fighting Apparatus, Hydrants or Equipment. Whoever willfully and maliciously cuts, injures, damages, tampers with or destroys or defaces any fire hydrant or any fire hose or any fire engine, or other public or private fire fighting equipment, or any apparatus appertaining to such equipment, or intentionally opens any fire hydrant without proper authorization, is guilty of a Class B misdemeanor.

§ 21-1.2. Institutional vandalism. (a) A person commits institutional vandalism when, by reason of the actual or perceived race, color, creed, religion, ancestry, gender, sexual orientation, physical or mental disability, or national origin of another individual or group of individuals, regardless of the existence of any other motivating factor or factors, he or she knowingly and without consent inflicts damage to any of the following properties:

(1) A church, synagogue, mosque, or other building, structure or place used for religious worship or other religious purpose;

(2) A cemetery, mortuary, or other facility used for the purpose of burial or memorializing the dead;

(3) A school, educational facility or community center;

(4) The grounds adjacent to, and owned or rented by, any institution, facility, building, structure or place described in paragraphs (1), (2) or (3) of this subsection (a); or

(5) Any personal property contained in any institution, facility, building, structure or place described in paragraphs (1), (2) or (3) of this subsection (a).

(b) Institutional vandalism is a Class 3 felony if the damage to the property does not exceed $ 300. Institutional vandalism is a Class 2 felony if the damage to the property exceeds $ 300. Institutional vandalism is a Class 2 felony for any second or subsequent offense.

(b-5) Upon imposition of any sentence, the trial court shall also either order restitution paid to the victim or impose a fine up to $ 1,000. In addition, any order of probation or conditional discharge entered following a conviction or an adjudication of delinquency shall include a condition that the offender perform public or community service of no less than 200 hours if that service is established in the county where the offender was convicted of institutional vandalism. The court may also impose any other condition of probation or conditional discharge under this Section.

(c) Independent of any criminal prosecution or the result of that prosecution, a person suffering damage to property or injury to his or her person as a result of institutional vandalism may bring a civil action for damages, injunction or other appropriate relief. The court may award actual damages, including damages for emotional distress, or punitive damages. A judgment may include attorney's fees and costs. The parents or legal guardians of an unemancipated minor, other than guardians appointed under the Juvenile Court Act or the Juvenile Court Act of 1987 [705 ILCS 405/1-1 et seq.], shall be liable for the amount of any judgment for actual damages rendered against the minor under this subsection in an amount not exceeding the amount provided under Section 5 of the Parental Responsibility Law [740 ILCS 115/5].

(d) As used in this Section, "sexual orientation" has the meaning ascribed to it in paragraph (O-1) of Section 1-103 of the Illinois Human Rights Act.

§ 21-1.3. Criminal defacement of property. (a) A person commits criminal defacement of property when the person knowingly damages the property of another by defacing, deforming, or otherwise damaging the property by the use of paint or any other similar substance, or by the use of a writing instrument, etching tool, or any other similar device. It is an affirmative defense to a violation of this Section that the owner of the property damaged consented to such damage.

(b) Criminal defacement of property is a Class A misdemeanor for a first offense if the aggregate value of the damage to the property does not exceed $ 300. Criminal defacement of property is a Class 4 felony if the aggregate value of the damage to property does not exceed $ 300 and the property damaged is a school building or place of worship. Criminal defacement of property is a Class 4 felony for a second or subsequent conviction or if the aggregate value of the damage to the property exceeds $ 300. Criminal defacement of property is a Class 3 felony if the aggregate value of the damage to property exceeds $ 300 and the property damaged is a school building or place of worship. In addition to any other sentence that may be imposed for a violation of this Section that is chargeable as a Class 3 or Class 4 felony, a person convicted of criminal defacement of property shall be subject to a mandatory minimum fine of $ 500 plus the actual costs incurred by the property owner or the unit of government to abate, remediate, repair, or remove the effect of the damage to the property. To the extent permitted by law, reimbursement for the costs of abatement, remediation, repair, or removal shall be payable to the person who incurred the costs. In addition to any other sentence that may be imposed, a court shall order any person convicted of criminal defacement of property to perform community service for not less than 30 and not more than 120 hours, if community service is available in the jurisdiction. The community service shall include, but need not be limited to, the cleanup and repair of the damage to property that was caused by the offense, or similar damage to property located in the municipality or county in which the offense occurred. If the property damaged is a school building, the community service may include cleanup, removal, or painting over the defacement. In addition, whenever any person is placed on supervision for an alleged offense under this Section, the supervision shall be conditioned upon the performance of the community service. For the purposes of this subsection (b), aggregate value shall be determined by adding the value of the damage to one or more properties if the offenses were committed as part of a single course of conduct.

§ 21-1.4. Jackrocks. (a) A person who knowingly sells, gives away, manufactures, purchases, or possesses a jackrock or who knowingly places, tosses, or throws a jackrock on public or private property commits a Class A misdemeanor.

(b) As used in this Section, "jackrock" means a caltrop or other object manufactured with one or more rounded or sharpened points, which when placed or thrown present at least one point at such an angle that it is peculiar to and designed for use in puncturing or damaging vehicle tires. It does not include a device designed to puncture or damage the tires of a vehicle driven over it in a particular direction, if a conspicuous and clearly visible warning is posted at the device's location, alerting persons to its presence.

(c) This Section does not apply to the possession, transfer, or use of jackrocks by any law enforcement officer in the course of his or her official duties.

§ 21-2. Criminal trespass to vehicles. Whoever knowingly and without authority enters any part of or operates any vehicle, aircraft, watercraft or snowmobile commits a Class A misdemeanor.

§ 21-2.5. Electronic tracking devices prohibited. a) As used in this Section:

"Electronic tracking device" means any device attached to a vehicle that reveals its location or movement by the transmission of electronic signals.

"State agency" means all departments, officers, commissions, boards, institutions, and bodies politic and corporate of the State. The term, however, does not mean the judicial branch, including, without limitation, the several courts of the State, the offices of the clerk of the supreme court and the clerks of the appellate court, and the Administrative Office of the Illinois Courts, nor does it mean the legislature or its committees or commissions.

"Telematics" includes, but is not limited to, automatic airbag deployment and crash notification, remote diagnostics, navigation, stolen vehicle location, remote door unlock, transmitting emergency and vehicle location information to public safety answering points, and any other service integrating vehicle location technology and wireless communications.

"Vehicle" has the meaning ascribed to it in Section 1-217 of the Illinois Vehicle Code.

(b) A person or entity in this State may not use an electronic tracking device to determine the location or movement of a person.

(c) This Section does not apply:

(1) when the registered owner, lessor, or lessee of a vehicle has consented to the use of the

electronic tracking device with respect to that vehicle;

(2) to the lawful use of an electronic tracking device by a law enforcement agency;

(3) when the vehicle is owned or leased by a business that is authorized to transact business in this State and the tracking device is used by the business for the purpose of tracking vehicles driven by employees of that business, its affiliates, or contractors of that business or its affiliates;

(4) when the vehicle is under the control of a State agency and the electronic tracking device is used by the agency, or the Inspector General appointed under the State Officials and Employees Ethics Act who has jurisdiction over that State agency, for the purpose of tracking vehicles driven by employees or contractors of that State agency; or

(5) telematic services that were installed by the manufacturer, or installed by or with the consent of the owner or lessee of the vehicle and to which the owner or lessee has subscribed. Consent by the owner or lessee of the vehicle constitutes consent for any other driver or passenger of that vehicle.

(d) Sentence. A violation of this Section is a Class A misdemeanor.

§ 21-3. Criminal trespass to real property. (a) Except as provided in subsection (a-5), whoever:

(1) knowingly and without lawful authority enters or remains within or on a building; or

(2) enters upon the land of another, after receiving, prior to such entry, notice from the owner or occupant that such entry is forbidden; or

(3) remains upon the land of another, after receiving notice from the owner or occupant to depart; or

(3.5) presents false documents or falsely represents his or her identity orally to the owner or occupant of a building or land in order to obtain permission from the owner or occupant to enter or remain in the building or on the land; or commits a Class B misdemeanor.

For purposes of item (1) of this subsection, this Section shall not apply to being in a building which is open to the public while the building is open to the public during its normal hours of operation; nor shall this Section apply to a person who enters a public building under the reasonable belief that the building is still open to the public.

(a-5) Except as otherwise provided in this subsection, whoever enters upon any of the following areas in or on a motor vehicle (including an off-road vehicle, motorcycle, moped, or any other powered two-wheel vehicle) after receiving, prior to that entry, notice from the owner or occupant that the entry is forbidden or remains upon or in the area after receiving notice from the owner or occupant to depart commits a Class A misdemeanor:

(1) A field that is used for growing crops or that is capable of being used for growing crops.

(2) An enclosed area containing livestock.

(3) An orchard.

(4) A barn or other agricultural building containing livestock.

(b) A person has received notice from the owner or occupant within the meaning of Subsection (a) if he has been notified personally, either orally or in writing including a valid court order as defined by subsection (7) of Section 112A-3 of the Code of Criminal Procedure of 1963 [725 ILCS 5/112A-3] granting remedy (2) of subsection (b) of Section 112A-14 of that Code [725 ILCS 5/112A-14], or if a printed or written notice forbidding such entry has been conspicuously posted or exhibited at the main entrance to such land or the forbidden part thereof.

(b-5) Subject to the provisions of subsection (b-10), as an alternative to the posting of real property as set forth in subsection (b), the owner or lessee of any real property may post the property by placing identifying purple marks on trees or posts around the area to be posted. Each purple mark shall be:

(1) A vertical line of at least 8 inches in length and the bottom of the mark shall be no less than 3 feet nor more than 5 feet high. Such marks shall be placed no more than 100 feet apart and shall be readily visible to any person approaching the property; or

(2) A post capped or otherwise marked on at least its top 2 inches. The bottom of the cap or mark shall be not less than 3 feet but not more than 5 feet 6 inches high. Posts so marked shall be placed not more than 36 feet apart and shall be readily visible to any person approaching the property. Prior to applying a cap or mark which is visible from both sides of a fence shared by different property owners or lessees, all such owners or lessees shall concur in the decision to post their own property.

Nothing in this subsection (b-5) shall be construed to authorize the owner or lessee of any real property to place any purple marks on any tree or post or to install any post or fence if doing so would violate any applicable law, rule, ordinance, order, covenant, bylaw, declaration, regulation, restriction, contract, or instrument.

(b-10) Any owner or lessee who marks his or her real property using the method described in subsection (b-5) must also provide notice as described in subsection (b) of this Section. The public of this State shall be informed of the provisions of subsection (b-5) of this Section by the Illinois Department of Agriculture and the Illinois Department of Natural Resources. These Departments shall conduct an information campaign for the general public concerning the interpretation and implementation of subsection (b-5). The information shall inform the public about the marking requirements and the applicability of subsection (b-5) including information regarding the size requirements of the markings as well as the manner in which the markings shall be displayed. The Departments shall also include information regarding the requirement that, until the date this subsection becomes inoperative, any owner or lessee who chooses to mark his or her property using paint, must also comply with one of the notice requirements listed in subsection (b). The Departments may prepare a brochure or may disseminate the information through agency websites. Non-governmental organizations including, but not limited to, the Illinois Forestry Association, Illinois Tree Farm and the Walnut Council may help to disseminate the information regarding the requirements and applicability of subsection (b-5) based on materials provided by the Departments. This subsection (b-10) is inoperative on and after January 1, 2013.

(b-15) Subsections (b-5) and (b-10) do not apply to real property located in a municipality of over 2,000,000 inhabitants.

(c) This Section does not apply to any person, whether a migrant worker or otherwise, living on the land with permission of the owner or of his agent having apparent authority to hire workers on such land and assign them living quarters or a place of accommodations for living thereon, nor to anyone living on such land at the request of, or by occupancy, leasing or other agreement or arrangement with the owner or his agent, nor to anyone invited by such migrant worker or other person so living on such land to visit him at the place he is so living upon the land.

(d) A person shall be exempt from prosecution under this Section if he beautifies unoccupied and abandoned residential and industrial properties located within any municipality. For the purpose of this subsection, "unoccupied and abandoned residential and industrial property" means any real estate (1) in which the taxes have not been paid for a period of at least 2 years; and (2) which has been left unoccupied and abandoned for a period of at least one year; and "beautifies" means to landscape, clean up litter, or to repair dilapidated conditions on or to board up windows and doors.

(e) No person shall be liable in any civil action for money damages to the owner of unoccupied and abandoned residential and industrial property which that person beautifies pursuant to subsection (d) of this Section.

(f) This Section does not prohibit a person from entering a building or upon the land of another for emergency purposes. For purposes of this subsection (f), "emergency" means a condition or circumstance in which an individual is or is reasonably believed by the person to be in imminent danger of serious bodily harm or in which property is or is reasonably believed to be in imminent danger of damage or destruction.

(g) Paragraph (3.5) of subsection (a) does not apply to a peace officer or other official of a unit of government who enters a building or land in the performance of his or her official duties.

(h) A person may be liable in any civil action for money damages to the owner of the land he or she entered upon with a motor vehicle as prohibited under subsection (a-5) of this Section. A person may also be liable to the owner for court costs and reasonable attorney's fees. The measure of damages shall be: (i) the actual damages, but not less than $ 250, if the vehicle is operated in a nature preserve or registered area as defined in Sections 3.11 and 3.14 of the Illinois Natural Areas Preservation Act [525 ILCS 30/3.11 and 525 ILCS 30/3.14]; (ii) twice the actual damages if the owner has previously notified the person to cease trespassing; or (iii) in any other case, the actual damages, but not less than $ 50. If the person operating the vehicle is under the age of 16, the owner of the vehicle and the parent or legal guardian of the minor are jointly and severally liable. For the purposes of this subsection (h):
"Land" includes, but is not limited to, land used for crop land, fallow land, orchard, pasture, feed lot, timber land, prairie land, mine spoil nature preserves and registered areas. "Land" does not include driveways or private roadways upon which the owner allows the public to drive.

"Owner" means the person who has the right to possession of the land, including the owner, operator or tenant.

"Vehicle" has the same meaning as provided under Section 1-217 of the Illinois Vehicle Code [625 ILCS 5/1-217].

(i) This Section does not apply to the following persons while serving process:

(1) a person authorized to serve process under Section 2-202 of the Code of Civil Procedure; or

(2) a special process server appointed by the circuit court.

§ 21-4. Criminal Damage to Government Supported Property. (1) Any of the following acts is a Class 4 felony when the damage to property is $ 500 or less, and any such act is a Class 3 felony when the damage to property exceeds $ 500 but does not exceed $ 10,000; a Class 2 felony when the damage to property exceeds $ 10,000 but does not exceed $ 100,000 and a Class 1 felony when the damage to property exceeds $ 100,000:

(a) Knowingly damages any property supported in whole or in part with State funds, funds of a unit of local government or school district, or Federal funds administered or granted through State agencies without the consent of the State; or

(b) Knowingly, by means of fire or explosive damages property supported in whole or in part with State funds, funds of a unit of local government or school district, or Federal funds administered or granted through State agencies; or

(c) Knowingly starts a fire on property supported in whole or in part with State funds, funds of a unit of local government or school district, or Federal funds administered or granted through State agencies without the consent of the State; or

(d) Knowingly deposits on land or in a building supported in whole or in part with State funds, funds of a unit of local government or school district, or Federal funds administered or granted through State agencies without the consent of the State, any stink bomb or any offensive smelling compound and thereby intends to interfere with the use by another of the land or building.

(2) When the damage to property exceeds $ 10,000, the court shall impose upon the offender a fine equal to the value of the damages to the property.

§ 21-5. Criminal Trespass to State Supported Land. (a) Whoever enters upon land supported in whole or in part with State funds, or Federal funds administered or granted through State agencies or any building on such land, after receiving, prior to such entry, notice from the State or its representative that such entry is forbidden, or remains upon such land or in such building after receiving notice from the State or its representative to depart, and who thereby interferes with another person's lawful use or enjoyment of such building or land, commits a Class A misdemeanor.

(a-5) A person commits criminal trespass to State supported land when he or she enters upon a right of way, including facilities and improvements thereon, owned, leased, or otherwise used by a public body or district organized under the Metropolitan Transit Authority Act, the Local Mass Transit District Act, or the Regional Transportation Authority Act, after receiving, prior to the entry, notice from the public body or district, or its representative, that the entry is forbidden, or the person remains upon the right of way after receiving notice from the public body or district, or its representative, to depart, and in either of these instances intends to compromise public safety by causing a delay in transit service lasting more than 15 minutes or destroying property.

A person has received notice from the public body or district within the meaning of this subsection if he or she has been notified personally, either orally or in writing, or if a printed or written notice forbidding entry to him or her has been conspicuously posted or exhibited at any point of entrance to the right of way or the forbidden part of the right of way.

As used in this subsection (a-5), "right of way" has the meaning ascribed to it in Section 18c-7502 of the Illinois Vehicle Code.

(b) A person has received notice from the State within the meaning of subsection (a) if he has been notified personally, either orally or in writing, or if a printed or written notice forbidding such entry to him or a group of which he is a part, has been conspicuously posted or exhibited at the main entrance to such land or the forbidden part thereof.

(c) Sentence. Criminal Trespass to State Supported Land is a Class A Misdemeanor, except a violation of subsection (a-5)of this Section is a Class A misdemeanor for a first violation and a Class 4 felony for a second or subsequent violation.

§ 21-6. Unauthorized Possession or Storage of Weapons. (a) Whoever possesses or stores any weapon enumerated in Section 33A-1 [720 ILCS 5/33A-1] in any building or on land supported in whole or in part with public funds or in any building on such land without prior written permission from the chief security officer for such land or building commits a Class A misdemeanor.

(b) The chief security officer must grant any reasonable request for permission under paragraph (a).

§ 21-7. Criminal trespass to restricted areas and restricted landing areas at airports; aggravated criminal trespass to restricted areas and restricted landing areas at airports. (a) Whoever enters upon, or remains in, any restricted area or restricted landing area used in connection with an airport facility, or part thereof, in this State, after such person has received notice from the airport authority that such entry is forbidden commits a Class 4 felony.

(b) Whoever enters upon, or remains in, any restricted area or restricted landing area used in connection with an airport facility, or part thereof, in this State, while in possession of a weapon, replica of a weapon, or ammunition, after the person has received notice from the airport authority that the entry is forbidden commits a Class 3 felony.

(c) Notice that the area is "restricted" and entry thereto "forbidden", for purposes of this Section, means that the person or persons have been notified personally, either orally or in writing, or by a printed or written notice forbidding such entry to him or a group or an organization of which he is a member, which has been conspicuously posted or exhibited at every usable entrance to such area or the forbidden part thereof.

(d) Whoever enters upon, or remains in, any restricted area or restricted landing area used in connection with an airport facility, or part thereof, in this State by presenting false documents or falsely representing his or her identity orally to the airport authority commits a Class A misdemeanor.

(e) Whoever enters upon, or remains in, any restricted area or restricted landing area as prohibited in subsection (a) of this Section, while dressed in the uniform of, improperly wearing the identification of, presenting false credentials of, or otherwise physically impersonating an airman, employee of an airline, employee of an airport, or contractor at an airport commits a Class 4 felony.

(f) The terms "Restricted area" or "Restricted landing area" in this Section are defined to incorporate the meaning ascribed to those terms in Section 8 of the "Illinois Aeronautics Act" [620 ILCS 5/8], approved July 24, 1945, as amended, and also include any other area of the airport that has been designated such by the airport authority.

The terms "airman" and "airport" in this Section are defined to incorporate the meaning ascribed to those terms in Sections 6 and 12 of the Illinois Aeronautics Act [620 ILCS 5/6 and 620 ILCS 5/12].

(g) Subsection (d) does not apply to a peace officer or other official of a unit of government who enters a restricted area or a restricted landing area used in connection with an airport facility, or part thereof, in the performance of his or her official duties.

§ 720 ILCS 5/21-8. Criminal trespass to a nuclear facility [Omitted.]

§ 720 ILCS 5/21-9. Criminal trespass to a place of public amusement. [Omitted.]

§ 720 ILCS 5/21-10. Criminal use of a motion picture exhibition facility.
[Omitted.]

Commentary – Trespassing Offenses

Trespassing Offenses. There are eight trespassing offenses. the first has been addressed in Article 19 – criminal trespass to a residence, and the other seven are set forth in Article 21 – criminal trespass to vehicles (Section 21-2), to real property (Section 21-3), to government supported property (Section 21-4), to state supported land (21-5), to restricted areas at airports (Section 21-7), to nuclear facilities (21-8) and to places of public amusement (21-9). [Note; the latter three offenses are rarely used and their text has been omitted.] All trespass offenses have in common the prohibition against the unauthorized entry or unauthorized remaining at certain locations after receiving notice that entry or remaining at that place is forbidden. Simply put, it is unlawful to come onto property when one has been told not to and it is equally impermissible to stay on property after being told to leave.

Mental state. Sections 21-2 (motor vehicles), 21-3 (real estate) generally require knowing entry without authority; however 21-3(c) and (d) and the other trespassing offenses have no stated mental state, thus one of the mental states of Sections 4-4 (intent), 4-5 (knowledge) or 4-6 (recklessness) would apply.

Invitation. Authorized presence at a location is not trespassing. If a defendant provides evidences of being invited to come to or stay, it is an affirmative defense that must be overcome by the prosecution just as any other affirmative defense.

In *People v. Washington* 326 Ill.App.3d 1089, 762 N.E.2d 698 (Ill. App. Ct. 4th Dist. 2002), the defendant was arrested at an apartment complex in Decatur. The owner had given the police a list of tenants and requested that warning notices be given to persons who had no authority to be present. The defendant had received a notice one month prior to his arrest but testified that he was at the complex every day to visit with his aunt, who was a tenant, and other relatives. The court reversed the defendant's conviction, holding that he had raised the affirmative defense of invitation and that the state was required to disprove invitation beyond a reasonable doubt once the defendant adduced evidence in support of that defense.

Article 21.1 – Residential Picketing
720 ILCS 5/21.1-1 *et seq.*

§ 720 ILCS 5/21.1-1. Legislative finding and declaration. the Legislature finds and declares that men in a free society have the right to quiet enjoyment of their homes; that the stability of community and family life cannot be maintained unless the right to privacy and a sense of security and peace in the home are respected and encouraged; that residential picketing, however just the cause inspiring it, disrupts home, family and communal life; that residential picketing is inappropriate in our society, where the jealously guarded rights of free speech and assembly have always been associated with respect for the rights of others. For these reasons the Legislature finds and declares this Article to be necessary.

§ 720 ILCS 5/21.1-2. [Picketing]. It is unlawful to picket before or about the residence or dwelling of any person, except when the residence or dwelling is used as a place of business. However, this Article does not apply to a person peacefully picketing his own residence or dwelling and does not prohibit the peaceful picketing of the place of holding a meeting or assembly on premises commonly used to discuss subjects of general public interest.

§ 720 ILCS 5/21.1-3. Sentence. Violation of Section 21.1-2 [*720 ILCS 5/21.1-2*] is a Class B misdemeanor.

Article 21.2 – Interference with a Public Institution of Higher Education
720 ILCS 5/21.2-2 *et seq.*

§ 720 ILCS 5/21.2-2. [Interference with public institution of learning]. a person commits interference with a public institution of education when, on the campus of a public institution of education, or at or in any building or other facility owned, operated or controlled by the institution, without authority from the institution he, through force or violence, actual or threatened:

(a) willfully denies to a trustee, school board member, superintendent, principal, employee, student or invitee of the institution:

(1) Freedom of movement at such place; or

(2) Use of the property or facilities of the institution; or

(3) The right of ingress or egress to the property or facilities of the institution; or

(b) willfully impedes, obstructs, interferes with or disrupts:

(1) the performance of institutional duties by a trustee, school board member, superintendent, principal, or employee of the institution; or

(2) the pursuit of educational activities, as determined or prescribed by the institution, by a trustee, school board member, superintendent, principal, employee, student or invitee of the institution; or

(c) knowingly occupies or remains in or at any building, property or other facility owned, operated or controlled by the institution after due notice to depart.

§ 720 ILCS 5/21.2-3. [Lawful assemblies; orderly petition for redress of grievances] Nothing in this Article prevents lawful assembly of the trustees, school board members, superintendent, principal, employees, students or invitees of a public institution of education, or prevents orderly petition for redress of grievances.

§ 720 ILCS 5/21.2-4. Sentence. a person convicted of violation of this Article commits a Class C misdemeanor for the first offense and for a second or subsequent offense commits a Class B misdemeanor. If the interference with the public institution of education is accompanied by a threat of personal injury or property damage, the person commits a Class 3 felony and may be sentenced to a term of imprisonment of not less than 2 years and not more than 10 years and may be prosecuted for intimidation in accordance with Section 12-6 of this Code [*720 ILCS 5/12-6*].

§ 720 ILCS 5/21.2-5. [Definitions] For the purposes of this Article the words and phrases described in this Section have the meanings designated in this Section, except when a particular context clearly requires a different meaning.

"Public institution of education" means an educational organization located in this State which provides an organized elementary, secondary, or post-high school educational program, and which is supported in whole or in part by appropriations of the General Assembly, a unit of local government or school district.

A person has received "due notice" if he, or the group of which he is a part, has been given oral or written notice from an authorized representative of the public institution of education in a manner reasonably designated to inform him, or the group of which he is a part, that he or they should cease such action or depart from such premises. The notice may also be given by a printed or written notice forbidding entry conspicuously posted or exhibited at the main entrance of the building or other facility, or the forbidden part thereof.

"Force or violence" includes, but is not limited to, use of one's person, individually or in concert with others, to impede access to or movement within or otherwise to interfere with the conduct of the authorized activities of the public institution of education, its trustees, school board members, superintendent, principal, employees, students or invitees.

§ 720 ILCS 5/21.2-6. [Severability] [Omitted.]

Article 21.3 – Solicitation on School Property
720 ILCS 5/21.3-1 *et seq.*

§ 720 ILCS 5/21.3-5. Distributing or delivering written or printed solicitation on school property. Distributing or delivering written or printed solicitation on school property. (a) Distributing or delivering written or printed solicitation on school property or within 1,000 feet of school property, for the purpose of inviting students to any event when a significant purpose of the event is to commit illegal acts or to solicit attendees to commit illegal acts, or to be held in or around abandoned buildings, is prohibited.

(b) A violation of this Section is a Class C misdemeanor.

(c) For the purposes of this Section, "school property" is defined as the buildings or grounds of any public or private elementary or secondary school.

(d)[Severability][Omitted.]

Title III : Part D Offenses Affecting Public Health, Safety and Decency
Article 24 – Deadly Weapons
720 ILCS 5/24-1 *et seq.*

§ 720 ILCS 5/24-1. Unlawful Use of Weapons. (a) A person commits the offense of unlawful use of weapons when he knowingly:

(1) Sells, manufactures, purchases, possesses or carries any bludgeon, black-jack, slung-shot, sand-club, sand-bag, metal knuckles or other knuckle weapon regardless of its composition, throwing star, or any knife, commonly referred to as a switchblade knife, which has a blade that opens automatically by hand pressure applied to a button, spring or other device in the handle of the knife, or a ballistic knife, which is a device that propels a knifelike blade as a projectile by means of a coil spring, elastic material or compressed gas; or

(2) Carries or possesses with intent to use the same unlawfully against another, a dagger, dirk, billy, dangerous knife, razor, stiletto, broken bottle or other piece of glass, stun gun or taser or any other dangerous or deadly weapon or instrument of like character; or

(3) Carries on or about his person or in any vehicle, a tear gas gun projector or bomb or any object containing noxious liquid gas or substance, other than an object containing a non-lethal noxious liquid gas or substance designed solely for personal defense carried by a person 18 years of age or older; or

(4) Carries or possesses in any vehicle or concealed on or about his person except when on his land or in his own abode, legal dwelling, or fixed place of business, or on the land or in the legal dwelling of another person as an invitee with that person's permission, any pistol, revolver, stun gun or taser or other firearm, except that this subsection (a)(4) does not apply to or affect transportation of weapons that meet one of the following conditions:

(i) are broken down in a non-functioning state; or

(ii) are not immediately accessible; or

(iii) are unloaded and enclosed in a case, firearm carrying box, shipping box, or other container by a person who has been issued a currently valid Firearm Owner's Identification Card; or

(iv) are carried or possessed in accordance with the Firearm Concealed Carry Act by a person who has been issued a currently valid license under the Firearm Concealed Carry Act; or

(5) Sets a spring gun; or

(6) Possesses any device or attachment of any kind designed, used or intended for use in silencing the report of any firearm; or

(7) Sells, manufactures, purchases, possesses or carries:

(i) a machine gun, which shall be defined for the purposes of this subsection as any weapon, which shoots, is designed to shoot, or can be readily restored to shoot, automatically more than one shot without manually reloading by a single function of the trigger, including the frame or receiver of any such weapon, or sells, manufactures, purchases, possesses, or carries any combination of parts designed or intended for use in converting any weapon into a machine gun, or any combination or parts from which a machine gun can be assembled if such parts are in the possession or under the control of a person;

(ii) any rifle having one or more barrels less than 16 inches in length or a shotgun having one or more barrels less than 18 inches in length or any weapon made from a rifle or shotgun, whether by alteration, modification, or otherwise, if such a weapon as modified has an overall length of less than 26 inches; or

(iii) any bomb, bomb-shell, grenade, bottle or other container containing an explosive substance of over one-quarter ounce for like purposes, such as, but not limited to, black powder bombs and Molotov cocktails or artillery projectiles; or

(8) Carries or possesses any firearm, stun gun or taser or other deadly weapon in any place which is licensed to sell intoxicating beverages, or at

any public gathering held pursuant to a license issued by any governmental body or any public gathering at which an admission is charged, excluding a place where a showing, demonstration or lecture involving the exhibition of unloaded firearms is conducted.

This subsection (a)(8) does not apply to any auction or raffle of a firearm held pursuant to a license or permit issued by a governmental body, nor does it apply to persons engaged in firearm safety training courses; or

(9) Carries or possesses in a vehicle or on or about his person any pistol, revolver, stun gun or taser or firearm or ballistic knife, when he is hooded, robed or masked in such manner as to conceal his identity; or

(10) Carries or possesses on or about his person, upon any public street, alley, or other public lands within the corporate limits of a city, village or incorporated town, except when an invitee thereon or therein, for the purpose of the display of such weapon or the lawful commerce in weapons, or except when on his land or in his own abode, legal dwelling, or fixed place of business, or on the land or in the legal dwelling of another person as an invitee with that person's permission, any pistol, revolver, stun gun or taser or other firearm, except that this subsection (a)(10) does not apply to or affect transportation of weapons that meet one of the following conditions:

(i) are broken down in a non-functioning state; or

(ii) are not immediately accessible; or

(iii) are unloaded and enclosed in a case, firearm carrying box, shipping box, or other container by a person who has been issued a currently valid Firearm Owner's Identification Card.

(iv) are carried or possessed in accordance with the Firearm Concealed Carry Act by a person who has been issued a currently valid license under the Firearm Concealed Carry Act.

A "stun gun or taser", as used in this paragraph (a) means (i) any device which is powered by electrical charging units, such as, batteries, and which fires one or several barbs attached to a length of wire and which, upon hitting a human, can send out a current capable of disrupting the person's nervous system in such a manner as to render him incapable of normal functioning or (ii) any device which is powered by electrical charging units, such as batteries, and which, upon contact with a human or clothing worn by a human, can send out current capable of disrupting the person's nervous system in such a manner as to render him incapable of normal functioning; or

(11) Sells, manufactures or purchases any explosive bullet. For purposes of this paragraph (a) "explosive bullet" means the projectile portion of an ammunition cartridge which contains or carries an explosive charge which will explode upon contact with the flesh of a human or an animal. "Cartridge" means a tubular metal case having a projectile affixed at the front thereof and a cap or primer at the rear end thereof, with the propellant contained in such tube between the projectile and the cap; or

(12) (Blank); or

(13) Carries or possesses on or about his or her person while in a building occupied by a unit of government, a billy club, other weapon of like character, or other instrument of like character intended for use as a weapon. For the purposes of this Section, "billy club" means a short stick or club commonly carried by police officers which is either telescopic or constructed of a solid piece of wood or other man-made material.

(b) Sentence. A person convicted of a violation of subsection 24-1(a)(1) through (5), subsection 24-1(a)(10), subsection 24-1(a)(11), or subsection 24-1(a)(13) commits a Class A misdemeanor. A person convicted of a violation of subsection 24-1(a)(8) or 24-1(a)(9) commits a Class 4 felony; a person convicted of a violation of subsection 24-1(a)(6) or 24-1(a)(7)(ii) or (iii) commits a Class 3 felony. A person convicted of a violation of subsection 24-1(a)(7)(i) commits a Class 2 felony and shall be sentenced to a term of imprisonment of not less than 3 years and not more than 7 years, unless the weapon is possessed in the passenger compartment of a motor vehicle as defined in Section 1-146 of the Illinois Vehicle Code [*625 ILCS 5/1-146*], or on the person, while the weapon is loaded, in which case it shall be a Class X felony. A person convicted of a second or subsequent violation of subsection 24-1(a)(4), 24-1(a)(8), 24-1(a)(9), or 24-1(a)(10) commits a Class 3 felony. The possession of each weapon in violation of this Section constitutes a single and separate violation.

(c) Violations in specific places.

(1) A person who violates subsection 24-1(a)(6) or 24-1(a)(7) in any school, regardless of the time of day or the time of year, in residential property owned, operated or managed by a public housing agency or leased by a public housing agency as part of a scattered site or mixed-income development, in a public park, in a courthouse, on the real property comprising any school, regardless of the time of day or the time of year, on residential property owned, operated or managed by a public housing agency or leased by a public housing agency as part of a scattered site or mixed-income development, on the real property comprising any public park, on the real property comprising any courthouse, in any conveyance owned, leased or contracted by a school to transport students to or from school or a school related activity, in any conveyance owned, leased, or contracted by a public transportation agency, or on any public way within 1,000 feet of the real property comprising any school, public park, courthouse, public transportation facility, or residential property owned, operated, or managed by a public housing agency or leased by a public housing agency as part of a scattered site or mixed-income development commits a Class 2 felony and shall be sentenced to a term of imprisonment of not less than 3 years and not more than 7 years.

(1.5) A person who violates subsection 24-1(a)(4), 24-1(a)(9), or 24-1(a)(10) in any school, regardless of the time of day or the time of year, in residential property owned, operated, or managed by a public housing agency or leased by a public housing agency as part of a scattered site or mixed-income development, in a public park, in a courthouse, on the real property comprising any school, regardless of the time of day or the time of year, on residential property owned, operated, or managed by a public housing agency or leased by a public housing agency as part of a scattered site or mixed-income development, on the real property comprising any public park, on the real property comprising any courthouse, in any conveyance owned, leased, or contracted by a school to transport students to or from school or a school related activity, in any conveyance owned, leased, or contracted by a public transportation agency, or on any public way within 1,000 feet of the real property comprising any school, public park, courthouse, public transportation facility, or residential property owned, operated, or managed by a public housing agency or leased by a public housing agency as part of a scattered site or mixed-income development commits a Class 3 felony.

(2) A person who violates subsection 24-1(a)(1), 24-1(a)(2), or 24-1(a)(3) in any school, regardless of the time of day or the time of year, in residential property owned, operated or managed by a public housing agency or leased by a public housing agency as part of a scattered site or mixed-income development, in a public park, in a courthouse, on the real property comprising any school, regardless of the time of day or the time of year, on residential property owned, operated or managed by a public housing agency or leased by a public housing agency as part of a scattered site or mixed-income development, on the real property comprising any public park, on the real property comprising any courthouse, in any conveyance owned, leased or contracted by a school to transport students to or from school or a school related activity, in any conveyance owned, leased, or contracted by a public transportation agency, or on any public way within 1,000 feet of the real property comprising any school, public park, courthouse, public transportation facility, or residential property owned, operated, or managed by a public housing agency or leased by a public housing agency as part of a scattered site or mixed-income development commits a Class 4 felony. "Courthouse" means any building that is used by the Circuit, Appellate, or Supreme Court of this State for the conduct of official business.

(3) Paragraphs (1), (1.5), and (2) of this subsection (c) shall not apply to law enforcement officers or security officers of such school, college, or university or to students carrying or possessing firearms for use in training courses, parades, hunting, target shooting on school ranges, or otherwise with the consent of school authorities and which firearms are transported unloaded enclosed in a suitable case, box, or transportation package.

(4) For the purposes of this subsection (c), "school" means any public or private elementary or secondary school, community college, college, or university.

(5) For the purposes of this subsection (c), "public transportation agency" means a public or private agency that provides for the transportation or conveyance of persons by means available to the general public, except for transportation by automobiles not used for conveyance of the general public as passengers; and "public transportation facility" means a terminal or other place where one may obtain public transportation.

(d) The presence in an automobile other than a public omnibus of any weapon, instrument or substance referred to in subsection (a)(7) is prima facie evidence that it is in the possession of, and is being carried by, all persons occupying such automobile at the time such weapon, instrument or substance is found, except under the following circumstances: (i) if such weapon, instrument or instrumentality is found upon the person of one of the occupants therein; or (ii) if such weapon, instrument or substance is found in an automobile operated for hire by a duly licensed driver in the due, lawful and proper pursuit of his trade, then such presumption shall not apply to the driver.

(e) Exemptions. Crossbows, Common or Compound bows and Underwater Spearguns are exempted from the definition of ballistic knife as defined in paragraph (1) of subsection (a) of this Section.

Commentary – Unlawful Use of Weapons (UUW)

Second Amendment Claims. After the United States Supreme Court's decisions in *District of Columbia v. Heller* 554 U.S. 570, 128 S.Ct. 2743 (U.S. S. Ct. 2008) and *McDonald v. City of Chicago* 561 U.S 742, 130 S.Ct. 3020 (U.S. S. Ct. 2010) which held that individuals had the constitutional right to possess certain firearms in their own homes, there were recurring claims that the unlawful use of weapons statutes Sections 24-1 and 24-1.6 are unconstitutional.

Weapons. Section 24-1 criminalizes the knowing manufacture, sale, delivery or possession of unlawful weapons. there is a significant variety of unlawful weapons encompassed by the statute – clubs, black jacks, daggers, dirks, spring guns, tasers, stun guns, pistols, rifles, shotguns, short barrel firearms, machine guns, bombs, grenades, Molotov cocktails and more. the weapons are unlawful by their nature (such as switchblade knives or sawed-off shotguns) or by where they are located (public streets, alleys or public lands), Note that weapons that are broken down to be inoperable, not immediately accessible to a person or if a firearm – unloaded and encased possessed by a person with a valid Firearm Owner ID, are not unlawful. (Section 24-1(a)(10(i), (ii) and (iii)). the offense is ordinarily a Class A misdemeanor.

In *People v. Perry* 397 Ill.App.3d 358, 923 N.e.2d 1247 (Ill. App. Ct. 4th Dist. 2010), the trial court dismissed a weapons charge against the defendant, a prison inmate. While waiting in line for a meal, the defendant struck another inmate in the face with a padlock that was inside of a sock, tied in place by a knot. the trial court held that as a matter of law, such a weapon could not be a "bludgeon" as that term is used in Section 24-1(a)(1) since a bludgeon was a short stick or club by common definition. The court on appeal held that the trial court was wrong – that a "black jack" is a weapon with a heavy head and a flexible handle and that a black jack was a form of bludgeon and that a reasonable jury could conclude after a trial that a padlock in a sock could be a "bludgeon" within the meaning of the unlawful use of weapons statute.

In *People v. Williams* 394 Ill.App.3d 286, 915 N.E.2d 815 (Ill. App. Ct. 1st Dist. 2010), the defendant was convicted for unlawful use of weapons for possessing a sawed-off shotgun, a 12 gauge shotgun having a 12 inch barrel. Testimony established that the gun was rusty, that the barrel fell off when the trigger was pulled and that the trigger failed to engage the firing pin. The defendant contended that it was a "piece of junk" and not an operable weapon. In affirming the defendant's conviction the court noted that a shotgun was "*any device by whatever name known, which is designed to expel a projectile or projectiles by the action of an explosion, expansion of gas or escape of gas.*" (430 ILCS 65/1.1 (West 2006). Since there was no evidence that the weapon could not be made to operate, the court held that it fit the definition of shotgun for purposes of Section 24-1(a)(7)(ii) of the UUW statute. See also *People v. Velez* 336 Ill. App. 3d 261, 270 Ill. Dec. 651, 783 N.E.2d 226 (Ill. App. Ct. 2nd Dist. 2003) where a malfunctioning switch-blade knife was held to be a prohibited weapon under Section 24-1(a)(1).

Possession by an Invitee. It is lawful to possess a pistol or in one's own home, or as a guest (invitee) in the home of another, 720 ILCS 5/24-1.6(a)(4). See also *People v. Brisco* 2012 IL App (1st) 101612 (defendant possessed a rifle on a public street and thus was not an invitee under exception provided by 720 ILCS 5/24-1.6(a)(4)). The continuing vitality of this analysis is suspect in light of the Second Amendment holdings discussed above.

§24-1.1. Unlawful Use or Possession of Weapons by Felons or Persons in the Custody of the Department of Corrections Facilities.
(a) It is unlawful for a person to knowingly possess on or about his person or on his land or in his own abode or fixed place of business any weapon prohibited under Section 24-1 of this Act or any firearm or any firearm ammunition if the person has been convicted of a felony under the laws of this State or any other jurisdiction. This Section shall not apply if the person has been granted relief by the Director of the Department of State Police under Section 10 of the Firearm Owners Identification Card Act.
(b) It is unlawful for any person confined in a penal institution, which is a facility of the Illinois Department of Corrections, to possess any weapon prohibited under Section 24-1 of this Code or any firearm or firearm ammunition, regardless of the intent with which he possesses it.

(c) It shall be an affirmative defense to a violation of subsection (b), that such possession was specifically authorized by rule, regulation, or directive of the Illinois Department of Corrections or order issued pursuant thereto.

(d) The defense of necessity is not available to a person who is charged with a violation of subsection (b) of this Section.

(e) Sentence. Violation of this Section by a person not confined in a penal institution shall be a Class 3 felony for which the person, shall be sentenced to no less than 2 years and no more than 10 years and any second or subsequent violation shall be a Class 2 felony for which the person shall be sentenced to a term of imprisonment of not less than 3 years and not more than 14 years. Violation of this Section by a person not confined in a penal institution who has been convicted of a forcible felony, a felony violation of Article 24 of this Code or of the Firearm Owners Identification Card Act, stalking or aggravated stalking, or a Class 2 or greater felony under the Illinois Controlled Substances Act, the Cannabis Control Act, or the Methamphetamine Control and Community Protection Act is a Class 2 felony for which the person shall be sentenced to not less than 3 years and not more than 14 years. Violation of this Section by a person who is on parole or mandatory supervised release is a Class 2 felony for which the person, shall be sentenced to not less than 3 years and not more than 14 years. Violation of this Section by a person not confined in a penal institution is a Class X felony when the firearm possessed is a machine gun. Any person who violates this Section while confined in a penal institution, which is a facility of the Illinois Department of Corrections, is guilty of a Class 1 felony, if he possesses any weapon prohibited under Section 24-1 of this Code regardless of the intent with which he possesses it, a Class X felony if he possesses any firearm, firearm ammunition or explosive, and a Class X felony for which the offender shall be sentenced to not less than 12 years and not more than 50 years when the firearm possessed is a machine gun. A violation of this Section while wearing or in possession of body armor as defined in Section 33F-1 is a Class X felony punishable by a term of imprisonment of not less than 10 years and not more than 40 years. The possession of each firearm or firearm ammunition in violation of this Section constitutes a single and separate violation.

Commentary – Unlawful Possession of a Weapon by a Felon

Section 24-1.1 prohibits the knowing possession of a weapon by a person with a prior felony conviction. Any weapon that would be criminally regulated by Section 24-1, including any firearm or ammunition, would likewise constitute criminal conduct if possessed by a felon on his person, at his home or place of business. It is also a crime for a person in custody at a jail or prison to possess a prohibited weapon, firearm or ammunition. Courts have continuously held this provision is constitutionally proper against a 2nd Amendment claim.

There is no limitation on the type of felony that is a predicate for this offense. At a trial for a violation of Section 24-1.1 if the defendant stipulates that he has the prior felony conviction it is error to permit the prosecution to introduce the precise name and details of the felony in evidence. See *People v. Walker* 211 Ill.2d 317, 812 N.E.2d 339 (Ill. S. Ct. 2004).

In *People v. Ingram* 389 IllApp.3d 897, 907 N.E.2d 110 (Ill. App. Ct. 2nd Dist. 2009), the defendant was a front seat passenger in a car stopped by the police in a high crime area. The defendant immediately got out of the car and started walking away, and did not stop until an officer grabbed him by the arm. He gave a false name and then corrected himself. The front passenger seat was broken and the back of the seat rested on the back seat. Behind and underneath the driver's seat there was a handgun that was easily accessible from the front passenger seat. The gun was plainly visible. There was a round of ammunition on the floor in front of the driver's seat. although there was a passenger in the rear seat on the driver's side of the car, the jury convicted the defendant of unlawful possession of a weapon by a felon (the defendant's felony conviction had been stipulated.) in affirming the conviction the appellate court noted the defendant's possession of the gun was constructive possession – he had immediate, exclusive control of the area where the gun was located and the circumstances of defendant's evasive conduct supported the conclusion that he knew about the presence of the gun. The fact that the rear seat passenger could also have possessed the gun did not mean that the defendant was not in possession.

In *People v. Almond* 2015 113817 (Ill. S. Ct. 2015), the defendant, a convicted felon, was held criminally responsible for possessing both the gun and the ammunition as separate crimes,

> "Under the plain meaning of this statutory language, the UUW by a felon statute unambiguously authorizes separate convictions when a felon possesses a loaded firearm, a conviction based on the firearm and a conviction based on the ammunition inside that firearm. The language not only criminalizes the possession of *any* firearm or *any* firearm ammunition by a felon, but also clarifies that the possession of each firearm or firearm ammunition by a felon constitutes *a single and separate* violation. *People v. Almond* 2015 113817, ¶36. (Court's emphasis)

§ 24-1.2. Aggravated discharge of a firearm.

(a) A person commits aggravated discharge of a firearm when he or she knowingly or intentionally:

(1) Discharges a firearm at or into a building he or she knows or reasonably should know to be occupied and the firearm is discharged from a place or position outside that building;

(2) Discharges a firearm in the direction of another person or in the direction of a vehicle he or she knows or reasonably should know to be occupied by a person;

(3) Discharges a firearm in the direction of a person he or she knows to be a peace officer, a community policing volunteer, a correctional institution employee, or a fireman while the officer, volunteer, employee or fireman is engaged in the execution of any of his or her official duties, or to prevent the officer, volunteer, employee or fireman from performing his or her official duties, or in retaliation for the officer, volunteer, employee or fireman performing his or her official duties;

(4) Discharges a firearm in the direction of a vehicle he or she knows to be occupied by a peace officer, a person summoned or directed by a peace officer, a correctional institution employee or a fireman while the officer, employee or fireman is engaged in the execution of any of his or her official duties, or to prevent the officer, employee or fireman from performing his or her official duties, or in retaliation for the officer, employee or fireman performing his or her official duties;

(5) Discharges a firearm in the direction of a person he or she knows to be an emergency medical technician-- ambulance, emergency medical technician -- intermediate, emergency medical technician -- paramedic, ambulance driver, or other medical assistance or first aid personnel, employed by a municipality or other governmental unit, while the emergency medical technician -- ambulance, emergency medical technician -- intermediate, emergency medical technician -- paramedic, ambulance driver, or other medical assistance or first aid personnel is engaged in the execution of any of his or her official duties, or to prevent the emergency medical technician -- ambulance, emergency medical technician--intermediate, emergency medical technician -- paramedic, ambulance driver, or other medical assistance or first aid personnel from performing his or her official duties, or in retaliation for the emergency medical technician -- ambulance, emergency medical technician -- intermediate, emergency medical technician -- paramedic, ambulance driver, or other medical assistance or first aid personnel performing his or her official duties;

(6) Discharges a firearm in the direction of a vehicle he or she knows to be occupied by an emergency medical technician -- ambulance, emergency medical technician -- intermediate, emergency medical technician -- paramedic, ambulance driver, or other medical assistance or first aid personnel, employed by a municipality or other governmental unit, while the emergency medical technician -- ambulance, emergency medical technician -- intermediate, emergency medical technician -- paramedic, ambulance driver, or other medical assistance or first aid personnel is engaged in the execution of any of his or her official duties, or to prevent the emergency medical technician -- ambulance, emergency medical technician -- intermediate, emergency medical technician -- paramedic, ambulance driver, or other medical assistance or first aid personnel from performing his or her official duties, or in retaliation for the emergency medical technician -- ambulance, emergency medical technician -- intermediate, emergency medical technician -- paramedic, ambulance driver, or other medical assistance or first aid personnel performing his or her official duties;

(7) Discharges a firearm in the direction of a person he or she knows to be a teacher or other person employed in any school and the teacher or other employee is upon the grounds of a school or grounds adjacent to a school, or is in any part of a building used for school purposes;

(8) Discharges a firearm in the direction of a person he or she knows to be an emergency management worker while the emergency management worker is engaged in the execution of any of his or her official duties, or to prevent the emergency management worker from performing his or her official duties, or in retaliation for the emergency management worker performing his or her official duties; or

(9) Discharges a firearm in the direction of a vehicle he or she knows to be occupied by an emergency management worker while the emergency management worker is engaged in the execution of any of his or her official duties, or to prevent the emergency management worker from performing his or her official duties, or in retaliation for the emergency management worker performing his or her official duties.

(b) A violation of subsection (a)(1) or subsection (a)(2) of this Section is a Class 1 felony. A violation of subsection (a)(1) or (a)(2) of this Section committed in a school, on the real property comprising a school, within 1,000 feet of the real property comprising a school, at a school related activity or on or within 1,000 feet of any conveyance owned, leased, or contracted by a school to transport students to or from school or a school related activity, regardless of the time of day or time of year that the offense was committed is a Class X felony. A violation of subsection (a)(3), (a)(4), (a)(5), (a)(6), (a)(7), (a)(8), or (a)(9) of this Section is a Class X felony for which the sentence shall be a term of imprisonment of no less than 10 years and not more than 45 years.

(c) For purposes of this Section:

"School" means a public or private elementary or secondary school, community college, college, or university.

"School related activity" means any sporting, social, academic, or other activity for which students' attendance or participation is sponsored, organized, or funded in whole or in part by a school or school district.

§24-1.2-5. Aggravated discharge of a machine gun or a firearm equipped with a device designed or used for silencing the report of a firearm. (a) A person commits aggravated discharge of a machine gun or a firearm equipped with a device designed or used for silencing the report of a firearm when he or she knowingly or intentionally:

(1) Discharges a machine gun or a firearm equipped with a device designed or used for silencing the report of a firearm at or into a building he or she knows to be occupied and the machine gun or the firearm equipped with a device designed or used for silencing the report of a firearm is discharged from a place or position outside that building;

(2) Discharges a machine gun or a firearm equipped with a device designed or used for silencing the report of a firearm in the direction of another person or in the direction of a vehicle he or she knows to be occupied;

(3) Discharges a machine gun or a firearm equipped with a device designed or used for silencing the report of a firearm in the direction of a person he or she knows to be a peace officer, a person summoned or directed by a peace officer, a correctional institution employee, or a fireman while the officer, employee or fireman is engaged in the execution of any of his or her official duties, or to prevent the officer, employee or fireman from performing his or her official duties, or in retaliation for the officer, employee or fireman performing his or her official duties;

(4) Discharges a machine gun or a firearm equipped with a device designed or used for silencing the report of a firearm in the direction of a vehicle he or she knows to be occupied by a peace officer, a person summoned or directed by a peace officer, a correctional institution employee or a fireman while the officer, employee or fireman is engaged in the execution of any of his or her official duties, or to prevent the officer, employee or fireman from performing his or her official duties, or in retaliation for the officer, employee or fireman performing his or her official duties;

(5) Discharges a machine gun or a firearm equipped with a device designed or used for silencing the report of a firearm in the direction of a person he or she knows to be an emergency medical technician--ambulance, emergency medical technician--intermediate, emergency medical technician--paramedic, ambulance driver, or other medical assistance or first aid

personnel, employed by a municipality or other governmental unit, while the emergency medical technician--ambulance, emergency medical technician--intermediate, emergency medical technician--paramedic, ambulance driver, or other medical assistance or first aid personnel is engaged in the execution of any of his or her official duties, or to prevent the emergency medical technician--ambulance, emergency medical technician--intermediate, emergency medical technician--paramedic, ambulance driver, or other medical assistance or first aid personnel from performing his or her official duties, or in retaliation for the emergency medical technician--ambulance, emergency medical technician--intermediate, emergency medical technician--paramedic, ambulance driver, or other medical assistance or first aid personnel performing his or her official duties;

(6) Discharges a machine gun or a firearm equipped with a device designed or used for silencing the report of a firearm in the direction of a vehicle he or she knows to be occupied by an emergency medical technician--ambulance, emergency medical technician--intermediate, emergency medical technician--paramedic, ambulance driver, or other medical assistance or first aid personnel, employed by a municipality or other governmental unit, while the emergency medical technician--ambulance, emergency medical technician--intermediate, emergency medical technician--paramedic, ambulance driver, or other medical assistance or first aid personnel is engaged in the execution of any of his or her official duties, or to prevent the emergency medical technician--ambulance, emergency medical technician--intermediate, emergency medical technician--paramedic, ambulance driver, or other medical assistance or first aid personnel from performing his or her official duties, or in retaliation for the emergency medical technician--ambulance, emergency medical technician--intermediate, emergency medical technician--paramedic, ambulance driver, or other medical assistance or first aid personnel performing his or her official duties;

(7) Discharges a machine gun or a firearm equipped with a device designed or used for silencing the report of a firearm in the direction of a person he or she knows to be an emergency management worker while the emergency management worker is engaged in the execution of any of his or her official duties, or to prevent the emergency management worker from performing his or her official duties, or in retaliation for the emergency management worker performing his or her official duties; or

(8) Discharges a machine gun or a firearm equipped with a device designed or used for silencing the report of a firearm in the direction of a vehicle he or she knows to be occupied by an emergency management worker while the emergency management worker is engaged in the execution of any of his or her official duties, or to prevent the emergency management worker from performing his or her official duties, or in retaliation for the emergency management worker performing his or her official duties.

(b) A violation of subsection (a)(1) or subsection (a)(2) of this Section is a Class X felony. A violation of subsection (a)(3), (a)(4), (a)(5), (a)(6), (a)(7), or (a)(8) of this Section is a Class X felony for which the sentence shall be a term of imprisonment of no less than 12 years and no more than 50 years.

(c) For the purpose of this Section, “machine gun” has the meaning ascribed to it in clause (i) of paragraph (7) of subsection (a) of Section 24-1 of this Code.

(d) This Section does not apply to a peace officer while serving as a member of a tactical response team or special operations team. A peace officer may not personally own or apply for ownership of a device or attachment of any kind designed, used, or intended for use in silencing the report of any firearm. These devices shall be owned and maintained by lawfully recognized units of government whose duties include the investigation of criminal acts.

Commentary – Aggravated Discharge of a Firearm

¶24-1.2 describes the elements of aggravated discharge of a firearm – the conduct focuses on the knowing or intentional shooting of a gun (1) at a house or building known or should be known to be occupied, (2) in the direction of another person or a motor vehicle that is known to be occupied or should be known to be occupied, (3) in the direction of a police officer fireman, emergency medical technician or emergency management employee or a motor vehicle that is known to be occupied or should be known to be occupied by a person of the listed categories or (4) in the direction of a teacher or school employee who is at or in a school building.

In *People v. Dawson* 403 Ill.App.3d 499, 934 N.E.2d 598 (Ill. App. Ct. 1st Dist. 2010), the victim, at trial, testified that the defendant was driving a van and fired shots at the victim while he was driving a truck. After the victim stopped the police, he drove to where the defendant lived and the defendant again fired at the victim. There were five bullet holes in the victim's truck. Police officers identified the defendant as shooting during the second incident and saw the defendant throwing guns from the premises. The guns were later recovered, as were bullet fragments that matched the guns. This evidence was sufficient to support the defendant's convictions for aggravated discharge of a firearm, however, his two convictions for shooting at the victim and shooting at the victim's van with the victim in it, were the same conduct, so that one conviction must be vacated.

§24-1.5. Reckless discharge of a firearm.
(a) A person commits reckless discharge of a firearm by discharging a firearm in a reckless manner which endangers the bodily safety of an individual.

(b) If the conduct described in subsection (a) is committed by a passenger of a moving motor vehicle with the knowledge and consent of the driver of the motor vehicle the driver is accountable for such conduct.

(c) Reckless discharge of a firearm is a Class 4 felony.
(d) This Section does not apply to a peace officer while in the performance of his or her official duties.

§24-1.6. Aggravated unlawful use of a weapon. (a) A person commits the offense of aggravated unlawful use of a weapon when he or she knowingly:
(1) Carries on or about his or her person or in any vehicle or concealed on or about his or her person except when on his or her land or in his or her abode, legal dwelling, or fixed place of business, or on the land or in the legal dwelling of another person as an invitee with that person's permission, any pistol, revolver, stun gun or taser or other firearm; or

(2) Carries or possesses on or about his or her person, upon any public street, alley, or other public lands within the corporate limits of a city, village or incorporated town, except when an invitee thereon or therein, for the purpose of the display of such weapon or the lawful commerce in weapons, or except when on his or her own land or in his or her own abode, legal dwelling, or fixed place of business, or on the land or in the legal dwelling of another person as an invitee with that person's permission, any pistol, revolver, stun gun or taser or other firearm; and

(3) One of the following factors is present:

(A) the firearm possessed was uncased, loaded and immediately accessible at the time of the offense; or

(B) the firearm possessed was uncased, unloaded and the ammunition for the weapon was immediately accessible at the time of the offense; or

(C) the person possessing the firearm has not been issued a currently valid Firearm Owner's Identification Card; or

(D) the person possessing the weapon was previously adjudicated a delinquent minor under the Juvenile Court Act of 1987 for an act that if committed by an adult would be a felony; or

(E) the person possessing the weapon was engaged in a misdemeanor violation of the Cannabis Control Act, in a misdemeanor violation of the Illinois Controlled Substances Act, or in a misdemeanor violation of the Methamphetamine Control and Community Protection Act; or

(F) (blank); or

(G) the person possessing the weapon had a order of protection issued against him or her within the previous 2 years; or

(H) the person possessing the weapon was engaged in the commission or attempted commission of a misdemeanor involving the use or threat of violence against the person or property of another; or

(I) the person possessing the weapon was under 21 years of age and in possession of a handgun as defined in Section 24-3, unless the person under 21 is engaged in lawful activities under the Wildlife Code or described in subsection 24-2(b)(1), (b)(3), or 24-2(f).

(b) "Stun gun or taser" as used in this Section has the same definition given to it in Section 24-1 of this Code.
(c) This Section does not apply to or affect the transportation or possession of weapons that:

(i) are broken down in a non-functioning state; or
(ii) are not immediately accessible; or
(iii) are unloaded and enclosed in a case, firearm carrying box, shipping box, or other container by a person who has been issued a currently valid Firearm Owner's Identification Card.

(d) Sentence.

(1) Aggravated unlawful use of a weapon is a Class 4 felony; a second or subsequent offense is a Class 2 felony for which the person shall be sentenced to a term of imprisonment of not less than 3 years and not more than 7 years.
(2) Except as otherwise provided in paragraphs (3) and (4) of this subsection (d), a first offense of aggravated unlawful use of a weapon committed with a firearm by a person 18 years of age or older where the factors listed in both items (A) and (C) of paragraph (3) of subsection (a) are present is a Class 4 felony, for which the person shall be sentenced to a term of imprisonment of not less than one year and not more than 3 years.

(3) Aggravated unlawful use of a weapon by a person who has been previously convicted of a felony in this State or another jurisdiction is a Class 2 felony for which the person shall be sentenced to a term of imprisonment of not less than 3 years and not more than 7 years.

(4) Aggravated unlawful use of a weapon while wearing or in possession of body armor as defined in Section 33F-1 by a person who has not been issued a valid Firearms Owner's Identification Card in accordance with Section 5 of the Firearm Owners Identification Card Act is a Class X felony.

(e) The possession of each firearm in violation of this Section constitutes a single and separate violation.

Commentary – Aggravated Unlawful Use of Weapons

AUUW elements. Section 24-1.6 (in the statutory text below) proscribes the more serious offense of Aggravated Unlawful Use of Weapons (AUUW). the offense occurs when (1) the offender knowingly carries a pistol, stun gun, taser, or other firearm on his person (including a concealed weapon) or in a vehicle, and is not on his own land, home or permanent place of business or a guest on another's property; or (2) the offender carries a pistol, stun gun, taser, or other firearm on his person on a public street or building and one of the following was present at the time of the offense: (a) the weapons was loaded, uncased and immediately accessible, (b) the weapon was unloaded, uncases and ammunition was immediately accessible, (c) the offender had no valid FOID, (d) the offender was an adjudicated on the basis of a felony offense as a juvenile delinquent, (e) the offender was committing a misdemeanor cannabis, controlled substance or methamphetamine offense, (f) the offender was a street gang member, (g)the offender was the subject of an order of protection, (h) the offender was committing a misdemeanor act that included use or threat of force or violence or (i) the offender was under 21 and possessed a handgun. Aggravated unlawful use of weapons is a Class 4 felony. In *People v. Mosley* 2015 IL 115872 (Ill. S. Ct. 2015), the AUUW statute was upheld against a 2nd Amendment challenge.

In *People v. Foster* 394 Ill.App.3d 163, 915 N.E.2d 153 (Ill. App. Ct. 4th Dist. 2009), the defendant was convicted of aggravated unlawful use of weapons where after being stopped for a traffic offense a loaded handgun was found in the console of the car he was driving. The court, in affirming the conviction, noted that the evidence proved that (1) he knowingly possessed a firearm in a vehicle; (2) he was not on his own land or at his home or business and (3) the gun was uncased, loaded and immediately accessible. The court rejected the defendant's argument that the state must prove that the weapon was operable at the time of the offense, and exception that may be raised by the defendant under Section 24-1.6(c)(i) since that was not an express element of the offense.

2nd Amendment Constitutional Challenges. In *People v. Aguilar* 2013 IL 112, 2 N.E.3d 321 (Ill. S.Ct. 2013), some aspects of the Class 4 form of Aggravated Unlawful Use of Weapons was held to violate the 2nd Amendment. The defendant was convicted of possessing a loaded weapon in public in violation of 24-1.6(a)(1) and (a)(3)(A) and argued that the statute was facially unconstitutional for criminalizing an individual's possession of a weapon in self-defense. The Illinois Supreme Court acknowledged persuasive reasoning of the 7th Circuit Court of Appeals decision in *Moore v. Madigan* 702 F.3d 933 (7th Cir. 2012) that the right to bear arms in self-defense under the 2nd Amendment to the Constitution of the United States is broader than just the possession of guns in the home. In *Aguilar* the Court stated:

> in this case, we are dealing not with a reasonable regulation but with a comprehensive ban. . . . . [I]n the form presently before us, the Class 4 form of section 24–1.6(a)(1), (a)(3)(A), (d) categorically prohibits the possession and use of an operable firearm for self-defense outside the home. In other words, the Class 4 form of section 24–1.6(a)(1), (a)(3)(A), (d) amounts to a wholesale statutory ban on the exercise of a personal right that is specifically named in and guaranteed by the United States Constitution, as construed by the United States Supreme Court. In no other context would we permit this, and we will not permit it here either.
>
> Accordingly, as the Seventh Circuit did in *Moore,* we here hold that, on its face, the Class 4 form of section 24–1.6(a)(1), (a)(3)(A), (d) violates the right to keep and bear arms, as guaranteed by the second amendment to the United States Constitution.[3] Defendant's conviction under that section therefore is reversed.
>
> *People v. Aguilar 2013 IL 112,* ¶¶21, 22, 2 N.E.3rd 327, 328.

On the other hand, the defendant in *Aguilar* also claimed that his conviction for Unlawful Possession of a Firearm (possession of a firearm by a person under 18 years of age – see below 725 ILCS 24-3.1(a)(1)) should also be reversed, claiming that this statute was also unconstitutional. The Illinois Supreme Court rejected this argument finding that 2nd Amendment protection did not extend to a minor's possession of a firearm. *People v. Aguilar* 2013 IL ¶27, 2 N.E.3rd at 329.

In response to the *Aguilar,* Public Act 98-63 was enacted (see text above). It will take time for cases to make their way through the system to test whether the criminal provisions of the Aggravated Unlawful Use of Weapons (AUUW) statute passes Constitutional muster. To illustrate this process of court review, two Illinois appellate decisions upheld the provision of prohibiting the possession of a firearm by a person with a felony conviction. For example, two appellate cases held that the "Class 2" form of AUUW was facially constitutional under the 2nd Amendment. See *People v. Burns*, 2013 IL App (1st) 120929, ¶ 27("[T]he Class 2 form of AUUW . . . merely regulates the possession of a firearm by a person who has been previously convicted of a felony" and, therefore, "defendant's constitutional challenge to the Class 2 form of the offense in the AUUW statute fails."); See also *People v. Soto*, 2014 IL App (1st) 121937, ¶ 14, 7 N.E.3d 823, 827 (Ill. App. Ct. 1st Dist 2014) ("[W]e agree that the Class 2 form of AUUW under section 24-1.6(a)(1), (a)(3)(A) is a reasonable regulation of the second amendment right to bear arms.").

The Illinois Supreme reviewed *People v. Burns* and reversed! In *People v. Burns*, 2015 IL 117387 (Ill. S. Ct. 2015), the Illinois Supreme Court recognized that the holding *Aguilar* was limited to the "Class 4" form of AUUW, but that under the facts in *Burns,* where possession of a firearm by a felon had not been listed as an essential element of the offense, concluded "section 24-1.6(a)(1), (a)(3)(A) of the statute is facially unconstitutional, without limitation." *See People v. Burns at 25*¶. The holding in *Burns* led to the *Soto* decision also being reversed.

In *People v. Williams* 2015 IL 117470 (Ill. S. Ct. 2015), the Court noted that a defendant who possessed a firearm in his home with no valid FOID would not be guilty of AUUW. AUUW requires that the possession be outside the home, on a public way or within a vehicle. In *People v. Grant* 2014 IL App (1st) 100174-B, the Court rejected the claim that possession of a loaded, uncased handgun outside the home without a valid FOID card violated the 2nd Amendment. The Defendant admitted to officers that he had no FOID and had purchased the gun from a crack head for $75.

§24-1.7. Armed habitual criminal.
(a) A person commits the offense of being an armed habitual criminal if he or she receives, sells, possesses, or transfers any firearm after having been convicted a total of 2 or more times of any combination of the following offenses:

(1) a forcible felony as defined in Section 2-8 of this Code;
(2) unlawful use of a weapon by a felon; aggravated unlawful use of a weapon; aggravated discharge of a firearm; vehicular hijacking; aggravated vehicular hijacking; aggravated battery of a child child as described in Section 12-4.3 or subdivision (b)(1) of Section 12-3.05; intimidation; aggravated intimidation; gunrunning; home invasion; or aggravated battery with a firearm as described in Section 12-4.2 or subdivision (e)(1), (e)(2), (e)(3), or (e)(4) of Section 12-3.05; or
(3) any violation of the Illinois Controlled Substances Act or the Cannabis Control Act that is punishable as a Class 3 felony or higher.

(b) Sentence. Being an armed habitual criminal is a Class X felony.

(c) For purposes of this Section:

"Street gang" or "gang" has the meaning ascribed to it in Section 10 of the Illinois Streetgang Terrorism Omnibus Prevention Act.

"Street gang member" or "gang member" has the meaning ascribed to it in Section 10 of the Illinois Streetgang Terrorism Omnibus Prevention Act.

Commentary – Armed Habitual Criminal

Section 24-1.7 created the offense of armed habitual offender, a Class X felony. To be convicted of this offense the defendant must have two or more convictions for forcible felonies or specified offenses involving weapons for crimes against person or serious (Class 3 or higher) controlled substance/cannabis offenses and knowingly possess, sell or transfer a firearm.

In *People v. Nesbit* 398 Ill.App.3d 200, 924 N.E.2d 517 (Ill. App. Ct. 3rd Dist. 2010), the defendant claimed that his conviction for Armed Habitual Criminal was not supported by the evidence. Peoria police officers responded to a domestic dispute call and gave chase to the defendant who was driving a black Corvette. The defendant eventually crashed, refused to obey commands to get out of the car with his hands up and was seen making furtive gestures inside the car. When he was removed, a .45 hand gun was found by the driver's seat. The defendant's mother testified that the gun was hers and that the defendant rarely drove the car. It was stipulated that the defendant had three prior burglary convictions – thus his only claim was that he did not know the gun was in the car and thus did not possess the gun. In affirming the conviction the court concluded that an inference of knowledge of the gun being in the car could be drawn from the defendant being the driver and the only occupant of the car. other circumstances of the defendant's conduct in driving away at an excessive speed when officers attempted to stop him, the movement of his hands and body inside the car when officers commanded him to get out and the location of the gun by the driver's seat were all circumstantial evidence that support the jury's decision to convict the defendant.

§24-1.8. Unlawful possession of a firearm by a street gang member. (a) A person commits unlawful possession of a firearm by a street gang member when he or she knowingly:

(1) possesses, carries, or conceals on or about his or her person a firearm and firearm ammunition while on any street, road, alley, gangway, sidewalk, or any other lands, except when inside his or her own abode or inside his or her fixed place of business, and has not been issued a currently valid Firearm Owner's Identification Card and is a member of a street gang; or

(2) possesses or carries in any vehicle a firearm and firearm ammunition which are both immediately accessible at the time of the offense while on any street, road, alley, or any other lands, except when inside his or her own abode or garage, and has not been issued a currently valid Firearm Owner's Identification Card and is a member of a street gang.

(b) Unlawful possession of a firearm by a street gang member is a Class 2 felony for which the person, if sentenced to a term of imprisonment, shall be sentenced to no less than 3 years and no more than 10 years. A period of probation, a term of periodic imprisonment or conditional discharge shall not be imposed for the offense of unlawful possession of a firearm by a street gang member when the firearm was loaded or contained firearm ammunition and the court shall sentence the offender to not less than the minimum term of imprisonment authorized for the Class 2 felony.

§24-2. Exemptions. (a) Subsections 24-1(a)(3), 24-1(a)(4), 24-1(a)(10), and 24-1(a)(13) and Section 24-1.6 do not apply to or affect any of the following:

(1) Peace officers, and any person summoned by a peace officer to assist in making arrests or preserving the peace, while actually engaged in assisting such officer.

(2) Wardens, superintendents and keepers of prisons, penitentiaries, jails and other institutions for the detention of persons accused or convicted of an offense, while in the performance of their official duty, or while commuting between their homes and places of employment.

(3) Members of the Armed Services or Reserve Forces of the United States or the Illinois National Guard or the Reserve Officers Training Corps, while in the performance of their official duty.

(4) Special agents employed by a railroad or a public utility to perform police functions, and guards of armored car companies, while actually engaged in the performance of the duties of their employment or commuting between their homes and places of employment; and watchmen while actually engaged in the performance of the duties of their employment.

(5) Persons licensed as private security contractors, private detectives, or private alarm contractors, or employed by an agency certified by the Department of Professional Regulation, if their duties include the carrying of a weapon under the provisions of the Private Detective, Private Alarm, Private Security, Fingerprint Vendor, and Locksmith Act of 2004, while actually engaged in the performance of the duties of their employment or commuting between their homes and places of employment, provided that such commuting is accomplished within one hour from departure from home or place of employment, as the case may be. Persons exempted under this subdivision (a)(5) shall be required to have completed a course of study in firearms handling and training approved and supervised by the Department of Professional Regulation as prescribed by Section 28 of the Private Detective, Private Alarm, Private Security, Fingerprint Vendor, and Locksmith Act of 2004, prior to becoming eligible for this exemption. The Department of Professional Regulation shall provide suitable documentation demonstrating the successful completion of the prescribed firearms training. Such documentation shall be carried at all times when such persons are in possession of a concealable weapon.

(6) Any person regularly employed in a commercial or industrial operation as a security guard for the protection of persons employed and private property related to such commercial or industrial operation, while actually engaged in the performance of his or her duty or traveling between sites or properties belonging to the employer, and who, as a security guard, is a member of a security force of at least 5 persons registered with the Department of Professional Regulation; provided that such security guard has successfully completed a course of study, approved by and supervised by the Department of Professional Regulation, consisting of not less than 40 hours of training that includes the theory of law enforcement, liability for acts, and the handling of weapons. A person shall be considered eligible for this exemption if he or she has completed the required 20 hours of training for a security officer and 20 hours of required firearm training, and has been issued a firearm control card by the Department of Professional Regulation. Conditions for the renewal of firearm control cards issued under the provisions of this Section shall be the same as for those cards issued under the provisions of the Private Detective, Private Alarm, Private Security, Fingerprint Vendor, and Locksmith Act of 2004. Such firearm control card shall be carried by the security guard at all times when he or she is in possession of a concealable weapon.

(7) Agents and investigators of the Illinois Legislative Investigating Commission authorized by the Commission to carry the weapons specified in subsections 24-1(a)(3) and 24-1(a)(4), while on duty in the course of any investigation for the Commission.

(8) Persons employed by a financial institution for the protection of other employees and property related to such financial institution, while actually engaged in the performance of their duties, commuting between their homes and places of employment, or traveling between sites or properties owned or operated by such financial institution, provided that any person so employed has successfully completed a course of study, approved by and supervised by the Department of Professional Regulation, consisting of not less than 40 hours of training which includes theory of law enforcement, liability for acts, and the handling of weapons. A person shall be considered to be eligible for this exemption if he or she has completed the required 20 hours of training for a security

officer and 20 hours of required firearm training, and has been issued a firearm control card by the Department of Professional Regulation. Conditions for renewal of firearm control cards issued under the provisions of this Section shall be the same as for those issued under the provisions of the Private Detective, Private Alarm, Private Security, Fingerprint Vendor, and Locksmith Act of 2004. Such firearm control card shall be carried by the person so trained at all times when such person is in possession of a concealable weapon. For purposes of this subsection, "financial institution" means a bank, savings and loan association, credit union or company providing armored car services.

(9) Any person employed by an armored car company to drive an armored car, while actually engaged in the performance of his duties.

(10) Persons who have been classified as peace officers pursuant to the Peace Officer Fire Investigation Act.

(11) Investigators of the Office of the State's Attorneys Appellate Prosecutor authorized by the board of governors of the Office of the State's Attorneys Appellate Prosecutor to carry weapons pursuant to Section 7.06 of the State's Attorneys Appellate Prosecutor's Act.

(12) Special investigators appointed by a State's Attorney under Section 3-9005 of the Counties Code.

(12.5) Probation officers while in the performance of their duties, or while commuting between their homes, places of employment or specific locations that are part of their assigned duties, with the consent of the chief judge of the circuit for which they are employed.

(13) Court Security Officers while in the performance of their official duties, or while commuting between their homes and places of employment, with the consent of the Sheriff.

(13.5) A person employed as an armed security guard at a nuclear energy, storage, weapons or development site or facility regulated by the Nuclear Regulatory Commission who has completed the background screening and training mandated by the rules and regulations of the Nuclear Regulatory Commission.

(14) Manufacture, transportation, or sale of weapons to persons authorized under subdivisions (1) through (13.5) of this subsection to possess those weapons.

(a-5) Subsections 24-1(a)(4) and 24-1(a)(10) do not apply to or affect any person carrying a concealed pistol, revolver, or handgun and the person has been issued a currently valid license under the Firearm Concealed Carry Act at the same time of the commission of the offense.

(b) Subsections 24-1(a)(4) and 24-1(a)(10) and Section 24-1.6 do not apply to or affect any of the following:

(1) Members of any club or organization organized for the purpose of practicing shooting at targets upon established target ranges, whether public or private, and patrons of such ranges, while such members or patrons are using their firearms on those target ranges.

(2) Duly authorized military or civil organizations while parading, with the special permission of the Governor.

(3) Hunters, trappers or fishermen with a license or permit while engaged in hunting, trapping or fishing.

(4) Transportation of weapons that are broken down in a non-functioning state or are not immediately accessible.

(5) Carrying or possessing any pistol, revolver, stun gun or taser or other firearm on the land or in the legal dwelling of another person as an invitee with that person's permission.

(c) Subsection 24-1(a)(7) does not apply to or affect any of the following:
(1) Peace officers while in performance of their official duties.

(2) Wardens, superintendents and keepers of prisons, penitentiaries, jails and other institutions for the detention of persons accused or convicted of an offense.

(3) Members of the Armed Services or Reserve Forces of the United States or the Illinois National Guard, while in the performance of their official duty.

(4) Manufacture, transportation, or sale of machine guns to persons authorized under subdivisions (1) through (3) of this subsection to possess machine guns, if the machine guns are broken down in a non-functioning state or are not immediately accessible.

(5) Persons licensed under federal law to manufacture any weapon from which 8 or more shots or bullets can be discharged by a single function of the firing device, or ammunition for such weapons, and actually engaged in the business of manufacturing such weapons or ammunition, but only with respect to activities which are within the lawful scope of such business, such as the manufacture, transportation, or testing of such weapons or ammunition. This exemption does not authorize the general private possession of any weapon from which 8 or more shots or bullets can be discharged by a single function of the firing device, but only such possession and activities as are within the lawful scope of a licensed manufacturing business described in this paragraph.

During transportation, such weapons shall be broken down in a non-functioning state or not immediately accessible.

(6) The manufacture, transport, testing, delivery, transfer or sale, and all lawful commercial or experimental activities necessary thereto, of rifles, shotguns, and weapons made from rifles or shotguns, or ammunition for such rifles, shotguns or weapons, where engaged in by a person operating as a contractor or subcontractor pursuant to a contract or subcontract for the development and supply of such rifles, shotguns, weapons or ammunition to the United States government or any branch of the Armed Forces of the United States, when such activities are necessary and incident to fulfilling the terms of such contract.

The exemption granted under this subdivision (c)(6) shall also apply to any authorized agent of any such contractor or subcontractor who is operating within the scope of his employment, where such activities involving such weapon, weapons or ammunition are necessary and incident to fulfilling the terms of such contract.

During transportation, any such weapon shall be broken down in a non-functioning state, or not immediately accessible.

(7) An active member of a bona fide, nationally recognized military re-enacting group ossessing a vintage rifle or modern reproduction thereof with a barrel or barrels less than 16 inches in length for the purpose of using the rifle during historical re-enactments if: (A) the person has been issued a Curios and Relics license from the U.S. Bureau of Alcohol, Tobacco, Firearms and Explosives; or (B) the modification is required and necessary to accurately portray the weapon for historical re-enactment purposes; the re-enactor is in possession of a valid and current re-enacting group membership credential; and the overall length of the weapon as modified is not less than 26 inches.

(d) Subsection 24-1(a)(1) does not apply to the purchase, possession or carrying of a black-jack or slung-shot by a peace officer.

(e) Subsection 24-1(a)(8) does not apply to any owner, manager or authorized employee of any place specified in that subsection nor to any law enforcement officer.

(f) Subsection 24-1(a)(4) and subsection 24-1(a)(10) and Section 24-1.6 do not apply to members of any club or organization organized for the purpose of practicing shooting at targets upon established target ranges, whether public or private, while using their firearms on those target ranges.

(g) Subsections 24-1(a)(11) and 24-3.1(a)(6) do not apply to:

(1) Members of the Armed Services or Reserve Forces of the United States or the Illinois National Guard, while in the performance of their official duty.

(2) Bonafide collectors of antique or surplus military ordinance.

(3) Laboratories having a department of forensic ballistics, or specializing in the development of ammunition or explosive ordinance.

(4) Commerce, preparation, assembly or possession of explosive bullets by manufacturers of ammunition licensed by the federal government, in connection with the supply of those organizations and persons exempted by subdivision (g)(1) of this Section, or like organizations and persons outside this State, or the transportation of explosive bullets to any organization or person exempted in this Section by a common carrier or by a vehicle owned or leased by an exempted manufacturer.

(g-5) Subsection 24-1(a)(6) does not apply to or affect persons licensed under federal law to manufacture any device or attachment of any kind designed, used, or intended for use in silencing the report of any firearm, firearms, or ammunition for those firearms equipped with those devices, and actually engaged in the business of manufacturing those devices, firearms, or ammunition, but only with respect to activities that are within the lawful scope of that business, such as the manufacture, transportation, or testing of those devices, firearms, or ammunition. This exemption does not authorize the general private possession of any device or attachment of any kind designed, used, or intended for use in silencing the report of any firearm, but only such possession and activities as are within the lawful scope of a licensed manufacturing business described in this subsection (g-5). During transportation, those devices shall be detached from any weapon or not immediately accessible.

(g-6) Subsections 24-1(a)(4) and 24-1(a)(10) and Section 24-1.6 do not apply to or affect any parole agent or parole supervisor who meets the qualifications and conditions prescribed in Section 3-14-1.5 of the Unified Code of Corrections.

(g-7) Subsection 24-1(a)(6) does not apply to a peace officer while serving as a member of a tactical response team or special operations team. A peace officer may not personally own or apply for ownership of a device or attachment of any kind designed, used, or intended for use in silencing the report of any firearm. These devices shall be owned and maintained by lawfully recognized units of government whose duties include the investigation of criminal acts.

(g-10) Subsections 24-1(a)(4), 24-1(a)(8), and 24-1(a)(10), and Sections 24-1.6 and 24-3.1 do not apply to an athlete's possession, transport on official Olympic and Paralympic transit systems established for athletes, or use of competition firearms sanctioned by the International Olympic Committee, the International Paralympic Committee, the International Shooting Sport Federation, or USA Shooting in connection with such athlete's training for and participation in shooting competitions at the 2016 Olympic and Paralympic Games and sanctioned test events leading up to the 2016 Olympic and Paralympic Games.

(h) An information or indictment based upon a violation of any subsection of this Article need not negative any exemptions contained in this Article. The defendant shall have the burden of proving such an exemption.

(i) Nothing in this Article shall prohibit, apply to, or affect the transportation, carrying, or possession, of any pistol or revolver, stun gun, taser, or other firearm consigned to a common carrier operating under license of the State of Illinois or the federal government, where such transportation, carrying, or possession is incident to the lawful transportation in which such common carrier is engaged; and nothing in this Article shall prohibit, apply to, or affect the transportation, carrying, or possession of any pistol, revolver, stun gun, taser, or other firearm, not the subject of and regulated by subsection 24-1(a)(7) or subsection 24-2(c) of this Article, which is unloaded and enclosed in a case, firearm carrying box, shipping box, or other container, by the possessor of a valid Firearm Owners Identification Card.

§24-2.1. Unlawful use of firearm projectiles. (a) A person commits the offense of unlawful use of firearm projectiles when he or she knowingly manufactures, sells, purchases, possesses, or carries any armor piercing bullet, dragon's breath shotgun shell, bolo shell, or flechette shell.

For the purposes of this Section:

"Armor piercing bullet" means any handgun bullet or handgun ammunition with projectiles or projectile cores constructed entirely (excluding the presence of traces of other substances) from tungsten alloys, steel, iron, brass, bronze, beryllium copper or depleted uranium, or fully jacketed bullets larger than 22 caliber designed and intended for use in a handgun and whose jacket has a weight of more than 25% of the total weight of the projectile, and excluding those handgun projectiles whose cores are composed of soft materials such as lead or lead alloys, zinc or zinc alloys, frangible projectiles designed primarily for sporting purposes, and any other projectiles or projectile cores that the U. S. Secretary of the Treasury finds to be primarily intended to be used for sporting purposes or industrial purposes or that otherwise does not constitute "armor piercing ammunition" as that term is defined by federal law.

The definition contained herein shall not be construed to include shotgun shells.

"Dragon's breath shotgun shell" means any shotgun shell that contains exothermic pyrophoric mesh metal as the projectile and is designed for the purpose of throwing or spewing a flame or fireball to simulate a flame-thrower.

"Bolo shell" means any shell that can be fired in a firearm and expels as projectiles 2 or more metal balls connected by solid metal wire.

"Flechette shell" means any shell that can be fired in a firearm and expels 2 or more pieces of fin-stabilized solid metal wire or 2 or more solid dart-type projectiles.

(b) Exemptions. This Section does not apply to or affect any of the following:

(1) Peace officers.

(2) Wardens, superintendents and keepers of prisons, penitentiaries, jails and other institutions for the detention of persons accused or convicted of an offense.

(3) Members of the Armed Services or Reserve Forces of the United States or the Illinois National Guard while in the performance of their official duties.

(4) Federal officials required to carry firearms, while engaged in the performance of their official duties.

(5) United States Marshals, while engaged in the performance of their official duties.

(6) Persons licensed under federal law to manufacture, import, or sell firearms and firearm ammunition, and actually engaged in any such business, but only with respect to activities which are within the lawful scope of such business, such as the manufacture, transportation, or testing of such bullets or ammunition.

This exemption does not authorize the general private possession of any armor piercing bullet, dragon's breath shotgun shell, bolo shell, or flechette shell, but only such possession and activities which are within the lawful scope of a licensed business described in this paragraph.

(7) Laboratories having a department of forensic ballistics or specializing in the development of ammunition or explosive ordnance.

(8) Manufacture, transportation, or sale of armor piercing bullets, dragon's breath shotgun shells, bolo shells, or flechette shells to persons specifically authorized under paragraphs (1)

through (7) of this subsection to possess such bullets or shells.

(c) An information or indictment based upon a violation of this Section need not negate any exemption herein contained. The defendant shall have the burden of proving such an exemption.

(d) Sentence. A person convicted of unlawful use of armor piercing bullets shall be guilty of a Class 3 felony.

§24-2.2. Manufacture, sale or transfer of bullets or shells represented to be armor piercing bullets, dragon's breath shotgun shells, bolo shells, or flechette shells.
(a) Except as provided in subsection (b) of this Section, it is unlawful for any person to knowingly manufacture, sell, offer to sell, or transfer any bullet or shell which is represented to be an armor piercing bullet, a dragon's breath shotgun shell, a bolo shell, or a flechette shell as defined in Section 24-2.1 of this Code.

(b) Exemptions. This Section does not apply to or affect any person authorized under Section 24-2.1 to manufacture, sell, purchase, possess, or carry any armor piercing bullet or any dragon's breath shotgun shell, bolo shell, or flechette shell with respect to activities which are within the lawful scope of the exemption therein granted.

(c) An information or indictment based upon a violation of this Section need not negate any exemption herein contained. The defendant shall have the burden of proving such an exemption and that the activities forming the basis of any criminal charge brought pursuant to this Section were within the lawful scope of such exemption.

(d) Sentence. A violation of this Section is a Class 4 felony.

§24-3. Unlawful sale or delivery of firearms.
(A) A person commits the offense of unlawful sale of firearms when he or she knowingly does any of the following:

(a) Sells or gives any firearm of a size which may be concealed upon the person to any person under 18 years of age.

(b) Sells or gives any firearm to a person under 21 years of age who has been convicted of a misdemeanor other than a traffic offense or adjudged delinquent.

(c) Sells or gives any firearm to any narcotic addict.

(d) Sells or gives any firearm to any person who has been convicted of a felony under the laws of this or any other jurisdiction.

(e) Sells or gives any firearm to any person who has been a patient in a mental hospital within the past 5 years.

(f) Sells or gives any firearms to any person who is a person with an intellectual disability.

(g) Delivers any firearm of a size which may be concealed upon the person, incidental to a sale, without withholding delivery of such firearm for at least 72 hours after application for its purchase has been made, or delivers any rifle, shotgun or other long gun, or a stun gun or taser, incidental to a sale, without withholding delivery of such rifle, shotgun or other long gun, or a stun gun or taser for at least 24 hours after application for its purchase has been made. However, this paragraph (g) does not apply to: (1) the sale of a firearm to a law enforcement officer if the seller of the firearm knows that the person to whom he or she is selling the firearm is a law enforcement officer or the sale of a firearm to a person who desires to purchase a firearm for use in promoting the public interest incident to his or her employment as a bank guard, armed truck guard, or other similar employment; (2) a mail order sale of a firearm from a federally licensed firearms dealer to a nonresident of Illinois under which the firearm is mailed to a federally licensed firearms dealer outside the boundaries of Illinois; (3) the sale of a firearm to a nonresident of Illinois while at a firearm showing or display recognized by the Illinois Department of State Police; ~~or~~ (4) the sale of a firearm to a dealer licensed as a federal firearms dealer under Section 923 of the federal Gun Control Act of 1968 (18 U.S.C. 923); or (5) the transfer or sale of any rifle, shotgun, or other long gun to a resident registered competitor or attendee or non-resident registered competitor or attendee by any dealer licensed as a federal firearms dealer under Section 923 of the federal Gun Control Act of 1968 at competitive shooting events held at the World Shooting Complex sanctioned by a national governing body. For purposes of transfers or sales under subparagraph (5) of this paragraph (g), the Department of Natural Resources shall give notice to the Department of State Police at least 30 calendar days prior to any competitive shooting events at the World Shooting Complex sanctioned by a national governing body. The notification shall be made on a form prescribed by the Department of State Police. The sanctioning body shall provide a list of all registered competitors and attendees at least 24 hours before the events to the Department of State Police. Any changes to the list of registered competitors and attendees shall be forwarded to the Department of State Police assoon as practicable. The Department of State Police must destroy the list of registered competitors and attendees no later than 30 days after the date of the event. Nothing in this paragraph (g) relieves a federally licensed firearm dealer from the requirements of conducting a NICS background check through the Illinois Point of Contact under 18 U.S.C. 922(t). For purposes of this paragraph (g), "application" means when the buyer and seller reach an agreement to purchase a firearm. For purposes of this paragraph (g), "national governing body" means a group of persons who adopt rules and formulate policy on behalf of a national firearm sporting organization.

(h) While holding any license as a dealer, importer, manufacturer or pawnbroker under the federal Gun Control Act of 1968, manufactures, sells or delivers to any unlicensed person a handgun having a barrel, slide, frame or receiver which is a die casting of zinc alloy or any other nonhomogeneous metal which will melt or deform at a temperature of less than 800 degrees Fahrenheit. For purposes of this paragraph, (1) “firearm” is defined as in the Firearm Owners Identification Card Act; and (2) “handgun” is defined as a firearm designed to be held and fired by the use of a single hand, and includes a combination of parts from which such a firearm can be assembled.

(i) Sells or gives a firearm of any size to any person under 18 years of age who does not possess a valid Firearm Owner's Identification Card.

(j) Sells or gives a firearm while engaged in the business of selling firearms at wholesale or retail without being licensed as a federal firearms dealer under Section 923 of the federal Gun Control Act of 1968. In this paragraph (j):

A person “engaged in the business” means a person who devotes time, attention, and labor to engaging in the activity as a regular course of trade or business with the principal objective of livelihood and profit, but does not include a person who makes occasional repairs of firearms or who occasionally fits special barrels, stocks, or trigger mechanisms to firearms.

“With the principal objective of livelihood and profit” means that the intent underlying the sale or disposition of firearms is predominantly one of obtaining livelihood and pecuniary gain, as opposed to other intents, such as improving or liquidating a personal firearms collection; however, proof of profit shall not be required as to a person who engages in the regular and repetitive purchase and disposition of firearms for criminal purposes or terrorism.

(k) Sells or transfers ownership of a firearm to a person who does not display to the seller or transferor of the firearm either: (1) a currently valid Firearm Owner's Identification Card that has previously been issued in the transferee's name by the Department of State Police under the provisions of the Firearm Owners Identification Card Act; or (2) a currently valid license to carry a concealed firearm that has previously been issued in the transferee's name by the Department of State Police under the Firearm Concealed Carry Act.This paragraph (k) does not apply to the transfer of a firearm to a person who is exempt from the requirement of possessing a Firearm Owner's Identification Card under Section 2 of the Firearm Owners Identification Card Act. For the purposes of this

Section, a currently valid Firearm Owner's Identification Card means (i) a Firearm Owner's Identification Card that has not expired or (ii) if the transferor is licensed as a federal firearms dealer under Section 923 of the federal Gun Control Act of 1968, an approval number issued in accordance with Section 3.1 of the Firearm Owners Identification Card Act shall be proof that the Firearm Owner's Identification Card was valid.

(l) Not being entitled to the possession of a firearm, delivers the firearm, knowing it to have been stolen or converted. It may be inferred that a person who possesses a firearm with knowledge that its serial number has been removed or altered has knowledge that the firearm is stolen or converted.

(B) Paragraph (h) of subsection (A) does not include firearms sold within 6 months after enactment of Public Act 78-355 (approved August 21, 1973, effective October 1, 1973), nor is any firearm legally owned or possessed by any citizen or purchased by any citizen within 6 months after the enactment of Public Act 78-355 subject to confiscation or seizure under the provisions of that Public Act. Nothing in Public Act 78-355 shall be construed to prohibit the gift or trade of any firearm if that firearm was legally held or acquired within 6 months after the enactment of that Public Act.

(C) Sentence. (1) Any person convicted of unlawful sale or delivery of firearms in violation of paragraph (c), (e), (f), (g), or (h) of subsection (A) commits a Class 4 felony.

(2) Any person convicted of unlawful sale or delivery of firearms in violation of paragraph (b) or (i) of subsection (A) commits a Class 3 felony.

(3) Any person convicted of unlawful sale or delivery of firearms in violation of paragraph (a) of subsection (A) commits a Class 2 felony.
(4) Any person convicted of unlawful sale or delivery of firearms in violation of paragraph (a), (b), or (i) of subsection (A) in any school, on the real property comprising a school, within 1,000 feet of the real property comprising a school, at a school related activity, or on or within 1,000 feet of any conveyance owned, leased, or contracted by a school or school district to transport students to or from school or a school related activity, regardless of the time of day or time of year at which the offense was committed, commits a Class 1 felony. Any person convicted of a second or subsequent violation of unlawful sale or delivery of firearms in violation of paragraph (a), (b), or (i) of subsection (A) in any school, on the real property comprising a school, within 1,000 feet of the real property comprising a school, at a school related activity, or on or within 1,000 feet of any conveyance owned, leased, or contracted by a school or school district to transport students to or from school or a school related activity, regardless of the time of day or time of year at which the offense was committed, commits a Class 1 felony for which the sentence shall be a term of imprisonment of no less than 5 years and no more than 15 years.

(5) Any person convicted of unlawful sale or delivery of firearms in violation of paragraph (a) or (i) of subsection (A) in residential property owned, operated, or managed by a public housing agency or leased by a public housing agency as part of a scattered site or mixed-income development, in a public park, in a courthouse, on residential property owned, operated, or managed by a public housing agency or leased by a public housing agency as part of a scattered site or mixed-income development, on the real property comprising any public park, on the real property comprising any courthouse, or on any public way within 1,000 feet of the real property comprising any public park, courthouse, or residential property owned, operated, or managed by a public housing agency or leased by a public housing agency as part of a scattered site or mixed-income development commits a Class 2 felony.
(6) Any person convicted of unlawful sale or delivery of firearms in violation of paragraph (j) of subsection (A) commits a Class A misdemeanor. A second or subsequent violation is a Class 4 felony.
(7) Any person convicted of unlawful sale or delivery of firearms in violation of paragraph (k) of subsection (A) commits a Class 4 felony. A

third or subsequent conviction for a violation of paragraph (k) of subsection (A) is a Class 1 felony.

(8) A person 18 years of age or older convicted of unlawful sale or delivery of firearms in violation of paragraph (a) or (i) of subsection (A), when the firearm that was sold or given to another person under 18 years of age was used in the commission of or attempt to commit a forcible felony, shall be fined or imprisoned, or both, not to exceed the maximum provided for the most serious forcible felony so committed or attempted by the person under 18 years of age who was sold or given the firearm.
(9) Any person convicted of unlawful sale of firearms in violation of paragraph (d) of subsection (A) commits a Class 3 felony.

(10) Any person convicted of unlawful sale or delivery of firearms in violation of paragraph (l) of subsection (A) commits a Class 2 felony if the delivery is of one firearm. Any person convicted of unlawful sale or delivery of firearms in violation of paragraph (l) of subsection (A) commits a Class 1 felony if the delivery is of not less than 2 and not more than 5 firearms at the same time or within a one year period. Any person convicted of unlawful sale or delivery of firearms in violation of paragraph (l) of subsection (A) commits a Class X felony for which he or she shall be sentenced to a term of imprisonment of not less than 6 years and not more than 30 years if the delivery is of not less than 6 and not more than 10 firearms at the same time or within a 2 year period. Any person convicted of unlawful sale or delivery of firearms in violation of paragraph (l) of subsection (A) commits a Class X felony for which he or she shall be sentenced to a term of imprisonment of not less than 6 years and not more than 40 years if the delivery is of not less than 11 and not more than 20 firearms at the same time or within a 3 year period. Any person convicted of unlawful sale or delivery of firearms in violation of paragraph (l) of subsection (A) commits a Class X felony for which he or she shall be sentenced to a term of imprisonment of not less than 6 years and not more than 50 years if the delivery is of not less than 21 and not more than 30 firearms at the same time or within a 4 year period. Any person convicted of unlawful sale or delivery of firearms in violation of paragraph (l) of subsection (A) commits a Class X felony for which he or she shall be sentenced to a term of imprisonment of not less than 6 years and not more than 60 years if the delivery is of 31 or more firearms at the same time or within a 5 year period.

(D) For purposes of this Section:

"School" means a public or private elementary or secondary school, community college, college, or university.
"School related activity" means any sporting, social, academic, or other activity for which students' attendance or participation is sponsored, organized, or funded in whole or in part by a school or school district.

(E) A prosecution for a violation of paragraph (k) of subsection (A) of this Section may be commenced within 6 years after the commission of the offense. A prosecution for a violation of this Section other than paragraph (g) of subsection (A) of this Section may be commenced within 5 years after the commission of the offense defined in the particular paragraph.

§24-3.1. Unlawful possession of firearms and firearm ammunition. (a) A person commits the offense of unlawful possession of firearms or firearm ammunition when:

(1) He is under 18 years of age and has in his possession any firearm of a size which may be concealed upon the person; or

(2) He is under 21 years of age, has been convicted of a misdemeanor other than a traffic offense or adjudged delinquent and has any firearms or firearm ammunition in his possession; or

(3) He is a narcotic addict and has any firearms or firearm ammunition in his possession; or

(4) He has been a patient in a mental hospital within the past 5 years and has any firearms or firearm ammunition in his possession; or

(5) He is a person with an intellectual disability and has any firearms or firearm ammunition in his possession; or

(6) He has in his possession any explosive bullet.

For purposes of this paragraph "explosive bullet" means the projectile portion of an ammunition cartridge which contains or carries an explosive charge which will explode upon contact with the flesh of a human or an animal. "Cartridge" means a tubular metal case having a projectile affixed at the front thereof and a cap or primer at the rear end thereof, with the propellant contained in such tube between the projectile and the cap.

(b) Sentence.

Unlawful possession of firearms, other than handguns, and firearm ammunition is a Class A misdemeanor. Unlawful possession of handguns is a Class 4 felony. The possession of each firearm or firearm ammunition in violation of this Section constitutes a single and separate violation.
(c) Nothing in paragraph (1) of subsection (a) of this Section prohibits a person under 18 years of age from participating in any lawful recreational activity with a firearm such as, but not limited to, practice shooting at targets upon established public or private target ranges or hunting, trapping, or fishing in accordance with the Wildlife Code or the Fish and Aquatic Life Code.

§24-3.2. Unlawful discharge of firearm projectiles. (a) A person commits the offense of unlawful discharge of firearm projectiles when he or she knowingly or recklessly uses an armor piercing bullet, dragon's breath shotgun shell, bolo shell, or flechette shell in violation of this Section.

For purposes of this Section:

"Armor piercing bullet" means any handgun bullet or handgun ammunition with projectiles or projectile cores constructed entirely (excluding the presence of traces of other substances) from tungsten alloys, steel, iron, brass, bronze, beryllium copper or depleted uranium, or fully jacketed bullets larger than 22 caliber whose jacket has a weight of more than 25% of the total weight of the projectile, and excluding those handgun projectiles whose cores are composed of soft materials such as lead or lead alloys, zinc or zinc alloys, frangible projectiles designed primarily for sporting purposes, and any other projectiles or projectile cores that the U. S. Secretary of the Treasury finds to be primarily intended to be used for sporting purposes or industrial purposes or that otherwise does not constitute "armor piercing ammunition" as that term is defined by federal law.

"Dragon's breath shotgun shell" means any shotgun shell that contains exothermic pyrophoric mesh metal as the projectile and is designed for the purpose of throwing or spewing a flame or fireball to simulate a flame-thrower.

"Bolo shell" means any shell that can be fired in a firearm and expels as projectiles 2 or more metal balls connected by solid metal wire. "Flechette shell" means any shell that can be fired in a firearm and expels 2 or more pieces of fin-stabilized solid metal wire or 2 or more solid dart-type projectiles.

(b) A person commits a Class X felony when he or she, knowing that a firearm, as defined in Section 1.1 of the Firearm Owners Identification Card Act, is loaded with an armor piercing bullet, dragon's breath shotgun shell, bolo shell, or flechette shell, intentionally or recklessly discharges such firearm and such bullet or shell strikes any other person.

(c) Any person who possesses, concealed on or about his or her person, an armor piercing bullet, dragon's breath shotgun shell, bolo shell, or flechette shell and a firearm suitable for the discharge thereof is guilty of a Class 2 felony.

(d) This Section does not apply to or affect any of the following:

(1) Peace officers;

(2) Wardens, superintendents and keepers of prisons, penitentiaries, jails and other institutions for the detention of persons accused or convicted of an offense;

(3) Members of the Armed Services or Reserve Forces of the United States or the Illinois National Guard while in the performance of their official duties;

(4) Federal officials required to carry firearms, while engaged in the performance of their official duties;

(5) United States Marshals, while engaged in the performance of their official duties.

Sec. 24-3.3. Unlawful Sale or Delivery of Firearms on the Premises of Any School, regardless of the time of day or the time of year, or any conveyance owned, leased or contracted by a school to transport students to or from school or a school related activity, or residential property owned, operated or managed by a public housing agency. Any person 18 years of age or older who sells, gives or delivers any firearm to any person under 18 years of age in any school, regardless of the time of day or the time of year or residential property owned, operated or managed by a public housing agency or leased by a public housing agency as part of a scattered site or mixed-income development, on the real property comprising any school, regardless of the time of day or the time of year or residential property owned, operated or managed by a public housing agency or leased by a public housing agency as part of a scattered site or mixed-income development commits a Class 3 felony. School is defined, for the purposes of this Section, as any public or private elementary or secondary school, community college, college or university. This does not apply to peace officers or to students carrying or possessing firearms for use in school training courses, parades, target shooting on school ranges, or otherwise with the consent of school authorities and which firearms are transported unloaded and enclosed in a suitable case, box or transportation package.

§24-3.4. Unlawful sale of firearms by liquor licensee. (a) It shall be unlawful for any person who holds a license to sell at retail any alcoholic liquor issued by the Illinois Liquor Control Commission or local liquor control commissioner under the Liquor Control Act of 1934 or an agent or employee of the licensee to sell or deliver to any other person a firearm in or on the real property of the establishment where the licensee is licensed to sell alcoholic liquors unless the sale or delivery of the firearm is otherwise lawful under this Article and under the Firearm Owners Identification Card Act.

(b) Sentence. A violation of subsection (a) of this Section is a Class 4 felony.

§24-3.5. Unlawful purchase of a firearm. (a) For purposes of this Section, "firearms transaction record form" means a form:

(1) executed by a transferee of a firearm stating: (i) the transferee's name and address (including county or similar political subdivision); (ii) whether the transferee is a citizen of the United States; (iii) the transferee's State of residence; and (iv) the date and place of birth, height, weight, and race of the transferee; and

(2) on which the transferee certifies that he or she is not prohibited by federal law from transporting or shipping a firearm in interstate or foreign commerce or receiving a firearm that has been shipped or transported in interstate or foreign commerce or possessing a firearm in or affecting commerce.

(b) A person commits the offense of unlawful purchase of a firearm who knowingly purchases or attempts to purchase a firearm with the intent to deliver that firearm to another person who is prohibited by federal or State law from possessing a firearm.

(c) A person commits the offense of unlawful purchase of a firearm when he or she, in purchasing or attempting to purchase a firearm, intentionally provides false or misleading information on a United States Department of the Treasury, Bureau of Alcohol, Tobacco and Firearms firearms transaction record form.

(d) Exemption. It is not a violation of subsection (b) of this Section for a person to make a gift or loan of a firearm to a person who is not prohibited by federal or State law from possessing a firearm if the transfer of the firearm is made in accordance with Section 3 of the Firearm Owners Identification Card Act.

(e) Sentence.

(1) A person who commits the offense of unlawful purchase of a firearm:

(A) is guilty of a Class 2 felony for purchasing or attempting to purchase one firearm;

(B) is guilty of a Class 1 felony for purchasing or attempting to purchase not less than 2 firearms and not more than 5 firearms at the same time or within a one year period;

(C) is guilty of a Class X felony for which the offender shall be sentenced to a term of imprisonment of not less than 9 years and not more than 40 years for purchasing or attempting to purchase not less than 6 firearms at the same time or within a 2 year period.

(2) In addition to any other penalty that may be imposed for a violation of this Section, the court may sentence a person convicted of a violation of subsection (c) of this Section to a fine not to exceed $250,000 for each violation.

(f) A prosecution for unlawful purchase of a firearm may be commenced within 6 years after the commission of the offense.

§24-3.6. Unlawful use of a firearm in the shape of a wireless telephone. (a) For the purposes of this Section, "wireless telephone" means a device that is capable of transmitting or receiving telephonic communications without a wire connecting the device to the telephone network.

(b) A person commits the offense of unlawful use of a firearm in the shape of a wireless telephone when he or she manufactures, sells, transfers, purchases, possesses, or carries a firearm shaped or designed to appear as a wireless telephone.

(c) This Section does not apply to or affect the sale to or possession of a firearm in the shape of a wireless telephone by a peace officer.

(d) Sentence. Unlawful use of a firearm in the shape of a wireless telephone is a Class 4 felony.

§24-3.7. Use of a stolen firearm in the commission of an offense.
(a) A person commits the offense of use of a stolen firearm in the commission of an offense when he or she knowingly uses a stolen firearm in the commission of any offense and the person knows that the firearm was stolen.

(b) Sentence. Use of a stolen firearm in the commission of an offense is a Class 2 felony.

§ 24-3.8. Possession of a stolen firearm.
(a) A person commits possession of a stolen firearm when he or she, not being entitled to the possession of a firearm, possesses or delivers the firearm, knowing it to have been stolen or converted. The trier of fact may infer that a person who possesses a firearm with knowledge that its serial number has been removed or altered has knowledge that the firearm is stolen or converted.

(b) Possession of a stolen firearm is a Class 2 felony.

§ 24-3.9. Aggravated possession of a stolen firearm. (a) A person commits aggravated possession of a stolen firearm when he or she:
(1) Not being entitled to the possession of not less than 2 and not more than 5 firearms, possesses or delivers those firearms at the same time or within a one-year period, knowing the firearms to have been stolen or converted.
(2) Not being entitled to the possession of not less than 6 and not more than 10 firearms, possesses or delivers those firearms at the same

time or within a 2-year period, knowing the firearms to have been stolen or converted.
(3) Not being entitled to the possession of not less than 11 and not more than 20 firearms, possesses or delivers those firearms at the same time or within a 3-year period, knowing the firearms to have been stolen or converted.
(4) Not being entitled to the possession of not less than 21 and not more than 30 firearms, possesses or delivers those firearms at the same time or within a 4-year period, knowing the firearms to have been stolen or converted.
(5) Not being entitled to the possession of more than 30 firearms, possesses or delivers those firearms at the same time or within a 5-year period, knowing the firearms to have been stolen or converted.

(b) The trier of fact may infer that a person who possesses a firearm with knowledge that its serial number has been removed or altered has knowledge that the firearm is stolen or converted.

(c) Sentence.
(1) A person who violates paragraph (1) of subsection (a) of this Section commits a Class 1 felony.
(2) A person who violates paragraph (2) of subsection (a) of this Section commits a Class X felony for which he or she shall be sentenced to a term of imprisonment of not less than 6 years and not more than 30 years.
(3) A person who violates paragraph (3) of subsection (a) of this Section commits a Class X felony for which he or she shall be sentenced to a term of imprisonment of not less than 6 years and not more than 40 years.
(4) A person who violates paragraph (4) of subsection (a) of this Section commits a Class X felony for which he or she shall be sentenced to a term of imprisonment of not less than 6 years and not more than 50 years.
(5) A person who violates paragraph (5) of subsection (a) of this Section commits a Class X felony for which he or she shall be sentenced to a term of imprisonment of not less than 6 years and not more than 60 years.

§24-3A. Gunrunning. (a) A person commits gunrunning when he or she transfers 3 or more firearms in violation of any of the paragraphs of Section 24-3 of this Code.

(b) Sentence. A person who commits gunrunning:

(1) is guilty of a Class 1 felony;

(2) is guilty of a Class X felony for which the sentence shall be a term of imprisonment of not less than 8 years and not more than 40 years if the transfer is of not less than 11 firearms and not more than 20 firearms;

(3) is guilty of a Class X felony for which the sentence shall be a term of imprisonment of not less than 10 years and not more than 50 years if the transfer is of more than 20 firearms.

A person who commits gunrunning by transferring firearms to a person who, at the time of the commission of the offense, is under 18 years of age is guilty of a Class X felony.

§24-4. Register of Sales by Dealer. (a) Any seller of firearms of a size which may be concealed upon the person, other than a manufacturer selling to a bona fide wholesaler or retailer or a wholesaler selling to a bona fide retailer, shall keep a register of all firearms sold or given away.

(b) Such register shall contain the date of the sale or gift, the name, address, age and occupation of the person to whom the weapon is sold or given, the price of the weapon, the kind, description and number of the weapon, and the purpose for which it is purchased and obtained.

(c) Such seller on demand of a peace officer shall produce for inspection the register and allow such peace officer to inspect such register and all stock on hand.

(d) Sentence. Violation of this Section is a Class B misdemeanor.

§24-4.1 Report of lost or stolen firearms. Report of lost or stolen firearms. (a) If a person who possesses a valid Firearm Owner's Identification Card and who possesses or acquires a firearm thereafter loses the firearm, or if the firearm is stolen from the person, the person must report the loss or theft to the local law enforcement agency within 72 hours after obtaining knowledge of the loss or theft.

(b) A law enforcement agency having jurisdiction shall take a written report and shall, as soon as practical, enter the firearm's serial number as stolen into the Law Enforcement Agencies Data System (LEADS).

(c) A person shall not be in violation of this Section if:

(1) the failure to report is due to an act of God, act of war, or inability of a law enforcement agency to receive the report;

(2) the person is hospitalized, in a coma, or is otherwise seriously physically or mentally impaired as to prevent the person from reporting; or

(3) the person's designee makes a report if the person is unable to make the report.

(d) Sentence. A person who violates this Section is guilty of a petty offense for a first violation. A second or subsequent violation of this Section is a Class A misdemeanor.

§24-5. Defacing identification marks of firearms. (a) Any person who shall knowingly or intentionally change, alter, remove or obliterate the name of the importer's or manufacturer's serial number of any firearm commits a Class 2 felony.

(b) A person who possesses any firearm upon which any such importer's or manufacturer's serial number has been changed, altered, removed or obliterated commits a Class 3 felony.

(c) Nothing in this Section shall prevent a person from making repairs, replacement of parts, or other changes to a firearm if those repairs, replacement of parts, or changes cause the removal of the name of the maker, model, or other marks of identification other than the serial number on the firearm's frame or receiver.

(d) A prosecution for a violation of this Section may be commenced within 6 years after the commission of the offense.

§24-6. Confiscation and disposition of weapons. (a) Upon conviction of an offense in which a weapon was used or possessed by the offender, any weapon seized shall be confiscated by the trial court.

(b) Any stolen weapon so confiscated, when no longer needed for evidentiary purposes, shall be returned to the person entitled to possession, if known. After the disposition of a criminal case or in any criminal case where a final judgment in the case was not entered due to the death of the defendant, and when a confiscated weapon is no longer needed for evidentiary purposes, and when in due course no legitimate claim has been made for the weapon, the court may transfer the weapon to the sheriff of the county who may proceed to destroy it, or may in its discretion order the weapon preserved as property of the governmental body whose police agency seized the weapon, or may in its discretion order the weapon to be transferred to the Department of State Police for use by the crime laboratory system, for training purposes, or for any other application as deemed appropriate by the Department. If, after the disposition of a criminal case, a need still exists for the use of the confiscated weapon for evidentiary purposes, the court may transfer the weapon to the custody of the State Department of Corrections for preservation. The court may not order the transfer of the weapon to any private individual or private organization other than to return a stolen weapon to its rightful owner.

The provisions of this Section shall not apply to violations of the Fish and Aquatic Life Code or the Wildlife Code. Confiscation of weapons for Fish and Aquatic Life Code and Wildlife Code violations shall be only as provided in those Codes.

(c) Any mental hospital that admits a person as an inpatient pursuant to any of the provisions of

the Mental Health and Developmental Disabilities Code shall confiscate any firearms in the possession of that person at the time of admission, or at any time the firearms are discovered in the person's possession during the course of hospitalization. The hospital shall, as soon as possible following confiscation, transfer custody of the firearms to the appropriate law enforcement agency. The hospital shall give written notice to the person from whom the firearm was confiscated of the identity and address of the law enforcement agency to which it has given the firearm.
The law enforcement agency shall maintain possession of any firearm it obtains pursuant to this subsection for a minimum of 90 days. Thereafter, the firearm may be disposed of pursuant to the provisions of subsection (b) of this Section.

§24-7. Weapons offenses; community service. In addition to any other sentence that may be imposed, a court shall order any person convicted of a violation of this Article to perform community service for not less than 30 and not more than 120 hours, if community service is available in the jurisdiction and is funded and approved by the county board of the county where the offense was committed. In addition, whenever any person is placed on supervision for an alleged offense under this Article, the supervision shall be conditioned upon the performance of the community service.

This Section does not apply when the court imposes a sentence of incarceration.

§24-8. Firearm tracing. (a) Upon recovering a firearm from the possession of anyone who is not permitted by federal or State law to possess a firearm, a local law enforcement agency shall use the best available information, including a firearms trace when necessary, to determine how and from whom the person gained possession of the firearm. Upon recovering a firearm that was used in the commission of any offense classified as a felony or upon recovering a firearm that appears to have been lost, mislaid, stolen, or otherwise unclaimed, a local law enforcement agency shall use the best available information, including a firearms trace when necessary, to determine prior ownership of the firearm.

(b) Local law enforcement shall, when appropriate, use the National Tracing Center of the Federal Bureau of Alcohol, Tobacco and Firearms in complying with subsection (a) of this Section.

(c) Local law enforcement agencies shall use the Illinois Department of State Police Law Enforcement Agencies Data System (LEADS) Gun File to enter all stolen, seized, or recovered firearms as prescribed by LEADS regulations and policies.

§24-9. Firearms; Child Protection.
(a) Except as provided in subsection (c), it is unlawful for any person to store or leave, within premises under his or her control, a firearm if the person knows or has reason to believe that a minor under the age of 14 years who does not have a Firearm Owners Identification Card is likely to gain access to the firearm without the lawful permission of the minor's parent, guardian, or person having charge of the minor, and the minor causes death or great bodily harm with the firearm, unless the firearm is:

(1) secured by a device or mechanism, other than the firearm safety, designed to render a firearm temporarily inoperable; or

(2) placed in a securely locked box or container; or

(3) placed in some other location that a reasonable person would believe to be secure from a minor under the age of 14 years.

(b) Sentence. A person who violates this Section is guilty of a Class C misdemeanor and shall be fined not less than $1,000. A second or subsequent violation of this Section is a Class A misdemeanor.

(c) Subsection (a) does not apply:

(1) if the minor under 14 years of age gains access to a firearm and uses it in a lawful act of self-defense or defense of another; or

(2) to any firearm obtained by a minor under the age of 14 because of an unlawful entry of the premises by the minor or another person.

(d) For the purposes of this Section, “firearm” has the meaning ascribed to it in Section 1.1 of the Firearm Owners Identification Card Act.

§24-9.5. Handgun safety devices. (a) It is unlawful for a person licensed as a federal firearms dealer under Section 923 of the federal Gun Control Act of 1968 to offer for sale, sell, or transfer a handgun to a person not licensed under that Act, unless he or she sells or includes with the handgun a device or mechanism, other than the firearm safety, designed to render the handgun temporarily inoperable or inaccessible. This includes but is not limited to:

(1) An external device that is:

(i) attached to the handgun with a key or combination lock; and

(ii) designed to prevent the handgun from being discharged unless the device has been deactivated.

(2) An integrated mechanical safety, disabling, or locking device that is:

(i) built into the handgun; and

(ii) designed to prevent the handgun from being discharged unless the device has been deactivated.

(b) Sentence. A person who violates this Section is guilty of a Class C misdemeanor and shall be fined not less than $1,000. A second or subsequent violation of this Section is a Class A misdemeanor.

(c) For the purposes of this Section, “handgun” has the meaning ascribed to it in clause (h)(2) of subsection (A) of Section 24-3 of this Code.

(d) This Section does not apply to:

(1) the purchase, sale, or transportation of a handgun to or by a federally licensed firearms dealer or manufacturer that provides or services a handgun for:
(i) personnel of any unit of the federal government;

(ii) members of the armed forces of the United States or the National Guard;
(iii) law enforcement personnel of the State or any local law enforcement agency in the State while acting within the scope of their official duties; and
(iv) an organization that is required by federal law governing its specific business or activity to maintain handguns and applicable ammunition;

(2) a firearm modified to be permanently inoperative;

(3) the sale or transfer of a handgun by a federally licensed firearms dealer or manufacturer described in item (1) of this subsection (d);

(4) the sale or transfer of a handgun by a federally licensed firearms dealer or manufacturer to a lawful customer outside the State; or

(5) an antique firearm.

§24-10. Municipal ordinance regulating firearms; affirmative defense to a violation. It is an affirmative defense to a violation of a municipal ordinance that prohibits, regulates, or restricts the private ownership of firearms if the individual who is charged with the violation used the firearm in an act of self-defense or defense of another as defined in Sections 7-1 and 7-2 of this Code when on his or her land or in his or her abode or fixed place of business.

Article 24.5. Nitrous Oxide

§24.5-5. Unlawful possession. any person who possesses nitrous oxide or any substance containing nitrous oxide, with the intent to breathe, inhale, or ingest for the purpose of causing a condition of intoxication, elation, euphoria, dizziness, stupefaction, or dulling of the senses or for the purpose of, in any manner, changing, distorting, or disturbing the audio, visual, or mental processes, or who knowingly and with the intent to do so is under the influence of nitrous oxide or any material containing nitrous oxide is guilty of a Class A misdemeanor. A person who commits a second or subsequent violation of this Section is guilty of a Class 4 felony. This Section shall not apply to any person who is under the influence of nitrous oxide or any material containing nitrous oxide pursuant to an administration for the purpose of medical, surgical, or dental care by a person duly licensed to administer such an agent.

§24.5-10. Unlawful manufacture or delivery. Any person, firm, corporation, co-partnership, limited liability company, or association that intentionally manufactures, delivers, or possesses with intent to manufacture or deliver nitrous oxide for any purpose prohibited under Section 24.5-5 is guilty of a Class 3 felony.

Article 24.6 Laser and Laser Pointers

§24.6-5. Definitions. In this Article:

"Aircraft" means any contrivance now known or hereafter invented, used, or designed for navigation of or flight in the air, but excluding parachutes.

"Laser" means both of the following:

(1) any device that utilizes the natural oscillations of atoms or molecules between energy levels for generating coherent electromagnetic radiation in the ultraviolet, visible, or infrared region of the spectrum and when discharged exceeds one milliwatt continuous wave;

(2) any device designed or used to amplify electromagnetic radiation by simulated emission that is visible to the human eye.

"Laser pointer" means a hand-held device that emits light amplified by the stimulated emission of radiation that is visible to the human eye.

"Laser sight" means a laser pointer that can be attached to a firearm and can be used to improve the accuracy of the firearm.

§24.6-20. Aiming a laser pointer at a peace officer. (a) A person commits aiming a laser pointer at a peace officer when he or she intentionally or knowingly aims an operating laser pointer at a person he or she knows or reasonably should know to be a peace officer.

(b) Sentence. Aiming a laser pointer at a peace officer is a Class A misdemeanor.

§Sec. 24.6-25. Discharging a laser at an aircraft. (a) A person commits discharging a laser at an aircraft when he or she intentionally or knowingly aims and discharges a laser or other device that creates visible light into the cockpit of an aircraft that is in the process of taking off,
landing, or is in flight.

(b) Exceptions. This Section does not apply to the following individuals who aim and discharge a laser or other device at an aircraft:

(1) an authorized individual in the conduct of research and development or flight test operations conducted by an aircraft manufacturer, the Federal Aviation Administration, or any other person authorized by the Federal Aviation Administration to conduct such research and development or flight test operations; or

(2) members or elements of the Department of Defense or Department of Homeland Security acting in an official capacity for the purpose of

research, development, operations, testing, or training.

(c) Sentence. Discharging a laser at an aircraft is a Class A misdemeanor.

ARTICLE 25. MOB ACTION AND RELATED OFFENSES

§25-1. Mob action. (a) A person commits the offense of mob action when he or she engages in any of the following:

(1) the knowing or reckless use of force or violence disturbing the public peace by 2 or more persons acting together and without authority of law;

(2) the knowing assembly of 2 or more persons with the intent to commit or facilitate the commission of a felony or misdemeanor; or

(3) the knowing assembly of 2 or more persons, without authority of law, for the purpose of doing violence to the person or property of anyone supposed to have been guilty of a violation of the law, or for the purpose of exercising correctional powers or regulative powers over any person by violence.

(b) Mob action as defined in paragraph (1) of subsection (a) is a Class 4 felony.

(c) Mob action as defined in paragraphs (2) and (3) of subsection (a) is a Class C misdemeanor.

(d) Any participant in a mob action that by violence inflicts injury to the person or property of another commits a Class 4 felony.

(e) Any participant in a mob action who does not withdraw on being commanded to do so by any peace officer commits a Class A misdemeanor.

(f) In addition to any other sentence that may be imposed, a court shall order any person convicted of mob action to perform community service for not less than 30 and not more than 120 hours, if community service is available in the jurisdiction and is funded and approved by the county board of the county where the offense was committed. In addition, whenever any person is placed on supervision for an alleged offense under this Section, the supervision shall be conditioned upon the performance of the community service.

This subsection does not apply when the court imposes a sentence of incarceration.

Commentary – Mob Action

Section 25-1 defines the offense of mob action. a mob is defined as actually only two or more individuals who have assembled (although it certainly can be a literal mob.) a member of the assembled "mob" commits the crime of mob action when he knowingly without lawful authority, (1) uses force to disturb the peace (can also be committed recklessly), or (2) acts with intent to commit a felony or misdemeanor or (3) acts for the purpose of doing violence to punish someone who is thought to have violated the law. Historically, the mental state was not defined by the statute and thus the general intent provisions of Section 4-3(b) applied so that a knowing, intentional or reckless mental state could be inferred. Effective July 1, 2010, the statute was amended to add mental states to each subsection defining the crime.

Mob action conjures up pictures of the mob trying to take a prisoner out of jail to hang him when he was accused of a crime, and that type of conduct would be covered by the statute. Indeed mob action has served as a predicate forcible felony offense for felony murder.

Mob action as predicate offense; mental state. In *People v. Davis* 213 Ill.2d102, 821 N.E.2d 1154 (Ill. S. Ct. 2004), the defendant was convicted of felony murder based on a death caused as a result of the forcible felony of mob action. A group of people went to a neighbor in an attempt to recover a stolen television set and went door to door asking if anyone had knowledge of the stolen TV. The members of the neighborhood were angry that the accusation was being made and formed a mob that attacked the TV people. One of them was killed when he was beaten. The defendant when questioned admitted that he got carried away and had hit the victim with a broom handle. The defendant argued that he was entitled to have the jury instructed on involuntary manslaughter because the mob action was done "recklessly", and thus had the same mental state for the manslaughter charge to permit the lesser included charge. the court noted that the felony murder charge was based on a "knowing" mob action, that his acts were not inherent in the murder of the victim, and that the evidence showed that the only reason the beating of the victim stopped was because the police arrived, the claim of recklessness of the mob action was not supported by the evidence. See also *People v. Davison* 236 Ill. 2d 232, 923 N.E.2d 781 (Ill. S. Ct. 2010) (felony murder properly based on mob action where two or more people use force to provoke a breach of the peace.)

§25-4. Looting by individuals. (a) A person commits the offense of looting when he or she knowingly without authority of law or the owner enters any home or dwelling or upon any premises of another, or enters any commercial, mercantile, business, or industrial building, plant, or establishment, in which normal security of property is not present by virtue of a hurricane, fire, or vis major of any kind or by virtue of a riot, mob, or other human agency, and obtains or exerts control over property of the owner.

(b) Sentence. Looting is a Class 4 felony. In addition to any other penalty imposed, the court shall impose a sentence of at least 100 hours of community service as determined by the court and shall require the defendant to make restitution to the owner of the property looted pursuant to Section 5-5-6 of the Unified Code of Corrections.

§25-5. Unlawful contact with streetgang members. (a) A person commits the offense of unlawful contact with streetgang members when:

(1) he or she knowingly has direct or indirect contact with a streetgang member as defined in Section 10 of the Illinois Streetgang Terrorism Omnibus Prevention Act after having been sentenced to probation, conditional discharge, or supervision for a criminal offense with a condition of that sentence being to refrain from direct or indirect contact with a streetgang member or members;

(2) he or she knowingly has direct or indirect contact with a streetgang member as defined in Section 10 of the Illinois Streetgang Terrorism Omnibus Prevention Act after having been released on bond for any criminal offense with a condition of that bond being to refrain from direct or indirect contact with a streetgang member or members;

(3) he or she knowingly has direct or indirect contact with a streetgang member as defined in Section 10 of the Illinois Streetgang Terrorism Omnibus Prevention Act after having been ordered by a judge in any non-criminal proceeding to refrain from direct or indirect contact with a streetgang member or members; or

(4) he or she knowingly has direct or indirect contact with a streetgang member as defined in Section 10 of the Streetgang Terrorism Omnibus Prevention Act after having been released from the Illinois Department of Corrections on a condition of parole or mandatory supervised release that he or she refrain from direct or indirect contact with a streetgang member or members.

(b) Unlawful contact with streetgang members is a Class A misdemeanor.

(c) This Section does not apply to a person when the only streetgang member or members he or she is with is a family or household member or members as defined in paragraph (3) of Section 112A-3 of the Code of Criminal Procedure of

1963 and the streetgang members are not engaged in any streetgang-related activity.

§25-6. Removal of chief of police or sheriff for allowing a person in his or her custody to be lynched. (a) If a prisoner is taken from the custody of any policeman or chief of police of any municipality and lynched, it shall be prima facie evidence of wrong-doing on the part of that chief of police and he or she shall be suspended. The mayor or chief executive of the municipality shall appoint an acting chief of police until he or she has ascertained whether the suspended chief of police had done all in his or her power to protect the life of the prisoner. If, upon hearing all evidence and argument, the mayor or chief executive finds that the chief of police had done his or her utmost to protect the prisoner, he or she may reinstate the chief of police; but, if he or she finds the chief of police guilty of not properly protecting the prisoner, a new chief of police shall be appointed. Any chief of police replaced is not be eligible to serve again in that office.

(b) If a prisoner is taken from the custody of any sheriff or his or her deputy and lynched, it is prima facie evidence of wrong-doing on the part of that sheriff and he or she shall be suspended. The Governor shall appoint an acting sheriff until he or she has ascertained whether the suspended sheriff had done all in his or her power to protect the life of the prisoner. If, upon hearing all evidence and argument, the Governor finds that the sheriff had done his or her utmost to protect the prisoner, he or she shall reinstate the sheriff; but, if he or she finds the sheriff guilty of not properly protecting the prisoner, a new sheriff shall be duly elected or appointed, pursuant to the existing law provided for the filling of vacancies in that office. Any sheriff replaced is not eligible to serve again in that office.

§25-7. Duty of internet service providers to report information to law enforcement. (a) Upon request of a law enforcement officer who has probable cause to believe that the services of an internet service provider were used to solict a violation of, conspiracy to violate attempt to violate, or otherwise facilitate a violation of, Section 25-1 of this Code, an internet service rprovider shall provide the identifying information related to e-mail addresses, instant messaging identities, chat room identities, text messaging identities, or other internet communications identies as requested. The identifying information shall include, at minimum, the name, e-mail address, internet service provider address, and location information (if available) of the person to which the communication identity is registered.

(b) Failure to timely provide the information upon request shall be a business offesnes with a fine of $1,000.

(c) An internet service provider or employee therof providing information under this Section is immune from any criminal, civil, or administrative liability in connection with providing the information, except for willful or wanton misconduct.
(d) For the purposes of this Section, “internet service provider” has the meaning provided in Section 2UU of the consumer Fraud and Deceptive Business Practices Act.

ARTICLE 26. DISORDERLY CONDUCT

§26-1. Elements of the Offense. (a) A person commits disorderly conduct when he knowingly:

(1) Does any act in such unreasonable manner as to alarm or disturb another and to provoke a breach of the peace; or

(2) Transmits or causes to be transmitted in any manner to the fire department of any city, town, village or fire protection district a false alarm of fire, knowing at the time of such transmission that there is no reasonable ground for believing that such fire exists; or

(3) Transmits or causes to be transmitted in any manner to another a false alarm to the effect that a bomb or other explosive of any nature or a container holding poison gas, a deadly biological

or chemical contaminant, or radioactive substance is concealed in such place that its explosion or release would endanger human life, knowing at the time of such transmission that there is no reasonable ground for believing that such bomb, explosive or a container holding poison gas, a deadly biological or chemical contaminant, or radioactive substance is concealed in such place; or

(4) Transmits or causes to be transmitted in any manner to any peace officer, public officer or public employee a report to the effect that an offense will be committed, is being committed, or has been committed, knowing at the time of such transmission that there is no reasonable ground for believing that such an offense will be committed, is being committed, or has been committed; or

(5) Enters upon the property of another and for a lewd or unlawful purpose deliberately looks into a dwelling on the property through any window or other opening in it; or

(6) While acting as a collection agency as defined in the "Collection Agency Act" or as an employee of such collection agency, and while attempting to collect an alleged debt, makes a telephone call to the alleged debtor which is designed to harass, annoy or intimidate the alleged debtor; or

(7) Transmits or causes to be transmitted a false report to the Department of Children and Family Services under Section 4 of the "Abused and Neglected Child Reporting Act"; or

(8) Transmits or causes to be transmitted a false report to the Department of Public Health under the Nursing Home Care Act, the MR/DD Community Care Act or the MC/DD Act; or

(9) Transmits or causes to be transmitted in any manner to the police department or fire department of any municipality or fire protection district, or any privately owned and operated ambulance service, a false request for an ambulance, emergency medical technician-ambulance or emergency medical technician-paramedic knowing at the time there is no reasonable ground for believing that such assistance is required; or

(10) Transmits or causes to be transmitted a false report under Article II of "An Act in relation to victims of violence and abuse", approved September 16, 1984, as amended; or

(11) Transmits or causes to be transmitted a false report to any public safety agency without the reasonable grounds necessary to believe that transmitting such a report is necessary for the safety and welfare of the public; or

(12) Calls the number "911" for the purpose of making or transmitting a false alarm or complaint and reporting information when, at the time the call or transmission is made, the person knows there is no reasonable ground for making the call or transmission and further knows that the call or transmission could result in the emergency response of any public safety agency; or

(13) Transmits or causes to be transmitted a threat of destruction of a school building or school property, or a threat of violence, death, or bodily harm directed against persons at a school, school function, or school event, whether or not school is in session.

(b) Sentence. A violation of subsection (a)(1) of this Section is a Class C misdemeanor. A violation of subsection (a)(5) or (a)(11) of this Section is a Class A misdemeanor. A violation of subsection (a)(8) or (a)(10) of this Section is a Class B misdemeanor. A violation of subsection (a)(2), (a)(4), (a)(7), (a)(9), (a)(12), or (a)(13) of this Section is a Class 4 felony. A violation of subsection (a)(3) of this Section is a Class 3 felony, for which a fine of not less than $3,000 and no more than $10,000 shall be assessed in addition to any other penalty imposed.

A violation of subsection (a)(6) of this Section is a Business Offense and shall be punished by a fine not to exceed $3,000. A second or subsequent violation of subsection (a)(7) or (a)(11) of this Section is a Class 4 felony. A third or subsequent violation of subsection (a)(5) of this Section is a Class 4 felony.

(c) In addition to any other sentence that may be imposed, a court shall order any person convicted of disorderly conduct to perform community service for not less than 30 and not more than 120 hours, if community service is available in the jurisdiction and is funded and approved by the county board of the county where the offense was committed. In addition, whenever any person is placed on supervision for an alleged offense under this Section, the supervision shall be conditioned upon the performance of the community service.

This subsection does not apply when the court imposes a sentence of incarceration.

(d) In addition to any other sentence that may be imposed, the court shall order any person convicted of disorderly conduct under paragraph (3) of subsection (a) involving a false alarm of a threat that a bomb or explosive device has been placed in a school to reimburse the unit of government that employs the emergency response officer or officers that were dispatched to the school for the cost of the search for a bomb or explosive device. For the purposes of this Section, "emergency response" means any incident requiring a response by a police officer, a firefighter, a State Fire Marshal employee, or an ambulance.

(e) In addition to any other sentence that may be imposed, the court shall order any person convicted of disorderly conduct under paragraph (6) of subsection (a) to reimburse the public agency for the reasonable costs of the emergency response by the public agency up to $10,000. If the court determines that the person convicted of disorderly conduct under paragraph (6) of subsection (a) is indigent, the provisions of this subsection (e) do not apply.

(f) For the purposes of this Section, "emergency response" means any condition that results in, or could result in, the response of a public official in an authorized emergency vehicle, any condition that jeopardizes or could jeopardize public safety and results in, or could result in, the evacuation of any area, building, structure, vehicle, or of any other place that any person may enter, or any incident requiring a response by a police officer, a firefighter, a State Fire Marshal employee, or an ambulance.

Sec. 26-1.1. False report of theft and other losses. (a) A person who knowingly makes a false report of a theft, destruction, damage or conversion of any property to a law enforcement agency or other governmental agency with the intent to defraud an insurer is guilty of a Class A misdemeanor.

(b) A person convicted of a violation of this Section a second or subsequent time is guilty of a Class 4 felony.

Commentary – Disorderly Conduct

Elements; words alone. Section 26-1 encompasses a variety of conduct that can be criminalized as "disorderly". the common crime of disorderly conduct is knowing, unreasonable action by the offender that alarms and disturbs the victim and tends to provoke a breach of the peace (Section 26-1(a)(1)), but there are several sections of the statute that focus on false alarms or reports to the public, to police or fire departments or other agencies Sections 26-1(a)(2) – (4) and (6)-(12). Creating false emergency or other highly emotional scenarios certainly alarms and disturbs employees of the agencies and people who are affected by the false information. Calling in a threat of violence at a school (Section 26-1(a)(13) would have the same effect. Window peeping (Section 26-1(a)(5) is also disorderly conduct. However, words alone are typically insufficient to establish disorderly conduct. They must rise to the level of "fighting words" so that the notion of physical threat or action is clearly involved. See *People v. Redwood* 335 Ill.App.3d 189, 780 N.E.2d 760 (Ill. App. Ct. 4th Dist. 2002)(insulting words, including name-calling are not necessarily "fighting words" and may be insufficient for the charge of disorderly conduct.)

False bomb threat. In *People v. Barron* 348 Ill.App.3d 149, 808 N.E.2d 1051 (Ill. App. Ct. 1st Dist. 2004), the defendant told ticket agents at Midway airport that he had a bomb in his shoe. The defendant appeared to be under the influence of alcohol, waived his arms and repeated his "bomb in my shoe" comment when the agent told him not to joke about it. A nearby agent also told the defendant not to joke about such things, but the defendant responded by laughing and saying that the agents should check his bag because they did not know what was in it. The police were notified and the defendant and his bags were searched. There was no bomb but the defendant admitted to the police that he had told the agents that he was carrying a bomb. The defendant was convicted of felony disorderly conduct (Section 26-1(a)(3)) and appealed claiming that the evidence clearly demonstrated that he was just joking and that his remarks were taken by the agents as a joke. In affirming the conviction, the appellate court was not amused:

> In line with our interpretation of section 26-1(a)(3), an individual may be found guilty of felony disorderly conduct upon transmission of a false alarm, regardless of the intention of the speaker or the effect the words have upon the person receiving them. Just as the false cry of "fire" in a crowded theater may cause panic and harm simply by its utterance, a false claim that a bomb or container holding a chemical, biological or radioactive agent is present in an airport may cause alarm and mass disruption. In light of our nation's recent history, this fact could not be more clear, nor the purpose behind section 26-1(a)(3) more necessary.
>
> *People v. Barron* 384 Ill.App.3d at 115, 808 N.E.2d at 1055.

Window peeping. In *People v. Rizzo* 362 Ill.App.3d 444, 842 N.E.2d 727 (Ill. App. Ct. 2nd Dist. 2005), the victim was sitting in her living room late at night and observed a flash at her bay window. When she saw it again, she went over and saw the defendant (who was a man with one arm), whose pants were unzipped, making movements with his hand. Physical evidence at the scene was consistent with her observations. The defendant's conviction for disorderly conduct pursuant to 26-1(a)(5) was affirmed.

False DCFS hotline report. In *People v. Marcotte* 337 Ill.App.3d 798, 787 N.E.2d 369 (Ill. App. Ct. 3rd Dist. 2005), the Department of Children and Family Services hotline received a call claiming that an act of sexual abuse to a five year old child had occurred at a daycare center in Bourbonnais, Illinois. The child was interviewed by police and it was determined the report was false. The child's mother told police that the defendant (who had in-home daycare) had told her of a DCFS hotline call about the Bourbonnais daycare center. A police officer talked to defendant who denied making the hotline call. The officer talked to the defendant by phone, had a lengthy conversation with her, in which he told her that he had checked the phone records and the call had come from her home. This was untrue, since 1-800 numbers do not appear on telephone records; however, the defendant ended the conversation admitting that she placed the DCFS sex abuse hotline call. at trial the defendant denied making the call and said that she only told the officer that she made the call to get him off the telephone after 1 ½ hours. The defendant's conviction of disorderly conduct for making a false report of abuse to DCFS under Section 26-1(a)(7) was affirmed.

§26-2. Interference with Emergency Communication. (a) A person commits the offense of interference with emergency communication when he knowingly, intentionally and without lawful justification interrupts, disrupts, impedes, or otherwise interferes with the transmission of a communication over a citizens band radio channel, the purpose of which communication is to inform or inquire about an emergency.

(b) For the purpose of this Section, "emergency" means a condition or circumstance in which an individual is or is reasonably believed by the person transmitting the communication to be in imminent danger of serious bodily injury or in which property is or is reasonably believed by the person transmitting the communication to be in imminent danger of damage or destruction.

(c) Sentence. (1) Interference with emergency communication is a Class B misdemeanor, except as otherwise provided in paragraph (2).

(2) Interference with emergency communication, where serious bodily injury or property loss in excess of $1,000 results, is a Class A misdemeanor.

§26-3. Use of a facsimile machine in unsolicited advertising or fund-raising.
(a) Definitions:

(1) "Facsimile machine" means a device which is capable of sending or receiving facsimiles of documents through connection with a telecommunications network.
(2) "Person" means an individual, public or private corporation, unit of government, partnership or unincorporated association.

(b) No person shall knowingly use a facsimile machine to send or cause to be sent to another person a facsimile of a document containing unsolicited advertising or fund-raising material, except to a person which the sender knows or under all of the circumstances reasonably believes has given the sender permission, either on a case by case or continuing basis, for the sending of such material.

(c) Sentence. Any person who violates subsection (b) is guilty of a petty offense and shall be fined an amount not to exceed $500.

§26-4. Unauthorized video recording and live video transmission. (a) It is unlawful for any person to knowingly make a video record or transmit live video of another person without that person's consent in a restroom, tanning bed, tanning salon, locker room, changing room, or hotel bedroom.

(a-5) It is unlawful for any person to knowingly make a video record or transmit live video of another person in that other person's residence without that person's consent.

(a-6) It is unlawful for any person to knowingly make a video record or transmit live video of another person in that other person's residence without that person's consent when the recording or transmission is made outside that person's residence by use of an audio or video device that records or transmits from a remote location.

(a-10) It is unlawful for any person to knowingly make a video record or transmit live video of another person under or through the clothing worn by that other person for the purpose of viewing the body of or the undergarments worn by that other person without that person's consent.

(a-15) It is unlawful for any person to place or cause to be placed a device that makes a video record or transmits a live video in a restroom, tanning bed, tanning salon, locker room, changing room, or hotel bedroom with the intent to make a video record or transmit live video of another person without that person's consent.

(a-20) It is unlawful for any person to place or cause to be placed a device that makes a video record or transmits a live video with the intent to make a video record or transmit live video of another person in that other person's residence without that person's consent.

(a-25) It is unlawful for any person to, by any means, knowingly disseminate, or permit to be disseminated, a video record or live video that he or she knows to have been made or transmitted in violation of (a), (a-5), (a-6), (a-10), (a-15), or (a-20).

(b) Exemptions. The following activities shall be exempt from the provisions of this Section:

(1) The making of a video record or transmission of live video by law enforcement

officers pursuant to a criminal investigation, which is otherwise lawful;

(2) The making of a video record or transmission of live video by correctional officials for security reasons or for investigation of alleged misconduct involving a person committed to the Department of Corrections.

(3) The making of a video record or transmission of live video in a locker room by a reporter or news medium, as those terms are defined in Section 8-902 of the Code of Civil Procedure, where the reporter or news medium has been granted access to the locker room by an appropriate authority for the purpose of conducting interviews.

(c) The provisions of this Section do not apply to any sound recording or transmission of an oral conversation made as the result of the making of a video record or transmission of live video, and to which Article 14 of this Code applies.

(d) Sentence.

(1) A violation of subsection (a-10), (a-15), or (a-20) is a Class A misdemeanor.

(2) A violation of subsection (a), (a-5), or (a-6) is a Class 4 felony.

(3) A violation of subsection (a-25) is a Class 3 felony.

(4) A violation of subsection (a), (a-5), (a-6), (a-10), (a-15) or (a-20) is a Class 3 felony if the victim is a person under 18 years of age or if the violation is committed by an individual who is required to register as a sex offender under the Sex Offender Registration Act.

(5) A violation of subsection (a-25) is a Class 2 felony if the victim is a person under 18 years of age or if the violation is committed by an individual who is required to register as a sex offender under the Sex Offender Registration Act.

(e) For purposes of this Section:

(1) "Residence" includes a rental dwelling, but does not include stairwells, corridors, laundry facilities, or additional areas in which the general public has access.

(2) "Video record" means and includes any videotape, photograph, film, or other electronic or digital recording of a still or moving visual image; and "live video" means and includes any real-time or contemporaneous electronic or digital transmission of a still or moving visual image.

§26-5. Dog fighting. (For other provisions that may apply to dog fighting, see the Humane Care for Animals Act. For provisions similar to this Section that apply to animals other than dogs, see in particular Section 4.01 of the Humane Care for Animals Act.)

(a) No person may own, capture, breed, train, or lease any dog which he or she knows is intended for use in any show, exhibition, program, or other activity featuring or otherwise involving a fight between the dog and any other animal or human, or the intentional killing of any dog for the purpose of sport, wagering, or entertainment.

(b) No person may promote, conduct, carry on, advertise, collect money for or in any other manner assist or aid in the presentation for purposes of sport, wagering, or entertainment of any show, exhibition, program, or other activity involving a fight between 2 or more dogs or any dog and human, or the intentional killing of any dog.

(c) No person may sell or offer for sale, ship, transport, or otherwise move, or deliver or receive any dog which he or she knows has been captured, bred, or trained, or will be used, to fight another dog or human or be intentionally killed for purposes of sport, wagering, or entertainment.

(c-5) No person may solicit a minor to violate this Section.

(d) No person may manufacture for sale, shipment, transportation, or delivery any device or equipment which he or she knows or should know is intended for use in any show, exhibition, program, or other activity featuring or otherwise involving a fight between 2 or more dogs, or any human and dog, or the intentional killing of any dog for purposes of sport, wagering, or entertainment.

(e) No person may own, possess, sell or offer for sale, ship, transport, or otherwise move any equipment or device which he or she knows or should know is intended for use in connection with any show, exhibition, program, or activity featuring or otherwise involving a fight between 2 or more dogs, or any dog and human, or the intentional killing of any dog for purposes of sport, wagering or entertainment.

(f) No person may knowingly make available any site, structure, or facility, whether enclosed or not, that he or she knows is intended to be used for the purpose of conducting any show, exhibition, program, or other activity involving a fight between 2 or more dogs, or any dog and human, or the intentional killing of any dog or knowingly manufacture, distribute, or deliver fittings to be used in a fight between 2 or more dogs or a dog and human.

(g) No person may knowingly attend or otherwise patronize any show, exhibition, program, or other activity featuring or otherwise involving a fight between 2 or more dogs, or any dog and human, or the intentional killing of any dog for purposes of sport, wagering, or entertainment.

(h) No person may tie or attach or fasten any live animal to any machine or device propelled by any power for the purpose of causing the animal to be pursued by a dog or dogs. This subsection (h) applies only when the dog is intended to be used in a dog fight.

(i) Penalties for violations of this Section shall be as follows:

(1) Any person convicted of violating subsection (a), (b), (c), or (h) of this Section is guilty of a Class 4 felony for a first violation and a Class 3 felony for a second or subsequent violation, and may be fined an amount not to exceed $50,000.

(1.5) A person who knowingly owns a dog for fighting purposes or for producing a fight between 2 or more dogs or a dog and human or who knowingly offers for sale or sells a dog bred for fighting is guilty of a Class 3 felony and may be fined an amount not to exceed $50,000, if the dog participates in a dogfight and any of the following factors is present:

(i) the dogfight is performed in the presence of a person under 18 years of age;
(ii) the dogfight is performed for the purpose of or in the presence of illegal wagering activity; or
(iii) the dogfight is performed in furtherance of streetgang related activity as defined in Section 10 of the Illinois Streetgang Terrorism Omnibus Prevention Act.

(1.7) A person convicted of violating subsection (c-5) of this Section is guilty of a Class 4 felony.

(2) Any person convicted of violating subsection (d) or (e) of this Section is guilty of a Class 4 felony for a first violation. A second or subsequent violation of subsection (d) or (e) of this Section is a Class 3 felony.

(2.5) Any person convicted of violating subsection (f) of this Section is guilty of a Class 4 felony. Any person convicted of violating subsection (f) of this Section in which the site, structure, or facility made available to violate subsection (f) is located within 1,000 feet of a school, public park, playground, child care institution, day care center, part day child care facility, day care home, group day care home, or a facility providing programs or services exclusively directed toward persons under 18 years of age is guilty of a Class 3 felony for a first violation and a Class 2 felony for a second or subsequent violation.

(3) Any person convicted of violating subsection (g) of this Section is guilty of a Class 4 felony for a first violation. A second or subsequent violation of subsection (g) of this Section is a Class 3 felony. If a person under 13 years of age is present at any show, exhibition, program, or other activity prohibited in

subsection (g), the parent, legal guardian, or other person who is 18 years of age or older who brings that person under 13 years of age to that show, exhibition, program, or other activity is guilty of a Class 3 felony for a first violation and a Class 2 felony for a second or subsequent violation.

(i-5) A person who commits a felony violation of this Section is subject to the property forfeiture provisions set forth in Article 124B of the Code of Criminal Procedure of 1963.

(j) Any dog or equipment involved in a violation of this Section shall be immediately seized and impounded under Section 12 of the Humane Care for Animals Act when located at any show, exhibition, program, or other activity featuring or otherwise involving a dog fight for the purposes of sport, wagering, or entertainment.

(k) Any vehicle or conveyance other than a common carrier that is used in violation of this Section shall be seized, held, and offered for sale at public auction by the sheriff's department of the proper jurisdiction, and the proceeds from the sale shall be remitted to the general fund of the county where the violation took place.

(l) Any veterinarian in this State who is presented with a dog for treatment of injuries or wounds resulting from fighting where there is a reasonable possibility that the dog was engaged in or utilized for a fighting event for the purposes of sport, wagering, or entertainment shall file a report with the Department of Agriculture and cooperate by furnishing the owners' names, dates, and descriptions of the dog or dogs involved. Any veterinarian who in good faith complies with the requirements of this subsection has immunity from any liability, civil, criminal, or otherwise, that may result from his or her actions. For the purposes of any proceedings, civil or criminal, the good faith of the veterinarian shall be rebuttably presumed.

(m) In addition to any other penalty provided by law, upon conviction for violating this Section, the court may order that the convicted person and persons dwelling in the same household as the convicted person who conspired, aided, or abetted in the unlawful act that was the basis of the conviction, or who knew or should have known of the unlawful act, may not own, harbor, or have custody or control of any dog or other animal for a period of time that the court deems reasonable.

(n) A violation of subsection (a) of this Section may be inferred from evidence that the accused possessed any device or equipment described in subsection (d), (e), or (h) of this Section, and also possessed any dog.

(o) When no longer required for investigations or court proceedings relating to the events described or depicted therein, evidence relating to convictions for violations of this Section shall be retained and made available for use in training peace officers in detecting and identifying violations of this Section. Such evidence shall be made available upon request to other law enforcement agencies and to schools certified under the Illinois Police Training Act.

(p) For the purposes of this Section, "school" has the meaning ascribed to it in Section 11-9.3 of this Code; and "public park", "playground", "child care institution", "day care center", "part day child care facility", "day care home", "group day care home", and "facility providing programs or services exclusively directed toward persons under 18 years of age" have the meanings ascribed to them in Section 11-9.4 of this Code.

§26-6. Disorderly conduct at a funeral or memorial service. (a) The General Assembly finds and declares that due to the unique nature of funeral and memorial services and the heightened opportunity for extreme emotional distress on such occasions, the purpose of this Section is to protect the privacy and ability to mourn of grieving families directly before, during, and after a funeral or memorial service.

(b) For purposes of this Section:

(1) "Funeral" means the ceremonies, rituals, processions, and memorial services held at a funeral site in connection with the burial, cremation, or memorial of a deceased person.

(2) "Funeral site" means a church, synagogue, mosque, funeral home, mortuary, cemetery, gravesite, mausoleum, or other place at which a funeral is conducted or is scheduled to be conducted within the next 30 minutes or has been conducted within the last 30 minutes.

(c) A person commits the offense of disorderly conduct at a funeral or memorial service when he or she:

(1) engages, with knowledge of the existence of a funeral site, in any loud singing, playing of music, chanting, whistling, yelling, or noisemaking with, or without, noise amplification including, but not limited to, bullhorns, auto horns, and microphones within 300 feet of any ingress or egress of that funeral site, where the volume of such singing, music, chanting, whistling, yelling, or noisemaking is likely to be audible at and disturbing to the funeral site;

(2) displays, with knowledge of the existence of a funeral site and within 300 feet of any ingress or egress of that funeral site, any visual images that convey fighting words or actual or veiled threats against any other person; or

(3) with knowledge of the existence of a funeral site, knowingly obstructs, hinders, impedes, or blocks another person's entry to or exit from that funeral site or a facility containing that funeral site, except that the owner or occupant of property may take lawful actions to exclude others from that property.

(d) Disorderly conduct at a funeral or memorial service is a Class C misdemeanor. A second or subsequent violation is a Class 4 felony.

(e) If any clause, sentence, section, provision, or part of this Section or the application thereof to any person or circumstance is adjudged to be unconstitutional, the remainder of this Section or its application to persons or circumstances other than those to which it is held invalid, is not affected thereby.

ARTICLE 28. GAMBLING AND RELATED OFFENSES

§28-1. Gambling. (a) A person commits gambling when he:

(1) Plays a game of chance or skill for money or other thing of value, unless excepted in subsection (b) of this Section; or

(2) Makes a wager upon the result of any game, contest, or any political nomination, appointment or election; or

(3) Operates, keeps, owns, uses, purchases, exhibits, rents, sells, bargains for the sale or lease of, manufactures or distributes any gambling device; or

(4) Contracts to have or give himself or another the option to buy or sell, or contracts to buy or sell, at a future time, any grain or other commodity whatsoever, or any stock or security of any company, where it is at the time of making such contract intended by both parties thereto that the contract to buy or sell, or the option, whenever exercised, or the contract resulting therefrom, shall be settled, not by the receipt or delivery of such property, but by the payment only of differences in prices thereof; however, the issuance, purchase, sale, exercise, endorsement or guarantee, by or through a person registered with the Secretary of State pursuant to Section 8 of the Illinois Securities Law of 1953, or by or through a person exempt from such registration under said Section 8, of a put, call, or other option to buy or sell securities which have been registered with the Secretary of State or which are exempt from such registration under Section 3 of the Illinois Securities Law of 1953 is not gambling within the meaning of this paragraph (4); or

(5) Knowingly owns or possesses any book, instrument or apparatus by means of which bets or wagers have been, or are, recorded or registered, or knowingly possesses any money which he has received in the course of a bet or wager; or

(6) Sells pools upon the result of any game or contest of skill or chance, political nomination, appointment or election; or

(7) Sets up or promotes any lottery or sells, offers to sell or transfers any ticket or share for any lottery; or

(8) Sets up or promotes any policy game or sells, offers to sell or knowingly possesses or transfers any policy ticket, slip, record, document or other similar device; or

(9) Knowingly drafts, prints or publishes any lottery ticket or share, or any policy ticket, slip, record, document or similar device, except for such activity related to lotteries, bingo games and raffles authorized by and conducted in accordance with the laws of Illinois or any other state or foreign government; or

(10) Knowingly advertises any lottery or policy game, except for such activity related to lotteries, bingo games and raffles authorized by and conducted in accordance with the laws of Illinois or any other state; or

(11) Knowingly transmits information as to wagers, betting odds, or changes in betting odds by telephone, telegraph, radio, semaphore or similar means; or knowingly installs or maintains equipment for the transmission or receipt of such information; except that nothing in this subdivision (11) prohibits transmission or receipt of such information for use in news reporting of sporting events or contests; or

(12) Knowingly establishes, maintains, or operates an Internet site that permits a person to play a game of chance or skill for money or other thing of value by means of the Internet or to make a wager upon the result of any game, contest, political nomination, appointment, or election by means of the Internet. This item (12) does not apply to activities referenced in items (6) and (6.1) of subsection (b) of this Section.

(b) Participants in any of the following activities shall not be convicted of gambling therefore:

(1) Agreements to compensate for loss caused by the happening of chance including without limitation contracts of indemnity or guaranty and life or health or accident insurance.

(2) Offers of prizes, award or compensation to the actual contestants in any bona fide contest for the determination of skill, speed, strength or endurance or to the owners of animals or vehicles entered in such contest.

(3) Pari-mutuel betting as authorized by the law of this State.

(4) Manufacture of gambling devices, including the acquisition of essential parts therefore and the assembly thereof, for transportation in interstate or foreign commerce to any place outside this State when such transportation is not prohibited by any applicable Federal law; or the manufacture, distribution, or possession of video gaming terminals, as defined in the Video Gaming Act, by manufacturers, distributors, and terminal operators licensed to do so under the Video Gaming Act.

(5) The game commonly known as “bingo”, when conducted in accordance with the Bingo License and Tax Act.

(6) Lotteries when conducted by the State of Illinois in accordance with the Illinois Lottery Law. This exemption includes any activity conducted by the Department of Revenue to sell lottery tickets pursuant to the provisions of the Illinois Lottery Law and its rules.

(6.1) The purchase of lottery tickets through the Internet for a lottery conducted by the State of Illinois under the program established in Section 7.12 of the Illinois Lottery Law.

(7) Possession of an antique slot machine that is neither used nor intended to be used in the operation or promotion of any unlawful gambling activity or enterprise. For the purpose of this subparagraph (b)(7), an antique slot machine is one manufactured 25 years ago or earlier.

(8) Raffles when conducted in accordance with the Raffles Act.

(9) Charitable games when conducted in accordance with the Charitable Games Act.

(10) Pull tabs and jar games when conducted under the Illinois Pull Tabs and Jar Games Act.

(11) Gambling games conducted on riverboats when authorized by the Riverboat Gambling Act.

(12) Video gaming terminal games at a licensed establishment, licensed truck stop establishment, licensed fraternal establishment, or licensed veterans establishment when conducted in accordance with the Video Gaming Act.

(13) Games of skill or chance where money or other things of value can be won but no payment or purchase is required to participate.

(c) Sentence. Gambling under subsection (a)(1) or (a)(2) of this Section is a Class A misdemeanor. Gambling under any of subsections (a)(3) through (a)(11) of this Section is a Class A misdemeanor. A second or subsequent conviction under any of subsections (a)(3) through (a)(11), is a Class 4 felony. Gambling under subsection (a)(12) of this Section is a Class A misdemeanor. A second or subsequent conviction under subsection (a)(12) is a Class 4 felony.

(d) Circumstantial evidence. In prosecutions under subsection (a)(1) through (a)(12) of this Section circumstantial evidence shall have the same validity and weight as in any criminal prosecution.

§28-1.1. Syndicated gambling. (a) Declaration of Purpose. Recognizing the close relationship between professional gambling and other organized crime, it is declared to be the policy of the legislature to restrain persons from engaging in the business of gambling for profit in this State. This Section shall be liberally construed and administered with a view to carrying out this policy.

(b) A person commits syndicated gambling when he operates a "policy game" or engages in the business of bookmaking.

(c) A person "operates a policy game" when he knowingly uses any premises or property for the purpose of receiving or knowingly does receive from what is commonly called "policy":

(1) money from a person other than the better or player whose bets or plays are represented by such money; or

(2) written "policy game" records, made or used over any period of time, from a person other than the better or player whose bets or plays are represented by such written record.

(d) A person engages in bookmaking when he receives or accepts more than five bets or wagers upon the result of any trials or contests of skill, speed or power of endurance or upon any lot, chance, casualty, unknown or contingent event whatsoever, which bets or wagers shall be of such size that the total of the amounts of money paid or promised to be paid to such bookmaker on account thereof shall exceed $2,000. Bookmaking is the receiving or accepting of such bets or wagers regardless of the form or manner in which the bookmaker records them.

(e) Participants in any of the following activities shall not be convicted of syndicated gambling:

(1) Agreements to compensate for loss caused by the happening of chance including without limitation contracts of indemnity or guaranty and life or health or accident insurance; and

(2) Offers of prizes, award or compensation to the actual contestants in any bona fide contest for the determination of skill, speed, strength or endurance or to the owners of animals or vehicles entered in such contest; and

(3) Pari-mutuel betting as authorized by law of this State; and

(4) Manufacture of gambling devices, including the acquisition of essential parts therefore and

the assembly thereof, for transportation in interstate or foreign commerce to any place outside this State when such transportation is not prohibited by any applicable Federal law; and

(5) Raffles when conducted in accordance with the Raffles Act; and

(6) Gambling games conducted on riverboats when authorized by the Riverboat Gambling Act; and

(7) Video gaming terminal games at a licensed establishment, licensed truck stop establishment, licensed fraternal establishment, or licensed veterans establishment when conducted in accordance with the Video Gaming Act.

(8) Savings promotion raffles authorized under Section 5g of the Illinois Banking Act, Section 7008 of the Savings Bank Act, Section 42.7 of the Illinois Credit Union Act, Section 5136B of the National Bank Act (12 U.S.C. 25a), or Section 4 of the Home Owners' Loan Act (12 U.S.C. 1463).

(f) Sentence. Syndicated gambling is a Class 3 felony.

§28-2. Definitions. (a) A "gambling device" is any clock, tape machine, slot machine or other machines or device for the reception of money or other thing of value on chance or skill or upon the action of which money or other thing of value is staked, hazarded, bet, won or lost; or any mechanism, furniture, fixture, equipment or other device designed primarily for use in a gambling place. A "gambling device" does not include:

(1) A coin-in-the-slot operated mechanical device played for amusement which rewards the player with the right to replay such mechanical device, which device is so constructed or devised as to make such result of the operation thereof depend in part upon the skill of the player and which returns to the player thereof no money, property or right to receive money or property.

(2) Vending machines by which full and adequate return is made for the money invested and in which there is no element of chance or hazard.

(3) A crane game. For the purposes of this paragraph (3), a "crane game" is an amusement device involving skill, if it rewards the player exclusively with merchandise contained within the amusement device proper and limited to toys, novelties and prizes other than currency, each having a wholesale value which is not more than $25.

(4) A redemption machine. For the purposes of this paragraph (4), a "redemption machine" is a single-player or multi-player amusement device involving a game, the object of which is throwing, rolling, bowling, shooting, placing, or propelling a ball or other object into, upon, or against a hole or other target, provided that all of the following conditions are met:

(A) The outcome of the game is predominantly determined by the skill of the player.
(B) The award of the prize is based solely upon the player's achieving the object of the game or otherwise upon the player's score.
(C) Only merchandise prizes are awarded.
(D) The wholesale value of prizes awarded in lieu of tickets or tokens for single play of the device does not exceed $25.
(E) The redemption value of tickets, tokens, and other representations of value, which may be accumulated by players to redeem prizes of greater value, does not exceed the amount charged for a single play of the device.

(a-5) "Internet" means an interactive computer service or system or an information service, system, or access software provider that provides or enables computer access by multiple users to a computer server, and includes, but is not limited to, an information service, system, or access software provider that provides access to a network system commonly known as the Internet, or any comparable system or service and also includes, but is not limited to, a World Wide Web page, newsgroup, message board, mailing list, or chat area on any interactive computer service or system or other online service.

(a-6) "Access" and "computer" have the meanings ascribed to them in Section 16D-2 of this Code.

(b) A "lottery" is any scheme or procedure whereby one or more prizes are distributed by chance among persons who have paid or promised consideration for a chance to win such prizes, whether such scheme or procedure is called a lottery, raffle, gift, sale or some other name, excluding savings promotion raffles authorized under Section 5g of the Illinois Banking Act, Section 7008 of the Savings Bank Act, Section 42.7 of the Illinois Credit Union Act, Section 5136B of the National Bank Act (12 U.S.C. 25a), or Section 4 of the Home Owners' Loan Act(12 U.S.C. 1463).

(c) A "policy game" is any scheme or procedure whereby a person promises or guarantees by any instrument, bill, certificate, writing, token or other device that any particular number, character, ticket or certificate shall in the event of any contingency in the nature of a lottery entitle the purchaser or holder to receive money, property or evidence of debt.

§28-3. Keeping a Gambling Place.
A "gambling place" is any real estate, vehicle, boat or any other property whatsoever used for the purposes of gambling other than gambling conducted in the manner authorized by the Riverboat Gambling Act or the Video Gaming Act. Any person who knowingly permits any premises or property owned or occupied by him or under his control to be used as a gambling place commits a Class A misdemeanor. Each subsequent offense is a Class 4 felony. When any premises is determined by the circuit court to be a gambling place:

(a) Such premises is a public nuisance and may be proceeded against as such, and

(b) All licenses, permits or certificates issued by the State of Illinois or any subdivision or public agency thereof authorizing the serving of food or liquor on such premises shall be void; and no license, permit or certificate so cancelled shall be reissued for such premises for a period of 60 days thereafter; nor shall any person convicted of keeping a gambling place be reissued such license for one year from his conviction and, after a second conviction of keeping a gambling place, any such person shall not be reissued such license, and

(c) Such premises of any person who knowingly permits thereon a violation of any Section of this Article shall be held liable for, and may be sold to pay any unsatisfied judgment that may be recovered and any unsatisfied fine that may be levied under any Section of this Article.

§28-4. Registration of Federal Gambling Stamps. (a) Every person who has purchased a Federal Wagering Occupational Tax Stamp, as required by the United States under the applicable provisions of the Internal Revenue Code, or a Federal Gaming Device Tax Stamp, as required by the United States under the applicable provisions of the Internal Revenue Code, shall register forthwith such stamp or stamps with the county clerk's office in which he resides and the county clerk's office of each and every county in which he conducts any business. A violation of this Section is a Class B misdemeanor. A subsequent violation is a Class A misdemeanor.

(b) To register a stamp as required by this Section, each individual stamp purchaser and each member of a firm or association which is a stamp purchaser and, if such purchaser is corporate, the registered agent of the purchasing corporation shall deliver the stamp to the county clerk for inspection and shall under oath or affirmation complete and sign a registration form which shall state the full name and residence and business address of each purchaser and of each member of a purchasing firm or association and of each person employed or engaged in gambling on behalf of such purchaser, shall state the registered agent and registered address of a corporate purchaser, shall state each place where gambling is to be performed by or on behalf of the purchaser, and shall state the duration of validity of the stamp and the federal registration number and tax return number thereof. Any false statement in the registration form is material and is evidence of perjury.

(c) Within 3 days after such registration the county clerk shall by registered mail forward notice of such registration and a duplicate copy of each registration form to the Attorney General of this State, to the Chairman of the Illinois Liquor Control Commission, to the State's Attorney and Sheriff of each county wherein the stamp is registered, and to the principal official of the department of police of each city, village and incorporated town in this State wherein the stamp is registered or wherein the registrant maintains a business address.

§28-5. Seizure of gambling devices and gambling funds. (a) Every device designed for gambling which is incapable of lawful use or every device used unlawfully for gambling shall be considered a "gambling device", and shall be subject to seizure, confiscation and destruction by the Department of State Police or by any municipal, or other local authority, within whose jurisdiction the same may be found. As used in this Section, a "gambling device" includes any slot machine, and includes any machine or device constructed for the reception of money or other thing of value and so constructed as to return, or to cause someone to return, on chance to the player thereof money, property or a right to receive money or property. With the exception of any device designed for gambling which is incapable of lawful use, no gambling device shall be forfeited or destroyed unless an individual with a property interest in said device knows of the unlawful use of the device.

(b) Every gambling device shall be seized and forfeited to the county wherein such seizure occurs. Any money or other thing of value integrally related to acts of gambling shall be seized and forfeited to the county wherein such seizure occurs.

(c) If, within 60 days after any seizure pursuant to subparagraph (b) of this Section, a person having any property interest in the seized property is charged with an offense, the court which renders judgment upon such charge shall, within 30 days after such judgment, conduct a forfeiture hearing to determine whether such property was a gambling device at the time of seizure. Such hearing shall be commenced by a written petition by the State, including material allegations of fact, the name and address of every person determined by the State to have any property interest in the seized property, a representation that written notice of the date, time and place of such hearing has been mailed to every such person by certified mail at least 10 days before such date, and a request for forfeiture. Every such person may appear as a party and present evidence at such hearing. The quantum of proof required shall be a preponderance of the evidence, and the burden of proof shall be on the State. If the court determines that the seized property was a gambling device at the time of seizure, an order of forfeiture and disposition of the seized property shall be entered: a gambling device shall be received by the State's Attorney, who shall effect its destruction, except that valuable parts thereof may be liquidated and the resultant money shall be deposited in the general fund of the county wherein such seizure occurred; money and other things of value shall be received by the State's Attorney and, upon liquidation, shall be deposited in the general fund of the county wherein such seizure occurred. However, in the event that a defendant raises the defense that the seized slot machine is an antique slot machine described in subparagraph (b)(7) of Section 28-1 of this Code and therefore he is exempt from the charge of a gambling activity participant, the seized antique slot machine shall not be destroyed or otherwise altered until a final determination is made by the Court as to whether it is such an antique slot machine. Upon a final determination by the Court of this question in favor of the defendant, such slot machine shall be immediately returned to the defendant. Such order of forfeiture and disposition shall, for the purposes of appeal, be a final order and judgment in a civil proceeding.

(d) If a seizure pursuant to subparagraph (b) of this Section is not followed by a charge pursuant to subparagraph (c) of this Section, or if the prosecution of such charge is permanently terminated or indefinitely discontinued without any judgment of conviction or acquittal (1) the State's Attorney shall commence an in rem proceeding for the forfeiture and destruction of a gambling device, or for the forfeiture and deposit in the general fund of the county of any seized money or other things of value, or both, in the circuit court and (2) any person having any property interest in such seized gambling device, money or other thing of value may commence separate civil proceedings in the manner provided by law.

(e) Any gambling device displayed for sale to a riverboat gambling operation or used to train occupational licensees of a riverboat gambling operation as authorized under the Riverboat Gambling Act is exempt from seizure under this Section.

(f) Any gambling equipment, devices and supplies provided by a licensed supplier in accordance with the Riverboat Gambling Act which are removed from the riverboat for repair are exempt from seizure under this Section.

§28-7. Gambling contracts void.
(a) All promises, notes, bills, bonds, covenants, contracts, agreements, judgments, mortgages, or other securities or conveyances made, given, granted, drawn, or entered into, or executed by any person whatsoever, where the whole or any part of the consideration thereof is for any money or thing of value, won or obtained in violation of any Section of this Article are null and void.
(b) Any obligation void under this Section may be set aside and vacated by any court of competent jurisdiction, upon a complaint filed for that purpose, by the person so granting, giving, entering into, or executing the same, or by his executors or administrators, or by any creditor, heir, legatee, purchaser or other person interested therein; or if a judgment, the same may be set aside on motion of any person stated above, on due notice thereof given.

(c) No assignment of any obligation void under this Section may in any manner affect the defense of the person giving, granting, drawing, entering into or executing such obligation, or the remedies of any person interested therein.

(d) This Section shall not prevent a licensed owner of a riverboat gambling operation from instituting a cause of action to collect any amount due and owing under an extension of credit to a riverboat gambling patron as authorized under the Riverboat Gambling Act.

§28-8. Gambling Losses Recoverable.
(a) Any person who by gambling shall lose to any other person, any sum of money or thing of value, amounting to the sum of $50 or more and shall pay or deliver the same or any part thereof, may sue for and recover the money or other thing of value, so lost and paid or delivered, in a civil action against the winner thereof, with costs, in the circuit court. No person who accepts from another person for transmission, and transmits, either in his own name or in the name of such other person, any order for any transaction to be made upon, or who executes any order given to him by another person, or who executes any transaction for his own account on, any regular board of trade or commercial, commodity or stock exchange, shall, under any circumstances, be deemed a "winner" of any moneys lost by such other person in or through any such transactions.

(b) If within 6 months, such person who under the terms of Subsection 28-8(a) is entitled to initiate action to recover his losses does not in fact pursue his remedy, any person may initiate a civil action against the winner. The court or the jury, as the case may be, shall determine the amount of the loss. After such determination, the court shall enter a judgment of triple the amount so determined.

§28-9. Prosecution by information
At the option of the prosecuting attorney any prosecution under this Article may be commenced by an information as defined in Section 102-12 of the Code of Criminal Procedure of 1963.

ARTICLE 29. BRIBERY IN CONTESTS

§29-1. Offering a bribe. (a) Any person who, with intent to influence any person participating in, officiating or connected with any professional or amateur athletic contest, sporting event or exhibition, gives, offers or promises any money, bribe or other thing of value or advantage to induce such participant, official or other person not to use his best efforts in connection with such contest, event or exhibition commits a Class 4 felony.

(b) Any person who, with the intent to influence the decision of any individual, offers or promises any money, bribe or other thing of value or advantage to induce such individual to attend, refrain from attending or continue to attend a particular public or private institution of secondary education or higher education for the purpose of participating or not participating in interscholastic athletic competition for such institution commits a Class A misdemeanor. This Section does not apply to the: (1) offering or awarding to an individual any type of scholarship, grant or other bona fide financial aid or employment; (2) offering of any type of financial assistance by such individual's family; or (3) offering of any item of de minimis value by such institution's authorities if such item is of the nature of an item that is commonly provided to any or all students or prospective students.

(c) Any person who gives any money, goods or other thing of value to an individual enrolled in an institution of higher education who participates in interscholastic competition and represents or attempts to represent such individual in future negotiations for employment with any professional sports team commits a Class A misdemeanor.

§29-2. Accepting a Bribe.
Any person participating in, officiating or connected with any professional or amateur athletic contest, sporting event or exhibition who accepts or agrees to accept any money, bribe or other thing of value or advantage with the intent, understanding or agreement that he will not use his best efforts in connection with such contest, event or exhibition commits a Class 4 felony.

§29-3. Failure to Report Offer of Bribe.
Any person participating, officiating or connected with any professional or amateur athletic contest, sporting event or exhibition who fails to report forthwith to his employer, the promoter of such contest, event or exhibition, a peace officer, or the local State's Attorney any offer or promise made to him in violation of Section 29-1 commits a Class A misdemeanor.

ARTICLE 29A. COMMERCIAL BRIBERY

§29A-1. Offering a bribe. a person commits commercial bribery when he confers, or offers or agrees to confer, any benefit upon any employee, agent or fiduciary without the consent of the latter's employer or principal, with intent to influence his conduct in relation to his employer's or principal's affairs.

§29A-2. Accepting a bribe. An employee, agent or fiduciary commits commercial bribe receiving when, without consent of his employer or principal, he solicits, accepts or agrees to accept any benefit from another person upon an agreement or understanding that such benefit will influence his conduct in relation to his employer's or principal's affairs.

§29A-3. Sentence. (a) If the benefit offered, conferred, or agreed to be conferred, solicited, accepted or agreed to be accepted is less than $500,000, commercial bribery or commercial bribe receiving is a Class A misdemeanor and the sentence shall include, but not be limited to, a fine not to exceed $5,000.

(b) If the benefit offered, conferred, or agreed to be conferred, solicited, accepted, or agreed to be accepted in violation of this Article is $500,000 or more, the offender is guilty of a Class 3 felony.

§29A-4. Corporate Crime Fund.
(a) In addition to any fines, penalties, and assessments otherwise authorized under this Code, any person convicted of a violation of this Article or Section 17-26 or 17-27 of this Code shall be assessed a penalty of not more than 3 times the value of all property involved in the criminal activity.

(b) The penalties assessed under subsection (a) shall be deposited into the Corporate Crime Fund, a special fund hereby created in the State treasury. Moneys in the Fund shall be used to make restitution to a person who has suffered property loss as a result of violations of this Article. The court may determine the reasonable amount, terms, and conditions of the restitution. In determining the amount and method of payment of restitution, the court shall take into account all financial resources of the defendant.

ARTICLE 29B. MONEY LAUNDERING

§29B-1. (a) A person commits the offense of money laundering:

(1) when, knowing that the property involved in a financial transaction represents the proceeds of some form of unlawful activity, he or she conducts or attempts to conduct such a financial transaction which in fact involves criminally derived property:

(A) with the intent to promote the carrying on of the unlawful activity from which the criminally derived property was obtained; or

(B) where he or she knows or reasonably should know that the financial transaction is designed in whole or in part:

(i) to conceal or disguise the nature, the location, the source, the ownership or the control of the criminally derived property; or

(ii) to avoid a transaction reporting requirement under State law; or

(1.5) when he or she transports, transmits, or transfers, or attempts to transport, transmit, or transfer a monetary instrument:

(A) with the intent to promote the carrying on of the unlawful activity from which the criminally derived property was obtained; or

(B) knowing, or having reason to know, that the financial transaction is designed in whole or in part:

(i) to conceal or disguise the nature, the location, the source, the ownership or the control of the criminally derived property; or

(ii) to avoid a transaction reporting requirement under State law; or

(2) when, with the intent to:

(A) promote the carrying on of a specified criminal activity as defined in this Article; or

(B) conceal or disguise the nature, location, source, ownership, or control of property believed to be the proceeds of a specified criminal activity as defined by subdivision (b)(6); or

(C) avoid a transaction reporting requirement under State law,

he or she conducts or attempts to conduct a financial transaction involving property he or she believes to be the proceeds of specified criminal activity as defined by subdivision (b)(6) or property used to conduct or facilitate specified criminal activity as defined by subdivision (b)(6).

(b) As used in this Section:

(0.5) "Knowing that the property involved in a financial transaction represents the proceeds of some form of unlawful activity" means that the person knew the property involved in the transaction represented proceeds from some form, though not necessarily which form, of activity that constitutes a felony under State, federal, or foreign law.

(1) "Financial transaction" means a purchase, sale, loan, pledge, gift, transfer, delivery or other disposition utilizing criminally derived property, and with respect to financial institutions, includes a deposit, withdrawal, transfer between accounts, exchange of currency, loan, extension of credit, purchase or sale of any stock, bond, certificate of deposit or other monetary instrument, use of safe deposit box, or any other payment, transfer or delivery by, through, or to a financial institution. For purposes of clause (a)(2) of this Section, the term "financial transaction" also means a transaction which without regard to whether the funds, monetary instruments, or real or personal property involved in the transaction are criminally derived, any transaction which in any way or degree: (1) involves the movement of funds by wire or any other means; (2) involves one or more monetary instruments; or (3) the transfer of title to any real or personal property. The receipt by an attorney of bona fide fees for the purpose of legal representation is not a financial transaction for purposes of this Section.

(2) "Financial institution" means any bank; saving and loan association; trust company; agency or branch of a foreign bank in the United States; currency exchange; credit union, mortgage banking institution; pawnbroker; loan or finance company; operator of a credit card system; issuer, redeemer or cashier of travelers checks, checks or money orders; dealer in precious metals, stones or jewels; broker or dealer in securities or commodities; investment banker; or investment company.

(3) "Monetary instrument" means United States coins and currency; coins and currency of a foreign country; travelers checks; personal checks, bank checks, and money orders; investment securities; bearer negotiable instruments; bearer investment securities; or bearer securities and certificates of stock in such form that title thereto passes upon delivery.

(4) "Criminally derived property" means: (A) any property, real or personal, constituting or derived from proceeds obtained, directly or indirectly, from activity that constitutes a felony under State, federal, or foreign law; or (B) any property represented to be property constituting or derived from proceeds obtained, directly or indirectly, from activity that constitutes a felony under State, federal, or foreign law.

(5) "Conduct" or "conducts" includes, in addition to its ordinary meaning, initiating, concluding, or participating in initiating or concluding a transaction.

(6) "Specified criminal activity" means any violation of Section 29D-15.1 and any violation of Article 29D of this Code.

(7) "Director" means the Director of State Police or his or her designated agents.

(8) "Department" means the Department of State Police of the State of Illinois or its successor agency.

(9) "Transaction reporting requirement under State law" means any violation as defined under the Currency Reporting Act.

(c) Sentence.

(1) Laundering of criminally derived property of a value not exceeding $10,000 is a Class 3 felony;

(2) Laundering of criminally derived property of a value exceeding $10,000 but not exceeding $100,000 is a Class 2 felony;

(3) Laundering of criminally derived property of a value exceeding $100,000 but not exceeding $500,000 is a Class 1 felony;

(4) Money laundering in violation of subsection (a)(2) of this Section is a Class X felony;

(5) Laundering of criminally derived property of a value exceeding $500,000 is a Class 1 non-probationable felony;

(6) In a prosecution under clause (a)(1.5)(B)(ii) of this Section, the sentences are as follows:

(A) Laundering of property of a value not exceeding $10,000 is a Class 3 felony;
(B) Laundering of property of a value exceeding $10,000 but not exceeding $100,000 is a Class 2 felony;

(C) Laundering of property of a value exceeding $100,000 but not exceeding $500,000 is a Class 1 felony;

(D) Laundering of property of a value exceeding $500,000 is a Class 1 non-probationable felony.

(d) Evidence. In a prosecution under this Article, either party may introduce the following evidence pertaining to the issue of whether the property or proceeds were known to be some form of criminally derived property or from some form of unlawful activity:

(1) A financial transaction was conducted or structured or attempted in violation of the reporting requirements of any State or federal law; or

(2) A financial transaction was conducted or attempted with the use of a false or fictitious name or a forged instrument; or

(3) A falsely altered or completed written instrument or a written instrument that contains any materially false personal identifying information was made, used, offered or presented, whether accepted or not, in connection with a financial transaction; or

(4) A financial transaction was structured or attempted to be structured so as to falsely report the actual consideration or value of the transaction; or

(5) A money transmitter, a person engaged in a trade or business or any employee of a money transmitter or a person engaged in a trade or business, knows or reasonably should know that false personal identifying information has been presented and incorporates the false personal identifying information into any report or record; or

(6) The criminally derived property is transported or possessed in a fashion inconsistent with the ordinary or usual means of transportation or possession of such property and where the property is discovered in the absence of any documentation or other indicia of legitimate origin or right to such property; or

(7) A person pays or receives substantially less than face value for one or more monetary instruments; or

(8) A person engages in a transaction involving one or more monetary instruments, where the physical condition or form of the monetary instrument or instruments makes it apparent that they are not the product of bona fide business or financial transactions.

(e) Duty to enforce this Article.

(1) It is the duty of the Department of State Police, and its agents, officers, and investigators, to enforce all provisions of this Article, except those specifically delegated, and to cooperate with all agencies charged with the enforcement of the laws of the United States, or of any state, relating to money laundering. Only an agent, officer, or investigator designated by the Director may be authorized in accordance with this Section to serve seizure notices, warrants, subpoenas, and summonses under the authority of this State.

(2) Any agent, officer, investigator, or peace officer designated by the Director may: (A) make seizure of property pursuant to the provisions of this Article; and (B) perform such other law enforcement duties as the Director designates. It is the duty of all State's Attorneys to prosecute violations of this Article and institute legal proceedings as authorized under this Article.

(f) Protective orders.

(1) Upon application of the State, the court may enter a restraining order or injunction, require the execution of a satisfactory performance bond, or take any other action to preserve the

availability of property described in subsection (h) for forfeiture under this Article:

(A) upon the filing of an indictment, information, or complaint charging a violation of this Article for which forfeiture may be ordered under this Article and alleging that the property with respect to which the order is sought would be subject to forfeiture under this Article; or

(B) prior to the filing of such an indictment, information, or complaint, if, after notice to persons appearing to have an interest in the property and opportunity for a hearing, the court determines that:

(i) there is probable cause to believe that the State will prevail on the issue of forfeiture and that failure to enter the order will result in the property being destroyed, removed from the jurisdiction of the court, or otherwise made unavailable for forfeiture; and

(ii) the need to preserve the availability of the property through the entry of the requested order outweighs the hardship on any party against whom the order is to be entered.

Provided, however, that an order entered pursuant to subparagraph (B) shall be effective for not more than 90 days, unless extended by the court for good cause shown or unless an indictment, information, complaint, or administrative notice has been filed.

(2) A temporary restraining order under this subsection may be entered upon application of the State without notice or opportunity for a hearing when an indictment, information, complaint, or administrative notice has not yet been filed with respect to the property, if the State demonstrates that there is probable cause to believe that the property with respect to which the order is sought would be subject to forfeiture under this Section and that provision of notice will jeopardize the availability of the property for forfeiture. Such a temporary order shall expire not more than 30 days after the date on which it is entered, unless extended for good cause shown or unless the party against whom it is entered consents to an extension for a longer period. A hearing requested concerning an order entered under this paragraph shall be held at the earliest possible time and prior to the expiration of the temporary order.

(3) The court may receive and consider, at a hearing held pursuant to this subsection (f), evidence and information that would be inadmissible under the Illinois rules of evidence.

(4) Order to repatriate and deposit.

(A) In general. Pursuant to its authority to enter a pretrial restraining order under this Section, the court may order a defendant to repatriate any property that may be seized and forfeited and to deposit that property pending trial with the Illinois State Police or another law enforcement agency designated by the Illinois State Police.

(B) Failure to comply. Failure to comply with an order under this subsection (f) is punishable as a civil or criminal contempt of court.

(g) Warrant of seizure. The State may request the issuance of a warrant authorizing the seizure of property described in subsection (h) in the same manner as provided for a search warrant. If the court determines that there is probable cause to believe that the property to be seized would be subject to forfeiture, the court shall issue a warrant authorizing the seizure of such property.

(h) Forfeiture.

(1) The following are subject to forfeiture:

(A) any property, real or personal, constituting, derived from, or traceable to any proceeds the person obtained directly or indirectly, as a result of a violation of this Article;

(B) any of the person's property used, or intended to be used, in any manner or part, to commit, or to facilitate the commission of, a violation of this Article;

(C) all conveyances, including aircraft, vehicles or vessels, which are used, or intended for use, to transport, or in any manner to facilitate the transportation, sale, receipt, possession, or

concealment of property described in subparagraphs (A) and (B), but:
(i) no conveyance used by any person as a common carrier in the transaction of business as a common carrier is subject to forfeiture under this Section unless it appears that the owner or other person in charge of the conveyance is a consenting party or privy to a violation of this Article;

(ii) no conveyance is subject to forfeiture under this Section by reason of any act or omission which the owner proves to have been committed or omitted without his or her knowledge or consent;
(iii) a forfeiture of a conveyance encumbered by a bona fide security interest is subject to the interest of the secured party if he or she neither had knowledge of nor consented to the act or omission;

(D) all real property, including any right, title, and interest (including, but not limited to, any leasehold interest or the beneficial interest in a land trust) in the whole of any lot or tract of land and any appurtenances or improvements, which is used or intended to be used, in any manner or part, to commit, or in any manner to facilitate the commission of, any violation of this Article or that is the proceeds of any violation or act that constitutes a violation of this Article.

(2) Property subject to forfeiture under this Article may be seized by the Director or any peace officer upon process or seizure warrant issued by any court having jurisdiction over the property. Seizure by the Director or any peace officer without process may be made:

(A) if the seizure is incident to a seizure warrant;

(B) if the property subject to seizure has been the subject of a prior judgment in favor of the State in a criminal proceeding, or in an injunction or forfeiture proceeding based upon this Article;

(C) if there is probable cause to believe that the property is directly or indirectly dangerous to health or safety;

(D) if there is probable cause to believe that the property is subject to forfeiture under this Article and the property is seized under circumstances in which a warrantless seizure or arrest would be reasonable; or

(E) in accordance with the Code of Criminal Procedure of 1963.

(3) In the event of seizure pursuant to paragraph (2), forfeiture proceedings shall be instituted in accordance with subsections (i) through (r).

(4) Property taken or detained under this Section shall not be subject to replevin, but is deemed to be in the custody of the Director subject only to the order and judgments of the circuit court having jurisdiction over the forfeiture proceedings and the decisions of the State's Attorney under this Article. When property is seized under this Article, the seizing agency shall promptly conduct an inventory of the seized property and estimate the property's value and shall forward a copy of the inventory of seized property and the estimate of the property's value to the Director. Upon receiving notice of seizure, the Director may:

(A) place the property under seal;

(B) remove the property to a place designated by the Director;

(C) keep the property in the possession of the seizing agency;

(D) remove the property to a storage area for safekeeping or, if the property is a negotiable instrument or money and is not needed for evidentiary purposes, deposit it in an interest bearing account;

(E) place the property under constructive seizure by posting notice of pending forfeiture on it, by giving notice of pending forfeiture to its owners and interest holders, or by filing notice of pending forfeiture in any appropriate public record relating to the property; or

(F) provide for another agency or custodian, including an owner, secured party, or lienholder, to take custody of the property upon the terms and conditions set by the Director.

(5) When property is forfeited under this Article, the Director shall sell all such property unless such property is required by law to be destroyed or is harmful to the public, and shall distribute the proceeds of the sale, together with any moneys forfeited or seized, in accordance with paragraph (6). However, upon the application of the seizing agency or prosecutor who was responsible for the investigation, arrest or arrests and prosecution which lead to the forfeiture, the Director may return any item of forfeited property to the seizing agency or prosecutor for official use in the enforcement of laws, if the agency or prosecutor can demonstrate that the item requested would be useful to the agency or prosecutor in its enforcement efforts. When any real property returned to the seizing agency is sold by the agency or its unit of government, the proceeds of the sale shall be delivered to the Director and distributed in accordance with paragraph (6).
(6) All monies and the sale proceeds of all other property forfeited and seized under this Article shall be distributed as follows:

(A) 65% shall be distributed to the metropolitan enforcement group, local, municipal, county, or State law enforcement agency or agencies which conducted or participated in the investigation resulting in the forfeiture. The distribution shall bear a reasonable relationship to the degree of direct participation of the law enforcement agency in the effort resulting in the forfeiture, taking into account the total value of the property forfeited and the total law enforcement effort with respect to the violation of the law upon which the forfeiture is based. Amounts distributed to the agency or agencies shall be used for the enforcement of laws.

(B)(i) 12.5% shall be distributed to the Office of the State's Attorney of the county in which the prosecution resulting in the forfeiture was instituted, deposited in a special fund in the county treasury and appropriated to the State's Attorney for use in the enforcement of laws. In counties over 3,000,000 population, 25% shall be distributed to the Office of the State's Attorney for use in the enforcement of laws. If the prosecution is undertaken solely by the Attorney General, the portion provided hereunder shall be distributed to the Attorney General for use in the enforcement of laws.

(ii) 12.5% shall be distributed to the Office of the State's Attorneys Appellate Prosecutor and deposited in the Narcotics Profit Forfeiture Fund of that office to be used for additional expenses incurred in the investigation, prosecution and appeal of cases arising under laws. The Office of the State's Attorneys Appellate Prosecutor shall not receive distribution from cases brought in counties with over 3,000,000 population.

(C) 10% shall be retained by the Department of State Police for expenses related to the administration and sale of seized and forfeited property.

Moneys and the sale proceeds distributed to the Department of State Police under this Article shall be deposited in the Money Laundering Asset Recovery Fund created in the State treasury and shall be used by the Department of State Police for State law enforcement purposes.

(i) Notice to owner or interest holder.

(1) Whenever notice of pending forfeiture or service of an in rem complaint is required under the provisions of this Article, such notice or service shall be given as follows:

(A) If the owner's or interest holder's name and current address are known, then by either personal service or mailing a copy of the notice by certified mail, return receipt requested, to that address. For purposes of notice under this Section, if a person has been arrested for the conduct giving rise to the forfeiture, then the address provided to the arresting agency at the time of arrest shall be deemed to be that person's known address. Provided, however, if an owner or interest holder's address changes prior to the effective date of the notice of pending forfeiture, the owner or interest holder shall promptly notify the seizing agency of the change in address or, if the owner or interest holder's address changes subsequent to the effective date of the notice of pending forfeiture, the owner or interest holder shall promptly notify the State's Attorney of the change in address; or

(B) If the property seized is a conveyance, to the address reflected in the office of the agency or official in which title or interest to the conveyance is required by law to be recorded, then by mailing a copy of the notice by certified mail, return receipt requested, to that address; or

(C) If the owner's or interest holder's address is not known, and is not on record as provided in paragraph (B), then by publication for 3 successive weeks in a newspaper of general circulation in the county in which the seizure occurred.

(2) Notice served under this Article is effective upon personal service, the last date of publication, or the mailing of written notice, whichever is earlier.

(j) Notice to State's Attorney. The law enforcement agency seizing property for forfeiture under this Article shall, within 90 days after seizure, notify the State's Attorney for the county, either where an act or omission giving rise to the forfeiture occurred or where the property was seized, of the seizure of the property and the facts and circumstances giving rise to the seizure and shall provide the State's Attorney with the inventory of the property and its estimated value. When the property seized for forfeiture is a vehicle, the law enforcement agency seizing the property shall immediately notify the Secretary of State that forfeiture proceedings are pending regarding such vehicle.

(k) Non-judicial forfeiture. If non-real property that exceeds $20,000 in value excluding the value of any conveyance, or if real property is seized under the provisions of this Article, the State's Attorney shall institute judicial in rem forfeiture proceedings as described in subsection (l) of this Section within 45 days from receipt of notice of seizure from the seizing agency under subsection (j) of this Section. However, if non-real property that does not exceed $20,000 in value excluding the value of any conveyance is seized, the following procedure shall be used:

(1) If, after review of the facts surrounding the seizure, the State's Attorney is of the opinion that the seized property is subject to forfeiture, then within 45 days after the receipt of notice of seizure from the seizing agency, the State's Attorney shall cause notice of pending forfeiture to be given to the owner of the property and all known interest holders of the property in accordance with subsection (i) of this Section.

(2) The notice of pending forfeiture must include a description of the property, the estimated value of the property, the date and place of seizure, the conduct giving rise to forfeiture or the violation of law alleged, and a summary of procedures and procedural rights applicable to the forfeiture action.

(3)(A) Any person claiming an interest in property which is the subject of notice under paragraph (1) of this subsection (k), must, in order to preserve any rights or claims to the property, within 45 days after the effective date of notice as described in subsection (i) of this Section, file a verified claim with the State's Attorney expressing his or her interest in the property. The claim must set forth:

(i) the caption of the proceedings as set forth on the notice of pending forfeiture and the name of the claimant;

(ii) the address at which the claimant will accept mail;

(iii) the nature and extent of the claimant's interest in the property;

(iv) the date, identity of the transferor, and circumstances of the claimant's acquisition of the interest in the property;

(v) the name and address of all other persons known to have an interest in the property;

(vi) the specific provision of law relied on in asserting the property is not subject to forfeiture;

(vii) all essential facts supporting each assertion; and

(viii) the relief sought.

(B) If a claimant files the claim and deposits with the State's Attorney a cost bond, in the form of a cashier's check payable to the clerk of the court, in the sum of 10% of the reasonable value of the property as alleged by the State's Attorney or the sum of $100, whichever is greater, upon condition that, in the case of forfeiture, the claimant must pay all costs and expenses of forfeiture proceedings, then the State's Attorney shall institute judicial in rem forfeiture proceedings and deposit the cost bond with the clerk of the court as described in subsection (l) of this Section within 45 days after receipt of the claim and cost bond. In lieu of a cost bond, a person claiming interest in the seized property may file, under penalty of perjury, an indigency affidavit which has been approved by a circuit court judge.

(C) If none of the seized property is forfeited in the judicial in rem proceeding, the clerk of the court shall return to the claimant, unless the court orders otherwise, 90% of the sum which has been deposited and shall retain as costs 10% of the money deposited. If any of the seized property is forfeited under the judicial forfeiture proceeding, the clerk of the court shall transfer 90% of the sum which has been deposited to the State's Attorney prosecuting the civil forfeiture to be applied to the costs of prosecution and the clerk shall retain as costs 10% of the sum deposited.

(4) If no claim is filed or bond given within the 45 day period as described in paragraph (3) of this subsection (k), the State's Attorney shall declare the property forfeited and shall promptly notify the owner and all known interest holders of the property and the Director of State Police of the declaration of forfeiture and the Director shall dispose of the property in accordance with law.

(l) Judicial in rem procedures. If property seized under the provisions of this Article is non-real property that exceeds $20,000 in value excluding the value of any conveyance, or is real property, or a claimant has filed a claim and a cost bond under paragraph (3) of subsection (k) of this Section, the following judicial in rem procedures shall apply:

(1) If, after a review of the facts surrounding the seizure, the State's Attorney is of the opinion that the seized property is subject to forfeiture, then within 45 days of the receipt of notice of seizure by the seizing agency or the filing of the claim and cost bond, whichever is later, the State's Attorney shall institute judicial forfeiture proceedings by filing a verified complaint for forfeiture and, if the claimant has filed a claim and cost bond, by depositing the cost bond with the clerk of the court. When authorized by law, a forfeiture must be ordered by a court on an action in rem brought by a State's Attorney under a verified complaint for forfeiture.

(2) During the probable cause portion of the judicial in rem proceeding wherein the State presents its case-in-chief, the court must receive and consider, among other things, all relevant hearsay evidence and information. The laws of evidence relating to civil actions apply to all other portions of the judicial in rem proceeding.

(3) Only an owner of or interest holder in the property may file an answer asserting a claim against the property in the action in rem. For purposes of this Section, the owner or interest holder shall be referred to as claimant. Upon motion of the State, the court shall first hold a hearing, wherein any claimant must establish by a preponderance of the evidence, that he or she has a lawful, legitimate ownership interest in the property and that it was obtained through a lawful source.

(4) The answer must be signed by the owner or interest holder under penalty of perjury and must set forth:

(A) the caption of the proceedings as set forth on the notice of pending forfeiture and the name of the claimant;

(B) the address at which the claimant will accept mail;

(C) the nature and extent of the claimant's interest in the property;

(D) the date, identity of transferor, and circumstances of the claimant's acquisition of the interest in the property;

(E) the name and address of all other persons known to have an interest in the property;
(F) all essential facts supporting each assertion; and

(G) the precise relief sought.

(5) The answer must be filed with the court within 45 days after service of the civil in rem complaint.

(6) The hearing must be held within 60 days after filing of the answer unless continued for good cause.

(7) The State shall show the existence of probable cause for forfeiture of the property. If the State shows probable cause, the claimant has the burden of showing by a preponderance of the evidence that the claimant's interest in the property is not subject to forfeiture.

(8) If the State does not show existence of probable cause, the court shall order the interest in the property returned or conveyed to the claimant and shall order all other property forfeited to the State. If the State does show existence of probable cause, the court shall order all property forfeited to the State.

(9) A defendant convicted in any criminal proceeding is precluded from later denying the essential allegations of the criminal offense of which the defendant was convicted in any proceeding under this Article regardless of the pendency of an appeal from that conviction. However, evidence of the pendency of an appeal is admissible.

(10) An acquittal or dismissal in a criminal proceeding does not preclude civil proceedings under this Article; however, for good cause shown, on a motion by the State's Attorney, the court may stay civil forfeiture proceedings during the criminal trial for a related criminal indictment or information alleging a money laundering violation. Such a stay shall not be available pending an appeal. Property subject to forfeiture under this Article shall not be subject to return or release by a court exercising jurisdiction over a criminal case involving the seizure of such property unless such return or release is consented to by the State's Attorney.

(11) All property declared forfeited under this Article vests in this State on the commission of the conduct giving rise to forfeiture together with the proceeds of the property after that time. Any such property or proceeds subsequently transferred to any person remain subject to forfeiture and thereafter shall be ordered forfeited.

(12) A civil action under this Article must be commenced within 5 years after the last conduct giving rise to forfeiture became known or should have become known or 5 years after the forfeitable property is discovered, whichever is later, excluding any time during which either the property or claimant is out of the State or in confinement or during which criminal proceedings relating to the same conduct are in progress.
(m) Stay of time periods. If property is seized for evidence and for forfeiture, the time periods for instituting judicial and non-judicial forfeiture proceedings shall not begin until the property is no longer necessary for evidence.

(n) Settlement of claims. Notwithstanding other provisions of this Article, the State's Attorney and a claimant of seized property may enter into an agreed-upon settlement concerning the seized property in such an amount and upon such terms as are set out in writing in a settlement agreement.

(o) Property constituting attorney fees. Nothing in this Article applies to property which constitutes reasonable bona fide attorney's fees paid to an attorney for services rendered or to be rendered in the forfeiture proceeding or criminal proceeding relating directly thereto where such property was paid before its seizure, before the issuance of any seizure warrant or court order prohibiting transfer of the property and where the attorney, at the time he or she received the property did not know that it was property subject to forfeiture under this Article.

(p) Construction. It is the intent of the General Assembly that the forfeiture provisions of this Article be liberally construed so as to effect their remedial purpose. The forfeiture of property and other remedies hereunder shall be considered to be in addition to, and not exclusive of, any sentence or other remedy provided by law.

(q) Judicial review. If property has been declared forfeited under subsection (k) of this Section, any person who has an interest in the property declared forfeited may, within 30 days after the effective date of the notice of the declaration of forfeiture, file a claim and cost bond as described in paragraph (3) of subsection (k) of this Section. If a claim and cost bond is filed under this Section, then the procedures described in subsection (l) of this Section apply.

(r) Burden of proof of exemption or exception. It is not necessary for the State to negate any exemption or exception in this Article in any complaint, information, indictment or other pleading or in any trial, hearing, or other proceeding under this Article. The burden of proof of any exemption or exception is upon the person claiming it.

(s) Review of administrative decisions. All administrative findings, rulings, final determinations, findings, and conclusions of the State's Attorney's Office under this Article are final and conclusive decisions of the matters involved. Any person aggrieved by the decision may obtain review of the decision pursuant to the provisions of the Administrative Review Law and the rules adopted pursuant to that Law. Pending final decision on such review, the administrative acts, orders, and rulings of the State's Attorney's Office remain in full force and effect unless modified or suspended by order of court pending final judicial decision. Pending final decision on such review, the acts, orders, and rulings of the State's Attorney's Office remain in full force and effect, unless stayed by order of court. However, no stay of any decision of the administrative agency shall issue unless the person aggrieved by the decision establishes by a preponderance of the evidence that good cause exists for the stay. In determining good cause, the court shall find that the aggrieved party has established a substantial likelihood of prevailing on the merits and that granting the stay will not have an injurious effect on the general public.

ARTICLE 29D. TERRORISM

§29D-5. Legislative findings. The devastating consequences of the barbaric attacks on the World Trade Center and the Pentagon on September 11, 2001 underscore the compelling need for legislation that is specifically designed to combat the evils of terrorism. Terrorism is inconsistent with civilized society and cannot be tolerated.

A comprehensive State law is urgently needed to complement federal laws in the fight against terrorism and to better protect all citizens against terrorist acts. Accordingly, the legislature finds that our laws must be strengthened to ensure that terrorists, as well as those who solicit or provide financial and other support to terrorists, are prosecuted and punished in State courts with appropriate severity. The legislature further finds that due to the grave nature and global reach of terrorism that a comprehensive law encompassing State criminal statutes and strong civil remedies is needed.

An investigation may not be initiated or continued for activities protected by the First Amendment to the United States Constitution, including expressions of support or the provision of financial support for the nonviolent political, religious, philosophical, or ideological goals or beliefs of any person or group.

§29D-10. Definitions. As used in this Article, where not otherwise distinctly expressed or manifestly incompatible with the intent of this Article:

(a) "Computer network" means a set of related, remotely connected devices and any communications facilities including more than one computer with the capability to transmit data among them through communication facilities.

(b) "Computer" means a device that accepts, processes, stores, retrieves, or outputs data, and includes, but is not limited to, auxiliary storage and telecommunications devices.

(c) "Computer program" means a series of coded instruction or statements in a form acceptable to a computer which causes the computer to process data and supply the results of data processing.

(d) "Data" means representations of information, knowledge, facts, concepts or instructions, including program documentation, that are prepared in a formalized manner and are stored or processed in or transmitted by a computer. Data may be in any form, including but not limited to magnetic or optical storage media, punch cards, or data stored internally in the memory of a computer.

(e) "Biological products used in or in connection with agricultural production" includes, but is not limited to, seeds, plants, and DNA of plants or animals altered for use in crop or livestock breeding or production or which are sold, intended, designed, or produced for use in crop production or livestock breeding or production.

(f) "Agricultural products" means crops and livestock.

(g) "Agricultural production" means the breeding and growing of livestock and crops.

(g-5) "Animal feed" means an article that is intended for use for food for animals other than humans and that is intended for use as a substantial source of nutrients in the diet of the animal, and is not limited to a mixture intended to be the sole ration of the animal.

(g-10) "Contagious or infectious disease" means a specific disease designated by the Illinois Department of Agriculture as contagious or infectious under rules pertaining to the Illinois Diseased Animals Act.

(g-15) "Processed food" means any food other than a raw agricultural commodity and includes any raw agricultural commodity that has been subject to processing, such as canning, cooking, freezing, dehydration, or milling.

(g-20) "Raw agricultural commodity" means any food in its raw or natural state, including all fruits that are washed, colored, or otherwise treated in their unpeeled natural form prior to marketing and honey that is in the comb or that is removed from the comb and in an unadulterated condition.

(g-25) "Endangering the food supply" means to knowingly:

(1) bring into this State any domestic animal that is affected with any contagious or infectious disease or any animal that has been exposed to any contagious or infectious disease;

(2) expose any animal in this State to any contagious or infectious disease;

(3) deliver any poultry that is infected with any contagious or infectious disease to any poultry producer pursuant to a production contract;

(4) except as permitted under the Insect Pest and Plant Disease Act, bring or release into this State any insect pest or expose any plant to an insect pest; or

(5) expose any raw agricultural commodity, animal feed, or processed food to any contaminant or contagious or infectious disease.

"Endangering the food supply" does not include bona fide experiments and actions related to those experiments carried on by commonly recognized research facilities or actions by agricultural producers and animal health professionals who may inadvertently contribute to the spread of detrimental biological agents while employing generally acceptable management practices.

(g-30) "Endangering the water supply" means to knowingly contaminate a public or private water well or water reservoir or any water supply of a public utility or tamper with the production of bottled or packaged water or tamper with bottled or packaged water at a retail or wholesale mercantile establishment. "Endangering the water supply" does not include contamination of a public or private well or water reservoir or any water supply of a public utility that may occur inadvertently as part of the operation of a public utility or electrical generating station.

(h) "Livestock" means animals bred or raised for human consumption.

(i) "Crops" means plants raised for: (1) human consumption, (2) fruits that are intended for human consumption, (3) consumption by livestock, and (4) fruits that are intended for consumption by livestock.

(j) "Communications systems" means any works, property, or material of any radio, telegraph, telephone, microwave, or cable line, station, or system.

(k) "Substantial damage" means monetary damage greater than $100,000.

(l) "Terrorist act" or "act of terrorism" means: (1) any act that is intended to cause or create a risk and does cause or create a risk of death or great bodily harm to one or more persons; (2) any act that disables or destroys the usefulness or operation of any communications system; (3) any act or any series of 2 or more acts committed in furtherance of a single intention, scheme, or design that disables or destroys the usefulness or operation of a computer network, computers, computer programs, or data used by any industry, by any class of business, or by 5 or more businesses or by the federal government, State government, any unit of local government, a public utility, a manufacturer of pharmaceuticals, a national defense contractor, or a manufacturer of chemical or biological products used in or in connection with agricultural production; (4) any act that disables or causes substantial damage to or destruction of any structure or facility used in or used in connection with ground, air, or water transportation; the production or distribution of electricity, gas, oil, or other fuel (except for acts that occur inadvertently and as the result of operation of the facility that produces or distributes electricity, gas, oil, or other fuel); the treatment of sewage or the treatment or distribution of water; or controlling the flow of any body of water; (5) any act that causes substantial damage to or destruction of livestock or to crops or a series of 2 or more acts committed in furtherance of a single intention, scheme, or design which, in the aggregate, causes substantial damage to or destruction of livestock or crops; (6) any act that causes substantial damage to or destruction of any hospital or any building or facility used by the federal government, State government, any unit of local government or by a national defense contractor or by a public utility, a manufacturer of pharmaceuticals, a manufacturer of chemical or biological products used in or in connection with agricultural production or the storage or processing of agricultural products or the preparation of agricultural products for food or food products intended for resale or for feed for livestock; (7) any act that causes substantial damage to any building containing 5 or more businesses of any type or to any building in which 10 or more people reside; (8) endangering the food supply; or (9) endangering the water supply.

(m) "Terrorist" and "terrorist organization" means any person who engages or is about to engage in a terrorist act with the intent to intimidate or coerce a significant portion of a civilian population.

(n) "Material support or resources" means currency or other financial securities, financial services, lodging, training, safe houses, false documentation or identification, communications equipment, facilities, weapons, lethal substances, explosives, personnel, transportation, any other kind of physical assets or intangible property, and expert services or expert assistance.

(o) "Person" has the meaning given in Section 2-15 of this Code and, in addition to that meaning, includes, without limitation, any charitable organization, whether incorporated or unincorporated, any professional fund raiser, professional solicitor, limited liability company, association, joint stock company, association, trust, trustee, or any group of people formally or informally affiliated or associated for a common purpose, and any officer, director, partner, member, or agent of any person.

(p) "Render criminal assistance" means to do any of the following with the intent to prevent, hinder, or delay the discovery or apprehension of, or the lodging of a criminal charge against, a person who he or she knows or believes has committed an offense under this Article or is being sought by law enforcement officials for the commission of an offense under this Article, or with the intent to assist a person in profiting or benefiting from the commission of an offense under this Article:

(1) harbor or conceal the person;

(2) warn the person of impending discovery or apprehension;

(3) provide the person with money, transportation, a weapon, a disguise, false identification documents, or any other means of avoiding discovery or apprehension;

(4) prevent or obstruct, by means of force, intimidation, or deception, anyone from performing an act that might aid in the discovery or apprehension of the person or in the lodging of a criminal charge against the person;

(5) suppress, by any act of concealment, alteration, or destruction, any physical evidence that might aid in the discovery or apprehension of the person or in the lodging of a criminal charge against the person;

(6) aid the person to protect or expeditiously profit from an advantage derived from the crime; or

(7) provide expert services or expert assistance to the person. Providing expert services or expert assistance shall not be construed to apply to: (1) a licensed attorney who discusses with a client the legal consequences of a proposed course of conduct or advises a client of legal or constitutional rights and (2) a licensed medical doctor who provides emergency medical treatment to a person whom he or she believes has committed an offense under this Article if, as soon as reasonably practicable either before or after providing such treatment, he or she notifies a law enforcement agency.

§29D-14.9. Terrorism. (a) A person commits the offense of terrorism when, with the intent to intimidate or coerce a significant portion of a civilian population:

(1) he or she knowingly commits a terrorist act as defined in Section 29D-10(1) of this Code within this State; or

(2) he or she, while outside this State, knowingly commits a terrorist act as defined in Section 29D-10(1) of this Code that takes effect within this State or produces substantial detrimental effects within this State.

(b) Sentence. Terrorism is a Class X felony. If no deaths are caused by the terrorist act, the sentence shall be a term of 20 years to natural life imprisonment; if the terrorist act caused the death of one or more persons, however, a mandatory term of natural life imprisonment shall be the sentence if the death penalty is not imposed and the person has attained the age of 18 years at the time of the commission of the offense. An offender under the age of 18 years at the time of the commission of the offense shall be sentenced under Section 5-4.5-105 of the Unified Code of Corrections.

§29D-15.1. Causing a catastrophe. (a) A person commits the offense of causing a catastrophe if he or she knowingly causes a catastrophe by explosion, fire, flood, collapse of a building, or release of poison, radioactive material, bacteria, virus, or other dangerous and difficult to confine force or substance.

(b) As used in this Section, "catastrophe" means serious physical injury to 5 or more persons, substantial damage to 5 or more buildings or inhabitable structures, or substantial damage to a vital public facility that seriously impairs its usefulness or operation; and "vital public facility" means a facility that is necessary to ensure or protect the public health, safety, or welfare, including, but not limited to, a hospital, a law enforcement agency, a fire department, a private or public utility company, a national defense contractor, a facility of the armed forces, or an emergency services agency.

(c) Sentence. Causing a catastrophe is a Class X felony.

§29D-15.2. Possession of a deadly substance. (a) A person commits the offense of possession of a deadly substance when he or she possesses, manufactures, or transports any poisonous gas, deadly biological or chemical contaminant or agent, or radioactive substance either with the intent to use that gas, biological or chemical contaminant or agent, or radioactive substance to commit a felony or with the knowledge that another person intends to use that gas, biological or chemical contaminant or agent, or radioactive substance to commit a felony.

(b) Sentence. Possession of a deadly substance is a Class 1 felony for which a person, if sentenced to a term of imprisonment, shall be sentenced to a term of not less than 4 years and not more than 30 years.

§29D-20. Making a terrorist threat. (a) A person is guilty of making a terrorist threat when, with the intent to intimidate or coerce a significant portion of a civilian population, he or she in any manner knowingly threatens to commit or threatens to cause the commission of a terrorist act as defined in Section 29D-10(1) and thereby causes a reasonable expectation or fear of the imminent commission of a terrorist act as defined in Section 29D-10(1) or of another terrorist act as defined in Section 29D-10(1).

(b) It is not a defense to a prosecution under this Section that at the time the defendant made the terrorist threat, unknown to the defendant, it was impossible to carry out the threat, nor is it a defense that the threat was not made to a person who was a subject or intended victim of the threatened act.

(c) Sentence. Making a terrorist threat is a Class X felony.

(d) In addition to any other sentence that may be imposed, the court shall order any person convicted of making a terrorist threat involving a threat that a bomb or explosive device has been placed in a school to reimburse the unit of government that employs the emergency response officer or officers that were dispatched to the school for the cost of the search for a bomb or explosive device. For the purposes of this Section, "emergency response" means any incident requiring a response by a police officer, a firefighter, a State Fire Marshal employee, or an ambulance.

§29D-25. Falsely making a terrorist threat. (a) A person commits the offense of falsely making a terrorist threat when in any manner he or she knowingly makes a threat to commit or cause to be committed a terrorist act as defined in Section 29D-10(1) or otherwise knowingly creates the impression or belief that a terrorist act is about to be or has been committed, or in any manner knowingly makes a threat to commit or cause to be committed a catastrophe as defined in Section 29D-15.1 of this Code that he or she knows is false.

(b) Sentence. Falsely making a terrorist threat is a Class 1 felony.

(c) In addition to any other sentence that may be imposed, the court shall order any person convicted of falsely making a terrorist threat, involving a threat that a bomb or explosive device has been placed in a school in which the offender knows that such bomb or explosive device was not placed in the school, to reimburse the unit of government that employs the emergency response officer or officers that were dispatched to the school for the cost of the search for a bomb or explosive device. For the purposes of this Section, "emergency response" means any incident requiring a response by a police officer, a firefighter, a State Fire Marshal employee, or an ambulance.

§29D-29.9. Material support for terrorism. (a) A person commits the offense of soliciting or providing material support for terrorism if he or she knowingly raises, solicits, collects, or provides material support or resources knowing that the material support or resources will be used, in whole or in part, to plan, prepare, carry out, facilitate, or avoid apprehension for committing terrorism as defined in Section 29D-14.9 or causing a catastrophe as defined in Section 29D-15.1 of this Code, or who knows and intends that the material support or resources so raised, solicited, collected, or provided will be used in the commission of a terrorist act as defined in Section 29D-10(1) of this Code by an organization designated under 8 U.S.C. 1189, as amended. It is not an element of the offense that the defendant actually knows that an organization has been designated under 8 U.S.C. 1189, as amended.

(b) Sentence. Soliciting or providing material support for terrorism is a Class X felony for which the sentence shall be a term of imprisonment of no less than 9 years and no more than 40 years.

§29D-35. Hindering prosecution of terrorism. (a) A person commits the offense of hindering prosecution of terrorism when he or she renders criminal assistance to a person who has committed terrorism as defined in Section 29D-14.9 or caused a catastrophe as defined in Section 29D-15.1 of this Code when he or she knows that the person to whom he or she rendered criminal assistance engaged in an act of terrorism or caused a catastrophe.

(b) Hindering prosecution of terrorism is a Class X felony, the sentence for which shall be a term of 20 years to natural life imprisonment if no death was caused by the act of terrorism committed by the person to whom the defendant rendered criminal assistance and a mandatory term of natural life imprisonment if death was caused by the act of terrorism committed by the person to whom the defendant rendered criminal assistance. An offender under the age of 18 years at the time of the commission of the offense shall be sentenced under Section 5-4.5-105 of the Unified Code of Corrections.

§29D-35.1. Boarding or attempting to board an aircraft with weapon. (a) It is unlawful for any person to board or attempt to board any commercial or charter aircraft, knowingly having in his or her possession any firearm, explosive of any type, or other lethal or dangerous weapon.

(b) This Section does not apply to any person authorized by either the federal government or any state government to carry firearms, but the person so exempted from the provisions of this Section shall notify the commander of any aircraft he or she is about to board that he or she does possess a firearm and show identification satisfactory to the aircraft commander that he or she is authorized to carry that firearm.

(c) Any person purchasing a ticket to board any commercial or charter aircraft shall by that purchase consent to a search of his or her person or personal belongings by the company selling the ticket to him or her. The person may refuse to submit to a search of his or her person or personal belongings by the aircraft company, but the person refusing may be denied the right to board the commercial or charter aircraft at the discretion of the carrier. Such a refusal creates no inference of unlawful conduct.
(d) Any evidence of criminal activity found during a search made pursuant to this Section shall be admissible in legal proceedings for the sole purpose of supporting a charge of violation of this Section and is inadmissible as evidence in any legal proceeding for any other purpose, except in the prosecution of offenses related to weapons as set out in Article 24 of this Code.

(e) No action may be brought against any commercial or charter airline company operating in this State for the refusal of that company to permit a person to board any aircraft if that person refused to be searched as set out in subsection (c) of this Section.

(f) Violation of this Section is a Class 4 felony.
§29D-40. Restitution. In addition to any other penalty that may be imposed, a court shall sentence any person convicted of any violation of this Article to pay all expenses incurred by the federal government, State government, or

any unit of local government in responding to any violation and cleaning up following any violation.

§29D-45. Limitations. A prosecution for any offense in this Article may be commenced at any time.

§29D-60. Injunctive relief. Whenever it appears to the Attorney General or any State's Attorney that any person is engaged in, or is about to engage in, any act that constitutes or would constitute a violation of this Article, the Attorney General or any State's Attorney may initiate a civil action in the circuit court to enjoin the violation.

§29D-65. Forfeiture of property acquired in connection with a violation of this Article; property freeze or seizure. (a) If there is probable cause to believe that a person used, is using, is about to use, or is intending to use property in a way that would violate this Article, then that person's assets may be frozen or seized pursuant to Part 800 of Article 124B of the Code of Criminal Procedure of 1963.

(b) Any person who commits any offense under this Article is subject to the property forfeiture provisions set forth in Article 124B of the Code of Criminal Procedure of 1963. Forfeiture under this subsection may be pursued in addition to or in lieu of proceeding under Section 124B-805 (property freeze or seizure; ex parte proceeding) of the Code of Criminal Procedure of 1963.

§29D-70. Severability. If any clause, sentence, Section, provision, or part of this Article or the application thereof to any person or circumstance shall be adjudged to be unconstitutional, the remainder of this Article or its application to persons or circumstances other than those to which it is held invalid, shall not be affected thereby.

§99. Effective date. This Act takes effect upon becoming law.

Part E. Offenses Affecting Governmental Functions
Article 30 – Treason and Related Offenses
720 ILCS 5/30-1 *et seq.*

§ 30-1. Treason. (a) A person owing allegiance to this State commits treason when he or she knowingly:

(1) levies war against this State; or

(2) adheres to the enemies of this State, giving them aid or comfort.

(b) No person may be convicted of treason except on the testimony of 2witnesses to the same overt act, or on his confession in open court.

(c) Sentence. Treason is a Class X felony for which an offender may be sentenced to death under Section 5-5-3 of the Unified Code of Corrections.

§ 30-2. Misprision of treason.
(a) A person owing allegiance to this State commits misprision of treason when he conceals or withholds his knowledge that another has committed treason against this State.

(b) Sentence. Misprision of treason is a Class 4 felony.

§ 30-3. Advocating overthrow of Government. a person who advocates, or with knowledge of its contents knowingly publishes, sells or distributes any document which advocates or with knowledge of its purpose, knowingly becomes a member of any organization which advocates the overthrow or reformation of the existing form of government of this State by violence or unlawful means commits a Class 3 felony.

Article 31 – Interference with Public Officers
720 ILCS 5/31-1 *et seq.*

§ 31-1. Resisting or obstructing a peace officer, firefighter, or correctional institution employee.
(a) A person who knowingly resists or obstructs the performance by one known to the person to be a peace officer, firefighter, or correctional institution employee of any authorized act within his official capacity commits a Class A misdemeanor.

(a-5) In addition to any other sentence that may be imposed, a court shall order any person convicted of resisting or obstructing a peace officer, firefighter, or correctional institution employee to be sentenced to a minimum of 48 consecutive hours of imprisonment or ordered to perform community service for not less than 100 hours as may be determined by the court. The person shall not be eligible for probation in order to reduce the sentence of imprisonment or community service.

(a-7) A person convicted for a violation of this Section whose violation was the proximate cause of an injury to a peace officer, firefighter, or correctional institution employee is guilty of a Class 4 felony.

(b) For purposes of this Section,

"correctional institution employee" means any person employed to supervise and control inmates incarcerated in a penitentiary, State farm, reformatory, prison, jail, house of correction, police detention area, half-way house, or other institution or place for the incarceration or custody of persons under sentence for offenses or awaiting trial or sentence for offenses, under arrest for an offense, a violation of probation, a violation of parole, or a violation of mandatory supervised release, or awaiting a bail setting hearing or preliminary hearing, or who are sexually dangerous persons or who are sexually violent persons; and

“firefighter" means any individual, either as an employee or volunteer, of a regularly constituted fire department of a municipality or fire protection district who performs fire fighting duties, including, but not limited to, the fire chief, assistant fire chief, captain, engineer, driver, ladder person, hose person, pipe person, and any other member of a regularly constituted fire department.

"Firefighter" also means a person employed by the Office of the State Fire Marshal to conduct arson investigations.

(c) It is an affirmative defense to a violation of this Section if a person resists or obstructs the performance of one known by the person to be a firefighter by returning to or remaining in a dwelling, residence, building, or other structure to rescue or to attempt to rescue any person.

§ 31-1a. Disarming a peace officer or correctional institution employee.
(a) A person who, without the consent of a peace officer or correctional institution employee as defined in subsection (b) of Section 31-1, takes a weapon from a person known to him or her to be a peace officer or correctional institution employee, while the peace officer or correctional institution employee is engaged in the performance of his or her official duties or from an area within the peace officer's or correctional institution employee's immediate presence is guilty of a Class 1 felony.

(b) A person who, without the consent of a peace officer or correctional institution employee as defined in subsection (b) of Section 31-1, attempts to take a weapon from a person known to him or her to be a peace officer or correctional institution employee, while the peace officer or correctional institution employee is engaged in the performance of his or her official duties or from an area within the peace officer's or correctional institution employee's immediate presence is guilty of a Class 2 felony.

§ 31-3. Obstructing service of process. Whoever knowingly resists or obstructs the authorized service or execution of any civil or criminal process or order of any court commits a Class B misdemeanor.

Commentary – Resisting or Obstructing a Peace Officer

Section 31-1 proscribes against resisting or obstructing a peace officer in the performance of his duties. The mental state of the offense is knowing, and that mental state requires proof that the defendant knew that the individual he was resisting was a peace officer. Knowledge may be proved by direct evidence, such as the defendant's own statements as to his knowledge, or it may be proved by circumstantial evidence, such as the officer being in uniform and the defendant acknowledging the officer's authority in responding to commands or orders from the officer. Obstruction occurs where the defendant interferes with the officer's performance of an official act. Resisting or obstructing ordinarily requires some form of physical act or omission that prevents, hinders or delays an officer from doing an authorized act such as letting one's body go limp to prevent an arrest or refusing to get out of a car when ordered to do so for purposes of a driving under the influence of alcohol investigation. However the focus of the act is on conduct that impedes or hinders an officer from performing his or duty. Firemen and correctional officers are also included within the scope of the statute.

In *People v. Baskerville* 2012 IL 111056, Section 31-1(a) was interpreted to apply to the making of a false material statement by a husband that might hinder or impede a police officer in locating the defendant's wife at her home. This was the first occasion the Illinois Supreme Court has recognized a non-physical act of obstructing a police officer. Nonetheless the court reversed the defendant's conviction, noting that the gravamen of the offense was the effect the obstructive conduct had on the administration of justice.

Resisting an authorized act. In *People v. Agnew-Downs* 404 Ill.App.3d 218, 936 N.E.2d 166 (Ill. App. Ct. 2nd Dist. 2010), the defendant was an NIU student attending a dance when a friend was intoxicated and became ill. In dealing with the friend, the defendant and Ward had a disagreement with an NIU police officer (Riddell) who told Ward he had to leave the dance. As Riddell was escorting Ward and his girlfriend from the gym, the defendant got between them and blocked the officer's action and held onto a door. Riddell grabbed the defendant's arm and tried to move him across the gym floor when the defendant broke free and made contact with another officer (Heard) knocking Heard to the floor. Concerned for Heard's safety, Riddell grabbed the defendant in a body hug, only to have the defendant attempt to buck himself free and force Riddell against some lockers. With others' help, Riddell finally forced the defendant to the floor where he was handcuffed. The defendant was charged with resisting a peace officer in the performance of his duties, namely; the arrest of the defendant under Section 31-1(a). There was no dispute that the defendant was not placed under arrest until he ended up on the floor handcuffed, but he had been told to stop or move in certain ways prior to that time. The defendant's conviction was affirmed with the court noting the unfortunate use of the word "arrest" to describe the official action of the NIU officer, which actually was to seize control over the defendant. This was an act the officer had authority to do, and even if the act had been unwarranted or unlawful, one is still guilty of resisting a police officer if he or she resists the command or order of a person known to be a police officer. See *People v. Bohannon* 403 Ill. App. 3d 1074, 936 N.E.2d 143 (Ill. App. Ct. 5th Dist. 2010)(refusal to display driver's license or insurance at roadside check was a traffic violation not resisting or obstructing a peace officer.) *People v. Jones* 2015 IL App (2d)

130387 (Defendant did not obstruct an authorized act where after initial entry into a home to investigate a domestic dispute, the officer found no evidence of a crime, but remained after being asked leave. The Defendant's resistance to the officer's use of force was not resisting or obstructing.)

Verbal arguments about authority insufficient. In *People v. Berardi* 407 Ill.App.3d 575, 948 N.E.2d 98 (Ill. App. Ct. 3rd Dist. 2011), the defendant was a Canton alderman who had come to the municipal building to obtain a copy of the city budget. When he was told that the budget would not be handed out, he remained outside the office, sometimes entering and videoed files that he believed were the budget. The Canton Chief of Police came to the office and told the defendant several times that he would have to leave. The defendant argued that he had a right to be at that location. Finally, the Chief told the defendant that if he did not leave, he would be arrested; so the defendant told the Chief he would have to arrest him. The Chief ordered the defendant to come with him and the defendant complied. The defendant's conviction for resisting or obstructing a police officer was reversed. The court held that mere argument or the correctness of an officer's act, without any other acts that hinder or prevent performance of an authorized act does not violate the statute.

Lesser-included Offense of Aggravated Battery to a Police Officer. In *People v. Sanchez* 2014 IL App (1st) 120514, the defendant was charged with Aggravated Battery to a Police Officer (720 ILCS 5/12-3.5(d)(4)(I)) for allegedly striking a police officer who had come to his parents' home to interview him about a homicide. The defendant was convicted of Resisting or Obstructing a Peace Officer when the prosecution asked that lesser-included jury instructions be given for the second offense. The defendant, on appeal claimed that since he was not being arrested but was to be interviewed, the conviction must be reversed since the officer's "official duties" element was not met. The court rejected this argument and affirmed the conviction, noting that when a police officer is engaged in official duties for any reason (including doing a witness interview) and a person resists or obstructs the performance of that duty, the evidence is sufficient to support the conviction for the resisting or obstructing offense.

§ 31-4 Obstructing justice. (a) A person obstructs justice when, with intent to prevent the apprehension or obstruct the prosecution or defense of any person, he or she knowingly commits any of the following acts:

(1) Destroys, alters, conceals or disguises physical evidence, plants false evidence, furnishes false information; or

(2) Induces a witness having knowledge material to the subject at issue to leave the State or conceal himself or herself; or

(3) Possessing knowledge material to the subject at issue, he or she leaves the State or conceals himself; or

(4) If a parent, legal guardian, or caretaker of a child under 13 years of age reports materially false information to a law enforcement agency, medical examiner, coroner, State's Attorney, or other governmental agency during an investigation of the disappearance or death of a child under circumstances described in subsection (a) or (b) of Section 10-10 of this Code.

(b) Sentence.

(1) Obstructing justice is a Class 4 felony, except as provided in paragraph (2) of this subsection (b).

(2) Obstructing justice in furtherance of streetgang related or gang-related activity, as defined in Section 10 of the Illinois Streetgang

Terrorism Omnibus Prevention Act, is a Class 3 felony.

§ 31-4.5. Obstructing identification. (a) A person commits the offense of obstructing identification when he or she intentionally or knowingly furnishes a false or fictitious name, residence address, or date of birth to a peace officer who has:

(1) lawfully arrested the person;

(2) lawfully detained the person; or

(3) requested the information from a person that the peace officer has good cause to believe is a witness to a criminal offense.

(b) Sentence. Obstructing identification is a Class A misdemeanor.

§ 31-5. Concealing or aiding a fugitive. Every person not standing in the relation of husband, wife, parent, child, brother or sister to the offender, who, with intent to prevent the apprehension of the offender, conceals his knowledge that an offense has been committed or harbors, aids or conceals the offender, commits a Class 4 felony.

Commentary – Obstructing Justice

Section 31- 4 sets forth the elements of obstructing justice, an offense that is much broader and more serious than resisting or obstructing a peace officer. The notion of obstructing justice is about the investigation, apprehension of a person and ultimately, the prosecution or defense of cases in court. The conduct that is criminalized is that conduct which is intended to interfere with the successful presentation of a case.

There are a variety of ways the crime can be committed, including knowingly (1) destroying or hiding physical evidence, planting false evidence or giving false information, (2) sending a material witness away so he is unavailable when needed, (3) being a material witness and leaving the state to be unavailable when needed. The crime, however, is a specific intent crime that requires proof that the acts were done to prevent apprehension of a person, or to prevent the prosecution of defense of a person in a legal proceeding. In *In re Q. P.* 2015 IL 118569 (Ill. S. Ct. 2015), the court recognized that a suspect who gave a false name to avoid being arrested on a warrant committed an obstruction of justice, noting that "the obstruction of justice statute is violated when a person knowingly provides false information with the intent to prevent his seizure or arrest on a criminal charge." *In re Q.P.* 2015 IL 118569 ¶25.

Concealment of physical evidence. In *People v. Comage* 241 Ill.2d 139, 946 N.E.2d 313 (Ill. S. Ct. 2011), the defendant was convicted of obstruction of justice. The defendant was stopped for questioning, and while a warrant check was being done, he ran. As he ran he threw a metal crack pipe and rod over a privacy fence. This conduct was observed by officers who recovered the item within minutes, although the items were out of the officers' view during this time. The defendant was charged with obstructing justice because he had "concealed "physical evidence, the crack pipe, from the officers with intent to prevent his prosecution for possession of drug paraphernalia. The trial court convicted him and the appellate court affirmed. the Illinois Supreme Court reversed - holding that "conceal" means to "withhold knowledge" and that permitting an obstructing justice charge in the context of an offense involving possession of contraband would lead to absurd results, since drugs, paraphernalia, cigarettes (minors' possession) and other contraband are routinely kept from view. Such objects are also thrown or dropped when officers come into view. The legislature in the obstructing justice statute aimed to address conduct that materially interferes with the administration of justice. Throwing the crack pipe over the fence in plain view of pursuing officers was not the type of conduct envisioned by the legislature to come within the coverage of the statute.

Preventing apprehension of a person. In *People v. Felton* 376 Ill.App.3d 1041, 879 N.E.2d 350 (Ill. App. Ct. 2nd Dist. 2007), the defendant loaned her car to her cousin, Carl King who later drove to a Road Ranger station. A passenger in the car driven by King, Marcus Jones, got into an altercation at the station and fled the scene in the car. Investigating officers traced the car to the defendant and interviewed her in an effort to identify the suspect involved in the incident (Jones). The defendant falsely told the officers that she never let others drive her car and that on the evening in question; the car was outside her residence. She admitted that there was a possibility that someone could have stolen her keys and taken the car, but said that as far as she knew that did not happen. She was indicted and convicted for obstructing justice (Section 31-4(a)) for knowingly providing false information with the intent to prevent the apprehension of Marcus Jones. On appeal, she challenged the sufficiency of the evidence because there was no showing that she obstructed the arrest of Jones or that she even knew who Jones was. In affirming her conviction, the court noted that her apparent fear for herself and her cousin instead of a specific person named Marcus Jones made no difference. Nor was it required that there be proof that she knew the person sought to be apprehended. It was enough to support her conviction that she knew that someone was a suspect and that her efforts to protect herself or her cousin would be advanced by preventing apprehension of the suspect.

False exculpatory "no" doctrine. In *People v. Ellis* 199 Ill.2d 28, 765 N.E.2d 991 (Ill. S. Ct. 2002), the defendant was stopped for a traffic violation and repeatedly gave false information as to his name and date of birth. He was convicted of obstructing justice; however his conviction on appeal was reversed on the basis of the false exculpatory no doctrine. This doctrine, which originally developed in the federal courts, had been followed by some Illinois appellate court and provided that the obstructing justice statute could not be applied to defendants who upon question by police denied their guilt but did not provide false affirmative information to investigating officers. On appeal to the Illinois Supreme Court, Ellis' conviction for obstructing justice was reinstated when the court rejected the "false exculpatory no" doctrine. The court determined that the doctrine was not consistent with the plain wording of the statute. While a suspect has the right to remain silent, the suspect has no right to lie. The choice of silence will be recognized and protected, but lying to police officers will not.

Immediate correction of false information. In *People v. Davis* 409 Ill. App.3d 457, 951 N.E.2d 230 (Ill. App. Ct. 4th Dist. 2011), the defendant was confronted at her home by officers looking for her ex-husband to arrest him on a warrant. the defendant falsely told the police that she had not seen him and that he was not present in her home (he was hiding in the attic.) as the defendant continued to talk, she began to cry and told the officers that she had seen her ex-husband but she believed he had left, and granted permission so the officers could search the house. In fact, the officers were able to execute the warrant and arrest the ex-husband. The defendant was charged and convicted for obstructing justice and on appeal argued that the evidence did not support her conviction since the totality of the evidence showed that she did not, in fact, prevent the apprehension of her ex-husband. The court rejected the defendant's claim that her almost immediate recantation of the false information was not a material impediment to the apprehension. The court held that her failure to immediately tell the truth slowed the progress of the apprehension and was obstructing justice. In contrast, see *People v. Taylor* 2012 IL App (2d) 110222 (defendant's giving false name and date-of-birth to officers was not sufficient to support conviction for Obstruction of Justice where officer suspected true identity and defendant gave correct information a few minutes later, thus not materially impeding an investigation).

§ 31-6. Escape; failure to report to a penal institution or to report for periodic imprisonment. (a) A person convicted of a felony or charged with the commission of a felony, or charged with or adjudicated delinquent for an act which, if committed by an adult, would constitute a felony, who intentionally escapes from any penal institution or from the custody of an employee of that institution commits a Class 2 felony; however, a person convicted of a felony, or adjudicated delinquent for an act which, if committed by an adult, would constitute a felony, who knowingly fails to report to a penal institution or to report for periodic imprisonment at any time or knowingly fails to return from furlough or from work and day release or who knowingly fails to abide by the terms of home confinement is guilty of a Class 3 felony.

(b) A person convicted of a misdemeanor or charged with the commission of a misdemeanor, or charged with or adjudicated delinquent for an act which, if committed by an adult, would constitute a misdemeanor, who intentionally escapes from any penal institution or from the custody of an employee of that institution commits a Class A misdemeanor; however, a person convicted of a misdemeanor, or adjudicated delinquent for an act which, if committed by an adult, would constitute a misdemeanor, who knowingly fails to report to a penal institution or to report for periodic imprisonment at any time or knowingly fails to return from furlough or from work and day release or who knowingly fails to abide by the terms of home confinement is guilty of a Class B misdemeanor.

(b-1) A person in the custody of the Department of Human Services under the provisions of the Sexually Violent Persons Commitment Act under a detention order, commitment order, conditional release order or other court order who intentionally escapes from any secure residential facility or from a Department employee or any of its agents commits a Class 2 felony.

(c) A person in the lawful custody of a peace officer for the alleged commission of a felony offense or an act which, if committed by an adult, would constitute a felony, and who intentionally escapes from custody commits a Class 2 felony; however, a person in the lawful custody of a peace officer for the alleged commission of a misdemeanor offense or an act which, if committed by an adult, would constitute a misdemeanor, who intentionally escapes from custody commits a Class A misdemeanor.

(c-5) A person in the lawful custody of a peace officer for an alleged violation of a term or condition of probation, conditional discharge, parole, or mandatory supervised release for a felony or an act which, if committed by an adult, would constitute a felony, who intentionally escapes from custody is guilty of a Class 2 felony.

(c-6) A person in the lawful custody of a peace officer for an alleged violation of a term or condition of supervision, probation, or conditional discharge for a misdemeanor or an act which, if committed by an adult, would constitute a misdemeanor, who intentionally escapes from custody is guilty of a Class A misdemeanor.

(d) A person who violates this Section while armed with a dangerous weapon commits a Class 1 felony.

§ 31-7. Aiding escape. (a) Whoever, with intent to aid any prisoner in escaping from any penal institution, conveys into the institution or transfers to the prisoner anything for use in escaping commits a Class A misdemeanor.

(b) Whoever knowingly aids a person convicted of a felony or charged with the commission of a felony, or charged with or adjudicated delinquent for an act which, if committed by an adult, would constitute a felony, in escaping from any penal institution or from the custody of any employee of that institution commits a Class

2 felony; however, whoever knowingly aids a person convicted of a felony or charged with the commission of a felony, or charged with or adjudicated delinquent for an act which, if committed by an adult, would constitute a felony, in failing to return from furlough or from work and day release is guilty of a Class 3 felony.

(c) Whoever knowingly aids a person convicted of a misdemeanor or charged with the commission of a misdemeanor, or charged with or adjudicated delinquent for an act which, if committed by an adult, would constitute a misdemeanor, in escaping from any penal institution or from the custody of an employee of that institution commits a Class A misdemeanor; however, whoever knowingly aids a person convicted of a misdemeanor or charged with the commission of a misdemeanor, or charged with or adjudicated delinquent for an act which, if committed by an adult, would constitute a misdemeanor, in failing to return from furlough or from work and day release is guilty of a Class B misdemeanor.

(d) Whoever knowingly aids a person in escaping from any public institution, other than a penal institution, in which he is lawfully detained, or from the custody of an employee of that institution, commits a Class A misdemeanor.

(e) Whoever knowingly aids a person in the lawful custody of a peace officer for the alleged commission of a felony offense or an act which, if committed by an adult, would constitute a felony, in escaping from custody commits a Class 2 felony; however, whoever knowingly aids a person in the lawful custody of a peace officer for the alleged commission of a misdemeanor offense or an act which, if committed by an adult, would constitute a misdemeanor, in escaping from custody commits a Class A misdemeanor.

(f) An officer or employee of any penal institution who recklessly permits any prisoner in his custody to escape commits a Class A misdemeanor.

(f-5) With respect to a person in the lawful custody of a peace officer for an alleged violation of a term or condition of probation, conditional discharge, parole, or mandatory supervised release for a felony, whoever intentionally aids that person to escape from that custody is guilty of a Class 2 felony.

(f-6) With respect to a person who is in the lawful custody of a peace officer for an alleged violation of a term or condition of supervision, probation, or conditional discharge for a misdemeanor, whoever intentionally aids that person to escape from that custody is guilty of a Class A misdemeanor.

(g) A person who violates this Section while armed with a dangerous weapon commits a Class 2 felony.

§ 31-8. Refusing to aid an officer. Whoever upon command refuses or knowingly fails reasonably to aid a person known by him to be a peace officer in:

(a) Apprehending a person whom the officer is authorized to apprehend; or

(b) Preventing the commission by another of any offense, commits a petty offense.

§ 31-9. Obstructing an emergency management worker. a person who knowingly obstructs the performance by one known to the person to be an emergency management worker of any authorized act within his or her official capacity commits a Class A misdemeanor.

Commentary – Escape

Under Section 31-6 the common way a person commits the offense of escape is if (1) having been convicted of or charged with a felony or misdemeanor (or as a juvenile adjudicated of an offense that would be a felony or misdemeanor if charged as an adult) he intentionally escapes from the custody of n jail or prison or an employee of such or (2) having been convicted of or charged with a felony or misdemeanor (or as a juvenile adjudicated of an offense that would be a felony or misdemeanor if charged as an adult) he intentionally escapes from the custody of a peace officer. A person can also commit the offense of escape if he fails to report to a detention center or other custodial circumstance based on an order for periodic imprisonment or work release. the classification of the escape offense is tied to the felony or misdemeanor conviction or charge in that the escape from a predicate felony case is a Class 2 felony offense, while the escape from a predicate misdemeanor case is a Class A misdemeanor offense.

In custody. In *People v. Howell* 388 Ill.App.3d 338, 902 N.E.2d 797 (Ill. App. Ct. 4th Dist. 2009), the defendant had been sentenced to 2 years imprisonment and was remanded to the custody of the sheriff. The court security officer escorted her from the courtroom without placing her in handcuffs. She asked the officer if she could give her purse to her mother, and after the officer said she could, the defendant pushed away and started down the stairs at the courthouse, only to be stopped (without resistance) three floors below. She was convicted of escape and sentenced to 4 years in prison consecutive to the prior sentence she had received. On appeal, she claimed that she was not in custody of an institution or a peace officer after her sentencing and had been granted permission to find her mother in the courthouse. Her conviction was affirmed because the court security officer was an employee of the Sheriff who ran the Macon County Jail and thus under the evidence the defendant had intentionally escaped from the custody an employee of a penal institution as proscribed by Section 31-6(a).

Article 31A – Interference with Penal Institution
720 ILCS 5/31A-1.1 *et seq.*

§ 31A-0.1. Definitions. For the purposes of this Article:
"Deliver" or "delivery" means the actual, constructive or attempted transfer of possession of an item of contraband, with or without consideration, whether or not there is an agency relationship.
"Employee" means any elected or appointed officer, trustee or employee of a penal institution or of the governing authority of the penal institution, or any person who performs services for the penal institution pursuant to contract with the penal institution or its governing authority.
"Item of contraband" means any of the following:
(i) "Alcoholic liquor" as that term is defined in Section 1-3.05 of the Liquor Control Act of 1934.
(ii) "Cannabis" as that term is defined in subsection (a) of Section 3 of the Cannabis Control Act.
(iii) "Controlled substance" as that term is defined in the Illinois Controlled Substances Act.
(iii-a) "Methamphetamine" as that term is defined in the Illinois Controlled Substances Act or the Methamphetamine Control and Community Protection Act.
(iv) "Hypodermic syringe" or hypodermic needle, or any instrument adapted for use of controlled substances or cannabis by subcutaneous injection.
(v) "Weapon" means any knife, dagger, dirk, billy, razor, stiletto, broken bottle, or other piece of glass which could be used as a dangerous weapon. This term includes any of the devices or implements designated in subsections (a)(1), (a)(3) and (a)(6) of Section 24-1 of this Code, or any other dangerous weapon or instrument of like character.
(vi) "Firearm" means any device, by whatever name known, which is designed to expel a projectile or projectiles by the action of an explosion, expansion of gas or escape of gas, including but not limited to:
(A) any pneumatic gun, spring gun, or B-B gun which expels a single globular projectile not exceeding .18 inch in diameter; or
(B) any device used exclusively for signaling or safety and required as recommended by the United States Coast Guard or the Interstate Commerce Commission; or

(C) any device used exclusively for the firing of stud cartridges, explosive rivets or industrial ammunition; or
(D) any device which is powered by electrical charging units, such as batteries, and which fires one or several barbs attached to a length of wire and which, upon hitting a human, can send out current capable of disrupting the person's nervous system in such a manner as to render him or her incapable of normal functioning, commonly referred to as a stun gun or taser.
(vii) "Firearm ammunition" means any self-contained cartridge or shotgun shell, by whatever name known, which is designed to be used or adaptable to use in a firearm, including but not limited to:
(A) any ammunition exclusively designed for use with a device used exclusively for signaling or safety and required or recommended by the United States Coast Guard or the Interstate Commerce Commission; or
(B) any ammunition designed exclusively for use with a stud or rivet driver or other similar industrial ammunition.
(viii) "Explosive" means, but is not limited to, bomb, bombshell, grenade, bottle or other container containing an explosive substance of over one-quarter ounce for like purposes such as black powder bombs and Molotov cocktails or artillery projectiles.
(ix) "Tool to defeat security mechanisms" means, but is not limited to, handcuff or security restraint key, tool designed to pick locks, popper, or any device or instrument used to or capable of unlocking or preventing from locking any handcuff or security restraints, doors to cells, rooms, gates or other areas of the penal institution.
(x) "Cutting tool" means, but is not limited to, hacksaw blade, wirecutter, or device, instrument or file capable of cutting through metal.
(xi) "Electronic contraband" for the purposes of Section 31A-1.1 of this Article means, but is not limited to, any electronic, video recording device, computer, or cellular communications equipment, including, but not limited to, cellular telephones, cellular telephone batteries, videotape recorders, pagers, computers, and computer peripheral equipment brought into or possessed in a penal institution without the written authorization of the Chief Administrative Officer. "Electronic contraband" for the purposes of Section 31A-1.2 of this Article, means, but is not limited to, any electronic, video recording device, computer, or cellular communications equipment, including, but not limited to, cellular telephones, cellular telephone batteries, videotape recorders, pagers, computers, and computer peripheral equipment.
"Penal institution" means any penitentiary, State farm, reformatory, prison, jail, house of correction, police detention area, half-way house or other institution or place for the incarceration or custody of persons under sentence for offenses awaiting trial or sentence for offenses, under arrest for an offense, a violation of probation, a violation of parole, a violation of aftercare release, or a violation of mandatory supervised release, or awaiting a bail setting hearing or preliminary hearing; provided that where the place for incarceration or custody is housed within another public building this Article shall not apply to that part of the building unrelated to the incarceration or custody of persons.

§ 31A-1.1. Bringing Contraband into a Penal Institution; Possessing Contraband in a Penal Institution. (a) A person commits the offense of bringing contraband into a penal institution when he knowingly and without authority of any person designated or authorized to grant such authority (1) brings an item of contraband into a penal institution or (2) causes another to bring an item of contraband into a penal institution or (3) places an item of contraband in such proximity to a penal institution as to give an inmate access to the contraband.

(b) A person commits the offense of possessing contraband in a penal institution when he possesses contraband in a penal institution, regardless of the intent with which he possesses it.

(c) For the purposes of this Section, the words and phrases listed below shall be defined as follows:

(1) "Penal institution" means any penitentiary, State farm, reformatory, prison, jail, house of correction, police detention area, half-way house

or other institution or place for the incarceration or custody of persons under sentence for offenses awaiting trial or sentence for offenses, under arrest for an offense, a violation of probation, a violation of parole, or a violation of mandatory supervised release, or awaiting a bail setting hearing or preliminary hearing; provided that where the place for incarceration or custody is housed within another public building this Act shall not apply to that part of such building unrelated to the incarceration or custody of persons.

(2) "Item of contraband" means any of the following:

(i) "Alcoholic liquor" as such term is defined in Section 1-3.05 of the Liquor Control Act of 1934.

(ii) "Cannabis" as such term is defined in subsection (a) of Section 3 of the Cannabis Control Act.

(iii) "Controlled substance" as such term is defined in the Illinois Controlled Substances Act.

(iii-a) "Methamphetamine" as such term is defined in the Illinois Controlled Substances Act or the Methamphetamine Control and Community Protection Act.

(iv) "Hypodermic syringe" or hypodermic needle, or any instrument adapted for use of controlled substances or cannabis by subcutaneous injection.

(v) "Weapon" means any knife, dagger, dirk, billy, razor, stiletto, broken bottle, or other piece of glass which could be used as a dangerous weapon. Such term includes any of the devices or implements designated in subsections (a)(1), (a)(3) and (a)(6) of Section 24-1 of this Act, or any other dangerous weapon or instrument of like character.

(vi) "Firearm" means any device, by whatever name known, which is designed to expel a projectile or projectiles by the action of an explosion, expansion of gas or escape of gas, including but not limited to:

(A) any pneumatic gun, spring gun, or B-B gun which expels a single globular projectile not exceeding .18 inch in diameter, or;

(B) any device used exclusively for signaling or safety and required as recommended by the United States Coast Guard or the Interstate Commerce Commission; or

(C) any device used exclusively for the firing of stud cartridges, explosive rivets or industrial ammunition; or
(D) any device which is powered by electrical charging units, such as batteries, and which fires one or several barbs attached to a length of wire and which, upon hitting a human, can send out current capable of disrupting the person's nervous system in such a manner as to render him incapable of normal functioning, commonly referred to as a stun gun or taser.

(vii) "Firearm ammunition" means any self-contained cartridge or shotgun shell, by whatever name known, which is designed to be used or adaptable to use in a firearm, including but not limited to:

(A) any ammunition exclusively designed for use with a device used exclusively for signaling or safety and required or recommended by the United States Coast Guard or the Interstate Commerce Commission; or

(B) any ammunition designed exclusively for use with a stud or rivet driver or other similar industrial ammunition.
(viii) "Explosive" means, but is not limited to, bomb, bombshell, grenade, bottle or other container containing an explosive substance of over one-quarter ounce for like purposes such as black powder bombs and Molotov cocktails or artillery projectiles.

(ix) "Tool to defeat security mechanisms" means, but is not limited to, handcuff or security restraint key, tool designed to pick locks, popper, or any device or instrument used to or capable of unlocking or preventing from locking any handcuff or security restraints, doors to cells, rooms, gates or other areas of the penal institution.

(x) "Cutting tool" means, but is not limited to, hacksaw blade, wire cutter, or device, instrument or file capable of cutting through metal.

(xi) "Electronic contraband" means, but is not limited to, any electronic, video recording device, computer, or cellular communications equipment, including, but not limited to, cellular telephones, cellular telephone batteries, videotape recorders, pagers, computers, and computer peripheral equipment brought into or possessed in a penal institution without the written authorization of the Chief Administrative Officer.

(d) Bringing alcoholic liquor into a penal institution is a Class 4 felony. Possessing alcoholic liquor in a penal institution is a Class 4 felony.

(e) Bringing cannabis into a penal institution is a Class 3 felony. Possessing cannabis in a penal institution is a Class 3 felony.

(f) Bringing any amount of a controlled substance classified in Schedules III, IV or V of Article II of the Controlled Substance Act into a penal institution is a Class 2 felony. Possessing any amount of a controlled substance classified in Schedule III, IV, or V of Article II of the Controlled Substance Act in a penal institution is a Class 2 felony.

(g) Bringing any amount of a controlled substance classified in Schedules I or II of Article II of the Controlled Substance Act into a penal institution is a Class 1 felony. Possessing any amount of a controlled substance classified in Schedules I or II of Article II of the Controlled Substance Act in a penal institution is a Class 1 felony.

(h) Bringing an item of contraband listed in paragraph (iv) of subsection (c)(2) into a penal institution is a Class 1 felony. Possessing an item of contraband listed in paragraph (iv) of subsection (c)(2) in a penal institution is a Class 1 felony.

(i) Bringing an item of contraband listed in paragraph (v), (ix), (x),or (xi) of subsection (c)(2) into a penal institution is a Class 1 felony. Possessing an item of contraband listed in paragraph (v), (ix), (x), or (xi) of subsection (c)(2) in a penal institution is a Class 1 felony.

(j) Bringing an item of contraband listed in paragraphs (vi), (vii) or (viii) of subsection (c)(2) in a penal institution is a Class X felony. Possessing an item of contraband listed in paragraphs (vi), (vii), or (viii) of subsection (c)(2) in a penal institution is a Class X felony.

(k) It shall be an affirmative defense to subsection (b) hereof, that such possession was specifically authorized by rule, regulation, or directive of the governing authority of the penal institution or order issued pursuant thereto.

(l) It shall be an affirmative defense to subsection (a)(1) and subsection (b) hereof that the person bringing into or possessing contraband in a penal institution had been arrested, and that that person possessed such contraband at the time of his arrest, and that such contraband was brought into or possessed in the penal institution by that person as a direct and immediate result of his arrest.

(m) Items confiscated may be retained for use by the Department of Corrections or disposed of as deemed appropriate by the Chief Administrative Officer in accordance with Department rules or disposed of as required by law.

§ 31A-1.2. Unauthorized bringing of contraband into a penal institution by an employee; unauthorized possessing of contraband in a penal institution by an employee; unauthorized delivery of contraband in a penal institution by an employee. (a) A person commits the offense of unauthorized bringing of contraband into a penal institution by an employee when a person who is an employee knowingly and without authority of any person designated or authorized to grant such authority:

(1) brings or attempts to bring an item of contraband listed in subsection (d)(4) into a penal institution, or

(2) causes or permits another to bring an item of contraband listed in subsection (d)(4) into a penal institution.

(b) A person commits the offense of unauthorized possession of contraband in a penal institution by an employee when a person who is an employee knowingly and without authority of any person designated or authorized to grant such authority possesses contraband listed in subsection (d)(4) in a penal institution, regardless of the intent with which he possesses it.

(c) A person commits the offense of unauthorized delivery of contraband in a penal institution by an employee when a person who is an employee knowingly and without authority of any person designated or authorized to grant such authority:

(1) delivers or possesses with intent to deliver an item of contraband to any inmate of a penal institution, or

(2) conspires to deliver or solicits the delivery of an item of contraband to any inmate of a penal institution, or

(3) causes or permits the delivery of an item of contraband to any inmate of a penal institution, or

(4) permits another person to attempt to deliver an item of contraband to any inmate of a penal institution.

(d) For purpose of this Section, the words and phrases listed below shall be defined as follows:
(1) "Penal Institution" shall have the meaning ascribed to it in subsection (c)(1) of Section 31A-1.1 of this Code;

(2) "Employee" means any elected or appointed officer, trustee or employee of a penal institution or of the governing authority of the penal institution, or any person who performs services for the penal institution pursuant to contract with the penal institution or its governing authority.

(3) "Deliver" or "delivery" means the actual, constructive or attempted transfer of possession of an item of contraband, with or without consideration, whether or not there is an agency relationship;

(4) "Item of contraband" means any of the following:

(i) "Alcoholic liquor" as such term is defined in Section 1-3.05 of the Liquor Control Act of 1934.

(ii) "Cannabis" as such term is defined in subsection (a) of Section 3 of the Cannabis Control Act.

(iii) "Controlled substance" as such term is defined in the Illinois Controlled Substances Act.

(iii-a) "Methamphetamine" as such term is defined in the Illinois Controlled Substances Act or the Methamphetamine Control and Community Protection Act.

(iv) "Hypodermic syringe" or hypodermic needle, or any instrument adapted for use of controlled substances or cannabis by subcutaneous injection.

(v) "Weapon" means any knife, dagger, dirk, billy, razor, stiletto, broken bottle, or other piece of glass which could be used as a dangerous weapon. Such term includes any of the devices or implements designated in subsections (a)(1), (a)(3) and (a)(6) of Section 24-1 of this Act, or any other dangerous weapon or instrument of like character.

(vi) "Firearm" means any device, by whatever name known, which is designed to expel a projectile or projectiles by the action of an explosion, expansion of gas or escape of gas, including but not limited to:

(A) any pneumatic gun, spring gun, or B-B gun which expels a single globular projectile not exceeding .18 inch in diameter; or

(B) any device used exclusively for signaling or safety and required or recommended by the United States Coast Guard or the Interstate Commerce Commission; or

(C) any device used exclusively for the firing of stud cartridges, explosive rivets or industrial ammunition; or

(D) any device which is powered by electrical charging units, such as batteries, and which fires one or several barbs attached to a length of wire and which, upon hitting a human, can send out current capable of disrupting the person's nervous system in such a manner as to render him incapable of normal functioning, commonly referred to as a stun gun or taser.

(vii) "Firearm ammunition" means any self-contained cartridge or shotgun shell, by whatever name known, which is designed to be used or adaptable to use in a firearm, including but not limited to:

(A) any ammunition exclusively designed for use with a device used exclusively for signaling or safety and required or recommended by the United States Coast Guard or the Interstate Commerce Commission; or

(B) any ammunition designed exclusively for use with a stud or rivet driver or other similar industrial ammunition.

(viii) "Explosive" means, but is not limited to, bomb, bombshell, grenade, bottle or other container containing an explosive substance of over one-quarter ounce for like purposes such as black powder bombs and Molotov cocktails or artillery projectiles.

(ix) "Tool to defeat security mechanisms" means, but is not limited to, handcuff or security restraint key, tool designed to pick locks, popper, or any device or instrument used to or capable of unlocking or preventing from locking any handcuff or security restraints, doors to cells, rooms, gates or other areas of the penal institution.

(x) "Cutting tool" means, but is not limited to, hacksaw blade, wire cutter, or device, instrument or file capable of cutting through metal.

(xi) "Electronic contraband" means, but is not limited to, any electronic, video recording device, computer, or cellular communications equipment, including, but not limited to, cellular telephones, cellular telephone batteries, videotape recorders, pagers, computers, and computer peripheral equipment.

For a violation of subsection (a) or (b) involving a cellular telephone or cellular telephone battery, the defendant must intend to provide the cellular telephone or cellular telephone battery to any inmate in a penal institution, or to use the cellular telephone or cellular telephone battery at the direction of an inmate or for the benefit of any inmate of a penal institution.

(e) A violation of paragraphs (a) or (b) of this Section involving alcohol is a Class 4 felony.

A violation of paragraph (a) or (b) of this Section involving cannabis is a Class 2 felony.

A violation of paragraph (a) or (b) involving any amount of a controlled substance classified in Schedules III, IV or V of Article II of the Illinois Controlled Substances Act is a Class 1 felony.

A violation of paragraph (a) or (b) of this Section involving any amount of a controlled substance classified in Schedules I or II of Article II of the Illinois Controlled Substances Act is a Class X felony.

A violation of paragraph (a) or (b) involving an item of contraband listed in paragraph (iv) of subsection (d)(4) is a Class X felony.

A violation of paragraph (a) or (b) involving an item of contraband listed in paragraph (v) or (xi) of subsection (d)(4) is a Class 1 felony.

A violation of paragraph (a) or (b) involving an item of contraband listed in paragraphs (vi), (vii) or (viii) of subsection (d)(4) is a Class X felony.

(f) A violation of paragraph (c) of this Section involving alcoholic liquor is a Class 3 felony.

A violation of paragraph (c) involving cannabis is a Class 1 felony.

A violation of paragraph (c) involving any amount of a controlled substance classified in Schedules III, IV or V of Article II of the Illinois Controlled Substances Act is a Class X felony.

A violation of paragraph (c) involving any amount of a controlled substance classified in Schedules I or II of Article II of the Illinois Controlled Substances Act is a Class X felony for which the minimum term of imprisonment shall be 8years.

A violation of paragraph (c) involving an item of contraband listed in paragraph (iv) of subsection (d)(4) is a Class X felony for which the minimum term of imprisonment shall be 8 years.

A violation of paragraph (c)involving an item of contraband listed in paragraph (v), (ix) or (x) of subsection (d)(4) is a Class X felony for which the minimum term of imprisonment shall be 10 years.

A violation of paragraph (c) involving an item of contraband listed in paragraphs (vi), (vii) or (viii) of subsection(d)(4) is a Class X felony for which the minimum term of imprisonment shall be 12 years.

(g) Items confiscated may be retained for use by the Department of Corrections or disposed of as deemed appropriate by the Chief Administrative Officer in accordance with Department rules or disposed of as required by law.

(h) For a violation of subsection (a) or (b) involving items described in clause (i), (v), (vi), (vii), (ix), (x), or (xi) of paragraph (4) of subsection (d), such items shall not be considered to be in a penal institution when they are secured in an employee's locked, private motor vehicle parked on the grounds of a penal institution.

Article 32 – Interference with Judicial Procedure
720 ILCS 5/32-1 *et seq.*

§ 32-1. Compounding a crime. (a) A person compounds a crime when he receives or offers to another any consideration for a promise not to prosecute or aid in the prosecution of an offender.

(b) Sentence. Compounding a crime is a petty offense.

§ 32-2. Perjury. (a) A person commits perjury when, under oath or affirmation, in a proceeding or in any other matter where by law such oath or affirmation is required, he makes a false statement, material to the issue or point in question, which he does not believe to be true.

(b) Proof of Falsity. an indictment or information for perjury alleging that the offender, under oath, has made contradictory statements, material to the issue or point in question, in the same or in different proceedings, where such oath or affirmation is required, need not specify which statement is false. At the trial, the prosecution need not establish which statement is false.

(c) Admission of Falsity. Where the contradictory statements are made in the same continuous trial, an admission by the offender in that same continuous trial of the falsity of a contradictory statement shall bar prosecution therefore under any provisions of this Code.
(d) A person shall be exempt from prosecution under subsection (a) of this Section if he is a peace officer who uses a false or fictitious name in the enforcement of the criminal laws, and such use is approved in writing as provided in Section 10-1 of "The Liquor Control Act of

1934", as amended, Section 5 of "An Act in relation to the use of an assumed name in the conduct or transaction of business in this State", approved July 17, 1941, as amended, or Section 2605-200 of the Department of State Police Law (20 ILCS 2605/2605-200). However, this exemption shall not apply to testimony in judicial proceedings where the identity of the peace officer is material to the issue, and he is ordered by the court to disclose his identity.

(e) Sentence. Perjury is a Class 3 felony.

Commentary – Perjury

Perjury, as defined by Section 31-2, is the making of a false, material statement which the offender does not believe to be true, in a proceeding or other matter where the law requires an oath or affirmation. If a person under oath, at different times, makes statements that contradict each other, in the same proceeding or in separate proceedings, that is evidence of falsehood, and the speaker may be prosecuted for perjury with the prosecution having no requirement to prove which contradictory statement was false

Proceeding or other matter; belief in truth. Perjured statements occur before a grand jury or at trials or hearings where witnesses are under oath or affirm to tell the truth. False sworn statements can occur in other settings such as depositions in civil cases, acknowledgements on election petitions or statements of candidacy.

In *People v. McCulloch* 404 Ill.App.3d 125, 936 N.E.2d 743 (Ill. App. Ct. 2nd Dist. 2010), the defendant was a paid political consultant who agreed to gather signatures necessary to place a candidate on an election ballot. He hired a group of people to gather signatures door-to-door, at the post office and in other locations. Some of the signatures were fake. The defendant turned in the petitions and signed a certification under oath on the election petitions that all the signatures were genuine, accurate and were taken in his presence. He explained to a notary that he was in his car watching his workers obtain the signatures. When the notary expressed concern about the requirements of the certification, he changed his story and said he was standing near the workers when the signatures were obtained, so she notarized his certification. He was prosecuted for perjury under a provision of the Illinois Election Code identical to Section 31-2(a) and convicted. He claimed on appeal that the evidence was insufficient to show that he did not believe in the truth of the certification language but the court rejected the claim in light of his changed story. The evidence in the case was largely circumstantial but showed the defendant's own knowledge of the falsity of his statements, since it would have been impossible for the defendant to observe multiple workers obtaining multiple signatures at multiple locations, at the same time.

Statements of fact or opinion. Perjury prosecutions cannot be based on matters of opinion or on statements that may be ambiguous or unclear. In *People ex rel Madigan v. Baumgartner* 355 Ill.App.3d 842, 823 N.E.2d 1144 (Ill. App. Ct. 4th Dist. 2005), the defendant was a candidate for county board in Moultrie County where he was born and where he maintained his address for voting and his driver's license. However for over 10 years he had attended the University of Illinois obtaining his bachelor's, masters and law degrees. He had also married and bought a house in Champaign. His wife used the Champaign home as her permanent address while the defendant continued to use an address in Windsor, Illinois. Nonetheless he had signed, under oath, a candidate's certification that he resided in Moultrie County. He was prosecuted for perjury for falsely stating that his permanent residence was in Windsor. He was convicted. His conviction was reversed on appeal with the court noting that a person cannot be convicted of perjury for a "statement, opinion or conclusion" that was inferred from other facts. Although the defendant had homes at two locations, he had the right to declare his intention about which was his permanent residence. There was no perjury.

On the other hand, untruthfully avoiding the question by giving a false answer can result in a prosecution for perjury. In *People v. Baltzer* 327 Ill.App.3d 222, 762 N.E.2d 1174 (Ill. App. Ct. 2nd Dist. 2002), the defendant had defaulted on a car loan, was sued by the bank and a civil judgment was entered against him. Also, an order to turn the car back into the bank was served on him. He falsely claimed the car was stolen, later transferring title to the car to his attorney in payment of attorney fees. He appeared at a citation to discover assets proceeding in court where the bank was trying to collect on the civil judgment and was placed under to oath. The following is a transcript of a portion of his testimony, with the italics representing the defendant's testimony that was contended to be perjury:

> "Q. What became of the title?
>
> A. For the car?
>
> Q. Right.
>
> A. I said I don't have it.
>
> Q. Well, when you last had it, where did it go? Did it get up and walk away?
>
> A. *I don't recall.*
>
> Q. Did you ever deliver the title to any other person or entity?
>
> A. *I don't recall.*
>
> Q. Was the title stolen?
>
> A. *I don't recall.*
>
> Q. Have you ever reported the title stolen?
>
> A. *I don't recall. If it was in the vehicle, perhaps it disappeared with that.* It has been a while.
>
> Q. Have you ever applied to the Secretary of State for a duplicate or a renewal title?
>
> A. Yes.
>
> Q. When did you do that?
>
> A. I don't recall.
>
> Q. What calendar year, Mr. Baltzer?
>
> A. I don't remember."

[As the examination continued, counsel for West Suburban Bank asked defendant additional questions about his application for a duplicate title and how and where defendant recovered the Corvette after it was allegedly stolen. The following colloquy occurred. Again, the italicized statements were alleged to constitute perjury.]

"Q. But it did come back into your possession; correct?

A. Yes.

Q. How long did you have it?

A. *I don't recall exactly.*

Q. Was it more than a week?

A. *Well, I have indicated to you I don't recall, so I am standing by that answer.*

Q. Okay. Was it more than a month?

A. *I don't recall.*

Q. Was it more than a day?

A. *I don't recall.*

Q. What did you do with the vehicle after it came back into your possession?

A. *That I don't recall.*

Q. But you no longer have it?

A. That's correct.

Q. Was it again stolen?

A. No.

Q. Did you sell the vehicle?

A. *I don't recall.*

Q. Did you transfer possession of the vehicle to some other person?

A. *I don't recall.*

Q. When did you last have possession of the vehicle?

A. *I have indicated I don't recall.*

Q. When was it that you last saw the vehicle?

A. *That I don't recall.*

Q. How did the vehicle come back into your possession?

A. *I don't recall.*

Q. What did you do with the vehicle after it came back into your possession?

A. *That I don't recall.*

Q. How did the vehicle come back into your possession?

A. *I don't recall.*

Q. When you say it was recovered, it was recovered by some police entity?

A. No.

Q. Who recovered it?

A. I did.

Q. And where did you find it?

A. *I don't recall.*

Q. Did you drive it after it came into your possession?

A. *I don't recall.*

Q. What was its condition when you found it?

A. *I don't recall.*

Q. Was it driveable?

A. *I don't recall.*

Q. Did it have its license plates still on it?

A. *I don't recall.*

* * *

Q. What did you do with the car itself, the actual physical vehicle? Did you sell it?

A. *I don't recall.*

Q. Do you know who has the vehicle?

A. I don't.

Q. Do you know to whom you gave the vehicle?

A. *I don't recall.*

Q. It was not stolen from you again, was it?

A. No.

Q. So you voluntarily gave it up?

A. I didn't say that.

Q. How did you last give up possession of it-

A. *I don't recall.*"

People v. Baltzer 327 Ill.App.3d at 224-226, 762 N.E.2d at 1175-1177. [Court's statement in brackets.]

On appeal the defendant claimed that his statements to the effect "I don't recall" could not be the subject of a perjury prosecution because they were either statements of opinion or conclusion or were ambiguous. an answer to a question that is literally true but evasive may not be perjury, and the ability of the questioner to narrow the question properly might avoid that issue. However, in *Baltzer* the court had no difficulty in concluding that the defendant was not telling the truth and did not believe he was telling the truth when he repeatedly said "I don't recall". His conviction for perjury was affirmed.

False material statement. The false statement that is the subject of perjury must be material that is the false statement must have a bearing on the matter presented. In court cases, the perjury must be capable of affecting the proceedings; although it need not actually have an effect to be material.

In *People v. Davis* 164 Ill.2d 309, 647 N.E.2d 977 (Ill. S. Ct. 1995), the defendant was a party to a civil case and gave a deposition where he was asked a series of eight questions about his sexual activities. The civil case was settled. The defendant was indicted and charged with eight counts of perjury, one count for each question and answer that was alleged to be false from the civil deposition. a motion to dismiss the indictment was filed and was heard by the trial judge who had also presided over the civil case, who said that the questions and answers from the civil deposition that were the subject of the criminal perjury prosecution were not considered by him in dealing with the civil case, and thus they were not material statements, even if they were false. The Illinois Supreme Court reversed and reinstated the indictment, stating:

> The language of the perjury statute does not require the alleged false statements to be before the trier of fact or anyone else. The law only requires that the statements be given under oath or affirmation in any type of matter where the law requires an oath or affirmation; that they be false; that they be material to the issue or point in question; and that the person making the statements believes them not to be true.

People v. Davis 164 Ill.2d at 311-312, 647 N.E.2d at 979.

In *People v. Acevedo* 275 Ill.App.3d 420, 656 N.E.2d 118 (Ill. App. Ct. 2nd Dist. 1995), the defendant testified as a witness at the murder trial of Robert "Droopy" Ranjel, who was acquitted. Afterward the defendant was charged with two counts of perjury (one each for separate questions and separate answers), in violation of Section 32-1(a) when he testified at the murder trial:

> "Q. At that time did you tell Wayne Biles, along with Investigator Powell of the Aurora Police Department, that a few minutes after Psycho [Alberto Gonzalez] got shot, Droopy, Loco, and Bam-Bam came by dressed in black with paint on their faces?
>
> A. No, I didn't."
>
> * * *
>
> "Q. Did you say-did you tell Detective Anderson on that date that you heard shots fired from the direction of Psycho's house, and five to ten minutes later Droopy, Loco, and Bam-Bam arrived with faces painted and they asked if they could wash em off at your place, did you tell him that, or words to that effect?
>
> A. No, I didn't."
>
> *People v. Acevedo,* 275 Ill.App.3d at 422, 656 N.E.2d at 120.

At the murder trial, the police officers did not testify to prove Acevedo's prior statements had been made, and the murder trial defendant presented an alibi defense.

At Acevedo's perjury trial, the police officers (Biles, Powell and Anderson) did testify that he made the statements he had denied at the murder trial. Acevedo was convicted of perjury and appealed, claiming that the testimony at the murder trial, even if false, was not material because the prosecution did not perfect the impeachment (i.e. have the officers testify that in fact he had made the prior statements) and thus the jury never heard the false testimony. Acevedo also claimed the murder trial testimony was not material in light of Ranjel's alibi evidence. The court rejected both claims and affirmed his conviction for perjury. The court reasoned that the testimonial denials were false statements and were before the jury, and that the testimony if truthfully given would have placed Ranjel within a few blocks of the murder soon after the crime. The false statements were material to points in issue in the murder trial and thus material in the sense of the perjury charges.

§ 32-3. Subornation of perjury. (a) A person commits subornation of perjury when he procures or induces another to make a statement in violation of Section 32-2 which the person knows to be false.

(b) Sentence. Subornation of perjury is a Class 4 felony.

§ 32-4. Communicating with jurors and witnesses. (a) A person who, with intent to influence any person whom he believes has been summoned as a juror, regarding any matter which is or may be brought before such juror, communicates, directly or indirectly, with such juror otherwise than as authorized by law commits a Class 4 felony.

(b) A person who, with intent to deter any party or witness from testifying freely, fully and truthfully to any matter pending in any court, or before a Grand Jury, Administrative agency or any other State or local governmental unit, forcibly detains such party or witness, or communicates, directly or indirectly, to such party or witness any knowingly false information or a threat of injury or damage to the property or person of any individual or offers or delivers or threatens to withhold money or another thing of value to any individual commits a Class 3 felony.

(c) A person who violates the Juror Protection Act commits a Class 4 felony.

§ 32-4a. Harassment of representatives for the child, jurors, witnesses and others.
(a) A person who, with intent to harass or annoy one who has served or is serving or who is a family member of a person who has served or is serving (1) as a juror because of the verdict returned by the jury in a pending legal proceeding or the participation of the juror in the verdict or (2) as a witness, or who may be expected to serve as a witness in a pending legal proceeding, or who was expected to serve as a witness but who did not serve as a witness because the charges against the defendant were dismissed or because the defendant pleaded guilty to the charges against him or her, because of the testimony or potential testimony of the witness or person who may be expected or may have been expected to serve as a witness, communicates directly or indirectly with the juror, witness or person who may be expected or may have been expected to serve as a witness, or family member of a juror or witness or person who may be expected or may have been expected to serve as a witness in such manner as to produce mental anguish or emotional distress or who conveys a threat of injury or damage to the property or person of any juror, witness or person who may be expected or may have been expected to serve as a witness, or family member of the juror or witness or person who may be expected or may have been expected to serve as a witness commits a Class 2 felony.

(b) A person who, with intent to harass or annoy one who has served or is serving or who is a family member of a person who has served or is serving as a representative for the child, appointed under Section 506 of the Illinois Marriage and Dissolution of Marriage Act or Section 2-502 of the Code of Civil Procedure, because of the representative service of that capacity, communicates directly or indirectly with the representative or a family member of the representative in such manner as to produce mental anguish or emotional distress or who conveys a threat of injury or damage to the property or person of any representative or a family member of the representative commits a Class A misdemeanor.

(c) For purposes of this Section, "family member" means a spouse, parent, child, stepchild or other person related by blood or by present marriage, a person who has, or allegedly has a child in common, and a person who shares or allegedly shares a blood relationship through a child.

§ 32-4b. Promise to excuse or excusing person from jury duty. A jury commissioner, or any other person acting on behalf of a jury commissioner, who requests, solicits, suggests, or accepts financial compensation or any other form of consideration in exchange for a promise to excuse or for excusing any person from jury duty commits a Class 3 felony.

In addition to any other penalty provided by law, any jury commissioner convicted under this Section shall forfeit the performance bond required by Section 1 of "An Act in relation to jury commissioners and authorizing judges to appoint such commissioners and to make rules concerning their powers and duties", approved June 15, 1887, as amended, 705 ILCS 310/1, and shall be excluded from further service as a jury commissioner.

Commentary – Communicating with Jurors and Witnesses

Influencing a witness. Words along are enough for criminal liability for attempting to influence a witness. In *People v. Stuckey*, 2011 IL App (1st) 0925350 (Ill. App. Ct. 1st Dist. 2011), the defendant was charged with violating §32-4(b) for approaching a woman who was a witness in a murder trial for the defendant's friend. The woman testified that the defendant asked her to do him a favor and not testify during trial, and that the defendant told her that if she testified against his friend, something bad would happen to her, but if she failed to testify, then his friend would give her $1,000. The defendant claimed that the statute only prohibited people from coercing witnesses into altering their testimony or testifying falsely and since he only wanted to deter the witness from showing up, he did not have the required *mens rea* for the crime. The Appellate Court affirmed the defendant's conviction, and found the evidence satisfied the *mens rea* element of 5/32-4(b) because not doing so would create an obvious loophole – allowing threatening witnesses to go unpunished. The *mens rea* of communicating with a witness includes the intent to deter a witness from appearing in court to testify.

§ 32-4c. Witnesses; prohibition on accepting payments before judgment or verdict.
(a) A person who, after the commencement of a criminal prosecution, has been identified in the criminal discovery process as a person who may be called as a witness in a criminal proceeding shall not accept or receive, directly or indirectly, any payment or benefit in consideration for providing information obtained as a result of witnessing an event or occurrence or having personal knowledge of certain facts in relation to the criminal proceeding.

(b) A violation of this Section is a Class B misdemeanor for which the court may impose a fine not to exceed 3 times the amount of compensation requested, accepted, or received.

(c) This Section remains applicable until the judgment of the court in the action if the defendant is tried by the court without a jury or the rendering of the verdict by the jury if the defendant is tried by jury in the action.

(d) This Section does not apply to any of the following circumstances:

(1) To the lawful compensation paid to expert witnesses, investigators, employees, or agents by a prosecutor, law enforcement agency, or an attorney employed to represent a person in a criminal matter.

(2) To the lawful compensation or benefits provided to an informant by a prosecutor or law enforcement agency.

(2.5) To the lawful compensation or benefits, or both, provided to an informant under a local anti-crime program, such as Crime Stoppers, We-Tip, and similar programs designed to solve crimes or that foster the detection of crime and encourage persons through the programs and otherwise to come forward with information about criminal activity.

(2.6) To the lawful compensation or benefits, or both, provided by a private individual to another private individual as a reward for information leading to the arrest and conviction of specified offenders.

(3) To the lawful compensation paid to a publisher, editor, reporter, writer, or other person connected with or employed by a newspaper, magazine, television or radio station or any other publishing or media outlet for disclosing information obtained from another person relating to an offense.

(e) For purposes of this Section, "publishing or media outlet" means a news gathering organization that sells or distributes news to newspapers, television, or radio stations, or a cable or broadcast television or radio network that disseminates news and information.

(f) The person referred to in subsection (a) of this Section may receive written notice from counsel for either the prosecution or defense of the fact that he or she has been identified as a person who may be called as a witness in a criminal proceeding and his or her responsibilities and possible penalties under this Section. This Section shall be applicable only if the person referred to in subsection (a) of this Section received the written notice referred to in this subsection (f).

§ 32-4d. Payment of jurors by parties prohibited. (a) After a verdict has been rendered in a civil or criminal case, a person who was a plaintiff or defendant in the case may not offer or pay an award or other fee to a juror

who was a member of the jury that rendered the verdict in the case.
(b) After a verdict has been rendered in a civil or criminal case, a member of the jury that rendered the verdict may not accept an award or fee from the plaintiff or defendant in that case.

(c) A violation of this Section is a Class A misdemeanor.

(d) This Section does not apply to the payment of a fee or award to a person who was a juror for purposes unrelated to the jury's verdict or to the outcome of the case.

§ 32-4e. Interfering with the duties of a judicial officer. (a) A person may not give or offer to give benefits, promises, pecuniary compensation, or any other form of compensation, either directly or indirectly, to a judicial officer or a member of the judicial officer's immediate family with the intent to:
(1) induce such judicial officer to do, or fail to do, any act in violation of the lawful execution of his or her official duties; or

(2) induce such judicial officer to commit or aid in the commission of any fraud, or to collude in, allow, or make available the opportunity for the commission of any fraud on the State of Illinois.

(b) A person may not give or offer to give benefits, promises, pecuniary compensation, or any other form of compensation, either directly or indirectly, to court employees and staff with the intent to interfere with the administration of the judicial process.

(c) Sentence. A person who violates this Section commits a Class 2 felony.

(d) Definitions. For purposes of this Section:

"Judicial officer" means a justice, judge, associate judge, or magistrate of a court of the United States of America or the State of Illinois.

"Immediate family" means a judicial officer's spouse or children.

§ 32-4f. Retaliating against a Judge by false claim, slander of title, or malicious recording of fictitious liens.
A person who files or causes to be filed, in any public record or in any private record that is generally available to the public, any false lien or encumbrance against the real or personal property of a Supreme, Appellate, Circuit, or Associate Judge of the State of Illinois with knowledge that such lien or encumbrance is false or contains any materially false, fictitious, or fraudulent statement or representation, and with the intent of retaliating against that Judge for the performance or non-performance of an official judicial duty, is guilty of a violation of this Section. A person is guilty of a Class A misdemeanor for a first offense and a Class 4 felony for a second or subsequent offense.

§32-5, 5.1-5.7 [Repealed.]

§ 32-6. Performance of unauthorized acts. A person who performs any of the following acts, knowing that his performance is not authorized by law, commits a Class 4 felony:

(a) Conducts a marriage ceremony; or

(b) Acknowledges the execution of any document which by law may be recorded; or

(c) Becomes a surety for any party in any civil or criminal proceeding, before any court or public officer authorized to accept such surety.

§ 32-7. Simulating legal process. A person who issues or delivers any document which he knows falsely purports to be or simulates any civil or criminal process commits a Class B misdemeanor

§ 32-8. Tampering with public records. As amended by P.A. 96-1508, effective June 1, 2011. (a) A person who knowingly, without lawful authority, and with the intent to defraud any party, public officer or entity, alters, destroys, defaces, removes or conceals any public record commits a Class 4 felony.

(b) "Public record" expressly includes, but is not limited to, court records, or documents, evidence, or exhibits filed with the clerk of the court and which have become a part of the official court record, pertaining to any civil or criminal proceeding in any court.

(c) Any judge, circuit clerk or clerk of court, public official or employee, court reporter, or other person who knowingly, without lawful authority, and with the intent to defraud any party, public officer or entity, alters, destroys, defaces, removes, or conceals any public record received or held by any judge or by a clerk of any court commits a Class 3 felony.

(d) Any person convicted under subsection (c) who at the time of the violation was responsible for making, keeping, storing, or reporting the record for which the tampering occurred :

(1) shall forfeit his or her public office or public employment, if any, and shall thereafter be ineligible for both State and local public office and public employment in this State for a period of 5 years after completion of any term of probation, conditional discharge, or incarceration in a penitentiary including the period of mandatory supervised release;

(2) shall forfeit all retirement, pension, and other benefits arising out of public office or public employment as may be determined by the court in accordance with the applicable provisions of the Illinois Pension Code;

(3) shall be subject to termination of any professional licensure or registration in this State as may be determined by the court in accordance with the provisions of the applicable professional licensing or registration laws;

(4) may be ordered by the court, after a hearing in accordance with applicable law and in addition to any other penalty or fine imposed by the court, to forfeit to the State an amount equal to any financial gain or the value of any advantage realized by the person as a result of the offense; and

(5) may be ordered by the court, after a hearing in accordance with applicable law and in addition to any other penalty or fine imposed by the court, to pay restitution to the victim in an amount equal to any financial loss or the value of any advantage lost by the victim as a result of the offense. For the purposes of this subsection (d), an offense under subsection (c) committed by a person holding public office or public employment shall be rebuttably presumed to relate to or arise out of or in connection with that public office or public employment.

(e) Any party litigant who believes a violation of this Section has occurred may seek the restoration of the court record as provided in the Court Records Restoration Act. Any order of the court denying the restoration of the court record may be appealed as any other civil judgment .

(f) When the sheriff or local law enforcement agency having jurisdiction declines to investigate, or inadequately investigates, the court or any interested party, shall notify the State Police of a suspected violation of subsection (a) or (c), who shall have the authority to investigate, and may investigate, the same, without regard to whether such local law enforcement agency has requested the State Police to do so.

(g) If the State's Attorney having jurisdiction declines to prosecute a violation of subsection (a) or (c), the court or interested party shall notify the Attorney General of such refusal. The attorney General shall, thereafter, have the authority to prosecute, and may prosecute, the same, without a referral from such State's Attorney.

(h) Prosecution of a violation of subsection (c) shall be commenced within 3 years after the act constituting the violation is discovered or reasonably should have been discovered.

§ 32-9. Tampering with public notice. A person who knowingly and without lawful authority alters, destroys, defaces, removes or conceals any public notice, posted according to law, during the time for which the notice was to remain posted, commits a petty offense.

§ 32-10. Violation of bail bond. (a) Whoever, having been admitted to bail for appearance before any court of this State, incurs a forfeiture of the bail and willfully fails to surrender himself within 30 days following the date of such forfeiture, commits, if the bail was given in connection with a charge of felony or pending appeal or certiorari after conviction of any offense, a felony of the next lower Class or a Class A misdemeanor if the underlying offense was a Class 4 felony; or, if the bail was given in connection with a charge of committing a misdemeanor, or for appearance as a witness, commits a misdemeanor of the next lower Class, but not less than a Class C misdemeanor.

(a-5) Any person who violates a condition of bail bond by possessing a firearm in violation of his or her conditions of bail commits a Class 4 felony for a first violation and a Class 3 felony for a second violation.

(b) Whoever, having been admitted to bail for appearance before any court of this State, while charged with a criminal offense in which the victim is a family or household member as defined in Article 112A of the Code of Criminal Procedure of 1963, knowingly violates a condition of that release as set forth in Section 110-10, subsection (d) of the Code of Criminal Procedure of 1963, commits a Class A misdemeanor.

(c) Whoever, having been admitted to bail for appearance before any court of this State for a felony, Class A misdemeanor or a criminal offense in which the victim is a family or household member as defined in Article112A of the Code of Criminal Procedure of 1963, is charged with any other felony, Class A misdemeanor, or a criminal offense in which the victim is a family or household member as defined in Article 112A of the Code of Criminal Procedure of 1963 while on such release, must appear before the court before bail is statutorily set.

(d) Nothing in this Section shall interfere with or prevent the exercise by any court of its power to punishment for contempt. Any sentence imposed for violation of this Section shall be served consecutive to the sentence imposed for the charge for which bail had been granted and with respect to which the defendant has been convicted.

§ 32-11. Barratry. If a person wickedly and willfully excites and stirs up actions or quarrels between the people of this State with a view to promote strife and contention, he or she is guilty of the petty offense of common barratry; and if he or she is an attorney at law, he or she shall be suspended from the practice of his or her profession, for any time not exceeding 6 months.

§ 32-12. Maintenance. If a person officiously intermeddles in an action that in no way belongs to or concerns that person, by maintaining or assisting either party, with money or otherwise, to prosecute or defend the action, with a view to promote litigation, he or she is guilty of maintenance and upon conviction shall be fined and punished as in cases of common barratry. It is not maintenance for a person to maintain the action of his or her relative or servant, or a poor person out of charity.

§ 32-13. Unlawful clouding of title. (a) Any person who intentionally records or files or causes to be recorded or filed any document in the office of the recorder or registrar of titles of any county of this State that is a cloud on the title of land in this State, knowing that the theory upon which the purported cloud on title is based is not recognized as a legitimate legal theory by the courts of this State or of the United States, commits the offense of unlawful clouding of title.

(b) Unlawful clouding of title is a Class A misdemeanor.

(c) In addition to any other sentence that may be imposed, the court shall order any person convicted of a violation of this Section, or placed on supervision for a violation of this Section, to execute a release of the purported cloud on title as may be requested by or on behalf of any person whose property is encumbered or potentially encumbered by the document filed.
Irrespective of whether or not a person charged under this Section is convicted of the offense of unlawful clouding of title, when the evidence

demonstrates that, as a matter of law, the cloud on title is not a type of cloud recognized or authorized by the courts of this State or the United States, the court shall forthwith direct the recorder or registrar of titles to expunge the cloud.

(c-5) This Section does not apply to an attorney licensed to practice law in this State who in good faith files a lien on behalf of his or her client and who in good faith believes that the validity of the lien is supported by statutory law, by a decision of a court of law, or by a good faith argument for an extension, modification, or reversal of existing court decisions relating to the validity of the lien.

(d) For purposes of this Section, "cloud on title" or "cloud on the title" means an outstanding claim or encumbrance that, if valid, would affect or impair the title of the owner of an estate in land and on its face has that effect, but can be shown by extrinsic proof to be invalid or inapplicable to that estate.

§ 32-14. Unlawful manipulation of a judicial sale. (a) A person commits the offense of unlawful manipulation of a judicial sale when he or she knowingly and by any means makes any contract with or engages in any combination or conspiracy with any other person who is, or but for a prior agreement is, a competitor of such person for the purpose of or with the effect of fixing, controlling, limiting, or otherwise manipulating (1) the participation of any person in, or (2) the making of bids, at any judicial sale.

(b) Penalties. Unlawful manipulation of a judicial sale is a Class 3 felony. A mandatory fine shall be imposed for a violation, not to exceed $1,000,000 if the violator is a corporation, or, if the violator is any other person, $100,000. A second or subsequent violation is a Class 2 felony.

(c) Injunctive and other relief. The State's Attorney shall bring suit in the circuit court to prevent and restrain violations of subsection (a). In such a proceeding, the court shall determine whether a violation has been committed, and shall enter such judgment as it considers necessary to remove the effects of any violation which it finds, and to prevent such violation from continuing or from being renewed in the future. The court, in its discretion, may exercise all powers necessary for this purpose, including, but not limited to, injunction and divestiture of property.

(d) Private right of action. Any person who has been injured by a violation of subsection (a) may maintain an action in the Circuit Court for damages, or for an injunction, or both, against any person who has committed such violation.

If, in an action for an injunction, the court issues an injunction, the plaintiff shall be awarded costs and reasonable attorney's fees. In an action for damages, the person injured shall be awarded 3 times the amount of actual damages. This State, counties, municipalities, townships, and any political subdivision organized under the authority of this State, and the United States, are considered a person having standing to bring an action under this subsection.

Any action for damages under this subsection is forever barred unless commenced within 4 years after the cause of action accrued. In any action for damages under this subsection, the court may, in its discretion, award reasonable fees to the prevailing defendant upon a finding that the plaintiff acted in bad faith, vexatiously, wantonly, or for oppressive reasons.

(e) Exclusion from subsequent judicial sales. Any person convicted of a violation of subsection (a) or any similar offense of any state or the United States shall be barred for 5 years from the date of conviction from participating as a bidding entity in any judicial sale.

No corporation shall be barred from participating in a judicial sale as a result of a conviction under subsection (a) of any employee or agent of such corporation if the employee so convicted is no longer employed by the corporation and: (1) it has been finally adjudicated not guilty or (2) it demonstrates to the circuit court conducting such judicial sale and the court so finds that the commission of the offense was neither authorized, requested, commanded, nor performed by a director, officer or a high managerial agent in behalf of the corporation as provided in paragraph (2) of subsection (a) of Section 5-4 of this Code.

(f) Definitions. As used in this Section, unless the context otherwise requires:

"Judicial sale" means any sale of real or personal property in accordance with a court order, including, but not limited to, judicial sales conducted pursuant to Section 15-1507 of the Code of Civil Procedure, sales ordered to satisfy judgments under Article XII of the Code of Civil Procedure, and enforcements of delinquent property taxes under Article XXI of the Property Tax Code.

"Person" means any natural person, or any corporation, partnership, or association of persons.

Article 33 – Official Misconduct
720 ILCS 5/33-1 *et seq.*

§ 33-1. Bribery. A person commits bribery when: (a) With intent to influence the performance of any act related to the employment or function of any public officer, public employee, juror or witness, he promises or tenders to that person any property or personal advantage which he is not authorized by law to accept; or

(b) With intent to influence the performance of any act related to the employment or function of any public officer, public employee, juror or witness, he promises or tenders to one whom he believes to be a public officer, public employee, juror or witness, any property or personal advantage which a public officer, public employee, juror or witness would not be authorized by law to accept; or

(c) With intent to cause any person to influence the performance of any act related to the employment or function of any public officer, public employee, juror or witness, he promises or tenders to that person any property or personal advantage which he is not authorized by law to accept; or

(d) He receives, retains or agrees to accept any property or personal advantage which he is not authorized by law to accept knowing that such property or personal advantage was promised or tendered with intent to cause him to influence the performance of any act related to the employment or function of any public officer, public employee, juror or witness; or

(e) He solicits, receives, retains, or agrees to accept any property or personal advantage pursuant to an understanding that he shall improperly influence or attempt to influence the performance of any act related to the employment or function of any public officer, public employee, juror or witness.

(f) As used in this Section, “tenders” means any delivery or proffer made with the requisite intent.

(g) Sentence. Bribery is a Class 2 felony.

§ 33-2. Failure to report a bribe. Any public officer, public employee or juror who fails to report forthwith to the local State's Attorney, or in the case of a State employee to the Department of State Police, any offer made to him in violation of Section 33-1 commits a Class A misdemeanor.

In the case of a State employee, the making of such report to the Department of State Police shall discharge such employee from any further duty under this Section. Upon receiving any such report, the Department of State Police shall forthwith transmit a copy thereof to the appropriate State's Attorney.

§ 33-3. Official Misconduct. (a) A public officer or employee or special government agent commits misconduct when, in his official capacity or capacity as a special government agent, he commits any of the following acts:

(1) intentionally or recklessly fails to perform any mandatory duty as required by law; or
(2) knowingly performs an act which he knows he is forbidden by law to perform; or
(3) with intent to obtain a personal advantage for himself or another, he performs an act in excess of his lawful authority; or
(4) solicits or knowingly accepts for the performance of any act a fee or reward which he knows is not authorized by law.

(b) An employee of a law enforcement agency commits misconduct when he or she knowingly uses or communicates, directly or indirectly, information acquired in the course of employment, with the intent to obstruct, impede, or prevent the investigation, apprehension, or prosecution of any criminal offense or person. Nothing in this subsection (b) shall be construed to impose liability for communicating to a confidential resource, who is participating or aiding law enforcement, in an ongoing investigation.

(c) A public officer or employee or special government agent convicted of violating any provision of this Section forfeits his office or employment or position as a special government agent. In addition, he commits a Class3 felony.

(d) For purposes of this Section, "special government agent" has the meaning ascribed to it in subsection (l) of Section 4A-101 of the Illinois Governmental Ethics Act.

§ 33-3.1. Solicitation misconduct (State government). (a) An employee of an executive branch constitutional officer commits solicitation misconduct (State government) when, at any time, he or she knowingly solicits or receives contributions, as that term is defined in Section 9-1.4 of the Election Code, from a person engaged in a business or activity over which the person has regulatory authority.

(b) For the purpose of this Section, "employee of an executive branch constitutional officer" means a full-time or part-time salaried employee, full-time or part-time salaried appointee, or any contractual employee of any office, board, commission, agency, department, authority, administrative unit, or corporate outgrowth under the jurisdiction of an executive branch constitutional officer; and "regulatory authority" means having the responsibility to investigate, inspect, license, or enforce regulatory measures necessary to the requirements of any State or federal statute or regulation relating to the business or activity.

(c) An employee of an executive branch constitutional officer, including one who does not have regulatory authority, commits a violation of this Section if that employee knowingly acts in concert with an employee of an executive branch constitutional officer who does have regulatory authority to solicit or receive contributions in violation of this Section.

(d) Solicitation misconduct (State government) is a Class A misdemeanor. An employee of an executive branch constitutional officer convicted of committing solicitation misconduct (State government) forfeits his or her employment.

(e) An employee of an executive branch constitutional officer who is discharged, demoted, suspended, threatened, harassed, or in any other manner discriminated against in the terms and conditions of employment because of lawful acts done by the employee or on behalf of the employee or others in furtherance of the enforcement of this Section shall be entitled to all relief necessary to make the employee whole.

(f) Any person who knowingly makes a false report of solicitation misconduct (State government) to the State Police, the Attorney General, a State's Attorney, or any law enforcement official is guilty of a Class C misdemeanor.

§ 33-3.2. Solicitation misconduct (local government). (a) An employee of a chief executive officer of a local government commits solicitation misconduct (local government) when, at any time, he or she knowingly solicits or receives contributions, as that term is defined in Section 9-1.4 of the Election Code, from a person engaged in a business or activity over which the person has regulatory authority.

(b) For the purpose of this Section,

"chief executive officer of a local government" means an executive officer of a county, township or municipal government or any administrative subdivision under jurisdiction of the county, township, or municipal government including but not limited to: chairman or president of a county board or commission, mayor or village president, township supervisor, county executive, municipal manager, assessor, auditor, clerk, coroner, recorder, sheriff or State's Attorney;

"employee of a chief executive officer of a local government" means a full-time or part-time salaried employee, full-time or part-time salaried appointee, or any contractual employee of any office, board, commission, agency, department, authority, administrative unit, or corporate outgrowth under the jurisdiction of a chief executive officer of a local government; and

"regulatory authority" means having the responsibility to investigate, inspect, license, or enforce regulatory measures necessary to the requirements of any State, local, or federal statute or regulation relating to the business or activity.

(c) An employee of a chief executive officer of a local government, including one who does not have regulatory authority, commits a violation of this Section if that employee knowingly acts in concert with an employee of a chief executive officer of a local government who does have regulatory authority to solicit or receive contributions in violation of this Section.

(d) Solicitation misconduct (local government) is a Class A misdemeanor. An employee of a chief executive officer of a local government convicted of committing solicitation misconduct (local government) forfeits his or her employment.

(e) An employee of a chief executive officer of a local government who is discharged, demoted, suspended, threatened, harassed, or in any other manner discriminated against in the terms and conditions of employment because of lawful acts done by the employee or on behalf of the employee or others in furtherance of the enforcement of this Section shall be entitled to all relief necessary to make the employee whole.

(f) Any person who knowingly makes a false report of solicitation misconduct (local government) to the State Police, the Attorney General, a State's Attorney, or any law enforcement official is guilty of a Class C misdemeanor.

§ 33-4. Peace officer or correctional officer; gang-related activity prohibited. (a) It is unlawful for a peace officer or correctional officer to knowingly commit any act in furtherance of gang-related activities, except when acting in furtherance of an undercover law enforcement investigation.

(b) In this Section, "gang-related" has the meaning ascribed to it in Section 10 of the Illinois Streetgang Terrorism Omnibus Prevention Act.

(c) Sentence. A violation of this Section is a Class 3 felony.

§ 33-5. Preservation of evidence. (a) It is unlawful for a law enforcement agency or an agent acting on behalf of the law enforcement agency to intentionally fail to comply with the provisions of subsection (a) of Section 116-4 of the Code of Criminal Procedure of 1963.

(b) Sentence. A person who violates this Section is guilty of a Class 4felony.

(c) For purposes of this Section, "law enforcement agency" has the meaning ascribed to it in subsection (e) of Section 116-4 of the Code of Criminal Procedure of 1963.

§ 33-6. Bribery to obtain driving privileges. (a) A person commits the offense of bribery to obtain driving privileges when:

(1) with intent to influence any act related to the issuance of any driver's license or permit by an employee of the Illinois Secretary of State's Office, or the owner or employee of any commercial driver training school licensed by the Illinois Secretary of State, or any other

individual authorized by the laws of this State to give driving instructions or administer all or part of a driver's license examination, he or she promises or tenders to that person any property or personal advantage which that person is not authorized by law to accept; or

(2) with intent to cause any person to influence any act related to the issuance of any driver's license or permit by an employee of the Illinois Secretary of State's Office, or the owner or employee of any commercial driver training school licensed by the Illinois Secretary of State, or any other individual authorized by the laws of this State to give driving instructions or administer all or part of a driver's license examination, he or she promises or tenders to that person any property or personal advantage which that person is not authorized by law to accept; or

(3) as an employee of the Illinois Secretary of State's Office, or the owner or employee of any commercial driver training school licensed by the Illinois Secretary of State, or any other individual authorized by the laws of this State to give driving instructions or administer all or part of a driver's license examination, solicits, receives, retains, or agrees to accept any property or personal advantage that he or she is not authorized by law to accept knowing that such property or personal advantage was promised or tendered with intent to influence the performance of any act related to the issuance of any driver's license or permit; or

(4) as an employee of the Illinois Secretary of State's Office, or the owner or employee of any commercial driver training school licensed by the Illinois Secretary of State, or any other individual authorized by the laws of this State to give driving instructions or administer all or part of a driver's license examination, solicits, receives, retains, or agrees to accept any property or personal advantage pursuant to an understanding that he or she shall improperly influence or attempt to influence the performance of any act related to the issuance of any driver's license or permit.

(b) Sentence. Bribery to obtain driving privileges is a Class 2 felony.

§ 33-7. Public contractor misconduct. (a) A public contractor; a person seeking a public contract on behalf of himself, herself, or another; an employee of a public contractor; or a person seeking a public contract on behalf of himself, herself, or another commits public contractor misconduct when, in the performance of, or in connection with, a contract with the State, a unit of local government, or a school district or in obtaining or seeking to obtain such a contract he or she commits any of the following acts:

(1) intentionally or knowingly makes, uses, or causes to be made or used a false record or statement to conceal, avoid, or decrease an obligation to pay or transmit money or property;
(2) knowingly performs an act that he or she knows he or she is forbidden by law to perform;

(3) with intent to obtain a personal advantage for himself, herself, or another, he or she performs an act in excess of his or her contractual responsibility;

(4) solicits or knowingly accepts for the performance of any act a fee or reward that he or she knows is not authorized bylaw; or

(5) knowingly or intentionally seeks or receives compensation or reimbursement for goods and services he or she purported to deliver or render, but failed to do so pursuant to the terms of the contract, to the unit of State or local government or school district.

(b) Sentence. Any person who violates this Section commits a Class 3 felony. Any person convicted of this offense or a similar offense in any state of the United States which contains the same elements of this offense shall be barred for 10 years from the date of conviction from contracting with, employment by, or holding public office with the State or any unit of local government or school district.
No corporation shall be barred as a result of a conviction under this Section of any employee or agent of such corporation if the employee so convicted is no longer employed by the

corporation and (1) it has been finally adjudicated not guilty or (2) it demonstrates to the government entity with which it seeks to contract, and that entity finds, that the commission of the offense was neither authorized, requested, commanded, nor performed by a director, officer or high managerial agent on behalf of the corporation as provided in paragraph (2) of subsection (a) of Section 5-4 of this Code.

(c) The Attorney General or the State's Attorney in the county where the principal office of the unit of local government or school district is located may bring a civil action on behalf of any unit of State or local government to recover a civil penalty from any person who knowingly engages in conduct which violates subsection (a)of this Section in treble the amount of the monetary cost to the unit of State or local government or school district involved in the violation.

The Attorney General or State's Attorney shall be entitled to recover reasonable attorney's fees as part of the costs assessed to the defendant. This subsection (c) shall in no way limit the ability of any unit of State or local government or school district to recover moneys or damages regarding public contracts under any other law or ordinance.

A civil action shall be barred unless the action is commenced within 6 years after the later of (1) the date on which the conduct establishing the cause of action occurred or (2) the date on which the unit of State or local government or school district knew or should have known that the conduct establishing the cause of action occurred.

(d) This amendatory Act of the 96th General Assembly shall not be construed to create a private right of action.

Title III. Part F: Certain Aggravated Offenses
Article 33A – Armed Violence
720 ILCS 33A *et seq.*

§ 33A-1. Legislative intent and definitions.
(a) Legislative findings. The legislature finds and declares the following:

(1) The use of a dangerous weapon in the commission of a felony offense poses a much greater threat to the public health, safety, and general welfare, than when a weapon is not used in the commission of the offense.

(2) Further, the use of a firearm greatly facilitates the commission of a criminal offense because of the more lethal nature of a firearm and the greater perceived threat produced in those confronted by a person wielding a firearm. Unlike other dangerous weapons such as knives and clubs, the use of a firearm in the commission of a criminal felony offense significantly escalates the threat and the potential for bodily harm, and the greater range of the firearm increases the potential for harm to more persons. Not only are the victims and bystanders at greater risk when a firearm is used, but also the law enforcement officers whose duty is to confront and apprehend the armed suspect.

(3) Current law does contain offenses involving the use or discharge of a gun toward or against a person, such as aggravated battery with a firearm, aggravated discharge of a firearm, and reckless discharge of a firearm; however, the General Assembly has legislated greater penalties for the commission of a felony while in possession of a firearm because it deems such acts as more serious.

(b) Legislative intent.

(1) In order to deter the use of firearms in the commission of a felony offense, the General Assembly deems it appropriate for a greater penalty to be imposed when a firearm is used or discharged in the commission of an offense than the penalty imposed for using other types of weapons and for the penalty to increase on more serious offenses.

(2) With the additional elements of the discharge of a firearm and great bodily harm inflicted by a firearm being added to armed violence and other serious felony offenses, it is the intent of the General Assembly to punish those elements more severely during commission of a felony offense than when those elements stand alone as the act of the offender.

(3) It is the intent of the 91st General Assembly that should Public Act 88-680 be declared unconstitutional for a violation of Article 4, Section 8 of the 1970 Constitution of the State of Illinois, the amendatory changes made by Public Act 88-680 to Article 33A of the Criminal Code of 1961 and which are set forth as law in this amendatory Act of the 91st General Assembly are hereby reenacted by this amendatory Act of the 91st General Assembly.

(c) Definitions.

(1) "Armed with a dangerous weapon". A person is considered armed with a dangerous weapon for purposes of this Article, when he or she carries on or about his or her person or is otherwise armed with a Category I, Category II, or Category III weapon.

(2) A Category I weapon is a handgun, sawed-off shotgun, sawed-off rifle, any other firearm small enough to be concealed upon the person, semiautomatic firearm, or machine gun. A Category II weapon is any other rifle, shotgun, spring gun, other firearm, stun gun or taser as defined in paragraph (a) of Section 24-1 of this Code, knife with a blade of at least 3 inches in length, dagger, dirk, switchblade knife, stiletto, axe, hatchet, or other deadly or dangerous weapon or instrument of like character.

As used in this subsection (b) "semiautomatic firearm" means a repeating firearm that utilizes a portion of the energy of a firing cartridge to extract the fired cartridge case and chamber the next round and that requires a separate pull of the trigger to fire each cartridge.

(3) A Category III weapon is a bludgeon, black-jack, slungshot, sand-bag, sand-club, metal knuckles, billy, or other dangerous weapon of like character.

§ 33A-2. Armed violence-Elements of the offense. (a) A person commits armed violence when, while armed with a dangerous weapon, he commits any felony defined by Illinois Law, except first degree murder, attempted first degree murder, intentional homicide of an unborn child, second degree murder, involuntary manslaughter, reckless homicide, predatory criminal sexual assault of a child, aggravated battery of a child as described in Section 12-4.3 or subdivision (b)(1) of Section 12-3.05, home invasion, or any offense that makes the possession or use of a dangerous weapon either an element of the base offense, an aggravated or enhanced version of the offense, or a mandatory sentencing factor that increases the sentencing range.

(b) A person commits armed violence when he or she personally discharges a firearm that is a Category I or Category II weapon while committing any felony defined by Illinois law, except first degree murder, attempted first degree murder, intentional homicide of an unborn child, second degree murder, involuntary manslaughter, reckless homicide, predatory criminal sexual assault of a child, aggravated battery of a child as described in Section 12-4.3 or subdivision (b)(1) of Section 12-3.05, home invasion, or any offense that makes the possession or use of a dangerous weapon either an element of the base offense, an aggravated or enhanced version of the offense, or a mandatory sentencing factor that increases the sentencing range.

(c) A person commits armed violence when he or she personally discharges a firearm that is a Category I or Category II weapon that proximately causes great bodily harm, permanent disability, or permanent disfigurement or death to another person while committing any felony defined by Illinois law, except first degree murder, attempted first degree murder, intentional homicide of an unborn child, second degree murder, involuntary manslaughter, reckless homicide, predatory criminal sexual assault of a child, aggravated battery of a child as described in Section 12-4.3

or subdivision (b)(1) of Section 12-3.05, home invasion, or any offense that makes the possession or use of a dangerous weapon either an element of the base offense, an aggravated or enhanced version of the offense, or a mandatory sentencing factor that increases the sentencing range.

(d) This Section does not apply to violations of the Fish and Aquatic Life Code or the Wildlife Code.

§ 33A-3. Sentence. (a) Violation of Section 33A-2(a) with a Category I weapon is a Class X felony for which the defendant shall be sentenced to a minimum term of imprisonment of 15 years.

(a-5) Violation of Section 33A-2(a) with a Category II weapon is a Class X felony for which the defendant shall be sentenced to a minimum term of imprisonment of 10 years.

(b) Violation of Section 33A-2(a) with a Category III weapon is a Class 2 felony or the felony classification provided for the same act while unarmed, whichever permits the greater penalty. A second or subsequent violation of Section 33A-2(a) with a Category III weapon is a Class 1 felony or the felony classification provided for the same act while unarmed, whichever permits the greater penalty.

(b-5) Violation of Section 33A-2(b) with a firearm that is a Category I or Category II weapon is a Class X felony for which the defendant shall be sentenced to a minimum term of imprisonment of 20 years.

(b-10) Violation of Section 33A-2(c) with a firearm that is a Category I or Category II weapon is a Class X felony for which the defendant shall be sentenced to a term of imprisonment of not less than 25 years nor more than 40 years.

(c) Unless sentencing under subsection (a) of Section 5-4.5-95 of the Unified Code of Corrections (730 ILCS 5/5-4.5-95) is applicable, any person who violates subsection (a) or (b) of Section 33A-2 with a firearm, when that person has been convicted in any state or federal court of 3 or more of the following offenses: treason, first degree murder, second degree murder, predatory criminal sexual assault of a child, aggravated criminal sexual assault, criminal sexual assault, robbery, burglary, arson, kidnapping, aggravated battery resulting in great bodily harm or permanent disability or disfigurement, a violation of the Methamphetamine Control and Community Protection Act, or a violation of Section 401(a) of the Illinois Controlled Substances Act, when the third offense was committed after conviction on the second, the second offense was committed after conviction on the first, and the violation of Section 33A-2 was committed after conviction on the third, shall be sentenced to a term of imprisonment of not less than 25 years nor more than 50 years.

(c-5) Except as otherwise provided in paragraph (b-10) or (c) of this Section, a person who violates Section 33A-2(a) with a firearm that is a Category I weapon or Section 33A-2(b) in any school, in any conveyance owned, leased, or contracted by a school to transport students to or from school or a school related activity, or on the real property comprising any school or public park, and where the offense was related to the activities of an organized gang, shall be sentenced to a term of imprisonment of not less than the term set forth in subsection (a) or (b-5) of this Section, whichever is applicable, and not more than 30 years. For the purposes of this subsection (c-5), "organized gang" has the meaning ascribed to it in Section 10 of the Illinois Streetgang Terrorism Omnibus Prevention Act.

(d) For armed violence based upon a predicate offense listed in this subsection (d) the court shall enter the sentence for armed violence to run consecutively to the sentence imposed for the predicate offense. The offenses covered by this provision are:

(i) solicitation of murder,

(ii) solicitation of murder for hire,

(iii) heinous battery as described in Section 12-4.1 or subdivision (a)(2) of Section 12-3.05,

(iv) aggravated battery of a senior citizen as described in Section 12-4.6 or subdivision (a)(4) of Section 12-3.05,

(v) (blank),

(vi) a violation of subsection (g) of Section 5 of the Cannabis Control Act,

(vii) cannabis trafficking,

(viii) a violation of subsection (a) of Section 401 of the Illinois Controlled Substances Act,

(ix) controlled substance trafficking involving a Class X felony amount of controlled substance under Section 401 of the Illinois Controlled Substances Act,

(x) calculated criminal drug conspiracy,

(xi) streetgang criminal drug conspiracy, or

(xii) a violation of the Methamphetamine Control and Community Protection Act.

Commentary – Armed Violence

Elements; Public policy behind armed violence. Section 33A-1 et seq. addresses the continuing concern of criminals committing felonies while armed with dangerous weapons. a person commits armed violence when (1) while armed with a dangerous weapon he commits another felony offense (2) he personally discharges a Category I or II firearm during the commission of another felony offense or (3) he personally discharges a Category I or II firearm and proximately causes great bodily harm, permanent disability or disfigurement or death during the commission of another felony. Certain offenses are excepted from the "another felony" predicate offenses for armed violence including first degree murder, attempted first degree murder, second degree murder, involuntary manslaughter, reckless homicide, predatory criminal sexual assault of a child, certain aggravated battery of a child offenses, home invasion, or any offense which has possession of a dangerous weapon as an element of the crime or as a specific sentencing enhancement.

As defined in the statute a person, is armed when he has upon his person or within his immediate access and control a Category I, Category II or Category III weapon. Category I weapons are guns that are small enough to be concealed on one's person – including pistols, sawed-off shotguns and sawed-off rifles. Category II weapons are larger guns, including shotguns, rifles and semi-automatic guns, stun guns and tasers, and knives, daggers, axes and hatchets. Category III weapons include clubs, bludgeons, brass knuckles and like weapons and are not proscribed under the armed violence statute. Weapons that are of like character (such as box cutters which are wielded as a knife, or a lead pipe that is wielded like a club) would also fall within the ambit of a dangerous weapon.

The statute addresses the concern of the criminal use of firearms, providing for more serious punishment for committing felony offenses while armed with firearms and even greater penalties for discharging a firearm during the commission of felony. If armed, the criminal will likely use the weapon during the commission of the offense or if there is resistance to the offense and law enforcement responds to a call for help, the weapon will be used against the victim, the police or the public in a natural cause and effect from the criminal having possession or immediate access to the weapon. The predicate felony offense must not have the possession or use of the weapon as an element of the offense; otherwise, there would be an impermissible double enhancement by charging armed violence. See *People v. Haron* 85 Ill.2d 261, 422 N.E.2d 627 (Ill. S. Ct. 1981).

Armed at the time of the commission of the offense. The importance of the offense is the presence of weapons in the hands of the criminal at the time of the commission of the offense. If there is not a nexus between access to a weapon and the commission of the predicate felony offense, there has not been a violation of the armed violence statute.

In *People v. Smith* 191 Ill.2d 408, 732 N.E.2d 513 (Ill. S. Ct. 2000), the defendant was present in his apartment when he saw police approaching to serve a search warrant. The defendant opened the window and threw out an unloaded hand gun. Once inside the police seized cocaine and cannabis. There was no other person, no other weapons and no ammunition inside the apartment. The defendant was convicted of unlawful possession of cannabis and unlawful possession of a controlled substance, unlawful possession of a firearm by a felon and armed violence. The Illinois Supreme Court agreed with the defendant that he had not been proved guilty of armed violence when he got rid of the firearm prior to the time of his arrest. The court stated:

> Defendant did not have " 'immediate access to' or 'timely control over' a weapon when the police entered" . . . because he dropped the gun out of the window as soon as he became aware that police were approaching. For this same reason, defendant also did not have the "intent and capability to maintain control and possession" of the weapon, as this court has required. . . . Permitting an armed violence conviction to stand against a felon such as defendant, who exhibited no propensity to violence and dropped the unloaded gun out of the window as the police approached his apartment to search for drugs, would not serve, but rather would frustrate, the statute's purpose of deterring criminals from involving themselves and others in potentially deadly situations.
>
> *People v. Smith* 191 Ill.2d at 412-13, 732 N.E.2d at 515 (citations omitted).

In *People v. Neylon* 327 Ill.App.3d 300, 762 N.E.2d 1127 (Ill. App. Ct. 4th Dist. 2002), the defendant was convicted of armed violence and controlled substance offenses. Police responded to a call about gunshots. When police arrived at a residence the defendant shared with his girlfriend, they found the defendant outside the residence. He was unarmed but five .38 shell casings were found on the ground outside the residence. A consent search was conducted and in a bedroom shared by the defendant and his girlfriend, the police discovered cannabis, an unloaded .38 pistol and drugs. In the defendant's car, police found a box of .38 ammunition. Forensic testing linked 3 of the 5 spent shells to the gun in the residence. The armed violence charge brought against the defendant was that he personally discharged a firearm during the commission of a controlled substance offence (possession of cocaine with intent to deliver). On appeal, the court affirmed the predicate controlled substance offense but reversed the defendant's conviction of armed violence reasoning that the circumstantial evidence did not prove that it was the defendant who fired the gun. There was no eye-witness testimony about the gunshots - no evidence as to where the gun was shot and no direct evidence as to who shot the gun. The court concluded that the circumstantial evidence could not exclude the reasonable hypothesis of the defendant's innocence.

Any felony under Illinois law. The predicate felony for an armed violence offense can be any felony defined by Illinois law, with the exception of the enumerated offenses mentioned above. Even a felony traffic offense can be a predicate offense.

In *People v. Brown* 362 Ill.App.3d 374, 839 N.E.2d 596 (Ill. App. Ct. 1st Dist. 2005), the defendant was observed by police shooting at a group of people from a black Lexus automobile. The police officers engaged their I-bar stop lights and gave chase for several blocks. During the chase the defendant's car traveled at speeds in excess of 70 mph in a 35 mph speed zone and the defendant was seen throwing a silver object out of the car. Another officer stopped at that location and picked up a .40 pistol that was loaded and had a shell in the chamber. When the defendant was finally stopped, .40 shell casings were found inside the Lexus. the defendant was charged and convicted for armed violence being armed with a dangerous weapon (a .40

automatic pistol) while committing a felony under Illinois law, aggravated fleeing or eluding a police officer, under the Illinois Motor Vehicle Code 625 ILCS 5/11-204(a)(1). His conviction was affirmed on appeal since the evidence clearly demonstrated he was attempting to avoid being stopped by the officers and he traveled in excess of 21 mph over the posted speed limit, the aggravating factor that made the traffic offense a felony.

Article 33D – Contributing to the Criminal Delinquency of a Juvenile 720 ILCS 33D-1 *et seq.*

§ 33D-1. (a) Contributing to the criminal delinquency of a juvenile. any person of the age of 21 years and upwards, who with the intent to promote or facilitate the commission of an offense that is either a felony or misdemeanor, solicits, compels or directs any person under the age of 17years in the commission of the offense commits the offense of contributing to the criminal delinquency of a juvenile.

(b) Sentence. Contributing to the criminal delinquency of a juvenile is a felony one grade higher than the offense committed, if the offense committed is a felony, except when the offense committed is first degree murder or a Class X felony.

When the offense committed is first degree murder or a Class X felony, the penalty for contributing to the criminal delinquency of a juvenile is the same as the penalty for first degree murder or a Class X felony, respectively. Contributing to the criminal delinquency of a juvenile is a misdemeanor one grade higher than the offense committed, if the offense committed is a misdemeanor, except when the offense committed is a Class A misdemeanor.

If the offense committed is a Class A misdemeanor, the penalty for contributing to the criminal delinquency of a juvenile is a Class 4 felony.

Article 33E – Public Contracts 720 ILCS 33E-1 *et seq.*

§ 33E-1. Interference with public contracting. It is the finding of the General Assembly that the cost to the public is increased and the quality of goods, services and construction paid for by public monies is decreased when contracts for such goods, services or construction are obtained by any means other than through independent noncollusive submission of bids or offers by individual contractors or suppliers, and the evaluation of those bids or offers by the governmental unit pursuant only to criteria publicly announced in advance.

§ 33E-2. Definitions. In this Act:

(a) "Public contract" means any contract for goods, services or construction let to any person with or without bid by any unit of State or local government.

(b) "Unit of State or local government" means the State, any unit of state government or agency thereof, any county or municipal government or committee or agency thereof, or any other entity which is funded by or expends tax dollars or the proceeds of publicly guaranteed bonds.

(c) "Change order" means a change in a contract term other than as specifically provided for in the contract which authorizes or necessitates any increase or decrease in the cost of the contract or the time to completion.

(d) "Person" means any individual, firm, partnership, corporation, joint venture or other entity, but does not include a unit of State or local government.

(e) "Person employed by any unit of State or local government" means any employee of a unit of State or local government and any person defined in subsection (d) who is authorized by such unit of State or local government to act on its behalf in relation to any public contract.

(f) "Sheltered market" has the meaning ascribed to it in Section 8b of the Business Enterprise for Minorities, Females, and Persons with Disabilities Act.

(g) "Kickback" means any money, fee, commission, credit, gift, gratuity, thing of value, or compensation of any kind which is provided, directly or indirectly, to any prime contractor, prime contractor employee, subcontractor, or subcontractor employee for the purpose of improperly obtaining or rewarding favorable treatment in connection with a prime contract or in connection with a subcontract relating to a prime contract.

(h) "Prime contractor" means any person who has entered into a public contract.

(i) "Prime contractor employee" means any officer, partner, employee, or agent of a prime contractor.

(i-5) "Stringing" means knowingly structuring a contract or job order to avoid the contract or job order being subject to competitive bidding requirements.

(j) "Subcontract" means a contract or contractual action entered into by a prime contractor or subcontractor for the purpose of obtaining goods or services of any kind under a prime contract.

(k) "Subcontractor" (1) means any person, other than the prime contractor, who offers to furnish or furnishes any goods or services of any kind under a prime contract or a subcontract entered into in connection with such prime contract; and (2) includes any person who offers to furnish or furnishes goods or services to the prime contractor or a higher tier subcontractor.
(l) "Subcontractor employee" means any officer, partner, employee, or agent of a subcontractor.

§ 33E-3. Bid-rigging. A person commits the offense of bid-rigging when he knowingly agrees with any person who is, or but for such agreement would be, a competitor of such person concerning any bid submitted or not submitted by such person or another to a unit of State or local government when with the intent that the bid submitted or not submitted will result in the award of a contract to such person or another and he either (1) provides such person or receives from another information concerning the price or other material term or terms of the bid which would otherwise not be disclosed to a competitor in an independent noncollusive submission of bids or (2) submits a bid that is of such a price or other material term or terms that he does not intend the bid to be accepted.
Bid-rigging is a Class 3 felony.

Any person convicted of this offense or any similar offense of any state or the United States which contains the same elements as this offense shall be barred for 5 years from the date of conviction from contracting with any unit of State or local government.
No corporation shall be barred from contracting with any unit of State or local government as a result of a conviction under this Section of any employee or agent of such corporation if the employee so convicted is no longer employed by the corporation and: (1) it has been finally adjudicated not guilty or (2) if it demonstrates to the governmental entity with which it seeks to contract and that entity finds that the commission of the offense was neither authorized, requested, commanded, nor performed by a director, officer or a high managerial agent in behalf of the corporation as provided in paragraph (2) of subsection (a) of Section 5-4 of this Code.

§ 33E-4. Bid rotating. A person commits the offense of bid rotating when, pursuant to any collusive scheme or agreement with another, he engages in a pattern over time (which, for the purposes of this Section, shall include at least 3 contract bids within a period of 10 years, the most recent of which occurs after the effective date of this amendatory Act of 1988) of submitting sealed bids to units of State or local government with the intent that the award of such bids rotates, or is distributed among, persons or business entities which submit bids

on a substantial number of the same contracts. Bid rotating is a Class 2 felony.
Any person convicted of this offense or any similar offense of any state or the United States which contains the same elements as this offense shall be permanently barred from contracting with any unit of State or local government.

No corporation shall be barred from contracting with any unit of State or local government as a result of a conviction under this Section of any employee or agent of such corporation if the employee so convicted is no longer employed by the corporation and: (1) it has been finally adjudicated not guilty or (2) if it demonstrates to the governmental entity with which it seeks to contract and that entity finds that the commission of the offense was neither authorized, requested, commanded, nor performed by a director, officer or a high managerial agent in behalf of the corporation as provided in paragraph (2) of subsection (a) of Section 5-4 of this Code.

§ 33E-5. Acquisition or disclosure of bidding information by public official.
(a) Any person who is an official of or employed by any unit of State or local government who knowingly opens a sealed bid at a time or place other than as specified in the invitation to bid or as otherwise designated by the State or unit of local government, or outside the presence of witnesses required by the applicable statute or ordinance, commits a Class 4 felony.

(b) Any person who is an official of or employed by any unit of State or local government who knowingly discloses to any interested person any information related to the terms of a sealed bid whether that information is acquired through a violation of subsection (a) or by any other means except as provided by law or necessary to the performance of such official's or employee's responsibilities relating to the bid, commits a Class 3 felony.

(c) It shall not constitute a violation of subsection (b) of this Section for any person who is an official of or employed by any unit of State or local government to make any disclosure to any interested person where such disclosure is also made generally available to the public.
(d) This Section only applies to contracts let by sealed bid. (Source: P.A. 86-150.)

§ 33E-6. Interference with contract submission and award by public official. (a) Any person who is an official of or employed by any unit of State or local government who knowingly conveys, either directly or indirectly, outside of the publicly available official invitation to bid, pre-bid conference, solicitation for contracts procedure or such procedure used in any sheltered market procurement adopted pursuant to law or ordinance by that unit of government, to any person any information concerning the specifications for such contract or the identity of any particular potential subcontractors, when inclusion of such information concerning the specifications or contractors in the bid or offer would influence the likelihood of acceptance of such bid or offer, commits a Class 4 felony.

It shall not constitute a violation of this subsection to convey information intended to clarify plans or specifications regarding a public contract where such disclosure of information is also made generally available to the public.

(b) Any person who is an official of or employed by any unit of State or local government who, either directly or indirectly, knowingly informs a bidder or offer or that the bid or offer will be accepted or executed only if specified individuals are included as subcontractors commits a Class 3felony.

(c) It shall not constitute a violation of subsection (a) of this Section where any person who is an official of or employed by any unit of State or local government follows procedures established by federal, State or local minority or female owned business enterprise programs.

(d) Any bidder or offer or who is the recipient of communications from the unit of government which he reasonably believes to be proscribed by subsections (a) or (b), and fails to inform either the Attorney General or the State's Attorney for the county in which the unit of

government is located, commits a Class A misdemeanor.
(e) Any public official who knowingly awards a contract based on criteria which were not publicly disseminated via the invitation to bid, when such invitation to bid is required by law or ordinance, the pre-bid conference, or any solicitation for contracts procedure or such procedure used in any sheltered market procurement procedure adopted pursuant to statute or ordinance, commits a Class 3 felony.

(f) It shall not constitute a violation of subsection (a) for any person who is an official of or employed by any unit of State or local government to provide to any person a copy of the transcript or other summary of any pre-bid conference where such transcript or summary is also made generally available to the public.

§ 33E-7. Kickbacks. (a) A person violates this Section when he knowingly either:

(1) provides, attempts to provide or offers to provide any kickback;

(2) solicits, accepts or attempts to accept any kickback; or

(3) includes, directly or indirectly, the amount of any kickback prohibited by paragraphs (1) or (2) of this subsection (a) in the contract price charged by a subcontractor to a prime contractor or a higher tier subcontractor or in the contract price charged by a prime contractor to any unit of State or local government for a public contract.

(b) Any person violates this Section when he has received an offer of a kickback, or has been solicited to make a kickback, and fails to report it to law enforcement officials, including but not limited to the Attorney General or the State's Attorney for the county in which the contract is to be performed.
(c) A violation of subsection (a) is a Class 3 felony. A violation of subsection (b) is a Class 4 felony.

(d) Any unit of State or local government may, in a civil action, recover a civil penalty from any person who knowingly engages in conduct which violates paragraph (3) of subsection (a) of this Section in twice the amount of each kickback involved in the violation.

This subsection (d) shall in no way limit the ability of any unit of State or local government to recover monies or damages regarding public contracts under any other law or ordinance. A civil action shall be barred unless the action is commenced within 6 years after the later of (1) the date on which the conduct establishing the cause of action occurred or (2) the date on which the unit of State or local government knew or should have known that the conduct establishing the cause of action occurred.

§ 33E-8. Bribery of inspector employed by contractor. (a) A person commits bribery of an inspector when he offers to any person employed by a contractor or subcontractor on any public project contracted for by any unit of State or local government any property or other thing of value with the intent that such offer is for the purpose of obtaining wrongful certification or approval of the quality or completion of any goods or services supplied or performed in the course of work on such project. Violation of this subsection is a Class 4 felony.

(b) Any person employed by a contractor or subcontractor on any public project contracted for by any unit of State or local government who accepts any property or other thing of value knowing that such was intentionally offered for the purpose of influencing the certification or approval of the quality or completion of any goods or services supplied or performed under subcontract to that contractor, and either before or afterwards issues such wrongful certification, commits a Class 3 felony.

Failure to report such offer to law enforcement officials, including but not limited to the Attorney General or the State's Attorney for the county in which the contract is performed, constitutes a Class 4 felony.

§ 33E-9. Change orders. Any change order authorized under this Section shall be made in writing. Any person employed by and authorized by any unit of State or local government to approve a change order to any public contract who knowingly grants that approval without first obtaining from the unit of State or local government on whose behalf the contract was signed, or from a designee authorized by that unit of State or local government, a determination in writing that (1) the circumstances said to necessitate the change in performance were not reasonably foreseeable at the time the contract was signed, or (2) the change is germane to the original contract as signed, or (3) the change order is in the best interest of the unit of State or local government and authorized by law, commits a Class 4 felony.

The written determination and the written change order resulting from that determination shall be preserved in the contract's file which shall be open to the public for inspection. This Section shall only apply to a change order or series of change orders which authorize or necessitate an increase or decrease in either the cost of a public contract by a total of $10,000 or more or the time of completion by a total of 30 days or more.

§ 33E-10. Rules of evidence. (a) The certified bid is *prima facie* evidence of the bid.

(b) It shall be presumed that in the absence of practices proscribed by this Article 33E, all persons who submit bids in response to an invitation to bid by any unit of State or local government submit their bids independent of all other bidders, without information obtained from the governmental entity outside the invitation to bid, and in a good faith effort to obtain the contract.

§ 33E-11. (a) Every bid submitted to and public contract executed pursuant to such bid by the State or a unit of local government shall contain a certification by the prime contractor that the prime contractor is not barred from contracting with any unit of State or local government as a result of a violation of either Section 33E-3 or 33E-4 of this Article.

The State and units of local government shall provide the appropriate forms for such certification.

(b) A contractor who makes a false statement, material to the certification, commits a Class 3 felony.

§ 33E-12. It shall not constitute a violation of any provisions of this Article for any person who is an official of or employed by a unit of State or local government to (1) disclose the name of any person who has submitted a bid in response to or requested plans or specifications regarding an invitation to bid or who has been awarded a public contract to any person or, (2) to convey information concerning acceptable alternatives or substitute to plans or specifications if such information is also made generally available to the public and mailed to any person who has submitted a bid in response to or requested plans or specifications regarding an invitation to bid on a public contract or, (3) to negotiate with the lowest responsible bidder a reduction in only the price term of the bid.

§ 33E-13. Contract negotiations under the Local Government Professional Services Selection Act shall not be subject to the provisions of this Article.

§ 33E-14. False statements on vendor applications. (a) A person commits false statements on vendor applications when he or she knowingly makes any false statement or report, with the intent to influence in any way the action of any unit of local government or school district in considering a vendor application.

(b) Sentence. False statements on vendor applications is a Class 3 felony.

§ 33E-15. False entries. Any officer, agent, or employee of, or anyone who is affiliated in any capacity with any unit of local government or school district and makes a false entry in any book, report, or statement of any unit of local government or school district with the intent to defraud the unit of local government or school district, is guilty of a Class 3 felony.

§ 33E-16. Misapplication of funds. Whoever, being an officer, director, agent, or employee of, or affiliated in any capacity with any unit of local government or school district, willfully misapplies any of the moneys, funds, or credits of the unit of local government or school district is guilty of a Class 3 felony.

§ 33E-17. Unlawful participation. Whoever, being an officer, director, agent, or employee of, or affiliated in any capacity with any unit of local government or school district participates, shares in, or receiving directly or indirectly any money, profit, property, or benefit through any contract with the unit of local government or school district, with the intent to defraud the unit of local government or school district is guilty of a Class 3 felony.

§ 33E-18. Unlawful stringing of bids. (a) A person commits unlawful stringing of bids when he or she, with the intent to evade the bidding requirements of any unit of local government or school district, knowingly strings or assists in stringing, or attempts to string any contract or job order with the unit of local government or school district.
(b) Sentence. Unlawful stringing of bids is a Class 4 felony.

Article 33F – Unlawful Use of Body Armor
720 ILCS 33F-1 *et seq.*

§ 33F-1. Definitions.

For purposes of this Article:

(a) "Body Armor" means any one of the following:

(1) A military style flak or tactical assault vest which is made of Kevlar or any other similar material or metal, fiberglass, plastic, and nylon plates and designed to be worn over one's clothing for the intended purpose of stopping not only missile fragmentation from mines, grenades, mortar shells and artillery fire but also fire from rifles, machine guns, and small arms.

(2) Soft body armor which is made of Kevlar or any other similar material or metal or any other type of insert and which is lightweight and pliable and which can be easily concealed under a shirt.

(3) A military style recon/surveillance vest which is made of Kevlar or any other similar material and which is lightweight and designed to be worn over one's clothing.

(4) Protective casual clothing which is made of Kevlar or any other similar material and which was originally intended to be used by undercover law enforcement officers or dignitaries and is designed to look like jackets, coats, raincoats, quilted or three piece suit vests.

(b) "Dangerous weapon" means a Category I, Category II, or Category III weapon as defined in Section 33A-1 of this Code.

§ 33F-2. Unlawful use of body armor. A person commits the offense of unlawful use of body armor when he knowingly wears body armor and is in possession of a dangerous weapon, other than a firearm, in the commission or attempted commission of any offense.

§ 33F-3. Sentence. A person convicted of unlawful use of body armor for a first offense shall be guilty of a Class A misdemeanor and for a second or subsequent offense shall be guilty of a Class 4 felony.

Article 33G –Illinois Street Gang and Racketeer Influenced and Corrupt Organizations Law (or "RICO") 720 ILCS 33G-1 *et seq.*

§ 33G-1. Short title. This Article may be cited as the Illinois Street Gang and Racketeer Influenced and Corrupt Organizations Law (or " RICO").

§ 33G-2. Legislative declaration. The substantial harm inflicted on the people and economy of this State by pervasive violent street gangs and other forms of enterprise criminality, is legitimately a matter of grave concern to the people of this State who have a basic right to be protected from that criminal activity and to be given adequate remedies to redress its harms. Whereas the current laws of this State provide inadequate remedies, procedures and punishments, the Illinois General Assembly hereby gives the supplemental remedies of the Illinois Street Gang and RacketeerInfluenced and Corrupt Organizations Law full force and effect under law for the common good of this State and its people.

§ 33G-3. Definitions. As used in this Article:
(a) "Another state" means any State of the United States (other than the State of Illinois), or the District of Columbia, or the Commonwealth of Puerto Rico, or any territory or possession of the United States, or any political subdivision, or any department, agency, or instrumentality thereof.

(b) "Enterprise" includes:
(1) any partnership, corporation, association, business or charitable trust, or other legal entity; and
(2) any group of individuals or other legal entities, or any combination thereof, associated in fact although not itself a legal entity. An association in fact must be held together by a common purpose of engaging in a course of conduct, and it may be associated together for purposes that are both legal and illegal. An association in fact must:
(A) have an ongoing organization or structure, either formal or informal;
(B) the various members of the group must function as a continuing unit, even if the group changes membership by gaining or losing members over time; and
(C) have an ascertainable structure distinct from that inherent in the conduct of a pattern of predicate activity.
As used in this Article, "enterprise" includes licit and illicit enterprises.
(c) "Labor organization" includes any organization, labor union, craft union, or any voluntary unincorporated association designed to further the cause of the rights of union labor that is constituted for the purpose, in whole or in part, of collective bargaining or of dealing with employers concerning grievances, terms or conditions of employment, or apprenticeships or applications for apprenticeships, or of other mutual aid or protection in connection with employment, including apprenticeships or applications for apprenticeships.

(d) "Operation or management" means directing or carrying out the enterprise's affairs and is limited to any person who knowingly serves as a leader, organizer, operator, manager, director, supervisor, financier, advisor, recruiter, supplier, or enforcer of an enterprise in violation of this Article.

(e) "Predicate activity" means any act that is a Class 2 felony or higher and constitutes a violation or violations of any of the following provisions of the laws of the State of Illinois (as amended or revised as of the date the activity occurred or, in the instance of a continuing offense, the date that charges under this Article are filed in a particular matter in the State of Illinois) or any act under the law of another jurisdiction for an offense that could be charged as a Class 2 felony or higher in this State:
(1) under the Criminal Code of 1961: 8-1.2 (solicitation of murder for hire), 9-1 (first degree murder), 9-3.3 (drug-induced homicide), 10-1 (kidnapping), 10-2 (aggravated kidnapping), 10-3.1 (aggravated unlawful restraint), 10-4 (forcible detention), 10-5(b)(10) (child

abduction), 10-9 (trafficking in persons, involuntary servitude, and related offenses), 11-1.20 (criminal sexual assault), 11-1.30 (aggravated criminal sexual assault), 11-1.40 (predatory criminal sexual assault of a child), 11-1.60 (aggravated criminal sexual abuse), 11-6 (indecent solicitation of a child), 11-6.5 (indecent solicitation of an adult), 11-14.3(a)(2)(A) and (a)(2)(B) (promoting prostitution), 11-14.4 (promoting juvenile prostitution), 11-18.1 (patronizing a minor engaged in prostitution; patronizing a juvenile prostitute), 12-3.05 (aggravated battery), 12-6.4 (criminal street gang recruitment), 12-6.5 (compelling organization membership of persons), 12-7.3 (stalking), 12-7.4 (aggravated stalking), 12-7.5 (cyberstalking), 12-11 (home invasion), 12-11.1 (vehicular invasion), 18-1 (robbery), 18-2 (armed robbery), 18-3 (vehicular hijacking), 18-4 (aggravated vehicular hijacking), 18-5 (aggravated robbery), 19-1 (burglary), 19-3 (residential burglary), 20-1 (arson), 20-1.1 (aggravated arson), 20-1.2 (residential arson), 20-1.3 (place of worship arson), 24-1.2 (aggravated discharge of a firearm), 24-1.2-5 (aggravated discharge of a machine gun or silencer equipped firearm), 24-1.8 (unlawful possession of a firearm by a street gang member), 24-3.2 (unlawful discharge of firearm projectiles), 24-3.9 (aggravated possession of a stolen firearm), 24-3A (gunrunning), 26-5 (dog-fighting), 29D-14.9 (terrorism), 29D-15 (soliciting support for terrorism), 29D-15.1 (causing a catastrophe), 29D-15.2 (possession of a deadly substance), 29D-20 (making a terrorist threat), 29D-25 (falsely making a terrorist threat), 29D-29.9 (material support for terrorism), 29D-35 (hindering prosecution of terrorism), 31A-1.2 (unauthorized contraband in a penal institution), or 33A-3 (armed violence);
(2) under the Cannabis Control Act: Sections 5 (manufacture or delivery of cannabis), 5.1 (cannabis trafficking), or 8 (production or possession of cannabis plants), provided the offense either involves more than 500 grams of any substance containing cannabis or involves more than 50 cannabis sativa plants;
(3) under the Illinois Controlled Substances Act: Sections 401 (manufacture or delivery of a controlled substance), 401.1 (controlled substance trafficking), 405 (calculated criminal drug conspiracy), or 405.2 (street gang criminal drug conspiracy); or
(4) under the Methamphetamine Control and Community Protection Act: Sections 15 (methamphetamine manufacturing), or 55 (methamphetamine delivery) .

(f) "Pattern of predicate activity" means:
(1) at least 3 occurrences of predicate activity that are in some way related to each other and that have continuity between them, and that are separate acts. Acts are related to each other if they are not isolated events, including if they have similar purposes, or results, or participants, or victims, or are committed a similar way, or have other similar distinguishing characteristics, or are part of the affairs of the same enterprise. There is continuity between acts if they are ongoing over a substantial period, or if they are part of the regular way some entity does business or conducts its affairs; and
(2) which occurs after the effective date of this Article, and the last of which falls within 3 years (excluding any period of imprisonment) after the first occurrence of predicate activity.
(g) "Unlawful death" includes the following offenses: under the Criminal Code of 1961: Sections 9-1 (first degree murder) or 9-2 (second degree murder).

§ 33G-4. Prohibited activities. (a) It is unlawful for any person, who intentionally participates in the operation or management of an enterprise, directly or indirectly, to:

(1) knowingly do so, directly or indirectly, through a pattern of predicate activity;

(2) knowingly cause another to violate this Article; or

(3) knowingly conspire to violate this Article. Notwithstanding any other provision of law, in any prosecution for a conspiracy to violate this Article, no person may be convicted of that conspiracy unless an overt act in furtherance of the agreement is alleged and proved to have been committed by him, her, or by a coconspirator, but the commission of the overt

act need not itself constitute predicate activity underlying the specific violation of this Article.

(b) It is unlawful for any person knowingly to acquire or maintain, directly or indirectly, through a pattern of predicate activity any interest in, or control of, to any degree, any enterprise, real property, or personal property of any character, including money.

(c) Nothing in this Article shall be construed as to make unlawful any activity which is arguably protected or prohibited by the National Labor Relations Act, the Illinois Educational Labor Relations Act, the Illinois Public Labor Relations Act, or the Railway Labor Act.

(d) The following organizations, and any officer or agent of those organizations acting in his or her official capacity as an officer or agent, may not be sued in civil actions under this Article:

(1) a labor organization; or
(2) any business defined in Division D, E, F, G, H, or I of the Standard Industrial Classification as established by the Occupational Safety and Health Administration, U.S. Department of Labor.

(e) Any person prosecuted under this Article may be convicted and sentenced either:

(1) for the offense of conspiring to violate this Article, and for any other particular offense or offenses that may be one of the objects of a conspiracy to violate this Article; or
(2) for the offense of violating this Article, and for any other particular offense or offenses that may constitute predicate activity underlying a violation of this Article.

(f) The State's Attorney, or a person designated by law to act for him or her and to perform his or her duties during his or her absence or disability, may authorize a criminal prosecution under this Article. Prior to any State's Attorney authorizing a criminal prosecution under this Article, the State's Attorney shall adopt rules and procedures governing the investigation and prosecution of any offense enumerated in this Article. These rules and procedures shall set forth guidelines which require that any potential prosecution under this Article be subject to an internal approval process in which it is determined, in a written prosecution memorandum prepared by the State's Attorney's Office, that (1) a prosecution under this Article is necessary to ensure that the indictment adequately reflects the nature and extent of the criminal conduct involved in a way that prosecution only on the underlying predicate activity would not, and (2) a prosecution under this Article would provide the basis for an appropriate sentence under all the circumstances of the case in a way that a prosecution only on the underlying predicate activity would not. No State's Attorney, or person designated by law to act for him or her and to perform his or her duties during his or her absence or disability, may authorize a criminal prosecution under this Article prior to reviewing the prepared written prosecution memorandum. However, any internal memorandum shall remain protected from disclosure under the attorney-client privilege, and this provision does not create any enforceable right on behalf of any defendant or party, nor does it subject the exercise of prosecutorial discretion to judicial review.

(g) A labor organization and any officer or agent of that organization acting in his or her capacity as an officer or agent of the labor organization are exempt from prosecution under this Article.

§ 33G-5. Penalties. Under this Article, notwithstanding any other provision of law:

(a) Any violation of subsection (a) of Section 33G-4 of this Article shall be sentenced as a Class X felony with a term of imprisonment of not less than 7 years and not more than 30 years, or the sentence applicable to the underlying predicate activity, whichever is higher, and the sentence imposed shall also include restitution, and/or a criminal fine, jointly and severally, up to $250,000 or twice the gross amount of any intended proceeds of the violation, if any, whichever is higher.

(b) Any violation of subsection (b) of Section 33G-4 of this Article shall be sentenced as a Class X felony, and the sentence imposed shall also include restitution, and/or a criminal fine, jointly and severally, up to $250,000 or twice the gross amount of any intended proceeds of the violation, if any, whichever is higher.

(c) Wherever the unlawful death of any person or persons results as a necessary or natural consequence of any violation of this Article, the sentence imposed on the defendant shall include an enhanced term of imprisonment of at least 25 years up to natural life, in addition to any other penalty imposed by the court, provided:
(1) the death or deaths were reasonably foreseeable to the defendant to be sentenced; and

(2) the death or deaths occurred when the defendant was otherwise engaged in the violation of this Article as a whole.

(d) A sentence of probation, periodic imprisonment, conditional discharge, impact incarceration or county impact incarceration, court supervision, withheld adjudication, or any pretrial diversionary sentence or suspended sentence, is not authorized for a violation of this Article.

§ 33G-6. Remedial proceedings, procedures, and forfeiture. Under this Article:

(a) The circuit court shall have jurisdiction to prevent and restrain violations of this Article by issuing appropriate orders, including:
(1) ordering any person to disgorge illicit proceeds obtained by a violation of this Article or divest himself or herself of any interest, direct or indirect, in any enterprise or real or personal property of any character, including money, obtained, directly or indirectly, by a violation of this Article;
(2) imposing reasonable restrictions on the future activities or investments of any person or enterprise, including prohibiting any person or enterprise from engaging in the same type of endeavor as the person or enterprise engaged in, that violated this Article; or
(3) ordering dissolution or reorganization of any enterprise, making due provision for the rights of innocent persons.

(b) Any violation of this Article is subject to the remedies, procedures, and forfeiture as set forth in subsections (f) through (s) of Section 29B-1 of this Code.

§ 33G-7. Construction. In interpreting the provisions of this Article, the court shall construe them in light of the applicable model jury instructions set forth in the Federal Criminal Jury Instructions for the Seventh Circuit (1999) for Title IX of Public Law, 91-452, 84 Stat. 922 (as amended in Title 18, United States Code, Sections 1961 through 1968), except to the extent that it is inconsistent with the plain language of this Article.

§ 33G-8. Limitations. Under this Article, notwithstanding any other provision of law, but otherwise subject to the periods of exclusion from limitation as provided in Section 3-7 of this Code, the following limitations apply:
(a) Any action, proceeding, or prosecution brought under this Article must commence within 5 years of one of the following dates, whichever is latest:
(1) the date of the commission of the last occurrence of predicate activity in a pattern of that activity, in the form of an act underlying the alleged violation of this Article; or
(2) in the case of an action, proceeding, or prosecution, based upon a conspiracy to violate this Article, the date that the last objective of the alleged conspiracy was accomplished, defeated or abandoned (whichever is later); or
(3) the date any minor victim of the violation attains the age of 18 years or the date any victim of the violation subject to a legal disability thereafter gains legal capacity.

(b) Any action, proceeding, or prosecution brought under this Article may be commenced at any time against all defendants if the conduct of any defendant, or any part of the overall violation, resulted in the unlawful death of any person or persons.

§ 33G-9. Repeal. This Article is repealed 5 years after it becomes law.

Article 36 – Seizure and Forfeiture of Vessels, Vehicles, and Aircraft
720 ILCS 36-1 et seq.

[Author's Note: This Article was substantially revised by Public Act 99-0078 and has been removed from text as beyond the purview of this text.]

Article 36.5 –Vehicles Impoundment
720 ILCS 36.5-5

§ 36.5-5. Vehicle impoundment. (a) In addition to any other penalty, fee or forfeiture provided by law, a peace officer who arrests a person for a violation of Section 10-9, 11-14, 11-14.1, 11-14.3, 11-14.4, 11-18, or 11-18.1 of this Code or related municipal ordinance, may tow and impound any vehicle used by the person in the commission of the violation. The person arrested for one or more such violations shall be charged a $1,000 fee, to be paid to the law enforcement agency that made the arrest or its designated representative. The person may recover the vehicle from the impound after a minimum of 2 hours after arrest upon payment of the fee.

(b) $500 of the fee shall be distributed to the law enforcement agency whose peace officers made the arrest, for the costs incurred by the law enforcement agency to investigate and to tow and impound the vehicle. Upon the defendant's conviction of one or more of the violations in connection with which the vehicle was impounded and the fee imposed under this Section, the remaining $500 of the fee shall be deposited into the DHS State Projects Fund and shall be used by the Department of Human Services to make grants to non-governmental organizations to provide services for persons encountered during the course of an investigation into any violation of Section 10-9, 11-14, 11-14.1, 11-14.3, 11-14.4, 11-15, 11-15.1, 11-16, 11-17, 11-17.1, 11-18, 11-18.1, 11-19, 11-19.1, or 11-19.2 of this Code, provided such persons constitute prostituted persons or other victims of human trafficking.

(c) Upon the presentation by the defendant of a signed court order showing that the defendant has been acquitted of all of the violations in connection with which a vehicle was impounded and a fee imposed under this Section, or that the charges against the defendant for those violations have been dismissed, the law enforcement agency shall refund the $1,000 fee to the defendant.

Chapter 2: Other Acts: Criminal Offenses and The Criminal Code of 1961
Offenses Against Persons

Hazing Act
720 ILCS 120/0.01 *et seq.* [Repealed]

Neglected Children Offense Act
720 ILCS 130/0.01 *et seq.* [Repealed]

Harassing and Obscene Communications Act
720 ILCS 135/0.01 *et seq.*

§135/0.01. Short title. This Act may be cited as the Harassing and Obscene Communications Act.

§135/1. [Sending obscene messages]. Any person in this State who sends messages or uses language or terms which are obscene, lewd or immoral with the intent to offend by means of or while using a telephone or telegraph facilities, equipment or wires of any person, firm or corporation engaged in the transmission of news or messages between states or within the State of Illinois is guilty of a Class B misdemeanor. The use of language or terms which are obscene, lewd or immoral is prima facie evidence of the intent to offend.

§135/1-1. Harassment by telephone. Harassment by telephone is use of telephone communication for any of the following purposes:

(1) Making any comment, request, suggestion or proposal which is obscene, lewd, lascivious, filthy or indecent with an intent to offend; or

(2) Making a telephone call, whether or not conversation ensues, with intent to abuse, threaten or harass any person at the called number; or

(3) Making or causing the telephone of another repeatedly to ring, with intent to harass any person at the called number; or

(4) Making repeated telephone calls, during which conversation ensues, solely to harass any person at the called number; or

(4.1) Making a telephone call or knowingly inducing a person to make a telephone call for the purpose of harassing another person who is under 13 years of age, regardless of whether the person under 13 years of age consents to the harassment, if the defendant is at least 16 years of age at the time of the commission of the offense; or

(5) Knowingly permitting any telephone under one's control to be used for any of the purposes mentioned herein. Every telephone directory published for distribution to members of the general public shall contain a notice setting forth a summary of the provisions of this Section. Such notice shall be printed in type which is no smaller than any other type on the same page and shall be preceded by the word "WARNING". All telephone companies in this State shall cooperate with law enforcement agencies in using their facilities and personnel to detect and prevent violations of this Act.

§135/1-2. Harassment through electronic communications. (a) Harassment through electronic communications is the use of electronic communication for any of the following purposes:

(1) Making any comment, request, suggestion or proposal which is obscene with an intent to offend;

(2) Interrupting, with the intent to harass, the telephone service or the electronic communication service of any person;

(3) Transmitting to any person, with the intent to harass and regardless of whether the communication is read in its entirety or at all, any file, document, or other communication which prevents that person from using his or her telephone service or electronic communications device;

(3.1) Transmitting an electronic communication or knowingly inducing a person to transmit an electronic communication for the purpose of harassing another person who is under 13 years of age, regardless of whether the person under 13 years of age consents to the harassment, if the defendant is at least 16 years of age at the time of the commission of the offense;

(4) Threatening injury to the person or to the property of the person to whom an electronic communication is directed or to any of his or her family or household members; or

(5) Knowingly permitting any electronic communications device to be used for any of the purposes mentioned in this subsection (a).

(b) As used in this Act:

(1) "Electronic communication" means any transfer of signs, signals, writings, images, sounds, data or intelligence of any nature transmitted in whole or in part by a wire, radio, electromagnetic, photoelectric or photo-optical system. "Electronic communication" includes transmissions through an electronic device including, but not limited to, a telephone, cellular phone, computer, or pager, which communication includes, but is not limited to, e-mail, instant message, text message, or voice mail .

(2) "Family or household member" includes spouses, former spouses, parents, children, stepchildren and other persons related by blood or by present or prior marriage, persons who share or formerly shared a common dwelling, persons who have or allegedly share a blood relationship through a child, persons who have or have had a dating or engagement relationship, and persons with disabilities and their personal assistants. For purposes of this Act, neither a casual acquaintanceship nor ordinary fraternization between 2 individuals in business or social contexts shall be deemed to constitute a dating relationship.
(c) Telecommunications carriers, commercial mobile service providers, and providers of information services, including, but not limited to, Internet service providers and hosting service providers, are not liable under this Section, except for willful and wanton misconduct, by virtue of the transmission, storage, or caching of electronic communications or messages of others or by virtue of the provision of other related telecommunications, commercial mobile services, or information services used by others in violation of this Section.

§135/1-3. Evidence inference. Evidence that a defendant made additional telephone calls or engaged in additional electronic communications after having been requested by a named complainant or by a family or household member of the complainant to stop may be considered as evidence of an intent to harass unless disproved by evidence to the contrary.

§135/1-4. Psychiatric examination. the court may order any person convicted under this Act to submit to a psychiatric examination.

§135/2. Sentence. (a) Except as provided in subsection (b), a person who violates any of the provisions of Section 1, 1-1, or 1-2 of this Act [*720 ILCS 135/1*, *720 ILCS 135/1-1*, or *720 ILCS 135/1-2*] is guilty of a Class B misdemeanor.

Except as provided in subsection (b), a second or subsequent violation of Section 1, 1-1, or 1-2 of this Act [*720 ILCS 135/1*, *720 ILCS 135/1-1*, or *720 ILCS 135/1-2*] is a Class A misdemeanor, for which the court shall impose a minimum of 14 days in jail or, if public or community service is established in the county in which the offender was convicted, 240 hours of public or community service.

(b) In any of the following circumstances, a person who violates Section 1, 1-1, or 1-2 of this Act [*720 ILCS 135/1*, *720 ILCS 135/1-1*, or *720 ILCS 135/1-2*] shall be guilty of a Class 4 felony:

(1) The person has 3 or more prior violations in the last 10 years of harassment by telephone under Section 1-1 of this Act [*720 ILCS 135/1-1*], harassment through electronic communications under Section 1-2 of this Act [*720 ILCS 135/1-2*], or any similar offense of any state;

(2) The person has previously violated the harassment by telephone provisions of Section 1-1 of this Act [*720 ILCS 135/1-1*] or the harassment through electronic communications provisions of Section 1-2 of this Act [*720 ILCS 135/1-2*] or committed any similar offense in any state with the same victim or a member of the victim's family or household;

(3) At the time of the offense, the offender was under conditions of bail, probation, mandatory supervised release or was the subject of an order of protection, in this or any other state, prohibiting contact with the victim or any member of the victim's family or household;

(4) In the course of the offense, the offender threatened to kill the victim or any member of the victim's family or household; or

(5) The person has been convicted in the last 10 years of a forcible felony as defined in Section 2-8 of the Criminal Code of 1961 [*720 ILCS 5/2-8*]; or

(6) The person violates paragraph (4.1) of Section 1-1 [*720 ILCS 135/1-1*] or paragraph (3.1) of subsection (a) of Section 1-2 [*720 ILCS 135/1-2*].

(7) The person was at least 18 years of age at the time of the commission of the offense and the victim was under 18 years of age at the time of the commission of the offense.

Commentary – Telephone Harassment

Elements; intent to harass. Section 135/1-1 criminalizes telephone harassment. Its various subsections address conduct that is made by telephone (1) leaving a message or engaging in conversation and (2) with intent to harass or offend. Because of first amendment considerations of free speech the statute has been narrowly construed to require more than bad or upsetting language. Indeed there must be either language that is so sexually explicit or of a nature to cause a reasonable person to feel threatened or grossly uncomfortable. Section 135/1-3 provides an inference of intent to harass if a caller continues to make calls after being warned about the harassing nature of prior calls.

In *People v. Taylor* 349 Ill.App.3d 839, 812 N.E.2d 759 (Ill. App. Ct. 2nd District 2004), the defendant was upset about some on-line postings made by the victim. She called and left a message at the victim's home that used the words "f**king and s**t" in describing her complaint about the on-line postings. When contacted by the police the defendant agreed that her choice of words was "wrong". She was convicted of harassment by telephone but her conviction was reversed on appeal. The appellate court held that even if the message was upsetting to the victim, who subjectively believed she was harassed, the use of vulgar language in a phone call with an otherwise proper purpose could not constitute harassment within the meaning of the statute.

Taxpreparer Disclosure of Information Act
720 ILCS 140/0.01 *et seq.*

§140/0.01. Short title. This Act may be cited as the Taxpreparer Disclosure of Information Act.

§140/1. [Disclosure of names prohibited]. It is a Class A misdemeanor for any person, including an individual, firm, corporation, association, partnership, joint venture, or any employee or agent thereof, to disclose, or to convey a list of names prepared on the basis of any information obtained in the business of preparing federal or state income tax returns or assisting taxpayers in preparing such returns, including the disclosure or conveyance of such information between separate departments of the same firm, corporation, association, partnership, or joint venture, unless such disclosure or conveyance is within any of the following:
(a) Consented to in writing by the taxpayer in a separate document.
(b) Expressly authorized by state or federal law.
(c) Necessary to the preparation of the return.
(d) Pursuant to court order.

§140/2. [Engaging in the business of preparing tax returns].
For the purposes of this Act, a person is engaged in the business of preparing federal or state income tax returns or assisting taxpayers in preparing such returns if he does either of the following: (a) Advertises, or gives publicity to

the effect that he prepares or assists others in the preparation of federal income tax returns.
(b) Prepares or assists others in the preparation of state or federal income tax returns for compensation.

§140/3. [Contacting taxpayer to obtain permission for disclosure].
Contacting a taxpayer to obtain his written consent to disclosure does not constitute a violation of this Act.

Wrongs to Children Act
720 ILCS 150/0.01 *et seq.*
[*Author's Note:* See Article 12C Harms to Children]

§ 150/0.01. Short title.
This Act may be cited as the Wrongs to Children Act.

§150/1. [Using or employing a child for injurious, dangerous or immoral purposes prohibited].
It shall be unlawful for any person having the care, custody or control of any child under the age of fourteen years, to exhibit, use or employ, or in any manner, or under any pretense, sell, apprentice, give away, let out, or otherwise dispose of any such child to any person in or for the vocation or occupation, service or purpose of singing, playing on musical instruments, rope or wire walking, dancing, begging, or peddling, or as a gymnast, contortionist, rider or acrobat in any place whatsoever, or for any obscene, indecent or immoral purpose, exhibition or practice whatsoever, or for, or in any business, exhibition or vocation injurious to the health or dangerous to the life or limb of such child, or cause, procure or encourage any such child to engage therein. Nothing in this section contained shall apply to or affect the employment or use of any such child as a singer or musician in any church, school or academy (or at any respectable entertainment), or the teaching or learning the science or practice of music.

§150/2. [Taking or employment of a child prohibited].
It shall also be unlawful for any person to take, receive, hire, employ, use, exhibit, or have in custody any child under the age and for the purposes prohibited in the first section of this act.

§150/3. [Placing a child in the custody of the court].
When upon examination before any court it appears that any child within the age previously mentioned in this Act was engaged or used for or in any business, exhibition, vocation, or purpose prohibited in this Act; and when upon the conviction of any person of a criminal assault upon a child in his custody, the court before whom such conviction is had, shall deem it desirable for the welfare of such child, that the person so convicted should be deprived of its custody; thereafter such child shall be deemed to be in the custody of court, and such court may in its discretion, make such order as to the custody thereof as now is, or hereafter may be, provided by law in cases of vagrant, truant, disorderly, pauper, or destitute children.

§150/3.1. [Single parents of children under 6; employment].
No agency of the State or unit of local government shall require a single parent or other person having the care, custody or control of any child under the age of 6 to accept employment that would unreasonably interfere with such responsibilities to the child. It is unlawful for any person acting under color of law to require or to attempt to require such employment of a parent or other person having the care, custody or control of such a child.

§3.5. Preliminary Review.
(a) Within 14 days of the seizure, the State shall seek a preliminary determination from the circuit court as to whether there is probable cause that the property may be subject to forfeiture.
(b) The rules of evidence shall not apply to any proceeding conducted under this Section.
(c) The court may conduct the review under subsection (a) simultaneously with a proceeding pursuant to Section 109-1 of the Code of Criminal Procedure of 1963 for a related criminal offense if a prosecution is commenced by information or complaint.
(d) The court may accept a finding of probable cause at a preliminary hearing following the filing of an information or complaint charging a related criminal offense or following the return of indictment by a grand jury charging the related offense as sufficient evidence of probable cause as required under subsection (a).
(e) Upon making a finding of probable cause as required under this Section, and after taking

into account the respective interests of all known claimants to the property including the State, the circuit court shall enter a restraining order or injunction, or take other appropriate action, as necessary to ensure that the property is not removed from the court's jurisdiction and is not concealed, destroyed, or otherwise disposed of by the property owner or interest holder before a forfeiture hearing is conducted.

§150/4.1. [Abandonment of school bus by driver].
It is unlawful for any school bus driver to willfully abandon the school bus while it contains any children who are without other adult supervision, except in an emergency where the driver is seeking help or otherwise acting in the best interests of the children.

§150/5. [Sentence].
Any person convicted under the provisions of the preceding sections, shall for the first offense be guilty of a Class A misdemeanor; and for a second or any subsequent offense shall be guilty of a Class 4 felony.

Ticket Sale and Resale Act
720 ILCS 375/0.01 *et seq.*

§375/0.01. Short title. This Act may be cited as the Ticket Sale and Resale Act.

§375/1. Sale of tickets other than at box office prohibited; exceptions. (a) It is unlawful for any person, firm or corporation, owner, lessee, manager, trustee, or any of their employees or agents, owning, conducting, managing or operating any theater, circus, baseball park, place of public entertainment or amusement where tickets of admission are sold for any such places of amusement or public entertainment to sell or permit the sale, barter or exchange of such admission tickets at any other place than in the box office or on the premises of such theater, circus, baseball park, place of public entertainment or amusement, but nothing herein prevents such theater, circus, baseball park, place of public entertainment or amusement from placing any of its admission tickets for sale at any other place at the same price such admission tickets are sold by such theater, circus, baseball park or other place of public entertainment or amusement at its box office or on the premises of such places, at the same advertised price or printed rate thereof.
(b) Any term or condition of the original sale of a ticket to any theater, circus, baseball park, or place of public entertainment or amusement where tickets of admission are sold that purports to limit the terms or conditions of resale of the ticket (including but not limited to the resale price of the ticket) is unenforceable, null, and void if the resale transaction is carried out by any of the means set forth in subsections (b), (c), (d), and (e) of Section 1.5 of this Act [*375/1.5*]. This subsection shall not apply to a term or condition of the original sale of a ticket to any theater, circus, baseball park, or place of public entertainment or amusement where tickets of admission are sold that purports to limit the terms or conditions of resale of a ticket specifically designated as seating in a special section for a person with a physical disability.

§375/1.5. Sale of tickets at more than face value prohibited; exceptions.
(a) Except as otherwise provided in subsections (b), (c), (d), and (e) of this Section and in Section 4 [*375/4*], it is unlawful for any person, persons, firm or corporation to sell tickets for baseball games, football games, hockey games, theatre entertainments, or any other amusement for a price more than the price printed upon the face of said ticket, and the price of said ticket shall correspond with the same price shown at the box office or the office of original distribution.

(b) This Act does not apply to the resale of tickets of admission to a sporting event, theater, musical performance, or place of public entertainment or amusement of any kind for a price in excess of the printed box office ticket price by a ticket broker who meets all of the following requirements: (1) The ticket broker is duly registered with the Office of the Secretary of State on a registration form provided by that

Office. The registration must contain a certification that the ticket broker:
(A) engages in the resale of tickets on a regular and ongoing basis from one or more permanent or fixed locations located within this State;
(B) maintains as the principal business activity at those locations the resale of tickets;
(C) displays at those locations the ticket broker's registration;
(D) maintains at those locations a listing of the names and addresses of all persons employed by the ticket broker;
(E) is in compliance with all applicable federal, State, and local laws relating to its ticket selling activities, and that neither the ticket broker nor any of its employees within the preceding 12 months have been convicted of a violation of this Act; and (F) meets the following requirements: (i) the ticket broker maintains a toll free number specifically dedicated for Illinois consumer complaints and inquiries concerning ticket sales;
(ii) the ticket broker has adopted a code that advocates consumer protection that includes, at a minimum:
(a-1) consumer protection guidelines;
(b-1) a standard refund policy. In the event a refund is due, the ticket broker shall provide that refund without charge other than for reasonable delivery fees for the return of the tickets; and
(c-1) standards of professional conduct;
(iii) the ticket broker has adopted a procedure for the binding resolution of consumer complaints by an independent, disinterested third party and thereby submits to the jurisdiction of the State of Illinois; and
(iv) the ticket broker has established and maintains a consumer protection rebate fund in Illinois in an amount in excess of $ 100,000, which must be cash available for immediate disbursement for satisfaction of valid consumer complaints. Alternatively, the ticket broker may fulfill the requirements of subparagraph (F) of this paragraph (1) if the ticket broker certifies that he or she belongs to a professional association organized under the laws of this State, or organized under the laws of any other state and authorized to conduct business in Illinois, that has been in existence for at least 3 years prior to the date of that broker's registration with the Office of the Secretary of State, and is specifically dedicated, for and on behalf of its members, to provide and maintain the consumer protection requirements of subparagraph (F) of this paragraph (1) to maintain the integrity of the ticket brokerage industry.
(2) (Blank).
(3) The ticket broker and his employees must not engage in the practice of selling, or attempting to sell, tickets for any event while sitting or standing near the facility at which the event is to be held or is being held unless the ticket broker or his or her employees are on property they own, lease, or have permission to occupy.
(4) The ticket broker must comply with all requirements of the Retailers' Occupation Tax Act [*35 ILCS 120/1* et seq.] and collect and remit all other applicable federal, State and local laws in connection with the ticket broker's ticket selling activities.
(5) Beginning January 1, 1996, no ticket broker shall advertise for resale any tickets within this State unless the advertisement contains the name of the ticket broker and the Illinois registration number issued by the Office of the Secretary of State under this Section.
(6) Each ticket broker registered under this Act shall pay an annual registration fee of $ 100.
(c) This Act does not apply to the sale of tickets of admission to a sporting event, theater, musical performance, or place of public entertainment or amusement of any kind for a price in excess of the printed box office ticket price by a reseller engaged in interstate or intrastate commerce on an Internet auction listing service duly registered with the Department of Financial and Professional Regulation under the Auction License Act [*225 ILCS 407/5-1* et seq.] and with the Office of the Secretary of State on a registration form provided by that Office.
This subsection (c) applies to both sales through an online bid submission process and sales at a fixed price on the same website or interactive computer service as an Internet auction listing service registered with the Department of Financial and Professional Regulation.
This subsection (c) applies to resales described in this subsection only if the operator of the

Internet auction listing service meets the following requirements:
(1) the operator maintains a listing of the names and addresses of its corporate officers;
(2) the operator is in compliance with all applicable federal, State, and local laws relating to ticket selling activities, and the operator's officers and directors have not been convicted of a violation of this Act within the preceding 12 months;
(3) the operator maintains, either itself or through an affiliate, a toll free number dedicated for consumer complaints;
(4) the operator provides consumer protections that include at a minimum:
(A) consumer protection guidelines;
(B) a standard refund policy that guarantees to all purchasers that it will provide and in fact provides a full refund of the amount paid by the purchaser (including, but not limited to, all fees, regardless of how characterized) if the following occurs:
(i) the ticketed event is cancelled and the purchaser returns the tickets to the seller or Internet auction listing service; however, reasonable delivery fees need not be refunded if the previously disclosed guarantee specifies that the fees will not be refunded if the event is cancelled;
(ii) the ticket received by the purchaser does not allow the purchaser to enter the ticketed event for reasons that may include, without limitation, that the ticket is counterfeit or that the ticket has been cancelled by the issuer due to non-payment, unless the ticket is cancelled due to an act or omission by such purchaser;
(iii) the ticket fails to conform to its description on the Internet auction listing service; or
(iv) the ticket seller willfully fails to send the ticket or tickets to the purchaser, or the ticket seller attempted to deliver the ticket or tickets to the purchaser in the manner required by the Internet auction listing service and the purchaser failed to receive the ticket or tickets; and
(C) standards of professional conduct;
(5) the operator has adopted an independent and disinterested dispute resolution procedure that allows resellers or purchasers to file complaints against the other and have those complaints mediated or resolved by a third party,
and requires the resellers or purchasers to submit to the jurisdiction of the State of Illinois for complaints involving a ticketed event held in Illinois;
(6) the operator either: (A) complies with all applicable requirements of the Retailers' Occupation Tax Act and collects and remits all applicable federal, State, and local taxes; or
(B) publishes a written notice on the website after the sale of one or more tickets that automatically informs the ticket reseller of the ticket reseller's potential legal obligation to pay any applicable local amusement tax in connection with the reseller's sale of tickets, and discloses to law enforcement or other government tax officials, without subpoena, the name, city, state, telephone number, e-mail address, user ID history, fraud complaints, and bidding and listing history of any specifically identified reseller or purchaser upon the receipt of a verified request from law enforcement or other government tax officials relating to a criminal investigation or alleged illegal activity; and
(7) the operator either: (A) has established and maintains a consumer protection rebate fund in Illinois in an amount in excess of $ 100,000, which must be cash available for immediate disbursement for satisfaction of valid consumer complaints; or
(B) has obtained and maintains in force an errors and omissions insurance policy that provides at least $ 100,000 in coverage and proof that the policy has been filed with the Department of Financial and Professional Regulation.

(d) This Act does not apply to the resale of tickets of admission to a sporting event, theater, musical performance, or place of public entertainment or amusement of any kind for a price in excess of the printed box office ticket price conducted at an auction solely by or for a not-for-profit organization for charitable purposes under clause (a)(1) of Section 10.-1 of the Auction License Act.

(e) This Act does not apply to the resale of a ticket for admission to a baseball game, football game, hockey game, theatre entertainment, or any other amusement for a price more than the price printed on the face of the ticket and for more than the price of the ticket at the box office if the resale is made through an Internet website whose operator meets the following requirements:

(1) the operator has a business presence and physical street address in the State of Illinois and clearly and conspicuously posts that address on the website;

(2) the operator maintains a listing of the names of the operator's directors and officers, and is duly registered with the Office of the Secretary of State on a registration form provided by that Office;

(3) the operator is in compliance with all applicable federal, State, and local laws relating to its ticket reselling activities regulated under this Act, and the operator's officers and directors have not been convicted of a violation of this Act within the preceding 12 months;

(4) the operator maintains a toll free number specifically dedicated for consumer complaints and inquiries regarding ticket resales made through the website;

(5) the operator either:

(A) has established and maintains a consumer protection rebate fund in Illinois in an amount in excess of $ 100,000, which must be cash available for immediate disbursement for satisfaction of valid consumer complaints; or

(B) has obtained and maintains in force an errors and omissions policy of insurance in the minimum amount of $ 100,000 for the satisfaction of valid consumer complaints;

(6) the operator has adopted an independent and disinterested dispute resolution procedure that allows resellers or purchasers to file complaints against the other and have those complaints mediated or resolved by a third party, and requires the resellers or purchasers to submit to the jurisdiction of the State of Illinois for complaints involving a ticketed event held in Illinois;

(7) the operator either:

(A) complies with all applicable requirements of the Retailers' Occupation Tax Act [35 ILCS 12/1 et seq.] and collects and remits all applicable federal, State, and local taxes; or

(B) publishes a written notice on the website after the sale of one or more tickets that automatically informs the ticket reseller of the ticket reseller's potential legal obligation to pay any applicable local amusement tax in connection with the reseller's sale of tickets, and discloses to law enforcement or other government tax officials, without subpoena, the name, city, state, telephone number, e-mail address, user ID history, fraud complaints, and bidding and listing history of any specifically identified reseller or purchaser upon the receipt of a verified request from law enforcement or other government tax officials relating to a criminal investigation or alleged illegal activity; and

(8) the operator guarantees to all purchasers that it will provide and in fact provides a full refund of the amount paid by the purchaser (including, but not limited to, all fees, regardless of how characterized) if any of the following occurs:

(A) the ticketed event is cancelled and the purchaser returns the tickets to the website operator; however, reasonable delivery fees need not be refunded if the previously disclosed guarantee specifies that the fees will not be refunded if the event is cancelled;

(B) the ticket received by the purchaser does not allow the purchaser to enter the ticketed event for reasons that may include, without limitation, that the ticket is counterfeit or that the ticket has been cancelled by the issuer due to non-payment, unless the ticket is cancelled due to an act or omission by the purchaser;

(C) the ticket fails to conform to its description on the website; or

(D) the ticket seller willfully fails to send the ticket or tickets to the purchaser, or the ticket seller attempted to deliver the ticket or tickets to the purchaser in the manner required by the website operator and the purchaser failed to receive the ticket or tickets. Nothing in this subsection (e) shall be deemed to imply any limitation on ticket sales made in accordance with subsections (b), (c), and (d) of this Section or any limitation on sales made in accordance with Section 4.

(f) The provisions of subsections (b), (c), (d), and (e) of this Section apply only to the resale of a ticket after the initial sale of that ticket. No reseller of a ticket may refuse to sell tickets to another ticket reseller solely on the basis that the purchaser is a ticket reseller or ticket broker authorized to resell tickets pursuant to this Act.

(g) The provisions of Public Act 89-406 [P.A. 89-406] are severable under Section 1.31 of the Statute on Statutes
(h) The provisions of this amendatory Act of the 94th General Assembly [P.A. 94-20] are severable under Section 1.31 of the Statute on Statutes [375/1.31].

§375/2. [Penalties].
(a) Whoever violates any of the provisions of Section 1.5 of this Act [*375/1.5*] shall be guilty of a Class A misdemeanor and may be fined up to $ 5,000.00 for each offense and whoever violates any other provision of this Act may be enjoined and be required to make restitution to all injured consumers upon application for injunctive relief by the State's Attorney or Attorney General and shall also be guilty of a Class A misdemeanor, and any owner, lessee, manager or trustee convicted under this Act shall, in addition to the penalty herein provided, forfeit the license of such theatre, circus, baseball park, place of public entertainment or amusement so granted and the same shall be revoked by the authorities granting the same.
(b) Tickets sold or offered for sale by a person, firm or corporation in violation of Section 1.5 of this Act [*375/1.5*] may be confiscated by a court on motion of the Attorney General, a State's Attorney, the sponsor of the event for which the tickets are being sold, or the owner or operator of the facility at which the event is to be held, and may be donated by order of the court to an appropriate organization as defined under Section 2 of the Charitable Games Act [*230 ILCS 30/2*].
(c) The Attorney General, a State's Attorney, the sponsor of an event for which tickets are being sold, or the owner or operator of the facility at which an event is to be held may seek an injunction restraining any person, firm or corporation from selling or offering for sale tickets in violation of the provisions of this Act. In addition, on motion of the Attorney General, a State's Attorney, the sponsor of an event for which tickets are being sold, or the owner or operator of the facility at which an event is to be held, a court may permanently enjoin a person, firm or corporation found guilty of violating Section 1.5 of this Act [*375/1.5*] from engaging in the offer or sale of tickets.

§375/3. [Civil action]. [Omitted.]

§375/4. [Service charges permitted].
Nothing contained in this Act was ever intended to prohibit nor shall ever be deemed to prohibit a ticket seller, with consent of the sponsor of such baseball game, football game, hockey game, theatre entertainment or other amusement, from collecting a reasonable service charge, in addition to the printed box office ticket price, from a ticket purchaser in return for service actually rendered.

Cannabis Control Act – Selected Provisions
720 ILCS § 550/1 *et seq.*

§550/1. The General Assembly recognizes that (1) the current state of scientific and medical knowledge concerning the effects of cannabis makes it necessary to acknowledge the physical, psychological and sociological damage which is incumbent upon its use; and (2) the use of cannabis occupies the unusual position of being widely used and pervasive among the citizens of Illinois despite its harmful effects; and (3) previous legislation enacted to control or forbid the use of cannabis has often unnecessarily and unrealistically drawn a large segment of our population within the criminal justice system without succeeding in deterring the expansion of cannabis use. It is, therefore, the intent of the General Assembly, in the interest of the health and welfare of the citizens of Illinois, to establish a reasonable penalty system which is responsive to the current state of knowledge concerning cannabis and which directs the greatest efforts of law enforcement agencies toward the commercial traffickers and large-scale purveyors of cannabis. To this end, this Act provides wide latitude in the sentencing discretion of the courts and establishes penalties in a sharply rising progression based on the amount of substances containing cannabis involved in each case.

§550/3. [Definitions]. As used in this Act, unless the context otherwise requires:
(a) "Cannabis" includes marihuana, hashish and other substances which are identified as including any parts of the plant Cannabis Sativa, whether growing or not; the seeds thereof, the resin extracted from any part of such plant; and any compound, manufacture, salt, derivative, mixture, or preparation of such plant, its seeds, or resin, including tetrahydrocannabinol (THC) and all other cannabinol derivatives, including its naturally occurring or synthetically produced ingredients, whether produced directly or indirectly by extraction, or independently by means of chemical synthesis or by a combination of extraction and chemical synthesis; but shall not include the mature stalks of such plant, fiber produced from such stalks, oil or cake made from the seeds of such plant, any other compound, manufacture, salt, derivative, mixture, or preparation of such mature stalks (except the resin extracted therefrom), fiber, oil or cake, or the sterilized seed of such plant which is incapable of germination.
(b) "Casual delivery" means the delivery of not more than 10 grams of any substance containing cannabis without consideration.
(c) "Department" means the Illinois Department of Human Services (as successor to the Department of Alcoholism and Substance Abuse) or its successor agency.
(d) "Deliver" or "delivery" means the actual, constructive or attempted transfer of possession of cannabis, with or without consideration, whether or not there is an agency relationship.
(e) "Department of State Police" means the Department of State Police of the State of Illinois or its successor agency.
(f) "Director" means the Director of the Department of State Police or his designated agent.
(g) "Local authorities" means a duly organized State, county, or municipal peace unit or police force.
(h) "Manufacture" means the production, preparation, propagation, compounding, conversion or processing of cannabis, either directly or indirectly, by extraction from substances of natural origin, or independently by means of chemical synthesis, or by a combination of extraction and chemical synthesis, and includes any packaging or repackaging of cannabis or labeling of its container, except that this term does not include the preparation, compounding, packaging, or labeling of cannabis as an incident to lawful research, teaching, or chemical analysis and not for sale.
(i) "Person" means any individual, corporation, government or governmental subdivision or agency, business trust, estate, trust, partnership or association, or any other entity.
(j) "Produce" or "production" means planting, cultivating, tending or harvesting.
(k) "State" includes the State of Illinois and any state, district, commonwealth, territory, insular possession thereof, and any area subject to the legal authority of the United States of America.
(l) "Subsequent offense" means an offense under this Act, the offender of which, prior to his conviction of the offense, has at any time been convicted under this Act or under any laws of the United States or of any state relating to cannabis, or any controlled substance as defined in the Illinois Controlled Substances Act [720 ILCS 570/100 et seq.].

§550/4. [Possession prohibited]. It is unlawful for any person knowingly to possess cannabis. Any person who violates this section with respect to:
(a) not more than 2.5 grams of any substance containing cannabis is guilty of a Class C misdemeanor;
(b) more than 2.5 grams but not more than 10 grams of any substance containing cannabis is guilty of a Class B misdemeanor;
(c) more than 10 grams but not more than 30 grams of any substance containing cannabis is guilty of a Class A misdemeanor; provided, that if any offense under this subsection (c) is a subsequent offense, the offender shall be guilty of a Class 4 felony;
(d) more than 30 grams but not more than 500 grams of any substance containing cannabis is guilty of a Class 4 felony; provided that if any offense under this subsection (d) is a subsequent offense, the offender shall be guilty of a Class 3 felony;

(e) more than 500 grams but not more than 2,000 grams of any substance containing cannabis is guilty of a Class 3 felony;
(f) more than 2,000 grams but not more than 5,000 grams of any substance containing cannabis is guilty of a Class 2 felony;
(g) more than 5,000 grams of any substance containing cannabis is guilty of a Class 1 felony.

§550/5. [Manufacture, delivery, or possession with intent to deliver or manufacture prohibited]. It is unlawful for any person knowingly to manufacture, deliver, or possess with intent to deliver, or manufacture, cannabis. Any person who violates this section with respect to:
(a) not more than 2.5 grams of any substance containing cannabis is guilty of a Class B misdemeanor;
(b) more than 2.5 grams but not more than 10 grams of any substance containing cannabis is guilty of a Class misdemeanor;
(c) more than 10 grams but not more than 30 grams of any substance containing cannabis is guilty of a Class 4 felony;
(d) more than 30 grams but not more than 500 grams of any substance containing cannabis is guilty of a Class 3 felony for which a fine not to exceed $ 50,000 may be imposed;
(e) more than 500 grams but not more than 2,000 grams of any substance containing cannabis is guilty of a Class 2 felony for which a fine not to exceed $ 100,000 may be imposed;
(f) more than 2,000 grams but not more than 5,000 grams of any substance containing cannabis is guilty of a Class 1 felony for which a fine not to exceed $ 150,000 may be imposed;
(g) more than 5,000 grams of any substance containing cannabis is guilty of a Class X felony for which a fine not to exceed $ 200,000 may be imposed.

§550/5.1. Cannabis Trafficking.
(a) Except for purposes authorized by this Act, any person who knowingly brings or causes to be brought into this State for the purpose of manufacture or delivery or with the intent to manufacture or deliver 2,500 grams or more of cannabis in this State or any other state or country is guilty of cannabis trafficking.
(b) A person convicted of cannabis trafficking shall be sentenced to a term of imprisonment not less than twice the minimum term and fined an amount as authorized by subsection (f) or (g) of Section 5 of this Act [720 ILCS § 550/5], based upon the amount of cannabis brought or caused to be brought into this State, and not more than twice the maximum term of imprisonment and fined twice the amount as authorized by subsection (f) or (g) of Section 5 of this Act [720 ILCS § 550/5], based upon the amount of cannabis brought or caused to be brought into this State.

§550/5.2. Delivery of cannabis on school grounds. (a) Any person who violates subsection (e) of Section 5 [720 ILCS § 550/5] in any school, on the real property comprising any school, or any conveyance owned, leased or contracted by a school to transport students to or from school or a school related activity, or on any public way within 1,000 feet of the real property comprising any school, or any conveyance owned, leased or contracted by a school to transport students to or from school or a school related activity, is guilty of a Class 1 felony, the fine for which shall not exceed $ 200,000;
(b) Any person who violates subsection (d) of Section 5 [720 ILCS § 550/5] in any school, on the real property comprising any school, or any conveyance owned, leased or contracted by a school to transport students to or from school or a school related activity, or on any public way within 1,000 feet of the real property comprising any school, or any conveyance owned, leased or contracted by a school to transport students to or from school or a school related activity, is guilty of a Class 2 felony, the fine for which shall not exceed $ 100,000;
(c) Any person who violates subsection (c) of Section 5 [720 ILCS § 550/5] in any school, on the real property comprising any school, or any conveyance owned, leased or contracted by a school to transport students to or from school or a school related activity, or on any public way within 1,000 feet of the real property comprising any school, or any conveyance owned, leased or contracted by a school to transport students to or from school or a school related activity, is guilty

of a Class 3 felony, the fine for which shall not exceed $ 50,000;
(d) Any person who violates subsection (b) of Section 5 [720 ILCS § 550/5] in any school, on the real property comprising any school, or any conveyance owned, leased or contracted by a school to transport students to or from school or a school related activity, or on any public way within 1,000 feet of the real property comprising any school, or any conveyance owned, leased or contracted by a school to transport students to or from school or a school related activity, is guilty of a Class 4 felony, the fine for which shall not exceed $ 25,000;
(e) Any person who violates subsection (a) of Section 5 [720 ILCS § 550/5] in any school, on the real property comprising any school, or any conveyance owned, leased or contracted by a school to transport students to or from school or a school related activity, on any public way within 1,000 feet of the real property comprising any school, or any conveyance owned, leased or contracted by a school to transport students to or from school or a school related activity, is guilty of a Class A misdemeanor.

§550/6. [Casual delivery of cannabis].
Any delivery of cannabis which is a casual delivery shall be treated in all respects as possession of cannabis for purposes of penalties.

§550/7. [Delivery to person under 18; violation by person under 18]. (a) Any person who is at least 18 years of age who violates Section 5 of this Act [720 ILCS § 550/5] by delivering cannabis to a person under 18 years of age who is at least 3 years his junior may be sentenced to imprisonment for a term up to twice the maximum term otherwise authorized by Section 5 [720 ILCS § 550/5].
(b) Any person under 18 years of age who violates Section 4 or 5 of this Act [720 ILCS § 550/4 or 720 ILCS § 550/5] may be treated by the court in accordance with the Juvenile Court Act of 1987 [705 ILCS 405/1-1 et seq.].

§550/8. [Production of cannabis plants].. It is unlawful for any person knowingly to produce the cannabis sativa plant or to possess such plants unless production or possession has been authorized pursuant to the provisions of Section 11 of the Act. Any person who violates this Section with respect to production or possession of:

(a) Not more than 5 plants is guilty of a Class A misdemeanor.

(b) More than 5, but not more than 20 plants, is guilty of a Class 4 felony.

(c) More than 20, but not more than 50 plants, is guilty of a Class 3 felony.

(d) More than 50, but not more than 200 plants, is guilty of a Class 2 felony for which a fine not to exceed $100,000 may be imposed and for which liability for the cost of conducting the investigation and eradicating such plants may be assessed. Compensation for expenses incurred in the enforcement of this provision shall be transmitted to and deposited in the treasurer's office at the level of government represented by the Illinois law enforcement agency whose officers or employees conducted the investigation or caused the arrest or arrests leading to the prosecution, to be subsequently made available to that law enforcement agency as expendable receipts for use in the enforcement of laws regulating controlled substances and cannabis. If such seizure was made by a combination of law enforcement personnel representing different levels of government, the court levying the assessment shall determine the allocation of such assessment. The proceeds of assessment awarded to the State treasury shall be deposited in a special fund known as the Drug Traffic Prevention Fund.

(e) More than 200 plants is guilty of a Class 1 felony for which a fine not to exceed $100,000 may be imposed and for which liability for the cost of conducting the investigation and eradicating such plants may be assessed. Compensation for expenses incurred in the enforcement of this provision shall be transmitted to and deposited in the treasurer's office at the level of government represented by the Illinois law enforcement agency whose officers or employees conducted the investigation or caused the arrest or arrests leading to the prosecution, to be subsequently made available to that law enforcement agency as expendable receipts for use in the enforcement of laws regulating controlled substances and cannabis. If such seizure was made by a combination of law enforcement personnel representing different levels of government, the court levying the assessment shall determine the allocation of such assessment. The proceeds of assessment awarded to the State treasury shall be deposited in a special fund known as the Drug Traffic Prevention Fund.

§550/9. [Calculated criminal cannabis conspiracy]. (a) Any person who engages in a calculated criminal cannabis conspiracy, as defined in subsection (b), is guilty of a Class 3 felony, and fined not more than $ 200,000 and shall be subject to the forfeitures prescribed in subsection (c); except that, if any person engages in such offense after one or more prior convictions under this Section, Section 4 (d), Section 5 (d), Section 8 (d) [720 ILCS § 550/4, 720 ILCS § 550/5 or 720 ILCS § 550/8] or any law of the United States or of any State relating to cannabis, or controlled substances as defined in the Illinois Controlled Substances Act [720 ILCS 570/100 et seq.], in addition to the fine and forfeiture authorized above, he shall be guilty of a Class 1 felony for which an offender may not be sentenced to death.

(b) For purposes of this section, a person engages in a calculated criminal cannabis conspiracy when: (1) he violates Section 4 (d), 4 (e), 5 (d), 5 (e), 8 (c) or 8 (d) of this Act [720 ILCS § 550/4, 720 ILCS § 550/5 or 720 ILCS § 550/8]; and

(2) such violation is a part of a conspiracy undertaken or carried on with 2 or more other persons; and

(3) he obtains anything of value greater than $ 500 from, or organizes, directs or finances such violation or conspiracy.

(c) Any person who is convicted under this Section of engaging in a calculated criminal cannabis conspiracy shall forfeit to the State of Illinois:

(1) the receipts obtained by him in such conspiracy; and

(2) any of his interests in, claims against, receipts from, or property or rights of any kind affording a source of influence over, such conspiracy.

(d) The circuit court may enter such injunctions, restraining orders, directions, or prohibitions, or take such other actions, including the acceptance of satisfactory performance bonds, in connection with any property, claim, receipt, right or other interest subject to forfeiture under this Section, as it deems proper.

§550/10. [First Offender Probation].

(a) Whenever any person who has not previously been convicted of, or placed on probation or court supervision for, any offense under this Act or any law of the United States or of any State relating to cannabis, or controlled substances as defined in the Illinois Controlled Substances Act [720 ILCS 570/100 et seq.], pleads guilty to or is found guilty of violating Sections 4(a), 4(b), 4(c), 5(a), 5(b), 5(c) or 8 of this Act [720 ILCS § 550/4, 720 ILCS § 550/5 or 720 ILCS § 550/8], the court may, without entering a judgment and with the consent of such person, sentence him to probation.

(b) When a person is placed on probation, the court shall enter an order specifying a period of probation of 24 months, and shall defer further proceedings in the case until the conclusion of the period or until the filing of a petition alleging violation of a term or condition of probation.

(c) The conditions of probation shall be that the person:

(1) not violate any criminal statute of any jurisdiction;

(2) refrain from possession of a firearm or other dangerous weapon;

(3) submit to periodic drug testing at a time and in a manner as ordered by the court, but no less than 3 times during the period of the probation, with the cost of the testing to be paid by the probationer; and

(4) perform no less than 30 hours of community service, provided community service is available in the jurisdiction and is funded and approved by the county board.

(d) The court may, in addition to other conditions, require that the person:

(1) make a report to and appear in person before or participate with the court or such courts,

person, or social service agency as directed by the court in the order of probation;
(2) pay a fine and costs;
(3) work or pursue a course of study or vocational training;
(4) undergo medical or psychiatric treatment; or treatment for drug addiction or alcoholism;
(5) attend or reside in a facility established for the instruction or residence of defendants on probation;
(6) support his dependents;
(7) refrain from possessing a firearm or other dangerous weapon;
(7-5) refrain from having in his or her body the presence of any illicit drug prohibited by the Cannabis Control Act [720 ILCS § 550/1 et seq.], the Illinois Controlled Substances Act [720 ILCS 570/100 et seq.], or the Methamphetamine Control and Community Protection Act [720 ILCS 646/1 et seq.], unless prescribed by a physician, and submit samples of his or her blood or urine or both for tests to determine the presence of any illicit drug;
(8) and in addition, if a minor:
(i) reside with his parents or in a foster home;
(ii) attend school;
(iii) attend a non-residential program for youth;
(iv) contribute to his own support at home or in a foster home.
(e) Upon violation of a term or condition of probation, the court may enter a judgment on its original finding of guilt and proceed as otherwise provided.
(f) Upon fulfillment of the terms and conditions of probation, the court shall discharge such person and dismiss the proceedings against him.
(g) A disposition of probation is considered to be a conviction for the purposes of imposing the conditions of probation and for appeal, however, discharge and dismissal under this Section is not a conviction for purposes of disqualification or disabilities imposed by law upon conviction of a crime (including the additional penalty imposed for subsequent offenses under Section 4(c), 4(d), 5(c) or 5(d) of this Act) [720 ILCS § 550/4 or 720 ILCS § 550/5].
(h) Discharge and dismissal under this Section, Section 410 of the Illinois Controlled Substances Act [720 ILCS § 550/410], or Section 70 of the Methamphetamine Control and Community Protection Act [720 ILCS 646/70] may occur only once with respect to any person.
(i) If a person is convicted of an offense under this Act, the Illinois Controlled Substances Act [720 ILCS 570/100 et seq.], or the Methamphetamine Control and Community Protection Act [720 ILCS 646/1 et seq.] within 5 years subsequent to a discharge and dismissal under this Section, the discharge and dismissal under this Section shall be admissible in the sentencing proceeding for that conviction as a factor in aggravation.

§550/10.1. [Fines]. (a) Whenever any person pleads guilty to, is found guilty of or is placed on supervision for an offense under this Act, a fine may be levied in addition to any other penalty imposed by the court.
(b) In determining whether to impose a fine under this Section and the amount, time for payment and method of payment of any fine so imposed, the court shall (1) consider the defendant's income, regardless of source, the defendant's earning capacity and the defendant's financial resources, as well as the nature of the burden the fine will impose on the defendant and any person legally or financially dependent upon the defendant;
(2) consider the proof received at trial, or as a result of a plea of guilty, concerning the full street value of the cannabis seized and any profits or other proceeds derived by the defendant from the violation of this Act;
(3) take into account any other pertinent equitable considerations; and
(4) give primary consideration to the need to deprive the defendant of illegally obtained profits or other proceeds from the offense. For the purpose of paragraph (2) of this subsection, "street value" shall be determined by the court on the basis of testimony of law enforcement personnel and the defendant as to the amount seized and such testimony as may be required by the court as to the current street value of the cannabis seized.
(c) As a condition of a fine, the court may require that payment be made in specified installments or within a specified period of time, but such period shall not be greater than the maximum applicable term of probation or imprisonment, whichever is greater. Unless

otherwise specified, payment of a fine shall be due immediately.
(d) If a fine for a violation of this Act is imposed on an organization, it is the duty of each individual authorized to make disbursements of the assets of the organization to pay the fine from assets of the organization.
(e) (1) A defendant who has been sentenced to pay a fine, and who has paid part but not all of such fine, may petition the court for an extension of the time for payment or modification of the method of payment.
(2) The court may grant a petition made pursuant to this subsection if it finds that (i) the circumstances that warranted payment by the time or method specified no longer exist; or (ii) it is otherwise unjust to require payment of the fine by the time or method specified.

§550/10.3. [Assessment upon conviction]. (a) Every person convicted of a violation of this Act, and every person placed on probation, conditional discharge, supervision or probation under Section 10 of this Act [720 ILCS § 550/10], shall be assessed for each offense a sum fixed at:
(1) $ 3,000 for a Class X felony;
(2) $ 2,000 for a Class 1 felony;
(3) $ 1,000 for a Class 2 felony;
(4) $ 500 for a Class 3 or Class 4 felony;
(5) $ 300 for a Class A misdemeanor;
(6) $ 200 for a Class B or Class C misdemeanor.

(b) The assessment under this Section is in addition to and not in lieu of any fines, restitution costs, forfeitures or other assessments authorized or required by law.

(c) As a condition of the assessment, the court may require that payment be made in specified installments or within a specified period of time. If the assessment is not paid within the period of probation, conditional discharge or supervision to which the defendant was originally sentenced, the court may extend the period of probation, conditional discharge or supervision pursuant to Section 5-6-2 or 5-6-3.1 of the Unified Code of Corrections, as applicable [730 ILCS 5/5-6-2 or 730 ILCS 5/5-6-3.1], until the assessment is paid or until successful completion of public or community service set forth in subsection (e) or the successful completion of the substance abuse intervention or treatment program set forth in subsection (f).
If a term of probation, conditional discharge or supervision is not imposed, the assessment shall be payable upon judgment or as directed by the court.
(d) If an assessment for a violation of this Act is imposed on an organization, it is the duty of each individual authorized to make disbursements of the assets of the organization to pay the assessment from assets of the organization.

(e) A defendant who has been ordered to pay an assessment may petition the court to convert all or part of the assessment into court-approved public or community service. One hour of public or community service shall be equivalent to $ 4 of assessment. The performance of this public or community service shall be a condition of the probation, conditional discharge or supervision and shall be in addition to the performance of any other period of public or community service ordered by the court or required by law.
(f) The court may suspend the collection of the assessment imposed under this Section; provided the defendant agrees to enter a substance abuse intervention or treatment program approved by the court; and further provided that the defendant agrees to pay for all or some portion of the costs associated with the intervention or treatment program. In this case, the collection of the assessment imposed under this Section shall be suspended during the defendant's participation in the intervention or treatment program.
Upon successful completion of the program, the defendant may apply to the court to reduce the assessment imposed under this Section by any amount actually paid by the defendant for his participation in the program. The court shall not reduce the penalty under this subsection unless the defendant establishes to the satisfaction of the court that he has successfully completed the intervention or treatment program. If the defendant's participation is for any reason terminated before his successful completion of the intervention or treatment program, collection of the entire assessment imposed under this

Section shall be enforced. Nothing in this Section shall be deemed to affect or suspend any other fines, restitution costs, forfeitures or assessments imposed under this or any other Act.

(g) The court shall not impose more than one assessment per complaint, indictment or information. If the person is convicted of more than one offense in a complaint, indictment or information, the assessment shall be based on the highest class offense for which the person is convicted.

(h) All moneys collected under this Section shall be forwarded by the clerk of the circuit court to the State Treasurer for deposit in the Drug Treatment Fund and expended as provided in Section 411.2 of the Illinois Controlled Substances Act [720 ILCS 570/411.2].

§550/12. [Forfeiture]. (a) The following are subject to forfeiture:
(1) all substances containing cannabis which have been produced, manufactured, delivered, or possessed in violation of this Act;
(2) all raw materials, products and equipment of any kind which are produced, delivered, or possessed in connection with any substance containing cannabis in violation of this Act;
(3) all conveyances, including aircraft, vehicles or vessels, which are used, or intended for use, to transport, or in any manner to facilitate the transportation, sale, receipt, possession, or concealment of property described in paragraph (1) or (2) that constitutes a felony violation of the Act, but:

(i) no conveyance used by any person as a common carrier in the transaction of business as a common carrier is subject to forfeiture under this Section unless it appears that the owner or other person in charge of the conveyance is a consenting party or privy to a violation of this Act;
(ii) no conveyance is subject to forfeiture under this Section by reason of any act or omission which the owner proves to have been committed or omitted without his knowledge or consent;
(iii) a forfeiture of a conveyance encumbered by a bona fide security interest is subject to the interest of the secured party if he neither had knowledge of nor consented to the act or omission;

(4) all money, things of value, books, records, and research products and materials including formulas, microfilm, tapes, and data which are used, or intended for use in a felony violation of this Act;
(5) everything of value furnished or intended to be furnished by any person in exchange for a substance in violation of this Act, all proceeds traceable to such an exchange, and all moneys, negotiable instruments, and securities used, or intended to be used, to commit or in any manner to facilitate any felony violation of this Act;
(6) all real property, including any right, title, and interest including, but not limited to, any leasehold interest or the beneficial interest to a land trust, in the whole of any lot or tract of land and any appurtenances or improvements, that is used or intended to be used to facilitate the manufacture, distribution, sale, receipt, or concealment of property described in paragraph (1) or (2) of this subsection (a) that constitutes a felony violation of more than 2,000 grams of a substance containing cannabis or that is the proceeds of any felony violation of this Act.

(b) Property subject to forfeiture under this Act may be seized by the Director or any peace officer upon process or seizure warrant issued by any court having jurisdiction over the property. Seizure by the Director or any peace officer without process may be made:
(1) if the property subject to seizure has been the subject of a prior judgment in favor of the State in a criminal proceeding or in an injunction or forfeiture proceeding based upon this Act or the Drug Asset Forfeiture Procedure Act [725 ILCS 150/1 et seq.];
(2) if there is probable cause to believe that the property is directly or indirectly dangerous to health or safety;
(3) if there is probable cause to believe that the property is subject to forfeiture under this Act and the property is seized under circumstances

in which a warrantless seizure or arrest would be reasonable; or
(4) in accordance with the Code of Criminal Procedure of 1963 [725 ILCS 5/100-1 et seq.].

(c) In the event of seizure pursuant to subsection (b), notice shall be given forthwith to all known interest holders
that forfeiture proceedings , including a preliminary review, shall be instituted in accordance with the Drug Asset Forfeiture Procedure Act [725 ILCS 150/1 et seq.] and such proceedings shall thereafter be instituted in accordance with that Act. Upon a showing of good cause, the notice required for a preliminary review under this Section may be postponed.
(c-1) In the event the State's Attorney is of the opinion that real property is subject to forfeiture under this Act, forfeiture proceedings shall be instituted in accordance with the Drug Asset Forfeiture Procedure Act [725 ILCS 150/1 et seq.]. The exemptions from forfeiture provisions of Section 8 of the Drug Asset Forfeiture Procedure Act [725 ILCS 150/1 et seq.] are applicable.

(d) Property taken or detained under this Section shall not be subject to replevin, but is deemed to be in the custody of the Director subject only to the order and judgments of the circuit court having jurisdiction over the
forfeiture proceedings and the decisions of the State's Attorney under the Drug Asset Forfeiture Procedure Act [725 ILCS 150/1 et seq.]. When property is seized under this Act, the seizing agency shall promptly conduct an inventory of the seized property, estimate the property's value, and shall forward a copy of the inventory of seized property and the estimate of the property's value to the Director. Upon receiving notice of seizure, the Director may:
(1) place the property under seal;
(2) remove the property to a place designated by him;
(3) keep the property in the possession of the seizing agency;
(4) remove the property to a storage area for safekeeping or, if the property is a negotiable instrument or money and is not needed for evidentiary purposes, deposit it in an interest bearing account;
(5) place the property under constructive seizure by posting notice of pending forfeiture on it, by giving notice of pending forfeiture to its owners and interest holders, or by filing notice of pending forfeiture in any appropriate
public record relating to the property; or
(6) provide for another agency or custodian, including an owner, secured party, or lienholder, to take custody of the property upon the terms and conditions set by the Director.
(e) No disposition may be made of property under seal until the time for taking an appeal has elapsed or until all appeals have been concluded unless a court, upon application therefore, orders the sale of perishable substances and the deposit of the proceeds of the sale with the court.
(f) When property is forfeited under this Act the Director shall sell all such property unless such property is required by law to be destroyed or is harmful to the public, and shall distribute the proceeds of the sale, together with any moneys forfeited or seized, in accordance with subsection (g).
However, upon the application of the seizing agency or prosecutor who was responsible for the investigation, arrest or arrests and prosecution which lead to the forfeiture, the Director may return any item of forfeited property to the seizing agency or prosecutor for official use in the enforcement of laws relating to cannabis or controlled substances, if the agency or prosecutor can demonstrate that
the item requested would be useful to the agency or prosecutor in their enforcement efforts.
When any forfeited conveyance, including an aircraft, vehicle, or vessel, is returned to the seizing agency or prosecutor, the
conveyance may be used immediately in the enforcement of the criminal laws of this State.
Upon disposal, all proceeds from the sale of the conveyance must be used for drug enforcement purposes.
When any real property returned to the seizing agency is sold by the agency or its unit of government, the proceeds of the sale shall be delivered to the Director and distributed in accordance with subsection (g).

(g) All monies and the sale proceeds of all other property forfeited and seized under this Act shall be distributed as follows:

(1) 65% shall be distributed to the metropolitan enforcement group, local, municipal, county, or state law enforcement agency or agencies which conducted or participated in the investigation resulting in the forfeiture. The distribution shall bear a reasonable relationship to the degree of direct participation of the law enforcement agency in the effort resulting in the forfeiture, taking into account the total value of the property forfeited and the total law enforcement effort with respect to the violation of the law upon which the forfeiture is based. Amounts distributed to the agency or agencies shall be used for the enforcement of laws governing cannabis and controlled substances or for security cameras used for the prevention or detection of violence, except that amounts distributed to the Secretary of State shall be deposited into the Secretary of State Evidence Fund to be used as provided in Section 2-115 of the Illinois Vehicle Code [625 ILCS 5/2-115].

(2)(i) 12.5% shall be distributed to the Office of the State's Attorney of the county in which the prosecution resulting in the forfeiture was instituted, deposited in a special fund in the county treasury and appropriated to the State's Attorney for use in the enforcement of laws governing cannabis and controlled substances. In counties over 3,000,000 population, 25% will be distributed to the Office of the State's Attorney for use in the enforcement of laws governing cannabis and controlled substances. If the prosecution is undertaken solely by the Attorney General, the portion provided hereunder shall be distributed to the Attorney General for use in the enforcement of laws governing cannabis and controlled substances.

(ii) 12.5% shall be distributed to the Office of the State's Attorneys Appellate Prosecutor and deposited in the Narcotics Profit Forfeiture Fund of that Office to be used for additional expenses incurred in the investigation, prosecution and appeal of cases arising under laws governing cannabis and controlled substances. The Office of the State's Attorneys Appellate Prosecutor shall not receive distribution from cases brought in counties with over 3,000,000 population.

(3) 10% shall be retained by the Department of State Police for expenses related to the administration and sale of seized and forfeited property.

§550/15. The Department shall encourage research on cannabis. In connection with the research, and in furtherance of the purposes of this Act, it may:

(1) establish methods to assess accurately the effect of cannabis;

(2) make studies and undertake programs of research to:
(i) develop new or improved approaches, techniques, systems, equipment and devices to strengthen the enforcement of this Act;

(ii) determine patterns of use of cannabis and its social effects; and

(iii) improve methods for preventing, predicting, understanding, and dealing with the use of cannabis;

(3) enter into contracts with public agencies, educational institutions, and private organizations or individuals for the purpose of conducting research, demonstrations, or special projects which relate to the use of cannabis.

§550/15.1 (a) If any cannabis derivative is designated or rescheduled as a controlled substance under federal law and notice thereof is given to the Department, the Department shall similarly control the substance under the Illinois Controlled Substances Act after the expiration of 30 days from publication in the Federal Register of a final order designating a substance as a controlled substance or rescheduling a substance unless within that 30 day period the Department objects, or a party adversely affected files with the Department substantial written objections to inclusion or rescheduling. In that case, the Department shall publish the reasons for objection or the substantial written objections and afford all interested parties an opportunity to be heard. At the conclusion of the hearing, the Department shall publish its decision, by means of a rule, which shall be final unless altered by statute. Upon publication of objections by the Department, similar control under the Illinois Controlled Substances Act whether by inclusion or rescheduling is suspended until the Department publishes its ruling.

(b) If any cannabis derivative is deleted as a controlled substance under Federal law and notice thereof is given to the Department, the Department shall similarly control the substance under this Act after the expiration of 30 days from publication in the Federal Register of a final order deleting a substance as a controlled substance or rescheduling a substance unless within that 30 day period the Department objects, or a party adversely affected files with the Department substantial written objections to inclusion or rescheduling. In that case, the Department shall publish the reasons for objection or the substantial written objections and afford all interested parties an opportunity to be heard. At the conclusion of the hearing, the Department shall publish its decision, by means of a rule, which shall be final unless altered by statute. Upon publication of objections by the Department, similar control under this Act whether by inclusion or rescheduling is suspended until the Department publishes its ruling.

(c) Cannabis derivatives are deemed to be regulated under this Act until such time as those derivatives are scheduled as provided for under the Illinois Controlled Substances Act. Following such scheduling, those derivatives shall be excepted from this Act and shall be regulated pursuant to the Illinois Controlled Substances Act. At such time that any derivative is deleted from schedules provided for under the Illinois Controlled Substance Act, that derivative shall be regulated pursuant to this Act.

§550/16. [Burden of proof as to exemption or exception].
It is not necessary for the State to negate any exemption or exception in this Act in any complaint, information, indictment or other pleading or in any trial, hearing, or other proceeding under this Act. The burden of proof of any exemption or exception is upon the person claiming it.

§550/16.1. [Affirmative defense of regulation as controlled substance].
In any prosecution for any violation of this Act, it shall be an affirmative defense that the substance possessed by the defendant was regulated as a controlled substance under the Illinois Controlled Substances Act [720 ILCS 570/100 et seq.]. In order to raise this affirmative defense, the defendant shall give notice thereof to the State not less than 7 days prior to trial.

§ 550/16.2. Preservation of cannabis or cannabis sativa plants for laboratory testing.
Preservation of cannabis or cannabis sativa plants for laboratory testing.
(a) Before or after the trial in a prosecution for a violation of Section 4, 5, 5.1, 5.2, 8, or 9 of this Act [720 ILCS § 550/4, 720 ILCS § 550/5, 720 ILCS § 550/5.1, 720 ILCS § 550/5.2, 720 ILCS § 550/8, or 720 ILCS § 550/9], a law enforcement agency or an agent acting on behalf of the law enforcement agency must preserve, subject to a continuous chain of custody, not less than 6,001 grams of any substance containing cannabis and not less than 51 cannabis sativa plants with respect to the offenses enumerated in this subsection (a) and must maintain sufficient documentation to locate that evidence. Excess quantities with respect to the offenses enumerated in this subsection (a) cannot practicably be retained by a law enforcement agency because of its size, bulk, and physical character.

(b) The court may before trial transfer excess quantities of any substance containing cannabis or cannabis sativa plants with respect to a prosecution for any offense enumerated in subsection (a) to the sheriff of the county, or may in its discretion transfer such evidence to the Department of State Police, for destruction after notice is given to the defendant's attorney of record or to the defendant if the defendant is proceeding pro se.

(c) After a judgment of conviction is entered and the charged quantity is no longer needed for evidentiary purposes with respect to a prosecution for any offense enumerated in subsection (a), the court may transfer any substance containing cannabis or cannabis sativa plants to the sheriff of the county, or may in its discretion transfer such evidence to the Department of State Police, for destruction after notice is given to the defendant's attorney of record or to the defendant if the defendant is proceeding pro se. No evidence shall be disposed of until 30 days after the judgment is entered, and if a notice of appeal is filed, no evidence shall be disposed of until the mandate has been received by the circuit court from the Appellate Court.

§550/17. [Duty to enforce Act].
It is hereby made the duty of the Department of State Police, all peace officers within the State and of all State's attorneys, to enforce all provisions of this Act and to cooperate with all agencies charged with the enforcement of the laws of the United States, of this State, and of all other states, relating to cannabis.

§550/18. [Saving clause].
Prosecution for any violation of law occurring prior to the effective date of this Act is not affected or abated by this Act. If the offense being prosecuted would be a violation of this Act, and has not reached the sentencing stage or a final adjudication, then for purposes of penalty the penalties under this Act apply if they are less than under the prior law upon which the prosecution was commenced.

§550/19. [Severability].
If any provision of this Act or the application thereof to any person or circumstance is held invalid, such invalidity shall not affect other provisions or applications of the Act which can be given effect without the invalid provision or application, and to this end the provisions of this Act are declared severable.

Commentary – Marijuana Offenses

Criminal Offenses – Cannabis Control Act. The Cannabis Control Act criminalizes the possession and sale of marijuana in Illinois. The classification of offenses is tied both to the type of criminal conduct and the amount or quantity of marijuana. The smallest quantities held for purpose of personal use are minor crimes. under section 550/4(a) the unlawful possession of less than 2.5 grams of cannabis is a Class C misdemeanor, while section 550/5(g) classifies the unlawful possession of more than 5000 grams as a Class 1 felony. Manufacture, delivery or possession with intent to deliver is more serious conduct and the classification scheme reflects that judgment, since manufacture or delivery of less than 2.5 grams is a Class B misdemeanor (Section 550/5(a)) and delivery or possession with intent to deliver more than 5000 grams is a Class X felony (Section 550/5(g)). Another variable in conduct that enhances the classification scheme is the location, so for example, the delivery of more than 500 but less than 2000 grams on school grounds or on a school bus is a Class 1 felony, an enhancement from a Class 2 felony for the same conduct if it occurred away from school property. (See Section 550/5(e) as compared to Section 550/5.2(a)). Cannabis trafficking (knowingly bringing 2500 grams or more of cannabis into the State of Illinois for purposes of manufacture or delivery) under Section 550/5.1 doubles the penalties for imprisonment or fine that would otherwise apply for the same quantities under Section 550/5(f) or 5(g). Thus a cannabis trafficker faces minimum sentences of 8 years imprisonment for 2500 grams and 12 years minimum imprisonment for 5000 or more grams of trafficked cannabis. As the classifications show, the primary cannabis offenses relate to concepts of possession, possession with intent to deliver, delivery and manufacture.

It should be noted that often cannabis offenses and controlled substance offenses go hand in hand. The cases regarding possession, possession with intent to deliver, and manufacture and delivery charges are easily applied to the same factual pattern, even if the drug-of-choice for the prosecution is different.

Possession. Possession is either actual or constructive. Actual possession is ordinarily proved by direct observation of the offender exercising physical control of the object (such as a bag or container with marijuana or other substances in it), by dropping it, throwing it or moving it to a concealed location. For actual possession the evidence must show that the defendant knew of the cannabis and that he had immediate, exclusive possession of it. Section 550/4 sets forth the elements of the offense of unlawful possession of cannabis.

Constructive possession means that the offender had the ability and opportunity to exercise control over the object and is normally proved by circumstantial evidence. The proof addresses the knowledge and ability to control the immediate area where the contraband object is found. the evidentiary factors that address constructive possession include (1) the location of the object within the vicinity of the person and the presence or lack of presence of others at the location, (2) the amount of time the person was in that position with the object, (3) any gestures or movements by the person who is in the vicinity of the object, and (4) the nature and size of the object. A person's mere presence in proximity to the object, standing alone, will not suffice to prove constructive possession. Possession can also be joint. In other words two or more persons can be shown to have possession of a single object by direct or circumstantial evidence. Because cannabis is contraband and has monetary value (i.e. it is bought, sold and of course used), it is not unusual for more than one person who is present with the object that is holding the cannabis to have a possessory interest in it.

In *People v. Love* 404 Ill.App.3d 784, 937 N.E.2d 752 (Ill. App. Ct. 2nd Dist. 2010), the defendant's probation was revoked because of a charge of possession of cannabis and unlawful possession of a weapon by a felon. The defendant was the back seat passenger of a car that was stopped for a traffic violation. When the defendant got out of the car at the request of the police, a brown paper bag with the top folded remained on the back seat in area where the defendant had been sitting. Inside the brown paper bag there was a pistol and some cannabis. Also in the back seat there was a wheel chair (for the front seat passenger) and some items of clothing. In and under the front seat, and in the console, there were baggies containing cannabis. The car had an odor of cannabis. The officer who made the stop testified that the defendant's right thigh was on top of the bag and so the officer could not see the bag when he first looked in the back seat. The defendant denied knowing that the bag was there and testified that he saw the wheel chair and articles of clothing in the back seat, but not the bag. The trial court found the officer credible and the defendant not credible. the court on appeal affirmed using the factors for circumstantial proof of constructive possession – the defendant was the only one in the back seat, he made actual contact with the bag, the bag had a hard metal object in it (the pistol), the defendant had been in the back seat for some time and the defendant denied seeing the bag although seeing every other object in the back seat.

In *People v. Kelly* 361 Ill.App.3d 515, 838 N.E.2d 236 (Ill. App. Ct. 4th Dist. 2005), the defendant was convicted of unlawful possession of more than 30 but less than 500 grams of cannabis. A drug task force executed a warrant at a residence in Pontiac and found the defendant and Williams in a bedroom smoking a "blunt" (a cigar containing cannabis). The officers looked around the premises and saw a backpack that had a plastic bag that contained approximately 90 grams of cannabis. The defendant initially denied any knowledge of the backpack but later said that he had taken the cannabis that was in the blunt from the plastic bag inside the backpack. There were no identifiable prints on the plastic bag in the backpack. Evidence at trial established that Williams was a dealer and regularly supplied Strong, who lived at the residence. The defendant contended on appeal that the proof was insufficient to establish his guilt of constructive possession. In affirming the defendant's conviction, the court concluded:

> Defendant was not in actual possession of the cannabis, and no contraband was found on his person. Although there was no evidence indicating who owned the backpack or who carried it into the residence, there *was* evidence connecting defendant to the plastic bag. According to [testimony], defendant said he had rolled a blunt using the cannabis in the plastic bag and was smoking that blunt at the time of the raid. Despite the fact that defendant's fingerprints did not appear on the bag, the evidence presented at trial was sufficient for a reasonable trier of fact to convict defendant of possession. The evidence indicated that defendant, at least temporarily, had physical and intentional control and dominion over the cannabis and had not attempted to abandon the bag to the exclusion of someone else's control. After viewing the evidence in a light most favorable to the prosecution, we affirm defendant's conviction.
>
> *People v. Kelly 361* Ill.App.3d at 520-521, 838 N.E.2d at 242.

Possession with intent to deliver. Simple possession of cannabis cases are typically associated with small quantities of marijuana that would be held for purposes of personal use (consumption). An offense that charges possession with intent to deliver naturally involves the (1) knowing (2) possession of cannabis (3) with intent to deliver. The last element (3) intent to deliver is almost always proved by circumstantial evidence. the factors that show intent to deliver include (1) the quantity and quality of the cannabis, (2) the presence of a large amount of cash, (3) the presence of weapons, (4) the packaging, (5) presence of police scanners or cell phones and the presence of scales or other paraphernalia. While not an exhaustive list, the same factors are also used in controlled substance "intent to deliver" cases and include a catch-all "any other relevant" factor in the list. See *People v. Robinson* 167 Ill.2d 397, 657 N.E.2d 1020 (Ill. S. Ct. 1995). Section 550/5 criminalizes possession with intent to deliver.

In *People v. Blakney* 366 Ill.App.3d 925, 853 N.E.2d 885 (Ill. App. Ct. 1st Dist. 2006), the defendant was standing halfway in a closet when officers served a search warrant at their residence. A girlfriend was also present in the residence. The searching officers found a large quantity of cannabis (over 2500 grams) and cocaine (almost 5 grams) and cash in various locations in the residence. Some of the cocaine was present in small quantities in numerous plastic bags (35 separate bags containing .1 grams each). Some of the cannabis was likewise present in small plastic bags (12 separate bags). An electronic scale was found. A letter addressed to defendant was found in the apartment. Applying the circumstantial evidence factors, the court on appeal affirmed the defendant's conviction for possession with intent to deliver cannabis and cocaine.

Manufacture or delivery. Section 550/5 also proscribes against the unlawful manufacture or delivery of cannabis. Delivery of cannabis (Section 550/3(d)) is the transfer of an amount of cannabis from one person to another. It could be hand to hand by the offender and thus be an "actual" delivery. It could be done through third parties where the offender has set up the transaction and may not be personally present. This would be a "constructive" delivery.

Manufacturing cannabis (Section 55/3(h is not growing it, it is doing something with an amount of cannabis to ready it for delivery. That would include altering the amount of cannabis chemically, or chopping it to change its texture or appearance, or manufacture is as simple as packaging the marijuana into more packages, less packages or different packages.

In *People v. Moreno* 334 Ill.App.3d 328, 778 N.E.2d 780 (Ill. App. Ct. 4th Dist. 2002), a large quantify of marijuana was shipped from El Paso, Texas to Springfield, Illinois in a U-Haul truck. The Hispanic drivers were stopped for a traffic offense in Oklahoma and agreed to cooperate with law enforcement. Under constant surveillance they checked into a Ramada Inn and called back to Texas. Soon other men showed up at the hotel, including the defendant. The truck was intentionally altered to make it inoperable, so the men discussed the problem in the presence of the defendant, under audio and video surveillance. The defendant made arrangements to obtain his sister's van and the cannabis was loaded from the U-Haul to the van. The defendant was not present at the scene; instead he was at a near-by fast food restaurant with the other men. After the van was completely loaded, the police effected an arrest on the driver of the van, as well as the individuals at the restaurant. The defendant was charged and convicted with delivery of cannabis and with cannabis trafficking under Section 550/9 (bring cannabis into the state for the purpose of delivery). On appeal, the defendant argued that the evidence did not prove him guilty of delivery since he never had possession of the cannabis and never did any physical act in the transfer of the marijuana from one vehicle to another. He also argued that since law enforcement acted in Oklahoma, in fact the police were in exclusive control of the cannabis since that time. The appellate court rejected the arguments noting that several people can possess the same quantity of drugs, and that by joining into the transaction, providing a car and by comments he made, the evidence proved both the defendant's intent to possess and intent to deliver.

Child Curfew Act
720 ILCS 555/0.01 *et seq.* [Repealed]

Illinois Controlled Substances Act
720 ILCS 570/100 *et seq.* – Selected Provisions

Article I

§102. Definitions. As used in this Act, unless the context otherwise requires:

(a) "Addict" means any person who habitually uses any drug, chemical, substance or dangerous drug other than alcohol so as to endanger the public morals, health, safety or welfare or who is so far addicted to the use of a dangerous drug or controlled substance other than alcohol as to have lost the power of self control with reference to his addiction.

(b) "Administer" means the direct application of a controlled substance, whether by injection, inhalation, ingestion, or any other means, to the body of a patient, research subject, or animal (as defined by the Humane Euthanasia in Animal Shelters Act) by: (1) a practitioner (or, in his presence, by his authorized agent),

(2) the patient or research subject at the lawful direction of the practitioner, or

(3) a euthanasia technician as defined by the Humane Euthanasia in Animal Shelters Act.

(c) "Agent" means an authorized person who acts on behalf of or at the direction of a manufacturer, distributor, or dispenser. It does not include a common or contract carrier, public warehouseman or employee of the carrier or warehouseman.

(c-1) "Anabolic Steroids" means any drug or hormonal substance, chemically and pharmacologically related to testosterone (other than estrogens, progestins, and corticosteroids) that promotes muscle growth, and includes:

(i) boldenone,

(ii) chlorotestosterone,

(iii) chostebol,

(iv) dehydrochlormethyltestosterone,

(v) dihydrotestosterone,

(vi) drostanolone,

(vii) ethylestrenol,

(viii) fluoxymesterone,

(ix) formebulone,

(x) mesterolone,

(xi) methandienone,

(xii) methandranone,

(xiii) methandriol,

(xiv) methandrostenolone,

(xv) methenolone,

(xvi) methyltestosterone,

(xvii) mibolerone,

(xviii) nandrolone,

(xix) norethandrolone,

(xx) oxandrolone,
(xxi) oxymesterone,

(xxii) oxymetholone,

(xxiii) stanolone,

(xxiv) stanozolol,

(xxv) testolactone,
(xxvi) testosterone,

(xxvii) trenbolone, and

(xxviii) any salt, ester, or isomer of a drug or substance described or listed in this paragraph, if that salt, ester, or isomer promotes muscle growth. any person who is otherwise lawfully in possession of an anabolic steroid, or who otherwise lawfully manufactures, distributes, dispenses, delivers, or possesses with intent to deliver an anabolic steroid, which anabolic steroid is expressly intended for and lawfully allowed to be administered through implants to livestock or other nonhuman species, and which is approved by the Secretary of Health and Human Services for such administration, and which the person intends to administer or have administered through such implants, shall not be considered to be in unauthorized possession or to unlawfully manufacture, distribute, dispense, deliver, or possess with intent to deliver such anabolic steroid for purposes of this Act.

(d) "Administration" means the Drug Enforcement Administration, United States Department of Justice, or its successor agency.

(e) "Control" means to add a drug or other substance, or immediate precursor, to a Schedule under Article II of this Act whether by transfer from another Schedule or otherwise.

(f) "Controlled Substance" means a drug, substance, or immediate precursor in the Schedules of Article II of this Act.

(g) "Counterfeit substance" means a controlled substance, which, or the container or labeling of which, without authorization bears the trademark, trade name, or other identifying mark, imprint, number or device, or any likeness thereof, of a manufacturer, distributor, or dispenser other than the person who in fact manufactured, distributed, or dispensed the substance.

(h) "Deliver" or "delivery" means the actual, constructive or attempted transfer of possession of a controlled substance, with or without consideration, whether or not there is an agency relationship.

(i) "Department" means the Illinois Department of Human Services (as successor to the Department of Alcoholism and Substance Abuse) or its successor agency.

(j) "Department of State Police" means the Department of State Police of the State of Illinois or its successor agency.

(k) "Department of Corrections" means the Department of Corrections of the State of Illinois or its successor agency.

(l) "Department of Professional Regulation" means the Department of Professional Regulation of the State of Illinois or its successor agency.

(m) "Depressant" or "stimulant substance" means: (1) a drug which contains any quantity of (i) barbituric acid or any of the salts of barbituric acid which has been designated as habit forming under section 502 (d) of the Federal Food, Drug, and Cosmetic Act (21 U.S.C. 352 (d)); or

(2) a drug which contains any quantity of (i) amphetamine or methamphetamine and any of their optical isomers; (ii) any salt of amphetamine or methamphetamine or any salt of an optical isomer of amphetamine; or (iii) any substance which the Department, after investigation, has found to be, and by rule designated as, habit forming because of its depressant or stimulant effect on the central nervous system; or

(3) lysergic acid diethylamide; or

(4) any drug which contains any quantity of a substance which the Department, after investigation, has found to have, and by rule designated as having, a potential for abuse because of its depressant or stimulant effect on the central nervous system or its hallucinogenic effect.

(n) (Blank).

(o) "Director" means the Director of the Department of State Police or the Department of Professional Regulation or his designated agents.

(p) "Dispense" means to deliver a controlled substance to an ultimate user or research subject by or pursuant to the lawful order of a prescriber, including the prescribing, administering, packaging, labeling, or compounding necessary to prepare the substance for that delivery.

(q) "Dispenser" means a practitioner who dispenses.

(r) "Distribute" means to deliver, other than by administering or dispensing, a controlled substance.

(s) "Distributor" means a person who distributes.

(t) "Drug" means

(1) substances recognized as drugs in the official United States Pharmacopoeia, Official Homeopathic Pharmacopoeia of the United States, or official National Formulary, or any supplement to any of them;

(2) substances intended for use in diagnosis, cure, mitigation, treatment, or prevention of disease in man or animals;

(3) substances

(other than food) intended to affect the structure of any function of the body of man or animals and

(4) substances intended for use as a component of any article specified in clause (1), (2), or (3) of this subsection. It does not include devices or their components, parts, or accessories.

(t-5) "Euthanasia agency" means an entity certified by the Department of Professional Regulation for the purpose of animal euthanasia that holds an animal control facility license or animal shelter license under the animal Welfare Act. A euthanasia agency is authorized to purchase, store, possess, and utilize Schedule II nonnarcotic and Schedule III nonnarcotic drugs for the sole purpose of animal euthanasia.

(t-10) "Euthanasia drugs" means Schedule II or Schedule III substances (nonnarcotic controlled substances) that are used by a euthanasia agency for the purpose of animal euthanasia.

(u) "Good faith" means the prescribing or dispensing of a controlled substance by a practitioner in the regular course of professional treatment to or for any person who is under his treatment for a pathology or condition other than that individual's physical or psychological dependence upon or addiction to a controlled substance, except as provided herein: and application of the term to a pharmacist shall mean the dispensing of a controlled substance pursuant to the prescriber's order which in the professional judgment of the pharmacist is lawful.

The pharmacist shall be guided by accepted professional standards including, but not limited to the following, in making the judgment:

(1) lack of consistency of doctor patient relationship,

(2) frequency of prescriptions for same drug by one prescriber for large numbers of patients,

(3) quantities beyond those normally prescribed,

(4) unusual dosages,

(5) unusual geographic distances between patient, pharmacist and prescriber,

(6) consistent prescribing of habit forming drugs.

(u-1) "Home infusion services" means services provided by a pharmacy in compounding solutions for direct administration to a patient in a private residence, long term care facility, or hospice setting by means of parenteral, intravenous, intramuscular, subcutaneous, or intraspinal infusion.

(v) "Immediate precursor" means a substance:
(1) which the Department has found to be and by rule designated as being a principal compound used, or produced primarily for use, in the manufacture of a controlled substance;

(2) which is an immediate chemical intermediary used or likely to be used in the manufacture of such controlled substance; and

(3) the control of which is necessary to prevent, curtail or limit the manufacture of such controlled substance.

(w) "Instructional activities" means the acts of teaching, educating or instructing by practitioners using controlled substances within educational facilities approved by the State Board of Education or its successor agency.

(x) "Local authorities" means a duly organized State, County or Municipal peace unit or police force.

(y) "Look alike substance" means a substance, other than a controlled substance which (1) by overall dosage unit appearance, including shape, color, size, markings or lack thereof, taste, consistency, or any other identifying physical characteristic of the substance, would lead a reasonable person to believe that the substance is a controlled substance, or

(2) is expressly or impliedly represented to be a controlled substance or is distributed under circumstances which would lead a reasonable person to believe that the substance is a controlled substance. For the purpose of determining whether the representations made or the circumstances of the distribution would lead a reasonable person to believe the substance to be a controlled substance under this clause (2) of subsection (y), the court or other authority may consider the following factors in addition to any other factor that may be relevant:

(a) statements made by the owner or person in control of the substance concerning its nature, use or effect;

(b) statements made to the buyer or recipient that the substance may be resold for profit;

(c) whether the substance is packaged in a manner normally used for the illegal distribution of controlled substances;

(d) whether the distribution or attempted distribution included an exchange of or demand for money or other property as consideration, and whether the amount of the consideration was substantially greater than the reasonable retail market value of the substance.

Clause (1) of this subsection (y) shall not apply to a noncontrolled substance in its finished dosage form that was initially introduced into commerce prior to the initial introduction into commerce of a controlled substance in its finished dosage form which it may substantially resemble.

Nothing in this subsection (y) prohibits the dispensing or distributing of noncontrolled substances by persons authorized to dispense and distribute controlled substances under this Act, provided that such action would be deemed to be carried out in good faith under subsection (u) if the substances involved were controlled substances.

Nothing in this subsection (y) or in this Act prohibits the manufacture, preparation, propagation, compounding, processing, packaging, advertising or distribution of a drug or drugs by any person registered pursuant to Section 510 of the Federal Food, Drug, and Cosmetic Act (21 U.S.C. 360).

(y-1) "Mail order pharmacy" means a pharmacy that is located in a state of the United States, other than Illinois, that delivers, dispenses or distributes, through the United States Postal Service or other common carrier, to Illinois residents, any substance which requires a prescription.

(z) "Manufacture" means the production, preparation, propagation, compounding, conversion or processing of a controlled substance other than methamphetamine, either directly or indirectly, by extraction from substances of natural origin, or independently by means of chemical synthesis, or by a combination of extraction and chemical synthesis, and includes any packaging or repackaging of the substance or labeling of its container, except that this term does not include:

(1) by an ultimate user, the preparation or compounding of a controlled substance for his own use; or

(2) by a practitioner, or his authorized agent under his supervision, the preparation, compounding, packaging, or labeling of a controlled substance: (a) as an incident to his administering or dispensing of a controlled substance in the course of his professional practice; or

(b) as an incident to lawful research, teaching or chemical analysis and not for sale.

(z-1) (Blank).

(aa) "Narcotic drug" means any of the following, whether produced directly or indirectly by extraction from substances of natural origin, or independently by means of chemical synthesis, or by a combination of extraction and chemical synthesis:

(1) opium and opiate, and any salt, compound, derivative, or preparation of opium or opiate;

(2) any salt, compound, isomer, derivative, or preparation thereof which is chemically equivalent or identical with any of the substances referred to in clause (1), but not including the isoquinoline alkaloids of opium;

(3) opium poppy and poppy straw;

(4) coca leaves and any salts, compound, isomer, salt of an isomer, derivative, or preparation of coca leaves including cocaine or ecgonine, and

any salt, compound, isomer, derivative, or preparation thereof which is chemically equivalent or identical with any of these substances, but not including decocainized coca leaves or extractions of coca leaves which do not contain cocaine or ecgonine (for the purpose of this paragraph, the term "isomer" includes optical, positional and geometric isomers).

(bb) "Nurse" means a registered nurse licensed under the Nurse Practice act.

(cc) (Blank).

(dd) "Opiate" means any substance having an addiction forming or addiction sustaining liability similar to morphine or being capable of conversion into a drug having addiction forming or addiction sustaining liability.

(ee) "Opium poppy" means the plant of the species Papaver somniferum L., except its seeds.

(ff) "Parole and Pardon Board" means the Parole and Pardon Board of the State of Illinois or its successor agency.

(gg) "Person" means any individual, corporation, mail order pharmacy, government or governmental subdivision or agency, business trust, estate, trust, partnership or association, or any other entity.

(hh) "Pharmacist" means any person who holds a license or certificate of registration as a registered pharmacist, a local registered pharmacist or a registered assistant pharmacist under the Pharmacy Practice Act.

(ii) "Pharmacy" means any store, ship or other place in which pharmacy is authorized to be practiced under the Pharmacy Practice Act.
(jj) "Poppy straw" means all parts, except the seeds, of the opium poppy, after mowing.

(kk) "Practitioner" means a physician licensed to practice medicine in all its branches, dentist, optometrist, podiatrist, veterinarian, scientific investigator, pharmacist, physician assistant, advanced practice nurse, licensed practical nurse, registered nurse, hospital, laboratory, or pharmacy, or other person licensed, registered, or otherwise lawfully permitted by the United States or this State to distribute, dispense, conduct research with respect to, administer or use in teaching or chemical analysis, a controlled substance in the course of professional practice or research.

(ll) "Pre printed prescription" means a written prescription upon which the designated drug has been indicated prior to the time of issuance.

(mm) "Prescriber" means a physician licensed to practice medicine in all its branches, dentist, optometrist, podiatrist or veterinarian who issues a prescription, a physician assistant who issues a prescription for a controlled substance in accordance with Section 303.05, a written delegation, and a written supervision agreement required under Section 7.5 of the Physician Assistant Practice Act of 1987, or an advanced practice nurse with prescriptive authority delegated under Section 65 40 of the Nurse Practice Act and in accordance with Section 303.05, a written delegation, and a written collaborative agreement under Section 65 35 of the Nurse Practice Act.

(nn) "Prescription" means a lawful written, facsimile, or verbal order of a physician licensed to practice medicine in all its branches, dentist, podiatrist or veterinarian for any controlled substance, of an optometrist for a Schedule III, IV, or V controlled substance in accordance with Section 15.1 of the Illinois Optometric Practice Act of 1987, of a physician assistant for a controlled substance in accordance with Section 303.05, a written delegation, and a written supervision agreement required under Section 7.5 of the Physician Assistant Practice Act of 1987, or of an advanced practice nurse with prescriptive authority delegated under Section 65 40 of the Nurse Practice Act who issues a prescription for a controlled substance in accordance with Section 303.05, a written delegation, and a written collaborative agreement under Section 65 35 of the Nurse Practice act.

(oo) "Production" or "produce" means manufacture, planting, cultivating, growing, or harvesting of a controlled substance other than methamphetamine.

(pp) "Registrant" means every person who is required to register under Section 302 of this Act.

(qq) "Registry number" means the number assigned to each person authorized to handle controlled substances under the laws of the United States and of this State.

(rr) "State" includes the State of Illinois and any state, district, commonwealth, territory, insular possession thereof, and any area subject to the legal authority of the United States of America.

(ss) "Ultimate user" means a person who lawfully possesses a controlled substance for his own use or for the use of a member of his household or for administering to an animal owned by him or by a member of his household.

Article II

§ 201. [Duties of Department relating to Schedules]. (a) The Department shall carry out the provisions of this Article. The Department or its successor agency may add substances to or delete or reschedule all controlled substances in the Schedules of Sections 204, 206, 208, 210 and 212 of this Act. In making a determination regarding the addition, deletion, or rescheduling of a substance, the Department shall consider the following:

(1) the actual or relative potential for abuse;

(2) the scientific evidence of its pharmacological effect, if known;

(3) the state of current scientific knowledge regarding the substance;

(4) the history and current pattern of abuse;

(5) the scope, duration, and significance of abuse;

(6) the risk to the public health;

(7) the potential of the substance to produce psychological or physiological dependence;

(8) whether the substance is an immediate precursor of a substance already controlled under this Article;

(9) the immediate harmful effect in terms of potentially fatal dosage; and

(10) the long-range effects in terms of permanent health impairment.

(b) (Blank).

(c) (Blank).

(d) If any substance is scheduled, rescheduled, or deleted as a controlled substance under Federal law and notice thereof is given to the Department, the Department shall similarly control the substance under this act after the expiration of 30 days from publication in the Federal Register of a final order scheduling a substance as a controlled substance or rescheduling or deleting a substance, unless within that 30 day period the Department objects, or a party adversely affected files with the Department substantial written objections objecting to inclusion, rescheduling, or deletion. In that case, the Department shall publish the reasons for objection or the substantial written objections and afford all interested parties an opportunity to be heard. At the conclusion of the hearing, the Department shall publish its decision, by means of a rule, which shall be final unless altered by statute. Upon publication of objections by the Department, similar control under this Act whether by inclusion, rescheduling or deletion is stayed until the Department publishes its ruling.

(e) The Department shall by rule exclude any non-narcotic substances from a schedule if such substance may, under the Federal Food, Drug, and Cosmetic Act, be lawfully sold over the counter without a prescription.

(f) (Blank).

(g) Authority to control under this section does not extend to distilled spirits, wine, malt beverages, or tobacco as those terms are defined or used in the Liquor Control Act and the Tobacco Products Tax Act.

(h) Persons registered with the Drug Enforcement Administration to manufacture or distribute controlled substances shall maintain adequate security and provide effective controls and procedures to guard against theft and diversion, but shall not otherwise be required to meet the physical security control requirements (such as cage or vault) for Schedule V controlled substances containing pseudoephedrine or Schedule II controlled substances containing dextromethorphan.

§ 202. [All names of substances are included]. The controlled substances listed or to be listed in the schedules in sections 204, 206, 208, 210 and 212 are included by whatever official, common, usual, chemical, or trade name designated.

§ 203. [Findings required for inclusion in Schedule I]. the Department shall issue a rule scheduling a substance in Schedule I if it finds that:

(1) the substance has high potential for abuse; and

(2) the substance has no currently accepted medical use in treatment in the United States or lacks accepted safety for use in treatment under medical supervision.

§ 204. [Schedule I]. (a) The controlled substances listed in this Section are included in Schedule I.

(b) Unless specifically excepted or unless listed in another schedule, any of the following opiates, including their isomers, esters, ethers, salts, and salts of isomers, esters, and ethers, whenever the existence of such isomers, esters, ethers and salts is possible within the specific chemical designation:

(1) Acetylmethadol;

(1.1) Acetyl–alpha–methylfentanyl (N–[1–(1–methyl–2–phenethyl)–4–piperidinyl]–N–phenylacetamide);

(2) Allylprodine;

(3) Alphacetylmethadol, except levo–alphacetylmethadol (also known as levo–alpha–acetylmethadol, levomethadyl acetate, or LAAM);

(4) Alphameprodine;

(5) Alphamethadol;

(6) Alpha–methylfentanyl (N–(1–alpha–methyl–beta–phenyl) ethyl–4–piperidyl) propionanilide; 1–(1–methyl–2–phenylethyl)–4–(N–propanilido) piperidine;

(6.1) Alpha–methylthiofentanyl (N–[1–methyl–2–(2–thienyl) ethyl–4–piperidinyl]–N–phenylpropanamide);

(7)1–methyl–4–phenyl–4–propionoxypiperidine (MPPP);

(7.1) PEPAP (1–(2–phenethyl)–4–phenyl–4–acetoxypiperidine);

(8) Benzethidine;

(9) Betacetylmethadol;

(9.1) Beta–hydroxyfentanyl (N–[1–(2–hydroxy–2–phenethyl)–4–piperidinyl]–N–phenylpropanamide);

(10) Betameprodine;

(11) Betamethadol;

(12) Betaprodine;

(13) Clonitazene;

(14) Dextromoramide;

(15) Diampromide;

(16) Diethylthiambutene;
(17) Difenoxin;

(18) Dimenoxadol;

(19) Dimepheptanol;

(20) Dimethylthiambutene;

(21) Dioxaphetylbutyrate;

(22) Dipipanone;

(23) Ethylmethylthiambutene;

(24) Etonitazene;

(25) Etoxeridine;

(26) Furethidine;

(27) Hydroxpethidine;

(28) Ketobemidone;

(29) Levomoramide;

(30) Levophenacylmorphan;

(31) 3–Methylfentanyl (N–[3–methyl–1–(2–phenylethyl)–4–piperidyl]–N–phenylpropanamide);

(31.1) 3–Methylthiofentanyl (N–[(3–methyl–1–(2–thienyl)ethyl–4–piperidinyl]–N–phenylpropanamide);

(32) Morpheridine;

(33) Noracymethadol;

(34) Norlevorphanol;

(35) Normethadone;

(36) Norpipanone;

(36.1) Para–fluorofentanyl (N–(4–fluorophenyl)–N–[1–(2–phenethyl)–4–piperidinyl] propanamide);

(37) Phenadoxone;

(38) Phenampromide;

(39) Phenomorphan;

(40) Phenoperidine;

(41) Piritramide;

(42) Proheptazine;

(43) Properidine;

(44) Propiram;

(45) Racemoramide;

(45.1) Thiofentanyl (N–phenyl–N–[1–(2–thienyl)ethyl–4–piperidinyl]–propanamide);

(46) Tilidine;

(47) Trimeperidine;

(48) Beta–hydroxy–3–methylfentanyl (other name: N–[1–(2–hydroxy–2–phenethyl)–3–methyl–4–piperidinyl]–N–phenylpropanamide).

(c) Unless specifically excepted or unless listed in another schedule, any of the following opium derivatives, its salts, isomers and salts of isomers, whenever the existence of such salts, isomers and salts of isomers is possible within the specific chemical designation:

(1) acetorphine;

(2) acetyldihydrocodeine;

(3) benzylmorphine;

(4) Codeine methylbromide;

(5) Codeine–N–Oxide;

(6) Cyprenorphine;

(7) Desomorphine;

(8) Diacetyldihydromorphine (Dihydroheroin);
(9) Dihydromorphine;

(10) Drotebanol;

(11) Etorphine (except hydrochloride salt);

(12) Heroin;

(13) Hydromorphinol;

(14) Methyldesorphine;

(15) Methyldihydromorphine;

(16) Morphine methylbromide;

(17) Morphine methylsulfonate;

(18) Morphine–N–Oxide;

(19) Myrophine;

(20) Nicocodeine;

(21) Nicomorphine;

(22) Normorphine;

(23) Pholcodine;

(24) thebacon.

(d) Unless specifically excepted or unless listed in another schedule, any material, compound, mixture, or preparation which contains any quantity of the following hallucinogenic substances, or which contains any of its salts, isomers and salts of isomers, whenever the existence of such salts, isomers, and salts of isomers is possible within the specific chemical designation (for the purposes of this paragraph only, the term "isomer" includes the optical, position and geometric isomers):

(1) 3,4–methylenedioxyamphetamine (alpha–methyl,3,4–methylenedioxyphenethylamine, methylenedioxyamphetamine, MDA);

(1.1) Alpha–ethyltryptamine (some trade or other names: etryptamine; MONASE; alpha–ethyl–1H–indole–3–ethanamine; 3–(2–aminobutyl)indole; a–ET; and AET);
(2) 3,4–methylenedioxymethamphetamine (MDMA);

(2.1) 3,4–methylenedioxy–N–ethylamphetamine (also known as: N–ethyl–alpha–methyl–3,4 (methylenedioxy) Phenethylamine, N–ethyl MDA, MDE, and MDEA);

(2.2) N–Benzylpiperazine (BZP);

(3) 3–methoxy–4,5–methylenedioxyamphetamine, (MMDA);

(4) 3,4,5–trimethoxyamphetamine (TMA);

(5) (Blank);

(6) Diethyltryptamine (DET);

(7) Dimethyltryptamine (DMT);

(8) 4–methyl–2,5–dimethoxyamphetamine (DOM, STP);

(9) Ibogaine (some trade and other names: 7–ethyl–6,6,beta,7,8,9,10,12,13–octahydro–2–methoxy–6,9–methano–5H–pyrido [1',2':1,2] azepino [5,4–b] indole; Tabernanthe iboga);

(10) Lysergic acid diethylamide;

(10.5) Salvia divinorum (meaning all parts of the plant presently classified botanically as Salvia divinorum, whether growing or not, the seeds thereof, any extract from any part of that plant, and every compound, manufacture, salts, isomers, and salts of isomers whenever the existence of such salts, isomers, and salts of isomers is possible within the specific chemical designation, derivative, mixture, or preparation of that plant, its seeds or extracts);

(11) 3,4,5–trimethoxyphenethylamine (Mescaline);

(12) Peyote (meaning all parts of the plant presently classified botanically as Lophophora williamsii Lemaire, whether growing or not, the seeds thereof, any extract from any part of that plant, and every compound, manufacture, salts, derivative, mixture, or preparation of that plant, its seeds or extracts);

(13) N–ethyl–3–piperidyl benzilate (JB 318);

(14) N–methyl–3–piperidyl benzilate;

(14.1) N–hydroxy–3,4–methylenedioxyamphetamine (also known as N–hydroxy–alpha–methyl–3,4 (methylenedioxy)phenethylamine and N–hydroxy MDA);

(15) Parahexyl; some trade or other names: 3–hexyl–1–hydroxy–7,8,9,10–tetrahydro–6,6,9–trimethyl–6H–dibenzo (b,d) pyran; Synhexyl;

(16) Psilocybin;

(17) Psilocyn;

(18) alpha–methyltryptamine (AMT);

(19) 2,5–dimethoxyamphetamine (2,5–dimethoxy–alpha–methylphenethylamine; 2,5–DMA);

(20) 4–bromo–2,5–dimethoxyamphetamine (4–bromo–2,5–dimethoxy–alpha–methylphenethylamine; 4–bromo–2,5–DMA);

(20.1) 4–Bromo–2,5 dimethoxyphenethylamine. Some trade or other names: 2–(4–bromo–2,5–dimethoxyphenyl)–1–aminoethane; alpha–desmethyl DOB, 2CB, Nexus;

(21) 4–methoxyamphetamine (4–methoxy–alpha–methylphenethylamine; paramethoxyamphetamine; PMA);

(22) (Blank);

(23) Ethylamine analog of phencyclidine. Some trade or other names: N–ethyl–1–phenylcyclohexylamine, (1–phenylcyclohexyl) ethylamine, N–(1–phenylcyclohexyl) ethylamine, cyclohexamine, PCE;

(24) Pyrrolidine analog of phencyclidine. Some trade or other names: 1–(1–phenylcyclohexyl) pyrrolidine, PCPy, PHP;

(25) 5–methoxy–3,4–methylenedioxy–amphetamine;
(26) 2,5–dimethoxy–4–ethylamphetamine

(another name: DOET);

(27) 1–[1–(2–thienyl)cyclohexyl] pyrrolidine (another name: TCPy);

(28) (Blank);

(29) Thiophene analog of phencyclidine (some trade or other names: 1–[1–(2–thienyl)–cyclohexyl]–piperidine;
2–thienyl analog of phencyclidine; TPCP; TCP);

(30) Bufotenine (some trade or other names: 3–(Beta–Dimethylaminoethyl)–5–hydroxyindole; 3–(2–dimethylaminoethyl)–5–indolol; 5–hydroxy–N,N–dimethyltryptamine; N,N–dimethylserotonin; mappine);

(31) 1–Pentyl–3–(1–naphthoyl) indole. Some trade or other names: JWH–018;

(32) 1–Butyl–3–(1–naphthoyl)indole
Some trade or other names: JWH–073

(33) Any compound structurally derived from 3-(1-naphthoyl)indole or 1H-indol-3-yl- (1-naphthyl)methane by substitution at the nitrogen atom of the indole ring by alkyl, haloalkyl, alkenyl, cycloalkylmethyl, cycloalkylethyl or 2-(4-morpholinyl)ethyl whether or not further substituted in the indole ring to any extent,

whether or not substituted in the naphthyl ring to any extent;

(34) Any compound structurally derived from 3-(1-naphthoyl)pyrrole by substitution at the nitrogen atom of the pyrrole ring by alkyl, haloalkyl, alkenyl, cycloalkylmethyl, cycloalkylethyl or 2- (4-morpholinyl)ethyl, whether or not further substituted in the pyrrole ring to any extent, whether or not substituted in the naphthyl ring to any extent;

(35) Any compound structurally derived from 1-(1-naphthylmethyl)indene by substitution at the 3-position of the indene ring by alkyl, haloalkyl, alkenyl, cycloalkylmethyl, cycloalkylethyl or 2- (4-morpholinyl)ethyl whether or not further substituted in the indene ring to any extent, whether or not substituted in the naphthyl ring to any extent;

(36) Any compound structurally derived from 3-phenylacetylindole by substitution at the nitrogen atom of the indole ring with alkyl, haloalkyl, alkenyl, cycloalkylmethyl, cycloalkylethyl or 2- (4-morpholinyl)ethyl, whether or not further substituted in the indole ring to any extent, whether or not substituted in the phenyl ring to any extent;

(37) Any compound structurally derived from 2-(3-ydroxycyclohexyl)phenol by substitution at the 5-position of the phenolic ring by alkyl, haloalkyl, alkenyl, cycloalkylmethyl, cycloalkylethyl or 2-(4-morpholinyl)ethyl, whether or not substituted in the cyclohexyl ring to any extent.

(e) Unless specifically excepted or unless listed in another schedule, any material, compound, mixture, or preparation which contains any quantity of the following substances having a depressant effect on the central nervous system, including its salts, isomers, and salts of isomers whenever the existence of such salts, isomers, and salts of isomers is possible within the specific chemical designation:

(1) mecloqualone;
(2) methaqualone; and
(3) gamma hydroxybutyric acid.

(f) Unless specifically excepted or unless listed in another schedule, any material, compound, mixture, or preparation which contains any quantity of the following substances having a stimulant effect on the central nervous system, including its salts, isomers, and salts of isomers:

(1) Fenethylline;

(2) N–ethylamphetamine;

(3) aminorex (some other names: 2–amino–5–phenyl–2–oxazoline; aminoxaphen; 4–5–dihydro–5–phenyl–2–oxazolamine) and its salts, optical isomers, and salts of optical isomers;

(4) Methcathinone (some other names: 2–methylamino–1–phenylpropan–1–one; Ephedrone; 2–(methylamino)–propiophenone; alpha–(methylamino)propiophenone; N–methylcathinone; methycathinone; Monomethylpropion; UR 1431) and its salts, optical isomers, and salts of optical isomers;

(5) Cathinone (some trade or other names: 2–aminopropiophenone; alpha–aminopropiophenone; 2–amino–1–phenyl–propanone; norephedrone);

(6) N,N–dimethylamphetamine (also known as: N,N–alpha–trimethyl–benzeneethanamine; N,N–alpha–trimethylphenethylamine);

(7) (+ or –) cis–4–methylaminorex ((+ or –) cis–4,5–dihydro–4–methyl–4–5–phenyl–2–oxazolamine).

(g) Temporary listing of substances subject to emergency scheduling. Any material, compound, mixture, or preparation that contains any quantity of the following substances:

(1) N–[1–benzyl–4–piperidyl]–N–phenylpropanamide (benzylfentanyl), its optical isomers, isomers, salts, and salts of isomers;

(2) N–[1(2–thienyl) methyl–4–piperidyl]–N–phenylpropanamide (thenylfentanyl), its optical isomers, salts, and salts of isomers.

§ 205. [Findings required for inclusion in Schedule II]. the Department shall issue a rule scheduling a substance in Schedule II if it finds that:

(1) the substance has high potential for abuse;

(2) the substance has currently accepted medical use in treatment in the United States, or currently accepted medical use with severe restrictions; and

(3) the abuse of the substance may lead to severe psychological or physiological dependence.

§ 206. [Schedule II.] (a) The controlled substances listed in this Section are included in Schedule II.

(b) Unless specifically excepted or unless listed in another schedule, any of the following substances whether produced directly or indirectly by extraction from substances of vegetable origin, or independently by means of chemical synthesis, or by combination of extraction and chemical synthesis:

(1) Opium and opiates, and any salt, compound, derivative or preparation of opium or opiate, excluding apomorphine, dextrorphan, levopropoxyphene, nalbuphine, nalmefene, naloxone, and naltrexone, and their respective salts, but including the following:

(i) Raw Opium;

(ii) Opium extracts;

(iii) Opium fluid extracts;

(iv) Powdered opium;

(v) Granulated opium;

(vi) Tincture of opium;

(vii) Codeine;
(viii) Ethylmorphine;

(ix) Etorphine Hydrochloride;

(x) Hydrocodone;

(xi) Hydromorphone;

(xii) Metopon;

(xiii) Morphine;

(xiv) Oxycodone;

(xv) Oxymorphone;

(xvi) Thebaine;

(xvii) Thebaine–derived butorphanol.

(xviii) Dextromethorphan, except drug products that may be dispensed pursuant to a prescription order of a practitioner and are sold in compliance with the safety and labeling standards as set forth by the United States Food and Drug Administration, or drug products containing dextromethorphan that are sold in solid, tablet, liquid, capsule, powder, thin film, or gel form and which are formulated, packaged, and sold in dosages and concentrations for use as an over–the–counter drug product. For the purposes of this Section, "over–the–counter drug product" means a drug that is available to consumers without a prescription and sold in compliance with the safety and labeling standards as set forth by the United States Food and Drug Administration.
(2) any salt, compound, isomer, derivative or preparation thereof which is chemically equivalent or identical with any of the substances referred to in subparagraph (1), but not including the isoquinoline alkaloids of opium;

(3) Opium poppy and poppy straw;

(4) Coca leaves and any salt, compound, isomer, salt of an isomer, derivative, or preparation of coca leaves including cocaine or ecgonine, and any salt, compound, isomer, derivative, or preparation thereof which is chemically equivalent or identical with any of these substances, but not including decocainized coca leaves or extractions of coca leaves which do not contain cocaine or ecgonine

(for the purpose of this paragraph, the term "isomer" includes optical, positional and geometric isomers);

(5) Concentrate of poppy straw
(the crude extract of poppy straw in either liquid, solid or powder form which contains the phenanthrine alkaloids of the opium poppy).

(c) Unless specifically excepted or unless listed in another schedule any of the following opiates, including their isomers, esters, ethers, salts, and salts of isomers, whenever the existence of these isomers, esters, ethers and salts is possible within the specific chemical designation, dextrorphan excepted:

(1) Alfentanil;

(1.1) Carfentanil;

(2) alphaprodine;

(3) anileridine;

(4) bezitramide;

(5) Bulk Dextropropoxyphene (non–dosage forms);

(6) Dihydrocodeine;

(7) Diphenoxylate;
(8) Fentanyl;

(9) Sufentanil;

(9.5) Remifentanil;

(10) isomethadone;
(11) Levomethorphan;

(12) Levorphanol (Levorphan);

(13) Metazocine;

(14) Methadone;
(15) Methadone–Intermediate, 4–cyano–2–dimethylamino–4,4–diphenyl–1–butane;

(16) Moramide–Intermediate, 2–methyl–3–morpholino–1,1–diphenylpropane–carboxylic acid;

(17) Pethidine (meperidine);

(18) Pethidine–Intermediate–A, 4–cyano–1–methyl–4–phenylpiperidine;

(19) Pethidine–Intermediate–B, ethyl–4–phenylpiperidine–4–carboxylate;

(20) Pethidine–Intermediate–C, 1–methyl–4–phenylpiperidine–4–carboxylic acid;

(21) Phenazocine;

(22) Piminodine;

(23) Racemethorphan;

(24) Racemorphan;

(25) Levo–alphacetylmethadol (some other names: levo–alpha–acetylmethadol, levomethadyl acetate, LAAM).

(d) Unless specifically excepted or unless listed in another schedule, any material, compound, mixture, or preparation which contains any quantity of the following substances having a stimulant effect on the central nervous system:

(1) amphetamine, its salts, optical isomers, and salts of its optical isomers;

(2) Methamphetamine, its salts, isomers, and salts of its isomers;

(3) Phenmetrazine and its salts;

(4) Methylphenidate.

(e) Unless specifically excepted or unless listed in another schedule, any material, compound, mixture, or preparation which contains any quantity of the following substances having a depressant effect on the central nervous system, including its salts, isomers, and salts of isomers whenever the existence of such salts, isomers, and salts of isomers is possible within the specific chemical designation:

(1) amobarbital;

(2) Secobarbital;

(3) Pentobarbital;

(4) Pentazocine;

(5) Phencyclidine;

(6) Gluthethimide;

(7) (Blank).

(f) Unless specifically excepted or unless listed in another schedule, any material, compound, mixture, or preparation which contains any quantity of the following substances:

(1) Immediate precursor to amphetamine and methamphetamine:

(i) Phenylacetone Some trade or other names: phenyl–2–propanone;P2P; benzyl methyl ketone; methyl benzyl ketone.

(2) Immediate precursors to phencyclidine:
(i) 1–phenylcyclohexylamine;

(ii) 1–piperidinocyclohexanecarbonitrile (PCC).
(3) Nabilone.

§ 207. [Findings required for inclusion in Schedule III]. the Department shall issue a rule scheduling a substance in Schedule III if it finds that:

(1) the substance has a potential for abuse less than the substances listed in Schedule I and II;

(2) the substance has currently accepted medical use in treatment in the United States; and

(3) abuse of the substance may lead to moderate or low physiological dependence or high psychological dependence.

§ 208. [Schedule III]. (a) The controlled substances listed in this Section are included in Schedule III.

(b) Unless specifically excepted or unless listed in another schedule, any material, compound, mixture, or preparation which contains any quantity of the following substances having a stimulant effect on the central nervous system, including its salts, isomers (whether optical position, or geometric), and salts of such isomers whenever the existence of such salts, isomers, and salts of isomers is possible within the specific chemical designation;

(1) Those compounds, mixtures, or preparations in dosage unit form containing any stimulant substances listed in Schedule II which compounds, mixtures, or preparations were listed on August 25,1971, as excepted compounds under Title 21, Code of Federal Regulations, Section 308.32, and any other drug of the quantitative e composition shown in that list for those drugs or which is the same except that it contains a lesser quantity of controlled substances;

(2) benzphetamine;

(3) Chlorphentermine;

(4) Clortermine;

(5) Phendimetrazine.

(c) Unless specifically excepted or unless listed in another schedule, any material, compound, mixture, or preparation which contains any quantity of the following substances having a potential for abuse associated with a depressant effect on the central nervous system:

(1) any compound, mixture, or preparation containing amobarbital, secobarbital, pentobarbital or any salt thereof and one or more other active medicinal ingredients which are not listed in any schedule;

(2) any suppository dosage form containing amobarbital, secobarbital, pentobarbital or any salt of any of these drugs and approved by the

Federal Food and Drug Administration for marketing only as a suppository;

(3) any substance which contains any quantity of a derivative of barbituric acid, or any salt thereof:

(4) Chlorhexadol;

(5) Methyprylon;

(6) Sulfondiethylmethane;

(7) Sulfonethylmethane;

(8) Sulfonmethane;

(9) Lysergic acid;

(10) Lysergic acid amide;

(10.1) Tiletamine or zolazepam or both, or any salt of either of them.
Some trade or other names for a tiletamine–zolazepam combination product: Telazol.
Some trade or other names for Tiletamine: 2–(ethylamino)–2–(2–thienyl)–cyclohexanone.
Some trade or other names for zolazepam: 4–(2–fluorophenyl)–6,8–dihydro–1,3,8–trimethylpyrazolo–[3,4–e], [1,4]–diazepin–7 (1H)–one, and flupyrazapon.

(11) any material, compound, mixture or preparation containing not more than 12.5 milligrams of pentazocine or any of its salts, per 325 milligrams of aspirin;

(12) any material, compound, mixture or preparation containing not more than 12.5 milligrams of pentazocine or any of its salts, per 325 milligrams of acetaminophen;

(13) any material, compound, mixture or preparation containing not more than 50 milligrams of pentazocine or any of its salts plus naloxone HCl USP 0.5 milligrams, per dosage unit;

(14) Ketamine.

(d) Nalorphine.

(e) Unless specifically excepted or unless listed in another schedule, any material, compound, mixture, or preparation containing limited quantities of any of the following narcotic drugs, or their salts calculated as the free anhydrous base or alkaloid, as set forth below:

(1) not more than 1.8 grams of codeine per 100milliliters or not more than 90 milligrams per dosage unit, with an equal or greater quantity of an isoquinoline alkaloid of opium;

(2) not more than 1.8 grams of codeine per 100 milliliters or not more than 90 milligrams per dosage unit, with one or more active non–narcotic ingredients in recognized therapeutic amounts;

(3) not more than 300 milligrams of dihydrocodeinoneper 100 milliliters or not more than 15 milligrams per dosage unit, with a fourfold or greater quantity of an isoquinoline alkaloid of opium;

(4) not more than 300 milligrams of dihydrocodeinone
per 100 milliliters or not more than 15 milligrams per dosage unit, with one or more active, non–narcotic ingredients in recognized therapeutic amounts;

(5) not more than 1.8 grams of dihydrocodeine per 100
milliliters or not more than 90 milligrams per dosage unit, with one or more active, non–narcotic ingredients in recognized therapeutic amounts;

(6) not more than 300 milligrams of ethylmorphine per 100 milliliters or not more than 15 milligrams per dosage unit, with one or more active, non–narcotic ingredients in recognized therapeutic amounts;

(7) not more than 500 milligrams of opium per 100 milliliters or per 100 grams, or not more than 25 milligrams per dosage unit, with one or more active, non–narcotic ingredients in recognized therapeutic amounts;

(8) not more than 50 milligrams of morphine per 100 milliliters or per 100 grams with one or more active, non–narcotic ingredients in recognized therapeutic amounts.

(f) Anabolic steroids, except the following anabolic steroids that are exempt:

(1) androgyn L.A.;

(2) andro–Estro 90–4;

(3) depANDROGYN;

(4) DEPO–T.E.;

(5) depTESTROGEN;

(6) Duomone;

(7) DURATESTRIN;

(8) DUO–SPAN II;

(9) Estratest;

(10) Estratest H.S.;

(11) PAN ESTRA TEST;

(12) Premarin with Methyltestosterone;

(13) TEST–ESTRO Cypionates;

(14) Testosterone Cyp 50 Estradiol Cyp 2;

(15) Testosterone Cypionate–Estradiol Cypionate injection; and

(16) Testosterone Enanthate–Estradiol Valerate injection.

(g) Hallucinogenic substances.

(1) Dronabinol (synthetic) in sesame oil and encapsulated in a soft gelatin capsule in a U.S. Food and Drug Administration approved product. Some other names for dronabinol: (6aR–trans)–6a,7,8,10a–tetrahydro–6,6,9–trimethyl–3–pentyl–6H–dibenzo (b,d) pyran–1–ol) or (–)–delta–9–(trans)–tetrahydrocannabinol.

(2) (Reserved).

(h) the Department may except by rule any compound, mixture, or preparation containing any stimulant or depressant substance listed in subsection (b) from the application of all or any part of this Act if the compound, mixture, or preparation contains one or more active medicinal ingredients not having a stimulant or depressant effect on the central nervous system, and if the admixtures are included therein in combinations, quantity, proportion, or concentration that vitiate the potential for abuse of the substances which have a stimulant or depressant effect on the central nervous system.

§ 209. [Findings required for inclusion in Schedule IV]. the Department shall issue a rule scheduling a substance in Schedule IV if it finds that:

(1) the substance has a low potential for abuse relative to substances in Schedule III;

(2) the substance has currently accepted medical use in treatment in the United States; and

(3) abuse of the substance may lead to limited physiological dependence or psychological dependence relative to the substances in Schedule III.

§ 210. [Schedule IV]. (a) the controlled substances listed in this Section are included in Schedule IV.

(b) Unless specifically excepted or unless listed in another schedule, any material, compound, mixture, or preparation containing limited quantities of any of the following narcotic drugs, or their salts calculated as the free anhydrous base or alkaloid, as set forth below:

(1) Not more than 1 milligram of difenoxin (DEA Drug Code No. 9618) and not less than 25

micrograms of atropine sulfate per dosage unit.

(2) Dextropropoxyphene (Alpha–(+)–4–dimethylamino–1, 2–diphenyl–3–methyl–2–propionoxybutane).

(c) Unless specifically excepted or unless listed in another schedule, any material, compound, mixture, or preparation which contains any quantity of the following substances having a potential for abuse associated with a depressant effect on the central nervous system:

(1) alprazolam;

(2) Barbital;

(2.1) Bromazepam;

(2.2) Camazepam;

(3) Chloral Betaine;

(4) Chloral Hydrate;

(5) Chlordiazepoxide;

(5.1) Clobazam;

(6) Clonazepam;

(7) Clorazepate;

(7.1) Clotiazepam;

(7.2) Cloxazolam;

(7.3) Delorazepam;

(8) Diazepam;

(8.1) Estazolam;

(9) Ethchlorvynol;

(10) Ethinamate;

(10.1) Ethyl loflazepate;

(10.2) Fludiazepam;

(10.3) Flunitrazepam;

(11) Flurazepam;

(12) Halazepam;

(12.1) Haloxazolam;

(12.2) Ketazolam;

(12.3) Loprazolam;

(13) Lorazepam;

(13.1) Lormetazepam;

(14) Mebutamate;

(14.1) Medazepam;

(15) Meprobamate;

(16) Methohexital;

(17) Methylphenobarbital (Mephobarbital);

(17.1) Midazolam;

(17.2) Nimetazepam;

(17.3) Nitrazepam;

(17.4) Nordiazepam;

(18) Oxazepam;

(18.1) Oxazolam;

(19) Paraldehyde;

(20) Petrichloral;

(21) Phenobarbital;

(21.1) Pinazepam;

(22) Prazepam;

(22.1) Quazepam;

(23) Temazepam;

(23.1) Tetrazepam;

(24) Triazolam;

(24.5) Zaleplon;

(25) Zolpidem.

(d) Any material, compound, mixture, or preparation which contains any quantity of the following substances, including its salts, isomers (whether optical, position, or geometric), and salts of such isomers, whenever the existence of such salts, isomers and salts of isomers is possible:

(1) Fenfluramine.

(e) Unless specifically excepted or unless listed in another schedule any material, compound, mixture, or preparation which contains any quantity of the following substances having a stimulant effect on the central nervous system, including its salts, isomers (whether optical, position or geometric), and salts of such isomers whenever the existence of such salts, isomers, and salts of isomers is possible within the specific chemical designation:

(1) Cathine ((+)–norpseudoephedrine);

(1.1) Diethylpropion;

(1.2) Fencamfamin;

(1.3) Fenproporex;

(2) Mazindol;

(2.1) Mefenorex;

(3) Phentermine;

(4) Pemoline (including organometallic complexes and chelates thereof);

(5) Pipradrol;

(6) SPA (–)–1–dimethylamino–1, 2–diphenylethane);

(7) Modafinil;

(8) Sibutramine.

(f) other Substances. Unless specifically excepted or unless listed in another schedule, any material, compound, mixture, or preparation that contains any quantity of the following substance, including its salts:

(1) Butorphanol (including its optical isomers).

(g) The Department may except by rule any compound, mixture, or preparation containing any depressant substance listed in subsection (b) from the application of all or any part of this Act if the compound, mixture, or preparation contains one or more active medicinal ingredients not having a depressant effect on the central nervous system, and if the admixtures are included therein in combinations, quantity, proportion, or concentration that vitiate the potential for abuse of the substances which have a depressant effect on the central nervous system.

(h) Except as otherwise provided in Section 216, any material, compound, mixture, or preparation that contains any quantity of the following substance having a stimulant effect on the central nervous system, including its salts, enantiomers (optical isomers) and salts of enantiomers (optical isomers):

(1) Ephedrine, its salts, optical isomers and salts of optical isomers.

§ 211. [Findings required for inclusion in Schedule V]. the Department shall issue a rule scheduling a substance in Schedule V if it finds that:

(1) the substance has low potential for abuse relative to the controlled substances listed in Schedule IV;

(2) the substance has currently accepted medical use in treatment in the United States; and

(3) abuse of the substance may lead to limited physiological dependence or psychological dependence relative to the substances in

Schedule IV, or the substance is a targeted methamphetamine precursor as defined in the Methamphetamine Precursor Control act.

§ 212. **[Schedule V].** (a) The controlled substances listed in this section are included in Schedule V.

(b) Any compound, mixture, or preparation containing limited quantities of any of the following narcotic drugs, or their salts calculated as the free anhydrous base or alkaloid which also contains one or more non narcotic active medicinal ingredients in sufficient proportion to confer upon the compound, mixture, or preparation, valuable medicinal qualities other than those possessed by the narcotic drug alone as set forth below:

(1) not more than 200 milligrams of codeine, or any of its salts, per 100 milliliters or per 100 grams;

(2) not more than 100 milligrams of dihydrocodeine; or any of its salts, per 100 milliliters or per 100 grams;

(3) not more than 100 milligrams of ethylmorphine, or any of its salts, per 100 milliliters or per 100 grams;

(4) not more than 2.5 milligrams of diphenoxylate and not less than 25 micrograms of atropine sulfate per dosage unit;

(5) not more than 100 milligrams of opium per 100 milliliters or per 100 grams;

(6) not more than 0.5 milligram of difenoxin

(DEA Drug Code No. 9618) and not less than 25 micrograms of atropine sulfate per dosage unit.

(c) Buprenorphine.
(d) Pyrovalerone.

(d-5) Any targeted methamphetamine precursor as defined in the Methamphetamine Precursor Control Act.

(e) Any compound, mixture or preparation which contains any quantity of any controlled substance when such compound, mixture or preparation is not otherwise controlled in Schedules I, II, III or IV.

§ 213. [Revision and republication of Schedules]. The Department shall revise and republish the Schedules semi-annually for two years from the effective date of this Act, and thereafter annually. If the Department fails to republish the Schedules, the last published Schedules shall remain in full force and effect.

§ **214. Excluded Substances.** (a) Products containing an anabolic steroid, that are expressly intended for administration through implants to cattle or other nonhuman species and that have been approved by the Secretary of Health and Human Services for that administration, and that are excluded from all schedules under Section 102 (41) (B)(1) of the federal Controlled Substances Act (21 U.S.C. 802 (41)(B)(1)) are also excluded from Sections 207 and 208 of this act.

(b) The non-narcotic substances excluded from all schedules of the Federal Controlled Substances Act (21 U.S.C. 801 et seq.) pursuant to Section 1308.22 of the Code of Federal Regulations (21 C.F.R. 1308.22), are excluded from all schedules of this Act.

§ **215. Excepted Compounds.** The compounds in the form excepted from application of certain specified sections of the Federal Controlled Substances Act (21 U.S.C. 801 et seq.), the Federal Controlled Substances Import and Export Act (21 U.S.C. 951 et seq.) and the Code of Federal Regulations, pursuant to Section 1308.32 of the Code of Federal Regulations (21 C.F.R. 1308.32) are excepted from the application of Sections 312 and 313 of this Act.

§ **216. Ephedrine.** (a) The following drug products containing ephedrine, its salts, optical isomers and salts of optical isomers shall be exempt from the application of Sections 312 and 313 of this Act if they:

(i) may lawfully be sold over-the-counter without a prescription under the Federal Food, Drug, and Cosmetic Act;

(ii) are labeled and marketed in a manner consistent with Section 341.76 of Title 21 of the Code of Federal Regulations;

(iii) are manufactured and distributed for legitimate medicinal use in a manner that reduces or eliminates the likelihood of abuse; and

(iv) are not marketed, advertised, or labeled for the indications of stimulation, mental alertness, weight loss, muscle enhancement, appetite control, or energy:

(1) Solid oral dosage forms, including soft gelatin caplets, which are formulated pursuant to 21 CFR 341 or its successor, and packaged in blister packs of not more than 2 tablets per blister.

(2) Anorectal preparations containing not more than 5% ephedrine.

(b) The marketing, advertising, or labeling of any product containing ephedrine, a salt of ephedrine, an optical isomer of ephedrine, or a salt of an optical isomer of ephedrine, for the indications of stimulation, mental alertness, weight loss, appetite control, or energy, is prohibited. in determining compliance with this requirement the Department may consider the following factors:

(1) The packaging of the drug product;

(2) The name and labeling of the product;

(3) The manner of distribution, advertising, and promotion of the product;

(4) Verbal representations made concerning the product;

(5) The duration, scope, and significance of abuse or misuse of the particular product.

(c) A violation of this Section is a Class A misdemeanor. A second or subsequent violation of this Section is a Class 4 felony.

(d) This Section does not apply to dietary supplements, herbs, or other natural products, including concentrates or extracts, which:

(1) are not otherwise prohibited by law; and

(2) may contain naturally occurring ephedrine, ephedrine alkaloids, or pseudoephedrine, or their salts, isomers, or salts of isomers, or a combination of these substances, that:

(i) are contained in a matrix of organic material; and

(ii) do not exceed 15% of the total weight of the natural product.

(e) Nothing in this Section limits the scope or terms of the Methamphetamine Precursor Control Act.

§ 217. Exempt anabolic steroid products. Compounds, mixtures, or preparations that contain an anabolic steroid that have been exempted by the Administrator of the federal Drug Enforcement Administration from application of Sections 302 through 309 and Sections 1002 through 1004 of the federal Controlled Substances Act (21 U.S.C. 822 through 829 and 952 through 954) and 21 CFR 1301.13, 1301.22, and 1301.71 through 1301.76 are also exempt from Sections 207 and 208 of this Act.

§ 218. Dextromethorphan. (a) (Blank).

(b) Possession of a drug product containing dextromethorphan in violation of this Act is a Class 4 felony. The sale, delivery, distribution, or possession with intent to sell, deliver, or distribute a drug product containing dextromethorphan in violation of this Act is a Class 2 felony.

(c) (Blank).

§ 219. Dietary supplements containing ephedrine or anabolic steroid precursors. (a) It is a Class A misdemeanor for any manufacturer, wholesaler, retailer, or other person to sell, transfer, or otherwise furnish any of the following to a person under 18 years of age:

(1) a dietary supplement containing an ephedrine group alkaloid; or

(2) a dietary supplement containing any of the following:
(A) Androstanediol;

(B) Androstanedione;

(C) Androstenedione;

(D) Norandrostenediol;

(E) Norandrostenedione; or

(F) Dehydroepiandrosterone.

(b) A seller shall request valid identification from any individual who attempts to purchase a dietary supplement set forth in subsection (a) if that individual reasonably appears to the seller to be under 18 years of age.

Article IV.

§ 401. [Manufacture of controlled or counterfeit substance or controlled substance analog prohibited]. Except as authorized by this Act, it is unlawful for any person knowingly to manufacture or deliver, or possess with intent to manufacture or deliver, a controlled substance other than methamphetamine, a counterfeit substance, or a controlled substance analog. A violation of this Act with respect to each of the controlled substances listed herein constitutes a single and separate violation of this Act. For purposes of this Section, "controlled substance analog" or "analog" means a substance which is intended for human consumption, other than a controlled substance, that has a chemical structure substantially similar to that of a controlled substance in Schedule I or II, or that was specifically designed to produce an effect substantially similar to that of a controlled substance in Schedule I or II.

Examples of chemical classes in which controlled substance analogs are found include, but are not limited to, the following: phenethylamines, N-substituted piperidines, morphinans, ecgonines, quinazolinones, substituted indoles, and arylcycloalkylamines. For purposes of this Act, a controlled substance analog shall be treated in the same manner as the controlled substance to which it is substantially similar.

(a) Any person who violates this Section with respect to the following amounts of controlled or counterfeit substances or controlled substance analogs, notwithstanding any of the provisions of subsections (c), (d), (e), (f), (g) or (h) to the contrary, is guilty of a Class X felony and shall be sentenced to a term of imprisonment as provided in this subsection (a) and fined as provided in subsection (b):
(1) (A) not less than 6 years and not more than 30 years with respect to 15 grams or more but less than 100 grams of a substance containing heroin, or an analog thereof;

(B) not less than 9 years and not more than 40 years with respect to 100 grams or more but less than 400 grams of a substance containing heroin, or an analog thereof;

(C) not less than 12 years and not more than 50 years with respect to 400 grams or more but less than 900 grams of a substance containing heroin, or an analog thereof;
(D) not less than 15 years and not more than 60 years with respect to 900 grams or more of any substance containing heroin, or an analog thereof;

(1.5) (A) not less than 6 years and not more than 30 years with respect to 15 grams or more but less than 100 grams of a substance containing fentanyl, or an analog thereof;

(B) not less than 9 years and not more than 40 years with respect to 100 grams or more but less than 400 grams of a substance containing fentanyl, or an analog thereof;

(C) not less than 12 years and not more than 50 years with respect to 400 grams or more but less than 900 grams of a substance containing fentanyl, or an analog thereof;

(D) not less than 15 years and not more than 60 years with respect to 900 grams or more of a substance containing fentanyl, or an analog thereof;
(2) (A) not less than 6 years and not more than 30 years with respect to 15 grams or more but less than 100 grams of a substance containing cocaine, or an analog thereof;

(B) not less than 9 years and not more than 40 years with respect to 100 grams or more but less than 400 grams of a substance containing cocaine, or an analog thereof;

(C) not less than 12 years and not more than 50 years with respect to 400 grams or more but less than 900 grams of a substance containing cocaine, or an analog thereof;

(D) not less than 15 years and not more than 60 years with respect to 900 grams or more of any substance containing cocaine, or an analog thereof;

(3) (A) not less than 6 years and not more than 30 years with respect to 15 grams or more but less than 100 grams of a substance containing morphine, or an analog thereof;

(B) not less than 9 years and not more than 40 years with respect to 100 grams or more but less than 400 grams of a substance containing morphine, or an analog thereof;

(C) not less than 12 years and not more than 50 years with respect to 400 grams or more but less than 900 grams of a substance containing morphine, or an analog thereof;

(D) not less than 15 years and not more than 60 years with respect to 900 grams or more of a substance containing morphine, or an analog thereof;

(4) 200 grams or more of any substance containing peyote, or an analog thereof;

(5) 200 grams or more of any substance containing a derivative of barbituric acid or any of the salts of a derivative of barbituric acid, or an analog thereof;

(6) 200 grams or more of any substance containing amphetamine or any salt of an optical isomer of amphetamine, or an analog thereof;
(6.5) (blank);

(6.6) (blank);

(7) (A) not less than 6 years and not more than 30 years with respect to:

(i) 15 grams or more but less than 100 grams of a substance containing lysergic acid diethylamide (LSD), or an analog thereof, or

(ii) 15 or more objects or 15 or more segregated parts of an object or objects but less than 200 objects or 200 segregated parts of an object or objects containing in them or having upon them any amounts of any substance containing lysergic acid diethylamide (LSD), or an analog thereof;

(B) not less than 9 years and not more than 40 years with respect to:

(i) 100 grams or more but less than 400 grams of a substance containing lysergic acid diethylamide (LSD), or an analog thereof, or

(ii) 200 or more objects or 200 or more segregated parts of an object or objects but less than 600 objects or less than 600 segregated parts of an object or objects containing in them or having upon them any amount of any substance containing lysergic acid diethylamide (LSD), or an analog thereof;

(C) not less than 12 years and not more than 50 years with respect to:

(i) 400 grams or more but less than 900 grams of a substance containing lysergic acid diethylamide (LSD), or an analog thereof, or

(ii) 600 or more objects or 600 or more segregated parts of an object or objects but less than 1500 objects or 1500 segregated parts of an object or objects containing in them or having upon them any amount of any substance containing lysergic acid diethylamide (LSD), or an analog thereof;

(D) not less than 15 years and not more than 60 years with respect to:
(i) 900 grams or more of any substance containing lysergic acid diethylamide (LSD), or an analog thereof, or

(ii) 1500 or more objects or 1500 or more segregated parts of an object or objects containing in them or having upon them any amount of a substance containing lysergic acid diethylamide (LSD), or an analog thereof;

(7.5) (A) not less than 6 years and not more than 30 years with respect to:

(i) 15 grams or more but less than 100 grams of a substance listed in paragraph (1), (2), (2.1), (2.2), (3), (14.1), (19), (20), (20.1), (21), (25), or (26) of subsection (d) of Section 204, or an analog or derivative thereof, or

(ii) 15 or more pills, tablets, caplets, capsules, or objects but less than 200 pills, tablets, caplets, capsules, or objects containing in them or having upon them any amounts of any substance listed in paragraph (1), (2), (2.1), (2.2), (3), (14.1), (19), (20), (20.1), (21), (25), or (26) of subsection (d) of Section 204, or an analog or derivative thereof;
(B) not less than 9 years and not more than 40 years with respect to:

(i) 100 grams or more but less than 400 grams of a substance listed in paragraph (1), (2), (2.1), (2.2), (3), (14.1), (19), (20), (20.1), (21), (25), or (26) of subsection (d) of Section 204, or an analog or derivative thereof, or

(ii) 200 or more pills, tablets, caplets, capsules, or objects but less than 600 pills, tablets, caplets, capsules, or objects containing in them or having upon them any amount of any substance listed in paragraph (1), (2), (2.1), (2.2), (3), (14.1), (19), (20), (20.1), (21), (25), or (26) of subsection (d) of Section 204, or an analog or derivative thereof;

(C) not less than 12 years and not more than 50 years with respect to:

(i) 400 grams or more but less than 900 grams of a substance listed in paragraph (1), (2), (2.1), (2.2), (3), (14.1), (19), (20), (20.1), (21), (25), or (26) of subsection (d) of Section 204, or an analog or derivative thereof, or

(ii) 600 or more pills, tablets, caplets, capsules, or objects but less than 1,500 pills, tablets, caplets, capsules, or objects containing in them or having upon them any amount of any substance listed in paragraph (1), (2), (2.1), (2.2), (3), (14.1), (19), (20), (20.1), (21), (25), or (26) of subsection (d) of Section 204, or an analog or derivative thereof;

(D) not less than 15 years and not more than 60 years with respect to:

(i) 900 grams or more of any substance listed in paragraph (1), (2), (2.1), (2.2), (3), (14.1), (19), (20), (20.1), (21), (25), or (26) of subsection (d) of Section 204, or an analog or derivative thereof, or

(ii) 1,500 or more pills, tablets, caplets, capsules, or objects containing in them or having upon them any amount of a substance listed in paragraph (1), (2), (2.1), (2.2), (3), (14.1), (19), (20), (20.1), (21), (25), or (26) of subsection (d) of Section 204, or an analog or derivative thereof;

(8) 30 grams or more of any substance containing pentazocine or any of the salts, isomers and salts of isomers of pentazocine, or an analog thereof;

(9) 30 grams or more of any substance containing methaqualone or any of the salts,

isomers and salts of isomers of methaqualone, or an analog thereof;

(10) 30 grams or more of any substance containing phencyclidine or any of the salts, isomers and salts of isomers of phencyclidine (PCP), or an analog thereof;

(10.5) 30 grams or more of any substance containing ketamine or any of the salts, isomers and salts of isomers of ketamine, or an analog thereof;

(11) 200 grams or more of any substance containing any other controlled substance classified in Schedules I or II, or an analog thereof, which is not otherwise included in this subsection.

(b) Any person sentenced with respect to violations of paragraph (1), (2), (3), (7), or (7.5) of subsection (a) involving 100 grams or more of the controlled substance named therein, may in addition to the penalties provided therein, be fined an amount not more than $500,000 or the full street value of the controlled or counterfeit substance or controlled substance analog, whichever is greater.

The term "street value" shall have the meaning ascribed in Section 110-5 of the Code of Criminal Procedure of 1963. Any person sentenced with respect to any other provision of subsection (a), may in addition to the penalties provided therein, be fined an amount not to exceed $500,000.

(b-1) Excluding violations of this Act when the controlled substance is fentanyl, any person sentenced to a term of imprisonment with respect to violations of Section 401, 401.1, 405, 405.1, 405.2, or 407, when the substance containing the controlled substance contains any amount of fentanyl, 3 years shall be added to the term of imprisonment imposed by the court, and the maximum sentence for the offense shall be increased by 3 years.

(c) Any person who violates this Section with regard to the following amounts of controlled or counterfeit substances or controlled substance analogs, notwithstanding any of the provisions of subsections (a), (b), (d), (e), (f), (g) or (h) to the contrary, is guilty of a Class 1 felony. the fine for violation of this subsection (c) shall not be more than $250,000:

(1) 1 gram or more but less than 15 grams of any substance containing heroin, or an analog thereof;

(1.5) 1 gram or more but less than 15 grams of any substance containing fentanyl, or an analog thereof;

(2) 1 gram or more but less than 15 grams of any substance containing cocaine, or an analog thereof;

(3) 10 grams or more but less than 15 grams of any substance containing morphine, or an analog thereof;

(4) 50 grams or more but less than 200 grams of any substance containing peyote, or an analog thereof;

(5) 50 grams or more but less than 200 grams of any substance containing a derivative of barbituric acid or any of the salts of a derivative of barbituric acid, or an analog thereof;

(6) 50 grams or more but less than 200 grams of any substance containing amphetamine or any salt of an optical isomer of amphetamine, or an analog thereof;

(6.5) (blank);

(7) (i) 5 grams or more but less than 15 grams of any substance containing lysergic acid diethylamide (LSD), or an analog thereof, or (ii) more than 10 objects or more than 10 segregated parts of an object or objects but less than 15 objects or less than 15 segregated parts of an object containing in them or having upon them any amount of any substance containing lysergic acid diethylamide (LSD), or an analog thereof;

(7.5) (i) 5 grams or more but less than 15 grams of any substance listed in paragraph (1), (2),

(2.1), (2.2), (3), (14.1), (19), (20), (20.1), (21), (25), or (26) of subsection (d) of Section 204, or an analog or derivative thereof, or

(ii) more than 10 pills, tablets, caplets, capsules, or objects but less than 15 pills, tablets, caplets, capsules, or objects containing in them or having upon them any amount of any substance listed in paragraph (1), (2), (2.1), (2.2), (3), (14.1), (19), (20), (20.1), (21), (25), or (26) of subsection (d) of Section 204, or an analog or derivative thereof;

(8) 10 grams or more but less than 30 grams of any substance containing pentazocine or any of the salts, isomers and salts of isomers of pentazocine, or an analog thereof;

(9) 10 grams or more but less than 30 grams of any substance containing methaqualone or any of the salts, isomers and salts of isomers of methaqualone, or an analog thereof;

(10) 10 grams or more but less than 30 grams of any substance containing phencyclidine or any of the salts, isomers and salts of isomers of phencyclidine (PCP), or an analog thereof;

(10.5) 10 grams or more but less than 30 grams of any substance containing ketamine or any of the salts, isomers and salts of isomers of ketamine, or an analog thereof;

(11) 50 grams or more but less than 200 grams of any substance containing a substance classified in Schedules I or II, or an analog thereof, which is not otherwise included in this subsection.

(c-5) (Blank).

(d) Any person who violates this Section with regard to any other amount of a controlled or counterfeit substance classified in Schedules I or II, or an analog thereof, which is (i) a narcotic drug,

(ii) lysergic acid diethylamide (LSD) or an analog thereof,

(iii) any substance containing amphetamine or fentanyl or any salt or optical isomer of amphetamine or fentanyl, or an analog thereof, or

(iv) any substance containing N-Benzylpiperazine (BZP) or any salt or optical isomer of N-Benzylpiperazine (BZP), or an analog thereof, is guilty of a Class 2 felony. The fine for violation of this subsection (d) shall not be more than $200,000.

(d-5) (Blank).

(e) Any person who violates this Section with regard to any other amount of a controlled substance other than methamphetamine or counterfeit substance classified in Schedule I or II, or an analog thereof, which substance is not included under subsection (d) of this Section, is guilty of a Class 3 felony. The fine for violation of this subsection (e) shall not be more than $150,000.

(f) Any person who violates this Section with regard to any other amount of a controlled or counterfeit substance classified in Schedule III is guilty of a Class 3 felony. The fine for violation of this subsection (f) shall not be more than $125,000.

(g) Any person who violates this Section with regard to any other amount of a controlled or counterfeit substance classified in Schedule IV is guilty of a Class 3 felony. The fine for violation of this subsection (g) shall not be more than $100,000.

(h) Any person who violates this Section with regard to any other amount of a controlled or counterfeit substance classified in Schedule V is guilty of a Class 3 felony. The fine for violation of this subsection (h) shall not be more than $75,000.

(i) This Section does not apply to the manufacture, possession or distribution of a substance in conformance with the provisions of an approved new drug application or an exemption for investigational use within the meaning of Section 505 of the Federal Food, Drug and Cosmetic act.

(j) (Blank).

§ 401.1. Controlled Substance Trafficking.
(a) Except for purposes as authorized by this Act, any person who knowingly brings or causes to be brought into this State for the purpose of manufacture or delivery or with the intent to manufacture or deliver a controlled substance other than methamphetamine or counterfeit substance in this or any other state or country is guilty of controlled substance trafficking.

(b) A person convicted of controlled substance trafficking shall be sentenced to a term of imprisonment not less than twice the minimum term and fined an amount as authorized by Section 401 of this Act, based upon the amount of controlled or counterfeit substance brought or caused to be brought into this State, and not more than twice the maximum term of imprisonment and fined twice the amount as authorized by Section 401 of this Act, based upon the amount of controlled or counterfeit substance brought or caused to be brought into this State.

(c) It shall be a Class 2 felony for which a fine not to exceed $100,000 may be imposed for any person to knowingly use a cellular radio telecommunication device in the furtherance of controlled substance trafficking. This penalty shall be in addition to any other penalties imposed by law.

§ 401.5. Chemical breakdown of illicit controlled substance. (a) It is unlawful for any person to manufacture a controlled substance other than methamphetamine prohibited by this Act by chemically deriving the controlled substance from one or more other controlled substances prohibited by this Act.

(a-5) It is unlawful for any person to possess any substance with the intent to use the substance to facilitate the manufacture of any controlled substance other than methamphetamine, any counterfeit substance, or any controlled substance analog other than as authorized by this Act.

(b) A violation of this Section is a Class 4 felony.

(c) (Blank).

§ 402. [Possession of controlled or counterfeit substance]. Except as otherwise authorized by this Act, it is unlawful for any person knowingly to possess a controlled or counterfeit substance or controlled substance analog a violation of this Act with respect to each of the controlled substances listed herein constitutes a single and separate violation of this Act.

For purposes of this Section, "controlled substance analog" or "analog" means a substance which is intended for human consumption, other than a controlled substance, that has a chemical structure substantially similar to that of a controlled substance in Schedule I or II, or that was specifically designed to produce an effect substantially similar to that of a controlled substance in Schedule I or II.

Examples of chemical classes in which controlled substance analogs are found include, but are not limited to, the following: phenethylamines, N-substituted piperidines, morphinans, ecgonines, quinazolinones, substituted indoles, and arylcycloalkylamines. For purposes of this Act, a controlled substance analog shall be treated in the same manner as the controlled substance to which it is substantially similar.

(a) Any person who violates this Section with respect to the following controlled or counterfeit substances and amounts, notwithstanding any of the provisions of subsections (c) and (d) to the contrary, is guilty of a Class 1 felony and shall, if sentenced to a term of imprisonment, be sentenced as provided in this subsection (a) and fined as provided in subsection (b):

(1) (A) not less than 4 years and not more than 15 years with respect to 15 grams or more but less than 100 grams of a substance containing heroin;

(B) not less than 6 years and not more than 30 years with respect to 100 grams or more but less than 400 grams of a substance containing heroin;

(C) not less than 8 years and not more than 40 years with respect to 400 grams or more but less than 900 grams of any substance containing heroin;

(D) not less than 10 years and not more than 50 years with respect to 900 grams or more of any substance containing heroin;

(2) (A) not less than 4 years and not more than 15 years with respect to 15 grams or more but less than 100 grams of any substance containing cocaine;

(B) not less than 6 years and not more than 30 years with respect to 100 grams or more but less than 400 grams of any substance containing cocaine;

(C) not less than 8 years and not more than 40 years with respect to 400 grams or more but less than 900 grams of any substance containing cocaine;

(D) not less than 10 years and not more than 50 years with respect to 900 grams or more of any substance containing cocaine;

(3) (A) not less than 4 years and not more than 15 years with respect to 15 grams or more but less than 100 grams of any substance containing morphine;

(B) not less than 6 years and not more than 30 years with respect to 100 grams or more but less than 400 grams of any substance containing morphine;

(C) not less than 6 years and not more than 40 years with respect to 400 grams or more but less than 900 grams of any substance containing morphine;

(D) not less than 10 years and not more than 50 years with respect to 900 grams or more of any substance containing morphine;

(4) 200 grams or more of any substance containing peyote;

(5) 200 grams or more of any substance containing a derivative of barbituric acid or any of the salts of a derivative of barbituric acid;

(6) 200 grams or more of any substance containing amphetamine or any salt of an optical isomer of amphetamine;

(6.5) (blank);

(7) (A) not less than 4 years and not more than 15 years with respect to: (i) 15 grams or more but less than 100 grams of any substance containing lysergic acid diethylamide (LSD), or an analog thereof, or

(ii) 15 or more objects or 15 or more segregated parts of an object or objects but less than 200 objects or 200 segregated parts of an object or objects containing in them or having upon them any amount of any substance containing lysergic acid diethylamide (LSD), or an analog thereof;

(B) not less than 6 years and not more than 30 years with respect to: (i) 100 grams or more but less than 400 grams of any substance containing lysergic acid diethylamide (LSD), or an analog thereof, or

(ii) 200 or more objects or 200 or more segregated parts of an object or objects but less than 600 objects or less than 600 segregated parts of an object or objects containing in them or having upon them any amount of any substance containing lysergic acid diethylamide (LSD), or an analog thereof;

(C) not less than 8 years and not more than 40 years with respect to: (i) 400 grams or more but less than 900 grams of any substance containing lysergic acid diethylamide (LSD), or an analog thereof, or

(ii) 600 or more objects or 600 or more segregated parts of an object or objects but less than 1500 objects or 1500 segregated parts of an object or objects containing in them or having upon them any amount of any substance containing lysergic acid diethylamide (LSD), or an analog thereof;

(D) not less than 10 years and not more than 50 years with respect to: (i) 900 grams or more of any substance containing lysergic acid diethylamide (LSD), or an analog thereof, or

(ii) 1500 or more objects or 1500 or more segregated parts of an object or objects containing in them or having upon them any amount of a substance containing lysergic acid diethylamide (LSD), or an analog thereof;

(7.5) (A) not less than 4 years and not more than 15 years with respect to: (i) 15 grams or more but less than 100 grams of any substance listed in paragraph (1), (2), (2.1), (2.2), (3), (14.1), (19), (20), (20.1), (21), (25), or (26) of subsection (d) of Section 204, or an analog or derivative thereof, or

(ii) 15 or more pills, tablets, caplets, capsules, or objects but less than 200 pills, tablets, caplets, capsules, or objects containing in them or having upon them any amount of any substance listed in paragraph (1), (2), (2.1), (2.2), (3), (14.1), (19), (20), (20.1), (21), (25), or (26) of subsection (d) of Section 204, or an analog or derivative thereof;

(B) not less than 6 years and not more than 30 years with respect to: (i) 100 grams or more but less than 400 grams of any substance listed in paragraph (1), (2), (2.1), (2.2), (3), (14.1), (19), (20), (20.1), (21), (25), or (26) of subsection (d) of Section 204, or an analog or derivative thereof, or

(ii) 200 or more pills, tablets, caplets, capsules, or objects but less than 600 pills, tablets, caplets, capsules, or objects containing in them or having upon them any amount of any substance listed in paragraph (1), (2), (2.1), (2.2), (3), (14.1), (19), (20), (20.1), (21), (25), or (26) of subsection (d) of Section 204, or an analog or derivative thereof;

(C) not less than 8 years and not more than 40 years with respect to: (i) 400 grams or more but less than 900 grams of any substance listed in paragraph (1), (2), (2.1), (2.2), (3), (14.1), (19), (20), (20.1), (21), (25), or (26) of subsection (d) of Section 204, or an analog or derivative thereof, or

(ii) 600 or more pills, tablets, caplets, capsules, or objects but less than 1,500 pills, tablets, caplets, capsules, or objects containing in them or having upon them any amount of any substance listed in paragraph (1), (2), (2.1), (2.2), (3), (14.1), (19), (20), (20.1), (21), (25), or (26) of subsection (d) of Section 204, or an analog or derivative thereof;

(D) not less than 10 years and not more than 50 years with respect to: (i) 900 grams or more of any substance listed in paragraph (1), (2), (2.1), (2.2), (3), (14.1), (19), (20), (20.1), (21), (25), or (26) of subsection (d) of Section 204, or an analog or derivative thereof, or

(ii) 1,500 or more pills, tablets, caplets, capsules, or objects containing in them or having upon them any amount of a substance listed in paragraph (1), (2), (2.1), (2.2), (3), (14.1), (19), (20), (20.1), (21), (25), or (26) of subsection (d) of Section 204, or an analog or derivative thereof;

(8) 30 grams or more of any substance containing pentazocine or any of the salts, isomers and salts of isomers of pentazocine, or an analog thereof;

(9) 30 grams or more of any substance containing methaqualone or any of the salts, isomers and salts of isomers of methaqualone;

(10) 30 grams or more of any substance containing phencyclidine or any of the salts, isomers and salts of isomers of phencyclidine (PCP);

(10.5) 30 grams or more of any substance containing ketamine or any of the salts, isomers and salts of isomers of ketamine;

(11) 200 grams or more of any substance containing any substance classified as a narcotic drug in Schedules I or II, or an analog thereof,

which is not otherwise included in this subsection.

(b) Any person sentenced with respect to violations of paragraph (1), (2), (3), (7), or (7.5) of subsection (a) involving 100 grams or more of the controlled substance named therein, may in addition to the penalties provided therein, be fined an amount not to exceed $200,000 or the full street value of the controlled or counterfeit substances, whichever is greater. The term "street value" shall have the meaning ascribed in Section 110-5 of the Code of Criminal Procedure of 1963. Any person sentenced with respect to any other provision of subsection (a), may in addition to the penalties provided therein, be fined an amount not to exceed $200,000.

(c) Any person who violates this Section with regard to an amount of a controlled substance other than methamphetamine or counterfeit substance not set forth in subsection (a) or (d) is guilty of a Class 4 felony. The fine for a violation punishable under this subsection (c) shall not be more than $25,000.

(d) Any person who violates this Section with regard to any amount of anabolic steroid is guilty of a Class C misdemeanor for the first offense and a Class B misdemeanor for a subsequent offense committed within 2 years of a prior conviction.

§ 404. [Look-alike substances].
(a) For the purposes of this Section:

(1) "Advertise" means the attempt, by publication, dissemination, solicitation or circulation, to induce directly or indirectly any person to acquire, or enter into an obligation to acquire, any substance within the scope of this Section.

(2) "Distribute" has the meaning ascribed to it in subsection (s) of Section 102 of this Act but as relates to look-alike substances.

(3) "Manufacture" means the producing, preparing, compounding, processing, encapsulating, packaging, repackaging, labeling or relabeling of a look-alike substance.

(b) It is unlawful for any person knowingly to manufacture, distribute, advertise, or possess with intent to manufacture or distribute a look-alike substance. Any person who violates this subsection

(b) shall be guilty of a Class 3 felony, the fine for which shall not exceed $150,000.

(c) It is unlawful for any person knowingly to possess a look-alike substance. Any person who violates this subsection (c) is guilty of a petty offense. Any person convicted of a subsequent offense under this subsection (c) shall be guilty of a Class C misdemeanor.

(d) In any prosecution brought under this Section, it is not a defense to a violation of this Section that the defendant believed the look-alike substance actually to be a controlled substance.

(e) Nothing in this Section applies to: (1) The manufacture, processing, packaging, distribution or sale of noncontrolled substances to licensed medical practitioners for use as placebos in professional practice or research.

(2) Persons acting in the course and legitimate scope of their employment as law enforcement officers.

(3) The retention of production samples of noncontrolled substances produced prior to the effective date of this amendatory Act of 1982, where such samples are required by federal law.
(f) Nothing in this Section or in this Act applies to the lawful manufacture, processing, packaging, advertising or distribution of a drug or drugs by any person registered pursuant to Section 510 of the Federal Food, Drug, and Cosmetic Act (21 U.S.C. 360).

§ 405. [Calculated criminal drug conspiracy].
(a) Any person who engages in a calculated criminal drug conspiracy, as defined in subsection (b), is guilty of a Class X felony. the

fine for violation of this Section shall not be more than $500,000, and the offender shall be subject to the forfeitures prescribed in subsection (c).

(b) For purposes of this section, a person engages in a calculated criminal drug conspiracy when: (1) he violates any of the provisions of subsection (a) or (c) of Section 401 or subsection (a) of Section 402; and

(2) such violation is a part of a conspiracy undertaken or carried on with two or more other persons; and

(3) he obtains anything of value greater than $500 from, or organizes, directs or finances such violation or conspiracy.

(c) Any person who is convicted under this section of engaging in a calculated criminal drug conspiracy shall forfeit to the State of Illinois:

(1) the receipts obtained by him in such conspiracy; and

(2) any of his interests in, claims against, receipts from, or property or rights of any kind affording a source of influence over, such conspiracy.

(d) The circuit court may enter such injunctions, restraining orders, directions or prohibitions, or to take such other actions, including the acceptance of satisfactory performance bonds, in connection with any property, claim, receipt, right or other interest subject to forfeiture under this Section, as it deems proper.

§ 405.1. [Elements of the offense; co-conspirators; sentence]. (a) Elements of the offense. A person commits criminal drug conspiracy when, with the intent that an offense set forth in Section 401, Section 402, or Section 407 of this Act be committed, he agrees with another to the commission of that offense. No person may be convicted of conspiracy to commit such an offense unless an act in furtherance of such agreement is alleged and proved to have been committed by him or by a co-conspirator.

(b) Co-conspirators. It shall not be a defense to conspiracy that the person or persons with whom the accused is alleged to have conspired:

(1) Has not been prosecuted or convicted, or

(2) Has been convicted of a different offense, or

(3) Is not amenable to justice, or

(4) Has been acquitted, or

(5) Lacked the capacity to commit an offense.

(c) Sentence. A person convicted of criminal drug conspiracy may be fined or imprisoned or both, but any term of imprisonment imposed shall be not less than the minimum nor more than the maximum provided for the offense which is the object of the conspiracy.

§ 405.2. Streetgang criminal drug conspiracy. (a) Any person who engages in a streetgang criminal drug conspiracy, as defined in this Section, is guilty of a Class X felony for which the offender shall be sentenced to a term of imprisonment as follows:

(1) not less than 15 years and not more than 60 years for a violation of subsection (a) of Section 401;

(2) not less than 10 years and not more than 30 years for a violation of subsection (c) of Section 401. for the purposes of this Section, a person engages in a streetgang criminal drug conspiracy when:

(i) he or she violates any of the provisions of subsection (a) or (c) of Section 401 of this Act or any provision of the Methamphetamine Control and Community Protection Act; and

(ii) such violation is part of a conspiracy undertaken or carried out with 2 or more other persons; and

(iii) such conspiracy is in furtherance of the activities of an organized gang as defined in the

Illinois Streetgang Terrorism Omnibus Prevention Act; and

(iv) he or she occupies a position of organizer, a supervising person, or any other position of management with those persons identified in clause

(ii) of this subsection (a). the fine for a violation of this Section shall not be more than $500,000, and the offender shall be subject to the forfeitures prescribed in subsection (b).
(b) Subject to the provisions of Section 8 of the Drug Asset Forfeiture Procedure Act, any person who is convicted under this Section of engaging in a streetgang criminal drug conspiracy shall forfeit to the State of Illinois:
(1) the receipts obtained by him or her in such conspiracy; and

(2) any of his or her interests in, claims against, receipts from, or property or rights of any kind affording a source of influence over, such conspiracy.

(c) The circuit court may enter such injunctions, restraining orders, directions or prohibitions, or may take such other actions, including the acceptance of satisfactory performance bonds, in connection with any property, claim, receipt, right or other interest subject to forfeiture under this Section, as it deems proper.

§ 406. [Additional violations]. (a) It is unlawful for any person:

(1) who is subject to Article III knowingly to distribute or dispense a controlled substance in violation of Sections 308 through 314 of this Act; or

(2) who is a registrant, to manufacture a controlled substance not authorized by his registration, or to distribute or dispense a controlled substance not authorized by his registration to another registrant or other authorized person; or

(3) to refuse or fail to make, keep or furnish any record, notification, order form, statement, invoice or information required under this Act; or

(4) to refuse an entry into any premises for any inspection authorized by this Act; or

(5) knowingly to keep or maintain any store, shop, warehouse, dwelling, building, vehicle, boat, aircraft, or other structure or place, which is resorted to by a person unlawfully possessing controlled substances, or which is used for possessing, manufacturing, dispensing or distributing controlled substances in violation of this Act.

Any person who violates this subsection (a) is guilty of a Class A misdemeanor for the first offense and a Class 4 felony for each subsequent offense. The fine for each subsequent offense shall not be more than $100,000. In addition, any practitioner who is found guilty of violating this subsection (a) is subject to suspension and revocation of his professional license, in accordance with such procedures as are provided by law for the taking of disciplinary action with regard to the license of said practitioner's profession.

(b) It is unlawful for any person knowingly:
(1) to distribute, as a registrant, a controlled substance classified in Schedule I or II, except pursuant to an order form as required by Section 307 of this Act; or

(2) to use, in the course of the manufacture or distribution of a controlled substance, a registration number which is fictitious, revoked, suspended, or issued to another person; or

(3) to acquire or obtain possession of a controlled substance by misrepresentation, fraud, forgery, deception or subterfuge; or

(4) to furnish false or fraudulent material information in, or omit any material information from, any application, report or other document required to be kept or filed under this Act, or any record required to be kept by this Act; or

(5) to make, distribute or possess any punch, die, plate, stone or other thing designed to print, imprint or reproduce the trademark, trade name or other identifying mark, imprint or device of another, or any likeness of any of the foregoing, upon any controlled substance or container or labeling thereof so as to render the drug a counterfeit substance; or

(6) (blank); or

(7) (blank). any person who violates this subsection (b) is guilty of a Class 4 felony for the first offense and a Class 3 felony for each subsequent offense. The fine for the first offense shall be not more than $100,000. the fine for each subsequent offense shall not be more than $200,000.

(c) A person who knowingly or intentionally violates Section 316, 317, 318, or 319 is guilty of a Class A misdemeanor.

§ 406.1. [Permitting unlawful use of building]. (a) Any person who controls any building and who performs the following act commits the offense of permitting unlawful use of a building: Knowingly grants, permits or makes the building available for use for the purpose of unlawfully manufacturing or delivering a controlled substance other than methamphetamine.

(b) Permitting unlawful use of a building is a Class 4 felony.

§ 406.2. Unauthorized possession of prescription form. (a) A person commits the offense of unauthorized possession of prescription form when he or she knowingly:
(1) alters a properly issued prescription form;

(2) possesses without authorization a blank prescription form or counterfeit prescription form; or

(3) possesses a prescription form not issued by a licensed prescriber.

(b) Knowledge shall be determined by an evaluation of all circumstances surrounding possession of a blank prescription or possession of a prescription altered or not issued by a licensed prescriber.

(c) Sentence. Any person who violates subsection (a) is guilty of a Class 4 felony for the first offense and a Class 3 felony for each subsequent offense. The fine for the first offense shall be not more than $100,000. The fine for each subsequent offense shall not be more than $200,000.

(d) For the purposes of this Section, "licensed prescriber" means a prescriber as defined in this Act or an optometrist licensed under the Illinois Optometric Practice Act of 1987.

§ 407. [Delivery to person under 18; violations on or near school or public housing agency property or public park]. (a) (1)(A) Any person 18 years of age or over who violates any subsection of Section 401 or subsection (b) of Section 404 by delivering a controlled, counterfeit or look-alike substance to a person under 18 years of age may be sentenced to imprisonment for a term up to twice the maximum term and fined an amount up to twice that amount otherwise authorized by the pertinent subsection of Section 401 and Subsection (b) of Section 404.

(B) (Blank).

(2) Except as provided in paragraph (3) of this subsection, any person who violates:

(A) subsection (c) of Section 401 by delivering or possessing with intent to deliver a controlled, counterfeit, or look-alike substance in or on, or within 1,000 feet of, a truck stop or safety rest area, is guilty of a Class 1 felony, the fine for which shall not exceed $250,000;

(B) subsection (d) of Section 401 by delivering or possessing with intent to deliver a controlled, counterfeit, or look-alike substance in or on, or within 1,000 feet of, a truck stop or safety rest area, is guilty of a Class 2 felony, the fine for which shall not exceed $200,000;

(C) subsection (e) of Section 401 or subsection (b) of Section 404 by delivering or possessing with intent to deliver a controlled, counterfeit, or look-alike substance in or on, or within 1,000 feet of, a truck stop or safety rest area, is guilty of a Class 3 felony, the fine for which shall not exceed $150,000;

(D) subsection (f) of Section 401 by delivering or possessing with intent to deliver a controlled, counterfeit, or look-alike substance in or on, or within 1,000 feet of, a truck stop or safety rest area, is guilty of a Class 3 felony, the fine for which shall not exceed $125,000;

(E) subsection (g) of Section 401 by delivering or possessing with intent to deliver a controlled, counterfeit, or look-alike substance in or on, or within 1,000 feet of, a truck stop or safety rest area, is guilty of a Class 3 felony, the fine for which shall not exceed $100,000;

(F) subsection (h) of Section 401 by delivering or possessing with intent to deliver a controlled, counterfeit, or look-alike substance in or on, or within 1,000 feet of, a truck stop or safety rest area, is guilty of a Class 3 felony, the fine for which shall not exceed $75,000;

(3) Any person who violates paragraph (2) of this subsection (a) by delivering or possessing with intent to deliver a controlled, counterfeit, or look-alike substance in or on, or within 1,000 feet of a truck stop or a safety rest area, following a prior conviction or convictions of paragraph (2) of this subsection (a) may be sentenced to a term of imprisonment up to 2 times the maximum term and fined an amount up to 2 times the amount otherwise authorized by Section 401.

(4) For the purposes of this subsection (a):

(A) "Safety rest area" means a roadside facility removed from the roadway with parking and facilities designed for motorists' rest, comfort, and information needs; and

(B) "Truck stop" means any facility (and its parking areas) used to provide fuel or service, or both, to any commercial motor vehicle as defined in Section 18b-101 of the Illinois Vehicle Code.

(b) Any person who violates: (1) subsection (c) of Section 401 in any school, or any conveyance owned, leased or contracted by a school to transport students to or from school or a school related activity, or residential property owned, operated or managed by a public housing agency or leased by a public housing agency as part of a scattered site or mixed-income development, or public park, on the real property comprising any school or residential property owned, operated or managed by a public housing agency or leased by a public housing agency as part of a scattered site or mixed-income development, or public park or within 1,000 feet of the real property comprising any school or residential property owned, operated or managed by a public housing agency or leased by a public housing agency as part of a scattered site or mixed-income development, or public park, on the real property comprising any church, synagogue, or other building, structure, or place used primarily for religious worship, or within 1,000 feet of the real property comprising any church, synagogue, or other building, structure, or place used primarily for religious worship, on the real property comprising any of the following places, buildings, or structures used primarily for housing or providing space for activities for senior citizens: nursing homes, assisted-living centers, senior citizen housing complexes, or senior centers oriented toward daytime activities, or within 1,000 feet of the real property comprising any of the following places, buildings, or structures used primarily for housing or providing space for activities for senior citizens: nursing homes, assisted-living centers, senior citizen housing complexes, or senior centers oriented toward daytime activities is guilty of a Class X felony, the fine for which shall not exceed $500,000;

(2) subsection (d) of Section 401 in any school, or any conveyance owned, leased or contracted by a school to transport students to or from school or a school related activity, or residential

property owned, operated or managed by a public housing agency or leased by a public housing agency as part of a scattered site or mixed-income development, or public park, on the real property comprising any school or residential property owned, operated or managed by a public housing agency or leased by a public housing agency as part of a scattered site or mixed-income development, or public park or within 1,000 feet of the real property comprising any school or residential property owned, operated or managed by a public housing agency or leased by a public housing agency as part of a scattered site or mixed-income development, or public park, on the real property comprising any church, synagogue, or other building, structure, or place used primarily for religious worship, or within 1,000 feet of the real property comprising any church, synagogue, or other building, structure, or place used primarily for religious worship, on the real property comprising any of the following places, buildings, or structures used primarily for housing or providing space for activities for senior citizens: nursing homes, assisted-living centers, senior citizen housing complexes, or senior centers oriented toward daytime activities, or within 1,000 feet of the real property comprising any of the following places, buildings, or structures used primarily for housing or providing space for activities for senior citizens: nursing homes, assisted-living centers, senior citizen housing complexes, or senior centers oriented toward daytime activities is guilty of a Class 1 felony, the fine for which shall not exceed $250,000;

(3) subsection (e) of Section 401 or Subsection (b) of Section 404 in any school, or any conveyance owned, leased or contracted by a school to transport students to or from school or a school related activity, or residential property owned, operated or managed by a public housing agency or leased by a public housing agency as part of a scattered site or mixed-income development, or public park, on the real property comprising any school or residential property owned, operated or managed by a public housing agency or leased by a public housing agency as part of a scattered site or mixed-income development, or public park or within 1,000 feet of the real property comprising any school or residential property owned, operated or managed by a public housing agency or leased by a public housing agency as part of a scattered site or mixed-income development, or public park, on the real property comprising any church, synagogue, or other building, structure, or place used primarily for religious worship, or within 1,000 feet of the real property comprising any church, synagogue, or other building, structure, or place used primarily for religious worship, on the real property comprising any of the following places, buildings, or structures used primarily for housing or providing space for activities for senior citizens: nursing homes, assisted-living centers, senior citizen housing complexes, or senior centers oriented toward daytime activities, or within 1,000 feet of the real property comprising any of the following places, buildings, or structures used primarily for housing or providing space for activities for senior citizens: nursing homes, assisted-living centers, senior citizen housing complexes, or senior centers oriented toward daytime activities is guilty of a Class 2 felony, the fine for which shall not exceed $200,000;

(4) subsection (f) of Section 401 in any school, or any conveyance owned, leased or contracted by a school to transport students to or from school or a school related activity, or residential property owned, operated or managed by a public housing agency or leased by a public housing agency as part of a scattered site or mixed-income development, or public park, on the real property comprising any school or residential property owned, operated or managed by a public housing agency or leased by a public housing agency as part of a scattered site or mixed-income development, or public park or within 1,000 feet of the real property comprising any school or residential property owned, operated or managed by a public housing agency or leased by a public housing agency as part of a scattered site or mixed-income development, or public park, on the real property comprising any church, synagogue, or other building, structure, or place used primarily for religious worship, or within 1,000 feet of the real property comprising

any church, synagogue, or other building, structure, or place used primarily for religious worship, on the real property comprising any of the following places, buildings, or structures used primarily for housing or providing space for activities for senior citizens: nursing homes, assisted-living centers, senior citizen housing complexes, or senior centers oriented toward daytime activities, or within 1,000 feet of the real property comprising any of the following places, buildings, or structures used primarily for housing or providing space for activities for senior citizens: nursing homes, assisted-living centers, senior citizen housing complexes, or senior centers oriented toward daytime activities is guilty of a Class 2 felony, the fine for which shall not exceed $150,000;

(5) subsection (g) of Section 401 in any school, or any conveyance owned, leased or contracted by a school to transport students to or from school or a school related activity, or residential property owned, operated or managed by a public housing agency or leased by a public housing agency as part of a scattered site or mixed-income development, or public park, on the real property comprising any school or residential property owned, operated or managed by a public housing agency or leased by a public housing agency as part of a scattered site or mixed-income development, or public park or within 1,000 feet of the real property comprising any school or residential property owned, operated or managed by a public housing agency or leased by a public housing agency as part of a scattered site or mixed-income development, or public park, on the real property comprising any church, synagogue, or other building, structure, or place used primarily for religious worship, or within 1,000 feet of the real property comprising any church, synagogue, or other building, structure, or place used primarily for religious worship, on the real property comprising any of the following places, buildings, or structures used primarily for housing or providing space for activities for senior citizens: nursing homes, assisted-living centers, senior citizen housing complexes, or senior centers oriented toward daytime activities, or within 1,000 feet of the real property comprising any of the following places, buildings, or structures used primarily for housing or providing space for activities for senior citizens: nursing homes, assisted-living centers, senior citizen housing complexes, or senior centers oriented toward daytime activities is guilty of a Class 2 felony, the fine for which shall not exceed $125,000;

(6) subsection (h) of Section 401 in any school, or any conveyance owned, leased or contracted by a school to transport students to or from school or a school related activity, or residential property owned, operated or managed by a public housing agency or leased by a public housing agency as part of a scattered site or mixed-income development, or public park, on the real property comprising any school or residential property owned, operated or managed by a public housing agency or leased by a public housing agency as part of a scattered site or mixed-income development, or public park or within 1,000 feet of the real property comprising any school or residential property owned, operated or managed by a public housing agency or leased by a public housing agency as part of a scattered site or mixed-income development, or public park, on the real property comprising any church, synagogue, or other building, structure, or place used primarily for religious worship, or within 1,000 feet of the real property comprising any church, synagogue, or other building, structure, or place used primarily for religious worship, on the real property comprising any of the following places, buildings, or structures used primarily for housing or providing space for activities for senior citizens: nursing homes, assisted-living centers, senior citizen housing complexes, or senior centers oriented toward daytime activities, or within 1,000 feet of the real property comprising any of the following places, buildings, or structures used primarily for housing or providing space for activities for senior citizens: nursing homes, assisted-living centers, senior citizen housing complexes, or senior centers oriented toward daytime activities is guilty of a Class 2 felony, the fine for which shall not exceed $100,000.

(c) Regarding penalties prescribed in subsection (b) for violations committed in a school or on or within 1,000 feet of school property, the time of day, time of year and whether classes were currently in session at the time of the offense is irrelevant.

§ 407.1. [Employing person under 18 to deliver substance]. Any person 18 years of age or over who violates any subsection of Section 401, Section 404 or Section 405 by using, engaging or employing a person under 18 years of age to deliver a controlled, counterfeit or look-alike substance may be sentenced to imprisonment for a term up to three times the maximum amount authorized by the pertinent subsection of Section 401, Section 404 or Section 405.

§ **407.2. Delivery of a controlled substance to a pregnant woman.** (a) Any person who violates subsection (a) of Section 401 of this Act by delivering a controlled substance to a woman he knows to be pregnant may be sentenced to imprisonment for a term twice the maximum amount authorized by Section 401 of this Act.

(b) Any person who delivers an amount of a controlled substance set forth in subsections (c) and (d) of Section 401 of this Act to a woman he knows to be pregnant commits a Class 1 felony. The fine for a violation of this subsection (b) shall not be more than $250,000.

§ 408. [Second or subsequent offenses].
(a) Any person convicted of a second or subsequent offense under this act may be sentenced to imprisonment for a term up to twice the maximum term otherwise authorized, fined an amount up to twice that otherwise authorized, or both.
(b) For purposes of this Section, an offense is considered a second or subsequent offense, if, prior to his conviction of the offense, the offender has at any time been convicted under this Act or under any law of the United States or of any State relating to controlled substances.

§ 409. [Bar to prosecution]. Except for convictions or acquittals which are the basis for a charge of narcotics racketeering under Section 4 of the Narcotics Profit forfeiture Act, a conviction or acquittal, under the laws of the United States or of any State relating to controlled substances, for the same act is a bar to prosecution in this State.

§ 410. [Probation]. (a) Whenever any person who has not previously been convicted of, or placed on probation or court supervision for any offense under this Act or any law of the United States or of any State relating to cannabis or controlled substances, pleads guilty to or is found guilty of possession of a controlled or counterfeit substance under subsection (c) of Section 402 or of unauthorized possession of prescription form under Section 406.2, the court, without entering a judgment and with the consent of such person, may sentence him to probation.

(b) When a person is placed on probation, the court shall enter an order specifying a period of probation of 24 months and shall defer further proceedings in the case until the conclusion of the period or until the filing of a petition alleging violation of a term or condition of probation.

(c) The conditions of probation shall be that the person: (1) not violate any criminal statute of any jurisdiction;

(2) refrain from possessing a firearm or other dangerous weapon;

(3) submit to periodic drug testing at a time and in a manner as ordered by the court, but no less than 3 times during the period of the probation, with the cost of the testing to be paid by the probationer; and
(4) perform no less than 30 hours of community service, provided community service is available in the jurisdiction and is funded and approved by the county board.

(d) The court may, in addition to other conditions, require that the person:

(1) make a report to and appear in person before or participate with the court or such courts, person, or social service agency as directed by the court in the order of probation;

(2) pay a fine and costs;

(3) work or pursue a course of study or vocational training;

(4) undergo medical or psychiatric treatment; or treatment or rehabilitation approved by the Illinois Department of Human Services;

(5) attend or reside in a facility established for the instruction or residence of defendants on probation;

(6) support his dependents;

(6-5) refrain from having in his or her body the presence of any illicit drug prohibited by the Cannabis Control Act, the Illinois Controlled Substances Act, or the Methamphetamine Control and Community Protection Act, unless prescribed by a physician, and submit samples of his or her blood or urine or both for tests to determine the presence of any illicit drug;

(7) and in addition, if a minor: (i) reside with his parents or in a foster home;

(ii) attend school;

(iii) attend a non-residential program for youth;

(iv) contribute to his own support at home or in a foster home.

(e) Upon violation of a term or condition of probation, the court may enter a judgment on its original finding of guilt and proceed as otherwise provided.

(f) Upon fulfillment of the terms and conditions of probation, the court shall discharge the person and dismiss the proceedings against him.

(g) A disposition of probation is considered to be a conviction for the purposes of imposing the conditions of probation and for appeal, however, discharge and dismissal under this Section is not a conviction for purposes of this Act or for purposes of disqualifications or disabilities imposed by law upon conviction of a crime.

(h) There may be only one discharge and dismissal under this Section, Section 10 of the Cannabis Control Act, or Section 70 of the Methamphetamine Control and Community Protection Act with respect to any person.

(i) If a person is convicted of an offense under this Act, the Cannabis Control Act, or the Methamphetamine Control and Community Protection Act within 5 years subsequent to a discharge and dismissal under this Section, the discharge and dismissal under this Section shall be admissible in the sentencing proceeding for that conviction as evidence in aggravation.

§ 411. [Offenses warranting most severe penalties]. in determining the appropriate sentence for any conviction under this Act, the sentencing court may consider the following as indicative of the type of offenses which the legislature deems most damaging to the peace and welfare of the citizens of Illinois and which warrants the most severe penalties:

(1) the unlawful delivery of the most highly toxic controlled substances, as reflected by their inclusion in Schedule I or II of this Act;

(2) offenses involving unusually large quantities of controlled substances, as measured by their wholesale value at the time of the offense;

(3) the unlawful delivery of controlled substances by a non-user to a user of controlled substances;

(4) non-possessory offenses by persons who have no other visible means of support;

(5) offenses involving the large-scale manufacture of controlled substances;

(6) offenses which indicate any immediate involvement whatsoever with organized crime in terms of the controlled substance's manufacture, importation, or volume distribution;

(7) the manufacture for, or the delivery of controlled substances to persons 3 years or more junior to the person(s) convicted under this Act;

(8) the unlawful delivery of anabolic steroids by an athletic trainer, coach, or health club personnel;

(9) the possession, delivery, or manufacture of controlled substances or cannabis in the presence of a child under 17 years of age. Nothing in this section shall be construed as limiting in any way the discretion of the court to impose any sentence authorized by this Act.

§ 411.1. [Fines]. (a) Whenever any person pleads guilty to, is found guilty of or is placed on supervision for an offense under this Article, a fine may be levied in addition to any other penalty imposed by the court.

(b) In determining whether to impose a fine under this Section and the amount, time for payment, and method of payment of any fine so imposed, the court shall:
(1) consider the defendant's income, regardless of source, the defendant's earning capacity and the defendant's financial resources, as well as the nature of the burden the fine will impose on the defendant and any person legally or financially dependent upon the defendant;

(2) consider the proof received at trial, or as a result of a plea of guilty, concerning the full street value of the controlled substances seized and any profits or other proceeds derived by the defendant from the violation of this Act;

(3) take into account any other pertinent equitable considerations; and
(4) give primary consideration to the need to deprive the defendant of illegally obtained profits or other proceeds from the offense. for the purpose of paragraph

(2) of this subsection, "street value" shall be determined by the court on the basis of testimony of law enforcement personnel and the defendant as to the amount seized and such testimony as may be required by the court as to the current street value of the controlled substances.

(c) As a condition of a fine, the court may require that payment be made in specified installments or within a specified period of time, but such period shall not be greater than the maximum applicable term of probation or imprisonment, whichever is greater. Unless otherwise specified, payment of a fine shall be due immediately.

(d) If a fine for a violation of this Act is imposed on an organization, it is the duty of each individual authorized to make disbursements of the assets of the organization to pay the fine from assets of the organization.

(e) (1) A defendant who has been sentenced to pay a fine, and who has paid part but not all of such fine, may petition the court for an extension of the time for payment or modification of the method of payment.

(2) The court may grant a petition made pursuant to this subsection if it finds that:

(i) the circumstances that warranted payment by the time or method specified no longer exist; or

(ii) it is otherwise unjust to require payment of the fine by the time or method specified.

§ 411.2. [Additional assessment]. (a) Every person convicted of a violation of this Act, and every person placed on probation, conditional discharge, supervision or probation under Section 410 of this Act, shall be assessed for each offense a sum fixed at:

(1) $3,000 for a Class X felony;
(2) $2,000 for a Class 1 felony;

(3) $1,000 for a Class 2 felony;

(4) $500 for a Class 3 or Class 4 felony;

(5) $300 for a Class A misdemeanor;
(6) $200 for a Class B or Class C misdemeanor.

(b) The assessment under this Section is in addition to and not in lieu of any fines, restitution costs, forfeitures or other assessments authorized or required by law.

(c) As a condition of the assessment, the court may require that payment be made in specified installments or within a specified period of time. If the assessment is not paid within the period of probation, conditional discharge or supervision to which the defendant was originally sentenced, the court may extend the period of probation, conditional discharge or supervision pursuant to Section 5-6-2 or 5-6-3.1 of the Unified Code of Corrections, as applicable, until the assessment is paid or until successful completion of public or community service set forth in subsection (e) or the successful completion of the substance abuse intervention or treatment program set forth in subsection (f). If a term of probation, conditional discharge or supervision is not imposed, the assessment shall be payable upon judgment or as directed by the court.

(d) If an assessment for a violation of this Act is imposed on an organization, it is the duty of each individual authorized to make disbursements of the assets of the organization to pay the assessment from assets of the organization.

(e) A defendant who has been ordered to pay an assessment may petition the court to convert all or part of the assessment into court-approved public or community service. One hour of public or community service shall be equivalent to $4 of assessment. The performance of this public or community service shall be a condition of the probation, conditional discharge or supervision and shall be in addition to the performance of any other period of public or community service ordered by the court or required by law.

(f) The court may suspend the collection of the assessment imposed under this Section; provided the defendant agrees to enter a substance abuse intervention or treatment program approved by the court; and further provided that the defendant agrees to pay for all or some portion of the costs associated with the intervention or treatment program. In this case, the collection of the assessment imposed under this Section shall be suspended during the defendant's participation in the approved intervention or treatment program. Upon successful completion of the program, the defendant may apply to the court to reduce the assessment imposed under this Section by any amount actually paid by the defendant for his participation in the program. The court shall not reduce the penalty under this subsection unless the defendant establishes to the satisfaction of the court that he has successfully completed the intervention or treatment program.
If the defendant's participation is for any reason terminated before his successful completion of the intervention or treatment program, collection of the entire assessment imposed under this Section shall be enforced. Nothing in this Section shall be deemed to affect or suspend any other fines, restitution costs, forfeitures or assessments imposed under this or any other Act.

(g) The court shall not impose more than one assessment per complaint, indictment or information. If the person is convicted of more than one offense in a complaint, indictment or information, the assessment shall be based on the highest class offense for which the person is convicted.

(h) In counties under 3,000,000, all moneys collected under this Section shall be forwarded by the clerk of the circuit court to the State Treasurer for deposit in the Drug Treatment Fund, which is hereby established as a special fund within the State Treasury. The Department of Human Services may make grants to persons licensed under Section 15-10 of the Alcoholism and Other Drug Abuse and Dependency Act or to municipalities or counties from funds appropriated to the Department from the Drug Treatment Fund for the treatment of pregnant women who are addicted to alcohol, cannabis or controlled substances and for the needed care of minor, unemancipated children of women undergoing residential drug treatment.

If the Department of Human Services grants funds to a municipality or a county that the Department determines is not experiencing a problem with pregnant women addicted to alcohol, cannabis or controlled substances, or with care for minor, unemancipated children of women undergoing residential drug treatment, or intervention, the funds shall be used for the treatment of any person addicted to alcohol, cannabis or controlled substances. The Department may adopt such rules as it deems appropriate for the administration of such grants.

(i) In counties over 3,000,000, all moneys collected under this Section shall be forwarded to the County Treasurer for deposit into the County Health Fund. The County Treasurer shall, no later than the 15th day of each month, forward to the State Treasurer 30 percent of all moneys collected under this Act and received into the County Health Fund since the prior remittance to the State Treasurer. Funds retained by the County shall be used for community-based treatment of pregnant women who are addicted to alcohol, cannabis, or controlled substances or for the needed care of minor, unemancipated children of these women. Funds forwarded to the State Treasurer shall be deposited into the State Drug Treatment Fund maintained by the State Treasurer from which the Department of Human Services may make grants to persons licensed under Section 15-10 of the Alcoholism and Other Drug Abuse and Dependency Act or to municipalities or counties from funds appropriated to the Department from the Drug Treatment Fund, provided that the moneys collected from each county be returned proportionately to the counties through grants to licensees located within the county from which the assessment was received and moneys in the State Drug Treatment Fund shall not supplant other local, State or federal funds.

If the Department of Human Services grants funds to a municipality or county that the Department determines is not experiencing a problem with pregnant women addicted to alcohol, cannabis or controlled substances, or with care for minor, unemancipated children or women undergoing residential drug treatment, the funds shall be used for the treatment of any person addicted to alcohol, cannabis or controlled substances. The Department may adopt such rules as it deems appropriate for the administration of such grants.

§ 412. [Penalties in addition to civil or administrative penalties].
Any penalty imposed for any violation of this Act is in addition to, and not in lieu of, any civil or administrative penalty or sanction otherwise authorized by this Act or any other law.

Commentary – Controlled Substance Offenses

Overview. Section 720 ILCS 570/401 *et seq* pronounces the criminal offenses relating to controlled substances. As indicated in Article II of the Controlled Substances Act the scheduled substances that may be the subject of criminal charges are complex in identity and there are a large number of them. It is lawful to possess a certain controlled substances if it is prescribed for purposes of medical treatment by a licensed physician.

The garden variety of criminal cases involves cocaine or heroin as narcotic street drugs, although, of course, there are others. (e.g. "ecstacy", "LSD" and "angel dust" are scheduled by their respective chemical names "3,4-methylendioxymethamphetamine", "lysergic acid diethylamide" and "phencyclidine" (PCP)(Sections 204(d)(1), (10) and (23)).

The possession, possession with intent to deliver and delivery of "look-alike" substances is also unlawful. (See 720 ILCS 570/404). This statute addresses the unscrupulous dealer who represents that he is selling illicit drugs, when he is really scamming for money. There are no scheduled controlled substances in look-alike drugs.

Field tests; forensic testimony. Every controlled substance offense requires proof of exactly what the controlled substance is, and a legal determination based on the conclusion that it is a prohibited substance. Sometimes police officers are trained and do conduct "field tests" to determine the substance, but at trial there is required proof of the nature of the compound that has been seized and is charged. This identity of the substance must be proved beyond a reasonable doubt in a criminal prosecution. At a trial, this is normally accomplished by expert testimony of a forensic chemist from a crime laboratory. "Field tests" on the other hand, can be used to establish probable cause or for probation violation proceedings where there is the lesser burden of proof of a preponderance of the evidence.

In *People v. Mocaby* 378 Ill.App.3d 1095, 882 N.E.2d 1162 (Ill. App. Ct. 5th Dist. 2008), the defendant was charged and convicted of delivery of three different types of controlled substances following an uncover sting operation. An officer and a confidential source went to the defendant's home on separate occasions and purchased different types of pills, being told that they were morphine, Valium and Vicodin. At trial two separate experts testified. As to the morphine pills, an expert testified that he did a chemical analysis using accepted testing procedures with a mass spectrometer and the pills he examined were morphine. A separate forensic chemist examined the Valium pills physically and compared their markings to photos in a pharmaceutical catalogue and determined that they contained diazepam. She also examined the Vicodin tablets physically and compared them to photos in a pharmaceutical catalogue, but that she also performed an "analytical analysis" on the pills and determined that they contained dihydrocodeinone. On appeal the defendant conceded that the forensic testimony as to the morphine charge was sufficient but claimed that the forensic testimony of the second chemist was insufficient for the prosecution to meet its burden of proof that the second and third counts were in fact controlled substance. The court agreed, stating:

> In the present case, there was no chemical analysis of the [Valium] tablets involved in count III. The sole analysis consisted of a physical identification. The only information we have regarding the physical identification is that the tablets were compared to pictures in a book. [The expert] did not describe the tablets, nor did she elaborate about which publication she used to make the physical identification. There is no indication that [she] did anything more than engage in conjecture that the tablets were diazepam based on her comparison with a depiction of tablets with similar characteristics, in some unknown publication. It is not enough to speculate that a substance is a controlled substance. The tablets could be look-alike substances. More conclusive evidence is needed. The State could have conducted a scientific analysis that would have conclusively determined that the tablets contained a controlled substance. Because the evidence regarding the composition of the tablets was not based on a conclusive scientific analysis, we find that the State failed to meet its burden of proof beyond a reasonable doubt that the tablets at issue in count III contained a controlled substance, and we therefore must reverse the defendant's conviction on count III.
>
> *People v. Mocaby* 378 Ill.App.3d at 1099-1100, 882 N.E.2d at 1167.

The court also concluded that the last count involving the Vicodin tablets should be reversed. Even though there apparently were chemical tests conducted, the expert's description was vague, with no indication of the type of test, how results were achieved and whether the results were conclusive. See also *People v. Hagberg* 192 Ill.2d 29, 733 N.E.2d 1271 (Ill. S. Ct. 2000) (officer conducted field testing was insufficient to prove identity of controlled substance where inadequate foundation laid for the conclusive nature of the tests).

In limited circumstances, over-the-counter drugs may be identified on the basis of admission of the contents of the label. there must be a foundational showing that the drugs are in their original packaging and have labels that identify their chemical components, as required by state or federal law. See *People v. Shevock* 335 Ill.App.3d 1031 (Ill. App. Ct. 4th Dist. 2003)(proper to admit contents of Sudafed label as an exception to the rule against hearsay).

Knowing possession; intent to deliver or manufacture. Just as with cannabis offenses, proof of the mental state required by offenses proscribed in the Controlled Substance Act is most often accomplished through circumstantial evidence. There need not be proof that the defendant knew the exact nature of the drug he possessed, if the evidence shows that he knew what he possessed was illegal. Rarely will the offender admit that he possessed the controlled substance (i.e. "it's mine") or that he intended to deliver or manufacture the drug. The factors of the quantity of the drugs, location, exclusive possession or control, access by others, furtive gestures or movements, the presence of large quantities of cash, the presence of weapons and other relevant proof will be relied upon by the prosecution to prove knowing possession and intent to deliver.

In *People v. Bush* 214 Ill.2d 318, 827 N.E.2d 855 (Ill. S. Ct. 2005), the defendant was charged and convicted of possession with intent to deliver crack cocaine. The evidence at trial established that undercover police officers observed the defendant receive money from a person, while standing behind a wrought iron fence the defendant then walked over to a brown paper bag on the ground, retrieved something and handed the item to the person who had given her the money. The officers approached the defendant, detained her and looked inside the bag that was still on the ground near her. Inside they found a chunk of a white substance and two ten-dollar bills. The evidence also showed that a forensic chemist weighed and tested the substance in accordance with proper lab techniques and determined that it was 0.1 gram of crack cocaine. On appeal, the defendant contended the evidence was insufficient to prove that she had intent to deliver because her conviction was based on evidence of sales of unidentified items to unknown persons and the quantity of drugs was so small that it could have been for personal use. The Illinois Supreme Court rejected this argument, stating:

> There is no question that, after viewing the evidence in this case in the light most favorable to the prosecution, a rational trier of fact could have found beyond a reasonable doubt that defendant intended to deliver the substance found in the brown paper bag. Officer Olsen observed defendant standing alone behind a wrought iron fence at 2 a.m. On two separate occasions, an unknown man approached defendant, spoke briefly to her, and handed her money. Defendant then retrieved an unknown item from a brown paper bag that she kept a short distance from herself, handed the item to the man who had just given her money, and returned to her post behind the fence while the unknown man walked away. After detaining defendant, the police looked inside the brown paper bag and found a substance later identified as cocaine. When construed in a light most favorable to the prosecution, these facts easily support an inference that defendant intended to deliver the remaining contents of the brown paper bag.
>
> *People v. Bush* 214 Ill.2d at 327, 827 N.E.2d 860-861.

In *People v. Bond* 405 Ill.App.3d 499, 942 N.E.2d 585 (Ill. App. Ct. 4th Dist. 2010), the defendant was charged and convicted of possession of crack cocaine with intent to deliver. He filed a post conviction petition claiming that his trial lawyer was ineffective in representing the defendant at trial. While the appellate court agreed that the trial lawyer had made mistakes, the court concluded that the errors were harmless because the testimony of the defendant showed that the evidence of his guilt was overwhelming:

> Defendant testified and admitted he possessed the cocaine. Thus, the only issue was his intent to deliver the drugs. Direct evidence of the intent to deliver a controlled substance is rare and the intent must usually be proved by circumstantial evidence... However, in this case, defendant testified the drugs were not for his personal use. In fact, defendant admitted when he got into the vehicle, the driver asked him to hold the drugs as a favor for him because the driver was on parole. Defendant testified he had no intention of selling the drugs or using them and admitted he was just holding them for the driver until defendant got home. In other words, defendant admitted he possessed the drugs with the intent to deliver them back to the driver.
>
> *People v. Bond* 405 Ill.App.3d at 512, 942 N.E.2d at 596. (Internal citation omitted.)

Weight of the controlled substance. A primary enhancement element in controlled substance offenses (again as with cannabis) is the weight to the substance. This essential element must be alleged in the charging document (information or indictment) and proved beyond a reasonable doubt. Where there is only one quantity of substance in one container, the issue is whether the quantity of substance contains the illicit chemical compound. Sometimes controlled substances are pure, but sometimes they are not – a form of "cut" (inositol, baking soda and other substances) can be used to cut cocaine and other drugs to make the quantity larger and thus bring a higher price on the street. A single package of one gram of cut cocaine is less pure than one gram of uncut cocaine but the penalties are the same for possession or possession with intent to deliver the package, because the weights are the same. On the other hand, if the controlled substance has a distinct identifiable form, such as tablets or pills, there is no requirement that each and every pill be tested. A representative sample being tested will suffice.

In *People v. Clinton* 397 Ill.App.3d 215, 922 N.E.2d 1118 (Ill. App. Ct. 1st Dist. 2010), the defendant was charged and convicted of possession with intent to deliver more than 1 gram but less than 15 grams of a substance containing heroin (Class 1 felony) and had been sentenced to 10 years imprisonment. At his trial a forensic chemist testified that he received a plastic bag with 13 individual tin foil packets inside. He determined the gross weight of all the packages, then unwrapped the packages and put the contents in a weighing container until the weight was more than 1 gram. He then performed chemical spectrometer tests and confirmed the presence of cocaine in the quantity. The defendant's conviction was reversed. The court reasoned that the testimony about combining all the bags before testing each of them, caused a significant proof issue. Since there was no proof that each bag contained a substance identified as cocaine before combining the contents of the bags, there could be no conclusion that the 1 gram quantity threshold had been achieved. Simply put if there were two bags, one with baking soda and one with cocaine that was sent to the lab, the chemist (or the police) would not be permitted to enhance the controlled substance offense by combining the two bags and then weighing them. The evidence in the defendant's case would lead to the same conclusion – the prosecution failed to prove the weight of the packages allegedly containing cocaine that had been found in the defendant's possession. While the prosecution did not successfully prove the over 1 gram weight, however, the evidence did prove the lesser offense of possession of some quantity of a controlled substance (Class 2 felony), so the case was remanded for imposition of a lesser sentence.

In contrast, in *People v. Fountain* 2011 IL App (1st) 083459 (the defendant was charged and convicted with possession with intent to deliver more than 1 gram but less than 15 grams of a substance containing heroin. The forensic chemist testified at trial that she received nine separate bags. Although her testimony was ambiguous, the defendant's conviction was affirmed based on the jury's reasonable inference that the lab scientist weighed the powder in each bag and tested the powder in each bag, concluding that the combined weight of the substance in the nine foil packages containing cocaine was 1.3 grams. Defendant's claim the prosecution failed to prove the weight of the controlled substance was rejected.

Sentencing Enhancements. Section 570/407 provides for significant enhancements to controlled substance offenses based on the location of the criminal conduct or if the drugs are distributed to persons under age 18.

The enhancing locations include schools, parks and public housing property. Charges can be "school" enhanced for public or private schools, including colleges and universities. The enhancement provisions go further to prohibit conduct within 1000 feet of a prohibited location. In every instance, the possession with intent to deliver or the delivery of a controlled substance at prohibited locations will increase the class of felony by one level. In *People v. White* 221 Ill.2d 1, 849 N.E.2d 406 (Ill. S. Ct. 2006), the defendant was first indicted for possession of cocaine with intent to deliver as a Class 1 felony. Immediately prior to trial, the prosecution filed an additional count, charging a violation of Section 407 in that the possession with intent to deliver occurred at a public housing location. The defendant was tried and convicted and sentenced on the basis of a Class X felony.

In *People v. Young* 2011 IL 111886, a "pre-school" was held not to be a school for purposes of the sentencing enhancement of Section 407.

Delivery to an underage person under Section 407 doubles the potential penalty that otherwise would apply to the criminal controlled offense transaction.

Article V.

§ 505. [Forfeiture]. (a) The following are subject to forfeiture:

(1) all substances which have been manufactured, distributed, dispensed, or possessed in violation of this Act;

(2) all raw materials, products and equipment of any kind which are used, or intended for use in manufacturing, distributing, dispensing, administering or possessing any substance in violation of this Act;

(3) all conveyances, including aircraft, vehicles or vessels, which are used, or intended for use, to transport, or in any manner to facilitate the transportation, sale, receipt, possession, or concealment of property described in paragraphs (1) and (2), but:

(i) no conveyance used by any person as a common carrier in the transaction of business as a common carrier is subject to forfeiture under this Section unless it appears that the owner or other person in charge of the conveyance is a consenting party or privy to a violation of this Act;

(ii) no conveyance is subject to forfeiture under this Section by reason of any act or omission which the owner proves to have been committed or omitted without his knowledge or consent;

(iii) a forfeiture of a conveyance encumbered by a bona fide security interest is subject to the interest of the secured party if he neither had knowledge of nor consented to the act or omission;

(4) all money, things of value, books, records, and research products and materials including formulas, microfilm, tapes, and data which are used, or intended to be used in violation of this act;

(5) everything of value furnished, or intended to be furnished, in exchange for a substance in violation of this Act, all proceeds traceable to such an exchange, and all moneys, negotiable instruments, and securities used, or

intended to be used, to commit or in any manner to facilitate any violation of this Act;

(6) all real property, including any right, title, and interest (including, but not limited to, any leasehold interest or the beneficial interest in a land trust) in the whole of any lot or tract of land and any appurtenances or improvements, which is used or intended to be used, in any manner or part, to commit, or in any manner to facilitate the commission of, any violation or act that constitutes a violation of Section 401 or 405 of this Act or that is the proceeds of any violation or act that constitutes a violation of Section 401 or 405 of this Act.

(b) Property subject to forfeiture under this Act may be seized by the Director or any peace officer upon process or seizure warrant issued by any court having jurisdiction over the property. Seizure by the Director or any peace officer without process may be made:

(1) if the seizure is incident to inspection under an administrative inspection warrant;

(2) if the property subject to seizure has been the subject of a prior judgment in favor of the State in a criminal proceeding, or in an injunction or forfeiture proceeding based upon this Act or the Drug Asset Forfeiture Procedure Act;

(3) if there is probable cause to believe that the property is directly or indirectly dangerous to health or safety;

(4) if there is probable cause to believe that the property is subject to forfeiture under this Act and the property is seized under circumstances in which a warrantless seizure or arrest would be reasonable; or

(5) in accordance with the Code of Criminal Procedure of 1963.

(c) In the event of seizure pursuant to subsection (b), forfeiture proceedings shall be instituted in accordance with the Drug Asset forfeiture Procedure Act.

(d) Property taken or detained under this Section shall not be subject to replevin, but is deemed to be in the custody of the Director subject only to the order and judgments of the circuit court having jurisdiction over the forfeiture proceedings and the decisions of the State's Attorney under the Drug Asset Forfeiture Procedure Act. When property is seized under this Act, the seizing agency shall promptly conduct an inventory of the seized property and estimate the property's value, and shall forward a copy of the inventory of seized property and the estimate of the property's value to the Director. Upon receiving notice of seizure, the Director may:

(1) place the property under seal;

(2) remove the property to a place designated by the Director;

(3) keep the property in the possession of the seizing agency;

(4) remove the property to a storage area for safekeeping or, if the property is a negotiable instrument or money and is not needed for evidentiary purposes, deposit it in an interest bearing account;

(5) place the property under constructive seizure by posting notice of pending forfeiture on it, by giving notice of pending forfeiture to its owners and interest holders, or by filing notice of pending forfeiture in any appropriate public record relating to the property; or

(6) provide for another agency or custodian, including an owner, secured party, or lienholder, to take custody of the property upon the terms and conditions set by the Director.

(e) If the Department of Professional Regulation suspends or revokes a registration, all controlled substances owned or possessed by the registrant at the time of suspension or the effective date of the revocation order may be placed under seal. No disposition may be made of substances under seal until the time for taking an appeal has elapsed or until all appeals have been concluded unless a court, upon application therefore, orders the sale of perishable substances and the deposit of the proceeds of the sale with the court. Upon a revocation rule becoming final, all substances may be forfeited to the Department of Professional Regulation.

(f) When property is forfeited under this Act the Director shall sell all such property unless such property is required by law to be destroyed or is harmful to the public, and shall distribute the proceeds of the sale, together with any moneys forfeited or seized, in accordance with subsection (g). However, upon the application of the seizing agency or prosecutor who was responsible for the investigation, arrest or arrests and prosecution which lead to the forfeiture, the Director may return any item of forfeited property to the seizing agency or prosecutor for official use in the enforcement of laws relating to cannabis or controlled substances, if the agency or prosecutor can demonstrate that the item requested would be useful to the agency or prosecutor in their enforcement efforts. When any forfeited conveyance, including an aircraft, vehicle, or vessel, is returned to the seizing agency or prosecutor, the conveyance may be used immediately in the enforcement of the criminal laws of this State. Upon disposal, all proceeds from the sale of the conveyance must be used for drug enforcement purposes. When any real property returned to the seizing agency is sold by the agency or its unit of government, the proceeds of the sale shall be delivered to the Director and distributed in accordance with subsection (g).

(g) All monies and the sale proceeds of all other property forfeited and seized under this Act shall be distributed as follows: (1) 65% shall be distributed to the metropolitan enforcement group, local, municipal, county, or state law enforcement agency or agencies which conducted or participated in the investigation resulting in the forfeiture. The distribution shall bear a reasonable relationship to the degree of direct participation of the law enforcement agency in the effort resulting in the forfeiture, taking into account the total value of the property forfeited and the total law enforcement effort with respect to the violation of the law upon which the forfeiture is based. Amounts distributed to the agency or agencies shall be used for the enforcement of laws governing cannabis and controlled substances or for security cameras used for the prevention or detection of violence, except that amounts distributed to the Secretary of State shall be deposited into the Secretary of State Evidence Fund to be used as provided in Section 2-115 of the Illinois Vehicle Code.

(2) (i) 12.5% shall be distributed to the Office of the State's Attorney of the county in which the prosecution resulting in the forfeiture was instituted, deposited in a special fund in the county treasury and appropriated to the State's Attorney for use in the enforcement of laws governing cannabis and controlled substances. In counties over 3,000,000 population, 25% will be distributed to the office of the State's Attorney for use in the enforcement of laws governing cannabis and controlled substances. If the prosecution is undertaken solely by the Attorney General, the portion provided hereunder shall be distributed to the Attorney General for use in the enforcement of laws governing cannabis and controlled substances.

(ii) 12.5% shall be distributed to the Office of the State's Attorneys Appellate Prosecutor and deposited in the Narcotics Profit Forfeiture Fund of that office to be used for additional expenses incurred in the investigation, prosecution and appeal of cases arising under laws governing cannabis and controlled substances. The office of the State's Attorneys Appellate Prosecutor shall not receive distribution from cases brought in counties with over 3,000,000 population.

(3) 10% shall be retained by the Department of State Police for expenses related to the administration and sale of seized and forfeited property.

(h) Species of plants from which controlled substances in Schedules I and II may be derived which have been planted or cultivated in violation of this Act, or of which the owners or cultivators are unknown, or which are wild growths, may be seized and summarily forfeited to the State. The failure, upon demand by the

Director or any peace officer, of the person in occupancy or in control of land or premises upon which the species of plants are growing or being stored, to produce registration, or proof that he is the holder thereof, constitutes authority for the seizure and forfeiture of the plants.

§ 506. [Burden of proof of exemption or exception]. It is not necessary for the State to negate any exemption or exception in this Act in any complaint, information, indictment or other pleading or in any trial, hearing, or other proceeding under this Act. The burden of proof of any exemption or exception is upon the person claiming it.

§ 509. [Testing as condition of probation]. Whenever any court in this State grants probation to any person that the court has reason to believe is or has been an addict or unlawful possessor of controlled substances, the court shall require, as a condition of probation, that the probationer submit to periodic tests by the Department of Corrections to determine by means of appropriate chemical detection tests whether the probationer is using controlled substances. The court may require as a condition of probation that the probationer enter an approved treatment program, if the court determines that the probationer is addicted to a controlled substance. Whenever the Parole and Pardon Board grants parole to a person whom the Board has reason to believe has been an unlawful possessor or addict of controlled substances, the Board shall require as a condition of parole that the parolee submit to appropriate periodic chemical tests by the Department of Corrections to determine whether the parolee is using controlled substances.

§ 510. Preservation of evidence for laboratory testing. (a) Before or after the trial in a prosecution for a violation of any Section of article IV of this Act, a law enforcement agency or an agent acting on behalf of the law enforcement agency must preserve, subject to a continuous chain of custody, not less than:

(1) 2 kilograms of any substance containing a detectable amount of heroin;

(2) 10 kilograms of any substance containing a detectable amount of: (A) coca leaves, except coca leaves and extract of coca leaves from which cocaine, ecgonine, and derivatives of ecgonine or their salts have been removed;

(B) cocaine, its salts, optical and geometric isomers, and salts of isomers;

(C) ecgonine, its derivatives, their salts, isomers, and salts of isomers; or

(D) any combination of the substances described in subdivisions (A) through (C) of this paragraph (a)(2);

(3) 10 kilograms of a mixture of substances described in subdivision (B) of paragraph (a)(2) that contains a cocaine base;

(4) 200 grams of phencyclidine (also referred to as "PCP") or 2 kilograms of any substance containing a detectable amount of phencyclidine;

(5) 20 grams of any substance containing a detectable amount of lysergic acid diethylamide (also referred to as "LSD");

(6) 800 grams of a mixture or substance containing a detectable amount of fentanyl, or 2 grams of any substance containing a detectable amount of any analog of fentanyl; with respect to the offenses enumerated in this subsection (a) and must maintain sufficient documentation to locate that evidence. Excess quantities with respect to the offenses enumerated in this subsection (a) cannot practicably be retained by a law enforcement agency because of its size, bulk, and physical character.

(b) The sheriff or seizing law enforcement agency must file a motion requesting destruction of bulk evidence before the trial judge in the courtroom where the criminal charge is pending. The sheriff or seizing law enforcement agency must give notice of the motion requesting destruction of bulk evidence to the prosecutor of the criminal charge and the defense attorney of record. The trial judge will conduct an evidentiary hearing in which all parties will be given the opportunity to present evidence and

arguments relating to whether the evidence should be destroyed, whether such destruction will prejudice the prosecution of the criminal case, and whether the destruction of the evidence will prejudice the defense of the criminal charge.
The court's determination whether to grant the motion for destruction of bulk evidence must be based upon the totality of all of the circumstances of the case presented at the evidentiary hearing, the effect such destruction would have upon the defendant's constitutional rights, and the prosecutor's ability to proceed with the prosecution of the criminal charge.
(c) The court may, before trial, transfer excess quantities of any substance containing any of the controlled substances enumerated in subsection (a) with respect to a prosecution for any offense enumerated in subsection (a) to the sheriff of the county, or may, in its discretion, transfer such evidence to the Department of State Police, for destruction after notice is given to the defendant's attorney of record or to the defendant if the defendant is proceeding *pro se*.

(d) After a judgment of conviction is entered and the charged quantity is no longer needed for evidentiary purposes with respect to a prosecution for any offense enumerated in subsection (a), the court may transfer any substance containing any of the controlled substances enumerated in subsection (a) to the sheriff of the county, or may, in its discretion, transfer such evidence to the Department of State Police, for destruction after notice is given to the defendant's attorney of record or to the defendant if the defendant is proceeding pro se. No evidence shall be disposed of until 30 days after the judgment is entered, and if a notice of appeal is filed, no evidence shall be disposed of until the mandate has been received by the circuit court from the Appellate Court.

Act 600: Drug Paraphernalia Control Act
720 ILCS 600 *et seq.*

§ 1. [Short title] This Act shall be known and may be cited as the "Drug Paraphernalia Control Act".

§ 2. [Definitions] As used in this Act, unless the context otherwise requires:

(a) The term "cannabis" shall have the meaning ascribed to it in Section 3 of the Cannabis Control Act, as if that definition were incorporated herein.

(b) The term "controlled substance" shall have the meaning ascribed to it in Section 102 of the Illinois Controlled Substances Act, as if that definition were incorporated herein.

(c) "Deliver" or "delivery" means the actual, constructive or attempted transfer of possession, with or without consideration, whether or not there is an agency relationship.

(d) "Drug paraphernalia" means all equipment, products and materials of any kind, other than methamphetamine manufacturing materials as defined in Section 10 of the Methamphetamine Control and Community Protection Act, which are intended to be used unlawfully in planting, propagating, cultivating, growing, harvesting, manufacturing, compounding, converting, producing, processing, preparing, testing, analyzing, packaging, repackaging, storing, containing, concealing, injecting, ingesting, inhaling or otherwise introducing into the human body cannabis or a controlled substance in violation of the Cannabis Control Act, the Illinois Controlled Substances Act, or the Methamphetamine Control and Community Protection Act. It includes, but is not limited to:

(1) kits intended to be used unlawfully in manufacturing, compounding, converting, producing, processing or preparing cannabis or a controlled substance;

(2) isomerization devices intended to be used unlawfully in increasing the potency of any species of plant which is cannabis or a controlled substance;

(3) testing equipment intended to be used unlawfully in a private home for identifying or in analyzing the strength, effectiveness or purity of cannabis or controlled substances;

(4) diluents and adulterants intended to be used unlawfully for cutting cannabis or a controlled substance by private persons;

(5) objects intended to be used unlawfully in ingesting, inhaling, or otherwise introducing cannabis, cocaine, hashish, or hashish oil into the human body including, where applicable, the following items:

(A) water pipes;

(B) carburetion tubes and devices;

(C) smoking and carburetion masks;

(D) miniature cocaine spoons and cocaine vials;

(E) carburetor pipes;

(F) electric pipes;

(G) air-driven pipes;

(H) chillums;

(I) bongs;

(J) ice pipes or chillers;
(6) any item whose purpose, as announced or described by the seller, is for use in violation of this Act.

§ 3. [Sale of drug paraphernalia] (a) Any person who keeps for sale, offers for sale, sells, or delivers for any commercial consideration any item of drug paraphernalia commits a Class 4 felony for which a minimum fine of $1,000 for each such item shall be imposed. Any person 18 years of age or older who sells or delivers for any commercial consideration any item of drug paraphernalia to a person under 18 years of age is guilty of a Class 3 felony.

(b) Any person who sells or delivers for a commercial consideration any item of drug paraphernalia to a woman he knows to be pregnant is guilty of a Class 2 felony.

(c) Any store, place, or premises from which or in which any item of drug paraphernalia is kept for sale, offered for sale, sold, or delivered for any commercial consideration is declared to be a public nuisance.

The State's Attorney of the county in which such a nuisance is located may commence an action in the circuit court, in the name of the People of the State of Illinois, to abate the public nuisance as described in this subsection (c).

Upon being satisfied by affidavits or other sworn evidence that an alleged public nuisance exists, the court may, without bond, enter a temporary restraining order to enjoin any defendant from maintaining the nuisance and may, without bond, enter a preliminary injunction restraining any defendant from removing or interfering with any property used in connection with the public nuisance.

If during the proceedings and hearings upon the merits the existence of the nuisance is established, and it is established that the nuisance was maintained with the intentional, knowing or reckless permission of the owner, or an agent of the owner managing the premises, the court shall enter an order restraining all persons from maintaining or permitting the nuisance and from using the premises for a period of one year thereafter. However an owner, lessee, or other occupant thereof may use the premises if the owner gives bond with sufficient security or surety, in an amount between $5,000 and $10,000 approved by the court, payable to the People of the State of Illinois. The bond shall include a condition that no offense specified in this Act shall be committed at, in, or upon the property described, and a condition that the principal obligor and surety assume responsibility for any fine, costs, or damages incurred by any person resulting from such an offense.

§ 3.5. Possession of drug paraphernalia.
(a) A person who knowingly possesses an item of drug paraphernalia with the intent to use it in

ingesting, inhaling, or otherwise introducing cannabis or a controlled substance into the human body, or in preparing cannabis or a controlled substance for that use, is guilty of a Class A misdemeanor for which the court shall impose a minimum fine of $750 in addition to any other penalty prescribed for a Class A misdemeanor. This subsection (a) does not apply to a person who is legally authorized to possess hypodermic syringes or needles under the Hypodermic Syringes and Needles Act.

(b) In determining intent under subsection (a), the trier of fact may take into consideration the proximity of the cannabis or controlled substances to drug paraphernalia or the presence of cannabis or a controlled substance on the drug paraphernalia.

§ 4. **Exemptions**. This Act does not apply to:

(a) Items used in the preparation, compounding, packaging, labeling, or other use of cannabis or a controlled substance as an incident to lawful research, teaching, or chemical analysis and not for sale.

(b) Items historically and customarily used in connection with the planting, propagating, cultivating, growing, harvesting, manufacturing, compounding, converting, producing, processing, preparing, testing, analyzing, packaging, repackaging, storing, containing, concealing, injecting, ingesting, or inhaling of tobacco or any other lawful substance.

Items exempt under this subsection include, but are not limited to, garden hoes, rakes, sickles, baggies, tobacco pipes, and cigarette-rolling papers.

(c) Items listed in Section 2 of this Act which are used for decorative purposes, when such items have been rendered completely inoperable or incapable of being used for any illicit purpose prohibited by this Act.

(d) A person who is legally authorized to possess hypodermic syringes or needles under the Hypodermic Syringes and Needles Act.

In determining whether or not a particular item is exempt under this Section, the trier of fact should consider, in addition to all other logically relevant factors, the following:

(1) the general, usual, customary, and historical use to which the item involved has been put;

(2) expert evidence concerning the ordinary or customary use of the item and the effect of any peculiarity in the design or engineering of the device upon its functioning;

(3) any written instructions accompanying the delivery of the item concerning the purposes or uses to which the item can or may be put;

(4) any oral instructions provided by the seller of the item at the time and place of sale or commercial delivery;

(5) any national or local advertising concerning the design, purpose or use of the item involved, and the entire context in which such advertising occurs;

(6) the manner, place and circumstances in which the item was displayed for sale, as well as any item or items displayed for sale or otherwise exhibited upon the premises where the sale was made;

(7) whether the owner or anyone in control of the object is a legitimate supplier of like or related items to the community, such as a licensed distributor or dealer of tobacco products;

(8) the existence and scope of legitimate uses for the object in the community.

§ 5. [Forfeiture] (a) All drug paraphernalia is subject to forfeiture.

(b) Property subject to forfeiture under this Act may be seized by any peace officer upon process issued by any court having jurisdiction over the property. Judgments in favor of the State in a criminal or forfeiture proceeding based upon this Act against a person's specific property shall serve as process authorizing a police officer to seize such property without further process.

Seizure by a police officer may be made without process:

(1) If there is probable cause to believe that the property is directly dangerous to health or safety and existing circumstances do not allow reasonable time for the officer to obtain lawful process; or

(2) In accordance with the provisions of The Code of Criminal Procedure of 1963, as amended.

(3) The presence of items which are deemed violative of this Act or are otherwise subject to its forfeiture provisions in an inventory shall not subject the entire inventory to seizure or forfeiture.

(c) Property taken or detained under this Section shall not be subject to replevin, but is deemed to be in the custody of the law enforcement department or agency employing the seizing officer, subject only to the order and judgments of the circuit court having jurisdiction over the forfeiture proceedings. When property is seized under this Act, the chief administrative officer of the seizing department or agency may place the property under seal, or remove the property to a place designated by him.
(d) No disposition may be made of property under seal until the validity of the seizure has been determined in a Circuit Court, unless such court upon application therefore, orders the sale of perishable substances and the deposit of the proceeds of the sale with the clerk of the court. The Circuit Court shall rule on the validity of the seizure within 30 days after the seizure, unless a continuance is obtained by a person from whom the items were seized or a person who otherwise has standing to complain, or by the State for good cause shown. In no event shall a continuance be granted to the State pursuant to this Section extend beyond 30 days. If judgment is entered in favor of the person from whom the property is seized, all seized property shall be returned immediately. Appeals from orders of the Circuit Court shall be heard within 60 days from the date judgment is entered. Judgments in favor of the person entitled to possession of the subject property shall serve as a mandate to the agency holding said property to return same forthwith.

(e) When property is forfeited under this Act the chief administrative officer of the seizing department or agency may retain it for official use, or forward it to the Bureau of Narcotics and Dangerous Drugs, United States Department of Justice, or its successor agency, for disposition.

§ 6. [Legislative intent]This Act is intended to be used solely for the suppression of the commercial traffic in and possession of items that, within the context of the sale or offering for sale, or possession, are clearly and beyond a reasonable doubt intended for the illegal and unlawful use of cannabis or controlled substances. To this end all reasonable and common-sense inferences shall be drawn in favor of the legitimacy of any transaction or item.

§ 7. [More restrictive ordinances permitted] The provisions of any ordinance enacted by any municipality or unit of local government which imposes the same or greater restrictions or limitations upon the availability of drug paraphernalia as defined herein, including the acquisition, sale or delivery of such items, are not invalidated or affected by this Act.

Act 602: Ephedra Prohibition Act
720 ILCS 602 *et seq.*

§ 5. Findings. The General Assembly finds the following:

(1) Over 3 billion servings of ephedra are consumed by Americans each year.

(2) Ephedra, or ma huang, has been associated with a wide range of severe adverse events, including death.

(3) The U.S. Food and Drug Administration has received over 18,000 reports of adverse reactions by ephedra users, including strokes, seizures, heart attacks, and deaths.

(4) The Inspector General of the U.S. Department of Health and Human Services noted in a report on ephedra adverse events that 60% of those adverse events were experienced by people under the age of 40.

(5) A study reported in the Annals of Internal Medicine concluded that, compared with other herbs, ephedra is associated with a greatly increased risk for adverse reactions and that the use of ephedra should be restricted.

(6) The American Medical Association and the consumer group, Public Citizen, have called for a nationwide ban on ephedra.

(7) The National Collegiate Athletics Association, the National Football League, and the International Olympic Committee have all banned ephedra use by their athletes because of concerns about the safety of this dietary supplement.

(8) The U.S. Army has banned the sale of ephedra products in army commissaries worldwide after 33 army personnel died from consuming ephedra products.

(9) Canada, Britain, Germany, and Australia have all taken steps to restrict the sale of ephedra products.

§ 10. Purpose. The purpose of this Act is to ban the sale of all dietary supplements containing ephedrine alkaloids in the State of Illinois regardless of the age of the purchaser in order to protect the health and public safety of Illinois residents.

§ 15. Definitions:

"Ephedra" means herbs and herbal products that contain ephedrine alkaloids, including ma huang, Chinese ephedra, ephedra sinica, ephedra herb powder, epitonin, or any extract of those substances, but does not include any drug that contains ephedrine and is lawfully sold, transferred, or furnished over the counter with or without a prescription pursuant to the federal Food, Drug, and Cosmetic Act (21 U.S.C. 301 and following) or regulations adopted under that Act.

"Person" means any natural person, individual, corporation, unincorporated association, proprietorship, firm, partnership, joint venture, joint stock association, or any other business organization or entity.

§ 20. Prohibition.

(a) No person may sell or offer for sale any dietary supplement containing any quantity of ephedra or ephedrine alkaloids to any person located within the State or to any person making the purchase from within the State.

(b) The prohibition in subsection (a) of this Section does not apply to the sale of any product that receives explicit approval as safe and effective for its intended use under the federal Food, Drug, and Cosmetic Act (21 U.S.C. 355) or is lawfully marketed under an over-the-counter monograph issued by the U.S. Food and Drug Administration.

§ 25. Penalties.

(a) Any person who violates this Act is guilty of a Class A misdemeanor. The penalty is imprisonment for less than one year or a fine of not more than $5,000 or both for a first offense.

(b) For a subsequent violation of this Act, a person is guilty of a Class 3 felony, and the penalty is imprisonment for less than 5 years or a fine of not more than $20,000 or both.

Act 635. Hypodermic Syringes and Needles Act
720 ILCS 635 *et. Al* – Selected Provisions

§ 1. Possession of hypodermic syringes and needles. (a) Except as provided in subsection (b), no person, not being a physician, dentist, chiropodist or veterinarian licensed under the laws of this State or of the state where he resides, or a registered professional nurse, or a registered embalmer, manufacturer or dealer in embalming supplies, wholesale druggist, manufacturing pharmacist, registered pharmacist, manufacturer of surgical instruments, industrial user, official of any government having possession of the articles hereinafter mentioned by reason of his official duties, nurse or a medical laboratory technician acting under the direction of a physician or dentist, employee of an incorporated hospital acting under the direction of its superintendent or officer in immediate charge, or a carrier or messenger engaged in the transportation of such articles, or the holder of a permit issued under Section 5 of this Act, or a farmer engaged in the use of such instruments on livestock, or a person engaged in chemical, clinical, pharmaceutical or other scientific research, shall have in his possession a hypodermic syringe, hypodermic needle, or any instrument adapted for the use of controlled substances or cannabis by subcutaneous injection.

(b) A person who is at least 18 years of age may purchase from a pharmacy and have in his or her possession up to 20 hypodermic syringes or needles.

§ 2. Sale of hypodermic syringes and needles. (a) Except as provided in subsection (b), no such syringe, needle or instrument shall be delivered or sold to, or exchanged with, any person except a registered pharmacist, physician, dentist, veterinarian, registered embalmer, manufacturer or dealer in embalming supplies, wholesale druggist, manufacturing pharmacist, industrial user, a nurse upon the written order of a physician or dentist, the holder of a permit issued under Section 5 of this Act, a registered chiropodist, or an employee of an incorporated hospital upon the written order of its superintendent or officer in immediate charge; provided that the provisions of this Act shall not prohibit the sale, possession or use of hypodermic syringes or hypodermic needles for treatment of livestock or poultry by the owner or keeper thereof or a person engaged in chemical, clinical, pharmaceutical or other scientific research.

(b) A pharmacist may sell up to 20 sterile hypodermic syringes or needles to a person who is at least 18 years of age. A syringe or needle sold under this subsection (b) must be stored at a pharmacy and in a manner that limits access to the syringes or needles to pharmacists employed at the pharmacy and any persons designated by the pharmacists. A syringe or needle sold at a pharmacy under this subsection (b) may be sold only from the pharmacy department of the pharmacy.

§ 4. Penalty. A person who violates any provision of Section 1 or 2 of this Act is guilty of a Class A misdemeanor for the first such offense; and a Class 4 felony for a second or any succeeding offense.

§ 5. Prescriptions. Except as provided under Section 2, a licensed physician may direct a patient under his immediate charge to have in possession any of the instruments specified in Sections 1 and 2 which may be dispensed by a registered pharmacist or assistant registered pharmacist in this state only (1) upon a written prescription of such physician, or (2) upon an oral order of such physician, which order is reduced promptly to writing and filed by the pharmacist, or (3) by refilling any such written or oral prescription if such refilling is authorized by the prescriber either in the original prescription or by oral order which is reduced promptly to writing and filed by the pharmacist in the same manner and under the same conditions as any other prescription issued by a practitioner licensed by law to write prescriptions, or (4) upon a signed statement of a patient, upon proper identification, stating that the prescriptions or instruments specified in Sections 1 and 2 were lost or broken, as the case may be, the name and address of the prescriber, the name and address of the patient and the purpose for which the prescription was ordered. Such written or oral prescriptions when reduced to writing for instruments specified in Sections 1 and 2 shall contain the date of such prescription, the name and address of the prescriber, the name and address of the patient, the purpose for which the prescription is ordered, the date when dispensed and by whom dispensed.

Provided, however, that a licensed physician or other allied medical practitioner, authorized by the laws of the State of Illinois to prescribe or administer controlled substances or cannabis to humans or animals, may authorize any person or the owner of any animal, to purchase and have in his possession any of the instruments specified in Sections 1 and 2, which may be sold to him without a specific written or oral prescription or order, by any person authorized by the laws of the State of Illinois to sell and dispense controlled substances or cannabis, if such authorization is in the form of a certificate giving the name and address of such licensed physician or other allied medical practitioner, the name, address and signature of the person, or of the owner of the animal, so authorized, the purpose or reason of such authorization, and the date of such certificate and in that event, no other prescription, writing or record shall be required to authorize the possession or sale of such instruments.

§ 6. Any prosecution under this Act may be commenced by an information as defined in Section 102-12 of the Code of Criminal Procedure of 1963.

Act 646 Methamphetamine Control and Community Protection Act – Selected Provisions

§ 1. Short title. This Act may be cited as the Methamphetamine Control and Community Protection Act.

§ 5. Purpose. The purpose of this Act is to reduce the damage that the manufacture, distribution, and use of methamphetamine are inflicting on children, families, communities, businesses, the economy, and the environment in Illinois. The General Assembly recognizes that methamphetamine is fundamentally different from other drugs regulated by the Illinois Controlled Substances Act because the harms relating to methamphetamine stem not only from the distribution and use of the drug, but also from the manufacture of the drug in this State. Because methamphetamine is not only distributed and used but also manufactured here, and because the manufacture of methamphetamine is extremely and uniquely harmful, the General Assembly finds that a separate Act is needed to address the manufacture, distribution, and use of methamphetamine in Illinois.

§ 10. Definitions. As used in this Act:
"Anhydrous ammonia" has the meaning provided in subsection (d) of Section 3 of the Illinois Fertilizer Act of 1961.

"Anhydrous ammonia equipment" means all items used to store, hold, contain, handle, transfer, transport, or apply anhydrous ammonia for lawful purposes.

"Booby trap" means any device designed to cause physical injury when triggered by an act of a person approaching, entering, or moving through a structure, a vehicle, or any location where methamphetamine has been manufactured, is being manufactured, or is intended to be manufactured.

"Deliver" or "delivery" has the meaning provided in subsection (h) of Section 102 of the Illinois Controlled Substances Act.

"Director" means the Director of State Police or the Director's designated agents.

"Dispose" or "disposal" means to abandon, discharge, release, deposit, inject, dump, spill, leak, or place methamphetamine waste onto or into any land, water, or well of any type so that the waste has the potential to enter the environment, be emitted into the air, or be discharged into the soil or any waters, including groundwater.

"Emergency response" means the act of collecting evidence, securing a methamphetamine laboratory site, methamphetamine waste site or other methamphetamine-related site and cleaning up the site, whether these actions are performed by public entities or private contractors paid by public entities.

"Emergency service provider" means a local, State, or federal peace officer, firefighter, emergency medical technician-ambulance, emergency medical technician-intermediate, emergency medical technician-paramedic, ambulance driver, or other medical or first aid personnel rendering aid, or any agent or designee of the foregoing.

"Finished methamphetamine" means methamphetamine in a form commonly used for personal consumption.

"Firearm" has the meaning provided in Section 1.1 of the Firearm Owners Identification Card Act.

"Manufacture" means to produce, prepare, compound, convert, process, synthesize, concentrate, purify, separate, extract, or package any methamphetamine, methamphetamine precursor, methamphetamine manufacturing catalyst, methamphetamine manufacturing reagent, methamphetamine manufacturing solvent, or any substance containing any of the foregoing.

"Methamphetamine" means the chemical methamphetamine (a Schedule II controlled substance under the Illinois Controlled Substances Act) or any salt, optical isomer, salt of optical isomer, or analog thereof, with the exception of 3,4-Methylenedioxymethamphetamine (MDMA) or any other scheduled substance with a separate listing under the Illinois Controlled Substances Act.

"Methamphetamine manufacturing catalyst" means any substance that has been used, is being used, or is intended to be used to activate, accelerate, extend, or improve a chemical reaction involved in the manufacture of methamphetamine.

"Methamphetamine manufacturing environment" means a structure or vehicle in which:

(1) methamphetamine is being or has been manufactured;

(2) chemicals that are being used, have been used, or are intended to be used to manufacture methamphetamine are stored;

(3) methamphetamine manufacturing materials that have been used to manufacture methamphetamine are stored; or

(4) methamphetamine manufacturing waste is stored.

"Methamphetamine manufacturing material" means any methamphetamine precursor, substance containing any methamphetamine precursor, methamphetamine manufacturing catalyst, substance containing any methamphetamine manufacturing catalyst, methamphetamine manufacturing reagent, substance containing any methamphetamine manufacturing reagent, methamphetamine manufacturing solvent, substance containing any methamphetamine manufacturing solvent, or any other chemical, substance, ingredient, equipment, apparatus, or item that is being used, has been used, or is intended to be used in the manufacture of methamphetamine.

"Methamphetamine manufacturing reagent" means any substance other than a methamphetamine manufacturing catalyst that has been used, is being used, or is intended to be used to react with and chemically alter any methamphetamine precursor.

"Methamphetamine manufacturing solvent" means any substance that has been used, is being used, or is intended to be used as a medium in which any methamphetamine precursor, methamphetamine manufacturing catalyst, methamphetamine manufacturing reagent, or any substance containing any of the foregoing is dissolved, diluted, or washed during any part of the methamphetamine manufacturing process.

"Methamphetamine manufacturing waste" means any chemical, substance, ingredient, equipment, apparatus, or item that is left over from, results from, or is produced by the process of manufacturing methamphetamine, other than finished methamphetamine.

"Methamphetamine precursor" means ephedrine, pseudoephedrine, benzyl methyl ketone, methyl benzyl ketone, phenylacetone, phenyl-2-propanone, P2P, or any salt, optical isomer, or salt of an optical isomer of any of these chemicals.

"Multi-unit dwelling" means a unified structure used or intended for use as a habitation, home, or residence that contains 2 or more condominiums, apartments, hotel rooms, motel rooms, or other living units.

"Package" means an item marked for retail sale that is not designed to be further broken down or subdivided for the purpose of retail sale.

"Participate" or "participation" in the manufacture of methamphetamine means to produce, prepare, compound, convert, process, synthesize, concentrate, purify, separate, extract, or package any methamphetamine, methamphetamine precursor, methamphetamine manufacturing catalyst, methamphetamine manufacturing reagent, methamphetamine manufacturing solvent, or any substance containing any of the foregoing, or to assist in any of these actions, or to attempt to take any of these actions, regardless of whether this action or these actions result in the production of finished methamphetamine.

"Person with a disability" means a person who suffers from a permanent physical or mental impairment resulting from disease, injury, functional disorder, or congenital condition which renders the person incapable of adequately providing for his or her own health and personal care.

"Procure" means to purchase, steal, gather, or otherwise obtain, by legal or illegal means, or to cause another to take such action.

"Second or subsequent offense" means an offense under this Act committed by an offender who previously committed an offense under this Act, the Illinois Controlled Substances Act, the Cannabis Control Act, or another Act of this State, another state, or the United States relating to methamphetamine, cannabis, or any other controlled substance.

"Standard dosage form", as used in relation to any methamphetamine precursor, means that the methamphetamine precursor is contained in a pill, tablet, capsule, caplet, gel cap, or liquid cap that has been manufactured by a lawful entity and contains a standard quantity of methamphetamine precursor.

"Unauthorized container", as used in relation to anhydrous ammonia, means any container that is not designed for the specific and sole purpose of holding, storing, transporting, or applying anhydrous ammonia. "Unauthorized container" includes, but is not limited to, any propane tank, fire extinguisher, oxygen cylinder, gasoline can, food or beverage cooler, or compressed gas cylinder used in dispensing fountain drinks. "Unauthorized container" does not encompass anhydrous ammonia manufacturing plants, refrigeration systems where anhydrous ammonia is used solely as a refrigerant, anhydrous ammonia transportation pipelines, anhydrous ammonia tankers, or anhydrous ammonia barges.

§ 15. Participation in methamphetamine manufacturing. (a) Participation in methamphetamine manufacturing.

(1) It is unlawful to knowingly participate in the manufacture of methamphetamine with the intent that methamphetamine or a substance containing methamphetamine be produced.

(2) A person who violates paragraph (1) of this subsection (a) is subject to the following penalties:

(A) A person who participates in the manufacture of less than 15 grams of methamphetamine or a substance containing methamphetamine is guilty of a Class 1 felony.

(B) A person who participates in the manufacture of 15 or more grams but less than 100 grams of methamphetamine or a substance containing methamphetamine is guilty of a Class X felony, subject to a term of imprisonment of not less than 6 years and not more than 30 years, and subject to a fine not to exceed $100,000 or the street value of the methamphetamine manufactured, whichever is greater.

(C) A person who participates in the manufacture of 100 or more grams but less than 400 grams of methamphetamine or a substance containing methamphetamine is guilty of a Class X felony, subject to a term of imprisonment of not less than 9 years and not more than 40 years, and subject to a fine not to exceed $200,000 or the street value of the methamphetamine manufactured, whichever is greater.

(D) A person who participates in the manufacture of 400 or more grams but less than 900 grams of methamphetamine or a substance containing methamphetamine is guilty of a Class X felony, subject to a term of imprisonment of not less than 12 years and not more than 50 years, and subject to a fine not to exceed $300,000 or the street value of the methamphetamine manufactured, whichever is greater.

(E) A person who participates in the manufacture of 900 grams or more of methamphetamine or a substance containing methamphetamine is guilty of a Class X felony, subject to a term of imprisonment of not less than 15 years and not more than 60 years, and subject to a fine not to exceed $400,000 or the street value of the methamphetamine, whichever is greater.

(b) Aggravated participation in methamphetamine manufacturing.

(1) It is unlawful to engage in aggravated participation in the manufacture of methamphetamine. A person engages in aggravated participation in the manufacture of methamphetamine when the person violates paragraph (1) of subsection (a) and:

(A) the person knowingly does so in a multi-unit dwelling;

(B) the person knowingly does so in a structure or vehicle where a child under the age of 18, a person with a disability, or a person 60 years of age or older who is incapable of adequately providing for his or her own health and personal care resides, is present, or is endangered by the manufacture of methamphetamine;

(C) the person does so in a structure or vehicle where a woman the person knows to be pregnant (including but not limited to the person herself) resides, is present, or is endangered by the methamphetamine manufacture;

(D) the person knowingly does so in a structure or vehicle protected by one or more firearms, explosive devices, booby traps, alarm systems, surveillance systems, guard dogs, or dangerous animals;

(E) the methamphetamine manufacturing in which the person participates is a contributing cause of the death, serious bodily injury, disability, or disfigurement of another person, including but not limited to an emergency service provider;

(F) the methamphetamine manufacturing in which the person participates is a contributing cause of a fire or explosion that damages property belonging to another person;

(G) the person knowingly organizes, directs, or finances the methamphetamine manufacturing or activities carried out in support of the methamphetamine manufacturing; or

(H) the methamphetamine manufacturing occurs within 1,000 feet of a place of worship or parsonage, or 1000 feet of the real estate comprising a school.

(2) A person who violates paragraph (1) of this subsection (b) is subject to the following penalties:

(A) A person who participates in the manufacture of less than 15 grams of methamphetamine or a substance containing methamphetamine is guilty of a Class X felony, subject to a term of imprisonment of not less than 6 years and not more than 30 years, and subject to a fine not to exceed $100,000 or the street value of the methamphetamine, whichever is greater.

(B) A person who participates in the manufacture of 15 or more grams but less than 100 grams of methamphetamine or a substance containing methamphetamine is guilty of a Class X felony, subject to a term of imprisonment of not less than 9 years and not more than 40 years, and subject to a fine not to exceed $200,000 or the street value of the methamphetamine, whichever is greater.

(C) A person who participates in the manufacture of 100 or more grams but less than 400 grams of methamphetamine or a substance containing methamphetamine is guilty of a Class X felony, subject to a term of imprisonment of not less than 12 years and not more than 50 years, and subject to a fine not to exceed $300,000 or the street value of the methamphetamine, whichever is greater.

(D) A person who participates in the manufacture of 400 grams or more of methamphetamine or a substance containing methamphetamine is guilty of a Class X felony, subject to a term of imprisonment of not less than 15 years and not more than 60 years, and subject to a fine not to exceed $400,000 or the street value of the methamphetamine, whichever is greater.

§ 20. Methamphetamine precursor.
(a) Methamphetamine precursor or substance containing any methamphetamine precursor in standard dosage form.

(1) It is unlawful to knowingly possess, procure, transport, store, or deliver any methamphetamine precursor or substance containing any methamphetamine precursor in standard dosage form with the intent that it be used to manufacture methamphetamine or a substance containing methamphetamine.

(2) A person who violates paragraph (1) of this subsection (a) is subject to the following penalties:

(A) A person who possesses, procures, transports, stores, or delivers less than 15 grams of methamphetamine precursor or substance containing any methamphetamine precursor is guilty of a Class 2 felony.

(B) A person who possesses, procures, transports, stores, or delivers 15 or more grams but less than 30 grams of methamphetamine precursor or substance containing any methamphetamine precursor is guilty of a Class 1 felony.

(C) A person who possesses, procures, transports, stores, or delivers 30 or more grams but less than 150 grams of methamphetamine precursor or substance containing any methamphetamine precursor is guilty of a Class X felony, subject to a term of imprisonment of not less than 6 years and not more than 30 years, and subject to a fine not to exceed $100,000.

(D) A person who possesses, procures, transports, stores, or delivers 150 or more grams but less than 500 grams of methamphetamine precursor or substance containing any methamphetamine precursor is guilty of a Class X felony, subject to a term of imprisonment of not less than 8 years and not more than 40 years, and subject to a fine not to exceed $200,000.

(E) A person who possesses, procures, transports, stores, or delivers 500 or more grams of methamphetamine precursor or substance containing any methamphetamine precursor is guilty of a Class X felony, subject to a term of imprisonment of not less than 10 years and not more than 50 years, and subject to a fine not to exceed $300,000.

(b) Methamphetamine precursor or substance containing any methamphetamine precursor in any form other than a standard dosage form.

(1) It is unlawful to knowingly possess, procure, transport, store, or deliver any methamphetamine precursor or substance containing any methamphetamine precursor in any form other than a standard dosage form with the intent that it be used to manufacture

methamphetamine or a substance containing methamphetamine.

(2) A person who violates paragraph (1) of this subsection (b) is subject to the following penalties:

(A) A person who violates paragraph (1) of this subsection (b) with the intent that less than 10 grams of methamphetamine or a substance containing methamphetamine be manufactured is guilty of a Class 2 felony.

(B) A person who violates paragraph (1) of this subsection (b) with the intent that 10 or more grams but less than 20 grams of methamphetamine or a substance containing methamphetamine be manufactured is guilty of a Class 1 felony.

(C) A person who violates paragraph (1) of this subsection (b) with the intent that 20 or more grams but less than 100 grams of methamphetamine or a substance containing methamphetamine be manufactured is guilty of a Class X felony, subject to a term of imprisonment of not less than 6 years and not more than 30 years, and subject to a fine not to exceed $100,000.

(D) A person who violates paragraph (1) of this subsection (b) with the intent that 100 or more grams but less than 350 grams of methamphetamine or a substance containing methamphetamine be manufactured is guilty of a Class X felony, subject to a term of imprisonment of not less than 8 years and not more than 40 years, and subject to a fine not to exceed $200,000.

(E) A person who violates paragraph (1) of this subsection (b) with the intent that 350 or more grams of methamphetamine or a substance containing methamphetamine be manufactured is guilty of a Class X felony, subject to a term of imprisonment of not less than 10 years and not more than 50 years, and subject to a fine not to exceed $300,000.

(c) Rule of evidence. The presence of any methamphetamine precursor in a sealed, factory imprinted container, including, but not limited to, a bottle, box, package, or blister pack, at the time of seizure by law enforcement, is prima facie evidence that the methamphetamine precursor located within the container is in fact the material so described and in the amount listed on the container. The factory imprinted container is admissible for a violation of this Act for purposes of proving the contents of the container.

§ 25. Anhydrous ammonia. (a) Possession, procurement, transportation, storage, or delivery of anhydrous ammonia with the intent that it be used to manufacture methamphetamine.

(1) It is unlawful to knowingly engage in the possession, procurement, transportation, storage, or delivery of anhydrous ammonia or to attempt to engage in any of these activities or to assist another in engaging in any of these activities with the intent that the anhydrous ammonia be used to manufacture methamphetamine.

(2) A person who violates paragraph (1) of this subsection (a) is guilty of a Class 1 felony.

(b) Aggravated possession, procurement, transportation, storage, or delivery of anhydrous ammonia with the intent that it be used to manufacture methamphetamine.

(1) It is unlawful to knowingly engage in the aggravated possession, procurement, transportation, storage, or delivery of anhydrous ammonia with the intent that it be used to manufacture methamphetamine. A person commits this offense when the person engages in the possession, procurement, transportation, storage, or delivery of anhydrous ammonia or attempts to engage in any of these activities or assists another in engaging in any of these activities with the intent that the anhydrous ammonia be used to manufacture methamphetamine and:

(A) the person knowingly does so in a multi-unit dwelling;

(B) the person knowingly does so in a structure or vehicle where a child under the age of 18, or a person with a disability, or a person who is 60 years of age or older who is incapable of adequately providing for his or her own health and personal care resides, is present, or is endangered by the anhydrous ammonia;

(C) the person's possession, procurement, transportation, storage, or delivery of anhydrous ammonia is a contributing cause of the death, serious bodily injury, disability, or disfigurement of another person; or

(D) the person's possession, procurement, transportation, storage, or delivery of anhydrous ammonia is a contributing cause of a fire or explosion that damages property belonging to another person.

(2) A person who violates paragraph (1) of this subsection (b) is guilty of a Class X felony, subject to a term of imprisonment of not less than 6 years and not more than 30 years, and subject to a fine not to exceed $100,000.

(c) Possession, procurement, transportation, storage, or delivery of anhydrous ammonia in an unauthorized container.

(1) It is unlawful to knowingly possess, procure, transport, store, or deliver anhydrous ammonia in an unauthorized container.

(1.5) It is unlawful to attempt to possess, procure, transport, store, or deliver anhydrous ammonia in an unauthorized container.

(2) A person who violates paragraph (1) of this subsection (c) is guilty of a Class 3 felony. A person who violates paragraph (1.5) of this subsection (c) is guilty of a Class 4 felony.

(3) Affirmative defense. It is an affirmative defense that the person charged possessed, procured, transported, stored, or delivered anhydrous ammonia in a manner that substantially complied with the rules governing anhydrous ammonia equipment found in 8 Illinois Administrative Code Section 215, in 92 Illinois Administrative Code Sections 171 through 180, or in any provision of the Code of Federal Regulations incorporated by reference into these Sections of the Illinois Administrative Code.

(d) Tampering with anhydrous ammonia equipment.

(1) It is unlawful to knowingly tamper with anhydrous ammonia equipment. A person tampers with anhydrous ammonia equipment when, without authorization from the lawful owner, the person:

(A) removes or attempts to remove anhydrous ammonia from the anhydrous ammonia equipment used by the lawful owner;

(B) damages or attempts to damage the anhydrous ammonia equipment used by the lawful owner; or

(C) vents or attempts to vent anhydrous ammonia into the environment.

(2) A person who violates paragraph (1) of this subsection (d) is guilty of a Class 3 felony.

§ 30. Methamphetamine manufacturing material. (a) It is unlawful to knowingly engage in the possession, procurement, transportation, storage, or delivery of any methamphetamine manufacturing material, other than a methamphetamine precursor, substance containing a methamphetamine precursor, or anhydrous ammonia, with the intent that it be used to manufacture methamphetamine.
(b) A person who violates subsection (a) of this Section is guilty of a Class 2 felony.

§ 35. Use of property. (a) It is unlawful for a person knowingly to use or allow the use of a vehicle, a structure, real property, or personal property within the person's control to help bring about a violation of this Act.

(b) A person who violates subsection (a) of this Section is guilty of a Class 2 felony.

§ 40. Protection of methamphetamine manufacturing. (a) It is unlawful to engage in the protection of methamphetamine manufacturing. A person engages in the protection of methamphetamine manufacturing when:

(1) the person knows that others have been participating, are participating, or will be participating in the manufacture of methamphetamine; and

(2) with the intent to help prevent detection of or interference with the methamphetamine manufacturing, the person serves as a lookout for or guard of the methamphetamine manufacturing.

(b) A person who violates subsection (a) of this Section is guilty of a Class 2 felony.

§ 45. Methamphetamine manufacturing waste. (a) It is unlawful to knowingly burn, place in a trash receptacle, or dispose of methamphetamine manufacturing waste, knowing that the waste was used in the manufacturing of methamphetamine.

(b) A person who violates subsection (a) of this Section is guilty of a Class 2 felony.

§ 50. Methamphetamine-related child endangerment. (a) Methamphetamine-related child endangerment.

(1) It is unlawful to engage in methamphetamine-related child endangerment. A person engages in methamphetamine-related child endangerment when the person knowingly endangers the life and health of a child by exposing or allowing exposure of the child to a methamphetamine manufacturing environment.

(2) A person who violates paragraph (1) of this subsection (a) is guilty of a Class 2 felony.

(b) Aggravated methamphetamine-related child endangerment.

(1) It is unlawful to engage in aggravated methamphetamine-related child endangerment. A person engages in aggravated methamphetamine-related child endangerment when the person violates paragraph (1) of this subsection (a) of this Section and the child experiences death, great bodily harm, disability, or disfigurement as a result of the methamphetamine-related child endangerment.

(2) A person who violates paragraph (1) of this subsection (b) is guilty of a Class X felony, subject to a term of imprisonment of not less than 6 years and not more than 30 years, and subject to a fine not to exceed $100,000.

§ 55. Methamphetamine delivery. (a) Delivery or possession with intent to deliver methamphetamine or a substance containing methamphetamine.

(1) It is unlawful knowingly to engage in the delivery or possession with intent to deliver methamphetamine or a substance containing methamphetamine.

(2) A person who violates paragraph (1) of this subsection (a) is subject to the following penalties:

(A) A person who delivers or possesses with intent to deliver less than 5 grams of methamphetamine or a substance containing methamphetamine is guilty of a Class 2 felony.

(B) A person who delivers or possesses with intent to deliver 5 or more grams but less than 15 grams of methamphetamine or a substance containing methamphetamine is guilty of a Class 1 felony.

(C) A person who delivers or possesses with intent to deliver 15 or more grams but less than 100 grams of methamphetamine or a substance containing methamphetamine is guilty of a Class X felony, subject to a term of imprisonment of not less than 6 years and not more than 30 years, and subject to a fine not to exceed $100,000 or the street value of the methamphetamine, whichever is greater.

(D) A person who delivers or possesses with intent to deliver 100 or more grams but less than 400 grams of methamphetamine or a substance containing methamphetamine is guilty of a Class X felony, subject to a term of imprisonment of not less than 9 years and not more than 40 years, and subject to a fine not to exceed $200,000 or the street value of the methamphetamine, whichever is greater.

(E) A person who delivers or possesses with intent to deliver 400 or more grams but less than 900 grams of methamphetamine or a substance containing methamphetamine is guilty of a Class X felony, subject to a term of imprisonment of not less than 12 years and not more than 50 years, and subject to a fine not to exceed $300,000 or the street value of the methamphetamine, whichever is greater.

(F) A person who delivers or possesses with intent to deliver 900 or more grams of methamphetamine or a substance containing methamphetamine is guilty of a Class X felony, subject to a term of imprisonment of not less than 15 years and not more than 60 years, and subject to a fine not to exceed $400,000 or the street value of the methamphetamine, whichever is greater.

(b) Aggravated delivery or possession with intent to deliver methamphetamine or a substance containing methamphetamine.

(1) It is unlawful to engage in the aggravated delivery or possession with intent to deliver methamphetamine or a substance containing methamphetamine. A person engages in the aggravated delivery or possession with intent to deliver methamphetamine or a substance containing methamphetamine when the person violates paragraph (1) of subsection (a) of this Section and:

(A) the person is at least 18 years of age and knowingly delivers or possesses with intent to deliver the methamphetamine or substance containing methamphetamine to a person under 18 years of age;

(B) the person is at least 18 years of age and knowingly uses, engages, employs, or causes another person to use, engage, or employ a person under 18 years of age to deliver the methamphetamine or substance containing methamphetamine;

(C) the person knowingly delivers or possesses with intent to deliver the methamphetamine or substance containing methamphetamine in any structure or vehicle protected by one or more firearms, explosive devices, booby traps, alarm systems, surveillance systems, guard dogs, or dangerous animals;

(D) the person knowingly delivers or possesses with intent to deliver the methamphetamine or substance containing methamphetamine in any school, on any real property comprising any school, or in any conveyance owned, leased, or contracted by a school to transport students to or from school or a school-related activity;

(E) the person delivers or causes another person to deliver the methamphetamine or substance containing methamphetamine to a woman that the person knows to be pregnant; or

(F) (blank).

(2) A person who violates paragraph (1) of this subsection (b) is subject to the following penalties:

(A) A person who delivers or possesses with intent to deliver less than 5 grams of methamphetamine or a substance containing methamphetamine is guilty of a Class 1 felony.

(B) A person who delivers or possesses with intent to deliver 5 or more grams but less than 15 grams of methamphetamine or a substance containing methamphetamine is guilty of a Class X felony, subject to a term of imprisonment of not less than 6 years and not more than 30 years, and subject to a fine not to exceed $100,000 or the street value of the methamphetamine, whichever is greater.

(C) A person who delivers or possesses with intent to deliver 15 or more grams but less than 100 grams of methamphetamine or a substance containing methamphetamine is guilty of a Class X felony, subject to a term of imprisonment of not less than 8 years and not more than 40 years, and subject to a fine not to exceed $200,000 or the street value of the methamphetamine, whichever is greater.

(D) A person who delivers or possesses with intent to deliver 100 or more grams of methamphetamine or a substance containing methamphetamine is guilty of a Class X felony, subject to a term of imprisonment of not less than 10 years and not more than 50 years, and subject to a fine not to exceed $300,000 or the street value of the methamphetamine, whichever is greater.

§ 56. Methamphetamine trafficking.
(a) Except for purposes as authorized by this Act, any person who knowingly brings, or causes to be brought, into this State methamphetamine, anhydrous ammonia, or a methamphetamine precursor for the purpose of manufacture or delivery of methamphetamine or with the intent to manufacture or deliver methamphetamine is guilty of methamphetamine trafficking.

(b) A person convicted of methamphetamine trafficking shall be sentenced to a term of imprisonment of not less than twice the minimum term and not more than twice the maximum term of imprisonment based upon the amount of methamphetamine brought or caused to be brought into this State, as provided in subsection (a) of Section 55 of this Act.

(c) A person convicted of methamphetamine trafficking based upon a methamphetamine precursor shall be sentenced to a term of imprisonment of not less than twice the minimum term and not more than twice the maximum term of imprisonment based upon the amount of methamphetamine precursor provided in subsection (a) or (b) of Section 20 of this Act brought or caused to be brought into this State.

(d) A person convicted of methamphetamine trafficking based upon anhydrous ammonia under paragraph (1) of subsection (a) of Section 25 of this Act shall be sentenced to a term of imprisonment of not less than twice the minimum term and not more than twice the maximum term of imprisonment provided in paragraph (1) of subsection (a) of Section 25 of this Act.

§ 60. Methamphetamine possession. (a) It is unlawful knowingly to possess methamphetamine or a substance containing methamphetamine.

(b) A person who violates subsection (a) is subject to the following penalties:

(1) A person who possesses less than 5 grams of methamphetamine or a substance containing methamphetamine is guilty of a Class 3 felony.
(2) A person who possesses 5 or more grams but less than 15 grams of methamphetamine or a substance containing methamphetamine is guilty of a Class 2 felony.

(3) A person who possesses 15 or more grams but less than 100 grams of methamphetamine or a substance containing methamphetamine is guilty of a Class 1 felony.

(4) A person who possesses 100 or more grams but less than 400 grams of methamphetamine or a substance containing methamphetamine is guilty of a Class X felony, subject to a term of imprisonment of not less than 6 years and not more than 30 years, and subject to a fine not to exceed $100,000.

(5) A person who possesses 400 or more grams but less than 900 grams of methamphetamine or a substance containing methamphetamine is guilty of a Class X felony, subject to a term of imprisonment of not less than 8 years and not more than 40 years, and subject to a fine not to exceed $200,000.

(6) A person who possesses 900 or more grams of methamphetamine or a substance containing methamphetamine is guilty of a Class X felony, subject to a term of imprisonment of not less than 10 years and not more than 50 years, and subject to a fine not to exceed $300,000.

§ 65. Methamphetamine conspiracy. (a) It is unlawful to engage in a methamphetamine conspiracy. A person engages in a methamphetamine conspiracy when:

(1) the person intends to violate one or more provisions of this Act;

(2) the person agrees with one or more persons to violate one or more provisions of this Act; and

(3) the person or any party to the agreement commits an act in furtherance of the agreement.

(b) A person convicted of engaging in a methamphetamine conspiracy shall face the penalty for the offense that is the object of the conspiracy and may be held accountable for the cumulative weight of any methamphetamine, substance containing methamphetamine, methamphetamine precursor, or substance containing methamphetamine precursor attributable to the conspiracy for the duration of the conspiracy.

(c) It is not a defense to a methamphetamine conspiracy charge that the person or persons with whom the person charged is alleged to have conspired have not been prosecuted or convicted, have been acquitted, have been convicted of a different offense, are not amenable to justice, or lacked the capacity to commit the offense.

(d) When any person is convicted under this Section of engaging in a methamphetamine conspiracy, the following shall be subject to forfeiture to the State of Illinois: the receipts the person obtained in the conspiracy and any of the person's interests in, claims against, receipts from, or property or rights of any kind affording a source of influence over, the conspiracy. The circuit court may enter such injunctions, restraining orders, directions, or prohibitions, or take such other actions, including the acceptance of satisfactory performance bonds, in connection with any property, claim, receipt, right, or other interest subject to forfeiture under this Section, as it deems proper.

§ 70. Probation. (a) Whenever any person who has not previously been convicted of, or placed on probation or court supervision for any offense under this Act, the Illinois Controlled Substances Act, the Cannabis Control Act, or any law of the United States or of any state relating to cannabis or controlled substances, pleads guilty to or is found guilty of possession of less than 15 grams of methamphetamine under paragraph (1) or (2) of subsection (b) of Section 60 of this Act, the court, without entering a judgment and with the consent of the person, may sentence him or her to probation.

(b) When a person is placed on probation, the court shall enter an order specifying a period of probation of 24 months and shall defer further proceedings in the case until the conclusion of the period or until the filing of a petition alleging violation of a term or condition of probation.

(c) The conditions of probation shall be that the person:

(1) not violate any criminal statute of any jurisdiction;

(2) refrain from possessing a firearm or other dangerous weapon;

(3) submit to periodic drug testing at a time and in a manner as ordered by the court, but no less than 3 times during the period of the probation, with the cost of the testing to be paid by the probationer; and

(4) perform no less than 30 hours of community service, if community service is available in the jurisdiction and is funded and approved by the county board.

(d) The court may, in addition to other conditions, require that the person take one or more of the following actions:

(1) make a report to and appear in person before or participate with the court or such courts, person, or social service agency as directed by the court in the order of probation;

(2) pay a fine and costs;

(3) work or pursue a course of study or vocational training;

(4) undergo medical or psychiatric treatment; or treatment or rehabilitation approved by the Illinois Department of Human Services;

(5) attend or reside in a facility established for the instruction or residence of defendants on probation;

(6) support his or her dependents;

(7) refrain from having in his or her body the presence of any illicit drug prohibited by this Act, the Cannabis Control Act, or the Illinois Controlled Substances Act, unless prescribed by a physician, and submit samples of his or her blood or urine or both for tests to determine the presence of any illicit drug; or

(8) if a minor:

(i) reside with his or her parents or in a foster home;

(ii) attend school;

(iii) attend a non-residential program for youth; or

(iv) contribute to his or her own support at home or in a foster home.

(e) Upon violation of a term or condition of probation, the court may enter a judgment on its original finding of guilt and proceed as otherwise provided.

(f) Upon fulfillment of the terms and conditions of probation, the court shall discharge the person and dismiss the proceedings against the person.

(g) A disposition of probation is considered to be a conviction for the purposes of imposing the conditions of probation and for appeal, however, discharge and dismissal under this Section is not a conviction for purposes of this Act or for purposes of disqualifications or disabilities imposed by law upon conviction of a crime.

(h) There may be only one discharge and dismissal under this Section, Section 410 of the Illinois Controlled Substances Act, or Section 10 of the Cannabis Control Act with respect to any person.

(i) If a person is convicted of an offense under this Act, the Cannabis Control Act, or the Illinois Controlled Substances Act within 5 years subsequent to a discharge and dismissal under this Section, the discharge and dismissal under this Section are admissible in the sentencing proceeding for that conviction as evidence in aggravation.

§ 75. Fines. (a) Whenever any person pleads guilty to, is found guilty of, or is placed on supervision for an offense under this Act, a fine may be levied in addition to any other penalty imposed by the court.

(b) In determining whether to impose a fine under this Section and the amount, time for payment, and method of payment of any fine so imposed, the court shall:

(1) consider the defendant's income, regardless of source, the defendant's earning capacity and the defendant's financial resources, as well as the nature of the burden the fine will impose on the defendant and any person legally or financially dependent upon the defendant;

(2) consider the proof received at trial, or as a result of a plea of guilty, concerning the full street value of the controlled substances seized and any profits or other proceeds derived by the defendant from the violation of this Act;

(3) take into account any other pertinent equitable considerations; and

(4) give primary consideration to the need to deprive the defendant of illegally obtained profits or other proceeds from the offense.

For the purpose of paragraph (2) of this subsection (b), "street value" shall be determined by the court on the basis of testimony of law enforcement personnel and the defendant as to the amount seized and such testimony as may be required by the court as to the current street value of the controlled substances.

(c) As a condition of a fine, the court may require that payment be made in specified installments or within a specified period of time, but the period shall not be greater than the maximum applicable term of probation or imprisonment, whichever is greater. Unless otherwise specified, payment of a fine shall be due immediately.

(d) If a fine for a violation of this Act is imposed on an organization, it is the duty of each individual authorized to make disbursements of the assets of the organization to pay the fine from the assets of the organization.

(e) A defendant who has been sentenced to pay a fine, and who has paid part but not all of the fine, may petition the court for an extension of the time for payment or modification of the method of payment. The court may grant the petition if it finds that:

(1) the circumstances that warranted payment by the time or method specified no longer exist; or
(2) it is otherwise unjust to require payment of the fine by the time or method specified.

§ 80. Assessment. (a) Every person convicted of a violation of this Act, and every person placed on probation, conditional discharge, supervision, or probation under this Act, shall be assessed for each offense a sum fixed at:

(1) $3,000 for a Class X felony;

(2) $2,000 for a Class 1 felony;

(3) $1,000 for a Class 2 felony;

(4) $500 for a Class 3 or Class 4 felony.

(b) The assessment under this Section is in addition to and not in lieu of any fines, restitution, costs, forfeitures, or other assessments authorized or required by law.

(c) As a condition of the assessment, the court may require that payment be made in specified installments or within a specified period of time. If the assessment is not paid within the period of probation, conditional discharge, or supervision to which the defendant was originally sentenced, the court may extend the period of probation, conditional discharge, or supervision pursuant to Section 5-6-2 or 5-6-3.1 of the Unified Code of Corrections, as applicable, until the assessment is paid or until successful completion of public or community service set forth in subsection (e) or the successful completion of the substance abuse intervention or treatment program set forth in subsection (f). If a term of probation, conditional discharge, or supervision is not imposed, the assessment shall be payable upon judgment or as directed by the court.

(d) If an assessment for a violation of this Act is imposed on an organization, it is the duty of each individual authorized to make disbursements of the assets of the organization to pay the assessment from assets of the organization.

(e) A defendant who has been ordered to pay an assessment may petition the court to convert all or part of the assessment into court-approved public or community service. One hour of public or community service shall be equivalent to $4 of assessment. The performance of this public or community service shall be a condition of the probation, conditional discharge, or supervision and shall be in addition to the performance of any other period of public or community service ordered by the court or required by law.

(f) The court may suspend the collection of the assessment imposed under this Section if the defendant agrees to enter a substance abuse intervention or treatment program approved by the court and the defendant agrees to pay for all or some portion of the costs associated with the intervention or treatment program. In this case, the collection of the assessment imposed under this Section shall be suspended during the defendant's participation in the approved intervention or treatment program. Upon successful completion of the program, the defendant may apply to the court to reduce the assessment imposed under this Section by any amount actually paid by the defendant for his or her participation in the program. The court shall not reduce the penalty under this subsection unless the defendant establishes to the satisfaction of the court that he or she has successfully completed the intervention or

treatment program. If the defendant's participation is for any reason terminated before his or her successful completion of the intervention or treatment program, collection of the entire assessment imposed under this Section shall be enforced. Nothing in this Section shall be deemed to affect or suspend any other fines, restitution costs, forfeitures, or assessments imposed under this or any other Act.
(g) The court shall not impose more than one assessment per complaint, indictment, or information. If the person is convicted of more than one offense in a complaint, indictment, or information, the assessment shall be based on the highest class offense for which the person is convicted.

(h) In counties with a population under 3,000,000, all moneys collected under this Section shall be forwarded by the clerk of the circuit court to the State Treasurer for deposit in the Drug Treatment Fund. The Department of Human Services may make grants to persons licensed under Section 15-10 of the Alcoholism and Other Drug Abuse and Dependency Act or to municipalities or counties from funds appropriated to the Department from the Drug Treatment Fund for the treatment of pregnant women who are addicted to alcohol, cannabis or controlled substances and for the needed care of minor, unemancipated children of women undergoing residential drug treatment. If the Department of Human Services grants funds to a municipality or a county that the Department determines is not experiencing a problem with pregnant women addicted to alcohol, cannabis or controlled substances, or with care for minor, unemancipated children of women undergoing residential drug treatment, or intervention, the funds shall be used for the treatment of any person addicted to alcohol, cannabis, or controlled substances. The Department may adopt such rules as it deems appropriate for the administration of such grants.

(i) In counties with a population of 3,000,000 or more, all moneys collected under this Section shall be forwarded to the County Treasurer for deposit into the County Health Fund. The County Treasurer shall, no later than the 15th day of each month, forward to the State Treasurer 30 percent of all moneys collected under this Act and received into the County Health Fund since the prior remittance to the State Treasurer. Funds retained by the County shall be used for community-based treatment of pregnant women who are addicted to alcohol, cannabis, or controlled substances or for the needed care of minor, unemancipated children of these women. Funds forwarded to the State Treasurer shall be deposited into the State Drug Treatment Fund maintained by the State Treasurer from which the Department of Human Services may make grants to persons licensed under Section 15-10 of the Alcoholism and Other Drug Abuse and Dependency Act or to municipalities or counties from funds appropriated to the Department from the Drug Treatment Fund, provided that the moneys collected from each county be returned proportionately to the counties through grants to licensees located within the county from which the assessment was received and moneys in the State Drug Treatment Fund shall not supplant other local, State or federal funds. If the Department of Human Services grants funds to a municipality or county that the Department determines is not experiencing a problem with pregnant women addicted to alcohol, cannabis or controlled substances, or with care for minor, unemancipated children or women undergoing residential drug treatment, the funds shall be used for the treatment of any person addicted to alcohol, cannabis or controlled substances. The Department may adopt such rules as it deems appropriate for the administration of such grants.

§ 85. Forfeiture. (a) The following are subject to forfeiture:

(1) all substances containing methamphetamine which have been produced, manufactured, delivered, or possessed in violation of this Act;

(2) all methamphetamine manufacturing materials which have been produced, delivered, or possessed in connection with any substance containing methamphetamine in violation of this Act;

(3) all conveyances, including aircraft, vehicles or vessels, which are used, or intended for use,

to transport, or in any manner to facilitate the transportation, sale, receipt, possession, or concealment of property described in paragraph (1) or (2) that constitutes a felony violation of the Act, but:

(i) no conveyance used by any person as a common carrier in the transaction of business as a common carrier is subject to forfeiture under this Section unless it appears that the owner or other person in charge of the conveyance is a consenting party or privy to a violation of this Act;

(ii) no conveyance is subject to forfeiture under this Section by reason of any act or omission which the owner proves to have been committed or omitted without his or her knowledge or consent;

(iii) a forfeiture of a conveyance encumbered by a bona fide security interest is subject to the interest of the secured party if he or she neither had knowledge of nor consented to the act or omission;

(4) all money, things of value, books, records, and research products and materials including formulas, microfilm, tapes, and data which are used, or intended for use in a felony violation of this Act;

(5) everything of value furnished or intended to be furnished by any person in exchange for a substance in violation of this Act, all proceeds traceable to such an exchange, and all moneys, negotiable instruments, and securities used, or intended to be used, to commit or in any manner to facilitate any felony violation of this Act.

(6) all real property, including any right, title, and interest (including, but not limited to, any leasehold interest or the beneficial interest in a land trust) in the whole of any lot or tract of land and any appurtenances or improvements, which is used, or intended to be used, in any manner or part, to commit, or in any manner to facilitate the commission of, any violation or act that constitutes a violation of this Act or that is the proceeds of any violation or act that constitutes a violation of this Act.

(b) Property subject to forfeiture under this Act may be seized by the Director or any peace officer upon process or seizure warrant issued by any court having jurisdiction over the property. Seizure by the Director or any peace officer without process may be made:

(1) if the property subject to seizure has been the subject of a prior judgment in favor of the State in a criminal proceeding or in an injunction or forfeiture proceeding based upon this Act or the Drug Asset Forfeiture Procedure Act;

(2) if there is probable cause to believe that the property is directly or indirectly dangerous to health or safety;

(3) if there is probable cause to believe that the property is subject to forfeiture under this Act and the property is seized under circumstances in which a warrantless seizure or arrest would be reasonable; or

(4) in accordance with the Code of Criminal Procedure of 1963.

(c) In the event of seizure pursuant to subsection (b), notice shall be given forthwith to all known interest holders that forfeiture proceedings, including a preliminary review, shall be instituted in accordance with the Drug Asset Forfeiture Procedure Act and such proceedings shall thereafter be instituted in accordance with that Act. Upon a showing of good cause, the notice required for a preliminary review under this section may be postponed.

(d) Property taken or detained under this Section is not subject to replevin, but is deemed to be in the custody of the Director subject only to the order and judgments of the circuit court having jurisdiction over the forfeiture proceedings and the decisions of the State's Attorney under the Drug Asset Forfeiture Procedure Act. When property is seized under this Act, the seizing agency shall promptly conduct an inventory of the seized property, estimate the property's value, and forward a copy of the inventory of seized property and the estimate of the property's value to the Director. Upon receiving notice of seizure, the Director may:

(1) place the property under seal;

(2) remove the property to a place designated by him or her;

(3) keep the property in the possession of the seizing agency;

(4) remove the property to a storage area for safekeeping or, if the property is a negotiable instrument or money and is not needed for evidentiary purposes, deposit it in an interest bearing account;

(5) place the property under constructive seizure by posting notice of pending forfeiture on it, by giving notice of pending forfeiture to its owners and interest holders, or by filing notice of pending forfeiture in any appropriate public record relating to the property; or

(6) provide for another agency or custodian, including an owner, secured party, or lienholder, to take custody of the property upon the terms and conditions set by the Director.

(e) No disposition may be made of property under seal until the time for taking an appeal has elapsed or until all appeals have been concluded unless a court, upon application therefore, orders the sale of perishable substances and the deposit of the proceeds of the sale with the court.

(f) When property is forfeited under this Act, the Director shall sell the property unless the property is required by law to be destroyed or is harmful to the public, and shall distribute the proceeds of the sale, together with any moneys forfeited or seized, in accordance with subsection (g). However, upon the application of the seizing agency or prosecutor who was responsible for the investigation, arrest or arrests and prosecution which lead to the forfeiture, the Director may return any item of forfeited property to the seizing agency or prosecutor for official use in the enforcement of laws relating to methamphetamine, cannabis, or controlled substances, if the agency or prosecutor demonstrates that the item requested would be useful to the agency or prosecutor in their enforcement efforts. When any forfeited conveyance, including an aircraft, vehicle, or vessel, is returned to the seizing agency or prosecutor, the conveyance may be used immediately in the enforcement of the criminal laws of this State. Upon disposal, all proceeds from the sale of the conveyance must be used for drug enforcement purposes. When any real property returned to the seizing agency is sold by the agency or its unit of government, the proceeds of the sale shall be delivered to the Director and distributed in accordance with subsection (g).

(g) All moneys and the sale proceeds of all other property forfeited and seized under this Act shall be distributed as follows:

(1) 65% shall be distributed to the metropolitan enforcement group, local, municipal, county, or State law enforcement agency or agencies which conducted or participated in the investigation resulting in the forfeiture. The distribution shall bear a reasonable relationship to the degree of direct participation of the law enforcement agency in the effort resulting in the forfeiture, taking into account the total value of the property forfeited and the total law enforcement effort with respect to the violation of the law upon which the forfeiture is based. Amounts distributed to the agency or agencies shall be used for the enforcement of laws governing methamphetamine, cannabis, and controlled substances or for security cameras used for the prevention or detection of violence, except that amounts distributed to the Secretary of State shall be deposited into the Secretary of State Evidence Fund to be used as provided in Section 2-115 of the Illinois Vehicle Code.

(2)(i) 12.5% shall be distributed to the Office of the State's Attorney of the county in which the prosecution resulting in the forfeiture was instituted, deposited in a special fund in the county treasury and appropriated to the State's Attorney for use in the enforcement of laws governing methamphetamine, cannabis, and controlled substances. In counties with a population over 3,000,000, 25% shall be distributed to the Office of the State's Attorney for use in the enforcement of laws governing methamphetamine, cannabis, and controlled substances. If the prosecution is undertaken solely by the Attorney General, the portion provided hereunder shall be distributed to the Attorney General for use in the enforcement of laws governing methamphetamine, cannabis, and controlled substances.

(ii) 12.5% shall be distributed to the Office of the State's Attorneys Appellate Prosecutor and deposited in the Narcotics Profit Forfeiture Fund of that Office to be used for additional expenses incurred in the investigation, prosecution and appeal of cases arising under laws governing methamphetamine, cannabis, and controlled substances. The Office of the State's Attorneys Appellate Prosecutor shall not receive distribution from cases brought in counties with a population over 3,000,000.

(3) 10% shall be retained by the Department of State Police for expenses related to the administration and sale of seized and forfeited property.

§ 90. Methamphetamine restitution.
(a) If a person commits a violation of this Act in a manner that requires an emergency response, the person shall be required to make restitution to all public entities involved in the emergency response, to cover the reasonable cost of their participation in the emergency response, including but not limited to regular and overtime costs incurred by local law enforcement agencies and private contractors paid by the public agencies in securing the site. The convicted person shall make this restitution in addition to any other fine or penalty required by law.

(b) Any restitution payments made under this Section shall be disbursed equitably by the circuit clerk in the following order:

(1) first, to the local agencies involved in the emergency response;
(2) second, to the State agencies involved in the emergency response; and
(3) third, to the federal agencies involved in the emergency response.

§ 100. Second or subsequent offenses.
(a) Any person convicted of a second or subsequent offense under this Act may be sentenced to imprisonment for a term up to twice the maximum term otherwise authorized, fined an amount up to twice that otherwise authorized, or both.

(b) Any penalty imposed for any violation of this Act is in addition to, and not in lieu of, any civil or administrative penalty or sanction otherwise authorized by this Act or any other law.

§ 105. Applicability. A prosecution for any violation of law occurring prior to the effective date of this Act is not affected or abated by this Act. If the offense being prosecuted would be a violation of this Act, and has not reached the sentencing stage or final adjudication, then for purposes of penalty the penalties under this Act apply if they are less than under the prior law upon which the prosecution was commenced.

§ 110. Scope of Act. Nothing in this Act limits any authority or activity authorized by the Illinois Controlled Substances Act, the Medical Practice Act of 1987, the Nurse Practice Act, the Pharmacy Practice Act, the Illinois Dental Practice Act, the Podiatric Medical Practice Act of 1987, or the Veterinary Medicine and Surgery Practice Act of 2004. Nothing in this Act limits the authority or activity of any law enforcement officer acting within the scope of his or her employment.

§ 9999. Effective date. This Act takes effect 30 days after becoming law.

Act 648. Methamphetamine Precursor Control Act – Selected Provisions

§ 1. Short title. This Act may be cited as the Methamphetamine Precursor Control Act.

§ 5. Purpose. The purpose of this Act is to reduce the harm that methamphetamine manufacturing and manufacturers are inflicting on individuals, families, communities, first responders, the economy, and the environment in Illinois, by making it more difficult for persons engaged in the unlawful manufacture of methamphetamine and related activities to obtain methamphetamine's essential ingredient, ephedrine or pseudoephedrine. It is the intent of the General Assembly that this Act operate in tandem with and be interpreted as consistent with federal laws and regulations relating to the subject matter of this Act to the greatest extent possible.

§ 10. Definitions. In this Act:

"Administer" or "administration" has the meaning provided in Section 102 of the Illinois Controlled Substances Act.

"Agent" has the meaning provided in Section 102 of the Illinois Controlled Substances Act.

"Authorized representative" means an employee or agent of a qualified outside entity who has been authorized in writing by his or her agency or office to receive confidential information from the Central Repository.

"Central Repository" means the entity chosen by the Illinois State Police to handle electronic transaction records as described in this Act.

"Convenience package" means any package that contains 360 milligrams or less of ephedrine or pseudoephedrine, their salts or optical isomers, or salts of optical isomers in liquid or liquid-filled capsule form.

"Covered pharmacy" means any pharmacy that distributes any amount of targeted methamphetamine precursor that is physically located in Illinois.

"Deliver" has the meaning provided in Section 102 of the Illinois Controlled Substances Act.

"Dispense" has the meaning provided in Section 102 of the Illinois Controlled Substances Act.

"Distribute" has the meaning provided in Section 102 of the Illinois Controlled Substances Act.

"Electronic transaction record" means, with respect to the distribution of a targeted methamphetamine precursor by a pharmacy to a recipient under Section 25 of this Act, an electronic record that includes: the name and address of the recipient; date and time of the transaction; brand and product name and total quantity distributed of ephedrine or pseudoephedrine, their salts, or optical isomers, or salts of optical isomers; identification type and identification number of the identification presented by the recipient; and the name and address of the pharmacy.

"Identification information" means identification type and identification number.

"Identification number" means the number that appears on the identification furnished by the recipient of a targeted methamphetamine precursor.

"Identification type" means the type of identification furnished by the recipient of a targeted methamphetamine precursor such as, by way of example only, an Illinois driver's license or United States passport.

"List I chemical" has the meaning provided in 21 U.S.C. Section 802.

"Methamphetamine precursor" has the meaning provided in Section 10 of the Methamphetamine Control and Community Protection Act.

"Package" means an item packaged and marked for retail sale that is not designed to be further broken down or subdivided for the purpose of retail sale.

"Pharmacist" has the meaning provided in Section 102 of the Illinois Controlled Substances Act.

"Pharmacy" has the meaning provided in Section 102 of the Illinois Controlled Substances Act.
"Practitioner" has the meaning provided in Section 102 of the Illinois Controlled Substances Act.

"Prescriber" has the meaning provided in Section 102 of the Illinois Controlled Substances Act.

"Prescription" has the meaning provided in Section 102 of the Illinois Controlled Substances Act.

"Qualified outside entity" means a law enforcement agency or prosecutor's office with authority to identify, investigate, or prosecute violations of this Act or any other State or federal law or rule involving a methamphetamine precursor, methamphetamine, or any other controlled substance.

"Readily retrievable" has the meaning provided in 21 C.F.R. part 1300.

"Recipient" means a person purchasing, receiving, or otherwise acquiring a targeted methamphetamine precursor from a pharmacy in Illinois, as described in Section 25 of this Act.

"Retail distributor" means a grocery store, general merchandise store, drug store, other merchandise store, or other entity or person whose activities as a distributor relating to drug products containing targeted methamphetamine precursor are limited exclusively or almost exclusively to sales for personal use by an ultimate user, both in number of sales and volume of sales, either directly to walk-in customers or in face-to-face transactions by direct sales.

"Sales employee" means any employee or agent, other than a pharmacist or pharmacy technician who at any time (a) operates a cash register at which convenience packages may be sold, (b) stocks shelves containing convenience packages, or (c) trains or supervises any other employee or agent who engages in any of the preceding activities.

"Single retail transaction" means a sale by a retail distributor to a recipient at a specific time.
"Targeted methamphetamine precursor" means any compound, mixture, or preparation that contains any detectable quantity of ephedrine or pseudoephedrine, their salts or optical isomers, or salts of optical isomers.

"Targeted package" means a package, including a convenience package, containing any amount of targeted methamphetamine precursor.

"Ultimate user" has the meaning provided in Section 102 of the Illinois Controlled Substances Act.

§ 15. Basic provisions. (a) No targeted methamphetamine precursor shall be purchased, received, or otherwise acquired in any manner other than that described in Section 20 of this Act.

(b) No targeted methamphetamine precursor shall be knowingly administered, dispensed, or distributed for any purpose other than a medical purpose.

(c) No targeted methamphetamine precursor shall be knowingly administered, dispensed, or distributed for the purpose of violating or evading this Act, the Illinois Controlled Substances Act, or the Methamphetamine Control and Community Protection Act.

(d) No targeted methamphetamine precursor shall be administered, dispensed, or distributed with knowledge that it will be used to manufacture methamphetamine or with reckless disregard of its likely use to manufacture methamphetamine.

(e) No targeted methamphetamine precursor shall be administered, dispensed, or distributed except by:

(1) a pharmacist pursuant to the valid order of a prescriber;

(2) any other practitioner authorized to do so by the Illinois Controlled Substances Act;

(3) a drug abuse treatment program, pursuant to subsection (d) of Section 313 of the Illinois Controlled Substances Act;

(4) a pharmacy pursuant to Section 25 of this Act;

(5) a retail distributor pursuant to Sections 30 and 35 of this Act; or

(6) a distributor authorized by the Drug Enforcement Administration to distribute bulk quantities of a list I chemical under the federal Controlled Substances Act and corresponding regulations, or the employee or agent of such a distributor acting in the normal course of business.

(f) Notwithstanding any provision of this Act to the contrary, it is lawful for persons to provide small quantities of targeted methamphetamine precursors to immediate family or household members for legitimate medical purposes, and it is lawful for persons to receive small quantities of targeted methamphetamine precursors from immediate family or household members for legitimate medical purposes.

§ 20. Restrictions on purchase, receipt, or acquisition. (a) Except as provided in subsection (e) of this Section, any person 18 years of age or older wishing to purchase, receive, or otherwise acquire a targeted methamphetamine precursor shall, prior to taking possession of the targeted methamphetamine precursor:

(1) provide a driver's license or other government-issued identification showing the person's name, date of birth, and photograph; and

(2) sign a log documenting the name and address of the person, date and time of the transaction, and brand and product name and total quantity distributed of ephedrine or pseudoephedrine, their salts, or optical isomers, or salts of optical isomers.

(b) Except as provided in subsection (e) of this Section, no person shall knowingly purchase, receive, or otherwise acquire, within any 30-day period products containing more than a total of 7,500 milligrams of ephedrine or pseudoephedrine, their salts or optical isomers, or salts of optical isomers.

(c) Except as provided in subsections (d) and (e) of this Section, no person shall knowingly purchase, receive, or otherwise acquire more than 2 targeted packages in a single retail transaction.

(d) Except as provided in subsection (e) of this Section, no person shall knowingly purchase, receive, or otherwise acquire more than one convenience package from a retail location other than a pharmacy counter in a 24-hour period.

(e) This Section shall not apply to any person who purchases, receives, or otherwise acquires a targeted methamphetamine precursor for the purpose of dispensing, distributing, or administering it in a lawful manner described in subsection (e) of Section 15 of this Act.

(f) A person shall not knowingly procure a targeted methamphetamine precursor for a third party for the purpose of evading this Act, the Illinois Controlled Substances Act, or the Methamphetamine Control and Community Protection Act.

§ 25. Pharmacies. (a) No targeted methamphetamine precursor may be knowingly distributed through a pharmacy, including a pharmacy located within, owned by, operated by, or associated with a retail distributor unless all terms of this Section are satisfied.

(b) Any targeted methamphetamine precursor other than a convenience package or a liquid, including but not limited to any targeted methamphetamine precursor in liquid-filled capsules, shall: be packaged in blister packs, with each blister containing not more than 2 dosage units, or when the use of blister packs is technically infeasible, in unit dose packets. Each targeted package shall contain no more than 3,000 milligrams of ephedrine or pseudoephedrine, their salts or optical isomers, or salts of optical isomers.

(c) The targeted methamphetamine precursor shall be stored behind the pharmacy counter and distributed by a pharmacist or pharmacy technician licensed under the Pharmacy Practice Act, or by an agent of the pharmacist or pharmacy technician.
(d) Any retail distributor operating a pharmacy, and any pharmacist or pharmacy technician involved in the transaction or transactions, shall ensure that any person purchasing, receiving, or otherwise acquiring the targeted methamphetamine precursor complies with subsection (a) of Section 20 of this Act.

(e) Any retail distributor operating a pharmacy, and any pharmacist or pharmacy technician involved in the transaction or transactions, shall verify that:
(1) The person purchasing, receiving, or otherwise acquiring the targeted methamphetamine precursor is 18 years of age or older and resembles the photograph of the person on the government-issued identification presented by the person; and
(2) The name entered into the log referred to in subsection (a) of Section 20 of this Act corresponds to the name on the government-issued identification presented by the person.

(f) The logs referred to in subsection (a) of Section 20 of this Act shall be kept confidential, maintained for not less than 2 years, and made available for inspection and copying by any law enforcement officer upon request of that officer. These logs shall be kept in an electronic format as required by the Methamphetamine Precursor Tracking Act.

(g) No retail distributor operating a pharmacy, and no pharmacist or pharmacy technician, shall knowingly distribute any targeted methamphetamine precursor to any person under 18 years of age.

(h) No retail distributor operating a pharmacy, and no pharmacist or pharmacy technician, shall knowingly distribute to a single person more than 2 targeted packages in a single retail transaction.

(i) No retail distributor operating a pharmacy, and no pharmacist or pharmacy technician, shall knowingly distribute to a single person in any 30-day period products containing more than a total of 7,500 milligrams of ephedrine or pseudoephedrine, their salts or optical isomers, or salts of optical isomers.
(j) A pharmacist or pharmacy technician may distribute a targeted methamphetamine precursor to a person who is without a form of identification specified in paragraph (1) of subsection (a) of Section 20 of this Act only if all other provisions of this Act are followed and either:
(1) the person presents a driver's license issued without a photograph by the State of Illinois pursuant to the Illinois Administrative Code, Title 92, Section 1030.90(b)(1); or
(2) the person is known to the pharmacist or pharmacy technician, the person presents some form of identification, and the pharmacist or pharmacy technician reasonably believes that the targeted methamphetamine precursor will be used for a legitimate medical purpose and not to manufacture methamphetamine.

(k) When a pharmacist or pharmacy technician distributes a targeted methamphetamine precursor to a person according to the procedures set forth in this Act, and the pharmacist or pharmacy technician does not have access to a working cash register at the pharmacy counter, the pharmacist or pharmacy technician may instruct the person to pay for the targeted methamphetamine precursor at a cash register located elsewhere in the retail establishment, whether that register is operated by a pharmacist, pharmacy technician, or other employee or agent of the retail establishment.

§ 30. Retail distributors; general requirements. (a) No retail distributor shall distribute any convenience package except in accordance with this Section and Section 35 of this Act.

(b) The convenience packages must be displayed behind store counters or in locked cases, so that customers are not able to reach the product without the assistance of a store employee or agent.

(c) The retailer distributor shall ensure that any person purchasing, receiving, or otherwise acquiring the targeted methamphetamine precursor complies with subsection (a) of Section 20 of this Act.

(d) The retail distributor shall verify that:

(1) The person purchasing, receiving, or otherwise acquiring the targeted methamphetamine precursor is 18 years of age or older and resembles the photograph of the person on the government-issued identification presented by the person; and

(2) The name entered into the log referred to in subsection (a) of Section 20 of this Act corresponds to the name on the government-issued identification presented by the person.

(e) The logs referred to in subsection (a) of Section 20 of this Act shall be kept confidential, maintained for not less than 2 years, and made available for inspection and copying by any law enforcement officer upon request of that officer. These logs may be kept in an electronic format if they include all the information specified in subsection (a) of Section 20 of this Act in a form that is readily retrievable.

(f) No retail distributor shall knowingly distribute any targeted methamphetamine precursor to any person under 18 years of age.

(g) No retail distributor shall knowingly distribute to a single person in any 24-hour period more than one convenience package.

(h) No retail distributor shall knowingly distribute to a single person in any 30-day period products containing more than a total of 7,500 milligrams of ephedrine or pseudoephedrine, their salts or optical isomers, or salts of optical isomers.

§ 35. Retail distributors; training requirements. (a) Every retail distributor of any targeted methamphetamine precursor shall train each sales employee on the topics listed on the certification form described in subsection (b) of this Section. This training may be conducted by a live trainer or by means of a computer-based training program. This training shall be completed within 30 days of the effective date of this Act or within 30 days of the date that each sales employee begins working for the retail distributor, whichever of these 2 dates comes later.

(b) Immediately after training each sales employee as required in subsection (a) of this Section, every retail distributor of any targeted methamphetamine precursor shall have each sales employee read, sign, and date a certification containing the following language:

(1) My name is (insert name of employee) and I am an employee of (insert name of business) at (insert street address).

(2) I understand that in Illinois there are laws governing the sale of certain over-the-counter medications that contain a chemical called ephedrine or a second chemical called pseudoephedrine. Medications that are subject to these laws are called "targeted methamphetamine precursors".

(3) I understand that "targeted methamphetamine precursors" can be used to manufacture the illegal and dangerous drug methamphetamine and that methamphetamine is causing great harm to individuals, families, communities, the economy, and the environment throughout Illinois.

(4) I understand that under Illinois law, unless they are at a pharmacy counter, customers can only purchase small "convenience packages" of " targeted methamphetamine precursors".

(5) I understand that under Illinois law, customers can only purchase these "convenience packages" if they are 18 years of age or older, show identification, and sign a log according to procedures that have been described to me.

(6) I understand that under Illinois law, I cannot sell more than one "convenience package" to a single customer in one 24-hour period.

(7) I understand that under Illinois law, I cannot sell "targeted methamphetamine precursors" to a person if I know that the person is going to use them to make methamphetamine.

(8) I understand that there are a number of ingredients that are used to make the illegal drug methamphetamine, including "targeted methamphetamine precursors" sold in "convenience packages". My employer has shown me a list of these various ingredients, and I have reviewed the list.

(9) I understand that there are certain procedures that I should follow if I suspect that a store customer is purchasing "targeted methamphetamine precursors" or other products for the purpose of manufacturing methamphetamine. These procedures have been described to me, and I understand them.

(c) A certification form of the type described in subsection (b) of this Section may be signed with a handwritten signature or an electronic signature that includes a unique identifier for each employee. The certification shall be retained by the retail distributor for each sales employee for the duration of his or her employment and for at least 30 days following the end of his or her employment. Any such form shall be made available for inspection and copying by any law enforcement officer upon request of that officer. These records may be kept in electronic format if they include all the information specified in this Section in a manner that is readily retrievable and reproducible in hard-copy format.

(d) The Office of the Illinois Attorney General shall make available to retail distributors the list of methamphetamine ingredients referred to in subsection (b) of this Section.

(e) The training requirements set forth in this Section apply to the distribution of convenience packages away from pharmacy counters as set forth in Section 30 of this Act but do not apply to the distribution of targeted methamphetamine precursors through a pharmacy as set forth in Section 25 of this Act.

§ 40. Penalties. (a) Violations of subsection (b) of Section 20 of this Act.

(1) Any person who knowingly purchases, receives, or otherwise acquires, within any 30-day period, products containing more than a total of 7,500 milligrams of ephedrine or pseudoephedrine, their salts or optical isomers, or salts of optical isomers in violation of subsection (b) of Section 20 of this Act is subject to the following penalties:

(A) More than 7,500 milligrams but less than 15,000 milligrams, Class B misdemeanor;

(B) 15,000 or more but less than 22,500 milligrams, Class A misdemeanor;

(C) 22,500 or more but less than 30,000 milligrams, Class 4 felony;

(D) 30,000 or more but less than 37,500 milligrams, Class 3 felony;

(E) 37,500 or more but less than 45,000 milligrams, Class 2 felony:

(F) 45,000 or more milligrams, Class 1 felony.

(2) Any person who knowingly purchases, receives, or otherwise acquires, within any 30-day period, products containing more than a total of 7,500 milligrams of ephedrine or pseudoephedrine, their salts or optical isomers, or salts of optical isomers in violation of subsection (b) of Section 20 of this Act, and who has previously been convicted of any methamphetamine-related offense under any State or federal law, is subject to the following penalties:

(A) More than 7,500 milligrams but less than 15,000 milligrams, Class A misdemeanor;

(B) 15,000 or more but less than 22,500 milligrams, Class 4 felony;

(C) 22,500 or more but less than 30,000 milligrams, Class 3 felony;

(D) 30,000 or more but less than 37,500 milligrams, Class 2 felony;

(E) 37,500 or more milligrams, Class 1 felony.

(3) Any person who knowingly purchases, receives, or otherwise acquires, within any 30-day period, products containing more than a total of 7,500 milligrams of ephedrine or pseudoephedrine, their salts or optical isomers, or salts of optical isomers in violation of subsection (b) of Section 20 of this Act, and who has previously been convicted 2 or more times of any methamphetamine-related offense under State or federal law, is subject to the following penalties:
(A) More than 7,500 milligrams but less than 15,000 milligrams, Class 4 felony;

(B) 15,000 or more but less than 22,500 milligrams, Class 3 felony;

(C) 22,500 or more but less than 30,000 milligrams, Class 2 felony;

(D) 30,000 or more milligrams, Class 1 felony.

(b) Violations of Section 15, 20, 25, 30, or 35 of this Act, other than violations of subsection (b) of Section 20 of this Act.

(1) Any pharmacy or retail distributor that violates Section 15, 20, 25, 30, or 35 of this Act, other than subsection (b) of Section 20 of this Act, is guilty of a petty offense and subject to a fine of $500 for a first offense; and $1,000 for a second offense occurring at the same retail location as and within 3 years of the prior offense. A pharmacy or retail distributor that violates this Act is guilty of a business offense and subject to a fine of $5,000 for a third or subsequent offense occurring at the same retail location as and within 3 years of the prior offenses.

(2) An employee or agent of a pharmacy or retail distributor who violates Section 15, 20, 25, 30, or 35 of this Act, other than subsection (b) of Section 20 of this Act, is guilty of a Class A misdemeanor for a first offense, a Class 4 felony for a second offense, and a Class 1 felony for a third or subsequent offense.

(3) Any other person who violates Section 15, 20, 25, 30, or 35 of this Act, other than subsection (b) of Section 20 of this Act, is guilty of a Class B misdemeanor for a first offense, a Class A misdemeanor for a second offense, and a Class 4 felony for a third or subsequent offense.

(c) (Blank).

(d) (Blank)

(e) Any person who, in order to acquire a targeted methamphetamine precursor, knowingly uses or provides the driver's license or government-issued identification of another person, or who knowingly uses or provides a fictitious or unlawfully altered driver's license or government-issued identification, or who otherwise knowingly provides false information, is guilty of a Class 4 felony for a first offense, a Class 3 felony for a second offense, and a Class 2 felony for a third or subsequent offense.

For purposes of this subsection (e), the terms "fictitious driver's license", "unlawfully altered driver's license", and "false information" have the meanings ascribed to them in Section 6-301.1 of the Illinois Vehicle Code.

§ 50. Scope of Act. (a) Nothing in this Act limits the scope, terms, or effect of the Methamphetamine Control and Community Protection Act.
(b) Nothing in this Act limits the lawful authority granted by the Medical Practice Act of 1987, the Nurse Practice Act, or the Pharmacy Practice Act.

(c) Nothing in this Act limits the authority or activity of any law enforcement officer acting within the scope of his or her employment.

§ 55. Preemption and home rule powers. The regulation of the sale of targeted methamphetamine precursors and targeted packages are exclusive powers and functions of the State. A county or municipality, including a home rule unit, may not regulate the sale of targeted methamphetamine precursors and targeted packages. This Section is a denial and limitation of home rule powers under subsection (h) of Section 6 of Article VII of the Illinois Constitution.

§ 60. Severability. The provisions of this Act are severable under Section 1.31 of the Statute on Statutes.

§ 999. Effective date. This Act takes effect January 15, 2006.

Act 675: Sale of Tobacco to Minors Act
720 ILCS 675 *et al.*

§ 1. Prohibition on sale to and possession of tobacco by minors; prohibition on the distribution of tobacco samples to any person; use of identification cards; vending machines; lunch wagons; out-of-package sales. (a) No minor under 18 years of age shall buy any tobacco product. No person shall sell, buy for, distribute samples of or furnish any tobacco product to any minor under 18 years of age.

(a-5) No minor under 16 years of age may sell any tobacco product at a retail establishment selling tobacco products. This subsection does not apply to a sales clerk in a family-owned business which can prove that the sales clerk is in fact a son or daughter of the owner.

(a-6) No minor under 18 years of age in the furtherance or facilitation of obtaining any tobacco product shall display or use a false or forged identification card or transfer, alter, or deface an identification card.

(a-7) No minor under 18 years of age shall possess any cigar, cigarette, smokeless tobacco, or tobacco in any of its forms.

(a-8) A person shall not distribute without charge samples of any tobacco product to any other person, regardless of age:

(1) within a retail establishment selling tobacco products, unless the retailer has verified the purchaser's age with a government issued identification;

(2) from a lunch wagon; or

(3) on a public way as a promotion or advertisement of a tobacco manufacturer or tobacco product.

This subsection (a-8) does not apply to the distribution of a tobacco product sample in any adult-only facility.

(a-9) For the purpose of this Section:

"Adult-only facility means a facility or restricted area (whether open-air or enclosed) where the operator ensures or has a reasonable basis to believe (such as by checking identification as required under State law, or by checking the identification of any person appearing to be under the age of 27) that no person under legal age is present. A facility or restricted area need not be permanently restricted to persons under legal age to constitute an adult-only facility, provided that the operator ensures or has a reasonable basis to believe that no person under legal age is present during the event or time period in question.

"Lunch wagon" means a mobile vehicle designed and constructed to transport food and from which food is sold to the general public.

"Smokeless tobacco" means any tobacco products that are suitable for dipping or chewing.

"Tobacco product" means any cigar, cigarette, smokeless tobacco, or tobacco in any of its forms.

(b) Tobacco products listed in this Section may be sold through a vending machine only if such tobacco products are not placed together with any non-tobacco product, other than matches, in the vending machine and the vending machine is in any of the following locations:

(1) (Blank).

(2) Places to which minors under 18 years of age are not permitted access.

(3) Places where alcoholic beverages are sold and consumed on the premises and vending machine operation is under the direct supervision of the owner or manager.

(4) (Blank).

(5) Places where the vending machine can only be operated by the owner or an employee over age 18 either directly or through a remote control device if the device is inaccessible to all customers.
(c) (Blank).

(d) The sale or distribution by any person of a tobacco product in this Section, including but not limited to a single or loose cigarette, that is not contained within a sealed container, pack, or package as provided by the manufacturer, which container, pack, or package bears the health warning required by federal law, is prohibited.

(e) It is not a violation of this Act for a person under 18 years of age to purchase or possess a cigar, cigarette, smokeless tobacco or tobacco in any of its forms if the person under the age of 18 purchases or is given the cigar, cigarette, smokeless tobacco or tobacco in any of its forms from a retail seller of tobacco products or an employee of the retail seller pursuant to a plan or action to investigate, patrol, or otherwise conduct a "sting operation" or enforcement action against a retail seller of tobacco products or a person employed by the retail seller of tobacco products or on any premises authorized to sell tobacco products to determine if tobacco products are being sold or given to persons under 18 years of age if the "sting operation" or enforcement action is approved by the Department of State Police, the county sheriff, a municipal police department, the Department of Public Health, or a local health department.

§1.5. Distribution of alternative nicotine products to persons under 18 years of age prohibited. (a) For the purposes of this Section, "alternative nicotine product" means a product or device not consisting of or containing tobacco that provides for the ingestion into the body of nicotine, whether by chewing, smoking, absorbing, dissolving, inhaling, snorting, sniffing, or by any other means. "Alternative nicotine product" excludes cigarettes, smokeless tobacco, or other tobacco products as these terms are defined in Section 1 of this Act and any product approved by the United States Food and Drug Administration as a non-tobacco product for sale as a tobacco cessation product, as a tobacco dependence product, or for other medical purposes, and is being marketed and sold solely for that approved purpose.

(b) A person, either directly or indirectly by an agent or employee, or by a vending machine owned by the person or located in the person's establishment, may not sell, offer for sale, give, or furnish any alternative nicotine product, or any cartridge or component of an alternative nicotine product, to a person under 18 years of age.
(c) Before selling, offering for sale, giving, or furnishing an alternative nicotine product, or any cartridge or component of an alternative nicotine product, to another person, the person selling, offering for sale, giving, or furnishing the alternative nicotine product shall verify that the person is at least 18 years of age by:

(1) examining from any person that appears to be under 27 years of age a government-issued photographic identification that establishes the person is at least 18 years of age or

(2) for sales made though the Internet or other remote sales methods, performing an age verification through an independent, third-party age verification service that compares information available from public records to the personal information entered by the person during the ordering process that establishes the person is 18 years of age or older.

§ 2. Penalties. (a) Any person who violates subsection (a), (a-5), or (a-6) of Section 1 of this Act is guilty of a petty offense and for the first offense shall be fined $200, $400 for the second offense in a 12-month period, and $600 for the third or any subsequent offense in a 12-month period.

(b) If a minor violates subsection (a-7) of Section 1 he or she is guilty of a petty offense and the court may impose a sentence of 15 hours of community service or a fine of $25 for a first violation.

(c) A second violation by a minor of subsection (a-7) of Section 1 that occurs within 12 months after the first violation is punishable by a fine of $50 and 25 hours of community service.

(d) A third or subsequent violation by a minor of subsection (a-7) of Section 1 that occurs within 12 months after the first violation is punishable by a $100 fine and 30 hours of community service.

(e) Any second or subsequent violation not within the 12-month time period after the first violation is punishable as provided for a first violation.

(f) If a minor is convicted of or placed on supervision for a violation of subsection (a-7) of Section 1, the court may, in its discretion, and upon recommendation by the State's Attorney, order that minor and his or her parents or legal guardian to attend a smoker's education or youth diversion program if that program is available in the jurisdiction where the offender resides. Attendance at a smoker's education or youth diversion program shall be time-credited against any community service time imposed for any first violation of subsection (a-7) of Section 1. In addition to any other penalty that the court may impose for a violation of subsection (a-7) of Section 1, the court, upon request by the State's Attorney, may in its discretion require the offender to remit a fee for his or her attendance at a smoker's education or youth diversion program.

(g) For purposes of this Section, "smoker's education program" or "youth diversion program" includes, but is not limited to, a seminar designed to educate a person on the physical and psychological effects of smoking tobacco products and the health consequences of smoking tobacco products that can be conducted with a locality's youth diversion program.

(h) All moneys collected as fines for violations of subsection (a), (a-5), (a-6), or (a-7) of Section 1 shall be distributed in the following manner:

(1) one-half of each fine shall be distributed to the unit of local government or other entity that successfully prosecuted the offender; and

(2) one-half shall be remitted to the State to be used for enforcing this Act.

Act 678: Prevention of Cigarette Sales to Minors Act

§ 2. Definitions. For the purpose of this Act:

"Cigarette", when used in this Act, means any roll for smoking made wholly or in part of tobacco irrespective of size or shape and whether or not the tobacco is flavored, adulterated, or mixed with any other ingredient, and the wrapper or cover of which is made of paper or any other substance or material except whole leaf tobacco.

"Clear and conspicuous statement" means the statement is of sufficient type size to be clearly readable by the recipient of the communication.

"Consumer" means an individual who acquires or seeks to acquire cigarettes for personal use.

"Delivery sale" means any sale of cigarettes to a consumer if:

(a) the consumer submits the order for such sale by means of a telephone or other method of voice transmission, the mails, or the Internet or other online service, or the seller is otherwise not in the physical presence of the buyer when the request for purchase or order is made; or

(b) the cigarettes are delivered by use of a common carrier, private delivery service, or the mails, or the seller is not in the physical presence of the buyer when the buyer obtains possession of the cigarettes.

"Delivery service" means any person (other than a person that makes a delivery sale) who delivers to the consumer the cigarettes sold in a delivery sale.

"Department" means the Department of Revenue.

"Government-issued identification" means a State driver's license, State identification card, passport, a military identification or an official naturalization or immigration document, such as an alien registration recipient card (commonly known as a "green card") or an immigrant visa.

"Mails" or "mailing" mean the shipment of cigarettes through the United States Postal Service.

"Out-of-state sale" means a sale of cigarettes to a consumer located outside of this State where the consumer submits the order for such sale by means of a telephonic or other method of voice transmission, the mails or any other delivery service, facsimile transmission, or the Internet or other online service and where the cigarettes are delivered by use of the mails or other delivery service.

"Person" means any individual, corporation, partnership, limited liability company, association, or other organization that engages in any for-profit or not-for-profit activities.

"Shipping package" means a container in which packs or cartons of cigarettes are shipped in connection with a delivery sale.

"Shipping documents" means bills of lading, air bills, or any other documents used to evidence the undertaking by a delivery service to deliver letters, packages, or other containers.

§ 5. Unlawful shipment or transportation of cigarettes. (a) It is unlawful for any person engaged in the business of selling cigarettes to ship or cause to be shipped any cigarettes unless the person shipping the cigarettes:
(1) is licensed as a distributor under either the Cigarette Tax Act, or the Cigarette Use Tax Act; or delivers the cigarettes to a distributor licensed under either the Cigarette Tax Act or the Cigarette Use Tax Act; or
(2) ships them to an export warehouse proprietor pursuant to Chapter 52 of the Internal Revenue Code, or an operator of a customs bonded warehouse pursuant to Section 1311 or 1555 of Title 19 of the United States Code.
For purposes of this subsection (a), a person is a licensed distributor if the person's name appears on a list of licensed distributors published by the Illinois Department of Revenue. The term cigarette has the same meaning as defined in Section 1 of the Cigarette Tax Act and Section 1 of the Cigarette Use Tax Act. Nothing in this Act prohibits a person licensed as a distributor under the Cigarette Tax Act or the Cigarette Use Tax Act from shipping or causing to be shipped any cigarettes to a registered retailer under the Retailers' Occupation Tax Act provided the cigarette tax or cigarette use tax has been paid.
(b) A common or contract carrier may transport cigarettes to any individual person in this State only if the carrier reasonably believes such cigarettes have been received from a person described in paragraph (a)(1). Common or contract carriers may make deliveries of cigarettes to licensed distributors described in paragraph (a)(1) of this Section. Nothing in this subsection (b) shall be construed to prohibit a person other than a common or contract carrier from transporting not more than 1,000 cigarettes at any one time to any person in this State.
(c) A common or contract carrier may not complete the delivery of any cigarettes to persons other than those described in paragraph (a)(1) of this Section without first obtaining from the purchaser an official written identification from any state or federal agency

that displays the person's date of birth or a birth certificate that includes a reliable confirmation that the purchaser is at least 18 years of age; that the cigarettes purchased are not intended for consumption by an individual who is younger than 18 years of age; and a written statement signed by the purchaser that certifies the purchaser's address and that the purchaser is at least 18 years of age. The statement shall also confirm: (1) that the purchaser understands that signing another person's name to the certification is illegal; (2) that the sale of cigarettes to individuals under 18 years of age is illegal; and (3) that the purchase of cigarettes by individuals under 18 years of age is illegal under the laws of Illinois.

(d) When a person engaged in the business of selling cigarettes ships or causes to be shipped any cigarettes to any person in this State, other than in the cigarette manufacturer's or tobacco products manufacturer's original container or wrapping, the container or wrapping must be plainly and visibly marked with the word "cigarettes".

(e) When a peace officer of this State or any duly authorized officer or employee of the Illinois Department of Public Health or Department of Revenue discovers any cigarettes which have been or which are being shipped or transported in violation of this Section, he or she shall seize and take possession of the cigarettes, and the cigarettes shall be subject to a forfeiture action pursuant to the procedures provided under the Cigarette Tax Act or Cigarette Use Tax Act.

§ 6. Prevention of delivery sales to minors.
(a) No person shall make a delivery sale of cigarettes to any individual who is under 18 years of age.

(b) Each person accepting a purchase order for a delivery sale shall comply with the provisions of this Act and all other laws of this State generally applicable to sales of cigarettes that occur entirely within this State.

§ 7. Age verification and shipping requirements to prevent delivery sales to minors. (a) No person, other than a delivery service, shall mail, ship, or otherwise cause to be delivered a shipping package in connection with a delivery sale unless the person:

(1) prior to the first delivery sale to the prospective consumer, obtains from the prospective consumer a written certification which includes a statement signed by the prospective consumer that certifies:

(A) the prospective consumer's current address; and

(B) that the prospective consumer is at least the legal minimum age;

(2) informs, in writing, such prospective consumer that:

(A) the signing of another person's name to the certification described in this Section is illegal;

(B) sales of cigarettes to individuals under 18 years of age are illegal;

(C) the purchase of cigarettes by individuals under 18 years of age is illegal; and

(D) the name and identity of the prospective consumer may be reported to the state of the consumer's current address under the Act of October 19, 1949 (15 U.S.C. § 375, et seq.), commonly known as the Jenkins Act;

(3) makes a good faith effort to verify the date of birth of the prospective consumer provided pursuant to this Section by:

(A) comparing the date of birth against a commercially available database; or

(B) obtaining a photocopy or other image of a valid, government-issued identification stating the date of birth or age of the prospective consumer;

(4) provides to the prospective consumer a notice that meets the requirements of subsection (b);

(5) receives payment for the delivery sale from the prospective consumer by a credit or debit card that has been issued in such consumer's name, or by a check or other written instrument in such consumer's name; and

(6) ensures that the shipping package is delivered to the same address as is shown on the government-issued identification or contained in the commercially available database.

(b) The notice required under this Section shall include:

(1) a statement that cigarette sales to consumers below 18 years of age are illegal;

(2) a statement that sales of cigarettes are restricted to those consumers who provide

verifiable proof of age in accordance with subsection (a);
(3) a statement that cigarette sales are subject to tax under Section 2 of the Cigarette Tax Act (35 ILCS 130/2), Section 2 of the Cigarette Use Tax Act, and Section 3 of the Use Tax Act and an explanation of how the correct tax has been, or is to be, paid with respect to such delivery sale.
(c) A statement meets the requirement of this Section if:
(1) the statement is clear and conspicuous;
(2) the statement is contained in a printed box set apart from the other contents of the communication;
(3) the statement is printed in bold, capital letters;
(4) the statement is printed with a degree of color contrast between the background and the printed statement that is no less than the color contrast between the background and the largest text used in the communication; and

(5) for any printed material delivered by electronic means, the statement appears at both the top and the bottom of the electronic mail message or both the top and the bottom of the Internet website homepage.

(d) Each person, other than a delivery service, who mails, ships, or otherwise causes to be delivered a shipping package in connection with a delivery sale shall:
(1) include as part of the shipping documents a clear and conspicuous statement stating: “Cigarettes: Illinois Law Prohibits Shipping to Individuals Under 18 and Requires the Payment of All Applicable Taxes”;
(2) use a method of mailing, shipping, or delivery that requires a signature before the shipping package is released to the consumer; and
(3) ensure that the shipping package is not delivered to any post office box.

§ 8. Registration and reporting requirements to prevent delivery sales to minors. (a) Not later than the 15th day of each month, each person making a delivery sale during the previous calendar month shall file a report with the Department containing the following information:
(1) the seller's name, trade name, and the address of such person's principal place of business and any other place of business;
(2) the name and address of the consumer to whom such delivery sale was made;
(3) the brand style or brand styles of the cigarettes that were sold in such delivery sale;
(4) the quantity of cigarettes that were sold in such delivery sale;

(5) an indication of whether or not the cigarettes sold in the delivery sale bore a tax stamp evidencing payment of the tax under Section 2 of the Cigarette Tax Act (35 ILCS 130/2); and
(6) such other information the Department may require.

(b) Each person engaged in business within this State who makes an out-of-state sale shall, for each individual sale, submit to the appropriate tax official of the state in which the consumer is located the information required in subsection (a).

(c) Any person that satisfies the requirements of 15 U.S.C. Section 376 shall be deemed to satisfy the requirements of subsections (a) and (b).
(d) The Department is authorized to disclose to the Attorney General any information received under this title and requested by the Attorney General. The Department and the Attorney General shall share with each other the information received under this title and may share the information with other federal, State, or local agencies for purposes of enforcement of this title or the laws of the federal government or of other states.
(e) This Section shall not be construed to impose liability upon any delivery service, or officers or employees thereof, when acting within the scope of business of the delivery service.
(f) The Department may establish procedures requiring electronic transmission of the information required by this Section directly to the Department on forms prescribed and furnished by the Department.

§ 9. Statements for delivery sales.
(a) Each person who makes a delivery sale shall collect and remit to the Department all excise taxes imposed by this State with respect to such

delivery sale and maintain evidence of such payment unless the person is located outside the State and includes a statement on the outside of the shipping package stating: "Illinois law requires the payment of state taxes on this shipment of cigarettes. You are legally responsible for all applicable unpaid state taxes on these cigarettes."

(b) A statement meets the requirements of subsection (a) if the statement is:

(1) clear and conspicuous;

(2) contained in a printed box set apart from the shipping label and other markings contained on the shipping package;

(3) printed in bold, capital letters;
(4) printed with a degree of color contrast between the background and the printed statement that is no less than the color contrast between the background and the largest text used on the shipping label; and

(5) located on the same side of the shipping package as the shipping label.

§ 10. Violation. (a) A person who violates subsection (a), (b), or (c) of Section 5 or Section 6, 7, 8, or 9 is guilty of a Class A misdemeanor. A second or subsequent violation of subsection (a), (b), or (c) of Section 5 or Section 6, 7, 8, or 9 is a Class 4 felony.

(b) The Department of Revenue shall impose a civil penalty not to exceed $5,000 on any person who violates subsection (a), (b), or (c) of Section 5 or Section 6, 7, 8, or 9. The Department of Revenue shall impose a civil penalty not to exceed $5,000 on any person engaged in the business of selling cigarettes who ships or causes to be shipped any such cigarettes to any person in this State in violation of subsection (d) of Section 5. Civil penalties imposed and collected by the Department shall be deposited into the Tax Compliance and Administration Fund.

(c) All cigarettes sold or attempted to be sold in a delivery sale that does not meet the requirements of this Act shall be forfeited to the State. All cigarettes forfeited to this State under this Act shall be destroyed or maintained and used in an undercover capacity. The Department may, prior to any destruction of cigarettes, permit the true holder of the trademark rights in the cigarette brand to inspect such contraband cigarettes, in order to assist the Department in any investigation regarding such cigarettes.

(d) Any person aggrieved by any decision of the Department of Revenue may, within 60 days after notice of that decision, protest in writing and request a hearing. The Department of Revenue shall give notice to the person of the time and place for the hearing and shall hold a hearing before it issues a final administrative decision. Absent a written protest within 60 days, the Department's decision shall become final without any further determination made or notice given.

(e) The penalties provided for in this Section are in addition to any other penalties provided for by law.

§ 20. Tip line. (a) Not later than 120 days after the effective date of this amendatory Act of the 95th General Assembly, the Department shall establish, publicize, and maintain a toll-free telephone number to receive information related to the sale and delivery of contraband cigarettes.
(b) The Attorney General may pay a reward of up to $5,000 to any person who furnishes information leading to the Department's collection of excise taxes imposed upon delivery sales which otherwise would not have been collected but for the information provided by the person.

§ 25. Construction. The requirements imposed by this Act shall not apply where such application would be contrary to the Constitution and laws of the United States.

§ 30. Severability. If any provision of this Act is for any reason held to be unconstitutional or invalid, such holding shall not affect the constitutionality or validity of the remaining provisions of this Act, and to this end the provisions of this Act are expressly declared to be severable.

Act 685. Tobacco Accessories and Smoking Herbs Control Act

§ 1. This Act shall be known and may be cited as the "Tobacco Accessories and Smoking Herbs Control Act".

§ 2. Purpose. The sale and possession of marijuana, hashish, cocaine, opium and their derivatives, is not only prohibited by Illinois Law, but the use of these substances has been deemed injurious to the health of the user.

It has further been determined by the Surgeon General of the United States that the use of tobacco is hazardous to human health.

The ready availability of smoking herbs to minors could lead to the use of tobacco and illegal drugs.

It is in the best interests of the citizens of the State of Illinois to seek to prohibit the spread of illegal drugs, tobacco or smoking materials to minors. The prohibition of the sale of tobacco and snuff accessories and smoking herbs to minors would help to curb the usage of illegal drugs and tobacco products, among our youth.

§ 3. Definitions. The following definitions shall apply to this Act:

(a) "Tobacco accessories" shall mean cigarette papers, pipes, holders of smoking materials of all types, cigarette rolling machines, and other items, designed primarily for the smoking or ingestion of tobacco products or of substances made illegal under any statute or of substances whose sale, gift, barter, or exchange is made unlawful under this Act.

(b) "Smoking herbs" shall mean all substances of plant origin and their derivatives, including but not limited to broom, calea, California poppy, damiana, hops, ginseng, lobelia, jimson weed and other members of the Datura genus, passion flower and wild lettuce, which are processed or sold primarily for use as smoking materials.

(c) "Bidi cigarette" means a product that contains tobacco that is wrapped in temburni or tendu leaf or that is wrapped in any other material identified by rules of the Department of Public Health that is similar in appearance or characteristics to the temburni or tendu leaf.

§ 4. Offenses. (a) Sale to minors. No person shall knowingly sell, barter, exchange, deliver or give away or cause or permit or procure to be sold, bartered, exchanged, delivered, or given away tobacco accessories or smoking herbs to any person under 18 years of age.
(a-5) Sale of bidi cigarettes. No person shall knowingly sell, barter, exchange, deliver, or give away a bidi cigarette to another person, nor shall a person cause or permit or procure a bidi cigarette to be sold, bartered, exchanged, delivered, or given away to another person.
(b) Sale of cigarette paper. No person shall knowingly offer, sell, barter, exchange, deliver or give away cigarette paper or cause, permit, or procure cigarette paper to be sold, offered, bartered, exchanged, delivered, or given away except from premises or an establishment where other tobacco products are sold. For purposes of this Section, "tobacco products" means cigarettes, cigars, smokeless tobacco, or tobacco in any of its forms.
(c) Sale of cigarette paper from vending machines. No person shall knowingly offer, sell, barter, exchange, deliver or give away cigarette paper or cause, permit, or procure cigarette paper to be sold, offered, bartered, exchanged, delivered, or given away by use of a vending or coin-operated machine or device. For purposes of this Section, "cigarette paper" shall not include any paper that is incorporated into a product to which a tax stamp must be affixed under the Cigarette Tax Act or the Cigarette Use Tax Act.
(d) Use of identification cards. No person in the furtherance or facilitation of obtaining smoking accessories and smoking herbs shall display or

use a false or forged identification card or transfer, alter, or deface an identification card.
(e) Warning to minors. Any person, firm, partnership, company or corporation operating a place of business where tobacco accessories and smoking herbs are sold or offered for sale shall post in a conspicuous place upon the premises a sign upon which there shall be imprinted the following statement, "SALE OF TOBACCO ACCESSORIES AND SMOKING HERBS TO PERSONS UNDER EIGHTEEN YEARS OF AGE OR THE MISREPRESENTATION OF AGE TO PROCURE SUCH A SALE IS PROHIBITED BY LAW". The sign shall be printed on a white card in red letters at least one-half inch in height.

§ 5. Penalty. (a) Any person who shall knowingly violate, or shall knowingly cause the violation of any provision of this Act other than subsection (a-5) of Section 4 shall be guilty of a Class C misdemeanor.

(b) Any person who knowingly violates or knowingly causes the violation of subsection (a-5) of Section 4 is guilty of a petty offense for which the offender may be fined an amount as follows:

(1) For a first offense, not less than $100 and not more than $500.

(2) For a second offense within a 2-year period, not less than $250 and not more than $500.

(3) For a third or subsequent offense within a 2-year period, not less than $500 and not more than $1,000.

Act 690. Use of Intoxicating Compounds Act

§ 1. Use prohibited. No person shall ingest, breathe, inhale or drink any compound, liquid, or chemical containing toluol, hexane, trichloroethylene, acetone, toluene, ethyl acetate, methyl ethyl ketone, trichloroethane, isopropanol, methyl isobutyl ketone, methyl cellosolve acetate, cyclohexanone, the alkaloids atropine, hyoscyamine, or scopolamine, or any other substance for the purpose of inducing a condition of intoxication, stupefaction, depression, giddiness, paralysis or irrational behavior, or in any manner changing, distorting or disturbing the auditory, visual or mental processes. For the purposes of this Act, any such condition so induced shall be deemed to be an intoxicated condition.

§ 2. Sale or delivery prohibited.
(a) No person shall knowingly sell or offer for sale, deliver or give to any person under 17 years of age, unless upon written order of such person's parent or guardian, any compound, liquid, or chemical containing toluol, hexane, trichloroethylene, acetone, toluene, ethyl acetate, methyl ethyl ketone, trichloroethane, isopropanol, methyl isobutyl ketone, methyl cellosolve acetate, cyclohexanone, or any other substance which will induce an intoxicated condition, as defined herein, when the seller, offeror, or deliverer knows or has reason to know that the compound is intended for use to induce such condition.

(b) No person shall knowingly sell or offer for sale, deliver, or give to any person any compound, liquid, or chemical containing alkaloids atropine, hyoscyamine, or scopolamine when the seller, offeror, or deliverer knows or has reason to know that the compound, liquid, or chemical is intended for use to induce an intoxicated condition.

§ 3. This Act shall not apply to any person who commits any act described herein pursuant to the direction or prescription of a practitioner authorized to so direct or prescribe. For purposes of this Section, practitioner shall mean any person authorized by law to practice medicine in all its branches in this State, to practice dentistry in this State, to practice veterinary medicine in this State, or to practice chiropody in this State.

§ 4. Sentence. (a) Except as otherwise provided in subsection (b), violation of this Act is a Class C misdemeanor for a first offense and a Class A misdemeanor for a second or subsequent offense.

(b)(1) The knowing ingestion of any compound, liquid, or chemical containing the alkaloids atropine, hyoscyamine, or scopolamine is a Class A misdemeanor.

(2) The sale, offer for sale, delivery, or giving to any person of a compound, liquid, or chemical containing the alkaloids atropine, hyoscyamine, or scopolamine is a Class 4 felony.

(3) This subsection (b) does not prohibit the sale, offer for sale, delivery, giving, or ingestion of a compound, liquid, or chemical containing the alkaloids atropine, hyoscyamine, or scopolamine under the direction or prescription of a practitioner authorized to so direct or prescribe as provided in Section 3.

§ 4.5. Exemption. This Act does not apply to the sale, offer for sale, delivery, or giving of any compound, liquid or chemical containing the alkaloids atropine, hyoscyamine, or scopolamine by a retail merchant.

Chapter 3: Illinois Criminal Procedure – Code of Criminal Procedure of 1963

Introduction to Illinois Criminal Procedure

The development of the law of criminal procedure in Illinois is one that has followed the development of American constitutional law regarding individual rights. to understand Illinois criminal procedure requires a basic understanding of the rights guaranteed by the 4th, 5th and 6th Amendments to the Constitution of the United States, and to understand that most of the criminal procedural protections of the Bill of Rights are also protections enjoyed by citizens and defendants in Illinois courts by virtue of the 14th Amendment to the U.S. Constitution and also by provisions of the Illinois Constitution of 1970.

Fourth Amendment Rights. The Fourth Amendment protects citizens against arbitrary arrests and searches and seizures. Peace officers must have probable cause to arrest someone – a reasoned basis to deprive one of his liberty even on a temporary basis to account for the claim that he has committed a crime. Similarly, to protect the security of one's home, property and person the Fourth Amendment requires that law enforcement obtain warrants based on probable cause from judges before searching and seizing an individual's property. By placing an impartial magistrate between the police and the people, the American system provides a prophylactic level of protection for individual freedom and privacy. These constitutional protections have been applied to state criminal prosecutions by virtue of the Fourteenth Amendment. The Illinois Constitution of 1970 has identical provisions regarding protection against unlawful searches and seizures in Article I, Section 6.

Exceptions to warrant requirement. There are numerous, and notable, exceptions to the requirement that searches and seizure occur only after the issuance of a warrant, based on probable cause. the exceptions have been recognized by U.S. Supreme Court judicial rulings in criminal cases and include: (1) consent searches, (2) searches incident to arrest, (3) motor vehicle searches, (4) inventory searches following arrest, (5) plain-view searches, (6) open fields, (7) border searches (8) public school searches and (9) exigent circumstances. If the police investigative activity results in the seizure of evidence and fits within one of these exceptions, it is deemed not to be in violation of the Fourth Amendment.

Terry stops and airport screening searches. Police officers who have an objective reason to suspect someone of criminal activity can approach the person to ask questions and "pat down" the person to be sure that he or she is not armed. Any object that would reasonably be discovered in such a limited search can be used as evidence against the individual. The nature of street policing and the need to check out unusual circumstances justify this type of limited interaction between police and citizens.

Recent instances of international terrorism have led to an increase in airport security. Anyone who seeks to use airline transportation thus may be searched to protect traveler and national security interests.

Fifth Amendment Rights. Individuals have the right to further protection in criminal prosecutions to require the government to prove their guilt without requiring the defendant to incriminate himself (self-incrimination), to have fair notice of charges (due process of law) so that there is a meaningful opportunity to defend himself and to not be placed in jeopardy for the same offense twice (double jeopardy). The right of an individual to be placed on trial for a felony only after grand jury indictment has not been held applicable to state criminal prosecutions. The Illinois Constitution of 1970, in Article I, Section 7 provides that Illinois criminal defendants must be brought to trial on the basis of a probable cause finding as a result of grand jury indictment or a preliminary hearing.

Sixth Amendment Rights. A person who is involved in the criminal justice system has further protective rights during the criminal process including (1) the right to a lawyer in representing the client, (2) the right to a fair trial which includes the right to the attorney's help and the right to confront and cross-examine witness that testify against the defendant, (3) the right to a speedy trial in the locale where the crime is allege to have occurred, (4) the right to subpoena witnesses to come to trial to testify on his behalf, (6) the right to a jury trial by an impartial jury, (7) the right to require the prosecution to prove guilt of a criminal offense by proof beyond a reasonable doubt. The Illinois Constitution likewise recognizes these rights in Article I, Section 8.

Miranda rights. Under the Fifth and Sixth Amendment, the right against self-incrimination has been tested in the context of a myriad of interrogation techniques and court decisions. The basic rule recognized that a confession, to be used against a defendant in a criminal trial in the United States, had to be a voluntary statement of the defendant. against a historical backdrop of beatings, torture and excessive psychological pressure, the United States Supreme Court sought to curb unlawful excesses and provide a significant measure of protection against improper police interrogation techniques. In *Miranda v. Arizona* 384 U.S. 436, 86 S.Ct. 1602 (U. S. S. Ct. 1966), the Court developed the now famous constitutional requirement that before in custodial interrogation a suspect must be warned that (1) he has a right to remain silent (2) anything that he says can and will be used against him in court and (3) he has a right to have an attorney to consult with and to be present during questioning, and if he cannot afford an attorney, one will be provided to him, free of charge. After being given these *Miranda* warnings, any statements made by a suspect would be deemed inadmissible unless the person waived his rights, typically in a signed waiver document. While the prosecution could not use the statements to prove the defendant's guilt (i.e. in the prosecution case-in-chief), the statements are admissible to contradict (impeach) the defendant's testimony to the contrary.

The exclusionary rule, pre-trial motions. To assure that law enforcement officials adhere to the constitutional rights of citizens, suspects and defendants, the United States Supreme Court developed the exclusionary rule to prohibit the use or admission of evidence at trial obtained in violation of the Constitutional guarantees of the 4th, 5th and 6th Amendments. This is a judicial remedy for violation of constitutional protections and is also adhered to by Illinois courts, as required by the United States Supreme Court (See *Mapp v. Ohio* 367 U.S.643, 81 S.Ct. 1684 (U.S. S. Ct. 1961) (exclusionary rule is binding on the states)).The inadmissibility of unlawfully obtained evidence applies to federal and state officials. In fact, if such unlawfully obtained evidence is used to further the investigation, additional evidence, even if obtained lawfully, can also be found to be inadmissible. This principle is call "fruit of the poisonous" tree, because the unlawfully obtained evidence has tainted the otherwise lawful evidence to render it unusable. The exclusionary rule does not apply to civil cases, grand jury, preliminary hearings, parole or probation revocation, bail hearings or other non-trial proceedings. In criminal cases, pre-trial motions to suppress evidence unlawfully seized, to suppress a confession, to quash an arrest or to return items wrongfully seized are common ways to raise the specter of the constitutional violation and seek application of the exclusionary rule.

Exceptions to the exclusionary rule. The exclusionary rule has significant impact on the criminal justice system. A person, who would otherwise be found guilty of a serious crime, may be set free and not prosecuted because of the constitutional errors of the police department. To mitigate that result certain doctrines have developed to prevent the exclusionary rule's application.

The main exception is the "good faith" exception where officers rely on what is believed to be a valid warrant to arrest or search, only to later find out that the warrant was lacking in probable cause or otherwise deficient so as to be invalid. The fact that the officers obtained a warrant demonstrated that they were interested in protecting the constitutional rights of the parties who were the subject of the warrant.

Another exception is the "inevitable discovery" rule. If the law enforcement officers can demonstrate to the court that the information obtained unlawfully, would have been obtained lawfully by the normal course of the case investigation and presentation, the fact that a constitutional violation occurred is more akin to a technical violation, and thus the evidence should not be suppressed.

The application of the exclusionary rule is also limited by the concept of "standing". Only the person whose constitutional rights have been directly affected may complain of the violation of those rights and obtain relief by use of the exclusionary rule. Other defendants who have criminal liability based on the evidence that may be suppressed do not enjoy the same protection. Thus, a traffic stop that was turned into a general search of all the passengers in a vehicle might result in suppression of something found in the trunk, in a case prosecuted against the driver, but would not protect a passenger with a prior felony conviction, riding in the vehicle, who was frisked and discovered in possession of a weapon. The Fourth Amendment violation may protect the driver, but not the passenger.

Illinois Implementation. The Illinois Supreme Court has historically been in lock-step with decisions of the United States Supreme Court in matters of fundamental rights of criminal procedure. Based on the supremacy clause of the U.S. Constitution, one would expect the Illinois courts to adhere to U.S. Supreme Court rulings; however there have been very few cases where Illinois has had more expansive protection under the state constitution than under federal constitutional provisions. Additionally, the Code of Criminal Procedure has been amended frequently to reflect procedural rulings of the U.S. Supreme Court.

Title I. General Provisions
Article 101 – General Purposes
725 ILCS 5/101-1 *et seq.*

§ 101-1. General purposes. The provisions of this Code shall be construed in accordance with the general purposes hereof, to:
(a) Secure simplicity in procedure;

(b) Ensure fairness of administration including the elimination of unjustifiable delay;

(c) Ensure the effective apprehension and trial of persons accused of crime;

(d) Provide for the just determination of every criminal proceeding by a fair and impartial trial and an adequate review; and
(e) Preserve the public welfare and secure the fundamental human rights of individuals.

Article 102 – General Definitions
725 ILCS 5/102-1 *et seq.*

§ 102-1. Meanings of words and phrases.
For the purposes of this Code, the words and phrases described in this Article have the meanings designated in this Article, except when a particular context clearly requires a different meaning.

§ 102-2. Reference to criminal code for words and phrases not described.
A word or phrase not described in this Code but which is described in Article 2 of the "Criminal Code of 1961", approved July 28, 1961, as heretofore and hereafter amended, shall have the meaning therein described, except when a particular context in this Code clearly requires a different meaning.

§ 102-3. Singular term includes plural-Gender.
A singular term shall include the plural and the masculine gender shall include the feminine except when a particular context clearly requires a different meaning.

§ 102-3.5. "Aftercare release".
"Aftercare release" means the conditional and revocable release of a person committed to the Department of Juvenile Justice under the Juvenile Court Act of 1987, under the supervision of the Department of Juvenile Justice.

§ 102-4. "Arraignment".
"Arraignment" means the formal act of calling the defendant into open court, informing him of the offense with which he is charged, and asking him whether he is guilty or not guilty.

§ 102-5. "Arrest".
"Arrest" means the taking of a person into custody.

§ 102-6. "Bail".
"Bail" means the amount of money set by the court which is required to be obligated and secured as provided by law for the release of a person in custody in order that he will appear before the court in which his appearance may be required and that he will comply with such conditions as set forth in the bail bond.

§ 102-7. "Bail bond".
"Bail bond" means an undertaking secured by bail entered into by a person in custody by which he binds himself to comply with such conditions as are set forth therein.

§ 102-8. "Charge".
"Charge" means a written statement presented to a court accusing a person of the commission of an offense and includes complaint, information and indictment.

§ 102-9. "Complaint".
"Complaint" means a verified written statement other than an information or an indictment, presented to a court, which charges the commission of an offense.

§ 102-10. "Court".

"Court" means a place where justice is judicially administered and includes a judge thereof.

§ 102-11. "Indictment".
"Indictment" means a written statement, presented by the Grand Jury to a court, which charges the commission of an offense.

§ 102-12. "Information".
"Information" means a verified written statement signed by a State's Attorney, and presented to a court, which charges the commission of an offense.

§ 102-13. "Judge".
"Judge" means a person who is invested by law with the power to perform judicial functions and includes a court when a particular context so requires.

§ 102-14. "Judgment".
"Judgment" means an adjudication by the court that the defendant is guilty or not guilty and if the adjudication is that the defendant is guilty it includes the sentence pronounced by the court.

§ 102-15. "Offense".
"Offense" means a violation of any penal statute of this State.

§ 102-16. "Parole".
"Parole" means the conditional and revocable release of a committed person under the supervision of a paroling authority.

§ 102-17. "Preliminary examination".
"Preliminary examination" means a hearing before a judge to determine if there is probable cause to believe that the person accused has committed an offense.

§ 102-18. "Probation".
"Probation" means a sentence or adjudication of conditional and revocable release under the supervision of a probation officer.

§ 102-19. "Recognizance".
"Recognizance" means an undertaking without security entered into by a person by which he binds himself to comply with such conditions as are set forth therein and which may provide for the forfeiture of a sum set by the court on failure to comply with the conditions thereof.

§ 102-20. "Sentence".
"Sentence" is the disposition imposed on the defendant by the court.

§ 102-21. Clinical psychologist; court-appointed examiner. (a) "Clinical psychologist" means a psychologist licensed under the Clinical Psychologist Licensing Act.

(b) "Court-appointed examiner" means a clinical social worker as defined in Section 9 of the Clinical Social Work and Social Work Practice Act.

§ 102-22. [“Facility Director”].
"Facility director", for the purposes of Article 104, means the chief officer of a mental health or developmental disabilities facility or his or her designee or the supervisor of a program of treatment or habilitation or his or her designee. "Designee" may include a physician, clinical psychologist, social worker, or nurse.

§ 102-23. [“Person with a moderate intellectual disability”].
"Person with a moderate intellectual disability" means a person whose intelligence quotient is between 41 and 55 and who does not suffer from significant mental illness to the extent that the person's ability to exercise rational judgment is impaired.

Article 103 - Rights of Accused
725 ILCS 5/103-1 *et seq.*

§ 103-1. Rights on arrest. (a) After an arrest on a warrant the person making the arrest shall inform the person arrested that a warrant has been issued for his arrest and the nature of the offense specified in the warrant.

(b) After an arrest without a warrant the person making the arrest shall inform the person arrested of the nature of the offense on which the arrest is based.

(c) No person arrested for a traffic, regulatory or misdemeanor offense, except in cases involving weapons or a controlled substance, shall be strip searched unless there is reasonable belief that the individual is concealing a weapon or controlled substance.

(d) "Strip search" means having an arrested person remove or arrange some or all of his or her clothing so as to permit a visual inspection of the genitals, buttocks, anus, female breasts or undergarments of such person.

(e) All strip searches conducted under this Section shall be performed by persons of the same sex as the arrested person and on premises where the search cannot be observed by persons not physically conducting the search.

(f) Every peace officer or employee of a police department conducting a strip search shall:

(1) Obtain the written permission of the police commander or an agent thereof designated for the purposes of authorizing a strip search in accordance with this Section.

(2) Prepare a report of the strip search. The report shall include the written authorization required by paragraph (1) of this subsection (f), the name of the person subjected to the search, the names of the persons conducting the search, and the time, date and place of the search. A copy of the report shall be provided to the person subject to the search.

(g) No search of any body cavity other than the mouth shall be conducted without a duly executed search warrant; any warrant authorizing a body cavity search shall specify that the search must be performed under sanitary conditions and conducted either by or under the supervision of a physician licensed to practice medicine in all of its branches in this State.

(h) Any peace officer or employee who knowingly or intentionally fails to comply with any provision of this Section is guilty of official misconduct as provided in Section 103-8; provided however, that nothing contained in this Section shall preclude prosecution of a peace officer or employee under another section of this Code.

(i) Nothing in this Section shall be construed as limiting any statutory or common law rights of any person for purposes of any civil action or injunctive relief.

(j) The provisions of subsections (c) through (h) of this Section shall not apply when the person is taken into custody by or remanded to the sheriff or correctional institution pursuant to a court order.

§ 103-2. Treatment while in custody.
(a) On being taken into custody every person shall have the right to remain silent.

(b) No unlawful means of any kind shall be used to obtain a statement, admission or confession from any person in custody.

(c) Persons in custody shall be treated humanely and provided with proper food, shelter and, if required, medical treatment.

§ 103-2.1. When statements by accused may be used. (a) In this Section, "custodial interrogation" means any interrogation during which

(i) a reasonable person in the subject's position would consider himself or herself to be in custody and

(ii) during which a question is asked that is reasonably likely to elicit an incriminating response.

In this Section, "place of detention" means a building or a police station that is a place of operation for a municipal police department or county sheriff department or other law enforcement agency, not a courthouse, that is owned or operated by a law enforcement agency at which persons are or may be held in detention in connection with criminal charges against those persons.

In this Section, "electronic recording" includes motion picture, audiotape, or videotape, or digital recording.

(b) An oral, written, or sign language statement of an accused made as a result of a custodial interrogation at a police station or other place of detention shall be presumed to be inadmissible as evidence against the accused in any criminal proceeding brought under Section 9-1, 9-1.2, 9-2, 9-2.1, 9-3, 9-3.2, or 9-3.3 of the Criminal Code of 1961 or under clause (d)(1)(F) of Section 11-501 of the Illinois Vehicle Code unless:

(1) an electronic recording is made of the custodial interrogation; and

(2) the recording is substantially accurate and not intentionally altered.

(c) Every electronic recording required under this Section must be preserved until such time as the defendant's conviction for any offense relating to the statement is final and all direct and habeas corpus appeals are exhausted, or the prosecution of such offenses is barred by law.

(d) If the court finds, by a preponderance of the evidence, that the defendant was subjected to a custodial interrogation in violation of this Section, then any statements made by the defendant during or following that non-recorded custodial interrogation, even if otherwise in compliance with this Section, are presumed to be inadmissible in any criminal proceeding against the defendant except for the purposes of impeachment.

(e) Nothing in this Section precludes the admission
(i) of a statement made by the accused in open court at his or her trial, before a grand jury, or at a preliminary hearing,
(ii) of a statement made during a custodial interrogation that was not recorded as required by this Section, because electronic recording was not feasible,
(iii) of a voluntary statement, whether or not the result of a custodial interrogation, that has a bearing on the credibility of the accused as a witness,
(iv) of a spontaneous statement that is not made in response to a question,
(v) of a statement made after questioning that is routinely asked during the processing of the arrest of the suspect,
(vi) of a statement made during a custodial interrogation by a suspect who requests, prior to making the statement, to respond to the interrogator's questions only if an electronic recording is not made of the statement, provided that an electronic recording is made of the statement of agreeing to respond to the interrogator's question, only if a recording is not made of the statement,
(vii) of a statement made during a custodial interrogation that is conducted out-of-state,
viii) of a statement given at a time when the interrogators are unaware that a death has in fact occurred, or
(ix) of any other statement that may be admissible under law. The State shall bear the burden of proving, by a preponderance of the evidence, that one of the exceptions described in this subsection(e) is applicable.

Nothing in this Section precludes the admission of a statement, otherwise inadmissible under this Section, that is used only for impeachment and not as substantive evidence.

(f) The presumption of inadmissibility of a statement made by a suspect at a custodial interrogation at a police station or other place of detention may be overcome by a preponderance of the evidence that the statement was voluntarily given and is reliable, based on the totality of the circumstances.

(g) Any electronic recording of any statement made by an accused during a custodial interrogation that is compiled by any law enforcement agency as required by this Section for the purposes of fulfilling the requirements of this Section shall be confidential and exempt from public inspection and copying, as provided under Section 7 of the Freedom of Information Act, and the information shall not be transmitted to anyone except as needed to comply with this Section.

§ 103-3. Right to communicate with attorney and family; transfers. (a) Persons who are arrested shall have the right to communicate with an attorney of their choice and a member of their family by making a reasonable number of telephone calls or in any other reasonable manner. Such communication shall be permitted within a reasonable time after arrival at the first place of custody.

(b) In the event the accused is transferred to a new place of custody his right to communicate with an attorney and a member of his family is renewed.

§ 103-4. Right to consult with attorney. Any person committed, imprisoned or restrained of his liberty for any cause whatever and whether or not such person is charged with an offense shall, except in cases of imminent danger of escape, be allowed to consult with any licensed attorney at law of this State whom such person may desire to see or consult, alone and in private at the place of custody, as many times and for such period each time as is reasonable. When any such person is about to be moved beyond the limits of this State under any pretense whatever the person to be moved shall be entitled to a reasonable delay for the purpose of obtaining counsel and of availing himself of the laws of this State for the security of personal liberty.

§ 103-5. Speedy trial. (a) Every person in custody in this State for an alleged offense shall be tried by the court having jurisdiction within 120 days from the date he was taken into custody unless delay is occasioned by the defendant, by an examination for fitness ordered pursuant to Section 104-13 of this Act, by a fitness hearing, by an adjudication of unfitness to stand trial, by a continuance allowed pursuant to Section 114-4 of this Act after a court's determination of the defendant's physical incapacity for trial, or by an interlocutory appeal. Delay shall be considered to be agreed to by the defendant unless he or she objects to the delay by making a written demand for trial or an oral demand for trial on the record. The provisions of this subsection (a) do not apply to a person on bail or recognizance for an offense but who is in custody for a violation of his or her parole or mandatory supervised release for another offense. The 120-day term must be one continuous period of incarceration. In computing the 120-day term, separate periods of incarceration may not be combined. If a defendant is taken into custody a second (or subsequent) time for the same offense, the term will begin again at day zero.

(b) Every person on bail or recognizance shall be tried by the court having jurisdiction within 160 days from the date defendant demands trial unless delay is occasioned by the defendant, by an examination for fitness ordered pursuant to Section 104-13 of this Act, by a fitness hearing, by an adjudication of unfitness to stand trial, by a continuance allowed pursuant to Section 114-4 of this Act after a court's determination of the defendant's physical incapacity for trial, or by an interlocutory appeal. The defendant's failure to appear for any court date set by the court operates to waive the defendant's demand for trial made under this subsection. For purposes of computing the 160 day period under this subsection (b), every person who was in custody for an alleged offense and demanded trial and is subsequently released on bail or recognizance and demands trial, shall be given credit for time spent in custody following the making of the demand while in custody. Any demand for trial made under this subsection (b) shall be in writing; and in the case of a defendant not in custody, the demand for trial shall include the date of any prior demand made under this provision while the defendant was in custody.

(c) If the court determines that the State has exercised without success due diligence to obtain evidence material to the case and that there are reasonable grounds to believe that such evidence may be obtained at a later day the court may continue the cause on application of the State for not more than an additional 60 days. If the court determines that the State has exercised without success due diligence to obtain results of DNA testing that is material to the case and that there are reasonable grounds to believe that such results may be obtained at a later day, the court may continue the cause on application of the State for not more than an additional 120 days.

(d) Every person not tried in accordance with subsections (a), (b) and (c) of this Section shall be discharged from custody or released from the obligations of his bail or recognizance.

(e) If a person is simultaneously in custody upon more than one charge pending against him in the same county, or simultaneously demands trial upon more than one charge pending against him in the same county, he shall be tried, or adjudged guilty after waiver of trial, upon at least one such charge before expiration relative to any of such pending charges of the period prescribed by subsections (a) and (b) of this Section.
Such person shall be tried upon all of the remaining charges thus pending within 160 days from the date on which judgment relative to the first charge thus prosecuted is rendered pursuant to the Unified Code of Corrections or, if such trial upon such first charge is terminated without judgment and there is no subsequent trial of, or adjudication of guilt after waiver of trial of, such first charge within a reasonable time, the person shall be tried upon all of the remaining charges thus pending within 160 days from the date on which such trial is terminated; if either such period of 160 days expires without the commencement of trial of, or adjudication of guilt after waiver of trial of, any of such remaining charges thus pending, such charge or charges shall be dismissed and barred for want of prosecution unless delay is occasioned by the defendant, by an examination for fitness ordered pursuant to Section 104-13 of this Act, by a fitness hearing, by an adjudication of unfitness for trial, by a continuance allowed pursuant to Section 114-4 of this Act after a court's determination of the defendant's physical incapacity for trial, or by an interlocutory appeal; provided, however, that if the court determines that the State has exercised without success due diligence to obtain evidence material to the case and that there are reasonable grounds to believe that such evidence may be obtained at a later day the court may continue the cause on application of the State for not more than an additional 60 days.

(f) Delay occasioned by the defendant shall temporarily suspend for the time of the delay the period within which a person shall be tried as prescribed by subsections (a),(b), or (e) of this Section and on the day of expiration of the delay the said period shall continue at the point at which it was suspended. Where such delay occurs within 21days of the end of the period within which a person shall be tried as prescribed by subsections (a), (b), or (e) of this Section, the court may continue the cause on application of the State for not more than an additional 21 days beyond the period prescribed by subsections (a), (b), or (e). This subsection (f) shall become effective on, and apply to persons charged with alleged offenses committed on or after, March 1, 1977.

§ 103-6. Waiver of jury trial. Every person accused of an offense shall have the right to a trial by jury unless (i) understandingly waived by defendant in open court or (ii) the offense is an ordinance violation punishable by fine only and the defendant either fails to file a demand for a trial by jury at the time of entering his or her plea of not guilty of fails to pay to the clerk of the circuit court at the time of entering his or her plea of not guilty any jury fee required to be paid to the clerk.

§ 103-7. Posting notice of rights. Every sheriff, chief of police or other person who is in charge of any jail, police station or other building where persons under arrest are held in custody pending investigation, bail or other criminal proceedings, shall post in every room, other than cells, of such buildings where persons are held in custody, in conspicuous places where it may be seen and read by persons in custody and others, a poster, printed in large type, containing a verbatim copy in the English language of the provisions of Sections 103-2, 103-3, 103-4, 109-1, 110-2, 110-4, and sub-parts (a) and (b) of Sections 110-7 and 113-3 of this Code. Each person who is in charge of any courthouse or other building in which any trial of an offense is conducted shall post in each room primarily used for such trials and in each room in which defendants are confined or wait, pending trial, in conspicuous places where it may be seen and read by persons in custody and others, a poster, printed in large type, containing a verbatim copy in the English language of the provisions of Sections 103-6, 113-1, 113-4 and 115-1 and of subparts (a) and (b) of Section 113-3 of this Code.

§ 103-8. Mandatory duty of officers. Any peace officer who intentionally prevents the exercise by an accused of any right conferred by this Article or who intentionally fails to perform any act required of him by this Article shall be guilty of official misconduct and may be punished in accordance with Section 33-3 of the "Criminal Code of 1961" approved July 28, 1961, as heretofore and hereafter amended.

§ 103-9. Bail bondsmen. No bail bondsman from any state may seize or transport unwillingly any person found in this State who is allegedly in violation of a bail bond posted in some other state. The return of any such person to another state may be accomplished only as provided by the laws of this State. Any bail bondsman who violates this Section is fully subject to the criminal and civil penalties provided by the laws of this State for his actions.

Commentary – Custodial Interrogation and Access to Attorneys

Strip Searches. 725 ILCS 5/103 addresses many of the constitutional protections for arrestees under the 4th, 5th and 6th Amendments to the United States Constitution (and the corollary provisions of the Illinois State Constitution of 1970). These statutory provisions codify that arrestees are going to be searched, but that "strip searches" will be limited to those who will have been charged with more serious offenses than traffic or misdemeanor violations, except for arrests for controlled substances or weapons, or there is a reasonable suspicion the arrestee has a controlled substance or weapon. Strip searches that do occur must be done by an officer of the same sex as the arrestee and the search process must be documented.

In *People v. Mitchell* 353 Ill. App. 838, 819 N.E.2d 1252 (Ill. App. Ct. 2nd Dist. 2004), the defendant, after a traffic stop, was arrested and taken into custody based on an outstanding misdemeanor warrant. At the jail, he was subjected to a strip search and a controlled substance was found on his person. He filed a motion to suppress the controlled substance, claiming that Section 103-1(c) prohibited the strip search. the court rejected his claim, noting that §103-1(j) provides that a strip search is permitted if the arrestee is remanded into custody pursuant to a court order, and that an arrest warrant counts as a court order. See *People v. Zayed* 2016 IL App (3d) 140780(Court found there was probable cause for a warrantless search following a traffic stop, but a strip search on a public roadway was an unreasonable search and seizure under the 4th Amendment.)

Custodial Interrogation. The arrestee has the right to remain silent (Section 103-2(a)) and also the right to consult with an attorney (§103-4). Illinois law addresses several scenarios that have been the subject of U.S. Supreme Court rulings to codify holdings of that court, and both Code of Criminal Procedure and court decisions are in lock-step with federal constitutional interpretations. Some examples will illustrate. A person is considered to be in custody (§103-2.1(a)) when a reasonable person in his circumstances would believe he is in custody. See *Berkemer v. McCarty* 468 U.S.420, 104 S.Ct. 3138 (U. S. S. Ct. 1984)(objective standard of whether a reasonable person would think he is in custody applies, not a subjective standard that the suspect thought he was in custody). A statement is considered to be in response to interrogation (§103-2.1(a) when it is in response to a question which would be reasonably likely to elicit a response. See *Rhode Island v. Innis* 446 U.S. 291, 100 S.Ct. 1682 (U. S. S. Ct. 1980)(volunteered statement was not elicited by interrogation, even if a psychological ploy is used to get a response). A person in custody has the right to consult with an attorney (§103-4) and if he requests an attorney, the interrogation (including attempts) must stop. See *Edwards v. Arizona* 451 U.S. 77, 101 S.Ct. 1880 (U. S. S. Ct. 1990)(when a suspect invokes his right to counsel, custodial interrogation must cease) and *Escobedo v. Illinois* 378 U.S. 478, 84 S.Ct.

1758 (1964)(defendant's 6th Amendment rights violated when he was prevented by police trickery from seeing his attorney who had come to police station during defendant's interrogation).

Illinois state constitutional protection broader. While Illinois court holdings are often in lock-step with United States Supreme Court criminal constitutional rulings, there have been occasions when Illinois courts have considered state constitutional protections to have broader affect. Illinois has developed a rule to protect individuals from tactics designed to undermine an attorney's role in the setting of police interrogations. This type of analysis that can result in a different result under state constitutional law than under federal constitutional law. In *Moran v. Burbine* 475 U.S. 412, 106 S.Ct. 1135 (1986), the Court ruled the defendant's rights against self-incrimination, to assistance of counsel and to due process were not violated by an in custodial interrogation that followed the denial of contact with his attorneys who had called with the detectives' division of the police department only to be told that her client would not be question. The defendant was not told of the attorney's contact with police nor that the attorney was told falsely that the defendant would not be questioned. Thereafter the defendant confessed after waiving his Miranda rights. The Supreme Court held that since the defendant did not know of the conversation between the attorney and the police, it could not have affected his understanding of his rights nor his waiver of those rights.

As a matter of state constitutional law in Illinois, however, law enforcement must notify defendants who are in custody of the presence of an attorney and any attempt by an attorney to contact a defendant who is in custody. In *People v. McCauley* 163 Ill.2d 414, 645 N.E.2d 923 (Ill. S. Ct. 1994), the contrary Moran holding was rejected for Illinois defendants under the Illinois State Constitution of 1970, when the court stated:

> The day is long past in Illinois, however, where attorneys must shout legal advice to their clients, held in custody, through the jailhouse door. In this case, we determine that our State constitutional guarantees afforded defendant a greater degree of protection. Our State constitutional guarantees simply do not permit police to delude custodial suspects, exposed to interrogation, into falsely believing they are without immediately available legal counsel and to also prevent that counsel from accessing and assisting their clients during the interrogation. (See Ill. Const.1970, art. I, §§ 2, 10.)It is apparent that when police are allowed to withhold information from custodial suspects that their attorneys are present and immediately available to offer assistance, enormous pressure builds upon the police to secure statements from those suspects before they either exercise their right to an attorney or somehow learn of their attorneys' presence. Further, by preventing those attorneys from accessing and assisting their clients, police improperly interfere with the suspects' right to their attorneys' presence as well as the attorney-client relationship, itself. The incommunicado interrogation and surrounding coercive environment likely to result from this objectionable practice is exactly the sort of scenario previously condemned by the United States Supreme Court in *Escobedo* and *Miranda.* See *Miranda v. Arizona* (1966), 384 U.S. 436, 457, 86 S.Ct. 1602, 1619 ("[t]his atmosphere carries its own badge of intimidation"); *Escobedo v. Illinois* (1964), 378 U.S. 478, 487, 84 S.Ct. 1758, 1763 ("it 'would be highly incongruous if our system of justice permitted the district attorney, the lawyer representing the State, to extract a confession from the accused while his own lawyer, seeking to speak with him, was kept from him by the police' ").
>
> *People v. McCauley* 163 Ill.2d at 423-424, 645 N.E.2d at 929.

However, a person in custody who talks to a cell mate is not protected by the 5th and 6th Amendment. In *Illinois v. Perkins* 496 U.S. 292, 110 S. Ct. 2394 (U. S. S. Ct. 1990) the court held that a defendant's conversations with cellmates do not implicate the same concerns that underlay *Miranda.* Police and prosecutors often use "informants" as snitches to offer testimony at trial that a defendant made admissions about the charged crime while in jail. In *People v. Hunt* 2012 IL 111089, 969 N.E.2d 819 (Ill. S. Ct. 2012), the Court held that the defendant's 6th Amendment rights were not violated when his conversation with an undercover informant (who was also in custody) was recorded, despite the presence of his attorney at the Chicago police station and the attempt by the attorney to get in contact with the defendant. The Court held that the setting was not a police interrogation and that the *McCauley* rule was not applicable. However, a parolee, having been convicted of a crime, still has 5th Amendment protection and the rights afforded by *Miranda* when being investigated and interrogated by parole agents for a new crime. *People v. Coleman* 2015 IL App (4th) 140730 (Defendant parolee was handcuffed and interrogated by agents based on a tip that he was dealing drugs, his statements were suppressed because a reasonable person would have believed he was in custody and he was not given his rights.)

Totality of circumstances. Juvenile interrogations. A custodial interrogation occurs where a reasonable person in the subjects position would feel that he or she was in custody and where questions asked are reasonably likely to elicit an incriminating response. Court will look to many factors in determining whether a custodial interrogation was voluntary or involuntary = age, intelligence and mental makeup of the subject, time, length, mood, and mode of the questioning, number of police officers present during the questioning, the presence or absence of family or friends; show of weapons, physical restraint, booking or fingerprinting or other indication of a formal arrest procedure. Applying these factors, would a reasonable person feel that he or she was free to leave? Able to stop questioning at any time? Looking at the totality of the circumstances the court will determine the voluntariness. For juvenile offenders, the reasonable person standard will focus on the reasonable juvenile of that age. Particularly, at home questioning in indicative but not conclusive, of a noncustodial interrogation. *In Re D.L.H* 2015 IL 117341 (Ill. S. Ct. 2015)(juvenile's statements to police at his home and in the presence of his father were voluntary.) A juvenile's confession will not be suppressed because he was denied the opportunity to confer with an adult, however police must make a reasonable effort to notify a concerned adult regarding an impending interrogation of a juvenile. *People v. Patterson* 2014 IL 115102 (Ill. S. Ct. 2014)(youth officer made a reasonable attempt to contact the residential director of defendant's residential facility by calling and leaving a message prior to the defendant's interrogation relating to an investigation for sexual assault.) In *People v. Murdock* 2012 IL 112362 (Ill. S. Ct. 2012), the court upheld the admission of the confession of 16 year-old in homicide investigation against a claim that it was constitutionally involuntary. The juvenile was not given access to an adult relative, even though his grandfather came to the police station during Murdock's question. The defendant showed no misunderstanding or stress about the process, waived his *Miranda* rights and otherwise acted voluntarily.

Waiver of Miranda Rights. Questioning suspects who are in custody requires obtaining a waiver of their *Miranda* rights. This is normally done orally and in writing. Whether the suspect has waived his rights is based on the totality of the circumstances. In *People v. Jones* 2014 IL App (1st) 120927, the defendant – suspect confessed to committing a murder and to the location of a hidden gun after receiving his *Miranda* warning sand waiving his rights. The homicide-required video recording showed that although the defendant –suspect had an IQ of 77, a forensic psychiatrist's evaluated the defendant and reviewed the video, testifying that the defendant – suspect understood his rights and manifested no difficulty during the interrogation. The trial courts finding of waiver by the defendant was upheld on appeal.

Custodial Interrogation in homicide cases. Section 103-2.1(b) requires that custodial statements taken from suspects accused of first degree murder, second degree murder and other homicide offenses must be electronically recorded. This enactment came as a result of legislative and Illinois Supreme Court commissioned studies into exonerations of defendants who had been sentenced to death in Illinois. In a homicide case, a statement taken from a defendant in violation of this section is presumed to be inadmissible. A custodial statement that is involuntarily given and recorded, of course, would be suppressed, as would a recorded custodial statement taken in violation of *Miranda.*

In *People v. Armstrong* 395 Ill.App.3d 606, 919 N.E.2d 57 (Ill. App. Ct. 2009), the defendant was convicted of involuntary manslaughter of his three-month-old son. The baby suffered massive external and internal head injuries on July 25, 2006 and was pronounced brain dead on July 27, 2006 at 4:15 p.m. Prior to that time, the defendant, who was in custody, gave two otherwise voluntary non-recorded statements to police that were incriminating. After the baby's death, the defendant gave a video-recorded confession which tracked his prior statements. His effort to suppress the statements under the electronic recording statute was rejected in the trial court and by the appellate court because § 103-2.1(e)(viii) provides that the recording requirements do not apply "when the interrogators are unaware that a death has in fact occurred". The evidence at the hearing on the motion to suppress established that the detectives were not told of the infant's death until after the second interrogation.

In *People v. Clayton* 2014 IL App (1st) 130743 the defendant was taken into custody and eventually two recorded interrogations appeared. Defense counsel learned that prior to the two recorded interrogations there had been a first, unrecorded interrogation. The Defendant moved to suppress all the Defendant's statements from all three of the interrogations claiming a violation of 725 ILCS 5/103-2.1(b). The trial court agreed and suppressed all three interrogations and their results. The prosecution appealed the suppression order claiming that by a preponderance of the evidence it had been shown the Defendant's statements were voluntary. In rejecting this claim and affirming the trial court's suppression order, the Court stated:

> We hold that the trial court's finding that Clayton was in custody under section 103-2.1(b) during the unrecorded first interview is not against the manifest weight of the evidence. Therefore, any statements which were made after the unrecorded interview were presumed inadmissible. 725 ILCS 5/103-2.1(d) (West 2012). Because the State failed to adduce any evidence sufficient to sustain its burden to prove that the later statements were voluntary and reliable, they were properly suppressed.
>
> *People v. Clayton* 2014 IL App (1st) 130743, ¶55

See also *People v. Little* 2016 IL App (3d) 140124 (suppression of an in custodial interrogation was required where police began an interrogation in a homicide investigation of Defendant and failed to record the first segment of the interview, only later turning on the recording system).

Corroboration of Confession. Courts have a general mistrust of confessions and therefore require additional independent proof of the commission of a crime in addition to an admitted confession In the absence of such independent proof, a confession may not be admissible. This is call the "*corpus delicti*" rule. See *People v. Lara* 2012 IL 112370 (Ill. S. Ct. 2012) (testimony of victim and corroboration by prior interviews of victim, were sufficient to support introduction of defendant's confession); *People v. Hurry* 2014 IL App.(3d)(victim's testimony corroborated defendant's confession as to all counts of his convictions for Predatory Criminal Sexual Assault).

§ 104-15. Report. (a) The person or persons conducting an examination of the defendant, pursuant to paragraph (a) or (b) of Section 104-13 shall submit a written report to the court, the State, and the defense within 30 days of the date of the order. The report shall include:

(1) A diagnosis and an explanation as to how it was reached and the facts upon which it is based;

(2) A description of the defendant's mental or physical disability, if any; its severity; and an opinion as to whether and to what extent it impairs the defendant's ability to understand the nature and purpose of the proceedings against him or to assist in his defense, or both.

(b) If the report indicates that the defendant is not fit to stand trial or to plead because of a disability, the report shall include an opinion as to the likelihood of the defendant attaining fitness within one year if provided with a course of treatment. If the person or persons preparing the report are unable to form such an opinion, the report shall state the reasons therefor. The report may include a general description of the type of treatment needed and of the least physically restrictive form of treatment therapeutically appropriate.

(c) The report shall indicate what information, if any, contained therein may be harmful to the mental condition of the defendant if made known to him.

§ 104-17. Commitment for Treatment; Treatment Plan. (a) If the defendant is eligible to be or has been released on bail or on his own recognizance, the court shall select the least physically restrictive form of treatment therapeutically appropriate and consistent with the treatment plan.

(b) If the defendant's disability is mental, the court may order him placed for treatment in the custody of the Department of Human Services, or the court may order him placed in the custody of any other appropriate public or private mental health facility or treatment program which has agreed to provide treatment to the defendant. If the defendant is placed in the custody of the Department of Human Services, the defendant shall be placed in a secure setting unless the court determines that there are compelling reasons why such placement is not necessary. During the period of time required to determine the appropriate placement the defendant shall remain in jail. If upon the completion of the placement process the Department of Human Services determines that the defendant is currently fit to stand trial, it shall immediately notify the court and shall submit a written report within 7 days. In that circumstance the placement shall be held pending a court hearing on the Department's report. Otherwise, upon completion of the placement process, the sheriff shall be notified and shall transport the defendant to the designated facility. The placement may be ordered either on an inpatient or an outpatient basis.

(c) If the defendant's disability is physical, the court may order him placed under the supervision of the Department of Human Services which shall place and maintain the defendant in a suitable treatment facility or program, or the court may order him placed in an appropriate public or private facility or treatment program which has agreed to provide treatment to the defendant. The placement may be ordered either on an inpatient or an outpatient basis.

(d) The clerk of the circuit court shall transmit to the Department, agency or institution, if any, to which the defendant is remanded for treatment, the following:

(1) a certified copy of the order to undergo treatment;

(2) the county and municipality in which the offense was committed;

(3) the county and municipality in which the arrest took place;

(4) a copy of the arrest report, criminal charges, arrest record, jail record, and the report prepared under Section 104-15; and

(5) all additional matters which the Court directs the clerk to transmit.

(e) Within 30 days of entry of an order to undergo treatment, the person supervising the defendant's treatment shall file with the court, the State, and the defense a report assessing the facility's or program's capacity to provide appropriate treatment for the defendant and indicating his opinion as to the probability of the defendant's attaining fitness within a period of one year from the date of the finding of unfitness. If the report indicates that there is a substantial probability that the defendant will attain fitness within the time period, the treatment supervisor shall also file a treatment plan which shall include:

(1) A diagnosis of the defendant's disability;

(2) A description of treatment goals with respect to rendering the defendant fit, a specification of the proposed treatment modalities, and an estimated timetable for attainment of the goals;

(3) An identification of the person in charge of supervising the defendant's treatment.

§ 104-18. Progress Reports. (a) The treatment supervisor shall submit a written progress report to the court, the State, and the defense:

(1) At least 7 days prior to the date for any hearing on the issue of the defendant's fitness;

(2) Whenever he believes that the defendant has attained fitness;

(3) Whenever he believes that there is not a substantial probability that the defendant will attain fitness, with treatment, within one year from the date of the original finding of unfitness.

(b) The progress report shall contain:

(1) The clinical findings of the treatment supervisor and the facts upon which the findings are based;

(2) The opinion of the treatment supervisor as to whether the defendant has attained fitness or as to whether the defendant is making progress, under treatment, toward attaining fitness within one year from the date of the original finding of unfitness;

(3) If the defendant is receiving medication, information from the prescribing physician indicating the type, the dosage and the effect of the medication on the defendant's appearance, actions and demeanor.

(c) Whenever the court is sent a report from the supervisor of the defendant's treatment under paragraph (2) of subsection (a) of this Section, the treatment provider shall arrange with the court for the return of the defendant to the county jail before the time frame specified in subsection (a) of Section 104-

20. This subsection (c) is inoperative on and after January 1, 2014.

§ 104-20. Ninety-Day Hearings; Continuing Treatment. (a) Upon entryor continuation of any order to undergo treatment, the court shall set a date for hearing to reexamine the issue of the defendant's fitness not more than 90 days thereafter. In addition, whenever the court receives a report from the supervisor of the defendant's treatment pursuant to subparagraph (2) or (3) of paragraph (a) of Section 104-18, the court shall forthwith set the matter for a first hearing within 14 days unless good cause is demonstrated why the hearing cannot be held. On the date set or upon conclusion of the matter then pending before it, the court, sitting without a jury, shall conduct a hearing, unless waived by the defense, and shall determine:

(1) Whether the defendant is fit to stand trial or to plead; and if not,
(2) Whether the defendant is making progress under treatment toward attainment of fitness within one year from the date of the original finding of unfitness.
(b) If the court finds the defendant to be fit pursuant to this Section, the court shall set the matter for trial; provided that if the defendant is in need of continued care or treatment and the supervisor of the defendant's treatment agrees to continue to provide it, the court may enter any order it deems appropriate for the continued care or treatment of the defendant by the facility or program pending the conclusion of the criminal proceedings.

(c) If the court finds that the defendant is still unfit but that he is making progress toward attaining fitness, the court may continue or modify its original treatment order entered pursuant to Section 104-17.

(d) If the court finds that the defendant is still unfit and that he is not making progress toward attaining fitness such that there is not a substantial probability that he will attain fitness within one year from the date of the original finding of unfitness, the court shall proceed pursuant to Section 104-23. However, if the defendant is in need of continued care and treatment and the supervisor of the defendant's treatment agrees to continue to provide it, the court may enter any order it deems appropriate for the continued care or treatment by the facility or program pending the conclusion of the criminal proceedings.

§ 21. Medication. (a) A defendant who is receiving psychotropic drugs shall not be presumed to be unfit to stand trial solely by virtue of the receipt of those drugs or medications.

(b) Whenever a defendant who is receiving medication under medical direction is transferred between a place of custody and a treatment facility or program, a written report from the prescribing physician shall accompany the defendant. The report shall state the type and dosage of the defendant's medication and the duration of the prescription. The chief officer of the place of custody or the treatment supervisor at the facility or program shall insure that such medication is provided according to the directions of the prescribing physician or until superseded by order of a physician who has examined the defendant.

§ 104-23. Unfit defendants. Cases involving an unfit defendant who demands a discharge hearing or a defendant who cannot become fit to stand trial and for whom no special provisions or assistance can compensate for his disability and render him fit shall proceed in the following manner:

(a) Upon a determination that there is not a substantial probability that the defendant will attain fitness within one year from the original finding of unfitness, a defendant or the attorney for the defendant may move for a discharge hearing pursuant to the provisions of Section 104-25. The discharge hearing shall be held within 120 days of the filing of a motion for a discharge hearing, unless the delay is occasioned by the defendant.

(b) If at any time the court determines that there is not a substantial probability that the defendant will become fit to stand trial or to plead within one year from the date of the original finding of unfitness, or if at the end of one year from that date the court finds the defendant still unfit and for whom no special provisions or assistance can compensate for his disabilities and render him fit, the State shall request the court:

(1) To set the matter for hearing pursuant to Section 104-25 unless a hearing has already been held pursuant to paragraph (a) of this Section; or

(2) To release the defendant from custody and to dismiss with prejudice the charges against him; or

(3) To remand the defendant to the custody of the Department of Human Services and order a hearing to be conducted pursuant to the provisions of the Mental Health and Developmental Disabilities Code, as now or hereafter amended. The Department of Human Services shall have 7 days from the date it receives the defendant to prepare and file the necessary petition and certificates that are required for commitment under the Mental Health and Developmental Disabilities Code. If the defendant is committed to the Department of Human Services pursuant to such hearing, the court having jurisdiction over the criminal matter shall dismiss the charges against the defendant, with the leave to reinstate. In such cases the Department of Human Services shall notify the court, the State's attorney and the defense attorney upon the discharge of the defendant. A former defendant so committed shall be treated in the same manner as any other civilly committed patient for all purposes including admission, selection of the place of treatment and the treatment modalities, entitlement to rights and privileges, transfer, and discharge. A defendant who is not committed shall be remanded to the court having jurisdiction of the criminal matter for disposition pursuant to subparagraph (1) or (2) of paragraph (b) of this Section.

(c) If the defendant is restored to fitness and the original charges against him are reinstated, the speedy trial provisions of Section 103-5 shall commence to run.

§ 104-31. No defendant placed in a setting of the Department of Human Services pursuant to the provisions of Sections 104-17, 104-25, or 104-26 shall be permitted outside the facility's housing unit unless escorted or accompanied by personnel of the Department of Human Services or authorized by court order. Any defendant placed in a secure setting pursuant to this Section, transported to court hearings or other necessary appointments off facility grounds by personnel of the Department of Human Services, may be placed in security devices or otherwise secured during the period of transportation to assure secure transport of the defendant and the safety of Department of Human Services personnel and others. These security measures shall not constitute restraint as defined in the Mental Health and Developmental Disabilities Code. Nor shall any defendant be permitted any off-grounds privileges, either with or without escort by personnel of the Department of Human Services, any unsupervised on-ground privileges, or placement in a non-secure setting unless such off-grounds or unsupervised on-grounds privileges, or placement in a non-secure setting have been approved by specific court order, which order may include such conditions on the defendant as the court may deem appropriate and necessary to reasonably assure the defendant's satisfactory progress in treatment and the safety of the defendant or others. Whenever the court receives a report from the supervisor of the defendant's treatment recommending the defendant for any off-grounds or unsupervised on-grounds privileges, or placement in a non-secure setting, the court shall set the matter for a first hearing within 21 days unless good cause is demonstrated why the hearing cannot be held. The changes made to this Section by this amendatory Act of the 96th General Assembly are declarative of existing law and shall not be construed as a new enactment.

Title II. Apprehension and Investigation
Selected Provisions of Article 107 – Arrest
725 ILCS 5/107-1 *et seq.*
Sections 107-1 through 107-3, 107-9 through 107-12

§ 107-1. Definitions. (a) A "warrant of arrest" is a written order from a court directed to a peace officer, or to some other person specifically named, commanding him to arrest a person.

(b) A "summons" is a written order issued by a court which commands a person to appear before a court at a stated time and place.

(c) A "notice to appear" is a written request issued by a peace officer that a person appear before a court at a stated time and place.

§ 107-2. (1) Arrest by Peace Officer. A peace officer may arrest a person when:

(a) He has a warrant commanding that such person be arrested; or

(b) He has reasonable grounds to believe that a warrant for the person's arrest has been issued in this State or in another jurisdiction; or

(c) He has reasonable grounds to believe that the person is committing or has committed an offense.

(2) Whenever a peace officer arrests a person, the officer shall question the arrestee as to whether he or she has any children under the age of 18 living with him or her who may be neglected as a result of the arrest or otherwise. The peace officer shall assist the arrestee in the placement of the children with a relative or other responsible person designated by the arrestee. If the peace officer has reasonable cause to believe that a child may be a neglected child as defined in the Abused and Neglected Child Reporting Act, he shall report it immediately to the Department of Children and Family Services as provided in that Act.

(3) A peace officer who executes a warrant of arrest in good faith beyond the geographical limitation of the warrant shall not be liable for false arrest.

§ 107-3. Arrest by private person.
Any person may arrest another when he has reasonable grounds to believe that an offense other than an ordinance violation is being committed.

§ 107-4. Arrest by peace officer from other jurisdiction. (a) As used in this Section:

(1) "State" means any State of the United States and the District of Columbia.

(2) "Peace Officer" means any peace officer or member of any duly organized State, County, or Municipal peace unit, any police force of another State, the United States Department of Defense, or any police force whose members, by statute, are granted and authorized to exercise powers similar to those conferred upon any peace officer employed by a law enforcement agency of this State.

(3) "Fresh pursuit" means the immediate pursuit of a person who is endeavoring to avoid arrest.

(4) "Law enforcement agency" means a municipal police department or county sheriff's office of this State.

(a-3) Any peace officer employed by a law enforcement agency of this State may conduct temporary questioning pursuant to Section 107-14 of this Code and may make arrests in any jurisdiction within this State:

(1) if the officer is engaged in the investigation of criminal activity that occurred in the officer's primary jurisdiction and the temporary questioning or arrest relates to, arises from, or is conducted pursuant to that investigation; or

(2) if the officer, while on duty as a peace officer, becomes personally aware of the immediate commission of a felony or misdemeanor violation of the laws of this State; or

(3) if the officer, while on duty as a peace officer, is requested by an appropriate State or local law enforcement official to render aid or assistance to the requesting law enforcement agency that is outside the officer's primary jurisdiction; or

(4) in accordance with Section 2605-580 of the Department of State Police Law of the Civil Administrative Code of Illinois. While acting pursuant to this subsection, an officer has the same authority as within his or her own jurisdiction.

(a-7) The law enforcement agency of the county or municipality in which any arrest is made under this Section shall be immediately notified of the arrest.

(b) Any peace officer of another State who enters this State in fresh pursuit and continues within this State in fresh pursuit of a person in order to arrest him on the ground that he has committed an offense in the other State has the same authority to arrest and hold the person in custody as peace officers of this State have to arrest and hold a person in custody on the ground that he has committed an offense in this State.

(c) If an arrest is made in this State by a peace officer of another State in accordance with the provisions of this Section he shall without unnecessary delay take the person arrested before the circuit court of the county in which the arrest was made. Such court shall conduct a hearing for the purpose of determining the lawfulness of the arrest. If the court determines that the arrest was lawful it shall commit the person arrested, to await for a reasonable time the issuance of an extradition warrant by the Governor of this State, or admit him to bail for such purpose. If the court determines that the arrest was unlawful it shall discharge the person arrested.

§ 107-5. Method of arrest.(a) An arrest is made by an actual restraint of the person or by his submission to custody.

(b) An arrest may be made on any day and at any time of the day or night.

(c) An arrest may be made anywhere within the jurisdiction of this State.

(d) All necessary and reasonable force may be used to effect an entry into any building or property or part thereof to make an authorized arrest.

§ 107-6. Release by officer of person arrested. A peace officer who arrests a person without a warrant is authorized to release the person without requiring him to appear before a court when the officer is satisfied that there are no grounds for criminal complaint against the person arrested.

§ 107-7. Persons exempt from arrest.
(a) Electors shall, in all cases except treason, felony or breach of the peace, be privileged from arrest during their attendance at election, and in going to and returning from the same.
(b) Senators and representatives shall, in all cases, except treason, felony or breach of the peace, be privileged from arrest during the session of the General Assembly, and in going to and returning from the same.

(c) The militia shall in all cases, except treason, felony, or breach of the peace, be privileged from arrest during their attendance at musters and elections, and in going to and returning from the same.

(d) Judges, attorneys, clerks, sheriffs, and other court officers shall be privileged from arrest while attending court and while going to and returning from court.

§ 107-8. Assisting peace officer. (a) A peace officer making a lawful arrest may command the aid of persons over the age of 18.

(b) A person commanded to aid a peace officer shall have the same authority to arrest as that peace officer.

(c) A person commanded to aid a peace officer shall not be civilly liable for any reasonable conduct in aid of the officer.

§ 107-9. Issuance of arrest warrant upon complaint. (a) When a complaint is presented to a court charging that an offense has been committed it shall examine upon oath or affirmation the complainant or any witnesses.

(b) The complaint shall be in writing and shall:

(1) State the name of the accused if known, and if not known the accused may be designated by any name or description by which he can be identified with reasonable certainty;

(2) State the offense with which the accused is charged;

(3) State the time and place of the offense as definitely as can be done by the complainant; and

(4) Be subscribed and sworn to by the complainant.
(c) A warrant shall be issued by the court for the arrest of the person complained against if it appears from the contents of the complaint and the examination of the complainant or other witnesses, if any, that the person against whom the complaint was made has committed an offense.

(d) The warrant of arrest shall:

(1) Be in writing;

2) Specify the name, sex and birth date of the person to be arrested or if his name, sex or birth date is unknown, shall designate such person by any name or description by which he can be identified with reasonable certainty;

(3) Set forth the nature of the offense;

(4) State the date when issued and the municipality or county where issued;

(5) Be signed by the judge of the court with the title of his office;

(6) Command that the person against whom the complaint was made be arrested and brought before the court issuing the warrant or if he is absent or unable to act before the nearest or most accessible court in the same county;

(7) Specify the amount of bail; and

(8) Specify any geographical limitation placed on the execution of the warrant, but such limitation shall not be expressed in mileage.

(e) The warrant shall be directed to all peace officers in the State. It shall be executed by the peace officer, or by a private person specially named therein, at any location within the geographic limitation for execution placed on the warrant. If no geographic limitation is placed on the warrant, then it may be executed anywhere in the State.

(f) The warrant may be issued electronically or electromagnetically by use of a facsimile transmission machine and any such warrant shall have the same validity as a written warrant.

§ 107-10. Defective warrant. A warrant of arrest shall not be quashed or abated nor shall any person in custody for an offense be discharged from such custody because of technical irregularities not affecting the substantial rights of the accused.

§ 107-11. When summons may be issued. (a) When authorized to issue a warrant of arrest, a court may instead issue a summons.
(b) The summons shall:

(1) Be in writing;

(2) State the name of the person summoned and his or her address, if known;

(3) Set forth the nature of the offense;
(4) State the date when issued and the municipality or county where issued;

(5) Be signed by the judge of the court with the title of his or her office; and

(6) Command the person to appear before a court at a certain time and place.

(c) The summons may be served in the same manner as the summons in a civil action, except that police officers may serve summons for violations of ordinances occurring within their municipalities.

§ 107-12. Notice to appear. (a) Whenever a peace officer is authorized to arrest a person without a warrant he may instead issue to such person a notice to appear.

(b) The notice shall:

(1) Be in writing;

(2) State the name of the person and his address, if known;

(3) Set forth the nature of the offense;

(4) Be signed by the officer issuing the notice; and

(5) Request the person to appear before a court at a certain time and place.

(c) Upon failure of the person to appear a summons or warrant of arrest may issue.

(d) In any case in which a person is arrested for a Class C misdemeanor or a petty offense and remanded to the sheriff other than pursuant to a court order, the sheriff may issue such person a notice to appear.

§ 107-13. Offenses committed by corporations. (a) When a corporation is charged with the commission of an offense the court shall issue a summons setting forth the nature of the offense and commanding the corporation to appear before a court at a certain time and place.

(b) The summons for the appearance of a corporation may be served in the manner provided for service of summons upon a corporation in a civil action.

(c) If, after being summoned, the corporation does not appear, a plea of not guilty shall be entered by the court having jurisdiction to try the offense for which the summons was issued, and such court shall proceed to trial and judgment without further process.

§107-14. Temporary questioning without arrest. (a) A peace officer, after having identified himself as a peace officer, may stop any person in a public place for a reasonable period of time when the officer reasonably infers from the circumstances that the person is committing, is about to commit or has committed an offense as defined in Section 102-15 of this Code, and may demand the name and address of the person and an explanation of his actions. Such detention and temporary questioning will be conducted in the vicinity of where the person was stopped.

(b) Upon completion of any stop under subsection (a) involving a frisk or search, and unless impractical, impossible, or under exigent circumstances, the officer shall provide the person with a stop receipt which provides the reason for the stop and contains the officer's name and badge number. This subsection (b) does not apply to searches or inspections for compliance with the Fish and Aquatic Life Code, the Wildlife Code, the Herptiles-Herps Act, or searches or inspections for routine security screenings at facilities or events. For the purposes of this subsection (b), "badge" means an officer's department issued identification number associated with his or her position as a police officer with that department.

§ 107-15. Fresh pursuit. When the fact that a felony has been committed comes to the knowledge of a sheriff or coroner, fresh pursuit shall be forthwith made after every person guilty of the felony, by the sheriff, coroner, and all other persons who is by any one of them commanded or summoned for that purpose; every such officer who does not do his or her duty in the premises is guilty of a Class B misdemeanor.

§ 107-16. Apprehension of offender.
It is the duty of every sheriff, coroner, and every marshal, policeman, or other officer of an incorporated city, town, or village, having the power of a sheriff, when a criminal offense or breach of the peace is committed or attempted in his or her presence, forthwith to apprehend the offender and bring him or her before a judge, to be dealt with according to law; to suppress all riots and unlawful assemblies, and to keep the peace, and without delay to serve and execute all warrants and other process to him or her lawfully directed.

Commentary – Arrests and Notices to Appear

Arrests. Section 102-5 defines "arrest" as the "taking of a person into custody". An arrest is an involuntary detention by the police, such that a reasonable person would feel that he or she was unable to leave. It is not the suspect's subjective belief that she has been arrested. In *People v. Washington* 363 Ill.App.3d 13, 842 N.E.2d 1193 (Ill. App. Ct. 1st Dist. 2006), the defendant voluntarily went to the police station but was held for interrogation in a separate interview room overnight, before making an investigation. In finding she had been arrested without probable cause, the court noted these criteria:

> Factors Illinois courts consider in determining whether a defendant was arrested include: (1) the time, place, length, mood, and mode of the encounter between the defendant and the police; (2) the number of police officers present; (3) any indicia of formal arrest or restraint, such as the use of handcuffs or drawing of guns; (4) the intention of the officers; (5) the subjective belief or understanding of the defendant; (6) whether the defendant was told he could refuse to accompany the police; (7) whether the defendant was transported in a police car; (8) whether the defendant was told he was free to leave; (9) whether the defendant was told he was under arrest; and (10) the language used by officers.
>
> *People v. Washington* 363 Ill.App.3d at 24, 842 N.E.2d at 1202 (citations omitted).

In concluding that the defendant had been arrested, applying these factors, the court noted that the police do not have to utter the words "you're under arrest" for a defendant to meet the test, even if she voluntarily went to the police station in the first instance.

In lieu of an arrest, an officer can issue a notice to appear. While the defendant has been detained and accused of committing a crime, he is released on the street and given notice that he must appear at a designated courtroom, on a specific date and time to answer the charge identified on the notice. An officer must have probable cause to issue the notice to appear. If the defendant does not appear in court at the identified time and place, a warrant for the defendant's arrest can issue.

Warrantless arrests. As Section 107-2 notes, a police officer has the power to arrest someone if he has a warrant for that person's arrest, if the officer is aware of an outstanding warrant for the person, or if the officer has reasonable grounds to believe the person has committed a crime. However, based on the 4th Amendment to the United States constitution, if the person to be arrested is at his own home, ordinarily an officer must have an arrest warrant. As with most circumstances, there are exceptions to the "home warrant" requirement, including consent by the owner or resident to enter the premises to make an arrest or search, or exigent circumstances. Exigent circumstances are reviewed based on many factors that include (1) hot pursuit of a person observed to have committed a crime, (2) the danger that evidence will be destroyed , (3) the danger that someone will be harmed (i.e. "armed and dangerous") or (4) the possibility the suspect will escape. The burden of proof is on the prosecution to show that an exception to the warrant requirement is present.

In other places – public places, open fields or someone else's residence the protection of the 4th Amendment warrant requirement is not available to a suspect where there is probable cause to believe he has committed a crime. The 4th Amendment emphasis is on the security and privacy of one's home.

In *People v. Davis* 398 Ill.App.3d 940, 924 N.E.2d 67 (Ill. App. Ct. 2nd Dist. 2010), the defendant was arrested in his own apartment, charged and convicted of cocaine, marijuana and another controlled substance offense. The defendant's motion to quash his arrest, suppress evidence seized (scales and drugs) and suppress his incriminating statements was denied by the trial court, and the defendant appealed. Evidence showed that police received a call from a victim who claimed she owed the defendant and his girlfriend money for drugs and that she had just been attacked and battered by them, along with another man. The victim told the police where the suspects lived and that there were drugs in the home. An officer (Willer) went to that apartment where he arrested the girlfriend on a battery charge, as she left the apartment building. Without consent, the police entered the apartment after seeing the defendant at the door and went room-to-room looking for others present. Two other individuals were arrested, and in the process the police seized a set of electronic scales and a white powdery substance that field tested for cocaine. The police did not have consent of the defendant or girlfriend to enter the apartment, and justified the law enforcement entry on the need to protect the welfare of children that were present in the apartment. The appellate court reversed, stating:

> In this case, it is undisputed that [officer] Willer had neither a warrant nor consent to enter the apartment. Our review of the record reveals that there did not exist exigent circumstances to justify Willer's entry into the apartment to arrest defendant for the battery committed against Harrison. The evidence presented by the State at the hearing on the motion to suppress does not support a finding of exigent circumstances because it does not suggest an immediacy or real threat of current danger or likelihood of flight.
>
> *People v. Davis* 398 Ill.App. 3d at 949, 924 N.E. 2d at 77.

See also, *Kentucky v. King* 563 U.S. ___, 131 S.Ct 1849 (U. S. S. Ct. 2011)(based on tip, police perceived suspicious movements inside the apartment and together with the smell of marijuana there were exigent circumstances present regarding possible destruction of evidence, even though officers went to the wrong apartment door and did not violate the 4th Amendment warrant requirement to enter home.)

Reasonable grounds and probable cause. Reasonable grounds to arrest in Section 107-2(b) is probable cause – an amount of evidence that would suggest that a crime was committed and the suspect to be arrested is responsible for the crime. A police officer need not witness the events that establish probable cause; he may rely upon citizen informants and other police officers; that is hearsay can be considered in deciding if there is probable cause to arrest, as well as an officer's experience. Probable cause is more than suspicion, and is evidence that would convince a reasonably prudent person that the suspect committed a crime. Courts will look at the totality of the circumstances in reviewing the existence of probable cause when confronted with a claim that a defendant's arrest was legally invalid. Probable cause deals with probabilities not certainties – there is no burden of proof on the police officer if the totality of the circumstances known to him at the time of the arrest would lead the reasonable officer to conclude an arrest was proper. See *People v. Wear* 229 Ill.2d 545, 893 N.E.2d 631 (Ill. S. Ct. 2008)(warrantless entry into defendant's home and arrest for DUI, following erratic driving, stumbling, odor of alcohol and other facts was based on probable cause and exigent circumstances of "hot pursuit" from public to private place).

Informant information used in making an arrest. In *People v. Arnold* 349 Ill.App.3d 668, 812 N.E.2d 696 (Ill. App. Ct. 1st Dist. 2004), police were investigating a murder where a woman was shot and killed in a blue Chevrolet while it sat in a parking lot between row houses. An informant told police that it was Brown and two others who shot three different weapons in that location, describing the shooting with accurate details. When questioned, Brown denied any involvement. On a second interview, the informant said it was the defendant who was the actual shooter, but the informant was afraid for his family's safety due to defendant's leadership as a general in a street gang. At the crime scene, police had discovered three different types of ammunition and recovered a .25 caliber gun in a dumpster where the informant said it had been thrown following the murder. The trial court and appellate court rejected the defendant's claim that his arrest had not been based on probable cause. The appellate court reasoned that the informant's information was sufficiently consistent with other facts known to the investigating officers, under the totality of circumstances, overwhelmingly established probable cause.

"Terry" stops Section 107-14 is the Illinois statutory provision that permits a police officer to temporarily detain someone for questioning, as was approved by the United States Supreme Court in *Terry v. Ohio* 392 U.S.1, 88 S.Ct. 1868 (U.S. S. Ct. 1969). the officer need only have a reasonable suspicion based on known facts that a crime has been committed or is about to be committed, to ask identifying questions, to inquire into the activities of the suspect and if the officer has reason to believe the suspect is armed and dangerous, to frisk the suspect for weapons to protect the officer's safety. (See 725 ILCS 5/108-1.1) Officers will use the opportunity afforded by a temporary detention to look for other facts that increase their authority to act. A *Terry* investigative stop is not a moment frozen in time and has the flexibility to ripen into probable cause.

In *People v. Allen* 409 Ill.App.3d 1058, 950 N.E.2d 1164, 2011 WL 1805368 (Ill. App. Ct. 4th Dist. 2011), the police received a tip from a known informant (who was not considered reliable) that a drug delivery was about to occur at his apartment from a person riding with two others in a white car. Officers observed the white car park in back of the informant's apartment, with the predicted occupants, and approached to identify the suspects and conduct a temporary detention stop. The driver and passengers were removed from the car, and the informant told officers to check the mouths of the individuals for drugs. Packets containing cocaine were found in the defendant's mouth. The trial and appellate court approved the initial *Terry* stop based on the informant's articulated facts, and found that the situation evolved into probable cause for arrest by independent verification of the informant's tip. Thus, the search and seizure was proper based on officers' questioning and investigative steps made during the temporary detention, as a search incident to the defendant's arrest. But see *People v. Boswell* 2014 IL App.(1st) 122275, ¶23 (*Terry* pat-down frisk search was not justified by the premise that all suspected narcotics transactions involve guns – articulated facts are necessary.)

However, *Terry* stops pursuant to Section 107-14 are limited. Such a temporary detention is not a license to search for drugs or other contraband. In *People v. Linley* 388 Ill.App.3d 747, 903 N.E.2d 791 (Ill. App. Ct. 2nd Dist. 2009), the defendant was standing in his driveway talking with two men inside a truck at 1:25 a.m. A police officer responded to a dispatch about gunshots in a nearby club and saw the defendant make a furtive gesture. The officer commanded the defendant to stand still with his hands on the truck and the defendant complied. The officer frisked the defendant and felt a lump in his pocket which he suspected to be drugs. The subsequent search resulted in the seizure of a package of cocaine and a digital scale. On appeal, the defendant's conviction was reversed, first on the basis of the lack of any articulated facts that the defendant was committing or about to commit a crime and second on the basis that the limited, permitted search for weapons was exceeded by the officer's search and seizure for drugs.

In *People v. Fields* 2014 IL App (1st) 130209 police respondent to complaints of drug dealing in a neighborhood at 2 a.m. and were told that dealers had run into an apartment building. Gaining access by ringing buzzers, two officer walked up the first two flights of stairs and saw no one. On the third floor landing they saw the Defendant who was seated on the floor and was shaking. The Defendant gave inconsistent answers about his age, where he lived and why he was there in the hall outside an apartment. He refused to stand up when requested to do so. The officers put handcuffs on the Defendant and when they raised him, a loaded handgun dropped to the ground. The Defendant was arrested and charged with a weapons crime. His motion to suppress was denied but was affirmed on appeal, with the Court holding that the officers had engaged in "community policing" but checking on the welfare of a young person, and that the Defendant's behaviors and statements turned the encounter into a *Terry* stop, permitting the handcuffs (for police protection) and the further detention to investigate reasonable suspicion of criminal behavior. The dropping of the gun established probable cause for Defendant's arrest and the evidence supported his conviction on the weapons charge. A dissenting judge concluded that the totaling of the circumstances did not support the seizure of the Defendant so that the motion to suppress should have been granted.

Custodial Arrests for Petty Offenses. In *People v. Fitzpatrick* 2013 IL 113449, the defendant was arrested and taken into custody for walking down the middle of a public street, a violation of the Illinois Traffic Code and of a local municipal ordinance. Both were petty offenses that could result only in the imposition of a fine. Following arrest a search at the police station disclosed the defendant was in possession of a controlled substance. The defendant challenged the search under Article I, §6 of the Illinois State Constitution of 1970, contending it was unconstitutional to make a custodial arrest for a petty offense. In *Atwater v. City of Lago Vista* 532 U.S. 318,121 S.Ct.1536 (U. S. S. Ct. 2001), the United States Supreme Court found that a custodial arrest for a petty traffic offense was not a violation of the Fourth Amendment to the U.S. Constitution. In *Fitzpatrick,* the Illinois Supreme Court followed the "limited lock-step" doctrine holding that a custodial arrest for a petty offense was not unlawful under Illinois Constitutional law, thus adhering to and in "lock-step" with the *Atwater* rule.

Selected Provisions of Article 107A - Lineup and Photo Spread Procedure
725 ILCS 5/725-5 *et seq.*

Sec. 107A-0.1. Definitions.
For the purposes of this Article:

"Eyewitness" means a person viewing the lineup whose identification by sight of another person may be relevant in a criminal proceeding.

"Filler" means a person or a photograph of a person who is not suspected of an offense and is included in a lineup.

"Independent administrator" means a lineup administrator who is not participating in the investigation of the criminal offense and is unaware of which person in the lineup is the suspected perpetrator.

"Lineup" includes a photo lineup or live lineup.

"Lineup administrator" means the person who conducts a lineup.

"Live lineup" means a procedure in which a group of persons is displayed to an eyewitness for the purpose of determining if the eyewitness is able to identify the perpetrator of a crime, but does not include a showup.

"Photo lineup" means a procedure in which photographs are displayed to an eyewitness for the purpose of determining if the eyewitness is able to identify the perpetrator of a crime.

"Sequential lineup" means a live or photo lineup in which each person or photograph is presented to an eyewitness separately, in a previously determined order, and removed from the eyewitness's view before the next person or photograph is presented, in order to determine if the eyewitness is able to identify the perpetrator of a crime.

"Showup" means a procedure in which a suspected perpetrator is presented to the eyewitness at, or near, a crime scene for the purpose of obtaining an immediate identification.

"Simultaneous lineup" means a live or photo lineup in which a group of persons or array of photographs is presented simultaneously to an eyewitness for the purpose of determining if the eyewitness is able to identify the perpetrator of a crime.

Sec. 107A-2. Lineup procedure.
(a) All lineups shall be conducted using one of the following methods:
(1) An independent administrator, unless it is not practical.
(2) An automated computer program or other device that can automatically display a photo lineup to an eyewitness in a manner that prevents the lineup administrator from seeing which photograph or photographs the eyewitness is viewing until after the lineup is completed. The automated computer program may present the photographs to the eyewitness simultaneously or sequentially, consistent with the law enforcement agency guidelines required under subsection (b) of this Section.
(3) A procedure in which photographs are placed in folders, randomly numbered, and shuffled and then presented to an eyewitness such that the lineup administrator cannot see or know which photograph or photographs are being presented to the eyewitness until after the procedure is completed. The photographs may be presented to the eyewitness simultaneously or sequentially, consistent with the law enforcement agency guidelines required under subsection (b) of this Section.
(4) Any other procedure that prevents the lineup administrator from knowing the identity of the suspected perpetrator or seeing or knowing the persons or photographs being presented to the eyewitness until after the procedure is completed.

(b) Each law enforcement agency shall adopt written guidelines setting forth when, if at all, simultaneous lineups shall be conducted and when, if at all, sequential lineups shall be conducted. This subsection does not establish a preference for whether a law enforcement agency should conduct simultaneous lineups or sequential lineups. Whether and when to conduct simultaneous lineups or sequential lineups is at the discretion of each law enforcement agency. If, after the effective date of this amendatory Act of the 98th General Assembly, a method of conducting a lineup different from a simultaneous or sequential lineup is determined by the Illinois Supreme Court to be sufficiently established to have gained general acceptance as a reliable method for eyewitness identifications and provides more accurate results than simultaneous or sequential lineups, a law enforcement agency may adopt written guidelines setting forth when, if at all, this different method of conducting lineups shall be used and, when feasible, the provisions of subsection (d) of this Section shall apply to the use of these methods.

(c) On and after the effective date of this amendatory Act of the 98th General Assembly, there is no preference as to whether a law enforcement agency conducts a live lineup or a photo lineup and to the extent that the common law directs otherwise, this direction is abrogated.

(d) If a lineup administrator conducts a sequential lineup, the following shall apply:
(1) Solely at the eyewitness's request, the lineup administrator may present a person or photograph to the eyewitness an additional time but only after the eyewitness has first viewed each person or photograph one time.
(2) If the eyewitness identifies a person as a perpetrator, the lineup administrator shall continue to sequentially present the remaining persons or photographs to the eyewitness until the eyewitness has viewed each person or photograph.

(e) Before a lineup is conducted:
(1) The eyewitness shall be instructed that:
(A) if recording the lineup is practical, an audio and video recording of the lineup will be made for the purpose of accurately documenting all statements made by the eyewitness, unless the eyewitness refuses to the recording of the lineup, and that if a recording is made it will be of the persons in the lineup and the eyewitness;
(B) the perpetrator may or may not be presented in the lineup;
(C) if an independent administrator is conducting the lineup, the independent administrator does not know the suspected perpetrator's identity or if the administrator conducting the lineup is not an independent administrator, the eyewitness should not assume that the lineup administrator knows which person in the lineup is the suspect;
(D) the eyewitness should not feel compelled to make an identification;
(E) it is as important to exclude innocent persons as it is to identify a perpetrator; and--
(F) the investigation will continue whether or not an identification is made.--
(2) The eyewitness shall acknowledge in writing the receipt of the instructions required under this subsection and, if applicable, the refusal to be recorded. If the eyewitness refuses to sign the acknowledgement, the lineup administrator shall note the refusal of the eyewitness to sign the acknowledgement and shall also sign the acknowledgement.

(f) In conducting a lineup:
(1) When practicable, the lineup administrator shall separate all eyewitnesses in order to prevent the eyewitnesses from conferring with one another before an during the lineup procedure. If separating the eyewitnesses is not practicable, the lineup administrator shall ensure that all eyewitnesses are monitored and that they do not confer with one another while waiting to view the lineup and during the lineup.
(2) Each eyewitness shall perform the identification procedures without any other eyewitness present. Each eyewitness shall be

given instructions regarding the identification procedures without other eyewitnesses present.

(3) The lineup shall be composed to ensure that the suspected perpetrator does not unduly stand out from the fillers. In addition:

(A) Only one suspected perpetrator shall be included in a lineup.

(B) The suspected perpetrator shall not be substantially different in appearance from the fillers based on the eyewitness's previous description of the perpetrator or based on other factors that would draw attention to the suspected perpetrator.

(C) At least 5 fillers shall be included in a photo lineup, in addition to the suspected perpetrator.

(D) When practicable, at least 5 fillers shall be included in a live lineup, in addition to the suspected perpetrator, but in no event shall there be less than 3 fillers in addition to the suspected perpetrator.

(E) If the eyewitness has previously viewed a photo lineup or live lineup in connection with the identification of another person suspected of involvement in the offense, the fillers in the lineup in which the current suspected perpetrator participates shall be different from the fillers used in the prior lineups.

(4) If there are multiple eyewitnesses, subject to the requirements in subsection (a) of this Section and to the extent possible, the suspected perpetrator shall be placed in a different position in the lineup or photo array for each eyewitness.

(5) Nothing shall be communicated to the eyewitness regarding the suspected perpetrator's position in the lineup or regarding anything that may influence the eyewitness's identification.

(6) No writings or information concerning any previous arrest, indictment, or conviction of the suspected perpetrator shall be visible or made known to the eyewitness.

(7) If a photo lineup, the photograph of the suspected perpetrator shall be contemporary in relation to the photographs of the fillers and, to the extent practicable, shall resemble the suspected perpetrator's appearance at the time of the offense.

(8) If a live lineup, any identifying actions, such as speech, gestures, or other movements, shall be performed by all lineup participants.

(9) If a live lineup, all lineup participants must be out of view of the eyewitness prior to the lineup.

(10) The lineup administrator shall obtain and document any and all statements made by the eyewitness during the lineup as to the perpetrator's identity. When practicable, an audio or video recording of the statements shall be made.

(11) If the eyewitness identifies a person as the perpetrator, the eyewitness shall not be provided any information concerning the person until after the lineup is completed.

(12) Unless otherwise allowed under subsection (a) of this Section, there shall not be anyone present during a lineup who knows the suspected perpetrator's identity, except the eyewitness and suspected perpetrator's counsel if required by law.

(g) The lineup administrator shall make an official report of all lineups, which shall include all of the following information:

(1) All identification and non-identification results obtained during the lineup, signed by the eyewitness, including any and all statements made by the eyewitness during the lineup as to the perpetrator's identity as required under paragraph (10) of subsection (f) of this Section. If the eyewitness refuses to sign, the lineup administrator shall note the refusal of the eyewitness to sign the results and shall also sign the notation.

(2) The names of all persons who viewed the lineup.

(3) The names of all law enforcement officers and counsel present during the lineup.

(4) The date, time, and location of the lineup.

(5) Whether it was a photo lineup or live lineup and how many persons or photographs were presented in the lineup.

(6) The sources of all persons or photographs used as fillers in the lineup.
(7) In a photo lineup, the actual photographs shown to the eyewitness.
(8) In a live lineup, a photograph or other visual recording of the lineup that includes all persons who participated in the lineup.
(9) If applicable, the eyewitness's refusal to be recorded.
(10) If applicable, the reason for any impracticability in strict compliance with this Section.

(h) Unless it is not practical or the eyewitness refuses, video record of all lineup procedures shall be made.
(1) If a video record is not practical or the eyewitness refuses to allow a video record to be made:
(A) the reasons or the refusal shall be documented in the official report required under subsection (g) of this Section;
(B) an audio record shall be made, if practical; and
(C) if a live lineup, the lineup shall be photographed.
(2) If an audio record is not practical, the reasons shall be documented in the official report required under subsection (g) of this Section.

(i) The photographs, recordings, and the official report of the lineup required by this Section shall be disclosed to counsel for the accused as provided by the Illinois Supreme Court Rules regarding discovery. All photographs of suspected perpetrators shown to an eyewitness during a lineup shall be disclosed to counsel for the accused as provided by the Illinois Supreme Court Rules regarding discovery. To protect-- the identity of the eyewitness and the identities of law enforcement officers used as fillers in the lineup from being disclosed to third parties, the State's Attorney shall petition the court for a protective order under Supreme Court Rule 415- upon disclosure of the photographs or recordings to the counsel of the accused.

(j) All of the following shall be available as consequences of compliance or noncompliance with the requirements of this Section:
(1) Failure to comply with any of the requirements of this Section shall be a factor to be considered by the court in adjudicating a motion to suppress an eyewitness identification or any other motion to bar an eyewitness identification. These motions shall be in writing and state facts showing how the identification procedure was improper. This paragraph (1) makes no change to existing applicable common law or statutory standards or burdens of proof.
(2) When warranted by the evidence presented at trial, the jury shall be instructed that it may consider all the facts and circumstances including compliance or noncompliance with this Section to assist in its weighing of the identification testimony of an eyewitness.

(k) Any electronic recording made during a lineup that is compiled by any law enforcement agency as required by this Section for the purposes of fulfilling the requirements of this Section shall be confidential and exempt from public inspection and copying, as provided under Section 7 of the Freedom of Information Act, and the recording shall not be transmitted to any person except as necessary to comply with this Section

Article 108 - Search and Seizure
725 ILCS 5/108-1 *et seq.*
§s 108-1, 108-1.01, 108-3 through 108-8

§ 108-1. Search without warrant.
(1) When a lawful arrest is effected a peace officer may reasonably search the person arrested and the area within such person's immediate presence for the purpose of:

(a) protecting the officer from attack; or

(b) preventing the person from escaping; or

(c) discovering the fruits of the crime; or

(d) discovering any instruments, articles, or things which may have been used in the commission of, or which may constitute evidence of, an offense.

(2) (Blank).

(3) A law enforcement officer may not search or inspect a motor vehicle, its contents, the driver, or a passenger solely because of a violation of Section 12-603.1 of the Illinois Vehicle Code.

§ 108-1.01. Search during temporary questioning. When a peace officer has stopped a person for temporary questioning pursuant to Section 107-14 of this Code and reasonably suspects that he or another is in danger of attack, he may search the person for weapons. If the officer discovers a weapon, he may take it until the completion of the questioning, at which time he shall either return the weapon, if lawfully possessed, or arrest the person so questioned.

§ 108-2. Custody and disposition of things seized. an inventory of all instruments, articles or things seized on a search without warrant shall be given to the person arrested and a copy thereof delivered to the judge before whom the person arrested is taken, and thereafter, such instruments, articles or things shall be handled and disposed of in accordance with Sections 108--11 and 108--12 of this Code. If the person arrested is released without a charge being preferred against him all instruments, articles or things seized, other than contraband, shall be returned to him upon release.

§ 108-3. Grounds for search warrant.
(a) Except as provided in subsection (b), upon the written complaint of any person under oath or affirmation which states facts sufficient to show probable cause and which particularly describes the place or person, or both, to be searched and the things to be seized, any judge may issue a search warrant for the seizure of the following:

(1) Any instruments, articles or things designed or intended for use or which are or have been used in the commission of, or which may constitute evidence of, the offense in connection with which the warrant is issued; or contraband, the fruits of crime, or things otherwise criminally possessed.

(2) Any person who has been kidnapped in violation of the laws of this State, or who has been kidnapped in another jurisdiction and is now concealed within this State, or any human fetus or human corpse.

(b) When the things to be seized are the work product of, or used in the ordinary course of business, and in the possession, custody, or control of any person known to be engaged in the gathering or dissemination of news for the print or broadcast media, no judge may issue a search warrant unless the requirements set forth in subsection (a) are satisfied and there is probable cause to believe that:

(1) such person has committed or is committing a criminal offense; or

(2) the things to be seized will be destroyed or removed from the State if the search warrant is not issued.

§ 108-4. Issuance of search warrant. (a) All warrants upon written complaint shall state the time and date of issuance and be the warrants of the judge issuing the same and not the warrants of the court in which he is then sitting and such warrants need not bear the seal of the court or clerk thereof. The complaint on which the warrant is issued need not be filed with the clerk of the court nor with the court if there is no clerk until the warrant has been executed or has been returned "not executed".

The search warrant upon written complaint may be issued electronically or electromagnetically by use of a facsimile transmission machine and any such warrant shall have the same validity as a written search warrant.

(b) Warrant upon oral testimony.

(1) General rule. When the offense in connection with which a search warrant is sought constitutes terrorism or any related offense as defined in Article 29D of the Criminal Code of 1961,and if the circumstances make it reasonable to dispense, in whole or in part, with a written affidavit, a judge may issue a warrant based upon sworn testimony communicated by telephone or other appropriate means, including facsimile transmission.

(2) Application. The person who is requesting the warrant shall prepare a document to be known as a duplicate original warrant and shall read such duplicate original warrant, verbatim, to the judge. The judge shall enter, verbatim, what is so read to the judge on a document to be known as the original warrant. The judge may direct that the warrant be modified.

(3) Issuance. If the judge is satisfied that the offense in connection with which the search warrant is sought constitutes terrorism or any related offense as defined in Article 29D of the Criminal Code of 1961, that the circumstances are such as to make it reasonable to dispense with a written affidavit, and that grounds for the application exist or that there is probable cause to believe that they exist, the judge shall order the issuance of a warrant by directing the person requesting the warrant to sign the judge's name on the duplicate original warrant. The judge shall immediately sign the original warrant and enter on the face of the original warrant the exact time when the warrant was ordered to be issued. The finding of probable cause for a warrant upon oral testimony may be based on the same kind of evidence as is sufficient for a warrant upon affidavit.

(4) Recording and certification of testimony. When a caller informs the judge that the purpose of the call is to request a warrant, the judge shall immediately place under oath each person whose testimony forms a basis of the application and each person applying for that warrant. If a voice recording device is available, the judge shall record by means of the device all of the call after the caller informs the judge that the purpose of the call is to request a warrant, otherwise a stenographic or longhand verbatim record shall be made. If a voice recording device is used or a stenographic record made, the judge shall have the record transcribed, shall certify the accuracy of the transcription, and shall file a copy of the original record and the transcription with the court. If a longhand verbatim record is made, the judge shall file a signed copy with the court.

(5) Contents. The contents of a warrant upon oral testimony shall be the same as the contents of a warrant upon affidavit.

(6) Additional rule for execution. The person who executes the warrant shall enter the exact time of execution on the face of the duplicate original warrant.
(7) Motion to suppress based on failure to obtain a written affidavit. Evidence obtained pursuant to a warrant issued under this subsection (b) is not subject to a motion to suppress on the ground that the circumstances were not such as to make it reasonable to dispense with a written affidavit, absent a finding of bad faith. All other grounds to move to suppress are preserved.

(8) This subsection (b) is inoperative on and after January 1, 2005.

(9) No evidence obtained pursuant to this subsection (b) shall be inadmissible in a court of law by virtue of subdivision (8).

§ 108-5. Persons authorized to execute search warrants. The warrant shall be issued in duplicate and shall be directed for execution to all peace officers of the State. However, the judge may direct the warrant to be executed by any person named specially therein.

§ 108-6. Execution of search warrants.
The warrant shall be executed within 96 hours from the time of issuance. If the warrant is executed the duplicate copy shall be left with any person from whom any instruments, articles or things are seized or if no person is available the copy shall be left at the place from which the instruments, articles or things were seized. Any warrant not executed within such time shall be

void and shall be returned to the court of the judge issuing the same as "not executed".

§ 108-7. Command of search warrant.
The warrant shall command the person directed to execute the same to search the place or person particularly described in the warrant and to seize the instruments, articles or things particularly described in the warrant.

§ 108-8. Use of force in execution of search warrant. (a) All necessary and reasonable force may be used to effect an entry into any building or property or part thereof to execute a search warrant.

(b) The court issuing a warrant may authorize the officer executing the warrant to make entry without first knocking and announcing his or her office if it finds, based upon a showing of specific facts, the existence of the following exigent circumstances:

(1) That the officer reasonably believes that if notice were given a weapon would be used:

(i) against the officer executing the search warrant; or

(ii) against another person.

(2) That if notice were given there is an imminent "danger" that evidence will be destroyed.

§ 108-9. Detention and search of persons on premises. in the execution of the warrant the person executing the same may reasonably detain to search any person in the place at the time:

(a) To protect himself from attack, or

(b) To prevent the disposal or concealment of any instruments, articles or things particularly described in the warrant.

108-10. Return to court of things seized.
A return of all instruments, articles or things seized shall be made without unnecessary delay before the judge issuing the warrant or before any judge named in the warrant or before any court of competent jurisdiction.
An inventory of any instruments, articles or things seized shall be filed with the return and signed under oath by the officer or person executing the warrant. The judge shall upon request deliver a copy of the inventory to the person from whom or from whose premises the instruments, articles or things were taken and to the applicant for the warrant.

§ 108-11. Disposition of things seized.
The court before which the instruments, articles or things are returned shall enter an order providing for their custody pending further proceedings.

§ 108-12. Disposition of obscene material.
In the case of any material seized which is alleged to have been possessed or used or intended to be used contrary to, or is evidence of a violation of, Section 11-20 of the "Criminal Code of 1961", approved July 28, 1961, as heretofore and hereafter amended, the court before which the material is returned shall, upon written request of any person from whom the material was seized or any person claiming ownership or other right to possession of such material, enter an order providing for a hearing to determine the obscene nature thereof not more than 10 days after such return. If the material is determined to be obscene it shall be held pending further proceedings as provided by Section 108-11 of this Code. If the material is determined not to be obscene it shall be returned to the person from whom or place from which it was seized, or to the person claiming ownership or other right to possession of such material; provided that enough of the record material may be retained by the State for purposes of appellate proceedings. The decision of the court upon this hearing shall not be admissible as evidence in any other proceeding nor shall it be *res judicata* of any question in any other proceeding.

§ 108-13. When warrant may be executed.
The warrant may be executed at any time of any day or night.

§ 108-14. No warrant quashed for technicality. No warrant shall be quashed nor evidence suppressed because of technical irregularities not affecting the substantial rights of the accused.

Commentary – Searches and Seizures

Search Warrants. The preferred and lawful course for officers who seek to conduct searches and seizures of evidence is for them to obtain a search warrant from a disinterested and objective judge. The process begins when under § 108-4 a sworn complaint for search warrant is prepared and presented to a judge. The judge will review the complaint for search warrant to determine whether probable cause exists to establish a crime that has been committed or is being committed, or that the fruits and instrumentalities of a crime, will be found at a named location or on an identified person. The warrant must describe the location or person to be searched with specificity so that executing officers will be limited in their authority to search and to seize objects, documents or other materials based on the command of the search warrant. If no exception to the requirement of a search warrant can be established, the seizure of evidence would be in violation of the statute (and thus the 4th Amendment to the U.S. Constitution and Article 1, § 6 of the Illinois Constitution of 1970). Evidence seized in violation of the statute and constitutional provisions will likely be suppressed and be inadmissible in evidence at a criminal trial. Modern technology has certainly come into play under the 4th Amendment. In *United States v. Jones* 565 U.S. ___, 132 S. Ct. 945 (U.S. S. Ct. 2012) the Court found a 4th Amendment violation for the use of a GPS device on a car without benefit of a search warrant. In *Riley v. California* 573 U.S. ____, 134 S.Ct. 2473 (U. S. S. Ct. 2014) the Court held that officers must generally obtain a search warrant before accessing data from a cell phone to comport with the warrant requirement of the 4th Amendment.

Validity of Search Warrants. A defendant, whose arrest and prosecution are based, in whole or in part, on evidence obtained by search warrant from his person, his home, his car or other place where he has an expectation of privacy, may still seek to suppress the evidence as being seized in violation of the defendant's rights. the defendant may claim that the information in the warrant did not establish probable cause, that the warrant was based on unreliable information from an unreliable informant, that the warrant did not specify the location to be searched or the objects to be seized or that the officers exceeded the command of the warrant when they executed the search and seizure. § 108-14 particularly notes that warrants should not be quashed and evidence suppressed based on technicalities that do not affect the defendant's substantial rights.

Sworn complaint. In *People v. Veras* 393 Ill.App.3d 94, 913 N.E.2d 86 (Ill. App. Ct. 1st Dist. 2009), a Chicago police officer submitted a complaint for search warrant based on informant information. according to the complaint for search warrant, the anonymous informant had worked with the officer on three prior successful investigations, had gone to the defendant's apartment under the officer's supervision and using money provided by the officer had entered the apartment, purchased cannabis from the defendant, returned the cannabis to the officer and also told the officer that a large bag of cannabis was still in the apartment. Based on this information the reviewing judge issued a search warrant for the defendant's apartment, which was executed and the bag of cannabis was seized. The defendant was indicted and filed a motion to quash the search warrant, on the basis that the officer had not signed the complaint for search warrant, and therefore the requirement of sworn evidence had not been met. The trial court granted the defendant's motion and suppressed the evidence, determining that a sworn affidavit and complaint for search warrant addressed a substantial right of the defendant, to have the officer be subject to penalties for perjury in obtaining authority to disturb the defendant's right to privacy. The appellate court reversed noting that the search warrant itself reflected a finding by the issuing judge that the officer appeared before him and provided a sworn complaint for search warrant. The failure of the officer to place his signature on the document was a technicality under Section 108-14.

General warrants. It is important that the search warrant specify the location to be searched and the items to be seized. Without such particular descriptions the warrant is vague and the scope of search is left to the discretion of the officers executing the warrant. Such a general warrant undermines the constitutional protection against unreasonable searches and seizures.

In *People v. Urbina* 393 Ill.App.3d 1074, 916 N.E.2d 1 (Ill. App. Ct. 2nd Dist. 2009), the search warrant commanded that the search for drugs and specific items be executed at a specific address, in apartment D. The supervising agent (Thomas) had been present when his informant had twice gone to that apartment to make supervised purchases of drugs, and the informant had told the officer that the defendants were in apartment D. When the warrant was executed, the agent realized that there was a mistake and that the proper address for the apartment was "apartment C". Nonetheless he had the executing officers enter apartment C, executed the warrant and seized drugs that tested to be cocaine. The defendants were charged with possession of cocaine with intent to deliver, but their motion to suppress the evidence seized, for being in violation of the command of the warrant, was denied by the trial court. On appeal their convictions were reversed, with the court stating:

> In this case . . . the executing officers searched a residence not listed on the search warrant and the warrant failed to describe with sufficient particularity the premises to be searched. There was a discrepancy in the search warrant, in that the warrant stated that apartment "D" was to the left at the top of the stairs. In actuality, apartment "C" was to the left at the top of the stairs.. . . [T]he warrant in this case was ambiguous when the officers attempted to execute it, leaving doubt in the officers' minds as to which apartment to search. Such doubt was manifested in the officers' request for direction from Thomas. Thomas used his discretion and directed the officers to search apartment "C" in contradiction to the express direction of the warrant. This was an impermissible use of discretion as a matter of law.
>
> *People v. Urbina* 393 Ill.App.3d at 1079, 916 N.E.2d at 7.

The court noted the proper course for the officers was to get authority from the judge to search the proper apartment, and not assume that they had the authority to enter the "wrong" unit. The court rejected the state's claims that the warrant error was a technicality and that the officers were acting in good faith. But see *People v. Elder* 392 Ill.App.3d 133, 910 N.E.2d 202 (Ill. App. Ct. 4th Dist. 2009)(search warrant's description of items to be seized as "any and all power tools, hand tools" was sufficiently particularized for the search of a storage unit owned by the defendant based on the information in the warrant of a large number of burglaries where tools and equipment were stolen).

Use of force in executing warrants; "Knock and announce". Section 108-8 addresses common problems with executing warrants where there is a danger that officers executing the warrants will be harmed or there is a serious risk that when the officers appear the evidence they are trying to seize will be destroyed. If the door is locked and the officers are not let in when they announce the warrant, force can be used to gain entry. If the officers can articulate reasons for fear of harm or the threat of the destruction of evidence in the complaint for search warrant, the judge can authorize a "no knock" entry, and permit going into the address without announcing the authority of the warrant. In *People v. Glorioso* 398 Ill.App.3d 975, 924 N.E.2d 1153 (Ill. App. Ct. 2nd Dist. 2010), the trial and appellate courts found a violation of the "knock and announce" requirement when officers knocked and almost simultaneously used a battering ram to gain entry, but held that the exclusionary rule did not apply to "knock and announce" violations based on the lock-step doctrine. See *Hudson v. Michigan* 547 U.S. 586, 126 S.Ct. 2169 (U.S. S. Ct. 2006)(exclusionary rule is not applicable to knock and announce violations).

Good faith exception. The application of the exclusionary rule is particularly harsh where law enforcement follows the preferred course and obtains a search warrant or obtains consent of a person who one would reasonably expect could give consent. What if the judge was wrong in granting the warrant, perhaps on the basis that a police informant's reliability had not been sufficiently shown in the application for warrant? Or what if the officers later find out the apparent authority of the person who consented to the search was illusory – there was no authority? If the premise behind the exclusionary rule is that there must be some remedy for unlawful actions by police, that policy is not advanced when the officers follow the rules, obtain the warrant or consent, properly execute the search and only later, find out some mistake has been made. Certainly the officers' good faith undermines the rationale behind the exclusionary rule. See *People v. LeFlore* 2015 IL 116799 (Ill. S. Ct. 2015)(trial court's denial of defendant's motion to suppress was proper where the investigating officer's relied on binding judicial precedent in performing a warrantless search with a GPS device place on defendant's vehicle was acting in objectively reasonable good faith. Later rulings establishing the wrongfulness of warrantless GPS searches established a 4th Amendment violation, but did not overcome the good faith exception to suppression of the evidence).

In *People v. Harris* 2015 IL App (1st) 132162 drug enforcement officers had obtained an "anticipatory search warrant" based on the installation of an electronic monitoring and breakaway filament device which would track the movement an opening of a Fed-ex package. Such a warrant assures that probable cause exits when a triggering event occurs. In *Harris* the triggering event was the movement and opening of the package as indicated by the device placed in the package. Officers followed the delivery of the package to a specific address where the Defendant picked it up off a doorstep and put it in the backseat of his car. Officers prematurely stopped Defendant and arrested his for the contents of the package (cannabis). The appellate Court reversed the trial courts denial of the Defendant's motion to suppress, and denied the prosecutions claim of good faith since the seizing officers were aware of the information in the search warrant documents, acted contrary to them and contrary to established law.

In *People v. LeFlore* 2015 IL 116799 (Ill. S. Ct. 2015) the Court held that officers acted in good faith in placing a GPS device on a vehicle and tracking that vehicle for a few days with the device, where existing 7th Circuit case law supported the officers' actions, despite the later holding in *United States v. Jones* 565 U.S. ___, 132 S. Ct. 945 (U.S. S. Ct. 2012) that GPS devices were invalid under the 4th Amendment to the Constitution in the absence of a search warrant. The *LeFlore* Court recognized the good faith of the officers in relying on existing court precedent. However, in *People v. Bravo* 2015 IL App (1st) 130145 drug enforcement officers heard that the defendant was a cocaine trafficker and place several GPS devices on the Defendant's vehicle for over a one month period and used the device to track him and arrest him for a drug offense. The Court held that reliance on the 7th Circuit case was misplaced and could not constitute good faith because of the unlimited use of GPS in the *Bravo* case.

Warrantless searches. While the rule may be to require search warrants, the exceptions to the warrant requirement virtually swallow the rule. The many categories of searches relating to traffic stops and arrests, consensual searches, plain view and inventory searches often merge into the facts of a given case. It is not unusual to have a temporary detention, a frisk, an arrest, a protective sweep, a search incident to arrest, a vehicle search and a consent search involved in the same incident. Well-trained officers recognize the applicable standards for each procedure and the limits of searching and seizing authority available to them.

In *People v. Lomax* 2012 IL App (1st) 103016, the appellate court recognized the "emergency aid exception" to the warrant requirement, reversing the trial court's grant of a motion to suppress physical evidence of a gun, ammunition and body armor from a home. The defendant was charged with unlawful use of weapon by a felon (720 ILCS 5/24-1.1) and as an armed habitual criminal (720 ILCS 5/24-1.7(a)). On appeal, the state argued the warrantless entry, search and seizure was constitutional valid as an exception to the warrant requirement. The emergency aid exception requires police to (1) have reasonable grounds to believe that an emergency exists at a location and (2) have some information that approximates probable cause that the area to be entered or searched is associated with the emergency that is being addressed by police action. In *Lomax*, there had been repeated but anonymous 911 calls that shots were being fired inside a residence, and the police responded and entered without obtaining consent of any adult resident. applying a totality-of-circumstances test to the "shots fired" situation left the court ruling that the police action should not be second guessed, upholding the warrantless entry to the residence to perform a safety check and help anyone who might be injured, even ordering the adult occupants out of the home before police review of the premises.

In *People v. Wells* 403 Ill.App.3d 839, 934 N.E.2d 1015 (Ill. App. Ct. 1st Dist. 2010), police responded to a domestic disturbance call at a woman's apartment. The dispatch related that she had been threatened by an ex-boyfriend, who was in the process of leaving her residence. When the police arrived the defendant was walking away down the street. No contact was made with him. Ten minutes later, a second call came from dispatch that the defendant had gone back to her apartment. When police arrived, the defendant was standing on the street in front of the apartment. He did not flee and cooperated with the police. The first action of the police was to put handcuffs on the defendant and pat him down. A handgun was found in his stocking. The defendant was taken to the station and charged as a felon in possession of a handgun. His car was on the street near the scene of the encounter with the police. It was illegally parked. Prior to towing the car, an inventory search resulted in the seizure of ammunition that fit the handgun found on the defendant's person. The defendant filed a motion to suppress. the state argued that the initial stop was a proper *Terry* stop, and the subsequent arrest and further search were justified by exceptions to the warrant requirement as well (search incident to arrest and a vehicle inventory search). The trial court and appellate court disagreed. The courts reasoned that when the officers first approached the defendant and handcuffed him, he was under arrest, but there was no specific criminal charge that police could describe. The further police actions that followed were fruit of the poisonous tree and thus the gun and ammunition were properly suppressed.

However, in *People v. O'Dell* 392 Ill.App.3d 979, 913 N.E.2d 107 (Ill. App. Ct. 5th Dist. 2009), a trooper saw the defendant pulling an old, junk trailer that had a brand new pick-up truck on it's back, on a rural road. The new truck still had the dealer's price sticker on it and was not properly strapped in the trailer. A chain on the trailer was dragging on the road behind it. The trooper made a traffic stop for unsafe equipment and inquired about the unusual nature of the new truck on the old trailer. The answers the defendant gave were suspicious claiming that he had purchased the new truck the day before and was taking it to his girlfriend's house in Effingham. The answers did not match and when the officer ran a check on the defendant and his vehicle, he discovered the defendant had prior theft and vehicle theft convictions. The trooper made calls to the dealer's town to determine if the truck had been sold as the defendant said or was stolen. In the meantime, he had the defendant sit in the police car and wrote him citations.

because he had not heard back on the inquiries about the status of the new truck, the trooper was about to let the defendant go on, but when he got the vehicle identification number from the new truck he noticed a piece of door trim was in the back, and when he looked inside the defendant's vehicle he saw a crowbar with paint on it that matched the new truck. After the passage of 90 minutes, the trooper heard from law enforcement that the truck was stolen. He arrested the defendant, gave him *Miranda* warnings and the defendant admitted he had stolen the truck. Looking at the totality of the circumstances both the trial court and the appellate court found every step the officer had taken was justified and proper, and that the defendant's motion to suppress on 4th Amendment grounds was properly denied.

In *People v. Lee* 2014 IL App (1st) 130507, a private contractor was requested to perform an unannounced audit of the defendant's business under the pretense of doing a Medicare audit. The trial court's grant of defendant's motion to suppress based on a prosecution-based warrantless search was affirmed on appeal. The appellate court noted that state and federal law enforcement agencies worked closely with the contractor ("TrustSolutions" whose investigator was "Pointer"), even to the point of asking for delay in the audit. In affirming the trial court's ruling grant of suppression, the Court's opinion noted:

> As the trial court found, "[a]ll evidence points to a tightly interwoven relationship between the FBI, OIG and Trust Solutions." From the very inception of TrustSolutions' involvement, the presence and influence of law enforcement controlled the investigation. Significantly, Poirier's request for an on-site audit stated that the objective was "[t]o further substantiate the allegations against this provider and to witness firsthand the daily operations in both facilities. Ultimately, this investigation will be referred to law enforcement based on all evidence gathered on the audit." This objective illustrates the clear purpose of the audit was to aid law enforcement.
>
> Further, the letter provided to [defendant's] offices explaining the audit indicated that TrustSolutions was investigating whether "Medicare claims have been billed and paid in the appropriate manner" and that the audit would include, but was not limited to, obtaining a random sample of medical records and interviewing staff. However, Poirier testified that in addition to the medical records, auditors obtained copies of personnel files, payroll records, and appointment books. These documents have little connection to the stated purpose of investigating Medicare billing practices. The record supports the trial court's conclusion that the audit served as a pretext for a criminal search.
>
> *People v. Lee* 2014 IL App (1st) 120507 ¶24-25, 7 N.E.3d at 858.

Consent to search. One of the major exceptions to the search warrant requirement is consent to search. If a police officer receives consent from, a person with a controlling interest in the property, who controls the property for purposes of access and who can permit law enforcement officers to affect the privacy interests of other people in the property, no warrant is required to search the property. Typical consent issues arise in the context of landlord-tenant, co-residents, parent-child and even husband and wife. In any property situation where multiple people have mutual rights of access and control of all or a portion of the premises, any one of them may be found to have common authority to give consent to a search of the premises. on the other hand, if a portion of the premises is segregated for control, or a closed container is in the location, for the use and privacy by only one person, and no authority is shown for a third party, who otherwise has an interest in the property, there may be a finding of a lack of consent to search. The scenarios about consent and the various forms of ownership, leaseholds, or other rights of possession to property do not lend themselves to a hard and fast rule. The courts will look to all the circumstances to determine whether the consent exception has been met. Ultimately whether a privacy interest of one person exists that can be affected by consent given by another person must be resolved for the consent exception to apply.

In *People v. London* 358 Ill.App.3d 567, 831 N.E.2d 1135 (Ill. App. Ct. 5th Dist. 2005), a woman who owned a vacant farmhouse asked a plumber to go winterize the home. While it had been rented in the past to private tenants, and the woman's grandson, it was then unoccupied. When they went into the farmhouse, the plumbers saw that furniture, a knife collection, other belongings and a person lying on a bed were present, so the owner was notified. She in turn, called the county sheriff and asked the farmhouse be cleared out. Several deputy sheriffs, a state trooper and another officer went to the farmhouse, based on the consent to enter that the owner had given. When they arrived they found several individuals present, and at first all of them, including the defendant claimed they did not live there and had not rented the premises. The officers conducted an allowable protective sweep to be sure that no one with weapons was present, and when they did so they saw evidence of methamphetamine manufacturing activity. Someone on the premises showed officers a receipt signed by the defendant and the owner's grandson for $100 as a deposit for the rental of the property. Nonetheless, the owner insisted that no one had authority to rent the place, except her, and she signed a consent to search form. When the officers searched they seized drugs, anhydrous ammonia and other components and equipment used in the methamphetamine manufacturing process. the defendant and others were charged with drug offenses and filed a motion to suppress claiming that the search and seizure was illegal because it was a search without warrant and no consent exception to the warrant requirement existed, because the grandson did have apparent authority to create a leasehold interest in the property with the defendant, who had never consented and thus, had never given up the expectation of privacy that she had in the farmhouse.

The trial judge and the appellate court found the owner's consent valid to make the search lawful, and the evidence of a lease interest in the defendant so inconsistent and improbable to reject her claim of a privacy interest in the property.

Plain view. If an officer is in a place where he lawfully may be, and sees drugs or other contraband, there is no requirement for a warrant to justify the observation and seizure of the object. This type of seizure is called "plain view". No Fourth Amendment interest is implicated in the procedure.

In *People v. Jones* 215 Ill.2d 251, 830 N.E.2d 541 (Ill. S. Ct. 2005), a police officer stopped the defendant's vehicle because of defective taillights. The defendant handed the officer his driver's license and when he did so, the officer saw a "one-hitter" box in the defendant's shirt pocket. Based on training and experience, the officer recognized the box as drug paraphernalia that contains a pipe and a cavity that holds cannabis. He ordered the defendant out of the car to arrest him and saw the defendant make a quick movement to his right with his right hand. When the defendant was out of the car, the officer saw the butt of a handgun between the seats. The handgun (which was loaded) was seized and after the defendant was secure in the police car, the officer searched the inside of the vehicle and found another loaded handgun and ammunition in the back seat. The defendant was charged and convicted for the drugs and weapons seized. The trial court denied a motion to suppress, the appellate court reversed and the Illinois Supreme Court reversed again, thus affirming the original conviction. The issues were (1) whether the "one-hitter" box was in plain view, and if it was, whether it established probable cause for the defendant's arrest or whether a search warrant would be required to open the box and (2) whether the guns could be seized as incident to the arrest or under the plain view doctrine. the Illinois Supreme Court upheld the seizure of the one-hitter box under the plain view doctrine, noting that police officers may rely on their experience and training, and that the officer's belief that the box was a container for drugs and probably did contain drugs was all that was required for him to seize it once he clearly saw it in defendant's shirt pocket. Further once the defendant left the vehicle the first gun was seen in plain view and the second gun and ammunition were properly seized incident to arrest. See also *People v. Sinegal* 409 Ill.App.3d 1130, 948 N.E.2d 1135 (Ill. App. Ct. 5th Dist. 2011)(following *Terry* stop, officer saw "one-hitter", seized and opened it based on his training and experience - all supported by plain view doctrine).

In *People v. Colyar* 2013 IL 111835, police officers approached a car that was parked in a hotel parking lot because it was blocking the entrance. As they approached a man walked out of the hotel and got into the car. When standing at the driver's side window, the officers inquired and learned that the car was parked to pick someone up, and while standing there the officers saw a plastic bag with a bullet in it, in the front console. The officers ordered the occupants out of the car, handcuffed them and frisked them, finding another bullet. Then the officers searched the car and found a handgun. The trial court granted the defendant's motion to suppress the bullets and gun and the appellate court affirmed. The Illinois Supreme Court reversed, holding that police officer who saw the bullet in plain view had sufficient support for their actions. Upon seeing a bullet in the passenger area police officers would naturally conduct a protective sweep of a vehicle in light of the finding that the approach to the car was a valid *Terry* stop. The court stated:

> Reviewing the actions of Officer Alcott and Detective Johnson under an objective standard, we believe that a reasonably cautious individual in a similar situation could reasonably suspect the presence of a gun, thus implicating officer safety, based on the bullet clearly visible in defendant's center console. Common sense and logic dictate that a bullet is often associated with a gun. Indeed, our appellate court has recognized that a bullet observed inside a vehicle may reasonably indicate the presence of a gun inside that vehicle. . . .
>
> Certainly, based on the presence of a bullet and a reasonable inference that a gun may be present in the vehicle, it was reasonable for Officer Alcott and Detective Johnson to suspect that their safety was in danger. As Terry instructs, "[t]he officer need not be absolutely certain that the individual is armed; the issue is whether a reasonably prudent man in the circumstances would be warranted in the belief that his safety or that of others was in danger." Terry, 392 U.S. at 27, 88 S.Ct. 1868. Based on the circumstances of this case, we believe that question must be answered affirmatively.
>
> *People v. Colyar* 2013 IL 11835 ¶43-44

Search Incident to Arrest. When a person is placed under arrest, it is legally permissible to search his person and to search the area within his immediate presence and control. *Chimel v. California* 395 U.S. 752,768, 89 S.Ct. 2034, 2048 (U.S.S.Ct. 1969)(impermissible search of arrestee's house exceeded reasonableness and was the equivalent to the use of a general warrant); *Arizona v. Gant* 556 U.S. 332, 129 S.Ct. 1710 (U.S.S.Ct.2009)(search of arrestees vehicle after he was arrested and in handcuffs could not be justified as a search incident to arrest when it exceeded the area of the defendant's control).

In *People v. Cregan*, 2014 IL 113600 (Ill. S. Ct. 2014), the defendant was wanted on an arrest warrant for failure to pay child support. He was also suspected of being a gang member and participating in drug trafficking. When he arrived at the airport, law enforcement agents were waiting for him and approached. The defendant had two pieces of luggage, one that he carried over his shoulder and a suitcase that was on rollers that he was pulling with him. Following his arrest, the defendant was handcuffed and officers searched his luggage and its contents. Inside the suitcase, the search uncovered a jar of hair gel. Inside the jar was a package of powder cocaine. The Illinois Supreme Court upheld the search as properly incident to arrest noting that the suitcase was within the defendant's immediate presence and control at the time of his arrest.

In *People v. Grant* 2013 IL 112734 (Ill. S. Ct. 2013), the defendant's conviction for cocaine possession was affirmed. The trial court properly denied defendant's motion to suppress where defendant was seen by police officers at the entrance of a public housing building yelling "dro, dro, dor" to a passing vehicle. The term "dro" was a solicitation of high quality marijuana and the solicitation of such a sale at the public housing building was in violation of a City of Chicago ordinance.)

Limited Lockstep. The Illinois law of search and seizure closely tracks holdings of the United States Supreme Court . While Illinois Constitution in Article 1, Section 6 protects Illinois citizens' privacy, Illinois courts construe the provision in the same manner at the Fourth Amendment to the U.S. Constitution unless state history, law and traditions indicate broader protection is proper (called "limited lockstep"). A search incident to an arrest for a petty offense has been held not in violation of the Fourth Amendment by the U.S. Supreme Court. See *Atwater v. City of Lago Vista* 532 U.S. 318, 121 S.Ct. 1536 (U.S. S. Ct. 2001)(search incident to arrest for seatbelt violation was valid under the Fourth Amendment). In *People v. Fitzpatrick* 2013 IL 113449, a search incident to a custodial arrest for a petty offense of walking in the roadway was upheld as valid in view of the longstanding authority of police officers to make custodial arrests for a violation of any criminal statute, including petty offenses. The Illinois Supreme Court rejected the claim that Illinois' right of privacy was broader than the 4th Amendment of the U.S. Constitution in this context.

Checkpoint vehicle stops. Police officers often establish traffic checkpoints and stop every vehicle, often to check for drivers who are under the influence of alcohol, or to determine if seatbelts are being properly used as required by law, or to check on the safety equipment of vehicles. Every stop of a vehicle under these types of checkpoint stops is a seizure that implicates Fourth Amendment concerns. To be lawful under the Fourth Amendment, such stops must have standardized procedures, must be designed to address the specific purpose claimed and should occur only for the period of time necessary to achieve its purpose. So long as these standards are being met, other evidence uncovered may be seized without violating the defendant's rights to proper searches and seizures. However, a roadside traffic checkpoint solely for the purpose of detecting evidence of crime, without any focus on a narrow and compelling state purpose is an overbroad search, not based on any suspicion that a particular vehicle or its occupant has committed or is committing a crime, and violates the Fourth Amendment. See *People v. Hacker* 388 Ill.App.3d 346, 902 N.E.2d 792 (Ill. App. Ct. 4th Dist. 2009)(Defendant did not prove his claim that the vehicle checkpoint was for impermissible drug-interdiction stops, as opposed to a DUI checkpoint).

In *Illinois v. Lidster* 540 U.S. 419, 124 S.Ct. 885 (U.S. S. Ct. 2004), a vehicle checkpoint was set up to gather information about a hit-and-run accident that had occurred at the same location one week earlier. Police officers stopped each vehicle for about 15 seconds, asked the driver if he or she knew anything about the prior incident and handed a flyer giving contact information if anything arose that would be of benefit to the investigation. The defendant when approaching the checkpoint veered his vehicle and almost hit the officer. At the checkpoint the defendant showed indicators that he was under the influence of alcohol, and a normal alcohol-suspected traffic stop procedure was executed by police resulting in DUI charges against the driver. The

Illinois Supreme Court had held that the traffic stop violated the defendant's Fourth Amendment rights, but this holding was reversed by the U.S. Supreme Court. That Court's ruling noted that the well-planned and executed checkpoint traffic stops were brief detentions that were reasonable in view of the compelling governmental interest in solving the hit-and-run crime under investigation.

Traffic Stops. An exception to the requirement of a search warrant is a traffic stop. Traffic stops are considered reasonable intrusions into a citizens life and are generally reviewed under the *Terry v. Ohio* principles. In *Illinois v. Caballes* 543 U.S. 405, 125 S. Ct. 34 (U.S. S.Ct. 2004), the U.S. Supreme Court recognized that where a lawful traffic stop was conducted for only such time as necessary to issue a warning ticket and make normal inquiries, there was no violation of the 4th Amendment when another officer arrived at the scene and conducted a routine dog-sniff search on the vehicle. The narcotics discovered by the further investigation was lawfully obtained by the police. Moreover, the reasonable traffic stop includes addressing issues of the reason for the stop and officer or public safety based on proper operation of the vehicle. Thus, asking to check a driver's license or to run a check for outstanding warrants is reasonable under the 4th Amendment. *Rodriguez v. United States,* 575 U.S. ___, 135 S. Ct. 1609 (U.S. S. Ct. 2015)(court approved under the 4th Amendment an 8 minute delay after the issuance of a warning ticket, during which a drug sniffing dog alerted, leading to the seizure of drug contraband). See also, *People v. Cummings*, 2016 IL 115769 (Ill. S. Ct. 2016), (while the initial traffic stop looking for a man would have been concluded once the driver was identified as a woman, running a driver's license check and determining the defendant was driving under suspension were proper police investigatory activities under the 4th Amendment to the Constitution); however, see *People v. Henderson* 2013 IL 114040 (Ill. S. Ct. 2013) (anonymous tip that there was a gun in a tan four door car was insufficient to support a *Terry* stop of a vehicle where police observed no traffic violations and there was no indicia of reliability of the tipster).

However clear or unclear Illinois law may be on *"Terry* traffic stops", matters were made more challenging by the holding in *Utah v. Strieff* 579 U.S. ____ (Case No. 14 – 1373, U.S. S. Ct. 2016). The defendant driver was stopped after leaving a suspected drug house. There was no probable cause for the stop, however a warrant check disclosed an outstand traffic warrant, so the officer arrested the defendant and searched him finding drug contraband. The defendant's motion to suppress based on an unlawful arrest was granted. The prosecution conceded that there was no probable cause for arrest and the state courts the suppression on the ground that the seizure was not incident to a lawful arrest. However Utah argued that the suppression was improper because it turned out there was a valid warrant for Strieff. In a 5-3 decision the U.S. Supreme Court agreed with the prosecution, stating "the evidence [the officer] seized as part of his search incident to arrest is admissible because his discovery of the arrest warrant attenuated the connection between the unlawful stop and the evidence seized from Strieff incident to arrest." (*Utah v. Strieff* , 579 at ____, slip opinion at p. 10).

Mistake of Law. If a police officer engages a suspect under the mistaken belief that a violation of the law has occurred, there is no 4th Amendment violation for a subsequent search and seizure that would otherwise be permissible. In *Heien v. North Carolina*, 574 U.S. ___, 135 S. Ct. 530 (2014), officers stopped a vehicle in the mistaken belief that having only one working taillight was a violation of the law. The Court held that the test was an objective one – whether a reasonable police officer under the same circumstances might mistakenly believe facts existed such to support the stop or might mistakenly believe that the law supported the stop. Under either circumstance, *Heien* stands for the proposition that reasonable suspicion to justify a stop can be present when an officer has an objective mistaken belief. See also *People v. Gaytan* 2015 116223 (Ill. S. Ct. 2015)(officer's mistaken belief that a trailer hitch was an impermissible obstruction of a vehicles license plate provided proper reasonable suspicion to justify a traffic stop).

In Car Videos. It is common for police cars to have video units that are used to record investigatory stops. Illinois law has required that law enforcement maintain the video recordings for a period of 90 days to see if criminal charges are filed and then the videos are to be retained thereafter. See 720 ILCS 5/14-3(h-15). However, in *People v. Wachholtz* 2013 IL App (4th) 110486, the Court noted that there is no remedy of suppressing evidence where the State admitted a video recording was improperly destroyed.

Title III. Proceedings After Arrest
Selected Provisions - Article 109 - Preliminary Examination
725 ILCS 5/109-1 – § 109-3

§ 109-1. Person arrested.
(a) A person arrested with or without a warrant shall be taken without unnecessary delay before the nearest and most accessible judge in that county, except when such county is a participant in a regional jail authority, in which event such person may be taken to the nearest and most accessible judge, irrespective of the county where such judge presides, and a charge shall be filed. Whenever a person arrested either with or without a warrant is required to be taken before a judge, a charge may be filed against such person by way of a two-way closed circuit television system, except that a hearing to deny bail to the defendant may not be conducted by way of closed circuit television.

(b) The judge shall:

(1) Inform the defendant of the charge against him and shall provide him with a copy of the charge.

(2) Advise the defendant of his right to counsel and if indigent shall appoint a public defender or licensed attorney at law of this State to represent him in accordance with the provisions of Section 113-3 of this Code.

(3) Schedule a preliminary hearing in appropriate cases;

(4) Admit the defendant to bail in accordance with the provisions of Article 110 of this Code: and

(5) Order the confiscation of the person's passport or impose travel restrictions on a defendant arrested for first degree murder or other violent crime as defined in Section 3 of the Rights of Crime Victims and Witnesses Act, if the judge determines based on the factors in Section 110-5 of this Code, that this will reasonably assure the appearance of the defendant and compliance by the defendant with all conditions of release.

(c) The court may issue an order of protection in accordance with the provisions of Article 112A of this Code.

§ 109-1.1. (1) Whenever a person arrested either with or without a warrant is taken before a judge as provided for in Sections 107-9(d) (6) and 109-1(a), the judge shall ask the arrestee whether he or she has any children under 18 years old living with him or her who may be neglected as a result of the arrest, incarceration or otherwise. If the judge has reasonable cause to believe that a child may be a neglected child as defined in the Abused and Neglected Child Care Reporting Act, he shall instruct a probation officer to report it immediately to the Department of Children and Family Services as provided in that Act.

§ 109-2. Person arrested in another county.
(a) Any person arrested in a county other than the one in which a warrant for his arrest was issued shall be taken without unnecessary delay

before the nearest and most accessible judge in the county where the arrest was made or, if no additional delay is created, before the nearest and most accessible judge in the county from which the warrant was issued. He shall be admitted to bail in the amount specified in the warrant or, for offenses other than felonies, in an amount as set by the judge, and such bail shall be conditioned on his appearing in the court issuing the warrant on a certain date. The judge may hold a hearing to determine if the defendant is the same person as named in the warrant.

(b) Notwithstanding the provisions of subsection (a), any person arrested in a county other than the one in which a warrant for his arrest was issued, may waive the right to be taken before a judge in the county where the arrest was made. If a person so arrested waives such right, the arresting agency shall surrender such person to a law enforcement agency of the county that issued the warrant without unnecessary delay. The provisions of Section 109-1 shall then apply to the person so arrested.

§ 109-3. Preliminary examination. (a) The judge shall hold the defendant to answer to the court having jurisdiction of the offense if from the evidence it appears there is probable cause to believe an offense has been committed by the defendant, as provided in Section 109-3.1 of this Code, if the offense is a felony.
(b) If the defendant waives preliminary examination the judge shall hold him to answer and may, or on the demand of the prosecuting attorney shall, cause the witnesses for the State to be examined. After hearing the testimony if it appears that there is not probable cause to believe the defendant guilty of any offense the judge shall discharge him.

(c) During the examination of any witness or when the defendant is making a statement or testifying the judge may and on the request of the defendant or State shall exclude all other witnesses. He may also cause the witnesses to be kept separate and to be prevented from communicating with each other until all are examined.

(d) If the defendant is held to answer the judge may require any material witness for the State or defendant to enter into a written undertaking to appear at the trial, and may provide for the forfeiture of a sum certain in the event the witness does not appear at the trial. Any witness who refuses to execute a recognizance may be committed by the judge to the custody of the sheriff until trial or further order of the court having jurisdiction of the cause. Any witness who executes a recognizance and fails to comply with its terms shall, in addition to any forfeiture provided in the recognizance, be subject to the penalty provided in Section 32-10 of the "Criminal Code of 1961", approved July 28, 1961, as heretofore and hereafter amended, for violation of bail bond.

(e) During preliminary hearing or examination the defendant may move for an order of suppression of evidence pursuant to Section 114-11 or 114-12 of this Act or for other reasons, and may move for dismissal of the charge pursuant to Section 114-1 of this Act or for other reasons.

§ 109-3.1. Persons Charged with Felonies. (a) In any case involving a person charged with a felony in this State, alleged to have been committed on or after January 1, 1984, the provisions of this Section shall apply.

(b) Every person in custody in this State for the alleged commission of a felony shall receive either a preliminary examination as provided in Section 109-3 or an indictment by Grand Jury as provided in Section 111-2,within 30 days from the date he or she was taken into custody. Every person on bail or recognizance for the alleged commission of a felony shall receive either a preliminary examination as provided in Section 109-3 or an indictment by Grand Jury as provided in Section 111-2, within 60 days from the date he or she was arrested. The provisions of this paragraph shall not apply in the following situations:

(1) when delay is occasioned by the defendant; or

(2) when the defendant has been indicted by the Grand Jury on the felony offense for which he or she was initially taken into custody or on an offense arising from the same transaction or conduct of the defendant that was the basis for the felony offense or offenses initially charged; or

(3) when a competency examination is ordered by the court; or

(4) when a competency hearing is held; or

(5) when an adjudication of incompetency for trial has been made; or

(6) when the case has been continued by the court under Section 114-4 of this Code after a determination that the defendant is physically incompetent to stand trial.

(c) Delay occasioned by the defendant shall temporarily suspend, for the time of the delay, the period within which the preliminary examination must be held. On the day of expiration of the delay the period in question shall continue at the point at which it was suspended.

Article 110 – Bail
725 ILCS 5/110-1 *et seq.*

§ 110-1. Definitions. (a) "Security" is that which is required to be pledged to insure the payment of bail.

(b) "Sureties" encompasses the monetary and nonmonetary requirements set by the court as conditions for release either before or after conviction. "Surety" is one who executes a bail bond and binds himself to pay the bail if the person in custody fails to comply with all conditions of the bail bond.

(c) The phrase "for which a sentence of imprisonment, without conditional and revocable release, shall be imposed by law as a consequence of conviction" means an offense for which a sentence of imprisonment, without probation, periodic imprisonment or conditional discharge, is required by law upon conviction.
(d) "Real and present threat to the physical safety of any person or persons", as used in this Article, includes a threat to the community, person, persons or class of persons.

§ 110-2. Release on own recognizance. When from all the circumstances the court is of the opinion that the defendant will appear as required either before or after conviction and the defendant will not pose a danger to any person or the community and that the defendant will comply with all conditions of bond, which shall include the defendant's current address with a written admonishment to the defendant that he or she must comply with the provisions of Section 110-12 of this Code regarding any change in his or her address, the defendant may be released on his or her own recognizance. The defendant's address shall at all times remain a matter of public record with the clerk of the court.

A failure to appear as required by such recognizance shall constitute an offense subject to the penalty provided in Section 32-10 of the "Criminal Code of 1961", approved July 28, 1961, as heretofore and hereafter amended, for violation of the bail bond, and any obligated sum fixed in the recognizance shall be forfeited and collected in accordance with subsection (g) of Section 110-7 of this Code.

This Section shall be liberally construed to effectuate the purpose of relying upon contempt of court proceedings or criminal sanctions instead of financial loss to assure the appearance of the defendant, and that the defendant will not pose a danger to any person or the community and that the defendant will comply with all conditions of bond. Monetary bail should be set only when it is determined that no other conditions of release will reasonably assure the defendant's appearance in court, that the defendant does not present a danger to any person or the community and that the defendant will comply with all conditions of bond. The State may appeal any order permitting release by personal recognizance.

§ 110-3. Issuance of warrant. Upon failure to comply with any condition of a bail bond or recognizance the court having jurisdiction at the time of such failure may, in addition to any other action provided by law, issue a warrant for the arrest of the person at liberty on bail or his own recognizance. The contents of such a warrant shall be the same as required for an arrest warrant issued upon complaint.

When a defendant is at liberty on bail or his own recognizance on a felony charge and fails to appear in court as directed, the court shall issue a warrant for the arrest of such person. Such warrant shall be noted with a directive to peace officers to arrest the person and hold such person without bail and to deliver such person before the court for further proceedings. A defendant who is arrested or surrenders within 30 days of the issuance of such warrant shall not be bailable in the case in question unless he shows by the preponderance of the evidence that his failure to appear was not intentional.

§ 110-4. Bailable Offenses. (a) All persons shall be bailable before conviction, except the following offenses where the proof is evident or the presumption great that the defendant is guilty of the offense: capital offenses; offenses for which a sentence of life imprisonment may be imposed as a consequence of conviction; felony offenses for which a sentence of imprisonment, without conditional and revocable release, shall be imposed by law as a consequence of conviction, where the court after a hearing, determines that the release of the defendant would pose a real and present threat to the physical safety of any person or persons; stalking or aggravated stalking, where the court, after a hearing, determines that the release of the defendant would pose a real and present threat to the physical safety of the alleged victim of the offense and denial of bail is necessary to prevent fulfillment of the threat upon which the charge is based; or unlawful use of weapons in violation of item (4) of subsection (a) of Section 24-1 of the Criminal Code of 1961 when that offense occurred in a school or in any conveyance owned, leased, or contracted by a school to transport students to or from school or a school-related activity, or on any public way within 1,000 feet of real property comprising any school, where the court, after a hearing, determines that the release of the defendant would pose a real and present threat to the physical safety of any person and denial of bail is necessary to prevent fulfillment of that threat; or making a terrorist threat in violation of Section 29D-20 of the Criminal Code of 1961 or an attempt to commit the offense of making a terrorist threat, where the court, after a hearing, determines that the release of the defendant would pose a real and present threat to the physical safety of any person and denial of bail is necessary to prevent fulfillment of that threat.

(b) A person seeking release on bail who is charged with a capital offense or an offense for which a sentence of life imprisonment may be imposed shall not be bailable until a hearing is held wherein such person has the burden of demonstrating that the proof of his guilt is not evident and the presumption is not great.

(c) Where it is alleged that bail should be denied to a person upon the grounds that the person presents a real and present threat to the physical safety of any person or persons, the burden of proof of such allegations shall be upon the State.

(d) When it is alleged that bail should be denied to a person charged with stalking or aggravated stalking upon the grounds set forth in Section 110-6.3 of this Code, the burden of proof of those allegations shall be upon the State.

§ 110-5. Determining the amount of bail and conditions of release. (a) In determining the amount of monetary bail or conditions of release, if any, which will reasonably assure the appearance of a defendant as required or the safety of any other person or the community and the likelihood of compliance by the defendant with all the conditions of bail, the court shall, on the basis of available information, take into account such matters as the nature and circumstances of the offense charged, whether the evidence shows that as part of the offense there was a use of violence or threatened use of violence, whether the offense involved corruption of public officials or employees, whether there was physical harm or threats of physical harm to any public official, public employee, judge, prosecutor, juror or witness, senior citizen, child or person with a disability, whether evidence shows that during the offense or during the arrest the defendant possessed or used a firearm, machine gun, explosive or metal piercing ammunition or explosive bomb device or any military or paramilitary armament, whether the evidence shows that the offense committed was related to or in furtherance of the criminal activities of an organized gang or was motivated by the defendant's membership in or allegiance to an organized gang, the condition of the victim, any written statement submitted by the victim or proffer or representation by the State regarding the impact which the alleged criminal conduct has had on the victim and the victim's concern, if any, with further contact with the defendant if released on bail, whether the offense was based on racial, religious, sexual orientation or ethnic hatred, the likelihood of the filing of a greater charge, the likelihood of conviction, the sentence applicable upon conviction, the weight of the evidence against such defendant, whether there exists motivation or ability to flee, whether there is any verification as to prior residence, education, or family ties in the local jurisdiction, in another county, state or foreign country, the defendant's employment, financial resources, character and mental condition, past conduct, prior use of alias names or dates of birth, and length of residence in the community, the consent of the defendant to periodic drug testing in accordance with Section 110-6.5, whether a foreign national defendant is lawfully admitted in the United States of America, whether the government of the foreign national maintains an extradition treaty with the United States by which the foreign government will extradite to the United States its national for a trial for a crime allegedly committed in the United States, whether the defendant is currently subject to deportation or exclusion under the immigration laws of the United States, whether the defendant, although a United States citizen, is considered under the law of any foreign state a national of that state for the purposes of extradition or non-extradition to the United States, the amount of unrecovered proceeds lost as a result of the alleged offense, the source of bail funds tendered or sought to be tendered for bail, whether from the totality of the court's consideration, the loss of funds posted or sought to be posted for bail will not deter the defendant from flight, whether the evidence shows that the defendant is engaged in significant possession, manufacture, or delivery of a controlled substance or cannabis, either individually or in consort with others, whether at the time of the offense charged he was on bond or pre-trial release pending trial, probation, periodic imprisonment or conditional discharge pursuant to this Code or the comparable Code of any other state or federal jurisdiction, whether the defendant is on bond or pre-trial release pending the imposition or execution of sentence or appeal of sentence for any offense under the laws of Illinois or any other state or federal jurisdiction, whether the defendant is under parole or mandatory supervised release or work release from the Illinois Department of Corrections or any penal institution or corrections department of any state or federal jurisdiction, the defendant's record of convictions, whether the defendant has been convicted of a misdemeanor or ordinance offense in Illinois or similar offense in other state or federal jurisdiction within the 10 years preceding the current charge or convicted of a felony in Illinois, whether the defendant was convicted of an offense in another state or federal jurisdiction that would be a felony if committed in Illinois within the 20 years preceding the current charge or has been convicted of such felony and released from the penitentiary within 20 years preceding the current charge if a penitentiary sentence was imposed in Illinois or other state or federal jurisdiction, the defendant's records of juvenile adjudication of delinquency in any jurisdiction, any record of appearance or failure to appear by the defendant at court proceedings, whether there was flight to avoid arrest or prosecution, whether the defendant escaped or attempted to escape to avoid arrest, whether the defendant refused to identify himself, or whether there was a refusal by the defendant to be fingerprinted as required by law. Information used by the court in its findings or stated in or offered in connection with this Section may be by way of proffer based upon reliable information offered by the State or defendant.

All evidence shall be admissible if it is relevant and reliable regardless of whether it would be admissible under the rules of evidence applicable at criminal trials. If the State presents evidence that the offense committed by the defendant was related to or in furtherance of the criminal activities of an organized gang or was motivated by the defendant's membership in or allegiance to an organized gang, and if the court determines that the evidence may be substantiated, the court shall prohibit the defendant from associating with other members of the organized gang as a condition of bail or release. For the purposes of this Section, "organized gang" has the meaning ascribed to it in Section 10 of the Illinois Streetgang Terrorism Omnibus Prevention Act.

(b) The amount of bail shall be:

(1) Sufficient to assure compliance with the conditions set forth in the bail bond, which shall include the defendant's current address with a written admonishment to the defendant that he or she must comply with the provisions of Section 110-12 regarding any change in his or her address. The defendant's address shall at all times remain a matter of public record with the clerk of the court.

(2) Not oppressive.

(3) Considerate of the financial ability of the accused.

(4) When a person is charged with a drug related offense involving possession or delivery of cannabis or possession or delivery of a controlled substance as defined in the Cannabis Control Act, the Illinois Controlled Substances Act, or the Methamphetamine Control and Community Protection Act, the full street value of the drugs seized shall be considered. "Street value" shall be determined by the court on the basis of a proffer by the State based upon reliable information of a law enforcement official contained in a written report as to the amount seized and such proffer may be used by the court as to the current street value of the smallest unit of the drug seized.

(b-5) Upon the filing of a written request demonstrating reasonable cause, the State's Attorney may request a source of bail hearing either before or after the posting of any funds. If the hearing is granted, before the posting of any bail, the accused must file a written notice requesting that the court conduct a source of bail hearing. The notice must be accompanied by justifying affidavits stating the legitimate and lawful source of funds for bail. At the hearing, the court shall inquire into any matters stated in any justifying affidavits, and may also inquire into matters appropriate to the determination which shall include, but are not limited to, the following:

(1) the background, character, reputation, and relationship to the accused of any surety; and

(2) the source of any money or property deposited by any surety, and whether any such money or property constitutes the fruits of criminal or unlawful conduct; and

(3) the source of any money posted as cash bail, and whether any such money constitutes the fruits of criminal or unlawful conduct; and

(4) the background, character, reputation, and relationship to the accused of the person posting cash bail.

Upon setting the hearing, the court shall examine, under oath, any persons who may possess material information.

The State's Attorney has a right to attend the hearing, to call witnesses and to examine any witness in the proceeding. The court shall, upon request of the State's Attorney, continue the proceedings for a reasonable period to allow the State's Attorney to investigate the matter raised in any testimony or affidavit. If the hearing is granted after the accused has posted bail, the court shall conduct a hearing consistent with this subsection (b-5). At the conclusion of the hearing, the court must issue an order either approving of disapproving the bail.

(c) When a person is charged with an offense punishable by fine only the amount of the bail shall not exceed double the amount of the maximum penalty.

(d) When a person has been convicted of an offense and only a fine has been imposed the amount of the bail shall not exceed double the amount of the fine.

(e) The State may appeal any order granting bail or setting a given amount for bail.

(f) When a person is charged with a violation of an order of protection under Section 12-3.4 or 12-30 of the Criminal Code of 1961,

(1) whether the alleged incident involved harassment or abuse, as defined in the Illinois Domestic Violence Act of 1986;

(2) whether the person has a history of domestic violence, as defined in the Illinois Domestic Violence Act, or a history of other criminal acts;

(3) based on the mental health of the person;

(4) whether the person has a history of violating the orders of any court or governmental entity;

(5) whether the person has been, or is, potentially a threat to any other person;

(6) whether the person has access to deadly weapons or a history of using deadly weapons;

(7) whether the person has a history of abusing alcohol or any controlled substance;

(8) based on the severity of the alleged incident that is the basis of the alleged offense, including, but not limited to, the duration of the current incident, and whether the alleged incident involved physical injury, sexual assault, strangulation, abuse during the alleged victim's pregnancy, abuse of pets, or forcible entry to gain access to the alleged victim;

(9) whether a separation of the person from the alleged victim or a termination of the relationship between the person and the alleged victim has recently occurred or is pending;

(10) whether the person has exhibited obsessive or controlling behaviors toward the alleged victim, including, but not limited to, stalking, surveillance, or isolation of the alleged victim or victim's family member or members;

(11) whether the person has expressed suicidal or homicidal ideations;

(12) based on any information contained in the complaint and any police reports, affidavits, or other documents accompanying the complaint, the court may, in its discretion, order the respondent to undergo a risk assessment evaluation conducted by an Illinois Department of Human Services approved partner abuse intervention program provider, pretrial service, probation, or parole agency. These agencies shall have access to summaries of the defendant's criminal history, which shall not include victim interviews or information, for the risk evaluation. Based on the information collected from the 12 points to be considered at a bail hearing for a violation of an order of protection, the results of any risk evaluation conducted and the other circumstances of the violation, the court may order that the person, as a condition of bail, be placed under electronic surveillance as provided in Section 5-8A-7 of the Unified Code of Corrections.

§ 110-5.1. Bail; certain persons charged with violent crimes against family or household members. (a) Subject to subsection (c), a person who is charged with a violent crime shall appear before the court for the setting of bail if the alleged victim was a family or household member at the time of the alleged offense, and if any of the following applies:

(1) the person charged, at the time of the alleged offense, was subject to the terms of an order of protection issued under Section 112A-14 of this Code or Section 214 of the Illinois Domestic Violence Act of 1986 or previously was convicted of a violation of an order of protection under Section 12-3.4 or 12-30 of the Criminal Code of 1961 or a violent crime if the victim was a family or household member at the time of the offense or a violation of a substantially similar municipal ordinance or law of this or any other state or the United States if the victim was a family or household member at the time of the offense;

(2) the arresting officer indicates in a police report or other document accompanying the complaint any of the following:

(A) that the arresting officer observed on the alleged victim objective manifestations of physical harm that the arresting officer reasonably believes are a result of the alleged offense;

(B) that the arresting officer reasonably believes that the person had on the person's person at the time of the alleged offense a deadly weapon;

(C) that the arresting officer reasonably believes that the person presents a credible threat of serious physical harm to the alleged victim or to any other person if released on bail before trial.

(b) To the extent that information about any of the following is available to the court, the court shall consider all of the following, in addition to any other circumstances considered by the court, before setting bail for a person who appears before the court pursuant to subsection (a):

(1) whether the person has a history of domestic violence or a history of other violent acts;

(2) the mental health of the person;

(3) whether the person has a history of violating the orders of any court or governmental entity;

(4) whether the person is potentially a threat to any other person;

(5) whether the person has access to deadly weapons or a history of using deadly weapons;

(6) whether the person has a history of abusing alcohol or any controlled substance;

(7) the severity of the alleged violence that is the basis of the alleged offense, including, but not limited to, the duration of the alleged violent incident, and whether the alleged violent incident involved serious physical injury, sexual assault, strangulation, abuse during the alleged victim's pregnancy, abuse of pets, or forcible entry to gain access to the alleged victim;

(8) whether a separation of the person from the alleged victim or a termination of the relationship between the person and the alleged victim has recently occurred or is pending;

(9) whether the person has exhibited obsessive or controlling behaviors toward the alleged victim, including, but not limited to, stalking, surveillance, or isolation of the alleged victim;

(10) whether the person has expressed suicidal or homicidal ideations;

(11) any information contained in the complaint and any police reports, affidavits, or other documents accompanying the complaint.

(c) Upon the court's own motion or the motion of a party and upon any terms that the court may direct, a court may permit a person who is required to appear before it by subsection (a) to appear by video conferencing equipment. If, in the opinion of the court, the appearance in person or by video conferencing equipment of a person who is charged with a misdemeanor and who is required to appear before the court by subsection (a) is not practicable, the court may waive the appearance and release the person on bail on one or both of the following types of bail in an amount set by the court:

(1) a bail bond secured by a deposit of 10% of the amount of the bond in cash;

(2) a surety bond, a bond secured by real estate or securities as allowed by law, or the deposit of cash, at the option of the person.

Subsection (a) does not create a right in a person to appear before the court for the setting of bail or prohibit a court from requiring any person charged with a violent crime who is not described in subsection (a) from appearing before the court for the setting of bail.

(d) As used in this Section:

(1) "Violent crime" has the meaning ascribed to it in Section 3 of the Rights of Crime Victims and Witnesses Act.

(2) "Family or household member" has the meaning ascribed to it in Section 112A-3 of this Code.

§ 110-6. [Alteration of amount of bail or conditions of release].

(a) Upon verified application by the State or the defendant or on its own motion the court before which the proceeding is pending may increase or reduce the amount of bail or may alter the conditions of the bail bond or grant bail where it has been previously revoked or denied. If bail has been previously revoked pursuant to subsection (f) of this Section or if bail has been denied to the defendant pursuant to subsection (e) of Section 110-6.1 or subsection (e) of Section 110-6.3, the defendant shall be required to present a verified application setting forth in detail any new facts not known or obtainable at the time of the previous revocation or denial of bail proceedings. If the court grants bail where it has been previously revoked or denied, the court shall state on the record of the proceedings the findings of facts and conclusion of law upon which such order is based.

(b) Violation of the conditions of Section 110-10 of this Code or any special conditions of bail as ordered by the court shall constitute grounds for the court to increase the amount of bail, or otherwise alter the conditions of bail, or, where the alleged offense committed on bail is a forcible felony in Illinois or a Class 2 or greater offense under the Illinois Controlled Substances Act, the Cannabis Control Act, or the Methamphetamine Control and Community Protection Act, revoke bail pursuant to the appropriate provisions of subsection (e) of this Section.

(c) Reasonable notice of such application by the defendant shall be given to the State.

(d) Reasonable notice of such application by the State shall be given to the defendant, except as provided in subsection (e).

(e) Upon verified application by the State stating facts or circumstances constituting a violation or a threatened violation of any of the conditions of the bail bond the court may issue a warrant commanding any peace officer to bring the defendant without unnecessary delay before the court for a hearing on the matters set forth in the application. If the actual court before which the proceeding is pending is absent or otherwise unavailable another court may issue a warrant pursuant to this Section. When the defendant is charged with a felony offense and while free on bail is charged with a subsequent felony offense and is the subject of a proceeding set forth in Section 109-1 or 109-3 of this Code, upon the filing of a verified petition by the State alleging a violation of Section 110-10 (a) (4) of this Code, the court shall without prior notice to the defendant, grant leave to file such application and shall order the transfer of the defendant and the application without unnecessary delay to the court before which the previous felony matter is pending for a hearing as provided in subsection (b) or this subsection of this Section.

The defendant shall be held without bond pending transfer to and a hearing before such court. At the conclusion of the hearing based on a violation of the conditions of Section 110-10 of this Code or any special conditions of bail as ordered by the court the court may enter an order increasing the amount of bail or alter the conditions of bail as deemed appropriate.

(f) Where the alleged violation consists of the violation of one or more felony statutes of any jurisdiction which would be a forcible felony in Illinois or a Class 2 or greater offense under the Illinois Controlled Substances Act, the Cannabis Control Act, or the Methamphetamine Control and Community Protection Act and the defendant is on bail for the alleged commission of a felony, or where the defendant is on bail for a felony domestic battery (enhanced pursuant to subsection (b) of Section 12-3.2 of the Criminal Code of 1961), aggravated domestic battery, aggravated battery, unlawful restraint, aggravated unlawful restraint or domestic battery in violation of item (1) of subsection (a) of Section 12-3.2 of the Criminal Code of 1961 against a family or household member as defined in Section 112A-3 of this Code and the violation is an offense of domestic battery against the same victim the court shall, on the motion of the State or its own motion, revoke bail in accordance with the following provisions:

(1) The court shall hold the defendant without bail pending the hearing on the alleged breach; however, if the defendant is not admitted to bail the hearing shall be commenced within 10 days from the date the defendant is taken into custody or the defendant may not be held any longer without bail, unless delay is occasioned by the defendant. Where defendant occasions the delay, the running of the 10 day period is temporarily suspended and resumes at the termination of the period of delay. Where defendant occasions the

delay with 5 or fewer days remaining in the 10 day period, the court may grant a period of up to 5 additional days to the State for good cause shown. The State, however, shall retain the right to proceed to hearing on the alleged violation at any time, upon reasonable notice to the defendant and the court.

(2) At a hearing on the alleged violation the State has the burden of going forward and proving the violation by clear and convincing evidence. The evidence shall be presented in open court with the opportunity to testify, to present witnesses in his behalf, and to cross-examine witnesses if any are called by the State, and representation by counsel and if the defendant is indigent to have counsel appointed for him. The rules of evidence applicable in criminal trials in this State shall not govern the admissibility of evidence at such hearing. Information used by the court in its findings or stated in or offered in connection with hearings for increase or revocation of bail may be by way of proffer based upon reliable information offered by the State or defendant.

All evidence shall be admissible if it is relevant and reliable regardless of whether it would be admissible under the rules of evidence applicable at criminal trials. A motion by the defendant to suppress evidence or to suppress a confession shall not be entertained at such a hearing. Evidence that proof may have been obtained as a result of an unlawful search and seizure or through improper interrogation is not relevant to this hearing.

(3) Upon a finding by the court that the State has established by clear and convincing evidence that the defendant has committed a forcible felony or a Class 2 or greater offense under the Illinois Controlled Substances Act, the Cannabis Control Act, or the Methamphetamine Control and Community Protection Act while admitted to bail, or where the defendant is on bail for a felony domestic battery (enhanced pursuant to subsection (b) of Section 12-3.2 of the Criminal Code of 1961), aggravated domestic battery, aggravated battery, unlawful restraint, aggravated unlawful restraint or domestic battery in violation of item (1) of subsection (a) of Section 12-3.2 of the Criminal Code of 1961 against a family or household member as defined in Section 112A-3 of this Code and the violation is an offense of domestic battery, against the same victim, the court shall revoke the bail of the defendant and hold the defendant for trial without bail. Neither the finding of the court nor any transcript or other record of the hearing shall be admissible in the State's case in chief, but shall be admissible for impeachment, or as provided in Section 115-10.1 of this Code or in a perjury proceeding.

(4) If the bail of any defendant is revoked pursuant to paragraph (f) (3) of this Section, the defendant may demand and shall be entitled to be brought to trial on the offense with respect to which he was formerly released on bail within 90 days after the date on which his bail was revoked. If the defendant is not brought to trial within the 90 day period required by the preceding sentence, he shall not be held longer without bail. In computing the 90 day period, the court shall omit any period of delay resulting from a continuance granted at the request of the defendant.

(5) If the defendant either is arrested on a warrant issued pursuant to this Code or is arrested for an unrelated offense and it is subsequently discovered that the defendant is a subject of another warrant or warrants issued pursuant to this Code, the defendant shall be transferred promptly to the court which issued such warrant. If, however, the defendant appears initially before a court other than the court which issued such warrant, the non-issuing court shall not alter the amount of bail heretofore set on such warrant unless the court sets forth on the record of proceedings the conclusions of law and facts which are the basis for such altering of another court's bond. The non-issuing court shall not alter another courts bail set on a warrant unless the interests of justice and public safety are served by such action.

(g) The State may appeal any order where the court has increased or reduced the amount of bail or altered the conditions of the bail bond or granted bail where it has previously been revoked.

§ 110-6.1. Denial of bail in non-probationable felony offenses. (a) Upon verified petition by the State, the court shall hold a hearing to determine whether bail should be denied to a defendant who is charged with a felony offense for which a sentence of imprisonment, without probation, periodic imprisonment or conditional discharge, is required by law upon conviction, when it is alleged that the defendant's admission to bail poses a real and present threat to the physical safety of any person or persons.

(1) A petition may be filed without prior notice to the defendant at the first appearance before a judge, or within the 21 calendar days, except as provided in Section 110-6, after arrest and release of the defendant upon reasonable notice to defendant; provided that while such petition is pending before the court, the defendant if previously released shall not be detained.

(2) The hearing shall be held immediately upon the defendant's appearance before the court, unless for good cause shown the defendant or the State seeks a continuance. A continuance on motion of the defendant may not exceed 5 calendar days, and a continuance on the motion of the State may not exceed 3 calendar days. The defendant may be held in custody during such continuance.

(b) The court may deny bail to the defendant where, after the hearing, it is determined that:

(1) the proof is evident or the presumption great that the defendant has committed an offense for which a sentence of imprisonment, without probation, periodic imprisonment or conditional discharge, must be imposed by law as a consequence of conviction, and

(2) the defendant poses a real and present threat to the physical safety of any person or persons, by conduct which may include, but is not limited to, a forcible felony, the obstruction of justice, intimidation, injury, physical harm, an offense under the Illinois Controlled Substances Act which is a Class X felony, or an offense under the Methamphetamine Control and Community Protection Act which is a Class X felony, and

(3) the court finds that no condition or combination of conditions set forth in subsection (b) of Section 110-10 of this Article, can reasonably assure the physical safety of any other person or persons.

(c) Conduct of the hearings.

(1) The hearing on the defendant's culpability and dangerousness shall be conducted in accordance with the following provisions:

(A) Information used by the court in its findings or stated in or offered at such hearing may be by way of proffer based upon reliable information offered by the State or by defendant. Defendant has the right to be represented by counsel, and if he is indigent, to have counsel appointed for him. Defendant shall have the opportunity to testify, to present witnesses in his own behalf, and to cross-examine witnesses if any are called by the State.

The defendant has the right to present witnesses in his favor. When the ends of justice so require, the court may exercises its discretion and compel the appearance of a complaining witness. The court shall state on the record reasons for granting a defense request to compel the presence of a complaining witness. Cross-examination of a complaining witness at the pretrial detention hearing for the purpose of impeaching the witness' credibility is insufficient reason to compel the presence of the witness. In deciding whether to compel the appearance of a complaining witness, the court shall be considerate of the emotional and physical well-being of the witness. The pre-trial detention hearing is not to be used for purposes of discovery, and the post arraignment rules of discovery do not apply. The State shall tender to the defendant, prior to the hearing, copies of defendant's criminal history, if any, if available, and any written or recorded statements and the substance of any oral statements made by any person, if relied upon by the State in its petition.

The rules concerning the admissibility of evidence in criminal trials do not apply to the presentation and consideration of information at the hearing. At the trial concerning the offense

for which the hearing was conducted neither the finding of the court nor any transcript or other record of the hearing shall be admissible in the State's case in chief, but shall be admissible for impeachment, or as provided in Section 115-10.1 of this Code, or in a perjury proceeding.
(B) A motion by the defendant to suppress evidence or to suppress a confession shall not be entertained. Evidence that proof may have been obtained as the result of an unlawful search and seizure or through improper interrogation is not relevant to this state of the prosecution.

(2) The facts relied upon by the court to support a finding that the defendant poses a real and present threat to the physical safety of any person or persons shall be supported by clear and convincing evidence presented by the State.

(d) Factors to be considered in making a determination of dangerousness. The court may, in determining whether the defendant poses a real and present threat to the physical safety of any person or persons, consider but shall not be limited to evidence or testimony concerning:

(1) The nature and circumstances of any offense charged, including whether the offense is a crime of violence, involving a weapon.

(2) The history and characteristics of the defendant including:

(A) Any evidence of the defendant's prior criminal history indicative of violent, abusive or assaultive behavior, or lack of such behavior. Such evidence may include testimony or documents received in juvenile proceedings, criminal, quasi-criminal, civil commitment, domestic relations or other proceedings.

(B) Any evidence of the defendant's psychological, psychiatric or other similar social history which tends to indicate a violent, abusive, or assaultive nature, or lack of any such history.

(3) The identity of any person or persons to whose safety the defendant is believed to pose a threat, and the nature of the threat;

(4) Any statements made by, or attributed to the defendant, together with the circumstances surrounding them;

(5) The age and physical condition of any person assaulted by the defendant;
(6) Whether the defendant is known to possess or have access to any weapon or weapons;

(7) Whether, at the time of the current offense or any other offense or arrest, the defendant was on probation, parole, mandatory supervised release or other release from custody pending trial, sentencing, appeal or completion of sentence for an offense under federal or state law;

(8) Any other factors, including those listed in Section 110-5 of this Article deemed by the court to have a reasonable bearing upon the defendant's propensity or reputation for violent, abusive or assaultive behavior, or lack of such behavior.

(e) Detention order. The court shall, in any order for detention:

(1) briefly summarize the evidence of the defendant's culpability and its reasons for concluding that the defendant should be held without bail;

(2) direct that the defendant be committed to the custody of the sheriff for confinement in the county jail pending trial;

(3) direct that the defendant be given a reasonable opportunity for private consultation with counsel, and for communication with others of his choice by visitation, mail and telephone; and

(4) direct that the sheriff deliver the defendant as required for appearances in connection with court proceedings.

(f) If the court enters an order for the detention of the defendant pursuant to subsection (e) of this Section, the defendant shall be brought to trial on the offense for which he is detained within 90 days after the date on which the order for detention was entered. If the defendant is not brought to trial within the 90 day period required by the preceding sentence, he shall not be held longer without bail. In computing the 90 day period, the court shall omit any period of delay resulting from a continuance granted at the request of the defendant.

(g) Rights of the defendant. Any person shall be entitled to appeal any order entered under this Section denying bail to the defendant.
(h) The State may appeal any order entered under this Section denying any motion for denial of bail.

(i) Nothing in this Section shall be construed as modifying or limiting in any way the defendant's presumption of innocence in further criminal proceedings.

§ 110-6.2. Post-conviction Detention.
(a) The court may order that a person who has been found guilty of an offense and who is waiting imposition or execution of sentence be held without bond unless the court finds by clear and convincing evidence that the person is not likely to flee or pose a danger to any other person or the community if released under Sections 110-5 and 110-10 of this Act.

(b) The court may order that person who has been found guilty of an offense and sentenced to a term of imprisonment be held without bond unless the court finds by clear and convincing evidence that:

(1) the person is not likely to flee or pose a danger to the safety of any other person or the community if released on bond pending appeal; and

(2) that the appeal is not for purpose of delay and raises a substantial question of law or fact likely to result in reversal or an order for a new trial.

§ 110-6.3. Denial of bail in stalking and aggravated stalking offenses. (a) Upon verified petition by the State, the court shall hold a hearing to determine whether bail should be denied to a defendant who is charged with stalking or aggravated stalking, when it is alleged that the defendant's admission to bail poses a real and present threat to the physical safety of the alleged victim of the offense, and denial of release on bail or personal recognizance is necessary to prevent fulfillment of the threat upon which the charge is based.

(1) A petition may be filed without prior notice to the defendant at the first appearance before a judge, or within 21 calendar days, except as provided in Section 110-6, after arrest and release of the defendant upon reasonable notice to defendant; provided that while the petition is pending before the court, the defendant if previously released shall not be detained.

(2) The hearing shall be held immediately upon the defendant's appearance before the court, unless for good cause shown the defendant or the State seeks a continuance. A continuance on motion of the defendant may not exceed 5 calendar days, and the defendant may be held in custody during the continuance. A continuance on the motion of the State may not exceed 3 calendar days; however, the defendant may be held in custody during the continuance under this provision if the defendant has been previously found to have violated an order of protection or has been previously convicted of, or granted court supervision for, any of the offenses set forth in Sections 11-1.20, 11-1.30, 11-1.40, 11-1.50, 11-1.60, 12-2, 12-3.05, 12-3.2, 12-3.3, 12-4, 12-4.1, 12-7.3, 12-7.4, 12-13, 12-14, 12-14.1, 12-15 or 12-16 of the Criminal Code of 1961, against the same person as the alleged victim of the stalking or aggravated stalking offense.

(b) The court may deny bail to the defendant when, after the hearing, it is determined that:

(1) the proof is evident or the presumption great that the defendant has committed the offense of stalking or aggravated stalking; and

(2) the defendant poses a real and present threat to the physical safety of the alleged victim of the offense; and

(3) the denial of release on bail or personal recognizance is necessary to prevent fulfillment of the threat upon which the charge is based; and

(4) the court finds that no condition or combination of conditions set forth in subsection (b) of Section 110-10 of this Code, including mental health treatment at a community mental health center, hospital, or facility of the Department of Human Services, can reasonably assure the physical safety of the alleged victim of the offense.

(c) Conduct of the hearings.

(1) The hearing on the defendant's culpability and threat to the alleged victim of the offense shall be conducted in accordance with the following provisions:

(A) Information used by the court in its findings or stated in or offered at the hearing may be by way of proffer based upon reliable information offered by the State or by defendant. Defendant has the right to be represented by counsel, and if he is indigent, to have counsel appointed for him. Defendant shall have the opportunity to testify, to present witnesses in his own behalf, and to cross-examine witnesses if any are called by the State. The defendant has the right to present witnesses in his favor. When the ends of justice so require, the court may exercise its discretion and compel the appearance of a complaining witness.

The court shall state on the record reasons for granting a defense request to compel the presence of a complaining witness. Cross-examination of a complaining witness at the pretrial detention hearing for the purpose of impeaching the witness' credibility is insufficient reason to compel the presence of the witness. In deciding whether to compel the appearance of a complaining witness, the court shall be considerate of the emotional and physical well-being of the witness. The pretrial detention hearing is not to be used for the purposes of discovery, and the post arraignment rules of discovery do not apply.

The State shall tender to the defendant, prior to the hearing, copies of defendant's criminal history, if any, if available, and any written or recorded statements and the substance of any oral statements made by any person, if relied upon by the State. The rules concerning the admissibility of evidence in criminal trials do not apply to the presentation and consideration of information at the hearing. At the trial concerning the offense for which the hearing was conducted neither the finding of the court nor any transcript or other record of the hearing shall be admissible in the State's case in chief, but shall be admissible for impeachment, or as provided in Section 115-10.1 of this Code, or in a perjury proceeding.

(B) A motion by the defendant to suppress evidence or to suppress a confession shall not be entertained. Evidence that proof may have been obtained as the result of an unlawful search and seizure or through improper interrogation is not relevant to this state of the prosecution.

(2) The facts relied upon by the court to support a finding that:

(A) the defendant poses a real and present threat to the physical safety of the alleged victim of the offense; and

(B) the denial of release on bail or personal recognizance is necessary to prevent fulfillment of the threat upon which the charge is based; shall be supported by clear and convincing evidence presented by the State.

(d) Factors to be considered in making a determination of the threat to the alleged victim of the offense. The court may, in determining whether the defendant poses, at the time of the hearing, a real and present threat to the physical safety of the alleged victim of the offense, consider but shall not be limited to evidence or testimony concerning:

(1) The nature and circumstances of the offense charged;

(2) The history and characteristics of the defendant including:

(A) Any evidence of the defendant's prior criminal history indicative of violent, abusive or assaultive behavior, or lack of that behavior. The evidence may include testimony or documents received in juvenile proceedings, criminal, quasi-criminal, civil commitment, domestic relations or other proceedings;

(B) Any evidence of the defendant's psychological, psychiatric or other similar social history that tends to indicate a violent, abusive, or assaultive nature, or lack of any such history.

(3) The nature of the threat which is the basis of the charge against the defendant;

(4) Any statements made by, or attributed to the defendant, together with the circumstances surrounding them;

(5) The age and physical condition of any person assaulted by the defendant;

(6) Whether the defendant is known to possess or have access to any weapon or weapons;

(7) Whether, at the time of the current offense or any other offense or arrest, the defendant was on probation, parole, mandatory supervised release or other release from custody pending trial, sentencing, appeal or completion of sentence for an offense under federal or state law;

(8) Any other factors, including those listed in Section 110-5 of this Code, deemed by the court to have a reasonable bearing upon the defendant's propensity or reputation for violent, abusive or assaultive behavior, or lack of that behavior.

(e) The court shall, in any order denying bail to a person charged with stalking or aggravated stalking:

(1) briefly summarize the evidence of the defendant's culpability and its reasons for concluding that the defendant should be held without bail;

(2) direct that the defendant be committed to the custody of the sheriff for confinement in the county jail pending trial;

(3) direct that the defendant be given a reasonable opportunity for private consultation with counsel, and for communication with others of his choice by visitation, mail and telephone; and

(4) direct that the sheriff deliver the defendant as required for appearances in connection with court proceedings.

(f) If the court enters an order for the detention of the defendant under subsection (e) of this Section, the defendant shall be brought to trial on the offense for which he is detained within 90 days after the date on which the order for detention was entered. If the defendant is not brought to trial within the 90 day period required by this subsection (f), he shall not be held longer without bail. In computing the 90 day period, the court shall omit any period of delay resulting from a continuance granted at the request of the defendant. The court shall immediately notify the alleged victim of the offense that the defendant has been admitted to bail under this subsection.

(g) Any person shall be entitled to appeal any order entered under this Section denying bail to the defendant.

(h) The State may appeal any order entered under this Section denying any motion for denial of bail.

(i) Nothing in this Section shall be construed as modifying or limiting in any way the defendant's presumption of innocence in further criminal proceedings.

§ 110-6.5. Drug testing program. The Chief Judge of the circuit may establish a drug testing program as provided by this Section in any county in the circuit if the county board has approved the establishment of the program and the county probation department or pretrial services agency has consented to administer it. The drug testing program shall be conducted under the following provisions:

(a) The court, in the case of a defendant charged with a felony offense or any offense involving the possession or delivery of cannabis or a controlled substance, shall:

(1) not consider the release of the defendant on his or her own recognizance, unless the defendant consents to periodic drug testing during the period of release on his or her own recognizance, in accordance with this Section;

(2) consider the consent of the defendant to periodic drug testing during the period of release on bail in accordance with this Section as a favorable factor for the defendant in determining the amount of bail, the conditions of release or in considering the defendant's motion to reduce the amount of bail.

(b) The drug testing shall be conducted by the pretrial services agency or under the direction of the probation department when a pretrial services agency does not exist in accordance with this Section.

(c) A defendant who consents to periodic drug testing as set forth in this Section shall sign an agreement with the court that, during the period of release, the defendant shall refrain from using illegal drugs and that the defendant will comply with the conditions of the testing program. The agreement shall be on a form prescribed by the court and shall be executed at the time of the bail hearing. This agreement shall be made a specific condition of bail.

(d) The drug testing program shall be conducted as follows:

(1) The testing shall be done by urinalysis for the detection of phencyclidine, heroin, cocaine, methadone and amphetamines.

(2) The collection of samples shall be performed under reasonable and sanitary conditions.

(3) Samples shall be collected and tested with due regard for the privacy of the individual being tested and in a manner reasonably calculated to prevent substitutions or interference with the collection or testing of reliable samples.

(4) Sample collection shall be documented, and the documentation procedures shall include:

(i) Labeling of samples so as to reasonably preclude the probability of erroneous identification of test results; and

(ii) An opportunity for the defendant to provide information on the identification of prescription or nonprescription drugs used in connection with a medical condition.

(5) Sample collection, storage, and transportation
to the place of testing shall be performed so as to reasonably preclude the probability of sample contamination or adulteration.

(6) Sample testing shall conform to scientifically accepted analytical methods and procedures. Testing shall include verification or confirmation of any positive test result by a reliable analytical method before the result of any test may be used as a basis for any action by the court.

(e) The initial sample shall be collected before the defendant's release on bail. Thereafter, the defendant shall report to the pretrial services agency or probation department as required by the agency or department. The pretrial services agency or probation department shall immediately notify the court of any defendant who fails to report for testing.

(f) After the initial test, a subsequent confirmed positive test result indicative of continued drug use shall result in the following:

(1) Upon the first confirmed positive test result, the pretrial services agency or probation department, shall place the defendant on a more frequent testing schedule and shall warn the defendant of the consequences of continued drug use.

(2) A second confirmed positive test result shall be grounds for a hearing before the judge who authorized the release of the defendant in accordance with the provisions of subsection (g) of this Section.

(g) The court shall, upon motion of the State or upon its own motion, conduct a hearing in connection with any defendant who fails to appear for testing, fails to cooperate with the persons conducting the testing program, attempts to submit a sample not his or her own or has had a confirmed positive test result indicative of continued drug use for the second or subsequent time after the initial test. The hearing shall be conducted in accordance with the procedures of Section 110-6.
Upon a finding by the court that the State has established by clear and convincing evidence that the defendant has violated the drug testing conditions of bail, the court may consider any of the following sanctions:

(1) increase the amount of the defendant's bail or conditions of release;

(2) impose a jail sentence of up to 5 days;

(3) revoke the defendant's bail; or

(4) enter such other orders which are within the

power of the court as deemed appropriate.

(h) The results of any drug testing conducted under this Section shall not be admissible on the issue of the defendant's guilt in connection with any criminal charge.

(i) The court may require that the defendant pay for the cost of drug testing.

§ 110-7. Deposit of Bail Security.
(a) The person for whom bail has been set shall execute the bail bond and deposit with the clerk of the court before which the proceeding is pending a sum of money equal to 10% of the bail, but in no event shall such deposit be less than $25. The clerk of the court shall provide a space on each form for a person other than the accused who has provided the money for the posting of bail to so indicate and a space signed by an accused who has executed the bail bond indicating whether a person other than the accused has provided the money for the posting of bail. The form shall also include a written notice to such person who has provided the defendant with the money for the posting of bail indicating that the bail may be used to pay costs, attorney's fees, fines, or other purposes authorized by the court and if the defendant fails to comply with the conditions of the bail bond, the court shall enter an order declaring the bail to be forfeited. The written notice must be:

(1) distinguishable from the surrounding text;

(2) in bold type or underscored; and

(3) in a type size at least 2 points larger than the surrounding type. When a person for whom bail has been set is charged with an offense under the Illinois Controlled Substances Act or the Methamphetamine Control and Community Protection Act which is a Class X felony, or making a terrorist threat in violation of Section 29D-20 of the Criminal Code of 1961 or an attempt to commit the offense of making a terrorist threat, the court may require the defendant to deposit a sum equal to 100% of the bail. Where any person is charged with a forcible felony while free on bail and is the subject of proceedings under Section 109-3 of this Code the judge conducting the preliminary examination may also conduct a hearing upon the application of the State pursuant to the provisions of Section 110-6 of this Code to increase or revoke the bail for that person's prior alleged offense.

(b) Upon depositing this sum and any bond fee authorized by law, the person shall be released from custody subject to the conditions of the bail bond.

(c) Once bail has been given and a charge is pending or is thereafter filed in or transferred to a court of competent jurisdiction the latter court shall continue the original bail in that court subject to the provisions of Section 110-6 of this Code.

(d) After conviction the court may order that the original bail stand as bail pending appeal or deny, increase or reduce bail subject to the provisions of Section 110-6.2.
(e) After the entry of an order by the trial court allowing or denying bail pending appeal either party may apply to the reviewing court having jurisdiction or to a justice thereof sitting in vacation for an order increasing or decreasing the amount of bail or allowing or denying bail pending appeal subject to the provisions of Section 110-6.2.

(f) When the conditions of the bail bond have been performed and the accused has been discharged from all obligations in the cause the clerk of the court shall return to the accused or to the defendant's designee by an assignment executed at the time the bail amount is deposited, unless the court orders otherwise, 90% of the sum which had been deposited and shall retain as bail bond costs 10% of the amount deposited. However, in no event shall the

amount retained by the clerk as bail bond costs be less than $5. Notwithstanding the foregoing, in counties with a population of 3,000,000 or more, in no event shall the amount retained by the clerk as bail bond costs exceed $100.Bail bond deposited by or on behalf of a defendant in one case may be used, in the court's discretion, to satisfy financial obligations of that same defendant incurred in a different case due to a fine, court costs, restitution or fees of the defendant's attorney of record. In counties with a population of 3,000,000 or more, the court shall not order bail bond deposited by or on behalf of a defendant in one case to be used to satisfy financial obligations of that same defendant in a different case until the bail bond is first used to satisfy court costs and attorney's fees in the case in which the bail bond has been deposited and any other unpaid child support obligations are satisfied. In counties with a population of less than 3,000,000, the court shall not order bail bond deposited by or on behalf of a defendant in one case to be used to satisfy financial obligations of that same defendant in a different case until the bail bond is first used to satisfy court costs in the case in which the bail bond has been deposited.
At the request of the defendant the court may order such 90% of defendant's bail deposit, or whatever amount is repayable to defendant from such deposit, to be paid to defendant's attorney of record.
(g) If the accused does not comply with the conditions of the bail bond the court having jurisdiction shall enter an order declaring the bail to be forfeited.

Notice of such order of forfeiture shall be mailed forthwith to the accused at his last known address. If the accused does not appear and surrender to the court having jurisdiction within 30 days from the date of the forfeiture or within such period satisfy the court that appearance and surrender by the accused is impossible and without his fault the court shall enter judgment for the State if the charge for which the bond was given was a felony or misdemeanor, or if the charge was quasi-criminal or traffic, judgment for the political subdivision of the State which prosecuted the case, against the accused for the amount of the bail and costs of the court proceedings; however, in counties with a population of less than 3,000,000, instead of the court entering a judgment for the full amount of the bond the court may, in its discretion, enter judgment for the cash deposit on the bond, less costs, retain the deposit for further disposition or, if a cash bond was posted for failure to appear in a matter involving enforcement of child support or maintenance, the amount of the cash deposit on the bond, less outstanding costs, may be awarded to the person or entity to whom the child support or maintenance is due.
The deposit made in accordance with paragraph (a) shall be applied to the payment of costs. If judgment is entered and any amount of such deposit remains after the payment of costs it shall be applied to payment of the judgment and transferred to the treasury of the municipal corporation wherein the bond was taken if the offense was a violation of any penal ordinance of a political subdivision of this State, or to the treasury of the county wherein the bond was taken if the offense was a violation of any penal statute of this State. The balance of the judgment may be enforced and collected in the same manner as a judgment entered in a civil action.

(h) After a judgment for a fine and court costs or either is entered in the prosecution of a cause in which a deposit had been made in accordance with paragraph (a) the balance of such deposit, after deduction of bail bond costs, shall be applied to the payment of the judgment.

(i) When a court appearance is required for an alleged violation of the Criminal Code of 1961, the Illinois Vehicle Code, the Wildlife Code, the Fish and Aquatic Life Code, the Child Passenger Protection Act, or a comparable offense of a unit of local government as specified in Supreme Court Rule 551, and if the accused does not appear in court on the date set for appearance or any date to which the case may be continued and the court issues an arrest warrant for the accused, based upon his or her failure to appear when having so previously been ordered to appear by the court, the accused upon his or her admission to bail shall be assessed by the court a fee of $75. Payment of the fee shall be a condition of release unless otherwise ordered by the court. The fee shall be in addition to any bail

that the accused is required to deposit for the offense for which the accused has been charged and may not be used for the payment of court costs or fines assessed for the offense. The clerk of the court shall remit $70 of the fee assessed to the arresting agency who brings the offender in on the arrest warrant. If the Department of State Police is the arresting agency, $70 of the fee assessed shall be remitted by the clerk of the court to the State Treasurer within one month after receipt for deposit into the State Police Operations
Assistance Fund. The clerk of the court shall remit $5 of the fee assessed to the Circuit Court Clerk Operation and Administrative Fund as provided in Section 27.3d of the Clerks of Courts Act.

§ 110-8. Cash, stocks, bonds and real estate as security for bail. (a) In lieu of the bail deposit provided for in Section 110-7 of this Code any person for whom bail has been set may execute the bail bond with or without sureties which bond may be secured:

(1) By a deposit, with the clerk of the court, of an amount equal to the required bail, of cash, or stocks and bonds in which trustees are authorized to invest trust funds under the laws of this State; or

(2) By real estate situated in this State with unencumbered equity not exempt owned by the accused or sureties worth double the amount of bail set in the bond.

(b) If the bail bond is secured by stocks and bonds the accused or sureties shall file with the bond a sworn schedule which shall be approved by the court and shall contain:

(1) A list of the stocks and bonds deposited describing each in sufficient detail that it may be identified;

(2) The market value of each stock and bond;

(3) The total market value of the stocks and bonds listed;

(4) A statement that the affiant is the sole owner of the stocks and bonds listed and they are not exempt from the enforcement of a judgment thereon;

(5) A statement that such stocks and bonds have not previously been used or accepted as bail in this State during the 12 months preceding the date of the bail bond; and

(6) A statement that such stocks and bonds are security for the appearance of the accused in accordance with the conditions of the bail bond.
(c) If the bail bond is secured by real estate the accused or sureties shall file with the bond a sworn schedule which shall contain:

(1) A legal description of the real estate;

(2) A description of any and all encumbrances on the real estate including the amount of each and the holder thereof;

(3) The market value of the unencumbered equity owned by the affiant;

(4) A statement that the affiant is the sole owner of such unencumbered equity and that it is not exempt from the enforcement of a judgment thereon;

(5) A statement that the real estate has not previously been used or accepted as bail in this State during the 12 months preceding the date of the bail bond; and

(6) A statement that the real estate is security for the appearance of the accused in accordance with the conditions of the bail bond.

(d) The sworn schedule shall constitute a material part of the bail bond. The affiant commits perjury if in the sworn schedule he makes a false statement which he does not believe to be true. He shall be prosecuted and punished accordingly, or, he may be punished for contempt.

(e) A certified copy of the bail bond and schedule of real estate shall be filed immediately in the office of the registrar of titles or recorder of the county in which the real estate is situated and the State shall have a lien on such real estate from the time such copies are filed in the office of the registrar of titles or recorder. The registrar of titles or recorder shall enter, index and record (or register as the case may be) such bail bonds and schedules without requiring any advance fee, which fee shall be taxed as costs in the proceeding and paid out of such costs when collected.

(f) When the conditions of the bail bond have been performed and the accused has been discharged from his obligations in the cause, the clerk of the court shall return to him or his sureties the deposit of any cash, stocks or bonds. If the bail bond has been secured by real estate the clerk of the court shall forthwith notify in writing the registrar of titles or recorder and the lien of the bail bond on the real estate shall be discharged.

(g) If the accused does not comply with the conditions of the bail bond the court having jurisdiction shall enter an order declaring the bail to be forfeited. Notice of such order of forfeiture shall be mailed forthwith by the clerk of the court to the accused and his sureties at their last known address.

If the accused does not appear and surrender to the court having jurisdiction within 30 days from the date of the forfeiture or within such period satisfy the court that appearance and surrender by the accused is impossible and without his fault the court shall enter judgment for the State against the accused and his sureties for the amount of the bail and costs of the proceedings; however, in counties with a population of less than 3,000,000, if the defendant has posted a cash bond, instead of the court entering a judgment for the full amount of the bond the court may, in its discretion, enter judgment for the cash deposit on the bond, less costs, retain the deposit for further disposition or, if a cash bond was posted for failure to appear in a matter involving enforcement of child support or maintenance, the amount of the cash deposit on the bond, less outstanding costs, may be awarded to the person or entity to whom the child support or maintenance is due.

(h) When judgment is entered in favor of the State on any bail bond given for a felony or misdemeanor, or judgment for a political subdivision of the state on any bail bond given for a quasi-criminal or traffic offense, the State's Attorney or political subdivision's attorney shall forthwith obtain a certified copy of the judgment and deliver same to the sheriff to be enforced by levy on the stocks or bonds deposited with the clerk of the court and the real estate described in the bail bond schedule.

Any cash forfeited under subsection (g) of this Section shall be used to satisfy the judgment and costs and, without necessity of levy, ordered paid into the treasury of the municipal corporation wherein the bail bond was taken if the offense was a violation of any penal ordinance of a political subdivision of this State, or into the treasury of the county wherein the bail bond was taken if the offense was a violation of any penal statute of this State, or to the person or entity to whom child support or maintenance is owed if the bond was taken for failure to appear in a matter involving child support or maintenance. The stocks, bonds and real estate shall be sold in the same manner as in sales for the enforcement of a judgment in civil actions and the proceeds of such sale shall be used to satisfy all court costs, prior encumbrances, if any, and from the balance a sufficient amount to satisfy the judgment shall be paid into the treasury of the municipal corporation wherein the bail bond was taken if the offense was a violation of any penal ordinance of a political subdivision of this State, or into the treasury of the county wherein the bail bond was taken if the offense was a violation of any penal statute of this State. The balance shall be returned to the owner. The real estate so sold may be redeemed in the same manner as real estate may be redeemed after judicial sales or sales for the enforcement of judgments in civil actions.

(i) No stocks, bonds or real estate may be used or accepted as bail bond security in this State more than once in any 12 month period.

§ 110-9. Taking of bail by peace officer. When bail has been set by a judicial officer for a particular offense or offender any sheriff or other peace officer may take bail in accordance with the provisions of Section 110-7 or 110-8 of this Code and release the offender to appear in accordance with the conditions of the bail bond, the Notice to Appear or the Summons. The officer shall give a receipt to the offender for the bail so taken and within a reasonable time deposit such bail with the clerk of the court having jurisdiction of the offense.

§ 110-10. Conditions of bail bond.

(a) If a person is released prior to conviction, either upon payment of bail security or on his or her own recognizance, the conditions of the bail bond shall be that he or she will:

(1) Appear to answer the charge in the court having jurisdiction on a day certain and thereafter as ordered by the court until discharged or final order of the court;

(2) Submit himself or herself to the orders and process of the court;

(3) Not depart this State without leave of the court;

(4) Not violate any criminal statute of any jurisdiction;

(5) At a time and place designated by the court, surrender all firearms in his or her possession to a law enforcement officer designated by the court to take custody of and impound the firearms and physically surrender his or her Firearm Owner's Identification Card to the clerk of the circuit court when the offense the person has been charged with is a forcible felony, stalking, aggravated stalking, domestic battery, any violation of the Illinois Controlled Substances Act, the Methamphetamine Control and Community Protection Act, or the Cannabis Control Act that is classified as a Class 2 or greater felony, or any felony violation of Article 24 of the Criminal Code of 1961; the court may, however, forgo the imposition of this condition when the circumstances of the case clearly do not warrant it or when its imposition would be impractical; if the Firearm Owner's Identification Card is confiscated, the clerk of the circuit court shall mail the confiscated card to the Illinois State Police; all legally possessed firearms shall be returned to the person upon the charges being dismissed, or if the person is found not guilty, unless the finding of not guilty is by reason of insanity; and

(6) At a time and place designated by the court, submit to a psychological evaluation when the person has been charged with a violation of item (4) of subsection (a) of Section 24-1 of the Criminal Code of 1961 and that violation occurred in a school or in any conveyance owned, leased, or contracted by a school to transport students to or from school or a school--related activity, or on any public way within 1,000 feet of real property comprising any school.

Psychological evaluations ordered pursuant to this Section shall be completed promptly and made available to the State, the defendant, and the court. As a further condition of bail under these circumstances, the court shall order the defendant to refrain from entering upon the property of the school, including any conveyance owned, leased, or contracted by a school to transport students to or from school or a school-related activity, or on any public way within 1,000 feet of real property comprising any school. Upon receipt of the psychological evaluation, either the State or the defendant may request a change in the conditions of bail, pursuant to Section 110-6 of this Code. The court may change the conditions of bail to include a requirement that the defendant follow the recommendations of the psychological evaluation, including undergoing psychiatric treatment. The conclusions of the psychological evaluation and any statements elicited from the defendant during its administration are not admissible as evidence of guilt during the course of any trial on the charged offense, unless the defendant places his or her mental competency in issue.

(b) The court may impose other conditions, such as the following, if the court finds that such conditions are reasonably necessary to assure the defendant's appearance in court, protect the public from the defendant, or prevent the defendant's unlawful interference with the orderly administration of justice:

(1) Report to or appear in person before such person or agency as the court may direct;

(2) Refrain from possessing a firearm or other dangerous weapon;

(3) Refrain from approaching or communicating with particular persons or classes of persons;
(4) Refrain from going to certain described geographical areas or premises;

(5) Refrain from engaging in certain activities or indulging in intoxicating liquors or in certain drugs;

(6) Undergo treatment for drug addiction or alcoholism;

(7) Undergo medical or psychiatric treatment;

(8) Work or pursue a course of study or vocational training;

(9) Attend or reside in a facility designated by the court;

(10) Support his or her dependents;

(11) If a minor resides with his or her parents or in a foster home, attend school, attend a non-residential program for youths, and contribute to his or her own support at home or in a foster home;

(12) Observe any curfew ordered by the court;

(13) Remain in the custody of such designated person or organization agreeing to supervise his release. Such third party custodian shall be responsible for notifying the court if the defendant fails to observe the conditions of release which the custodian has agreed to monitor, and shall be subject to contempt of court for failure so to notify the court;

(14) Be placed under direct supervision of the Pretrial Services Agency, Probation Department or Court Services Department in a pretrial bond home supervision capacity with or without the use of an approved electronic monitoring device subject to Article 8A of Chapter V of the Unified Code of Corrections;

(14.1) The court shall impose upon a defendant who is charged with any alcohol, cannabis, methamphetamine, or controlled substance violation and is placed under direct supervision of the Pretrial Services Agency, Probation Department or Court Services Department in a pretrial bond home supervision capacity with the use of an approved monitoring device, as a condition of such bail bond, a fee that represents costs incidental to the electronic monitoring for each day of such bail supervision ordered by the court, unless after determining the inability of the defendant to pay the fee, the court assesses a lesser fee or no fee as the case may be. The fee shall be collected by the clerk of the circuit court. The clerk of the circuit court shall pay all monies collected from this fee to the county treasurer for deposit in the substance abuse services fund under Section 5-1086.1 of the Counties Code;

(14.2) The court shall impose upon all defendants, including those defendants subject to paragraph (14.1) above, placed under direct supervision of the Pretrial Services Agency, Probation Department or Court Services Department in a pretrial bond home supervision capacity with the use of an approved monitoring device, as a condition of such bail bond, a fee which shall represent costs incidental to such electronic monitoring for each day of such bail supervision ordered by the court, unless after determining the inability of the defendant to pay the fee, the court assesses a lesser fee or no fee as the case may be. The fee shall be collected by the clerk of the circuit court. The clerk of the circuit court shall pay all monies collected from this fee to the county treasurer who shall use the monies collected to defray the costs of corrections. The county treasurer shall deposit the fee collected in the county working cash fund under Section 6-27001 or Section 6-29002 of the Counties Code, as the case may be;

(14.3) The Chief Judge of the Judicial Circuit may establish reasonable fees to be paid by a person receiving pretrial services while under supervision of a pretrial services agency, probation department, or court services department. Reasonable fees may be charged for pretrial services including, but not limited to, pretrial supervision, diversion programs, electronic monitoring, victim impact services, drug and alcohol testing, DNA testing, GPS electronic monitoring, assessments and evaluations related to domestic violence and other victims, and victim mediation services. The person receiving pretrial services may be ordered to pay all costs incidental to pretrial services in accordance with his or her ability to pay those costs;

(14.4) For persons charged with violating Section 11-501 of the Illinois Vehicle Code, refrain from operating a motor vehicle not equipped with an ignition interlock device, as defined in Section 1-129.1 of the Illinois Vehicle Code, pursuant to the rules promulgated by the Secretary of State for the installation of ignition interlock devices. Under this condition the court may allow a defendant who is not self-employed to operate a vehicle owned by the defendant's employer that is not equipped with an ignition interlock device in the course and scope of the defendant's employment;

(15) Comply with the terms and conditions of an order of protection issued by the court under the Illinois Domestic Violence Act of 1986 or an order of protection issued by the court of another state, tribe, or United States territory;

(16) Under Section 110-6.5 comply with the conditions of the drug testing program; and

(17) Such other reasonable conditions as the court may impose.

(c) When a person is charged with an offense under Section 11-1.20, 11-1.30, 11-1.40, 11-1.50, 11-1.60, 12-13, 12-14, 12-14.1, 12-15 or 12-16 of the "Criminal Code of 1961", involving a victim who is a minor under 18 years of age living in the same household with the defendant at the time of the offense, in granting bail or releasing the defendant on his own recognizance, the judge shall impose conditions to restrict the defendant's access to the victim which may include, but are not limited to conditions that he will:

1. Vacate the Household.

2. Make payment of temporary support to his dependents.

3. Refrain from contact or communication with the child victim, except as ordered by the court.
(d) When a person is charged with a criminal offense and the victim is a family or household member as defined in Article 112A, conditions shall be imposed at the time of the defendant's release on bond that restrict the defendant's access to the victim. Unless provided otherwise by the court, the restrictions shall include requirements that the defendant do the following:

(1) refrain from contact or communication with the victim for a minimum period of 72 hours following the defendant's release; and

(2) refrain from entering or remaining at the victim's residence for a minimum period of 72 hours following the defendant's release.

(e) Local law enforcement agencies shall develop standardized bond forms for use in cases involving family or household members as defined in Article 112A, including specific conditions of bond as provided in subsection (d). Failure of any law enforcement department to develop or use those forms shall in no way limit the applicability and enforcement of subsections (d) and (f).

(f) If the defendant is admitted to bail after conviction the conditions of the bail bond shall be that he will, in addition to the conditions set forth in subsections (a) and (b) hereof:

(1) Duly prosecute his appeal;

(2) Appear at such time and place as the court may direct;

(3) Not depart this State without leave of the court;

(4) Comply with such other reasonable conditions as the court may impose; and

(5) If the judgment is affirmed or the cause reversed and remanded for a new trial, forthwith surrender to the officer from whose custody he was bailed.

(g) Upon a finding of guilty for any felony offense, the defendant shall physically surrender, at a time and place designated by the court, any and all firearms in his or her possession and his or her Firearm Owner's Identification Card as a condition of remaining on bond pending sentencing.

§ 110-11. Bail on a new trial. If the judgment of conviction is reversed and the cause remanded for a new trial the trial court may order that the bail stand pending such trial, or reduce or increase bail.

§ 110-12. Notice of change of address. A defendant who has been admitted to bail shall file a written notice with the clerk of the court before which the proceeding is pending of any change in his or her address within 24 hours after such change, except that a defendant who has been admitted to bail for a forcible felony as defined in Section 2-8 of the Criminal Code of 1961 shall file a written notice with the clerk of the court before which the proceeding is pending and the clerk shall immediately deliver a time stamped copy of the written notice to the State's Attorney charged with the prosecution within 24 hours prior to such change. The address of a defendant who has been admitted to bail shall at all times remain a matter of public record with the clerk of the court.

§ 110-13. Persons prohibited from furnishing bail security. No attorney at law practicing in this State and no official authorized to admit another to bail or to accept bail shall furnish any part of any security for bail in any criminal action or any proceeding nor shall any such person act as surety for any accused admitted to bail.

§ 110-14. Credit for Incarceration on Bailable Offense. (a) Any person incarcerated on a bailable offense who does not supply bail and against whom a fine is levied on conviction of such offense shall be allowed a credit of $5 for each day so incarcerated upon application of the defendant. However, in no case shall the amount so allowed or credited exceed the amount of the fine.

(b) Subsection (a) does not apply to a person incarcerated for sexual assault as defined in paragraph (1) of subsection (a) of Section 5-9-1.7 of the Unified Code of Corrections.

§ 110-15. Applicability of provisions for giving and taking bail. The provisions of Sections 110-7 and 110-8 of this Code are exclusive of other provisions of law for the giving, taking, or enforcement of bail. In all cases where a person is admitted to bail the provisions of Sections 110-7 and 110-8 of this Code shall be applicable.

However, the Supreme Court may, by rule or order, prescribe a uniform schedule of amounts of bail in specified traffic and conservation cases, quasi-criminal offenses, and misdemeanors. Such uniform schedule may provide that the cash deposit provisions of Section 110-7 shall not apply to bail amounts established for alleged violations punishable by fine alone, and the schedule may further provide that in specified traffic cases a valid Illinois chauffeur's or operator's license must be deposited, in addition to 10% of the amount of the bail specified in the schedule.

§ 110-16. Bail bond-forfeiture in same case or absents self during trial-not bailable. If a person admitted to bail on a felony charge forfeits his bond and fails to appear in court during the 30 days immediately after such forfeiture, on being taken into custody thereafter he shall not be bailable in the case in question, unless the court finds that his absence was not for the purpose of obstructing justice or avoiding prosecution.

§ 110-17. Unclaimed Bail Deposits. Notwithstanding the provisions of the Uniform Disposition of Unclaimed Property Act, any sum of money deposited by any person to secure his release from custody which remains unclaimed by the person entitled to its return for 3 years after the conditions of the bail bond have been performed and the accused has been discharged from all obligations in the cause shall be presumed to be abandoned.

(a) The clerk of the circuit court, as soon thereafter as practicable, shall cause notice to be published once, in English, in a newspaper or newspapers of general circulation in the county wherein the deposit of bond was received.

(b) The published notice shall be entitled "Notice of Persons Appearing to be Owners of Abandoned Property" and shall contain:

(1) The names, in alphabetical order, of persons to whom the notice is directed.

(2) A statement that information concerning the amount of the property may be obtained by any persons possessing an interest in the property by making an inquiry at the office of the clerk of the circuit court at a location designated by him.

(3) A statement that if proof of claim is not presented by the owner to the clerk of the circuit court and if the owner's right to receive the property is not established to the satisfaction of the clerk of the court within 65 days from the date of the published notice, the abandoned property will be placed in the custody of the treasurer of the county, not later than 85 days after such publication, to whom all further claims must thereafter be directed. If the claim is established as aforesaid and after deducting an amount not to exceed $20 to cover the cost of notice publication and related clerical expenses, the clerk of the court shall make payment to the person entitled thereto.

(4) The clerk of the circuit court is not required to publish in such notice any items of less than $100 unless he deems such publication in the public interest.

(c) Any clerk of the circuit court who has caused notice to be published as provided by this Section shall, within 20 days after the time specified in this Section for claiming the property from the clerk of the court, pay or deliver to the treasurer of the county having jurisdiction of the offense, whether the bond was taken there or any other county, all sums deposited as specified in this section less such amounts as may have been returned to the persons whose rights to receive the sums deposited have been established to the satisfaction of the clerk of the circuit court. Any clerk of the circuit court who transfers such sums to the county treasury including sums deposited by persons whose names are not required to be set forth in the published notice aforesaid, is relieved of all liability for such sums as have been transferred as unclaimed bail deposits or any claim which then exists or which thereafter may arise or be made in respect to such sums.

(d) The treasurer of the county shall keep just and true accounts of all moneys paid into the treasury, and if any person appears within 5 years after the deposit of moneys by the clerk of the circuit court and claims any money paid into the treasury, he shall file a claim therefore on the form prescribed by the treasurer of the county who shall consider any claim filed under this Act and who may, in his discretion, hold a hearing and receive evidence concerning it. The treasurer of the county shall prepare a finding and the decision in writing on each hearing, stating the substance of any evidence heard by him, his findings of fact in respect thereto, and the reasons for his decision. The decision shall be a public record.

(e) All claims which are not filed within the 5 year period shall be forever barred.

§ 110-18. Reimbursement. The sheriff of each county shall certify to the treasurer of each county the number of days that persons had been detained in the custody of the sheriff without a bond being set as a result of an order entered pursuant to Section 110-6.1 of this Code. The county treasurer shall, no later than January 1, annually certify to the Supreme Court the number of days that persons had been detained without bond during the twelve-month period ending November 30. The Supreme Court shall reimburse, from funds appropriated to it by the General Assembly for such purposes, the treasurer of each county an amount of money for deposit in the county general revenue fund at a rate of $50 per day for each day that persons were detained in custody without bail as a result of an order entered pursuant to Section 110-6.1 of this Code.

Title IV. Proceedings to Commence Prosecution
Article 111 – Charging an Offense
725 ILCS 111-8

§ 111-1. Methods of prosecution. When authorized by law a prosecution may be commenced by:

(a) A complaint;

(b) An information;

(c) An indictment.

Upon commencement of a prosecution for a violation of Section 11-501 of The Illinois Vehicle Code, or a similar provision of a local ordinance, or Section 9-3 of the Criminal Code of 1961, as amended, relating to the offense of reckless homicide, the victims of these offenses shall have all the rights under this Section as they do in Section 4 of the Bill of Rights for Victims and Witnesses of Violent Crime Act.

For the purposes of this Section "victim" shall mean an individual who has suffered personal injury as a result of the commission of a violation of Section 11-501 of The Illinois Vehicle Code, or a similar provision of a local ordinance, or Section 9-3 of the Criminal Code of 1961, as amended, relating to the offense of reckless homicide. In regard to a violation of Section 9-3 of the Criminal Code of 1961, as amended, relating to the offense of reckless homicide, "victim" shall also include, but not be limited to, spouse, guardian, parent, or other family member.

§ 111-2. Commencement of prosecutions. (a) All prosecutions of felonies shall be by information or by indictment. No prosecution may be pursued by information unless a preliminary hearing has been held or waived in accordance with Section 109-3 and at that hearing probable cause to believe the defendant committed an offense was found, and the provisions of Section 109-3.1 of this Code have been complied with.

(b) All other prosecutions may be by indictment, information or complaint.

(c) Upon the filing of an information or indictment in open court charging the defendant with the commission of a sex offense defined in any Section of Article 11 of the Criminal Code of 1961, as amended, and a minor as defined in Section 1-3 of the Juvenile Court Act of 1987, as amended, is alleged to be the victim of the commission of the acts of the defendant in the commission of such offense, the court may appoint a guardian ad litem for the minor as provided in Section 2-17, 3-19, 4-16 or 5-610 of the Juvenile Court Act of 1987.

(d) Upon the filing of an information or indictment in open court, the court shall immediately issue a warrant for the arrest of each person charged with an offense directed to a peace officer or some other person specifically named commanding him to arrest such person.

(e) When the offense is bailable, the judge shall endorse on the warrant the amount of bail required by the order of the court, and if the court orders the process returnable forthwith, the warrant shall require that the accused be arrested and brought immediately into court.

(f) Where the prosecution of a felony is by information or complaint after preliminary hearing, or after a waiver of preliminary hearing in accordance with paragraph (a) of this Section, such prosecution may be for all offenses, arising from the same transaction or conduct of a defendant even though the complaint or complaints filed at the preliminary hearing charged only one or some of the offenses arising from that transaction or conduct.

§ 111-3. Form of charge. (a) A charge shall be in writing and allege the commission of an offense by:

(1) Stating the name of the offense;

(2) Citing the statutory provision alleged to have been violated;
(3) Setting forth the nature and elements of the offense charged;

(4) Stating the date and county of the offense as definitely as can be done; and

(5) Stating the name of the accused, if known, and if not known, designate the accused by any name or description by which he can be identified with reasonable certainty.

(b) An indictment shall be signed by the foreman of the Grand Jury and an information shall be signed by the State's Attorney and sworn to by him or another. A complaint shall be sworn to and signed by the complainant; provided, that when a peace officer observes the commission of a misdemeanor and is the complaining witness, the signing of the complaint by the peace officer is sufficient to charge the defendant with the commission of the offense, and the complaint need not be sworn to if the officer signing the complaint certifies that the statements set forth in the complaint are true and correct and are subject to the penalties provided by law for false certification under Section 1-109 of the Code of Civil Procedure and perjury under Section 32-2 of the Criminal Code of 1961; and further provided , however, that when a citation is issued on a Uniform Traffic Ticket or Uniform Conservation Ticket (in a form prescribed by the Conference of Chief Circuit Judges and filed with the Supreme Court), the copy of such Uniform Ticket which is filed with the circuit court constitutes a complaint to which the defendant may plead, unless he specifically requests that a verified complaint be filed.

(c) When the State seeks an enhanced sentence because of a prior conviction, the charge shall also state the intention to seek an enhanced sentence and shall state such prior conviction so as to give notice to the defendant. However, the fact of such prior conviction and the State's intention to seek an enhanced sentence are not elements of the offense and may not be disclosed to the jury during trial unless otherwise permitted by issues properly raised during such trial. For the purposes of this Section, "enhanced sentence" means a sentence which is increased by a prior conviction from one classification of offense to another higher level classification of offense set forth in Section 5-4.5-10 of the Unified Code of Corrections (730 ILCS 5/5-4.5-10); it does not include an increase in the sentence applied within the same level of classification of offense.

(c-5) Notwithstanding any other provision of law, in all cases in which the imposition of the death penalty is not a possibility, if an alleged fact (other than the fact of a prior conviction) is not an element of an offense but is sought to be used to increase the range of penalties for the offense beyond the statutory maximum that could otherwise be imposed for the offense, the alleged fact must be included in the charging instrument or otherwise provided to the defendant through a written notification before trial, submitted to a trier of fact as an aggravating factor, and proved beyond a reasonable doubt. Failure to prove the fact beyond a reasonable doubt is not a bar to a conviction for commission of the offense, but is a bar to increasing, based on that fact, the range of penalties for the offense beyond the statutory maximum that could otherwise be imposed for that offense.

Nothing in this subsection (c-5) requires the imposition of a sentence that increases the range of penalties for the offense beyond the statutory maximum that could otherwise be imposed for the offense if the imposition of that sentence is not required by law.

(d) At any time prior to trial, the State on motion shall be permitted to amend the charge, whether brought by indictment, information or complaint, to make the charge comply with subsection (c) or (c-5) of this Section. Nothing in Section 103-5 of this Code precludes such an amendment or a written notification made in accordance with subsection (c-5) of this Section.

(e) The provisions of subsection (a) of Section 5-4.5-95 of the Unified Code of Corrections (730 ILCS 5/5-4.5-95) shall not be affected by this Section.

§ 111-4. Joinder of offenses and defendants.
(a) Two or more offenses may be charged in the same indictment, information or complaint in a separate count for each offense if the offenses charged, whether felonies or misdemeanors or both, are based on the same act or on 2 or more acts which are part of the same comprehensive transaction.
(b) Two or more defendants may be charged in the same indictment, information or complaint if they are alleged to have participated in the same act or in the same comprehensive transaction out of which the offense or offenses arose. Such defendants may be charged in one or more counts together or separately and all of the defendants need not be charged in each count.
(c) Two or more acts or transactions in violation of any provision or provisions of Sections 8A-2, 8A-3, 8A-4, 8A-4A and 8A-5 of the Illinois Public Aid Code, Section 14 of the Illinois Wage Payment and Collection Act, Sections 16-1, 16-1.3, 16-2, 16-3, 16-5, 16-7, 16-8, 16-10, 16-25, 16-30,16A-3, 16B-2, 16G-15, 16G-20, 16H-15, 16H-20, 16H-25, 16H-30, 16H-45, 16H-50, 16H-55, 17-1, 17-3, 17-6, 17-30, or 17-60, or item (ii) of subsection (a) or (b) of Section 17-9, or subdivision (a)(2) of Section 17-10.5, of the Criminal Code of 1961 and Section 118 of Division I of the Criminal Jurisprudence Act, may be charged as a single offense in a single count of the same indictment, information or complaint, if such acts or transactions by one or more defendants are in furtherance of a single intention and design or if the property, labor or services obtained are of the same person or are of several persons having a common interest in such property, labor or services.

In such a charge, the period between the dates of the first and the final such acts or transactions may be alleged as the date of the offense and, if any such act or transaction by any defendant was committed in the county where the prosecution was commenced, such county may be alleged as the county of the offense.

§ 111-5. Formal defects in a charge.
An indictment, information or complaint which charges the commission of an offense in accordance with Section 111-3 of this Code shall not be dismissed and may be amended on motion by the State's Attorney or defendant at any time because of formal defects, including:

(a) Any miswriting, misspelling or grammatical error;

(b) Any misjoinder of the parties defendant;

(c) Any misjoinder of the offense charged;

(d) The presence of any unnecessary allegation;

(e) The failure to negative any exception, any excuse or proviso contained in the statute defining the offense; or

(f) The use of alternative or disjunctive allegations as to the acts, means, intents or results charged.

§ 111-6. Bill of particulars.
When an indictment, information or complaint charges an offense in accordance with the provisions of Section 111-3 of this Code but fails to specify the particulars of the offense sufficiently to enable the defendant to prepare his defense the court may, on written motion of the defendant, require the State's Attorney to furnish the defendant with a Bill of Particulars containing such particulars as may be necessary for the preparation of the defense. At the trial of the cause the State's evidence shall be confined to the particulars of the bill.

§ 111-7. Loss of charge. When an indictment, information or complaint which has been returned or presented to a court as authorized by law has become illegible or cannot be produced at the arraignment or trial the defendant may be arraigned and tried on a copy thereof certified by the clerk of the court.

§ 111-8. Orders of protection to prohibit domestic violence. (a) Whenever a violation of Section 9-1, 9-2, 9-3, 10-3, 10-3.1, 10-4, 10-5, 11-1.20, 11-1.30, 11-1.40, 11-1.50, 11-1.60, 11-14.3 that involves soliciting for a prostitute, 11-14.4 that involves soliciting for a juvenile prostitute, 11-15, 11-15.1, 11-20.1, 11-20.1B, 11-20.3, 11-20a, 12-1, 12-2, 12-3, 12-3.05, 12-3.2, 12-3.3, 12-3.5, 12-4, 12-4.1, 12-4.3, 12-4.6, 12-5, 12-6, 12-6.3, 12-7.3, 12-7.4, 12-7.5, 12-11, 12-13, 12-14, 12-14.1, 12-15, 12-16, 19-4, 21-1, 21-2, or 21-3 of the Criminal Code of 1961 or Section 1-1 of the Harassing and Obscene Communications Act is alleged in an information, complaint or indictment on file, and the alleged offender and victim are family or household members, as defined in the Illinois Domestic Violence Act, as now or hereafter amended, the People through the respective State's Attorneys may by separate petition and upon notice to the defendant, except as provided in subsection (c) herein, request the court to issue an order of protection.

(b) In addition to any other remedies specified in Section 208 of the Illinois Domestic Violence Act, as now or hereafter amended, the order may direct the defendant to initiate no contact with the alleged victim or victims who are family or household members and to refrain from entering the residence, school or place of business of the alleged victim or victims.

(c) The court may grant emergency relief without notice upon a showing of immediate and present danger of abuse to the victim or minor children of the victim and may enter a temporary order pending notice and full hearing on the matter.

Commentary – Proceedings following arrest and before trial

First appearance; arraignment. A defendant who is arrested with or without a warrant and taken into custody, must be taken before a judge who will admonish the defendant about the charges that have been made against him, advise him of his right to counsel and conduct a hearing about whether the defendant will be admitted to bail. If the defendant is indigent, a lawyer (usually the public defender) will be appointed for him. If the defendant is not indigent or indicates he will hire a private attorney, the court will set another date for a private attorney to appear. If counsel appears at the first appearance date, the judge will advise the defendant of his right to a preliminary hearing if charged with a felony, or if charged with a misdemeanor will hear the defendant enter a plea of not guilty to the charge and also enter a demand to have a trial by jury. The difference between a "first appearance" and an arraignment is the defendant entering a plea of not guilty and either demanding a jury or waiving a jury so the case can be set for bench trial. as part of the arraignment procedure, most Illinois courts now enter standard discovery orders requiring the prosecution to comply with discovery requirements under Illinois Supreme Court Rule 412 and the defense to comply with discovery requirements under Illinois Supreme Court Rule 413 (those rules are set forth at pp. 594 - 596). The court may also set a deadline for filing pre-trial motions.

At this first court appearance, the States Attorney's Office has reviewed the reports and filed the criminal charges against the defendant in an Information. The Information can be in multiple counts setting forth by date, location and proper elements the charges against the defendant. When the defendant enters a plea of not guilty, he is saying that the state must prove that he is guilty of the charges.

A felony case (i.e. after first appearance) will be set for a date that is less than 30 days away for a preliminary hearing. Typically, a misdemeanor case will be set for a status or pre-trial date before being set for an actual trial date. If the defendant has had counsel prior to his arrest or prior to his arraignment, there is a possibility that plea bargaining has occurred. The entire process, in some jurisdictions, can result in the presentation of a negotiated plea and a disposition by entry of a sentencing order at one court appearance. This is especially true in smaller counties.

Bail hearing; setting bail; bail conditions; release from custody pending trial. When the defendant is arrested pursuant to warrant, the judge will set bail on the warrant, unless the offense is not bailable. A defendant who is arrested on a warrant has the option of posting the bail set on the warrant and being released from custody until the date of the first appearance, which usually is a pre-set date set by court administration. If the defendant in custody is unable to post the bail set on the warrant, the court at the first appearance date, or at some other time, can entertain a motion to reduce bail or modify the conditions of bail. Upon the state's request, the court may also increase the amount of bail or modify the conditions of bail. The judge will consider arguments and information from 725 ILCS 5/110-1 *et seq.* in addressing these matters.

The judge has the power to release the defendant on recognizance, signing a bond promising to appear in court subject to having a judgment entered against the defendant if he fails to appear or otherwise violates conditions that have been set in the order admitting him to bail. Conditions of bail may include (1) remaining within the jurisdiction of the court; (2) having no contact with a named victim; (3) having no contact with a particular property – residence, school or business premises; (4) refraining from consuming alcohol or obtaining treatment; (5) obtain or maintain employment; (6) supporting dependants or (7) not possessing firearms.

Bail requirements can be met by posting 10% of the amount of bail (i.e. a $100,000 bail is met by making a bail deposit of $10,000 as required by 725 ILCS 5/110-7) and once the deposit is made, the defendant is released from custody subject to the conditions of bail that have been set. there is a cost of posting a deposit – typically 10% of the bail deposit (i.e. the bond fee for a $100,000 bail is $1,000 which is 10% of the $10,000 posted as a deposit.) a defendant can post the entire bail amount by cash or other security and not incur the bond fee. Often a defense attorney will accept a bond assignment on the bail deposited, which at the conclusion of the case can result in a court order that the clerk pay the money on deposit after applicable fees and costs over to the named attorney.

Felony charges – preliminary hearing or indictment. If the defendant is charged with a felony, he is entitled to have a determination that there is probable cause to believe that he committed the felony offense. At his first appearance, the defendant can waive a preliminary hearing or request one. If the defendant waives his preliminary hearing, he is considered to have been arraigned on the information, since he has been admonished about the charges against him, the possible penalties if found guilty and of course, has either hired a lawyer or had one appointed for him.

If the defendant requests a preliminary hearing, he may indeed appear on an assigned date and the prosecutor will present evidence, typically in the form of an investigating police officer who gives in court testimony about the investigation of the case. Hearsay evidence is admissible, so one officer can testify about the knowledge of all officers about the investigation in the case. Sometimes other occurrence witnesses, including the victim, could be asked to testify, but such occasions are rare. The defendant, through his attorney will be able to cross examine the testifying officer or the other witness. The defendant can testify himself or herself, or call other witnesses to contest the claim of probable cause, but such defense evidence is a rare occurrence as well. Since the burden of proof is probable cause (i.e. a reasonable person would believe the defendant committed a felony crime), preliminary hearings are often short, to the point and result in the finding of probable cause, to set the matter over for a trial call or trial date. Some cases can be cleared if the judge does not find probable cause, but that finding does not mean the defendant cannot still be prosecuted if additional evidence can be provided to a grand jury that the court did not hear.

Indictment by grand jury. The prosecution can bypass the preliminary hearing by presenting its evidence to a grand jury so that an indictment is returned. the standard of proof before a grand jury is the same (probable cause), the rules of evidence are the same (hearsay is admissible) and the witnesses are normally the same (police officer, sometimes the victim and others) as at a preliminary hearing. However, the defendant is not present, his lawyer is not present, and he has no right to cross-examine witnesses or present proof at the grand jury. Many counties have gone to a system where there are no preliminary hearings and only grand jury indictments to determine probable cause.

Pre-trial hearings, discovery and plea negotiations. Most courts set cases for pre-trial calls – misdemeanor pre-trials are usually on a different date from felony pre-trials. At those hearings, cases that are ready for trial are set for jury trials or bench trials (if juries are waived) or if the cases are not ready for trial, the case may be continued on motion of the state or the defense. A defendant who is in custody and who has made a demand for a speedy trial must be brought to trial within 120 days. A defendant who is not in custody and who has made a demand for speedy trial must be brought to trial within 160 days.

While the cases are pending, the parties engage in discovery production as required by the order entered after arraignment. Strengths, weaknesses and misunderstandings about the evidence, witnesses and facts are discussed between the states attorney's office and the defense attorneys. The defendant's criminal history, the victim's wishes, the standard policies of the states attorney's office and other factors all come into play. If a plea agreement is reached, courts sometimes have specific dates set for pleas to be presented. lawyers can set their clients cases for pleas on those dates through court administration or await attendance at a pre-trial hearing to advise the court the case will be presented by a plea agreement and have the case assigned to a date and time for presentation of the plea. Most courts require the defendant to be present at the pre-trial hearings.

Plea negotiations can be agreements for pleas to a single count of a multicounty indictment or information, to multiple counts, to a lesser charge that will be filed as an additional count. Typically in return for a plea to charge or charges, other courts or cases are dismissed and an agreed sentence is recommended to the court who accepts the plea agreement, admonishes the defendant of his rights under Illinois Supreme Court Rule 601, makes a record of required trial rights waivers (jury trial, confrontation of witnesses, etc.) and sentences the defendant according the plea agreement. Other plea agreements may involve "open pleas" where the prosecution and the defense agree on the charge or charges but not on the sentence, so that the court accepts the guilty plea and has a separate sentencing hearing where the court determines the sentence and either the prosecution or defense can argue what the fair and proper sentence should be. A hybrid plea agreement is for the prosecution to agree to a "cap", that is a maximum sentence that the prosecution will recommend.

Most state court judges accept plea bargaining as an essential component of the criminal justice system, and accordingly accept the agreements. Some judges may feel that the plea agreement is too lenient on the defendant and refuse to accept the agreement. Again practice varies from county to county. It is theoretically possible that a judge could feel that a plea agreement is too harsh on the defendant, however, in the author's experience this has never happened, and the author has never heard of it happening. Indeed, an unauthorized promise made by law enforcement officials regarding a plea agreement or even a charging decision may be enforced under the 14th Amendment due process clause. If the defendant relied on the promise and acted to his detriment, the government may be made to honor such an agreement. *People v. Stapinski* 2015 IL 117242 (Ill. S. Ct. 2015)(following defendant's arrest he agreed to cooperate in return for a no-prosecution promise; the due process clause of the 14th amendment required enforcement of the promise.)

ARTICLE 112. GRAND JURY

§112-1. Selection and qualification. The grand jurors shall be summoned, drawn, qualified and certified according to law.

§112-2. Impaneling the Grand Jury. (a) The Grand Jury shall consist of 16 persons, 12 of whom shall be necessary to constitute a quorum.

(b) The Grand Jury shall be impaneled, sworn and instructed as to its duties by the court. The court shall select and swear one of the grand jurors to serve as foreman.

(c) Before the Grand Jury shall enter upon the discharge of their duties the following oath shall be administered to the jurors: "You and each of you do solemnly swear (or affirm, as the case may be), that you will diligently inquire into and true presentment make of all such matters and things as shall be given you in charge, or shall otherwise come to your knowledge, touching the present service; you shall present no person through malice, hatred or ill-will; nor shall you leave any unpresented through fear, favor, affection, or for any fee or reward, or for any hope or promise thereof; but in all of your presentments, you shall present the truth, the whole truth, and nothing but the truth, according to the best of your skill and understanding; so help you God."

§112-3. Duration of Grand Jury. (a) In counties with a population in excess of 1,000,000 a Grand Jury shall be convened, impaneled and sworn, and shall commence the performance of its duties for an indeterminate period, on the first Monday of each month. In such counties a Grand Jury shall serve until discharged by the court, except that no Grand Jury shall serve in excess of 18 months and not more than 6 Grand Juries shall sit at the same time. In counties with a population in excess of 225,000 but less than 1,000,000 a Grand Jury may be convened, empaneled, and sworn and may sit at such times and for such periods as the circuit court may order on its own motion or that of the State's Attorney. No Grand Jury shall serve in excess of 18 months and not more than 2 Grand Juries shall sit at the same time.
(b) In all other counties the Grand Jury shall be called and sit at such times and for such periods as the circuit court may order on its own motion or that of the State's Attorney; provided, that no Grand Jury shall sit for a period in excess of 18 months and, provided further, that no more than one Grand Jury shall sit at the same time.

(c) At any time for cause shown the court may excuse a grand juror either temporarily or permanently and, if permanently, may impanel another person in place of the grand juror excused.

§112-4. Duties of Grand Jury and State's Attorney.) (a) The Grand Jury shall hear all evidence presented by the State's Attorney.

(b) The Grand Jury has the right to subpoena and question any person against whom the State's Attorney is seeking a Bill of Indictment, or any other person, and to obtain and examine any documents or transcripts relevant to the matter being prosecuted by the State's Attorney. Prior to the commencement of its duties and, again, before the consideration of each matter or charge before the Grand Jury, the State's Attorney shall inform the Grand Jury of these rights. In cases where the initial charge has been commenced by information or complaint and a finding of no probable cause has resulted as to any offense charged therein, the Grand Jury shall be informed of the finding entered at the preliminary hearing and further advised that such finding shall not bar the State from initiating new charges by indictment, information or complaint if the State's Attorney has reasonable grounds to believe that the evidence available at that time is sufficient to establish probable cause. In such cases, the Grand Jury shall be further advised that it has the right to subpoena and question any witness who testified at the preliminary hearing, or who is believed to have knowledge of such offense, and of its right to obtain and examine the testimony heard at the preliminary hearing, either through the production of a transcript of the proceedings, or through the verbatim testimony of the court reporter who attended the preliminary hearing. The State's Attorney shall file an affidavit as part of the Grand Jury record indicating whether the jurors were advised of such previous findings of no probable cause and of their rights based upon such previous finding.

Any person subpoenaed who is already charged with an offense or against whom the State's Attorney is seeking a Bill of Indictment shall have the right to be accompanied by counsel who shall advise him of his rights during the proceedings but may not participate in any other way. Before any testimony is given by such a person, he shall be informed that he has the right to refuse to answer any question that will tend to incriminate him, that anything he says may be used against him in a court of law, that he has the right to be accompanied and advised of his rights by counsel, and that he will have counsel appointed for him if he cannot afford one.

(c) The foreman shall preside over all hearings and swear all witnesses. Except where otherwise provided by this Article, the foreman may delegate duties to other grand jurors and determine rules of procedure.

(d) If 9 grand jurors concur that the evidence before them constitutes probable cause that a person has committed an offense the State's Attorney shall prepare a Bill of Indictment charging that person with such offense. The foreman shall sign each Bill of Indictment which shall be returned in open court.

(e) When the evidence presented to the Grand Jury does not warrant the return of a Bill of Indictment, the State's Attorney may prepare a written memorandum to such effect, entitled, "No Bill".
(Source: P.A. 85-690.)

§112-4.1. Any person appearing before the grand jury shall have the right to be accompanied by counsel who shall advise him of his rights but shall not participate in any other way.
(Source: P.A. 81-1112.)

Article 112A – Domestic Violence: Order of Protection
725 ILCS 5/112A-1 *et seq.*

§ 112A-1. Construction. This Article shall be interpreted in accordance with the purposes and rules of construction set forth in Section 102 of the Illinois Domestic Violence Act of 1986. Each of the provisions of the Illinois Domestic Violence Act of 1986 which are included in this Article shall govern the issuance, recording and enforcement of orders of protection in criminal proceedings.

§ 112A-2. Commencement of Actions.
(a) Actions for orders of protection are commenced in conjunction with a delinquency petition or a criminal prosecution by filing a petition for an order of protection, under the same case number as the delinquency petition or the criminal prosecution, to be granted during pre-trial release of a defendant, with any dispositional order issued under Section 5-710 of the Juvenile Court Act of 1987, or as a condition of release, supervision, conditional discharge, probation, periodic imprisonment, parole or mandatory supervised release, or in conjunction with imprisonment or a bond forfeiture warrant, provided that:

(i) the violation is alleged in an information, complaint, indictment or delinquency petition on file, and the alleged offender and victim are family or household members; and

(ii) the petition, which is filed by the State's Attorney, names a victim of the alleged crime as a petitioner.

(b) Withdrawal or dismissal of any petition for an order of protection prior to adjudication where the petitioner is represented by the state shall operate as a dismissal without prejudice.

(c) Voluntary dismissal or withdrawal of any delinquency petition or criminal prosecution or a finding of not guilty shall not require dismissal of the action for the order of protection; instead, in the discretion of the State's Attorney, it may be treated as an independent action and, if necessary and appropriate, transferred to a different court or division.

Dismissal of any delinquency petition or criminal prosecution shall not affect the validity of any previously issued order of protection, and thereafter subsection (b) of Section 112A-20 shall be inapplicable to that order.

[§ **112A-3 to** § **112A-29** omitted.]

§ **112A-30. Assistance by law enforcement officers.** (a) Whenever a law enforcement officer has reason to believe that a person has been abused by a family or household member, the officer shall immediately use all reasonable means to prevent further abuse, including:

(1) Arresting the abusing party, where appropriate;

(2) If there is probable cause to believe that particular weapons were used to commit the incident of abuse, subject to constitutional limitations, seizing and taking inventory of the weapons;

(3) Accompanying the victim of abuse to his or her place of residence for a reasonable period of time to remove necessary personal belongings and possessions;

(4) Offering the victim of abuse immediate and adequate information (written in a language appropriate for the victim or in Braille or communicated in appropriate sign language), which shall include a summary of the procedures and relief available to victims of abuse under subsection (c) of Section 112A-17 and the officer's name and badge number;

(5) Providing the victim with one referral to an accessible service agency;

(6) Advising the victim of abuse about seeking medical attention and preserving evidence (specifically including photographs of injury or damage and damaged clothing or other property); and

(7) Providing or arranging accessible transportation for the victim of abuse (and, at the victim's request, any minors or dependents in the victim's care) to a medical facility for treatment of injuries or to a nearby place of shelter or safety; or, after the close of court business hours, providing or arranging for transportation for the victim (and, at the victim's request, any minors or dependents in the victim's care) to the nearest available circuit judge or associate judge so the victim may file a petition for an emergency order of protection under subsection (c) of Section 112A-17.

When a victim of abuse chooses to leave the scene of the offense, it shall be presumed that it is in the best interests of any minors or dependents in the victim's care to remain with the victim or a person designated by the victim, rather than to remain with the abusing party.

(b) Whenever a law enforcement officer does not exercise arrest powers or otherwise initiate criminal proceedings, the officer shall:

(1) Make a police report of the investigation of any bona fide allegation of an incident of abuse and the disposition of the investigation, in accordance with subsection (a) of Section 112A-29;

(2) Inform the victim of abuse of the victim's right to request that a criminal proceeding be initiated where appropriate, including specific times and places for meeting with the State's

Attorney's office, a warrant officer, or other official in accordance with local procedure; and

(3) Advise the victim of the importance of seeking medical attention and preserving evidence (specifically including photographs of injury or damage and damaged clothing or other property).

(c) Except as provided by Section 24-6 of the Criminal Code of 1961 or under a court order, any weapon seized under subsection (a)(2) shall be returned forthwith to the person from whom it was seized when it is no longer needed for evidentiary purposes.

§ 112A-31. Limited law enforcement liability. Any act of omission or commission by any law enforcement officer acting in good faith in rendering emergency assistance or otherwise enforcing this Article shall not impose civil liability upon the law enforcement officer or his or her supervisor or employer, unless the act is a result of willful or wanton misconduct.

Title V. Proceedings Prior to Trial
Article 113 – Arraignment
725 ILCS 5/113-1 *et seq.*

§ 113-1. Procedure on arraignment. before any person is tried for the commission of an offense he shall be called into open court, informed of the charge against him, and called upon to plead thereto. If the defendant so requests the formal charge shall be read to him before he is required to plead. An entry of the arraignment shall be made of record.

§ 113-2. Joint defendants. Defendants who are jointly charged may be arraigned separately or together in the discretion of the court.

§ 113-3. [Right to counsel; court-appointed counsel]. (a) Every person charged with an offense shall be allowed counsel before pleading to the charge. If the defendant desires counsel and has been unable to obtain same before arraignment the court shall recess court or continue the cause for a reasonable time to permit defendant to obtain counsel and consult with him before pleading to the charge. If the accused is a dissolved corporation, and is not represented by counsel, the court may, in the interest of justice, appoint as counsel a licensed attorney of this State.

(b) In all cases, except where the penalty is a fine only, if the court determines that the defendant is indigent and desires counsel, the Public Defender shall be appointed as counsel. If there is no Public Defender in the county or if the defendant requests counsel other than the Public Defender and the court finds that the rights of the defendant will be prejudiced by the appointment of the Public Defender, the court shall appoint as counsel a licensed attorney at law of this State, except that in a county having a population of 2,000,000 or more the Public Defender shall be appointed as counsel in all misdemeanor cases where the defendant is indigent and desires counsel unless the case involves multiple defendants, in which case the court may appoint counsel other than the Public Defender for the additional defendants. The court shall require an affidavit signed by any defendant who requests court-appointed counsel. Such affidavit shall be in the form established by the Supreme Court containing sufficient information to ascertain the assets and liabilities of that defendant. The Court may direct the Clerk of the Circuit Court to assist the defendant in the completion of the affidavit.

Any person who knowingly files such affidavit containing false information concerning his assets and liabilities shall be liable to the county where the case, in which such false affidavit is filed, is pending for the reasonable value of the services rendered by the public defender or other court-appointed counsel in the case to the extent that such services were unjustly or falsely procured.

(c) Upon the filing with the court of a verified statement of services rendered the court shall order the county treasurer of the county of trial to pay counsel other than the Public Defender a reasonable fee. The court shall consider all relevant circumstances, including but not limited to the time spent while court is in session, other time spent in representing the defendant, and expenses reasonably incurred by counsel. In counties with a population greater than 2,000,000, the court shall order the county treasurer of the county of trial to pay counsel other than the Public Defender a reasonable fee stated in the order and based upon a rate of compensation of not more than $40 for each hour spent while court is in session and not more than $30 for each hour otherwise spent representing a defendant, and such compensation shall not exceed $150 for each defendant represented in misdemeanor cases and $1250 in felony cases, in addition to expenses reasonably incurred as hereinafter in this Section provided, except that, in extraordinary circumstances, payment in excess of the limits herein stated may be made if the trial court certifies that such payment is necessary to provide fair compensation for protracted representation.

A trial court may entertain the filing of this verified statement before the termination of the cause, and may order the provisional payment of sums during the pendency of the cause.

(d) In capital cases, in addition to counsel, if the court determines that the defendant is indigent the court may, upon the filing with the court of a verified statement of services rendered, order the county Treasurer of the county of trial to pay necessary expert witnesses for defendant reasonable compensation stated in the order not to exceed $250 for each defendant.

(e) If the court in any county having a population greater than 2,000,000 determines that the defendant is indigent the court may, upon the filing with the court of a verified statement of such expenses, order the county treasurer of the county of trial, in such counties having a population greater than 2,000,000 to pay the general expenses of the trial incurred by the defendant not to exceed $50 for each defendant.

(f) The provisions of this Section relating to appointment of counsel, compensation of counsel, and payment of expenses in capital cases apply except when the compensation and expenses are being provided under the Capital Crimes Litigation Act.

§ 113-3.1. Payment for Court-Appointed Counsel. (a) Whenever under either Section 113-3 of this Code or Rule 607 of the Illinois Supreme Court the court appoints counsel to represent a defendant, the court may order the defendant to pay to the Clerk of the Circuit Court a reasonable sum to reimburse either the county or the State for such representation. In a hearing to determine the amount of the payment, the court shall consider the affidavit prepared by the defendant under Section 113-3 of this Code and any other information pertaining to the defendant's financial circumstances which may be submitted by the parties. Such hearing shall be conducted on the court's own motion or on motion of the State's Attorney at any time after the appointment of counsel but no later than 90 days after the entry of a final order disposing of the case at the trial level.

(b) Any sum ordered paid under this Section may not exceed $500 for a defendant charged with a misdemeanor, $5,000 for a defendant charged with a felony, or $2,500 for a defendant who is appealing a conviction of any class offense.

(c) The method of any payment required under this Section shall be as specified by the Court. The court may order that payments be made on a monthly basis during the term of representation; however, the sum deposited as money bond shall not be used to satisfy this court order. Any sum deposited as money bond with the Clerk of the Circuit Court under Section 110-7 of this Code may be used in the court's discretion in whole or in part to comply with any payment order entered in accordance with paragraph (a) of this Section. The court may give special consideration to the interests of relatives or other third parties who may have posted a money bond on the behalf of the defendant to secure his release.

At any time prior to full payment of any payment order the court on its own motion or the motion of any party may reduce, increase, or suspend the ordered payment, or modify the method of payment, as the interest of fairness may require. No increase, suspension, or reduction may be ordered without a hearing and notice to all parties.

(d) The Supreme Court or the circuit courts may provide by rule for procedures for the enforcement of orders entered under this Section. Such rules may provide for the assessment of all costs, including attorneys' fees which are required for the enforcement of orders entered under this Section when the court in an enforcement proceeding has first found that the defendant has willfully refused to pay. The Clerk of the Circuit Court shall keep records and make reports to the court concerning funds paid under this Section in whatever manner the court directs.

(e) Whenever an order is entered under this Section for the reimbursement of the State due to the appointment of the State Appellate Defender as counsel on appeal, the order shall provide that the Clerk of the Circuit Court shall retain all funds paid pursuant to such order until the full amount of the sum ordered to be paid by the defendant has been paid. When no balance remains due on such order, the Clerk of the Circuit Court shall inform the court of this fact and the court shall promptly order the Clerk of the Circuit Court to pay to the State Treasurer all of the sum paid.

(f) The Clerk of the Circuit Court shall retain all funds under this Section paid for the reimbursement of the county, and shall inform the court when no balance remains due on an order entered hereunder. The Clerk of the Circuit Court shall make payments of funds collected under this Section to the County Treasurer in whatever manner and at whatever point as the court may direct, including payments made on a monthly basis during the term of representation.

(g) A defendant who fails to obey any order of court entered under this Section may be punished for contempt of court. Any arrearage in payments may be reduced to judgment in the court's discretion and collected by any means authorized for the collection of money judgments under the law of this State.

§ 113-4. Plea. (a) When called upon to plead at arraignment the defendant shall be furnished with a copy of the charge and shall plead guilty, guilty but mentally ill, or not guilty.

(b) If the defendant stands mute a plea of not guilty shall be entered for him and the trial shall proceed on such plea.
(c) If the defendant pleads guilty such plea shall not be accepted until the court shall have fully explained to the defendant the consequences of such plea and the maximum penalty provided by law for the offense which may be imposed by the court. After such explanation if the defendant understandingly persists in his plea it shall be accepted by the court and recorded.

(d) If the defendant pleads guilty but mentally ill, the court shall not accept such a plea until the defendant has undergone examination by a clinical psychologist or psychiatrist and the judge has examined the psychiatric or psychological report or reports, held a hearing on the issue of the defendant's mental condition and is satisfied that there is a factual basis that the defendant was mentally ill at the time of the offense to which the plea is entered.

(e) If a defendant pleads not guilty, the court shall advise him at that time or at any later court date on which he is present that if he escapes from custody or is released on bond and fails to appear in court when required by the court that his failure to appear would constitute a waiver of his right to confront the witnesses against him and trial could proceed in his absence.

§ 113-4.1. Plea of *nolo contendere*. a defendant who is charged with a violation of the Illinois Income Tax Act may plead not guilty, guilty or, with the consent of the court, *nolo contendere*. The court may refuse to accept a plea of guilty, and shall not accept such plea or a plea of *nolo contendere* without first addressing the defendant personally and determining that the plea is made voluntarily with understanding of the nature of the charge and the consequences of the plea. If a defendant refuses to plead or if the court refuses to accept a plea of guilty or if a defendant corporation fails to appear, the court shall enter a plea of not guilty. The court shall not enter a judgment upon a plea of guilty unless it is satisfied that there is a factual basis for the plea.

§ 113-5. Plea and Waiver of Jury by Person under 18. No person under the age of 18 years shall be permitted to plead guilty, guilty but mentally ill or waive trial by jury in any case except where the penalty is by fine only unless he is represented by counsel in open court.

§ 113-6. Effect of failure to arraign and irregularity of arraignment. Neither a failure to arraign nor an irregularity in the arraignment shall effect the validity of any proceeding in the cause if the defendant pleads to the charge or proceeds to trial without objecting to such failure or irregularity.

§ 113-8. Advisement concerning status as an alien. before the acceptance of a plea of guilty, guilty but mentally ill, or *nolo contendere* to a misdemeanor or felony offense, the court shall give the following advisement to the defendant in open court:

"If you are not a citizen of the United States, you are hereby advised that conviction of the offense for which you have been charged may have the consequences of deportation, exclusion from admission to the United States, or denial of naturalization under the laws of the United States.".

Article 114 – Pre-trial Motions
725 ILCS 5/114/ *et seq.*

§ 114-1. Motion to dismiss charge. (a) Upon the written motion of the defendant made prior to trial before or after a plea has been entered the court may dismiss the indictment, information or complaint upon any of the following grounds:

(1) The defendant has not been placed on trial in compliance with Section 103-5 of this Code.

(2) The prosecution of the offense is barred by Sections 3-3 through 3-8 of the Criminal Code of 1961, as heretofore and hereafter amended.

(3) The defendant has received immunity from prosecution for the offense charged.

(4) The indictment was returned by a Grand Jury which was improperly selected and which results in substantial injustice to the defendant.

(5) The indictment was returned by a Grand Jury which acted contrary to Article 112 of this Code and which results insubstantial injustice to the defendant.

(6) The court in which the charge has been filed does not have jurisdiction.

(7) The county is an improper place of trial.

(8) The charge does not state an offense.

(9) The indictment is based solely upon the testimony of an incompetent witness.

(10) The defendant is misnamed in the charge and the misnomer results in substantial injustice to the defendant.

(11) The requirements of Section 109-3.1 have not been complied with.

(b) The court shall require any motion to dismiss to be filed within a reasonable time after the defendant has been arraigned. Any motion not filed within such time or an extension thereof shall not be considered by the court and the grounds therefore, except as to subsections (a)(6) and(a)(8) of this Section, are waived.

(c) If the motion presents only an issue of law the court shall determine it without the necessity of further pleadings. If the motion alleges facts not of record in the case the State shall file an answer admitting or denying each of the factual allegations of the motion.

(d) When an issue of fact is presented by a motion to dismiss and the answer of the State the court shall conduct a hearing and determine the issues.

(d-5) When a defendant seeks dismissal of the charge upon the ground set forth in subsection (a)(7) of this Section, the defendant shall make a *prima facie* showing that the county is an improper place of trial. Upon such showing, the State shall have the burden of proving, by a preponderance of the evidence, that the county is the proper place of trial.

(e) Dismissal of the charge upon the grounds set forth in subsections(a)(4) through (a)(11) of this Section shall not prevent the return of a new indictment or the filing of a new charge, and upon such dismissal the court may order that the defendant be held in custody or, if the defendant had been previously released on bail, that the bail be continued for a specified time pending the return of a new indictment or the filing of anew charge.

(f) If the court determines that the motion to dismiss based upon the grounds set forth in subsections (a)(6) and (a)(7) is well founded it may, instead of dismissal, order the cause transferred to a court of competent jurisdiction or to a proper place of trial.

§ 114-2. Motion for a bill of particulars. (a) A written motion for a bill of particulars shall be filed before or within a reasonable time after arraignment and shall specify the particulars of the offense necessary to enable the defendant to prepare his defense.

(b) A bill of particulars may be amended at any time before trial subject to such conditions as justice may require.

§ 114-3. Motion to discharge jury panel.
(a) Any objection to the manner in which a jury panel has been selected or drawn shall be raised by a motion to discharge the jury panel prior to the void dire examination. For good cause shown the court may entertain the motion after the voir dire has begun but such motion shall not be heard after a jury has been sworn to hear the cause.

(b) The motion shall be in writing supported by affidavit and shall state facts which show that the jury panel was improperly selected or drawn.

(c) If the motion states facts which show that the jury panel has been improperly selected or drawn it shall be the duty of the court to conduct a hearing. The burden of proving that the jury panel was improperly selected or drawn shall be upon the movant.

(d) If the court finds that the jury panel was improperly selected or drawn the court shall order the jury panel discharged and the selection or drawing of a new panel in the manner provided by law.

§ 114-4. Motion for continuance.
(a) The defendant or the State may move for a continuance. If the motion is made more than 30 days after arraignment the court shall require that it be in writing and supported by affidavit.

(b) A written motion for continuance made by defendant more than 30 days after arraignment may be granted when:

(1) Counsel for the defendant is ill, has died, or is held to trial in another cause; or

(2) Counsel for the defendant has been unable to prepare for trial because of illness or because he has been held to trial in another cause; or

(3) A material witness is unavailable and the defense will be prejudiced by the absence of his testimony; however, this shall not be a ground for continuance if the State will stipulate that the testimony of the witness would be as alleged; or

(4) The defendant cannot stand trial because of physical or mental incompetency; or

(5) Pre-trial publicity concerning the case has caused a prejudice against defendant on the part of the community; or

(6) The amendment of a charge or a bill of particulars has taken the defendant by surprise and he cannot fairly defend against such an amendment without a continuance.
(c) A written motion for continuance made by the State more than 30 days after arraignment may be granted when:

(1) The prosecutor assigned to the case is ill, has died, or is held to trial in another cause; or

(2) A material witness is unavailable and the prosecution will be prejudiced by the absence of his testimony; however this shall not be a ground for continuance if the defendant will stipulate that the testimony of the witness would be as alleged; or

(3) Pre-trial publicity concerning the case has caused a prejudice against the prosecution on the part of the community.
(d) The court may upon the written motion of either party or upon the court's own motion order a continuance for grounds not stated in subsections (b) and (c) of this Section if he finds that the interests of justice so require.

(e) All motions for continuance are addressed to the discretion of the trial court and shall be considered in the light of the diligence shown on the part of the movant. Where 1 year has expired since the filing of an information or indictments, filed after January 1, 1980, if the court finds that the State has failed to use due diligence in bringing the case to trial, the court may, after a hearing had on the cause, on its own motion, dismiss the information or indictment. Any demand that the defendant had made for a speedy trial under Section 103-5 of this code shall not abate if the State files a new information or the grand jury reindicts in the cause. After a hearing has been held upon the issue of the State's diligence and the court has found that the State has failed to use due diligence in pursuing the prosecution, the court may not dismiss the indictment or information without granting the State one more court date upon which to proceed. Such date shall be not less than 14 nor more than 30 days from the date of the court's finding. If the State is not prepared to proceed upon that date, the court shall dismiss the indictment or information, as provided in this Section.

(f) After trial has begun a reasonably brief continuance may be granted to either side in the interests of justice.

(g) During the time the General Assembly is in session, the court shall, on motion of either party or on its own motion, grant a continuance where the party or his attorney is a member of either house of the General Assembly whose presence is necessary for the full, fair trial of the cause and, in the case of an attorney, where the attorney was retained by the party before the cause was set for trial.

(h) This Section shall be construed to the end that criminal cases are tried with due diligence consonant with the rights of the defendant and the State to a speedy, fair and impartial trial.
(i) Physical incapacity of a defendant may be grounds for a continuance at any time. If, upon written motion of the defendant or the State or upon the court's own motion, and after presentation of affidavits or evidence, the court determines that the defendant is physically unable to appear in court or to assist in his defense, or that such appearance would endanger his health or result in substantial prejudice, a continuance shall be granted. If such continuance precedes the appearance of counsel for such defendant the court shall simultaneously appoint counsel in the manner prescribed by Section 113-3 of this Act. Such continuance shall suspend the provisions of Section 103-5 of this Act, which periods of time limitation shall commence anew when the court, after presentation of additional affidavits or evidence, has determined that such physical incapacity has been substantially removed.
(j) In actions arising out of building code violations or violations of municipal ordinances caused by the failure of a building or structure to conform to the minimum standards of health and safety, the court shall grant a continuance only upon a written motion by the party seeking the continuance specifying the reason why such continuance should be granted.

(k) In prosecutions for violations of Section 10-1, 10-2, 11-1.20, 11-1.30, 11-1.40, 11-1.50, 11-1.60, 12-13, 12-14, 12-14.1, 12-15 or 12-16 of the "Criminal Code of 1961" involving a victim or witness who is a minor under 18 years of age, the court shall, in ruling on any motion or other request for a delay or continuance of proceedings, consider and give weight to the adverse impact the delay or continuance may have on the well-being of a child or witness.

(l) The court shall consider the age of the victim and the condition of the victim's health when ruling on a motion for a continuance.

§ **114-5. Substitution of judge.** (a) Within 10 days after a cause involving only one defendant has been placed on the trial call of a judge the defendant may move the court in writing for a substitution of that judge on the ground that such judge is so prejudiced against him that he cannot receive a fair trial. Upon the filing of such a motion the court shall proceed no further in the cause but shall transfer it to another judge not named in the motion. the defendant may name only one judge as prejudiced, pursuant to this subsection; provided, however, that in a case in which the offense charged is a Class X felony or may be punished by death or life imprisonment, the defendant may name two judges as prejudiced.

(b) Within 24 hours after a motion is made for substitution of judge in a cause with multiple defendants each defendant shall have the right to move in accordance with subsection (a) of this Section for a substitution of one judge. The total number of judges named as prejudiced by all defendants shall not exceed the total number of defendants. The first motion for substitution of judge in a cause with multiple defendants shall be made within 10 days after the cause has been placed on the trial call of a judge.

(c) Within 10 days after a cause has been placed on the trial call of a judge the State may move the court in writing for a substitution of that judge on the ground that such judge is prejudiced against the State. Upon the filing of such a motion the court shall proceed no further in the cause but shall transfer it to another judge not named in the motion. The State may name only one judge as prejudiced, pursuant to this subsection.

(d) In addition to the provisions of subsections (a), (b) and (c) of this Section the State or any defendant may move at any time for substitution of judge for cause, supported by affidavit. Upon the filing of such motion a hearing shall be conducted as soon as possible after its filing by a judge not named in the motion; provided, however, that the judge named in the motion need not testify, but may submit an affidavit if the judge wishes. If the motion is allowed, the case shall be assigned to a judge not named in the motion. If the motion is denied the case shall be assigned back to the judge named in the motion.

§ **114-6. Change of place of trial.** (a) A defendant may move the court for a change of place of trial on the ground that there exists in the county in which the charge is pending such prejudice against him on the part of the inhabitants that he cannot receive a fair trial in such county.

(b) The motion shall be in writing and supported by affidavit which shall state facts showing the nature of the prejudice alleged. The State may file
counter-affidavits. The court shall conduct a hearing and determine the merits of the motion.

(c) If the court determines that there exists in the county where the prosecution is pending such prejudice against the defendant that he cannot receive a fair trial it shall transfer the cause to the circuit court in any county where a fair trial may be had.

(d) In all cases of change of place of trial the clerk of the court from which the change is granted shall immediately prepare a full transcript of the record and proceedings in the case, and of the petition, affidavits and order for the change of place of trial, and transmit the same, together with all papers filed in the case, including the indictment and recognizances of the defendant and all witnesses, to the proper court. If the change is granted to a part but not all of several defendants, a certified copy of the indictment or information, and of the other papers in the case, shall be transmitted to the court to which the change of place of trial is ordered, and such certified copies shall stand as the originals. Such transcript and papers may be transmitted by mail, or in such other way as the court may direct.

(e) When the applicant is in custody or confined in jail, the court shall enter an order directed to the sheriff or other officer having custody of the applicant, to remove his body to the common jail of the county to which the place of trial is changed, and there deliver him to the keeper of the jail, together with the warrant by virtue of which he is confined or held in custody, not more than 3 days next before the day upon which the trial is to commence in the court; and the sheriff shall obey such order and shall endorse on such warrant of commitment the reason of the change of custody, and shall deliver such warrant, with the body of the prisoner, to the keeper of the jail of the proper county, who shall receive the same and give to the sheriff a receipt therefore, and shall take charge of and keep the prisoner in the same manner as if he had originally been committed to his custody.
(f) When the place of trial is changed in any criminal case, the parties and witnesses, and all others who may have entered recognizances to attend the trial of such cause, having notice of the change of place of trial, must attend at the time and place at which the trial is to be had according to such change, and a failure to do so shall operate as a forfeiture of the recognizance.

(g) When the place of trial is changed the State's attorney shall have all the witnesses on the part of the prosecution recognized to appear at the court to which the change is ordered on the day upon which the trial is to commence.

(h) Upon the termination of any trial, when a change of place of trial has been obtained, the clerk of the court in which the trial is had shall submit a certified statement of all costs, fees, charges, claims and expenses resulting from such change of place of trial and necessarily incurred in connection with or incident to the trial of the case, or any appeal therefrom, or required in executing any and all orders of the court made in the case, but shall not include charges for the use of the courtroom or the facilities thereof, nor shall it include fees or salaries paid to employees of the county in which the trial is held, unless it is made necessary by reason of such trial, and when so certified, the items thereof shall be paid by the county in which such indictment or information was found to the officers and persons entitled thereto.
All fines imposed and collected in the county where the trial is had, shall be paid over to the county in which the indictment or information was found.

§ **114-7. Joinder of related prosecutions.** The court may order 2 or more charges to be tried together if the offenses and the defendants could have been joined in a single charge. The procedure shall be the same as if the prosecution were under a single charge.

§ **114-8. Motion for severance.** (a) If it appears that a defendant or the State is prejudiced by a joinder of related prosecutions or defendants in a single charge or by joinder of separate charges or defendants for trial the court may order separate trials, grant a severance of defendants, or provide any other relief as justice may require.

(b) In the case of a prosecution of multiple defendants for criminal sexual assault, aggravated criminal sexual assault, predatory criminal sexual assault of a child, criminal sexual abuse, or aggravated criminal sexual abuse arising out of the same course of conduct, the court, in deciding a motion to sever the charges and try the defendants separately, must consider, subject to constitutional limitations, the impact upon the alleged victim of multiple trials requiring the victim's testimony.

§ **114-9. Motion for a list of witnesses.**
(a) On motion of the defendant the court shall order the State to furnish the defense with a list of prosecution witnesses and their last known addresses, except the home address of any peace officer witness shall not be required to be so

furnished, the address of his assignment station being sufficient for the purposes of this statute.

(b) The court may permit witnesses not named in an original or amended list to testify when the names of the additional witnesses were not known and could not have been obtained by the exercise of due diligence prior to trial.

(c) The requirements of subsection (a) of this Section shall not apply to rebuttal witnesses.

§ **114-10. Motion to produce confession.** (a) On motion of a defendant in any criminal case made prior to trial the court shall order the State to furnish the defendant with a copy of any written confession made to any law enforcement officer of this State or any other State and a list of the witnesses to its making and acknowledgment. If the defendant has made an oral confession a list of the witnesses to its making shall be furnished.

(b) The list of witnesses may upon notice and motion be amended by the State prior to trial.

(c) No such confession shall be received in evidence which has not been furnished in compliance with subsection (a) of this Section unless the court is satisfied that the prosecutor was unaware of the existence of such confession prior to trial and that he could not have become aware of such in the exercise of due diligence.

§ **114-11. Motion to Suppress Confession.** (a) Prior to the trial of any criminal case a defendant may move to suppress as evidence any confession given by him on the ground that it was not voluntary.

(b) The motion shall be in writing and state facts showing wherein the confession is involuntary.

(c) If the allegations of the motion state facts which, if true, show that the confession was not voluntarily made the court shall conduct a hearing into the merits of the motion.

(d) The burden of going forward with the evidence and the burden of proving that a confession was voluntary shall be on the State. Objection to the failure of the State to call all material witnesses on the issue of whether the confession was voluntary must be made in the trial court.

(e) The motion shall be made only before a court with jurisdiction to try the offense.
(f) The issue of the admissibility of the confession shall not be submitted to the jury. The circumstances surrounding the making of the confession may be submitted to the jury as bearing upon the credibility or the weight to be given to the confession.

(g) The motion shall be made before trial unless opportunity therefore did not exist or the defendant was not aware of the grounds for the motion. If the motion is made during trial, and the court determines that the motion is not untimely, and the court conducts a hearing on the merits and enters an order suppressing the confession, the court shall terminate the trial with respect to every defendant who was a party to the hearing and who was within the scope of the order of suppression, without further proceedings, unless the State files a written notice that there will be no interlocutory appeal from such order of suppression. In the event of such termination, the court shall proceed with the trial of other defendants not thus affected. Such termination of trial shall be proper and shall not bar subsequent prosecution of the identical charges and defendants; however, if after such termination the State fails to prosecute the interlocutory appeal until a determination of the merits of the appeal by the reviewing court, the termination shall be improper within the meaning of subparagraph (a) (3) of Section 3--4 of the "Criminal Code of 1961", approved July 28, 1961, as amended, and subsequent prosecution of such defendants upon such charges shall be barred.

§ **114-12. Motion to Suppress Evidence Illegally Seized.** (a) A defendant aggrieved by an unlawful search and seizure may move the court for the return of property and to suppress as evidence anything so obtained on the ground that:

(1) The search and seizure without a warrant was illegal; or

(2) The search and seizure with a warrant was illegal because the warrant is insufficient on its face; the evidence seized is not that described in the warrant; there was not probable cause for the issuance of the warrant; or, the warrant was illegally executed.

(b) The motion shall be in writing and state facts showing wherein the search and seizure were unlawful. The judge shall receive evidence on any issue of fact necessary to determine the motion and the burden of proving that the search and seizure were unlawful shall be on the defendant. If the motion is granted the property shall be restored, unless otherwise subject to lawful detention, and it shall not be admissible in evidence against the movant at any trial.

(1) If a defendant seeks to suppress evidence because of the conduct of a peace officer in obtaining the evidence, the State may urge that the peace officer's conduct was taken in a reasonable and objective good faith belief that the conduct was proper and that the evidence discovered should not be suppressed if otherwise admissible. The court shall not suppress evidence which is otherwise admissible in a criminal proceeding if the court determines that the evidence was seized by a peace officer who acted in good faith.

(2) "Good faith" means whenever a peace officer obtains evidence:

(i) pursuant to a search or an arrest warrant obtained from a neutral and detached judge, which warrant is free from obvious defects other than non-deliberate errors in preparation and contains no material misrepresentation by any agent of the State, and the officer reasonably believed the warrant to be valid; or

(ii) pursuant to a warrantless search incident to an arrest for violation of a statute or local ordinance which is later declared unconstitutional or otherwise invalidated.

(3) This amendatory Act of 1987 shall not be construed to limit the enforcement of any appropriate civil remedy or criminal sanction in actions pursuant to other provisions of law against any individual or government entity found to have conducted an unreasonable search or seizure.

(4) This amendatory Act of 1987 does not apply to unlawful electronic eavesdropping or wiretapping.

(c) The motion shall be made before trial unless opportunity therefore did not exist or the defendant was not aware of the grounds for the motion. If the motion is made during trial, and the court determines that the motion is not untimely, and the court conducts a hearing on the merits and enters an order suppressing the evidence, the court shall terminate the trial with respect to every defendant who was a party to the hearing and who was within the scope of the order of suppression, without further proceedings, unless the State files a written notice that there will be no interlocutory appeal from such order of suppression. In the event of such termination, the court shall proceed with the trial of other defendants not thus affected. such termination of trial shall be proper and shall not bar subsequent prosecution of the identical charges and defendants; however, if after such termination the State fails to prosecute the interlocutory appeal until a determination of the merits of the appeal by the reviewing court, the termination shall be improper within the meaning of subparagraph (a) (3) of Section 3-4 of the "Criminal Code of 1961", approved July 28,1961, as amended, and subsequent prosecution of such defendants upon such charges shall be barred.

(d) The motion shall be made only before a court with jurisdiction to try the offense.

(e) The order or judgment granting or denying the motion shall state the findings of facts and conclusions of law upon which the order or judgment is based.

§ **114-13. Discovery in criminal cases.**
(a) Discovery procedures in criminal cases

shall be in accordance with Supreme Court Rules.

(b) Any public investigative, law enforcement, or other public agency responsible for investigating any homicide offense or participating in an investigation of any homicide offense, other than defense investigators, shall provide to the authority prosecuting the offense all investigative material, including but not limited to reports, memoranda, and field notes, that have been generated by or have come into the possession of the investigating agency concerning the homicide offense being investigated. In addition, the investigating agency shall provide to the prosecuting authority any material or information, including but not limited to reports, memoranda, and field notes, within its possession or control that would tend to negate the guilt of the accused of the offense charged or reduce his or her punishment for the homicide offense.

Every investigative and law enforcement agency in this State shall adopt policies to ensure compliance with these standards. Any investigative, law enforcement, or other public agency responsible for investigating any "non-homicide felony" offense or participating in an investigation of any "non-homicide felony" offense, other than defense investigators, shall provide to the authority prosecuting the offense all investigative material, including but not limited to reports and memoranda that have been generated by or have come into the possession of the investigating agency concerning the "non-homicide felony" offense being investigated. In addition, the investigating agency shall provide to the prosecuting authority any material or information, including but not limited to reports and memoranda, within its possession or control that would tend to negate the guilt of the accused of the "non-homicide felony" offense charged or reduce his or her punishment for the "non-homicide felony" offense. This obligation to furnish exculpatory evidence exists whether the information was recorded or documented in any form. Every investigative and law enforcement agency in this State shall adopt policies to ensure compliance with these standards.

§ 114-13.5. Evidence deposition; elder abuse. In a prosecution for abuse, neglect, or financial exploitation of an eligible adult as defined in the Elder Abuse and Neglect Act, the eligible adult may give testimony in the form of an evidence deposition and not be required to appear in court to testify.

§ 114-15. Intellectual Disability.
(a) In a first degree murder case in which the State seeks the death penalty as an appropriate sentence, any party may raise the issue of the defendant's intellectual disabilities by motion. A defendant wishing to raise the issue of his or her intellectual disabilities shall provide written notice to testate and the court as soon as the defendant reasonably believes such issue will be raised.

(b) The issue of the defendant's intellectual disabilities shall be determined in a pretrial hearing. The court shall be the fact finder on the issue of the defendant's intellectual disabilities and shall determine the issue by a preponderance of evidence in which the moving party has the burden of proof. The court may appoint an expert in the field of intellectual disabilities. The defendant and the State may offer experts from the field of intellectual disabilities. The court shall determine admissibility of evidence and qualification as an expert.

(c) If after a plea of guilty to first degree murder, or a finding of guilty of first degree murder in a bench trial, or a verdict of guilty for first degree murder in a jury trial, or on a matter remanded from the Supreme Court for sentencing for first degree murder, and the State seeks the death penalty as an appropriate sentence, the defendant may raise the issue of defendant's intellectual disabilities not at eligibility but at aggravation and mitigation. The defendant and the State may offer experts from the field of intellectual disabilities. The court shall determine admissibility of evidence and qualification as an expert.

(d) In determining whether the defendant is a person with an intellectual disability, the intellectual disability must have manifested itself by the age of 18. IQ tests and psychometric tests administered to the defendant must be the kind and type recognized by experts in the field of intellectual disabilities. In order for the defendant to be considered a person with an intellectual disability, a low IQ must be accompanied by significant deficits in adaptive behavior in at least 2 of the following skill areas: communication, self-care, social or interpersonal skills, home living, self-direction, academics, health and safety, use of community resources, and work. An intelligence quotient (IQ) of 75 or below is presumptive evidence of intellectual disabilities.

(e) Evidence of intellectual disabilities that did not result in disqualifying the case as a capital case, may be introduced as evidence in mitigation during a capital sentencing hearing. A failure of the court to determine that the defendant is a person with an intellectual disability does not preclude the court during trial from allowing evidence relating to mental disability should the court deem it appropriate.

(f) If the court determines at a pretrial hearing or after remand that a capital defendant is a person with an intellectual disability, and the State does not appeal pursuant to Supreme Court Rule 604, the case shall no longer be considered a capital case and the procedural guidelines established for capital cases shall no longer be applicable to the defendant. In that case, the defendant shall be sentenced under the sentencing provisions of Chapter V of the Unified Code of Corrections.

Commentary – Pre-trial motions

Motions to suppress. The method for bring a defendant's claims that his constitutional rights regarding improper searches and seizure and improper police interrogation were violated is to file motions to suppress evidence (and sometimes motions to quash arrests or search warrants). Such matters are set for hearing. The defendant has the burden of showing by *prima facie* evidence that there was a constitutional violation (e.g. a warrantless seizure), and once met, the prosecution must rebut the evidence to show the search and seizure was proper. However, the ultimate burden on a motion to suppress evidence from an unlawful search remains with the defendant. See *People v. Gipson* 203 Ill.2d 298, 786 N.E. 2d 540 (Ill. S. Ct. 2003)(defendant's prima facie showing of a warrantless search of his trunk was rebutted by proof of the routine practice of inventory searches of towed vehicles, with defendant not proving any constitutional violation thereafter).

Burden to prove good faith exception to exclusionary rule. In *United States v. Leon* 468 U.S. 897, 104 S.Ct. 3405 (U.S. S. Ct. 1984), the Court recognized a good-faith exception to the exclusionary rule where officers relied on a defective warrant. Illinois law codified the good-faith exception in 725 ILCS 5/114-12(b). If a defendant establishes a violation of his rights based on an unlawful search and seizure, the burden is on the prosecution to prove that the good faith exception applies. In *People v. Morgan* 388 Ill.App.3d 252, 901 N.E.2d 1049 (Ill. App. Ct. 4th Dist. 2009), police officers made a warrantless entry into the defendant's home based on an invalid arrest warrant. The warrant was several days old and had been recalled. The officers were met at the door by the defendant's father who told them that the arrest warrant they had was invalid, because he had posted bail for the defendant that same morning. The defendant's father refused to consent to the officers entering the home, so officers shoved open the door, knocking the father to the floor and entered the home, seizing the defendant and placing him in handcuffs. When officers were shown the bail documents, they took the handcuffs off, although later, they again handcuffed the defendant and took him away from his home. After confirming that the warrant was invalid, the defendant was again returned to his home. The defendant's father refused to consent to a search of the home, but the officers searched anyway and seized drugs and drug paraphernalia found in an upstairs bedroom. The appellate court held that the staleness of the warrant and the officers' failure to check on the validity of the warrant meant the good-faith exception had not been established and that the purpose of the exclusionary rule to deter police officer gross negligence was achieved by suppression in the case.

Motions to suppress confessions. If a motion to suppress addresses admissions or confessions, the prosecution has the burden of going forward with the evidence and establishing voluntariness of any defendant statements by a preponderance of the evidence, but the burden of proving *Miranda* violations is on the defendant. The motion hearings routinely require in court testimony from police officers who participated in the investigative activity being attacked. Defendants will often testify at these hearings and the judge who is presiding has to make credibility determinations in disputed fact situations about who to believe and what weight to give to testimony.

Motions to dismiss. Often a pre-trial motion to dismiss will be filed by a defendant, claiming that the charge filed against him does not properly state a crime or that there has been some type of procedural irregularity or violation of a required time limit. Normally, there is no factual dispute about the matters raised and the court will hear arguments from the prosecution and defense at a motion hearing and rule on the legal issues presented. There can be motions to dismiss that have factual disputes such as claim violation of due process for the failure to keep a promised plea agreement. In *People v. Nunn* 2014 IL App (3d) 120614 the Appellate Court held the trial court erred in failing to grant a motion to dismiss charges of Aggravated Battery at the close of the prosecution's case where it was shown that eye witnesses to an altercation between a police officer and the Defendant were threatened with arrest and jail if they did not stop recording the incident on their cell phones or deleting recordings that had been made.

Discharge based on speedy trial violation. In the speedy trial case, there are exceptions to times, required to bring the case for trial based on delays caused by the defendant, such as pre-trial motions, or delays that have occurred on the prosecution side because of forensic laboratory testing that has caused delays. The prosecution will usually be careful to document delays, making a record so that precise calculations of elapsed time toward the speedy trial deadlines can be readily made and understood by the court. A motion for discharge under 725 ILCS 5/103-5 asks the court to release the defendant from custody and/or dismiss the case on the non-custodial defendant who have made speedy trial demands, because the 120 day and 160 day time limits, respectively have passed and the defendant's trial has not commenced.

Motion to change place of trial. This is commonly called a motion for change of venue. The defendant's right to a fair trial by jurors of his peers would be violated if as a result of pre-trial publicity or community knowledge there was a preconceived notion about his guilt. A motion to change venue typically includes media (print and broadcast) information about the pre-trial publicity and in infamous cases, sometimes evidence based on public opinion polling is brought forward, all to show the judge that the defendant cannot receive a fair trial. The recent view is that the best way to measure community prejudice is to conduct jury selection (known as "*voir dire*") to determine whether the defendant can receive a fair trial.

In *People v. Pelo* 404 Ill.App.3d 839, 942 N.E.2d 463 (Ill. App. Ct 4th Dist. 2010), the defendant, a former police officer, was charged and convicted as a serial rapist with five female victims in his home community, over a 3 ½ year period. The publicity surrounding his arrest, leading up to the time of his trial was extensive, but the trial court denied the defendant's motion to change venue brought claiming potential juror prejudice. During voir dire examination, two jurors indicated they had formed opinions that the defendant was guilty, recognized that they had to set aside those opinions and be open-minded if selected as jurors and thought they would be able to do so with some difficulty. The defendant renewed his motion to change venue, but it was denied. Following his conviction and appeal, the appellate court affirmed the trial court's denial of the motion to change venue, holding that the trial judge was in the best position to determine whether jurors can be fair and impartial to the defendant, stating:

> In this case, although a number of the jurors eventually empaneled had heard about the case, only two jurors, Larson and Willenborg, claimed to have formed an opinion about the case. During *voir dire,* the trial court inquired about these jurors' ability to set aside their respective opinions and render a verdict based upon the evidence at trial. The court first addressed Larson, as follows:
>
> "THE COURT: Okay, [a]ll right. Based on the information that you have heard in the past through the news media and so forth, have you formed any opinions about this case or about [d]efendant's guilt as you sit here today?
>
> MR. LARSON: Well, it's, the way they gloss up a case, it's hard to say that he's innocent.
>
> THE COURT: Okay. So you have heard things and * * * you may have formed some opinions based upon what you have previously heard?
>
> MR. LARSON: Correct.
>
> THE COURT: Okay. All right. If you were to be selected as a juror in this case, the [c]ourt would instruct you that you are to decide the case only on the basis of the evidence that you hear in the courtroom and the instructions of law that are presented to the jury at the end of the case; that is, you are to disregard anything that you may have heard or read about the case outside of the evidence presented here in the courtroom. If you were selected as a juror in this case, do you believe that you could disregard what you may have heard or read about the case and decide the case only on the evidence presented in court and the law that you will be given by the [c]ourt? Do you believe that you could do that?
>
> MR. LARSON: It would be difficult but I think I can.
>
> THE COURT: All right. Now, when you say it would be difficult but you think you can do that, [is the court] to understand that what you are saying is you have some opinions, but you believe you could set those aside, listen to * * * all the evidence, and then decide the case based on the evidence that you hear? You believe you could do that?
>
> MR. LARSON: That's correct."
>
> The court then turned its attention to Willenborg, as follows:
>
> "THE COURT: Okay. As you sit hear today, do you have an opinion as to whether * * * [d]efendant is guilty in this case?
>
> MS. WILLENBORG: Yes.
>
> THE COURT: If you were selected to serve as a juror in this case, do you believe that you could disregard what you may have heard or read or talked about with others and set aside that opinion and decide this case only on the evidence which will be presented in open court and the law that the [c]ourt will give you? Do you think you could do that?
>
> MS. WILLENBORG: Yes.
>
> THE COURT: In other words, do you think you could be fair and impartial to both sides without regard to the opinion you may have formed:

MS. WILLENBORG: Yes."

As this exchange demonstrates, each of the panelists in this case convinced the trial court that he or she could be fair and impartial—that is, each agreed that he or she could determine whether defendant was guilty based only upon the evidence presented at trial. Accordingly, we conclude that the court did not err by denying defendant's motion for a change of venue. In so concluding, we note that the court's analysis of this issue was entirely correct, particularly its observation that the actual *voir dire* examination of potential jurors is the best method for determining whether pretrial publicity has resulted in prejudice against a defendant so as to warrant granting his motion for a change of venue.

People v. Pelo 404 Ill.App.3d at 873-874, 942 N.E.2d at 491-492 (court's edited brackets)

Title VI. Proceedings At Trial
Article 115 – Trial
725 ILCS 5/115 *et seq.*

§ **115-1. Method of Trial.** All prosecutions except on a plea of guilty or guilty but mentally ill shall be tried by the court and a jury unless the defendant waives a jury trial in writing.

§ 115-1.5. Waiver of counsel by persons under 17 years of age prohibited. A person under 17 years of age may not waive the right to the assistance of counsel in his or her defense in any judicial proceeding. This Section does not apply to a minor charged with an offense for which the penalty is a fine only. Except for violations of Sections 11-401, 11-402, 11-501, and 11-503 of the Illinois Vehicle Code, this Section does not apply to proceedings involving violations of the Illinois Vehicle Code.

§ **115-2. Pleas of Guilty and guilty but mentally ill.** (a) Before or during trial a plea of guilty may be accepted when:

(1) The defendant enters a plea of guilty in open court;

(2) The court has informed the defendant of the consequences of his plea and of the maximum penalty provided by law which may be imposed upon acceptance of such plea. Upon acceptance of a plea of guilty the court shall determine the factual basis for the plea.

(b) Before or during trial a plea of guilty but mentally ill may be accepted by the court when:

(1) the defendant has undergone an examination by a clinical psychologist or psychiatrist and has waived his right to trial; and

(2) the judge has examined the psychiatric or psychological report or reports; and

(3) the judge has held a hearing, at which either party may present evidence, on the issue of the defendant's mental health and, at the conclusion of such hearing, is satisfied that there is a factual basis that the defendant was mentally ill at the time of the offense to which the plea is entered.

§ **115-3. Trial by the Court.** (a) A trial shall be conducted in the presence of the defendant unless he waives the right to be present.

(b) Upon conclusion of the trial the court shall enter a general finding, except that, when the affirmative defense of insanity has been presented during the trial and acquittal is based solely upon the defense of insanity, the court shall enter a finding of not guilty by reason of insanity. In the event of a finding of not guilty by reason of insanity, a hearing shall be held pursuant to the Mental Health and Developmental Disabilities Code to determine whether the defendant is subject to involuntary admission.

(c) When the defendant has asserted a defense of insanity, the court may find the defendant guilty but mentally ill if, after hearing all of the evidence, the court finds that:

(1) the State has proven beyond a reasonable doubt that the defendant is guilty of the offense charged; and

(2) the defendant has failed to prove his insanity as required in subsection (b) of Section 3-2 of the Criminal Code of 1961, as amended, and subsections (a), (b) and (e) of Section 6-2 of the Criminal Code of 1961, as amended; and

(3) the defendant has proven by a preponderance of the evidence that he was mentally ill, as defined in subsections (c) and (d) of Section 6-2 of the Criminal Code of 1961, as amended, at the time of the offense.

§ 115-4. Trial by Court and Jury.
(a) Questions of law shall be decided by the court and questions of fact by the jury.

(b) The jury shall consist of 12 members.

(c) Upon request the parties shall be furnished with a list of prospective jurors with their addresses if known.

(d) Each party may challenge jurors for cause. If a prospective juror has a physical impairment, the court shall consider such prospective juror's ability to perceive and appreciate the evidence when considering a challenge for cause.

(e) A defendant tried alone shall be allowed 20 peremptory challenges in a capital case, 10 in a case in which the punishment may be imprisonment in the penitentiary, and 5 in all other cases; except that, in a single trial of more than one defendant, each defendant shall be allowed 12 peremptory challenges in a capital case, 6 in a case in which the punishment may be imprisonment in the penitentiary, and 3 in all other cases. If several charges against a defendant or defendants are consolidated for trial, each defendant shall be allowed peremptory challenges upon one charge only, which single charge shall be the charge against that defendant authorizing the greatest maximum penalty. The State shall be allowed the same number of peremptory challenges as all of the defendants.

(f) After examination by the court the jurors may be examined, passed upon, accepted and tendered by opposing counsel as provided by Supreme Court rules.

(g) After the jury is impaneled and sworn the court may direct the selection of 2 alternate jurors who shall take the same oath as the regular jurors. Each party shall have one additional peremptory challenge for each alternate juror. If before the final submission of a cause a member of the jury dies or is discharged he shall be replaced by an alternate juror in the order of selection.
(h) A trial by the court and jury shall be conducted in the presence of the defendant unless he waives the right to be present.

(i) After arguments of counsel the court shall instruct the jury as to the law.

(j) Unless the affirmative defense of insanity has been presented during the trial, the jury shall return a general verdict as to each offense charged. When the affirmative defense of insanity has been presented during the trial, the court shall provide the jury not only with general verdict forms but also with a special verdict form of not guilty by reason of insanity, as to each offense charged, and in such event the court shall separately instruct the jury that a special verdict of not guilty by reason of insanity may be returned instead of a general verdict but such special verdict requires a unanimous finding by the jury that the defendant committed the acts charged but at the time of the commission of those acts the defendant was insane. in the event of a verdict of not guilty by reason of insanity, a hearing shall be held pursuant to the Mental Health and Developmental Disabilities Code to determine whether the defendant is subject to involuntary admission. When the affirmative defense of insanity has been presented during the trial, the court, where warranted by the evidence, shall also provide the jury with a special verdict form of guilty but mentally ill, as to each offense charged and shall separately instruct the jury that a special verdict of guilty but mentally ill may be returned instead of a general verdict, but that such special verdict requires a unanimous finding by the jury that:

(1) the State has proven beyond a reasonable doubt that the defendant is guilty of the offense charged; and

(2) the defendant has failed to prove his insanity as required in subsection (b) of Section 3-2 of the Criminal Code of 1961, as amended, and subsections (a), (b) and (e) of Section 6-2 of the Criminal Code of 1961, as amended; and

(3) the defendant has proven by a preponderance of the evidence that he was mentally ill, as defined in subsections (c) and (d) of Section 6-2 of the Criminal Code of 1961, as amended, at the time of the offense.

(k) When, at the close of the State's evidence or at the close of all of the evidence, the evidence is insufficient to support a finding or verdict of guilty the court may and on motion of the defendant shall make a finding or direct the jury to return a verdict of not guilty, enter a judgment of acquittal and discharge the defendant.

(l) When the jury retires to consider its verdict an officer of the court shall be appointed to keep them together and to prevent conversation between the jurors and others; however, if any juror is deaf, the jury may be accompanied by and may communicate with a court-appointed interpreter during its deliberations. Upon agreement between the State and defendant or his counsel the jury may seal and deliver its verdict to the clerk of the court, separate, and then return such verdict in open court at its next session.

(m) In the trial of a capital or other offense, any juror who is a member of a panel or jury which has been impaneled and sworn as a panel or as a jury shall be permitted to separate from other such jurors during every period of adjournment to a later day, until final submission of the cause to the jury for determination, except that no such separation shall be permitted in any trial after the court, upon motion by the defendant or the State or upon its own motion, finds a probability that prejudice to the defendant or to the State will result from such separation.

(n) The members of the jury shall be entitled to take notes during the trial, and the sheriff of the county in which the jury is sitting shall provide them with writing materials for this purpose. Such notes shall remain confidential, and shall be destroyed by the sheriff after the verdict has been returned or a mistrial declared.

(o) A defendant tried by the court and jury shall only be found guilty, guilty but mentally ill, not guilty or not guilty by reason of insanity, upon the unanimous verdict of the jury.

§ 115-4.1. Absence of defendant.

(a) When a defendant after arrest and an initial court appearance for a non-capital felony or a misdemeanor, fails to appear for trial, at the request of the State and after the State has affirmatively proven through substantial evidence that the defendant is willfully avoiding trial, the court may commence trial in the absence of the defendant. Absence of a defendant as specified in this Section shall not be a bar to indictment of a defendant, return of information against a defendant, or arraignment of a defendant for the charge for which bail has been granted. If a defendant fails to appear at arraignment, the court may enter a plea of "not guilty" on his behalf. If a defendant absents himself before trial on a capital felony, trial may proceed as specified in this Section provided that the State certifies that it will not seek a death sentence following conviction. Trial in the defendant's absence shall be by jury unless the defendant had previously waived trial by jury. the absent defendant must be represented by retained or appointed counsel. The court, at the conclusion of all of the proceedings, may order the clerk of the circuit court to pay counsel such sum as the court deems reasonable, from any bond monies which were posted by the defendant with the clerk, after the clerk has first deducted all court costs. If trial had previously commenced in the presence of the defendant and the defendant willfully absents himself for two successive court days, the court shall proceed to trial.

All procedural rights guaranteed by the United States Constitution, Constitution of the State of Illinois, statutes of the State of Illinois, and rules of court shall apply to the proceedings the same as if the defendant were present in court and had not either forfeited his bail bond or escaped from custody. The court may set the case for a trial which may be conducted under this Section despite the failure of the defendant to appear at the hearing at which the trial date is set. When such trial date is set the clerk shall send to the defendant, by certified mail at his last known address indicated on his bond slip, notice of the new date which has been set for trial. Such notification shall be required when the defendant was not personally present in open court at the time when the case was set for trial.
(b) The absence of a defendant from a trial conducted pursuant to this Section does not operate as a bar to concluding the trial, to a judgment of conviction resulting there from, or to a final disposition of the trial in favor of the defendant.

(c) Upon a verdict of not guilty, the court shall enter judgment for the defendant. Upon a verdict of guilty, the court shall set a date for the hearing of post-trial motions and shall hear such motion in the absence of the defendant. If post-trial motions are denied, the court shall proceed to conduct a sentencing hearing and to impose a sentence upon the defendant.

(d) A defendant who is absent for part of the proceedings of trial, post-trial motions, or sentencing, does not thereby forfeit his right to be present at all remaining proceedings.

(e) When a defendant who in his absence has been either convicted or sentenced or both convicted and sentenced appears before the court, he must be granted a new trial or new sentencing hearing if the defendant can establish that his failure to appear in court was both without his fault and due to circumstances beyond his control. A hearing with notice to the State's Attorney on the defendant's request for a new trial or a new sentencing hearing must be held before any such request may be granted. At any such hearing both the defendant and the State may present evidence.

(f) If the court grants only the defendant's request for a new sentencing hearing, then a new sentencing hearing shall be held in accordance with the provisions of the Unified Code of Corrections. At any such hearing, both the defendant and the State may offer evidence of the defendant's conduct during his period of absence from the court. The court may impose any sentence authorized by the Unified Code of Corrections and is not in any way limited or restricted by any sentence previously imposed.

(g) A defendant whose motion under paragraph (e) for a new trial or new sentencing hearing has been denied may file a notice of appeal therefrom. Such notice may also include a request for review of the judgment and sentence not vacated by the trial court.

§ 115-5. Business records as evidence.
(a) Any writing or record, whether in the form of an entry in a book or otherwise, made as a memorandum or record of any act, transaction, occurrence, or event, shall be admissible as evidence of such act, transaction, occurrence, or event, if made in regular course of any business, and if it was the regular course of such business to make such memorandum or record at the time of such act, transaction, occurrence, or event or within a reasonable time thereafter. all other circumstances of the making of such writing or record, including lack of personal knowledge by the entrant or maker, may be shown to affect its weight, but such circumstances shall not affect its admissibility. the term "business," as used in this Section, includes business, profession, occupation, and calling of every kind.
(b) If any business, institution, member of a profession or calling, or any department or agency of government, in the regular course of business or activity has kept or recorded any memorandum, writing, entry, print, representation or combination thereof, of any act, transaction, occurrence, or event, and in the regular course of business has caused any or all of the same to be recorded, copied, or reproduced by any photographic, photostatic, microfilm, micro-card, miniature photographic, optical imaging, or other process which accurately reproduces or forms a medium for so reproducing the original, the original may be

destroyed in the regular course of business unless its preservation is required by law. Such reproduction, when satisfactorily identified, is as admissible in evidence as the original itself in any proceeding whether the original is in existence or not and an enlargement or facsimile of such reproduction is likewise admissible in evidence if the original reproduction is in existence and available for inspection under direction of court. The introduction of a reproduced record, enlargement, or facsimile does not preclude admission of the original.
This Section shall not be construed to exclude from evidence any document or copy thereof which is otherwise admissible under the rules of evidence.

(c) No writing or record made in the regular course of any business shall become admissible as evidence by the application of this Section if:

(1) Such writing or record has been made by anyone in the regular course of any form of hospital or medical business; or

(2) Such writing or record has been made by anyone during an investigation of an alleged offense or during any investigation relating to pending or anticipated litigation of any kind, except during a hearing to revoke a sentence of probation or conditional discharge or an order of court supervision that is based on a technical violation of a sentencing order when the hearing involves a probationer or defendant who has transferred or moved from the county having jurisdiction over the original charge or sentence. For the purposes of this subsection (c), "technical violation" means a breach of a sentencing order but does not include an allegation of a subsequent criminal act asserted in a formal criminal charge.

(d) Upon request of the moving party and with reasonable notice given to the opposing party, in a criminal prosecution in which the defendant is accused of an offense under Article 16 or 17 of the Criminal Code of 1961 or the Criminal Code of 2012, the court may, after a hearing, for good cause and upon appropriate safeguards, permit live foundational testimony business records as evidence, subject to cross-examination, in open court by means of a contemporaneous audio and video transmission from outside this State.

§ **115-5.1.** In any civil or criminal action the records of the coroner's medical or laboratory examiner summarizing and detailing the performance of his or her official duties in performing medical examinations upon deceased persons or autopsies, or both, and kept in the ordinary course of business of the coroner's office, duly certified by the county coroner or chief supervisory coroner's pathologist or medical examiner, shall be received as competent evidence in any court of this State, to the extent permitted by this Section. These reports, specifically including but not limited to the pathologist's protocol, autopsy reports and toxicological reports, shall be public documents and thereby may be admissible as prima facie evidence of the facts, findings, opinions, diagnoses and conditions stated therein. A duly certified coroner's protocol or autopsy report, or both, complying with the requirements of this Section may be duly admitted into evidence as an exception to the hearsay rule as prima facie proof of the cause of death of the person to whom it relates. The records referred to in this Section shall be limited to the records of the results of post-mortem examinations of the findings of autopsy and toxicological laboratory examinations. persons who prepare reports or records offered in evidence hereunder may be subpoenaed as witnesses in civil or criminal cases upon the request of either party to the cause. However, if such person is dead, the county coroner or a duly authorized official of the coroner's office may testify to the fact that the examining pathologist, toxicologist or other medical or laboratory examiner is deceased and that the offered report or record was prepared by such deceased person. The witness must further attest that the medical report or record was prepared in the ordinary and usual course of the deceased person's duty or employment in conformity with the provisions of this Section.

§ **115-6. Appointment of Psychiatrist or Clinical Psychologist.** If the defendant has given notice that he may rely upon the defense of insanity as defined in Section 6-2 of the

Criminal Code of 1961 or the defendant indicates that he intends to plead guilty but mentally ill or the defense of intoxicated or drugged condition as defined in Section 6-3 of the Criminal Code of 1961 or if the facts and circumstances of the case justify a reasonable belief that the aforesaid defenses may be raised, the Court shall, on motion of the State, order the defendant to submit to examination by at least one clinical psychologist or psychiatrist, to be named by the prosecuting attorney.
The Court shall also order the defendant to submit to an examination by one neurologist, one clinical psychologist and one electroencephalographer to be named by the prosecuting attorney if the State asks for one or more of such additional examinations. The Court may order additional examinations if the Court finds that additional examinations by additional experts will be of substantial value in the determination of issues of insanity or drugged conditions. The reports of such experts shall be made available to the defense. Any statements made by defendant to such experts shall not be admissible against the defendant unless he raises the defense of insanity or the defense of drugged condition, in which case they shall be admissible only on the issue of whether he was insane or drugged. The refusal of the defendant to cooperate in such examinations shall not automatically preclude the raising of the aforesaid defenses but shall preclude the defendant from offering expert evidence or testimony tending to support such defenses if the expert evidence or testimony is based upon the expert's examination of the defendant.
If the Court, after a hearing, determines to its satisfaction that the defendant's refusal to cooperate was unreasonable it may, in its sound discretion, bar any or all evidence upon the defense asserted.

§115-6.1. Prostitution; affirmative defense. (a) In prosecutions for prostitution, when the accused intends to raise at trial the affirmative defense provided in subsection (c-5) of Section 11-14 of the Criminal Code of 2012 and has reason to believe that the evidence presented in asserting that defense may jeopardize the safety of the accused, courtroom personnel, or others impacted by human trafficking, the accused may file under seal a motion for an in camera hearing to review the accused's safety concerns. Upon receipt of the motion and notice to the parties, the court shall conduct an in camera hearing, with counsel present, limited to review of potential safety concerns. The court shall cause an official record of the in camera hearing to be made, which shall be kept under seal. The court shall not consider the merits of the affirmative defense during the in camera review.

(b) If the court finds by a preponderance of the evidence that the assertion of an affirmative defense under subsection (c-5) of Section 11-14 of the Criminal Code of 2012 by the accused in open court would likely jeopardize the safety of the accused, court personnel, or other persons, the court may clear the courtroom with the agreement of the accused, order additional in camera hearings, seal the records, prohibit court personnel from disclosing the proceedings without prior court approval, or take any other appropriate measure that in the court's discretion will enhance the safety of the proceedings and ensure the accused a full and fair opportunity to assert his or her affirmative defense.

(c) Statements made by the accused during the in camera hearing to review safety concerns shall not be admissible against the accused for the crimes charged.

§ 115-7. Prior sexual activity or reputation of victim of sexual offense. (a) In prosecutions for predatory criminal sexual assault of a child, aggravated criminal sexual assault, criminal sexual assault, aggravated criminal sexual abuse, criminal sexual abuse, or criminal transmission of HIV; and in prosecutions for battery and aggravated battery, when the commission of the offense involves sexual penetration or sexual conduct as defined in Section 11-0.1 of the Criminal Code of 1961; and with the trial or retrial of the offenses formerly known as rape, deviate sexual assault, indecent liberties with a child, and aggravated indecent liberties with a child, the prior sexual activity or the reputation of the alleged victim or corroborating witness under Section 115-7.3 of this Code is inadmissible except

(1) as evidence concerning the past sexual conduct of the alleged victim or corroborating witness under Section 115-7.3 of this Code with the accused when this evidence is offered by the accused upon the issue of whether the alleged victim or corroborating witness under Section 115-7.3 of this Code consented to the sexual conduct with respect to which the offense is alleged; or

(2) when constitutionally required to be admitted.

(b) No evidence admissible under this Section shall be introduced unless ruled admissible by the trial judge after an offer of proof has been made at a hearing to be held in camera in order to determine whether the defense has evidence to impeach the witness in the event that prior sexual activity with the defendant is denied. Such offer of proof shall include reasonably specific information as to the date, time and place of the past sexual conduct between the alleged victim or corroborating witness under Section 115-7.3 of this Code and the defendant. Unless the court finds that reasonably specific information as to date, time or place, or some combination thereof, has been offered as to prior sexual activity with the defendant, counsel for the defendant shall be ordered to refrain from inquiring into prior sexual activity between the alleged victim or corroborating witness under Section 115-7.3 of this Code and the defendant. the court shall not admit evidence under this Section unless it determines at the hearing that the evidence is relevant and the probative value of the evidence outweighs the danger of unfair prejudice. The evidence shall be admissible at trial to the extent an order made by the court specifies the evidence that may be admitted and areas with respect to which the alleged victim or corroborating witness under Section 115-7.3 of this Code may be examined or cross examined.

§ 115-7.1. Court may not order mental examination of sex victim. Except where explicitly authorized by this Code or by the Rules of the Supreme Court of Illinois, no court may require or order a witness who is the victim of an alleged sex offense to submit to or undergo either a psychiatric or psychological examination.

§ 115-7.2. [Expert testimony as evidence in trial for sexual offense In a prosecution for an illegal sexual act perpetrated upon a victim, including but not limited to prosecutions for violations of Sections 11-1.20 through 11-1.60 or 12-13 through 12-16 of the Criminal Code of 1961, or ritualized abuse of a child under Section 12-33 of the Criminal Code of 1961, testimony by an expert, qualified by the court relating to any recognized and accepted form of post-traumatic stress syndrome shall be admissible as evidence.

§ 115-7.3. Evidence in certain cases. (a) This Section applies to criminal cases in which:

(1) the defendant is accused of predatory criminal sexual assault of a child, aggravated criminal sexual assault, criminal sexual assault, aggravated criminal sexual abuse, criminal sexual abuse, child pornography, aggravated child pornography, or criminal transmission of HIV;

(2) the defendant is accused of battery, aggravated battery, first degree murder, or second degree murder when the commission of the offense involves sexual penetration or sexual conduct as defined in Section 12-12 of the Criminal Code of 1961; or

(3) the defendant is tried or retried for any of the offenses formerly known as rape, deviate sexual assault, indecent liberties with a child, or aggravated indecent liberties with a child.

(b) If the defendant is accused of an offense set forth in paragraph (1) or (2) of subsection (a) or the defendant is tried or retried for any of the offenses set forth in paragraph (3) of subsection (a), evidence of the defendant's commission of another offense or offenses set forth in paragraph (1), (2), or (3) of subsection (a), or evidence to rebut that proof or an inference from that proof, may be admissible (if that evidence is otherwise admissible under the rules of evidence) and may be considered for its bearing on any matter to which it is relevant.

(c) In weighing the probative value of the evidence against undue prejudice to the defendant, the court may consider:

(1) the proximity in time to the charged or predicate offense;

(2) the degree of factual similarity to the charged or predicate offense; or

(3) other relevant facts and circumstances.

(d) In a criminal case in which the prosecution intends to offer evidence under this Section, it must disclose the evidence, including statements of witnesses or a summary of the substance of any testimony, at a reasonable time in advance of trial, or during trial if the court excuses pretrial notice on good cause shown.

(e) In a criminal case in which evidence is offered under this Section, proof may be made by specific instances of conduct, testimony as to reputation, or testimony in the form of an expert opinion, except that the prosecution may offer reputation testimony only after the opposing party has offered that testimony.

(f) In prosecutions for a violation of Section 10-2, 12-3.05, 12-4, 12-13, 12-14, 12-14.1, 12-15, 12-16, or 18-5 of the Criminal Code of 1961,involving the involuntary delivery of a controlled substance to a victim, no inference may be made about the fact that a victim did not consent to a test for the presence of controlled substances.

§ 115-7.4. Evidence in domestic violence cases. (a) In a criminal prosecution in which the defendant is accused of an offense of domestic violence as defined in paragraphs (1) and (3) of Section 103 of the Illinois Domestic Violence Act of 1986, evidence of the defendant's commission of another offense or offenses of domestic violence is admissible, and may be considered for its bearing on any matter to which it is relevant.

(b) In weighing the probative value of the evidence against undue prejudice to the defendant, the court may consider:

(1) the proximity in time to the charged or predicate offense;

(2) the degree of factual similarity to the charged or predicate offense; or

(3) other relevant facts and circumstances.

(c) In a criminal case in which the prosecution intends to offer evidence under this Section, it must disclose the evidence, including statements of witnesses or a summary of the substance of any testimony, at a reasonable time in advance of trial, or during trial if the court excuses pretrial notice on good cause shown.

(d) In a criminal case in which evidence is offered under this Section, proof may be made by specific instances of conduct, testimony as to reputation, or testimony in the form of an expert opinion, except that the prosecution may offer reputation testimony only after the opposing party has offered that testimony.

§ 115-8. A defendant may waive his right to be present during trial. However, upon motion of the State's Attorney made prior to or during trial, the court shall order the defendant to present himself in open court for the purpose of identification.

§ 115-9. [Photographs as evidence in trials for theft or related offense]. (a) In a prosecution for theft, retail theft, deceptive practice, robbery, armed robbery, burglary or residential burglary, the court shall receive as competent evidence, a photograph of property over which the accused is alleged to have exerted unauthorized control or to have otherwise obtained unlawfully, if the photograph:

(1) will serve the purpose of demonstrating the nature of the property; and

(2) is otherwise admissible into evidence under all other rules of law governing the admissibility of photographs into evidence.

The fact that it is impractical to introduce into evidence the actual property for any reason, including its size, weight, or unavailability, need not be established for the court to find a photograph of that property to be competent evidence. If a photograph is found to be competent evidence under this subsection, it is admissible into evidence in place of the property and to the same extent as the property itself.

(b) A law enforcement agency that is holding as evidence property over which a person is alleged to have exerted unauthorized control or to have otherwise obtained unlawfully, shall return that property to its owner if:

(1) the property has been photographed in a manner that will serve the purpose of demonstrating the nature of the property, and if these photographs are filed with or retained by the law enforcement agency in place of the property;

(2) receipt for the property is obtained from the owner upon delivery by the law enforcement agency;

(3) the prosecuting attorney who is prosecuting a case that involves the property furnishes the law enforcement agency with a written request for return of the property to its owner; and

(4) the property may be lawfully possessed by the owner.

(c) Notwithstanding the provisions of subsection (b) of this Section a court may, if a motion so requesting is filed by defendant before expiration of the time period specified in subsection (d) of this Section, order the law enforcement agency to hold such property as evidence pending completion of trial.

(d) The time period during which the defendant may file a motion with the court for retention of the property as evidence shall be as follows:

(1) if the property was being displayed, held, stored or offered for sale to the public by a person or entity holding a Retailers Occupation Tax Number issued by the State of Illinois, the time period shall expire 14days after the arrest of the defendant;

(2) for all other property, the time period shall expire 30 days after the filing of an information or indictment, or in the case of misdemeanor charges within 30 days after the filing of a complaint.

§ **115-10. Certain hearsay exceptions.** a) In a prosecution for a physical or sexual act perpetrated upon or against a child under the age of 13, or a person with a moderate, severe or profound intellectual disability as defined in this Code and in Section 2-10.1 of the Criminal Code of 1961 at the time the act was committed, including but not limited to prosecutions for violations of Sections 11-1.20 through 11-1.60 or 12-13 through 12-16 of the Criminal Code of 1961 and prosecutions for violations of Sections 10-1 (kidnapping), 10-2 (aggravated kidnapping), 10-3 (unlawful restraint), 10-3.1 (aggravated unlawful restraint), 10-4 (forcible detention), 10-5 (child abduction), 10-6 (harboring a runaway), 10-7 (aiding or abetting child abduction), 11-9 (public indecency), 11-11 (sexual relations within families), 11-21 (harmful material), 12-1 (assault), 12-2 (aggravated assault), 12-3 (battery), 12-3.2 (domestic battery), 12-4 (aggravated battery), 12-4.1 (heinous battery), 12-4.2 (aggravated battery with a firearm), 12-4.3 (aggravated battery of a child), 12-4.7 (drug induced infliction of great bodily harm), 12-5 (reckless conduct), 12-6 (intimidation), 12-6.1 (compelling organization membership of persons), 12-7.1 (hate crime), 12-7.3 (stalking), 12-7.4 (aggravated stalking), 12-10 (tattooing body of minor), 12-11 (home invasion), 12-21.5 (child abandonment), 12-21.6 (endangering the life or health of a child) or 12-32 (ritual mutilation) of the Criminal Code of 1961 or any sex offense as defined in subsection (B) of Section 2 of the Sex Offender Registration Act, the following evidence shall be admitted as an exception to the hearsay rule:
(1) testimony by the victim of an out of court statement made by the victim that he or she complained of such act to another; and

(2) testimony of an out of court statement made by the victim describing any complaint of such act or matter or detail pertaining to any act which is an element of an offense which is the

subject of a prosecution for a sexual or physical act against that victim.

(b) Such testimony shall only be admitted if:

(1) The court finds in a hearing conducted outside the presence of the jury that the time, content, and circumstances of the statement provide sufficient safeguards of reliability; and

(2) The child or person with a moderate, severe, or profound intellectual disability either:

(A) testifies at the proceeding; or

(B) is unavailable as a witness and there is corroborative evidence of the act which is the subject of the statement; and

(3) In a case involving an offense perpetrated against a child under the age of 13, the out of court statement was made before the victim attained 13 years of age or within 3 months after the commission of the offense, whichever occurs later, but the statement may be admitted regardless of the age of the victim at the time of the proceeding.

(c) If a statement is admitted pursuant to this Section, the court shall instruct the jury that it is for the jury to determine the weight and credibility to be given the statement and that, in making the determination, it shall consider the age and maturity of the child, or the intellectual capabilities of the person with a moderate, severe, or profound intellectual disability, the nature of the statement, the circumstances under which the statement was made, and any other relevant factor.

(d) The proponent of the statement shall give the adverse party reasonable notice of his intention to offer the statement and the particulars of the statement.

(e) Statements described in paragraphs (1) and (2) of subsection (a) shall not be excluded on the basis that they were obtained as a result of interviews conducted pursuant to a protocol adopted by a Child Advocacy Advisory Board as set forth in subsections (c), (d), and (e) of Section 3 of the Children's Advocacy Center Act or that an interviewer or witness to the interview was or is an employee, agent, or investigator of a State's Attorney's office.

§ 115-10.1. Admissibility of Prior Inconsistent Statements. In all criminal cases, evidence of a statement made by a witness is not made inadmissible by the hearsay rule if

(a) the statement is inconsistent with his testimony at the hearing or trial, and

(b) the witness is subject to cross-examination concerning the statement, and

(c) the statement-

(1) was made under oath at a trial, hearing, or other proceeding, or

(2) narrates, describes, or explains an event or condition of which the witness had personal knowledge, and

(A) the statement is proved to have been written or signed by the witness, or

(B) the witness acknowledged under oath the making of the statement either in his testimony at the hearing or trial in which the admission into evidence of the prior statement is being sought, or at a trial, hearing, or other proceeding, or

(C) the statement is proved to have been accurately recorded by a tape recorder, videotape recording, or any other similar electronic means of sound recording.

Nothing in this Section shall render a prior inconsistent statement inadmissible for purposes of impeachment because such statement was not recorded or otherwise fails to meet the criteria set forth herein.

§ 115-10.2. Admissibility of prior statements when witness refused to testify despite a court order to testify. (a) A statement not specifically covered by any other hearsay exception but having equivalent circumstantial guarantees of trustworthiness, is not excluded by the hearsay rule if the declarant is unavailable as defined in subsection (c) and if the court determines that:

(1) the statement is offered as evidence of a material fact; and

(2) the statement is more probative on the point for which it is offered than any other evidence which the proponent can procure through reasonable efforts; and

(3) the general purposes of this Section and the interests of justice will best be served by admission of the statement into evidence.

(b) A statement may not be admitted under this exception unless the proponent of it makes known to the adverse party sufficiently in advance of the trial or hearing to provide the adverse party with a fair opportunity to prepare to meet it, the proponent's intention to offer the statement, and the particulars of the statement, including the name and address of the declarant.

(c) Unavailability as a witness is limited to the situation in which the declarant persists in refusing to testify concerning the subject matter of the declarant's statement despite an order of the court to do so.

(d) A declarant is not unavailable as a witness if exemption, refusal, claim or lack of memory, inability or absence is due to the procurement or wrongdoing of the proponent of a statement for purpose of preventing the witness from attending or testifying.

(e) Nothing in this Section shall render a prior statement inadmissible for purposes of impeachment because the statement was not recorded or otherwise fails to meet the criteria set forth in this Section.

(f) Prior statements are admissible under this Section only if the statements were made under oath and were subject to cross-examination by the adverse party in a prior trial, hearing, or other proceeding.

§ 115-10.2a. Admissibility of prior statements in domestic violence prosecutions when the witness is unavailable to testify. (a) In a domestic violence prosecution, a statement, made by an individual identified in Section 201 of the Illinois Domestic Violence Act of 1986 as a person protected by that Act, that is not specifically covered by any other hearsay exception but having equivalent circumstantial guarantees of trustworthiness, is not excluded by the hearsay rule if the declarant is identified as unavailable as defined in subsection (c) and if the court determines that:

(1) the statement is offered as evidence of a material fact; and

(2) the statement is more probative on the point for which it is offered than any other evidence which the proponent can procure through reasonable efforts; and

(3) the general purposes of this Section and the interests of justice will best be served by admission of the statement into evidence.

(b) A statement may not be admitted under this exception unless the proponent of it makes known to the adverse party sufficiently in advance of the trial or hearing to provide the adverse party with a fair opportunity to prepare to meet it, the proponent's intention to offer the statement, and the particulars of the statement, including the name and address of the declarant.

(c) Unavailability as a witness includes circumstances in which the declarant:

(1) is exempted by ruling of the court on the ground of privilege from testifying concerning the subject matter of the declarant's statement; or

(2) persists in refusing to testify concerning the subject matter of the declarant's statement despite an order of the court to do so; or

(3) testifies to a lack of memory of the subject matter of the declarant's statement; or

(4) is unable to be present or to testify at the hearing because of health or then existing physical or mental illness or infirmity; or

(5) is absent from the hearing and the proponent of the statement has been unable to procure the declarant's attendance by process or other reasonable means; or

(6) is a crime victim as defined in Section 3 of the Rights of Crime Victims and Witnesses Act and the failure of the declarant to testify is caused by the defendant's intimidation of the declarant as defined in Section 12-6 of the Criminal Code of 1961.

(d) A declarant is not unavailable as a witness if exemption, refusal, claim of lack of memory, inability, or absence is due to the procurement or wrongdoing of the proponent of a statement for purpose of preventing the witness from attending or testifying.
(e) Nothing in this Section shall render a prior statement inadmissible for purposes of impeachment because the statement was not recorded or otherwise fails to meet the criteria set forth in this Section.

§ 115-10.3. Hearsay exception regarding elder adults. (a) In a prosecution for a physical act, abuse, neglect, or financial exploitation perpetrated upon or against an eligible adult, as defined in the Elder Abuse and Neglect Act, who has been diagnosed by a physician to suffer from

(i) any form of dementia, developmental disability, or other form of mental incapacity or

(ii) any physical infirmity,

including but not limited to prosecutions for violations of Sections 10-1, 10-2, 10-3, 10-3.1, 10-4, 11-1.20, 11-1.30, 11-1.40, 11-1.50, 11-1.60, 11-11, 12-1, 12-2, 12-3, 12-3.2, 12-4, 12-4.1, 12-4.2, 12-4.5, 12-4.6, 12-4.7, 12-5, 12-6, 12-7.3, 12-7.4, 12-11, 12-11.1, 12-13, 12-14, 12-15, 12-16, 12-21, 16-1, 16-1.3, 17-1, 17-3, 18-1, 18-2, 18-3, 18-4, 18-5, 20-1.1, 24-1.2, and 33A-2 of the Criminal Code of 1961, the following evidence shall be admitted as an exception to the hearsay rule:

(1) testimony by an eligible adult, of an out of court statement made by the eligible adult, that he or she complained of such act to another; and

(2) testimony of an out of court statement made by the eligible adult, describing any complaint of such act or matter or detail pertaining to any act which is an element of an offense which is the subject of a prosecution for a physical act, abuse, neglect, or financial exploitation perpetrated upon or against the eligible adult.
(b) Such testimony shall only be admitted if:

(1) The court finds in a hearing conducted outside the presence of the jury that the time, content, and circumstances of the statement provide sufficient safeguards of reliability; and

(2) The eligible adult either:

(A) testifies at the proceeding; or

(B) is unavailable as a witness and there is corroborative evidence of the act which is the subject of the statement.

(c) If a statement is admitted pursuant to this Section, the court shall instruct the jury that it is for the jury to determine the weight and credibility to be given the statement and that, in making the determination, it shall consider the condition of the eligible adult, the nature of the statement, the circumstances under which the statement was made, and any other relevant factor.

(d) The proponent of the statement shall give the adverse party reasonable notice of his or her intention to offer the statement and the particulars of the statement.

§ 115-10.4. Admissibility of prior statements when witness is deceased.
(a) A statement not specifically covered by any other hearsay exception but having equivalent circumstantial guarantees of trustworthiness is not excluded by the hearsay rule if the declarant is deceased and if the court determines that:

(1) the statement is offered as evidence of a material fact; and

(2) the statement is more probative on the point for which it is offered than any other evidence which the proponent can procure through reasonable efforts; and

(3) the general purposes of this Section and the interests of justice will best be served by admission of the statement into evidence.

(b) A statement may not be admitted under this exception unless the proponent of it makes known to the adverse party sufficiently in advance of the trial or hearing to provide the adverse party with a fair opportunity to prepare to meet it, the proponent's intention to offer the statement, and the particulars of the statement, including the name of the declarant.

(c) Unavailability as a witness under this Section is limited to the situation in which the declarant is deceased.

(d) Any prior statement that is sought to be admitted under this Section must have been made by the declarant under oath at a trial, hearing, or other proceeding and been subject to cross-examination by the adverse party.

(e) Nothing in this Section shall render a prior statement inadmissible for purposes of impeachment because the statement was not recorded or otherwise fails to meet the criteria set forth in this Section.

§ 115-10.5. Hearsay exception regarding safe zone testimony. (a) In any prosecution for any offense charged as a violation of Section 407 of the Illinois Controlled Substances Act, Section 55 of the Methamphetamine Control and Community Protection Act, or Section 5-130 of the Juvenile Court Act of 1987 the following evidence shall be admitted as an exception to the hearsay rule any testimony by any qualified individual regarding the status of any property as:

(1) a truck stop or safety rest area, or

(2) a school or conveyance owned, leased or contracted by a school to transport students to or from school, or

(3) residential property owned, operated, and managed by a public housing agency, or

(4) a public park, or

(5) the real property comprising any church, synagogue, or other building, structure, or place used primarily for religious worship, or
(6) the real property comprising any of the following places, buildings, or structures used primarily for housing or providing space for activities for senior citizens: nursing homes, assisted-living centers, senior citizen housing complexes, or senior centers oriented toward daytime activities.
(b) As used in this Section, "qualified individual" means any person who (i) lived or worked within the territorial jurisdiction where the offense took place when the offense took place; and (ii) is familiar with various public places within the territorial jurisdiction where the offense took place when the offense took place.

(c) For the purposes of this Section, "qualified individual" includes any peace officer, or any member of any duly organized State, county, or municipal peace unit, assigned to the territorial jurisdiction where the offense took place when the offense took place.

(d) This Section applies to all prosecutions pending at the time this amendatory Act of the 91st General Assembly takes effect and to all prosecutions commencing on or after its effective date.

§ 115-10.6. Hearsay exception for intentional murder of a witness. (a) A statement is not rendered inadmissible by the hearsay rule if it is offered against a party that has killed the declarant in violation of clauses (a)(1) and (a)(2) of Section 9-1 of the Criminal Code of 1961 intending to procure the unavailability of the declarant as a witness in a criminal or civil proceeding.

(b) While intent to procure the unavailability of the witness is a necessary element for the introduction of the statements, it need not be the sole motivation behind the murder which procured the unavailability of the declarant as a witness.

(c) The murder of the declarant may, but need not, be the subject of the trial at which the statement is being offered. If the murder of the declarant is not the subject of the trial at which the statement is being offered, the murder need not have ever been prosecuted.

(d) The proponent of the statements shall give the adverse party reasonable written notice of its intention to offer the statements and the substance of the particulars of each statement of the declarant. For purposes of this Section, identifying the location of the statements in tendered discovery shall be sufficient to satisfy the substance of the particulars of the statement.

(e) The admissibility of the statements shall be determined by the court at a pretrial hearing. At the hearing, the proponent of the statement bears the burden of establishing 3 criteria by a preponderance of the evidence:

(1) first, that the adverse party murdered the declarant and that the murder was intended to cause the unavailability of the declarant as a witness;

(2) second, that the time, content, and circumstances of the statements provide sufficient safeguards of reliability;

(3) third, the interests of justice will best be served by admission of the statement into evidence.

(f) The court shall make specific findings as to each of these criteria on the record before ruling on the admissibility of said statements.

(g) This Section in no way precludes or changes the application of the existing common law doctrine of forfeiture by wrongdoing.

§ 115-10.7. Admissibility of prior statements of an unavailable witness whose absence was wrongfully procured. (a) Legislative intent. The Illinois General Assembly finds that no party to a criminal case who wrongfully procures the unavailability of a witness should be allowed to benefit from such wrongdoing by depriving the trier of fact of relevant testimony.

(b) A statement of a witness is not excluded at the trial or hearing of any defendant by the hearsay rule or as a violation of any right to confront witnesses if the witness was killed, bribed, kidnapped, secreted, intimidated, or otherwise induced by a party, or one for whose conduct such party is legally responsible, to prevent the witness from being available to testify at such trial or hearing.
(c) The party seeking to introduce the statement shall disclose the statement sufficiently in advance of trial or hearing to provide the opposing party with a fair opportunity to meet it. The disclosure shall include notice of an intent to offer the statement, including the identity of the declarant.
(d) Prior to ruling on the admissibility of a statement under this Section, the court shall conduct a hearing outside the presence of the jury. During the course of the hearing the court may allow the parties to proceed by way of proffer. Except in cases where a preponderance of the evidence establishes that the defendant killed the declarant, the party seeking to introduce the statement shall be required to show by a reponderance of the evidence that the party who caused the unavailability of the witness did so with the intent or motive that the witness be unavailable for trial or hearing. The court is not required to find that the conduct or wrongdoing amounts to a criminal act.
(e) Nothing in this Section shall be construed to prevent the admissibility of Statements under existing hearsay exceptions.

§ 115-11. [Closed trial during testimony of child victim of a sexual offense permitted]. in a prosecution for a criminal offense defined in Article 11 or in Section 11-1.20, 11-1.30, 11-1.40, 11-1.50, 11-1.60, 12-13, 12-14, 12-14.1, 12-15 or 12-16 of the "Criminal Code of 1961", where the alleged victim of the offense is a minor under 18 years of age, the court may exclude from the proceedings while the victim is testifying, all persons, who, in the opinion of the court, do not have a direct interest in the case, except the media.

§ **115-11.1. Use of "Rape".** The use of the word "rape", "rapist", or any derivative of "rape" by any victim, witness, State's Attorney, defense attorney, judge or other court personnel in any prosecutions of offenses in Sections 11-1.20 through 11-1.60 or 12-13 through 12-16 of the Criminal Code of 1961, as amended, is not inadmissible.

§ **115-12. Substantive Admissibility of Prior Identification.** A statement is not rendered inadmissible by the hearsay rule if :
(a) the declarant testifies at the trial or hearing, and

(b) the declarant is subject to cross-examination concerning the statement, and

(c) the statement is one of identification of a person made after perceiving him.

§ 115-13. [Medical records as evidence in trial for sexual offense]. In a prosecution for violation of Section 11-1.20, 11-1.30, 11-1.40, 11-1.50, 11-1.60, 12-13, 12-14, 12-14.1, 12-15 or 12-16 of the "Criminal Code of 1961", statements made by the victim to medical personnel for purposes of medical diagnosis or treatment including descriptions of the cause of symptom, pain or sensations, or the inception or general character of the cause or external source thereof insofar as reasonably pertinent to diagnosis or treatment shall be admitted as an exception to the hearsay rule.

§ **115-14. Witness Competency.**
(a) Every person, irrespective of age, is qualified to be a witness and no person is disqualified to testify to any matter, except as provided in subsection (b).

(b) A person is disqualified to be a witness if he or she is:
(1) Incapable of expressing himself or herself concerning the matter so as to be understood, either directly or through interpretation by one who can understand him or her; or

(2) Incapable of understanding the duty of a witness to tell the truth.

(c) A party may move the court prior to a witness' testimony being received in evidence, requesting that the court make a determination if a witness is competent to testify. The hearing shall be conducted outside the presence of the jury and the burden of proof shall be on the moving party.

§ **115-15. Laboratory reports.** (a) In any criminal prosecution for a violation of the Cannabis Control Act, the Illinois Controlled Substances Act, or the Methamphetamine Control and Community Protection Act, a laboratory report from the Department of State Police, Division of Forensic Services, that is signed and sworn to by the person performing an analysis and that states

(1) that the substance that is the basis of the alleged violation has been weighed and analyzed, and

(2) the person's findings as to the contents, weight and identity of the substance, and

(3) that it contains any amount of a controlled substance or cannabis is prima facie evidence of the contents, identity and weight of the substance. Attached to the report shall be a copy of a notarized statement by the signer of the report giving the name of the signer and stating

(i) that he or she is an employee of the Department of State Police, Division of Forensic Services,

(ii) the name and location of the laboratory where the analysis was performed,

(iii) that performing the analysis is apart of his or her regular duties, and

(iv) that the signer is qualified by education, training and experience to perform the analysis. The signer shall also allege that scientifically accepted tests were performed with due caution and that the evidence was handled in accordance with established and accepted procedures while in the custody of the laboratory.

(a-5) In any criminal prosecution for reckless homicide under Section 9-3 of the Criminal Code of 1961 or driving under the influence of alcohol, other drug, or combination of both, in violation of Section 11-501 of the Illinois Vehicle Code or in any civil action held under a statutory summary suspension or revocation hearing under Section 2-118.1 of the Illinois Vehicle Code, a laboratory report from the Department of State Police, Division of Forensic Services, that is signed and sworn to by the person performing an analysis, and that states that the sample of blood or urine was tested for alcohol or drugs, and contains the person's findings as to the presence and amount of alcohol or drugs and type of drug is prima facie evidence of the presence, content, and amount of the alcohol or drugs analyzed in the blood or urine.
Attached to the report must be a copy of a notarized statement by the signer of the report giving the name of the signer and stating

(1) that he or she is an employee of the Department of State Police, Division of Forensic Services,

(2) the name and location of the laboratory where the analysis was performed,

(3) that performing the analysis is a part of his or her regular duties,

(4) that the signer is qualified by education, training, and experience to perform the analysis, and

(5) that scientifically accepted tests were performed with due caution and that the evidence was handled in accordance with established and accepted procedures while in the custody of the laboratory.

(b) The State's Attorney shall serve a copy of the report on the attorney of record for the accused, or on the accused if he or she has no attorney, before any proceeding in which the report is to be used against the accused other than at a preliminary hearing or grand jury hearing when the report may be used without having been previously served upon the accused.

(c) The report shall not be prima facie evidence if the accused or his or her attorney demands the testimony of the person signing the report by serving the demand upon the State's Attorney within 7 days from the accused or his or her attorney's receipt of the report.

§ **115-16. Witness disqualification.** No person shall be disqualified as a witness in a criminal case or proceeding by reason of his or her interest in the event of the case or proceeding, as a party or otherwise, or by reason of his or her having been convicted of a crime; but the interest or conviction may be shown for the purpose of affecting the credibility of the witness. A defendant in a criminal case or proceeding shall only at his or her own request be deemed a competent witness, and the person's neglect to testify shall not create a presumption against the person, nor shall the court permit a reference or comment to be made to or upon that neglect.
In criminal cases, husband and wife may testify for or against each other. Neither, however, may testify as to any communication or admission made by either of them to the other or as to any conversation between them during marriage, except in cases in which either is charged with an offense against the person or property of the other, in case of spouse abandonment, when the interests of their child or children or of any child or children in either spouse's care, custody, or control are directly involved, when either is charged with or under investigation for an offense under Section 11-1.20, 11-1.30, 11-1.40, 11-1.50, 11-1.60, 12-13, 12-14, 12-14.1, 12-15, or 12-16 of the Criminal Code of 1961 and the victim is a minor under 18 years of age in either spouse's care, custody, or control at the time of the offense, or as to matters in which either has acted as agent of the other.

Commentary – Marital Privilege

In Illinois, a husband or wife may testify for or against each other. Neither is deemed to be incompetent as a witness by virtue of the marital relationship. However, conversations between husband and wife have long been the subject of protection by the marital conversation privilege under the common law, which was codified in 725 ILCS 5/115-16. However, in an unusual case, a divided Illinois Supreme Court found the marital conversation privilege abrogated. In *People v. Trzeciak* 2013 IL 114491 (Ill. S. Ct. 2013), the Illinois marital conversation privilege was held not to apply to a conversation between a defendant and his wife, even where the conversations occurred during their marriage. In the conversation the defendant threatened his wife and decedent. Evidence at trial showed that the decedent protected the wife and provided a place of refuse from the defendant's domestic violence. Decedent was killed two months after the conversation. The majority of the Court held the privilege did not apply because the conversation was not intended to be confidential, in spite of the lack of express qualifying language of the Illinois marital privilege statute 725 ILCS 5/115-16. The court relied upon foreign state court decisions as persuasive authority in the face of no direct Illinois case on point. (Three dissenting justices and one concurring justice).

§ **115-17. Clerk; issuance of subpoenas.** It is the duty of the clerk of the court to issue subpoenas, either on the part of the people or of the accused, directed to the sheriff or coroner of any county of this State. An attorney admitted to practice in the State of Illinois, as an officer of the court, may also issue subpoenas in a pending action. A witness who is duly subpoenaed who neglects or refuses to attend any court, under the requisitions of the subpoena, shall be proceeded against and punished for contempt of the court. Attachments against witnesses who live in a different county from that where the subpoena is returnable may be served in the same manner as warrants are directed to be served out of the county from which they issue.

§ **115-17a. Subpoenas to crime victims.** In a post conviction proceeding, before the crime victim may be subpoenaed by the defendant, the defendant must first petition the court and give notice to the victim. At the hearing on the petition, the victim shall be given the opportunity to appear and object to the requested subpoena. At the request of the victim, the State's Attorney shall represent the victim in the proceeding. The court shall grant the request for the subpoena only if and to the extent it determines that the subpoena seeks evidence that is material and relevant to the post conviction hearing. For the purposes of this Section, "crime victim" has the meaning ascribed to it in Section 3 of the Rights of Crime Victims and Witnesses Act.

Sec. 115-17b. Administrative subpoenas.

(a) Definitions. As used in this Section:

"Electronic communication services" and "remote computing services" have the same meaning as provided in the Electronic Communications Privacy Act in Chapter 121 (commencing with Section 2701) of Part I of Title 18 of the United States Code Annotated.

"Offense involving the sexual exploitation of children" means an offense under Section 11-6, 11-6.5, 11-6.6, 11-9.1, 11-15.1, 11-17.1, 11-18.1, 11-19.1, 11-19.2, 11-20.1, 11-20.3, 11-21, 11-23, 11-25, 11-26, 12-13, 12-14, 12-14.1, 12-15, or 12-16 of the Criminal Code of 1961 or any attempt to commit any of these offenses when the victim is under 18 years of age.

(b) Subpoenas duces tecum. In any criminal investigation of an offense involving the sexual exploitation of children, the Attorney General, or his or her designee, or a State's Attorney, or his or her designee, may issue in writing and cause to be served subpoenas duces tecum to providers of electronic communication services or remote computing services requiring the production of records relevant to the investigation. Any such request for records shall not extend beyond requiring the provider to disclose the information specified in 18 U.S.C. 2703(c)(2). Any subpoena duces tecum issued under this Section shall be made returnable to the Chief Judge of the Circuit Court for the Circuit in which the State's Attorney resides, or his or her designee, or for subpoenas issued by the Attorney General, the subpoena shall be made returnable to the Chief Judge of the Circuit Court for the Circuit to which the investigation pertains, or his or her designee, to determine whether the documents are privileged and whether the subpoena is unreasonable or oppressive.

(c) Contents of subpoena. A subpoena under this Section shall describe the records or other things required to be produced and prescribe a return date within a reasonable period of time within which the objects or records can be assembled and made available.

(c-5) Contemporaneous notice to Chief Judge. Whenever a subpoena is issued under this Section, the Attorney General or his or her designee or the State's Attorney or his of her designee shall be required to provide a copy of the subpoena to the Chief Judge of the county in which the subpoena is returnable.

(d) Modifying or quashing subpoena. At any time before the return date specified in the subpoena, the person or entity to whom the subpoena is directed may petition for an order modifying or quashing the subpoena on the grounds that the subpoena is oppressive or unreasonable or that the subpoena seeks privileged documents or records.

(e) Ex parte order. An Illinois circuit court for the circuit in which the subpoena is or will be issued, upon application of the Attorney General, or his or her designee, or State's Attorney, or his or her designee, may issue an ex parte order that no person or entity disclose to any other person or entity (other than persons necessary to comply with the subpoena) the existence of such subpoena for a period of up to 90 days.

(1) Such order may be issued upon a showing that the things being sought may be relevant to the investigation and there is reason to believe that such disclosure may result in:

(A) endangerment to the life or physical safety of any person;

(B) flight to avoid prosecution;

(C) destruction of or tampering with evidence;

(D) intimidation of potential witnesses; or

(E) otherwise seriously jeopardizing an investigation or unduly delaying a trial.

(2) An order under this Section may be renewed for additional periods of up to 90 days upon a showing that the circumstances described in paragraph (1) of this subsection (e) continue to exist.

(f) Enforcement. A witness who is duly subpoenaed who neglects or refuses to comply with the subpoena shall be proceeded against and punished for contempt of the court. A subpoena duces tecum issued under this Section may be enforced pursuant to the Uniform Act to Secure the Attendance of Witnesses from Within or Without a State in Criminal Proceedings.

(g) Immunity from civil liability. Notwithstanding any federal, State, or local law, any person, including officers, agents, and employees, receiving a subpoena under this Section, who complies in good faith with the subpoena and thus produces the materials sought, shall not be liable in any court of Illinois to any customer or other person for such production or for nondisclosure of that production to the customer.

§ **115-18. Employee protected.** No employer shall discharge or terminate, or threaten to discharge or terminate, from his or her employment, or otherwise punish or penalize his or her employee who is a witness to a crime, because of time lost from regular employment resulting from his or her attendance at a proceeding under subpoena issued in any criminal proceeding relative to the crime. An employer who knowingly or intentionally violates this Section shall be proceeded against and punished for contempt of court.
This Section shall not be construed as requiring an employer to pay an employee for time lost resulting from attendance at any proceeding.

§ **115-19. Polygraph.** In the course of a criminal trial the court shall not require, request, or suggest that the defendant submit to a polygraphic detection deception test, commonly known as a lie detector test, to questioning under the effect of thiopental sodium, or to any other test or questioning by means of a mechanical device or chemical substance.

§ **115-20. Evidence of prior conviction.** (a) Evidence of a prior conviction of a defendant for domestic battery, aggravated battery committed against a family or household member as defined in Section 112A-3, stalking, aggravated stalking, or violation of an order of protection is admissible in a later criminal prosecution for any of these types of offenses when the victim is the same person who was the victim of the previous offense that resulted in conviction of the defendant.

(b) If the defendant is accused of an offense set forth in subsection (a) or the defendant is tried or retried for any of the offenses set forth in subsection (a), evidence of the defendant's conviction for another offense or offenses set forth in subsection (a) may be admissible (if that evidence is otherwise admissible under the rules of evidence) and may be considered for its bearing on any matter to which it is relevant if the victim is the same person who was the victim of the previous offense that resulted in conviction of the defendant.

(c) In weighing the probative value of the evidence against undue prejudice to the defendant, the court may consider:

(1) the proximity in time to the charged or predicate offense;

(2) the degree of factual similarity to the charged or predicate offense; or
(3) other relevant facts and circumstances.

(d) In a criminal case in which the prosecution intends to offer evidence under this Section, it must disclose the evidence, including statements of witnesses or a summary of the substance of any testimony, at a reasonable time in advance of trial, or during trial if the court excuses pretrial notice on good cause shown.

(e) In a criminal case in which evidence is offered under this Section, proof may be made by specific instances of conduct as evidenced by proof of conviction, testimony as to reputation, or testimony in the form of an expert opinion, except that the prosecution may offer reputation testimony only after the opposing party has offered that testimony.

§ **115-21. Informant testimony.** (a) For the purposes of this Section, "informant" means someone who is purporting to testify about admissions made to him or her by the accused while incarcerated in a penal institution contemporaneously.

(b) This Section applies to any capital case in which the prosecution attempts to introduce evidence of incriminating statements made by the accused to or overheard by an informant.

(c) In any case under this Section, the prosecution shall timely disclose in discovery:

(1) the complete criminal history of the informant;

(2) any deal, promise, inducement, or benefit that the offering party has made or will make in the future to the informant;

(3) the statements made by the accused;

(4) the time and place of the statements, the time and place of their disclosure to law enforcement officials, and the names of all persons who were present when the statements were made;

(5) whether at any time the informant recanted that testimony or statement and, if so, the time and place of the recantation, the nature of the recantation, and the names of the persons who were present at the recantation;

(6) other cases in which the informant testified, provided that the existence of such testimony can be ascertained through reasonable inquiry and whether the informant received any promise, inducement, or benefit in exchange for or subsequent to that testimony or statement; and

(7) any other information relevant to the informant's credibility.
(d) In any case under this Section, the prosecution must timely disclose its intent to

introduce the testimony of an informant. The court shall conduct a hearing to determine whether the testimony of the informant is reliable, unless the defendant waives such a hearing. If the prosecution fails to show by a preponderance of the evidence that the informant's testimony is reliable, the court shall not allow the testimony to be heard at trial. At this hearing, the court shall consider the factors enumerated in subsection (c) as well as any other factors relating to reliability.

(e) A hearing required under subsection (d) does not apply to statements covered under subsection (b) that are lawfully recorded.

(f) This Section applies to all death penalty prosecutions initiated on or after the effective date of this amendatory Act of the 93rd General Assembly.

§ **115-22. Witness inducements.** When the State intends to introduce the testimony of a witness in a capital case, the State shall, before trial, disclose to the defendant and to his or her defense counsel the following information, which shall be reduced to writing:

(1) whether the witness has received or been promised anything, including pay, immunity from prosecution, leniency in prosecution, or personal advantage, in exchange for testimony;

(2) any other case in which the witness testified or offered statements against an individual but was not called, and whether the statements were admitted in the case, and whether the witness received any deal, promise, inducement, or benefit in exchange for that testimony or statement; provided that the existence of such testimony can be ascertained through reasonable inquiry;

(3) whether the witness has ever changed his or her testimony;

(4) the criminal history of the witness; and

(5) any other evidence relevant to the credibility of the witness.

Commentary – Trial

Jury Trial or Bench Trial. Section 115-1 provides that the defendant will have a jury trial unless he waives jury, in which case, he will have a bench trial. Section 115-3 relates that the defendant will be present, unless he absents himself or waives appearing, along with his attorney for the trial. At the conclusion of the trial, the judge will enter a general finding of guilty or not guilty, unless the defendant has raised an insanity defense, in which case the judge could find him not guilty by reason of insanity. To waive a jury, the defendant must appear in front of the judge personally, be admonished as to his right to jury trial, knowingly waive jury trial and show his waiver by executing a written jury waiver form. Section 115-4 describes the procedure for a jury trial, where the judge determines questions of law and the jury determines questions of fact. The jury consists of 12 jurors (plus two alternates if deemed necessary by the court) who are summoned to court from a randomly composed jury pool, who fill out juror questionnaires and who are called to the courtroom for jury selection. During the jury selection process, the judge and attorneys will ask questions of jurors to determine if they can be fair and impartial. Illinois Supreme Court Rule 431(b) requires the court to inquire of jurors about fundamental principles of law and determine that each juror understands the principles and accepts them. The rule provides:

> The court shall ask each potential juror, individually or in a group, whether that juror understands and accepts the following principles:
>
> (1) that the defendant is presumed innocent of the charge(s) against him or her;

(2) that before a defendant can be convicted the State must prove the defendant guilty beyond a reasonable doubt;

(3) that the defendant is not required to offer any evidence on his or her own behalf; and

(4) that the defendant's failure to testify cannot be held against him or her; however, no inquiry of a prospective juror shall be made into the defendant's failure to testify when the defendant objects.

The court's method of inquiry shall provide each juror an opportunity to respond to specific questions concerning the principles set out in this section.

Illinois Supreme Court Rule 431(b)

Under Section 115-4(d), the judge, on motion of either the prosecution or defense, may excuse jurors for cause – the determination that the juror would not follow the fundamental principles or if for any other reason the judge determines that the juror could not be fair and impartial. Pursuant to Section 115-4(e), the prosecution and defense are allowed to use peremptory challenges to excuse up to a certain number of jurors for any non-discriminatory reason. In a single defendant felony trial, the state and defense each would have 10 peremptory challenges and 5 peremptory challenges in a single-defendant misdemeanor case. Jurors cannot be discharged on the basis of race or gender. See *Batson v. Kentucky* 476 U.S.79, 106 S.Ct. 1712 (U.S. S. Ct. 1986)(violation of equal protection of law for prosecutor to use peremptory challenges to remove black jurors in a case involving a black defendant). Jurors are generally selected in panels of four in accordance with Illinois Supreme Court Rule 434.

Opening Statements. After the jury is selected, they are sworn in. The prosecution and defense are each permitted to make opening statements. These are summary statements that discuss what the evidence will prove in the case. These are to be free from argument.

Prosecution case-in-chief. The prosecution must go forward with the evidence first. Witnesses are sworn in and are questioned by a prosecutor. These witnesses usually include police officers, lay witnesses and expert witnesses. This direct examination questioning generally uses open-ended questions (e.g. "What was the defendant wearing?") that require the witness to say more than "yes" or "no", as opposed to leading questions (e.g. "The defendant wore a black leather jacket, correct?) that seeks agreement from the witness about the point of the question. Some leading question form is commonly used in direct examination to lay foundation for exhibits (e.g. "Is this photograph and fair and accurate portrayal of the scene that day?") or for other purposes. The primary goal of direct examination is to let the witness talk. Exhibits that are admitted into evidence may also be published (shown) to the jury during a witness's examination, depending on local practices.

When the prosecutor has concluded with direct examination, the defendant, through his attorney, has the right to confront and cross-examine the witness. While not required, effective lawyers normally ask only leading questions on cross-examination to emphasis points of testimony that are favorable to the defendant or to attack the credibility of the witness to show that his observations were poor, mistaken or even false. Following cross-examination, the prosecutor may ask re-direct questions, designed to permit further explanation of matters brought out on cross examination. The back-and-forth of further cross-examination and re-direct examination can continue, but is controlled by the discretion of the judge.

This process goes on for every prosecution witness, including the admission of exhibits, until the prosecution rests its case. The prosecution will select witnesses and present testimony and exhibits to prove the essential elements of each of the crimes charged. Depending on the case, a prosecution's case-in-chief could last for hours, a day, many days, or a month or longer.

Objections and Defense motions. If during the presentation of evidence, the prosecution asks questions or the witness gives responses that would be in violation of the law of evidence, the defendant's attorney may choose to object to have the evidence barred from admission or stricken so that it may not be considered. Typical grounds for objection include relevancy, privilege, hearsay or improper opinion. Defendants can also object to the form of the question since direct examination is supposed to be the witness testifying and leading questions undermine that principle. The judge will rule on objections, ordinarily without extended argument. If the matter involves a more complicated consideration of the law of evidence, the court may discuss it at the bench (at sidebar) with the lawyers out of the jury's hearing, or may send the jury to wait in the jury room while extended discussion happens. The judge will either sustain (agree with the objection) or overrule (disagree with the objection) the legal matter rose. Prosecutors may also object to questions or answers given during cross-examination.

If the issue is a fundamental threat to a fair trial (e.g. surprise evidence, commenting on the defendant's right to remain silent or offering evidence that has been excluded by prior order), the defendant may move for a mistrial. To grant a mistrial, the judge must be convinced that whatever has occurred has irreversibly damaged the prospect that the defendant will be tried based on proper evidence so that the trial can conclude fairly. If a mistrial is granted, the court must determine if the error by the prosecution or its witnesses occurred intentionally. In a rare case, the court would determine that the defendant could not be re-tried on the charges that brought him to trial. Normally, the matter would be re-set for trial.

At the conclusion of the prosecution's case, the defendant may make a motion for a directed finding of not-guilty. This motion argues that the prosecution's evidence, considered in the light most favorable to the prosecution, has failed to prove a prima facie case concerning the crime or crimes charged. If the court agrees, the defendant is discharged as not guilty. If the motion for directed verdict is denied, the defendant is afforded the opportunity to present evidence.

Defendant's case-in chief. Because the defendant typically has no burden of proof, the defendant can choose to present no evidence and of course, choose not to testify. If the defendant presents evidence, it is presented through the process of direct and cross-examination as was followed in the prosecution's case-in-chief. The defendant may also offer exhibits through his witnesses. The process of objecting to claimed improper questions, testimony or exhibits is the same as what occurred during the prosecution's case. The judge will have a conversation with the defendant, outside the presence of the jury, about his right to testify or not testify as he chooses.

After the defendant has rested, the prosecution has the opportunity to present limited rebuttal evidence, and thereafter, sur-rebuttal evidence by the defense. When the proof is closed, the defendant may renew the motion for judgment of acquittal as a matter of law.

Evidence. One of the most significant areas of law that apply to trials is the law of evidence. On January 1, 2011, the Illinois Supreme Court implemented the Illinois Rules of Evidence (See Chapter 5). These rules incorporated decades of case law holdings and some statutory enactments about the law of evidence in Illinois. A separate commentary follows the rules in this book.

Jury Instructions and Jury Instruction Conference. The law that is given to the jury by the court is prepared by the parties and tendered to the court at a jury instruction conference, as required by Illinois Supreme Court Rule 451. This is typically held at the close of the evidence. Illinois Pattern Instructions – Criminal are required to be given, as modified, under the facts and charges of each case. If there is no "IPI" instruction on a subject, then a non-pattern instruction that accurately states the law may be given by the court. Instructions govern such matters and the role of the jury, witness credibility, fundamental criminal defendant's rights, definitions of offenses, elements required to be proved for each offense, witness credibility issues and of course, verdict forms. A "guilty" and a "not guilty" verdict form is provided for the jury's use as to each charge.

Closing arguments. The prosecution gives a closing argument to persuade the jury that it has met the burden of proof beyond a reasonable doubt, discussing the evidence and the law in the course of argument. The defense follows with closing argument that the prosecution has failed to meet the burden of proof and the prosecution has the last word with a rebuttal argument to respond to the points made by the defendant's attorney. Opening statements and closing arguments often follow a theme, and are an opportunity in public speaking that can and do make a difference in many cases. Ultimately, the cases with the strongest evidence result in guilty verdicts and cases with weaknesses result in acquittals.

Sentencing upon conviction. If the defendant is convicted the judge will normally order the court services (probation) department to prepare a pre-sentence report. A separate sentencing hearing is held where the court considers the pre-sentence report, evidence in aggravation offered by the prosecution and evidence in mitigation offered by the defense. Victims of crimes have the right and opportunity (as set forth in 725 ILCS 5/120/1 *et seq.*) to present statements about the impact of the crime on the victim and the victim's family. The court hears arguments from both the prosecution and the defense, based on the applicable factors in aggravation and in mitigation, then recommends an appropriate sentence under the Unified Code of Corrections 730 ILCS 5/1/1 et seq. Sentences include issues of probation, imprisonment, fines and costs and restitution to victims.

Article 116 – Post-Trial Motions
725 ILCS 5/116 *et seq.*

§ 116-1. Motion for new trial.
(a) Following a verdict or finding of guilty the court may grant the defendant a new trial.

(b) A written motion for a new trial shall be filed by the defendant within 30 days following the entry of a finding or the return of a verdict. Reasonable notice of the motion shall be served upon the State.

(c) The motion for a new trial shall specify the grounds therefore.

§ 116-2. Motion in arrest of judgment.
(a) A written motion in arrest of judgment shall be filed by the defendant within 30 days following the entry of a verdict or finding of guilty. Reasonable notice of the motion shall be served upon the State.

(b) The court shall grant the motion when:

(1) The indictment, information or complaint does not charge an offense, or

(2) The court is without jurisdiction of the cause.

(c) A motion in arrest of judgment attacking the indictment, information, or complaint on the ground that it does not charge an offense shall be denied if the indictment, information or complaint apprised the accused of the precise offense charged with sufficient specificity to prepare his defense and allow pleading a resulting conviction as a bar to future prosecution out of the same conduct.

Sec. 116-2.1. Motion to vacate prostitution convictions for sex trafficking victims.
(a) A motion under this Section may be filed at any time following the entry of a verdict or finding of guilty where the conviction was under Section 11-14 (prostitution) or Section 11-14.2 (first offender; felony prostitution) of the Criminal Code of 1961 or a similar local ordinance and the defendant's participation in the offense was a result of having been a trafficking victim under Section 10-9 (involuntary servitude, involuntary sexual servitude of a minor, or trafficking in persons for forced labor or services) of the Criminal Code of 1961; or a victim of a severe form of trafficking under the federal Trafficking Victims Protection Act (22 U.S.C. Section 7102(13)); provided that:

(1) a motion under this Section shall state why the facts giving rise to this motion were not presented to the trial court, and shall be made with due diligence, after the defendant has ceased to be a victim of such trafficking or has sought services for victims of such trafficking, subject to reasonable concerns for the safety of the defendant, family members of the defendant, or other victims of such trafficking that may be jeopardized by the bringing of such motion, or for other reasons consistent with the purpose of this Section; and

(2) reasonable notice of the motion shall be served upon the State.

(b) The court may grant the motion if, in the discretion of the court, the violation was a result of the defendant having been a victim of human trafficking. Evidence of such may include, but is not limited to:

(1) certified records of federal or State court proceedings which demonstrate that the defendant was a victim of a trafficker charged with a trafficking offense under Section 10-9 of the Criminal Code of 1961 or under 22 U.S.C. Chapter 78;

(2) certified records of "approval notices" or "law enforcement certifications" generated from federal immigration proceedings available to such victims; or

(3) a sworn statement from a trained professional staff of a victim services organization, an attorney, a member of the clergy, or a medical or other professional from whom the defendant has sought assistance in addressing the trauma associated with being trafficked. Alternatively, the court may consider such other evidence as it deems of sufficient credibility and probative value in determining whether the defendant is a trafficking victim or victim of a severe form of trafficking.

(c) If the court grants a motion under this Section, it must vacate the conviction and may take such additional action as is appropriate in the circumstances.

§ 116-3. Motion for fingerprint, Integrated Ballistic Identification System, or forensic testing not available at trial regarding actual innocence. (a) A defendant may make a motion before the trial court that entered the judgment of conviction in his or her case for the performance of fingerprint, Integrated Ballistic Identification System, or forensic DNA testing, including comparison analysis of genetic marker groupings of the evidence collected by criminal justice agencies pursuant to the alleged offense, to those of the defendant, to those of other forensic evidence, and to those maintained under subsection (f) of Section 5-4-3 of the Unified Code of Corrections, on evidence that was secured in relation to the trial which resulted in his or her conviction, and:
(1) was not subject to the testing which is now requested at the time of trial; or
(2) although previously subjected to testing, can be subjected to additional testing utilizing a method that was not scientifically available at the time of trial that provides a reasonable likelihood of more probative results. Reasonable notice of the motion shall be served upon the State.

(b) The defendant must present a prima facie case that:

(1) identity was the issue in the trial which resulted in his or her conviction; and

(2) the evidence to be tested has been subject to a chain of custody sufficient to establish that it has not been substituted, tampered with, replaced, or altered in any material aspect.

(c) The trial court shall allow the testing under reasonable conditions designed to protect the State's interests in the integrity of the evidence and the testing process upon a determination that:
(1) the result of the testing has the scientific potential to produce new, noncumulative evidence materially relevant to the defendant's assertion of actual innocence even though the results may not completely exonerate the defendant;

(2) the testing requested employs a scientific method generally accepted within the relevant scientific community.

(d) If evidence previously tested pursuant to this Section reveals an unknown fingerprint from the crime scene that does not match the defendant or the victim, the order of the Court shall direct the prosecuting authority to request the Illinois State Police Bureau of Forensic Science to submit the unknown fingerprint evidence into the FBI's Integrated Automated Fingerprint Identification System (AIFIS) for identification.

§ 116-4. Preservation of evidence for forensic testing (a) Before or after the trial in a prosecution for a violation of Section 11-1.20, 11-1.30, 11-1.40, 11-1.50, 11-1.60, 12-13, 12-14, 12-14.1, 12-15, or 12-16 of the Criminal Code of 1961 or in a prosecution for an offense defined in Article 9 of that Code, or in a prosecution for an attempt in violation of Section 8-4 of that Code of any of the above-enumerated offenses, unless otherwise provided herein under subsection (b) or (c), a law enforcement agency or an agent acting on behalf of the law enforcement agency shall preserve, subject to a continuous chain of custody, any physical evidence in their possession or control that is reasonably likely to contain forensic evidence, including, but not limited to, fingerprints or biological material secured in relation to a trial and with sufficient documentation to locate that evidence.

(b) After a judgment of conviction is entered, the evidence shall either be impounded with the Clerk of the Circuit Court or shall be securely retained by a law enforcement agency. Retention shall be permanent in cases where a sentence of death is imposed. Retention shall be until the completion of the sentence, including the period of mandatory supervised release for the offense, or January 1, 2006, whichever is later, for any conviction for an offense or an attempt of an offense defined in Article 9 of the Criminal Code of 1961 or in Section 11-1.20, 11-1.30, 11-1.40, 11-1.50, 11-1.60, 12-13, 12-14, 12-14.1, 12-15, or 12-16 of the Criminal Code of 1961 or for 7 years following any conviction for any other felony for which the defendant's genetic profile may be taken by a law enforcement agency and submitted for comparison in a forensic DNA database for unsolved offenses.
(c) After a judgment of conviction is entered, the law enforcement agency required to retain evidence described in subsection (a) may petition the court with notice to the defendant or, in cases where the defendant has died, his estate, his attorney of record, or an attorney appointed for that purpose by the court for entry of an order allowing it to dispose of evidence if, after a hearing, the court determines by a preponderance of the evidence that:

(1) it has no significant value for forensic science analysis and should be returned to its rightful owner, destroyed, used for training purposes, or as otherwise provided by law; or

(2) it has no significant value for forensic science analysis and is of a size, bulk, or physical character not usually retained by the law enforcement agency and cannot practicably be retained by the law enforcement agency; or

(3) there no longer exists a reasonable basis to require the preservation of the evidence because of the death of the defendant; however, this paragraph (3) does not apply if a sentence of death was imposed.

(d) The court may order the disposition of the evidence if the defendant is allowed the opportunity to take reasonable measures to remove or preserve portions of the evidence in question for future testing.

(d-5) Any order allowing the disposition of evidence pursuant to subsection (c) or (d) shall be a final and appealable order. No evidence shall be disposed of until 30 days after the order is entered, and if a notice of appeal is filed, no evidence shall be disposed of until the mandate has been received by the circuit court from the appellate court.

(d-10) All records documenting the possession, control, storage, and destruction of evidence and all police reports, evidence control or inventory records, and other reports cited in this Section, including computer records, must be retained for as long as the evidence exists and may not be disposed of without the approval of the Local Records Commission.

(e) In this Section, "law enforcement agency" includes any of the following or an agent acting on behalf of any of the following: a municipal police department, county sheriff's office, any prosecuting authority, the Department of State Police, or any other State, university, county, federal, or municipal police unit or police force. "Biological material" includes, but is not limited to, any blood, hair, saliva, or semen from which genetic marker groupings may be obtained.

§ 116-5. Motion for DNA database search (genetic marker groupings comparison analysis). (a) Upon motion by a defendant charged with any offense where DNA evidence may be material to the defense investigation or relevant at trial, a court may order a DNA database search by the Department of State Police. Such analysis may include comparing:

(1) the genetic profile from forensic evidence that was secured in relation to the trial against the genetic profile of the defendant,
(2) the genetic profile of items of forensic evidence secured in relation to trial to the genetic profile of other forensic evidence secured in relation to trial, or
(3) the genetic profiles referred to in subdivisions (1) and (2) against:

(i) genetic profiles of offenders maintained under subsection (f) of Section 5-4-3 of the Unified Code of Corrections, or
(ii) genetic profiles, including but not limited to, profiles from unsolved crimes maintained in state or local DNA databases by law enforcement agencies.

(b) If appropriate federal criteria are met, the court may order the Department of State Police to request the National DNA index system to search its database of genetic profiles.

(c) If requested by the defense, a defense representative shall be allowed to view any genetic marker grouping analysis conducted by the Department of State Police. The defense shall be provided with copies of all documentation, correspondence, including digital correspondence, notes, memoranda, and reports generated in relation to the analysis.

(d) Reasonable notice of the motion shall be served upon the State.

Commentary – DNA Analysis and Post-Conviction Proceedings

DNA and its impact. Since the late 1980's, the use of DNA (deoxyribonucleic acid) analysis in the investigation and trial of criminal offenses has increased dramatically. All living organisms have a unique DNA profile that is identifiable and comparable as a "genetic fingerprint". The use of DNA testing can clear a wrongly convicted person. In *People v. Davis* 2012 IL App (4th) 110305, the defendant was convicted of murder while committing rape (now called "aggravated criminal sexual assault") of a 3-year-old girl in 1981. At the crime scene, semen was found on bed sheets combined with the victim's blood. Utilizing the post-conviction procedure found in 725 ILCS 116-3, in 2004 and 2005, DNA testing excluded the defendant as the donor of any blood or semen at the crime scene. Further, the DNA testing identified Maurice Tucker as a donor of some of the forensic evidence. Tucker had been a witness who testified against the defendant at the original trial. In 2012, Davis was granted a new trial in a post-conviction proceeding utilizing the DNA test results to demonstrate that the outcome of his original trial would have been different if the DNA evidence had been available and presented at that trial.

DNA evidence is now being used in the investigative phases of criminal cases, but like other scientific evidence, it must be used in a methodological and analytically sound way. In *People v. Wright* 2012 IL App (1st) 073106, the Court recognized the defendant's pre-trial right to seek DNA testing pursuant to §116-5. The defendant was convicted of two counts of sexual assault, based solely on a "cold case" analysis of forensic DNA evidence from swabs taken from a female victim's underwear and from a rectal swab. Testing of the underwear could not exclude the defendant, and testing of the rectal swab had only 9 *loci* instead of the standard 13 *loci* that were consistent with an identification of the defendant. Nonetheless, the DNA "expert" testified that there was a "match" of the defendant with the DNA profile from the rectal swab. The defendant requested that the State of Illinois identify the number of all *9-loci* "matches" within the state's convicted DNA database system, but the trial court denied the request. The defendant was convicted even though the victim could not identify the perpetrator and there was no other evidence, forensic or otherwise, that linked the defendant to the crime.

In *People v. Watson* 2012 IL App (2d) 091328, the appellate court granted the defendant a new trial, finding that the defendant was denied effective assistance of counsel at his trial where the lawyer did not contest the admission of DNA results in evidence, even in the face of testimony that a partial-profile did not meet investigative standards for forensic use (need for a sufficient number of identification *loci for* acceptable DNA interpretation).

In *People v Zapata* 2014 IL App (2d) 120825, the defendant's conviction for criminal sexual assault was affirmed. The Court rejected the defendant's contention that Y-STR DNA testing lacked general scientific acceptance.

Illinois Supreme Court Rules
Article 4 – Rules on Criminal Proceedings in the Trial Court
Part A – Waivers and Pleas
Rules 401 – 410

Rule 401. Waiver of Counsel
(a) Waiver of Counsel. Any waiver of counsel shall be in open court. The court shall not permit a waiver of counsel by a person accused of an offense punishable by imprisonment without first, by addressing the defendant personally in open court, informing him of and determining that he understands the following:

(1) the nature of the charge;

(2) the minimum and maximum sentence prescribed by law, including, when applicable, the penalty to which the defendant may be subjected because of prior convictions or consecutive sentences; and

(3) that he has a right to counsel and, if he is indigent, to have counsel appointed for him by the court.

(b) Transcript. The proceedings required by this rule to be in open court shall be taken verbatim, and upon order of the trial court transcribed, filed and made a part of the common law record.

Rule 402. Pleas of Guilty or Stipulations Sufficient to Convict In hearings on pleas of guilty, or in any case in which the defense offers to stipulate that the evidence is sufficient to convict, there must be substantial compliance with the following:

(a) Admonitions to Defendant. The court shall not accept a plea of guilty or a stipulation that the evidence is sufficient to convict without first, by addressing the defendant personally in open court, informing him or her of and determining that he or she understands the following:

(1) the nature of the charge;
(2) the minimum and maximum sentence prescribed by law, including, when applicable, the penalty to which the defendant may be subjected because of prior convictions or consecutive sentences;
(3) that the defendant has the right to plead not guilty, or to persist in that plea if it has already been made, or to plead guilty; and
(4) that if he or she pleads guilty there will not be a trial of any kind, so that by pleading guilty he or she waives the right to a trial by jury and the right to be confronted with the witnesses against him or her; or that by stipulating the evidence is sufficient to convict, he or she waives the right to a trial by jury and the right to be confronted with any witnesses against him or her who have not testified.

(b) Determining Whether the Plea is Voluntary. The court shall not accept a plea of guilty without first determining that the plea is voluntary. If the tendered plea is the result of a plea agreement, the agreement shall be stated in open court. The court, by questioning the defendant personally in open court, shall confirm the terms of the plea agreement, or that there is no agreement, and shall determine whether any force or threats or any promises, apart from a plea agreement, were used to obtain the plea.

(c) Determining Factual Basis for Plea. The court shall not enter final judgment on a plea of guilty without first determining that there is a factual basis for the plea.

(d) Plea Discussions and Agreements. When there is a plea discussion or plea agreement, the following provisions, in addition to the preceding paragraph of this rule, shall apply:

(1) The trial judge shall not initiate plea discussions. Upon request by the defendant and with the agreement of the prosecutor, the trial judge may participate in plea discussions. Prior to participating in the plea discussions, the trial judge shall admonish the defendant and inquire as to the defendant's understanding of the following:

That the defendant's attorney has requested that the trial judge participate in the conference to determine whether or not the charge(s) which is/are pending against the defendant can be resolved by a plea of guilty;

That during the course of the conference the prosecutor will be present and advise the judge of the facts of the case as contained in the police reports or conversations with witnesses, that the defendant's attorney will also be present and will advise the judge of any information the defendant may have concerning the circumstances which led to the defendant's arrest in the case.

That without the conference, the judge would not learn about this information unless the case proceeded to trial.

That the judge will also learn whether the defendant has a prior criminal history, his or her driving record, whether the defendant has any alcohol or drug problem, the defendant's work history, family situation, and other things which would bear on what, if any punishment should be imposed upon the defendant as a result of his or her plea of guilty to one or more of these charges. That these are things that the judge would not learn about unless the case went to trial and the defendant was found guilty.
That at the end of the conference, the judge may make a recommendation as to what an appropriate sentence would be.

That the defendant or the prosecutor is free to accept or reject the judge's recommendation. However, if the defendant rejects the judge's recommendation and he or she wishes to have a trial on the charges, the defendant may not obtain another judge solely on the basis that the judge participated in the conference and is aware of the facts and circumstances surrounding the incident as well as the defendant's background. This means that the defendant will be waiving his or her right to request a substitution of judge based upon the judge's knowledge of the case.

That knowing all of these things the defendant still wishes that the judge participate in this conference.

(2) If a tentative plea agreement has been reached by the parties which contemplates entry of a plea of guilty in the expectation that a specified sentence will be imposed or that other charges before the court will be dismissed, the trial judge may permit, upon request of the parties, the disclosure to him or her of the tentative agreement and the reasons therefore in advance of the tender of the plea. At the same time ~~he~~ the trial judge may also receive, with the consent of the defendant, evidence in aggravation or mitigation. The judge may then indicate to the parties whether he or she will concur in the proposed disposition; and if ~~he~~ the judge has not yet received evidence in aggravation or mitigation, he or she may indicate that his or her concurrence is conditional on that evidence being consistent with the representations made ~~to him~~. If ~~he~~ the judge has indicated his or her concurrence or conditional concurrence, ~~he~~ the judge shall so state in open court at the time the agreement is stated as required by paragraph (b) of this rule. If the defendant thereupon pleads guilty, but the trial judge later withdraws his or her concurrence or conditional concurrence, the judge shall so advise the parties and then call upon the defendant either to affirm or to withdraw his or her plea of guilty. If the defendant thereupon withdraws his or her plea, the trial judge shall recuse himself or herself.

(3) If the parties have not sought or the trial judge has declined to give his or her concurrence or conditional concurrence to a plea agreement, the judge shall inform the defendant in open court at the time the agreement is stated as required by paragraph (b) of this rule that the court is not bound by the plea agreement, and that if the defendant persists in his or her plea the disposition may be different from that contemplated by the plea agreement.

(e) Transcript. In cases in which the defendant is charged with a crime punishable by imprisonment in the penitentiary, the proceedings required by this rule to be in open court shall be taken verbatim, and upon order of the trial court transcribed, filed, and made a part of the common law record.

(f) Plea Discussions, Plea Agreements, Pleas of Guilty Inadmissible Under Certain Circumstances. If a plea discussion does not result in a plea of guilty, or if a plea of guilty is not accepted or is withdrawn, or if judgment on a plea of guilty is reversed on direct or collateral review, neither the plea discussion nor any resulting agreement, plea, or judgment shall be admissible against the defendant in any criminal proceeding.

Plea negotiations, Pleas of Guilty and Stipulated Dispositions

Plea negotiations. Since fully 90% of the criminal cases filed are resolved by plea negotiation process, the method of presenting pleas needs to be well organized and predictable. 715 ILCS 5/113-4(c) provides that the court must explain the potential consequences of a plea, including the maximum possible penalty. However, Illinois Supreme Court Rule 402 details the admonishments and waivers that must be made on the court's record of proceedings for a plea to be accepted.

Improper admonishments. Trial courts must comply with Illinois law in handling guilty pleas. If a judge accepts a guilty plea and enters a judgment when there has not been substantial compliance with both procedural and substantive law, the judgment of conviction can be declared void. In *People v. White* 2011 IL 109616 (Ill. S. Ct. 2011), the defendant pled guilty to murder and received a sentence of 28 years imprisonment, however, the factual basis presented during the plea procedure identified the defendant as having been armed with a firearm during the crime, requiring a mandatory 15 year consecutive enhancement. The Illinois Supreme Court held that the judgment of conviction should be vacated, noting that the factual basis for the plea demonstrated the mandatory sentencing enhancement applied and that since the defendant was not admonished about that punishment, and the entire plea agreement was void. In *People v. Snyder* 2011 IL 111382 (Ill. S. Ct. 2011), the failure to admonish a defendant about the potential of restitution would require vacating a judgment based on a partial plea agreement.

Rule 402A. Admissions or Stipulations in Proceedings to Revoke Probation, Conditional Discharge or Supervision. in proceedings to revoke probation, conditional discharge or supervision in which the defendant admits to a violation of probation, conditional discharge or supervision, or offers to stipulate that the evidence is sufficient to revoke probation, conditional discharge or supervision, there must be substantial compliance with the following.

(a) Admonitions to Defendant. The court shall not accept an admission to a violation, or a stipulation that the evidence is sufficient to revoke, without first addressing the defendant personally in open court, and informing the defendant of and determining that the defendant understands the following:

(1) the specific allegations in the petition to revoke probation, conditional discharge or supervision;

(2) that the defendant has the right to a hearing with defense counsel present, and the right to appointed counsel if the defendant is indigent and the underlying offense is punishable by imprisonment;>

(3) that at the hearing, the defendant has the right to confront and cross-examine adverse witnesses and to present witnesses and evidence in his or her behalf;

(4) that at the hearing, the State must prove the alleged violation by a preponderance of the evidence;

(5) that by admitting to a violation, or by stipulating that the evidence is sufficient to revoke, there will not be a hearing on the petition to revoke probation, conditional discharge or supervision, so that by admitting to a violation, or by stipulating that the evidence is sufficient to revoke, the defendant waives the right to a hearing and the right to confront and cross-examine adverse witnesses, and the right to present witnesses and evidence in his or her behalf; and

(6) the sentencing range for the underlying offense for which the defendant is on probation, conditional discharge or supervision.

(b) Determining Whether Admission Is Voluntary. The court shall not accept an admission to a violation, or a stipulation sufficient to revoke without first determining that the defendant's admission is voluntary and not made on the basis of any coercion or promise. If the admission or tendered stipulation is the result of an agreement as to the disposition of the defendant's case, the agreement shall be stated in open court. The court, by questioning the defendant personally in open court, shall confirm the terms of the agreement, or that there is no agreement, and shall determine whether any coercion or promises, apart from an agreement as to the disposition of the defendant's case, were used to obtain the admission.

(c) Determining Factual Basis for Admission. The court shall not revoke probation, conditional discharge or supervision on an admission or a stipulation without first determining that there is a factual basis for the defendant's admission or stipulation.
(d) Application of Rule 402. The provisions of Rules 402(d), (e), and (f) shall apply to proceedings on a petition to revoke probation, conditional discharge or supervision.

Rule 403. Pleas and Waivers by Persons Under 18 A person under the age of 18 years shall not, except in cases in which the penalty is by fine only, be permitted to enter a plea of guilty or to waive trial by jury, unless he is represented by counsel in open court.

Rules 404-410. Reserved

Part B – Discovery
Rules 411 - 415, 417

Rule 411. Applicability of Discovery Rules
These rules shall be applied in all criminal cases wherein the accused is charged with an offense for which, upon conviction, he might be imprisoned in the penitentiary. If the accused is charged with an offense for which, upon conviction, he might be sentenced to death, these rules shall be applied to the separate sentencing hearing provided for in section 9-1(d) of the Criminal Code of 1961 (720 ILCS 5/9-1(d)). they shall become applicable following indictment or information and shall not be operative prior to or in the course of any preliminary hearing.

Rule 412. Disclosure to Accused
(a) Except as is otherwise provided in these rules as to matters not subject to disclosure and protective orders, the State shall, upon written motion of defense counsel, disclose to defense counsel the following material and information within its possession or control:

(i) the names and last known addresses of persons whom the State intends to call as witnesses, together with their relevant written or recorded statements, memoranda containing substantially verbatim reports of their oral statements, and a list of memoranda reporting or summarizing their oral statements. Upon written motion of defense counsel memoranda reporting or summarizing oral statements shall be examined by the court *in camera* and if found to be substantially verbatim reports of oral statements shall be disclosed to defense counsel;

(ii) any written or recorded statements and the substance of any oral statements made by the accused or by a codefendant, and a list of witnesses to the making and acknowledgment of such statements;

(iii) a transcript of those portions of grand jury minutes containing testimony of the accused and relevant testimony of persons whom the prosecuting attorney intends to call as witnesses at the hearing or trial;

(iv) any reports or statements of experts, made in connection with the particular case, including results of physical or mental examinations and of scientific tests, experiments, or comparisons, and a statement of qualifications of the expert;

(v) any books, papers, documents, photographs or tangible objects which the prosecuting attorney intends to use in the hearing or trial or which were obtained from or belong to the accused; and

(vi) any record of prior criminal convictions, which may be used for impeachment, of persons whom the State intends to call as witnesses at the hearing or trial.
If the State has obtained from the defendant, pursuant to Rule 413(d), information regarding defenses the defendant intends to make, it shall provide to defendant not less than 7 days before the date set for the hearing or trial, or at such other time as the court may direct, the names

and addresses of witnesses the State intends to call in rebuttal, together with the information required to be disclosed in connection with other witnesses by subdivisions (i), (iii), and (vi), above, and a specific statement as to the substance of the testimony such witnesses will give at the trial of the cause.

(b) The State shall inform defense counsel if there has been any electronic surveillance (including wiretapping) of conversations to which the accused was a party, or of his premises.

(c) Except as is otherwise provided in these rules as to protective orders, the State shall disclose to defense counsel any material or information within its possession or control which tends to negate the guilt of the accused as to the offense charged or which would tend to reduce his punishment therefore. the State shall make a good-faith effort to specifically identify by description or otherwise any material disclosed pursuant to this section based upon the information available to the State at the time the material is disclosed to the defense. at trial, the defendant may not offer evidence or otherwise communicate to the trier of fact the State's identification of any material or information as tending to negate the guilt of the accused or reduce his punishment.

(d) The State shall perform its obligations under this rule as soon as practicable following the filing of a motion by defense counsel.

(e) The State may perform these obligations in any manner mutually agreeable to itself and defense counsel or by:

(i) notifying defense counsel that material and information, described in general terms, may be inspected, obtained, tested, copied, or photographed, during specified reasonable times; and

(ii) making available to defense counsel at the time specified such material and information, and suitable facilities or other arrangements for inspection, testing, copying and photographing of such material and information.

(f) The State should ensure that a flow of information is maintained between the various investigative personnel and its office sufficient to place within its possession or control all material and information relevant to the accused and the offense charged.

(g) Upon defense counsel's request and designation of material or information which would be discoverable if in the possession or control of the State, and which is in the possession or control of other governmental personnel, the State shall use diligent good-faith efforts to cause such material to be made available to defense counsel; and if the State's efforts are unsuccessful and such material or other governmental personnel are subject to the jurisdiction of the court, the court shall issue suitable subpoenas or orders to cause such material to be made available to defense counsel.

(h) Discretionary Disclosures. Upon a showing of materiality to the preparation of the defense, and if the request is reasonable, the court, in its discretion, may require disclosure to defense counsel of relevant material and information not covered by this rule.

(i) Denial of Disclosure. The court may deny disclosure authorized by this rule and Rule 413 if it finds that there is substantial risk to any person of physical harm, intimidation, bribery, economic reprisals, or unnecessary annoyance or embarrassment resulting from such disclosure which outweighs any usefulness of the disclosure to counsel.

(j) Matters Not Subject to Disclosure.
(i) *Work Product.* Disclosure under this rule and Rule 413 shall not be required of legal research or of records, correspondence, reports or memoranda to the extent that they contain the opinions, theories or conclusions of the State or members of its legal or investigative staffs, or of defense counsel or his staff.

(ii) *Informants.* Disclosure of an informant's identity shall not be required where his identity is a prosecution secret and a failure to disclose will not infringe the constitutional rights of the accused. Disclosure shall not be denied hereunder of the identity of witnesses to be produced at a hearing or trial.

(iii) *National Security.* Disclosure shall not be required where it involves a substantial risk of grave prejudice to national security and where a failure to disclose will not infringe the constitutional rights of the accused. Disclosure shall not thus be denied hereunder regarding witnesses or material to be produced at a hearing or trial.

Rule 413. Disclosure to Prosecution
(a) The Person of the Accused. Notwithstanding the initiation of judicial proceedings, and subject to constitutional limitations, a judicial officer may require the accused, among other things, to:

(i) appear in a lineup;

(ii)speak for identification by witnesses to an offense;

(iii) be fingerprinted;

(iv) pose for photographs not involving reenactment of a scene;

(v) try on articles of clothing;

(vi) permit the taking of specimens of material under his fingernails;

(vii) permit the taking of samples of his blood, hair and other materials of his body which involve no unreasonable intrusion thereof;

(viii) provide a sample of his handwriting; and
(ix) submit to a reasonable physical or medical inspection of his body.

(b) Whenever the personal appearance of the accused is required for the foregoing purposes, reasonable notice of the time and place of such appearance shall be given by the State to the accused and his counsel, who shall have the right to be present. Provision may be made for appearances for such purposes in an order admitting the accused to bail or providing for his release.

(c) Medical and Scientific Reports. Subject to constitutional limitations, the trial court shall, on written motion, require that the State be informed of, and permitted to inspect and copy or photograph, any reports or results, or testimony relative thereto, of physical or mental examinations or of scientific tests, experiments or comparisons, or any other reports or statements of experts which defense counsel has in his possession or control, including a statement of the qualifications of such experts, except that those portions of reports containing statements made by the defendant may be withheld if defense counsel does not intent to use any of the material contained in the report at a hearing or trial.

(d) Defenses. Subject to constitutional limitations and within a reasonable time after the filing of a written motion by the State, defense counsel shall inform the State of any defenses which he intends to make at a hearing or trial and shall furnish the State with the following material and information within his possession or control:

(i) the names and last known addresses of persons he intends to call as witnesses, together with their relevant written or recorded statements, including memoranda reporting or summarizing their oral statements, and record of prior criminal convictions known to him; and

(ii) any books, papers, documents, photographs, or tangible objects he intends to use as evidence or for impeachment at a hearing or trial;

(iii) and if the defendant intends to prove an alibi, specific information as to the place where he maintains he was at the time of the alleged offense.

(e) Additional Disclosure. Upon a showing of materiality, and if the request is reasonable, the court in its discretion may require disclosure to the State of relevant material and information not covered by this rule.

Rule 414. Evidence Depositions
(a) If it appears to the court in which a criminal charge is pending that the deposition of any person other than the defendant is necessary for the preservation of relevant testimony because of the substantial possibility it would be unavailable at the time of hearing or trial, the court may, upon motion and notice to both parties and their counsel, order the taking of such person's deposition under oral examination or written questions for use as evidence at a hearing or trial.

(b) The taking of depositions shall be in accordance with rules providing for the taking of depositions in civil cases, and the order for the taking of a deposition may provide that any designated books, papers, documents or tangible objects, not privileged, be produced at the same time and place.

(c) If a witness is committed for failure to execute a recognizance to appear to testify at a hearing or trial, the court, on written motion of the witness and upon notice to the State and defense counsel, may order that his deposition be taken, and after the deposition has been subscribed, the court may discharge the witness.

(d) Rule 207--Signing and Filing Depositions--shall apply to the signing and filing of depositions taken pursuant to this rule.
(e) The defendant and defense counsel shall have the right to confront and cross-examine any witness whose deposition is taken. The defendant and defense counsel may waive such right in writing, filed with the clerk of the court.

(f) If the defendant is indigent, all costs of taking depositions shall be paid by the county wherein the criminal charge is initiated. If the defendant is not indigent the costs shall be allocated as in civil cases.

Rule 415. Regulation of Discovery
(a) Investigations Not to be Impeded. Except as is otherwise provided as to matters not subject to disclosure and protective orders, neither the counsel for the parties nor other prosecution or defense personnel shall advise persons having relevant material or information (except the accused) to refrain from discussing the case with opposing counsel or showing opposing counsel any relevant material, nor shall they otherwise impede opposing counsel's investigation of the case.

(b) Continuing Duty to Disclose. If, subsequent to compliance with these rules or orders pursuant thereto, a party discovers additional material or information which is subject to disclosure, he shall promptly notify the other party or his counsel of the existence of such additional material, and if the additional material or information is discovered during trial, the court shall also be notified.

(c) Custody of Materials. Any materials furnished to an attorney pursuant to these rules shall remain in his exclusive custody and be used only for the purposes of conducting his side of the case, and shall be subject to such other terms and conditions as the court may provide.

(d) Protective Orders. Upon a showing of cause, the court may at any time order that specified disclosures be restricted or deferred, or make such other order as is appropriate, provided that all material and information to which a party is entitled must be disclosed in time to permit counsel to make beneficial use thereof.

(e) Excision. When some parts of certain material are discoverable under these rules, and other parts not discoverable, as much of the material should be disclosed as is consistent with the rules. Excision of certain material and disclosure of the balance is preferable to withholding the whole. Material excised pursuant to judicial order shall be sealed, impounded and preserved in the records of the court, to be made available to the reviewing court in the event of an appeal.

(f) In Camera Proceedings. Upon request of any person, the court may permit any showing of cause for denial or regulation of disclosures, or portion of such showing, to be made *in camera*. A record shall be made of such proceedings. If the court enters an order granting relief following a showing *in camera*, the entire record of such showing shall be sealed, impounded, and preserved in the records of the court, to be made available to the reviewing court in the event of an appeal.

(g) Sanctions.

(i) If at any time during the course of the proceedings it is brought to the attention of the court that a party has failed to comply with an applicable discovery rule or an order issued pursuant thereto, the court may order such party to permit the discovery of material and information not previously disclosed, grant a continuance, exclude such evidence, or enter such other order as it deems just under the circumstances.

(ii) Willful violation by counsel of an applicable discovery rule or an order issued pursuant thereto may subject counsel to appropriate sanctions by the court.

Rule 417. DNA Evidence (a) Statement of Purpose. This rule is promulgated to produce uniformly sufficient information to allow a proper, well-informed determination of the admissibility of DNA evidence and to insure that such evidence is presented competently and intelligibly. The rule is designed to provide a minimum standard for compliance concerning DNA evidence, and is not intended to limit the production and discovery of material information.

(b) Obligation to Produce. In all felony prosecutions, post-trial and post-conviction proceedings, the proponent of the DNA evidence, whether prosecution or defense, shall provide or otherwise make available to the adverse party all relevant materials, including, but not limited to the following:

(i) Copies of the case file including all reports, memoranda, notes, phone logs, contamination records, and data relating to the testing performed in the case.

(ii) Copies of any autoradiographs, lumigraphs, DQ Alpha Polymarker strips, PCR gel photographs and electropherogams, tabular data, electronic files and other data needed for full evaluation of DNA profiles produced and an opportunity to examine the originals, if requested.

(iii) Copies of any records reflecting compliance with quality control guidelines or standards employed during the testing process utilized in the case.

(iv) Copies of DNA laboratory procedure manuals, DNA testing protocols, DNA quality assurance guidelines or standards, and DNA validation studies.

(v) Proficiency testing results, proof of continuing professional education, current curriculum vitae and job description for examiners, or analysts and technicians involved in the testing and analysis of DNA evidence in the case.

(vi) Reports explaining any discrepancies in the testing, observed defects or laboratory errors in the particular case, as well as the reasons for those and the effects thereof.

(vii) Copies of all chain of custody documents for each item of evidence subjected to DNA testing.

(viii) A statement by the testing laboratory setting forth the method used to calculate the statistical probabilities in the case.

(ix) Copies of the allele frequencies or database for each locus examined.

(x) A list of all commercial or in-house software programs used in the DNA testing, including the name of the software program, manufacturer and version used in the case.

(xi) Copies of all DNA laboratory audits relating to the laboratory performing the particular tests.

Part C – Trials
Rules 431 – 451

Rule 431. Voir Dire Examination
(a) The court shall conduct *voir dire* examination of prospective jurors by putting to them questions it thinks appropriate, touching upon their qualifications to serve as jurors in the case at trial. The court may permit the parties to submit additional questions to it for further inquiry if it thinks they are appropriate and shall permit the parties to supplement the examination by such direct inquiry as the court deems proper for a reasonable period of time depending upon the length of examination by the court, the complexity of the case, and the nature of the charges. Questions shall not directly or indirectly concern matters of law or instructions. The court shall acquaint prospective jurors with the general duties and responsibilities of jurors.

(b) The court shall ask each potential juror, individually or in a group, whether that juror understands and accepts the following principles:
(1) that the defendant is presumed innocent of the charge(s) against him or her;

(2) that before a defendant can be convicted the State must prove the defendant guilty beyond a reasonable doubt;

(3) that the defendant is not required to offer any evidence on his or her own behalf; and

(4) that the defendant's failure to testify cannot be held against him or her; however, no inquiry of a prospective juror shall be made into the defendant's failure to testify when the defendant objects.

The court's method of inquiry shall provide each juror an opportunity to respond to specific questions concerning the principles set out in this section.

Rule 432. Opening Statements. Opening statements in criminal cases are governed by Rule 235.

Rule 433. Impeachment of Witnesses; Hostile Witnesses. the impeachment of witnesses and the examination of hostile witnesses in criminal cases is governed by Rule 238.

Rule 434. Jury Selection
(a) Impaneling Juries. In criminal cases the parties shall pass upon and accept the jury in panels of four, commencing with the State, unless the court, in its discretion, directs otherwise, and alternate jurors shall be passed upon separately.

(b) Names and Addresses of Prospective Jurors. Upon request, the parties shall be furnished with a list of prospective jurors with their addresses, if known.

(c) Challenging Prospective Jurors for Cause. Each party may challenge jurors for cause. If a prospective juror has a physical impairment, the court shall consider such prospective juror's ability to perceive and appreciate the evidence when considering a challenge for cause.

(d) Peremptory Challenges. A defendant tried alone shall be allowed 14 peremptory challenges in a capital case, 7 in a case in which the punishment may be imprisonment in the penitentiary, and 5 in all other cases; except that, in a single trial of more than one defendant, each defendant shall be allowed 8 peremptory challenges in a capital case, 5 in a case in which the punishment may be imprisonment in the penitentiary, and 3 in all other cases. If several charges against a defendant or defendants are consolidated for trial, each defendant shall be allowed peremptory challenges upon one charge only, which single charge shall be the charge against that defendant authorizing the greatest maximum penalty. The State shall be allowed the same number of peremptory challenges as all of the defendants.

(e) Selection of Alternate Jurors. After the jury is impaneled and sworn the court may direct the selection of alternate jurors, who shall take the same oath as the regular jurors. Each party shall have one additional peremptory challenge for each alternate juror. If before the final submission of a cause a member of the jury dies or is discharged he shall be replaced by an alternate juror in the order of election.

Rules 435. Reserved.

Rule 436. Separation and Sequestration of Jury in Criminal Cases; Admonition by Court. (a) In criminal cases, either before or after submission of the cause to the jury for determination, the trial court may, in its discretion, keep the jury together in the charge of an officer of the court, or the court may allow the jurors to separate temporarily outside the presence of a court officer, overnight, on weekends, on holidays, or in emergencies.

(b) The jurors shall, whether permitted to separate or kept in charge of officers, be admonished by the trial court that it is their duty

(1) not to converse with anyone else on any subject connected with the trial until they are discharged;

(2) not to knowingly read or listen to outside comments or news accounts of the procedure until they are discharged;

(3) not to discuss among themselves any subject connected with the trial, or form or express any opinion on the cause until it is submitted to them for deliberation; and

(4) not to view the place where the offense was allegedly committed.

Rules 437-450. Reserved

Rule 451. Instructions (a) Use of IPI Criminal Instructions; Requirements of Other Instructions. Whenever Illinois Pattern Jury Instructions, Criminal (4th ed. 2000) (IPI Criminal 4th), contains an instruction applicable in a criminal case, giving due consideration to the facts and the governing law, and the court determines that the jury should be instructed on the subject, the IPI Criminal 4th instruction shall be used, unless the court determines that it does not accurately state the law. Whenever IPI Criminal 4th does not contain an instruction on a subject on which the court determines that the jury should be instructed, the instruction given on that subject should be simple, brief, impartial, and free from argument.

(b) Court's Instructions. At any time before or during the trial, the court may direct counsel to prepare designated instructions. Counsel shall comply with the direction, and copies of instructions so prepared shall be marked "Court's Instructions." Counsel may object at the conference on instructions to any instruction prepared at the court's direction, regardless of who prepared it, and the court shall rule on these objections as well as objections to other instructions. The grounds of the objections shall be particularly specified.

(c) Section 2-1107 of the Code of Civil Procedure to Govern. Except as otherwise provided in these rules, instructions in criminal cases shall be tendered, settled, and given in accordance with section 2-1107 of the Code of Civil Procedure, but substantial defects are not waived by failure to make timely objections thereto if the interests of justice require. The court shall instruct the jury after the arguments are completed, or, in its discretion, at the close of all the evidence.

(d) Procedure. The court shall be provided an original and a copy of each instruction, and a copy shall be delivered to each opposing counsel. In addition to numbering the copies and indicating who tendered them, as required by section 2-1107 of the Code of Civil Procedure, the copy shall contain a notation substantially as follows:
"IPI Criminal 4th No. _____" or "IPI Criminal No. _____ Modified" or "Not in IPI Criminal" as the case may be. All objections made at the conference and the rulings thereon shall be shown in the report of proceedings.

(e) Instructions Before Opening Statements. After the jury is selected and before opening statements, the court may orally instruct the jury as follows:

(i) On cautionary or preliminary matters, including, but not limited to, the burden of proof, the believability of witnesses, and the receipt of evidence for a limited purpose.

(ii) On the issue of substantive law applicable to the case, including, but not limited to, the elements of the offense. When requested by the defendant, the court may instruct the jury on the elements of an affirmative defense. Nothing in this rule is intended to eliminate the giving of written instructions at the close of the trial in accord with paragraph (c).

(f) Instructions During Trial. Nothing in the rule is intended to restrict the court's authority to give any appropriate instruction during the course of the trial.

(g) Proceedings When an Enhanced Sentence is Sought. When the death penalty is not being sought and the State intends, for the purpose of sentencing, to rely on one or more sentencing enhancement factors which are subject to the notice and proof requirements of section 111-3(c-5) of the Code of Criminal Procedure, the court may, within its discretion, conduct a unitary trial through verdict on the issue of guilt and on the issue of whether a sentencing enhancement factor exists. The court may also, within its discretion, upon motion of a party, conduct a bifurcated trial. In deciding whether to conduct such a bifurcated trial, the court must first hold a pretrial hearing to determine if proof of the sentencing enhancement factor is not relevant to the question of guilt or if undue prejudice outweighs the factor's probative value. Such bifurcated trial shall be conducted subject to the following:

(1) The court shall first conduct a trial through verdict on the issue of guilt under the procedures applicable to trials in other cases.

Rights of Crime Victims and Witnesses Act
725 ILCS 120/1 *et seq.*

§ 1. Short title. This Article I may be cited as the Rights of Crime Victims and Witnesses Act.

§ 2. The purpose of this Act is to implement, preserve and protect the rights guaranteed to crime victims by Article I, Section 8.1 of the Illinois Constitution to ensure that crime victims are treated with fairness and respect for their dignity and privacy throughout the criminal justice system and to increase the effectiveness of the criminal justice system by affording certain basic rights and considerations to the witnesses of violent crime who are essential to prosecution.

§ 3. The terms used in this Act, unless the context clearly requires otherwise, shall have the following meanings:

(a) "Crime victim" and "victim" mean

(1) a person physically injured in this State as a result of a violent crime perpetrated or attempted against that person or

(2) a person who suffers injury to or loss of property as a result of a violent crime perpetrated or attempted against that person or

(3) a single representative who may be the spouse, parent, child or sibling of a person killed as a result of a violent crime perpetrated against the person killed or the spouse, parent, child or sibling of any person granted rights under this Act who is physically or mentally incapable of exercising such rights, except where the spouse, parent, child or sibling is also the defendant or prisoner or

(4) any person against whom a violent crime has been committed or

(5) any person who has suffered personal injury as a result of a violation of Section 11-501 of the Illinois Vehicle Code, or of a similar provision of a local ordinance, or of Section 9-3 of the Criminal Code of 1961, as amended or

(6) in proceedings under the Juvenile Court Act of 1987, both parents, legal guardians, foster parents, or a single adult representative of a minor or disabled person who is a crime victim.

(b) "Witness" means any person who personally observed the commission of a violent crime and who will testify on behalf of the State of Illinois in the criminal prosecution of the violent crime.

(c) "Violent Crime" means any felony in which force or threat of force was used against the victim, or any offense involving sexual exploitation, sexual conduct or sexual penetration, or a violation of Section 11-20.1, 11-20.1B, or 11-20.3 of the Criminal Code of 1961, domestic battery, violation of an order of protection, stalking, or any misdemeanor which results in death or great bodily harm to the victim or any violation of Section 9-3 of the Criminal Code of 1961, or Section 11-501 of the Illinois Vehicle Code, or a similar provision of a local ordinance, if the violation resulted in personal injury or death, and includes any action committed by a juvenile that would be a violent crime if committed by an adult. For the purposes of this paragraph, "personal injury" shall include any Type A injury as indicated on the traffic accident report completed by a law enforcement officer that requires immediate professional attention in either a doctor's office or medical facility. A type A injury shall include severely bleeding wounds, distorted extremities, and injuries that require the injured party to be carried from the scene.

(d) "Sentencing Hearing" means any hearing where a sentence is imposed by the court on a convicted defendant and includes hearings conducted pursuant to Sections 5-6-4, 5-6-4.1, 5-7-2 and 5-7-7 of the Unified Code of Corrections except those cases in which both parties have agreed to the imposition of a specific sentence.

(e) "Court proceedings" includes the preliminary hearing, any hearing the effect of which may be the release of the defendant from custody or to alter the conditions of bond, the trial, sentencing hearing, notice of appeal, any modification of sentence, probation revocation hearings or parole hearings.

(f) "Concerned citizen" includes relatives of the victim, friends of the victim, witnesses to the crime, or any other person associated with the victim or prisoner.

§ 4. Rights of crime victims.

(a) Crime victims shall have the following rights:

(1) The right to be treated with fairness and respect for their dignity and privacy throughout the criminal justice process.

(2) The right to notification of court proceedings.

(3) The right to communicate with the prosecution.

(4) The right to make a statement to the court at sentencing.

(5) The right to information about the conviction, sentence, imprisonment and release of the accused.

(6) The right to the timely disposition of the case following the arrest of the accused.

(7) The right to be reasonably protected from the accused through the criminal justice process.

(8) The right to be present at the trial and all other court proceedings on the same basis as the accused, unless the victim is to testify and the court determines that the victim's testimony would be materially affected if the victim hears other testimony at the trial.

(9) the right to have present at all court proceedings, including proceedings under the Juvenile Court Act of 1987, subject to the admonition of the rules of confidentiality and subject to the rules of evidence, a victim-witness specialist, an advocate or other support person of the victim's choice.

(10) The right to restitution.

(b) A statement and explanation of the rights of crime victims set forth in paragraph (a) of this Section shall be given to a crime victim at the initial contact with the criminal justice system by the appropriate authorities and shall be conspicuously posted in all court facilities.

§ 4.5. Procedures to implement the rights of crime victims. To afford crime victims their rights, law enforcement, prosecutors, judges and corrections will provide information, as appropriate of the following procedures:

(a) At the request of the crime victim, law enforcement authorities investigating the case shall provide notice of the status of the investigation, except where the State's attorney determines that disclosure of such information would unreasonably interfere with the investigation, until such time as the alleged assailant is apprehended or the investigation is closed.

(b) The office of the State's Attorney:

(1) shall provide notice of the filing of information, the return of an indictment by which a prosecution for any violent crime is commenced, or the filing of a petition to adjudicate a minor as a delinquent for a violent crime;

(2) shall provide notice of the date, time, and place of trial;
(3) or victim advocate personnel shall provide information of social services and financial assistance available for victims of crime, including information of how to apply for these services and assistance;

(4) shall assist in having any stolen or other personal property held by law enforcement authorities for evidentiary or other purposes returned as expeditiously as possible, pursuant to the procedures set out in Section 115-9 of the Code of Criminal Procedure of 1963;

(5) or victim advocate personnel shall provide appropriate employer intercession services to ensure that employers of victims will cooperate with the criminal justice system in order to minimize an employee's loss of pay and other benefits resulting from court appearances;

(6) shall provide information whenever possible, of a secure waiting area during court proceedings that does not require victims to be in close proximity to defendant or juveniles accused of a violent crime, and their families and friends;

(7) shall provide notice to the crime victim of the right to have a translator present at all court proceedings and, in compliance with the federal Americans with Disabilities Act of 1990, the right to communications access through a sign language interpreter or by other means;

(8) in the case of the death of a person, which death occurred in the same transaction or occurrence in which acts occurred for which a defendant is charged with an offense, shall notify the spouse, parent, child or sibling of the decedent of the date of the trial of the person or persons allegedly responsible for the death;

(9) shall inform the victim of the right to have present at all court proceedings, subject to the rules of evidence, an advocate or other support person of the victim's choice, and the right to retain an attorney, at the victim's own expense, who, upon written notice filed with the clerk of the court and State's Attorney, is to receive copies of all notices, motions and court orders filed thereafter in the case, in the same manner as if the victim were a named party in the case;

(10) at the sentencing hearing shall make a good faith attempt to explain the minimum amount of time during which the defendant may actually be physically imprisoned. The Office of the State's Attorney shall further notify the crime victim of the right to request from the Prisoner Review Board information concerning the release of the defendant under subparagraph (d)(1) of this Section;

(11) shall request restitution at sentencing and shall consider restitution in any plea negotiation, as provided by law; and

(12) shall, upon the court entering a verdict of not guilty by reason of insanity, inform the victim of the notification services available from the Department of Human Services, including the statewide telephone number, under subparagraph (d)(2) of this Section.

(c) At the written request of the crime victim, the office of the State's Attorney shall:

(1) provide notice a reasonable time in advance of the following court proceedings: preliminary hearing, any hearing the effect of which may be the release of defendant from custody, or to alter the conditions of bond and the sentencing hearing. The crime victim shall also be notified of the cancellation of the court proceeding in sufficient time, wherever possible, to prevent an unnecessary appearance in court;

(2) provide notice within a reasonable time after receipt of notice from the custodian, of the release of the defendant on bail or personal recognizance or the release from detention of a minor who has been detained for a violent crime;

(3) explain in nontechnical language the details of any plea or verdict of a defendant, or any adjudication of a juvenile as a delinquent for a violent crime;

(4) where practical, consult with the crime victim before the Office of the State's Attorney makes an offer of a plea bargain to the defendant or enters into negotiations with the defendant concerning a possible plea agreement, and shall consider the written victim impact statement, if prepared prior to entering into a plea agreement;

(5) provide notice of the ultimate disposition of the cases arising from an indictment or an information, or a petition to have a juvenile adjudicated as a delinquent for a violent crime;

(6) provide notice of any appeal taken by the defendant and information on how to contact the appropriate agency handling the appeal;

(7) provide notice of any request for post-conviction review filed by the defendant under Article 122 of the Code of Criminal Procedure of 1963, and of the date, time and place of any hearing concerning the petition. Whenever possible, notice of the hearing shall be given in advance;

(8) forward a copy of any statement presented under Section 6 to the Prisoner Review Board to be considered by the Board in making its determination under subsection (b) of Section 3-3-8 of the Unified Code of Corrections.

(d) (1) The Prisoner Review Board shall inform a victim or any other concerned citizen, upon written request, of the prisoner's release on parole, mandatory supervised release, electronic detention, work release, international transfer or exchange, or by the custodian of the discharge of any individual who was adjudicated a delinquent for a violent crime from State custody and by the sheriff of the appropriate county of any such person's final discharge from county custody. The Prisoner Review Board, upon written request, shall provide to a victim or any other concerned citizen a recent photograph of any person convicted of a felony, upon his or her release from custody. The Prisoner Review Board, upon written request, shall inform a victim or any other concerned citizen when feasible at least 7 days prior to the prisoner's release on furlough of the times and dates of such furlough. Upon written request by the victim or any other concerned citizen, the State's Attorney shall notify the person once of the times and dates of release of a prisoner sentenced to periodic imprisonment. Notification shall be based on the most recent information as to victim's or other concerned citizen's residence or other location available to the notifying authority.

(2) When the defendant has been committed to the Department of Human Services pursuant to Section 5-2-4 or any other provision of the Unified Code of Corrections, the victim may request to be notified by the releasing authority of the defendant's furloughs, temporary release, or final discharge from State custody. The Department of Human Services shall establish and maintain a statewide telephone number to be used by victims to make notification requests under these provisions and shall publicize this telephone number on its website and to the State's Attorney of each county.

(3) In the event of an escape from State custody, the Department of Corrections or the Department of Juvenile Justice immediately shall notify the Prisoner Review Board of the escape and the Prisoner Review Board shall notify the victim. The notification shall be based upon the most recent information as to the victim's residence or other location available to the Board. When no such information is available, the Board shall make all reasonable efforts to obtain the information and make the notification. When the escapee is apprehended, the Department of Corrections or the Department of Juvenile Justice immediately shall notify the Prisoner Review Board and the Board shall notify the victim.

(4) The victim of the crime for which the prisoner has been sentenced shall receive reasonable written notice not less than 30 days prior to the parole interview and may submit, in writing, on film, videotape or other electronic means or in the form of a recording or in person at the parole interview or if a victim of a violent crime, by calling the toll-free number established in subsection (f) of this Section, information for consideration by the Prisoner Review Board.

The victim shall be notified within 7 days after the prisoner has been granted parole and shall be informed of the right to inspect the registry of parole decisions, established under subsection (g) of Section 3-3-5 of the Unified Code of Corrections. The provisions of this paragraph (4) are subject to the Open Parole Hearings Act.

(5) If a statement is presented under Section 6, the Prisoner Review Board shall inform the victim of any order of discharge entered by the Board pursuant to Section 3-3-8 of the Unified Code of Corrections.

(6) At the written request of the victim of the crime for which the prisoner was sentenced or the State's Attorney of the county where the person seeking parole was prosecuted, the Prisoner Review Board shall notify the victim and the State's Attorney of the county where the person seeking parole was prosecuted of the death of the prisoner if the prisoner died while on parole or mandatory supervised release.

(7) When a defendant who has been committed to the Department of Corrections, the Department of Juvenile Justice, or the Department of Human Services is released or discharged and subsequently committed to the Department of Human Services as a sexually violent person and the victim had requested to be notified by the releasing authority of the defendant's discharge from State custody, the releasing authority shall provide to the Department of Human Services such information that would allow the Department of Human Services to contact the victim.

(8) When a defendant has been convicted of a sex offense as defined in Section 2 of the Sex Offender Registration Act and has been sentenced to the Department of Corrections or the Department of Juvenile Justice, the Prisoner Review Board shall notify the victim of the sex offense of the prisoner's eligibility for release on parole, mandatory supervised release, electronic detention, work release, international transfer or exchange, or by the custodian of the discharge of any individual who was adjudicated a delinquent for a sex offense from State custody and by the sheriff of the appropriate county of any such person's final discharge from county custody. The notification shall be made to the victim at least 30 days, whenever possible, before release of the sex offender.

(e) The officials named in this Section may satisfy some or all of their obligations to provide notices and other information through participation in a statewide victim and witness notification system established by the Attorney General under Section 8.5 of this Act.

(f) To permit a victim of a violent crime to provide information to the Prisoner Review Board for consideration by the Board at a parole hearing of a person who committed the crime against the victim in accordance with clause (d)(4) of this Section or at a proceeding to determine the conditions of mandatory supervised release of a person sentenced to a determinate sentence or at a hearing on revocation of mandatory supervised release of a person sentenced to a determinate sentence, the Board shall establish a toll-free number that may be accessed by the victim of a violent crime to present that information to the Board.

§ 5. Rights of Witnesses. (a) Witnesses as defined in subsection (b) of Section 3 of this Act shall have the following rights:
(1) to be notified by the Office of the State's attorney of all court proceedings at which the witness' presence is required in a reasonable amount of time prior to the proceeding, and to be notified of the cancellation of any scheduled court proceeding in sufficient time to prevent an unnecessary appearance in court, where possible;

(2) to be provided with appropriate employer intercession services by the Office of the State's Attorney or the victim advocate personnel to ensure that employers of witnesses will cooperate with the criminal justice system in order to minimize an employee's loss of pay and other benefits resulting from court appearances;

(3) to be provided, whenever possible, a secure waiting area during court proceedings that does not require witnesses to be in close proximity to defendants and their families and friends;

(4) to be provided with notice by the Office of the State's Attorney, where necessary, of the right to have a translator present whenever the witness' presence is required and, in compliance with the federal Americans with Disabilities Act of 1990, to be provided with notice of the right to communications access through a sign language interpreter or by other means.

(b) At the written request of the witness, the witness shall:

(1) receive notice from the office of the State's attorney of any request for post-conviction review filed by the defendant under Article 122 of the Code of Criminal Procedure of 1963, and of the date, time, and place of any hearing concerning the petition for post-conviction review; whenever possible, notice of the hearing on the petition shall be given in advance;

(2) receive notice by the releasing authority of the defendant's discharge from State custody if the defendant was committed to the Department of Human Services under Section 5-2-4 or any other provision of the Unified Code of Corrections;

(3) receive notice from the Prisoner Review Board of the prisoner's escape from State custody, after the Board has been notified of the escape by the Department of Corrections or the Department of Juvenile Justice; when the escapee is apprehended, the Department of Corrections or the Department of Juvenile Justice shall immediately notify the Prisoner Review Board and the Board shall notify the witness;

(4) receive notice from the Prisoner Review Board of the prisoner's release on parole, electronic detention, work release or mandatory supervised release and of the prisoner's final discharge from parole, electronic detention, work release, or mandatory supervised release.

§ 6. Rights to present victim impact statement. (a) In any case where a defendant has been convicted of a violent crime or a juvenile has been adjudicated a delinquent for a violent crime and a victim of the violent crime or the victim's spouse, guardian, parent, grandparent, or other immediate family or household member is present in the courtroom at the time of the sentencing or the disposition hearing, the victim or his or her representative shall have the right and the victim's spouse, guardian, parent, grandparent, and other immediate family or household member upon his, her, or their request may be permitted by the court to address the court regarding the impact that the defendant's criminal conduct or the juvenile's delinquent conduct has had upon them and the victim. The court has discretion to determine the number of oral presentations of victim impact statements.

Any impact statement must have been prepared in writing in conjunction with the Office of the State's Attorney prior to the initial hearing or sentencing, before it can be presented orally or in writing at the sentencing hearing. In conjunction with the Office of the State's Attorney, a victim impact statement that is presented orally may be done so by the victim or the victim's spouse, guardian, parent, grandparent, or other immediate family or household member or his, her, or their representative. At the sentencing hearing, the prosecution may introduce that evidence either in its case in chief or in rebuttal. The court shall consider any impact statement admitted along with all other appropriate factors in determining the sentence of the defendant or disposition of such juvenile.

(a-5) In any case where a defendant has been found not guilty by reason of insanity of a violent crime and a hearing has been ordered by the court under the Mental Health and Developmental Disabilities Code to determine if the defendant is:

(1) in need of mental health services on an inpatient basis;

(2) in need of mental health services on an outpatient basis; or

(3) not in need of mental health services and a victim of the violent crime or the victim's spouse, guardian, parent, grandparent, or other immediate family or household member is present in the courtroom at the time of the initial commitment hearing, the victim or his or her representative shall have the right and the victim's spouse, guardian, parent, grandparent, and other immediate family or household members upon their request may be permitted by the court to address the court regarding the impact that the defendant's criminal conduct has had upon them and the victim. The court has discretion to determine the number of oral presentations of victim impact statements.

Any impact statement must have been prepared in writing in conjunction with the Office of the State's Attorney prior to the initial commitment hearing, before it may be presented orally or in writing at the commitment hearing. In conjunction with the Office of the State's Attorney, a victim impact statement that is presented orally may be presented so by the victim or the victim's spouse, guardian, parent, grandparent, or other immediate family or household member or his or her representative. At the initial commitment hearing, the State's Attorney may introduce the statement either in its case in chief or in rebuttal. The court may only consider the impact statement along with all other appropriate factors in determining the:

(1) threat of serious physical harm poised by the respondent to himself or herself, or to another person;

(2) location of inpatient or outpatient mental health services ordered by the court, but only after complying with all other applicable administrative, rule, and statutory requirements;

(3) maximum period of commitment for inpatient mental health services; and

(4) conditions of release for outpatient mental health services ordered by the court.

(b) The crime victim has the right to prepare a victim impact statement and present it to the Office of the State's Attorney at any time during the proceedings. Any written victim impact statement submitted to the Office of the State's Attorney shall be considered by the court during its consideration of aggravation and mitigation in plea proceedings under Supreme Court Rule 402.

(c) This Section shall apply to any victims of a violent crime during any dispositional hearing under Section 5-705 of the Juvenile Court Act of 1987 which takes place pursuant to an adjudication or trial or plea of delinquency for any such offense.

§ 7. Responsibilities of victims and witnesses. Victims and witnesses shall have the following responsibilities to aid in the prosecution of violent crime:

(a) To make a timely report of the violent crime;

(b) To cooperate with law enforcement authorities throughout the investigation, prosecution, and trial;

(c) To testify at trial;

(d) To notify law enforcement authorities of any change of address.

§ 8. Privately operated crime victim and witness notification service.
A county sheriff with the approval of the county board in counties with 3,000,000 or fewer inhabitants, or a county department of corrections with the approval of the county board of commissioners and under the direction of the sheriff in counties with more than 3,000,000 inhabitants, and the office of the State's Attorney with the approval of the respective county board or county board of commissioners may contract with a private entity to operate a crime victim and witness notification service.

The county sheriff, the county department of corrections, and the State's attorney shall make available to the private entity the information to implement the notification procedure in a timely manner. The private entity shall immediately deliver the notification information to the requesting crime victim or witness according to the requirements of this Act for certain offenses determined by the county board upon the release or discharge of a defendant or prisoner in county custody.

The release of information to the private entity to implement the contract shall be limited to the extent necessary to comply with the provisions of this Act.

§ 8.5. Statewide victim and witness notification system. (a) The Attorney General may establish a crime victim and witness notification system to assist public officials in carrying out their duties to notify and inform crime victims and witnesses under Section 4.5 of this Act or under subsections (a), (a-2), and (a-3) of Section 120 of the Sex Offender Community Notification Law as the Attorney General specifies by rule. The system shall download necessary information from participating officials into its computers, where it shall be maintained, updated, and automatically transmitted to victims and witnesses by telephone, computer, or written notice.

(b) The Illinois Department of Corrections, the Department of Juvenile Justice, the Department of Human Services, and the Prisoner Review Board shall cooperate with the attorney General in the implementation of this Section and shall provide information as necessary to the effective operation of the system.

(c) State's attorneys, circuit court clerks, and local law enforcement and correctional authorities may enter into agreements with the Attorney General for participation in the system. The Attorney General may provide those who elect to participate with the equipment, software, or training necessary to bring their offices into the system.

(d) The provision of information to crime victims and witnesses through the Attorney General's notification system satisfies a given State or local official's corresponding obligation to provide the information.

(e) The Attorney General may provide for telephonic, electronic, or other public access to the database established under this Section.

(f) The Attorney General shall adopt rules as necessary to implement this Section. the rules shall include, but not be limited to, provisions for the scope and operation of any system the Attorney General may establish and procedures, requirements, and standards for entering into agreements to participate in the system and to receive equipment, software, or training.

(g) There is established in the Office of the Attorney General a Crime Victim and Witness Notification Advisory Committee consisting of those victims advocates, sheriffs, State's Attorneys, circuit court clerks, Illinois Department of Corrections, the Department of Juvenile Justice, and Prisoner Review Board employees that the Attorney General chooses to appoint. The Attorney General shall designate one member to chair the Committee.

(1) The Committee shall consult with and advise the attorney General as to the exercise of the Attorney General's authority under this Section, including, but not limited to:

(i) the design, scope, and operation of the notification system;

(ii) the content of any rules adopted to implement this Section;

(iii) the procurement of hardware, software, and support for the system, including choice of supplier or operator; and

(iv) the acceptance of agreements with and the award of equipment, software, or training to officials that seek to participate in the system.

(2) The Committee shall review the status and operation of the system and report any findings and recommendations for changes to the Attorney General and the General Assembly by November 1 of each year.

(3) The members of the Committee shall receive no compensation for their services as members of the Committee, but may be reimbursed for their actual expenses incurred in serving on the Committee.

§ 9. This Act does not limit any rights or responsibilities otherwise enjoyed by or imposed upon victims or witnesses of violent crime, nor does it grant any person a cause of action for damages or attorneys fees.

Any act of omission or commission by any law enforcement officer, circuit court clerk, or State's Attorney, by the Attorney General, Prisoner Review Board, Department of Corrections, the Department of Juvenile Justice, Department of Human Services, or other State agency, or private entity under contract pursuant to Section 8, or by any employee of any State agency or private entity under contract pursuant to Section 8 acting in good faith in rendering crime victim's assistance or otherwise enforcing this Act shall not impose civil liability upon the individual or entity or his or her supervisor or employer.

Nothing in this Act shall create a basis for vacating a conviction or a ground for appellate relief in any criminal case. Failure of the crime victim to receive notice as required, however, shall not deprive the court of the power to act regarding the proceeding before it; nor shall any such failure grant the defendant the right to seek a continuance.

Article 122 - Post Conviction Hearings
725 ILCS 5/122-1 *et seq.*

§ 122-1. Petition in the trial court. (a) Any person imprisoned in the penitentiary may institute a proceeding under this Article if the person asserts that:

(1) in the proceedings which resulted in his or her conviction there was a substantial denial of his or her rights under the Constitution of the United States or of the State of Illinois or both; or

(2) the death penalty was imposed and there is newly discovered evidence not available to the person at the time of the proceeding that resulted in his or her conviction that establishes a substantial basis to believe that the defendant is actually innocent by clear and convincing evidence.

(a-5) A proceeding under paragraph (2) of subsection (a) may be commenced within a reasonable period of time after the person's conviction notwithstanding any other provisions of this Article. In such a proceeding regarding actual innocence, if the court determines the petition is frivolous or is patently without merit, it shall dismiss the petition in a written order, specifying the findings of fact and conclusions of law it made in reaching its decision. Such order of dismissal is a final judgment and shall be served upon the petitioner by certified mail within 10 days of its entry.

(b) The proceeding shall be commenced by filing with the clerk of the court in which the conviction took place a petition (together with a copy thereof) verified by affidavit. Petitioner shall also serve another copy upon the State's Attorney by any of the methods provided in Rule 7 of the Supreme Court. The clerk shall docket the petition for consideration by the court pursuant to Section 122-2.1 upon his or her receipt thereof and bring the same promptly to the attention of the court.

(c) Except as otherwise provided in subsection (a-5), if the petitioner is under sentence of death and a petition for writ of certiorari is filed, no proceedings under this Article shall be commenced more than 6 months after the conclusion of proceedings in the United States Supreme Court, unless the petitioner alleges facts showing that the delay was not due to his or her culpable negligence. If a petition for certiorari is not filed, no proceedings under this Article shall be commenced more than 6 months from the date for filing a certiorari petition, unless the petitioner alleges facts showing that the delay was not due to his or her culpable negligence. When a defendant has a sentence other than death, no proceedings under this Article shall be commenced more than 6 months after the conclusion of proceedings in the United States Supreme Court, unless the petitioner alleges facts showing that the delay was not due to his or her culpable negligence. If a petition for certiorari is not filed, no proceedings under this Article shall be commenced more than 6 months from the date for filing a certiorari petition, unless the petitioner alleges facts showing that the delay was not due to his or her culpable negligence. If a defendant does not file a direct appeal, the post-conviction petition shall be filed no later than 3 years from the date of conviction, unless the petitioner alleges facts showing that the delay was not due to his or her culpable negligence. this limitation does not apply to a petition advancing a claim of actual innocence.

(d) A person seeking relief by filing a petition under this Section must specify in the petition or its heading that it is filed under this Section. A trial court that has received a petition complaining of a conviction or sentence that fails to specify in the petition or its heading that it is filed under this Section need not evaluate the petition to determine whether it could otherwise have stated some grounds for relief under this Article.

(e) A proceeding under this Article may not be commenced on behalf of a defendant who has been sentenced to death without the written consent of the defendant, unless the defendant, because of a mental or physical condition, is incapable of asserting his or her own claim.

(f) Only one petition may be filed by a petitioner under this Article without leave of the court. Leave of court may be granted only if a petitioner demonstrates cause for his or her failure to bring the claim in his or her initial post-conviction proceedings and prejudice results from that failure. For purposes of this subsection (f):

(1) a prisoner shows cause by identifying an objective factor that impeded his or her ability to raise a specific claim during his or her initial post-conviction proceedings; and

(2) a prisoner shows prejudice by demonstrating that the claim not raised during his or her initial post-conviction proceedings so infected the trial that the resulting conviction or sentence violated due process.

§ 122-2. Contents of petition. the petition shall identify the proceeding in which the petitioner was convicted, give the date of the rendition of the final judgment complained of, and clearly set forth the respects in which petitioner's constitutional rights were violated. The petition shall have attached thereto affidavits, records, or other evidence supporting its allegations or shall state why the same are not attached. The petition shall identify any previous proceedings that the petitioner may have taken to secure relief from his conviction. Argument and citations and discussion of authorities shall be omitted from the petition.

§ 122-2.1. [Examination of petition; order]. (a) Within 90 days after the filing and docketing of each petition, the court shall examine such petition and enter an order thereon pursuant to this Section.

(1) If the petitioner is under sentence of death and is without counsel and alleges that he is without means to procure counsel, he shall state whether or not he wishes counsel to be appointed to represent him. If appointment of counsel is so requested, the court shall appoint counsel if satisfied that the petitioner has no means to procure counsel.

(2) If the petitioner is sentenced to imprisonment and the court determines the petition is frivolous or is patently without merit, it shall dismiss the petition in a written order, specifying the findings of fact and conclusions of law it made in reaching its decision. Such order of dismissal is a final judgment and shall be served upon the petitioner by certified mail within 10 days of its entry.

(b) If the petition is not dismissed pursuant to this Section, the court shall order the petition to be docketed for further consideration in accordance with Sections 122-4 through 122-6. If the petitioner is under sentence of death, the court shall order the petition to be docketed for further consideration and hearing within one year of the filing of the petition. Continuances may be granted as the court deems appropriate.

(c) In considering a petition pursuant to this Section, the court may examine the court file of the proceeding in which the petitioner was convicted, any action taken by an appellate court in such proceeding and any transcripts of such proceeding.

§ 122-2.2. Intellectual disabilities and post-conviction relief. (a) In cases where no determination of intellectual disabilities was made and a defendant has been convicted of first-degree murder, sentenced to death, and is in custody pending execution of the sentence of death, the following procedures shall apply:

(1) Notwithstanding any other provision of law or rule of court, a defendant may seek relief from the death sentence through a petition for post-conviction relief under this Article alleging that the defendant was a person with an intellectual disability as defined in Section 114-15 at the time the offense was alleged to have been committed.

(2) The petition must be filed within 180 days of the effective date of this amendatory Act of the 93rd General Assembly or within 180 days of the issuance of the mandate by the Illinois Supreme court setting the date of execution, whichever is later.

(3) All other provisions of this Article governing petitions for post-conviction relief shall apply to a petition for post-conviction relief alleging intellectual disabilities.

§ 122-3. Waiver of claims. Any claim of substantial denial of constitutional rights not raised in the original or an amended petition is waived.

§ 122-4. Pauper Petitions. If the petition is not dismissed pursuant to Section 122-2.1, and alleges that the petitioner is unable to pay the costs of the proceeding, the court may order that the petitioner be permitted to proceed as a poor person and order a transcript of the proceedings delivered to petitioner in accordance with Rule of the Supreme court. If the petitioner is without counsel and alleges that he is without means to procure counsel, he shall state whether or not he wishes counsel to be appointed to represent him. If appointment of counsel is so requested, and the petition is not dismissed pursuant to Section 122-2.1, the court shall appoint counsel if satisfied that the petitioner has no means to procure counsel.

A petitioner who is a prisoner in an Illinois Department of Corrections facility who files a pleading, motion, or other filing that purports to be a legal document seeking post-conviction relief under this Article against the State, the Illinois Department of Corrections, the Prisoner Review Board, or any of their officers or employees in which the court makes a specific finding that the pleading, motion, or other filing that purports to be a legal document is frivolous shall not proceed as a poor person and shall be liable for the full payment of filing fees and actual court costs as provided in Article XXII of the Code of Civil Procedure. a Circuit Court or the Illinois Supreme Court may appoint the State appellate Defender to provide post-conviction representation in a case in which the defendant is sentenced to death. Any attorney assigned by the office of the State Appellate Defender to provide post-conviction representation for indigent defendants in cases in which a sentence of death was imposed in the trial court may, from time to time submit bills and time sheets to the Office of the State Appellate Defender for payment of services rendered and the Office of the State Appellate Defender shall pay bills from funds appropriated for this purpose in accordance with rules promulgated by the State Appellate Defender.

The court, at the conclusion of the proceedings upon receipt of a petition by the appointed counsel, shall determine a reasonable amount to be allowed an indigent defendant's counsel other than the Public Defender or the State Appellate Defender for compensation and reimbursement of expenditures necessarily incurred in the proceedings. The compensation shall not exceed $500 in each case, except that, in extraordinary circumstances, payment in excess of the limits herein stated may be made if the trial court certifies that the payment is necessary to provide fair compensation for protracted representation, and the amount is approved by the chief judge of the circuit. The court shall enter an order directing the county treasurer of the county where the case was tried to pay the amount thereby allowed by the court. The court may order the provisional payment of sums during the pendency of the cause.

§ 122-5. Proceedings on petition. Within 30 days after the making of an order pursuant to subsection (b) of Section 122-2.1, or within such further time as the court may set, the State shall answer or move to dismiss. In the event that a motion to dismiss is filed and denied, the State must file an answer within 20 days after such denial. No other or further pleadings shall be filed except as the court may order on its own motion or on that of either party.

The court may in its discretion grant leave, at any stage of the proceeding prior to entry of judgment, to withdraw the petition. The court may in its discretion make such order as to amendment of the petition or any other pleading, or as to pleading over, or filing further pleadings, or extending the time of filing any pleading other than the original petition, as shall be appropriate, just and reasonable and as is generally provided in civil cases.

§ 122-6. Disposition in trial court.
The court may receive proof by affidavits, depositions, oral testimony, or other evidence. In its discretion the court may order the petitioner brought before the court for the hearing. If the court finds in favor of the petitioner, it shall enter an appropriate order with respect to the judgment or sentence in the former proceedings and such supplementary orders as to rearraignment, retrial, custody, bail or discharge as may be necessary and proper.
§ **122-7.** Any final judgment entered upon such petition shall be reviewed in a manner pursuant to the rules of the Supreme Court.

Selected Provisions of the Code of Civil Procedure
Article 2 - Civil Practice
Part 14 - Post-Judgment
735 ILCS 5/2 – 1401

§ 2-1401. Relief from judgments.
(a) Relief from final orders and judgments, after 30 days from the entry thereof, may be had upon petition as provided in this Section. Writs of error *coram nobis* and *coram vobis*, bills of review and bills in the nature of bills of review are abolished. All relief heretofore obtainable and the grounds for such relief heretofore available, whether by any of the foregoing remedies or otherwise, shall be available in every case, by proceedings hereunder, regardless of the nature of the order or judgment from which relief is sought or of the proceedings in which it was entered. Except as provided in Section 6 of the Illinois Parentage Act of 1984, there shall be no distinction between actions and other proceedings, statutory or otherwise, as to availability of relief, grounds for relief or the relief obtainable.

(b) The petition must be filed in the same proceeding in which the order or judgment was entered but is not a continuation thereof. The petition must be supported by affidavit or other appropriate showing as to matters not of record. All parties to the petition shall be notified as provided by rule.

(c) Except as provided in Section 20b of the Adoption Act and Section 2-32 of the Juvenile Court Act of 1987 or in a petition based upon Section 116-3 of the Code of Criminal Procedure of 1963, the petition must be filed not later than 2 years after the entry of the order or judgment. Time during which the person seeking relief is under legal disability or duress or the ground for relief is fraudulently concealed shall be excluded in computing the period of 2 years.
(d) The filing of a petition under this Section does not affect the order or judgment, or suspend its operation.

(e) Unless lack of jurisdiction affirmatively appears from the record proper, the vacation or modification of an order or judgment pursuant to the provisions of this Section does not affect the right, title or interest in or to any real or personal property of any person, not a party to the original action, acquired for value after the entry of the order or judgment but before the filing of the petition, nor affect any right of any person not a party to the original action under any certificate of sale issued before the filing of the petition, pursuant to a sale based on the order or judgment.

(f) Nothing contained in this Section affects any existing right to relief from a void order or judgment, or to employ any existing method to procure that relief.

Article 10 - Habeas Corpus
735 ILCS 5/10 – 101 *et seq.*

§ 10-101. Action commenced by plaintiff. In all proceedings commenced under Article X of this Act, the name of the person seeking the relief afforded by this Article shall be set out as plaintiff without the use of the phrase "People ex rel." or "People on the relation of".

§ 10-102. Who may file. Every person imprisoned or otherwise restrained of his or her liberty, except as herein otherwise provided, may apply for habeas corpus in the manner provided in Article X of this Act, to obtain relief from such imprisonment or restraint, if it proves to be unlawful.

§ 10-103. Application. Application for the relief shall be made to the Supreme Court or to the circuit court of the county in which the person in whose behalf the application is made, is imprisoned or restrained, or to the circuit court of the county from which such person was sentenced or committed. Application shall be made by complaint signed by the person for whose relief it is intended, or by some person in his or her behalf, and verified by affidavit. Application for relief under this Article may not be commenced on behalf of a person who has been sentenced to death without the written consent of that person, unless the person, because of a mental or physical condition, is incapable of asserting his or her own claim.

§ **10-104. Substance of complaint.** The complaint shall state in substance:
1. That the person in whose behalf the relief is applied for is imprisoned or restrained of his or her liberty, and the place where - naming all the parties if they are known, or describing them if they are not known.

2. The cause or pretense of the restraint, according to the best knowledge and belief of the applicant, and that such person is not committed or detained by virtue of any process, or judgment, specified in Section 10-123 of this Act.
3. If the commitment or restraint is by virtue of any warrant or process, a copy thereof shall be annexed, or it shall be stated that by reason of such prisoner being removed or concealed before application, a demand of such copy could not be made, or that such demand was made, and the legal fees therefore tendered to the officer or person having such prisoner in his or her custody, and that such copy was refused.

§ **10-105. Copy of process.** Any sheriff or other officer or person having custody of any prisoner committed on any civil or criminal process of any court who shall neglect to give such prisoner a copy of the process or order of commitment by which he or she is imprisoned within 6 hours after demand made by the prisoner, or any one on behalf of the prisoner, shall forfeit to the prisoner or party affected not exceeding $500. This Section shall not apply to the Illinois Department of Corrections.

§ **10-106. Grant of relief - Penalty.** Unless it shall appear from the complaint itself, or from the documents thereto annexed, that the party can neither be discharged, admitted to bail nor otherwise relieved, the court shall forthwith award relief by habeas corpus.

Any judge empowered to grant relief by habeas corpus who shall corruptly refuse to grant the relief when legally applied for in a case where it may lawfully be granted, or who shall for the purpose of oppression unreasonably delay the granting of such relief shall, for every such offense, forfeit to the prisoner or party affected a sum not exceeding $1,000.

§ **10-107. Form of orders.** If the relief is allowed by an order of a court it shall be certified by the clerk under the seal of the court; if by a judge, it shall be under the judge's signature, and shall be directed to the person in whose custody or under whose restraint the prisoner is, and may be substantially in the following form:

The People of the State of Illinois, to the Sheriff of .... County (or, "to A B," as the case may be): You are hereby commanded to have the body of C D, imprisoned and detained by you, together with the time and cause of such imprisonment and detention by whatsoever name C D is called or charged, before .... court of .... County (or before E F, judge of, etc.), at, etc., immediately after being served with a certified copy of this order, to be dealt with according to law; and you are to deliver a certified copy of this order with a return thereon of your performance in carrying out this order.

§ **10-108. Indorsement.** With the intent that no officer or person to whom such order is directed may pretend ignorance thereof, every such order shall be indorsed with these words: "By the habeas corpus law."

§ **10-109. Subpoena-Service.** When the party has been committed upon a criminal charge, unless the court deems it unnecessary, a subpoena shall also be issued to summon the witnesses whose names have been endorsed upon the warrant of commitment, to appear before such court at the time and place when and where such order of habeas corpus is returnable, and it shall be the duty of the sheriff, or other officer to whom the subpoena is issued, to serve the same, if it is possible, in time to enable such witnesses to attend.

§ **10-110. Service of order.** The habeas corpus order may be served by the sheriff, coroner or any person appointed for that purpose by the court which entered the order; if served by a person not an officer, he or she shall have the same power, and be liable to the same penalty for non-performance of his or her duty, as though he or she were sheriff.

§ **10-111. Manner of service.** Service shall be made by leaving a copy of the order with the person to whom it is directed, or with any of his or her under officers who may be at the place where the prisoner is detained; or if he or she cannot be found, or has not the person imprisoned or restrained in custody, the service may be made upon any person who has the person in custody with the same effect as though he or she had been made a defendant therein.

§ **10-112. Expense involved.** When the person confined or restrained is in the custody of a civil officer, the court entering the order shall certify thereon the sum to be paid for the expense of bringing the person from the place of imprisonment, not exceeding 10 cents per mile, and the officer shall not be bound to obey it unless the sum so certified is paid or tendered to him or her, and security is given to pay the charges of carrying the party back if he or she should be remanded.

If the court is satisfied that the party so confined or restrained is a poor person and unable to pay such expense, then the court shall so state in the order, and in such case no tender or payment of expenses need be made or security given but the officer shall be bound to obey such order.

§ **10-113. Form of return.** The officer or person upon whom such order is served shall state in his or her return, plainly and unequivocally:

1. Whether he or she has or has not the party in his or her custody or control, or under his or her restraint, and if he or she has not, whether he or she has had the party in his or her custody or control, or under his or her restraint, at any and what time prior or subsequent to the date of the order.

2. If he or she has the party in his or her custody or control, or under his or her restraint, the authority and true cause of such imprisonment or restraint, setting forth the same in detail.

3. If the party is detained by virtue of any order, warrant or other written authority, a copy thereof shall be attached to the return, and the original shall be produced and exhibited on the return of the order to the court before whom the same is returnable.

4. If the person upon whom the order is served has had the party in his or her custody or control or under his or her restraint, at any time prior or subsequent to the date of the order but has transferred such custody or restraint to another, the return shall state particularly to whom, at what time, for what cause and by what authority such transfer took place. The return shall be signed by the person making the same, and except where such person is a sworn public officer and makes the return in his or her official capacity, it shall be verified by oath.

§ **10-114. Bringing of body.** The officer or person making the return, shall, at the same time, bring the body of the party, if in his or her custody or power or under his or her restraint, according to the command of the order unless prevented by the sickness or infirmity of the party.

§ **10-115. Sickness or infirmity.**
When, from the sickness or infirmity of the party, he or she cannot without danger, be brought to the place designated for the return of the order, that fact shall be stated in the return, and if it is proved to the satisfaction of the judge, he or she may proceed to the jail or other place where the party is confined, and there make an examination, or the judge may adjourn the same to such other time, or make such other order in the case as law and justice require.

§ **10-116. Neglect to obey order.**
If the officer or person upon whom such order is served refuses or neglects to obey the same, by producing the party named in the order and making a full and explicit return thereto within the time required by Article X of this Act, and no sufficient excuse is shown for such refusal or

neglect, the court before whom the order is returnable, upon proof of the service thereof, shall enforce obedience by attachment as for contempt, and the officer or person so refusing or neglecting shall forfeit to the party a sum not exceeding $500, and be incapable of holding office.

§ **10-117. Order in case of neglect.** The court may also, at the same time or afterwards, enter an order to the sheriff or other person to whom such attachment is directed, commanding him or her to bring forthwith before the court the party for whose benefit the habeas corpus order was entered, who shall thereafter remain in the custody of such sheriff, or other person, until the party is discharged, bailed or remanded, as the court directs.

§ **10-118. Proceedings in case of emergency.** Whenever it appears by the complaint, or by affidavit, that any one is illegally held in custody or restraint, and that there is good reason to believe that such person will be taken out of the jurisdiction of the court in which the application for a habeas corpus is made, or will suffer some irreparable injury before compliance with the order can be enforced, the court may enter an order directed to the sheriff or other proper officer, commanding him or her to take the prisoner thus held in custody or restraint, and forthwith bring him or her before the court to be dealt with according to law.

The court may also, if it is deemed necessary, order the apprehension of the person charged with causing the illegal restraint. The officer shall execute the order by bringing the person therein named before the court, and the like return and proceedings shall be had as in other orders of habeas corpus.

§ **10-119. Examination.** Upon the return of an order of habeas corpus, the court shall, without delay, proceed to examine the cause of the imprisonment or restraint, but the examination may be adjourned from time to time as circumstances require.

§ **10-120. Denial of allegations in return.** The party imprisoned or restrained may file a reply to the return and deny any of the material facts set forth in the return, and may allege any other facts that may be material in the case, which denial or allegation shall be on oath; and the court shall proceed promptly to examine the cause of the imprisonment or restraint, hear the evidence produced by any person interested or authorized to appear, both in support of such imprisonment or restraint and against it, and thereupon shall determine the matter according to law.

§ **10-121. Seeking wrong remedy not fatal.** Where relief is sought under Article X of this Act and the court determines, on motion directed to the pleadings, or on motion for summary judgment or upon trial, that the plaintiff has pleaded or established facts which entitle the plaintiff to relief but that the plaintiff has sought the wrong remedy, the court shall permit the pleadings to be amended, on just and reasonable terms, and the court shall grant the relief to which the plaintiff is entitled on the amended pleadings or upon the evidence.

In considering whether a proposed amendment is just and reasonable, the court shall consider the right of the defendant to assert additional defenses, to demand a trial by jury, to plead a counterclaim or third party complaint, and to order the plaintiff to take additional steps which were not required under the pleadings as previously filed.

§ **10-122. Amendments.** The return, as well as any denial or allegation, may be amended at any time by leave of the court.

§ **10-123. When prisoner not entitled to discharge.** No person shall be discharged under the provisions of this Act, if he or she is in custody:

1. By virtue of process of any court of the United States, in a case where such court has exclusive jurisdiction; or,

2. By virtue of a final judgment of any circuit court, or of any proceeding for the enforcement of such judgment, unless the time during which such party may be legally detained has expired; or,

3. For any treason, felony or other crime committed in any other state or territory of the United States, for which such person ought, by the Constitution and laws of the United States, to be delivered to the executive power of such state or territory.

§ 10-124. Causes for discharge when in custody on process of court. If it appears that the prisoner is in custody by virtue of process from any court legally constituted, he or she may be discharged only for one or more of the following causes:

1. Where the court has exceeded the limit of its jurisdiction, either as to the matter, place, sum or person.

2. Where, though the original imprisonment was lawful, nevertheless, by some act, omission or event which has subsequently taken place, the party has become entitled to be discharged.

3. Where the process is defective in some substantial form required by law.

4. Where the process, though in proper form, has been issued in a case or under circumstances where the law does not allow process to issue or orders to be entered for imprisonment or arrest.

5. Where, although in proper form, the process has been issued in a case or under circumstances unauthorized to issue or execute the same, or where the person having the custody of the prisoner under such process is not the person empowered by law to detain him or her.

6. Where the process appears to have been obtained by false pretense or bribery.

7. Where there is no general law, nor any judgment or order of a court to authorize the process if in a civil action, nor any conviction if in a criminal proceeding. No court, on the return of a habeas corpus, shall, in any other matter, inquire into the legality or justice of a judgment of a court legally constituted.

§ 10-125. New commitment. In all cases where the imprisonment is for a criminal, or supposed criminal matter, if it appears to the court that there is sufficient legal cause for the commitment of the prisoner, although such commitment may have been informally made, or without due authority, or the process may have been executed by a person not duly authorized, the court shall make a new commitment in proper form, and direct it to the proper officer, or admit the party to bail if the case is bailable. The court shall also, when necessary, take the recognizance of all material witnesses against the prisoner, as in other cases. The recognizances shall be in the form provided by law, and returned as other recognizances.
If any judge shall neglect or refuse to bind any such prisoner or witness by recognizance, or to return a recognizance when taken as hereinabove stated, he or she shall be guilty of a Class A misdemeanor in office, and be proceeded against accordingly.

§ 10-126. Remand. When any prisoner brought up on a habeas corpus is remanded to prison, it shall be the duty of the court remanding the prisoner to deliver to the sheriff, or other person to whose custody the prisoner is remanded, an order in writing, stating the cause of remanding the prisoner. If such prisoner obtains a second order of habeas corpus, it shall be the duty of such sheriff, or other person to whom the same is directed, to return therewith the order above stated; and if it appears that the prisoner was remanded for an offense adjudged not bailable, it shall be taken and received as conclusive, and the prisoner shall be remanded without further proceedings.

§ 10-127. Grant of habeas corpus.
It is not lawful for any court, on a second order of habeas corpus obtained by such prisoner, to discharge the prisoner, if he or she is clearly and specifically charged in the warrant of commitment with a criminal offense; but the court shall, on the return of such second order,

have power only to admit such prisoner to bail where the offense is bailable by law, or remand him or her to prison where the offense is not bailable, or being bailable, where such prisoner fails to give the bail required.

§ 10-128. Person discharged again imprisoned. No person who has been discharged by order of the court on a habeas corpus, shall be again imprisoned, restrained or kept in custody for the same cause, unless he or she is afterwards indicted for the same offense, nor unless by the legal order or process of the court wherein he or she is bound by recognizance to appear. The following shall not be deemed to be the same cause:

1. If, after a discharge for a defect of proof, or any material defect in the commitment, in a criminal case, the prisoner is again arrested on sufficient proof, and committed by legal process for the same offense.

2. If, in a civil action, the party has been discharged for any illegality in the judgment or process, and is afterwards imprisoned by legal process for the same cause of action.

3. Generally, whenever the discharge is ordered on account of the non-observance of any of the forms required by law, the party may be a second time imprisoned if the cause is legal and the forms required by law observed.

§ 10-129. Penalty for rearrest of person discharged.
Any person who, knowing that another has been discharged by order of a competent court on a habeas corpus, shall, contrary to the provisions of Article X of this Act, arrest or detain him or her again for the same cause which was shown on the return to such order, shall forfeit $500 for the first offense, and $1,000 for every subsequent offense.

§ 10-130. Prisoner not to be removed from county. To prevent any person from avoiding or delaying his or her trial, it shall not be lawful to remove any prisoner on habeas corpus under Article X of this Act out of the county in which he or she is confined, within 15 days next preceding the first day of the calendar month in which such person ought to be tried unless it is done to convey him or her into the county where the offense with which he or she stands charged is properly cognizable.

§ 10-131. Custody not to be changed. Any person being committed to any prison, or in the custody of any sheriff or other officer or person for any criminal or supposed criminal matter, shall not be removed therefrom into any other prison or custody, unless it is done by habeas corpus order or some other legal process or when it is expressly allowed by law.

If any person removes, or causes to be removed any prisoner so committed, except as above provided, he or she shall forfeit to the party affected a sum not exceeding $300.

§ 10-132. Avoidance of order - Punishment.
Any one having a person in his or her custody, or under his or her restraint, power or control, for whose relief an order of habeas corpus is entered, who, with intent to avoid the effect of such order, transfers such person to the custody or places him or her under the control of another, or conceals him or her, or changes the place of his or her confinement, with intent to avoid the operation of such order, or with intent to remove him or her out of the State, shall, for every such offense, be guilty of a Class 4 felony.

In any prosecution for the penalty incurred under this Section it shall not be necessary to show that the order of habeas corpus had been entered at the time of the removal, transfer or concealment therein mentioned, if it is proven that the acts therein forbidden were done with the intent to avoid the operation of such order.

§ 10-133. Penalties - How recovered.
All the pecuniary forfeitures incurred under this Act shall inure to the use of the party for whose benefit the order of habeas corpus was entered, and shall be sued for and recovered with costs, by the Attorney General or State's Attorney, in the name of the State, by complaint; and the

amount, when recovered, shall, without any deduction, be paid to the party entitled thereto.

§ 10-134. **No bar to civil damages.** The recovery of the penalties shall be no bar to a civil action for damages.

§ **10-135. Habeas corpus to testify.** The several courts having authority to grant relief by habeas corpus, may enter orders, when necessary, to bring before them any prisoner to testify, or to be surrendered in discharge of bail, or for trial upon any criminal charge lawfully pending in the same court or to testify in a criminal proceeding in another state as provided for by Section 2 of the "Uniform Act to secure the attendance of witnesses from within or without a state in criminal proceedings", approved July 23, 1959, as heretofore or hereafter amended; and the order may be directed to any county in the State, and there be served and returned by any officer to whom it is directed.

§ **10-136. Prisoner remanded or punished.** After a prisoner has given his or her testimony, or been surrendered, or his or her bail discharged, or he or she has been tried for the crime with which he or she is charged, he or she shall be returned to the jail or other place of confinement from which he or she was taken for that purpose.

If such prisoner is convicted of a crime punishable with death or imprisonment in the penitentiary, he or she may be punished accordingly; but in any case where the prisoner has been taken from the penitentiary, and his or her punishment is by imprisonment, the time of such imprisonment shall not commence to run until the expiration of the time of service under any former sentence.

§ **10-137. Contempt - Discharge.** Any person imprisoned for any contempt of court for the non-performance of any order or judgment for the payment of money, is entitled to relief by habeas corpus, and if it appears, on full examination of such person and such witnesses, and other evidence as may be adduced, that he or she is unable to comply with such order or judgment, or to endure the confinement, and that all persons interested in the order or judgment have had reasonable notice of the time and place of trial, the court may discharge him or her from imprisonment, but no such discharge shall operate to release the lien of such order or judgment, but the same may be enforced against the property of such person as other orders and judgments are enforced in civil cases.

Chapter 4 – Evidence in Illinois Courts
Illinois Rules of Evidence

Article I: General Provisions

Rule 101. Scope. these rules govern proceedings in the courts of Illinois to the extent and with the exceptions stated in Rule 1101. A statutory rule of evidence not in conflict with these rules or other rules adopted by the Supreme Court is effective unless superseded by rule or decision of the Supreme Court.

Rule 102. Purpose and Construction. these rules shall be construed to secure fairness in administration, elimination of unjustifiable expense and delay, and promotion of growth and development of the law of evidence to the end that the truth may be ascertained and proceedings justly determined.

Rule 103. Rulings on Evidence.
(a) *Effect of Erroneous Ruling.* Error may not be predicated upon a ruling which admits or excludes evidence unless a substantial right of the party is affected, and

(1) *Objection.* In case the ruling is one admitting evidence, a timely objection or motion to strike appears of record, stating the specific ground of objection, if the specific ground was not apparent from the context; or

(2) *Offer of Proof.* In case the ruling is one excluding evidence, the substance of the evidence was made known to the court by offer or was apparent from the context within which questions were asked.

(b) *Record of Offer and Ruling.* The court may add any other or further statement which shows the character of the evidence, the form in which it was offered, the objection made, and the ruling thereon. It may direct the making of an offer in question and answer form.

(c) *Hearing of Jury.* In jury cases, proceedings shall be conducted, to the extent practicable, so as to prevent inadmissible evidence from being suggested to the jury by any means, such as making statements or offers of proof or asking questions in the hearing of the jury.

(d) *Plain Error.* Nothing in this rule precludes taking notice of plain errors affecting substantial rights although they were not brought to the attention of the court.

Rule 104. Preliminary Questions
(a) *Questions of admissibility generally.* Preliminary questions concerning the qualification of a person to be a witness, the existence of a privilege, or the admissibility of evidence shall be determined by the court, subject to the provisions of subdivision

(b). In making its determination, the court is not bound by the rules of evidence except those with respect to privileges.

(b) *Relevancy conditioned on fact.* When the relevancy of evidence depends upon the fulfillment of a condition of fact, the court shall admit it upon, or subject to, the introduction of evidence sufficient to support a finding of the fulfillment of the condition.

(c) *Hearing of jury.* Hearings on the admissibility of confessions shall in all cases be conducted out of the hearing of the jury. Hearings on other preliminary matters shall be so conducted when the interests of justice require, or when an accused is a witness and so requests.

(d) *Testimony by accused.* The accused does not, by testifying upon a preliminary matter, become subject to cross-examination as to other issues in the case.

(e) *Weight and credibility.* This rule does not limit the right of a party to introduce before the jury evidence relevant to weight or credibility.

Rule 105. Limited Admissibility. When evidence which is admissible as to one party or for one purpose but not admissible as to another party or for another purpose is admitted, the court, upon request, shall restrict the evidence to its proper purpose or scope and instruct the jury accordingly.

Rule 106. Remainder of or Related Writings or Recorded Statements. When a writing or recorded statement or part thereof is introduced by a party, an adverse party may require the introduction at that time of any other part or any other writing or recorded statement which ought in fairness to be considered contemporaneously with it.

Article II: Judicial Notice

Rule 201. Judicial Notice of Adjudicative Facts.
(a) *Scope of Rule.* This rule governs only judicial notice of adjudicative facts.

(b) *Kinds of Facts.* A judicially noticed fact must be one not subject to reasonable dispute in that it is either
(1) generally known within the territorial jurisdiction of the trial court or
(2) capable of accurate and ready determination by resort to sources whose accuracy cannot reasonably be questioned.

(c) *When Discretionary.* A court may take judicial notice, whether requested or not.

(d) *When Mandatory.* A court shall take judicial notice if requested by a party and supplied with the necessary information.

(e) *Opportunity to be Heard.* A party is entitled upon timely request to an opportunity to be heard as to the propriety of taking judicial notice and the tenor of the matter noticed. In the absence of prior notification, the request may be made after judicial notice has been taken.

(f) *Time of Taking Notice.* Judicial notice may be taken at any stage of the proceeding

(g) *Informing the Jury.* In a civil action or proceeding, the court shall inform the jury to accept as conclusive any fact judicially noticed. In a criminal case, the court shall inform the jury that it may, but is not required to, accept as conclusive any fact judicially noticed.

Article III: Presumptions In Civil Actions and Proceedings

Rule 301. Presumptions in General in civil Actions and Proceedings. In all civil actions and proceedings not otherwise provided for by rule, statute or court decision, a presumption imposes on the party against whom it is directed the burden of going forward with evidence to rebut or meet the presumption, but does not shift to such party the burden of proof in the sense of the risk of nonpersuasion, which remains throughout the trial upon the party on whom it was originally cast.

Article IV: Relevancy and Its Limits

Rule 401. Definition of "Relevant Evidence". "Relevant evidence" means evidence having any tendency to make the existence of any fact that is of consequence to the determination of the action more probable or less probable than it would be without the evidence.

Rule 402. Relevant Evidence Generally Admissible; Irrelevant Evidence Inadmissible.
(a) *Scope of rule.* All relevant evidence is admissible, except as otherwise provided by law. Evidence which is not relevant is not admissible.

Rule 403. Exclusion of Relevant Evidence on Grounds of Prejudice, Confusion, or Waste of Time. although relevant, evidence may be excluded if its probative value is substantially outweighed by the danger of unfair prejudice, confusion of the issues, or misleading the jury, or by considerations of undue delay, waste of time, or needless presentation of cumulative evidence.

Rule 404. Character Evidence Not Admissible to Prove Conduct; Exceptions; Other Crimes.
(a) *Character Evidence Generally.* Evidence of a person's character or a trait of character is not admissible for the purpose of proving action in conformity therewith on a particular occasion, except:

(1) *Character of Accused.* In a criminal case, evidence of a pertinent trait of character offered by an accused, or by the prosecution to rebut the same;

(2) *Character of Alleged Victim.* In a criminal case, and subject to the limitations imposed by section 115-7 of the Code of Criminal Procedure (*725 ILCS 5/115-7*), evidence of a pertinent trait of character of the alleged victim of the crime offered by an accused, or by the prosecution to rebut the same, or evidence of a character trait of peacefulness of the alleged victim offered by the prosecution in a homicide or battery case to rebut evidence that the alleged victim was the first aggressor;

(3) *Character of Witness.* Evidence of the character of a witness, as provided in Rules 607, 608, and 609.

(b) *Other Crimes, Wrongs, or Acts.* Evidence of other crimes, wrongs, or acts is not admissible to prove the character of a person in order to show action in conformity therewith except as

provided by sections 115-7.3, 115-7.4, and 115-20 of the Code of Criminal Procedure (*725 ILCS 5/115-7.3*, *725 ILCS 5/115-7.4*, and *725 ILCS 5/115-20*). Such evidence may also be admissible for other purposes, such as proof of motive, opportunity, intent, preparation, plan, knowledge, identity, or absence of mistake or accident.
(c) In a criminal case in which the prosecution intends to offer evidence under subdivision (b), it must disclose the evidence, including statements of witnesses or a summary of the substance of any testimony, at a reasonable time in advance of trial, or during trial if the court excuses pretrial notice on good cause shown.

Rule 405. Methods of Proving Character.
(a) *Reputation or Opinion.* In all cases in which evidence of character or a trait of character of a person is admissible, proof may be made by testimony as to reputation, or by testimony in the form of an opinion.

(b) *Specific Instances of Conduct.*

(1) In cases in which character or a trait of character of a person is an essential element of a charge, claim, or defense, proof may also be made of specific instances of that person's conduct; and

(2) In criminal homicide or battery cases when the accused raises the theory of self-defense and there is conflicting evidence as to whether the alleged victim was the aggressor, proof may also be made of specific instances of the alleged victim's prior violent conduct.

Rule 406. Habit; Routine Practice. Evidence of the habit of a person or of the routine practice of an organization, whether corroborated or not and regardless of the presence of eyewitnesses, is relevant to prove that the conduct of the person or organization on a particular occasion was in conformity with the habit or routine practice.

Rule 407. RESERVED [Subsequent Remedial Measures].

Rule 408. Compromise and Offers to Compromise. (a) *Prohibited Uses.* Evidence of the following is not admissible on behalf of any party, when offered to prove liability for, invalidity of, or amount of a claim that was disputed as to validity or amount, or to impeach through a prior inconsistent statement or contradiction:

(1) furnishing or offering or promising to furnish --or accepting or offering or promising to accept --a valuable consideration in compromising or attempting to compromise the claim; and

(2) conduct or statements made in compromise negotiations regarding the claim.

(b) *Permitted Uses.* This rule does not require the exclusion of any evidence otherwise discoverable merely because it is presented in the course of settlement negotiations. This rule also does not require exclusion if the evidence is offered for purposes not prohibited by subdivision

(a). Examples of permissible purposes include proving a witness' bias or prejudice; negating an assertion of undue delay; establishing bad faith; and proving an effort to obstruct a criminal investigation or prosecution.

Rule 409. Payment of Medical and Similar Expenses.
In addition to the provisions of section 8-1901 of the Code of Civil Procedure (*735 ILCS 5/8-1901*), evidence of furnishing or offering or promising to pay medical, hospital, or similar expenses occasioned by an injury is not admissible to prove liability for the injury.
Rule 410. Inadmissibility of Pleas, Plea Discussions, and Related Statements. Except as otherwise provided in this rule, evidence of the following is not admissible in any criminal proceeding against the defendant who made the plea or was a participant in the plea discussions:

(1) a plea of guilty which was later withdrawn;

(2) a plea of nolo contendere;

(3) any statement made in the course of any

proceedings under *Illinois Supreme Court Rule 402* regarding either of the foregoing pleas; or

(4) any statement made in the course of plea discussions which do not result in a plea of guilty or which result in a plea of guilty later withdrawn.
However, such a statement is admissible
(i) in any proceeding wherein another statement made in the course of the same plea or plea discussions has been introduced and the statement ought in fairness be considered contemporaneously with it, or
(ii) in a criminal proceeding for perjury or false statement if the statement was made by the defendant under oath, on the record and in the presence of counsel.

Rule 411. Liability Insurance. Evidence that a person was or was not insured against liability is not admissible upon the issue whether the person acted negligently or otherwise wrongfully. This rule does not require the exclusion of evidence of insurance against liability when offered for another purpose, such as proof of agency, ownership, or control, or bias or prejudice of a witness.

Article V: Privileges

Rule 501. General Rule.
Except as otherwise required by the Constitution of the United States, the Constitution of Illinois, or provided by applicable statute or rule prescribed by the Supreme Court, the privilege of a witness, person, government, state, or political subdivision thereof shall be governed by the principles of the common law as they may be interpreted by Illinois courts in the light of reason and experience.

Article VI: Witnesses

Rule 601. General Rule of Competency.
Every person is competent to be a witness, except as otherwise provided by these rules, by other rules prescribed by the Supreme Court, or by statute.

Rule 602. Lack of Personal Knowledge. a witness may not testify to a matter unless evidence is introduced sufficient to support a finding that the witness has personal knowledge of the matter. Evidence to prove personal knowledge may, but need not, consist of the witness' own testimony. This rule is subject to the provisions of Rule 703, relating to opinion testimony by expert witnesses.

Rule 603. Oath or Affirmation. before testifying, every witness shall be required to declare that the witness will testify truthfully, by oath or affirmation, administered in a form calculated to awaken the witness' conscience and impress the witness' mind with the duty to do so.

Rule 604. Interpreters. an interpreter is subject to the provisions of these rules relating to qualification as an expert and the administration of an oath or affirmation to make a true translation.

Rule 605. Competency of Judge as Witness. the judge presiding at the trial may not testify in that trial as a witness. No objection need be made in order to preserve the point.

Rule 606. Competency of Juror as Witness.
(a) *At the Trial.* A member of the jury may not testify as a witness before that jury in the trial of the case in which the juror is sitting. If the juror is called so to testify, the opposing party shall be afforded an opportunity to object out of the presence of the jury.

(b) *Inquiry Into Validity of Verdict or Indictment.* Upon an inquiry into the validity of a verdict or indictment, a juror may not testify as to any matter or statement occurring during the course of the jury's deliberations or to the effect of anything upon that or any other juror's mind or emotions as influencing the juror to assent to or dissent from the verdict or indictment or concerning the juror's mental processes in connection therewith. But a juror may testify

(1) whether any extraneous prejudicial information was improperly brought to the jury's attention,

(2) whether any outside influence was improperly brought to bear upon any juror, or

(3) whether there was a mistake in entering the verdict onto the verdict form. A juror's affidavit or evidence of any statement by the juror may not be received concerning a matter about which the juror would be precluded from testifying.

Rule 607. Who May Impeach the credibility of a witness may be attacked by any party, including the party calling the witness, except that the credibility of a witness may be attacked by the party calling the witness by means of a prior inconsistent statement only upon a showing of affirmative damage. The foregoing exception does not apply to statements admitted pursuant to Rules 801 (d)(1)(A), 801(d)(1)(C), 801(d)(2), or 803.

Rule 608. Evidence of Character Witness. the credibility of a witness may be attacked or supported by evidence in the form of opinion or reputation, but subject to these limitations:
(1) the evidence may refer only to character for truthfulness or untruthfulness, and

(2) evidence of truthful character is admissible only after the character of the witness for truthfulness has been attacked by opinion or reputation evidence or otherwise.

Rule 609. Impeachment by Evidence of Conviction of Crime. (a) *General Rule.* For the purpose of attacking the credibility of a witness, evidence that the witness has been convicted of a crime, except on a plea of nolo contendere, is admissible but only if the crime,

(1) was punishable by death or imprisonment in excess of one year under the law under which the witness was convicted, or

(2) involved dishonesty or false statement regardless of the punishment unless

(3), in either case, the court determines that the probative value of the evidence of the crime is substantially outweighed by the danger of unfair prejudice.

(b) *Time Limit.* Evidence of a conviction under this rule is not admissible if a period of more than 10 years has elapsed since the date of conviction or of the release of the witness from confinement, whichever is the later date.

(c) *Effect of Pardon, Annulment, or Certificate of Rehabilitation.* Evidence of a conviction is not admissible under this rule if

(1) the conviction has been the subject of a pardon, annulment, certificate of rehabilitation, or other equivalent procedure, and

(2) the procedure under which the same was granted or issued required a substantial showing of rehabilitation or was based on innocence.

(d) *Juvenile Adjudications.* Evidence of juvenile adjudications is generally not admissible under this rule. The court may, however, allow evidence of a juvenile adjudication of a witness other than the accused if conviction of the offense would be admissible to attack the credibility of an adult and the court is satisfied that admission in evidence is necessary for a fair determination of the issue of guilt or innocence.
(e) *Pendency of Appeal.* The pendency of an appeal therefrom does not render evidence of a conviction inadmissible. Evidence of the pendency of an appeal is admissible.

Rule 610. Religious Beliefs or Opinions. Evidence of the beliefs or opinions of a witness on matters of religion is not admissible for the purpose of showing that by reason of their nature the witness' credibility is impaired or enhanced.

Rule 611. Mode and Order of Interrogation and Presentation.
(a) *Control by Court.* The court shall exercise reasonable control over the mode and order of

interrogating witnesses and presenting evidence so as to

(1) make the interrogation and presentation effective for the ascertainment of the truth,

(2) avoid needless consumption of time, and

(3) protect witnesses from harassment or undue embarrassment.

(b) *Scope of Cross-Examination.* Cross-examination should be limited to the subject matter of the direct examination and matters affecting the credibility of the witness. The court may, in the exercise of discretion, permit inquiry into additional matters as if on direct examination.

(c) *Leading Questions.* Leading questions should not be used on the direct examination of a witness except as may be necessary to develop the witness' testimony. Ordinarily leading questions should be permitted on cross-examination. When a party calls a hostile witness, an adverse party, or a witness identified with an adverse party, interrogation may be by leading questions.

Rule 612. Writing Used to Refresh Memory. If a witness uses a writing to refresh memory for the purpose of testifying, either -

(1) while testifying, or

(2) before testifying,

an adverse party is entitled to have the writing produced at the hearing, to inspect it, to cross-examine the witness thereon, and to introduce in evidence for the purpose of impeachment those portions which relate to the testimony of the witness. If it is claimed that the writing contains matters not related to the subject matter of the testimony the court shall examine the writing in camera, excise any portions not so related, and order delivery of the remainder to the party entitled thereto. Any portion withheld over objections shall be preserved and made available to the appellate court in the event of an appeal. If a writing is not produced or delivered pursuant to order under this rule, the court shall make any order justice requires, except that in criminal cases when the prosecution elects not to comply, the order shall be one striking the testimony or, if the court in its discretion determines that the interests of justice so require, declaring a mistrial.

Rule 613. Prior Statements of Witness.
(a) *Examining Witness Concerning Prior Statement.* In examining a witness concerning a prior statement made by the witness, whether written or not, the statement need not be shown nor its contents disclosed to the witness at that time, but on request the same shall be shown or disclosed to opposing counsel.

(b) *Extrinsic Evidence of Prior Inconsistent Statement of Witness.* Extrinsic evidence of a prior inconsistent Statement by a witness is not admissible unless the witness is first afforded an opportunity to explain or deny the same and the opposing party is afforded an opportunity to interrogate the witness thereon, or the interests of justice otherwise require. This provision does not apply to admissions of a party-opponent as defined in Rule 801(d)(2).

Rule 614. Calling and Interrogation of Witnesses by Court.
(a) *Calling by Court.* The court may, on its own motion or at the suggestion of a party, call witnesses, and all parties are entitled to cross-examine witnesses thus called.

(b) *Interrogation by Court.* The court may interrogate witnesses, whether called by itself or by a party.

(c) *Objections.* Objections to the calling of witnesses by the court or to interrogation by it may be made at the time or at the next available opportunity when the jury is not present.

Rule 615. Exclusion of Witnesses. at the request of a party the court shall order witnesses excluded so that they cannot hear the testimony of other witnesses, and it may make the order of its own motion. This rule does not authorize exclusion of (1) a party who is a natural person, or (2) an officer or employee of a party which is not a natural person designated as its representative by its attorney, or (3) a person whose presence is shown by a party to be essential to the presentation of the party's cause, or (4) a person authorized by law to be present.

Article VII: Opinions and Expert Testimony

Rule 701. Opinion Testimony by Lay Witnesses. If the witness is not testifying as an expert, the witness' testimony in the form of opinions or inferences is limited to those opinions or inferences which are (a) rationally based on the perception of the witness, and (b) helpful to a clear understanding of the witness' testimony or the determination of a fact in issue, and (c) not based on scientific, technical, or other specialized knowledge within the scope of Rule 702.

Rule 702. Testimony by Experts. If scientific, technical, or other specialized knowledge will assist the trier of fact to understand the evidence or to determine a fact in issue, a witness qualified as an expert by knowledge, skill, experience, training, or education, may testify thereto in the form of an opinion or otherwise.

Rule 703. Bases of Opinion Testimony by Experts. the facts or data in the particular case upon which an expert bases an opinion or inference may be those perceived by or made known to the expert at or before the hearing. If of a type reasonably relied upon by experts in the particular field in forming opinions or inferences upon the subject, the facts or data need not be admissible in evidence.

Rule 704. Opinion on Ultimate Issue. Testimony in the form of an opinion or inference otherwise admissible is not objectionable because it embraces an ultimate issue to be decided by the trier of fact.

Rule 705. Disclosure of Facts or Data Underlying Expert Opinion. the expert may testify in terms of opinion or inference and give reasons therefore without first testifying to the underlying facts or data, unless the court requires otherwise. The expert may in any event be required to disclose the underlying facts or data on cross-examination.

Article VIII: Hearsay

Rule 801. Definitions.
(a) *Statement.* A "statement" is

(1) an oral or written assertion or

(2) nonverbal conduct of a person, if it is intended by the person as an assertion.

(b) *Declarant.* A "declarant" is a person who makes a statement.

(c) *Hearsay.* "Hearsay" is a statement, other than one made by the declarant while testifying at the trial or hearing, offered in evidence to prove the truth of the matter asserted.

(d) *Statements Which Are Not Hearsay.* A statement is not hearsay if

(1) *Prior statement by Witness.* The declarant testifies at the trial or hearing and is subject to cross-examination concerning the statement, and the statement
(A) in a civil case is inconsistent with the declarant's testimony, and was given under oath subject to the penalty of perjury at a trial, hearing, or other proceeding, or in a deposition; or in a criminal case is
(a) inconsistent with the declarant's testimony,

(b) the declarant is subject to cross-examination concerning the statement, and

(c) the statement -

(1) was made under oath at trial, hearing, or other proceeding, or in a deposition, or

(2) narrates, describes, or explains an event or condition of which the declarant had personal

knowledge, and

(A) the statement is proved to have been written or signed by the declarant, or

(B) the declarant acknowledged under oath the making of the statement either in the declarant's testimony at the hearing or trial in which the admission into evidence of the prior statement is being sought or at a trial, hearing, or other proceeding, or in a deposition, or

(C) the statement is proved to have been accurately recorded by a tape recorder, videotape recording, or any other similar electronic means of sound recording; or

(B) is consistent with the declarant's testimony and is offered to rebut an express or implied charge against the declarant of recent fabrication or improper influence or motive, or

(C) is one of identification of a person made after perceiving the person.

(2) *Admission by Party-Opponent.* The statement is offered against a party and is

(A) the party's own statement, in either an individual or a representative capacity, or

(B) a statement of which the party has manifested an adoption or belief in its truth, or

(C) a statement by a person authorized by the party to make a statement concerning the subject, or

(D) a statement by the party's agent or servant concerning a matter within the scope of the agency or employment, made during the existence of the relationship, or

(E) a statement by a coconspirator of a party during the course and in furtherance of the conspiracy, or

(F) a statement by a person, or a person on behalf of an entity, in privity with the party or jointly interested with the party.

Rule 802. Hearsay Rule. Hearsay is not admissible except as provided by these rules, by other rules prescribed by the Supreme Court, or by statute as provided in Rule 101.

Rule 803. Hearsay Exceptions; Availability of Declarant Immaterial. the following are not excluded by the hearsay rule, even though the declarant is available as a witness:

(1) *Reserved. [Present Sense Impressions]*

(2) *Excited Utterance.* A statement relating to a startling event or condition made while the declarant was under the stress of excitement caused by the event or condition.

(3) *Then Existing Mental, Emotional, or Physical Condition.* A statement of the declarant's then existing state of mind, emotion, sensation, or physical condition

(such as intent, plan, motive, design, mental feeling, pain, and bodily health), but not including:

(A) a statement of memory or belief to prove the fact remembered or believed unless it relates to the execution, revocation, identification, or terms of declarant's will; or

(B) a statement of declarant's then existing state of mind, emotion, sensation, or physical condition to prove the state of mind, emotion, sensation, or physical condition of another declarant at that time or at any other time when such state of the other declarant is an issue in the action.

(4) *Statements for purposes of medical diagnosis or treatment.*

(A) Statements made for purposes of medical treatment, or medical diagnosis in contemplation of treatment, and describing medical history, or past or present symptoms, pain, or sensations, or the inception or general character of the cause or external source thereof insofar as reasonably pertinent to diagnosis or treatment but, subject to Rule 703, not including statements made to a health care provider consulted solely for the purpose of preparing for litigation or obtaining testimony for trial, or

(B) in a prosecution for violation of sections 12-13, 12-14, 12-14.1, 12-15, or 12-16 of the Criminal Code of 1961 statements made by the victim to medical personnel for purposes of medical diagnoses or treatment including descriptions of the cause of symptom, pain or sensations, or the inception or general character of the cause or external source thereof insofar as reasonably pertinent to diagnosis or treatment.

(5) *Recorded recollection.* A memorandum or record concerning a matter about which a witness once had knowledge but now has insufficient recollection to enable the witness to testify fully and accurately, shown to have been made or adopted by the witness when the matter was fresh in the witness' memory and to reflect that knowledge correctly.

(6) *Records of regularly conducted activity.* A memorandum, report, record, or data compilation, in any form, of acts, events, conditions, opinions, or diagnoses, made at or near the time by, or from information transmitted by, a person with knowledge, if kept in the course of a regularly conducted business activity, and if it was the regular practice of that business activity to make the memorandum, report, record or data compilation, all as shown by the testimony of the custodian or other qualified witness, or by certification that complies with Rule 902(11), unless the source of information or the method or circumstances of preparation indicate lack of trustworthiness, but not including in criminal cases medical records. The term 'business" as used in this paragraph includes business, institution, association, profession, occupation, and calling of every kind, whether or not conducted for profit.

(7) *Absence of Entry in Records Kept in Accordance With the Provisions of Paragraph (6).* Evidence that a matter is not included in the memoranda reports, records, or data compilations, in any form, kept in accordance with the provisions of paragraph (6), to prove the nonoccurrence or nonexistence of the matter, if the matter was of a kind of which a memorandum, report, record, or data compilation was regularly made and preserved, unless the sources of information or other circumstances indicate lack of trustworthiness.

(8) *Public records and reports.* Records, reports, statements, or data compilations, in any form, of public offices or agencies, setting forth

(A) the activities of the office or agency, or

(B) matters observed pursuant to duty imposed by law as to which matters there was a duty to report, excluding, however, police accident reports and in criminal cases medical records and matters observed by police officers and other law enforcement personnel, unless the sources of information or other circumstances indicate lack of trustworthiness.

(9) *Records of Vital Statistics.* Facts contained in records or data compilations, in any form, of births, fetal deaths, deaths, or marriages, if the report thereof was made to a public office pursuant to requirements of law.

(10) *Absence of Public Record or Entry.* To prove the absence of a record, report, statement, or data compilation, in any form, or the nonoccurrence or nonexistence of a matter of which a record, report, statement, or data compilation, in any form, was regularly made and preserved by a public office or agency, evidence in the form of a certification in accordance with Rule 902, or testimony, that diligent search failed to disclose the record, report, statement, or data compilation, or entry.

(11) *Records of Religious Organizations.* Statements of births, marriages, divorces, deaths, legitimacy, ancestry, relationship by blood or marriage, or other similar facts of personal or family history, contained in a regularly kept record of a religious organization.

(12) *Marriage, Baptismal, and Similar Certificates.* Statements of fact contained in a certificate that the maker performed a marriage or other ceremony or administered a sacrament, made by a clergyman, public official, or other

person authorized by the rules or practices of a religious organization or by law to perform the act certified, and purporting to have been issued at the time of the act or within a reasonable time thereafter.

(13) *Family Records.* Statements of fact concerning personal or family history contained in family Bibles, genealogies, charts, engravings on rings, inscriptions on family portraits, engravings on urns, crypts, or tombstones, or the like.

(14) *Records of Documents Affecting an Interest in Property.* The record of a document purporting to establish or affect an interest in property, as proof of the content of the original recorded document and its execution and delivery by each person by whom it purports to have been executed, if the record is a record of a public office and an applicable statute authorizes the recording of documents of that kind in that office.

(15) *Statements in Documents Affecting an Interest in Property.* A statement contained in a document purporting to establish or affect an interest in property if the matter stated was relevant to the purpose of the document, unless dealings with the property since the document was made have been inconsistent with the truth of the statement or the purport of the document.

(16) *Statements in Ancient Documents.* Statements in a document in existence 20 years or more the authenticity of which is established.

(17) *Market Reports, Commercial Publications.* Market quotations, tabulations, lists, directories, or other published compilations, generally used and relied upon by the public or by persons in particular occupations.

(18) *Reserved. [Learned Treatises]*

(19) *Reputation Concerning Personal or Family History.* Reputation among members of a person's family by blood, adoption, or marriage, or among a person's associates, or in the community, concerning a person's birth, adoption, marriage, divorce, death, legitimacy, relationship by blood, adoption, or marriage, ancestry, or other similar fact of personal or family history.

(20) *Reputation Concerning Boundaries or General History.* Reputation in a community, arising before the controversy, as to boundaries of or customs affecting lands in the community, and reputation as to events of general history important to the community or State or nation in which located.

(21) *Reputation as to Character.* Reputation of a person's character among associates or in the community.

(22) *Judgment of Previous Conviction.* Evidence of a final judgment, entered after a trial or upon a plea of guilty, adjudging a person guilty of a crime punishable by death or imprisonment in excess of one year, to prove any fact essential to sustain the judgment, but not including, when offered by the Government in a criminal prosecution for purposes other than impeachment, judgments against persons other than the accused. The pendency of an appeal may be shown but does not affect admissibility.

(23) *Judgment as to Personal, Family or General History, or Boundaries.* Judgments as proof of matters of personal, family or general history, or boundaries, essential to the judgment, if the same would be provable by evidence of reputation.

(24) *Receipt or Paid Bill.* A receipt or paid bill as prima facie evidence of the fact of payment and as prima facie evidence that the charge was reasonable.

Rule 804. Hearsay Exceptions; Declarant Unavailable. (a) *Definition of unavailability.* "Unavailability as a witness" includes situations in which the declarant -

(1) is exempted by ruling of the court on the ground of privilege from testifying concerning the subject matter of the declarant's statement; or

(2) persists in refusing to testify concerning the subject matter of the declarant's statement

despite an order of the court to do so; or

(3) testifies to a lack of memory of the subject matter of the declarant's statement; or
(4) is unable to be present or to testify at the hearing because of death or then existing physical or mental illness or infirmity; or

(5) is absent from the hearing and the proponent of a statement has been unable to procure the declarant's attendance (or in the case of a hearsay exception under subdivision (b)(2), (3), or (4), the declarant's attendance or testimony) by process or other reasonable means. A declarant is not unavailable as a witness if exemption, refusal, claim of lack of memory, inability, or absence is due to the procurement or wrongdoing of the proponent of a statement for the purpose of preventing the witness from attending or testifying.

(b) *Hearsay Exceptions.* The following are not excluded by the hearsay rule if the declarant is unavailable as a witness:

(1) *Former Testimony.* Testimony given as a witness

(A) at another hearing of the same or a different proceeding, or in an evidence deposition taken in compliance with law in the course of the same or another proceeding, if the party against whom the testimony is now offered, or, in a civil action or proceeding, a predecessor in interest, had an opportunity and similar motive to develop the testimony by direct, cross, or redirect examination, or

(B) in a discovery deposition as provided for in Supreme Court Rule 212(a)(5).

(2) *Statement Under Belief of Impending Death.* In a prosecution for homicide, a statement made by a declarant while believing that the declarant's death was imminent, concerning the cause or circumstances of what the declarant believed to be impending death.

(3) *Statement Against Interest.* A statement which was at the time of its making so far contrary to the declarant's pecuniary or proprietary interest, or so far tended to subject the declarant to civil or criminal liability, or to render invalid a claim by the declarant against another, that a reasonable person in the declarant's position would not have made the statement unless believing it to be true. A statement tending to expose the declarant to criminal liability and offered in a criminal case is not admissible unless corroborating circumstances clearly indicate the trustworthiness of the statement.

(4) *Statement of Personal of Family History.*

(A) A statement concerning the declarant's own birth, adoption, marriage, divorce, legitimacy, relationship by blood, adoption, or marriage, ancestry, or other similar fact of personal or family history, even though declarant had no means of acquiring personal knowledge of the matter stated; or

(B) a statement concerning the foregoing matters, and death also, of another person, if the declarant was related to the other by blood, adoption, or marriage or was so intimately associated with the other's family as to be likely to have accurate information concerning the matter declared.

(5) *Forfeiture by Wrongdoing.* A statement offered against a party that has engaged or acquiesced in wrongdoing that was intended to, and did, procure the unavailability of the declarant as a witness.

Rule 805. Hearsay Within Hearsay. Hearsay within hearsay is not excluded under the hearsay rule if each part of the combined statements conforms with an exception to the hearsay rule provided in these rules.

Rule 806. Attacking and Supporting Credibility of Declarant. When a hearsay statement, or a statement defined in Rule 801(d)(2)(C), (D), (E), or (F), has been admitted in evidence, the credibility of the declarant may be attacked, and if attacked may be supported, by any evidence which would be admissible for those purposes if declarant had testified as a witness. Evidence of a statement or conduct by the declarant at any time, inconsistent with the declarant's hearsay statement, is not subject to any requirement that the declarant may have been afforded an opportunity to deny or explain. If the party against whom a hearsay statement has been admitted calls the declarant as a witness, the party is entitled to examine the declarant on the statement as if under cross-examination.

Article IX: AUTHENTICATION AND IDENTIFICATION

Rule 901. Requirement of Authentication or Identification.

(a) *General Provision.* The requirement of authentication or identification as a condition precedent to admissibility is satisfied by evidence sufficient to support a finding that the matter in question is what its proponent claims.

(b) *Illustrations.* By way of illustration only, and not by way of limitation, the following are examples of authentication or identification conforming with the requirements of this rule:

(1) Testimony of Witness With Knowledge. Testimony that a matter is what it is claimed to be.

(2) Nonexpert Opinion on Handwriting. Nonexpert opinion as to the genuineness of handwriting, based upon familiarity not acquired for purposes of the litigation.

(3) Comparison by Trier or Expert Witness. Comparison by the trier of fact or by expert witnesses with specimens which have been authenticated.

(4) Distinctive Characteristics and the Like. Appearance, contents, substance, internal patterns, or other distinctive characteristics, taken in conjunction with circumstances.

(5) Voice Identification. Identification of a voice, whether heard firsthand or through mechanical or electronic transmission or recording, by opinion based upon hearing the voice at any time under circumstances connecting it with the alleged speaker.

(6) Telephone Conversations. Telephone conversations, by evidence that a call was made to the number assigned at the time by the telephone company to a particular person or business, if

(A) in the case of a person, circumstances, including self-identification, show the person answering to be the one called, or

(B) in the case of a business, the call was made to a place of business and the conversation related to business reasonably transacted over the telephone.

(7) Public Records or Reports. Evidence that a writing authorized by law to be recorded or filed and in fact recorded or filed in a public office, or a purported public record, report, statement, or data compilation, in any form, is from the public office where items of this nature are kept.

(8) Ancient Documents or Data Compilation. Evidence that a document or data compilation, in any form,

(A) is in such condition as to create no suspicion concerning its authenticity,

(B) was in a place where it, if authentic, would likely be, and

(C) has been in existence 20 years or more at the time it is offered.

(9) Process or System. Evidence describing a process or system used to produce a result and showing that the process or system produces an accurate result.

(10) Methods Provided by Statute or Rule. Any method of authentication or identification provided by statute or by other rules prescribed by the Supreme Court.

Rule 902. Self-Authentication. Extrinsic evidence of authenticity as a condition precedent to admissibility is not required with respect to the following:

(1) *Domestic Public Documents Under Seal.* A document bearing a seal purporting to be that of the United States, or of any State, district, Commonwealth, territory, or insular possession thereof, or the Panama Canal Zone, or the Trust Territory of the Pacific Islands, or of a political subdivision, department, officer, or agency thereof, and a signature purporting to be an attestation or execution.

(2) *Domestic Public Documents Not Under Seal.* A document purporting to bear the signature in the official capacity of an officer or employee of any entity included in paragraph

(1) hereof, having no seal, if a public officer having a seal and having official duties in the district or political subdivision of the officer or employee certifies under seal that the signer has the official capacity and that the signature is genuine.

(3) *Foreign Public Documents.* A document purporting to be executed or attested in an official capacity by a person authorized by the laws of a foreign country to make the execution or attestation, and accompanied by a final certification as to the genuineness of the signature and official position

(A) of the executing or attesting person, or

(B) of any foreign official whose certificate of genuineness of signature and official position relates to the execution or attestation or is in a chain of certificates of genuineness of signature and official position relating to the execution or attestation. A final certification may be made by a secretary of an embassy or legation, consul general, consul, vice consul, or consular agent of the United States, or a diplomatic or consular official of the foreign country assigned or accredited to the United States. If reasonable opportunity has been given to all parties to investigate the authenticity and accuracy of official documents, the court may, for good cause shown, order that they be treated as presumptively authentic without final certification or permit them to be evidenced by an attested summary with or without final certification.

(4) *Certified Copies of Public Records.* A copy of an official record or report or entry therein, or of a document authorized by law to be recorded or filed and actually recorded or filed in a public office, including data compilations in any form, certified as correct by the custodian or other person authorized to make the certification, by certificate complying with paragraph (1), (2), or (3) of this rule or complying with any statute or rule prescribed by the Supreme Court.

(5) *Official Publications.* Books, pamphlets, or other publications purporting to be issued by public authority.

(6) *Newspapers and Periodicals.* Printed materials purporting to be newspapers or periodicals.

(7) *Trade Inscriptions and the Like.* Inscriptions, signs, tags, or labels purporting to have been affixed in the course of business and indicating ownership, control, content, ingredients, or origin.

(8) *Acknowledged Documents.* Documents accompanied by a certificate of acknowledgement executed in the manner provided by law by a notary public or other officer authorized by law to take acknowledgments.

(9) *Commercial Paper and Related Documents.* Commercial paper, signatures thereon, and documents relating thereto to the extent provided by general commercial law.

(10) *Presumptions Under Statutes.* Any signature, document, or other matter declared by statutes to be presumptively or prima facie genuine or authentic.

(11) *Certified Records of Regularly Conducted Activity.* The original or a duplicate of a record of regularly conducted activity that would be admissible under Rule 803(6) if accompanied by a written certification of its custodian or other qualified person that the record (A) was made at or near the time of the occurrence of the

matters set forth by, or from information transmitted by, a person with knowledge of these matters; (B) was kept in the course of the regularly conducted activity; and (C) was made by the regularly conducted activity as a regular practice.

The word "certification" as used in this subsection means with respect to a domestic record, a written declaration under oath subject to the penalty of perjury and, with respect to a record maintained or located in a foreign country, a written declaration signed in a country which, if falsely made, would subject the maker to criminal penalty under the laws of the country. A party intending to offer a record into evidence under this paragraph must provide written notice of that intention to all adverse parties, and must make the record and declaration available for inspection sufficiently in advance of their offer into evidence to provide an adverse party with a fair opportunity to challenge them.

Rule 903. Subscribing Witness' Testimony Unnecessary. the testimony of a subscribing witness is not necessary to authenticate a writing unless required by the laws of the jurisdiction whose laws govern the validity of the writing.

Article X: CONTENTS OF WRITINGS, RECORDINGS AND PHOTOGRAPHS

Rule 1002. Requirement of Original. to prove the content of a writing, recording, or photograph, the original writing, recording, or photograph is required, except as otherwise provided in these rules or by statute.

Rule 1004. Admissibility of Other Evidence of Contents. the original is not required and other evidence of the contents of a writing, recording, or photograph is admissible if

(1) *Originals Lost or Destroyed.* All originals are lost or have been destroyed, unless the proponent lost or destroyed them in bad faith; or
(2) *Original Not Obtainable.* No original can be obtained by any available judicial process or procedure; or

(3) *Original in Possession of Opponent.* At a time when an original was under the control of the party against whom offered, that party was put on notice, by the pleadings or otherwise, that the contents would be a subject of proof at the hearing; or

(4) *Collateral Matters.* The writing, recording, or photograph is not closely related to a controlling issue.

Rule 1005. Public records. the contents of an official record, or of a document authorized to be recorded or filed and actually recorded or filed, including data compilations in any form, if otherwise admissible, may be proved by copy, certified as correct in accordance with Rule 902 or testified to be correct by a witness who has compared it with the original. If a copy which complies with the foregoing cannot be obtained by the exercise of reasonable diligence, then other evidence of the contents may be given.

Rule 1006. Summaries. the contents of voluminous writings, recordings, or photographs which cannot conveniently be examined in court may be presented in the form of a chart, summary, or calculation. The originals, or duplicates, shall be made available for examination or copying, or both, by other parties at reasonable time and place. The court may order that they be produced in court.

Rule 1007. Testimony or Written Admission of Party. Contents of writings, recordings, or photography may be proved by the testimony or deposition of the party against whom offered or by that party's written admission, without accounting for the nonproduction of the original.

Rule 1008. Functions of Court and Jury. When the admissibility of other evidence of contents of writings, recordings, or photographs under these rules depends upon the fulfillment of a condition of fact, the question whether the condition has been fulfilled is ordinarily for the court to determine in accordance with the provisions of Rule 104(a). However, when an issue is raised

(a) whether the asserted writing ever existed, or
(b) whether another writing, recording, or photograph produced at the trial is the original, or
(c) whether other evidence of contents correctly reflects the contents, the issue is for the trier of fact to determine as in the case of other issues of fact.

Article XI: MISCELLANEOUS RULES

Rule 1101. Applicability of Rules. (a) Except as otherwise provided in paragraphs (b) and (c), these rules govern proceedings in the courts of Illinois.

(b) *Rules inapplicable.* These rules (other than with respect to privileges) do not apply in the following situations:

(1) *Preliminary questions of fact.* The determination of questions of fact preliminary to admissibility of evidence when the issue is to be determined by the court under Rule 104.

(2) *Grand jury.* Proceedings before grand juries.

(3) *Miscellaneous proceedings.* Proceedings for extradition or rendition; preliminary examinations in criminal cases; sentencing, or granting or revoking probation, conditional discharge or supervision; issuance of warrants for arrest, criminal summonses, and search warrants; and proceedings with respect to release on bail or otherwise, and contempt proceedings in which the court may act summarily.

(c) These rules apply to small claims actions, subject to the application of Supreme Court Rule 286 (b).

Commentary – Overview of New Illinois Rules of Evidence

No formal rules of evidence before 2011. A trial is a process that seeks to recreate an event that happened outside the courtroom to set the stage for a legal decision. In the case of a criminal trial, some conduct has occurred outside the courtroom (e.g. a murder, a rape, a robbery, a burglary, etc.). A defendant has been accused of conduct that if proved in court would subject him to sanctions (prison, probation, restitution, etc.). Because of the potential loss of liberty, the defendant has fundamental rights that protect him from arbitrary action by the government.

To recreate the outside incident, the law of evidence permits competent evidence in the form of witnesses and exhibits to establish the courtroom image of the events. Some of the witnesses are occurrence witnesses, some are investigative reporters (i.e. the police) and some are witnesses with special forensic skill (i.e. experts) – all must take an oath or affirmation to tell the truth, all must have perceived something, all must have memory to repeat what they know and all must have the ability to communicate in some form to the judge or jury – depending on the type of criminal trial.

The law of evidence will not let just any information in about the case – the evidence must be relevant. The admitted evidence must have some tendency in logic to prove a fact that is important to the outcome of the case. This "relevant" evidence will be limited further, however, because there is a problem with evidence that shocks, misleads, confuses, or is inefficient in its use. The trial process will also permit evidence that addresses the credibility of the witnesses to determine if they have always been consistent in their description of events, if they have a motive or interest in the trial that would cause them to exaggerate or minimize their testimony, or even if they have something in their background (such as criminal convictions) that the judge or jury might use to decide how much weight to give to their testimony.

The exhibits that are used must also be shown to be accurate and relevant to the case on trial. If the exhibits are copies, why is the original not available, and would the original exhibit be important to a proper presentation of the story of the case?

The law of evidence will bar use of privileged information – matters said between lawyers and clients, patients and doctors and other similar relationships. Other decisions about limiting the reach of otherwise relevant evidence may also come into play in the criminal trial, such as the extent of attempts at plea negotiation to resolve the case that may have failed.

The law of evidence will be especially careful about hearsay – the out-of-court statement of a person that is being offered in court by a different witness for the truth of the things said in that statement. Some hearsay is going to be admitted, because historically it has been deemed to be safe and reliable to use in trials. However, a good deal of hearsay will be excluded, either because it is not trustworthy evidence, or because the 6th Amendment to the U.S. Constitution guarantees that the defendant will have the right to cross examine witnesses who claim that he has committed a crime, by their direct or indirect statements.

For about 175 years, Illinois has been a hodge-podge of common law – cases, statutes, Supreme Court rules, local legends and stories about Illinois evidence – what to admit and what not to admit, how to admit it, how to object. Trial judges have been able to make decisions about what evidence to admit or deny based on the accumulation of wisdom about evidence from these sources. In recent years, politics has entered the fray and there have been some enactments accompanied by press releases. Some of the enactments about evidence have even been the subject of political office election campaigns. So, it just made sense to codify all these components into the Illinois Rules of Evidence (IRE). To move away from this system of evidence, to modernize the law of Illinois evidence and to improve the system of Illinois justice, the Illinois Supreme Court appointed a special committee to study and then recommend rules of evidence for Illinois courts, largely in the same fashion that Federal Rules of Evidence were adopted by Congress for use in United States Federal courts.

The Federal Rules of Evidence (FRE) are well-established, are working well in the Federal Courts, have been adopted by many states in lieu of that state's common law of evidence, and certainly have been a solid evidence template with which to work. Having done its work, the special committee made its recommendations to the Illinois Supreme Court in 2010. On September 27, 2010 Chief Justice Thomas Fitzgerald, in accepting the work of the Special Supreme Court Committee on Evidence and announcing its adoption to be effective January 1, 2011, said, "Trial proceedings for litigants and the judiciary . . . will become even more efficient."

In most respects, the law of criminal evidence for Illinois courts remains unchanged under the new rules. It is beyond the scope of this book to discuss each and every rule or the nuance of change. Illinois evidence law is not the same, in many respects, as the Federal Rules of Evidence (FRE), although the IRE and the FRE track with some consistency.

Differences between the IRE and the FRE. Committee Comments note that the IRE, Illinois statutory enactments and Supreme Court Rules on evidence are not in conflict save one – about use of a juvenile conviction as an impeaching offense. However, there are many differences between IRE and FRE – almost too many to count. Some are procedural due to the difference between the federal and state systems, but by far, most are substantive because the federal rules of evidence have not been the law in Illinois. Although, the adoption of the IRE has brought with it an upgrade of the Illinois law of evidence. The Supreme Court Committee noted that it believed these upgrades, which were labeled "modernization", were non-controversial and were consistent with the law of evidence nationwide based on a survey of 44 other jurisdictions.

Changes in Illinois Evidence. The new Illinois Rules of Evidence did work some changes in Illinois evidence and differences with the Federal Rules of Evidence that should be noted.

IRE 103(a) and FRE 103(a). Under the Federal Rules, there is no need to renew an objection to a prior ruling on evidence at trial (such as a ruling on a motion in limine). However under IRE 103(a), the failure to renew an objection means that the error of the prior ruling is deemed waived. Presenting the issue in a post-trial motion is required in criminal cases by 725 ILCS 5/116-1 to preserve error for appeal, but the failure to renew an objection when evidence is presented at trial under IRE 103(a) is waiver.

IRE 106 is the completeness rule in which the parts of the remainder of a writing or some other writing are admissible out of fairness when one party seeks to admit only part of a writing. ISR 212(c) permitted the reading of additional parts of a deposition when a party admitted only one part. This rule goes beyond that rule and permits other writings that would complete the context or understanding of the admitted writing. The IRE comments suggest that this is a "modernization" of the prior practice about completeness in Illinois.

IRE 201 is the rule regarding judicial notice and is virtually identical to its FRE counterpart, except that under IRE 201(g) the court is to "inform" the jury instead of "instruct" the jury about the judicially-noticed fact. This certainly is less formal. In criminal cases, the jury may accept the fact as established in contrast to civil cases where the jury is to accept the fact as established.

IRE 405(a) and 608(a) change prior Illinois law regarding the method of proof of admissible evidence regarding character traits. In the past, a relevant character trait, such as a witness's truthfulness, could be proved only by reputation evidence with proper foundation (knowledge of the person, knowledge of a relevant community, the opportunity to determine reputation and a statement that "based on the foundation" the witness's reputation was "good" or "bad"). This differed from FRE where opinion testimony about the character trait was admissible with the foundation that the opinion witness has sufficient opportunity to form the opinion about the character trait. The FRE commentary suggests that in some sense the "opinion witness" is superior to the "reputation witness" because the latter can be based on rumors or gossip and the former tends to be more direct evidence. Of course, IRE 405(b)(1) permits evidence probative of a substantive character trait (i.e. incompetence as a driver in a negligent entrustment) by specific instances of conduct.

IRE 410 says that statements made during a plea of guilty that is later withdrawn are inadmissible. This applies only to criminal cases and thus would have potential admissibility in an associated civil case.

No IRE 412-415 - FRE 412 - 415 as these were not adopted. Instead the statutes with similar provisions as to criminal and civil cases remain. The criminal evidence statute is 725 ILCS 5/115-7, a "rape shield" law which bars evidence about a victim's sexual behavior or sexual predisposition, except for prior instances between the parties (defense of consent) or to show that the source of forensic evidence (i.e. semen, hair, etc.) was from a source other than the accused person. There are special pre-trial notice and hearing requirements for such evidence.

Propensity evidence of the defendant committing other sexual offenses similar to the charged offense is admissible under 725 ILCS 5/115-7.3. If the prosecution intends to offer such evidence, pre-trial disclosure is required and the trial court must conduct a pretrial hearing. At that hearing, the judge must consider (1) the similarity between the prior criminal sexual conduct and the charge on trial, (2) the proximity in time between the prior acts and the charged conduct and (3) any other facts and circumstances. If the court determines that the probative value is not substantially outweighed by its prejudicial effect, the prior conduct is admissible. But see *People v. Ward* 2011 IL 108690 (Ill. S. Cr. 2011) (Reversible error under 725 ILCS 5/115-7.3 to admit evidence of prior claimed sexual assault of defendant by alleged victim and refuse admitting into evidence that defendant was acquitted by a jury of the charge).

Propensity evidence of prior domestic assaults is also admissible in domestic violence cases, pursuant to 725 ILCS5/115-7.4, using the same factors and procedure.

FRE 415 permits evidence of acts of prior sexual molestation by a defendant to be admitted against that defendant in civil cases seeking money damages for sexual molestation claims. Illinois has no counterpart rule or statutory provision for FRE 415.

NOTE: the failure to create or include IRE 412-415 to comprehensively codify the criminal and civil provisions on matters relating to sexual conduct regarding civil claims and criminal offenses involving sexual conduct undermines the purpose of the Illinois Rules of Evidence. Instead of finding all things in one place, one must go looking for it.

IRE 501 is a placeholder rule which notes that the law of privilege in Illinois exists by virtue of statutory provisions 735 ILCS 5/8-802 *et seq.* (physician patient, informant, union member – union leader, husband and wife, penitent-priest, etc.), common law and the constitution. Thus, there is no IRE 502 (as there is an FRE 502) to address the issue of inadvertent disclosure under the attorney-client privilege, which in Illinois is a common law privilege.

IRE 601 states that competency of witnesses is a question of law for the court. The rule presumes that everyone is presumed to be competent (meet minimum requirement of (1) oath; (2) perception; (3) memory and (4) communication). IRE is different than FRE because Illinois has statutory incompetence. In criminal law, it is 725 ILCS 115/5-14, and in civil law, it is The Dead Man's Act 735 ILCS 5/8-201.

IRE 607 is Illinois' law about impeaching one's own witness and is different than FRE. FRE plainly states that witness credibility can be attacked by any party, including the party that called the witness. There is no FRE limitation. The IRE requires that if a witness called by a party is to be impeached by a prior inconsistent statement, there must be "a showing of affirmative damage", an Illinois common law requirement. Affirmative damage means that the witness has given evidence that assists the opponent's case. The prior inconsistent statement, in this setting, is to attack witness credibility as to that matter, not to get the truth of the prior statement before the jury. Thus, the impeachment is limited purpose evidence. Considerations of whether the impeachment relates to a collateral or non-collateral matter arise under this rule, and of course, a good-faith basis for the impeaching question is also required. There is no requirement of "affirmative damage" for a prior inconsistent statement admitted pursuant to IRE 801(d)(1)(A)(prior testimony given under oath in a hearing or deposition), 801(d)(1)(B)(prior consistent statement to rebut claim of recent fabrication), 801(d)(2)(admissions by a party opponent) or 803(hearsay exceptions).

IRE 608 allows evidence of the character of a witness to be presented in the form of opinion or reputation testimony, but this evidence must relate to the character trait of truthfulness. The addition of opinion witnesses as to character for truthfulness or untruthfulness is a change in Illinois law (see IRE 405 as to opinion witnesses as to other character traits). Just as FRE 608 requires, Illinois only permits such truthfulness character evidence in support of the witness if truthfulness has been attacked. IRE 608 is different than FRE 608 in that Illinois has not adopted the "prior bad act" rule of FRE 608(b) that permits an attack on witness credibility by questions on cross examination about acts probative of untruthfulness, but bars introduction of extrinsic evidence when the witness denies the specific instance questions.

IRE 609 is Illinois' rule on admissibility of the prior conviction of a crime by a witness and is consistent with the ruling in *People v. Montgomery* 47 Ill.2d 510, 268 N.E.2d 695 (1971). IRE 609 differs from FRE 609 in several respects. IRE 609(a) applies to all witnesses, including criminal defendants ("accused"), in the same way. Thus, the balancing test for admissibility of the prior conviction is the same as articulated in IRE 403 ("probative value is substantially outweighed by the danger of unfair prejudice") and this balancing test is expressly noted in IRE 609(a). The balancing test in IRE 609(a) applies also to both felony impeachment and dishonest or false statement crime impeachment, while FRE 609(a) applies the FRE 403 balancing test to felony impeachment. FRE 609(a) also has the "probative value" weighed against "unfair prejudice" for defendants who testify – a test that is more sensitive to the impact of prior convictions on testifying defendants. IRE 609(a) permits admission of conviction as to witness "credibility", while the FRE 609(a) admission is to attack witness "truthfulness". FRE 609 permits impeachment by any type of conviction, but IRE 609 makes inadmissible convictions based on pleas of *nolo contendre*. While both IRE 609(b) and FRE 609(b) have the same time limit permitting introduction of prior convictions, they differ in the calculation of that limit. Both states that only if the convictions were within ten (10) years of the date the witness testifies are admissible. For purposes of calculating the ten years under FRE, the time limit begins to run when the witness is released from confinement for the impeaching offense. Under IRE, the time limit starts to run when the witness is released from confinement generally. Thus, the 10-year window for purposes of IRE 609 impeachment is potentially extended. FRE 609 permits impeachment by conviction of eligible crimes older than 10 years with the application a harsher balancing test (unfair prejudice substantially outweighed by probative value); however, IRE 609's 10-year rule is absolute. It should also be noted that Illinois does not permit "mere fact" as a method of conviction (i.e. that the witness has a prior felony conviction in 2008), and instead requires that prior conviction impeachment must recite the named crime of the impeaching conviction. Finally, although worded differently, IRE 609(c) and FRE 609(c) are substantially similar in precluding impeachment by prior conviction where the conviction has been the subject of a pardon, clemency, certificate of rehabilitation, or other such action that rely upon findings of rehabilitation or innocence.

IRE 611(a) and (b) and FRE 611(a) and (b) are identical. So are the first two sentences of IRE 611(c) and FRE 611(c). All relate to the court's control over the examination of witnesses, the scope of cross examination and the use of leading questions during examination. IRE 611(c) and FRE 611(c) differ in what constitutes an adverse witness for purposes of examination as if on cross examination. FRE 611(c) includes the power of the court to permit cross examination of "a witness identified with an adverse party" and IRE 611(c) continues the limitation of Illinois law (735 ILCS 5/2-1102 and ISCR 238(b)) to permit cross examination of "hostile or unwilling witnesses" and "examination of a party or agent of a party". IRE 611 provisions do not expand current Illinois law on adverse examination.

IRE 612 is the equivalent of FRE 612 and concerns the use of writing to refresh memory. If a witness uses a writing to his refresh memory before or during trial, the opponent is entitled to see and review the writing (at least the portion relating to the witness's testimony) and to introduce portions of the writing. In Illinois, portions of the writing are admissible as impeachment. There is no such provision in FRE.

IRE 613 (a) and FRE 613(a), regarding prior statements of witness, are the same but confirm a clarification in Illinois law that a witness need not be shown or told the content of a prior statement before being asked about its content. IRE 613(b) also confirms Illinois' existing practice that a witness confronted by a prior inconsistent statement must have the opportunity to "explain or deny" the statement, followed by opposing counsel's opportunity to ask questions about the prior statement.

IRE 702 is on the subject of expert opinion testimony. IRE 702 differs significantly from FRE 702. Illinois remains a "*Frye"* state. *United States v. Frye* 293 F. 1013 (Ct. of App. D.C. Cir. 1923). The *Frye* principle underlying the determination of the admissibility of an expert opinion is on the basis of "general acceptance in the field." The *Frye* standard is expressly in IRE 702 in place of FRE 702's recitation of *Daubert* principles ("(1) the testimony is based on sufficient facts and data, (2) the testimony is based on reliable principles and methods, and (3) the witness has applied the principles and methods reliably to the facts of the case").

IRE 703 and **FRE 703** regarding the bases of expert testimony, also have significant differences. Under FRE 703, the content of the bases of expert opinion that would otherwise be inadmissible are generally precluded from disclosure to the jury. Disclosure occurs only when the court makes a "reverse FRE 403" finding (i.e. that disclosure of the facts or data has probative value in assisting the jury to evaluate the expert opinion which substantially outweighs the prejudicial effect). IRE 703 has no prohibition against disclosure of the facts or data relied upon by the expert witness and thus it would be subject to the normal IRE 403 balancing test – which is tipped in favor of admissibility.

IRE 706 not FRE 706 is the Illinois standard. Illinois has not adopted FRE 706 regarding the court's appointment of experts. Illinois courts have the power to appoint experts in several situations and thus, Illinois statutory law is more limited than the FRE. (See ISCR 215(d) regarding court appointment of an independent medical examiner).

IRE 801 states that the hearsay definitions under IRE 801(a), (b) and (c) are identical to their FRE counterparts. This gives hope that someday the hearsay analysis in Illinois will be the same as the FRE, but that is in the future – not now!

IRE 801(d)(1) - Illinois had a statutory criminal law counterpart where prior inconsistent testimony of a witness who is now testifying at trial, which was (1) given under oath at a prior proceeding, or (2) describes something the witness has personal knowledge about and (i) was written or signed by the witness, or (ii) the witness has acknowledged under oath the prior was made, or (iii) the statement is shown to have been accurately recorded by electronic means, was not inadmissible by the hearsay rule (thus the statement was admissible as substantive evidence (See 725 ILCS 5/115-10.1)). This statutory "not hearsay" rule was adopted in IRE 801(d)(1)(A)(1) and (2).

There is a civil differentiation that is significant in that IRE 801(d)(1)(A) does not adopt the language of FRE 801(d)(1)(A) about prior testimony of a witness now testifying at trial, which was given under oath at other proceedings (trials or depositions). This is not considered hearsay because it was the subject of examination by the opponent to its admission and thus does not meet the underlying principle of hearsay – that the out-of-court statement that is offered for its truth was not confronted by the party opposing its admission. Nonetheless, in civil cases, Illinois only permits this kind of evidence to be admitted on the basis of attacking witness credibility (e.g. IRE 607), not for its truth since this was the Illinois common law. FRE 801(d)(1)(A) permits such evidence to be admitted as "not hearsay".

IRE 801(d)(1)(B) did not adopt this rule even though FRE 801(d)(1)(B) provides that prior statements made that are consistent with a witness' testimony at trial are admissible as "not hearsay" if they corroborate the witness' testimony at trial and are offered to rebut claim of recent fabrication by the witness. Illinois did not adopt this rule – instead the common law rule is that the evidence of a prior consistent statement can only be used to corroborate the witness' credibility, not as substantive evidence. In Illinois, prior consistent statements are admissible only to rehabilitate a witness and not for substantive truthfulness. See *People v. Randolph* 2014 IL App (1st) 113624 (error to permit police reports' use as prior consistent statements when testifying officers' credibility had been impeached by omissions in their reports. Officers testified that defendant looked "big eyed" and "fidgety" and that he dropped bag containing narcotics when an officer got out of the squad car and none of these facts were in the police reports. The reports were not admissible as substantive evidence or as prior consistent statements that the defendant had indeed dropped the bag).

IRE 801(d)(1)(B) - To add to the hearsay evidence confusion, IRE 801(d)(1)(B) is identical with FRE 801(d)(1)(C) in that the prior statements of identification made out-of-court by a witness who testifies in court are not hearsay. The additional difference, beyond numbering, is that the Illinois rule is limited to criminal cases, and the Federal rule has no such limitation. Note that another person who heard the out-of-court statement of perceived identification can testify to the statement so long as the identifying witness also testifies.

IRE 801(d)(2) states party admissions are considered not to be hearsay, but IRE 801(d)(2) and FRE 801(d)(2) are again not identical. They match up in labeling "statements" as admissions when made by the party-opponent (IRE 801(d)(2)(A)), or adopted by the party-opponent (IRE 801(d)(2)(B)), or made by a person authorized to make the statement (IRE 801(d)(2)(C)), made by a party's agent during and authorized by the scope of agency (IRE 801(d)(2)(D)), or made by a co-conspirator of the party-opponent (IRE 801(d)(2)(E)). However, Illinois adds an additional category of party admission with "a statement made by a person or a person on behalf of an entity, in privity with the party or jointly interested with the party" in IRE 801(d)(2)(F). Section F of "admissions of party-opponents" is consistent with Illinois common law. Illinois does not include language at the end of FRE 801(d)(2) which provides the contents of the statements under review may be considered in determining whether the foundation for admissibility in each subsection are met, but the content alone cannot provide the foundation. Illinois common law required independent proof (i.e. no consideration of the content of the statement) for the necessary foundational relationship for the statement of an agent or co-conspirator and so that is continued with the new rules. However, under prior common law, "authorized" statements of an agent required proof of specific authorization to make the statement. This may now be implied as being within the scope of the agency during the existence of the relationship, because there is no express proof of authorization required by the language of the new rule.

IRE 802 lays out which hearsay is inadmissible. Hearsay is declared inadmissible under IRE 802, just as it is under FRE 802, unless permitted by the rules (ISCR 101) or statute. This leads directly into a comparative analysis of what are permissible exceptions to hearsay that permit out-of-court statements to be admitted for their truth – remembering that if not admitted for its truth, a statement is not hearsay.

IRE 803 lays out the hearsay objections for the unavailability of the declarant and states that there is no IRE 803(1) Present Sense Impression. The premise of FRE 803 is that certain evidence is historically reliable and is admissible hearsay regardless of the availability of the declarant. But the very first "reliable" FRE 803 exception, Present Sense Impression – FRE 803(1) is not adopted by the IRE and has not been a recognized exception to the rule against hearsay under Illinois law. At least, the IRE has reserved 803(1) for the eventuality that it could be adopted as a hearsay exception.

IRE 803(2) – Illinois has long recognized the "excited utterance" exception to the hearsay rule, which requires a startling or exciting event and a statement made within a close time where the declarant is still under the influence of the event. This was most recently recognized in *People v. Connolly* 406 Ill.App.3d 1022, 942 N.E.2d 71 (Ill. App. Ct. 1st Dist. 2011)(wife's spontaneous statements to police that her husband beat her on the head and put her child in the middle of street were admissible as excited utterances).

IRE 803(3)(A) is identical to FRE 803(3) in permitting admission of statements probative of the "then existing state of mind, emotion, sensation or physical condition" of the declarant, but not a statement of memory or belief to prove the fact remembered or believed. However, IRE 803(3)(B) goes further to make express what has been held to be implicit in FRE 803(3) – that the declarant's statement of then existing state of mind, etc. is not admissible to prove the then existing state of mind, etc. of another declarant whose state of mind, etc. is in issue. Thus, what declarant A says he intends to do is admissible to prove that A did what he said he intended, but what declarant A says he and declarant B intended to do cannot be used to prove that B did what A said B was going to do. This is the current expression of the limitations of the doctrine of *Mutual Life Ins. Co. v. Hillman* 145 U.S. 285 (1892).

Note: Adoption of IRE 803(3) also ends a contradiction in the Illinois law of evidence which had required that, for this hearsay exception to apply, the declarant had to be unavailable and there had to be a reasonable probability that the statement was truthful. One would have expected this to be an 804 exception under prior law.

IRE 803(4)(A) is virtually identical to FRE 803(4) in admitting statements made for purposes of medical treatment or medical diagnosis, except for the added limitation that statements made to a consulting health care provider in preparation for litigation or obtaining testimony for trial are inadmissible (with the possible exception of a IRE 703 statement customarily relied upon for purposes of an expert's opinion).

IRE 803(4)(B) reflects current Illinois criminal law (725 ILCS5/115-13) that victims' statements made for purposes of medical diagnosis or treatment are admissible to prove the assault actually occurred and to prove the identity of the perpetrator (the cause of the victim's injuries) if the matter is pertinent to the diagnosis and treatment of sexual abuse. See *People v. Freeman* 404 Ill.App.3d 978, 936 N.E.2d 1110 (Ill. App. Ct. 1st Dist. 2010)(emergency room physician's testimony that child said she "never had sex before" was admissible as an exception to the hearsay rule since it a statement made to medical personnel for purposes of diagnosis and treatment).

IRE 803(5) regarding past recollection recorded, has the same foundational elements as FRE 803(5) and permits the admission of the content of a writing made or adopted by the witness when the matter was fresh in his memory. Under FRE, the rule includes the proviso that the writing's content is given as testimony but the writing itself is not admitted. The IRE provision does not have this limitation, and thus, the proponent of the evidence in Illinois can mark the writing as an exhibit and admit it into evidence.

IRE 803(6) permits the admission of "business records" in both civil and criminal. This is consistent with existing Illinois law in both criminal (725 ILCS 5/115-5) and civil (ISCR 236) venues. What is new is the addition of "certification" foundation for such records of regularly conducted activity in IRE 901(11). The records custodian or other qualified witness may testify to the foundation requirements in court, but by certification, the same witness in a written declaration, subject to the penalty for perjury in the place where the declaration was executed, can recite the elements of foundation to admit the records. Note, however, that medical records are not admissible "business records" in a criminal case. This includes both hospital and medical business records. (See 725 ILCS 5/115-5(c)(1)).

IRE 803(8) permits the admission of public records and reports. It differs from FRE 803(8) in holding inadmissible police accident reports in both civil and criminal cases (again see ISCR 236) and medical records in criminal cases (again see 725 ILCS 5/115-5(c)(1)). Also IRE does not contain the element of FRE 803(8)(C) which provides for admission of factual findings made by a lawful body in civil "actions and proceedings", and in criminal cases, factual findings made against the government. Illinois law has never permitted such evidence. However, records, statements, data compilations of public offices or agencies which involve the activities of the agency or matters consistent with the observations and recordings pursuant to duty imposed by law, except as noted, are admissible. The key to this exception is "official duty" because it is thought that public officials will not have a motive to falsify, and thus the recognized exception to the hearsay rule.

IRE 803 (9) vital statistics is identical to FRE 803(9), except for the introductory phrase "facts contained in" ("records or data compilations . . . . of births, deaths, or marriages if the report there of was made to a public officer pursuant to requirements of law"). 725 ILCS 5.115-5.1 permits the admission into evidence as an exception to the hearsay rule, business records from results of autopsies in both civil and criminal cases. However, a civil statute, 735 ILCS 5/8-2201, bars introduction into evidence of a coroner's verdict as proof in a civil action.

IRE 803(13) says information from family bibles, engravings, grave stone inscriptions and the like are admissible. Old Illinois requirements that the declarant be identified as related by blood or marriage and that the inscription or information must have been entered before any motive to falsify arose are not longer prerequisites. This is a "modern view".

IRE 803(14), (15) and (16) – documents and statements in documents affecting an interest in property and ancient documents – these are identical to FRE counterparts. There were few or no Illinois cases on the subject matter of these rules, except that at Illinois common law an "ancient document" was 30 years old. That has now been relaxed to 20 years in IRE 803(16), so newspapers that are older than 1991 are now "ancient documents". There is no limitation that these documents be about property.

IRE 803 (18) Learned treatises – reserved. Under FRE 803(18) the text of a treatise or publication can be admitted into evidence if there is a foundation for the work as a "reliable authority". This foundation can be established from a witness on cross examination, by another expert witness or by judicial notice. Illinois does not have this rule to permit the admission of such text as substantive evidence, but IRE does reserve the rule, so that the Illinois Supreme Court or the legislature could adopt it in the future.

IRE 803(24) Receipt or Paid Bill – there is no FRE 803(24). This rule codifies Illinois common law that a receipt from a third party or a paid bill is *prima facie* evidence that the charge was reasonable and that the bill was in fact paid.

IRE 804 Declarant unavailable – the IRE and FRE are identical in addressing the issue of unavailability (IRE 804(a)). IRE 804(b)(1) is the "former testimony" exception. The only difference with FRE 804(b)(1) is that Illinois law has both "evidence" and "discovery" depositions. Evidence depositions are obviously "former testimony" in the case on trial, and discovery depositions from that case may be admissible under ISCR 212(a)(5) for certain witnesses.

A number of Illinois criminal statutes provide for the admission of hearsay for absent witnesses. There are constitutional questions concerning the validity of those statutes that permit introduction of testimony of unavailable witnesses. 725 ILCS 5/115-10 (child victim under age 13), 115-10.2 (witness how refuses to testify despite court order), 115-10.2a (domestic assault victim), 115-10.3 (elder witnesses) and 115-10.4 (deceased witnesses). This will be discussed in a separate commentary below.

.

IRE 804(b)(1)(B) Statement under belief of impending death – "dying declarations are only admissible in homicide cases in Illinois, unlike FRE 804(b)(2), which permits such evidence in both civil and criminal cases.

IRE 804(b)(3) Statement against penal interest – almost identical to FRE to the old 804(b)(3) to the extent that a statement by the declarant is admissible if against his/her proprietary or penal interest and would not have been said by a reasonable person unless it were believed true. However, in a criminal case, the requirement of corroborating circumstances for a statement implicating the declarant applies to both the prosecution and the defense. In the FRE statements exculpating the defendant require corroboration of the declarant who is taking the blame, whose statement is exculpatory of the defendant.

IRE 804(b)(5) Forfeiture by wrongdoing. If a party is responsible for the witness being unavailable, then he cannot benefit by having those witness statements excluded – he forfeits the hearsay claim. There are provisions in the Code of Criminal Procedure that express the same forfeiture rule, 725 ILCS 5/115-10.6 (dead witness's statements are admissible against defendant in murder trial, who murdered the witness to prevent testimony when part of the motivation was to prevent the witness from testifying) and 725 ILCS 5/115-10.7 (witness statements are admissible in trial of defendant, where the witness' absence was wrongly procured by defendant). In both situations, there are pretrial disclosure, hearing and ruling requirements for the trial court.

IRE 807 Residual hearsay - not adopted. The FRE 807 provision permits introduction into evidence of hearsay that is relevant and reliable and needed, upon disclosure to the opponent prior to trial and a finding by the court about its admissibility. Illinois has not express counterpart.

IRE 902(11) Certified Record of Regularly Conducted Activity – the IRE authentication approach to business records is different than the FRE approach. FRE 902(11) and 902(12) provide for a "declaration" consistent with an act of Congress or a U.S. Supreme Court rule that meet the foundation requirements for admissibility of "domestic" or "foreign" records of regularly conducted activity. Illinois combines the two into one rule and adopts the concept of "certification", which is a writing under penalty of perjury that the foundational requirements have been met. These requirements are that the record was: (1) made at or near the time of the matters recorded by or from a person with knowledge; (2) kept in the ordinary course of business (regularly conducted activity); and (3) as a regular practice of the business or organization.

IRE 1004 Secondary evidence of originals – this is identical to FRE 1004 and relaxes Illinois' secondary evidence requirements to the Best Evidence Rule. Now, unless there is a showing of bad faith that caused the original to be missing, secondary evidence is admissible upon a showing that the original at one time existed and either (1) all the originals have been lost or destroyed (but not in bad faith); or (2) the originals are in the hands of third parties and cannot be reasonably procured by process; or (3) the original is in the possession of the opponent who has failed to produce the original; or (4) the content of the original is a collateral issue in the proceeding.

Confrontation of witnesses. Perhaps the most significant constitutional issue presented by the law of Illinois evidence is hearsay and the right of witness confrontation in criminal cases. In 2004, the U.S. Supreme Court decided *Crawford v. Washington* 541 U.S. 36, 124 S.Ct. 1354 (U.S. S. Ct. 2004), which held that admitting testimonial hearsay evidence without the right of cross examination violated the defendant's right to confront and cross-examine witnesses under the 6th Amendment to the U.S. Constitution. Prior case law had seemed to suggest that states were free to admit hearsay evidence in criminal cases and it was permissible so long as the evidence was determined to be reliable. Illinois had adopted a number of statutory criminal evidence reforms under the "reliability" standard. More recently, the U.S. Supreme Court decided *Melendez-Diaz v. Massachusetts* 557 U.S.305, 129 S.Ct. 2527 (2009), which found constitutional error in admitting a chemist report as reliable hearsay evidence under a state statute. This evidence had not been subjected to cross examination and was offered as proof of the type and weight of the cocaine that was the subject of criminal charges. The court found constitutional error in admitting this evidence, since it was offered for the truth assert in the chemist's reports – that the substance was cocaine and the weight of the substance.

Note: Illinois has an almost identical criminal statute – 725 ILCS 5/115-15 (Laboratory Reports) – that would permit the admission of laboratory reports in controlled substance, cannabis and other such cases without actually calling the forensic scientist who had conducted the testing. This statute is plainly invalid after *Melendez-Diaz.* The other special hearsay-based statutes for child victims (725 ILCS 5/115-10) or elder victims (725 ILCS 5/115-10.3) have the potential for violating the *Crawford v. Washington,* unless the victim actually testifies at trial.

In 2012, the U.S. Supreme Court, in a 5-4 decision, held in *Williams v. Illinois* 567 U.S. ___, 132 S.Ct. 2221 (U. S. S. Ct. 2012), that there was no *Crawford* violation where an Illinois lab analyst relied upon of the work of an out-of-state lab report creating a DNA profile from a forensic sample in a sexual assault investigation. The plurality opinion found that the defendant's right to confrontation was not violated where the Illinois witness was relying on otherwise inadmissible evidence pursuant to IRE 703 as the basis of her opinion. See also *People v. Barner* 2015 IL 116949 (Ill. S. Ct. 2015)(forensic DNA analyst's reliance on reports written by others proper in the face of a confrontation cause challenge. The reports of other analysts were nontestimonial if produced before any suspect was identified in the case).

In 2015, the U.S. Supreme Court in a unanimous decision held in *Ohio v. Clark* 576 U.S. ____, 135 S.Ct. 2153 (U.S. S. Ct. 2015) that a 3 year old child's statement to a pre-school teacher describing domestic battery by Defendant Clark was non-testimonial. The Court noted that the child's statement related to the care-taking function of his pre-school and was not obtained for law enforcement purposes, so that the principles underlying the confrontation clause protections were not present.

In *People v. Torres* 2012 IL 111302 (Ill. S. Ct. 2012), the Court found a violation of the defendant's right to confront witnesses where a transcript of a 1983 preliminary hearing was admitted at his 2007 trial. The witness at the hearing had been deported and was thus "unavailable", but the defendant's attorney at the time of the preliminary hearing had not received discovery, did not know of the witness' status as a deportable alien and was rushed to conclude his cross examination by a judge with a congested docket. Thus, under *Crawford v. Washington*, a prior opportunity to cross examine is insufficient to meet 6th Amendment confrontation requirements if it is not a meaningful opportunity to cross examine the later-unavailable witness.

In *People v. Leach* 2012 IL 111534, the Court held that an autopsy report prepared by a coroner or medical examiner pursuant to a duty in law required of a public office was not testimonial for purposes of confrontation analysis.

Commentary for Evidence Cases 2011 - 2016

Foundation for video recordings. In *People v. Taylor* 2011 IL 110067 (Ill. S. Ct. 2011), the Court held that video recordings from surveillance camera systems were admissible upon a showing that the system was reliable and operated properly, the evidence was preserved in an acceptable chain of custody and the video recording was properly copied and edited for presentation in court. The Court particularly noted that making a VHS copy of a recording from a DVR (digital video recording) system still produced an "original" for Best Evidence Rule (IRE 1002 and 1004) purposes.

Prior conviction as proper propensity evidence. Prior convictions are ordinarily admissible only to impeach the credibility of a witness as set forth in IRE 609. However, 725 ILCS 5/115-20 permits the admission a prior convictions for domestic battery as proof of propensity for later offenses. *People v. Chapman* 2012 IL 111896 (Ill. S. Ct. 2012)(defendant's prior conviction for domestic battery involving same victim was admissible as proper propensity evidence in his subsequent trial for murder).

Prior conviction of same character as charged offense as impeachment. In *People v. Raney* 2014 IL App (4th) 130551, the defendant was charged with Aggravated Battery, Domestic Battery and Violation of an Order of Protection. When the defendant testified, the prosecution was permitted to impeach him by having the Court inform the jury of his prior felony conviction for Domestic Battery. The defendant argued that this conviction was of the same character as the charges he faced and thus its prejudicial impact was significant – the jury would consider it as propensity evidence of his continuing domestic violence. The appellate court noted that a number of factors must be used in analyzing the use of the balancing test to determine the admission of prior convictions against a testifying defendant, but held it was not an abuse of discretion for the trial court to admit the prior Domestic Battery conviction, particularly where the trial judge gave the jury a limiting instruction that it was to consider the prior conviction only as to the defendant's credibility as a witness and not for guilt.

Forfeiture by Wrongdoing. The common law rule was that a person could not prevent a witness from testifying, and then object to the admission of other witnesses' testimony about the statements of the missing witness on the basis of hearsay. This rule which permits the admission of the hearsay testimony is called "forfeiture by wrongdoing". The General Assembly enacted 725 ILCS 5/115-10.6 to create a procedure to deal with "missing witness" testimony where there was foundation evidence to show that the defendant in a criminal case had murdered a witness to prevent the witness from testifying. That procedure included a required finding of "reliability" by the trial court before overruling a hearsay objection and admitting the statements of the dead witness. However, in 2011, the Illinois Supreme Court adopted the Illinois Rules of Evidence. One of the "new rules" was IRE 804(b)(5) which expressly adopted the common law rule of forfeiture by wrongdoing. In *People v. Peterson* 2012 IL App (3d) 1005514-B, the defendant was charged with murdering his wife. Oral and written statements of his deceased wife and of two prior wives were identified by the prosecution to be offered in evidence. The defendant's pre-trial *Motion in Limine* on hearsay grounds was granted in part with the trial court sustaining hearsay objections on "lack of reliability" grounds based on the provisions of 725 ILCS 5/115-10.6. The appellate court reversed, holding that the adoption of FRE 805(b)(5) by the Illinois Supreme Court, specifically adopted the common law rule, and thus, the statutory requirement of "reliability" did not apply to the forfeiture by wrongdoing decision of trial courts.

Other bad act contrasted with admissible propensity evidence. Some of the most troubling, and sometimes controversial, rules of evidence concern "other bad acts" – evidence of crimes or misconduct of a defendant for which he is not charged – being offered at a trial for a different charge. IRE 404(a) prohibits the introduction of "other crime" evidence in a criminal trial for "propensity", or that the defendant "did it before, so he must be guilty of doing it again", or that the fact-finding judge or jury thinks the defendant must be guilty because he is a bad person. Thus, under IRE 404(b), evidence of other crimes has limited admissibility on such issues as motive, identity, knowledge, plan or *modus operandi.* The trial court has discretion and uses a balancing test (IRE 403) to determine that the probative value of such evidence on the limited issue is not substantially outweigh by its prejudicial effect. On the other hand, in trials involving certain crimes, such as sexual assault or sexual abuse (720 ILCS 5/11-1.20 *et seq*) or domestic violence (720 ILCS 5/12-3.2), the Illinois Rules of Evidence authorize trial courts to admit evidence of a similar crimes for any purpose including propensity. See 725 ILCS 5/115-7.3 and 5/115-7.4). Simply put, the defendant can be found guilty of a charged crime because of evidence of other similar crimes.

In *People v. Perez* 2012 IL App (2d) 100865, the defendant was tried on two counts of criminal sexual abuse of a victim "S.C." The two counts alleged that the acts had been committed several times when, for purposes of his sexual gratification, (2) the defendant was in bed with S.C. and fondled her breasts and placed his penis against her buttocks and (2) an incident when S.C. was in the basement at an ironing board when the defendant again fondled her breasts and placed his penis against her buttocks. S.C. and other witnesses testified about these incidents, but also testified, over objection, about other incidents of a similar nature with S.C. for which the defendant was not charged. There was also evidence, also admitted despite the defendant's objection, about another alleged victim "D.W." D.W. testified herself about two other incidents where the defendant touched her in a sexual way. The D.W. charges were the subject of separate counts charged as criminal sexual abuse that had been severed for trial on another date. Finally, there was evidence that when officers came to arrest the defendant, he gave them a false name, ran away and had to be apprehended by a taser. Again, the defendant was not charged with the false statement to police of misconduct in attempting to evade arrest. The defendant was convicted of the two counts of sexual abuse. Since this case involves all types of the other crimes evidence, used for both a limited purpose (the false statement and flight from police) and propensity evidence (other crimes with S.C. and D.W), it illustrates that the scope of investigation definitely includes "other act" events. The appellate court in affirming the defendant's conviction and six year prison sentence summarized the "other acts and crimes" law of evidence:

> Other-crimes evidence is unquestionably prejudicial to a defendant. Generally, the risk associated with the admission of other-crimes evidence is that it might prove "too much," rendering a jury inclined to convict the defendant simply because it believes that he or she is a bad person deserving of punishment. . . . *under* certain circumstances, however, the probative value of other-crimes evidence is considered to outweigh its prejudicial effect, rendering it admissible. For example, under the common law, other-crimes evidence may be admissible for limited purposes, such as establishing motive, identity, presence, *modus operandi*, knowledge, intent, common design, or absence of mistake. . . . Regardless of probative value, however, under the common law the introduction of other-crimes evidence is *not* permitted for the purpose of establishing the defendant's propensity to commit crimes. . . .
>
> In contrast, section 115-7.3 of the Code permits evidence of a defendant's prior sexual activity with a child complainant to be admitted for *any purpose*, including the defendant's propensity to commit sex offenses. . . .Like the common law, however, section 115-7.3 permits other-crimes evidence only if: (1) it is relevant; and (2) its probative value is not outweighed by its prejudicial effect. . . . Section 115-7.3 further provides that, in weighing probative value against prejudicial effect, a court may consider: "(1) the proximity in time to the charged or predicate offense; (2) the degree of factual similarity to the charged or predicate offense; or (3) other relevant facts and circumstances."
>
> *People v. Perez* 2012 IL App (2d) 100865 ¶¶46-47,. 969 N.E.2d at 906-907 (Internal citations omitted)

The Court affirmed the trial court's ruling admitting all of the other act evidence, and also affirmed the defendant's conviction and sentence.

Business Records; Public Records. An autopsy report in a homicide case was held admissible as either an IRE 803(6) business record or an IRE 803(8) public record. See *People v. Leach* 2012 IL 111534.

Gruesome Photographs. Frequently, objections will be raised to crime scene or autopsy photographs or video recording that have images of blood, tissue and other severe injuries. Typically, under IRE 403, the trial court must weigh the probative value of this photographic evidence against the possible prejudice that the jury will be emotionally shocked about what is depicted and will potentially find the defendant guilty out of disgust, instead of reason. In *People v. Slack* 2014 IL App (5th) 120216, the prosecution admitted gruesome photographs in a First Degree Murder case. The defense was justified use of force. The Court found no error in the trial court's ruling admitting autopsy photos which displayed scenes of internal injuries:

> People's Exhibit 42 is an internal photograph of the victim's ribs after his chest plate was removed, and People's Exhibit 57 is a photograph of the victim's head after the scalp was peeled back. Both photographs were relevant to show the nature and extent of the victim's injuries and the amount of force used by defendant in inflicting the injuries upon the victim.. . . . Therefore, the photographs were relevant not only to show the amount of force used by defendant but also to assist the jury in understanding . . . [the medical examiner's] testimony. Under these circumstances, we cannot say the trial court abused its discretion in admitting either People's Exhibit 42 or 57

People v. Slack 2014 IL App (5th) 120216, ¶28.

Expert Testimony on Eyewitness Identification. In *People v. Lerma* 2016 IL 118496 (Ill. S. Ct. 2016), the Court noted that expert witness testimony should not be allowed where matters of common knowledge are concerned, but that it was error to refuse to admit defendant's proffered expert testimony on the reliability of eyewitness identification where the only evidence of the defendant's guilt was eyewitness identifications of the victim and his friend.

GENERAL INDEX

(Commentary index in *italics*)

Commentaries